1. Cost per Unit = Total Cost/Total Units

2. Standard Cost per Unit = Quantity Standard × Price Standard

3. SQ = Unit Quantity Standard × Actual Output

4. SH = Unit Labor Standard × Actual Output

5. Total Variance = Actual Cost – Planned Cost = $(AP \times AQ) - (SP \times SQ)$

6. Total Materials Variance = Actual Cost – Planned Cost = $(AP \times AQ) - (SP \times SQ)$

7. $MPV = (AP - SP) \times AQ$

8. $MUV = (AQ - SQ) \times SP$

9. $MPV = (AP \times AQ) - (SP \times AQ)$

10. $MUV = (SP \times AQ) - (SP \times SQ)$

11. Total Labor Variance = $(AR \times AH) - (SR \times SH)$

12. Total Labor Variance = Labor Rate Variance + Labor Efficiency Variance

13. $LRV = (AR \times AH) - (SR \times AH)$

14. $LRV = (AR - SR) \times AH$

15. $LEV = (SR \times AH) - (SR \times SH)$

16. $LEV = (AH - SH) \times SR$

17. Target Cost per Unit = Expected Sales Price per Unit – Desired Profit per Unit

18. VOH Spending Variance = Actual VOH – $(AH \times SVOR)$

19. VOH Efficiency Variance = $(AH - SH) \times SVOR$

20. Practical Capacity at Standard = SH_p

21. $SFOR = BFOH/SH_p$

22. Applied $FOH = SH \times SFOR$

23. Total FOH Variance = Actual FOH – Applied FOH

24. FOH Spending Variance = $AFOH - BFOH$

25. Volume Variance = $BFOH$ – Applied FOH
$$= BFOH - (SH \times SFOR)$$

Chapter 11

1. ROI = Operating Income/Average Operating Assets

2. Average Operating Assets = (Beginning Assets + Ending Assets)/2

3.   **Margin**   **Turnover**
   ROI = Operating Income/Sales × Sales/Average Operating Assets

4. Residual Income = Operating Income – (Minimum Rate of Return × Average Operating Assets)

5. EVA = After-Tax Operating Income – (Actual Percentage Cost of Capital × Total Capital Employed)

6. MCE = Processing Time/(Processing Time + Move Time + Inspection Time + Waiting Time)

Chapter 12

1. Payback Period = $\dfrac{\text{Original Investment}}{\text{Annual Cash Flow}}$

2. Accounting Rate of Return = $\dfrac{\text{Average Income}}{\text{Initial Investment}}$

3. $NPV = \left[\sum CF_t /(1+i)^t\right] - I$
$$= \left[\sum CF_t df_t\right] - I$$
$$= P - I$$

4. $I = \sum\left[CF_t /(1+i)^t\right]$

5. $I = CF(df)$

6. $df = I/CF$
$$= \dfrac{\text{Investment}}{\text{Annual Cash Flow}}$$

7. $F = P(1 + i)^n$

8. $P = F/(1 + i)^n$

Chapter 13

1. Risk Response Benefit = Inherent Risk – Residual Risk

2. Risk Response Net Benefit = Response Benefit – Response Cost

3. Value-Stream Product Cost = Total Actual Value-Stream Costs/Units Shipped

4. Value-Stream Product Cost = Unit Materials Cost + Average Conversion Cost

5. Unit Materials Cost (for each product) = Actual Materials Cost/Units Shipped

6. Average Conversion Cost = Total Actual Conversion Costs/Units Shipped

7. Conversion Cost Rate = Total Actual Conversion Costs/Total Net Production Hours

8. Conversion Cost per Unit = Conversion Cost Rate × Cycle Time

Chapter 15

Liquidity ratios:

1. Current Ratio = Current Assets/Current Liabilities

2. Quick Ratio = (Cash + Marketable Securities + Accounts Receivable)/Current Liabilities

3. Accounts Receivable Turnover Ratio = Net Sales/Average Accounts Receivable

4. Average Accounts Receivable = (Beginning Receivables + Ending Receivables)/2

5. Accounts Receivable Turnover in Days = 365/Accounts Receivable Turnover Ratio

6. Inventory Turnover Ratio = Cost of Goods Sold/Average Inventory

7. Average Inventory = (Beginning Inventory + Ending Inventory)/2

8. Inventory Turnover in Days = 365/Inventory Turnover Ratio

9. Times-Interest-Earned Ratio = (Income Before Taxes + Interest Expense)/Interest Expense

10. Debt Ratio = Total Liabilities/Total Assets

11. Debt-to-Equity Ratio = Total Liabilities/Total Stockholder' Equity

Profitability ratios:

12. Return on Sales = Net Income/Sales

13. Return on Total Assets = {Net Income + [Interest Expense(1 – Tax Rate)]}/Average Total Assets

14. Average Total Assets = (Beginning Total Assets + Ending Total Assets)/2

15. Return on Stockholders' Equity = (Net Income – Preferred Dividends)/Average Common Stockholders' Equity

16. Earnings per Share = (Net Income – Preferred Dividends)/Average Common Shares

17. Price-Earnings Ratio = Market Price per Share/Earnings per Share

18. Dividend Yield = Dividends per Common Share/Market Price per Common Share

19. Dividend Payout Ratio = Common Dividends/(Net Income – Preferred Dividends)

SEVENTH EDITION

Managerial Accounting

THE CORNERSTONE OF BUSINESS DECISION MAKING

Maryanne M. Mowen
Oklahoma State University

Don R. Hansen
Oklahoma State University

Dan L. Heitger
Miami University

CENGAGE
Learning™

Australia • Brazil • Mexico • Singapore • United Kingdom • United States

Managerial Accounting: The Cornerstone of Business Decision Making, Seventh Edition

Maryanne M. Mowen, Don R. Hansen, Dan L. Heitger

Sr. Vice President, General Manager,
    Social Science and Qualitative Business: Erin Joyner

Executive Product Director: Mike Schenk

Product Director: Jason Fremder

Product Manager: Matt Filimonov

Content Development Manager: Daniel Celenza

Product Assistant: Audrey Jacobs

Executive Marketing Manager: Robin LeFevre

Sr. Content Project Manager: Martha Conway

Manufacturing Planner: Doug Wilke

Production Service: Cenveo

Sr. Art Director: Michelle Kunkler

Cover and Internal Designer: Harasymczuk Design

Cover Image: © Digital Storm/Shutterstock.com

Kicker Icon: Courtesy of Kicker

Kicker Speaker Image: © dencg/Shutterstock.com

Intellectual Property Analyst: Brittani Morgan

Intellectual Property Project Manager: Reba Frederics

Microsoft Excel® is a registered trademark of Microsoft Corporation. © 2017 Microsoft.

Library of Congress Control Number: 2016958236
ISBN: 978-1-337-11577-3

Cengage Learning
20 Channel Center Street
Boston, MA 02210
USA

Cengage Learning is a leading provider of customized learning solutions with employees residing in nearly 40 different countries and sales in more than 125 countries around the world. Find your local representative at **www.cengage.com**.

Cengage Learning products are represented in Canada by Nelson Education, Ltd.

To learn more about Cengage Learning solutions, visit **www.cengage.com**

Purchase any of our products at your local college store or at our preferred online store **www.cengagebrain.com**

Printed in the United States of America
Print Number: 03   Print Year: 2018

This book is dedicated to our students—past, present, and future—
who are at the heart of our passion for teaching.

Brief Contents

Dear Colleague,

We have been teaching managerial accounting for decades. We love it and believe strongly that managerial accounting is one of the most important courses in the business curriculum! Since it is one of the first business courses students take, we work to share our love and enthusiasm for the material and to show each student that managerial accounting is both FUN and RELATABLE to their current life, as well as to their future.

We wrote this book because there was no other book available that helped us reach the wide variety of students we see each term. Reaching students is a challenge because:

- There is so much material to teach that instructors don't have time for the "fun stuff;"

- Students don't connect the detail with the big picture;

- Many students juggle jobs, family, and so on, so they have little time—their time in the class must be optimized for understanding;

- Managerial accounting is not as straightforward as financial, and students must develop judgment skills in addition to absorbing material;

- There is a tremendous diversity of students (incoming skills, language, etc.); and

- There is no standard road map to teach the course (a.k.a., the balance sheet).

Our approach is to make the entire managerial accounting experience for instructors and students *timely, meaningful, fun, and relatable*. This edition contains numerous new features that achieve these goals in a way that positively sets our book apart from all other managerial accounting books. For instance, our new chapter, "Emerging Topics in Managerial Accounting," addresses timeliness by covering cutting-edge topics. Our unique *"Here's How It's Used"* pedagogy enables students to enjoy the process of developing a deeper understanding of managerial accounting and its implications for themselves, as well as businesses. Our watchwords are "Here's How:"

1. *Here's How It's Used Concept Clip Animations* for many major topics portray the most difficult concepts in a brief and fun animated cartoon. They present the information in a logical, entertaining, and relatable way that pertains not only to businesses, but also to students' everyday lives.

2. *Here's How It's Used Examples* (formerly Cornerstones) *throughout the text* walk students through the most important managerial accounting models and help them solve computations. Students say these examples really get them started on their homework and help them understand the material before class. As a result, the Examples allow the instructor to focus valuable class time on the "why," and allow students to understand the big picture—helping students see the relevance and importance of what they are learning.

3. *Here's Why It's Important* highlights for students the reason that key topics within each chapter are important. This new feature significantly helps students better understand the big picture of why managerial accounting is important.

4. *Experience Managerial Accounting Videos* focus on real companies, such as Coldstone Creamery, Second City Comedy Club, and Boyne USA ski resorts, and the integrated real-world examples of Kicker Speakers provide students with inside access into how management accounting is used to make real-world business decisions.

Using our text, you don't need to spend as much valuable class time teaching "how," you can focus on "why."

- Examples are built around how students work, summarizing key procedures to help students complete homework independently.

- Because students are able to complete homework independently, they do not bombard the instructor with "How do I do this?" type questions.

Students who want to go farther can use:

- ***Blueprint Problems.*** We wrote these expressly to accompany this book and help students expand their understanding.

- ***Blueprint Problems Using Excel.*** We wrote these to help develop students' spreadsheet skills. Students are required to develop their own Excel formulas to solve the problems.

- ***Analyzing Relationships.*** We developed these to help students use a graphical approach to see exactly how changing one or more underlying variables affects a model. These allow students to engage in sensitivity analysis and to consider the related analytical questions. These help to foster analytical skills and to develop judgment and understanding.

Our goal is to improve student understanding and preparedness while allowing you to focus on meaningful applications of managerial accounting to important real-world topics. We believe it will work in your classroom and look forward to teaming up with you to improve your students' success and make managerial accounting *meaningful, fun, and relatable.*

Sincerely,

Maryanne Mowen, Don Hansen, Dan Heitger

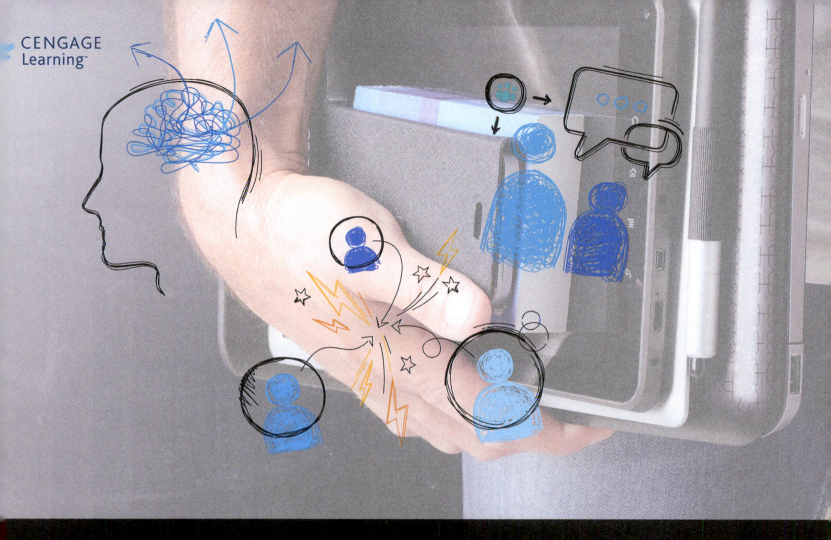

Close the Gap

Between Homework and Exam Performance

with **CengageNOWv2**

We've talked with hundreds of accounting instructors across the country and we are learning that online homework systems have created a new challenge in the accounting course.

We are hearing that students perform well on the homework but poorly on the exam, which leads instructors to believe that students are not truly learning the content, but rather memorizing their way through the system.

CengageNOWv2 better prepares students for the exam by providing an online homework experience that is similar to what students will experience on the exam and in the real world.

Read on to see how CengageNOWv2 helps close this gap.

 CENGAGENOWv2

Closing the gap, one step at a time.

Multi-Panel View

One of the biggest complaints students have about online homework is the scrolling, which prevents students from seeing the big picture and understanding the accounting system. This new Multi-Panel View in CengageNOWv2 enables students to see all the elements of a problem on one screen.

- Students make connections and see the tasks as connected components in the accounting process.
- Dramatically reduced scrolling eliminates student frustration.

Blank Sheet of Paper Experience

Many students perform well on homework but struggle when it comes to exams. Now, with the new Blank Sheet of Paper Experience, students must problem-solve on their own, just as they would if taking a test on a blank sheet of paper. This discourages overreliance on the system.

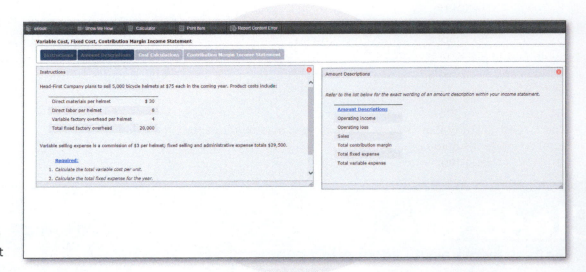

From Motivation to Mastery

MOTIVATION:
Engage students and better prepare them for class.

Concept Clips
Written by the authors, these clips provide students with a deeper explanation into the why and the how of managerial accounting concepts.

Video: Tell Me More
Tell Me More lecture activities explain the core concepts of the chapter through an engaging auditory and visual presentation that is ideal for all class formats—flipped mode, online, hybrid, face-to-face.

Adaptive Study Plan
The Adaptive Study Plan is an assignable/gradable study center that adapts to each student's unique needs and provides a remediation pathway to keep students progressing.

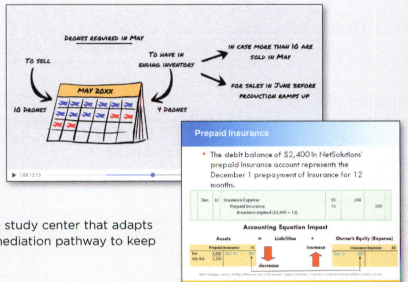

APPLICATION:
Help students apply accounting concepts.

Video: Show Me How
Linked to end-of-chapter problems in CengageNOWv2, Show Me How problem demonstration videos provide a step-by-step model of a similar problem.

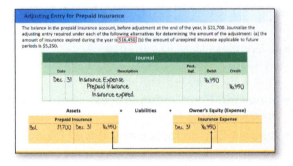

MASTERY:
Teach students to go beyond memorization to true understanding.

Mastery Problems for *Managerial Accounting, 7e*
These problems allow students to see the interrelationships among core concepts.

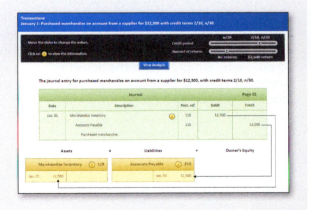

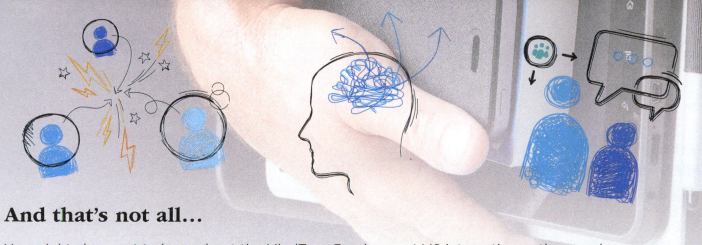

And that's not all...

You might also want to learn about the MindTap eReader, our LMS integration options, and more.

MindTap eReader

The MindTap eReader is the most robust digital reading experience available.

- Fully optimized for the iPad.
- Note-taking, highlighting, and more.
- Off-line access on smartphones.

The MindTap eReader also features ReadSpeaker®, an online text-to-speech application that vocalizes, or "speechenables," online educational content.

LMS Integration

CengageNOWv2 can be seamlessly integrated with most learning management systems. Adopters will enjoy:

- **A Seamless User Experience**—Access your Cengage resources seamlessly using only your LMS login credentials.
- **Simplified Registration Process**—Get students up and running faster!
- **Content Customization and Deep Linking**—Use our Content Selector to create a unique learning path for students that blends your content with Cengage Learning activities, eText, and more within your LMS course.
- **Automatic Grade Synchronization***—Need to have your course grades recorded in your LMS gradebook? No problem. Simply select the activities you want synched and grades will automatically be recorded in your LMS gradebook.

* Grade synchronization is currently available with Blackboard, Brightspace (powered by D2L), Angel 8, and Canvas.

ADA Accessibility

Cengage Learning is committed to making its educational materials accessible to users of all abilities. We are steadily working to increase accessibility and create a full spectrum of usable tools, features, and choices that are accessible for users of all abilities. All new Cengage Learning products and services are designed with accessibility in mind.

- With the latest release of CengageNOWv2:
  - Images and graphics have been converted to HTML tables so that they can be read by screen readers.
  - The assignment experience now offers proper heading structure to support easy navigation with assistive technology.
- CengageNOWv2 solutions offer high contrast and well-structured HTML, which helps support screen reader interactivity.
- All videos are created with closed captioning and transcripts available for download.
- The MindTap eReader is HTML-based and compatible with most screen reading assistive software. The eReader supports browser settings for high-contrast narrative text, variable font sizes, and multiple foreground and background color options.

For more information on accessibility, please visit www.cengage.com/accessibility.

IPAD Tablet Compatibility

CengageNOWv2 is fully compatible with the iPad and other tablet devices, with the exception of General Ledger (CLGL) and Excel Tutorials, which are flash based.

New to this Edition

I. New Additions to Each Chapter

A number of **meaningful features** were added to *each chapter* in this edition, including:

✳ ***Here's How It's Used:*** Several Here's How It's Used boxes in each chapter tell students how managerial concepts are used in a variety of businesses and in their own lives. This exciting new feature makes the material more relatable and meaningful. Here's How It's Used features include:

- In Your Life
- Data Analytics
- Sustainability
- At Kicker
- At Real Companies

✳ ***Here's Why It's Important:*** Brief explanations of why the concepts are important are highlighted in the text to motivate students in their study.

✳ ***New A and B sets of Brief Exercises:*** These new sets of brief exercises give instructors more options for using illustrative exercises in class and then assigning very similar material to get students started with homework.

✳ ***Animated Concept Clip:*** All new brief animated video clips help students understand concepts and see them in a visual way.

✳ ***Check Point questions at the conclusion of each learning objective section:*** Check Point questions help students perform quick self-checks while reading chapter material.

✳ ***Key Term Definitions:*** To facilitate study and review, definitions for each key term are now found at the end of each chapter (in addition to the glossary at the end of the text).

II. Creation of a New Chapter

The growing importance of managerial accounting in several critical areas led to the creation of a *completely new chapter*, **Emerging Topics in Managerial Accounting**, that provides students with exciting insights and cutting-edge perspectives on *Enterprise Risk Management, Business Sustainability, Quality Cost Management, Lean Accounting, International Issues in Management Accounting, and the Role of Cost and Managerial Accounting in Fraud and Forensic Accounting.*

III. Restructuring of Chapter Content and Organization

A restructuring of the text tightened and aligned topics in a natural sequence. In this edition:

- **Reduction in chapters.** *The total number of chapters was reduced from 16 to 15.* By streamlining, eliminating, and realigning topics, the number of chapters was reduced, but the number of topics available to cover was actually increased.

- **Chapter elimination.** *The chapter on variable and absorption costing and inventory management was eliminated* and the basic material on absorption costing and variable costing was added to Chapter 3 on Cost Behavior and Forecasting. Locating these topics in this chapter provides a good foundation for the costing chapters that follow. It also allows students the opportunity to see an immediate application of cost behavior. The inventory management topic was eliminated and its coverage deferred to a higher level course.

- **Chapter elimination.** *The chapter on flexible budgeting and overhead analysis was eliminated and its topics moved to other chapters.* The flexible budgeting material was added to Chapter 9 on Profit Planning to give students an overview of both static and flexible budgets in the same chapter. The overhead analysis material was added to the standard costing chapter (Chapter 10) to give students a complete picture of a standard costing system.

- **Chapters relocated.** *Cost-Volume-Profit Analysis has been moved to Chapter 7* to allow instructors to explain the basics of job-order, activity-based (moved to follow job order costing), and process costing. This relocation enables students to develop a richer understanding of costs used in CVP.

- **Chapter relocated.** *The Tactical Decision Making and Relevant Analysis chapter is positioned immediately after CVP **and now includes material on segmented income statements to provide students with a more logical and impactful understanding of how to prepare and interpret Keep-or-Drop decisions.***

- **Topic depth increased and new chapter added.** *The basic introduction to quality costing and environmental issues was removed from the chapter on activity based costing and management.* A much deeper treatment of these topics, as well as Enterprise Risk Management, Business Sustainability, Issues in International Managerial Accounting, and the Role of Cost and Managerial Accounting in Fraud and Forensic Accounting, is now found in the new chapter, Emerging Topics in Managerial Accounting (Chapter 13).

Our strong belief is that these additions and changes maintain all of the positive aspects of our previous editions that current users enjoy and appreciate, while significantly improving the managerial accounting experience for students and instructors alike. This new edition helps students to learn firsthand that managerial accounting is ***timely, meaningful, fun***, and ***relatable*** to their everyday lives!

Acknowledgments and Thanks

Thank you to the following instructors who contributed to the development of the 7th edition of *Managerial Accounting: The Cornerstone of Business Decision Making*. By reviewing, verifying, or participating in focus groups, you allowed us to create a text that will benefit all of our students and instructors that use this text.

Janice Akao, *Butler Community College*

Michael Alles, *Rutgers Business School*

Cornelia Alsheimer, *Santa Barbara City College*

Linda Amann, *University of Wisconsin–Whitewater*

Julie Armstrong, *St. Clair County Community College*

Elise Bartley, *Westminster College*

Nancy Batch, *Texas A&M–San Antonio*

Robert Beatty, *Anne Arundel Community College*

Connie Belden, *Butler Community College*

Pamela S. Benner, *Stark State College*

Debbie Benson, *Kennesaw State University*

Dr. Timothy B. Biggart, *Berry College*

Eric Blazer, *Millersville University*

Cindy Bleasdale, *Hilbert College*

Marie Blouin, *Ithaca College*

Maryann Bolton, *Central Community College–Hastings Campus*

Marian W. Boscia, *King's College*

Anna Boulware, *St. Charles Community College*

Amy Bourne, *Oregon State University*

Thomas J. Bradley, *Ashford University*

Rachel Brassine, *East Carolina University*

Jerold K. Braun, *Daytona State College*

Jeff Brennan, *Austin Community College*

Ann K. Brooks, *University of New Mexico*

Patti Brown, *The University of Texas at Austin*

Richard Buchanan, *Oklahoma State University*

Esther Bunn, *Stephen F Austin State University*

Kelley Butler, *Ivy Tech Community College*

Marci Butterfield, *University of Utah*

Edward Bysiek, *St. Bonaventure*

Leonor M. Cabrera, *Canada College*

Don Campodonico, *Notre Dame de Namur University*

Tongyu Cao, *University College Cork, Ireland*

Rodney Carmack, *Arkansas State University*

Sandra Cereola, *James Madison University*

Richard Chen, *Eastern Kentucky University*

Bea Chiang, *The College of New Jersey*

Linda Christiansen, *Indiana University Southeast*

Lisa Church, *Rhode Island College*

Jay Cohen, *Oakton Community College*

Kelley Colston, *University of Toledo*

Margaret Combs, *University of the Cumberlands*

Stephanie Comer, *Cornerstone University*

Rita Kingery Cook, *University of Delaware*

Dixon Cooper, *Henderson State University*

Sandra Copa, *North Hennepin Community College*

Karen Crisonino, *County College of Morris*

Anthony Daly-Leonard, *Delaware County Community College*

David Dearman, *University of Arkansas–Little Rock*

Charlene Deno, *SUNY Oneonta*

Harry DeWolf, *Mt. Hood Community College*

Patricia A. Doherty, *Boston University*

David Doyon, *Southern NH University*

Barbara Durham, *University of Central Florida*

Howard Eskew, *San Diego Mesa College*

Diane Eure, *Texas State University*

Jade Fang, *Marist College*

Christopher Ferro, *College of DuPage*

Clayton Forester, *University of Minnesota*

Robert Foster, *California State University, Northridge*

Shari Fowler, *Briar Cliff University*

Sheri Geddes, *Hope College*

Joe Gerard, *University of Wisconsin–Whitewater*

Daniel J. Gibbons, *Waubonsee Community College*

Paul Goodchild, *University of Central Missouri*

Julie Goodin, *Immaculata University*

Andrea Gouldman, *Weber State University*

Bob Gutschick, *College of Southern Nevada*

Joohyung Ha, *University of San Francisco*

Wilbert Harri, *Pima Community College*

Bob Hartung, *Metro Community College*

Haihong He, *California State University, Los Angeles*

Candice Heino, *Anoka Ramsey Community College*

Youngwon Her, *California State University, Northridge*

Dave Hinrichs, *Lehigh*

Jan Hlavaty, *Lakeland Community College*

Dr. Louann Hofheins, *The University of Findlay*

Steve Horan, *University of Sioux Falls*

Melvin Houston, *Wayne State University*

Wayne Ingalls, *University of Maine*

Marianne James, *California State University, Los Angeles*

Steve Johnson, *Minnesota State University, Mankato*

Jeffrey Jones, *The College of Southern Nevada*

Stani Kantcheva, *Cincinnati State Technical and Community College*

Kathryn W. Kapka, *The University of Texas at Tyler*

Ben Kaplan, *Johnson & Wales University*

Howard Keller, *IUPUI*

Marie Kelly, *Stephen F Austin State University*

Dr. Bhagwan Khanna, *Ball State University*

Garry Kirk, *Southwest Wisconsin Technical College*

Christine Kloezeman, *Glendale Community College*

Barbara Kren, *Marquette University*

Marco Lam, *Western Carolina University*

Meg Costello Lambert, *Oakland Community College–Auburn Hills*

Donna Larner, *Cornerstone University*

John Lauck, *Louisiana Tech University*

Dr. Mark Lawrence, *University of North Alabama*

Rose Layton, *University of Southern California*

Brian R. Lazarus, *Baltimore City Community College*

Chuohsuan Lee, *SUNY Plattsburgh*

Michael Lee, *Boise State University*

Cedric Lewis, *UNF*

Ping Lin, *California State University, Long Beach*

Danny Litt, *UCLA*

Harold Little, *Western Kentucky University*

William Lloyd, *Lock Haven University*

John Logsdon, *Webber International University*

Dennis M. Lopez, *University of Texas at San Antonio*

Suzanne Lowensohn, *Colorado State University*

Claudia A. Lubaski, *Lorain County Community College*

Susan Lynn, *University of Baltimore*

Ajay Maindiratta, *NYU–Stern*

Diane Marker, *University of Toledo*

Maureen McBeth, *College of DuPage*

Dawn McKinley, *Harper College*

Roger McMillian, *Mineral Area College*

Tammy Metzke, *Milwaukee Area Technical College*

Michael Meyer, *University of Notre Dame*

Linda Miller, *Northeast Community College*

Stephanie Morris, *Mercer University*

Kenneth Mullins, *University of Wisconsin–Stevens Point*

Gerald F. Murphy, *Capital Community College*

Pam Neely, *SUNY Brockport*

Mary Beth Nelson, *North Shore Community College*

Mary Netzler, *University of Maryland–University College*

Richard Newmark, *University of Northern Colorado*

Joseph Malino Nicassio, *Westmoreland County Community College*

Barbara A. Norris, *Johnson & Wales University*

Kalpana Pai, *Notre Dame de Namur University*

Angela Pannell, *Mississippi State University*

Laurel Parrilli, *Cornell University*

Richard Pettit, *Mountain View College*

Kristen Quinn, *Northern Essex Community College*

Rama Ramamurthy, *Georgetown University*

Paulette Ratliff-Miller, *Grand Valley State University*

Barbara Reider, *University of Montana*

Barbara Rice, *Gateway Community and Technical College*

Vernon Richardson, *University of Arkansas*

Constance Rodriguez, *SUNY Brockport*

Paulette Rodriguez, *The University of Texas at El Paso*

Molly Rogers, *University of Cincinnati*

Katrina Rowe, *Schenectady County Community College*

Paul San Miguel, *Western Michigan University*

Christine Schalow, *University of Wisconsin–Stevens Point*

Erica Scheidecker, *University of Dubuque*

Lee Schiffel, *Valparaiso University*

Pamela Schwer, *St. Xavier University*

Randy Serrett, *University of Houston–Downtown*

Carlo Silvesti, *Gwynedd Mercy University*

James Sinclair, *Georgetown University*

Ercan Sinmaz, *Houston Community College*

Harshini Siriwardane, *University of Cincinnati*

Jennifer Smith, *Chattahoochee Technical College*

Stephan Smith, *Nicholls State University*

Mohsen Souissi, *Fayetteville State University*

Vicki Splawn, *Mid-America Christian University*

Jason Stanfield, *Purdue*

George Starbuck, *McMurry University*

Dr. J. William Stinde, *Glendale Community College*

James Sundberg, *Eastern Michigan University*

Kenton Swift, *University of Montana*

Karen Tabak, *Maryville University*

Diane Tanner, *University of North Florida*

Glade Tew, *BYU–Idaho*

Todd Thornock, *Iowa State University*

Sarah Thorrick, *Loyola University New Orleans*

Donald Trippeer, *SUNY Oneonta*

Hugh Van Seaton, *Jacksonville University*

Glenn Walberg, *University of Vermont*

Joe Welker, *College of Western Idaho*

Wendy Wilson, *Texas Christian University*

Maef Woods, *Heidelberg University*

Patricia Worsham, *Norco College*

Gail Wright, *Castleton University*

Jennifer Yin, *University of Texas at San Antonio*

Xiaoli Yuan, *ECSU*

Benny Zachry, *Tulane University*

Syed Zaidi, California State University, *Santa Monica*

Ronald Zullo, *Northeastern University*

About the Authors

Dr. Maryanne M. Mowen is Associate Professor Emerita of Accounting at Oklahoma State University. She currently teaches online classes in cost and management accounting for Oklahoma State University. She received her Ph.D. from Arizona State University. She brings an interdisciplinary perspective to teaching and writing in cost and management accounting, with degrees in history and economics. She has taught classes in ethics and the impact of the Sarbanes-Oxley Act on accountants. Her scholarly research is in the areas of management accounting, behavioral decision theory, and compliance with the Sarbanes-Oxley Act. She has published articles in journals such as Decision Science, The Journal of Economics and Psychology, and The Journal of Management Accounting Research. Dr. Mowen has served as a consultant to mid-sized and Fortune 100 companies and works with corporate controllers on management accounting issues. She is a member of the Northern New Mexico chapter of SCORE and serves as a counselor, assisting small and start-up businesses. Outside the classroom, she enjoys hiking, traveling, reading mysteries, and working crossword puzzles.

Dr. Don R. Hansen is Professor Emeritus of Oklahoma State University. He received his Ph.D. from the University of Arizona in 1977. He has an undergraduate degree in mathematics from Brigham Young University. He has published articles in both accounting and engineering journals including The Accounting Review, The Journal of Management Accounting Research, Accounting Organizations and Society, Accounting Horizons, and IIE Transactions. He has served on the editorial board of *The Accounting Review*. His outside interests include family, church activities, reading, movies, and watching sports.

Dr. Dan L. Heitger is the Deloitte Professor of Accounting and Co-Director of the William Isaac & Michael Oxley Center for Business Leadership at Miami University. He received his Ph.D. from Michigan State University and his undergraduate degree in accounting from Indiana University. He actively works with executives and students of all levels in developing and teaching courses in managerial accounting, business sustainability, risk management, stakeholder management, governance, and business reporting. He co-founded an organization that provides executive education for large international organizations. His interactions with business professionals, through executive education and the Center, allow him to bring a current and real-world perspective to his writing. His published research focuses on managerial accounting and risk management issues and has appeared in Harvard Business Review, Behavioral Research in Accounting, Accounting Horizons, Issues in Accounting Education, Journal of Accountancy, and Management Accounting Quarterly. His outside interests include hiking with his family in the National Park system.

Contents

SEVENTH EDITION

Managerial Accounting

THE CORNERSTONE OF BUSINESS DECISION MAKING

1

Introduction to Managerial Accounting

After studying Chapter 1, you should be able to:

1 ▸ Explain the meaning of managerial accounting.

2 ▸ Explain the differences between managerial accounting and financial accounting.

3 ▸ Identify and explain the current focus of managerial accounting.

4 ▸ Describe the role of managerial accountants in an organization.

5 ▸ Explain the importance of ethical behavior for managers and managerial accountants.

6 ▸ Identify three forms of certification available to managerial accountants.

Nico Traut/Shutterstock.com

EXPERIENCE MANAGERIAL DECISIONS

with BuyCostumes.com

The greatest benefit of managerial accounting is also its biggest challenge—to provide managers with information that improves decisions and creates organizational value. This information helps inform managers about the impact of various strategic and operational decisions on key nonfinancial performance measures and their eventual impact on the organization's financial performance. The information is challenging to prepare and analyze because it requires an understanding of all value chain components that affect the organization, including research and development, production, marketing, distribution, and customer service.

Since its inception in 1999, **BuyCostumes.com** has blended the right managerial accounting information and an innovative business model to provide over 10 billion costume combinations to millions of customers all over the world. Using the Internet and marketing creativity, BuyCostumes.com serves a growing market of consumers. For example, U.S. consumers spend over $2.5 billion each year on Halloween costumes for adults, children and even pets (who account for $350 million of this amount)!

> "Using the Internet and marketing creativity, BuyCostumes.com serves a market of 150 million U.S. consumers who spend $2.5 billion on Halloween costumes each year."

According to BuyCostumes.com's CEO, the company measures key performance indicators to guide its decision making. For example, managerial accountants analyze measures of customer satisfaction, average time between order placement and costume arrival for each shipping method, and the profitability of individual customer types. As customer trends change, competitors emerge, and technological advances occur, BuyCostumes.com's managerial accounting information adapts to provide crucial insight into the company's performance and how its strategy should evolve to remain one of the world's largest Internet costume retailers.

Here's **Why It's important**

CONCEPT CLIP

THE MEANING OF MANAGERIAL ACCOUNTING

What do we mean by managerial accounting? Quite simply, **managerial accounting** is the provision of accounting information for a company's internal users. More specifically, managerial accounting represents the firm's internal accounting system designed to provide the necessary financial and nonfinancial information that helps company managers make the best possible decisions. Unlike financial accounting, managerial accounting is not bound by any formal criteria such as generally accepted accounting principles (GAAP). Managerial accounting has three broad objectives:

- To provide information for planning the organization's actions.
- To provide information for controlling the organization's actions.
- To provide information for making effective decisions.

Using recent examples from many companies in both the for-profit and not-for-profit sectors, this textbook explains how all manufacturing (e.g., aircraft producer—**Boeing Corporation**), merchandising (e.g., clothing retailer—**American Eagle Outfitters**), and service (e.g., healthcare provider—**Cleveland Clinic**, or online retailer **Amazon.com**) organizations use managerial accounting information and concepts. People in all types of positions—from corporate presidents to graphic designers to hospital administrators—can improve their managerial skills by being well-grounded in the basic concepts and use of managerial accounting information for planning, controlling, and decision making.

The exciting reality is that the importance and scope of managerial accounting information is growing rapidly around the globe. As a result, the demand for businesspeople who possess the ability to create, understand, use, and communicate managerial accounting information continues to grow. Chapter 13 explores special and emerging managerial accounting areas, such as enterprise risk management, lean and quality accounting, corporate sustainability reporting, and fraud and forensic accounting.

Here's How It's Used: SUSTAINABILITY

One of the fastest growing needs in business is the area of corporate sustainability measurement and reporting. Managerial accounting plays an important role in this exciting aspect of business. Thousands of companies increasingly release to the public (i.e., suppliers, regulators, employees, human rights organizations, environmental groups, customers, etc.) very large quantities of managerial accounting information that traditionally either did not exist or was released only internally. This information is released through optional reports known as corporate sustainability reports (e.g., **Coca-Cola**, **McDonald's**), social responsibility reports (e.g., **Starbucks**, **Target**), or citizenship reports (e.g., **ExxonMobil**, **General Electric**). The release of these reports often occurs because firms want to manage their reputation by preparing and releasing such information themselves, rather than having Internet bloggers, newspapers, and cable news networks publish their own estimates of such information. Some leading companies (e.g., **Clorox**, **Eli Lilly**, **Novo Nordisk**) have even moved so far as to combine their sustainability report with their annual report, thereby resulting in a single, integrated report containing both traditional financial accounting information as well as managerial accounting information.[1] Measuring the nonfinancial aspects of corporate business sustainability, including economic, social, environmental, legal, and political issues, and then linking their impact on the company's financial performance requires the unique insights and expertise of managerial accountants!

---

1 For a more in-depth discussion of the future of sustainability accounting, see "Currents of Change: The KPMG Survey of Corporate Responsibility Reporting 2015," taken from KPMG's website, www.kpmg.com/crreporting; or Brian Ballou, Dan Heitger, and Chuck Landes, "Accounting for the Sustainability Cycle," 2013, taken from the American Institute of Certified Public Accountants' website, www.aicpa.org/interestareas/frc/assuranceadvisoryservices/downloadabledocuments/sustainability/whitepaper_accounting_for_the_sustainability_cycle.pdf.

Information Needs of Managers and Other Users

Managerial accounting information is needed by a number of individuals. In particular, managers and empowered workers need comprehensive, up-to-date information for the following activities:

- planning
- controlling
- decision making

Planning

The detailed formulation of action to achieve a particular end is the management activity called **planning**. Planning requires setting objectives and identifying methods to achieve those objectives. For example, a firm may set the objective of increasing its short- and long-term profitability by improving the overall quality of its products. **DaimlerChrysler** drastically improved the quality and profitability of its **Chrysler** automobile division in the early 21st century to the point where its quality surpassed that of **Mercedes-Benz** (also owned by DaimlerChrysler). By improving product quality, firms like DaimlerChrysler (now Daimler AG) should be able to reduce scrap and rework, decrease the number of customer complaints and warranty work, reduce the resources currently assigned to inspection, and so on, thus increasing profitability. To realize these benefits, management must develop some specific methods that, when implemented, will lead to the achievement of the desired objective. A plant manager, for example, may start a supplier evaluation program to identify and select suppliers who are willing and able to supply defect-free parts. Empowered workers may be able to identify production causes of defects and to create new methods for producing a product that will reduce scrap and rework and the need for inspection. The new methods should be clearly specified and detailed.

Controlling

Planning is only half the battle. Once a plan is created, it must be implemented and its implementation monitored by managers and workers to ensure that the plan is being carried out as intended. The managerial activity of monitoring a plan's implementation and taking corrective action as needed is referred to as **controlling**. Control is usually achieved by comparing actual performance with expected performance. This information can be used to evaluate or to correct the steps being taken to implement a plan. Based on the feedback, a manager (or worker) may decide to let the plan continue as is, take corrective action of some type to put the actions back in harmony with the original plan, or do some midstream replanning.

The managerial accounting information used for planning and control purposes can be either financial or nonfinancial in nature. For example, **Duffy Tool and Stamping** saved $14,300 per year by redesigning a press operation. In one department, completed parts (made by a press) came down a chute and fell into a parts tub. When the tub became full, press operators had to stop operation while the stock operator removed the full tub and replaced it with an empty one. Workers redesigned the operation so that each press had a chute with two branches—each leading to a different tub. Now when one tub is full, completed parts are routed into the other tub. The $14,300 savings are a financial measure of the success of the redesign. The redesign also eliminated machine downtime and increased the number of units produced per hour (operational feedback), both of which are examples of nonfinancial performance. Both types of measures convey important information. Often, financial and nonfinancial feedback is given to managers in the form of performance reports that compare the actual data with planned data or other benchmarks.

Decision Making

The process of choosing among competing alternatives is called **decision making**. This managerial function is intertwined with planning and control in that a manager cannot successfully plan or control the organization's actions without making decisions regarding competing alternatives. For instance, if **BMW** contemplates the possibility of offering a car that runs on gasoline and hydrogen, its ultimate decision would be improved if information about the alternatives (e.g., pertaining to gasoline versus hydrogen versus hybrid combinations of these two automobile fuel options) is gathered and made available to managers. One of the major roles of the managerial accounting information system is to supply information that facilitates decision making. For example, based on managerial accounting information concerning current market size and potential growth opportunities in the costume market, **BuyCostumes.com** decided to sell many different types of costumes internationally in order to best meet customer demand. As a result, the company offers a selection of exclusive and licensed costumes and accessories that equate to over 10 billion costume combinations! This important strategic decision allows BuyCostumes.com to serve as a premier destination for the 10 million global partiers that visit its website each Halloween. Interestingly, since its creation, BuyCostumes.com management has correctly predicted the outcome of each presidential election based on the sales data from its presidential candidate mask collection.

Here's How It's Used: AT COSTCO

What Constitutes Managerial Accounting Information?

You are the **Costco** executive who has been chosen to decide whether or not the company should continue its policy of sourcing its finest coffee from Rwanda.

What types of information should you consider as you decide how best to structure and analyze this important long-term strategic decision? What challenges do you expect to face in making this decision?

What constitutes managerial accounting information is growing considerably as organizations must make decisions that include the global consequences of their actions, as well as the impact on an increasingly large number of vocal, well-informed, and powerful stakeholders. Stakeholders include the company's customers, suppliers, employees, regulators, politicians, lawmakers, and local community members. Generally speaking, managerial accounting information can be *financial* in nature, such as sales revenue or cost of sales, or *nonfinancial* in nature, such as the number of quality defects or the percentage of manufacturing plants that are inspected for compliance with human rights policies. One of the most exciting—and yet daunting—aspects of managerial accounting is that one can choose to measure *anything*, assuming the resources, information technology, and creativity exist to capture the desired performance measure.

As a Costco executive, one of the first nonfinancial factors you likely would consider measuring is the quality of the Rwandan coffee to ensure that it fulfills Costco's strategic goal of creating a competitive advantage by providing premium coffee to customers. Quality could be defined by the beans' taste, shelf life longevity, or other factors valued by customers. Other important nonfinancial performance measures might include the time required to ship the harvested beans from Rwanda to Costco stores around North America and the presence of a local farming workforce in Rwanda critical to successfully sustaining a long-term supply chain between Rwandan fields and Costco customers.

One of the most important financial items to measure would be the importance to Costco's customers of purchasing premium quality coffee, which could be measured by the additional price they are willing to pay for Rwandan coffee over and above more average quality coffee. Other financial measures might include the cost of harvesting, inspecting, and shipping beans, as well as investments in Rwandan farming communities (e.g., physical infrastructure and schools) that ensure the relationship is sustainable for future generations.

Finally, you should consider how the decision to continue sourcing premium coffee from Rwanda will be perceived by Costco's important stakeholders, including its customers who buy the coffee, suppliers who provide the coffee beans, and government officials in the United States and Rwanda who set trading policies between the two countries. Accurately measuring issues like stakeholder perceptions of such decisions can be difficult because the managerial accountant oftentimes must invent new measures, figure out where the data to create such measures might come from, and estimate how accurate these measures will be once collected.

The managerial accountant's ability to inform executive decision makers by providing innovative, accurate, and timely performance measures can create an important competitive advantage for the organization by improving its key decisions.

1. **Which activity generally occurs first: decision making, planning, or control?**

Answer:

Planning usually occurs first to set objectives, followed by controlling to monitor implementation of the planned objectives, and, finally, decision making to choose the best alternative(s).

2. **The desire to attract and retain the most talented workers in a given industry is an example of which activity: decision making, planning, or control?**

Answer:

Planning. Setting an objective to improve workforce quality is an example of an important planning activity.

FINANCIAL ACCOUNTING AND MANAGERIAL ACCOUNTING

OBJECTIVE ◀ 2
Explain the differences between managerial accounting and financial accounting.

Here's **Why It's important**

There are two basic kinds of accounting information systems: financial accounting and managerial accounting. The company's accounting system should be designed to provide both financial and managerial accounting information. The key point is flexibility—the system should be able to supply different *information* for different *purposes*.

Financial Accounting

Financial accounting is primarily concerned with producing information (financial statements) for *external* users, including investors, creditors, customers, suppliers, government agencies (Food and Drug Administration, Federal Communications Commission, etc.), and labor unions. This information has a historical orientation and is used for such things as investment decisions, stewardship evaluation, monitoring activity, and regulatory measures. Financial statements must conform to certain rules and conventions that are defined by various agencies, such as the Securities and Exchange Commission (SEC), the Financial Accounting Standards Board (FASB), and the International Accounting Standards Board (IASB). These rules pertain to issues such as the recognition of revenues; timing of expenses; and recording of assets, liabilities, and stockholders' equity.

Managerial Accounting

The managerial accounting system produces information for *internal* users, such as managers, executives, and workers. Thus, managerial accounting could be properly called *internal accounting*, and financial accounting could be called *external accounting*. Specifically, managerial accounting identifies, collects, measures, classifies, and reports financial and nonfinancial information that is useful to internal users in planning, controlling, and decision making.

Comparison of Financial and Managerial Accounting

When comparing financial accounting to managerial accounting, several differences can be identified. Some of the more important differences follow and are summarized in Exhibit 1.1.

- *Targeted users.* Managerial accounting focuses on providing information for internal users, while financial accounting focuses on providing information for external users.
- *Restrictions on inputs and processes.* Managerial accounting is not subject to the requirements of generally accepted accounting principles set by the SEC and the FASB that must be followed for financial reporting. The inputs and processes of financial accounting are well defined. Only certain kinds of economic events qualify as inputs, and processes must follow generally accepted methods. Unlike financial accounting, managerial accounting has no official body that prescribes the format, content, and rules for selecting inputs and processes and preparing reports.
- *Type of information.* The restrictions imposed by financial accounting tend to produce objective and verifiable financial information. For managerial accounting, information may be financial and nonfinancial and may be much more subjective in nature.
- *Time orientation.* Financial accounting has a historical orientation (i.e., looking through the rearview mirror). It records and reports events that have already happened. Although managerial accounting also records and reports events that have already occurred, it strongly emphasizes providing information about future events (i.e., looking through the front windshield). Management, for example, may want to know what it will cost to produce a product next year. This future orientation is necessary for planning and decision making.
- *Degree of aggregation.* Managerial accounting provides measures and internal reports used to evaluate the performance of entities, product lines, departments, and managers. Essentially, detailed information is needed and provided. Financial accounting, on the other hand, focuses on overall firm performance, providing a more aggregated viewpoint.
- *Breadth.* Managerial accounting is much broader than financial accounting. It includes aspects of managerial economics, industrial engineering, and management science as well as numerous other areas.

Exhibit 1.1

Comparison of Financial and Managerial Accounting

Financial Accounting	Managerial Accounting
• Externally focused	• Internally focused
• Must follow externally imposed rules	• No mandatory rules
• Objective financial information	• Financial and nonfinancial information; subjective information possible
• Historical orientation	• Emphasis on the future
• Information about the firm as a whole	• Internal evaluation and decisions based on very detailed information
• More self-contained	• Broad, multidisciplinary

Check Point

1. **Is the preparation of financial statements for the annual report a task more suited to managerial accounting or financial accounting?**

Answer:
Financial accounting. While managerial accounting provides important inputs (such as work-in-process inventory or cost of goods sold) to external financial statements, financial accounting focuses most heavily on producing financial statements for use by external parties.

2. **Is performance measurement information concerning internal product failure rates an example of financial accounting information or managerial accounting information?**

Answer:
Managerial accounting. Product failure rates are an example of important internal managerial accounting information that would be helpful in forecasting future financial accounting performance measures such as sales revenue.

CURRENT FOCUS OF MANAGERIAL ACCOUNTING

OBJECTIVE 3

Identify and explain the current focus of managerial accounting.

The business environment in which companies operate has changed dramatically over the past several decades. For instance, advances in technology, the Internet, the opening of markets around the world, increased competitive pressures, and increased complexity of strategy (e.g., alliances between **McDonald's** and **The Walt Disney Company** for promotional tie-ins) and operations all have combined to produce a global business environment. Effective managerial accounting systems also have changed in order to provide information that helps improve companies' planning, control, and decision-making activities. Several important uses of managerial accounting resulting from these advances include new methods of estimating product and service cost and profitability, understanding customer orientation, evaluating the business from a cross-functional perspective, and providing information useful in improving total quality.

Here's **Why It's important**

New Methods of Costing Products and Services

Today's companies need focused, accurate information on the cost of the products and services they produce. In the past, a company might have produced a few products that were roughly similar to one another. Only the cost of materials and labor might have differed from one product to another, and figuring out the cost of each unit was relatively easy. Now, with the increase in technology and automation, it is more difficult to generate the costing information needed by management. As Peter Drucker, internationally respected management guru, points out:

> Traditional cost accounting in manufacturing does not record the cost of nonproducing such as the cost of faulty quality, or of a machine being out of order, or of needed parts not being on hand. Yet these unrecorded and uncontrolled costs in some plants run as high as the costs that traditional accounting does record. By contrast, a new method of cost accounting developed in the last 10 years—called "activity-based" accounting—records all costs. And it relates them, as traditional accounting cannot, to value-added.[2]

Activity-based costing (ABC) is a more detailed approach to determining the cost of goods and services. ABC improves costing accuracy by emphasizing the cost of the many activities or tasks that must be done to produce a product or offer a service. **United Parcel Service Inc. (UPS)** used ABC to discover and manage the cost of the activities involved with shipping packages by truck, rather than by plane, in order to beat **FedEx** at its overnight delivery business in quick mid-distance (up to 500 miles) overnight deliveries.[3] Process-value analysis focuses on the way in which companies create value for customers. The objective is to find ways to perform necessary activities more efficiently and to eliminate those that do not create customer value.

Customer Orientation

Customer value is a key focus because firms can establish a competitive advantage by creating better customer value for the same or lower cost than competitors or creating equivalent value for lower cost than that of competitors. Customer value is the difference between what a customer receives and what the customer gives up when buying a product or service. When we talk about customer value, we consider the complete range of tangible and intangible benefits that a customer receives from a purchased product. Customers receive basic and special product features, service, quality, instructions for use, reputation, brand name, and other important factors. On the other hand, customers give up the cost of purchasing the product, the time and

---

2 Peter F. Drucker, "We Need to Measure, Not Count," *The Wall Street Journal* (April 13, 1993): A14.

3 Charles Haddad and Jack Ewing, "Ground Wars: UPS's Rapid Ascent Leaves FedEx Scrambling," *BusinessWeek* (May 21, 2001): 64–68.

Here's How It's Used: DATA ANALYTICS

UPS invested hundreds of millions of dollars in its Orion computer platform—a 1,000-page algorithm written by a team of 50 UPS engineers—to help managers and drivers determine the best delivery routes from both a fuel and time efficiency perspective, as well as a driver and customer preference perspective.[4] For example, many UPS customers prefer to receive their packages at approximately the same time each day regardless of the efficiency implications.

Similarly, most UPS drivers like to follow approximately the same path each day, regardless of the nature and variation of the day's particular customer orders. Experts estimate that UPS will earn back its hefty investment by reducing annual costs by approximately $300 million! The ability to integrate such "big data" analytics, financial impact factors, and human behavioral preferences represents a growing role and opportunity for managerial accountants to create value for their organization.

CONCEPT CLIP

effort spent acquiring and learning to use the product, and the costs of using, maintaining, and disposing of it.

Strategic Positioning Effective cost information can help the company identify strategies that increase customer value and, in so doing, create a sustainable competitive advantage.[5] Generally, firms choose one of two general strategies:

- *Cost leadership*: The objective of the cost leadership strategy is to provide the same or better value to customers at a *lower* cost than competitors.
- *Superior products through differentiation (e.g., highest performance quality, most desired product features, best customer service, etc.)*: A differentiation strategy strives to increase customer value by providing something to customers not provided by competitors. For example, **Best Buy**'s Geek Squad of computer technicians creates a competitive advantage for Best Buy by providing 24-hour in-home technical assistance for its customers. Accurate cost information is important to see whether or not the additional service provided by the Geek Squad adds more to revenue than it does to cost.

The Value Chain Successful pursuit of cost leadership and/or differentiation strategies requires an understanding of a firm's value chain. The **value chain** is the set of activities required to design, develop, produce, market, and deliver products and services, as well as provide support services to customers. Exhibit 1.2 illustrates the value chain.

A managerial accounting system should track information about a wide variety of activities that span the value chain. For example, **Apple** spends considerable effort researching the cost of developing, manufacturing, and servicing each new iteration of its iPhone and iPad products. Also, customer value can be increased by improving the speed of delivery and response, as many

Exhibit 1.2

The Value Chain

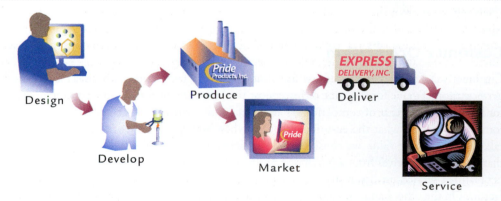

---

4 Steven Rosenbush and Laura Stevens, "At UPS, the Algorithm Is the Driver: Turn Right, Turn Left: Inside Orion, the 10-Year Effort to Squeeze Every Penny from Delivery Routes," *The Wall Street Journal* (February 16, 2015). Taken from http://www.wsj.com/articles/at-ups-the-algorithm-is-the-driver-1424136536.

5 Deloitte Insights, "Cutting Costs to Drive Growth," *CFO Journal* (August 27, 2013). Taken from http://deloitte.wsj.com/cfo/2013/08/27/cutting-costs-to-drive-growth-trends-among-the-fortune-1000/ on January 14, 2014.

customers believe that delivery delayed is delivery denied. **FedEx** exploited this part of the value chain and successfully developed a service that was not being offered by the **U.S. Postal Service**.

It is important to note that companies have internal customers as well. For example, the procurement process acquires and delivers parts and materials to producing departments. Providing high-quality parts on a timely basis to managers of producing departments is just as vital for procurement as it is for the company as a whole to provide high-quality goods to external customers. The emphasis on managing the internal value chain and servicing internal customers has revealed the importance of a cross-functional perspective.

Cross-Functional Perspective

In managing the value chain, a managerial accountant must understand and measure many functions of the business. Contemporary approaches to costing may include initial design and engineering costs, as well as manufacturing costs, and the costs of distribution, sales, and service. An individual well-schooled in the various definitions of cost, who understands the shifting definitions of cost from the short run to the long run, can be invaluable in determining what information is relevant in decision making. For example, strategic decisions may require a cost definition that assigns the costs of all value chain activities. In a long-run decision environment, companies in industries ranging from banking to retail to consumer products (e.g., **Bank of America**, **Kraft**) collectively spend billions of dollars per year across all functional areas to perform customer profitability analyses that identify their most, and least, profitable customers.[6] However, a short-run decision to determine the profitability of a special order (e.g., an offer made to **Bridgestone Firestone North American Tire** at year-end to use idle machinery to produce 1,000 extra tires for a local tire distributor) may require only the incremental costs of the special order in a single functional area.

Why try to relate managerial accounting to marketing, management, engineering, finance, and other business functions? When a value chain approach is taken and customer value is emphasized, we see that these disciplines are interrelated. For example, salespeople may offer deep discounts at the end of the year to meet their sales targets. If customers buy more product, the company's factories may have to work double shifts, incurring overtime pay, to meet this sudden increase in demand. A cross-functional perspective allows us to see the big picture—to see that the increased revenue came at the expense of much higher product costs. This broader vision allows managers to increase quality, reduce the time required to service customers (both internal and external), and improve efficiency.

Total Quality Management

Continuous improvement is the continual search for ways to increase the overall efficiency and productivity of activities by reducing waste, increasing quality, and managing costs. Managerial accounting information about the costs of products, customers, processes, and other objects of management interest can be the basis for identifying problems and alternative solutions.

---

6 E. Yoon, S. Carlotti, and D. Moore, "Make Your Best Customers Even Better," *Harvard Business Review* (March 2014).

Continuous improvement is fundamental for establishing excellence. A philosophy of **total quality management**, in which manufacturers strive to create an environment that will enable workers to manufacture perfect (zero-defect) products, has replaced the "acceptable quality" attitudes of the past. This emphasis on quality has also created a demand for a managerial accounting system that provides information about quality, including quality cost measurement and reporting for both manufacturing and service industries. For example, in response to increasing customer complaints regarding its laptop computer repair process, **Toshiba** formed an alliance with **UPS** in which UPS picks up the broken laptop, Toshiba fixes it, and UPS returns the repaired laptop to the customer. In order for this alliance to work effectively, both Toshiba and UPS require relevant managerial accounting information regarding the cost of existing poor quality and efforts to improve future quality.[7]

Increasingly, companies such as **Chrysler** are using techniques like Six Sigma and Design for Six Sigma (DFSS), together with various types of cost information, to achieve improved quality performance. Chrysler's goal is "to meet customer requirements and improve vehicle and system reliability while reducing development costs and cultivating innovation." On a related note, many companies attempt to increase organizational value by eliminating wasteful activities that exist throughout the value chain. In eliminating such waste, companies usually find that their accounting must also change. This change in accounting, referred to as **lean accounting**, organizes costs according to the value chain and collects both financial and nonfinancial information. The objective is to provide information to managers that supports their waste reduction efforts and to provide financial statements that better reflect overall performance, using both financial and nonfinancial information.

Finally, one of the more recent charges of managerial accountants is to help carry out the company's approach to enterprise risk management (ERM) and/or corporate sustainability reporting (CSR). ERM is a formal way for managerial accountants to identify and respond to the most important threats and business opportunities facing the organization. ERM is becoming increasingly important for long-term success. For example, it is well recognized that **Walmart**'s expert crisis management processes and teams repeatedly responded to the aftermath of Hurricane Katrina throughout Louisiana and Mississippi better and faster than did either local or federal government agencies (e.g., FEMA).[8] CSR represents the ways in which organizations choose to communicate the results of their various *business sustainability* practices to key internal and external stakeholders. The results of many public accounting firm surveys, as well as the *Institute of Management Accountants*, highlight the growing importance that organizations place on conducting effective risk management and corporate sustainability reporting practices.[9, 10]

Time as a Competitive Element

Time is a crucial element in all phases of the value chain. World-class firms reduce time to market by compressing design, implementation, and production cycles. These firms deliver products or services quickly by eliminating nonvalue-added time, which is time of no value to the customer (e.g., the time a product spends on the loading dock). Interestingly, decreasing nonvalue-added time appears to go hand in hand with increasing quality.

What about the relationship between time and product life cycles? The rate of technological innovation has increased for many industries, and the life of a particular product can be quite short. Managers must be able to respond quickly and decisively to changing market conditions

---

7 T. Friedman, *The World Is Flat: A Brief History of the Twenty-First Century* (New York: Farrar, Straus and Giroux, 2005).
8 A. Zimmerman and V. Bauerlein, "At Walmart, Emergency Plan Has Big Payoff," *The Wall Street Journal* (September 12, 2005): B1.
9 *Enterprise Risk Management: Tools and Techniques for Effective Implementation* (Montvale, NJ: Institute of Management Accountants, 2007), 1–31.
10 Ernst & Young and Boston College Center for Corporate Citizenship, *"Value of Sustainability Reporting,"* 2013. EYGM Limited.

and will rely on managerial accounting information to accomplish this. For example, **Hewlett-Packard** has found that it is better to be 50% over budget in new product development than to be six months late.

Efficiency

Improving efficiency is also a vital concern. Both financial and nonfinancial measures of efficiency are needed. Cost is a critical measure of efficiency. Trends in costs over time and measures of productivity changes can provide important measures of the efficacy of continuous improvement decisions. For these efficiency measures to be of value, costs must be properly defined, measured, and assigned; furthermore, production of output must be related to the inputs required, and the overall financial effect of productivity changes should be calculated.

Check Point

1. **Does Walmart more heavily emphasize a cost leadership or a product differentiation strategy?**

Answer:
Cost leadership. While Walmart likely attempts to differentiate its products from other discount retailers, its primary strategic focus is to continually reduce its costs in order to provide customers with products at the lowest price.

2. **The notion of "continuous improvement" is most closely associated with which of the following areas of managerial accounting focus: cross-functional perspective, customer orientation, or total quality management?**

Answer:
Total quality management. Continuous improvement in finding new and better ways to increase the overall efficiency and productivity of work activities is critical to improving product or service quality.

THE ROLE OF THE MANAGERIAL ACCOUNTANT

OBJECTIVE 4
Describe the role of managerial accountants in an organization.

 Here's **Why It's important**

Managerial accountants play a critically important decision-making support role in an organization. They assist those individuals who are responsible for carrying out an organization's basic objectives by providing them with various types of performance measurement information. Positions that have direct responsibility for the basic objectives of an organization are referred to as **line positions**. Positions that are supportive in nature and have only indirect responsibility for an organization's basic objectives are called **staff positions**. For **Kicker**, an organization that designs, produces, and sells audio equipment, the president, general manager, and vice presidents for sales and marketing and operations hold line positions. The purchasing manager and the cost accountant hold staff positions. Kicker's organization chart is shown in Exhibit 1.3.

Managerial accounting helps to improve a wide range of business decisions for organizations. For example, **Kicker**, a real company that makes car stereo systems, relies heavily on managerial accounting information, as we learned in extensive interviews with its top management. Boxes titled "Here's How It's Used at Kicker," like the one that follows, detail how the company has used managerial accounting information in its operations.

Exhibit 1.3   Kicker Inc. Organizational Chart

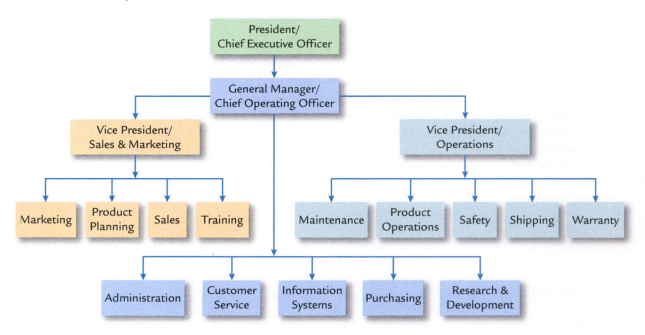

Here's How It's Used: AT KICKER

A division of **Stillwater Designs** and **Audio Inc.**, **Kicker** makes car stereo systems. Its signature logo, "Livin' Loud," gives you a hint as to the capabilities of the system. As the company website says, "Livin' Loud has always been the KICKER way—staying one step ahead of the pack—driven to create components that consistently raise the world's expectations for car stereo performance."

Forty years ago, car stereos were underpowered tinny affairs. They could power a radio or an 8-track tape deck. But the in-home listening experience coveted by audio buffs eluded the automobile market. In 1980, Stillwater Designs' founder and president Steve Irby developed the first full-range speaker enclosure designed specifically for automotive use—the Original Kicker®.

Stillwater Designs began in 1973 as a two-person operation, custom designing and building professional sound and musical instrument speaker systems for churches, auditoriums, and entertainers. Building upon the success of the Original Kicker, the company concentrated on the car audio market, applying the same research and design skills that made its first product so successful to the development of a complete line of high-performance components for car audio. What was once a company with two employees in a single-car garage is now a corporation with more than 200 employees in facilities totaling more than 500,000 square feet.

The Kicker brand includes many high-performance car stereo products, including subwoofers, midrange and midbass drivers, tweeters, crossovers, matched component systems, speakers, and power amplifiers. Kicker is proud to have won the prestigious Audio Video International Auto Sound Grand Prix Award, sponsored annually by *Audio-Video International* magazine. Winners are selected by retailers based on fidelity of sound reproduction, design engineering, reliability, craftsmanship and product integrity, and cost/performance ratio. In 2003, seven Kicker products earned Grand Prix awards. Awards emphasizing the performance of the company include the Governor's Award for Excellence in Exporting (2000) and the 1996 Oklahoma City International Trade Association designation as its International Business of the Year.

While Stillwater Designs originally handled research and design (R&D), manufacturing, and sales, it now concentrates primarily on R&D and sales. The bulk of manufacturing has been outsourced (performed by outside firms on a contract basis), although the company still builds some product and plans to build even more as it moves into its new facility for factory-installed audio systems. Engineering and audio research is Kicker president and chief executive officer Steve Irby's first love, and he still heads its design team. The day-to-day involvement of top management, coupled with an energetic workforce of talented individuals in all areas of the company's operations and an innate ability to create truly musical components, has been the reason for the company's remarkable success.

The **controller**, or chief accounting officer, for **Kicker** is located in the administration department. She supervises all accounting functions and reports directly to the general manager and chief operating officer (COO). Although managerial accountants, such as controllers and cost accounting managers, may wield considerable influence in the organization, they have no authority over the managers in the production area. The managers in line positions are the ones who set policy and make the decisions that impact the company. However, by supplying and interpreting accounting information, managerial accountants can have significant input into policies and decisions.

Because of the critical role that managerial accounting plays in the operation of an organization, the controller is often viewed as a member of the top management team and is encouraged to participate in planning, controlling, and decision-making activities. As the chief accounting officer, the controller has responsibility for both internal and external accounting requirements. In larger firms, this charge may include direct responsibility for internal auditing, cost accounting, financial accounting (including SEC reports and financial statements), systems accounting (including analysis, design, and internal controls), and taxes. The duties and organization of the controller's office vary from firm to firm. For example, in some firms, the internal audit department may report directly to the financial vice president; similarly, the systems department may report directly to the financial vice president or some other vice president.

In larger companies, the controller is separate from the treasury department. The **treasurer** is responsible for the finance function. Specifically, the treasurer raises capital and manages cash and investments. The treasurer may also be in charge of credit and collection and insurance.

No matter which position managerial accountants hold, they must support management in all phases of business decision making. As specialists in accounting, they must be intelligent, well prepared, up to date with new developments, and familiar with the customs and practices of all countries in which their firms operate. They also should be knowledgeable about the legal environment of business including important financial laws and regulations, such as the Dodd-Frank Act and the Sarbanes-Oxley Act.

Check Point

1. **Is the controller or the treasurer responsible for the finance function in large organizations?**

Answer:

In larger organizations, the controller is separate from the treasury department; thus, the treasurer is responsible for the finance function.

2. **Which position sits atop Kicker's organizational chart?**

Answer:

The president or chief executive officer.

MANAGERIAL ACCOUNTING AND ETHICAL CONDUCT

OBJECTIVE 5

Explain the importance of ethical behavior for managers and managerial accountants.

Here's **Why It's important**

Virtually all managerial accounting practices were developed to assist managers in maximizing profits. Traditionally, actions regarding the economic performance of the firm have been the overriding concern. Yet managers and managerial accountants should not become so focused on profits that they develop a belief that the only goal of a business is maximizing its net worth. The objective of profit maximization should be constrained by the requirement that profits be achieved through legal and ethical means.

Here's How It's Used: IN YOUR LIFE

Most students and young professionals rarely think about *ethics* until they are in the middle of a potential personal or professional crisis. Ethical conflicts often are assumed—incorrectly—to arise only for executives negotiating international business deals or employees working in "shady" industries. However, these commonly held sentiments could not be further from your student reality! For example, you might already have been asked to sign a student honor code at your university. If so, you likely realized that in order to comply, you are not allowed to cheat on exams or to turn in anything that is not 100% your own original work. But you might be surprised to realize that compliance often also requires that you share with university officials any and all knowledge you possess regarding cheating by *other* people! As another example, students can find themselves in an ethical quandary when they excitedly accept a full-time job offer as a sophomore or junior but then stumble into an even better job offer as a graduating senior. While many students might believe that they ultimately are entitled to the most lucrative or prestigious job they can find—even after they have accepted a full-time offer—most employers consider students reneging on a job offer acceptance to be unethical behavior. Finally, turning to your young professional life, managerial accounting students sometimes decide to work for various consulting organizations, such as **Bain**, **McKinsey**, **Deloitte Consulting**, **EY Parthenon**, **Boston Consulting Group**, or **Protiviti**. New hires often are asked to sign a "noncompete" agreement stating they will not start their own competing consulting organization and attempt to lure away (i.e., "poach") their former clients. As you can see, everyone must understand ethics!

Ethical Behavior

CONCEPT CLIP

Ethical behavior involves choosing actions that are right, proper, and just. Behavior can be right or wrong; it can be proper or improper; and the decisions we make can be fair or unfair. Though people often differ in their views of the meaning of the ethical terms cited, there seems to be a common principle underlying all ethical systems. This principle is expressed by the belief that each member of a group bears some responsibility for the well-being of other members. Willingness to sacrifice one's self-interest for the well-being of the group is the heart of ethical action.

This notion of sacrifice produces some core values—values that describe what is meant by right and wrong in more concrete terms. James W. Brackner, writing for the "Ethics Column" in *Management Accounting*, made the following observation:

> *For moral or ethical education to have meaning, there must be agreement on the values that are considered "right." Ten of these values are identified and described by Michael Josephson in "Teaching Ethical Decision Making and Principled Reasoning." The study of history, philosophy, and religion reveals a strong consensus as to certain universal and timeless values essential to the ethical life.*
>
> *These 10 core values yield a series of principles that delineate right and wrong in general terms. Therefore, they provide a guide to behavior.[11]*

The 10 core values referred to in the quotation include the following:

1. Honesty
2. Integrity
3. Promise keeping
4. Fidelity
5. Fairness
6. Caring for others

---

11 James W. Brackner, "Consensus Values Should Be Taught," *Management Accounting* (August 1992): 19. For a more complete discussion of the 10 core values, see also Michael Josephson, *Teaching Ethical Decision Making and Principled Reasoning, Ethics Easier Said Than Done* (Winter Los Angeles, CA: The Josephson Institute, 1988): 29–30.

7. Respect for others
8. Responsible citizenship
9. Pursuit of excellence
10. Accountability

Many of the well-known accounting scandals, such as those involving **Adelphia**, **WorldCom**, **HealthSouth**, **Parmalat**, and **McKesson**, provide evidence of the pressures faced by top managers and accountants to produce large net income numbers, especially in the short term. Unfortunately, such individuals often give in to these pressures when faced with questionable revenue- and cost-related judgments. For example, the scandal at WorldCom was committed because the CEO, Bernie Ebbers, coerced several of the top accountants at WorldCom to wrongfully record journal entries in the company's books that capitalized millions of dollars in costs as assets (i.e., on the balance sheet) rather than as expenses (i.e., on the income statement) that would have dramatically lowered current period net income. Eventually, WorldCom was forced to pay hundreds of millions of dollars to the U.S. government and to shareholders for its illegal and unethical actions. In addition, several of the top executives were sentenced to extensive prison time for their actions. The recent subprime mortgage crisis also highlights the importance of ethical considerations as some banks tried to increase their profits either by lending individuals more money than they could reasonably afford or using terms that were intentionally less clear, or transparent, than many outsiders thought they should be.[12]

Congress passed the **Sarbanes-Oxley Act (SOX)** in an attempt to limit securities frauds and accounting misconduct scandals like those associated with **Enron**, **WorldCom**, **Adelphia**, and **HealthSouth**. SOX led to increased attention on corporate ethics. While successful on many fronts, SOX has not prevented all subsequent frauds. Evidence is in the Allen Stanford securities fraud and the Bernard Maddoff ponzi scheme, which at the time was the world's biggest fraud, allegedly swindling investors out of a total of $50 billion.

Although it may seem contradictory, sacrificing self-interest for the collective good might not only be right and bring a sense of individual worth but might also make good business sense. Companies with a strong code of ethics can create strong customer and employee loyalty. While liars and cheats may win on occasion, their victories often are short-lived. Companies in business for the long term find that it pays to treat all of their constituents with honesty and loyalty.

Company Codes of Ethical Conduct

One needs only to hear the names "**Enron**, **FIFA**, **Toshiba**, or **Volkswagen**" to be reminded of the importance of ethical conduct.[13] To promote ethical behavior by managers and employees, organizations commonly establish standards of conduct referred to as Company Codes of Conduct. A quick review of various corporate codes of conduct shows some common ground. For example, **Coca-Cola**'s list of corporate values[14] includes leadership, collaboration, integrity, accountability, passion, diversity, and quality. **Boeing**'s Code of Conduct[15] states that it will "conduct its business fairly, impartially, in an ethical and proper manner, and in full compliance with all applicable laws and regulations." All employees must sign the code, and the company "requires that they understand the code, and ask questions, seek guidance, report

---

12 Jane Sasseen, "FBI Widens Net Around Subprime Industry: With 14 Companies Under Investigation, the Bureau's Scope Is the Entire Securitization Process," *BusinessWeek Online* (January 30, 2008). Taken from http://www. businessweek.com/stories/2008-01-30/fbi-widens-net-around-subprime-industrybusinessweek-business-news -stock-market-and-financial-advice on February 27, 2016.
13 C. Matthews and S. Gandel, "The 5 Biggest Corporate Scandals of 2015," *Fortune* (December 27, 2015).
14 Taken from Coca-Cola's website, http://www.coca-colacompany.com/our-company/mission-vision-values on February 27, 2016.
15 Taken from Boeing's website, http://www.boeing.com/resources/boeingdotcom/principles/ethics_and_compliance/ pdf/english.pdf on February 27, 2016.

suspected violations, and express concerns regarding compliance with this policy and the related procedures."

Important parts of corporate codes of conduct are integrity, performance of duties, and compliance with the rule of law. They also uniformly prohibit the acceptance of kickbacks and improper gifts, insider trading, and misappropriation of corporate information and assets. Some such as **Google**[16] outline employee responsibilities to each other, customers, suppliers, business partners, shareholders, governments, communities, and competitors, as well as the process and personnel to contact when they have a code-related question or concern.

Standards of Ethical Conduct for Managerial Accountants

In addition to organizations establishing standards of conduct for their managers and employees, professional associations also establish ethical standards. Both the American Institute of Certified Public Accountants (AICPA) and the Institute of Management Accountants (IMA) have established ethical standards for accountants. Professional accountants are bound by these codes of conduct.[17] Both the AICPA and IMA stress the importance of competence, confidentiality, integrity, and credibility or objectivity. The IMA's Ethics Center helps professionals and students understand and adhere to the highest standards of ethical business practices by offering numerous resources, such as its IMA Statement of Ethical Professional Practice, its Ethics Helpline, and various cases and other teaching materials.[18]

The IMA's Standards of Ethical Conduct for Management Accountants reflects the impact of the Sarbanes-Oxley Act. Now called the Statement of Ethical Professional Practice, the revised code considers global issues and incorporates the principles of the code of the International Federation of Accountants, which is the global association of professional accounting groups. In this statement, managerial accountants are told that "they shall not commit acts contrary to these standards nor shall they condone the commission of such acts by others in their organizations." The standards and the recommended resolution of ethical conflicts are presented in Exhibit 1.4.

Suppose a manager's bonus is linked to reported profits, with the bonus increasing as profits increase. Thus, the manager has an incentive to find ways to increase profits, including unethical approaches. A manager could delay promotions of deserving employees or use cheaper parts to produce a product. In either case, if the motive is simply to increase the bonus, the behavior could be labeled as unethical. Neither action is in the best interest of the company or its employees. Yet where should the blame be assigned? After all, the reward system strongly encourages the manager to increase profits. Is the reward system at fault, or is the manager who chooses to increase profits at fault? Or both?

In reality, both the manager and the reward system are probably at fault. It is important to design evaluation and reward systems so that incentives to pursue undesirable behavior are minimized. Yet designing a perfect reward system is not a realistic expectation. Managers also have an obligation to avoid abusing the system. Standard III-1 of the code reminds us that members have "a responsibility to (1) mitigate actual conflicts of interest … [and to] advise all parties of any potential conflicts." Basically, the prospect of an increased bonus (e.g., a favor) should not influence a manager to engage in unethical actions.

Can ethics be taught? Philosophers and ethicists from Socrates to those studying business ethics today agree that ethics can be taught and, even more importantly, learned. In fact, the IMA now requires continuing education in ethics, as do many of the state boards

---

16 Taken from Google's website, https://www.google.com/intl/en/about/company/philosophy/ on February 27, 2016.

17 The AICPA Code of Professional Conduct can be found at http://www.aicpa.org/Research/Standards/
    CodeofConduct/Pages/default.aspx.

18 Taken from the IMA Ethics Center's website, http://www.imanet.org/resources-publications/ethics-center on
    February 22, 2016.

Members of IMA shall behave ethically. A commitment to ethical professional practice includes overarching principles that express our values, and standards that guide our conduct.

PRINCIPLES

IMA's overarching ethical principles include: Honesty, Fairness, Objectivity, and Responsibility. Members shall act in accordance with these principles and shall encourage others within their organizations to adhere to them.

STANDARDS

A member's failure to comply with the following standards may result in disciplinary action.

I. COMPETENCE

Each member has a responsibility to:

1. Maintain an appropriate level of professional expertise by continually developing knowledge and skills.
2. Perform professional duties in accordance with relevant laws, regulations, and technical standards.
3. Provide decision support information and recommendations that are accurate, clear, concise, and timely.
4. Recognize and communicate professional limitations or other constraints that would preclude responsible judgment or successful performance of an activity.

II. CONFIDENTIALITY

Each member has a responsibility to:

1. Keep information confidential except when disclosure is authorized or legally required.
2. Inform all relevant parties regarding appropriate use of confidential information. Monitor subordinates' activities to ensure compliance.
3. Refrain from using confidential information for unethical or illegal advantage.

III. INTEGRITY

Each member has a responsibility to:

1. Mitigate actual conflicts of interest, regularly communicate with business associates to avoid apparent conflicts of interest. Advise all parties of any potential conflicts.
2. Refrain from engaging in any conduct that would prejudice carrying out duties ethically.
3. Abstain from engaging in or supporting any activity that might discredit the profession.

IV. CREDIBILITY

Each member has a responsibility to:

1. Communicate information fairly and objectively.
2. Disclose all relevant information that could reasonably be expected to influence an intended user's understanding of the reports, analyses, or recommendations.
3. Disclose delays or deficiencies in information, timeliness, processing, or internal controls in conformance with organization policy and/or applicable law.

RESOLUTION OF ETHICAL CONFLICT

In applying the Standards of Ethical Professional Practice, you may encounter problems identifying unethical behavior or resolving an ethical conflict. When faced with ethical issues, you should follow your organization's established policies on the resolution of such conflict. If these policies do not resolve the ethical conflict, you should consider the following courses of action:

1. Discuss the issue with your immediate supervisor except when it appears that the supervisor is involved. In that case, present the issue to the next level. If you cannot achieve a satisfactory resolution, submit the issue to the next management level. If your immediate superior is the chief executive officer or equivalent, the acceptable reviewing authority may be a group such as the audit committee, executive committee, board of directors, board of trustees, or owners. Contact with levels above the immediate superior should be initiated only with your superior's knowledge, assuming he or she is not involved. Communication of such problems to authorities or individuals not employed or engaged by the organization is not considered appropriate, unless you believe there is a clear violation of the law.
2. Clarify relevant ethical issues by initiating a confidential discussion with an IMA Ethics Counselor or other impartial advisor to obtain a better understanding of possible courses of action.
3. Consult your own attorney as to legal obligations and rights concerning the ethical conflict.

Source: Derived from the IMA website. Copyright © 2006 by Institute of Management Accountants, Inc. Reprint permission granted by Institute of Certified Management Accountants, Inc.

Exhibit 1.4

Statement of Ethical Professional Practice

of accountancy. Perhaps the biggest challenge with ethical dilemmas is that when they arise, employees frequently do not realize (1) that such a dilemma has arisen or (2) the "correct" action that should be taken to rectify the dilemma. Therefore, rather than attempt to study numerous ethical issues in one place, each chapter of this text includes an ethical dilemma or situation designed to increase awareness of the types of conduct considered unethical in business.

Check Point

1. **Which of the following items is *not* a common core value of ethical behavior as defined by James Brackner's "Ethics Column" in *Management Accounting*?**

   (a) Fairness, (b) Integrity, (c) Immediacy, (d) Accountability

   Answer:
   (c) Immediacy.

2. **How do groups like the IMA attempt to teach ethics?**

   Answer:
   Groups like the IMA attempt to help individuals learn ethics by requiring continuing education in ethics. Many state boards of accountancy also require ethics training.

OBJECTIVE 6

Identify three forms of certification available to managerial accountants.

 Why It's important

CERTIFICATION

As with the legal and medical professions, the accounting profession relies on certification to help promote ethical behavior, as well as to provide evidence that the certificate holder has achieved a minimum level of professional competence. The accounting profession offers three major forms of certification to managerial accountants:

- Certificate in Management Accounting
- Certificate in Public Accounting
- Certificate in Internal Auditing

Each certification offers particular advantages to a managerial accountant. In each case, an applicant must meet specific educational and experience requirements and pass a qualifying examination to become certified. Thus, all three certifications offer evidence that the holder has achieved a minimum level of professional competence. Furthermore, all three certifications require the holders to engage in continuing professional education in order to maintain certification. Because certification reveals a commitment to professional competency, most organizations encourage their managerial accountants to become certified. In addition, an increasing number of accountants also consider becoming a Certified Fraud Examiner (CFE),[19] which allows them to conduct expert work in the areas of fraud prevention, detection, and deterrence.[20]

The Certified Management Accountant

The Certificate in Management Accounting is designed to meet the specific needs of managerial accountants. A **Certified Management Accountant (CMA)** has passed a rigorous qualifying examination, met an experience requirement, and participates in continuing education.

---

19 For more information about the CFE process, see http://www.acfe.com/cfe-credential.aspx?gclid=CMm8vKO__ rsCFcsRMwodCWcAlQ (accessed January 15, 2014).

20 To learn more about the growing world of forensic accounting, see Crumbley, Heitger, and Smith, *"Forensic and Investigative Accounting,"* 6th edition, CCH.

One of the key requirements for obtaining the CMA is passing a qualifying examination. The following four areas are emphasized:

- economics, finance, and management
- financial accounting and reporting
- management reporting, analysis, and behavioral issues
- decision analysis and information systems

The parts to the examination reflect the needs of managerial accounting and underscore the earlier observation that managerial accounting has more of an interdisciplinary flavor than other areas of accounting.

One of the main purposes of the CMA was to establish managerial accounting as a recognized, professional discipline, separate from the profession of public accounting. Since its inception, the CMA program has been quite successful. Many firms now sponsor and pay for classes that prepare their managerial accountants for the qualifying examination as well as provide other financial incentives to encourage acquisition of the CMA.

The Certified Public Accountant

The Certificate in Public Accounting is the oldest and most well-known certification in accounting. The purpose of the certificate is to provide minimal professional qualification for external auditors. The responsibility of auditors is to provide assurance concerning the reliability of a firm's financial statements. Only a **Certified Public Accountant (CPA)** is permitted (by law) to serve as an external auditor. CPAs must pass a national examination and be licensed by the state in which they practice. Although the Certificate in Public Accounting does not have a managerial accounting orientation, many managerial accountants also hold this certificate.

The Certified Internal Auditor

The other certification available to internal accountants is the Certificate in Internal Auditing. Internal auditing differs from external auditing and managerial accounting, and many internal auditors felt a need for a specialized certification. The **Certified Internal Auditor (CIA)** has passed a comprehensive examination designed to ensure technical competence and has 2 years' experience.

Check Point

1. **Which of the following groups requires members to pass an examination as part of becoming a member?**

   (a) Certified Management Accountant, (b) Certified Internal Auditor, (c) Certified Public Accountant, (d) All three require an examination, (e) None of these requires an examination

   Answer:
   (d).

2. **What term is associated with accountants who meet certain requirements to conduct expert work in the areas of fraud prevention, detection, and deterrence?**

   Answer:
   These accountants are referred to as Certified Fraud Examiners.

SUMMARY OF LEARNING OBJECTIVES

LO1. Explain the meaning of managerial accounting.
- Managerial accounting information is used to identify problems and opportunities, solve problems and exploit opportunities, and assess organizational strategy and evaluate performance.
- Managerial accounting information helps managers in planning, controlling, and decision making.
- Planning is the detailed formulation of action to achieve a particular end.
- Controlling is the monitoring of a plan's implementation.
- Decision making is choosing among competing alternatives.

LO2. Explain the differences between managerial accounting and financial accounting.
- Managerial accounting is:
  - intended for internal users.
  - not subject to rules for external financial reporting (e.g., GAAP and SEC regulations).
  - subjective.
  - able to use both financial and nonfinancial measures of performance.
  - able to give a broader, interdisciplinary perspective.
- Financial accounting is:
  - directed toward external users.
  - subject to externally imposed rules (e.g., GAAP and SEC regulations).
  - able to provide audited, objective financial information.

LO3. Identify and explain the current focus of managerial accounting.
- It supports management focus on customer value, total quality management, and time-based competition.
- Information about value chain activities and customer sacrifice (such as post-purchase costs) is collected and made available.
- Activity-based management is a major innovative response to the demand for more accurate and relevant managerial accounting information.
- The nature of managerial accounting information system may depend on the strategic position of the firm:
  - Cost leadership strategy
  - Product differentiation strategy
  - Lean accounting

LO4. Describe the role of managerial accountants in an organization.
- They are responsible for identifying, collecting, measuring, analyzing, preparing, interpreting, and communicating information.
- They must be sensitive to the information needs of managers.
- They serve as staff members of the organization and are part of the management team.

LO5. Explain the importance of ethical behavior for managers and managerial accountants.
- A strong ethical sense is needed to resist efforts to change economic information that may present an untrue picture of firm performance.
- Many firms have a written code of ethics or code of conduct.
- The IMA has a code of ethics for managerial accountants.

LO6. Identify three forms of certification available to managerial accountants.
- The Certificate of Management Accounting serves managerial accountants.
- The Certificate of Public Accounting serves and is required for those who practice public accounting.
- The Certificate of Internal Auditing serves internal auditors.

KEY TERMS

Certified Internal Auditor (CIA), 21, has passed a comprehensive examination designed to ensure technological competence and has 2 years of experience.

Certified Management Accountant (CMA), 20, has passed a rigorous qualifying examination, met an experience requirement, and participates in continuing education.

Certified Public Accountant (CPA), 21, has passed a national examination and must be licensed by the state in which he or she wishes to practice accounting (e.g., in audit, tax, etc.).

Continuous improvement, 11, searching for ways to increase the overall efficiency and productivity of activities by decreasing waste, increasing quality, and reducing costs.

Controller, 15, the chief accounting officer in an organization.

Controlling, 5, the managerial activity of monitoring a plan's implementation and taking corrective action as needed.

Decision making, 6, the process of choosing among competing alternatives.

Ethical behavior, 16, choosing actions that are right, proper, and just.

Financial accounting, 7, a type of accounting focused primarily on the creation of financial information for external users.

Lean accounting, 12, an accounting practice that organizes costs according to the value chain to help managers eliminate waste and, ultimately, reduce costs and improve financial performance.

Line positions, 13, positions that have direct responsibility for the basic objectives of an organization.

Managerial accounting, 4, a type of accounting focused primarily on providing internal users with the necessary financial and nonfinancial information to help them make the best possible decisions for the company.

Planning, 5, a management activity that involves the detailed formulation of action to achieve a particular end.

Sarbanes-Oxley Act (SOX), 17, passed in response to revelations of misconduct and fraud by several well-known firms, this legislation established stronger governmental regulation of public companies in the United States, from enhanced oversight (PCAOB) to increased auditor independence and tightened regulation of corporate governance.

Staff positions, 13, positions that are supportive in nature and have only indirect responsibility for an organization's basic objectives.

Total quality management, 12, a management philosophy in which manufacturers strive to create an environment that will enable workers to manufacture perfect (zero-defect) products.

Treasurer, 15, the individual responsible for the finance function; raises capital and manages cash and investments.

Value chain, 10, the set of activities required to design, develop, produce, market (and deliver), and service products and services to customers.

DISCUSSION QUESTIONS

1. What is managerial accounting?
2. What are the three broad objectives of managerial accounting?
3. Who are the users of managerial accounting information?

4. Should a managerial accounting system provide both financial and nonfinancial information? Explain.
5. What is meant by controlling?
6. Describe the connection between planning, feedback, and controlling.
7. How do managerial accounting and financial accounting differ?
8. Explain the role of financial reporting in the development of managerial accounting. Why has this changed in recent years?
9. Explain the meaning of customer value. How is focusing on customer value changing managerial accounting?
10. What is the value chain? Why is it important?
11. Explain why today's managerial accountant must have a cross-functional perspective.
12. Briefly explain the practice of enterprise risk management and the role that can be played by managerial accountants in enterprise risk management.
13. What is the difference between a staff position and a line position?
14. The controller should be a member of the top management staff. Do you agree or disagree? Explain.
15. What is ethical behavior? Is it possible to teach ethical behavior in a managerial accounting course?
16. Briefly describe some of the common themes or pressures faced by executives who commit corporate fraud.
17. Identify the three forms of accounting certification. Which form of certification do you believe is best for a managerial accountant? Why?

MULTIPLE-CHOICE QUESTIONS

1-1 The provision of accounting information for internal users is known as

a. accounting.
b. financial accounting.
c. managerial accounting.
d. information provision.
e. accounting for planning and control.

1-2 The use and importance of managerial accounting is growing in each of the following areas except for

a. enterprise risk management.
b. nanotechnology advancements.
c. corporate sustainability reporting.
d. quality accounting.
e. lean accounting.

1-3 Setting objectives and identifying methods to achieve those objectives is called

a. planning.
b. decision making.
c. controlling.
d. performance evaluation.
e. None of these.

1-4 The process of choosing among competing alternatives is called

a. planning.
b. decision making.
c. controlling.
d. performance evaluation.
e. None of these.

1-5 Which of the following is a characteristic of managerial accounting?

    a. There is an internal focus.
    b. Subjective information may be used.
    c. There is an emphasis on the future.
    d. It is broad-based and multidisciplinary.
    e. All of these.

1-6 An effective managerial accounting system should track information about an organization's activities in which of the following areas?

    a. Development
    b. Marketing
    c. Production
    d. Design
    e. All of these.

1-7 In terms of strategic positioning, which two general strategies may be chosen by a company?

    a. Revenue production and cost enhancement
    b. Activity-based costing and value chain emphasis
    c. Increasing customer value and decreasing supplier orientation
    d. Cost leadership and product differentiation
    e. Product differentiation and cost enhancement

1-8 Which of the following is *not* a common form of certification for managerial accountants?

    a. Certificate in Internal Auditing
    b. Certificate in External Auditing
    c. Certificate in Public Accounting
    d. Certificate in Management Accounting

1-9 The chief accounting officer for a firm is the

    a. chief executive officer.
    b. chief operating officer.
    c. vice president of sales.
    d. production head.
    e. controller.

1-10 The objective of profit maximization should be constrained by the requirement that profits be achieved through

    a. legal means only.
    b. ethical means only.
    c. any means possible.
    d. both legal and ethical means.
    e. None of these.

EXERCISES

Exercise 1-11 The Managerial Process

OBJECTIVE ▸ 1

Each of the following scenarios requires the use of accounting information to carry out one or more managerial accounting objectives.

    a. **Laboratory Manager:** An HMO approached me recently and offered us its entire range of blood tests. It provided a price list revealing the amount it is willing to pay for each test.

(Continued)

In many cases, the prices are below what we normally charge. I need to know the costs of the individual tests to assess the feasibility of accepting its offer and perhaps suggest price adjustments on some of the tests.

b. **Operating Manager:** This report indicates that we have 30% more defects than originally targeted. An investigation into the cause has revealed the problem. We were using a lower-quality material than expected, and the waste has been higher than normal. By switching to the quality level originally specified, we can reduce the defects to the planned level.

c. **Divisional Manager:** Our market share has increased because of higher-quality products. Current projections indicate that we should sell 25% more units than last year. I want a projection of the effect that this increase in sales will have on profits. I also want to know our expected cash receipts and cash expenditures on a month-by-month basis. I have a feeling that some short-term borrowing may be necessary.

d. **Plant Manager:** Foreign competitors are producing goods with lower costs and delivering them more rapidly than we can to customers in our markets. We need to decrease the cycle time and increase the efficiency of our manufacturing process. There are two proposals that should help us accomplish these goals, both of which involve investing in computer-aided manufacturing. I need to know the future cash flows associated with each system and the effect each system has on unit costs and cycle time.

e. **Manager:** At the last board meeting, we established an objective of earning a 25% return on sales. I need to know how many units of our product we need to sell to meet this objective. Once I have the estimated sales in units, we need to outline a promotional campaign that will take us where we want to be. However, in order to compute the targeted sales in units, I need to know the expected unit price and a lot of cost information.

f. **Manager:** Perhaps the Harrison Medical Clinic should not offer a full range of medical services. Some services seem to be having a difficult time showing any kind of profit. I am particularly concerned about the mental health service. It has not shown a profit since the clinic opened. I want to know what costs can be avoided if I drop the service. I also want some assessment of the impact on the other services we offer. Some of our patients may choose this clinic because we offer a full range of services.

Required:

Select the managerial accounting objective(s) that are applicable for each scenario: planning, controlling (including performance evaluation), or decision making.

OBJECTIVE **2** ▶ **Exercise 1-12 Differences between Managerial Accounting and Financial Accounting**

Jenna Suarez, the controller for Arben Company, has faced the following situations in the past 2 weeks:

a. Ben Heald, head of production, wondered whether it would be more cost effective to buy parts partially assembled or to buy individual parts and assemble them at the Arben factory.

b. The president of Arben reminded Jenna that the stockholders' meeting was coming up, and he needed her to prepare a PowerPoint® presentation showing the income statement and balance sheet information for last year.

c. Ellen Johnson, vice president of sales, has decided to expand the sales offices for next year. She sent Jenna the information on next year's rent and depreciation information for budgeting purposes.

d. Jenna's assistant, Mike, received the information from Ellen on depreciation and added it to depreciation expenses and accumulated depreciation on office equipment.

e. Jenna compared the budgeted spending on materials used in production with the actual spending on materials used in production. Materials spending was significantly higher than expected. She set up a meeting to discuss this outcome with Ben Heald so that he could explain it.

Required:

Determine whether each request is relatively more *managerial accounting oriented* or *financial accounting oriented*.

Exercise 1-13 Customer Value, Strategic Positioning

OBJECTIVE ▶ 3

Adriana Alvarado has decided to purchase a personal computer. She has narrowed the choices to two: Drantex and Confiar. Both brands have the same processing speed, 6.4 gigabytes of hard-disk capacity, two USB ports, and a DVDRW drive, and each comes with the same basic software support package. Both come from mail-order companies with good reputations. The selling price for each is identical. After some review, Adriana discovers that the cost of operating and maintaining Drantex over a 3-year period is estimated to be $300. For Confiar, the operating and maintenance cost is $600. The sales agent for Drantex emphasized the lower operating and maintenance costs. The agent for Confiar, however, emphasized the service reputation of the product and the faster delivery time (Confiar can be purchased and delivered 1 week sooner than Drantex). Based on all the information, Adriana has decided to buy Confiar.

Required:

1. What is the total product purchased by Adriana?
2. **CONCEPTUAL CONNECTION** How does the strategic positioning differ for the two companies?
3. **CONCEPTUAL CONNECTION** When asked why she decided to buy Confiar, Adriana responded, "I think that Confiar offers more value than Drantex." What are the possible sources of this greater value? What implications does this have for the managerial accounting information system?
4. **CONCEPTUAL CONNECTION** Suppose that Adriana's decision was prompted mostly by the desire to receive the computer quickly. Informed that it was losing sales because of the longer time to produce and deliver its products, the management of the company producing Drantex decided to improve delivery performance by improving its internal processes. These improvements decreased the number of defective units and the time required to produce its product. Consequently, delivery time and costs both decreased, and the company was able to lower its prices on Drantex. Explain how these actions translate into strengthening the competitive position of the Drantex PC relative to the Confiar PC. Also discuss the implications for the managerial accounting information system.

Exercise 1-14 Line versus Staff

OBJECTIVE ▶ 4

The following describes the job responsibilities of two employees of Barney Manufacturing.

Joan Dennison, Cost Accounting Manager. Joan is responsible for measuring and collecting costs associated with the manufacture of the garden hose product line. She is also responsible for preparing periodic reports that compare the actual costs with planned costs. These reports are provided to the production line managers and the plant manager. Joan helps to explain and interpret the reports.

Steven Swasey, Production Manager. Steven is responsible for the manufacture of the high-quality garden hose. He supervises the line workers, helps to develop the production schedule, and is responsible for seeing that production quotas are met. He is also held accountable for controlling manufacturing costs.

Required:

CONCEPTUAL CONNECTION Identify Joan and Steven as line or staff and explain your reasons.

OBJECTIVE 5

Exercise 1-15 Ethical Behavior

Consider the following scenario between Dave, a printer, and Steve, an assistant in the local university's athletic department.

Steve: Dave, our department needs to have 10,000 posters printed for the basketball team for next year. Here's the mock-up, and we'll need them in a month. How much will you charge?

Dave: Well, given the costs I have for ink and paper, I can come in at around $5,000.

Steve: Great, here's what I want you to do. Print me up an invoice for $7,500. That's our budget.

Then, when they pay you, you give me a check for $2,500. I'll make sure that you get the job.

Required:

CONCEPTUAL CONNECTION Is Steve's proposal ethical? What should Dave do?

OBJECTIVE 5

Exercise 1-16 Ethical Behavior

Manager: If I can reduce my costs by $40,000 during this last quarter, my division will show a profit that is 10% above the planned level, and I will receive a $10,000 bonus. However, given the projections for the fourth quarter, it does not look promising. I really need that $10,000. I know of one way that I can qualify. All I have to do is lay off my three most expensive salespeople. After all, most of the orders are in for the fourth quarter, and I can always hire new sales personnel at the beginning of the next year.

Required:

CONCEPTUAL CONNECTION What is the right choice for the manager to make? Why did the ethical dilemma arise? Is there any way to redesign the accounting reporting system to discourage the type of behavior that the manager is contemplating?

OBJECTIVE 5

Exercise 1-17 Ethical Issues

The following statements have appeared in newspaper editorials:

1. Business students come from all segments of society. If they have not been taught ethics by their families and by their elementary and secondary schools, a business school can have little effect.
2. Sacrificing self-interest for the collective good won't happen unless a majority of Americans also accept this premise.
3. Competent executives manage people and resources for the good of society. Monetary benefits and titles are simply the by-products of doing a good job.
4. Unethical firms and individuals, like high rollers in Las Vegas, are eventually wiped out financially.

Required:

CONCEPTUAL CONNECTION Assess and comment on each of the statements.

OBJECTIVE 5

Exercise 1-18 Ethical Issues

Bedron Company is a closely held investment service group that has been quite successful over the past 5 years, consistently providing most members of the top management group with 50% bonuses. In addition, both the chief financial officer and the chief executive officer have received 100% bonuses. Bedron expects this trend to continue.

Recently, Bedron's top management group, which holds 35% of the outstanding shares of common stock, has learned that a major corporation is interested in acquiring Bedron. The other corporation's initial offer is attractive and is several dollars per share higher than Bedron's current share price. One member of management told a group of employees under him about the potential offer. He suggested that they might want to purchase more Bedron stock at the current price in anticipation of the takeover offer.

Required:

CONCEPTUAL CONNECTION Do you think that the employees should take the action suggested by their boss? Suppose the action is prohibited by Bedron's code of ethics. Now suppose that it is not prohibited by Bedron's code of ethics. Is the action acceptable in that case?

Exercise 1-19 Company Codes of Conduct   OBJECTIVE ▸ 5

Using the Internet, locate the code of conduct for three different companies.

Required:

CONCEPTUAL CONNECTION Briefly describe each code of conduct. How are they similar? How are they different?

2 Basic Managerial Accounting Concepts

After studying Chapter 2, you should be able to:

1 ▶ Explain the meaning of cost and how costs are assigned to products and services.

2 ▶ Define the various costs of manufacturing products and providing services as well as the costs of selling and administration.

3 ▶ Prepare income statements for manufacturing and service organizations.

Yuri Arcurs/Shutterstock.com

EXPERIENCE MANAGERIAL DECISIONS

with Little Guys Home Electronics

An 80-inch, 4K ultra high-definition television creates an aura of intense realism for sports aficionados as they watch with unparalleled clarity the fuzz on the tennis ball as it barely catches the line during a night match at the U.S. Open or the insignia on the football as Tom Brady throws yet another spiral touchdown pass. Using a combination of effective cost-plus pricing and marketplace knowledge, **Little Guys Home Electronics** has, for years, helped to bring such exciting sporting events to life for its thousands of customers. Correct pricing decisions are crucial in the home entertainment market, where the profit margin on video products is only 2 to 3%.

Little Guys sets prices by marking up full costs and ensuring that the final price falls within a range between the suggested retail price and the minimum advertised price, both of which are affected by the manufacturer and the marketplace. Its managerial accountants must understand cost behavior to be able to predict costs accurately in order for effective markup and pricing decisions to be made. What types of costs does Little Guys consider in its markups? Several examples include product purchases and shipping costs, warehousing costs, labor (including employee health care and retirement benefits as well as other labor support costs), store insurance, advertising, delivery truck investments and maintenance, and customer service trips. Also, future demand must be estimated so that Little Guys can figure out how much to charge for each television, receiver, and the like, such that all costs across the value chain are covered and the desired profit is achieved. Armed with an effective pricing strategy involving judgment about costs, markup percentages, and future market trends, Little Guys hopes to continue delivering exciting home electronics products and services to Chicago-area families for years to come.

> "Using a combination of effective cost-plus pricing and marketplace knowledge, Little Guys Home Electronics has, for years, helped to bring such exciting sporting events to life for its thousands of customers."

OBJECTIVE

Explain the meaning of cost and how costs are assigned to products and services.

Here's **Why It's important**

THE MEANING AND USES OF COST

One of the most important yet difficult tasks of managerial accounting is to determine the cost of products, services, customers, and other items of interest to managers. Therefore, we need to understand the meaning of cost and the ways in which costs can be used to make decisions, both for small entrepreneurial businesses and large international businesses. For example, consider a small gourmet restaurant and its owner Courtney, who also is the head chef. In addition to understanding the complexities of gourmet food preparation, Courtney needs to understand the breakdown of the restaurant's costs into various categories in order to make effective operating decisions. Cost categories of particular interest include:

- direct costs (food and beverages)
- indirect costs (laundry of linens)

On a larger scale, local banks operating in college communities often look at the cost of providing basic checking account services to students. These accounts typically lose money—that is, the accounts cost more to service than they yield in fees and interest revenue. However, the bank finds that students already banking with them are more likely to take out student loans through the bank, and these loans are very profitable. As a result, the bank may actually decide to expand its offerings to students when the related loan business is considered.

Cost

Cost is the amount of cash or cash equivalent sacrificed for goods and/or services that are expected to bring a current or future benefit to the organization. If a furniture manufacturer buys lumber for $10,000, then the cost of that lumber is $10,000 cash. Sometimes, one asset is traded for another asset. Then the cost of the new asset is measured by the value of the asset given up (the cash equivalent). If the same manufacturer trades office equipment valued at $8,000 for a forklift, then the cost of the forklift is the $8,000 value of the office equipment traded for it. Cost is a dollar measure of the resources used to achieve a given benefit. Managers strive to minimize the cost of achieving benefits. Reducing the cost required to achieve a given benefit means that a firm is becoming more efficient.

Here's How It's Used: **IN YOUR LIFE**

Making financially sound decisions requires that the costs associated with those decisions be clearly identified and accurately estimated. The exact purpose, or decision, for which the costs are being estimated must be determined—this purpose is referred to as a "cost object." *Individuals*, as well as businesses, must understand cost objects for various personal decisions. For example, as a prospective college student, Hannah wanted to know *how much it costs to obtain a college education*. Therefore, Hannah asked this question of her parents, her friends, and a family friend who works in a bank. However, she soon learned that this question was much more complicated than she had realized. Every time she asked this exact **same** question, she received a very **different** answer. Hannah quickly became concerned as she wondered if she could afford college. So she went back and asked everyone for a specific breakdown of the costs that went into their estimates. Hannah heard many specific costs including tuition, food, dormitory housing, gas for driving home on weekends, books and online access licenses, apartment utilities, plane fare for spring break vacations, clothes, scholarship offsets, computer, bar money, and weekend entertainment funds. Hannah realized that everyone had made very different assumptions. Some people assumed an out-of-state university, others used an in-state university, and yet others an online education. In addition, some people assumed that Hannah wanted a *total* cost analysis for food, gas, and *all* living expenses, while others assumed she wanted an *incremental* cost analysis for costs that she would incur *only* if she pursued college (e.g., tuition, fees). Finally, her banking friend also included the *opportunity cost* of college, or the wages she would give up by not being able to work a full-time job while in college.[1] This experience taught her the importance of understanding cost objects. Hannah now feels much better about her college selection process, including the steps she should take to prepare financially and enjoy her college experience!

---

1 The concept of opportunity cost will be discussed more fully later in this chapter, as well as in Chapter 8.

Costs are incurred to produce future benefits. In a profit-making firm, those benefits usually mean revenues. As costs are used up in the production of revenues, they are said to expire. Expired costs are called **expenses**. On the income statement, expenses are deducted from revenues to determine income (also called *profit*). For a company to remain in business, revenues must be larger than expenses. In addition, the income earned must be large enough to satisfy the owners of the firm.

We can look more closely at the relationship between cost and revenue by focusing on the units sold. The revenue per unit is called **price**. In everyday conversation, we have a tendency to use cost and price as synonyms, because the price of an item (e.g., an iPhone) is the cost to us. However, accounting courses take the viewpoint of the owner of the company. In that case, cost and price are *not* the same. Instead, for the company, revenue and price are the same. Price must be greater than cost in order for the firm to earn income. Hence, managers need to know cost and trends in cost. For example, the price a consumer pays for a fleece jacket from **The North Face** might be $250, while the total cost that the company incurs to design, manufacture, deliver, and service that jacket is much lower than the $250 price it charges consumers. Remember that **Little Guys Home Electronics** must be especially careful to set prices above its costs because profit margins (i.e., price minus cost) on most products and services in the home entertainment industry are extremely small (e.g., only 2 to 3%).

Cost Objects

Managerial accounting systems are structured to measure and assign costs to entities called *cost objects*. A **cost object** is any item such as a product, customer, department, project, geographic region, plant, and so on, for which costs are measured and assigned. For example, if **Fifth Third Bank** wants to determine the cost of a platinum credit card, then the cost object is the platinum credit card. All costs related to the platinum card are added in, such as the cost of mailings to potential customers, the cost of employee labor and information technology software programs dedicated to receiving and resolving credit card customers' calls, the portion of the computer department that processes platinum card transactions and bills, and so on.

CONCEPT CLIP

Accumulating and Assigning Costs

Accumulating costs is the way that costs are measured and recorded. The accounting system typically does this job quite well. When the company receives a phone bill, for example, the bookkeeper records an addition to the telephone expense account and an addition to the liability account, Accounts Payable. In this way, the cost is *accumulated*. It would be easy to tell, at the end of the year, the total spending on phone calls. Accumulating costs tells the company what was spent. However, that usually is not enough information. The company also wants to know why the money was spent. In other words, it wants to know how costs were assigned to cost objects.

Assigning costs is the way that a cost is linked to some cost object. A cost object is something for which a company wants to know the cost. For example, of the total phone expense, how much was for the sales department, and how much was for manufacturing? *Assigning* costs tells the company why the money was spent. In this case, cost assignment tells whether the money spent on phone calls was to support the manufacturing or the selling of the product. As we will discuss in later chapters, cost assignment typically is more difficult than cost accumulation.

Assigning Costs to Cost Objects

Costs can be assigned to cost objects in a number of ways. Relatively speaking, some methods are more accurate, and others are simpler. The choice of a method depends on a number of factors, such as the need for accuracy. The notion of accuracy is a relative concept and has to do with the reasonableness and logic of the cost assignment methods used. The objective is to

Here's How It's Used: AT DELTA

For Which Business Activities Do We Need an Estimate of Cost?

You are the chief financial officer for **Delta Air Lines**. Managing the company's numerous costs is critically important in the fiercely competitive airline industry. Therefore, one of your major tasks is deciding which costs to manage in order to achieve the company's profitability targets. In other words, you must identify the airline's most important cost objects to track, measure, and control.

Which cost objects would you select as critical to the company's success?

Certain airline cost objects are obvious, such as the cost of operating a flight, which includes jet fuel (**Delta** spends over $10 billion annually for jet fuel)[2] and labor costs for pilots, flight crews, and maintenance staffs. However, even the costs of these obvious cost objects can become challenging. For example, when an airline operates multiple types of aircraft, it incurs additional costs to train workers and store spare parts for each aircraft type (i.e., the total cost of training and maintaining 100 aircraft of two different types is greater than the same number of aircraft all of one type). Airlines might be even more specific with certain cost objects, such as when they focus on the cost per available seat mile (or CASM as industry experts refer to it), which typically falls in the 6 to 10 cent range for most airlines.

Other airline cost objects are even more challenging. For example, you likely did not include the cost of managing crises as an important cost object. However, according to the International Air Transit Association, the airline industry took an estimated $1.7 billion hit from disrupted airline travel resulting from the volcanic ash cloud caused by the eruption of the Icelandic volcano Eyjafjallajokull.[3]

Finally, you might consider the cost object of processing customers, such as loading and unloading passengers and their baggage on and off of flights. For example, airlines have charged fees for using curbside check-in services, consuming soft drinks during flight, using pillows and blankets while onboard, selecting seats prior to the day of the flight, and checking bags. **Spirit Airlines** raised many customer (and even regulator) eyebrows by being the first airline to charge passengers ($45) for their carry-on bags.[4]

Like any company, an airline can identify and manage any cost objects it so desires. Sometimes the most difficult part of effective cost management is the first step—deciding on the exact items for which one needs to understand the cost. Mistakes in selecting the cost objects almost always lead to poor decisions and subpar performance.

measure and assign costs as well as possible, given management objectives. For example, suppose you and three of your friends go out to dinner at a local pizza parlor. When the bill comes, everything has been added together for a total of $36. How much is your share? One easy way to find your share is to divide the bill evenly among you and your friends. In that case, you each owe $9 ($36/4). But suppose that one of you had a small salad and drink (totaling $5), while another had a specialty pizza, appetizer, and beer (totaling $15). Clearly, it is possible to identify what each person had and assign costs that way. The second method is more accurate, but also more work. Which method you choose will depend on how important it is to you to assign the specific meal costs to each individual. It is the same way in accounting. There are a number of ways to assign costs to cost objects. Some methods are quick and easy but may be inaccurate. Other methods are much more accurate, but involve much more work. (In business, more work equals more expense.)

Direct Costs   **Direct costs** are those costs that can be easily and accurately traced to a cost object. When we say that a cost is easy to trace, we often mean that the relationship between the cost and the object can be physically observed and is easy to track. The more costs that can be traced to the object, the more accurate are the cost assignments. For example, suppose that Chef Courtney, from our earlier discussion, wants to know the cost of emphasizing fresh, in-season fruits and vegetables in her entrees. The purchase cost of the fruits and vegetables would be relatively easy to determine.

---

2 From Delta Air Lines' 2015 Annual Report.

3 www.guardian.co.uk/business/2010/apr/21/airline-industry-cost-volcanic-ash (accessed May 8, 2010).

4 Joan Lowy, "Spirit CEO Says Carry-on Fees Will Be Disclosed," *NBCNews.com* (May 6, 2010). Taken from www.msnbc.msn.com/id/37004725/ns/travel-news/.

Indirect Costs Some costs, however, are hard to trace. **Indirect costs** are costs that cannot be easily and accurately traced to a cost object. For example, Courtney incurs additional costs in scouting the outlying farms and farmers' markets (as opposed to simply ordering fruits and vegetables from a distributor). She must use her own time and automobile to make the trips. Farmers' markets may not deliver, so Courtney must arrange for a coworker with a van to pick up the produce. By definition, fruits and vegetables that are currently in season will be out of season (i.e., unavailable) in a few weeks. This seasonality means that Courtney must spend more time revising menus and developing new recipes that can be adapted to restaurant conditions. In addition, waste and spoilage may increase until Courtney and the kitchen staff learn just how much to order. These costs are difficult to assign to the meals prepared and sold. Therefore, they are indirect costs. Some businesses refer to indirect costs as overhead costs or support costs. Exhibit 2.1 shows direct and indirect costs being assigned to cost objects.

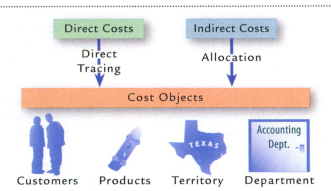

Exhibit 2.1

Object Costing

Assigning Indirect Costs Even though indirect costs cannot be traced to cost objects, it is still important to assign them. This assignment usually is accomplished by using allocation. **Allocation** means that an indirect cost is assigned to a cost object by using a reasonable and convenient method. Since no clearly observable causal relationship exists, allocating indirect costs is based on convenience or some assumed causal linkage. For example, consider the cost of heating and lighting a plant in which five products are manufactured. Suppose that this utility cost is to be assigned to these five products. It is difficult to see any causal relationship between utility costs and each unit of product manufactured. Therefore, a convenient way to allocate this cost is to assign it in proportion to the direct labor hours used by each product. This method is relatively easy and accomplishes the purpose of ensuring that all costs are assigned to units produced. Allocating indirect costs is important for a variety of reasons. For example, allocating indirect costs to products is needed to determine the value of inventory and of cost of goods

Here's How It's Used: AT LITTLE GUYS HOME ELECTRONICS

Returning briefly to the **Little Guys Home Electronics** business from the chapter opening, the prices set by Little Guys management are heavily dependent on understanding the company's costs, both traced direct and allocated indirect, for each product. The more difficult costs to estimate and, therefore, use appropriately in setting prices are the indirect, or overhead, costs. According to David, a partner in Little Guys, the most difficult part of pricing is deciding how accurately the indirect costs—such as inventory warehousing, support role employee labor, store insurance, delivery truck maintenance and rental (when the store owned trucks are in the shop for repair), and health care—have been allocated to each home electronics product. For example, if management believes that too few indirect costs have been allocated to a set of Klipsch speakers, then the speaker cost is marked up by a greater percentage than if the correct amount of indirect costs has been assigned. Therefore, accurately tracing direct costs and allocating indirect costs to products and services are important for many management decisions.

sold. Perhaps more importantly, as companies become more complex in the number and types of products and services they offer to customers, the need to understand, allocate, and effectively control indirect costs becomes increasingly important. In addition, indirect costs represent an increasingly large percentage of total costs for many companies.

Direct and indirect costs occur in service businesses as well. For example, a bank's cost of printing and mailing monthly statements to checking account holders is a direct cost of the product—checking accounts. However, the cost of office furniture in the bank is an indirect cost for the checking accounts.

Ethical Decisions

Tracking costs can also act as an early warning system for unauthorized activity and possible ethical problems. For example, **Metropolitan Life Insurance Company** was dismayed to learn that some of its agents were selling policies as retirement plans. This practice is illegal, and it cost the company more than $20 million in fines as well as $50 million in refunds to policyholders. More accurate and comprehensive data tracking regarding sales, individual agents, types of policies, and policyholders could have alerted Metropolitan Life to a potential problem. Thus, we can see that tracking costs can serve many different and important purposes. ●

Other Categories of Cost   In addition to being categorized as either direct or indirect, costs often are analyzed with respect to their behavior patterns, or the way in which a cost changes when the level of the output changes.

Variable Cost   A **variable cost** is one that increases in total as output increases and decreases in total as output decreases. For example, the denim used in making jeans is a variable cost. As the company makes more jeans, it needs more denim.

Fixed Cost   A **fixed cost** is a cost that does not increase in total as output increases and does not decrease in total as output decreases. For example, the cost of property taxes on the factory building stays the same no matter how many pairs of jeans the company makes. How can that be, since property taxes can and do change yearly? While the cost changes, it is not because output changes. Rather, it changes because the city or county government decides to raise taxes.

Variable and fixed costs, as well as other important types of cost behavior, are covered more extensively in Chapter 3.

Check Point

1. **How are direct costs handled from a product/service costing perspective?**
   a. **Allocated to products/services**
   b. **Traced to products/services**
   c. **Neither allocated nor traced to products/services**
   d. **Both allocated and traced to products/services**

Answer:
b. Direct costs are those costs that can be TRACED to their respective cost object (e.g., product, service, project, geographic region, plant, product line, etc.) in a reasonably easy and accurate manner.

2. *Fixed* **and** *variable* **are used to describe what aspects of costs?**

Answer:
Fixed and *variable* are key words used in describing basic, yet very important, cost behavior patterns. A cost behavior pattern describes how a particular cost behaves, or changes, as output volume increases or decreases.

Opportunity Cost An **opportunity cost** is the benefit given up or sacrificed when one alternative is chosen over another. For example, an opportunity cost of you participating in a summer study abroad program might include the wages you would have earned during that time if you had stayed home to work rather than participating in the overseas program. On the other hand, an opportunity cost of your staying home to work rather than participating in the study abroad program might include the value that future employers would have placed on the knowledge and experience you would have gathered had you participated in the overseas program. Opportunity cost differs from accounting cost in that the opportunity cost is never included in the accounting records because it is the cost of something that did not occur. Opportunity costs are important to decision making, as we will see more clearly in Chapter 8.

PRODUCT AND SERVICE COSTS

Output represents one of the most important cost objects. There are two types of output: products and services.

- **Products** are goods produced by converting raw materials through the use of labor and indirect manufacturing resources, such as the manufacturing plant, land, and machinery. Televisions, hamburgers, automobiles, computers, clothes, and furniture are examples of products.
- **Services** are tasks or activities performed for a customer or an activity performed by a customer using an organization's products or facilities. Medical care, teaching, dental care, spa activities, insurance coverage, and accounting are examples of service activities performed for customers. Car rental, video rental, and skiing are examples of services where the customer uses an organization's products or facilities.

Organizations that produce products are called **manufacturing organizations**. Organizations that provide services are called **service organizations**. Managers of both types of organizations need to know how much individual products or services cost. Accurate cost information is vital for profitability analysis and strategic decisions concerning product design, pricing, and product mix. Incidentally, retail organizations, such as J. Crew, buy finished products from other organizations, such as manufacturers, and then sell them to customers. The accounting for inventory and cost of goods sold for retail organizations, often referred to as merchandisers, is much simpler than for manufacturing organizations and is usually covered extensively in introductory financial accounting courses. Therefore, the focus here is on manufacturing and service organizations.

Here's **Why It's important**

Services differ from products in many ways, including the following:

- *Services are intangible:* The buyers of services cannot see, feel, hear, or taste a service before it is bought.
- *Services are perishable:* Services cannot be stored for future use by a consumer but must be consumed when performed. Inventory valuation, so important for products, is not an issue for services. In other words, because service organizations do not produce and sell products as part of their regular operations, they have no inventory asset on the balance sheet.
- *Services require direct contact between providers and buyers:* An eye examination, for example, requires both the patient and the optometrist to be present. However, producers of products need not have direct contact with the buyers of their goods. Thus, buyers of automobiles never need to have contact with the engineers and assembly line workers that produced their automobiles.

The overall way in which a company costs services in terms of classifying related costs as either direct or indirect is very similar to the way in which it costs products. The main difference in costing is that products have inventories, and services do not.

Here's How It's Used: AT KICKER

Kicker collects and analyzes many types of costs and breaks cost information into a series of accounts that helps Kicker's management in budgeting and decision making. The sales function, for example, is broken down into three areas: selling, customer service, and marketing. Consider the marketing department, which is responsible for advertising, promotions, and tent shows.

Tent shows are small-scale affairs held several times a year in the central and south-central United States. Kicker brings its semitrailer full of products and sound equipment as well as a couple of show trucks. Then, a large tent is set up to sell Kicker merchandise, explain products, showcase new models, and

sell the previous year's models at greatly reduced prices. The cost of each tent show is carefully tracked and compared with that show's revenue. Sites that don't provide sales revenue greater than cost are not booked for the coming year.

Like many of today's companies, Kicker tracks costs carefully for use in decision making. The general cost categories discussed in this chapter help the company to organize cost information and relate it to decision making.

Providing Cost Information

Managerial accountants must decide what types of managerial accounting information to provide to managers, how to measure such information, and when and to whom to communicate the information. For example, when making most strategic and operating decisions, managers typically rely on managerial accounting information that is prepared in whatever manner the managerial accountant believes provides the best analysis for the decision at hand. Therefore, the majority of the managerial accounting issues explained in this book do not reference a formal set of external rules, but instead consider the context of the given decision (e.g., relevant versus irrelevant cost information for make-or-buy decisions, full cost versus functional cost information for pricing decisions, etc.).

However, there is one major exception. Managerial accountants must follow specific external reporting rules (i.e., generally accepted accounting principles) when their companies provide outside parties with cost information about the amount of ending inventory on the balance sheet and the cost of goods sold on the income statement. In order to calculate these two amounts, managerial accountants must subdivide costs into functional categories: production and period (i.e., nonproduction). The following section describes the process for categorizing costs as either product or period in nature.

Determining Product Cost

Product (manufacturing) costs are those costs, both direct and indirect, of producing a product in a manufacturing firm or of acquiring a product in a merchandising firm and preparing it for sale. Therefore, only costs in the *production* section of the value chain are included in product costs. A key feature of product costs is that they are inventoried. Product costs initially are added to an inventory account and remain in inventory until they are sold, at which time they are transferred to cost of goods sold (COGS). Product costs can be further classified as direct materials, direct labor, and manufacturing overhead, which are the three cost elements that can be assigned to products for external financial reporting (e.g., inventories or COGS). Exhibit 2.2 shows how direct materials, direct labor, and overhead become product costs.

Direct Materials   **Direct materials** are those materials that are a part of the final product and can be directly traced to the goods being produced. The cost of these materials can be directly charged to products because physical observation can be used to measure the quantity used by each product. Materials that become part of a product usually are classified as direct materials.

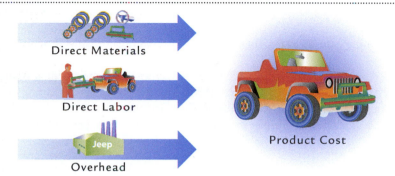

For example, tires on a new **Porsche** automobile, wood in an **Ethan Allen** dining room table, alcohol in a **Gucci** cologne, and denim in a pair of **American Eagle** jeans are all part of direct materials for manufacturers of these products.

A closely related term is raw materials. Often, the inventory of materials is called the raw materials account. Materials in the raw materials account do not become direct materials until they are withdrawn from inventory for use in production. The raw materials inventory account can include indirect materials as well as direct materials. Indirect materials are used in the production process, but the amount used by each unit cannot be easily determined and, as a result, these costs are treated as indirect costs (as discussed later).

Direct Labor **Direct labor** is the labor that can be directly traced to the goods being produced. Physical observation can be used to measure the amount of labor used to produce a product. Those employees who convert direct materials into a product are classified as direct labor. For example, workers on a computer assembly line at **Hewlett-Packard** are classified as direct labor.

Just as there were indirect materials in a company, there may also be indirect labor. This labor is not direct labor since these workers do not actually make the product. However, their contribution is necessary to production. An example of indirect labor in a production setting is the maintenance crew who performs regularly scheduled preventative maintenance every other Wednesday morning in **Georgia Pacific**'s plywood manufacturing plants. Indirect labor is included in overhead and, therefore, is an indirect cost rather than a direct cost.

Manufacturing Overhead All product costs other than direct materials and direct labor are put into a category called **manufacturing overhead**. In a manufacturing firm, manufacturing overhead also is known as *factory burden, support,* or *indirect* manufacturing costs. Costs are included as manufacturing overhead if they cannot be traced to the cost object of interest (e.g., unit of product). The manufacturing overhead cost category contains a wide variety of items. Examples of manufacturing overhead costs include depreciation on plant buildings and equipment, janitorial and maintenance labor, plant supervision, materials handling, power for plant utilities, and plant property taxes.

The important thing to remember is that all costs in the factory are classified as direct materials, direct labor, or manufacturing overhead. No product cost can be omitted from classification, no matter how far removed you might think it is from the actual production of a product. Earlier we mentioned that indirect materials and indirect labor are included in overhead. In manufacturing, the glue used in furniture or toys is an example, as is the cost of oil to grease cookie sheets for producing cookies.

Total Product Cost The total product cost equals the sum of direct materials, direct labor, and manufacturing overhead:

Total Product Cost = Direct Materials + Direct Labor + Manufacturing Overhead

The unit product cost equals total product cost divided by the number of units produced:

> Per-Unit Product Cost = Total Product Cost/Number of Units Produced

Here's **Why It's important**   Product costs are essential to management control and decision making. Managers use product costs to create budgets and analyses. Product costs within manufacturing can then be contrasted with period costs incurred outside of manufacturing.

Example 2.1 shows how to calculate total product cost and per-unit product cost.

EXAMPLE 2.1

How to Calculate Product Cost in Total and Per Unit

BlueDenim Company makes blue jeans. Last week, direct materials (denim, thread, zippers, and rivets) costing $48,000 were put into production. Direct labor of $30,000 (50 workers × 40 hours × $15 per hour) was incurred. Manufacturing overhead equaled $72,000. By the end of the week, BlueDenim had manufactured 30,000 pairs of jeans.

Required:

1. Calculate the total product cost for last week.
2. Calculate the cost of one pair of jeans that was produced last week.

Solution:

1.
Direct materials	$ 48,000
Direct labor	30,000
Manufacturing overhead	72,000
Total product cost	$150,000

2. Per-Unit Product Cost = $150,000/30,000 = $5

Product costs include direct materials, direct labor, and manufacturing overhead. Once the product is finished, no more costs attach to it. That is, any costs associated with storing, selling, and delivering the product are not product costs, but instead are period costs.

Prime and Conversion Costs   Product costs of direct materials, direct labor, and manufacturing overhead are sometimes grouped into prime cost and conversion cost:

- **Prime cost** is the sum of direct materials cost and direct labor cost:

> Prime Cost = Direct Materials + Direct Labor

- **Conversion cost** is the sum of direct labor cost and manufacturing overhead cost:

> Conversion Cost = Direct Labor + Manufacturing Overhead

Here's **Why It's important**   For a manufacturing firm, conversion cost can be interpreted as the cost of converting raw materials into a final product. Managers often categorize product costs into either prime or conversion in nature to compare the relative cost of manufacturing inputs (i.e., direct materials and direct labor) versus processing (i.e., direct labor and manufacturing overhead).

Example 2.2 shows how to calculate prime cost and conversion cost for a manufactured product.

Refer to the information in Example 2.1 (p. 40) for BlueDenim Company.

Required:

1. Calculate the total prime cost for last week.
2. Calculate the per-unit prime cost.
3. Calculate the total conversion cost for last week.
4. Calculate the per-unit conversion cost.

Solution:

1.
Direct materials	$48,000
Direct labor	30,000
Total prime cost	$78,000

2. Per-Unit Prime Cost = $78,000/30,000 = $2.60

3.
Direct labor	$ 30,000
Manufacturing overhead	72,000
Total conversion cost	$102,000

4. Per-Unit Conversion Cost = $102,000/30,000 units = $3.40

Note: Remember that prime cost and conversion cost do NOT equal total product cost. This is because direct labor is part of BOTH prime cost and conversion cost.

Period Costs The costs of production are assets that are carried in inventories until the goods are sold. There are other costs of running a company, referred to as *period costs*, that are not carried in inventory. Thus, **period costs** are all costs that are not product costs (i.e., all areas of the value chain except for production). The cost of office supplies, research and development activities, the CEO's salary, and advertising are examples of period costs. For instance, **Jaguar** spent an estimated $8 million to air its 60 seconds of air time during the Super Bowl, which included $5 million to produce its commercial. In addition, Jaguar spent an additional $5 million to advertise in advance its subsequent Super Bowl advertisement! Not to be outdone, Arnold Schwarzenegger enjoyed his Mobile Strike in his Super Bowl ad. These types of sporting events often draw massive television audiences, thereby tempting many organization executives to pull the trigger and incur breathtakingly large advertising costs for such a short period of exposure.[5] For example, the Patriots' last play interception to beat the Seahawks in Super Bowl XLIX was watched by more viewers (an average of 114.4 million) than any television show in history![6] Despite these record ratings, however, some people consider this $8 million period expense to be excessive. Managerial accountants help executives at companies like **Jaguar** and **Victoria's Secret** determine whether or not such costly advertising campaigns generate enough additional sales revenue over the long run to make them profitable.

Period costs cannot be assigned to products or appear as part of the reported values of inventories on the balance sheet. Instead, period costs typically are expensed in the period in which they are incurred. However, if a period cost is expected to provide an economic benefit (i.e., revenues) beyond the next year, then it is recorded as an asset (i.e., capitalized) and allocated to expense through depreciation throughout its useful life. The cost associated with the purchase of a delivery truck is an example of a period cost that would be capitalized when

---

5 Suzanne Vranica, "And Now, Ads for the Super Bowl Ads," *The Wall Street Journal* (January 28, 2014). http://online.wsj.com/news/article_email/SB10001424052702304856504579338704254890072-lMyQjAxMTA0MDIwNzEyNDcyWj (accessed January 27, 2014).

6 Catherine Taibi, "Super Bowl XLIX Was Most-Watched Show in U.S. Television History," *The Huffington Post* (February 2, 2015). http://www.huffingtonpost.com/2015/02/02/super-bowl-tv-ratings-2015-patriots-seahawks_n_6595690.html (accessed March 6, 2016).

incurred and then recognized as an expense over the useful life of the truck. Exhibit 2.3 depicts the distinction between product and period costs and how each type of cost eventually becomes an expense on the income statement. As shown in the exhibit, product costs, which are capitalized as an inventory asset, are expensed on the income statement as cost of goods sold to match against the revenues generated from the sale of the inventory. However, capitalized period costs are depreciated to expense on the income statement over the asset's useful life to match against the revenues generated by the asset over its useful life.

Exhibit 2.3

The Impact of Product versus Period Costs on the Financial Statements

CONCEPT CLIP

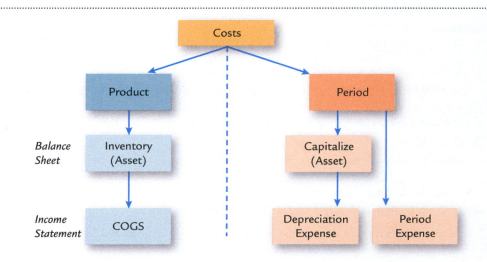

In a manufacturing organization, the level of period costs can be significant (often greater than 25% of sales revenue), and controlling them may bring greater cost savings than the same effort exercised in controlling production costs. For example, **Nike**'s period expenses are 35% of its revenue ($10,794,000,000/$30,601,000,000).[7] For service organizations, the relative importance of selling and administrative costs depends on the nature of the service produced. Physicians and dentists, for example, do relatively little marketing and thus have very low selling costs. On the other hand, a grocery chain may incur substantial marketing costs. Period costs often are divided into selling costs and administrative costs.

Selling Costs   Those costs necessary to market, distribute, and service a product or service are **selling costs**. They are often referred to as *order-getting* and *order-filling* costs. Examples of selling costs include salaries and commissions of sales personnel, advertising, warehousing, shipping, and customer service. The first two items are examples of order-getting costs; the last three are order-filling costs.

Administrative Costs   All costs associated with research, development, and general administration of the organization that cannot reasonably be assigned to either selling or production are **administrative costs**. General administration has the responsibility of ensuring that the various activities of the organization are properly integrated so that the overall mission of the firm is realized. The president of the firm, for example, is concerned with the efficiency of selling, production, and research and development activities. Proper integration of these activities is essential to maximizing the overall profits of a firm. Examples of general administrative costs are executive salaries, legal fees, printing the annual report, and general accounting. Research and development costs are the costs associated with designing and developing new products and must be expensed in the period incurred.

Direct and Indirect Period Costs   As with product costs, it is often helpful to distinguish between direct period costs and indirect period costs. Service companies also make this important distinction. For example, a surgical center would show that surgical gauze and anesthesia are direct costs used for an operation because it could be determined how much gauze or anesthesia was used for each procedure or patient. Other examples of direct costs in service industries include the chef in a restaurant, a surgical nurse attending an open heart operation, and a pilot for **Southwest Airlines**.

---

7 From Nike's 2015 Annual Report.

Here's How It's Used: DATA ANALYTICS

Increasingly, accountants use data analytics tools to help define, access, and utilize industry benchmark data for evaluating their own performance against that of other key competitors and industry leaders. Specifically, benchmarking allows managerial accountants to help management better understand how the organization's accounting performance metrics, ratios, and results compare to the performance of similar companies (e.g., operate in the same industry, are of comparable size, face common risks such as regulatory scrutiny, etc.). With the rapid growth in data analytics, managerial accountants can access larger quantities of benchmarking data from a much wider set of data sources (e.g., domestic vs. multinational organizations) at a considerably lower investment of time and money. As a result,

trends and patterns in how the organization's performance compares to that of other important benchmarked organizations can be more quickly and accurately detected. In addition, the associated management decisions can be made to improve performance to stay ahead of (or catch up to) the competition. For example, **Twitter** can use data analytics to gauge how its expenses as a relatively young and publicly traded technology company compare to other companies in the technology industry, such as **Facebook** and **LinkedIn**. Twitter can choose to adjust its spending on research and development (R&D) if the analytics it performs show that various trends in its R&D expenses—both in total and as a percentage of sales revenue—differ significantly from that of its key comparison companies.

Alternately, although shampoo and hair spray are used in a health spa and salon, the exact amount used in each individual's haircut is not easily determinable. As a result, the costs associated with shampoo and hair spray would be considered indirect, or overhead, costs and allocated, rather than traced, to individual haircuts. Examples of indirect labor costs in a service setting include the surgical assistants in a hospital who clean up the operating room after surgery, dispose of certain used materials, and sterilize the reusable instruments. Indirect labor is included in overhead. The rental of a Santa suit for the annual company Christmas party would be an example of an indirect cost that would be expensed in the period incurred. Although these costs do not affect the calculation of inventories or COGS (i.e., because they are service companies), their correct classification nonetheless affects numerous decisions and planning and control activities for managers, as we will discuss in detail in future chapters.

Check Point

1. **Which of the following items should be included as part of product cost?**
   a. **Manufacturing overhead**
   b. **Direct materials**
   c. **Direct labor**
   d. **All of the above**
   e. **None of the above**

Answer:

d. Direct materials, direct labor, and manufacturing overhead costs should all be included as part of product cost because they meet the definition of product cost, which is "any cost, direct or indirect, of producing a product in a manufacturing firm or of acquiring a product in a merchandising firm and preparing it for sale."

2. **What is the main difference between product costs and period costs?**

Answer:

The most important difference between these two types of costs is that *all* product costs flow through inventory (a current asset on the balance sheet) and then are expensed as cost of goods sold (an expense on the income statement) as finished goods inventory items are sold. *No* period costs flow through inventory. Instead, period costs are either expensed in the current period as incurred (e.g., research and development expenses) or are capitalized as long-term assets and then allocated to expense over time (e.g., a new building appears as a long-lived asset on the balance sheet and is depreciated to expense on the income statement over time). Refer to Exhibit 2.3 for a graphical depiction of these relationships.

OBJECTIVE 3

Prepare income statements for manufacturing and service organizations.

 **Why It's important**

PREPARING INCOME STATEMENTS

The earlier definitions of product, selling, and administrative costs provide a good conceptual overview of these important costs. However, the actual calculation of these costs in practice is a bit more complicated. Managers need to understand how the financial statements are affected by product costs (e.g., cost of goods sold on the income statement; inventory on the balance sheet) and by period costs (e.g., advertising expense on the income statement; warehouse facility long-lived asset on the balance sheet). In addition, many managers and investors pay special attention to cost of goods sold and inventory because they affect key ratios, such as gross margin and return on assets, respectively. Let's take a closer look at just how costs are calculated for purposes of preparing the external financial statements, focusing first on manufacturing firms.

Cost of Goods Manufactured

The **cost of goods manufactured** represents the total product cost of goods *completed* during the current period and transferred to finished goods inventory. The only costs assigned to goods completed are the manufacturing costs of direct materials, direct labor, and manufacturing overhead. So, why don't we just add together the current period's costs of direct materials, direct labor, and manufacturing overhead to arrive at cost of goods sold? The reason is inventories of materials and work in process. For instance, some of the materials purchased in the current period likely were used in production (i.e., transferred from materials inventory to work-in-process inventory during the period). However, other materials likely were not used in production, and thus remain in materials inventory at period-end. Also, some of the units that were worked on (and thus allocated labor and manufacturing overhead costs) in the current period likely were completed during the period (i.e., transferred from work-in-process inventory to finished goods inventory during the period). However, other units worked on during the period likely were not completed during the period, and thus remain in work-in-process inventory at period-end. In calculating cost of goods sold, we need to distinguish between the total manufacturing cost for the current period and the manufacturing costs associated with the units that were completed during the current period (i.e., cost of goods manufactured).

Let's take a look at direct materials. Suppose a company had no materials on hand at the beginning of the month, then bought $15,000 of direct materials during the month, and used all of them in production. The entire $15,000 would be properly called *direct materials*. Usually, though, the company has some materials on hand at the beginning of the month. These materials are the beginning inventory of materials. Let's say that this beginning inventory of materials cost $2,500. Then during the month, the company would have a total of $17,500 of materials that could be used in production ($2,500 from beginning inventory and $15,000 purchased during the month). Typically, the company would not use the entire amount of materials on hand in production. Perhaps it uses only $12,000 of materials. Then, the cost of direct materials used in production this month is $12,000, and the remaining $5,500 of materials is the ending inventory of materials. This reasoning can be easily expressed in a formula:

$$\begin{array}{c} \text{Beginning Inventory} \\ \text{of Materials} \end{array} + \text{Purchases} - \begin{array}{c} \text{Direct Materials} \\ \text{Used in Production} \end{array} = \begin{array}{c} \text{Ending Inventory} \\ \text{of Materials} \end{array}$$

While this computation is logical and simple, it does not express the result for which we usually are looking. We are usually trying to figure out the amount of direct materials used in production—not the amount of ending inventory. **Example 2.3** shows how to compute the amount of direct materials used in production.

 **Why It's important**
The primary use of calculating the direct materials used in production is to serve as the first number in calculating the cost of goods manufactured. Direct materials used in production also show managers the difference between the amount of materials purchased and the amount of materials used in manufacturing for the period.

EXAMPLE 2.3

How to Calculate the
Direct Materials Used
in Production

BlueDenim Company makes blue jeans. On May 1, BlueDenim had $68,000 of materials in inventory. During the month of May, BlueDenim purchased $210,000 of materials. On May 31, materials inventory equaled $22,000.

Required:
Calculate the cost of direct materials used in production for the month of May.

Solution:

Materials inventory, May 1	$ 68,000
Purchases	210,000
Materials inventory, May 31	(22,000)
Direct materials used in production	$256,000

Once the direct materials are calculated, the direct labor and manufacturing overhead *for the time period* can be added to get the total manufacturing cost for the period. Now we need to consider the second type of inventory—work in process. **Work in process (WIP)** is the cost of the partially completed goods that are still on the factory floor at the end of a time period. These are units that have been started, but are not finished. They have value, but not as much as they will when they are completed. Just as there are beginning and ending inventories of materials, there are beginning and ending inventories of WIP. We must adjust the total manufacturing cost for the time period for the inventories of WIP. After this adjustment, we will have the total cost of the goods that were completed and transferred from work-in-process inventory to finished goods inventory during the current time period, which is the cost of goods manufactured. The primary use for the statement of cost of goods manufactured is to help facilitate external financial reporting because cost of goods manufactured must be calculated before cost of goods sold can be determined, which is one of the most important components of the income statement for manufacturers.

Example 2.4 shows how to calculate the cost of goods manufactured for a particular time period.

Here's **Why It's important**

EXAMPLE 2.4

How to Calculate
Cost of Goods
Manufactured

BlueDenim Company makes blue jeans. During the month of May, BlueDenim purchased $210,000 of materials and incurred direct labor cost of $135,000 and manufacturing overhead of $150,000. On May 31, materials inventory equaled $22,000. Inventory information is as follows:

	May 1	May 31
Materials	$68,000	$22,000
Work in process	50,000	16,000

Required:
Calculate the cost of goods manufactured for the month of May.

Solution:

Direct materials used in production*	$256,000
Direct labor	135,000
Manufacturing overhead	150,000
Total manufacturing cost for May	$541,000
WIP, May 1	50,000
WIP, May 31	(16,000)
Cost of goods manufactured	$575,000

*Direct Materials = $68,000 + $210,000 − $22,000 = $256,000

Cost of Goods Sold

To meet external reporting requirements, costs must be classified into three categories:

- production
- selling
- administration

Here's **Why It's important**

Remember that product costs are initially put into inventory. They become expenses only when the products are sold, which matches the expenses of manufacturing the product to the sales revenue generated by the product at the time it is sold. Therefore, the expense of manufacturing is not the cost of goods manufactured; instead, it is the cost of the goods that are sold. **Cost of goods sold** represents the cost of goods that were sold during the period and, therefore, transferred from finished goods inventory on the balance sheet to cost of goods sold on the income statement (i.e., as an inventory expense). The primary use for the statement of cost of goods sold is for external financial reporting. It is a critical input to the income statement.

Example 2.5 shows how to calculate the cost of goods sold.

EXAMPLE 2.5

How to Calculate Cost of Goods Sold

BlueDenim Company makes blue jeans. During the month of May, 115,000 pairs of jeans were completed at a cost of goods manufactured of $575,000. Suppose that on May 1, BlueDenim had 10,000 units in the finished goods inventory costing $50,000 and on May 31, the company had 26,000 units in the finished goods inventory costing $130,000.

Required:

1. Prepare a cost of goods sold statement for the month of May.

2. Calculate the number of pairs of jeans that were sold during May.

Solution:

1.

BlueDenim Company
Cost of Goods Sold Statement
For the Month of May

Cost of goods manufactured	$ 575,000
Finished goods inventory, May 1	50,000
Finished goods inventory, May 31	(130,000)
Cost of goods sold	$ 495,000

2.

Number of units sold:	
Finished goods inventory, May 1	10,000
Units finished during May	115,000
Finished goods inventory, May 31	(26,000)
Units sold during May	99,000

The ending inventories of materials, WIP, and finished goods are important because they are assets and appear on the balance sheet (as current assets). The cost of goods sold is an expense that appears on the income statement. Selling and administrative costs are period costs and also appear on the income statement as an expense. Collectively, Examples 2.3, 2.4, and 2.5 (pp. 45–46) depict the flow of costs through the three inventories (materials, work in process, and finished goods) and finally into cost of goods sold.

Exhibit 2.4 uses the information in Examples 2.3, 2.4, and 2.5 to illustrate how the manufacturing costs—direct materials, direct labor, and manufacturing overhead—flow through the inventories—direct materials, work in process, and finished goods—and eventually into cost

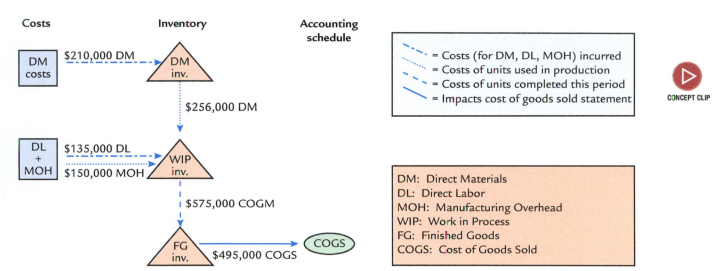

Exhibit 2.4 Relationship between the Flow of Costs, Inventories, and Cost of Goods Sold

of goods sold on the income statement. Exhibit 2.4 also shows the difference between when direct materials are purchased (or incurred and put into direct materials inventory—$210,000) versus when they are used in production (i.e., placed into WIP inventory—$256,000). There is no difference between when direct labor and manufacturing overhead costs are incurred versus when they are used in production because they cannot be stored in inventory before use (as can direct materials).

Income Statement: Manufacturing Firm

The income statement for a manufacturing firm is displayed in Example 2.6. This income statement follows the traditional format taught in an introductory financial accounting course. Notice that the income statement covers a certain period of time (i.e., the month of May in **Example 2.6**). However, the time period may vary. The key point is that all sales revenue and expenses attached to that period of time appear on the income statement. The primary use for the income statement is for external financial reporting. Investors and outside parties use it to determine the financial health of a firm, including the calculation of various important financial ratios. For example, gross margin (sales revenue minus cost of goods sold) represents one of the most frequently calculated ratios for manufacturers.

Here's **Why It's important**

Look at the income statement in Example 2.6. First, the heading tells us what type of statement it is, for what firm, and for what period of time. Then, the income statement itself always begins with "sales revenue" (or "sales" or "revenue"). The sales revenue is calculated as follows:

$$\text{Sales Revenue} = \text{Price} \times \text{Units Sold}$$

After the sales revenue is determined, the firm must calculate expenses for the period. Notice that the expenses are separated into three categories: production (cost of goods sold), selling, and administrative. The first type of expense is the cost of producing the units sold, or the cost of goods sold. This amount was computed and explained in Example 2.5 (p. 46). Remember that the cost of goods sold is the cost of producing the units that were sold during the time period. It includes direct materials, direct labor, and manufacturing overhead. It does *not* include any selling or administrative expense. In the case of a retail (i.e., a merchandising) firm, the cost of goods sold represents the total cost of the goods sold when they were purchased from an outside supplier. Therefore, the cost of goods sold for a retailer equals the purchase costs adjusted for the beginning and ending balances in its single inventory account. A merchandising firm, such as **American Eagle Outfitters** or **J. Crew**, has only one inventory account because

---

EXAMPLE 2.6

How to Prepare an Income Statement for a Manufacturing Firm

Recall that BlueDenim Company sold 99,000 pairs of jeans during the month of May at a total cost of $495,000. Each pair sold at a price of $8. BlueDenim also incurred two types of selling costs: commissions equal to 10% of the sales price and fixed selling expense of $120,000. Administrative expense totaled $85,000.

Required:

Prepare an income statement for BlueDenim for the month of May.

Solution:

BlueDenim Company
Income Statement
For the Month of May

Sales revenue (99,000 × $8)		$792,000
Cost of goods sold		495,000
Gross margin		$297,000
Less:		
Selling expenses		
Commissions ($792,000 × 0.10)	$ 79,200	
Fixed selling expenses	120,000	199,200
Administrative expenses		85,000
Operating income		$ 12,800

---

it does not transform the purchased good into a different form by adding materials, labor, and overhead, as does a manufacturing firm.

Recall **Little Guys Home Electronics** from the chapter opener. Little Guys is an example of a retail merchandising company specializing in home electronics. As a merchandiser, Little Guys has only one inventory account and computes cost of goods sold simply by adjusting its purchase costs for its beginning and ending inventory balances. The company's various period expenses, such as advertising, warehousing activities, home delivery, and customer service trips, are subtracted from gross margin to arrive at operating income.

Gross margin is the difference between sales revenue and cost of goods sold:

Gross Margin = Sales Revenue − Cost of Goods Sold

It shows how much the firm is making over and above the cost of the units sold. Gross margin does *not* equal operating income or profit. Selling and administrative expenses have not yet been subtracted. However, gross margin does provide useful information. If gross margin is positive, the firm at least charges prices that cover the product cost. In addition, the firm can calculate its gross margin percentage (gross margin/sales revenue), as shown in Example 2.7, and compare it with the average gross margin percentage for the industry to see if its experience is in the ballpark with other firms in the industry. Calculating the percentage of revenue for each line on the income statement informs managers of the size of each income statement line item relative to sales revenue. This calculation also enables comparisons between fiscal periods (i.e., trend analysis) and with other firms in the industry (i.e., competitor benchmarking).

Gross margin percentage varies significantly by industry. For instance, **Kroger**'s gross margin percentage as determined from the income statement in its annual report is 21.2% ($22,953,000,000/$108,465,000,000).[8] However, **Merck**'s gross margin percentage as

Here's Why It's important

---

8 Per Kroger's 2014 Annual Report.

Refer to the income statement for BlueDenim Company in Example 2.6.

Required:
Calculate the percentage of sales revenue represented by each line of the income statement.

Solution:

EXAMPLE 2.7

**How to Calculate the
Percentage of Sales
Revenue for Each
Line on the Income
Statement**

**BlueDenim Company
Income Statement
For the Month of May**

			Percent*
Sales revenue (99,000 × $8)		$792,000	100.0
Cost of goods sold		495,000	62.5
Gross margin		$297,000	37.5
Less:			
Selling expenses			
Commissions ($792,000 × 0.10)	$ 79,200		
Fixed selling expenses	120,000	199,200	25.2
Administrative expenses		85,000	10.7
Operating income		$ 12,800	1.6

*Steps in calculating the percentages:
1. Sales Revenue Percent = $792,000/$792,000 = 1.00 or 100% (sales revenue is always 100% of itself)
2. Cost of Goods Sold Percent = $495,000/$792,000 = 0.625, or 62.5%
3. Gross Margin Percent = $297,000/$792,000 = 0.375, or 37.5%
4. Selling Expenses Percent = $199,200/$792,000 = 0.252, or 25.2% (rounded)
5. Administrative Expenses Percent = $85,000/$792,000 = 0.107, or 10.7% (rounded)
6. Operating Income Percent = $12,800/$792,000 = 0.016, or 1.6% (rounded)

determined from the income statement in its annual report is 62.2% ($24,564,000,000/ $39,498,000,000).[9] One reason for Merck's extremely high gross margin percent is that a large percentage of its costs is related to marketing (e.g., advertising) and research and development ($10.3 billion and $6.7 billion, respectively) and, as such, is expensed as period costs in the period incurred. Thus, Merck's cost of goods sold was relatively small.

Finally, selling expense and administrative expense for the period are subtracted from gross margin to arrive at operating income:

> Operating Income = Gross Margin – Selling and Administrative Expense

Operating income is the key figure from the income statement; it is profit, and shows how much the owners are actually earning from the company. Again, calculating the percentage of operating income (i.e., operating income/sales revenue) and comparing it to the average for the industry gives the owners valuable information about relative profitability.

The income statement can be analyzed further by calculating the percentage of sales revenue represented by each line of the statement, as was done in Example 2.7. How can management use this information? The first thing that jumps out is that operating income is less than 2% of sales revenue. That's a very small percentage. Unless this is common for the blue jeans manufacturing business, BlueDenim's management should work hard to increase the percentage. Selling expense is a whopping 25.2% of sales. Do commissions really need to be that high? Or is the price too low (compared to competitors' prices)? Can cost

---

9 Per Merck's 2015 Annual Report.

Here's How It's Used: SUSTAINABILITY

As noted earlier, service organizations, such as **UPS**, do not show a cost of goods sold on their income statement because they make money by providing services rather than manufacturing physical products. In essence, UPS makes money by delivering packages (approximately 5 billion packages annually!) all over the globe on a schedule that meets its 10 million consumers' constantly changing business needs. As a result, UPS's "license to operate"—to sustain itself as an organization—involves the emission of considerable amounts of costly greenhouse gases (GHG) into the atmosphere from its gigantic fleet of trucks and aircraft. Not surprisingly, UPS's income statement contains an extremely large fuel expense—typically around $4 billion in total and oftentimes larger than its net income! While UPS faced vastly different sustainability challenges during its 1907 founding, its management today increasingly must understand how best to measure and manage its fuel consumption and GHG emissions. Various external parties can look to UPS's income statement to evaluate management's ability to maintain the company's license to operate with regulators and to produce acceptable financial returns to shareholders. In addition, UPS discloses numerous global performance metrics involving its environmental footprint, such as its switch to alternative fuel vehicles and the increase in its natural gas-powered vehicle fleet.[10]

of goods sold be reduced? Is 62.5% reasonable? These are questions that are suggested by Example 2.7, but not answered. Answering the questions is the job of management.

Income Statement: Service Firm

Here's **Why It's important**

In a service organization, there is no product to purchase (e.g., a merchandiser like **American Eagle Outfitters**) or to manufacture (e.g., **Toshiba**) and, therefore, there are no beginning or ending inventories. As a result, there is no cost of goods sold or gross margin on the income statement. Instead, the cost of providing services appears along with the other operating expenses of the company. The primary use for the income statement is for external financial reporting. Investors and outside parties use it to determine the financial health of a firm. Cost of goods sold typically does not exist on the income statement of service organizations because such organizations generate sales by providing services rather than selling products. Therefore, the income statement for a service provider is important because it showcases how the major expenses incurred to provide key services compare to the organization's overall sales revenue. For example, **Southwest Airlines**' income statement begins with total operating revenues of $18,605,000,000 and subtracts total operating expenses of $16,380,000,000 to arrive at an operating income of $2,225,000,000.[11]

An income statement for a service firm is shown in Example 2.8.

EXAMPLE 2.8

How to Prepare an Income Statement for a Service Organization

Komala Information Systems designs and installs human resources software for small companies. Last month, Komala had software licensing costs of $5,000, service technicians' costs of $35,000, and research and development costs of $55,000. Selling expenses were $5,000, and administrative expenses equaled $7,000. Sales totaled $130,000.

Required:

Prepare an income statement for Komala Information Systems for the past month.

---

10 Taken from http://sustainability.ups.com/sustainability-reporting/.
11 Per Southwest Airlines' 2014 Annual Report.

EXAMPLE 2.8

(Continued)

Solution:

Komala Information Systems
Income Statement
For the Past Month

Sales revenues:		$130,000
Less operating expenses:		
Software licensing	$ 5,000	
Service technicians	35,000	
Research and development	55,000	
Selling expenses	5,000	
Administrative expenses	7,000	107,000
Operating income		$ 23,000

Check Point

1. **What item is subtracted from the sum of purchases and beginning materials inventory to arrive at ending materials inventory?**
   a. **Direct materials used in production**
   b. **Cost of goods sold**
   c. **Direct labor**
   d. **Cost of goods manufactured**

Answer:

a. Beginning materials inventory plus purchases represents the amount of materials available for production. Therefore, subtracting the direct materials used in production results in the amount of ending materials inventory.

2. **Why does cost of goods sold not appear on the income statement of a service firm?**

Answer:

Cost of goods sold represents the cost of goods that were sold during the period and, therefore, transferred from finished goods inventory on the balance sheet to cost of goods sold on the income statement. In essence, cost of goods sold is an inventory expense. However, service firms generate a net income by providing services, rather than selling physical products. As a result, service firms have no inventory expense, or cost of goods sold.

SUMMARY OF LEARNING OBJECTIVES

LO1. Explain the meaning of cost and how costs are assigned to products and services.
- Cost is the cash or cash equivalent sacrificed for goods and services that are expected to bring a current or future benefit to the organization.
- Managers use cost information to determine the cost of objects such as products, projects, plants, and customers.
- Direct costs are traced to cost objects based on cause-and-effect relationships.
- Indirect (i.e., overhead) costs are allocated to cost objects based on assumed relationships and convenience.

LO2. Define the various costs of manufacturing products and providing services as well as the costs of selling and administration.
- Products are goods that either are purchased or produced by converting raw materials through the use of labor and indirect manufacturing resources, such as plants, land, and machinery. Services are tasks performed for a customer or activities performed by a customer using an organization's products or facilities.
- Product costs are those costs, both direct and indirect, of acquiring a product in a merchandising business and preparing it for sale or of producing a product in a manufacturing business. Product costs are classified as inventory on the balance sheet and then expensed as cost of goods sold on the income statement when the inventory is sold.
- Selling costs are the costs of marketing and distributing goods and services, and administrative costs are the costs of organizing and running a company.
- Both selling and administrative costs are period costs.

LO3. Prepare income statements for manufacturing and service organizations.
- The cost of goods manufactured (COGM) represents the total product cost of goods completed during the period and transferred to finished goods inventory. The cost of goods sold (COGS) represents the cost of goods that were sold during the period and, therefore, transferred from finished goods inventory to cost of goods sold. For a retailer, there is no COGM, and COGS equals the beginning inventory plus net purchases minus ending inventory.
- For manufacturing and merchandising firms, cost of goods sold is subtracted from sales revenue to arrive at gross margin. In addition, for manufacturing firms, cost of goods manufactured must first be calculated before calculating cost of goods sold.
- Service firms do not calculate gross margin because they do not purchase or produce inventory for sale and, as a result, do not have a cost of goods sold (i.e., inventory expense).
- All firms next subtract selling and administrative expense to arrive at net income.

SUMMARY OF IMPORTANT EQUATIONS

1. Total Product Cost = Direct Materials + Direct Labor + Manufacturing Overhead

2. Per-Unit Product Cost = Total Product Cost/Number of Units Produced

3. Prime Cost = Direct Materials + Direct Labor

4. Conversion Cost = Direct Labor + Manufacturing Overhead

5. Beginning Inventory of Materials + Purchases − Direct Materials Used in Production = Ending Inventory of Materials

6. Gross Margin = Sales Revenue − Cost of Goods Sold

7. Operating Income = Gross Margin − Selling and Administrative Expense

EXAMPLE 2.1	How to calculate product cost in total and per unit, page 40
EXAMPLE 2.2	How to calculate prime cost and conversion cost in total and per unit, page 41
EXAMPLE 2.3	How to calculate the direct materials used in production, page 45
EXAMPLE 2.4	How to calculate cost of goods manufactured, page 45
EXAMPLE 2.5	How to calculate cost of goods sold, page 46
EXAMPLE 2.6	How to prepare an income statement for a manufacturing firm, page 48
EXAMPLE 2.7	How to calculate the percentage of sales revenue for each line on the income statement, page 49
EXAMPLE 2.8	How to prepare an income statement for a service organization, page 50

KEY TERMS

Accumulating costs, 33, the way that costs are measured and recorded.

Administrative costs, 42, all costs associated with research, development, and general administration of the organization that cannot reasonably be assigned to either selling or production.

Allocation, 35, when an indirect cost is assigned to a cost object using a reasonable and convenient method.

Assigning costs, 33, the way that a cost is linked to some cost object.

Conversion cost, 40, the sum of direct labor cost and overhead cost.

Cost, 32, the amount of cash or cash equivalent sacrificed for goods and/or services that are expected to bring a current or future benefit to the organization.

Cost object, 33, any item such as products, customers, departments, projects, and so on, for which costs are measured and assigned.

Cost of goods manufactured, 44, the total product cost of goods completed during the current period.

Cost of goods sold, 46, the total product cost of goods sold during the period.

Direct costs, 34, costs that can be easily and accurately traced to a cost object.

Direct labor, 39, the labor that can be directly traced to the goods or services being produced.

Direct materials, 38, materials that are a part of the final product and can be directly traced to the goods or services being produced.

Expenses, 33, costs that are used up (expired) in the production of revenue.

Fixed cost, 36, costs that, in total, are constant within the relevant range as the level of output increases or decreases.

Gross margin, 48, the difference between sales revenue and cost of goods sold.

Indirect costs, 35, costs that cannot be easily and accurately traced to a cost object.

Manufacturing organizations, 37, an organization that produces tangible products.

Manufacturing overhead, 39, all product costs other than direct materials and direct labor. In a manufacturing firm, manufacturing overhead also is known as factory burden or indirect manufacturing costs. Costs are included as manufacturing overhead if they cannot be traced to the cost object of interest (e.g., unit of product).

Opportunity cost, 37, the benefit given up or sacrificed when one alternative is chosen over another.

Period costs, 41, costs that are not product costs (i.e., all areas of the value chain except for production).

Price, 33, the revenue per unit.

Prime cost, 40, the sum of direct materials cost and direct labor cost.

Product (manufacturing) costs, 38, costs of producing a product in a manufacturing firm or of acquiring a product in a merchandising firm and preparing it for sale. Product costs include direct materials, direct labor, and manufacturing overhead.

Products, 37, goods produced by converting raw materials through the use of labor and indirect manufacturing resources, such as the manufacturing plant, land, and machinery.

Selling costs, 42, those costs necessary to market, distribute, and service a product or service.

Service organizations, 37, an organization that produces intangible products.

Services, 37, tasks or activities performed for a customer or an activity performed by a customer using an organization's products or facilities.

Variable cost, 36, costs that, in total, vary in direct proportion to changes in output within the relevant range.

Work in process (WIP), 45, the cost of the partially completed goods that are still being worked on at the end of a time period.

REVIEW PROBLEM

I. Product Costs, Cost of Goods Manufactured Statement, and the Income Statement

Brody Company makes industrial cleaning solvents. Various chemicals, detergent, and water are mixed together and then bottled in 10-gallon drums. Brody provided the following information for last year:

Raw materials purchases	$250,000
Direct labor	140,000
Depreciation on factory equipment	45,000
Depreciation on factory building	30,000
Depreciation on headquarters building	50,000
Factory insurance	15,000
Property taxes:	
Factory	20,000
Headquarters	18,000
Utilities for factory	34,000
Utilities for sales office	1,800
Administrative salaries	150,000
Indirect labor salaries	156,000
Sales office salaries	90,000
Beginning balance, Raw materials	124,000
Beginning balance, WIP	124,000
Beginning balance, Finished goods	84,000
Ending balance, Raw materials	102,000
Ending balance, WIP	130,000
Ending balance, Finished goods	82,000

Last year, Brody completed 100,000 units. Sales revenue equaled $1,200,000, and Brody paid a sales commission of 5% of sales.

Required:

1. Calculate the direct materials used in production for last year.
2. Calculate total prime cost.
3. Calculate total conversion cost.
4. Prepare a cost of goods manufactured statement for last year. Calculate the unit product cost.
5. Prepare a cost of goods sold statement for last year.
6. Prepare an income statement for last year. Show the percentage of sales that each line item represents.

Solution:

1. Direct Materials = $124,000 + $250,000 − $102,000 = $272,000
2. Prime Cost = $272,000 + $140,000 = $412,000
3. First, calculate total overhead cost:

Depreciation on factory equipment	$ 45,000
Depreciation on factory building	30,000
Factory insurance	15,000
Factory property taxes	20,000
Factory utilities	34,000
Indirect labor salaries	156,000
Total overhead	$300,000

Conversion Cost = $140,000 + $300,000 = $440,000

4.

Direct materials	$272,000
Direct labor	140,000
Overhead	300,000
Total manufacturing cost	$712,000
+ Beginning WIP	124,000
− Ending WIP	130,000
Cost of goods manufactured	$706,000

$$\text{Unit Product Cost} = \frac{\$706,000}{100,000 \text{ units}} = \$7.06$$

5.

Cost of goods manufactured	$706,000
+ Beginning inventory, Finished goods	84,000
− Ending inventory, Finished goods	82,000
Cost of goods sold	$708,000

6. First, compute selling expense and administrative expense:

Utilities, sales office	$ 1,800
Sales office salaries	90,000
Sales commissions ($1,200,000 × 0.05)	60,000
Total selling expenses	$151,800
Depreciation on headquarters building	$ 50,000
Property taxes, headquarters	18,000
Administrative salaries	150,000
Total administrative expenses	$218,000

Brody Company
Income Statement
For Last Year

		Percent
Sales	$1,200,000	100.00
Cost of goods sold	708,000	59.00
Gross margin	$ 492,000	41.00
Less:		
Selling expenses	151,800	12.65
Administrative expenses	218,000	18.17*
Operating income	$ 122,200	10.18*

*Rounded

DISCUSSION QUESTIONS

1. Explain the difference between cost and expense.
2. What is the difference between accumulating costs and assigning costs?
3. What is a cost object? Give some examples.
4. What is a direct cost? An indirect cost? Can the same cost be direct for one purpose and indirect for another? Give an example.
5. What is allocation?
6. What is the difference between a product and a service? Give an example of each.
7. Define *manufacturing overhead*.
8. Explain the difference between direct materials purchased in a month and direct materials used for the month.
9. Define *prime cost* and *conversion cost*. Why can't prime cost be added to conversion cost to get total product cost?
10. How does a period cost differ from a product cost?
11. Define *selling cost*. Give five examples of selling cost.
12. What is the cost of goods manufactured?
13. What is the difference between cost of goods manufactured and cost of goods sold?
14. What is the difference between the income statement for a manufacturing firm and the income statement for a service firm?
15. Why do firms like to calculate a percentage column on the income statement (in which each line item is expressed as a percentage of sales)?

MULTIPLE-CHOICE QUESTIONS

2-1   Accumulating costs means that

a. costs must be summed and entered on the income statement.
b. each cost must be linked to some cost object.
c. costs must be measured and tracked.
d. costs must be allocated to units of production.
e. costs have expired and must be transferred from the balance sheet to the income statement.

2-2   Product (or manufacturing) costs consist of

a. direct materials, direct labor, and selling costs.
b. direct materials, direct labor, manufacturing overhead, and operating expense.
c. administrative costs and conversion costs.
d. prime costs and manufacturing overhead.
e. selling and administrative costs.

Use the following information for Multiple-Choice Questions 2-3 and 2-4:
Wachman Company produces a product with the following per-unit costs:

Direct materials	$15
Direct labor	6
Manufacturing overhead	19

Last year, Wachman produced and sold 2,000 units at a price of $75 each. Total selling and administrative expense was $30,000.

2-3   Refer to the information for Wachman Company on the previous page. Conversion cost per unit was

    a. $21.
    b. $25.
    c. $34.
    d. $40.
    e. None of these.

2-4   Refer to the information for Wachman Company on the previous page. Total gross margin for last year was

    a. $40,000.
    b. $70,000.
    c. $80,000.
    d. $88,000.
    e. $100,000.

2-5   The accountant in a factory that produces biscuits for fast-food restaurants wants to assign costs to boxes of biscuits. Which of the following costs can be traced directly to boxes of biscuits?

    a. The cost of flour and baking soda
    b. The wages of the mixing labor
    c. The cost of the boxes
    d. The cost of packing labor
    e. All of these.

2-6   Which of the following is an indirect cost?

    a. The cost of denim in a jeans factory
    b. The cost of mixing labor in a factory that makes over-the-counter pain relievers
    c. The cost of bottles in a shampoo factory
    d. The cost of restriping the parking lot at a perfume factory
    e. All of these.

2-7   Bobby Dee's is an owner-operated company that details (thoroughly cleans—inside and out) automobiles. Bobby Dee's is which of the following?

    a. Wholesaler
    b. Retailer
    c. Service firm
    d. Manufacturing firm
    e. None of these.

2-8   **Kellogg's** makes a variety of breakfast cereals. Kellogg's is which of the following?

    a. Wholesaler
    b. Retailer
    c. Service firm
    d. Manufacturing firm
    e. None of these.

2-9   **Target** is which of the following?

    a. Wholesaler
    b. Retailer
    c. Service firm
    d. Manufacturing firm
    e. None of these.

2-10 Stone Inc. is a company that purchases goods (e.g., chess sets, pottery) from overseas and resells them to gift shops in the United States. Stone Inc. is which of the following?

    a. Wholesaler

    b. Retailer

    c. Service firm

    d. Manufacturing firm

    e. None of these.

2-11 JackMan Company produces die-cast metal bulldozers for toy shops. JackMan estimated the following average costs per bulldozer:

Direct materials	$8.65
Direct labor	1.10
Manufacturing overhead	0.95

Prime cost per unit is

    a. $8.65.

    b. $1.10.

    c. $0.95.

    d. $2.05.

    e. $9.75.

2-12 Which of the following is a period expense?

    a. Factory insurance

    b. CEO salary

    c. Direct labor

    d. Factory maintenance

    e. All of these.

Use the following information for Multiple-Choice Questions 2-13 through 2-18:
Last year, Barnard Company incurred the following costs:

Direct materials	$ 50,000
Direct labor	20,000
Manufacturing overhead	130,000
Selling expense	40,000
Administrative expense	36,000

Barnard produced and sold 10,000 units at a price of $31 each.

2-13 Refer to the information for Barnard Company above. Prime cost per unit is

    a. $7.00.

    b. $20.00.

    c. $15.00.

    d. $5.00.

    e. $27.60.

2-14 Refer to the information for Barnard Company above. Conversion cost per unit is

    a. $7.00.

    b. $20.00.

    c. $15.00.

    d. $5.00.

    e. $27.60.

2-15   Refer to the information for Barnard Company on the previous page. The cost of goods sold per unit is

    a. $7.00.

    b. $20.00.

    c. $15.00.

    d. $5.00.

    e. $27.60.

2-16   Refer to the information for Barnard Company on the previous page. The gross margin per unit is

    a. $24.00.

    b. $11.00.

    c. $16.00.

    d. $26.00.

    e. $3.40.

2-17   Refer to the information for Barnard Company on the previous page. The total period expense is

    a. $276,000.

    b. $200,000.

    c. $76,000.

    d. $40,000.

    e. $36,000.

2-18   Refer to the information for Barnard Company on the previous page. Operating income is

    a. $34,000.

    b. $110,000.

    c. $234,000.

    d. $270,000.

    e. $74,000.

BRIEF EXERCISES: SET A

> *Use the following information for Brief Exercises 2-19 and 2-20:*
> Slapshot Company makes ice hockey sticks. Last week, direct materials (wood, paint, Kevlar, and resin) costing $32,000 were put into production. Direct labor of $28,000 (10 workers × 200 hours × $14 per hour) was incurred. Manufacturing overhead equaled $60,000. By the end of the week, the company had manufactured 500 hockey sticks.

Brief Exercise 2-19 Total Product Cost and Per-Unit Product Cost

OBJECTIVE ▶ **2**

Example 2.1

Refer to the information for Slapshot Company above.

Required:

1. Calculate the total product cost for last week.
2. Calculate the per-unit cost of one hockey stick that was produced last week.

OBJECTIVE ▶ **2**
Example 2.2

Brief Exercise 2-20 Prime Cost and Conversion Cost

Refer to the information for Slapshot Company on the previous page.

Required:

1. Calculate the total prime cost for last week.
2. Calculate the per-unit prime cost.
3. Calculate the total conversion cost for last week.
4. Calculate the per-unit conversion cost.

OBJECTIVE ▶ **3**
Example 2.3

Brief Exercise 2-21 Direct Materials Used in Production

Slapshot Company makes ice hockey sticks. On June 1, Slapshot had $48,000 of materials in inventory. During the month of June, the company purchased $132,000 of materials. On June 30, materials inventory equaled $45,000.

Required:

Calculate the direct materials used in production for the month of June.

OBJECTIVE ▶ **3**
Example 2.4

Brief Exercise 2-22 Cost of Goods Manufactured

Slapshot Company makes ice hockey sticks. During the month of June, the company purchased $132,000 of materials. Also during the month of June, Slapshot Company incurred direct labor cost of $113,000 and manufacturing overhead of $187,000. Inventory information is as follows:

	June 1	June 30
Materials	$48,000	$45,000
Work in process	65,000	63,000

Required:

1. Calculate the cost of goods manufactured for the month of June.
2. Calculate the cost of one hockey stick assuming that 1,900 sticks were completed during June.

OBJECTIVE ▶ **3**
Example 2.5

Brief Exercise 2-23 Cost of Goods Sold

Slapshot Company makes ice hockey sticks. During the month of June, 1,900 sticks were completed at a cost of goods manufactured of $437,000. Suppose that on June 1, Slapshot had 350 units in finished goods inventory costing $80,000 and on June 30, 370 units in finished goods inventory costing $84,000.

Required:

1. Prepare a cost of goods sold statement for the month of June.
2. Calculate the number of sticks that were sold during June.

Use the following information for Brief Exercises 2-24 and 2-25:
Slapshot Company makes ice hockey sticks and sold 1,880 sticks during the month of June at a total cost of $433,000. Each stick sold at a price of $400. Slapshot also incurred two types of selling costs: commissions equal to 10% of the sales price and other selling expense of $65,000. Administrative expense totaled $53,800.

Brief Exercise 2-24 Manufacturing Firm Income Statement

OBJECTIVE ▶ 3
Example 2.6

Refer to the information for Slapshot Company on the previous page.

Required:

Prepare an income statement for Slapshot for the month of June.

Brief Exercise 2-25 Income Statement Percentages

OBJECTIVE ▶ 3
Example 2.7

Refer to the information for Slapshot Company above.

Required:

Prepare an income statement for Slapshot for the month of June and calculate the percentage of sales revenue represented by each line of the income statement. (*Note*: Round answers to one decimal place.)

Brief Exercise 2-26 Service Organization Income Statement

OBJECTIVE ▶ 3
Example 2.8

Allstar Exposure designs and sells advertising services to small, relatively unknown companies. Last month, Allstar had sales commissions costs of $50,000, technology costs of $75,000, and research and development costs of $200,000. Selling expenses were $10,000, and administrative expenses equaled $35,000. Sales totaled $410,000.

Required:

1. Prepare an income statement for Allstar for the past month.
2. Briefly explain why Allstar's income statement has no line item for cost of goods sold.

BRIEF EXERCISES: SET B

Use the following information for Brief Exercises 2-27 and 2-28:
Morning Smiles Coffee Company manufactures Stoneware French Press coffee makers for use in dorm rooms, apartments, homes, and travel situations where customers desire high-quality coffee in small amounts. Last week, direct materials (stoneware, paint, enamel, and steel) costing $100,000 were put into production. Direct labor of $18,000 (10 workers × 100 hours × $18 per hour) was incurred. Manufacturing overhead equaled $50,000. By the end of the week, Morning Smiles had manufactured 2,000 Stoneware French Press coffee makers.

Brief Exercise 2-27 Total Product Cost and Per-Unit Product Cost

OBJECTIVE ▶ 2
Example 2.1

Refer to the information for Morning Smiles Coffee Company above.

Required:

1. Calculate the total product cost for last week.
2. Calculate the per-unit cost of one coffee maker that was produced last week.

OBJECTIVE ▶ 2
Example 2.2

Brief Exercise 2-28 Prime Cost and Conversion Cost

Refer to the information for Morning Smiles Coffee Company on the previous page.

Required:

1. Calculate the total prime cost for last week.
2. Calculate the per-unit prime cost.
3. Calculate the total conversion cost for last week.
4. Calculate the per-unit conversion cost.

OBJECTIVE ▶ 3
Example 2.3

Brief Exercise 2-29 Direct Materials Used in Production

Morning Smiles Coffee Company manufactures Stoneware French Press coffee makers. On March 1, Morning Smiles had $25,000 of materials in inventory. During the month of March, the company purchased $350,000 of materials. On March 31, materials inventory equaled $40,000.

Required:

Calculate the direct materials used in production for the month of March.

OBJECTIVE ▶ 3
Example 2.4

Brief Exercise 2-30 Cost of Goods Manufactured

Morning Smiles Coffee Company manufactures Stoneware French Press coffee makers. During the month of March, the company purchased $350,000 of materials. Also during the month of March, Morning Smiles incurred direct labor cost of $74,000 and manufacturing overhead of $190,000. Inventory information is as follows:

	March 1	March 31
Materials	$25,000	$40,000
Work in process	55,000	46,500

Required:

1. Calculate the cost of goods manufactured for the month of March.
2. Calculate the cost of one coffee maker assuming that 8,100 coffee makers were completed during March.

OBJECTIVE ▶ 3
Example 2.5

Brief Exercise 2-31 Cost of Goods Sold

Morning Smiles Coffee Company manufactures Stoneware French Press coffee makers. During the month of March, 8,100 coffee makers were completed at a cost of goods manufactured of $607,500. Suppose that on March 1, Morning Smiles had 1,000 units in finished goods inventory costing $70,000 and on March 31, 1,100 units in finished goods inventory costing $65,000.

Required:

1. Prepare a cost of goods sold statement for the month of March.
2. Calculate the number of coffee makers that were sold during March.

> *Use the following information for Brief Exercises 2-32 and 2-33:*
> Morning Smiles Coffee Company manufactures Stoneware French Press coffee makers and sold 8,000 coffee makers during the month of March at a total cost of $612,500. Each coffee maker sold at a price of $100. Morning Smiles also incurred two types of selling costs: commissions equal to 5% of the sales price and other selling expense of $45,000. Administrative expense totaled $47,500.

Brief Exercise 2-32 Manufacturing Firm Income Statement

OBJECTIVE ▶ 3

Example 2.6

Refer to the information for Morning Smiles Coffee Company on the previous page.

Required:

Prepare an income statement for Morning Smiles for the month of March.

Brief Exercise 2-33 Income Statement Percentages

OBJECTIVE ▶ 3

Example 2.7

Refer to the information for Morning Smiles Coffee Company on the previous page.

Required:

Prepare an income statement for Morning Smiles for the month of March and calculate the percentage of sales revenue represented by each line of the income statement. (*Note*: Round answers to one decimal place.)

Brief Exercise 2-34 Service Organization Income Statement

OBJECTIVE ▶ 3

Example 2.8

Healing Hands Massage Hut offers high-end, specialized massages and grooming services, including manicures, pedicures, facials, and full-body massages. Healing Hands is a new start-up service organization that generates monthly sales of $200,000. As a startup organization, Healing Hands spends $5,000 a month on advertising in local newspapers and on social media sites. In addition, each month Healing Hands spends $100,000 to pay its team of highly specialized massage therapists, and $10,000 to a technology company (to handle the company's website, massage appointment scheduling activities, and customer communications). Further, the company incurs a $15,000 monthly expense to rent its hut space in a hip new retail market. Finally, Healing Hands incurs $20,000 of monthly administrative expenses.

Required:

1. Prepare an income statement for Healing Hands for the past month.
2. Briefly explain why Healing Hands' income statement has no line item for cost of goods sold.

EXERCISES

Exercise 2-35 Cost Assignment

OBJECTIVE ▶ 1

EXCEL

The sales staff of Central Media (a locally owned radio and cable television station) consists of two salespeople, Derek and Lawanna. During March, the following salaries and commissions were paid:

	Derek	Lawanna
Salaries	$25,000	$30,000
Commissions	6,000	1,500

Derek spends 100% of his time selling advertising. Lawanna spends two-thirds of her time selling advertising and the remaining one-third on administrative work. Commissions are paid only on sales.

(Continued)

Required:

1. Accumulate these costs by account by filling in the following table:

Cost	Salaries	Commissions
Derek		
Lawanna		
Total		

2. Assign the costs of salaries and commissions to selling expense and administrative expense by filling in the following table:

Cost	Selling Costs	Administrative Costs
Derek's salary		
Lawanna's salary		
Derek's commissions		
Lawanna's commissions		
Total		

OBJECTIVE 1 ▶ **Exercise 2-36 Products versus Services, Cost Assignment**

Holmes Company produces wooden playhouses. When a customer orders a playhouse, it is delivered in pieces with detailed instructions on how to put it together. Some customers prefer that Holmes put the playhouse together. Therefore, these customers purchase the playhouse, as well as pay an additional fee for Holmes to install the playhouse. Holmes then pulls two workers off the production line and sends them to construct the playhouse on site.

Required:

1. What two products does Holmes sell? Classify each one as a product or a service.
2. **CONCEPTUAL CONNECTION** Do you think Holmes assigns costs individually to each product or service? Why or why not?
3. **CONCEPTUAL CONNECTION** Describe the opportunity cost of the installation process.

OBJECTIVE 1 ▶ **Exercise 2-37 Assigning Costs to a Cost Object, Direct and Indirect Costs**

Hummer Company uses manufacturing cells to produce its products (a *cell* is a manufacturing unit dedicated to the production of subassemblies or products). One manufacturing cell produces small motors for lawn mowers. Suppose that the motor manufacturing cell is the cost object. Assume that all or a portion of the following costs must be assigned to the cell.

a. Salary of cell supervisor
b. Power to heat and cool the plant in which the cell is located
c. Materials used to produce the motors
d. Maintenance for the cell's equipment (provided by the maintenance department)
e. Labor used to produce motors
f. Cafeteria that services the plant's employees
g. Depreciation on the plant
h. Depreciation on equipment used to produce the motors
i. Ordering costs for materials used in production
j. Engineering support (provided by the engineering department)
k. Cost of maintaining the plant and grounds
l. Cost of the plant's personnel office
m. Property tax on the plant and land

Required:

Classify each of the costs as a direct cost or an indirect cost to the motor manufacturing cell.

Exercise 2-38 Total and Unit Product Cost

OBJECTIVE 2

Martinez Manufacturing Inc. showed the following costs for last month:

Direct materials	$7,000
Direct labor	3,000
Manufacturing overhead	2,000
Selling expense	8,000

Last month, 4,000 units were produced and sold.

Required:

1. Classify each of the costs as product cost or period cost.
2. What is the total product cost for last month?
3. What is the unit product cost for last month?

Exercise 2-39 Cost Classification

OBJECTIVE 2

Loring Company incurred the following costs last year:

Direct materials	$ 216,000	Sales salaries	$ 65,000
Factory rent	24,000	Advertising	37,000
Direct labor	120,000	Depreciation on the headquarters	
Factory utilities	6,300	building	10,000
Supervision in the factory	50,000	Salary of the corporate receptionist	30,000
Indirect labor in the factory	30,000	Other administrative costs	175,000
Depreciation on factory equipment	9,000	Salary of the factory receptionist	28,000
Sales commissions	27,000		

Required:

1. Classify each of the costs using the following table format. Be sure to total the amounts in each column. *Example:* Direct materials, $216,000.

	Product Cost			Period Cost	
Costs	Direct Materials	Direct Labor	Manufacturing Overhead	Selling Expense	Administrative Expense
Direct materials	$216,000				

2. What was the total product cost for last year?
3. What was the total period cost for last year?
4. If 30,000 units were produced last year, what was the unit product cost?

Exercise 2-40 Classifying Cost of Production

OBJECTIVE 2

A factory manufactures jelly. The jars of jelly are packed six to a box, and the boxes are sold to grocery stores. The following types of cost were incurred:

Jars	Receptionist's wages
Sugar	Telephone
Fruit	Utilities
Pectin (thickener used in jams and jellies)	Rental of Santa Claus suit (for Christmas
Boxes	party for children of factory workers)
Depreciation on the factory building	Supervisory labor salaries
Cooking equipment operators' wages	Insurance on factory building
Filling equipment operators' wages	Depreciation on factory equipment
Packers' wages	Oil to lubricate filling equipment
Janitors' wages	

(Continued)

Required:

Classify each of the costs as direct materials, direct labor, or overhead by using the following table. The row for "Jars" is filled in as an example.

Costs	Direct Materials	Direct Labor	Manufacturing Overhead
Jars	X		

Use the following information for Exercises 2-41 and 2-42:
Grin Company manufactures digital cameras. In January, Grin produced 4,000 cameras with the following costs:

Direct materials	$400,000
Direct labor	80,000
Manufacturing overhead	320,000

There were no beginning or ending inventories of WIP.

OBJECTIVE 2

Exercise 2-41 **Product Cost in Total and Per Unit**

Refer to the information for Grin Company above.

Required:

1. What was the total product cost in January?
2. What was the product cost per unit in January?

OBJECTIVE 2

Exercise 2-42 **Prime Cost and Conversion Cost**

Refer to the information for Grin Company above.

Required:

1. What was the total prime cost in January?
2. What was the prime cost per unit in January?
3. What was the total conversion cost in January?
4. What was the conversion cost per unit in January?

OBJECTIVE 3

Exercise 2-43 **Direct Materials Used**

Hannah Banana Bakers makes chocolate chip cookies for cafe restaurants. In June, Hannah Banana purchased $15,500 of materials. On June 1, the materials inventory was $3,700. On June 30, $1,600 of materials remained in materials inventory.

Required:

1. What is the cost of the direct materials used in production during June?
2. **CONCEPTUAL CONNECTION** Briefly explain why there is a difference between the cost of direct materials that were *purchased* during the month and the cost of direct materials that were *used* in production during the month.

Exercise 2-44 Cost of Goods Sold

OBJECTIVE ◀ 3

Allyson Ashley makes jet skis. During the year, Allyson manufactured 94,000 jet skis. Finished goods inventory had the following units:

January 1	6,800
December 31	7,200

Required:

1. How many jet skis did Allyson sell during the year?
2. If each jet ski had a product cost of $2,200, what was the cost of goods sold last year?

Use the following information for Exercises 2-45 and 2-46:

In September, Lauren Ashley Company purchased materials costing $200,000 and incurred direct labor cost of $120,000. Overhead totaled $325,000 for the month. Information on inventories was as follows:

	September 1	September 30
Materials	$120,000	$130,000
Work in process	80,000	90,000
Finished goods	70,000	65,000

Exercise 2-45 Direct Materials Used, Cost of Goods Manufactured

OBJECTIVE ◀ 3

Refer to the information for Lauren Ashley above.

EXCEL

Required:

1. What was the cost of direct materials used in September?
2. What was the total manufacturing cost in September?
3. What was the cost of goods manufactured for September?

Exercise 2-46 Cost of Goods Sold

OBJECTIVE ◀ 3

Refer to the information for Lauren Ashely Company above.

Required:

What was the cost of goods sold for September?

Use the following information for Exercises 2-47 through 2-49.
Jasper Company provided the following information for last year:

Sales in units	280,000
Selling price	$ 12
Direct materials	180,000
Direct labor	505,000
Manufacturing overhead	110,000
Selling expense	437,000
Administrative expense	854,000

Last year, beginning and ending inventories of work in process and finished goods equaled zero.

OBJECTIVE 3   **Exercise 2-47 Cost of Goods Sold, Sales Revenue, Income Statement**

Refer to the information for Jasper Company on the previous page.

Required:

Calculate the cost of goods sold for last year.

OBJECTIVE 3   **Exercise 2-48 Income Statement**

Refer to the information for Jasper Company on the previous page.

Required:

1. Calculate the sales revenue for last year.
2. Prepare an income statement for Jasper for last year.

OBJECTIVE 3   **Exercise 2-49 Income Statement**

EXCEL

Refer to the information for Jasper Company on the previous page.

Required:

1. Prepare an income statement for Jasper for last year. Calculate the percentage of sales for each line item on the income statement. (*Note*: Round percentages to the nearest tenth of a percent.)
2. **CONCEPTUAL CONNECTION** Briefly explain how a manager could use the income statement created for Requirement 1 to better control costs.

OBJECTIVE 3   **Exercise 2-50 Understanding the Relationship between Cost Flows, Inventories, and Cost of Goods Sold**

Ivano Company has collected cost accounting information for the following subset of items for Years 1 and 2.

	Year 1	Year 2
Item:		
Direct materials used in production	a	$50,000
Direct materials: Beginning inventory	$ 10,000	c
Direct materials purchases	45,000	d
Direct materials: Ending inventory	15,000	17,000
Direct labor used in production	b	53,000
Manufacturing overhead costs used in production	80,000	76,000
Work in process: Beginning inventory	17,000	14,000
Work in process: Ending inventory	14,000	19,000
Finished goods: Beginning inventory	8,000	7,000
Finished goods: Ending inventory	7,000	11,000
Cost of goods sold	169,000	e

Required:

Calculate the values of the missing Items a through e.

PROBLEMS

Problem 2-51 Manufacturing, Cost Classification, Product Costs and Selling and Administrative Costs, Income Statement

OBJECTIVE ◄ 2 ◄ 3

Pop's Drive-Thru Burger Heaven produces and sells quarter-pound hamburgers. Each burger is wrapped and put in a "burger bag," which also includes a serving of fries and a soft drink. The price for the burger bag is $3.50. During December, 10,000 burger bags were sold. The restaurant employs college students part time to cook and fill orders. There is one supervisor (the owner, John Peterson). Pop's maintains a pool of part-time employees so that the number of employees scheduled can be adjusted to the changes in demand. Demand varies on a weekly as well as a monthly basis.

A janitor is hired to clean the building early each morning. Cleaning supplies are used by the janitor, as well as the staff, to wipe counters, wash cooking equipment, and so on. The building is leased from a local real estate company; it has no seating capacity. All orders are filled on a drive-thru basis.

The supervisor schedules work, opens the building, counts the cash, advertises, and is responsible for hiring and firing. The following costs were incurred during December:

Hamburger meat	$ 4,500	Rent	$ 1,800
Buns, lettuce, pickles, and onions	800	Depreciation, cooking equipment	
Frozen potato strips	1,250	and fixtures	600
Wrappers, bags, and condiment		Advertising	500
packages	600	Janitor's wages	520
Other ingredients	660	Janitorial supplies	150
Part-time employees' wages	7,250	Accounting fees	1,500
John Peterson's salary	3,000	Taxes	4,250
Utilities	1,500		

Pop's accountant, Elena DeMarco, does the bookkeeping, handles payroll, and files all necessary taxes. She noted that there were no beginning or ending inventories of materials. To simplify accounting for costs, Elena assumed that all part-time employees are production employees and that John Peterson's salary is selling and administrative expense. She further assumed that all rent and depreciation expense on the building and fixtures are part of product cost. Finally, she decided to put all taxes into one category, taxes, and to treat them as administrative expense.

Required:

1. Classify each of the costs for Pop's December operations using the table format given below. Be sure to total the amounts in each column.

   Example: Hamburger meat, $4,500.

Cost	Direct Materials	Direct Labor	Manufacturing Overhead	Selling and Administrative
Hamburger meat	$4,500			
Totals				

2. Prepare an income statement for the month of December.
3. **CONCEPTUAL CONNECTION** Elena made some simplifying assumptions. Were those reasonable? Suppose a good case could be made that the portion of the employees' time spent selling the burger bags was really a part of sales. In that case, would it be better to divide their time between production and selling? Should John Peterson's time be divided between marketing and administrative duties? What difference (if any) would that make on the income statement?

OBJECTIVE **1**   **Problem 2-52 Cost Assignment, Direct Costs**

Harry Whipple, owner of an inkjet printer, has agreed to allow Mary and Natalie, two friends who are pursuing master's degrees, to print several papers for their graduate courses. However, he has imposed two conditions. First, they must supply their own paper. Second, they must pay Harry a fair amount for the usage of the ink cartridge. Harry's printer takes two types of cartridges, a black one and a color one that contains the inks necessary to print in color. Black replacement cartridges cost $25.50 each and print approximately 850 pages. The color cartridge replacement cost $31 and prints approximately 310 color pages. One ream of paper costs $2.50 and contains 500 sheets. Mary's printing requirements are for 500 pages, while Natalie's are for 1,000 pages.

Required:

1. Assuming that both women write papers using text only (i.e., black ink), what is the total amount owed to Harry by Mary? By Natalie?
2. What is the total cost of printing (ink and paper) for Mary? For Natalie?
3. Now suppose that Natalie illustrates her writing with many large colorful pie charts and pictures and that about 20% of her total printing is primarily color. Mary uses no color illustrations. What is the total amount owed to Harry by Natalie? What is the total cost of printing (ink and paper) for Natalie?

OBJECTIVE **3**   **Problem 2-53 Cost of Direct Materials, Cost of Goods Manufactured, Cost of Goods Sold**

Bisby Company manufactures fishing rods. At the beginning of July, the following information was supplied by its accountant:

Raw materials inventory	$40,000
Work-in-process inventory	21,000
Finished goods inventory	23,200

During July, the direct labor cost was $43,500, raw materials purchases were $64,000, and the total overhead cost was $108,750. The inventories at the end of July were:

Raw materials inventory	$19,800
Work-in-process inventory	32,500
Finished goods inventory	22,100

Required:

1. What is the cost of the direct materials used in production during July?
2. What is the cost of goods manufactured for July?
3. What is the cost of goods sold for July?

OBJECTIVE **3**   **Problem 2-54 Preparation of Income Statement: Manufacturing Firm**

Laworld Inc. manufactures small camping tents. Last year, 200,000 tents were made and sold for $60 each. Each tent includes the following costs:

Direct materials	$18
Direct labor	12
Manufacturing overhead	16

The only selling expenses were a commission of $2 per unit sold and advertising totaling $100,000. Administrative expenses, all fixed, equaled $300,000. There were no beginning or ending finished goods inventories. There were no beginning or ending work-in-process inventories.

Required:

1. Calculate the product cost for one tent. Calculate the total product cost for last year.
2. **CONCEPTUAL CONNECTION** Prepare an income statement for external users. Did you need to prepare a supporting statement of cost of goods manufactured? Explain.
3. **CONCEPTUAL CONNECTION** Suppose 200,000 tents were produced (and 200,000 sold) but that the company had a beginning finished goods inventory of 10,000 tents produced in the prior year at $40 per unit. The company follows a first-in, first-out policy for its inventory (meaning that the units produced first are sold first for purposes of cost flow). What effect does this have on the income statement? Show the new statement.

Problem 2-55 Cost of Goods Manufactured, Cost of Goods Sold

OBJECTIVE ◀ 3

EXCEL

Hayward Company, a manufacturing firm, has supplied the following information from its accounting records for the month of May:

Direct labor cost	$10,500	Material handling	$ 3,750
Purchases of raw materials	15,000	Materials inventory, May 1	3,475
Supplies used	675	Work-in-process inventory, May 1	12,500
Factory insurance	350	Finished goods inventory, May 1	6,685
Commissions paid	2,500	Materials inventory, May 31	9,500
Factory supervision	2,225	Work-in-process inventory, May 31	14,250
Advertising	800	Finished goods inventory, May 31	4,250

Required:

1. Prepare a statement of cost of goods manufactured.
2. Prepare a statement of cost of goods sold.

Problem 2-56 Cost Identification

OBJECTIVE ◀ 1 ◀ 2

Following is a list of cost terms described in the chapter as well as a list of brief descriptive settings for each item.

Cost terms:

a. Opportunity cost
b. Period cost
c. Product cost
d. Direct labor cost
e. Selling cost

f. Conversion cost
g. Prime cost
h. Direct materials cost
i. Manufacturing overhead cost
j. Administrative cost

Settings:

1. Marcus Armstrong, manager of Timmins Optical, estimated that the cost of plastic, wages of the technician producing the lenses, and overhead totaled $30 per pair of single-vision lenses.
2. Linda was having a hard time deciding whether to return to school. She was concerned about the salary she would have to give up for the next 4 years.
3. Randy Harris is the finished goods warehouse manager for a medium-sized manufacturing firm. He is paid a salary of $90,000 per year. As he studied the financial statements prepared by the local certified public accounting firm, he wondered how his salary was treated.
4. Jamie Young is in charge of the legal department at company headquarters. Her salary is $95,000 per year. She reports to the chief executive officer.
5. All factory costs that are not classified as direct materials or direct labor.

(Continued)

6. The new product required machining, assembly, and painting. The design engineer asked the accounting department to estimate the labor cost of each of the three operations. The engineer supplied the estimated labor hours for each operation.

7. After obtaining the estimate of direct labor cost, the design engineer estimated the cost of the materials that would be used for the new product.

8. The design engineer totaled the costs of materials and direct labor for the new product.

9. The design engineer also estimated the cost of converting the raw materials into their final form.

10. The auditor for a soft drink bottling plant pointed out that the depreciation on the delivery trucks had been incorrectly assigned to product cost (through overhead). Accordingly, the depreciation charge was reallocated on the income statement.

Required:

Match the cost terms with the settings. More than one cost classification may be associated with each setting; however, select the setting that seems to fit the item best. When you are done, each cost term will be used just once.

OBJECTIVE 2 ▶ 3 ▶ **Problem 2-57 Income Statement, Cost of Services Provided, Service Attributes**

Berry Company is an architectural firm located in Detroit, Michigan. The company works with small and medium-size construction businesses to prepare building plans according to the client's contract. The following data are provided for the previous year:

Number of designs completed and sold	700	Direct labor	$ 800,000
Beginning inventory of direct materials	$ 20,000	Manufacturing overhead	100,000
Beginning inventory of designs in		Administrative expense	150,000
process	60,000	Selling expense	60,000
Ending inventory of direct materials	10,000	Beginning inventory of finished	
Ending inventory of designs in process	100,000	designs	300,000
Purchases, direct materials	40,000	Ending inventory of finished designs	280,000

Required:

1. Calculate the cost of goods manufactured.

2. Calculate the cost of goods sold.

3. Assume that the average fee for a design is $2,100. Prepare an income statement for Berry.

4. **CONCEPTUAL CONNECTION** Refer to the cost of goods sold (calculated in Requirement 2). What is the dominant cost? Briefly explain why this cost is the dominant one for Berry.

OBJECTIVE 3 ▶ **Problem 2-58 Cost of Goods Manufactured, Income Statement**

W. W. Phillips Company produced 4,000 leather recliners during the year. These recliners sell for $400 each. Phillips had 500 recliners in finished goods inventory at the beginning of the year. At the end of the year, there were 700 recliners in finished goods inventory. Phillips' accounting records provide the following information:

Purchases of raw materials	$320,000	Salary, sales supervisor	$ 90,000
Beginning materials inventory	46,800	Commissions, salespersons	180,000
Ending materials inventory	66,800	General administration	300,000
Direct labor	200,000	Beginning work-in-process	
Indirect labor	40,000	inventory	13,040
Rent, factory building	42,000	Ending work-in-process inventory	14,940
Depreciation, factory equipment	60,000	Beginning finished goods inventory	80,000
Utilities, factory	11,900	Ending finished goods inventory	114,100

Required:

1. Prepare a statement of cost of goods manufactured.
2. Compute the average cost of producing one unit of product in the year.
3. Prepare an income statement for external users.

Problem 2-59 Cost Definitions

OBJECTIVE ◀ 1

Luisa Giovanni is a student at New York University. To help pay her way through college, Luisa started a dog walking service. She has 12 client dogs—six are walked on the first shift (6:30 A.M. and 5:00 P.M.), and six are walked on the second shift (7:30 A.M. and 6:00 P.M.).

Last month, Luisa noted the following:

1. Purchase of three leashes at $10 each (she carries these with her in case a leash breaks during a walk).
2. Internet service cost of $40 a month. This enables her to keep in touch with the owners, bill them by email, and so on.
3. Dog treats of $50 to reward each dog at the end of each walk.
4. A heavy-duty raincoat and hat for $100.
5. Partway through the month, Luisa's friend, Jason, offered her a chance to play a bit role in a movie that was shooting on location in New York City. The job paid $100 and would have required Luisa to be on location at 6:00 A.M. and to remain for 12 hours. Regretfully, Luisa turned it down.
6. The dog owners pay Luisa $250 per month per dog for her services.

Required:

1. At the end of the month, how would Luisa classify her Internet payment of $40—as a cost on the balance sheet or as an expense on the income statement?
2. **CONCEPTUAL CONNECTION** Which of the above items is an opportunity cost? Why?
3. What price is charged? What is Luisa's total revenue for a month?

Problem 2-60 Cost Identification and Analysis, Cost Assignment, Income Statement

OBJECTIVE ◀ 1 ◀ 2 ◀ 3

Melissa Vassar has decided to open a printing shop. She has secured two contracts. One is a 5-year contract to print a popular regional magazine. This contract calls for 5,000 copies each month. The second contract is a 3-year agreement to print tourist brochures for the state. The state tourist office requires 10,000 brochures per month.

Melissa has rented a building for $1,400 per month. Her printing equipment was purchased for $40,000 and has a life expectancy of 20,000 hours with no salvage value. Depreciation is assigned to a period based on the hours of usage. Melissa has scheduled the delivery of the products so that two production runs are needed. In the first run, the equipment is prepared for the magazine printing. In the second run, the equipment is reconfigured for brochure printing. It takes twice as long to configure the equipment for the magazine setup as it does for the brochure setup. The total setup costs per month are $600.

Insurance costs for the building and equipment are $140 per month. Power to operate the printing equipment is strongly related to machine usage. The printing equipment causes virtually all the power costs. Power costs will run $350 per month. Printing materials will cost $0.40 per copy for the magazine and $0.08 per copy for the brochure. Melissa will hire workers to run the presses as needed (part-time workers are easy to hire). She must pay $10 per hour. Each worker can produce 20 copies of the magazine per printing hour or 100 copies of the brochure. Distribution costs are $500 per month. Melissa will receive a salary of $1,500 per month. She is responsible for personnel, accounting, sales, and production—in effect, she is responsible for administering all aspects of the business.

(Continued)

Required:

1. What are the total monthly manufacturing costs?
2. What are the total monthly prime costs? What are the total monthly prime costs for the regional magazine? For the brochure?
3. What are the total monthly conversion costs? Suppose Melissa wants to determine monthly conversion costs for each product. Assign monthly conversion costs to each product using direct tracing and driver tracing whenever possible. For those costs that cannot be assigned using a tracing approach, you may assign them using direct labor hours.
4. Melissa receives $1.80 per copy of the magazine and $0.45 per brochure. Prepare an income statement for the first month of operations.

Problem 2-61 Cost Analysis, Income Statement

Five to six times a year, **Kicker** puts on tent sales in various cities throughout Oklahoma and the surrounding states. The tent sales are designed to show Kicker customers new products, engender enthusiasm about those products, and sell soon to be out-of-date products at greatly reduced prices. Each tent sale lasts 1 day and requires parking lot space to set up the Kicker semitrailer, a couple of show cars, a disc jockey playing music, and a tent to sell Kicker merchandise, distribute brochures, and so on.

Last year, the Austin tent sale was held in a far corner of the parking lot outside the city exhibition hall where the automotive show was in progress. Because most customers were interested more in the new model cars than in the refurbishment of their current cars, foot traffic was low. In addition, customers did not want to carry speakers and amplifiers all the way back to where they had originally parked. Total direct costs for this tent sale were $14,300. Direct costs included gasoline and fuel for three pickup trucks and the semitrailer; wages and per diem for the five Kicker personnel who traveled to the show, rent on the parking lot space, and depreciation on the semitrailer, pickups, tent, tables (in tent), sound equipment, and the like. Revenue was $20,000. Cost of goods sold for the speakers was $7,000.

Required:

1. **CONCEPTUAL CONNECTION** How do you suppose Kicker accounts for the costs of the tent sales? What income statement items are affected by the tent sales?
2. **CONCEPTUAL CONNECTION** What was the profit (loss) from the Austin tent sale? What do you think Kicker might do to make it more profitable in the future?

CASES

Case 2-62 Cost Classification, Income Statement

Gateway Construction Company, run by Jack Gateway, employs 25 to 30 people as subcontractors for laying gas, water, and sewage pipelines. Most of Gateway's work comes from contracts with city and state agencies in Nebraska. The company's sales volume averages $3 million, and profits vary between 0 and 10% of sales.

Sales and profits have been somewhat below average for the past 3 years due to a recession and intense competition. Because of this competition, Jack constantly reviews the prices that other companies bid for jobs. When a bid is lost, he analyzes the reasons for the differences between his bid and that of his competitors and uses this information to increase the competitiveness of future bids.

Jack believes that Gateway's current accounting system is deficient. Currently, all expenses are simply deducted from revenues to arrive at operating income. No effort is made to distinguish among the costs of laying pipe, obtaining contracts, and administering the company. Yet all bids are based on the costs of laying pipe.

With these thoughts in mind, Jack looked more carefully at the income statement for the previous year (see below). First, he noted that jobs were priced on the basis of equipment hours, with an average price of $165 per equipment hour. However, when it came to classifying and assigning costs, he needed some help. One thing that really puzzled him was how to classify his own $114,000 salary. About half of his time was spent in bidding and securing contracts, and the other half was spent in general administrative matters.

Gateway Construction Company
Income Statement
For the Year Ended December 31, 2017

Sales (18,200 equipment hours @ $165 per hour)		$3,003,000
Less expenses:		
Utilities	$ 24,000	
Machine operators	218,000	
Rent, office building	24,000	
CPA fees	20,000	
Other direct labor	265,700	
Administrative salaries	114,000	
Supervisory salaries	70,000	
Pipe	1,401,340	
Tires and fuel	418,600	
Depreciation, equipment	198,000	
Salaries of mechanics	50,000	
Advertising	15,000	
Total expenses		2,818,640
Operating income		$ 184,360

Required:

1. Classify the costs in the income statement as (1) costs of laying pipe (production costs), (2) costs of securing contracts (selling costs), or (3) costs of general administration. For production costs, identify direct materials, direct labor, and overhead costs. The company never has significant work in process (most jobs are started and completed within a day).
2. Assume that a significant driver is equipment hours. Identify the expenses that would likely be traced to jobs using this driver. Explain why you feel these costs are traceable using equipment hours. What is the cost per equipment hour for these traceable costs?

Case 2-63 Cost Information and Ethical Behavior, Service Organization

OBJECTIVE 1 2

Jean Erickson, manager and owner of an advertising company in Charlotte, North Carolina, arranged a meeting with Leroy Gee, the chief accountant of a large, local competitor. The two are lifelong friends. They grew up together in a small town and attended the same university. Leroy is a competent, successful accountant but is having some personal financial difficulties after some of his investments turned sour, leaving him with a $15,000 personal loan to pay off— just when his oldest son is starting college.

Jean, on the other hand, is struggling to establish a successful advertising business. She had recently acquired the rights to open a branch office of a large regional advertising firm headquartered in Atlanta, Georgia. During her first 2 years, she was able to build a small, profitable practice. However, the chance to gain a significant foothold in Charlotte hinged on the success of winning a bid to represent the state of North Carolina in a major campaign to attract new industry and tourism. The meeting she had scheduled with Leroy concerned the bid she planned to submit.

(Continued)

Jean: Leroy, I'm at a critical point in my business venture. If I can win the bid for the state's advertising dollars, I'll be set. Winning the bid will bring $600,000 to $700,000 of revenues into the firm. On top of that, I estimate that the publicity will bring another $200,000 to $300,000 of new business.

Leroy: I understand. My boss is anxious to win that business as well. It would mean a huge increase in profits for my firm. It's a competitive business, though. As new as you are, I doubt that you'll have much chance of winning.

Jean: You're forgetting two very important considerations. First, I have the backing of all the resources and talent of a regional firm. Second, I have some political connections. Last year, I was hired to run the publicity side of the governor's campaign. He was impressed with my work and would like me to have this business. I am confident that the proposals I submit will be very competitive. My only concern is to submit a bid that beats your firm. If I come in with a lower bid and good proposals, the governor can see to it that I get the work.

Leroy: Sounds promising. If you do win, however, there will be a lot of upset people. After all, they are going to claim that the business should have been given to local advertisers, not to some out-of-state firm. Given the size of your office, you'll have to get support from Atlanta. You could take a lot of heat.

Jean: True. But I am the owner of the branch office. That fact alone should blunt most of the criticism. Who can argue that I'm not a local? Listen, with your help, I think I can win this bid. Furthermore, if I do win it, you can reap some direct benefits. With that kind of business, I can afford to hire an accountant, and I'll make it worthwhile for you to transfer jobs. I can offer you an up-front bonus of $15,000. On top of that, I'll increase your annual salary by 20%. That should solve most of your financial difficulties. After all, we have been friends since day one—and what are friends for?

Leroy: Jean, my wife would be ecstatic if I were able to improve our financial position as quickly as this opportunity affords. I certainly hope that you win the bid. What kind of help can I provide?

Jean: Simple. To win, all I have to do is beat the bid of your firm. Before I submit my bid, I would like you to review it. With the financial skills you have, it should be easy for you to spot any excessive costs that I may have included. Or perhaps I included the wrong kind of costs. By cutting excessive costs and eliminating costs that may not be directly related to the project, my bid should be competitive enough to meet or beat your firm's bid.

Required:

1. What would you do if you were Leroy? Fully explain the reasons for your choice. What do you suppose the code of conduct for Leroy's company would say about this situation?
2. What is the likely outcome if Leroy agrees to review the bid? Is there much risk to him personally if he reviews the bid? Should the degree of risk have any bearing on his decision?

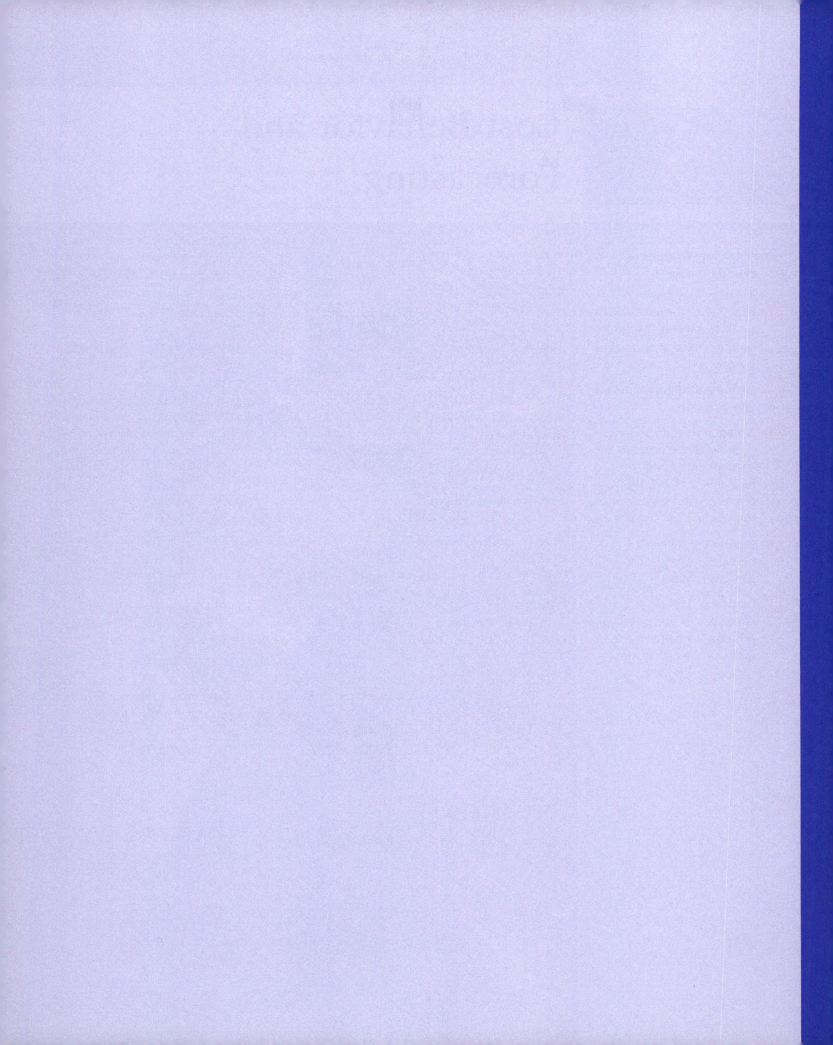

3

Cost Behavior and Forecasting

After studying Chapter 3, you should be able to:

1 Explain the meaning of cost behavior, and define and describe fixed and variable costs.

2 Define and describe mixed and step costs.

3 Separate mixed costs into their fixed and variable components using the high-low method, the scattergraph method, and the method of least squares.

4 Explain the difference between absorption and variable costing.

5 (*Appendix 3A*) Use a computer spreadsheet program to perform the method of least squares.

Steven Pepple/Shutterstock.com

EXPERIENCE MANAGERIAL DECISIONS

with Zingerman's

Have you ever walked by a bakery counter, or even Mom's kitchen, and been stopped in your tracks by the unmistakable aroma of freshly baked bread or homemade cookies? If so, cost behavior was probably the furthest thing from your mind. However, for the owners of **Zingerman's** deli and bakery, founded in 1982 in Ann Arbor, Michigan, cost behavior is critical in making decisions that improve Zingerman's profitability.

In total, Zingerman's tracks and manages over 3,000 distinct costs! For example, Zingerman's pays close attention to variable costs, such as the all-natural, non-alkalized cocoa powder ingredient used in its signature Hot Cocoa Cake, and the size of its hourly workforce, which varies by season. Zingerman's also closely manages its numerous fixed costs, such as ovens and recipe "research and development" creation, across different production and sales levels to be sure that it doesn't make decisions that increase costs to a greater extent than revenues. Still other costs are mixed in nature, and the variable and fixed components must be disentangled before Zingerman's owners can budget for future periods, set prices, and plan for growth in the businesses. So, the next time you bite into a warm chocolate chip cookie, think about—if only for a brief moment—all of the cost behaviors that went into producing, packaging, selling, and distributing that tasty bite of joy!

> "Zingerman's also closely manages its numerous fixed costs, such as ovens and recipe "research and development" creation, across different production and sales levels to be sure that it doesn't make decisions that increase costs to a greater extent than revenues."

Chapter 2 discussed various types of costs and looked closely at manufacturing and service costs. The primary concern of the chapter was organizing costs into production, selling, and administrative costs and building related schedules of the cost of goods manufactured, cost of goods sold, and income statements. Now let's focus on cost behavior—the way costs change as the related activity changes.

Cost behavior is the *foundation* upon which managerial accounting is built. In financial accounting, the theoretical pyramid contains critical assumptions (e.g., going concern assumption) and principles (e.g., matching principle) necessary for helping financial accountants properly record transactions and prepare financial statements. In much the same way, managers must properly understand cost behavior in order to make wise decisions. For example, **Deloitte**'s fourth biennial cost survey of 210 senior executives from Fortune 1000 companies reports the critical importance of understanding and managing various costs to achieve key business objectives, such as creating growth, retaining top employee talent and profitable customers, and gaining competitive advantage.[1]

Costs can be variable, fixed, mixed, or even semi-variable or semi-fixed in more complex business environments. Knowing how costs change as output changes—from various business actions such **Procter &Gamble**'s decision to sell off half its brands[2]—is essential to planning, controlling, and decision making. For example, suppose that BlueDenim Company expects demand for its jeans product to increase by 10% next year. How will that affect the total costs budgeted for the factory? Clearly, BlueDenim will need 10% more raw materials (denim, thread, zippers, and so on). It will also need more cutting and sewing labor because someone will need to make the additional jeans. These costs are variable. But the factory building will probably not need to be expanded. Neither will the factory need an additional receptionist or plant manager. Those costs are fixed. As long as BlueDenim's accountant understands the behavior of the fixed and variable costs, it will be possible to develop a fairly accurate budget for the next year.

Budgeting, deciding to keep or drop a product line (e.g., **Nike**'s ongoing decision to keep, drop, or alter its LeBron shoe line), and evaluating the performance of a segment (e.g., **FOX**'s decision to discontinue its once top-rated show, *American Idol*, after 15 seasons) all benefit from knowledge of cost behavior. In fact, failure to know and understand cost behavior can lead to poor—even disastrous—decisions. This chapter discusses cost behavior in depth so that a proper foundation is laid for its use in studying other cost management topics.

OBJECTIVE 1

Explain the meaning of cost behavior, and define and describe fixed and variable costs.

BASICS OF COST BEHAVIOR

$Here's$ **Why It's important**

CONCEPT CLIP

Cost behavior is the general term for describing whether and how a cost changes when the level of output changes. A cost that does not change in total as output changes is a *fixed cost*. A *variable cost*, on the other hand, increases in total with an increase in output and decreases in total with a decrease in output. As illustrated with numerous examples throughout this chapter, many critical business decisions require a thorough understanding of cost behavior. As discussed in the opening company scenario, even a relatively small family-run business like **Zingerman's** tracks and manages over 3,000 distinct costs! A failure to predict and manage simple cost behavior, such as variable and fixed costs, as well as more complex cost behavior, such as mixed, step, and semi-variable costs, can significantly damage business performance and even lead to business failure. Therefore, let's first review the basics of cost and output measures. Then we will look at fixed and variable costs.

---

1 Deloitte, "Thriving in Uncertainty: Cost Improvement Practices and Trends in the Fortune 1000" (April 2016). Taken from http://www2.deloitte.com/content/dam/Deloitte/us/Documents/process-and-operations/us-deloitte-cost-survey-report-2016.pdf.

2 Alexander Coolidge, "P&G Sells Off Shampoo Brands" (March 3, 2016). Taken from http://www.cincinnati.com/story/money/2016/03/03/pg-sells-off-shampoo-brands/81259498/.

Measures of Output and the Relevant Range

In order to determine the behavior of a cost, we need to have a good grasp of the cost under consideration and a measure of the output associated with the activity. The terms *fixed cost* and *variable cost* do not exist in a vacuum; they only have meaning when related to some output measure. In other words, a cost is fixed or variable with respect to some output measure or driver. In order to understand the behavior of costs, we must first determine the underlying business activity and ask "What causes the cost of this particular activity to go up (or down)?" A **cost driver** is a causal factor that measures the output of the activity that leads (or causes) costs to change. Identifying and managing drivers helps managers better predict and control costs. For instance, weather is a significant driver in the airline industry, especially when storms concentrate in the country's busiest flight corridors such as the Northeast and Midwest. One analyst estimated that the particularly cold weather caused by a week of polar vortex conditions led to the cancellation of about 20,000 flights nationwide at a cost of $100 million to the U.S. airline industry as measured by lost revenue and incremental costs for items such as rotating in well-rested pilots after repeated airport delays![3]

Suppose that BlueDenim Company wants to classify its product costs as either variable or fixed with respect to the number of jeans produced. In this case, the number of jeans produced is the driver. Clearly, the use of raw materials (denim, thread, zippers, and buttons) varies with the number of jeans produced. So, materials costs are variable with respect to the number of units produced. How about electricity to run the sewing machines? That, too, is variable with respect to the number of jeans produced because the more jeans that are produced, the more sewing machine time is needed, and the more electricity it takes. Finally, what about the cost of supervision for the sewing department? Whether the company produces many pairs of jeans or fewer pairs of jeans, the cost of supervision is unchanged. So, we would say that supervision is fixed with respect to the number of jeans produced.

How does the relevant range fit into cost relationships? The **relevant range** is the range of output over which the assumed cost relationship is valid for the normal operations of a firm. The relevant range limits the cost relationship to the range of operations that the firm normally expects to occur. Let's consider BlueDenim's cost relationships more carefully. We said that the salary of the supervisor is strictly fixed. But is that true? If the company produced just a few pairs of jeans a year, it would not even need a supervisor. Surely the owner could handle that task (and probably a good number of other tasks as well). On the other hand, suppose that BlueDenim increased its current production by two or three times, perhaps by adding a second and third shift. One supervisor could not possibly handle all three shifts. So, when we talk about supervision cost, we are implicitly talking about it for the range of production that normally occurs. We now take a closer look at fixed, variable, and mixed costs. In each case, the cost is related to only one driver and is defined within the relevant range.

Fixed Costs

Fixed costs are costs that *in total* are constant within the relevant range as the level of output increases or decreases. For example, Southwest Airlines operates a large fleet of 737s. The cost of these planes represents a fixed cost to the airline because, within the relevant range, the cost does not change as the number of flights or the number of passengers changes. Similarly, the rental cost of warehouse space by a wholesaler is fixed for the term of the lease. If the wholesaler's sales go up or down, the cost of the leased warehouse stays the same.

---

3 Chris Isidore, "Storm Costs Airlines Up to $100 Million," CNNMoney (January 8, 2014). http://money.cnn.com/2014/01/08/news/companies/storm-cost-airlines/(accessed January 28, 2014).

Here's How It's Used: AT KICKER

Kicker uses information on cost behavior to guide new programs. For example, the variable cost of manufacturing speakers led Kicker to work with its manufacturers to both increase quality and decrease cost. Fixed costs at the Stillwater location also received attention. Several years ago Safety Director Terry Williams faced a problem with worker safety. Cost information based on a number of indicators revealed the problem:

- The cost of workmen's compensation insurance was high.
- The workmen's compensation experience rating was high.
- The number of injuries was up.
- The number of injuries requiring time off was up.
- The number of back injuries (the most serious type) was up.
- The average cost per injury was up.

Terry looked for the root cause of the problem and discovered that improper lifting led to the more serious back injuries. He instituted a comprehensive safety program emphasizing 20 minutes of stretching exercises each day (five minutes before work, five minutes after each break, and five minutes after lunch).

Was the program a success? At first, the workers resisted the stretching, so Terry got them weight belts. The workers hated them. They went back to stretching. But this time, any worker who refused to stretch had to wear the weight belt for 30 days. This was a highly visible sign of failure to adhere to the program. In addition, Kicker's president was a big proponent of the safety program. He explained the impact of the increased insurance premiums and lost work time on the Kicker profit-sharing program. The profit-sharing program is an important extra for Kicker employees. Each employee makes it his or her job to contribute to the bottom line whenever possible.

Over several months, workers bought into the program. The indicators decreased dramatically. The cost of workmen's compensation insurance decreased by nearly 50%, the average cost per injury is less than 5% of the pre-safety program cost, and there is no lost work time.

Here's Why It's important

Fixed costs are extremely important to understand because they usually are relatively large in amount. Therefore, effective business decisions involving financial estimations often include fixed costs. Managers who understand when and if fixed costs will change as a result of various business decisions usually fare much better than managers who fail to understand fixed cost behavior.

To illustrate fixed cost behavior, consider a factory operated by Colley Computers Inc., a company that produces unlabeled personal computers for small computer stores across the Midwest. The assembly department of the factory assembles components into a completed personal computer. Assume that Colley Computers wants to look at the cost relationship between supervision cost and the number of computers processed and has the following information:

- The assembly department can process up to 50,000 computers per year.
- The assemblers (direct labor) are supervised by a production-line manager who is paid $32,000 per year.
- The company was established 5 years ago.
- Currently, the factory produces 40,000 to 50,000 computers per year.
- Production has never fallen below 20,000 computers in a year.

The cost of supervision for several levels of production is as follows:

Colley Computers Inc.
Cost of Supervision

Number of Computers Produced	Total Cost of Supervision	Unit Cost
20,000	$32,000	$1.60
30,000	32,000	1.07
40,000	32,000	0.80
50,000	32,000	0.64

The cost relationship considered is between supervision cost and the number of computers processed. The number of computers processed is called the *output measure*, or *driver*. Since Colley Computers has been processing between 20,000 and 50,000 computers per year, the relevant range is 20,000 to 50,000. Notice that the *total* cost of supervision remains constant within this range as more computers are processed. Colley Computers pays $32,000 for supervision regardless of whether it processes 20,000, 40,000, or 50,000 computers.

Pay particular attention to the words *in total* in the definition of fixed costs. While the total cost of supervision remains unchanged as more computers are processed, the unit cost does change as the level of output changes. As the example in the table shows, within the relevant range, the unit cost of supervision decreases from $1.60 to $0.64. Because of the behavior of per-unit fixed costs, it is easy to get the impression that the fixed costs themselves are affected by changes in the level of output. But that is not true. Instead, higher output means that the fixed costs can be spread over more units and are thus smaller per unit. Unit fixed costs can often be misleading and may lead to poor decisions. It is often safer to work with total fixed costs.

Let's take a look at the graph of fixed costs given in **Exhibit 3.1**. For the relevant range, the horizontal line indicates fixed cost behavior. Notice that at 40,000 computers processed, supervision cost is $32,000; at 50,000 computers processed, supervision is also $32,000. This line visually demonstrates that cost remains unchanged as the level of the activity driver varies. For the relevant range, total fixed costs are simply an amount. For Colley Computers, supervision cost amounted to $32,000 for any level of output between 20,000 and 50,000 computers processed. Thus, supervision is a fixed cost and can be expressed as:

$$\text{Supervision Cost} = \$32,000$$

Strictly speaking, this equation assumes that the fixed costs are $32,000 for all levels (as if the line extends to the vertical axis as indicated by the dashed portion in Exhibit 3.1). Although this assumption is not true, it is harmless if the operating decisions are confined to the relevant range.

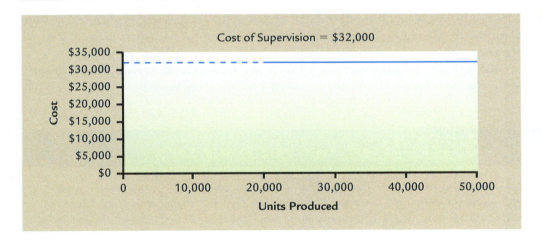

Exhibit 3.1

Colley Computers Fixed Cost of Supervision

Can fixed costs change? Of course, but this possibility does not make them variable. They are fixed at a new higher (or lower) rate. Going back to Colley Computers, suppose that the company gives a raise to the assembly department supervisor. Instead of being paid $32,000 per year, the salary is $34,000 per year. The cost of supervision within the relevant range is $34,000 per year. However, supervision cost is still *fixed* with respect to the number of computers produced.

Discretionary Fixed Costs Versus Committed Fixed Costs By their nature, fixed costs are difficult to change quickly—that is why they are considered fixed. Two types of fixed costs are commonly recognized: discretionary fixed costs and committed fixed costs. **Discretionary fixed costs** are fixed costs that can be changed or avoided relatively easily in the short run at management discretion. For example, advertising is a discretionary fixed cost. Advertising cost depends on the decision by management to purchase print, radio, or video advertising. This cost might depend on the size of the ad or the number of times it runs, but it does *not* depend on the number of units produced and sold. Management can easily decide to increase or decrease dollars spent on advertising.

As another example, just before a new season, the **National Football League (NFL)** was forced to make a decision involving discretionary costs when it realized that **Wilson Sporting Goods** had already manufactured 500,000 footballs (of the 900,000 footballs needed for the entire season) with the signature of the outgoing NFL commissioner—Paul Tagliabue—instead of the incoming commissioner—Roger Goodell. The NFL had to decide whether to play the entire season or only half of the season with the incoming commissioner's signature on the balls. In the end, the NFL decided to give the 500,000 existing balls away to high schools. In this case, the $250,000 additional cost to produce another 500,000 balls with the new signature is a discretionary cost because it could be changed (i.e., avoided) relatively easily. The $250,000 is a discretionary cost that is entirely fixed because the NFL needed to purchase the additional footballs regardless of the number of games played (the driver for football cost).

Committed fixed costs, on the other hand, are fixed costs that cannot be easily changed. Often, committed fixed costs are those that involve a long-term contract (e.g., leasing of machinery or warehouse space) or the purchase of property, plant, and equipment. For example, a construction company may lease heavy-duty earth-moving equipment for a period of 3 years. The lease cost is a committed fixed cost.

Variable Costs

Variable costs are costs that in total vary in direct proportion to changes in output within the relevant range. The costs of producing and assembling the propeller on each boat manufactured by **Boston Whaler** represent variable costs for a manufacturer. In a dentist's office, certain supplies, such as floss, X-ray film, and the disposable bib used on each patient, vary with the number of patients seen. **Binney & Smith**, the maker of Crayola crayons, finds that the cost of wax and pigments varies with the number of crayons produced.

Here's **Why It's important**

Variable costs are part of several critically important performance measures used throughout managerial accounting, including contribution margin (see Chapter 7 on cost-volume-profit

Here's How It's Used: AT ZINGERMAN'S

Recall **Zingerman's** from the chapter opening feature. Zingerman's management uses its understanding of discretionary and nondiscretionary fixed costs to make wise decisions during brief periods of peak demand. The deli's labor and food costs—both variable in nature—go up when business volume increases. Other costs, including some of its larger fixed costs, also can increase when volume pushes the company beyond its relevant range. As a result, management has to be creative to manage its costs in the most effective manner possible. For example, Zingerman's bakeshop manager, Katie,

explains that she needs considerable extra freezer capacity for the Christmas holidays, but management does not want to permanently incur the added fixed cost of another large freezer (i.e., a *nondiscretionary* fixed cost). Instead, Zingerman's rents two freezer trucks for the short time Katie needs them (i.e., a *discretionary* fixed cost). Of course, in order to make wise choices regarding these important cost decisions, Katie has to be able to forecast customer demand and costs, which requires that she understand the idea of discretionary and nondiscretionary costs.

behavior), segment margin (see Chapter 8 on segmented income statements for keep-or-drop decisions), and variable costing (discussed later in this chapter and useful in various decisions such as predatory pricing scenarios).

To illustrate, let's expand the Colley Computers example to include the cost of the DVD-ROM drive that is installed in each computer. Here the cost is the cost of direct materials—the DVD-ROM drive—and the output measure is the number of computers processed. Each computer requires one DVD-ROM drive costing $40. The cost of DVD-ROM drives for various levels of production is as follows:

Colley Computers Inc.
Cost of DVD-ROM Drives

Number of Computers Produced	Total Cost of DVD-ROM Drives	Unit Cost
20,000	$ 800,000	$40
30,000	1,200,000	40
40,000	1,600,000	40
50,000	2,000,000	40

As more computers are produced, the total cost of DVD-ROM drives increases in direct proportion. For example, as production doubles from 20,000 to 40,000 units, the *total* cost of DVD-ROM drives doubles from $800,000 to $1,600,000. Notice also that the unit cost of direct materials is constant.

Variable costs can also be represented by a linear equation. Here, total variable cost depends on the level of output. This relationship can be described by the following equation:

Total Variable Cost = Variable Rate × Units of Output

The relationship that describes the cost of disk drives is:

Total Variable Cost = $40 × Number of Computers

Applying this to Colley, at 50,000 computers processed, the total cost of disk drives is:

$2,000,000 = $40 × 50,000 computers processed

At 30,000 computers processed, the total cost would be $1,200,000.

Exhibit 3.2 shows graphically that variable cost behavior is represented by a straight line extending out from the origin. Notice that at zero units processed, total variable cost is zero. However, as units produced increase, the total variable cost also increases. Total cost increases in direct proportion to increases in the number of computers processed; the rate of increase is measured by the slope of the line.

Similar to some fixed costs, certain variable costs also can be discretionary. **Discretionary variable costs** are variable costs that can be changed or avoided relatively easily in the short run at management discretion. For example, by offering free gift wrapping with every purchase during the holiday shopping season, **Athleta Clothing** would incur discretionary variable costs. Athleta incurs more total gift wrapping cost as it makes more sales; it can choose to end its policy at any time, thereby making this cost both variable and discretionary. On the other hand, an author textbook royalty is a nondiscretionary (i.e., unavoidable) variable cost. Royalty cost increases (decreases) as the number of textbooks sold increases (decreases) and, therefore, is a variable cost. However, the textbook publisher cannot reduce its royalty cost by simply no longer paying authors their full royalty because such costs are required by the author–publisher contract—in other words, they are nondiscretionary in nature.

Exhibit 3.2

Colley Computers Variable Cost of
DVD-ROM Drives

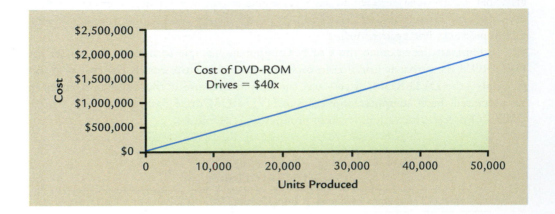

More Advanced Cost Behavior: The Reasonableness of Straight-Line Cost Relationships

The graphs of fixed and variable costs that were just reviewed show cost relationships that are straight lines. Are real-world cost relationships linear? This section examines this premise for variable costs, while the next section examines the linearity assumption for fixed costs.

Semi-Variable Costs

For Colley Computers, the DVD-ROM drives cost $40 each—no matter how many were purchased. However, if only a few drives were bought, the per-unit cost likely would be higher. So, there are economies of scale in producing larger quantities of output. For example, at extremely low levels of output, workers often use more materials per unit or require more time per unit than they do at higher levels of output. Then, as the level of output increases, workers learn how to use materials and time more efficiently so that the variable cost per unit decreases as more and more output is produced. As such, when economies of scale are present, the true total cost function is increasing at a *decreasing* rate, as shown by the nonlinear cost curve in **Exhibit 3.3**. Some managers refer to costs that behave in this manner as semi-variable costs. Therefore, a **semi-variable cost** is a cost that is variable in nature but whose rate of change is not constant.

Exhibit 3.3

Semi-Variable Cost: Decreasing
Rate

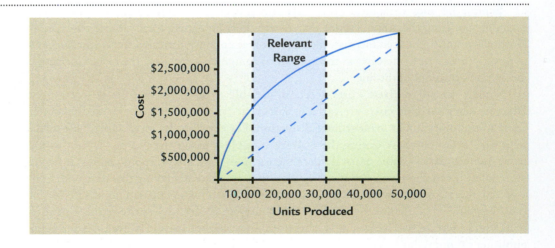

Alternately, a semi-variable cost might behave such that the total cost function is increasing at an *increasing* rate. A direct materials cost might behave in this manner when the supply of the raw material becomes increasingly scarce as the total industry output (or consumption)

grows particularly large. For example, electric car battery production requires certain rare earth minerals, such as terbium, dysprosium, and cobalt, that have a per-unit cost that can increase significantly as output reaches high levels. This particular type of cost behavior is not as common as traditional fixed or variable cost behavior. However, failing to recognize and predict semi-variable costs that increase at an increasing rate can lead to disastrous outcomes for businesses because total costs increase considerably over a relatively short output range, as shown by the nonlinear cost curve in **Exhibit 3.4**.

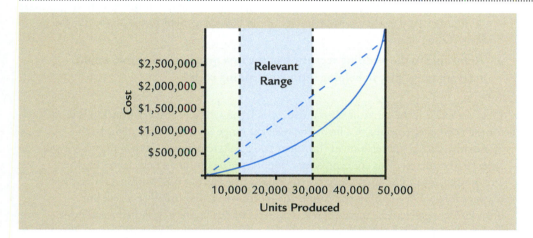

Exhibit 3.4
Semi-Variable Cost: Increasing Rate

CONCEPT CLIP

When unit costs change in this semi-variable way, how do we choose the correct variable rate? Fortunately, the relevant range can help. Recall that *relevant range* is defined as the range of activity for which the assumed cost relationships are valid. Exhibits 3.3 and 3.4 show how the relevant range can be used to see how well a straight line approximates variable cost. Note in Exhibit 3.3 that for units of output below 10,000 on the *x*-axis, the approximation appears to break down (i.e., the curved actual semi-variable cost curve does not match the dotted straight line as closely as it does for *higher* levels of output within the relevant range). Similarly, in Exhibit 3.4, note that for units of output above 30,000 on the *x*-axis, the approximation also appears to break down but in the opposite direction (i.e., the curved actual semi-variable cost curve does not match the dotted straight line as closely as it does for *lower* levels of output within the relevant range). Therefore, managers must be extremely careful in applying cost behavior assumptions to decision making whenever the output level falls outside of—either below or above—the company's relevant range of operations.

Here's How It's Used: SUSTAINABILITY

Not surprisingly, companies manage their use of oil to control costs and improve profitability. Increasingly, they are turning their attention toward the semi-variable costs associated with managing an additional scarce resource—water. For example, **Levi Strauss & Co.** discloses in its sustainability report that a single pair of 501® jeans uses 3,781 liters of water in its full lifecycle! This lifecycle spans from growing cotton for materials, through manufacturing the finished product, consumer washing, and eventual end of life disposal. Changing industries, **Guinness** notes that 90% of beer is actually water and, as a result, it has worked hard to reduce its water usage

in the production process by 6 billion liters! However, despite such conservation efforts, given the scarcity of water, many government water districts set the price of water such that the more a business uses, the more the district charges it per unit. Furthermore, some districts charge even higher starting per-unit rates—and increase them more steeply as usage increases—during various stages of drought than during normal conditions. Therefore, in order to make financially sound decisions, managers must recognize when a decision entails semi-variable costs such as water usage, especially when the total semi-variable cost increases at an increasing rate!

1. **Consider the costs of a wedding reception. Which costs are fixed? Which costs are variable? What output measure did you use in classifying the costs as fixed or variable?**

Answer:

Often, the number of guests is the output measure for a wedding reception. Variable costs might include the cost of food and drinks as their total cost likely varies with the number of guests. Fixed costs might include rental of the reception venue, gratuity paid to the priest or Justice of the Peace, payment to the band, and the bride's wedding dress.

2. **Returning to the wedding reception in the first question, what role would relevant range play in helping estimate wedding costs?**

Answer:

Relevant range is the range of output over which the assumed cost relationship is valid for the normal operations of a firm. The relevant range for a wedding might be the approximate size—perhaps small (less than 100 guests), medium (100–300 guests), and large (300+ guests). This concept is very important to consider when estimating the wedding costs as some costs are likely to be fixed in total, but only within a respective relevant range. For example, the cost of the reception facility usually is fixed, but only within a particular range. Therefore, a $10,000 fee might be charged to rent one banquet room within the reception facility that holds a maximum of 100 guests. If the number of wedding guests increases beyond 100, then this cost would jump up to a higher level as the wedding party would need to rent a larger room within the facility thereby increasing the total rental fee (e.g., perhaps to $20,000). Similarly, the cost of the wedding cake is fixed in total; however, this fixed cost would be greater for a wedding with 500 guests than it would be for 75 guests.

OBJECTIVE **2**

Define and describe mixed and step costs.

 Why It's important

MIXED COSTS AND STEP COSTS

While strictly fixed and variable costs are easy to handle, many costs do not fall into those categories. Often, costs are a combination of fixed and variable costs (mixed costs) or have an increased fixed component at specified intervals (step costs).

Mixed Costs

Mixed costs are costs that have both a fixed and a variable component. For example, sales representatives often are paid a salary plus a commission on sales. The formula for a mixed cost is as follows:

> Total Cost = Total Fixed Cost + Total Variable Cost

Suppose that Colley Computers has 10 sales representatives, each earning a salary of $30,000 per year plus a commission of $25 per computer sold. The activity is selling, and the output measure is units sold. If 50,000 computers are sold, then the total cost associated with the sales representatives is:

= (10 sales reps × $30,000 salary) + ($25 per-unit commission × 50,000 computers sold)
= $300,000 + $1,250,000 = $1,550,000

The cost of Colley's sales representatives is therefore represented by the following equation:

$$\text{Total Cost} = \$300,000 + (\$25 \times \text{Number of Computers Sold})$$

The following table shows the selling cost for different levels of sales activity:

Colley Computers Inc.				
Fixed Cost of Selling	Variable Cost of Selling	Total Cost	Computers Sold	Selling Cost per Unit
$300,000	$ 500,000	$ 800,000	20,000	$40.00
300,000	750,000	1,050,000	30,000	35.00
300,000	1,000,000	1,300,000	40,000	32.50
300,000	1,250,000	1,550,000	50,000	31.00

The graph for our mixed cost example is given in **Exhibit 3.5** (assuming a relevant range of 0 to 50,000 units). Costs are represented in the following ways:

- Mixed costs are represented by a line that intercepts the vertical axis (at $300,000 for this example).
- Fixed costs correspond with the *y*-intercept.
- Variable cost per unit of activity driver is given by the slope of the line ($25 for this example).

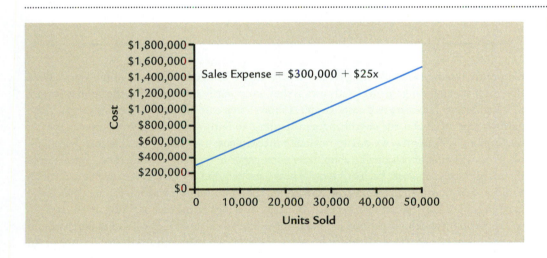

Exhibit 3.5

Mixed Cost Behavior

Step Cost Behavior

So far, we have assumed that the cost function is continuous. In reality, some cost functions may be discontinuous. These costs are known as *step costs* (or semi-fixed). **Step costs** display a constant level of total cost for a range of output and then jump to a higher level (or step) of total cost at some point, where they remain for a similar range of output. The width of the step defines the range of output for which a particular amount of the resource applies. Such step function costs often are very difficult to recognize because predicting the exact output level at which a step cost will next jump up (i.e., increase) or step down (i.e., decrease) can be unclear. In addition, remember from the opening vignette that Zingerman's—a relatively small family-run business—measures and tracks over 3,000 costs! Having to keep track of the various cost behavior patterns of so many costs also adds to the difficulty in predicting and managing step cost behavior.

Here's Why It's important

Recall that Zingerman's experiences significant increases in its sales volume during the Christmas holiday season. Because the extra sales demand is temporary, management chooses not to purchase additional freezers, which would permanently increase its fixed costs year-round. Instead, management rents the necessary number of freezer trucks to accommodate its

Here's How It's Used: IN YOUR LIFE

Roommates! You likely have had at least one at some point in your life. Whether you ended the year as best friends or refusing to speak to each other, you probably discussed how to split bills. Assume that you and three roommates are deciding how best to allocate the monthly utility bill for your rental house. Having taken managerial accounting, you consider cost behavior and believe that utilities expense is a variable cost. Therefore, you simply divide the monthly bill equally across the four of you as each of you spends about the same amount of time using the house. Also, each of you loves the environment and tries to use less electricity, which suggests your bill will decrease over time. As the holidays approach, one of your roommates has become very serious with her boyfriend and another has taken a 6-month internship job far away. As a result, neither of them will be spending much time in your house during the remaining 6 months of the lease. Given that utilities is a variable cost, these two roommates argue that future utility bills be split only between yourself and the one remaining roommate because their absence will result in less electricity being consumed, thereby reducing the utility bill by approximately 50%. You wonder, "Is this an accurate assessment of the spring utility bill?" To answer this question, you look carefully at your utility bill for the first time and notice that while your monthly use of total kilowatt-hours (i.e., electricity) has been decreasing, your utility bill has changed very little. You also discover that your monthly bill includes a fixed charge that does not vary with the number of kilowatt-hours consumed. When you ask a utility company representative about this fixed fee, he tells you that as conservation efforts cause customers to use less electricity, the company has been forced to add a large fixed fee to customers' monthly utility bills to ensure it has money for utility grid maintenance. Armed with this new cost behavior knowledge that utility expense is a mixed cost—not a variable cost—you realize that your monthly bill is unlikely to change much as a result of your two absent roommates. Therefore, you all agree to continue splitting the utility bill equally for the remainder of the lease, which makes you all laugh because you realize that a proper understanding of mixed cost behavior has saved the day by helping avoid a potential roommate conflict!

temporary requirements. Renting freezer trucks on an "as-needed" basis is an innovative decision for managing Zingerman's fixed costs as they temporarily step up during the holiday season.

Exhibit 3.6 illustrates step costs. Graph A shows a step cost with relatively narrow steps. These narrow steps mean that the cost changes in response to fairly small changes in output. Often, if the steps are very narrow, we can approximate the step cost as a strictly variable cost. For example, Copy-2-Go, a photocopying shop, buys copy paper in large boxes. The shop typically uses three large boxes per week. Each box is quite heavy and requires the Copy-2-Go owner to incur an additional cost for help in moving the box around the shop and into position for use. The cost of handling paper is a step cost with very narrow steps. Specifically, the cost of taking on an extra job will cause an increase in paper box handling only if the job requires Copy-2-Go to purchase and handle a new box of paper. Graph B, however, shows a step cost with relatively wide steps. An example of this type of cost is a factory that leases production machinery. Suppose that each machine can produce 1,000 units per month. If production ranges from 0 to 1,000 units, only one machine is needed. However, if production increases to amounts between 1,001 and 2,000 units, a second machine must be leased. Many so-called fixed costs may be, in reality, step costs.

Exhibit 3.6

Step Costs: Narrow Steps and Wide Steps

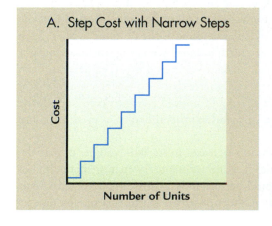

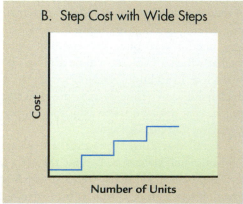

Accounting Records and Need for Cost Separation

Sometimes it is easy to identify the variable and fixed components of a mixed cost, as in the example given earlier for Colley Computers' sales representatives. Many times, however, the only information available is the total cost and a measure of output. For example, the accounting system will usually record both the total cost of maintenance and the number of maintenance hours provided during a given period of time. How much of the total maintenance cost represents a fixed cost and how much represents a variable cost is not revealed by the accounting records. (In fact, the accounting records may not even reveal the breakdown of costs in the sales representative example.)

Therefore, it is necessary to separate the total cost into its fixed and variable components. Only through a formal effort to separate costs can all costs be classified into the appropriate cost behavior categories.

If mixed costs are a very small percentage of total costs, formal cost separation may be more trouble than it's worth. In this case, mixed costs could be assigned to either the fixed or variable cost category without much concern for the classification error or its effect on decision making. Alternatively, the total mixed cost could be arbitrarily divided between the two cost categories. However, this option is seldom available. Mixed costs for many firms are large enough to call for separation.

Check Point

1. A mixed cost is comprised of which of the following items?
   (a) A variable cost component
   (b) A fixed cost component
   (c) Both a variable and a fixed cost component
   (d) Neither a variable nor a fixed cost component

Answer:
(c).

2. Step costs also are known as:
   (a) semi-fixed costs.
   (b) mixed costs.
   (c) range costs.
   (d) total costs.

Answer:
(a).

METHODS FOR SEPARATING MIXED COSTS INTO FIXED AND VARIABLE COMPONENTS

Managers use cost functions to help them better understand mixed costs. Specifically, the purpose of creating a cost formula is to provide a quantitative estimate of both total fixed costs and the variable cost per unit of the cost driver(s). After these cost formula components are determined, managers can predict total costs at various levels of output.

Three commonly used methods of separating a mixed cost into its fixed and variable components are:

- the high-low method
- the scattergraph method
- the method of least squares

OBJECTIVE 3

Separate mixed costs into their fixed and variable components using the high-low method, the scattergraph method, and the method of least squares.

Here's **Why It's important**

CONCEPT CLIP

Each method requires the simplifying assumption of a linear cost relationship. Let's review the expression of cost as an equation for a straight line.

Total Cost = Total Fixed Cost + (Variable Rate × Units of Output)

The **dependent variable** is a variable whose value depends on the value of another variable. In the previous equation, total cost is the dependent variable; it is the cost we are trying to predict. The **independent variable** explains changes in the dependent variable and, as such, its value does not depend on the value of another variable. A good independent variable is one that causes or is closely associated with the dependent variable. Therefore, many managers refer to an independent variable as a cost driver. The **intercept** corresponds to fixed cost. Graphically, the intercept is the point at which the cost line intercepts the cost (vertical) axis. The **slope** of the cost line corresponds to the variable rate (the variable cost per unit of output). **Example 3.1** shows how to create and use a cost formula.

EXAMPLE 3.1

How to Create and Use a Cost Formula

The art and graphics department of State College decided to equip each faculty office with an inkjet color printer (computers were already in place). Sufficient color printers had monthly depreciation of $250. The department purchased paper in boxes of 10,000 sheets (20 reams of 500 sheets each) for $35 per box. Ink cartridges cost $30 and will print, on average, 300 pages.

Required:

1. Create a formula for the monthly cost of inkjet printing in the department.
2. If the department expects to print 4,400 pages next month, what is the expected total fixed cost? Total variable cost? Total printing cost?

Solution:

1. The cost formula takes the following form:

    Total Cost = Fixed Cost + (Variable Rate × Number of Pages)

    The monthly fixed cost is $250 (the cost of printer depreciation), as it does not vary according to the number of pages printed. The variable costs are paper and ink, as both vary with the number of pages printed.

    Cost of paper per page is $35/10,000 = $0.0035

    Cost of ink per page is $30/300 = $0.10

    Variable rate per page is $0.0035 + $0.10 = $0.1035

    The cost formula is:

    Total Cost of Printing = $250 + ($0.1035 × Number of Pages)

2. Expected fixed cost for next month is $250.

    Expected variable cost for next month is $0.1035 × 4,400 pages = $455.40

    Expected total printing cost for next month is $250 + $455.40 = $705.40

Since the accounting records reveal only total cost and output, those values must be used to estimate the fixed cost and variable rate. To do so, we'll illustrate the high-low method, the scattergraph method, and the method of least squares (i.e., regression) with the following example. The same data will be used with each method so that comparisons among them can be made. The example focuses on materials handling cost for Anderson Company, a manufacturer of household cleaning products. Materials handling involves moving materials from one area of the factory, say the raw materials storeroom, to another area, such as Workstation 6. Large, complex organizations have found that the cost of moving materials can be quite large. Understanding the behavior of this cost is an important part of deciding how to reduce the cost.

Anderson's controller has accumulated data for the materials handling activity. The plant manager believes that the number of material moves is a good activity driver for the activity. Assume that the accounting records of Anderson Company disclose the following materials handling costs and number of material moves for the past 10 months:

Month	Materials Handling Cost	Number of Moves
January	$2,000	100
February	3,090	125
March	2,780	175
April	1,990	200
May	7,500	500
June	5,300	300
July	3,800	250
August	6,300	400
September	5,600	475
October	6,240	425

The High-Low Method

From basic geometry, we know that two points are needed to determine a line. Once we know the two points on a line, then its equation can be determined. Recall that the fixed cost is the *intercept* of the total cost line and that the variable rate is the *slope* of the line. Given two points, the slope and the intercept can be determined. The **high-low method** is a method of separating mixed costs into fixed and variable components by using just the high and low data points. The high-low method provides managers with a quick way to estimate cost behavior. Only two data points are needed (i.e., the high and low activity, or driver, points). This method is relatively easy and inexpensive for companies to incorporate.

Here's **Why It's important**

Four steps must be taken in the high-low method.

Step 1: Find the high point and the low point for a given data set. The *high point* is defined as the point with the *highest* activity or output level. The *low point* is defined as the point with the *lowest* activity or output level. It is important to note that the high and low points are identified by looking at the activity levels and not the costs. In some cases, the highest (or lowest) activity level might also be associated with the highest (or lowest) cost, whereas in other cases it is not. Therefore, regardless of cost, the managerial accountant must be careful to use the activity level in identifying the high and low data points for the analysis. In the data for maintenance cost, the high output occurred in May, with 500 material moves and total cost of $7,500. The low output was in January with 100 material moves and total cost of $2,000.

Step 2: Using the high and low points, calculate the variable rate. The variable rate, or slope, is the change in the total cost divided by the change in output.

Variable Rate = (High Point Cost – Low Point Cost)/(High Point Output – Low Point Output)

Using the high and low points for our example, the variable rate would be as follows:

$$\text{Variable Rate} = \frac{\$7,500 - \$2,000}{500 - 100} = \frac{\$5,500}{400} = \$13.75$$

Step 3: Calculate the fixed cost using the variable rate (from Step 2) and either the high point or low point.

Fixed Cost = Total Cost at High Point – (Variable Rate × Output at High Point)

OR

Fixed Cost = Total Cost at Low Point – (Variable Rate × Output at Low Point)

Let's use the high point to calculate fixed cost.

$$\text{Fixed Cost} = \$7,500 - (\$13.75 \times 500) = \$625$$

Step 4: Form the cost formula for materials handling based on the high-low method.

$$\text{Total Cost} = \$625 + (\$13.75 \times \text{Number of Moves})$$

Example 3.2 shows how to use the high-low method to construct a cost formula.

EXAMPLE 3.2

How to Use the High-Low Method to Calculate Fixed Cost and the Variable Rate and to Construct a Cost Formula

BlueDenim Company makes blue jeans. The company controller wants to calculate the fixed and variable costs associated with electricity used in the factory. Data for the past 8 months were collected:

Month	Electricity Cost	Machine Hours
January	$3,255	460
February	3,485	500
March	4,100	600
April	3,300	470
May	3,312	470
June	2,575	350
July	3,910	570
August	4,200	590

Required:

Using the high-low method, calculate the fixed cost of electricity, calculate the variable rate per machine hour, and construct the cost formula for total electricity cost.

Solution:

Step 1: Find the high and low points:

The high number of machine hours is in March, and the low number of machine hours is in June. August is not the high point because its number of machine hours is not the highest activity level.

Step 2: Calculate the variable rate:

$$\begin{aligned} \text{Variable Rate} &= (\text{High Cost} - \text{Low Cost})/(\text{High Machine Hours} - \text{Low Machine Hours}) \\ &= (\$4,100 - \$2,575)/(600 - 350) = \$1,525/250 \\ &= \$6.10 \text{ per machine hour} \end{aligned}$$

Step 3: Calculate the fixed cost:

$$\text{Fixed Cost} = \text{Total Cost} - (\text{Variable Rate} \times \text{Machine Hours})$$

Let's choose the high point with cost of $4,100 and machine hours of 600.

$$\text{Fixed Cost} = \$4,100 - (\$6.10 \times 600) = \$4,100 - \$3,660 = \$440$$

(*Hint:* Check your work by computing fixed cost using the low point.)

Step 4: Construct a cost formula: If the variable rate is $6.10 per machine hour and fixed cost is $440 per month, then the formula for monthly electricity cost is:

$$\text{Total Electricity Cost} = \$440 + (\$6.10 \times \text{Machine Hours})$$

After the cost formula is constructed, its components can be used to predict either total variable costs, total fixed costs, or total costs (i.e., both variable and fixed). For example, the cost formula can be used in budgeting and in performance control. As determined earlier, the cost formula for materials handling based on the high-low method is:

$$\text{Total Cost} = \$625 + (\$13.75 \times \text{Number of Moves})$$

Suppose that the number of moves for November is expected to be 350. Budgeted materials handling cost would be:

$$\$5,437.50 = \$625 + (\$13.75 \times 350)$$

Alternatively, suppose that the controller wondered whether October's materials handling cost of $6,240 was reasonably close to what would have been predicted. Our cost formula would predict October's cost of:

$$\$6,469(\text{rounded}) = \$625 + (\$13.75 \times 425)$$

The actual cost is just $229 different from the predicted cost and probably would be judged to be reasonably close to the budgeted cost. **Example 3.3** shows how to use the high-low method to calculate predicted total variable cost and total cost for budgeted output.

EXAMPLE 3.3

How to Use the High-Low Method to Calculate Predicted Total Variable Cost and Total Cost for Budgeted Output

Recall that BlueDenim Company constructed the following formula for monthly electricity cost. (Refer to Example 3.2 to see how the fixed cost per month and the variable rate were computed.)

$$\text{Total Electricity Cost} = \$440 + (\$6.10 \times \text{Machine Hours})$$

Required:
Assume that 550 machine hours are budgeted for the month of October. Use the previous cost formula to calculate (1) total variable electricity cost for October and (2) total electricity cost for October.

Solution:

1. Total Variable Electricity Cost = Variable Rate × Machine Hours
   $$= \$6.10 \times 550$$
   $$= \$3,355$$

2. Total Electricity Cost = Fixed Cost + (Variable Rate × Machine Hours)
   $$= \$440 + (\$6.10 \times 550)$$
   $$= \$440 + \$3,355$$
   $$= \$3,795$$

A cost formula can help managers predict total costs for time periods of varying lengths. This flexibility is important because managers often must predict costs for periods of a week, month, quarter, or year in length.

For example, let's look at one last point. Notice that monthly data were used to find the high and low points and to calculate the fixed cost and variable rate. This means that the cost formula is the fixed cost *for the month*. Suppose, however, that the company wants to use that formula to predict cost for a different period of time, say a year. In that case, the variable cost rate is just multiplied by the budgeted amount of the independent variable for the year. The intercept, or fixed cost, must be adjusted. To convert monthly fixed cost to yearly fixed cost, simply multiply the monthly fixed cost by 12 (because there are 12 months in a year). If weekly data were used to calculate the fixed and variable costs, one would multiply the weekly fixed cost by 52 to convert it to yearly fixed cost, and so on. **Example 3.4** shows how to use the high-low method to calculate predicted total variable cost and total cost for budgeted output in which the time period differs from the data period.

EXAMPLE 3.4

How to Use the High-Low Method to Calculate Predicted Total Variable Cost and Total Cost for a Time Period That Differs from the Data Period

Recall that BlueDenim Company constructed the following formula for *monthly* electricity cost. (Refer to Example 3.2 (p. 94) to see how the fixed cost per month and variable rate were computed.)

$$\text{Total Electricity Cost} = \$440 + (\$6.10 \times \text{Machine Hours})$$

Required:

Assume that 6,500 machine hours are budgeted for the coming year. Use the previous cost formula to calculate (1) total variable electricity cost for the year, (2) total fixed electricity cost for the year, and (3) total electricity cost for the coming year.

Solution:

1. Total Variable Electricity Cost = Variable Rate × Machine Hours
    $$= \$6.10 \times 6,500$$
    $$= \$39,650$$

2. *Note:* The cost formula is for the month, but we need to budget electricity for the year. Thus, we need to multiply the fixed cost for the month by 12 (the number of months in a year).

    Total Fixed Electricity Cost = Fixed Cost × 12 Months in a Year
    $$= \$440 \times 12$$
    $$= \$5,280$$

3. Total Electricity Cost = 12($440) + ($6.10 × 6,500)
    $$= \$5,280 + \$39,650$$
    $$= \$44,930$$

The high-low method has several important advantages, including the following:

-   **Objectivity:** Any two people using the high-low method on a particular data set will arrive at the same answer.
-   **Quick overview:** The high-low method allows a manager to get a quick fix on a cost relationship by using only two data points. For example, a manager may have only 2 months of data. Sometimes this will be enough to get a crude approximation of the cost relationship.
-   **Ease of use:** The high-low method is simple, inexpensive, and easily communicated to other individuals, even those who are not comfortable with numerical analyses.

For these reasons, managerial accountants use the high-low method.

However, the high-low method also has several disadvantages that lead some managers to believe that it is not as good as the other methods at separating mixed costs into fixed and variable components.

- **Occurrence of outliers:** The high and low points often can be what are known as outliers. They may represent atypical cost-activity relationships. For instance, if in the Anderson Company example the high output had been 1,000 moves (rather than 500) due to some extremely unusual business activity during a given month, then this high point likely would have fallen outside of the company's relevant range of operations. It would, therefore, represent an outlier. In the case of outliers, the cost formula computed using these two points will not represent what usually takes place. The scattergraph method can help a manager avoid this trap by selecting two points that appear to be representative of the general cost-activity pattern.
- **Potential for misrepresentative data:** Even if the high and low points are not outliers, other pairs of points may be more representative. To stress the likelihood of this possibility, a high-low analysis of 50 weeks of data would ignore 96% (i.e., 48 out of the 50 weeks) of the data! Again, the scattergraph method allows the choice of more representative points.

Scattergraph Method

The **scattergraph method** is a way to see the cost relationship by plotting the data points on a graph. The first step in applying the scattergraph method is to plot the data points so that the relationship between materials handling costs and activity output can be seen. This plot is referred to as a scattergraph and is shown in Exhibit 3.7. The vertical axis is total cost (materials handling cost), and the horizontal axis is the driver or output measure (number of moves).

Exhibit 3.7 Anderson Company's Materials Handling Cost

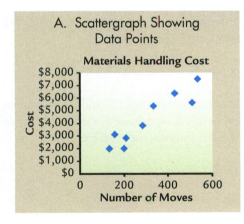

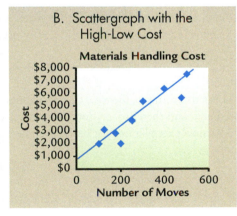

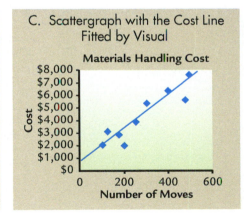

Looking at Graph A, we see that the relationship between materials handling costs and number of moves is reasonably linear. Cost goes up as the number of moves goes up and vice versa.

Now let's examine Graph B to see if the line determined by the high and low points is representative of the overall relationship. Notice that three points lie above the high-low line and five lie below it. This does not give us confidence in the high-low results for fixed and variable costs. In particular, we might wonder if the variable cost (slope) is somewhat higher than it should be and the fixed cost is somewhat lower than it should be.

Thus, one purpose of a scattergraph is to see whether or not a straight line reasonably describes the cost relationship. Additionally, inspecting the scattergraph may reveal one or more points that do not seem to fit the general pattern of behavior. Upon investigation, it may be discovered that these points (the outliers) were due to some irregular occurrences that are not expected to happen again. This knowledge might justify their elimination and perhaps lead to a better estimate of the underlying cost function.

We can use the scattergraph to visually fit a line to the data points on the graph. Of course, the manager or cost analyst will choose the line that appears to fit the points the best, and perhaps that choice will take into account past experience with the behavior of the cost item. Experience may provide a good intuitive sense of how materials handling costs behave. The scattergraph then becomes a useful tool to quantify this intuition. Fitting a line to the points in this way is how the scattergraph method works. Keep in mind that the scattergraph and other statistical aids are tools that can help managers improve their judgment. Using the tools does not restrict the manager from using judgment to alter any of the estimates produced by formal methods.

Examine Graph A carefully. Based only on the information contained in the graph, how would you fit a line to the points in it? Of course, an infinite number of lines might go through the data, but let's choose one that goes through the point for January (100, $2,000) and intersects the y-axis at $800. This gives us the straight line shown in Graph C. The fixed cost, of course, is $800, the intercept. We can use the high-low method to determine the variable rate.

First, remember that our two points are (100, $2,000) and (0, $800). Next, use these two points to compute the variable rate (the slope):

$$\text{Variable Rate} = \frac{(\text{High Point Cost} - \text{Low Point Cost})}{(\text{High Point Number of Moves} - \text{Low Point Number of Moves})}$$

$$= (\$2,000 - \$800)/(100 - 0)$$
$$= \$1,200/100$$
$$= \$12$$

Thus, the variable rate is $12 per material move.

The fixed cost and variable rate for materials handling cost have now been identified. The cost formula for the materials handling activity can be expressed as:

$$\text{Total Cost} = \$800 + (\$12 \times \text{Number of Moves})$$

Using this formula, the total cost of materials handling for between 100 and 500 moves can be predicted and then broken down into fixed and variable components. For example, assume that 350 moves are planned for November. Using the cost formula, the predicted cost is:

$$\$5,000 = \$800 + (\$12 \times 350)$$

Of this total cost, $800 is fixed, and $4,200 is variable.

The cost formula for materials handling was obtained by fitting a line to two points [(0, $800) and (100, $2,000)] in Graph C. Judgment was used to select the line. Whereas one person may decide that the best-fitting line is the one passing through those points, others, using their own judgment, may decide that the best line passes through other pairs of points.

A significant advantage of the scattergraph method is that it allows a cost analyst to inspect the data visually. Exhibit 3.8 illustrates cost behavior situations that are not appropriate for the simple application of the high-low method. Graph A shows a nonlinear relationship between cost and output. An example of this type of relationship is a volume discount given on direct materials or evidence of learning by workers (e.g., as more hours are worked, the total cost increases at a decreasing rate due to the increased efficiency of the workers). Graph B shows an upward shift in cost if more than X_1 units are made—perhaps because an additional supervisor must be hired or a second shift run. Graph C shows outliers that do not represent the overall cost relationship.

Exhibit 3.8

Scattergraphs with Nonlinear Cost

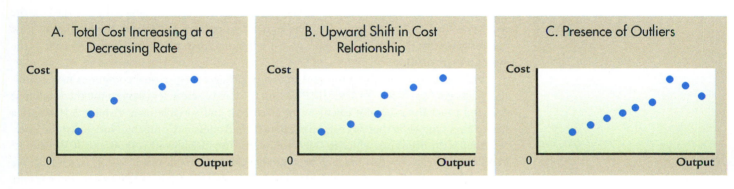

The scattergraph method suffers from the lack of any objective criterion for choosing the best-fitting line. The quality of the cost formula depends on the quality of the subjective judgment of the analyst. The high-low method removes the subjectivity in the choice of the line. Regardless of who uses the method, the same line will result.

Looking again at Graphs B and C in Exhibit 3.7 (p. 97), we can compare the results of the scattergraph method with those of the high-low method. There is a difference between the fixed cost components and the variable rates. The predicted materials handling cost for 350 moves is $5,000 according to the scattergraph method and $5,438 according to the high-low method. Which is correct? Since the two methods can produce significantly different cost formulas, the question of which method is the best arises. Ideally, a method that is objective and, at the same time, produces the best-fitting line is needed.

The Method of Least Squares

The **method of least squares (regression)** is a statistical way to find the *best-fitting* line through a set of data points. One advantage of the method of least squares is that for a given set of data, it will always produce the same cost formula. Basically, the best-fitting line is the one in which the data points are closer to the line than to any other line. What do we mean by closest? Let's take a look at Exhibit 3.9.

Exhibit 3.9

Line Deviations

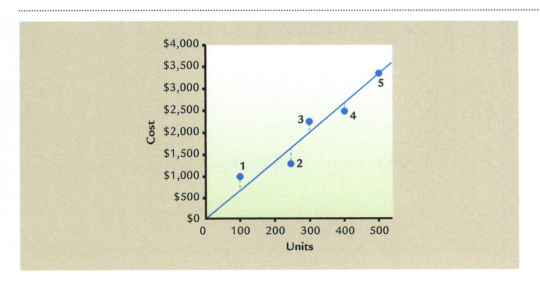

Notice that there are a series of data points and a line—we'll assume that it is the regression line calculated by the method of least squares. The data points do not all lie directly on the line; this is typical. However, the regression line better describes the pattern of the data than other possible lines. This description results because the squared deviations between the regression line and each data point are, in total, smaller than the sum of the squared deviations of the data points and any other line. The least squares statistical formulas can find the one line with the smallest sum of squared deviations. In other words, this method identifies the regression line that minimizes the cost prediction errors or differences between predicted costs (i.e., on the regression line) and actual costs (i.e., the actual data points). Given that the method of least squares generates the smallest possible cost prediction errors, many managers refer to it as the most accurate method.

Various spreadsheet programs and software packages for personal computers have regression packages (e.g., Excel XLstat®, JMP®, Minitab®, Citrix®, etc.). It is easy to use them to input data and to let the programs calculate the fixed cost and variable rate.[4] Exhibit 3.10 shows a spreadsheet regression that was run on the data from Anderson Company. Notice that the intercept term is the fixed cost, which is $789 (rounded). The variable rate is shown as "X Variable 1." In other words, it is the first independent variable. So, the variable rate is $12.38 (rounded). We can use the output of regression in budgeting and control the same way that we used the results of the high-low and scattergraph methods.

Suppose that Anderson Company expects the number of moves for November to be 350. Budgeted materials handling cost would be:

$$\begin{aligned}
\text{Total Cost} &= \text{Fixed Cost} + (\text{Variable Rate} \times \text{Output}) \\
&= \$789(\text{rounded}) + [\$12.38(\text{rounded}) \times 350 \text{ moves}] \\
&= \$789 + \$4{,}333 \\
&= \$5{,}122
\end{aligned}$$

Alternatively, suppose the controller wondered whether October's materials handling cost of $6,240 was reasonably close to what would have been predicted. Our cost formula would predict October cost of $6,051 (rounded):

$$\$6{,}051 \text{ (rounded)} = \$789 + (\$12.38 \times 425)$$

The actual cost is just $189 different from the predicted cost and probably would be judged to be reasonably close to the budgeted cost. **Example 3.5** shows how to use results of regression to construct a cost formula.

Exhibit 3.10

A Portion of the Summary Output from Excel for Anderson Company

	A	B	C	D	
1	Coefficients:				
2	Intercept	788.7806			
3	X Variable 1	12.38058			
4					
5					
6					
7					
8					
9					

Sheet1 / Sheet2 / Sheet3

4 See Appendix 3A at the end of this chapter for more information on how to use regression programs in Microsoft Excel®.

BlueDenim Company makes blue jeans. The company controller wanted to calculate the fixed and variable costs associated with electricity used in the factory. Data for the past 8 months were collected:

EXAMPLE 3.5

How to Use the Regression Method to Calculate Fixed Cost and the Variable Rate and to Construct a Cost Formula and to Determine Budgeted Cost

Month	Electricity Cost	Machine Hours
January	$3,255	460
February	3,485	500
March	4,100	600
April	3,300	470
May	3,312	470
June	2,575	350
July	3,910	570
August	4,200	590

Coefficients shown by a regression program are:

Intercept	321
X Variable 1	6.38

Required:

Use the results of regression to perform the following:

1. Calculate the fixed cost of electricity and the variable rate per machine hour.
2. Construct the cost formula for total electricity cost.
3. Calculate the budgeted cost for next month, assuming that 550 machine hours are budgeted.

Solution:

1. The fixed cost and the variable rate are given directly by regression.

$$\text{Fixed Cost} = \$321$$
$$\text{Variable Rate} = \$6.38$$

2. The cost formula is:

$$\text{Total Electricity Cost} = \$321 + (\$6.38 \times \text{Machine Hours})$$

3. Budgeted Electricity Cost = $321 + ($6.38 × 550) = $3,830

Comparison of Methods

Selecting the most appropriate cost estimation technique requires judgment. As discussed earlier, the high-low method can yield sufficiently accurate cost estimates when neither the high nor low point is an outlier. However, when the need for accuracy is high (e.g., competition is fierce, the product or service has a very small profit margin, etc.), the regression method has considerable appeal, because it uses *all* of the given data points, thereby producing the best (i.e., most accurate) estimates possible of the intercept (total fixed cost) and slope (variable cost per unit). The value of such potential greater accuracy must be weighed against the cost of greater complexity to perform the cost analysis and to explain it to other managers as compared to less sophisticated methods such as the high-low method.

Knowing how costs change in relation to changes in output is essential to planning, controlling, and decision making. Each of the methods for separating mixed costs into fixed and variable components helps managers understand cost behavior and consequently make good business decisions. Exhibit 3.11 (p. 102) provides an overview of each of these methods, along with the advantages and disadvantages of each.

Here's **Why It's important**

Exhibit 3.11

Overview of Methods for Separating Mixed Costs into Fixed and Variable Components

Method	Overview	Advantages	Disadvantages
High-low method	A method for separating mixed costs into fixed and variable components by using just the low and high data points	• Objective • Quick • Simple • Inexpensive • Easily communicated to others	• Occurrence of outliers • Potential for misrepresentative data
Scattergraph method	A method for separating mixed costs into fixed and variable components by fitting a line to a set of data using two points that are selected by judgment	• Simple • Visual representation of the data	• Subjective (choosing the best-fitting line)
Method of least squares (regression)	A method for separating mixed costs into fixed and variable components by statistically finding the best-fitting line through a set of data points	• Objective • Regression packages can quickly and easily calculate the fixed cost and variable rate	• Relatively more complicated method to perform and/or to explain to the managerial users of the regression output

Managerial Judgment

Managerial judgment is critically important in determining cost behavior and is by far the most widely used method in practice. Many managers simply use their experience and past observation of cost relationships to determine fixed and variable costs. This method, however, may take a number of forms. Some managers simply assign some costs to the fixed category and others to the variable category. They ignore the possibility of mixed costs. Thus, a chemical firm may regard materials and utilities as strictly variable, with respect to pounds of chemical produced, and all other costs as fixed. Even labor, the textbook example of a strictly variable cost, may be fixed for this firm. The appeal of using a managerial judgment method is simplicity. Before opting for this method, however, management would do well to make sure that each cost is predominantly fixed or variable and that the decisions being made are not highly sensitive to errors in classifying costs as fixed or variable.

Here's **Why It's important**

The use of quantitative analysis—whether relatively simple techniques such as the high-low method or relatively complex techniques such as the regression method—can add helpful insights into variable and fixed costs beyond what judgment alone might provide. Therefore, effective managers often estimate the costs associated with important decisions by using a *combination* of judgment and some form of quantitative analysis.

To illustrate the use of judgment in assessing cost behavior, consider companies like **Honda** that use large quantities of manufacturing labor hours in China. Some companies might assume that hourly manufacturing labor cost is strictly variable and, therefore, not worthy of careful cost analysis. However, as workers in China begin to demand significantly higher wages and more lucrative labor deals, some resulting labor costs might (1) increase significantly in amount and (2) change their behavior pattern to become more similar to other countries in which labor unions can guarantee that workers receive certain wages even when manufacturing levels fall dramatically (i.e., labor becomes a mixed, semi-fixed, or even fixed cost). Or more specifically, consider **Elgin Sweeper Company**, a leading manufacturer of motorized street sweepers. Using production volume as the measure of activity output, Elgin revised its chart of accounts to organize costs into fixed and variable components. Elgin's accountants used their knowledge of the company to assign expenses to either a fixed or variable category, using a decision rule that categorized an expense as fixed if it were fixed 75% of the time and as variable if it were variable 75% of the time.

Management may instead identify mixed costs and divide these costs into fixed and variable components by deciding what the fixed and variable parts are. That is, they may use experience to say that a certain amount of a cost is fixed and that the rest therefore must be variable. Suppose that a small business had a photocopier with a fixed cost of $3,000 per year. The variable

Here's How It's Used: DATA ANALYTICS

Managerial accountants increasingly use *data analytics* to improve business decisions, many of which involve cost behavior patterns. Most accountants consider data analytics to be much broader than simply a particular software program or quantitative technique. For example, a recent study that surveyed over 400 business professionals from a wide range of work experiences and industry backgrounds found that data analytics in accounting includes an array of knowledge and skills necessary for using large data sets to improve decision making.[5] Specifically, these professionals reported that effective data analytics requires that managerial accountants must understand **what** issues to measure (i.e., how a measure would help inform management on the company's strategy); **how** to measure a given issue (e.g., using a qualitative measure, nonfinancial measure, financial measure, etc.); **where** to obtain the data for the desired measures (e.g., from an existing information system operating within the organization, from a new enterprise-wide resource planning system—such as SAP® or Oracle®—that would need to be purchased and installed, etc.); **which** statistical tool or software package to use in analyzing the collected data (e.g., Excel XLstat®, JMP®, Minitab®, etc.); and finally, how best to **communicate** the analytical findings to interested parties (e.g., quantitatively oriented engineers who might lack sophisticated accounting knowledge, marketing personnel who understand the business but might not be as comfortable with high-level quantitative analyses, or external stakeholders). Thus, while accountants need to become increasingly familiar with statistical software packages, they also must be sure they understand these other critical elements in order to fully utilize data analytics to help managers improve business decision making.

component could be computed by using one or more cost/volume data points. This approach has the advantage of accounting for mixed costs but is subject to a similar type of error as the strict fixed/variable dichotomy. That is, management may be wrong in its assessment.

CONCEPT CLIP

Finally, management may use experience and judgment to refine statistical estimation results. Perhaps the experienced manager might "eyeball" the data and throw out several points as being highly unusual or revise the results of estimation to account for projected changes in cost structure or technology. For example, **Tecnol Medical Products Inc.** radically changed its method of manufacturing medical face masks. Traditionally, face-mask production was labor intensive, requiring hand stitching. Tecnol developed its own highly automated equipment and became the industry's low-cost supplier—beating both **Johnson & Johnson** and **3M**. Tecnol's rapid expansion into new product lines and European markets means that historical data on costs and revenues are for the most part irrelevant. Tecnol's management must look forward, not back, to predict the impact of changes on profit. Statistical techniques are highly accurate in depicting the past, but they cannot foresee the future, which, of course, is what management really wants.

The advantage of using managerial judgment to separate fixed and variable costs is its simplicity. In situations in which the manager has a deep understanding of the firm and its cost patterns, this method can give good results. However, if the manager does not have good judgment, errors will occur. Therefore, it is important to consider the experience of the manager, the potential for error, and the effect that error could have on related decisions.

Ethical Decisions

There are ethical implications to the use of managerial judgment. Managers use their knowledge of fixed and variable costs to make important decisions, such as whether to switch suppliers, expand or contract production, or lay off workers. These decisions affect the lives of workers, suppliers, and customers. Ethical managers will make sure that they have the best information possible when making these decisions. In addition, managers will not let personal factors affect the use of cost information. For example, suppose that the purchasing department manager has a good friend who wants to supply some materials for production. The price of the friend's materials is slightly lower than that of the current supplier. However, the friend's company will not ensure 100% quality control—and that will lead to additional costs for rework and warranty

---

5 See Stoel, Ballou, and Heitger, "Data-Driven Decision-Making and Its Impact on Accounting Curriculum," *Issues in Accounting Education*.

repair. The ethical manager will include these additional costs along with the purchase price to calculate the full cost of purchasing from the friend's company. ●

Check Point

1. **Draw a straight line through the high and low points on each graph in Exhibit 3.7. Can you see that these lines, the high-low lines, could give misleading information on fixed and variable costs?**

Answer:

Yes, it is quite important to consider the relevant range.

2. **Suppose that you own a small business with a photocopier that a neighboring business owner asks to use occasionally. What is the average cost of copying one page? What cost items would you include? Now consider FedEx Office. What cost items do you think that it would include?**

Answer:

If a neighboring business owner only needed a copy rarely, you might consider it a favor and not charge at all. If it happened several times a month, you might charge the variable cost of paper and toner. Finally, if the neighboring business owner used your copier frequently, you might charge 10¢ to 20¢ per page—a price similar to that of an outside photocopying shop. Alternatively, the neighbor might buy you a ream of paper from time to time. FedEx Office must include all costs in determining the cost of copies, including paper, toner, depreciation on equipment, cost of electricity and utilities, wages of staff, and so on.

Here's How It's Used: AT ROYAL CARIBBEAN CRUISES

Assume that you work as a financial analyst for **Royal Caribbean Cruises Ltd.** The company operates some of the world's biggest cruise ships, such as *The Allure of the Seas*, which weighs 222,000 tons and carries 5,400 guests, as well as 1,650 crew members. As an internal financial analyst, one of your most important tasks is to estimate the costs that Royal will incur on the many cruises it offers to customers each year. The accuracy with which you predict Royal's most important cruise-related costs will affect many of the strategic and operating decisions made by management. You are familiar with several common cost estimation methods, including scattergraph, high-low, and regression. However, you also are aware that each method has its advantages and disadvantages.

Which cost estimation method should you employ?

If the scattergraph method were used, the analysis would be quite easy as you could employ Excel to quickly create a plot of the important costs against various potential cost drivers. However, this method does not involve quantitative analysis, which some individuals believe is a significant weakness. If the high-low method were adopted, the analysis would be quantitative in nature and relatively easy to conduct and explain to management. However, this method can be subject to considerable inaccuracy if one or both of the two data points used to construct the cost formula is an outlier. Finally, regression overcomes many of the weaknesses of high-low because it incorporates all of the data into its estimate of the cost formula. Nevertheless, regression can require considerably more time than other methods to collect the necessary input data, ensure their accuracy, and explain the results to the ultimate users of the results.

To determine which method to employ, you would be wise to consult the managers who will be using your analysis. For example, does management need a general "ball park" estimate or does it need the most accurate estimate possible? The results from your cost analysis, along with the competitive pressures facing Royal, will affect important decisions such as how much to pay cruise ship employees to ensure a high-quality customer experience, the prices to charge customers to ensure affordability yet exclusivity, and the types and quantities of food, beverages, and shopping to offer onboard the ships. **There is no obvious, one-size-fits-all answer as to the best cost estimation method to employ. Regardless of the cost estimation method ultimately selected, you likely will supplement the results with a dose of managerial judgment to help management make the best decisions possible.**

VARIABLE AND ABSORPTION INCOME STATEMENTS: TWO WAYS OF MEASURING INCOME

Two methods of computing income have been developed: one based on variable costing and the other based on absorption costing. These are costing methods because they refer to the way in which product costs are determined. Recall that *product costs* are inventoried; they include direct materials, direct labor, and overhead. *Period costs*, such as selling and administrative expense, are expensed in the period incurred. The difference between variable and absorption costing hinges on the treatment of one particular cost: fixed factory overhead.

Here's **Why It's important**

Absorption Costing

Absorption costing (sometimes called full costing) assigns *all* manufacturing costs to the product. Direct materials, direct labor, variable overhead, and fixed overhead define the cost of a product. Thus, under absorption costing, fixed overhead is viewed as a product cost, not a period cost. Under this method, fixed overhead is assigned to the product through the use of a predetermined fixed overhead rate and is not expensed until the product is sold. In other words, fixed overhead is an inventoriable cost. Understanding absorption-costing income statements is important because they are used for external reporting (i.e., contained in the financial statements).

Here's **Why It's important**

Variable Costing

Variable costing stresses the difference between fixed and variable manufacturing costs. **Variable costing** assigns only variable manufacturing costs to the product; these costs include direct materials, direct labor, and variable overhead. Fixed overhead is treated as a period expense and is *excluded* from the product cost. The rationale for excluding fixed overhead from period costs when preparing variable-costing income statements is that fixed overhead is a cost of capacity—or staying in business—such as the lease cost on a manufacturing plant. Therefore, while not used for external financial reporting, understanding variable-costing income statements is important because they can provide useful insights into various capacity cost management decisions. Once the period is over, any benefits provided by capacity have expired and should not be inventoried. Under variable costing, fixed overhead of a period is seen as expiring that period and is charged in total against the revenues of the period.

Here's **Why It's important**

Comparison of Variable and Absorption Costing Methods

Exhibit 3.12 illustrates the classification of costs as product or period costs under absorption and variable costing.

	Absorption Costing	**Variable Costing**
Product costs	Direct materials Direct labor Variable overhead Fixed overhead	Direct materials Direct labor Variable overhead
Period costs	Selling expenses Administrative expenses	Fixed overhead Selling expenses Administrative expenses

Exhibit 3.12

Classification of Costs under Absorption and Variable Costing as Product or Period Costs

Generally accepted accounting principles (GAAP) require absorption costing for external reporting. The Financial Accounting Standards Board (FASB), the Internal Revenue Service (IRS), and other regulatory bodies do not accept variable costing as a product-costing method for external reporting. Yet variable costing can supply vital cost information for decision making and control, information not supplied by absorption costing. For *internal* application, variable costing is an important managerial tool.

Inventory Valuation

Inventory is valued at product or manufacturing cost. (Recall that inventory cost *never* includes the period costs of selling or administration.) Under absorption costing, product cost includes direct materials, direct labor, variable overhead, and fixed overhead. Therefore, under absorption costing, all product costs are included in cost of goods sold.

> Absorption-Costing Product Cost = Direct Materials + Direct Labor
> + Variable Overhead + Fixed Overhead

Under variable costing, the product cost includes only direct materials, direct labor, and variable overhead.

> Variable-Costing Product Cost = Direct Materials + Direct Labor + Variable Overhead

Example 3.6 shows how to compute inventory cost under absorption costing.

EXAMPLE 3.6

How to Compute Inventory Cost under Absorption Costing

During the most recent year, Fairchild Company had the following data associated with the product it makes:

Units in beginning inventory	—
Units produced	10,000
Units sold ($300 per unit)	8,000
Variable costs per unit:	
Direct materials	$50
Direct labor	100
Variable overhead	50
Fixed costs:	
Fixed overhead per unit produced	$25
Fixed selling and administrative	100,000

Required:

1. How many units are in ending inventory?
2. Using absorption costing, calculate the per-unit product cost.
3. What is the value of ending inventory?

Solution:

1. Ending Inventory Units = Beginning Inventory Units + Units Produced − Units Sold
    = 0 + 10,000 − 8,000
    = 2,000 units

EXAMPLE 3.6

(*Continued*)

2. Absorption-costing unit cost:

Direct materials	$ 50
Direct labor	100
Variable overhead	50
Fixed overhead	25
Unit product cost	$225

3. Value of Ending Inventory = Ending Inventory Units × Absorption Unit Product Cost
   = 2,000 units × $225
   = $450,000

As noted earlier and reflected in Example 3.6, the inventory cost computed under absorption costing is the traditional product cost used for external financial statements under GAAP. Each unit includes all variable manufacturing costs as well as a portion of fixed factory overhead. **Example 3.7** shows how to calculate inventory cost under variable costing.

EXAMPLE 3.7

How to Compute Inventory Cost under Variable Costing

Refer to the data in Example 3.6 for Fairchild Company (p. 106).

Required:

1. How many units are in ending inventory?
2. Using variable costing, calculate the per-unit product cost.
3. What is the value of ending inventory?

Solution:

1. Ending Inventory Units = Beginning Inventory Units + Units Produced − Units Sold
   = 0 + 10,000 − 8,000
   = 2,000 units

2. Variable-costing unit cost:

Direct materials	$ 50
Direct labor	100
Variable overhead	50
Unit product cost	$200

3. Value of Ending Inventory = Ending Inventory Units × Variable Unit Product Cost
   = 2,000 units × $200
   = $400,000

Looking carefully at Examples 3.6 and 3.7 we can see that the only difference between the two approaches is the treatment of fixed factory overhead. Thus, the unit product cost under absorption costing is always greater than the unit product cost under variable costing. Exhibit 3.13 shows this difference pictorially for a simplified example.

CONCEPT CLIP

Exhibit 3.13

Product Cost under Absorption and Variable Costing

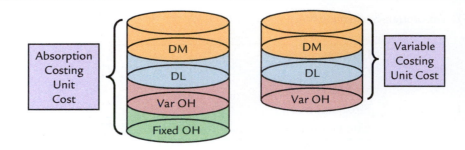

Income Statements Using Variable and Absorption Costing

Here's **Why It's important**

Because unit product costs are the basis for cost of goods sold, the variable- and absorption-costing methods can lead to different operating income figures. The difference arises because of the amount of fixed overhead recognized as an expense under the two methods. **Example 3.8** shows how to develop cost of goods sold and income statements for absorption costing.

EXAMPLE 3.8

How to Prepare an Absorption-Costing Income Statement

Refer to the data in Example 3.6 for Fairchild Company (p. 106).

Required:

1. Calculate the cost of goods sold under absorption costing.
2. Prepare an income statement using absorption costing.

Solution:

1. Cost of Goods Sold = Absorption Unit Product Cost × Units Sold
   $$= \$225 \times 8{,}000$$
   $$= \$1{,}800{,}000$$

2.

Fairchild Company
Absorption-Costing Income Statement

Sales ($300 × 8,000)	$2,400,000
Less: Cost of goods sold	1,800,000
Gross margin	$ 600,000
Less: Selling and administrative expenses	100,000
Operating income	$ 500,000

As we see in Example 3.8, the cost of goods sold includes some but not all fixed factory overhead. Total fixed factory overhead is $250,000 ($25 × 10,000 units produced). However, only $200,000 ($25 × 8,000 units sold) of fixed overhead was expensed in cost of goods sold. Where did the other $50,000 of fixed overhead go? It is included in the cost of ending inventory. **Example 3.9** shows how to prepare a variable-costing income statement.

Compare Examples 3.8 and 3.9. Operating income under absorption costing is $500,000, whereas operating income under variable costing is only $450,000. Remember that $50,000 of fixed factory overhead went into inventory under absorption costing. However, all of the fixed factory overhead is included in the costs for variable costing. Notice that selling and administrative expenses are never included in product cost. They are always expensed on the income statement and never appear on the balance sheet.

EXAMPLE 3.9

**How to Prepare a
Variable-Costing
Income Statement**

Refer to the data in Example 3.6 for Fairchild Company (p. 106).

Required:

1. Calculate the cost of goods sold under variable costing.

2. Prepare an income statement using variable costing.

Solution:

1. Cost of Goods Sold = Variable Unit Product Cost × Units Sold

    $$= \$200 \times 8{,}000$$
    $$= \$1{,}600{,}000$$

2.

Fairchild Company
Variable-Costing Income Statement

Sales ($300 × 8,000)		$2,400,000
Less variable expenses:		
Variable cost of goods sold		1,600,000
Contribution margin		$ 800,000
Less fixed expenses:		
Fixed overhead	$250,000	
Fixed selling and administrative	100,000	350,000
Operating income		$ 450,000

Production, Sales, and Income Relationships

The relationship between variable-costing income and absorption-costing income changes as the relationship between production and sales changes. If more (fewer) units are sold than were produced, variable-costing income is greater (less) than absorption-costing income. For example, selling more than was produced means that at least some beginning inventory and all units produced are sold. Under absorption costing, units coming out of inventory include fixed overhead from a prior period. In addition, units produced and sold have all of the current period's fixed overhead attached. Thus, the amount of fixed overhead expensed by absorption costing is greater than the current period's fixed overhead by the amount of fixed overhead flowing out of inventory. Accordingly, variable-costing income is greater than absorption-costing income by the amount of fixed overhead flowing out of beginning inventory.

If production and sales are equal, of course, no difference exists between the two reported incomes. Since the units produced are all sold, absorption costing, like variable costing, will recognize the total fixed overhead of the period as an expense. No fixed overhead flows into or out of inventory.

The relationships between production, sales, and the two reported incomes are summarized in Exhibit 3.14. Note that if production is greater than sales, then inventory has increased. If production is less than sales, then inventory must have decreased. If production is equal to sales, then the number of units in beginning inventory is equal to the number of units in ending inventory.

Here's **Why It's important**

If	Then
1. Production > Sales	Absorption income > Variable income
2. Production < Sales	Absorption income < Variable income
3. Production = Sales	Absorption income = Variable income

Exhibit 3.14

Production, Sales, and Income Relationships

The difference between absorption and variable costing centers on the recognition of expense associated with fixed factory overhead. Under absorption costing, fixed factory overhead must be assigned to units produced. This presents two problems that we have not explicitly considered.

- First, how do we convert factory overhead applied on the basis of direct labor hours or machine hours into factory overhead applied to units produced?
- Second, what is done when actual factory overhead does not equal applied factory overhead?

The solution to these problems is reserved for a more advanced accounting course.

Check Point

1. **Selwidge Company produced 1,000 units with costs as follows:**

Direct materials	**$4,500**
Direct labor	**2,300**
Variable overhead	**1,100**
Fixed overhead	**5,000**

What is the unit product cost under absorption costing? Under variable costing?

Answer:

Direct materials	$ 4,500
Direct labor	2,300
Variable overhead	1,100
Fixed overhead	5,000
Total absorption cost	$12,900
÷ Number of units	1,000
Unit absorption cost	$ 12.90
Direct materials	$ 4,500
Direct labor	2,300
Variable overhead	1,100
Total absorption cost	$ 7,900
÷ Number of units	1,000
Unit variable cost	$ 7.90

2. **Last year, Turing Company produced 12,000 units and sold 12,400 units. Will absorption-costing income be higher or lower than variable-costing income? Why?**

Answer:

Absorption-costing income will be lower because the 400 units that came out of ending inventory to be sold come with fixed factory overhead attached. So, not only is all fixed overhead for the period expensed under both absorption and variable costing, but there will also be additional fixed factory overhead attached to the units coming out of ending inventory under absorption costing. Thus, total cost will be higher and income lower under absorption costing.

OBJECTIVE **5**

Use a computer spreadsheet program to perform the method of least squares.

ere's **Why It's important**

APPENDIX 3A: USING THE REGRESSION PROGRAMS

Computing the regression formula manually is tedious, even with only a few data points. As the number of data points increases, manual computation becomes impractical. Fortunately, software packages such as Excel XLstat®, Minitab®, JMP®, and Citrix® have regression routines that will perform the computations. All you need to do is input the data. The spreadsheet regression program supplies more than the estimates of the coefficients. It also provides information that can be used to see how reliable the cost equation is—a feature that is not available for the scattergraph and high-low methods.

The first step in using the computer to calculate regression coefficients is to enter the data. Exhibit 3.15 shows the computer screen that you would see if you entered the Anderson Company data on material moves into a spreadsheet. It is a good idea to label your variables as is done in the exhibit. The months are labeled, as are column B for moving costs and column C for number of moves. The next step is to run the regression. In Excel, if the regression feature needs to be installed, press the Office button, click the Excel Options button at the bottom of the drop-down menu, and click Add-Ins from the menu at the left. Click the Go button to the right of the Manage list box at the bottom of the dialog box, click to add a check mark beside Analysis ToolPak, and click OK. Click Yes to install. When the data analysis tools have been added, Data Analysis will appear in the Analysis group on the Data tab. Click on Data Analysis and then choose Regression.

	A	B	C	D
1	**Month**	**Cost**	**# Moves**	
2	January	$2,000	100	
3	February	3,090	125	
4	March	2,780	175	
5	April	1,990	200	
6	May	7,500	500	
7	June	5,300	300	
8	July	3,800	250	
9	August	6,300	400	
10	September	5,600	475	
11	October	6,240	425	
12				
13				
14				

Sheet1 Sheet2 Sheet3

Exhibit 3.15

Spreadsheet Data for Anderson Company

When the regression screen pops up, you can tell the program where the dependent and independent variables are located. Place the cursor at the beginning of the independent rectangle and then (again using the cursor) drag down to select the values under the independent variable column—in this case, cells C2 through C11. Then, move the cursor to the beginning of the dependent rectangle, and select the values in cells B2 through B11. Finally, you need to tell the computer where to place the output. Block a nice-size rectangle, say cells A13 through F20, and click OK. In less than the blink of an eye, the regression output is complete. The regression output is shown in Exhibit 3.16.

Now, let's take a look at the output in Exhibit 3.16. First, let's locate the fixed cost and variable rate coefficients. At the bottom of the exhibit, the intercept and X Variable 1 are shown, and the next column gives their coefficients. Rounding, the fixed cost is 789 and the variable rate is 12.38. Now we can construct the cost formula for materials handling cost. It is:

$$\text{Materials Handling Cost} = \$789 + (\$12.38 \times \text{Number of Moves})$$

We can use this formula to predict the materials handling cost for future months as we did with the formulas for the high-low and scattergraph methods.

Since the regression cost formula is the best-fitting line, it should produce better predictions of materials handling costs. For 350 moves, the total materials handling cost predicted by the least squares line is:

$$\$5,122 = \$789 + (\$12.38 \times 350)$$

Exhibit 3.16

Regression Output for Anderson Company

	A	B	C	D	
1	SUMMARY OUTPUT				∧
2					
3	*Regression Statistics*				
4	Multiple R	0.92436			
5	R Square	0.854442			
6	Standard Error	810.1969			
7	Observations	9			
8					
9					
10	*Coefficients*				
11	Intercept	788.7806			
12	X Variable 1	12.38058			≡
13					
14					
15					∨

Sheet1 / Sheet2 / Sheet3

Of the total materials handling cost, $789 is fixed and $4,333 is variable. Using this prediction as a standard, the scattergraph line most closely approximates the least squares line.

While the computer output in Exhibit 3.16 can give us the fixed and variable cost coefficients, its major usefulness lies in its ability to provide information about reliability of the estimated cost formula. This is a feature not provided by either the scattergraph or high-low methods.

Goodness of Fit

Regression routines provide information on goodness of fit. Goodness of fit tells us how well the independent variable(s) predict(s) the dependent variable. This information can be used to assess reliability of the estimated cost formula, a feature not provided by either the scattergraph or high-low methods. The summary output in Exhibit 3.16 provides a wealth of statistical information. However, we will look at just one more feature—the coefficient of determination, or R^2. (The remaining information is discussed in statistics classes and higher-level accounting classes.)

The Anderson Company example suggests that the number of moves can explain changes in materials handling costs. The scattergraph shown in Graph A in Exhibit 3.7 (p. 97) confirms this belief because it reveals that materials handling costs and activity output (as measured by number of moves) seem to move together. It is quite likely that a significant percentage of the total variability in cost is explained by our output variable. We can determine statistically just how much variability is explained by looking at the coefficient of determination. The percentage of variability in the dependent variable explained by an independent variable (in this case, a measure of activity output) is called the **coefficient of determination (R^2)**. The higher the percentage of cost variability explained, the better job the independent variable does of explaining the dependent variable. Since R^2 is the percentage of variability explained, it always has a value between 0 and 1.00. In the summary output in Exhibit 3.16, the coefficient of determination is labeled R Square (R^2). The value given is 0.85 (rounded), which means that 85% of the variability in the materials handling cost is explained by the number of moves. This is not bad. However, something else explains the remaining 15%.

How good is this result? There is no cutoff point for a good versus bad coefficient of determination. Clearly, the closer R^2 is to 1.00, the better. Is 85% good enough? How about 73%? Or even 46%? The answer is that it depends. If your cost equation yields a coefficient of determination of 75%, you know that your independent variable explains three-fourths of the variability in cost. You also know that some other factor or combination of factors explains the remaining one-fourth. Depending on your tolerance for error, you may want to improve the equation by trying different independent variables (e.g., materials handling hours worked rather than number of moves) or by trying multiple regressions. (Multiple regressions use two or more independent variables. This topic is saved for later courses.)

SUMMARY OF LEARNING OBJECTIVES

LO1. Explain the meaning of cost behavior, and define and describe fixed and variable costs.
- Cost behavior is the way a cost changes in relation to changes in activity output.
- Time horizon is important because costs can change from fixed to variable depending on whether the decision takes place over the short run or the long run.
- Variable costs change *in total* as the driver, or output measure, changes. Usually, we assume that variable costs increase in direct proportion to increases in activity output.
- Fixed costs do not change *in total* as activity output changes.

LO2. Define and describe mixed and step costs.
- Mixed costs have both a variable and a fixed component.
- Step costs remain at a constant level of cost for a range of output and then jump to a higher level of cost at some point, where they remain for a similar range of output.
- Cost objects that display a step cost behavior must be purchased in chunks.
- The width of the step defines the range of output for which a particular amount of the resource applies.

LO3. Separate mixed costs into their fixed and variable components using the high-low method, the scattergraph method, and the method of least squares.
- In the high-low method, only two data points are used—the high point and the low point with respect to activity level. These two points then are used to compute the intercept and the slope of the line on which they lie.
- The high-low method is objective and easy, but a nonrepresentative high or low point will lead to an incorrectly estimated cost relationship.

- The scattergraph method involves inspecting a graph showing total mixed cost at various output levels and selecting two points that seem to best represent the relationship between cost and output, and drawing a straight line. The intercept gives an estimate of the fixed cost component and the slope an estimate of the variable cost per unit of activity.
- The scattergraph method is a good way to identify nonlinearity, the presence of outliers, and the presence of a shift in the cost relationship. Its disadvantage is that it is subjective.
- The method of least squares uses all of the data points (except outliers) on the scattergraph and produces a line that best fits all of the points.
- The method of least squares offers ways to assess the reliability of cost equations.
- Managers use their experience and knowledge of cost and activity-level relationships to identify outliers, understand structural shifts, and adjust parameters due to anticipated changing conditions.

LO4. Explain the difference between absorption and variable costing.
- Absorption costing treats fixed factory overhead as a product cost. Unit product cost consists of direct materials, direct labor, variable factory overhead, and fixed factory overhead.
- The absorption-costing income statement groups expenses according to function:
  - Production cost—cost of goods sold, including variable and fixed product cost.
  - Selling expense—variable and fixed cost of selling and distributing product.
  - Administrative expense—variable and fixed cost of administration.
- Variable costing treats fixed factory overhead as a period expense. Unit product cost consists of direct materials, direct labor, and variable factory overhead.
- The variable-costing income statement groups expenses according to cost behavior:
  - Variable expenses of manufacturing, selling, and administration.
  - Fixed expenses of manufacturing (fixed factory overhead), selling, and administration.
- Impact of units produced and units sold on absorption-costing income and variable-costing income:
  - If units produced > units sold, then absorption-costing income > variable-costing income.
  - If units produced < units sold, then absorption-costing income < variable-costing income.
  - If units produced = units sold, then absorption-costing income = variable-costing income.

LO5. (*Appendix 3A*) Use a computer spreadsheet program to perform the method of least squares.

SUMMARY OF IMPORTANT EQUATIONS

1. Total Variable Costs = Variable Rate × Units of Output
2. Total Cost = Total Fixed Cost + Total Variable Cost
3. Total Cost = Total Fixed Cost + (Variable Rate × Units of Output)
4. Variable Rate = (High Point Cost − Low Point Cost)/(High Point Output − Low Point Output)
5. Fixed Cost = Total Cost at High Point − (Variable Rate × Output at High Point)
6. Fixed Cost = Total Cost at Low Point − (Variable Rate × Output at Low Point)
7. Absorption Costing Product Cost = Direct Materials + Direct Labor + Variable Overhead + Fixed Overhead
8. Variable Costing Product Cost = Direct Materials + Direct Labor + Variable Overhead

EXAMPLE 3.1	How to create and use a cost formula, page 92
EXAMPLE 3.2	How to use the high-low method to calculate fixed cost and the variable rate and to construct a cost formula, page 94
EXAMPLE 3.3	How to use the high-low method to calculate predicted total variable cost and total cost for budgeted output, page 95
EXAMPLE 3.4	How to use the high-low method to calculate predicted total variable cost and total cost for a time period that differs from the data period, page 96
EXAMPLE 3.5	How to use the regression method to calculate fixed cost and the variable rate and to construct a cost formula and to determine budgeted cost, page 101
EXAMPLE 3.6	How to compute inventory cost under absorption costing, page 106
EXAMPLE 3.7	How to compute inventory cost under variable costing, page 107
EXAMPLE 3.8	How to prepare an absorption-costing income statement, page 108
EXAMPLE 3.9	How to prepare a variable-costing income statement, page 109

KEY TERMS

Absorption costing, 105, assigns *all* manufacturing costs to the product and includes direct materials, direct labor, variable overhead, and fixed overhead.

Coefficient of determination (R^2), 112 (*Appendix 3A*), the percentage of total variability in a dependent variable that is explained by an independent variable. It assumes a value between 0 and 1.

Committed fixed costs, 84, a fixed cost that cannot be easily changed.

Cost behavior, 80, the way in which a cost changes when the level of output changes.

Cost driver, 81, a causal factor that measures the output of the activity that leads (or causes) costs to change.

Dependent variable, 92, a variable whose value depends on the value of another variable.

Discretionary fixed costs, 84, fixed costs that can be changed relatively easily in the short run at management discretion.

Discretionary variable costs, 85, variable costs that can be changed or avoided relatively easily in the short run at management discretion.

Fixed costs, 81, costs that, in total, are constant within the relevant range as the level of output increases or decreases.

High-low method, 93, a method for separating mixed costs into fixed and variable components by using just the high and low data points. [*Note:* The high (low) data point corresponds to the high (low) output level.]

Independent variable, 92, explains changes in the dependent variable and, as such, its value does not depend on the value of another variable.

Intercept, 92, the fixed cost, representing the point where the cost formula intercepts the vertical axis.

Method of least squares (regression), 99, a statistical method to find the best-fitting line through a set of data points. It is used to break out the fixed and variable components of a mixed cost.

Mixed costs, 88, costs that have both a fixed and a variable component.

Relevant range, 81, the range of output over which an assumed cost relationship is valid for the normal operations of a firm.

Scattergraph method, 97, a method to fit a line to a set of data using two points that are selected by judgment. It is used to break out the fixed and variable components of a mixed cost.

Semi-variable costs, 86, a cost that is variable in nature but whose rate of change is not constant (i.e., total cost increases at either a decreasing or an increasing rate) as output increases.

Slope, 92, the variable cost per unit of activity usage.

Step cost, 89, a cost that displays a constant level of total cost for a range of output and then jumps to a higher level of total cost at some point, where it remains for a similar range of output.

Variable costing, 105, assigns all variable manufacturing costs to the product and includes direct materials, direct labor, and variable overhead.

Variable costs, 84, costs that, in total, vary in direct proportion to changes in output within the relevant range.

REVIEW PROBLEMS

I. Using High-Low and Method of Least Squares to Separate Mixed Costs into Their Fixed and Variable Components

Kim Wilson, controller for Max Enterprises, has decided to estimate the fixed and variable components associated with the company's shipping activity. She has collected the following data for the past 6 months:

Packages Shipped	Total Shipping Costs
10	$ 800
20	1,100
15	900
12	900
18	1,050
25	1,250

Required:

1. Estimate the fixed and variable components for the shipping costs using the high-low method. Using the cost formula, predict the total cost of shipping if 14 packages are shipped.
2. Estimate the fixed and variable components using the method of least squares. Using the cost formula, predict the total cost of shipping if 14 packages are shipped.
3. (*Appendix 3A*) For the method of least squares, explain what the coefficient of determination tells us.

Solution:

1. The estimate of fixed and variable costs using the high-low method is as follows:

$$\text{Variable Rate} = \frac{\$1,250 - \$800}{25 - 10}$$

$$= \$450/15 \text{ packages}$$

$$= \$30 \text{ per package}$$

$$\text{Fixed Amount} = \$1,250 - \$30(25) = \$500$$

$$\text{Total Cost} = \$500 + \$30X$$

$$= \$500 + \$30(14)$$

$$= \$920$$

2. The output of a spreadsheet regression routine is as follows:
   Regression output:

Constant (intercept)	509.911894273125
R Squared	0.96928536465981
No. of Observations	6
X Coefficient(s)	29.4052863436125

   $$Y = \$509.91 + \$29.41(14) = \$921.65$$

3. The coefficient of determination (R^2) tells us that about 96.9% of total shipping cost is explained by the number of packages shipped.

II. Absorption and Variable Costing

Fine Leathers Company produces a ladies' wallet and a men's wallet. Selected data for the past year follow:

	Ladies' Wallet	Men's Wallet
Production (units)	100,000	200,000
Sales (units)	90,000	210,000
Selling price	$5.50	$4.50
Direct labor hours	50,000	80,000
Manufacturing costs:		
Direct materials	$ 75,000	$100,000
Direct labor	250,000	400,000
Variable overhead	20,000	24,000
Fixed overhead:		
Direct	$ 50,000	$ 40,000
Common[a]	20,000	20,000
Nonmanufacturing costs:		
Variable selling	$ 30,000	$ 60,000
Direct fixed selling	35,000	40,000
Common fixed selling[b]	25,000	25,000

[a] Common overhead totals $40,000 and is divided equally between the two products.

[b] Common fixed selling costs total $50,000 and are divided equally between the two products.

Budgeted fixed overhead for the year, $130,000, equaled the actual fixed overhead. Fixed overhead is assigned to products using a plantwide rate based on expected direct labor hours, which were 130,000. The company had 10,000 men's wallets in inventory at the beginning of the year. These wallets had the same unit cost as the men's wallets produced during the year.

(Continued)

Required:

1. Compute the unit cost for the ladies' and men's wallets using the variable-costing method. Compute the unit cost using absorption costing.
2. Prepare an income statement using absorption costing.
3. Prepare an income statement using variable costing.

Solution:

1. Unit cost for the ladies' wallet is as follows:

Direct materials ($75,000/100,000)	$0.75
Direct labor ($250,000/100,000)	2.50
Variable overhead ($20,000/100,000)	0.20
Variable cost per unit	**$3.45**
Fixed overhead [(50,000 × $1.00)/100,000]	0.50
Absorption cost per unit	**$3.95**

The unit cost for the men's wallet is as follows:

Direct materials ($100,000/200,000)	$0.50
Direct labor ($400,000/200,000)	2.00
Variable overhead ($24,000/200,000)	0.12
Variable cost per unit	**$2.62**
Fixed overhead [(80,000 × $1.00)/200,000]	0.40
Absorption cost per unit	**$3.02**

Notice that the only difference between the two unit costs is the assignment of the fixed overhead cost. Notice also that the fixed overhead unit cost is assigned using the predetermined fixed overhead rate ($130,000/130,000 hours = $1 per hour). For example, the ladies' wallets used 50,000 direct labor hours and so receive $1 × 50,000, or $50,000, of fixed overhead. This total, when divided by the units produced, gives the $0.50 per-unit fixed overhead cost. Finally, observe that variable nonmanufacturing costs are not part of the unit cost under variable costing. For both approaches, only manufacturing costs are used to compute the unit costs.

2. The income statement under absorption costing is as follows:

Sales [($5.50 × 90,000) + ($4.50 × 210,000)]	$1,440,000
Less: Cost of goods sold [($3.95 × 90,000) + ($3.02 × 210,000)]	989,700
Gross margin	$ 450,300
Less: Selling expenses*	215,000
Operating income	$ 235,300

* The sum of selling expenses for both products.

3. The income statement under variable costing is as follows:

Sales [($5.50 × 90,000) + ($4.50 × 210,000)]	$1,440,000
Less variable expenses:	
Variable cost of goods sold [($3.45 × 90,000) + ($2.62 × 210,000)]	860,700
Variable selling expenses	90,000
Contribution margin	$ 489,300
Less fixed expenses:	
Fixed overhead	130,000
Fixed selling	125,000
Operating income	$ 234,300

DISCUSSION QUESTIONS

1. Why is knowledge of cost behavior important for managerial decision making? Give an example to illustrate your answer.
2. What is a driver? Give an example of a cost and its corresponding output measure or driver.
3. Suppose a company finds that shipping cost is $3,560 each month plus $6.70 per package shipped. What is the cost formula for monthly shipping cost? Identify the independent variable, the dependent variable, the fixed cost per month, and the variable rate.
4. Some firms assign mixed costs to either the fixed or variable cost categories without using any formal methodology to separate them. Explain how this practice can be defended.
5. Explain the difference between committed and discretionary fixed costs. Give examples of each.
6. Explain why the concept of relevant range is important when dealing with step costs.
7. Why do mixed costs pose a problem when it comes to classifying costs into fixed and variable categories?
8. Describe the cost formula for a strictly fixed cost such as depreciation of $15,000 per year.
9. Describe the cost formula for a strictly variable cost such as electrical power cost of $1.15 per machine hour (i.e., every hour the machinery is run, electrical power cost goes up by $1.15).
10. What is the scattergraph method, and why is it used? Why is a scattergraph a good first step in separating mixed costs into their fixed and variable components?
11. Describe how the scattergraph method breaks out the fixed and variable costs from a mixed cost. Now describe how the high-low method works. How do the two methods differ?
12. What are the advantages of the scattergraph method over the high-low method? The high-low method over the scattergraph method?
13. Describe the method of least squares. Why is this method better than either the high-low method or the scattergraph method?
14. What is meant by the best-fitting line?
15. What is the difference between the unit cost of a product under absorption costing and variable costing?
16. If a company produces 10,000 units and sells 8,000 units during a period, which method of computing operating income (absorption costing or variable costing) will result in the higher operating income? Why?
17. (Appendix 3A) Explain the meaning of the coefficient of determination.

MULTIPLE-CHOICE EXERCISES

3-1 A factor that causes or leads to a change in a cost or activity is a(n)

    a. slope.
    b. intercept.
    c. driver.
    d. variable term.
    e. cost object.

3-2 Which of the following would probably be a variable cost in a soda bottling plant?

    a. Direct labor
    b. Bottles
    c. Carbonated water
    d. Power to run the bottling machine
    e. All of these.

3-3   Which of the following would probably be a fixed cost in an automobile insurance company?

a. Application forms
b. The salary of customer service representatives
c. Time spent by adjusters to evaluate accidents
d. All of these.
e. None of these.

Use the following information for Multiple-Choice Questions 3-4 through 3-7:
The following cost formula was developed by using monthly data for a hospital.

Total Cost = $128,000,000 + ($12,000 × Number of Patient Days)

3-4   In the cost formula, the term $128,000,000

a. is the total variable cost.
b. is the dependent variable.
c. is the variable rate.
d. is the total fixed cost.
e. cannot be determined from the above formula.

3-5   In the cost formula, the term $12,000

a. is the variable rate.
b. is the dependent variable.
c. is the independent variable.
d. is the intercept.
e. cannot be determined from the above formula.

3-6   In the cost formula, the term "Number of Patient Days"

a. is the variable rate.
b. is the intercept.
c. is the dependent variable.
d. is the independent variable.
e. cannot be determined from the above formula.

3-7   In the cost formula, the term "Total Cost"

a. is the variable rate.
b. is the intercept.
c. is the dependent variable.
d. is the independent variable.
e. cannot be determined from the above formula.

3-8   The following cost formula for total purchasing cost in a factory was developed using monthly data.

Total Cost = $235,000 + ($75 × Number of Purchase Orders)

Next month, 8,000 purchase orders are predicted. The total cost predicted for the purchasing department next month

a. is $8,000.
b. is $235,000.
c. is $600,000.
d. is $835,000.
e. cannot be determined from the above formula.

3-9 An advantage of the high-low method is that it

    a. is subjective.
    b. is objective.
    c. is the most accurate method.
    d. removes outliers.
    e. is descriptive of nonlinear data.

Use the following information for Multiple-Choice Questions 3-10 and 3-11:
The following 6 months of data were collected on maintenance cost and the number of machine hours in a factory:

Month	Maintenance Cost	Machine Hours
January	$16,900	5,600
February	13,900	4,500
March	10,900	3,800
April	11,450	3,700
May	13,050	4,215
June	16,990	4,980

3-10 Select the independent and dependent variables.

	Independent Variable	Dependent Variable
a.	Maintenance cost	Machine hours
b.	Machine hours	Maintenance cost
c.	Maintenance cost	Month
d.	Machine hours	Month
e.	Month	Maintenance cost

3-11 Select the correct set of high and low months.

	High	Low
a.	January	April
b.	January	March
c.	June	March
d.	June	April

3-12 An advantage of the scattergraph method is that it

    a. is objective.
    b. is easier to use than the high-low method.
    c. is the most accurate method.
    d. removes outliers.
    e. is descriptive

3-13 The total cost for monthly supervisory cost in a factory is $4,500 regardless of how many hours the supervisor works or the quantity of output achieved. This cost

    a. is strictly variable.
    b. is strictly fixed.
    c. is a mixed cost.
    d. is a step cost.
    e. cannot be determined from this information.

3-14 Yates Company shows the following unit costs for its product:

Direct materials	$40
Direct labor	30
Variable overhead	2
Fixed overhead	5

Yates started the year with 8,000 units in inventory, produced 50,000 units during the year, and sold 55,000 units. The value of ending inventory is

a. greater under variable costing than absorption costing.
b. greater under absorption costing than variable costing.
c. the same under both variable and absorption costing.
d. There is no ending inventory.
e. This situation cannot happen.

3-15 (*Appendix 3A*) In the method of least squares, the coefficient that tells the percentage of variation in the dependent variable that is explained by the independent variable is

a. the intercept term.
b. the *x*-coefficient.
c. the coefficient of correlation.
d. the coefficient of determination.
e. None of these.

BRIEF EXERCISES: SET A

Brief Exercise 3-16 Creating and Using a Cost Formula

Big Thumbs Company manufactures portable flash drives for computers. Big Thumbs incurs monthly depreciation costs of $15,000 on its plant equipment. Also, each drive requires materials and manufacturing overhead resources. On average, the company uses 10,000 ounces of materials to manufacture 5,000 flash drives per month. Each ounce of material costs $3.00. In addition, manufacturing overhead resources are driven by machine hours. On average, the company incurs $22,500 of variable manufacturing overhead resources to produce 5,000 flash drives per month.

Required:

1. Create a formula for the monthly cost of flash drives for Big Thumbs.
2. If the department expects to manufacture 6,000 flash drives next month, what is the expected fixed cost (assuming that 6,000 units is within the company's current relevant range)? Total variable cost? Total manufacturing cost (i.e., both fixed and variable)?

Use the following information for Brief Exercises 3-17 through 3-20:
Pizza Vesuvio makes specialty pizzas. Data for the past 8 months were collected:

Month	Labor Cost	Employee Hours
January	$7,000	360
February	8,140	550
March	9,899	630
April	9,787	610
May	8,490	480
June	7,450	350
July	9,490	570
August	7,531	310

Brief Exercise 3-17 Using High-Low to Calculate Fixed Cost, Calculate the Variable Rate, and Construct a Cost Function

OBJECTIVE ▶3

Example 3.2

Refer to the information for Pizza Vesuvio on the previous page. Pizza Vesuvio's controller wants to calculate the fixed and variable costs associated with labor used in the restaurant.

Required:

Using the high-low method, calculate the fixed cost of labor, calculate the variable rate per employee hour, and construct the cost formula for total labor cost.

Brief Exercise 3-18 Using High-Low to Calculate Predicted Total Variable Cost and Total Cost for Budgeted Output

OBJECTIVE ▶3

Example 3.3

Refer to the information for Pizza Vesuvio on the previous page. Assume that this information was used to construct the following formula for monthly labor cost.

$$\text{Total Labor Cost} = \$5{,}237 + (\$7.40 \times \text{Employee Hours})$$

Required:

Assume that 675 employee hours are budgeted for the month of September. Use the total labor cost formula for the following calculations:
1. Calculate total variable labor cost for September.
2. Calculate total labor cost for September.

Brief Exercise 3-19 Using High-Low to Calculate Predicted Total Variable Cost and Total Cost for a Time Period That Differs from the Data Period

OBJECTIVE ▶3

Example 3.4

Refer to the information for Pizza Vesuvio on the previous page. Assume that this information was used to construct the following formula for monthly labor cost.

$$\text{Total Labor Cost} = \$5{,}237 + (\$7.40 \times \text{Employee Hours})$$

Required:

Assume that 4,000 employee hours are budgeted for the coming year. Use the total labor cost formula to make the following calculations:
1. Calculate total variable labor cost for the year.
2. Calculate total fixed labor cost for the year.
3. Calculate total labor cost for the coming year.

Brief Exercise 3-20 Using Regression to Calculate Fixed Cost, Calculate the Variable Rate, Construct a Cost Formula, and Determine Budgeted Cost

OBJECTIVE ▶3

Example 3.5

Refer to the information for Pizza Vesuvio on the previous page. Coefficients shown by a regression program for Pizza Vesuvio's data are:

Intercept	4,517
X Variable	8.20

Required:

Use the results of regression to make the following calculations:
1. Calculate the fixed cost of labor and the variable rate per employee hour.
2. Construct the cost formula for total labor cost.
3. Calculate the budgeted cost for next month, assuming that 675 employee hours are budgeted. (*Note:* Round answers to the nearest dollar.)

Use the following information for Brief Exercises 3-21 and 3-22:
During the most recent year, Judson Company had the following data associated with the product it makes:

Units in beginning inventory	300
Units produced	15,000
Units sold ($300 per unit)	12,700
Variable costs per unit:	
Direct materials	$20
Direct labor	$60
Variable overhead	$12
Fixed costs:	
Fixed overhead per unit produced	$30
Fixed selling and administrative	$140,000

OBJECTIVE 4
Example 3.6

Brief Exercise 3-21 Inventory Valuation under Absorption Costing

Refer to the data for Judson Company above.

Required:

1. How many units are in ending inventory?
2. Using absorption costing, calculate the per-unit product cost.
3. What is the value of ending inventory under absorption costing?

OBJECTIVE 4
Example 3.7

Brief Exercise 3-22 Inventory Valuation under Variable Costing

Refer to the data for Judson Company above.

Required:

1. How many units are in ending inventory?
2. Using variable costing, calculate the per-unit product cost.
3. What is the value of ending inventory under variable costing?

Use the following information for Brief Exercises 3-23 and 3-24:
During the most recent year, Osterman Company had the following data:

Units in beginning inventory	—
Units produced	10,000
Units sold ($47 per unit)	9,300
Variable costs per unit:	
Direct materials	$9
Direct labor	$6
Variable overhead	$4
Fixed costs:	
Fixed overhead per unit produced	$5
Fixed selling and administrative	$138,000

OBJECTIVE 4
Example 3.8

Brief Exercise 3-23 Absorption-Costing Income Statement

Refer to the data for Osterman Company above.

Required:

1. Calculate the cost of goods sold under absorption costing.
2. Prepare an income statement using absorption costing.

Brief Exercise 3-24 Variable-Costing Income Statement

OBJECTIVE ▶ 4
Example 3.9

Refer to the data for Osterman Company on the previous page.

Required:

1. Calculate the cost of goods sold under variable costing.
2. Prepare an income statement using variable costing.

BRIEF EXERCISES: SET B

Brief Exercise 3-25 Creating and Using a Cost Formula

OBJECTIVE ▶ 3
Example 3.1

Kleenaire Motors manufactures hybrid sports utility vehicles (SUVs). Kleenaire incurs monthly depreciation costs of $10,000,000 on its highly automated plant machinery and warehousing facility. Also, each SUV requires materials and manufacturing overhead resources. On average, the company uses 75,000,000 pounds of steel to manufacture 50,000 SUVs per month. Each pound of steel costs $0.20. In addition, manufacturing overhead resources are driven by machine hours. On average, the company incurs $200,000,000 of variable manufacturing overhead resources to produce 50,000 SUVs per month.

Required:

1. Create a formula for the monthly cost of SUVs for Kleenaire.
2. If Kleenaire expects to manufacture 55,000 SUVs next month, what is the expected fixed cost (assuming that 55,000 units is within the company's current relevant range)? Total variable cost? Total manufacturing cost (i.e., both fixed and variable)?

Use the following information for Brief Exercises 3-26 through 3-29:

Speedy Pete's is a small start-up company that delivers high-end coffee drinks to large metropolitan office buildings via a cutting-edge motorized coffee cart to compete with other premium coffee shops. Data for the past 8 months were collected as follows:

Month	Delivery Cost	Number of Deliveries
May	$63,450	1,800
June	67,120	2,010
July	66,990	2,175
August	68,020	2,200
September	73,400	2,550
October	72,850	2,630
November	75,450	2,800
December	73,300	2,725

Brief Exercise 3-26 Using High-Low to Calculate Fixed Cost, Calculate the Variable Rate, and Construct a Cost Function

OBJECTIVE ▶ 3
Example 3.2

Refer to the information for Speedy Pete's above. Speedy Pete's controller wants to calculate the fixed and variable costs associated with its cutting-edge delivery service.

Required:

Using the high-low method, calculate the fixed cost of deliveries, calculate the variable rate per delivery, and construct the cost formula for total delivery cost.

Brief Exercise 3-27 Using High-Low to Calculate Predicted Total Variable Cost and Total Cost for Budgeted Output

OBJECTIVE ▶ 3
Example 3.3

Refer to the information for Speedy Pete's above. Assume that this information was used to construct the following formula for monthly delivery cost.

$$\text{Total Delivery Cost} = \$41,850 + (\$12.00 \times \text{Number of Deliveries})$$

(*Continued*)

Required:

Assume that 3,000 deliveries are budgeted for the following month of January. Use the total delivery cost formula for the following calculations:

1. Calculate total variable delivery cost for January.
2. Calculate total delivery cost for January.

OBJECTIVE ▶3
Example 3.4

Brief Exercise 3-28 Using High-Low to Calculate Predicted Total Variable Cost and Total Cost for a Time Period that Differs from the Data Period

Refer to the information for Speedy Pete's on the previous page. Assume that this information was used to construct the following formula for monthly delivery cost.

$$\text{Total Delivery Cost} = \$41{,}850 + (\$12.00 \times \text{Number of Deliveries})$$

Required:

Assume that 3,000 deliveries are budgeted for the coming year. Use the total delivery cost formula to make the following calculations:

1. Calculate total variable delivery cost for the coming year.
2. Calculate total fixed delivery cost for the year.
3. Calculate total delivery cost for the year.

OBJECTIVE ▶3
Example 3.5

Brief Exercise 3-29 Using Regression to Calculate Fixed Cost, Calculate the Variable Rate, Construct a Cost Formula, and Determine Budgeted Cost

Refer to the information for Speedy Pete's on the previous page. Coefficients shown by a regression program for Speedy Pete's data are:

Intercept	43,293
X Variable	11.34

Required:

Use the results of regression to make the following calculations:

1. Calculate the fixed cost of deliveries and the variable rate per delivery.
2. Construct the cost formula for total delivery cost.
3. Calculate the budgeted cost for next month, assuming that 3,000 deliveries are budgeted. (*Note:* Round answers to the nearest dollar.)

Use the following information for Brief Exercises 3-30 and 3-31:
During the most recent year, Pelham Company had the following data associated with the product it makes:

Units in beginning inventory	400
Units produced	14,000
Units sold ($300 per unit)	13,700
Variable costs per unit:	
Direct materials	$15
Direct labor	$36
Variable overhead	$9
Fixed costs:	
Fixed overhead per unit produced	$40
Fixed selling and administrative	$140,000

Brief Exercise 3-30 Inventory Valuation under Absorption Costing

OBJECTIVE ◀ 4
Example 3.6

Refer to the data for Pelham Company on the previous page.

Required:

1. How many units are in ending inventory?
2. Using absorption costing, calculate the per-unit product cost.
3. What is the value of ending inventory under absorption costing?

Brief Exercise 3-31 Inventory Valuation under Variable Costing

OBJECTIVE ◀ 4
Example 3.7

Refer to the data for Pelham Company on the previous page.

Required:

1. How many units are in ending inventory?
2. Using variable costing, calculate the per-unit product cost.
3. What is the value of ending inventory under variable costing?

Use the following information for Brief Exercises 3-32 and 3-33:
During the most recent year, Beyta Company had the following data:

Units in beginning inventory	—
Units produced	10,000
Units sold ($60 per unit)	8,800
Variable costs per unit:	
Direct materials	$12
Direct labor	$7
Variable overhead	$5
Fixed costs:	
Fixed overhead per unit produced	$8
Fixed selling and administrative	$138,000

Brief Exercise 3-32 Absorption-Costing Income Statement

OBJECTIVE ◀ 4
Example 3.8

Refer to the data for Beyta Company above.

Required:

1. Calculate the cost of goods sold under absorption costing.
2. Prepare an income statement using absorption costing.

Brief Exercise 3-33 Variable-Costing Income Statement

OBJECTIVE ◀ 4
Example 3.9

Refer to the data for Beyta Company above.

Required:

1. Calculate the cost of goods sold under variable costing.
2. Prepare an income statement using variable costing.

EXERCISES

Exercise 3-34 Variable and Fixed Costs

OBJECTIVE ◀ 1

What follows are a number of resources that are used by a manufacturer of futons. Assume that the output measure or cost driver is the number of futons produced. All direct labor is paid

(Continued)

on an hourly basis, and hours worked can be easily changed by management. All other factory workers are salaried.

a. Power to operate a drill (to drill holes in the wooden frames of the futons)
b. Cloth to cover the futon mattress
c. Salary of the factory receptionist
d. Cost of food and decorations for the annual Fourth of July party for all factory employees
e. Fuel for a forklift used to move materials in a factory
f. Depreciation on the factory
g. Depreciation on a forklift used to move partially completed goods
h. Wages paid to workers who assemble the futon frame
i. Wages paid to workers who maintain the factory equipment
j. Cloth rags used to wipe the excess stain off the wooden frames

Required:

Classify the resource costs as variable or fixed.

OBJECTIVE ▶**1**▶   **Exercise 3-35** **Cost Behavior, Classification**

Smith Concrete Company owns enough ready-mix trucks to deliver up to 100,000 cubic yards of concrete per year (considering each truck's capacity, weather, and distance to each job). Total truck depreciation is $200,000 per year. Raw materials (cement, gravel, and so on) cost about $25 per cubic yard of cement.

Required:

1. Prepare a graph for truck depreciation. Use the vertical axis for depreciation cost and the horizontal axis for cubic yards of cement.
2. Prepare a graph for raw materials. Use the vertical axis for cost and the horizontal axis for cubic yards of cement.
3. Assume that the normal operating range for the company is 90,000 to 96,000 cubic yards per year. Classify truck depreciation and raw materials as variable or fixed costs.
4. **CONCEPTUAL CONNECTION** Briefly describe actions that Smith management could take to reduce the truck depreciation cost from year to year.
5. **CONCEPTUAL CONNECTION** Briefly describe actions that Smith management could take to reduce the total raw materials cost from year to year.

OBJECTIVE ▶**1**▶   **Exercise 3-36** **Classifying Costs as Fixed and Variable in a Service Organization**

Alva Community Hospital has five laboratory technicians who are responsible for doing a series of standard blood tests. Each technician is paid a salary of $30,000. The lab facility represents a recent addition to the hospital and cost $300,000. It is expected to last 20 years. Equipment used for the testing cost $10,000 and has a life expectancy of 5 years. In addition to the salaries, facility, and equipment, Alva expects to spend $200,000 for chemicals, forms, power, and other supplies. This $200,000 is enough for 200,000 blood tests.

Required:

Assuming that the driver (measure of output) for each type of cost is the number of blood tests run, classify the costs by completing the following table. Put an X in the appropriate box for variable cost, discretionary fixed cost, or committed fixed cost.

Cost Category	Variable Cost	Discretionary Fixed Cost	Committed Fixed Cost
Technician salaries			
Laboratory facility			
Laboratory equipment			
Chemicals and other supplies			

> *Use the following information for Exercises 3-37 and 3-38:*
> Alisha Incorporated manufactures medical stents for use in heart bypass surgery. Based on past experience, Alisha has found that its total maintenance costs can be represented by the following formula: Maintenance Cost = $1,750,000 + $125X, where X = Number of Heart Stents. Last year, Alisha produced 50,000 stents. Actual maintenance costs for the year were as expected. (*Note:* Round all answers to two decimal places.)

Exercise 3-37 Cost Behavior

OBJECTIVE 1

Refer to the information for Alisha Incorporated above.

Required:

1. What is the total maintenance cost incurred by Alisha last year?
2. What is the total fixed maintenance cost incurred by Alisha last year?
3. What is the total variable maintenance cost incurred by Alisha last year?
4. What is the maintenance cost per unit produced?
5. What is the fixed maintenance cost per unit?
6. What is the variable maintenance cost per unit?
7. **CONCEPTUAL CONNECTION** Briefly explain how Alisha management could improve its cost function to better understand past maintenance costs and predict future maintenance costs.

Exercise 3-38 Cost Behavior

OBJECTIVE 1

Refer to the information for Alisha Incorporated above. However, now assume that Alisha produced 25,000 medical stents (rather than 50,000).

Required:

1. What is the total maintenance cost incurred by Alisha last year?
2. What is the total fixed maintenance cost incurred by Alisha last year?
3. What is the total variable maintenance cost incurred by Alisha last year?
4. What is the maintenance cost per unit produced?
5. What is the fixed maintenance cost per unit?
6. What is the variable maintenance cost per unit?
7. **CONCEPTUAL CONNECTION** The number of stents produced in **Exercise 3-38** (25,000) is only half of the number produced in **Exercise 3-37** (50,000), yet the maintenance cost per unit (see Requirement 4) is larger in Exercise 3-38 than in Exercise 3-37. Briefly explain why Alisha's maintenance cost per unit in Exercise 3-38 is different than in Exercise 3-37. Should Alisha's management use maintenance cost per unit to make decisions?

Exercise 3-39 Step Costs, Relevant Range

OBJECTIVE 2

Bellati Inc. produces large industrial machinery. Bellati has a machining department and a group of direct laborers called machinists. Each machinist can machine up to 500 units per year. Bellati also hires supervisors to develop machine specification plans and oversee production within the machining department. Given the planning and supervisory work, a supervisor can oversee, at most, three machinists. Bellati's accounting and production history shows the following relationships between number of units produced and the annual costs of supervision and materials handling (by machinists):

(Continued)

Units Produced	Direct Labor	Supervision
0–500	$ 36,000	$ 40,000
501–1,000	72,000	40,000
1,001–1,500	108,000	40,000
1,501–2,000	144,000	80,000
2,001–2,500	180,000	80,000
2,501–3,000	216,000	80,000
3,001–3,500	252,000	120,000
3,501–4,000	288,000	120,000

Required:

1. Prepare a graph that illustrates the relationship between direct labor cost and number of units produced in the machining department. (Let cost of direct labor be the vertical axis and number of units be the horizontal axis.) Would you classify this cost as a strictly variable cost, a fixed cost, or a step cost?
2. Prepare a graph that illustrates the relationship between the cost of supervision and the number of units produced. (Let cost of supervision be the vertical axis and number of units be the horizontal axis.) Would you classify this cost as a strictly variable cost, a fixed cost, or a step cost?
3. Suppose that the normal range of production is between 1,400 and 1,500 units and that the exact number of machinists is currently hired to support this level of activity. Further suppose that production for the next year is expected to increase by an additional 500 units. What is the increase in the cost of direct labor? Cost of supervision?

OBJECTIVE **1** ▶ **2** ▶   **Exercise 3-40** Matching Cost Behavior Descriptions to Cost Behavior Graphs

Select the graph (A through L) that best matches the numbered (1 through 7) italicized descriptions of various cost behavior. For each graph, the vertical (y) axis represents total dollars of cost, and the horizontal (x) axis represents output units during the period. The graphs may be used more than once.

1. *The cost of depreciation.* The asset being depreciated is a large piece of production machinery equipment where the straight-line depreciation method is used.
   letter _____
2. *The cost of operating a forklift.* The forklift is used to move work-in-process inventory in groups of 100 units across the factory floor.
   letter _____
3. *The cost of direct materials.* The first 2,000 pounds of direct materials are free because they are donated by the local city government. After that, the direct materials cost consists of a per-unit amount that decreases after a threshold of 2,500 total pounds is reached.
   letter _____
4. *The cost of inspecting finished goods inventory.* Each unit is inspected by a quality expert who is paid the same amount for each unit inspected.
   letter _____
5. *The cost of product shipping for all output shipped in the period.* The shipping cost per unit decreases with each unit shipped up to a certain number of units, at which time the shipping cost per unit remains constant.
   letter _____
6. *The cost of compliance with Environmental Protection Agency (EPA) regulations.* An electric car plant manufactures car batteries. Part of the manufacturing process involves the emission of toxic chemicals into the environment, which is regulated by the EPA in the form

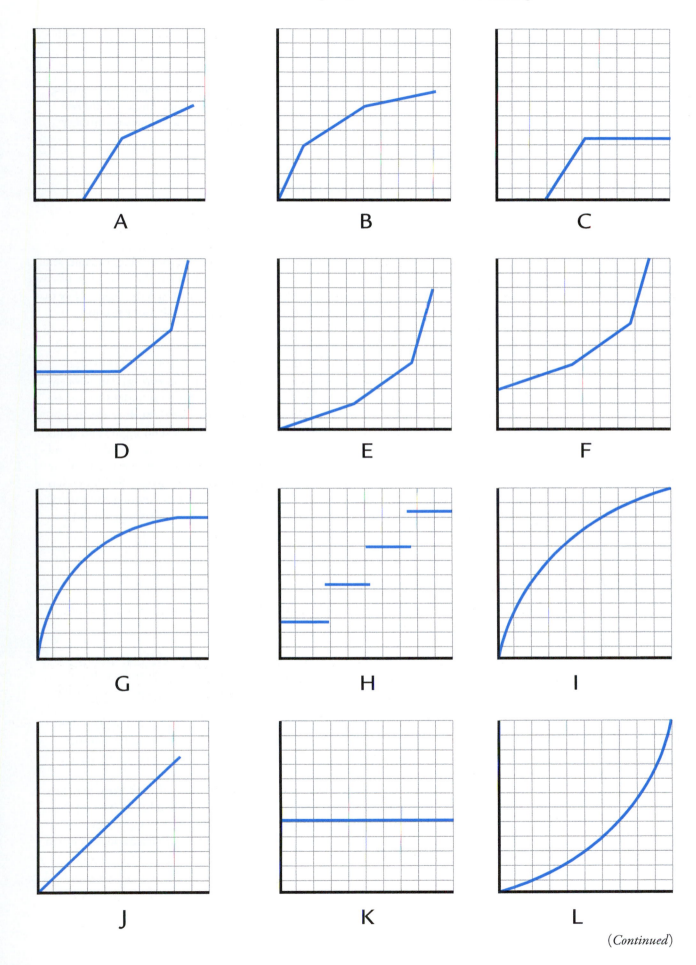

(*Continued*)

of a fee assessed on a per-unit manufactured basis. The per-unit cost of complying with these regulations increases with every fifth battery produced.

letter _____

7. *The cost of customer energy consumption.* The local electric utility company uses a pricing system designed to encourage customers to conserve energy usage. Therefore, the rate per kilowatt-hour that is charged to customers increases with each hour the customer consumes.

letter _____

OBJECTIVE ❶ ❷

Exercise 3-41 Interpreting Cost Behavior Graphs

Examine the graphs in Exercise 3-40.

Required:

As explained in the chapter, cost behavior patterns can be described as fixed, variable, semi-variable, mixed, or step function (i.e., semi-fixed) in nature. Explain the exact type of cost behavior pattern represented by each of the cost curves shown in graphs A through L. Note that some of the graphs might represent a combination of multiple cost behavior patterns.

> *Use the following information for Exercises 3-42 and 3-43:*
> Ben Palman owns an art gallery. He accepts paintings and sculpture on consignment and then receives 20% of the price of each piece as his fee. Space is limited, and there are costs involved, so Ben is careful about accepting artists. When he does accept one, he arranges for an opening show (usually for 3 hours on a weekend night) and sends out invitations to his customer list. At the opening, he serves wine, soft drinks, and appetizers to create a comfortable environment for prospective customers to view the new works and to chat with the artist. On average, each opening costs $500. Ben has given as many as 20 opening shows in a year. The total cost of running the gallery, including rent, furniture and fixtures, utilities, and a part-time assistant, amounts to $80,000 per year.

OBJECTIVE ❷

Exercise 3-42 Mixed Costs

Refer to the information for Ben Palman's art gallery above.

Required:

1. Prepare a graph that illustrates the relationship between the cost of giving opening shows and the number of opening shows given. (Let cost be the vertical axis and number of opening shows be the horizontal axis.) Would you classify this cost as a strictly variable cost, a fixed cost, or a mixed cost?

2. Prepare a graph that illustrates the relationship between the cost of running the gallery and the number of opening shows given. (Let cost be the vertical axis and number of opening shows be the horizontal axis.) Would you classify this cost as a strictly variable cost, a fixed cost, or a mixed cost?

3. Prepare a graph that illustrates the relationship between Ben's total costs (the sum of the costs of giving opening shows and running the gallery) and the number of opening shows given. (Let total cost be the vertical axis and number of opening shows given the horizontal axis.) Would you classify this cost as a strictly variable cost, a fixed cost, or a mixed cost?

Exercise 3-43 Mixed Costs and Cost Formula

OBJECTIVE ▶ 3

Refer to the information for Ben Palman's art gallery on the previous page.

Required:

1. Assume that the cost driver is number of opening shows. Develop the cost formula for the gallery's costs for a year.
2. Using the formula developed in Requirement 1, what is the total cost for Ben in a year with 12 opening shows? With 14 opening shows?

Use the following information for Exercises 3-44 through 3-46:

Luisa Crimini has been operating a beauty shop in a college town for the past 10 years. Recently, Luisa rented space next to her shop and opened a tanning salon. She anticipated that the costs for the tanning service would primarily be fixed, but found that tanning salon costs increased with the number of appointments. Costs for this service over the past 8 months are as follows:

Month	Tanning Appointments	Total Cost
January	1,600	$1,754
February	2,000	2,140
March	3,500	2,790
April	2,500	2,400
May	1,500	1,790
June	2,300	2,275
July	2,150	2,200
August	3,000	2,640

Exercise 3-44 High-Low Method

OBJECTIVE ▶ 3

Refer to the information for Luisa Crimini above.

Required:

1. Which month represents the high point? The low point?
2. Using the high-low method, compute the variable rate for tanning. Compute the fixed cost per month.
3. Using your answers to Requirement 2, write the cost formula for tanning services.
4. Calculate the total predicted cost of tanning services for September for 2,500 appointments using the formula found in Requirement 3. Of that total cost, how much is the total fixed cost for September? How much is the total predicted variable cost for September?
5. CONCEPTUAL CONNECTION Identify and briefly explain any additional issues that Luisa might be wise to consider when using the high-low method to estimate the costs of her tanning salon.

Exercise 3-45 Scattergraph Method

OBJECTIVE ▶ 3

Refer to the information for Luisa Crimini above.

Required:

CONCEPTUAL CONNECTION Prepare a scattergraph based on Luisa's data. Use monthly cost for the vertical axis and number of appointments for the horizontal axis. Based on an examination of the scattergraph, does there appear to be a linear relationship between the cost of tanning services and the number of appointments?

OBJECTIVE 3

EXCEL

Exercise 3-46 Method of Least Squares

Refer to the information for Luisa Crimini on the previous page.

Required:

1. Using a computer spreadsheet program such as Excel, run a regression on these data. Based on the regression output, write the cost formula for tanning. (*Note:* Round the fixed cost to the nearest dollar and the variable rate to the nearest cent.)
2. Using the formula computed in Requirement 1, what is the predicted cost of tanning services for September for 2,500 appointments?

Use the following information for Exercises 3-47 and 3-48:
During the past year, the high and low use of three different resources for Fly High Airlines occurred in July and April. The resources are airplane depreciation, fuel, and airplane maintenance. The number of airplane flight hours is the driver. The total costs of the three resources and the related number of airplane flight hours are as follows:

Resource	Airplane Flight Hours	Total Cost
Airplane depreciation:		
High	44,000	$ 18,000,000
Low	28,000	18,000,000
Fuel:		
High	44,000	445,896,000
Low	28,000	283,752,000
Airplane maintenance:		
High	44,000	15,792,000
Low	28,000	11,504,000

OBJECTIVE 3

EXCEL

Exercise 3-47 High-Low Method, Cost Formulas

Refer to the information for Fly High Airlines above.

Required:

Use the high-low method to answer the following questions.

1. What is the variable rate for airplane depreciation? The fixed cost?
2. What is the cost formula for airplane depreciation?
3. What is the variable rate for fuel? The fixed cost?
4. What is the cost formula for fuel?
5. What is the variable rate for airplane maintenance? The fixed cost?
6. What is the cost formula for airplane maintenance?
7. Using the three cost formulas that you developed, predict the cost of each resource in a month with 36,000 airplane flight hours.

OBJECTIVE 3

Exercise 3-48 Changing the Cost Formula for a Month to the Cost Formula for a Year

Refer to the information for Fly High Airlines above.

Required:

1. Develop annual cost formulas for airplane depreciation, fuel, and airplane maintenance.
2. Using the three annual cost formulas that you developed, predict the cost of each resource in a year with 480,000 airline flight hours.

Exercise 3-49 **Method of Least Squares, Developing and Using the Cost Formula**

OBJECTIVE 3

The method of least squares was used to develop a cost equation to predict the cost of receiving purchased parts at a video game manufacturer. Ninety-six data points from monthly data were used for the regression. The following computer output was received:

Intercept	147,400
Slope	210

The cost driver used was number of parts inspected.

Required:

1. What is the cost formula?
2. Using the cost formula from Requirement 1, identify each of the following: independent variable, dependent variable, variable rate, and fixed cost per month.
3. Using the cost formula, predict the cost of receiving for a month in which 6,800 parts are inspected.

Exercise 3-50 **Method of Least Squares, Budgeted Time Period Is Different from Time Period Used to Generate Results**

OBJECTIVE 3

Refer to the company information in **Exercise 3-49**.

Required:

1. What is the cost formula for a year?
2. Using the cost formula from Requirement 1, predict the cost of parts inspection for a year in which 70,000 parts are inspected.

Exercise 3-51 **Identifying the Parts of the Cost Formula; Calculating Monthly, Quarterly, and Yearly Costs Using a Cost Formula Based on Monthly Data**

OBJECTIVE 3

Gordon Company's controller, Eric Junior, estimated the following formula, based on monthly data, for overhead cost:

$$\text{Overhead Cost} = \$150,000 + (\$52 \times \text{Direct Labor Hours})$$

Required:

1. Link each term in column A to the corresponding term in column B.

Column A	Column B
Overhead cost	Fixed cost (intercept)
$150,000	Dependent variable
$52	Independent variable
Direct labor hours	Variable rate (slope)

2. If next month's budgeted direct labor hours equal 8,000, what is the budgeted overhead cost?
3. If next quarter's budgeted direct labor hours equal 23,000, what is the budgeted overhead cost?
4. If next year's budgeted direct labor hours equal 99,000, what is the budgeted overhead cost?

Exercise 3-52 **Inventory Valuation under Absorption Costing**

OBJECTIVE 4

Amiens Company produced 20,000 units during its first year of operations and sold 18,900 at $17 per unit. The company chose practical activity—at 20,000 units—to compute its predetermined overhead rate. Manufacturing costs are as follows:

(Continued)

Direct materials	$ 80,000
Direct labor	101,400
Variable overhead	15,600
Fixed overhead	54,600

Required:

1. Calculate the unit cost for each of these four costs.
2. Calculate the cost of one unit of product under absorption costing.
3. How many units are in ending inventory?
4. Calculate the cost of ending inventory under absorption costing.

OBJECTIVE 4 **Exercise 3-53** Inventory Valuation under Variable Costing

Lane Company produced 50,000 units during its first year of operations and sold 47,300 at $12 per unit. The company chose practical activity—at 50,000 units—to compute its predetermined overhead rate. Manufacturing costs are as follows:

Direct materials	$123,000
Direct labor	93,000
Variable overhead	65,000
Fixed overhead	51,000

Required:

1. Calculate the cost of one unit of product under variable costing.
2. Calculate the cost of ending inventory under variable costing.

OBJECTIVE 4 **Exercise 3-54** Income Statements under Absorption and Variable Costing

In the coming year, Kalling Company expects to sell 28,700 units at $32 each. Kalling's controller provided the following information for the coming year:

Units production	30,000
Unit direct materials	$ 9.95
Unit direct labor	$ 2.75
Unit variable overhead	$ 1.65
Unit fixed overhead*	$ 2.50
Unit selling expense (variable)	$ 2.00
Total fixed selling expense	$ 65,500
Total fixed administrative expense	$231,000

* The unit fixed overhead is based on 30,000 units produced.

Required:

1. Calculate the cost of one unit of product under absorption costing.
2. Calculate the cost of one unit of product under variable costing.
3. Calculate operating income under absorption costing for next year.
4. Calculate operating income under variable costing for next year.

OBJECTIVE 5 **Exercise 3-55** *(Appendix 3A)* Method of Least Squares Using Computer Spreadsheet Program

EXCEL

The controller for Beckham Company believes that the number of direct labor hours is associated with overhead cost. He collected the following data on the number of direct labor hours and associated factory overhead cost for the months of January through August.

Month	Number of Direct Labor Hours	Overhead Cost
January	689	$5,550
February	700	5,590
March	720	5,650
April	690	5,570
May	680	5,570
June	590	5,410
July	750	5,720
August	675	5,608

Required:

1. Using a computer spreadsheet program such as Excel, run a regression on these data. Print out your results.
2. Using your results from Requirement 1, write the cost formula for overhead cost. (*Note*: Round the fixed cost to the nearest dollar and the variable rate to the nearest cent.)
3. **CONCEPTUAL CONNECTION** What is R^2 based on your results? Do you think that the number of direct labor hours is a good predictor of factory overhead cost?
4. Assuming that expected September direct labor hours are 700, what is expected factory overhead cost using the cost formula in Requirement 2?

Exercise 3-56 *(Appendix 3A)* Method of Least Squares Using Computer Spreadsheet Program

OBJECTIVE ◄ 5

EXCEL

Susan Lewis, owner of a florist shop, is interested in predicting the cost of delivering floral arrangements. She collected monthly data on the number of deliveries and the total monthly delivery cost (depreciation on the van, wages of the driver, and fuel) for the past year.

Month	Number of Deliveries	Delivery Cost
January	100	$1,200
February	550	1,800
March	85	1,100
April	115	1,050
May	160	1,190
June	590	1,980
July	500	1,800
August	520	1,700
September	100	1,100
October	200	1,275
November	260	1,400
December	450	2,200

Required:

1. Using a computer spreadsheet program such as Excel, run a regression on these data. Print out your results.
2. Using your results from Requirement 1, write the cost formula for delivery cost. (*Note*: Round the fixed cost to the nearest dollar and the variable rate to the nearest cent.)
3. **CONCEPTUAL CONNECTION** What is R^2 based on your results? Do you think that the number of direct labor hours is a good predictor of delivery cost?
4. Using the cost formula in Requirement 2, what would predicted delivery cost be for a month with 300 deliveries?

PROBLEMS

OBJECTIVE ▸ 1 ▸ 2

Problem 3-57 Identifying Fixed, Variable, Mixed, and Step Costs

Consider each of the following independent situations:

a. A computer service agreement in which a company pays $150 per month and $15 per hour of technical time
b. Fuel cost of the company's fleet of motor vehicles
c. The cost of beer for a bar
d. The cost of computer printers and copiers at your college
e. Rent for a dental office
f. The salary of a receptionist in a law firm
g. The wages of counter help in a fast-food restaurant
h. The salaries of dental hygienists in a three-dentist office. One hygienist can take care of 120 cleanings per month.
i. Electricity cost which includes a $15 per month billing charge and an additional amount depending on the number of kilowatt-hours used

Required:

1. For each situation, describe the cost as one of the following: fixed cost, variable cost, mixed cost, or step cost. (*Hint:* First, consider what the driver or output measure is. If additional assumptions are necessary to support your cost type decision, be sure to write them down.)

    Example: Raw materials used in production—Variable cost

2. **CONCEPTUAL CONNECTION** Change your assumption(s) for each situation so that the cost type changes to a different cost type. List the new cost type and the changed assumption(s) that gave rise to it.
    Example: Raw materials used in production. Changed assumption—the materials are difficult to obtain, and a year's worth must be contracted for in advance. Now, this is a fixed cost. (This is the case with diamond sales by **DeBeers Inc.** to its sightholders. See the following website for information: www.keyguide.net/sightholders/.)

OBJECTIVE ▸ 3

Problem 3-58 Identifying Use of the High-Low, Scattergraph, and Least Squares Methods

Consider each of the following independent situations:

a. Shaniqua Boyer just started her new job as controller for St. Matthias General Hospital. She wants to get a feel for the cost behavior of various departments of the hospital. Shaniqua first looks at the radiology department. She has annual data on total cost and the number of procedures that have been run for the past 15 years. However, she knows that the department upgraded its equipment substantially 2 years ago and is doing a wider variety of tests. So, Shaniqua decides to use data for just the past 2 years.
b. Francis Hidalgo is a summer intern in the accounting department of a manufacturing firm. His boss assigned him a special project to determine the cost of manufacturing a special order. Francis needs information on variable and fixed overhead, so he gathers monthly data on overhead cost and machine hours for the past 60 months and enters them into his personal computer. A few keystrokes later, he has information on fixed and variable overhead costs.
c. Ron Wickstead sighed and studied his computer printout again. The results made no sense to him. He seemed to recall that sometimes it helped to visualize the cost relationships. He reached for some graph paper and a pencil.

d. Lois March had hoped that she could find information on the actual cost of promoting new products. Unfortunately, she had spent the weekend going through the files and was only able to find data on the total cost of the sales department by month for the past 3 years. She was also able to figure out the number of new product launches by month for the same time period. Now, she had just 15 minutes before a staff meeting in which she needed to give the vice president of sales an expected cost of the average new product launch. A light bulb went off in her head, and she reached for paper, pencil, and a calculator.

Required:

Determine which of the following cost separation methods is being used: the high-low method, the scattergraph method, or the method of least squares.

Problem 3-59 Identifying Variable Costs, Committed Fixed Costs, and Discretionary Fixed Costs

OBJECTIVE ◀ 1

Required:

Classify each of the following costs for a jeans manufacturing company as a variable cost, committed fixed cost, or discretionary fixed cost.

a. The cost of buttons
b. The cost to lease warehouse space for completed jeans—the lease contract runs for 2 years at $5,000 per year
c. The salary of a summer intern
d. The cost of landscaping and mowing the grass—the contract with a local mowing company runs from month to month
e. Advertising in a national magazine for teenage girls
f. Electricity to run the sewing machines
g. Oil and spare needles for the sewing machines
h. Quality training for employees—typically given for 4 hours at a time, every 6 months
i. Food and beverages for the company Fourth of July picnic
j. Natural gas to heat the factory during the winter

Use the following information for Problems 3-60 and 3-61:
Farnsworth Company has gathered data on its overhead activities and associated costs for the past 10 months. Tracy Heppler, a member of the controller's department, has convinced management that overhead costs can be better estimated and controlled if the fixed and variable components of each overhead activity are known. One such activity is receiving raw materials (unloading incoming goods, counting goods, and inspecting goods), which she believes is driven by the number of receiving orders. Ten months of data have been gathered for the receiving activity and are as follows:

Month	Receiving Orders	Receiving Cost
1	1,000	$18,000
2	700	15,000
3	1,500	28,000
4	1,200	17,000
5	1,300	25,000
6	1,100	21,000
7	1,600	29,000
8	1,400	24,000
9	1,700	27,000
10	900	16,000

OBJECTIVE **3**

EXCEL

Problem 3-60 Scattergraph, High-Low Method, and Predicting Cost for a Different Time Period from the One Used to Develop a Cost Formula

Refer to the information for Farnsworth Company on the previous page.

Required:

1. Prepare a scattergraph based on the 10 months of data. Does the relationship appear to be linear?
2. Using the high-low method, prepare a cost formula for the receiving activity. Using this formula, what is the predicted cost of receiving for a month in which 1,450 receiving orders are processed?
3. Prepare a cost formula for the receiving activity for a quarter. Based on this formula, what is the predicted cost of receiving for a quarter in which 4,650 receiving orders are anticipated? Prepare a cost formula for the receiving activity for a year. Based on this formula, what is the predicted cost of receiving for a year in which 18,000 receiving orders are anticipated?

OBJECTIVE **3**

Problem 3-61 Method of Least Squares, Predicting Cost for Different Time Periods from the One Used to Develop a Cost Formula

Refer to the information for Farnsworth Company on the previous page. However, assume that Tracy has used the method of least squares on the receiving data and has gotten the following results:

Intercept	3,212
Slope	15.15

Required:

1. Using the results from the method of least squares, prepare a cost formula for the receiving activity.
2. Using the formula from Requirement 1, what is the predicted cost of receiving for a month in which 1,450 receiving orders are processed? (*Note:* Round your answer to the nearest dollar.)
3. Prepare a cost formula for the receiving activity for a quarter. Based on this formula, what is the predicted cost of receiving for a quarter in which 4,650 receiving orders are anticipated? Prepare a cost formula for the receiving activity for a year. Based on this formula, what is the predicted cost of receiving for a year in which 18,000 receiving orders are anticipated?

OBJECTIVE **1** **2** **3**

Problem 3-62 Cost Behavior, High-Low Method, Pricing Decision

Fonseca, Ruiz, and Dunn is a large, local accounting firm located in a southwestern city. Carlos Ruiz, one of the firm's founders, appreciates the success his firm has enjoyed and wants to give something back to his community. He believes that an inexpensive accounting services clinic could provide basic accounting services for small businesses located in the barrio. He wants to price the services at cost.

Since the clinic is brand new, it has no experience to go on. Carlos decided to operate the clinic for 2 months before determining how much to charge per hour on an ongoing basis. As a temporary measure, the clinic adopted an hourly charge of $25, half the amount charged by Fonseca, Ruiz, and Dunn for professional services.

The accounting services clinic opened on January 1. During January, the clinic had 120 hours of professional service. During February, the activity was 150 hours. Costs for these two levels of activity usage are as follows:

	120 Professional Hours	150 Professional Hours
Salaries:		
Senior accountant	$2,500	$2,500
Office assistant	1,200	1,200
Internet and software subscriptions	700	850
Consulting by senior partner	1,200	1,500
Depreciation (equipment)	2,400	2,400
Supplies	905	1,100
Administration	500	500
Rent (offices)	2,000	2,000
Utilities	332	365

Required:

1. Classify each cost as fixed, variable, or mixed, using hours of professional service as the activity driver.
2. Use the high-low method to separate the mixed costs into their fixed and variable components. (*Note:* Round variable rates to two decimal places and fixed amounts to the nearest dollar.)
3. Luz Mondragon, the chief paraprofessional of the clinic, has estimated that the clinic will average 140 professional hours per month. If the clinic is to be operated as a non-profit organization, how much will it need to charge per professional hour? How much of this charge is variable? How much is fixed? (*Note:* Round answers to two decimal places.)
4. **CONCEPTUAL CONNECTION** Suppose the accounting center averages 170 professional hours per month. How much would need to be charged per hour for the center to cover its costs? Explain why the per-hour charge decreased as the activity output increased. (*Note:* Round answers to two decimal places.)

Problem 3-63 Flexible and Committed Resources, Capacity Usage for a Service

OBJECTIVE ▸1 ▸2 ▸3

Jana Morgan is about to sign up for cellular telephone service. She is primarily interested in the safety aspect of the phone; she wants to have one available for emergencies. She does not want to use it as her primary phone. Jana has narrowed her options down to two plans:

	Plan 1	Plan 2
Monthly fee	$ 20	$ 30
Free local minutes	60	120
Additional charges per minute:		
Airtime	$0.40	$0.30
Long distance	0.15	—
Regional roaming	0.60	—
National roaming	0.60	0.60

Both plans are subject to a $25 activation fee and a $120 cancellation fee if the service is cancelled before 1 year. Jana's brother will give her a cell phone that he no longer needs. It is not the latest version (and is not Internet capable) but will work well with both plans.

Required:

1. Classify the charges associated with the cellular phone service as (a) committed resources or (b) flexible resources.
2. **CONCEPTUAL CONNECTION** Assume that Jana will use, on average, 45 minutes per month in local calling. For each plan, split her minute allotment into used and unused capacity. Which plan will be most cost effective? Why?

(Continued)

3. **CONCEPTUAL CONNECTION** Assume that Jana loves her cell phone and ends up talking frequently with friends while traveling within her region. On average, she uses 60 local minutes a month and 30 regional minutes. For each plan, split her minute allotment into used and unused capacity. Which plan will be most cost effective? Why?

4. **CONCEPTUAL CONNECTION** Analyze your own cellular phone plan by comparing it with other possible options.

OBJECTIVE ▶ 1 ▶ 3

Problem 3-64 Variable and Fixed Costs, Cost Formula, High-Low Method

Li Ming Yuan and Tiffany Shaden are the department heads for the accounting department and human resources department, respectively, at a large textile firm in the southern United States. They have just returned from an executive meeting at which the necessity of cutting costs and gaining efficiency has been stressed. After talking with Tiffany and some of her staff members, as well as his own staff members, Li Ming discovered that there were a number of costs associated with the claims processing activity. These costs included the salaries of the two paralegals who worked full time on claims processing, the salary of the accountant who cut the checks, the cost of claims forms, checks, envelopes, and postage, and depreciation on the office equipment dedicated to the processing. Some of the paralegals' time appears to vary with the routine processing of uncontested claims, but considerable time also appears to be spent on the claims that have incomplete documentation or are contested. The accountant's time appears to vary with the number of claims processed.

Li Ming was able to separate the costs of processing claims from the costs of running the departments of accounting and human resources. He gathered the data on claims processing cost and the number of claims processed per month for the past 6 months. These data are as follows:

Month	Claims Processing Cost	Number of Claims Processed
February	$34,907	5,700
March	31,260	4,900
April	37,950	6,100
May	38,250	6,500
June	44,895	7,930
July	44,055	7,514

Required:

1. Classify the claims processing costs that Li Ming identified as variable and fixed.
2. What is the independent variable? The dependent variable?
3. Use the high-low method to find the fixed cost per month and the variable rate. What is the cost formula?
4. **CONCEPTUAL CONNECTION** Suppose that an outside company bids on the claims processing business. The bid price is $4.60 per claim. If Tiffany expects 75,600 claims next year, should she outsource the claims processing or continue to do it in-house?

OBJECTIVE ▶ 1

Problem 3-65 Cost Separation

About 8 years ago, **Kicker** faced the problem of rapidly increasing costs associated with workplace accidents. The costs included the following:

State unemployment insurance premiums	$100,000
Average cost per injury	$1,500
Number of injuries per year	15
Number of serious injuries	4
Number of workdays lost	30

A safety program was implemented with the following features: hiring a safety director, new employee orientation, stretching required four times a day, and systematic monitoring of adherence to the program by directors and supervisors. A year later, the indicators were as follows:

State unemployment insurance premiums	$50,000
Average cost per injury	$ 50
Number of injuries per year	10
Number of serious injuries	0
Number of workdays lost	0
Safety director's starting salary	$60,000

Required:

1. **CONCEPTUAL CONNECTION** Discuss the safety-related costs listed. Are they variable or fixed with respect to speakers sold? With respect to other independent variables (describe)?
2. **CONCEPTUAL CONNECTION** Did the safety program pay for itself? Discuss your reasoning.

Problem 3-66 Variable-Costing and Absorption-Costing Income

OBJECTIVE 4

EXCEL

Borques Company produces and sells wooden pallets that are used for moving and stacking materials. The operating costs for the past year were as follows:

Variable costs per unit:	
Direct materials	$ 2.85
Direct labor	$ 1.92
Variable overhead	$ 1.60
Variable selling	$ 0.90
Fixed costs per year:	
Fixed overhead	$180,000
Selling and administrative	$ 96,000

During the year, Borques produced 200,000 wooden pallets and sold 204,300 at $9 each. Borques had 8,200 pallets in beginning finished goods inventory; costs have not changed from last year to this year. An actual costing system is used for product costing.

Required:

1. What is the per-unit inventory cost that is acceptable for reporting on Borques's balance sheet at the end of the year? How many units are in ending inventory? What is the total cost of ending inventory?
2. Calculate absorption-costing operating income.
3. **CONCEPTUAL CONNECTION** What would the per-unit inventory cost be under variable costing? Does this differ from the unit cost computed in Requirement 1? Why?
4. Calculate variable-costing operating income.
5. Suppose that Borques Company had sold 196,700 pallets during the year. What would absorption-costing operating income have been? Variable-costing operating income?

Problem 3-67 *(Appendix 3A)* Method of Least Squares

OBJECTIVE 5

EXCEL

Refer to the information for Farnsworth Company (p. 139) for the first 10 months of data on receiving orders and receiving cost. Now suppose that Tracy has gathered 2 more months of data:

Month	Receiving Orders	Receiving Cost
11	1,200	$28,000
12	950	17,500

Note: For the following requirements, round the intercept terms to the nearest dollar, round the variable rates to the nearest cent, and R^2 to two decimal places.

(*Continued*)

Required:

1. Run two regressions using a computer spreadsheet program such as Excel. First, use the method of least squares on the first 10 months of data. Then, use the method of least squares on all 12 months of data. Write down the results for the intercept, slope, and R^2 for each regression. Compare the results.

2. **CONCEPTUAL CONNECTION** Prepare a scattergraph using all 12 months of data. Do any points appear to be outliers? Suppose Tracy has learned that the factory suffered severe storm damage during Month 11 that required extensive repairs to the receiving area—including major repairs on a forklift. These expenses, included in Month 11 receiving costs, are not expected to recur. What step might Tracy, using her judgment, take to amend the results from the method of least squares?

3. **CONCEPTUAL CONNECTION** Rerun the method of least squares, using all the data except for Month 11. (You should now have 11 months of data.) Prepare a cost formula for receiving based on these results, and calculate the predicted receiving cost for a month with 1,450 receiving orders. Discuss the results from this regression versus those from the regression for 12 months of data.

OBJECTIVE 3 ▶ 5 ▶

Problem 3-68 *(Appendix 3A)* **Scattergraph, High-Low Method, Method of Least Squares, Use of Judgment**

The management of Wheeler Company has decided to develop cost formulas for its major overhead activities. Wheeler uses a highly automated manufacturing process, and power costs are a significant manufacturing cost. Cost analysts have decided that power costs are mixed. The costs must be broken into their fixed and variable elements so that the cost behavior of the power usage activity can be properly described. Machine hours have been selected as the activity driver for power costs. The following data for the past 8 quarters have been collected:

Quarter	Machine Hours	Power Cost
1	20,000	$26,000
2	25,000	38,000
3	30,000	42,500
4	22,000	37,000
5	21,000	34,000
6	18,000	29,000
7	24,000	36,000
8	28,000	40,000

Note: For the following requirements, round the fixed cost to the nearest dollar, round the variable rates to three decimal places, and the R^2 to two decimal places.

Required:

1. Prepare a scattergraph by plotting power costs against machine hours. Does the scattergraph show a linear relationship between machine hours and power cost?

2. Using the high and low points (i.e., the high-low method), compute a power cost formula. (*Note:* Round answers to three decimal places.)

3. Use the method of least squares to compute a power cost formula. Evaluate the coefficient of determination.

4. **CONCEPTUAL CONNECTION** Rerun the regression, and drop the point (20,000, $26,000) as an outlier. Compare the results from this regression to those for the regression in Requirement 3. Which is better?

OBJECTIVE 3 ▶ 5 ▶

Problem 3-69 *(Appendix 3A)* **Separating Fixed and Variable Costs, Service Setting**

Louise McDermott, controller for the Galvin plant of Veromar Inc., wanted to determine the cost behavior of moving materials throughout the plant. She accumulated the following data on the number of moves (from 100 to 800 in increments of 100) and the total cost of moving materials at those levels of moves:

Number of Moves	Total Cost
100	$ 3,000
200	4,650
300	3,400
400	8,500
500	10,000
600	12,600
700	13,600
800	14,560

Required:

1. Prepare a scattergraph based on these data. Use cost for the vertical axis and number of moves for the horizontal axis. Based on an examination of the scattergraph, does there appear to be a linear relationship between the total cost of moving materials and the number of moves?

2. Compute the cost formula for moving materials by using the high-low method. Calculate the predicted cost for a month with 550 moves by using the high-low formula. (*Note:* Round the answer for the variable rate to three decimal places and the answer for total fixed cost and total cost to the nearest dollar.)

3. **CONCEPTUAL CONNECTION** Compute the cost formula for moving materials using the method of least squares. (*Note:* For the method of least squares, round the variable rate to two decimal places and total fixed cost and total cost to the nearest dollar.) Using the regression cost formula, what is the predicted cost for a month with 550 moves? What does the coefficient of determination tell you about the cost formula computed by regression?

4. **CONCEPTUAL CONNECTION** Evaluate the cost formula using the least squares coefficients. Could it be improved? Try dropping the third data point (300, $3,400), and rerun the regression.

CASES

Case 3-70 (*Appendix 3A*) Cost Formulas, Single and Multiple Cost Drivers

OBJECTIVE 1 2 3 5

For the past 5 years, Garner Company has had a policy of producing to meet customer demand. As a result, finished goods inventory is minimal, and for the most part, units produced equal units sold.

Recently, Garner's industry entered a recession, and the company is producing well below capacity (and expects to continue doing so for the coming year). The president is willing to accept orders that at least cover its variable costs so that the company can keep its employees and avoid layoffs. Also, any orders above variable costs will increase overall profitability of the company. Toward that end, the president of Garner Company implemented a policy that any special orders will be accepted if they cover the costs that the orders cause.

To help implement the policy, Garner's controller developed the following cost formulas:

Direct Materials Usage = $94X,	$R^2 = 0.90$
Direct Labor Usage = $16X,	$R^2 = 0.92$
Overhead = $350,000 + $80X,	$R^2 = 0.56$
Selling Costs = $50,000 + $7X,	$R^2 = 0.86$

where X = direct labor hours.

(Continued)

Required:

1. Compute the total unit variable cost. Suppose that Garner has an opportunity to accept an order for 20,000 units at $212 per unit. Each unit uses 1 direct labor hour for production. Should Garner accept the order? (The order would not displace any of Garner's regular orders.)
2. (*Appendix 3A*) Explain the significance of the coefficient of determination measures for the cost formulas. Did these measures have a bearing on your answer in Requirement 1? Should they have a bearing? Why?
3. (*Appendix 3A*) Suppose that a multiple regression equation is developed for overhead costs: $Y = \$100,000 + \$85X1 + \$5,000X2 + \$300X3$, where X1 = Direct Labor Hours, X2 = Number of Setups, and X3 = Engineering Hours. The coefficient of determination for the equation is 0.89. Assume that the order of 20,000 units requires 12 setups and 600 engineering hours. Given this new information, should the company accept the special order referred to in Requirement 1? Is there any other information about cost behavior that you would like to have? Explain.

OBJECTIVE ▶ 1

Case 3-71 Suspicious Acquisition of Data, Ethical Issues

Bill Lewis, manager of the Thomas Electronics Division, called a meeting with his controller, Brindon Peterson, and his marketing manager, Patty Fritz. The following is a transcript of the conversation that took place during the meeting:

Bill: Brindon, the variable costing system that you developed has proved to be a big plus for our division. Our success in winning bids has increased, and as a result our revenues have increased by 25%. However, if we intend to meet this year's profit targets, we are going to need something extra—am I right, Patty?

Patty: Absolutely. While we have been able to win more bids, we still are losing too many, particularly to our major competitor, Kilborn Electronics. If we knew more about their bidding strategy, we could be more successful at competing with them.

Brindon: Would knowing their variable costs help?

Patty: Certainly. It would give me their minimum price. With that knowledge, I'm sure that we could find a way to beat them on several jobs, particularly on those jobs where we are at least as efficient. It would also help us to identify where we are not cost competitive. With this information, we might be able to find ways to increase our efficiency.

Brindon: Well, I have good news. I've been talking with Carl Penobscot, Kilborn's assistant controller. Carl doesn't feel appreciated by Kilborn and wants to make a change. He could easily fit into our team here. Plus, Carl has been preparing for a job switch by quietly copying Kilborn's accounting files and records. He's already given me some data that reveal bids that Kilborn made on several jobs. If we can come to a satisfactory agreement with Carl, he'll bring the rest of the information with him. We'll easily be able to figure out Kilborn's prospective bids and find ways to beat them. Besides, I could use another accountant on my staff. Bill, would you authorize my immediate hiring of Carl with a favorable compensation package?

Bill: I know that you need more staff, Brindon, but is this the right thing to do? It sounds like Carl is stealing those files, and surely Kilborn considers this information confidential. I have real ethical and legal concerns about this. Why don't we meet with Laurie, our attorney, and determine any legal problems?

Required:

1. Is Carl's behavior ethical? What would Kilborn think?
2. Is Bill correct in supposing that there are ethical and/or legal problems involved with the hiring of Carl? (Reread the section on corporate codes of conduct in Chapter 1.) What would you do if you were Bill? Explain.

4

Job-Order Costing and Overhead Application

After studying Chapter 4, you should be able to:

1 ▶ Describe the differences between job-order costing and process costing, and identify the types of firms that would use each method.

2 ▶ Compute the predetermined overhead rate, and use the rate to assign overhead to units or services produced.

3 ▶ Identify and set up the source documents used in job-order costing.

4 ▶ Describe the cost flows associated with job-order costing.

5 ▶ *(Appendix 4A)* Prepare the journal entries associated with job-order costing.

6 ▶ *(Appendix 4B)* Allocate support department costs to producing departments.

iStockphoto.com/Kemter

EXPERIENCE MANAGERIAL DECISIONS

with Washburn Guitars

Since 1883, **Washburn Guitars** has manufactured high-quality acoustic and electric guitars. Washburn's guitar buyers include musicians ranging from garage bands to some of the world's most famous bands.

Washburn produces many guitar series, and each has many different models requiring the use of varied resources.[1] For example, in 2006 Washburn introduced the Damen Idol, retailing for $2,249. The Damen, named after Damen Avenue in Chicago's Wicker Park—a known hot spot for alternative, pop, and punk musicians—illustrates the complexity and individuality of specialized guitars. It featured a mahogany body, flame maple top, mahogany neck with cream binding, rosewood fingerboard, Seymour Duncan Custom pickups in the bridge and a Seymour Duncan '59 in the neck, a Tone Pros Bridge and Tailpiece, and numerous other options for frets, scaling, finishing, and tuning. Joe Trohman from Fall Out Boy, Aaron Dugan of Matisyahu, Mike Kennerty from The All American Rejects, Shaun Glass from Soil, Marty Casey from the Lovehammers, and INXS all played the Damen Idol at one time or another.

Many guitar buyers, including most professionals, request various product customizations. For example, Washburn's Custom Shop Pilsen guitar was made especially for Billy Sawilchik to play the National Anthem at Game 2 of the 2005 American League Championship Series between the White Sox and Angels. While customization created great publicity for Washburn, it led to significant design and product differences between guitars, even those within the same model line of a given series. These differences meant that different materials and labor were needed, requiring Washburn to estimate the cost of each guitar job according to the desired degree of customization. Washburn managers relied heavily on their job-order costing system to help them understand the costs of such product changes. The costs were factored into the price set, ensuring that Washburn earned a profit after all costs were covered.

> "While customization created great publicity for Washburn, it led to significant design and product differences between guitars, even those within the same model line of a given series. These differences meant that different materials and labor were needed, requiring Washburn to estimate the cost of each guitar job according to the desired degree of customization."

---

1 By 2009, Washburn stopped making the customized guitars favored by top rock musicians. It now concentrates on guitars for a mass audience. While the Damen Idol is no longer in production, it is still an excellent example of job-order production.

OBJECTIVE

Describe the differences between job-order costing and process costing, and identify the types of firms that would use each method.

CHARACTERISTICS OF THE JOB-ORDER ENVIRONMENT

Companies can be divided into two major types, depending on whether their products/services are unique. Manufacturing and service firms producing unique products or services require a job-order accounting system. When **Washburn Guitars** was producing its custom guitars, it fell into this category. On the other hand, those firms producing similar products or services can use a process-costing accounting system. **Ben & Jerry's Homemade, Inc.**, maker of premium ice creams with the whimsical flavor names, falls into this latter category. Each pint of a particular flavor of ice cream, say Cherry Garcia or Triple Caramel Chunk, is indistinguishable from the other pints. The characteristics of a company's actual production process determine whether it needs a job-order or a process-costing accounting system.

Job-Order Production and Costing

Firms operating in job-order industries produce a wide variety of services or products that are quite distinct from each other. Customized or built-to-order products fit into this category, as do services that vary from customer to customer, like **Sky Limo Corporation**, which provides air charter services. A **job** is one distinct unit or set of units. For example, a job might be a kitchen remodel for the Ruiz family, or a set of 12 tables for the children's reading room at the local library. Common job-order processes include:

- printing
- construction
- furniture making
- medical and dental services
- automobile repair
- beautician services

Often, a job is associated with a particular customer order. The key feature of job-order costing is that the cost of one job differs from that of another and must be kept track of separately.

For job-order production systems, costs are accumulated by job. This approach to assigning costs is called a **job-order costing system**. In a job-order firm, collecting costs by job provides vital information for management. For example, prices frequently are based on costs in a job-order environment.

Here's **Why It's important**

Here's How It's Used: **AT KICKER**

In the 1970s, **Kicker** began operations in Steve Irby's garage. Steve was an engineering student at Oklahoma State University and a keyboard player with a local band. The band needed speakers but couldn't afford new ones. Steve and his father built wooden boxes and fitted them with secondhand components. Word spread, and other bands asked for speakers. Steve partnered with a friend to fill the orders. Then, an oil-field worker asked if Steve could rig up speakers for his pickup truck. Long days bouncing over rough fields went more smoothly with music, but the built-in audio systems at the time were awful. Steve designed and built a speaker to fit behind the driver's seat, and Kicker was born.

At first, each job was made to order to fit a particular truck or car. The price Steve charged depended heavily on the cost of the job. Since each job was different, the various costs had to be computed individually. Clearly, the costs of wood, fabric, glue, and components were traceable to each job. Steve could also trace labor time. But the other costs of design time, use of power tools, and space were combined to create an overhead rate. To the extent that the price of a job was greater than its costs, Steve earned a profit.

KICKER
Livin' Loud

Process Production and Costing

Firms in process industries mass-produce large quantities of similar or homogeneous products. Examples of process manufacturers include:

- food canning and manufacturing
- cement
- petroleum
- pharmaceutical and chemical manufacturing

One gallon of paint is the same as another gallon; one bottle of aspirin is the same as another bottle. The important point is that the cost of one unit of a product is identical to the cost of another. Service firms can also use a process-costing approach. For example, check-clearing departments of banks incur a uniform cost to clear a check, no matter the size of the check or the name of the payee.

Process firms accumulate production costs by process or by department for a given period of time. The output for the process for that period of time is measured. Unit costs are computed by dividing the process costs for the given period by the output of the period:

$$\text{Unit Costs} = \frac{\text{Process Costs}}{\text{Output}}$$

This approach to cost accumulation is known as a **process-costing system** and is examined in detail in Chapter 6. A comparison of job-order costing and process costing is given in Exhibit 4.1.

Job-Order Costing	Process Costing
• Wide variety of distinct products	• Homogeneous products
• Costs accumulated by job	• Costs accumulated by process or department
• Unit Cost = Total Job Costs/Output	• Unit Cost = Process Costs/Output

Exhibit 4.1

Comparison of Job-Order and Process Costing

Check Point

1. **Give some examples of businesses in your community that would use job-order costing and process costing.**

Answer:

Answers will vary. One possible example: A tax accounting firm would keep track of costs by job because some tax returns are relatively simple while others are complex and require time to fill out additional forms and to do necessary research. A "while you wait" oil change shop would use process costing (but cost the oil required separately) since each car would take about the same amount of time and supplies to perform the oil change.

2. **Explain how one firm could use both job-order and process costing.**

Answer:

If a firm makes a standard product for sale to a large number of customers, it would use process costing. If it also made custom versions of that product for sale to individual customers, it would use job-order costing for those products. **Washburn Guitars** is a good example of this type of business. A jewelry maker that produces some standard designs for sale to large jewelry stores such as **Zales** or **Kay Jewelers** would use a process-costing approach. If that same jewelry maker also produced custom designs (e.g., a one-of-a-kind ring for the Simpsons' 25th anniversary), it would use job-order costing for that order.

Production Costs in Job-Order Costing

While the variety of product-costing definitions discussed in Chapter 2 applies to both job-order and process costing, we will use the traditional definition to illustrate job-order costing procedures. That is, production costs consist of direct materials, direct labor, and overhead. Direct materials and direct labor are typically fairly easy to trace to individual jobs, while overhead, because it consists of all production costs other than direct materials and direct labor, is not always as simple.

OBJECTIVE

Compute the predetermined overhead rate, and use the rate to assign overhead to units or services produced.

NORMAL COSTING AND OVERHEAD APPLICATION

Unit costs are very important because managers need accurate cost information on materials, labor, and overhead when making decisions. For example, **Bechtel Construction**, whose projects include Boston's "Big Dig" and the Channel Tunnel ("Chunnel") connecting England and France, typically bills its clients at set points throughout construction. As a result, it is important that the unit cost be generated in a timely fashion. Job-order costing using a normal cost system will give the company the unit cost information it needs.

Actual Costing versus Normal Costing

Two ways are commonly used to measure the costs associated with production: actual costing and normal costing.

Actual Costing In an **actual cost system**, only actual costs of direct materials, direct labor, and overhead are used to determine unit cost. However, several issues are involved in using actual costing.

Defining Overhead Costs Per-unit computation of the direct materials and direct labor costs is relatively easy to determine. However, defining overhead is much more difficult. Overhead items do not have the direct relationship with units produced that direct materials and direct labor do. For example, how much of a security guard's salary should be assigned to a unit of product or service? Even if the firm averages overhead cost by totaling manufacturing overhead costs for a given period and then divides this total by the number of units produced, distorted costs can occur. The distortion can be traced to uneven incurrence of overhead costs and uneven production from period to period.

Uneven Overhead Costs Many overhead costs are not incurred uniformly throughout the year. For example, actual repair cost occurs whenever a machine breakdown occurs. This timing can make overhead costs in the month of a machine breakdown higher than in other months.

Uneven Production The second problem, nonuniform production levels, can mean that low production in one month would give rise to high unit overhead costs, and high production in another month would give rise to low unit overhead costs. Yet the production process and total overhead costs may remain unchanged. One solution would be to wait until the end of the year to total the actual overhead costs and divide by the total actual production, an option that is not realistic for most companies.

Strict actual cost systems are rarely used because they cannot provide accurate unit cost information on a timely basis. A company needs unit cost information throughout the year. This information is needed to prepare interim financial statements and to help managers make decisions such as pricing. Managers must react to day-to-day conditions in the marketplace in order to maintain a sound competitive position. Therefore, they need timely information.

Normal Costing Normal costing solves the problems associated with actual costing. A **normal cost system** determines unit cost by adding actual direct materials, actual direct labor, and estimated overhead. Overhead can be estimated by approximating the year's actual overhead at the *beginning* of the year and then using a predetermined rate throughout the year to obtain the needed unit cost information. Virtually all firms use normal costing.

Here's **Why It's important**

CONCEPT CLIP

Importance of Unit Costs to Manufacturing Firms

Unit cost is a critical piece of information for a manufacturer. Unit costs are essential for valuing inventory, determining income, and making numerous important decisions.

Disclosing the cost of inventories and determining income are financial reporting requirements that a firm faces at the end of each period. In order to report the cost of its inventories, a firm must know the number of units on hand and the unit cost. The cost of goods sold (COGS), used to determine income, requires knowledge of the units sold and their unit cost.

Note that full cost information is useful as an input for a number of important internal decisions as well as for financial reporting. In the long run, for any product to be viable, its price must cover its full cost. Decisions to introduce a new product, to continue a current product, and to analyze long-run prices are examples of important internal decisions that rely on full unit cost information.

Importance of Unit Costs to Service Firms

Like manufacturing firms, service and nonprofit firms also require unit cost information. Conceptually, the way companies accumulate and assign costs is the same whether or not the firm is a manufacturer. The service firm must first identify the service "unit" being provided. A hospital would accumulate costs by patient, patient day, and type of procedure (e.g., X-ray, complete blood count test). A governmental agency must also identify the service provided. For example, city government might provide household trash collection and calculate the cost by truck run or number of houses served.

Here's How It's Used: IN YOUR LIFE

It's close to the end of the month and you need $400 for your share of the rent. What do you do? If you have a four-door car, you might consider signing up for a few hours of driving for **Uber**. Part of the so-called peer-to-peer economy, Uber matches you with people who need rides in your area. You keep 80% of the fare, and Uber keeps the remaining 20%. But how do you know how much profit you are making? Profit is the difference between the price charged and all costs of providing the ride. Let's say you give a ride to someone whose fare is $25. Your share is 80% of that, or $20. So, did you just make $20? That depends on what your costs for the trip were. Clearly, the cost of gasoline is a direct cost. You can figure that by multiplying the miles driven times the cost of gas per mile using the actual cost of your most recent fill-up. However, there are many other costs,

and you may need to allocate costs between your personal use of the car and the Uber, or business, use. The cost of maintenance and tires can be smoothed out over total miles driven in a year. What about the cost of the car itself (or depreciation on it)—how much should be allocated to business use? Here we can take a page from normal costing and overhead application. Total indirect costs will be in the numerator, and total miles driven in the denominator. This will give you a cost per mile. Multiply that cost times the miles driven for Uber and you get a sense of the part of your costs that are applicable to the Uber use. Different Uber drivers will get different cost amounts, depending on their car's model and make, fuel economy, and so on. In the end, is it worth it? That's something you can determine once you know all the costs and benefits.

Service firms use cost data in much the same way that manufacturing firms do. They use costs to determine profitability, the feasibility of introducing new services, and so on. However, because service firms do not produce physical products, they do not need to value work-in-process and finished goods inventories. (Inventories of supplies are simply valued at historical cost.)

Ethical Decisions

Nonprofit firms must track costs to be sure that they provide their services in a cost-efficient way. Governmental agencies have a fiduciary responsibility to taxpayers to use funds wisely, and that requires accurate accounting for costs. Without such responsibility, questionable results can occur, such as the alleged overcharges by several pharmaceutical firms for common prescription drugs used by Medicaid patients. Under Medicaid rules, the government reimburses companies for the average wholesale price of the drugs used. **Sandoz Pharmaceuticals**, among others, allegedly inflated the prices charged by up to 60,000%.[2] ●

A cost accounting system measures and assigns costs so that the unit cost of a product or service can be determined. Unit cost is a critical piece of information for both manufacturing and service firms. Bidding is a common requirement in the markets for specialized products and services (e.g., bids for special tools, audits, legal services, and medical tests and procedures). For example, it would be virtually impossible for **KPMG** to submit a meaningful bid to one of its large audit clients without knowing the unit costs of its services.

Normal Costing and Estimating Overhead

In normal costing, overhead is estimated and applied to production. The basics of overhead application can be described in three steps:

Step 1: Calculate the predetermined overhead rate.
Step 2: Apply overhead to production throughout the year.
Step 3: Reconcile the difference between the total actual overhead incurred during the year and the total overhead applied to production.

Here's Why It's important

Predetermined overhead rates help companies maintain a constant application of overhead throughout the year. These rates do not allow seasonality or variations in production to affect unit cost.

CONCEPT CLIP

Step 1: Calculating the Predetermined Overhead Rate The **predetermined overhead rate** is calculated at the beginning of the year by dividing the total estimated annual overhead by the total estimated level of associated activity or cost driver:

$$\text{Predetermined Overhead Rate} = \frac{\text{Estimated Annual Overhead}}{\text{Estimated Annual Activity Level}}$$

Notice that the predetermined overhead rate includes estimated amounts in *both* the numerator and the denominator. This estimation is necessary because the predetermined overhead rate is calculated in advance, usually at the beginning of the year. It is impossible to use actual overhead or actual activity level for the year because at that time the company does not know what the actual levels will be.

Estimated overhead is the firm's best estimate of the amount of overhead (utilities, indirect labor, depreciation, etc.) to be incurred in the coming year. The estimate is often based on last year's figures and is adjusted for anticipated changes in the coming year.

The associated activity level depends on which activity is best associated with overhead. Often, the activity chosen is the number of direct labor hours or the direct labor cost. This

---

2   Jim Edwards, "Sandoz Overcharged Medicaid by 60,000% in $13B Pricing Scam, Says Judge," *BNET* (January 28, 2010). Taken from http://industry.bnet.com/pharma/10006357/sandoz-overcharged-medicaid-by-60000-in-13b-pricing-scam-says-judge/.

makes sense when much of overhead cost is associated with direct labor (e.g., fringe benefits, worker safety training programs, the cost of running the personnel department). The number of machine hours could be a good choice for a company with automated production. Then, much of the overhead cost might consist of equipment maintenance, depreciation on machinery, electricity to run the machinery, and so on. The estimated activity level is the number of direct labor hours, or machine hours, expected for the coming year. **Washburn Guitars** found that much of its overhead was connected to the use of direct labor (e.g., body and neck sanding, fret board assembly, neck joint sanding, taping and painting, wiring and assembly) and of machinery (e.g., CNC body and neck roughing, fret board inlay programming and cutting). Therefore, direct labor and machine hours were good activity choices for overhead application.

Step 2: Applying Overhead to Production Once the overhead rate has been computed, the company can begin to apply overhead to production. **Applied overhead** is found by multiplying the predetermined overhead rate by the actual use of the associated activity for the period:

$$\text{Applied Overhead} = \text{Predetermined Overhead Rate} \times \text{Actual Activity Level}$$

Suppose that a company has an overhead rate of $5 per machine hour. In the first week of January, the company used 9,000 hours of machine time. The overhead applied to the week's production is computed as:

$$\$5 \times 9,000 = \$45,000$$

The concept is the same for any time period. So, if the company runs its machines for 50,000 hours in the month of January, applied overhead for January would be $250,000 ($5 × 50,000).

The total cost of product for the period is the actual direct materials and direct labor, plus the applied overhead:

$$\text{Total Normal Product Costs} = \text{Actual Direct Materials} + \text{Actual Direct Labor} + \text{Applied Overhead}$$

Example 4.1 shows how to calculate the predetermined overhead rate and how to use that rate to apply overhead to production.

EXAMPLE 4.1

How to Calculate the Predetermined Overhead Rate and Apply Overhead to Production

At the beginning of the year, Argus Company estimated the following costs:

Overhead	$360,000
Direct labor cost	720,000

Argus uses normal costing and applies overhead on the basis of direct labor cost. (Direct labor cost equals total direct labor hours worked multiplied by the wage rate.) For the month of February, direct labor cost was $56,000.

Required:

1. Calculate the predetermined overhead rate for the year.
2. Calculate the overhead applied to production in February.

Solution:

1. Predetermined Overhead Rate = $\dfrac{\$360,000}{\$720,000}$

   = 0.50, or 50% of direct labor cost

2. Overhead Applied to February Production = 0.50 × $56,000 = $28,000

CONCEPT CLIP

Step 3: Reconciling Actual Overhead with Applied Overhead Recall that two types of overhead are recorded:

- *Actual overhead:* Costs are tracked throughout the year in the overhead account.
- *Applied overhead:* Costs are computed throughout the year and added to actual direct materials and actual direct labor to get total product cost.

At the end of the year, any difference between actual and applied overhead must be recognized and closed to the cost of goods sold account so that it reflects actual overhead spending.

Suppose that Proto Company had actual overhead of $400,000 for the year but had applied $390,000 to production. Proto Company has *underapplied* overhead by $10,000. If applied overhead had been $410,000, too much overhead would have been applied to production. The firm would have *overapplied* overhead by $10,000. The difference between actual overhead and applied overhead is called an **overhead variance**:

$$\text{Overhead Variance} = \text{Actual Overhead} - \text{Applied Overhead}$$

If actual overhead is greater than applied overhead, then the variance is called **underapplied overhead**. If actual overhead is less than applied overhead, then the variance is called **overapplied overhead**. If overhead has been underapplied, then product cost has been understated. In this case, the cost appears lower than it really is. Conversely, if overhead has been overapplied, then product cost has been overstated. In this case, the cost appears higher than it really is. Exhibit 4.2 illustrates the concepts of over- and underapplied overhead.

Exhibit 4.2   Actual and Applied Overhead

Here's **Why It's important**

Because it is impossible to perfectly estimate future overhead costs and production activity, overhead variances are virtually inevitable. However, at year-end, costs reported on the financial statements must be actual amounts. Since the costs of units sold and of units kept in inventory are carried at historical cost, the difference between actual and applied overhead must be recognized and total cost must be adjusted. Thus, something must be done with the overhead variance. Usually, the entire overhead variance is assigned to Cost of Goods Sold. This practice is justified on the basis of materiality, the same principle used to justify expensing the entire cost of a stapler in the period acquired rather than depreciating its cost over the life of the stapler. Since the overhead variance is usually relatively small, and all production costs should appear in cost of goods sold eventually, the method of disposition is not a critical matter. Thus,

- Underapplied overhead is added to Cost of Goods Sold.
- Overapplied overhead is subtracted from Cost of Goods Sold.

> Adjusted Cost of Goods Sold = Unadjusted Cost of Goods Sold ± Overhead Variance

Suppose Proto Company has an ending balance in its cost of goods sold account equal to $607,000. The underapplied overhead variance of $10,000 would be added to produce a new adjusted balance of $617,000. (Since applied overhead was $390,000, and actual overhead was $400,000, production costs were *understated* by $10,000. Cost of Goods Sold must be increased to correct the problem.) If the variance had been overapplied, it would have been subtracted from Cost of Goods Sold to produce a new balance of $597,000. **Example 4.2** shows how to reconcile actual overhead with applied overhead for Argus Company.

EXAMPLE 4.2

How to Reconcile Actual Overhead with Applied Overhead

Recall that Argus Company's predetermined overhead rate was 0.50 or 50% of direct labor cost. By the end of the year, actual data are:

Overhead	$375,400
Direct labor cost	750,000

Cost of Goods Sold (before adjusting for any overhead variance) is $632,000.

Required:

1. Calculate the overhead variance for the year.
2. Dispose of the overhead variance by adjusting Cost of Goods Sold.

Solution:

1. Overhead Applied for the Year = 0.50 × $750,000 = $375,000

Actual overhead	$375,400
Applied overhead	375,000
Overhead variance—underapplied	$ 400

2.

Unadjusted cost of goods sold	$ 632,000
Add: Overhead variance—underapplied	400
Adjusted cost of goods sold	$ 632,400

If the overhead variance is material, or large, another approach would be taken. That approach, allocating the variance among the ending balances of Work in Process, Finished Goods, and Cost of Goods Sold, is discussed in more detail in later accounting courses.

Departmental Overhead Rates

The description of overhead application so far has emphasized the plantwide overhead rate. A **plantwide overhead rate** is a single overhead rate calculated by using all estimated overhead for a factory divided by the estimated activity level across the entire factory. However, some companies believe that multiple overhead rates give more accurate costing information. Service firms, or service departments of manufacturing firms, can also use separate overhead rates to charge out their services. Departmental overhead rates allow companies to recognize that different producing departments have different overhead costs. These rates allow more precise application of overhead as units pass through one or more departments.

Here's **Why It's important**

Departmental overhead rates are a widely used type of multiple overhead rate. A **departmental overhead rate** is estimated overhead for a department divided by the estimated activity level for that same department:

$$\text{Departmental Overhead Rate} = \frac{\text{Estimated Department Overhead}}{\text{Estimated Departmental Activity Level}}$$

The steps involved in calculating and applying overhead are the same as those involved for one plantwide overhead rate. The company has as many overhead rates as it has departments. **Example 4.3** shows how to calculate and apply departmental overhead rates.

EXAMPLE 4.3

How to Calculate Predetermined Departmental Overhead Rates and Apply Overhead to Production

At the beginning of the year, Sorrel Company estimated the following:

	Machining Department	Assembly Department	Total
Overhead	$240,000	$360,000	$600,000
Direct labor hours	135,000	240,000	375,000
Machine hours	200,000	—	200,000

Sorrel uses departmental overhead rates. In the machining department, overhead is applied on the basis of machine hours. In the assembly department, overhead is applied on the basis of direct labor hours. Actual data for the month of June are as follows:

	Machining Department	Assembly Department	Total
Overhead	$22,500	$30,750	$53,250
Direct labor hours	11,000	20,000	31,000
Machine hours	17,000	—	17,000

Required:

1. Calculate the predetermined overhead rates for the machining and assembly departments.
2. Calculate the overhead applied to production in each department for the month of June.
3. By how much has each department's overhead been overapplied? Underapplied?

Solution:

1. $\text{Machining Department Overhead Rate} = \dfrac{\$240,000}{200,000 \text{ mhrs}}$

   $= \$1.20$ per machine hour

   $\text{Assembly Department Overhead Rate} = \dfrac{\$360,000}{240,000 \text{ DLH}}$

   $= \$1.50$ per direct labor hour

2. Overhead Applied to Machining in June = $1.20 × 17,000 = $20,400

   Overhead Applied to Assembly in June = $1.50 × 20,000 = $30,000

	Machining Department	Assembly Department
Actual overhead	$22,500	$30,750
Applied overhead	20,400	30,000
Underapplied overhead	$ 2,100	$ 750

It is important to realize that departmental overhead rates simply carve total overhead into two or more parts. The departments can be added back to get plantwide overhead, as illustrated in **Example 4.4**.

At the beginning of the year, Sorrel Company estimated the following:

	Machining Department	Assembly Department	Total
Overhead	$240,000	$360,000	$600,000
Direct labor hours	135,000	240,000	375,000
Machine hours	200,000	—	200,000

Sorrel has decided to use a plantwide overhead rate based on direct labor hours. Actual data for the month of June are as follows:

	Machining Department	Assembly Department	Total
Overhead	$22,500	$30,750	$53,250
Direct labor hours	11,000	20,000	31,000
Machine hours	17,000	—	17,000

Required:

1. Calculate the predetermined plantwide overhead rate.
2. Calculate the overhead applied to production for the month of June.
3. Calculate the overhead variance for the month of June.

Solution:

1. Predetermined Plantwide Overhead Rate $= \dfrac{\$600,000}{375,000 \text{ DLH}}$

   $= \$1.60$ per direct labor hour

2. Overhead Applied in June $= \$1.60 \times 31,000 = \$49,600$

3. Overhead Variance = Actual Overhead − Applied Overhead

   $= \$53,250 - \$49,600$

   $= \$3,650$ underapplied

Considerable emphasis has been placed on describing how overhead costs are treated because this is the key to normal costing. Now, it is time to see how normal costing is used to develop unit costs in the job-order costing system.

Unit Costs in the Job-Order System

In a job-order environment, predetermined overhead rates are always used because the completion of a job rarely coincides with the completion of a fiscal year. Therefore, in the remainder of this chapter, normal costing is used.

The unit cost of a job is the total cost of the job (materials used on the job, labor worked on the job, and applied overhead) divided by the number of units in the job:

$$\text{Unit Product Cost} = \frac{\text{Total Product Cost}}{\text{Number of Units}}$$

Although the concept is simple, in practice, calculating job cost can be somewhat more complex because of the recordkeeping involved.

For example, suppose that Stan Johnson forms a new company, Johnson Leathergoods, which produces custom leather products. Stan believes that there is a market for one-of-a-kind leather purses, briefcases, and backpacks. In January, its first month of operation, he obtains two orders. The first order is for 20 leather backpacks for a local sporting goods store. The second order is for 10 distinctively tooled briefcases for the coaches of a local college. The price of each order is cost plus 50% of cost. The first order, the backpacks, requires direct materials (leather, thread, buckles), direct labor (cutting, sewing, assembling), and overhead. Assume that overhead is applied using direct labor hours. Suppose that the materials cost $1,000 and the direct labor costs $1,080 (60 hours at $18 per hour). If the predetermined overhead rate is $4 per direct labor hour, then the overhead applied to this job is $240 (60 hours at $4 per hour). The total cost of the backpacks is $2,320, and the unit cost is $116, computed as follows:

Direct materials	$1,000
Direct labor	1,080
Overhead	240
Total cost	$2,320
÷ Number of units	÷ 20
Unit cost	$ 116

Since cost is so closely linked to price in this case, it is easy to see that Stan will charge the sporting goods store $3,480 (cost of $2,320 plus 50% of $2,320), or $174 per backpack.

Check Point

1. A company had the following data for last year:

	Budgeted	Actual
Overhead	**$31,200**	**$31,500**
Direct labor hours	**12,000**	**12,200**

What is the overhead rate per direct labor hour? What is overhead applied for the year? What is the overhead variance?

Answer:
Overhead Rate = Budgeted Overhead/Budgeted Direct Labor Hours
        = $31,200/12,000 = $2.60
Applied Overhead = Overhead Rate × Actual Direct Labor Hours
        = $2.60 × 12,200 = $31,720
Overhead Variance = Applied Overhead − Actual Overhead
        = $31,720 − $31,500 = $220 overapplied

2. Now suppose the actual overhead for the company for last year was $32,000. What is the overhead variance? Why is it different from the answer in question 1?

Answer:
Overhead Variance = Actual Overhead − Applied Overhead
        = $32,000 − $31,720 = $280 underapplied
The applied overhead remains the same because the budgeted numbers have not changed, nor has the amount of actual direct labor hours. In this case, however, actual overhead is more than the applied overhead so the variance is underapplied.

KEEPING TRACK OF JOB COSTS WITH SOURCE DOCUMENTS

OBJECTIVE ◀ 3
Identify and set up the source documents used in job-order costing.

Accounting for job-order production begins by preparing the source documents that are used to keep track of the costs of jobs. In a job-order firm, where price is so often based on cost, it is critically important to keep careful track of the costs of a job.

Here's **Why It's important**

Ethical Decisions

Ethics

Ethical issues arise when a firm adds costs from one job to the job-order sheet of another job. The first job is undercosted and underpriced, while the second job is overcosted and overpriced. Customers rely on the professionalism and honesty of the job-order firm in recordkeeping. ●

Job-Order Cost Sheet

How does Stan know that actual materials will cost $1,000 or that actual direct labor for this particular job will come to $1,080? In order to determine those figures, Stan will need to keep track of costs. One way to do so is to prepare a job-order cost sheet every time a new job is started. The earlier computation for Stan's backpack job, which lists the total cost of materials, labor, and overhead for a single job, is the simplest example of a job-order cost sheet. The **job-order cost sheet** is prepared for every job. It is subsidiary to the work-in-process account and is the primary document for accumulating all costs related to a particular job. Exhibit 4.3 illustrates a simple job-order cost sheet.

Johnson Leathergoods
Job-Order Cost Sheet

Job Name: Backpacks   Date Started: Jan. 3, 20XX   Date Completed: Jan. 29, 20XX

Direct materials	$1,000
Direct labor	1,080
Applied overhead	240
Total cost	$2,320
÷ Number of units	÷ 20
Unit cost	$ 116

Exhibit 4.3
Job-Order Cost Sheet

The job-order cost sheet contains all information pertinent to a job. For a simple job, the job-order cost sheet is quite brief, containing only the job description (backpacks) and cost of materials, labor, and overhead added during the month.

Johnson Leathergoods had only two jobs in January. These could be easily identified by calling them "Backpacks" and "Briefcases." Some companies may find that the customer's name is sufficient to identify a job. For example, a construction company may identify its custom houses as the "Kumar Residence" or the "Malkovich House."

As more and more jobs are produced, a company will usually find it more convenient to number them. For example, it may number them as Job 13, Job 5776, or Job ALM67. Perhaps the job number starts with the year so that the first job of 2017 is 2017-001, the second is 2017-002, and so on. The key point is that each job is unique and must have a uniquely identifiable name. This name, or job-order number, heads the job-order cost sheet.

Work in process consists of all incomplete work. In a job-order system, this will be all of the unfinished jobs. The balance in Work in Process at the end of the month will be the total of all the job-order cost sheets for the incomplete jobs.

A job-order costing system must have the ability to identify the quantity of direct materials, direct labor, and overhead consumed by each job. That is, documentation and procedures are needed to associate the manufacturing inputs used by a job with the job itself. This need is satisfied through the use of materials requisitions for direct materials, time tickets for direct labor, and source documents for other activity drivers that might be used in applying overhead.

Materials Requisitions

The cost of direct materials is assigned to a job by the use of a source document known as a **materials requisition form**, which is illustrated in Exhibit 4.4. Notice that the form asks for the type, quantity, and unit price of the direct materials issued and, most importantly, the name or number of the job. Using this form, the cost accounting department can enter the cost of direct materials onto the correct job-order cost sheet.

Exhibit 4.4

Materials Requisition Form

Materials Requisition Number: 012

Date: January 11, 20XX
Department: Assembly
Job: Briefcases

Description	Quantity	Cost/Unit	Total Cost
Buckles	10	$3	$30

Authorized Signature ___*Jim Lawson*___

If the accounting system is automated, this posting may entail directly entering the data at a computer terminal, using the materials requisition forms as source documents. A program enters the cost of direct materials into the record for each job. In addition to providing essential information for assigning direct materials costs to jobs, the materials requisition form may also include other data items, such as a requisition number, a date, and a signature. These items are useful for maintaining proper control over a firm's inventory of direct materials. The signature, for example, transfers responsibility for the materials from the storage area to the person receiving the materials, usually a production supervisor.

No attempt is made to trace the cost of other materials, such as supplies, lubricants, and the like, to a particular job. These indirect materials are assigned to jobs through the predetermined overhead rate.

Time Tickets

Direct labor must be associated with each particular job. The means by which direct labor costs are assigned to individual jobs is the source document known as a **time ticket** (Exhibit 4.5, p. 163). Each day, the employee fills out a time ticket that identifies his or her name, wage rate, and the hours worked on each job. These time tickets are collected and transferred to the cost accounting department where the information is used to post the cost of direct labor to individual jobs. Again, in an automated system, posting involves entering the data into the computer.

Exhibit 4.5
Time Ticket

Job Time Ticket #: _008_

Employee Name: _Ed Wilson_____
Date: _January 12, 20XX_____

Start Time	Stop Time	Total Time	Hourly Rate	Amount	Job Number
8:00	10:00	2	$18	$36	Backpacks
10:00	11:00	1	18	18	Briefcases
11:00	12:00	1	18	18	Backpacks
1:00	5:00	4	18	72	Backpacks

Approved by: ___*Jim Lawson*_____
(Department Supervisor)

Time tickets are used only for direct laborers. Since indirect labor is common to all jobs, these costs belong to overhead and are allocated using one or more predetermined overhead rates.

All completed job-order cost sheets of a firm can serve as a subsidiary ledger for the finished goods inventory. Then, the work-in-process account consists of all of the job-order cost sheets for the unfinished jobs. The finished goods inventory account consists of all the job-order cost sheets for jobs that are complete but not yet sold. As finished goods are sold and shipped, the cost records will be pulled (or deleted) from the finished goods inventory file. These records then form the basis for calculating a period's cost of goods sold. We will examine the flow of costs through these accounts next.

Here's How It's Used: TO CREATE SOURCE DOCUMENTS FOR A PHOTOGRAPHY BUSINESS

Suppose you are the cost accounting manager for a company that provides photography services for special events, such as weddings, bar mitzvahs, anniversary parties, and corporate functions. The cost of the services varies from job to job. The time of the photographers assigned to the job is already kept track of using labor time tickets. However, your company now wants to reimburse the photographers for mileage and may want to include an additional charge to clients for mileage.

What type of source document could serve to accumulate miles driven?

In this case, your company needs to know not only the number of miles each photographer drives, but also to which job the mileage pertains. A relatively simple mileage log listing the date, starting mileage, ending mileage, and purpose of the trip should suffice. This will allow you to compute the miles driven (ending mileage minus beginning mileage) and assign them to the specific photographic job. In addition, total miles

for each photographer can be computed on a monthly basis and multiplied by your company's mileage reimbursement rate for purposes of reimbursing each photographer for automotive operating costs. Some companies might have other specific needs. For example, perhaps the company has a fleet of different vehicles and wants to compute different rates depending on the vehicle. Using a van might require a higher rate than using a small automobile. In this case, an additional column to record the type of vehicle or vehicle's license plate would be necessary.

Still other companies may use an overhead application base other than direct labor hours. Perhaps machine hours may be used to apply overhead. Then, a new document must be developed. A source document that will track the machine hours used by each job can be modeled on job time tickets.

As a result, different firms may have different source documents to support their specialized needs for accounting information.

OBJECTIVE **4**

Describe the cost flows associated with job-order costing.

THE FLOW OF COSTS THROUGH THE ACCOUNTS

Cost flow describes the way costs are accounted for from the point at which they are incurred to the point at which they are recognized as an expense on the income statement. The principal interest in a job-order costing system is the flow of manufacturing costs. Accordingly, we begin with a description of exactly how the three manufacturing cost elements—direct materials, direct labor, and overhead—flow through Work in Process, into Finished Foods, and, finally, into Cost of Goods Sold. Exhibit 4.6 illustrates the flow of costs through the accounts of a job-order costing firm.

The simplified job-shop environment provided by Johnson Leathergoods continues to serve as an example. To start the business, Stan leased a small building and bought the necessary production equipment. Recall that he obtained two orders for January: one for 20 backpacks

Exhibit 4.6   Flow of Costs through the Accounts of a Job-Order Costing Firm

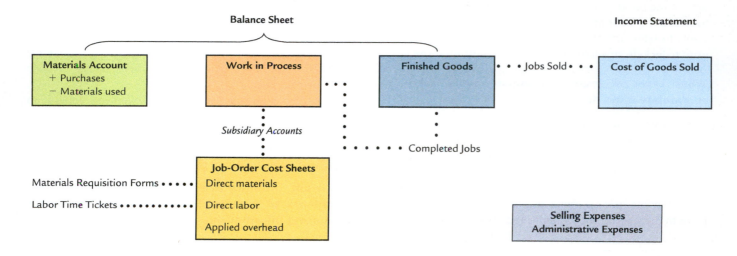

for a local sporting goods store and a second for 10 briefcases for the coaches of a local college. Both orders will be sold for manufacturing costs plus 50%. Stan expects to average two orders per month for the first year of operation.

Stan created two job-order cost sheets, the first of which is for the backpacks; the second is for the briefcases.

Accounting for Materials

Since the company is just starting business, it has no beginning inventories. To produce the backpacks and briefcases in January and to have a supply of materials on hand at the beginning of February, Stan purchases, on account, $2,500 of raw materials (leather, webbing for backpack straps, heavy-duty thread, buckles). Physically, the materials are put in a materials storeroom. In the accounting records, the raw materials and the accounts payable accounts are each increased by $2,500. Raw Materials is an inventory account (it appears on the balance sheet under current assets). It also is the controlling account for all raw materials. Any purchase increases the raw materials account.

When the production supervisor needs materials for a job, materials are removed from the storeroom. The cost of the materials is removed from the raw materials account and added to the work-in-process account. Of course, in a job-order environment, the materials moved from the storeroom to work stations on the factory floor must be "tagged" with the appropriate job name. Suppose that Stan needs $1,000 of materials for the backpacks and $500 for the briefcases. Then the job-order cost sheet for the backpacks would show $1,000 for direct materials, and the job-order cost sheet for the briefcases would show $500 for direct materials. Exhibit 4.7 summarizes the raw materials cost flow into these two jobs.

	A	B	C	D	E	F	G	H
1	Raw Materials Account							
2	Beginning balance		$ 0					
3	Add: Purchases		2,500					
4	Less: Direct materials charged to jobs		1,500					
5	Ending balance		$1,000					
6								
7			Work-in-Process Account					
8	Job: Backpacks				Job: Briefcases			
9	Direct materials		$1,000		Direct materials		$500	
10	Direct labor				Direct labor			
11	Applied overhead				Applied overhead			
12	Total cost				Total cost			
13	Number of units		÷ 20		Number of units		÷ 10	
14	Unit cost				Unit cost			
15								

Exhibit 4.7

Summary of Materials Cost Flows

The raw materials account increased by $2,500 due to purchases and decreased by $1,500 as materials were withdrawn for use in production. So, the balance in the raw materials account after these two transactions would be:

Raw Materials Beginning Balance + Purchases − Materials Used = Raw Materials Balance
$$\$0 + \$2,500 - \$1,500 = \$1,000$$

Accounting for Direct Labor Cost

Since two jobs were in process during January, Stan must determine not only the total number of direct labor hours worked but also the time worked on each job. The backpacks required

60 hours at an average wage rate of $18 per hour, for a total direct labor cost of $1,080. For the briefcases, the total was $450, based on 25 hours at an average hourly wage of $18. These amounts are posted to each job's cost sheet. The summary of the labor cost flows is given in Exhibit 4.8. Notice that the direct labor costs assigned to the two jobs exactly equal the total labor costs assigned to Work in Process. Remember that the labor cost flows reflect only direct labor cost. Indirect labor is assigned as part of overhead.

Exhibit 4.8

Summary of Direct Labor Cost Flows

	A	B	C	D	E	F	G	H
1	**Wages Payable Account**							
2	Direct labor hours for backpacks		60					
3	Direct labor hours for briefcases		25					
4	Total direct labor hours		85					
5	Wage rate		× $18					
6	Total direct labor		$1,530					
7								
8			Work-in-Process Account					
9	Job: Backpacks				Job: Briefcases			
10	Direct materials		$1,000		Direct materials		$500	
11	Direct labor		1,080		Direct labor		450	
12	Applied overhead				Applied overhead			
13	Total cost				Total cost			
14	Number of units		÷ 20		Number of units		÷ 10	
15	Unit cost				Unit cost			
16								

More accounts are involved in this transaction than meet the eye in Exhibit 4.8. Accounting for labor cost is a complex process because the company must keep track of FICA, Medicare, federal and state unemployment taxes, vacation time, and so on. We will concentrate on the concept that direct labor adds to the cost of the product or service and not on the details of the various labor-related accounts.

Accounting for Overhead

The use of normal costing means that overhead is applied to each job by using a predetermined rate. Actual overhead costs incurred must be accounted for as well, but on an overall (not a job-specific) basis.

Overhead costs can be assigned using a single plantwide overhead rate or departmental rates. Typically, direct labor hours is the measure used to calculate a plantwide overhead rate, and departmental rates are based on drivers such as direct labor hours, machine hours, or direct materials dollars. The use of a plantwide rate has the virtue of being simple and reduces data collection requirements. To illustrate these two features, assume that total estimated overhead cost for Johnson Leathergoods is $9,600, and the estimated direct labor hours total 2,400 hours. Accordingly, the predetermined overhead rate is:

$$\text{Overhead Rate} = \frac{\$9,600}{2,400} = \$4 \text{ per direct labor hour}$$

For the backpacks, with a total of 60 hours worked, the amount of applied overhead cost posted to the job-order cost sheet is $240 ($4 × 60). For the briefcases, the applied overhead cost is $100 ($4 × 25). Note that assigning overhead to jobs only requires a rate and the direct labor hours used by the job. Since direct labor hours are already being collected to assign direct labor costs to jobs, overhead assignment will not demand any additional data collection.

Accounting for Actual Overhead Costs

Overhead has been applied to the jobs, but what about the actual overhead incurred? To illustrate how actual overhead costs are recorded, assume that Johnson Leathergoods incurred the following indirect costs for January:

Lease payment	$200
Utilities	50
Equipment depreciation	100
Indirect labor	65
Total overhead costs	$415

It is important to understand that the actual overhead costs never enter the work-in-process account. The usual procedure is to record actual overhead to the overhead control account. Then, at the end of a period (typically a year), actual overhead is reconciled with applied overhead, and, if the overhead variance is immaterial, it is closed to Cost of Goods Sold.

For Johnson Leathergoods at the end of January, actual overhead incurred is $415, while applied overhead is $340. Therefore, the overhead variance of $75 ($415 − $340) means that overhead is underapplied for the month of January.

The flow of overhead costs is summarized in Exhibit 4.9. Notice that the total overhead applied from all jobs is entered in the work-in-process account.

	A	B	C	D	E	F	G	H
1	**Actual Overhead Account**				**Applied Overhead Account**			
2	Lease		$200		Direct labor hours		85	
3	Utilities		50		Overhead rate		× $4	
4	Equipment depreciation		100		Total applied overhead		340	
5	Indirect labor		65					
6	Total actual overhead		$415					
7								
8				**Work-in-Process Account**				
9	Job: Backpacks				Job: Briefcases			
10	Direct materials		$1,000		Direct materials		$500	
11	Direct labor		1,080		Direct labor		450	
12	Applied overhead		240		Applied overhead		100	
13	Total cost				Total cost			
14	Number of units		÷ 20		Number of units		÷ 10	
15	Unit cost				Unit cost			
16								

Exhibit 4.9

Summary of Overhead Cost Flows

Let's take a moment to recap. The cost of a job includes direct materials, direct labor, and applied overhead. These costs are entered on the job-order cost sheet. Work in Process, at any point in time, is the total of the costs on all open job-order cost sheets. When the job is complete, it must leave Work in Process and be entered into Finished Goods or Cost of Goods Sold.

Accounting for Finished Goods

When a job is complete, direct materials, direct labor, and applied overhead amounts are totaled to yield the manufacturing cost of the job. Simultaneously, the costs of the completed job are transferred from the work-in-process account to the finished goods account.

For example, assume that the backpacks were finished in January with the completed cost sheet shown in Exhibit 4.9. Since the backpacks are finished, the total manufacturing costs of

$2,320 must be transferred from the work-in-process account to the finished goods account. A summary of the cost flows occurring when a job is finished is shown in Exhibit 4.10.

Exhibit 4.10

Summary of Cost Flows from Work in Process to Finished Goods

	A	B	C	D	E	F	G	H
1	**Work-in-Process Account BEFORE Transfer of Backpacks to Finished Goods**							
2	**Job: Backpacks**				**Job: Briefcases**			
3	Direct materials		$1,000		Direct materials		$ 500	
4	Direct labor		1,080		Direct labor		450	
5	Applied overhead		240		Applied overhead		100	
6	Total cost		$2,320		Total cost		$1,050	
7	Number of units		÷ 20		Number of units			
8	Unit cost*		$ 116		Unit cost*			
9								
10	**Work-in-Process Account AFTER Transfer of Backpacks to Finished Goods**							
11	**Job: Briefcases**							
12	Direct materials		$ 500					
13	Direct labor		450					
14	Applied overhead		100					
15	Total cost		$1,050					
16	Number of units							
17	Unit cost							
18								
19	**Finished Goods Account**							
20	Beginning balance		$ 0					
21	Add: Completed backpacks		2,320					
22	Less: Jobs sold		0					
23	Ending balance		$2,320					
24								

*Unit cost information is included for backpacks because they are finished. The briefcases are still in process, so no unit cost is calculated.

The completion of a job is an important step in the flow of manufacturing costs. The cost of the finished job is removed from Work in Process, added to Finished Goods, and, eventually, added to cost of goods sold on the income statement. To ensure accuracy in computing these costs, a cost of goods manufactured statement is prepared. Exhibit 4.11 (p. 169) shows the schedule of cost of goods manufactured for Johnson Leathergoods for January. Notice that applied overhead is used to obtain the cost of goods manufactured. Both work-in-process and finished goods inventories are carried at normal cost rather than actual cost.

The balance of ending work in process is $1,050. Where did this figure come from? Of the two jobs, the backpacks were finished and transferred to finished goods. The briefcases are still in process, however, and the manufacturing costs assigned thus far are direct materials, $500; direct labor, $450; and overhead applied, $100. The total of these costs gives the cost of ending work in process. Check these figures against the job-order cost sheet for briefcases shown at the top right of Exhibit 4.10.

Accounting for Cost of Goods Sold

In a job-order firm, units can be produced for a particular customer, or they can be produced with the expectation of selling the units later. If a job is produced especially for a customer (as with the backpacks) and then shipped to the customer, then the cost of the finished job becomes the cost of goods sold. When the backpacks are finished, Cost of Goods Sold increases by $2,320, while Work in Process decreases by the same amount. (The job is no longer incomplete, so its costs cannot stay in Process.) Then, the sale is recognized by increasing both Sales Revenue and Accounts Receivable by $3,480 (cost plus 50% of cost, or $2,320 + $1,160).

Exhibit 4.11

Schedule of Cost of Goods Manufactured

Johnson Leathergoods
Schedule of Cost of Goods Manufactured
For the Month of January

Direct materials:		
Beginning raw materials inventory	$ 0	
Purchases of raw materials	2,500	
Total raw materials available	$2,500	
Ending raw materials	1,000	
Total raw materials used		$1,500
Direct labor		1,530
Overhead:		
Lease	$ 200	
Utilities	50	
Depreciation	100	
Indirect labor	65	
	$ 415	
Less: Underapplied overhead	75	
Overhead applied		340
Current manufacturing costs		$3,370
Add: Beginning work in process		0
Total manufacturing costs		$3,370
Less: Ending work in process		1,050
Cost of goods manufactured		$2,320

A schedule of cost of goods sold usually is prepared at the end of each reporting period (e.g., monthly and quarterly), as shown in Exhibit 4.12 for Johnson Leathergoods for January. Typically, the overhead variance is not material and, therefore, is closed to the cost of goods sold account. The cost of goods sold before an adjustment for an overhead variance is called **normal cost of goods sold**. After the adjustment for the period's overhead variance takes place, the result is called the **adjusted cost of goods sold**. This latter figure appears as an expense on the income statement.

Exhibit 4.12

Statement of Cost of Goods Sold

Statement of Cost of Goods Sold	
Beginning finished goods inventory	$ 0
Cost of goods manufactured	2,320
Goods available for sale	$2,320
Less: Ending finished goods inventory	0
Normal cost of goods sold	$2,320
Add: Underapplied overhead	75
Adjusted cost of goods sold	$2,395

Typically, the overhead variance is closed to the cost of goods sold account at the end of the year. Variances occur each month because of nonuniform production and nonuniform actual overhead costs. As the year unfolds, these monthly variances should about offset each other so that the year-end variance is small. However, to illustrate how the year-end overhead variance would be treated, we will close out the overhead variance for Johnson Leathergoods in January.

Notice that there are two cost of goods sold figures in Exhibit 4.12. The first is normal cost of goods sold and is equal to actual direct materials, actual direct labor, and applied overhead for the jobs that were sold. The second figure is adjusted cost of goods sold. The adjusted cost of goods sold is equal to normal cost of goods sold plus or minus the overhead variance. In this case, overhead has been underapplied (actual overhead of $415 is $75 higher than the applied overhead of $340), so this amount is added to normal cost of goods sold. If the overhead variance shows overapplied overhead, then that amount would be subtracted from normal cost of goods sold.

Suppose that the backpacks had not been ordered by a customer but had been produced with the expectation that they could be sold through a subsequent marketing effort. Then all 20 units might not be sold at the same time. Assume that on January 31, there were 15 backpacks sold. In this case, the cost of goods sold figure is the unit cost times the number of units sold ($116 × 15, or $1,740). The unit cost figure is found on the cost sheet in Exhibit 4.10.

Sometimes it is simpler to use a briefer version of the job-order cost sheet in order to calculate ending Work in Process, Finished Goods, and Cost of Goods Sold. (This is particularly true when working homework and test questions.) Job-order cost sheets are crucial organizing tools. They are the way that companies keep track of the cost of unique jobs. **Example 4.5** shows how to set up such a version to calculate account balances.

Here's **Why It's important**

EXAMPLE 4.5

How to Prepare Brief Job-Order Cost Sheets

At the beginning of June, Galway Company had two jobs in process, Job 78 and Job 79, with the following accumulated cost information:

	Job 78	Job 79
Direct materials	$1,000	$ 800
Direct labor	600	1,000
Applied overhead	750	1,250
Balance, June 1	$2,350	$3,050

During June, two more jobs (80 and 81) were started. The following direct materials and direct labor costs were added to the four jobs during the month of June:

	Job 78	Job 79	Job 80	Job 81
Direct materials	$500	$1,110	$ 900	$100
Direct labor	400	1,400	2,000	320

At the end of June, Jobs 78, 79, and 80 were completed. Only Job 79 was sold. On June 1, the balance in Finished Goods was zero.

EXAMPLE 4.5

(*Continued*)

Required:

1. Calculate the overhead rate based on direct labor cost.

2. Prepare a brief job-order cost sheet for the four jobs. Show the balance as of June 1 as well as direct materials and direct labor added in June. Apply overhead to the four jobs for the month of June, and show the ending balances.

3. Calculate the ending balances of Work in Process and Finished Goods as of June 30.

4. Calculate Cost of Goods Sold for June.

Solution:

1. While the predetermined overhead rate is calculated using estimated overhead and estimated direct labor cost, those figures were not given. However, we can work backward from the applied overhead and direct labor cost given in the June 1 balance for Job 78.

$$\text{Applied Overhead} = \text{Predetermined Overhead Rate} \times \text{Actual Activity Level for Job 78,}$$
$$\$750 = \text{Predetermined Overhead Rate} \times \$600$$
$$\text{Predetermined Overhead Rate} = \frac{\$750}{\$600}$$
$$= 1.25, \text{ or } 125\% \text{ of direct labor cost}$$

(The predetermined overhead rate using Job 79 is identical.)

2.

	Job 78	Job 79	Job 80	Job 81
Beginning balance, June 1	$2,350	$3,050	$ 0	$ 0
Direct materials	500	1,110	900	100
Direct labor	400	1,400	2,000	320
Applied overhead	500*	1,750*	2,500*	400*
Total, June 30	$3,750	$7,310	$ 5,400	$820

*$500 = $400 × 1.25; $1,750 = $1,400 × 1.25; $2,500 = $2,000 × 1.25; $400 = $320 × 1.25

3. By the end of June, Jobs 78, 79, and 80 have been transferred out of Work in Process. Thus, the ending balance in Work in Process consists only of Job 81.

Work in process, June 30	$820

While three jobs (78, 79, and 80) were transferred out of Work in Process and into Finished Goods during June, only two jobs remain (Jobs 78 and 80).

Finished goods, June 1	$ 0
Job 78	3,750
Job 80	5,400
Finished goods, June 30	$9,150

4. One job, Job 79, was sold during June.

Cost of Goods Sold	$7,310

Accounting for Nonmanufacturing Costs

Manufacturing costs are not the only costs experienced by a firm. Nonmanufacturing, or period, costs are also incurred. These include selling and general administrative costs, which are never assigned to the product; they are not part of the manufacturing cost flows.

To illustrate how these costs are accounted for, assume Johnson Leathergoods had the following additional transactions in January:

Advertising circulars	$ 75
Sales commission	125
Office salaries	500
Depreciation, office equipment	50

The first two transactions are selling expenses and the last two are administrative expenses. Therefore, the selling expense account would increase by $200 ($75 + $125), and the administrative expense account would increase by $550 ($500 + $50).

Controlling accounts accumulate all of the selling and administrative expenses for a period. At the end of the period, all of these costs flow to the period's income statement. An income statement for Johnson Leathergoods is shown in Exhibit 4.13.

Exhibit 4.13

Income Statement

Johnson Leathergoods		
Income Statement		
For the Month Ended January 31, 20XX		
Sales		$3,480
Less: Cost of goods sold		2,395
Gross margin		$1,085
Less selling and administrative expenses:		
Selling expenses	$200	
Administrative expenses	550	750
Net operating income		$ 335

With the preparation of the income statement, the flow of costs through the manufacturing, selling, and administrative expense accounts is complete. A more detailed look at the actual accounting for these cost flows is undertaken in Appendix 4A.

Here's How It's Used: AT WASHBURN GUITARS

Creating a made-to-order guitar for an artist is demanding. The artisans in the various **Washburn** departments must execute the artist's vision in every particular. Of course, the materials specified are kept track of and assigned to the job, as are the hours of labor in each department. Overhead is assigned using predetermined overhead rates; however, these are adjusted to take into account the special aspects of a project. For example, the Maya guitar, created for artist Dan Donegan, used a variety of materials including maple, mahogany, rosewood, and abalone. These woods are not used in the standard guitars Washburn makes for the mass

market. Not only must the materials be assigned to the Donegan job, but the overhead is also adjusted due to the scrap created when using these special materials. Think of the abalone used to create the dot inlays—much of the rest of the sheet of abalone is scrap. This is an overhead cost not incurred by the mass-market guitars. In addition, some copies of the guitar are available for purchase by others. As a result, these special order guitars required more administrative and marketing (both print and web design) resources than the mass-market guitars. This additional cost was factored into determining the price.

Check Point

1. **A company had three jobs in Work in Process on June 1: Job 43, Job 44, and Job 46. During June, two more jobs were started, Jobs 47 and 48. At the end of June, Jobs 43, 44, and 48 had been completed and sold. The company always sells every job as soon as it is completed. Which jobs were in Work in Process on June 30?**

Answer:
Since all jobs completed are sold, there are no jobs in Finished Goods. Therefore, Jobs 46 and 47 were not completed in June and must be in ending work-in-process inventory.

2. **Suppose a job was in process on March 31 and was worked on in April but was unfinished as of April 30. What costs are included in the job's total costs as of April 30?**

Answer:
The beginning inventory costs of the job on March 31, the direct materials and direct labor costs added in April, and applied overhead for April make up the job cost total.

APPENDIX 4A: JOURNAL ENTRIES ASSOCIATED WITH JOB-ORDER COSTING

OBJECTIVE 5
Prepare the journal entries associated with job-order costing.

The transactions that flow through the accounts in job-order costing are entered into the accounting system by making journal entries and posting them to the accounts. Let's complete this process for the various transactions that occurred during the month of January for Johnson Leathergoods.

1. Purchased raw materials costing $2,500 on account.

Raw Materials	2,500	
Accounts Payable		2,500

This journal entry shows that the purchase of materials increases the raw materials account as well as the accounts payable account. In other words, the company has increased both assets (materials on hand) and liabilities (through Accounts Payable).

2. Requisitioned materials costing $1,500 for use in production.

Work in Process	1,500	
Raw Materials		1,500

This entry shows the transfer from the materials storeroom to the factory floor. That is, the materials are no longer awaiting requisition; they are being used. So, the work-in-process account goes up, but the raw materials account goes down.

3. Recognized direct labor costing $1,530 (i.e., it was not paid in cash but was shown as a liability in the wages payable account).

Work in Process	1,530	
Wages Payable		1,530

This entry recognizes the cost of direct labor. The amount of direct labor wages is added to Work in Process and to the liability account, Wages Payable.

4.   Applied overhead to production at the rate of $4 per direct labor hour. A total of 85
     direct labor hours were worked.

Work in Process	340	
Overhead Control		340

This entry recognizes the application of overhead to the jobs. Since 85 hours of direct labor
were worked, and the overhead rate is $4 per direct labor hour, then $340 has been applied
to overhead. The application of overhead increases the work-in-process account and is
credited to Overhead Control.

5.   Incurred actual overhead costs of $415.

Overhead Control	415	
Lease Payable		200
Utilities Payable		50
Accumulated Depreciation		100
Wages Payable		65

This entry shows that the actual overhead incurred is debited to Overhead Control. The
credit is to the various payable accounts and Accumulated Depreciation.

6.   Completed the backpack job and transferred it to Finished Goods.

Finished Goods	2,320	
Work in Process		2,320

This entry shows the transfer of the backpack job from Work in Process to Finished
Goods. We find the appropriate cost by referring to the job-order cost sheet in
Exhibit 4.10 (p. 168).

7.   Sold the backpack job at cost plus 50%.

Cost of Goods Sold	2,320	
Finished Goods		2,320
Accounts Receivable	3,480	
Sales Revenue		3,480

First, we recognize the cost of the backpack job by debiting Cost of Goods Sold for the
cost and crediting Finished Goods. This entry mirrors the physical movement of the
backpacks out of the warehouse and to the customer. Second, the sales price is shown. It
is very important to separate the cost of the job from the sale. This always requires two
entries.

8.   Closed underapplied overhead to Cost of Goods Sold.

Cost of Goods Sold	75	
Overhead Control		75

Finally, we check the overhead control account. It has a debit balance of $75,
indicating that the overhead variance is $75 underapplied. To bring the balance to
zero, then, Overhead Control must be credited $75, and Cost of Goods Sold must be
debited $75.

Exhibit 4.14 (p. 175) summarizes these journal entries and posts them to the appropriate
accounts.

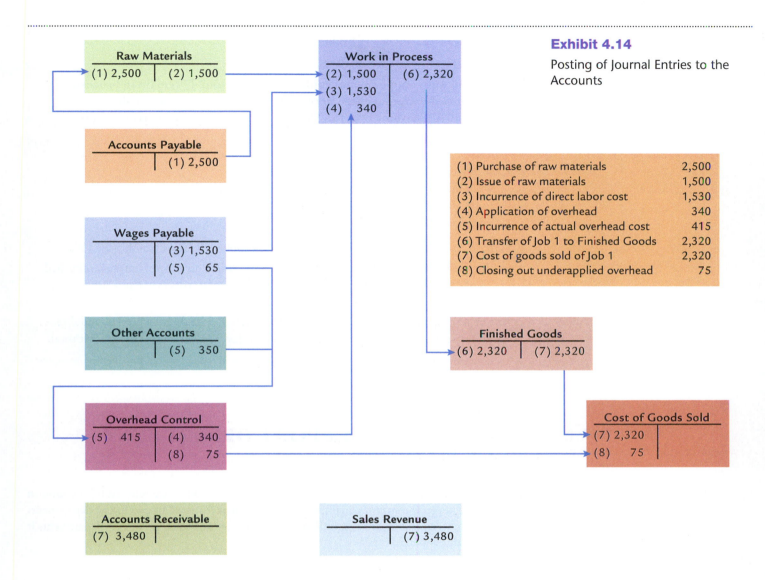

Exhibit 4.14

Posting of Journal Entries to the Accounts

(1) Purchase of raw materials	2,500
(2) Issue of raw materials	1,500
(3) Incurrence of direct labor cost	1,530
(4) Application of overhead	340
(5) Incurrence of actual overhead cost	415
(6) Transfer of Job 1 to Finished Goods	2,320
(7) Cost of goods sold of Job 1	2,320
(8) Closing out underapplied overhead	75

Check Point

1. During the month, direct labor cost of $1,300 was charged to Job 88, $1,000 to Job 89, and $2,500 to Job 90. Direct labor is paid $15 per hour, and overhead is applied at the rate of $6 per direct labor hour. What is the journal entry for overhead applied during the month?

Answer:

Total Direct Labor Cost for the Month = $1,300 + $1,000 + $2,500 = $4,800
Total Direct Labor Hours Worked = $4,800/$15 per hour = 320 direct labor hours
Overhead Applied = 320 × $6 = $1,920

Work in Process   1,920
    Overhead Control   1,920

2. The following are total job costs by April 30:

Job 45	$4,500
Job 46	$2,000

(*Continued*)

| Job 47 | $1,000 |
| Job 50 | $5,500 |

Job 50 was completed and sold; Jobs 45, 46, and 47 remain in process. What is the journal entry to record the sale of Job 50 on account at cost plus 30%? (Assume that Job 50 was sold directly to the customer upon completion.)

Answer:

Cost of Goods Sold	5,500	
Work in Process		5,500
Accounts Receivable	7,150	
Sales Revenue		7,150

Note: Sales Revenue = Cost + (0.30 × Cost) = $5,500 + (0.30 × $5,500) = $7,150

3. **Suppose a job was in process on March 31 and worked on in April but was unfinished as of April 30. What costs are included in the job's total costs as of April 30?**

Answer:

The beginning inventory costs of the job on March 31, the direct materials and direct labor costs added in April, and applied overhead for April make up the job cost total.

 OBJECTIVE 6

Allocate support department costs to producing departments.

APPENDIX 4B: SUPPORT DEPARTMENT COST ALLOCATION

The costs of resources shared by two or more services or products are referred to as **common costs**. For example, the cost of a maintenance department is shared by producing departments that use these services. How to assign these shared costs to individual producing departments is the focus of this appendix.

Types of Departments

CONCEPT CLIP

Nearly every company or factory has producing departments and support departments.

- **Producing departments** are directly responsible for creating the products or services sold to customers. For example, a public accounting firm might have producing departments devoted to auditing, tax, and management advisory services. In a factory, producing departments are those that work directly on the products being manufactured, such as the grinding and assembly departments.
- **Support departments** provide essential services for producing departments, but they do not actually make the product or service being sold. Examples include the maintenance, grounds, engineering, housekeeping, personnel, and photocopying departments.

Once producing and support departments have been identified, overhead costs that belong exclusively to each department are identified—these are direct overhead costs. For example, direct costs of a factory cafeteria include food, salaries of cooks and servers, depreciation on dishwashers and stoves, and supplies (e.g., dishwasher detergent, napkins, plastic forks). Direct overhead costs of a producing department include supplies, supervisory salaries, and depreciation on equipment used in that department. Overhead that cannot easily be assigned to a producing or support department is assigned to a catchall department such as "general factory."

Once the direct overhead costs of each department are determined, the next step is to assign the support department costs to producing departments. These costs are assigned to producing departments by using **causal factors** (drivers) that measure the consumption of the services. Each producing department's share of the support department costs is added to the producing department's direct overhead cost. This total estimated overhead is then divided by a unit-level driver to obtain a predetermined overhead rate for each producing department. Overhead rates are calculated only for producing departments because products only pass through producing departments. Exhibit 4.15 summarizes the steps involved. Steps 1 through 4 are explained in this appendix; Steps 5 and 6 are explained in Example 4.3 (p. 158) of this chapter.

1. Departmentalize the firm.
2. Classify each department as a support department or a producing department.
3. Trace all overhead costs in the firm to a support department or a producing department.
4. Assign support department costs to the producing departments using drivers that measure the consumption of support department services.
5. Calculate predetermined overhead rates for producing departments.
6. Assign overhead costs to the units of individual products using the predetermined overhead rates.

Exhibit 4.15

Steps for Determining Product Costs by Using Predetermined Departmental Overhead Rates

Ethical Decisions

Deliberations about discontinuing a support department need to be kept confidential. Ethical professional practice requires this and more. For example, it may be tempting to use confidential information about the discontinuance of a support department to provide an unfair advantage to a friend or relative who may be the owner of an outside service firm that essentially would be replacing the support department. ●

Ethics

Methods of Support Department Cost Allocation

In order to calculate departmental overhead rates (as opposed to plantwide overhead rates), it is necessary to allocate support department costs to the producing departments. The three methods of assigning costs of multiple support departments to producing departments are the *direct method*, the *sequential method*, and the *reciprocal method*. In determining which support department cost allocation method to use, companies must determine the extent of support department interaction and weigh the individual costs and benefits of each method. In the next three sections, the direct, sequential, and reciprocal methods are discussed.

CONCEPT CLIP

Direct Method All factory costs must be included in product cost. Since support departments do not make the product sold, their costs would not be added to unit cost if they were not included in the cost of producing departments. The direct method is the quickest and easiest way to do this. The **direct method** ignores support department interactions and assigns support department costs *only* to the producing departments. No cost from one support department is given to another support department. Thus, no support department interaction is recognized. Exhibit 4.16 (p. 178) illustrates the way support department costs are allocated to producing departments using the direct method.

Here's **Why It's important**

Example 4.6 (p. 178) shows how the direct method is used to assign the costs of two support departments to two producing departments.

Exhibit 4.16

Illustration of the Direct Method

Suppose there are two support departments, Power and Maintenance, and two producing departments, Grinding and Assembly, each with a "bucket" of directly traceable overhead cost.

Objective: Distribute all maintenance and power costs to Grinding and Assembly using the direct method.

Direct method—Allocate maintenance and power costs only to Grinding and Assembly.

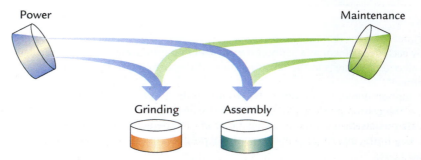

After allocation—Zero cost in Maintenance and Power; all overhead cost is in Grinding and Assembly.

EXAMPLE 4.6

How to Assign Support Department Costs by Using the Direct Method

Departmental data:

	Support Departments		Producing Departments	
	Power	**Maintenance**	**Grinding**	**Assembly**
Direct overhead costs*	$250,000	$160,000	$100,000	$ 60,000
Expected activity:				
Kilowatt-hours	—	200,000	600,000	200,000
Maintenance hours	1,000	—	4,500	4,500

*Overhead costs that are directly traceable to the department.

Required:

Using the direct method, assign the support department costs to the producing departments.

Solution:

Calculate usage or allocation ratios:

	Grinding	Assembly
Power: 600,000/(600,000 + 200,000)	0.75	—
200,000/(600,000 + 200,000)	—	0.25
Maintenance: 4,500/(4,500 + 4,500)	0.50	—
4,500/(4,500 + 4,500)	—	0.50

EXAMPLE 4.6

(*Continued*)

	Support Departments		Producing Departments	
	Power	**Maintenance**	**Grinding**	**Assembly**
Direct costs	$ 250,000	$ 160,000	$100,000	$ 60,000
Power[a]	(250,000)	—	187,500	62,500
Maintenance[b]		(160,000)	80,000	80,000
Total	$ 0	$ 0	$367,500	$202,500

[a] Using the allocation ratios for Power: 0.75 × $250,000; 0.25 × $250,000.

[b] Using the allocation ratios for Maintenance: 0.50 × $160,000; 0.50 × $160,000.

Ignoring department interactions and allocating service costs directly to producing departments may produce unfair and inaccurate cost assignments. For example, the power department, although a support department, may use 30% of the services of the maintenance department. By not assigning some maintenance costs to the power department, its costs are understated. As a result, a producing department that is a heavy user of power and an average or below-average user of maintenance may then receive, under the direct method, a cost allocation that is understated.

Sequential Method of Allocation The **sequential (or step) method** of allocation recognizes that interactions among support departments occur. However, the sequential method does not fully account for support department interaction. Therefore, it is somewhat more accurate than the direct method. Cost allocations are performed in a step-down fashion, following a predetermined ranking procedure. Usually, the sequence is defined by ranking the support departments in order of the amount of service rendered, from the greatest to the least, where degree of service is measured by the direct costs of each support department.

Here's **Why It's important**

Exhibit 4.17 (p. 180) provides a visual portrayal of the sequential method. First, the support departments are ranked, usually in accordance with direct costs; here, the power department is first, then the maintenance department. Next, power costs are allocated to the maintenance department and the two producing departments. Finally, the costs of the maintenance department are allocated only to producing departments.

The costs of the support department rendering the greatest service are assigned to all support departments below it in the sequence and to all producing departments. The costs of the support department next in sequence are similarly allocated, and so on. *In the sequential method, once a support department's costs are allocated, it never receives a subsequent allocation from another support department.* In other words, costs of a support department are never allocated to support departments above it in the sequence. *Note that the costs allocated from a support department are its direct costs plus any costs it receives in allocations from other support departments.*

Example 4.7 (p. 181) shows how to assign support department costs to producing departments by using the sequential method. The power department will be allocated first since its direct cost is higher, followed by the maintenance department. Note that the allocation ratios for the maintenance department ignore the usage by the power department because Power is above Maintenance in the allocation sequence. Unlike the direct method, the sequential method recognizes some interactions among the support departments.

Reciprocal Method of Allocation The **reciprocal method** of allocation recognizes all interactions among support departments. Under the reciprocal method, one support department's use by another figures in determining the total cost of each support department, where the total cost reflects interactions among the support departments. Then, the new total of support department costs is allocated to the producing departments. This method fully accounts for support department interaction by using a system of simultaneous linear equations. The reciprocal method is not widely used due to its complexity. This method will not be illustrated. Rather, its complete description is left to a more advanced course.

Technology and Support Department Cost Allocation Another factor in allocating support department cost is the rapid change in technology. Many firms currently find that support department cost allocation is useful for them. However, the move toward activity-based costing and just-in-time manufacturing can virtually eliminate the need for support department cost allocation.

Exhibit 4.17

Illustration of the Sequential Method

Suppose there are two support departments, Power and Maintenance, and two producing departments, Grinding and Assembly, each with a "bucket" of directly traceable overhead cost.

Objective: Distribute all maintenance and power costs to Grinding and Assembly using the sequential method.

Sequential—Step 1: Rank service departments—#1 Power, #2 Maintenance.
          Step 2: Distribute power to Maintenance, Grinding, and Assembly.

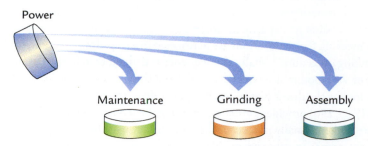

Then, distribute maintenance to Grinding and Assembly.

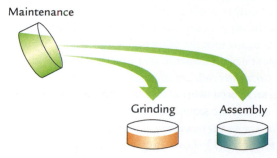

After allocation—Zero cost in Maintenance and Power; all overhead cost is in Grinding and Assembly.

EXAMPLE 4.7

Departmental data:

How to Assign Support Department Costs by Using the Sequential Method

	Support Departments		Producing Departments	
	Power	**Maintenance**	**Grinding**	**Assembly**
Direct costs*	$250,000	$160,000	$100,000	$ 60,000
Expected activity:				
Kilowatt-hours	—	200,000	600,000	200,000
Maintenance hours	1,000	—	4,500	4,500

*Overhead costs that are directly traceable to the department.

Required:
Using the sequential method, assign the support department costs to the producing departments.

Solution:
Calculate usage ratios:

	Maintenance	Grinding	Assembly
Power: 200,000/(200,000 + 600,000 + 200,000)	0.20	—	—
600,000/(200,000 + 600,000 + 200,000)	—	0.60	—
200,000/(200,000 + 600,000 + 200,000)	—	—	0.20
Maintenance: 4,500/(4,500 + 4,500)	—	0.50	—
4,500/(4,500 + 4,500)	—	—	0.50

	Support Departments		Producing Departments	
	Power	**Maintenance**	**Grinding**	**Assembly**
Direct costs	$ 250,000	$ 160,000	$100,000	$ 60,000
Power[a]	(250,000)	50,000	150,000	50,000
Maintenance[b]	—	(210,000)	105,000	105,000
	$ 0	$ 0	$355,000	$215,000

[a] Using the usage ratios for Power: 0.20 × $250,000; 0.60 × $250,000; 0.20 × $250,000.
[b] Using the usage ratios for Maintenance: 0.50 × $210,000; 0.50 × $210,000.

Check Point

1. **Why is the sequential method considered to be more accurate than the direct method?**

Answer:
The sequential method considers some of the interactions among service departments, whereas the direct method ignores these interactions.

2. **A company has two departments: Department A and Department B. Overhead costs of $30,000 are allocated on the basis of machine hours using the direct method. Department A has 1,000 machine hours, and Department B has 4,000 machine hours. How much overhead is allocated to Department A? To Department B?**

Answer:
Total Machine Hours = 1,000 + 4,000 = 5,000
Proportion of Machine Hours Used by Department A = 1,000/5,000 = 0.2
Proportion of Machine Hours Used by Department B = 4,000/5,000 = 0.8
Overhead Allocated to Department A = 0.2 × $3,000 = $6,000
Overhead Allocated to Department B = 0.8 × $3,000 = $24,000

SUMMARY OF LEARNING OBJECTIVES

LO1. Describe the differences between job-order costing and process costing, and identify the types of firms that would use each method.
- Job-order firms collect costs by job.
- Job-order firms produce heterogeneous products/services—each unit or batch has a different total cost.
- Job-order firms include construction, custom cabinetry, dentistry, medical services, and automotive repair.
- Process firms produce homogeneous products.
- In process firms, the cost of one batch or unit is the same as another batch or unit.
- Process firms include paint manufacturing, check clearing, and toy manufacturing.

LO2. Compute the predetermined overhead rate, and use the rate to assign overhead to units or services produced.
- Most firms use normal costing, where total product cost equals actual direct materials, actual direct labor, and applied overhead.
- Predetermined overhead is total budgeted overhead divided by total budgeted activity level.
- Overhead is applied by multiplying the rate by the actual activity usage.
- Applied overhead is added to total actual direct materials and direct labor cost, which is divided by number of units to yield unit cost.

LO3. Identify and set up the source documents used in job-order costing.
- Job-order cost sheets summarize all costs associated with a job.
- Materials requisition forms are used to request direct materials for a job.
- Time tickets show the number of labor hours worked on a job.

LO4. Describe the cost flows associated with job-order costing.
- The job-order cost sheet is subsidiary to the work-in-process account.
- The balance in Work in Process consists of the balances of all incomplete jobs.
- The cost of a finished job is transferred out of Work in Process and into Finished Goods.
- The cost of jobs sold is transferred out of Finished Goods and into Cost of Goods Sold.

LO5. *(Appendix 4A)* Prepare the journal entries associated with job-order costing.
- Direct materials and direct labor are charged to Work in Process.
- Applied overhead costs are charged to Work in Process. Actual overhead costs are charged to Overhead Control.
- When units are completed, their total cost is debited to Finished Goods and credited to Work in Process.
- When units are sold, their total cost is debited to Cost of Goods Sold and credited to Finished Goods.

LO6. *(Appendix 4B)* Allocate support department costs to producing departments.
- Producing departments actually make the products or services. Support departments provide service to the producing departments.
- When departmental overhead rates are used, the costs of support departments must be allocated to the producing departments.
- Three methods of support department cost allocation are direct method, sequential method, and reciprocal method.

SUMMARY OF IMPORTANT EQUATIONS

1. $\text{Predetermined Overhead Rate} = \dfrac{\text{Estimated Annual Overhead}}{\text{Estimated Annual Activity Level}}$

2. Applied Overhead = Predetermined Overhead Rate × Actual Activity Level
3. Total Normal Product Costs = Actual Direct Materials + Actual Direct Labor + Applied Overhead
4. Overhead Variance = Actual Overhead - Applied Overhead
5. Adjusted COGS = Unadjusted COGS ± Overhead Variance
   (*Note*: Applied Overhead > Actual Overhead means Overapplied Overhead; subtract from COGS
   Applied Overhead < Actual Overhead means Underapplied Overhead; add to COGS)

6. $\text{Departmental Overhead Rate} = \dfrac{\text{Estimated Department Overhead}}{\text{Estimated Departmental Activity Level}}$

EXAMPLE 4.1	How to calculate the predetermined overhead rate and apply overhead to production, page 155
EXAMPLE 4.2	How to reconcile actual overhead with applied overhead, page 157
EXAMPLE 4.3	How to calculate predetermined departmental overhead rates and apply overhead to production, page 158
EXAMPLE 4.4	How to convert departmental data to plantwide data to calculate the overhead rate and apply overhead to production, page 159
EXAMPLE 4.5	How to prepare brief job-order cost sheets, page 170
EXAMPLE 4.6	*(Appendix 4B)* How to assign support department costs by using the direct method, page 178
EXAMPLE 4.7	*(Appendix 4B)* How to assign support department costs by using the sequential method, page 181

KEY TERMS

Actual cost system, 152, an actual cost system uses only actual costs of direct materials, direct labor, and overhead to determine unit cost.

Adjusted cost of goods sold, 169, normal cost of goods sold (actual direct materials, actual direct labor, and applied overhead) is adjusted for the overhead variance. Underapplied overhead is added back; overapplied overhead is subtracted. This is an expense on the income statement.

Applied overhead, 155, calculated by multiplying the predetermined overhead rate by the actual amount of the base or driver used.

Causal factors, 177 *(Appendix 4B)*, drivers that are directly associated with the actual use of the services.

Common costs, 176 *(Appendix 4B)*, the costs of resources shared by two or more services or products.

Departmental overhead rate, 158, estimated overhead for a department divided by the estimated activity level for that same department. There are as many rates as there are producing departments. This allows firms to more accurately cost products that only pass through a few departments.

Direct method, 177 *(Appendix 4B)*, method that assigns support department costs *only* to the producing departments. No cost from one support department is given to another support department; thus, it ignores support department interaction.

Job, 150, one distinct unit or set of units. The costs for that unit are unique and must be kept track of on an individual job basis.

Job-order cost sheet, 161, document prepared for every job; it is subsidiary to the work-in-process account and is the primary document for accumulating all costs related to a particular job.

Job-order costing system, 150, a costing system in which costs are accumulated by job.

Materials requisition form, 162, a source document that assigns the cost of direct materials to a job.

Normal cost of goods sold, 169, cost of goods sold before any adjustment for an overhead variance.

Normal cost system, 153, a system in which the cost of production consists of actual direct materials, actual direct labor, and applied (not actual) overhead.

Overapplied overhead, 156, overhead that occurs when the applied overhead is greater than the actual overhead.

Overhead variance, 156, difference between applied overhead and actual overhead.

Plantwide overhead rate, 157, a single overhead rate calculated by using all estimated overhead for a factory divided by the estimated activity level across the entire factory.

Predetermined overhead rate, 154, the overhead rate calculated at the beginning of the year by dividing the total estimated annual overhead by the total estimated level of associated activity or cost driver.

Process-costing system, 151, a costing system that accumulates production costs by process or by department for a given period of time. Unit costs are computed by dividing the process costs for the given period by the output of the period.

Producing departments, 176 *(Appendix 4B),* departments in a factory or service firm that make the product or service that is sold to customers.

Reciprocal method, 179 *(Appendix 4B),* a support department allocation method that recognizes all interactions among support departments.

Sequential (or step) method, 179 *(Appendix 4B),* a support department allocation method that recognizes that interactions among support departments occur, but does not fully account for support department interaction.

Support departments, 176 *(Appendix 4B),* departments that provide essential services for producing departments, but do not actually make the product or service being sold.

Time ticket, 162, a source document that records time spent on each job by each employee. It is used to assign direct labor costs to jobs.

Underapplied overhead, 156, overhead that occurs when the applied overhead is less than the actual overhead.

REVIEW PROBLEMS

I. Job Cost Using Plantwide and Departmental Overhead Rates

Lindberg Company uses a normal job-order costing system. There are two departments, Assembly and Finishing, through which most jobs pass. Selected budgeted and actual data for the past year follow:

	Assembly	Finishing
Budgeted overhead	$330,000	$1,000,000
Actual overhead	110,000	520,000
Expected activity (direct labor hours)	150,000	25,000
Expected machine hours	25,000	125,000

During the year, several jobs were completed. Data pertaining to one such job, Job 330, follow:

Direct materials	$730,000
Direct labor cost:	
Assembly (5,000 hours @ $12 per hr.)	$60,000
Finishing (400 hours @ $12 per hr.)	$4,800
Machine hours used:	
Assembly	100
Finishing	1,200
Units produced	10,000

Lindberg uses a plantwide predetermined overhead rate based on direct labor hours (DLH) to assign overhead to jobs.

Required:

1. Compute the predetermined overhead rate.
2. Using the predetermined rate, compute the per-unit manufacturing cost for Job 330. (*Note:* Round the unit cost to the nearest cent.)
3. Recalculate the unit manufacturing cost for Job 330 using departmental overhead rates. Use direct labor hours for Assembly and machine hours for Finishing.

Solution:

1. Predetermined Overhead Rate = $1,330,000/175,000 DLH = $7.60 per DLH. Add the budgeted overhead for the two departments, and divide by the total expected direct labor hours (DLH = 150,000 + 25,000).

2.

Direct materials	$730,000
Direct labor ($12 × 5,400 DLH)	64,800
Overhead ($7.60 × 5,400 DLH)	41,040
Total manufacturing costs	$835,840
Unit cost ($835,840/10,000 units)	$ 83.58

3. Predetermined Rate for Assembly $= \dfrac{\$330,000}{150,000 \text{ DLH}} = \$2.20$ per direct labor hour

Predetermined Rate for Finishing $= \dfrac{\$1,000,000}{125,000 \text{ mhrs}} = \$8.00$ per machine hour

Direct materials	$730,000
Direct labor	64,800
Overhead:	
Assembly ($2.20 × 5,000 DLH)	11,000
Finishing ($8.00 × 1,200 mhrs)	9,600
Total manufacturing costs	$815,400
Unit cost ($815,400/10,000 units)	$ 81.54

II. Calculation of Work in Process and Cost of Goods Sold with Multiple Jobs

Kennedy Kitchen and Bath (KKB) Company designs and installs upscale kitchens and bathrooms. On May 1, there were three jobs in process, Jobs 77, 78, and 79. During May, two more jobs were started, Jobs 80 and 81. By May 31, Jobs 77, 78, and 80 were completed. The following data were gathered:

	Job 77	Job 78	Job 79	Job 80	Job 81
May 1 balance	$875	$1,140	$410	$ 0	$ 0
Direct materials	690	320	500	3,500	2,750
Direct labor	450	420	80	1,800	1,300

Overhead is applied at the rate of 150% of direct labor cost. Jobs are sold at cost plus 30%. Operating expenses for May totaled $2,700.

Required:

1. Prepare job-order cost sheets for each job as of May 31.
2. Calculate the ending balance in Work in Process (as of May 31) and Cost of Goods Sold for May.
3. Construct an income statement for KKB for the month of May.

Solution:

1.

	Job 77	Job 78	Job 79	Job 80	Job 81
May 1 balance	$ 875	$1,140	$ 410	$ 0	$ 0
Direct materials	690	320	500	3,500	2,750
Direct labor	450	420	80	1,800	1,300
Applied overhead	675	630	120	2,700	1,950
Totals	$2,690	$2,510	$1,110	$8,000	$6,000

2. Ending Balance in Work in Process = Job 79 + Job 81
$$= \$1,110 + \$6,000$$
$$= \$7,110$$

Cost of Goods Sold for May = Job 77 + Job 78 + Job 80
$$= \$2,690 + \$2,510 + \$8,000$$
$$= \$13,200$$

3.

Kennedy Kitchen and Bath Company
Income Statement
For the Month Ended May 31, 20XX

Sales*	$17,160
Cost of goods sold	13,200
Gross margin	$ 3,960
Less: Operating expenses	2,700
Operating income	$ 1,260

*Sales = $13,200 + 0.30($13,200) = $17,160

III. Allocation: Direct and Sequential Methods

Barok Manufacturing produces machine parts on a job-order basis. Most business is obtained through bidding. Most firms competing with Barok bid full cost plus a 20% markup. Recently, with the expectation of gaining more sales, Barok reduced its markup from 25% to 20%.

The company operates two service departments and two producing departments. The budgeted costs and the normal activity levels for each department are given below.

	Service Departments		Producing Departments	
	A	B	C	D
Direct overhead costs	$100,000	$200,000	$100,000	$50,000
Number of employees	8	7	30	30
Maintenance hours	2,000	200	6,400	1,600
Machine hours	—	—	10,000	1,000
Labor hours	—	—	1,000	10,000

The direct costs of Department A are allocated on the basis of employees. The direct costs of Department B are allocated on the basis of maintenance hours. Departmental overhead rates are used to assign costs to products. Department C uses machine hours, and Department D uses labor hours.

The firm is preparing to bid on a job (Job K) that requires three machine hours per unit produced in Department C and no time in Department D. The expected prime costs per unit are $67.

Required:

1. Allocate the service costs to the producing departments by using the direct method.
2. What will the bid be for Job K if the direct method of allocation is used?
3. Allocate the service costs to the producing departments by using the sequential method.
4. What will the bid be for Job K if the sequential method is used?

Solution:

1.

	Service Departments		Producing Departments	
	A	B	C	D
Direct overhead costs	$ 100,000	$ 200,000	$100,000	$ 50,000
Department A[a]	(100,000)	—	50,000	50,000
Department B[b]	—	(200,000)	160,000	40,000
Total	$ 0	$ 0	$310,000	$140,000

[a] Department A costs are allocated on the basis of the number of employees in the producing departments, Departments C and D. The percentage of Department A cost allocated to Department C = 30/(30 + 30) = 0.50. Cost of Department A allocated to Department C = 0.50 × $100,000 = $50,000. The percentage of Department A cost allocated to Department D = 30/(30 + 30) = 0.50. Cost of Department A allocated to Department D = 0.50 × $100,000 = $50,000.

[b] Department B costs are allocated on the basis of maintenance hours used in the producing departments, Departments C and D. The percentage of Department B cost allocated to Department C = 6,400/(6,400 + 1,600) = 0.80. Cost of Department B allocated to Department C = 0.80 × $200,000 = $160,000. The percentage of Department B cost allocated to Department D = 1,600/(6,400 + 1,600) = 0.20. Cost of Department B allocated to Department D = 0.20 × $200,000 = $40,000.

2. Department C: Overhead Rate = $310,000/10,000 mhrs = $31 per machine hour. Product cost and bid price:

Prime cost	$ 67
Overhead (3 × $31)	93
Total unit cost	$160

Bid Price = $160 × 1.20 = $192

(*Continued*)

3.

	Service Departments		Producing Departments	
	A	**B**	**C**	**D**
Direct overhead costs	$ 100,000	$ 200,000	$100,000	$ 50,000
Department Bª	40,000	(200,000)	128,000	32,000
Department Aᵇ	(140,000)	—	70,000	70,000
Total	$ 0	$ 0	$298,000	$152,000

ª Department B ranks first because its direct costs are higher than those of Department A. Department B costs are allocated on the basis of maintenance hours used in Department A, and producing Departments C and D. Percent of Department B cost allocated to Department A is 0.20 [2,000/(2,000 + 6,400 + 1,600)]; cost of Department B allocated to Department A = 0.20 × $200,000 = $40,000. The percentage of Department B cost allocated to Department C = 6,400/(2,000 + 6,400 + 1,600) = 0.64. Cost of Department B allocated to Department C = 0.64 × $200,000 = $128,000. The percentage of Department B cost allocated to Department D = 1,600/(2,000 + 6,400 + 1,600) = 0.16. Cost of Department B allocated to Department D = 0.16 × $200,000 = $32,000.

ᵇ Department A costs are allocated on the basis of number of employees in the producing departments, Departments C and D. The percentage of Department A cost allocated to Department C = 30/(30 + 30) = 0.50. Cost of Department A allocated to Department C = 0.50 × $140,000 = $70,000. The percentage of Department A cost allocated to Department D = 30/(30 + 30) = 0.50. Cost of Department A allocated to Department D = 0.50 × $140,000 = $70,000. (*Note:* Department A cost is no longer $100,000. It is $140,000 due to the $40,000 that was allocated from Department B.)

4. Department C: Overhead Rate = $298,000/10,000 mhrs = $29.80 per machine hour. Product cost and bid price:

Prime cost	$ 67.00
Overhead (3 × $29.80)	89.40
Total unit cost	$156.40

Bid Price = $156.40 × 1.20 = $187.68

DISCUSSION QUESTIONS

1. What are job-order costing and process costing? What types of firms use job-order costing? Process costing?
2. Give some examples of service firms that might use job-order costing, and explain why it is used in those firms.
3. What is normal costing? How does it differ from actual costing?
4. Why are actual overhead rates seldom used in practice?
5. Explain how overhead is assigned to production when a predetermined overhead rate is used.
6. What is underapplied overhead? When Cost of Goods Sold is adjusted for underapplied overhead, will the cost increase or decrease? Why?
7. What is overapplied overhead? When Cost of Goods Sold is adjusted for overapplied overhead, will the cost increase or decrease? Why?
8. Suppose that you and a friend decide to set up a lawn mowing service next summer. Describe the source documents that you would need to account for your activities.
9. Why might a company decide to use departmental overhead rates instead of a plantwide overhead rate?
10. What is the role of materials requisition forms in a job-order costing system? Time tickets? Predetermined overhead rates?
11. Carver Company uses a plantwide overhead rate based on direct labor cost. Suppose that during the year, Carver raises its wage rate for direct labor. How would that affect overhead applied? The total cost of jobs?
12. What is an overhead variance? How is it accounted for typically?
13. Is the cost of a job related to the price charged? Explain.

14. If a company decides to increase advertising expense by $25,000, how will that affect the predetermined overhead rate? Eventual cost of goods sold?

15. How can a departmental overhead system be converted to a plantwide overhead system?

16. *(Appendix 4B)* Describe the difference between producing and support departments.

17. *(Appendix 4B)* Assume that a company has decided not to allocate any support department costs to producing departments. Describe the likely behavior of the managers of the producing departments. Would this be good or bad? Explain why allocation would correct this type of behavior.

18. *(Appendix 4B)* Why is it important to identify and use causal factors to allocate support department costs?

19. *(Appendix 4B)* Identify some possible causal factors for the following support departments:
    a. Cafeteria
    b. Custodial services
    c. Laundry
    d. Receiving, shipping, and storage
    e. Maintenance
    f. Personnel
    g. Accounting

20. *(Appendix 4B)* Explain the difference between the direct method and the sequential method.

MULTIPLE-CHOICE QUESTIONS

4-1 Which of the following statements is true?

  a. Job-order costing is used only in manufacturing firms.
  b. Process costing is used only for services.
  c. Job-order costing is simpler to use than process costing because the recordkeeping requirements are less.
  d. The job cost sheet is subsidiary to the work-in-process account.
  e. All of these.

4-2 The ending balance of which of the following accounts is calculated by summing the totals of the open (unfinished) job-order cost sheets?

  a. Raw Materials
  b. Overhead Control
  c. Work in Process
  d. Finished Goods
  e. Cost of Goods Sold

4-3 In a normal costing system, the cost of a job includes

  a. actual direct materials, actual direct labor, and estimated (applied) overhead.
  b. estimated direct materials, estimated direct labor, and estimated overhead.
  c. actual direct materials, actual direct labor, actual overhead, and actual selling cost.
  d. actual direct materials, actual direct labor, and actual overhead.
  e. None of these. Job-order costing requires the use of actual, not normal, costing.

4-4 The predetermined overhead rate equals

  a. actual overhead divided by actual activity level for a period.
  b. estimated overhead divided by estimated activity level for a period.
  c. actual overhead minus estimated overhead.
  d. actual overhead multiplied by actual activity level for a period.
  e. one-twelfth of estimated overhead.

4-5   The job-order cost sheet is a subsidiary account to

   a. Raw Materials.
   b. Work in Process.
   c. Finished Goods.
   d. Cost of Goods Sold.
   e. Jobs Started.

4-6   Applied overhead is

   a. an important part of normal costing.
   b. never used in normal costing.
   c. an important part of actual costing.
   d. the predetermined overhead rate multiplied by estimated activity level.
   e. the predetermined overhead rate multiplied by estimated activity level for the month.

4-7   The overhead variance is overapplied if

   a. actual overhead is less than applied overhead.
   b. actual overhead is more than applied overhead.
   c. applied overhead is less than actual overhead.
   d. estimated overhead is less than applied overhead.
   e. estimated overhead is more than applied overhead.

4-8   Which of the following is typically a job-order costing firm?

   a. Paint manufacturer
   b. Pharmaceutical manufacturer
   c. Cleaning products manufacturer
   d. Cement manufacturer
   e. Large regional medical center

4-9   Which of the following is typically a process-costing firm?

   a. Paint manufacturer
   b. Custom cabinetmaker
   c. Large regional medical center
   d. Law office
   e. Custom framing shop

4-10   When materials are requisitioned for use in production in a job-order costing firm, the cost of materials is added to the

   a. raw materials account.
   b. work-in-process account.
   c. finished goods account.
   d. accounts payable account.
   e. cost of goods sold account.

4-11   When a job is completed, the total cost of the job is

   a. subtracted from the raw materials account.
   b. added to the work-in-process account.
   c. added to the finished goods account.
   d. added to the accounts payable account.
   e. subtracted from the cost of goods sold account.

4-12   The costs of a job are accounted for on the

   a. materials requisition sheet.
   b. time ticket.
   c. requisition for overhead application.
   d. sales invoice.
   e. job-order cost sheet.

4-13 Wilson Company has a predetermined overhead rate of $5 per direct labor hour. The job-order cost sheet for Job 145 shows 500 direct labor hours costing $10,000 and materials requisitions totaling $17,500. Job 145 had 1,000 units completed and transferred to Finished Goods. What is the cost per unit for Job 145?

    a. $20
    b. $17.50
    c. $25
    d. $30
    e. $22,500

4-14 *(Appendix 4A)* When a job costing $2,000 is finished but not sold, the following journal entry is made:

a. Cost of Goods Sold	2,000	
Finished Goods		2,000
b. Finished Goods	2,000	
Cost of Goods Sold		2,000
c. Finished Goods	2,000	
Work in Process		2,000
d. Work in Process	2,000	
Finished Goods		2,000
e. Cost of Goods Sold	2,000	
Sales		2,000

4-15 *(Appendix 4B)* Those departments responsible for creating products or services that are sold to customers are referred to as

    a. profit-making departments.
    b. producing departments.
    c. cost centers.
    d. support departments.
    e. None of these.

4-16 *(Appendix 4B)* Those departments that provide essential services to producing departments are referred to as

    a. revenue-generating departments.
    b. support departments.
    c. profit centers.
    d. production departments.
    e. None of these.

4-17 *(Appendix 4B)* An example of a producing department is

    a. a materials storeroom.
    b. the maintenance department.
    c. engineering design.
    d. assembly.
    e. All of these.

4-18 *(Appendix 4B)* An example of a support department is

    a. data processing.
    b. personnel.
    c. a materials storeroom.
    d. payroll.
    e. All of these.

4-19   *(Appendix 4B)* The method that assigns support department costs only to producing departments in proportion to each department's usage of the service is known as
a. the sequential method.
b. the proportional method.
c. the reciprocal method.
d. the direct method.
e. None of these.

4-20   *(Appendix 4B)* The method that assigns support department costs by giving partial recognition to support department interactions is known as
a. the sequential method.
b. the proportional method.
c. the reciprocal method.
d. the direct method.
e. None of these.

4-21   *(Appendix 4B)* The method that assigns support department costs by giving full recognition to support department interactions is known as
a. the sequential method.
b. the proportional method.
c. the reciprocal method.
d. the direct method.
e. None of these.

BRIEF EXERCISES: SET A

OBJECTIVE ▶2▶
Example 4.1

Brief Exercise 4-22 Predetermined Overhead Rate, Overhead Application

At the beginning of the year, Ilberg Company estimated the following costs:

Overhead	$416,000
Direct labor cost	520,000

Ilberg uses normal costing and applies overhead on the basis of direct labor cost. (Direct labor cost is equal to total direct labor hours worked multiplied by the wage rate.) For the month of December, direct labor cost was $43,700.

Required:

1. Calculate the predetermined overhead rate for the year.
2. Calculate the overhead applied to production in December.

OBJECTIVE ▶2▶
Example 4.2

Brief Exercise 4-23 Overhead Variance (Over- or Underapplied), Closing to Cost of Goods Sold

At the end of the year, Ilberg Company provided the following actual information:

Overhead	$423,600
Direct labor cost	532,000

Ilberg uses normal costing and applies overhead at the rate of 80% of direct labor cost. At the end of the year, Cost of Goods Sold (before adjusting for any overhead variance) was $1,890,000.

Required:

1. Calculate the overhead variance for the year.
2. Dispose of the overhead variance by adjusting Cost of Goods Sold.

Use the following information for Brief Exercises 4-24 and 4-25:
At the beginning of the year, Hallett Company estimated the following:

	Cutting Department	Sewing Department	Total
Overhead	$240,000	$350,000	$590,000
Direct labor hours	31,200	100,000	131,200
Machine hours	150,000	—	150,000

Brief Exercise 4-24 **Predetermined Departmental Overhead Rates, Applying Overhead to Production**

OBJECTIVE 2
Example 4.3

Refer to the information for Hallett Company above. Hallett uses departmental overhead rates. In the cutting department, overhead is applied on the basis of machine hours. In the sewing department, overhead is applied on the basis of direct labor hours. Actual data for the month of June are as follows:

	Cutting Department	Sewing Department	Total
Overhead	$20,610	$35,750	$56,360
Direct labor hours	2,800	8,600	11,400
Machine hours	13,640	—	13,640

Required:

1. Calculate the predetermined overhead rates for the cutting and sewing departments.
2. Calculate the overhead applied to production in each department for the month of June.
3. By how much has each department's overhead been overapplied? Underapplied?

Brief Exercise 4-25 **Convert Departmental Data to Plantwide Data, Plantwide Overhead Rate, Apply Overhead to Production**

OBJECTIVE 2
Example 4.4

Refer to the information in **Brief Exercise 4-24** for data. Now, assume that Hallett has decided to use a plantwide overhead rate based on direct labor hours.

Required:

1. Calculate the predetermined plantwide overhead rate. (*Note:* Round to the nearest cent.)
2. Calculate the overhead applied to production for the month of June.
3. Calculate the overhead variance for the month of June.

Brief Exercise 4-26 **Prepare Job-Order Cost Sheets, Predetermined Overhead Rate, Ending Balance of WIP, Finished Goods, and COGS**

OBJECTIVE 3
Example 4.5

At the beginning of June, Rhone Company had two jobs in process, Job 44 and Job 45, with the following accumulated cost information:

	Job 44	Job 45
Direct materials	$5,100	$1,500
Direct labor	1,200	3,000
Applied overhead	780	1,950
Balance, June 1	$7,080	$6,450

During June, two more jobs (46 and 47) were started. The following direct materials and direct labor costs were added to the four jobs during the month of June:

	Job 44	Job 45	Job 46	Job 47
Direct materials	$2,500	$7,110	$1,800	$1,700
Direct labor	800	6,400	900	560

(*Continued*)

At the end of June, Jobs 44, 45, and 47 were completed. Only Job 45 was sold. On June 1, the balance in Finished Goods was zero.

Required:

1. Calculate the overhead rate based on direct labor cost. (*Note:* Round to three decimal places.)
2. Prepare a brief job-order cost sheet for the four jobs. Show the balance as of June 1 as well as direct materials and direct labor added in June. Apply overhead to the four jobs for the month of June, and show the ending balances.
3. Calculate the ending balances of Work in Process and Finished Goods as of June 30.
4. Calculate the Cost of Goods Sold for June.

Use the following information for Brief Exercises 4-27 and 4-28:

Quillen Company manufactures a product in a factory that has two producing departments, Cutting and Sewing, and two support departments, S1 and S2. The activity driver for S1 is number of employees, and the activity driver for S2 is number of maintenance hours. The following data pertain to Quillen:

	Support Departments		Producing Departments	
	S1	**S2**	**Cutting**	**Sewing**
Direct costs	$180,000	$150,000	$122,000	$90,500
Normal activity:				
Number of employees	—	30	63	147
Maintenance hours	1,200	—	16,000	4,000

OBJECTIVE 6
Example 4.6

Brief Exercise 4-27 *(Appendix 4B)* **Assigning Support Department Costs by Using the Direct Method**

Refer to the information for Quillen Company above.

Required:

1. Calculate the cost assignment ratios to be used under the direct method for Departments S1 and S2. (*Note:* Each support department will have two ratios—one for Cutting and the other for Sewing.)
2. Allocate the support department costs to the producing departments by using the direct method.

OBJECTIVE 6
Example 4.7

EXCEL

Brief Exercise 4-28 *(Appendix 4B)* **Sequential Method**

Refer to the information for Quillen Company above. Now assume that Quillen uses the sequential method to allocate support department costs. S1 is allocated first, then S2.

Required:

1. Calculate the cost assignment ratios to be used under the sequential method for S2, Cutting, and Sewing. Carry out your answers to four decimal places.
2. Allocate the overhead costs to the producing departments by using the sequential method.

BRIEF EXERCISES: SET B

OBJECTIVE 2
Example 4.1

Brief Exercise 4-29 **Predetermined Overhead Rate, Overhead Application**

At the beginning of the year, Estes Company estimated the following costs:

Overhead	$450,000
Direct labor cost	600,000

Estes uses normal costing and applies overhead on the basis of direct labor cost. (Direct labor cost is equal to total direct labor hours worked multiplied by the wage rate.) For the month of September, direct labor cost was $46,300.

Required:

1. Calculate the predetermined overhead rate for the year.
2. Calculate the overhead applied to production in September.

Brief Exercise 4-30 Overhead Variance (Over- or Underapplied), Closing to Cost of Goods Sold

OBJECTIVE ▶ 2
Example 4.2

At the end of the year, Estes Company provided the following actual information:

Overhead	$412,600
Direct labor cost	532,000

Estes uses normal costing and applies overhead at the rate of 75% of direct labor cost. At the end of the year, Cost of Goods Sold (before adjusting for any overhead variance) was $1,670,000.

Required:

1. Calculate the overhead variance for the year.
2. Dispose of the overhead variance by adjusting Cost of Goods Sold.

Use the following information for Brief Exercises 4-31 and 4-32:
At the beginning of the year, Jonson Company estimated the following:

	Firing Department	**Polishing Department**	**Total**
Overhead	$405,000	$110,000	$515,000
Direct labor hours	28,750	100,000	128,750
Kiln hours	90,000	—	90,000

Brief Exercise 4-31 Predetermined Departmental Overhead Rates, Applying Overhead to Production

OBJECTIVE ▶ 2
Example 4.3

Refer to the information for Jonson Company above. Jonson uses departmental overhead rates. In the firing department, overhead is applied on the basis of kiln hours (number of hours spent in the gas-fired kiln). In the polishing department, overhead is applied on the basis of direct labor hours. Actual data for the month of July are as follows:

	Firing Department	**Polishing Department**	**Total**
Overhead	$34,000	$9,370	$43,370
Direct labor hours	2,350	8,600	10,950
Kiln hours	7,400	—	7,400

Required:

1. Calculate the predetermined overhead rates for the firing and polishing departments.
2. Calculate the overhead applied to production in each department for the month of July.
3. By how much has each department's overhead been overapplied? Underapplied?

Brief Exercise 4-32 Convert Departmental Data to Plantwide Data, Plantwide Overhead Rate, Apply Overhead to Production

OBJECTIVE ▶ 2
Example 4.4

Refer to the information in **Brief Exercise 4-31** for data. Now, assume that Jonson has decided to use a plantwide overhead rate based on direct labor hours.

(Continued)

Required:

1. Calculate the predetermined plantwide overhead rate. (*Note:* Round to the nearest cent.)
2. Calculate the overhead applied to production for the month of July.
3. Calculate the overhead variance for the month of July.

 OBJECTIVE 3
Example 4.5

Brief Exercise 4-33 Prepare Job-Order Cost Sheets, Predetermined Overhead Rate, Ending Balance of WIP, Finished Goods, and COGS

At the beginning of March, Mendez Company had two jobs in process, Job 86 and Job 87, with the following accumulated cost information:

	Job 86	Job 87
Direct materials	$4,800	$1,600
Direct labor	1,200	3,000
Applied overhead	888	2,220
Balance, March 1	$6,888	$6,820

During March, two more jobs (88 and 89) were started. The following direct materials and direct labor costs were added to the four jobs during the month of March:

	Job 86	Job 87	Job 88	Job 89
Direct materials	$3,000	$7,000	$2,100	$1,500
Direct labor	800	6,000	900	500

At the end of March, Jobs 86, 87, and 89 were completed. Only Job 87 was sold. On March 1, the balance in Finished Goods was zero.

Required:

1. Calculate the overhead rate based on direct labor cost. (*Note:* Round to three decimal places.)
2. Prepare a brief job-order cost sheet for the four jobs. Show the balance as of March 1 as well as direct materials and direct labor added in March. Apply overhead to the four jobs for the month of March, and show the ending balances.
3. Calculate the ending balances of Work in Process and Finished Goods as of March 31.
4. Calculate the Cost of Goods Sold for March.

Use the following information for Brief Exercises 4-34 and 4-35:
Sanjay Company manufactures a product in a factory that has two producing departments, Assembly and Painting, and two support departments, S1 and S2. The activity driver for S1 is square footage, and the activity driver for S2 is number of machine hours. The following data pertain to Sanjay:

	Support Departments		Producing Departments	
	S1	S2	Assembly	Painting
Direct costs	$200,000	$140,000	$115,000	$96,000
Normal activity:				
Square footage	—	500	1,875	625
Machine hours	337	—	3,200	12,800

OBJECTIVE 6
Example 4.6

Brief Exercise 4-34 *(Appendix 4B)* Assigning Support Department Costs by Using the Direct Method

Refer to the information for Sanjay Company above.

Required:

1. Calculate the cost assignment ratios to be used under the direct method for Departments S1 and S2. (*Note:* Each support department will have two ratios—one for Assembly and the other for Painting.)
2. Allocate the support department costs to the producing departments by using the direct method.

Brief Exercise 4-35 *(Appendix 4B)* Sequential Method

Refer to the information for Sanjay Company on the previous page. Now assume that Sanjay uses the sequential method to allocate support department costs. S1 is allocated first, then S2.

OBJECTIVE 6

Example 4.7

EXCEL

Required:

1. Calculate the cost assignment ratios to be used under the sequential method for S2, Assembly, and Painting. Carry out your answers to four decimal places.
2. Allocate the overhead costs to the producing departments by using the sequential method.

EXERCISES

Exercise 4-36 Job-Order Costing versus Process Costing

OBJECTIVE 1

a. Hospital services
b. Custom cabinet making
c. Toy manufacturing
d. Soft-drink bottling
e. Airplane manufacturing (e.g., 767s)
f. Personal computer assembly
g. Furniture making (e.g., computer desks sold at discount stores)
h. Custom furniture making
i. Dental services
j. Paper manufacturing
k. Nut and bolt manufacturing
l. Auto repair
m. Architectural services
n. Landscape design services
o. Flashlight manufacturing

Required:

Identify each of these preceding types of businesses as using either job-order or process costing.

Exercise 4-37 Job-Order Costing versus Process Costing

OBJECTIVE 1

a. Auto manufacturing
b. Dental services
c. Auto repair
d. Costume making

Required:

CONCEPTUAL CONNECTION For each of the given types of industries, give an example of a firm that would use job-order costing. Then, give an example of a firm that would use process costing.

OBJECTIVE **2** **Exercise 4-38** Calculating the Predetermined Overhead Rate, Applying Overhead to Production

At the beginning of the year, Debion Company estimated the following:

Overhead	$522,900
Direct labor hours	83,000

Debion uses normal costing and applies overhead on the basis of direct labor hours. For the month of March, direct labor hours were 7,600.

Required:

1. Calculate the predetermined overhead rate for Debion.
2. Calculate the overhead applied to production in March.

OBJECTIVE **2** **Exercise 4-39** Calculating the Predetermined Overhead Rate, Applying Overhead to Production, Reconciling Overhead at the End of the Year, Adjusting Cost of Goods Sold for Under- and Overapplied Overhead

At the beginning of the year, Han Company estimated the following:

Overhead	$582,400
Direct labor hours	80,000

Han uses normal costing and applies overhead on the basis of direct labor hours. For the month of January, direct labor hours were 6,950. By the end of the year, Han showed the following actual amounts:

Overhead	$613,320
Direct labor hours	84,100

Assume that unadjusted Cost of Goods Sold for Han was $927,000.

Required:

1. Calculate the predetermined overhead rate for Han.
2. Calculate the overhead applied to production in January. (*Note:* Round to the nearest dollar.)
3. Calculate the total applied overhead for the year. Was overhead over- or underapplied? By how much?
4. Calculate adjusted Cost of Goods Sold after adjusting for the overhead variance.

OBJECTIVE **2** **Exercise 4-40** Calculating Departmental Overhead Rates and Applying Overhead to Production

At the beginning of the year, Glaser Company estimated the following:

	Assembly Department	Testing Department	Total
Overhead	$338,000	$630,000	$968,000
Direct labor hours	130,000	40,000	170,000
Machine hours	45,000	120,000	165,000

Glaser uses departmental overhead rates. In the assembly department, overhead is applied on the basis of direct labor hours. In the testing department, overhead is applied on the basis of machine hours. Actual data for the month of March are as follows:

	Assembly Department	Testing Department	Total
Overhead	$29,850	$58,000	$87,850
Direct labor hours	11,700	3,450	15,150
Machine hours	4,100	10,900	15,000

Required:

1. Calculate the predetermined overhead rates for the assembly and testing departments.
2. Calculate the overhead applied to production in each department for the month of March.
3. By how much has each department's overhead been overapplied? Underapplied?

Exercise 4-41 Job-Order Costing Variables

OBJECTIVE ▸ 3

On July 1, Job 46 had a beginning balance of $1,235. During July, prime costs added to the job totaled $560. Of that amount, direct materials were three times as much as direct labor. The ending balance of the job was $1,921.

Required:

1. What was overhead applied to the job during July?
2. What was direct materials for Job 46 for July? Direct labor?
3. Assuming that overhead is applied on the basis of direct labor cost, what is the overhead rate for the company? (*Note:* Round your answer to two decimal places.)

Exercise 4-42 Source Documents

OBJECTIVE ▸ 3

For each of the following independent situations, give the source document that would be referred to for the necessary information.

Required:

1. Direct materials costing $460 are requisitioned for use on a job.
2. Greiner's Garage uses a job-order costing system. Overhead is applied to jobs based on direct labor hours. Which source document gives the number of direct labor hours worked on Job 2004-276?
3. Pasilla Investigative Services bills clients on a monthly basis for costs to date. Job 3-48 involved an investigator following the client's business partner for a week by automobile. Mileage is billed at number of miles times $0.75.
4. The foreman on the Jackson job wonders what the actual direct materials cost was for that job.

Exercise 4-43 Applying Overhead to Jobs, Costing Jobs

OBJECTIVE ▸ 4

Jagjit Company designs and builds retaining walls for individual customers. On August 1, there were two jobs in process: Job 93 with a beginning balance of $8,750 and Job 94 with a beginning balance of $7,300. Jagjit applies overhead at the rate of $8 per direct labor hour. Direct labor wages average $18 per hour.

Data on August costs for all jobs are as follows:

	Job 93	Job 94	Job 95	Job 96
Direct materials	$ 950	$4,500	$3,300	$1,300
Direct labor cost	2,160	5,400	2,610	900

During August, Jobs 95 and 96 were started. Job 93 was completed on August 17, and the client was billed at cost plus 40%. All other jobs remained in process.

Required:

1. Calculate the number of direct labor hours that were worked on each job in August.
2. Calculate the overhead applied to each job during the month of August.
3. Prepare job-order cost sheets for each job as of the end of August.
4. Calculate the balance in Work in Process on August 31.
5. What is the price of Job 93?

(*Continued*)

6. **CONCEPTUAL CONNECTION** Partway though the year, Jagjit bought a bulldozer to handle larger jobs. The bulldozer cost $38,000 and is needed for larger commercial jobs. Smaller residential jobs can still be done with the smaller bobcat tractor. How could the bulldozer's cost be applied to only those jobs that need the larger equipment?

OBJECTIVE **4**   **Exercise 4-44** Applying Overhead to Jobs, Costing Jobs

Gorman Company builds internal conveyor equipment to client specifications. On October 1, Job 877 was in process with a cost of $18,640 to date.

During October, Jobs 878, 879, and 880 were started. Data on costs added during October for all jobs are as follows:

	Job 877	**Job 878**	**Job 879**	**Job 880**
Direct materials	$14,460	$6,000	$3,500	$1,800
Direct labor	14,800	8,500	1,750	2,150

Overhead is applied to production at the rate of 80% of direct labor cost. Job 877 was completed on October 28, and the client was billed at cost plus 50%. All other jobs remained in process.

Required:

1. Prepare a brief job-order cost sheet showing the October 1 balances of all four jobs, plus the direct materials and direct labor costs during October. (*Note:* There is no need to calculate applied overhead at this point or to total the costs.)
2. Calculate the overhead applied to each job during October.
3. Calculate the balance in Work in Process on October 31.
4. What is the price of Job 877?

OBJECTIVE **4**   **Exercise 4-45** Balance of Work in Process and Finished Goods, Cost of Goods Sold

Derry Company uses job-order costing. At the end of the month, the following information was gathered:

Job #	Total Cost	Complete?	Sold?
301	$1,600	Yes	No
302	1,240	Yes	Yes
303	780	No	No
304	2,300	Yes	No
305	4,150	Yes	No
306	350	No	No
307	710	Yes	Yes
308	620	No	No
309	1,200	No	No
310	515	No	No

The beginning balance of Finished Goods was $300, consisting of Job 300, which was not sold by the end of the month.

Required:

1. Calculate the balance in Work in Process at the end of the month.
2. Calculate the balance in Finished Goods at the end of the month.
3. Calculate Cost of Goods Sold for the month.

Exercise 4-46 Job-Order Cost Sheets, Balance in Work in Process and Finished Goods

OBJECTIVE ▶ 4

EXCEL

Prull Company, a job-order costing firm, worked on three jobs in July. Data are as follows:

	Job 86	Job 87	Job 88
Balance, July 1	$15,310	$ 4,250	$ 0
Direct materials	$ 4,450	$10,300	$13,150
Direct labor	$16,000	$12,200	$24,000
Machine hours	500	300	1,000

Overhead is applied to jobs at the rate of $10 per machine hour. By July 31, Jobs 86 and 88 were completed. Jobs 82 and 86 were sold. Job 87 remained in process. On July 1, the balance in Finished Goods was $49,000 (consisting of Job 82 for $25,600 and Job 84 for $23,400).

Prull prices its jobs at cost plus 20%. During July, variable marketing expenses were 4% of sales, and fixed marketing expenses were $1,275; administrative expenses were $3,900. (Round all amounts to the nearest dollar.)

Required:

1. Prepare job-order cost sheets for all jobs in process during July, showing all costs through July 31.
2. Calculate the balance in Work in Process on July 31.
3. Calculate the balance in Finished Goods on July 31.
4. Calculate Cost of Goods Sold for July.
5. Calculate operating income for Prull Company for the month of July.

Exercise 4-47 Cost Flows

OBJECTIVE ▶ 4

Consider the following independent jobs. Overhead is applied in Department 1 at the rate of $6 per direct labor hour. Overhead is applied in Department 2 at the rate of $8 per machine hour. Direct labor wages average $10 per hour in each department.

	Job 213	Job 214	Job 217	Job 225
Total sales revenue	$?	$4,375	$5,600	$1,150
Price per unit	$ 12	$?	$ 14	$ 5
Materials used in production	$ 365	$?	$ 488	$ 207
Department 1, direct labor cost	$?	$ 700	$2,000	$ 230
Department 1, machine hours	15	35	50	12
Department 2, direct labor cost	$ 50	$ 100	$?	$ 0
Department 2, machine hours	25	50	?	?
Department 1, overhead applied	$ 90	$?	$1,200	$ 138
Department 2, overhead applied	$?	$ 400	$ 160	$ 0
Total manufacturing cost	$ 855	$3,073	$?	$ 575
Number of units	?	350	400	?
Unit cost	$8.55	$?	$ 9.87	$?

Required:

Fill in the missing data for each job.

Exercise 4-48 Job Cost Flows

OBJECTIVE ▶ 4

Roseler Company uses a normal job-order costing system. The company has two departments through which most jobs pass. Overhead is applied using a plantwide overhead rate of $10 per direct labor hour. During the year, several jobs were completed. Data pertaining to one such job, Job 9-601, follow:

(*Continued*)

Direct materials	$12,000
Direct labor cost:	
Department A (450 hours @ $18)	$ 8,100
Department B (120 hours @ $18)	$ 2,160
Machine hours used:	
Department A	200
Department B	800
Units produced	1,000

Required:

1. Compute the total cost of Job 9-601.
2. Compute the per-unit manufacturing cost for Job 9-601.

> *For Requirements 3 and 4, assume that Roseler uses departmental overhead rates. In Department A, overhead is applied at the rate of $3 per direct labor hour. In Department B, overhead is applied at the rate of $7 per machine hour.*

3. Compute the total cost of Job 9-601.
4. Compute the per-unit manufacturing cost for Job 9-601.

OBJECTIVE 4

Exercise 4-49   Calculation of Work in Process and Cost of Goods Sold with Multiple Jobs

Ensign Landscape Design designs landscape plans and plants the material for clients. On April 1, there were three jobs in process, Jobs 39, 40, and 41. During April, two more jobs were started, Jobs 42 and 43. By April 30, Jobs 40, 41, and 43 were completed and sold. The following data were gathered:

	Job 39	Job 40	Job 41	Job 42	Job 43
Balance, April 1	$540	$3,400	$2,990	—	—
Direct materials	700	560	375	$3,500	$6,900
Direct labor	500	600	490	2,500	3,000

Overhead is applied at the rate of 110% of direct labor cost. Jobs are sold at cost plus 30%. Selling and administrative expenses for April totaled $4,575. (Round all amounts to the nearest dollar.)

Required:

1. Prepare job-order cost sheets for each job as of April 30.
2. Calculate the ending balance in Work in Process (as of April 30) and Cost of Goods Sold for April.
3. Construct an income statement for Ensign Landscape Design for the month of April.

OBJECTIVE 5

Exercise 4-50   *(Appendix 4A)* Journal Entries

Yurman Inc. uses a job-order costing system. During the month of May, the following transactions occurred:

a. Purchased materials on account for $29,670.
b. Requisitioned materials totaling $24,500 for use in production. Of the total, $9,200 was for Job 58, $8,900 for Job 59, and the remainder for Job 60.
c. Incurred direct labor of $32,400, with an average wage of $18 per hour. Job 58 used 800 hours; Job 59, 600 hours; and Job 60, 400 hours.
d. Incurred and paid actual overhead of $17,880 (credit Various Payables).
e. Charged overhead to production at the rate of $4.80 per direct labor hour.

f. Completed and transferred Jobs 58 and 59 to Finished Goods.
g. Sold Job 57 (see beginning balance of Finished Goods) and Job 58 to their respective clients on account for a price of cost plus 40%.

Beginning balances as of May 1 were:

Materials	$ 2,300
Work in Process	0
Finished Goods (Job 57)	25,600

Required:

1. Prepare the journal entries for Transactions a through g.
2. Prepare brief job-order cost sheets for Jobs 58, 59, and 60.
3. Calculate the ending balance of Raw Materials.
4. Calculate the ending balance of Work in Process.
5. Calculate the ending balance of Finished Goods.

Exercise 4-51 *(Appendix 4B)* Direct Method of Support Department Cost Allocation

OBJECTIVE ▶ 6

Stevenson Company is divided into two operating divisions: Battery and Small Motors. The company allocates power and general factory costs to each operating division using the direct method. Power costs are allocated on the basis of the number of machine hours and general factory costs on the basis of square footage. Support department cost allocations using the direct method are based on the following data:

	Support Departments		Operating Divisions	
	Power	**General Factory**	**Battery**	**Small Motors**
Overhead costs	$160,000	$430,000	$163,000	$84,600
Machine hours	2,000	2,000	7,000	1,000
Square footage	1,000	1,500	5,000	15,000
Direct labor hours			18,000	60,000

Required:

1. Calculate the allocation ratios for Power and General Factory. (*Note:* Carry these calculations out to four decimal places.)
2. Allocate the support service costs to the operating divisions. (*Note:* Round all amounts to the nearest dollar.)
3. Assume divisional overhead rates are based on direct labor hours. Calculate the overhead rate for the Battery Division and for the Small Motors Division. (*Note:* Round overhead rates to the nearest cent.)

Exercise 4-52 *(Appendix 4B)* Sequential Method of Support Department Cost Allocation

OBJECTIVE ▶ 6

Refer to **Exercise 4-51** for data. Now assume that Stevenson uses the sequential method to allocate support department costs to the operating divisions. General Factory is allocated first in the sequential method for the company.

Required:

1. Calculate the allocation ratios for Power and General Factory. (*Note:* Carry these calculations out to four decimal places.)
2. Allocate the support service costs to the operating divisions. (*Note:* Round all amounts to the nearest dollar.)
3. Assume divisional overhead rates are based on direct labor hours. Calculate the overhead rate for the Battery Division and for the Small Motors Division. (*Note:* Round overhead rates to the nearest cent.)

PROBLEMS

OBJECTIVE 2 ▶ 4

Problem 4-53 Overhead Application and Job-Order Costing

Heurion Company is a job-order costing firm that uses a plantwide overhead rate based on direct labor hours. Estimated information for the year is as follows:

Overhead	$789,000
Direct labor hours	100,000

Heurion worked on five jobs in July. Data are as follows:

	Job 741	Job 742	Job 743	Job 744	Job 745
Balance, July 1	$29,870	$55,215	$27,880	$ 0	$ 0
Direct materials	$25,500	$39,800	$14,450	$13,600	$ 8,420
Direct labor cost	$61,300	$48,500	$28,700	$24,500	$21,300
Direct labor hours	4,000	3,400	1,980	1,600	1,400

By July 31, Jobs 741 and 743 were completed and sold. The remaining jobs were in process.

Required:

1. Calculate the plantwide overhead rate for Heurion Company. (*Note:* Round to the nearest cent.)
2. Prepare job-order cost sheets for each job showing all costs through July 31. (*Note:* Round all amounts to the nearest dollar.)
3. Calculate the balance in Work in Process on July 31.
4. Calculate Cost of Goods Sold for July.

OBJECTIVE 1 ▶ 3

Problem 4-54 Job Cost, Source Documents

Spade Millhone Detective Agency performs investigative work for a variety of clients. Recently, Alban Insurance Company asked Spade Millhone to investigate a series of suspicious claims for whiplash. In each case, the claimant was driving on a freeway and was suddenly rear-ended by an Alban-insured client. The claimants were all driving old, uninsured automobiles. The Alban clients reported that the claimants suddenly changed lanes in front of them, and the accidents were unavoidable. Alban suspected that these "accidents" were the result of insurance fraud. Basically, the claimants cruised the freeways in virtually worthless cars, attempting to cut in front of expensive late-model cars that would surely be insured. Alban believed that the injuries were faked.

Rex Spade spent 37 hours shadowing the claimants and taking pictures as necessary. His surveillance methods located the office of a doctor used by all claimants. He also took pictures of claimants performing tasks that they had sworn were now impossible to perform due to whiplash injuries. Victoria Millhone spent 48 hours using the Internet to research court records in surrounding states to locate the names of the claimants and their doctors. She found a pattern of similar insurance claims for each of the claimants.

Spade Millhone Detective Agency bills clients for detective time at $120 per hour. Mileage is charged at $0.50 per mile. The agency logged in 510 miles on the Alban job. The film and developing amounted to $120.

Required:

1. Prepare a job-order cost sheet for the Alban job.
2. **CONCEPTUAL CONNECTION** Why is overhead not specified in the charges? How does Spade Millhone charge clients for the use of overhead (e.g., the ongoing costs of their office—supplies, paper for notes and reports, telephone, utilities)?
3. The mileage is tallied from a source document. Design a source document for this use, and make up data for it that would total the 510 miles driven on the Alban job.

Problem 4-55 Calculating Ending Work in Process, Income Statement

OBJECTIVE ▶ 4

Pavlovich Prosthetics Company produces artificial limbs for individuals. Each prosthetic is unique. On January 1, three jobs, identified by the name of the person being fitted with the prosthetic, were in process with the following costs:

	Carter	Pelham	Tillson
Direct materials	$ 210	$ 615	$1,290
Direct labor	440	700	1,260
Applied overhead	374	595	1,071
Total	$1,024	$1,910	$3,621

During the month of January, two more jobs were started, Jasper and Dashell. Materials and labor costs incurred by each job in January are as follows:

	Materials	Direct Labor
Carter	$ 600	$ 300
Pelham	550	200
Tillson	770	240
Jasper	2,310	2,100
Dashell	190	240

Tillson and Jasper's prosthetics were completed and sold by January 31.

Required:

1. If overhead is applied on the basis of direct labor dollars, what is the overhead rate? (*Note:* Round your answer to four decimal places.)
2. Prepare simple job-order cost sheets for each of the five jobs in process during January. (*Note:* Round all amounts to the nearest dollar.)
3. What is the ending balance of Work in Process on January 31? What is the Cost of Goods Sold in January?
4. Suppose that Pavlovich Prosthetics Company prices its jobs at cost plus 30%. In addition, during January, marketing and administrative expenses of $2,635 were incurred. Prepare an income statement for the month of January.

Problem 4-56 Overhead Applied to Jobs, Departmental Overhead Rates

OBJECTIVE ▶ 2

Xania Inc. uses a normal job-order costing system. Currently, a plantwide overhead rate based on machine hours is used. Xania's plant manager has heard that departmental overhead rates can offer significantly better cost assignments than a plantwide rate can offer. Xania has the following data for its two departments for the coming year:

	Department A	Department B
Overhead costs (expected)	$75,000	$33,000
Normal activity (machine hours)	10,000	8,000

Required:

1. Compute a predetermined overhead rate for the plant as a whole based on machine hours.
2. Compute predetermined overhead rates for each department using machine hours. (*Note:* Carry your calculations out to three decimal places.)
3. **CONCEPTUAL CONNECTION** Job 73 used 20 machine hours from Department A and 50 machine hours from Department B. Job 74 used 50 machine hours from Department A and 20 machine hours from Department B. Compute the overhead cost assigned to each job using the plantwide rate computed in Requirement 1. Repeat the computation using the departmental rates found in Requirement 2. Which of the two approaches gives the fairer assignment? Why? (*Note:* Round cost to the nearest cent.)

(Continued)

4. **CONCEPTUAL CONNECTION** Repeat Requirement 3, assuming the expected overhead cost for Department B is $60,000 (not $33,000). For this company, would you recommend departmental rates over a plantwide rate? (*Note:* Round overhead rates to the nearest cent.)

OBJECTIVE **2**

EXCEL

Problem 4-57 Overhead Rates, Unit Costs

Folsom Company manufactures specialty tools to customer order. There are three producing departments. Departmental information on budgeted overhead and various activity measures for the coming year is as follows:

	Welding	Assembly	Finishing
Estimated overhead	$220,000	$ 62,000	$150,000
Direct labor hours	4,500	10,000	6,000
Direct labor cost	$ 90,000	$150,000	$120,000
Machine hours	5,000	1,000	2,000

Currently, overhead is applied on the basis of machine hours using a plantwide rate. However, Janine, the controller, has been wondering whether it might be worthwhile to use departmental overhead rates. She has analyzed the overhead costs and drivers for the various departments and decided that Welding and Finishing should base their overhead rates on machine hours and that Assembly should base its overhead rate on direct labor hours.

Janine has been asked to prepare bids for two jobs with the following information:

	Job 1	Job 2
Direct materials	$6,725	$9,340
Direct labor cost	$1,800	$3,100
Direct labor hours:		
Welding	20	10
Assembly	60	20
Finishing	20	70
Number of machine hours:		
Welding	50	50
Assembly	60	25
Finishing	90	125

The typical bid price includes a 35% markup over full manufacturing cost. Round all overhead rates to the nearest cent. Round all bid prices to the nearest dollar.

Required:

1. Calculate a plantwide rate for Folsom Company based on machine hours. What is the bid price of each job using this rate?
2. Calculate departmental overhead rates for the producing departments. What is the bid price of each job using these rates?

OBJECTIVE **2** **4**

Problem 4-58 Calculate Job Cost and Use It to Calculate Price

Suppose that back in the 1970s, Steve was asked to build speakers for two friends. The first friend, Jan, needed a speaker for her band. The second friend, Ed, needed a speaker built into the back of his hatchback automobile. Steve figured the following costs for each:

	Jan's Job	Ed's Job
Materials	$50	$75
Labor hours	10	20

Steve knew that Jan's job would be easier, since he had experience in building the type of speaker she needed. Her job would not require any special equipment or specialized fitting. Ed's job, on the other hand, required specialized design and precise fitting. Steve thought he might need to build a mock-up of the speaker first, to fit it into the space. In addition, he might have to add to his tool collection to complete the job. Normally, Steve figured a wage rate of $6 per hour and charged 20% of labor and materials as an overhead rate.

Required:

1. Prepare job-order cost sheets for the two jobs, showing total cost.
2. **CONCEPTUAL CONNECTION** Which cost do you think is more likely to be accurate? How might Steve build in some of the uncertainty of Ed's job into a budgeted cost?

Problem 4-59 *(Appendix 4A)* Unit Cost, Ending Work in Process, Journal Entries

OBJECTIVE 4 5

During August, Leming Inc. worked on two jobs. Data relating to these two jobs follow:

	Job 64	Job 65
Units in each order	50	80
Units sold	50	—
Materials requisitioned	$3,560	$ 785
Direct labor hours	410	583
Direct labor cost	$6,720	$9,328

Overhead is assigned on the basis of direct labor hours at a rate of $11. During August, Job 64 was completed and transferred to Finished Goods. Job 65 was the only unfinished job at the end of the month.

Required:

1. Calculate the per-unit cost of Job 64.
2. Compute the ending balance in the work-in-process account.
3. Prepare the journal entries reflecting the completion and sale on account of Job 64. The selling price is 175% of cost. (*Note:* Round all journal entry amounts to the nearest dollar.)

Problem 4-60 *(Appendix 4A)* Journal Entries, Job Costs

OBJECTIVE 4 5

The following transactions occurred during the month of April for Nelson Company:

a. Purchased materials costing $4,610 on account.
b. Requisitioned materials totaling $4,800 for use in production, $3,170 for Job 518 and the remainder for Job 519.
c. Recorded 65 hours of direct labor on Job 518 and 90 hours on Job 519 for the month. Direct laborers are paid at the rate of $14 per hour.
d. Applied overhead using a plantwide rate of $6.20 per direct labor hour.
e. Incurred and paid in cash actual overhead for the month of $973.
f. Completed and transferred Job 518 to Finished Goods.
g. Sold on account Job 517, which had been completed and transferred to Finished Goods in March, for cost ($2,770) plus 25%.

Required:

1. Prepare journal entries for Transactions a through e.
2. Prepare job-order cost sheets for Jobs 518 and 519. Prepare journal entries for Transactions f and g. (*Note:* Round to the nearest dollar.)
3. Prepare a schedule of cost of goods manufactured for April. Assume that the beginning balance in the raw materials account was $1,025 and that the beginning balance in the work-in-process account was zero.

Problem 4-61 *(Appendix 4A)* Predetermined Overhead Rates, Variances, Cost Flows

OBJECTIVE 2 4 5

Barrymore Costume Company, located in New York City, sews costumes for plays and musicals. Barrymore considers itself primarily a service firm, as it never produces costumes without

(Continued)

a preexisting order and only purchases materials to the specifications of the particular job. Any finished goods ending inventory is temporary and is zeroed out as soon as the show producer pays for the order. Overhead is applied on the basis of direct labor cost. During the first quarter of the year, the following activity took place in each of the accounts listed:

Work in Process			
Bal.	17,000	Complete	245,000
DL	80,000		
OH	140,000		
DM	40,000		
Bal.	32,000		

Finished Goods			
Bal.	40,000	Sold	210,000
Complete	245,000		
Bal.	75,000		

Overhead			
	138,500		140,000
		Bal.	1,500

Cost of Goods Sold	
210,000	

Job 32 was the only job in process at the end of the first quarter. A total of 1,000 direct labor hours at $10 per hour were charged to Job 32.

Required:

1. Assuming that overhead is applied on the basis of direct labor cost, what was the overhead rate used during the first quarter of the year?
2. What was the applied overhead for the first quarter? The actual overhead? The under- or overapplied overhead?
3. What was the cost of goods manufactured for the quarter?
4. Assume that the overhead variance is closed to the cost of goods sold account. Prepare the journal entry to close out the overhead control account. What is the adjusted balance in Cost of Goods Sold?
5. For Job 32, identify the costs incurred for direct materials, direct labor, and overhead.

OBJECTIVE ▶ 2 ▶ 4 ▶ 5

EXCEL

Problem 4-62 *(Appendix 4A)* **Overhead Application, Journal Entries, Job Cost**

At the beginning of the year, Smith Company budgeted overhead of $129,600 as well as 13,500 direct labor hours. During the year, Job K456 was completed with the following information: direct materials cost, $2,750; direct labor cost, $5,355. The average wage for Smith Company employees is $17 per hour.

By the end of the year, 18,100 direct labor hours had actually been worked, and Smith incurred the following actual overhead costs for the year:

Equipment lease	$ 6,800
Depreciation on building	19,340
Indirect labor	90,400
Utilities	14,560
Other overhead	41,400

Required:

1. Calculate the overhead rate for the year.
2. Calculate the total cost of Job K456.
3. Prepare the journal entries to record actual overhead and to apply overhead to production for the year.
4. Is overhead overapplied or underapplied? By how much?
5. Assuming that the normal cost of goods sold for the year is $635,600, what is the adjusted cost of goods sold?

Problem 4-63 *(Appendix 4A)* Journal Entries, T-Accounts

OBJECTIVE ◀ 1 ◀ 4 ◀ 5

Lowder Inc. builds custom conveyor systems for warehouses and distribution centers. During the month of July, the following occurred:

a. Purchased materials on account for $42,630.
b. Requisitioned materials totaling $27,000 for use in production: $12,500 for Job 703 and the remainder for Job 704.
c. Recorded direct labor payroll for the month of $26,320 with an average wage of $14 per hour. Job 703 required 780 direct labor hours; Job 704 required 1,100 direct labor hours.
d. Incurred and paid actual overhead of $19,950.
e. Charged overhead to production at the rate of $10 per direct labor hour.
f. Completed Job 703 and transferred it to Finished Goods.
g. Kept Job 704, which was started during July, in process at the end of the month.
h. Sold Job 700, which had been completed in May, on account for cost plus 30%.
   Beginning balances as of July 1 were:

Raw Materials	$ 6,070
Work in Process (for Job 703)	10,000
Finished Goods (for Job 700)	6,240

Required:

1. Prepare the journal entries for transactions a through e.
2. Prepare simple job-order cost sheets for Jobs 703 and 704.
3. Prepare the journal entries for transactions f and h.
4. Calculate the ending balances of the following: (a) Raw Materials, (b) Work in Process, and (c) Finished Goods.

Problem 4-64 *(Appendix 4B)* Support Department Cost Allocation

OBJECTIVE ◀ 6

MedServices Inc. is divided into two operating departments: Laboratory and Tissue Pathology. The company allocates delivery and accounting costs to each operating department. Delivery costs include the costs of a fleet of vans and drivers that drive throughout the state each day to clinics and doctors' offices to pick up samples and deliver them to the centrally located laboratory and tissue pathology offices. Delivery costs are allocated on the basis of number of samples. Accounting costs are allocated on the basis of the number of transactions processed. No effort is made to separate fixed and variable costs; however, only budgeted costs are allocated. Allocations for the coming year are based on the following data:

	Support Departments		Operating Departments	
	Delivery	Accounting	Laboratory	Pathology
Overhead costs	$240,000	$270,000	$345,000	$456,000
Number of samples	—	—	70,200	46,800
Transactions processed	2,000	—	24,700	13,300

Required:

1. Assign the support department costs by using the direct method. (*Note:* Round allocation ratios to four decimal places.)
2. Assign the support department costs by using the sequential method, allocating accounting costs first. (*Note:* Round allocation ratios to four decimal places.)

Problem 4-65 *(Appendix 4B)* Support Department Cost Allocation: Comparison of Methods of Allocation

OBJECTIVE ◀ 6

Bender Automotive Works Inc. manufactures a variety of front-end assemblies for automobiles. A front-end assembly is the unified front of an automobile that includes the headlamps, fender,

EXCEL

(Continued)

and surrounding metal/plastic. Bender has two producing departments: Drilling and Assembly. Usually, the front-end assemblies are ordered in batches of 100.

Two support departments provide support for Bender's producing departments: Maintenance and Power. Budgeted data for the coming quarter follow. The company does not separate fixed and variable costs.

| | Support Departments | | Producing Departments | |
	Maintenance	Power	Drilling	Assembly
Overhead costs	$320,000	$400,000	$163,000	$ 90,000
Machine hours	—	22,500	30,000	7,500
Kilowatt-hours	40,000	—	36,000	324,000
Direct labor hours	—	—	5,000	40,000

The predetermined overhead rate for Drilling is computed on the basis of machine hours. Direct labor hours are used for Assembly.

Recently, a truck manufacturer requested a bid on a 3-year contract that would supply front-end assemblies to a nearby factory. The prime costs for a batch of 100 front-end assemblies are $1,817. It takes two machine hours to produce a batch in the drilling department and 50 direct labor hours to assemble the 100 front-end assemblies in the assembly department.

Bender's policy is to bid full manufacturing cost, plus 15%. (*Note:* Round allocation ratios to four decimal places, allocated support department cost to the nearest dollar, and the job cost components to the nearest cent.)

Required:

1. Prepare bids for Bender by using each of the following allocation methods: (a) direct method and (b) sequential method, allocating power costs first. (*Note:* Round allocation ratios to four decimal places, allocated support department cost to the nearest dollar, and the job cost components to the nearest cent.)
2. **CONCEPTUAL CONNECTION** Which method most accurately reflects the cost of producing the front-end assemblies? Why?

CASES

OBJECTIVE **1 ▶ 2**

Case 4-66 Overhead Assignment: Actual and Normal Activity Compared

Reynolds Printing Company specializes in wedding announcements. Reynolds uses an actual job-order costing system. An actual overhead rate is calculated at the end of each month using actual direct labor hours and overhead for the month. Once the actual cost of a job is determined, the customer is billed at actual cost plus 50%.

During April, Mrs. Lucky, a good friend of owner Jane Reynolds, ordered three sets of wedding announcements to be delivered May 10, June 10, and July 10, respectively. Reynolds scheduled production for each order on May 7, June 7, and July 7, respectively. The orders were assigned job numbers 115, 116, and 117, respectively.

Reynolds assured Mrs. Lucky that she would attend each of her daughters' weddings. Out of sympathy and friendship, she also offered a lower price. Instead of cost plus 50%, she gave her a special price of cost plus 25%. Additionally, she agreed to wait until the final wedding to bill for the three jobs.

On August 15, Reynolds asked her accountant to bring her the completed job-order cost sheets for Jobs 115, 116, and 117. She also gave instructions to lower the price as had been agreed upon. The cost sheets revealed the following information:

	Job 115	Job 116	Job 117
Cost of direct materials	$250.00	$250.00	$250.00
Cost of direct labor (5 hours)	25.00	25.00	25.00
Cost of overhead	200.00	400.00	400.00
Total cost	$475.00	$675.00	$675.00
Total price	$593.75	$843.75	$843.75
Number of announcements	500	500	500

Reynolds could not understand why the overhead costs assigned to Jobs 116 and 117 were so much higher than those for Job 115. She asked for an overhead cost summary sheet for the months of May, June, and July, which showed that actual overhead costs were $20,000 each month. She also discovered that direct labor hours worked on all jobs were 500 hours in May and 250 hours each in June and July.

Required:

1. How do you think Mrs. Lucky will feel when she receives the bill for the three sets of wedding announcements?
2. Explain how the overhead costs were assigned to each job.
3. Assume that Reynolds's average activity is 500 hours per month and that the company usually experiences overhead costs of $240,000 each year. Can you recommend a better way to assign overhead costs to jobs? Recompute the cost of each job and its price, given your method of overhead cost assignment. Which method do you think is best? Why?

Case 4-67 Assigning Overhead to Jobs—Ethical Issues

OBJECTIVE ▶ 2 ◀ 5

Tonya Martin, CMA and controller of the Parts Division of Gunderson Inc., was meeting with Doug Adams, manager of the division. The topic of discussion was the assignment of overhead costs to jobs and their impact on the division's pricing decisions. Their conversation was as follows:

Tonya: Doug, as you know, about 25% of our business is based on government contracts, with the other 75% based on jobs from private sources won through bidding. During the last several years, our private business has declined. We have been losing more bids than usual. After some careful investigation, I have concluded that we are overpricing some jobs because of improper assignment of overhead costs. Some jobs are also being underpriced. Unfortunately, the jobs being overpriced are coming from our higher-volume, labor-intensive products, so we are losing business.

Doug: I think I understand. Jobs associated with our high-volume products are being assigned more overhead than they should be receiving. Then when we add our standard 40% markup, we end up with a higher price than our competitors, who assign costs more accurately.

Tonya: Exactly. We have two producing departments, one labor-intensive and the other machine-intensive. The labor-intensive department generates much less overhead than the machine-intensive department. Furthermore, virtually all of our high-volume jobs are labor-intensive. We have been using a plantwide rate based on direct labor hours to assign overhead to all jobs. As a result, the high-volume, labor-intensive jobs receive a greater share of the machine-intensive department's overhead than they deserve. This problem can be greatly alleviated by switching to departmental overhead rates. For example, an average high-volume job would be assigned $100,000 of overhead using a plantwide rate and only $70,000 using departmental rates. The change would lower our bidding price on high-volume jobs by an average of $42,000 per job. By increasing the accuracy of our product costing, we can make better pricing decisions and win back much of our private-sector business.

Doug: Sounds good. When can you implement the change in overhead rates?

Tonya: It won't take long. I can have the new system working within four to six weeks—certainly by the start of the new fiscal year.

(Continued)

Doug: Hold it. I just thought of a possible complication. As I recall, most of our government contract work is done in the labor-intensive department. This new overhead assignment scheme will push down the cost on the government jobs, and we will lose revenues. They pay us full cost plus our standard markup. This business is not threatened by our current costing procedures, but we can't switch our rates for only the private business. Government auditors would question the lack of consistency in our costing procedures.

Tonya: You do have a point. I thought of this issue also. According to my estimates, we will gain more revenues from the private sector than we will lose from our government contracts. Besides, the costs of our government jobs are distorted. In effect, we are overcharging the government.

Doug: They don't know that and never would unless we switch our overhead assignment procedures. I think I have the solution. Officially, let's keep our plantwide overhead rate. All of the official records will reflect this overhead costing approach for both our private and government business. Unofficially, I want you to develop a separate set of books that can be used to generate the information we need to prepare competitive bids for our private-sector business.

Required:

1. Do you believe that the solution proposed by Doug is ethical? Explain.
2. Suppose that Tonya decides that Doug's solution is not right and objects strongly. Further suppose that, despite Tonya's objections, Doug insists strongly on implementing the action. What should Tonya do?

5

Activity-Based Costing and Management

After studying Chapter 5, you should be able to:

1 ▶ Explain why functional (or volume)-based costing approaches may produce distorted costs.

2 ▶ Explain how an activity-based costing system works for product costing.

3 ▶ Describe activity-based customer costing and activity-based supplier costing.

4 ▶ Explain how activity-based management can be used for cost reduction.

Madlen/Shutterstock.com

EXPERIENCE MANAGERIAL DECISIONS

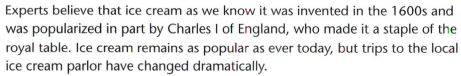

with Cold Stone Creamery

Experts believe that ice cream as we know it was invented in the 1600s and was popularized in part by Charles I of England, who made it a staple of the royal table. Ice cream remains as popular as ever today, but trips to the local ice cream parlor have changed dramatically.

Cold Stone Creamery, founded in 1988 in Tempe, Arizona, has helped to lead this change with its innovative business model focused on making the ice cream trip an entertainment experience for the entire family. Cold Stone operates nearly 1,500 stores worldwide. Cold Stone executives must understand and control the company's complex cost structure in order to profitably manage its ice cream empire. For example, its most popular product line—ice cream with "mix in" ingredients—boasts 16 basic ice cream flavors with 30 different ingredients and three sizes, which represent thousands of possible ice cream product options! These options are great for customers with varied tastes, but are challenging for Cold Stone to manage, given the different types of activities associated with different types of product orders. Therefore, Cold Stone adopted activity-based costing (ABC) to identify the activity drivers associated with each type of ice cream order and to estimate the costs of these activities.

Two important drivers of costs for Cold Stone include ingredients and time, both of which vary significantly across different ice cream product orders. With the insights gained from its ABC analysis, Cold Stone understands the cost of various orders' preparation time, which is measured in seconds. In addition to labor, Cold Stone's ABC system considers the costs associated with training, uniforms, and employee benefits when estimating the cost of each second required in making each product. When combined with other costs, the ABC analysis provides an estimate of profit margin by product type. If a particular product is not making its expected margin, Cold Stone managers know to look at the activities involved in creating the product and to fine-tune that activity. This understanding of Cold Stone's complex cost structure has provided the company with a valuable competitive advantage to become one of the most profitable and fastest-growing franchises in America.

> "These options are great for customers with varied tastes, but are challenging for Cold Stone to manage, given the different types of activities associated with different types of product orders. Therefore, Cold Stone adopted activity-based costing (ABC) to identify the activity drivers associated with each type of ice cream order and to estimate the costs of these activities."

OBJECTIVE

Explain why functional (or volume)-based costing approaches may produce distorted costs.

LIMITATIONS OF FUNCTIONAL-BASED COST ACCOUNTING SYSTEMS

Plantwide and departmental rates based on direct labor hours, machine hours, or other volume-based measures have been used for decades to assign overhead costs to products and continue to be used successfully by many organizations. However, for many settings, this approach to costing is equivalent to an averaging approach and may produce distorted, or inaccurate, costs. For example, assume two friends, Lisa and Jessie, go to **Cold Stone Creamery** for dessert. Lisa orders a small chocolate ice cream in a plastic cup with no mix-ins, costing $3.00, and Jessie orders a medium strawberry banana rendezvous in a waffle dish (which has four mix-ins: graham cracker pie crust, white chocolate chips, strawberries, and bananas), costing $10.00. If the total bill is split evenly between the two, each individual would pay $6.50, which doesn't accurately represent the actual cost of each dessert. Lisa's dessert is overstated by $3.50, and Jessie's is understated by $3.50. If it is important to know the cost of each dessert, the averaging approach is not suitable.

In the same way, plantwide and departmental rates can produce average costs that severely understate or overstate individual product costs. Thus, **Cold Stone Creamery** would be very interested in knowing the cost of its numerous products and likely would not be satisfied with an averaging approach. Without accurate costing, Cold Stone would not be able to properly price its various products. Product cost distortions can be damaging, particularly for those firms whose business environment is characterized by the following:

- intense or increasing competitive pressures (often on a worldwide level)
- small profit margins
- continuous improvement
- total quality management
- total customer satisfaction
- sophisticated technology

Firms operating in these types of business environments in particular need accurate cost information in order to make effective decisions.

In order for accurate cost information to be produced, it is important that the firm's cost system accurately reflect the firm's underlying business, or economic, reality. Thus, it is important that the managerial accountant continually ask the question, "How well does the cost system's *representation* of my business match the economic *reality* of my business?" If the answer is "not very well," then the cost system needs to be changed. Therefore, in much the same way that financial statements must be transparent for external users, the cost system must be transparent in its assignment of costs for internal users.

The need for more accurate product costs has forced many companies to take a serious look at their costing procedures. Two major factors impair the ability of unit-based plantwide and departmental rates to assign overhead costs accurately:

- The proportion of nonunit-related overhead costs to total overhead costs is large.
- The degree of product diversity is great.

Nonunit-Related Overhead Costs

The use of either plantwide rates or departmental rates assumes that a product's consumption of overhead resources is related strictly to the units produced. For **unit-level activities**—activities that are performed each time a unit is produced—this assumption makes sense. Traditional, volume-based cost systems label the costs associated with these activities as variable in nature, because they increase or decrease in direct proportion to increases or decreases in the levels of these unit-level activities. All other costs (i.e., ones that are not unit-level) are considered fixed by volume-based cost systems.

But what if there are *nonunit-level activities*—activities that are not performed each time a unit of product is produced? The costs associated with these nonunit-level activities are unlikely to vary (i.e., increase or decrease) with units produced. These costs vary with other factor(s), besides units, and identifying such factor(s) is helpful in predicting and managing these costs. Proponents of activity-based costing (ABC) refer to the ABC cost hierarchy that categorizes costs either as *unit-level* (i.e., vary with output volume), *batch-level* (i.e., vary with the number of groups or batches that are run), *product-sustaining* (i.e., vary with the diversity of the product or service line), or *facility-sustaining* (i.e., do not vary with any factor but are necessary in operating the plant).[1] Exhibit 5.1 shows the activity-based costing hierarchy.

Type of Cost	Description of Cost Driver	Example
Unit-level	Varies with output volume (e.g., units); traditional variable costs	Cost of indirect materials for labeling each bottle of **Victoria's Secret** perfume
Batch-level	Varies with the number of batches produced	Cost of setting up laser engraving equipment for each batch of **Epilog** key chains
Product-sustaining	Varies with the number of product lines	Cost of inventory handling and warranty servicing of different brands carried by **Best Buy** electronics store
Facility-sustaining	Necessary to operate the plant facility but does not vary with units, batches, or product lines	Cost of **General Motors** plant manager salary

Exhibit 5.1

ABC Hierarchy

Nonunit-Level Activity Drivers Setting up equipment is one example of a nonunit-level activity because, often, the same equipment is used to produce different products. Setting up equipment means preparing it for the particular type of product being made. For example, a vat may be used to dye t-shirts. After completing a batch of 1,000 red t-shirts, the vat must be carefully cleaned before a batch of 3,000 green t-shirts is produced. Thus, setup costs are incurred each time a batch of products is produced. A batch may consist of 1,000 or 3,000 units, and the cost of setup is the same. Yet as more setups are done, setup costs increase. The number of setups (a batch-level cost), not the number of units produced (a unit-level cost), is a much better measure of the consumption of the setup activity.

Another example of a nonunit-level activity is reengineering products. At times, based on customer feedback, firms face the necessity of redesigning their products. This product reengineering activity is authorized by a document called an *engineering work order*. For example, **Multibras S.A. Electrodomesticos**, a Brazilian appliance manufacturer (and subsidiary of **Whirlpool**), may issue engineering work orders to correct design flaws of its refrigerators, freezers, and washers. Product reengineering costs may depend on the number of different engineering work orders (a product-sustaining cost) rather than the units produced of any given product.

Similarly, **JetBlue**'s decision to add a second type of jet, the Embraer 190, to its existing fleet of Airbus A320s, caused it to incur significant additional product-sustaining costs that it would not have incurred had it stayed with only one type of plane. These additional product-sustaining costs included the costs for doubling the spare parts inventory, maintenance programs, and separate pilot-training tracks.[2]

---

1 R. Cooper, "Cost Classification in Unit-Based and Activity-Based Manufacturing Cost Systems," *Journal of Cost Management* for the Manufacturing Industry (Fall 1990): 4–14.

2 S. Carey, "Balancing Act: Amid JetBlue's Rapid Ascent, CEO Adopts Big Rivals' Traits," *The Wall Street Journal* (August 25, 2005).

Therefore, **nonunit-level activity drivers** (i.e., batch, product-sustaining, and facility-sustaining) are factors that measure the consumption of nonunit-level activities by products and other cost objects, whereas **unit-level activity drivers** measure the consumption of unit-level activities. **Activity drivers**, then, are factors that measure the consumption of activities by products and other cost objects and can be classified as either *unit-level* or *nonunit-level*.

Using only unit-based activity drivers to assign nonunit-related overhead costs can create distorted product costs. The severity of this distortion depends on what proportion of total overhead costs these nonunit-based costs represent. For many companies, this percentage can be significant, so care should be exercised in assigning nonunit-based overhead costs. If nonunit-based overhead costs are only a small percentage of total overhead costs, then the distortion of product costs will be quite small. In such a case, using unit-based activity drivers to assign overhead costs is acceptable.

Product Diversity

The presence of significant nonunit overhead costs is a necessary but not sufficient condition for plantwide and departmental rate failure (i.e., distorted costs). For example, if products consume the nonunit-level overhead activities in the same proportion as the unit-level overhead activities, then no product-costing distortion will occur (with the use of traditional overhead assignment methods). The presence of product diversity is also necessary for product cost distortion to occur. **Product diversity** means that products consume overhead activities in systematically different proportions. This may occur for several reasons, including differences in:

- product size
- product complexity
- setup time
- size of batches

Illustrating the Failure of Unit-Based Overhead Rates

To illustrate how traditional unit-based overhead rates can distort product costs, refer to the data for Rio Novo's Porto Behlo plant in Exhibit 5.2 (assume that the measures are expected and actual outcomes). The Porto Behlo plant produces two models of washers: a deluxe and a regular model. Because the quantity of regular models produced is 10 times greater than that of the deluxe, the regular model is a high-volume product and the deluxe model is a low-volume product. The models are produced in batches.

Remember that prime costs represent direct materials and direct labor. Given that these costs are direct in nature, they can be traced to each individual unit produced. It is the indirect, or overhead, costs that typically are treated differently by different types of cost systems. Usually, activity-based cost systems generate more accurate cost data than unit-based cost systems because of their more appropriate treatment of overhead costs. For simplicity, only four types of overhead activities, performed by four distinct support departments, are assumed:

- setting up the equipment for each batch (different configurations are needed for the electronic components associated with each model)
- moving a batch
- machining
- assembly (performed after each department's operations)

Problems with Costing Accuracy   The activity usage data in Exhibit 5.2 reveal some serious problems with either plantwide or departmental rates for assigning overhead costs. The main problem with either procedure is the assumption that unit-level drivers such as machine hours or direct labor hours drive or cause all overhead costs.

Here's How It's Used: IN YOUR LIFE

Carsen, Kambry, and Joseph had each just won the individual championship in their conference's wrestling tournament. Carsen wrestled in the heavyweight class (183 to 285 pounds), Kambry in the 105-pound class for women, and Joseph in the 149-pound class. The three were friends from high school and agreed to meet for lunch at a well-known pizzeria. Upon arriving, they each ordered a salad. Kambry ordered a small salad ($2.00), Joseph ordered a medium salad ($3.00), and Carsen ordered a large salad ($4.00). For drinks, Carsen ordered a fruit smoothie ($3.50) and a glass of water ($0.00), Kambry ordered only water to drink ($0.00), and Joseph ordered a soft drink ($1.50). They then ordered a large supreme pizza ($18.00) and agreed to share the cost of the pizza. The pizza came with 12 slices. Carsen ate eight slices of the pizza, Joseph ate three slices, and Kambry ate one slice.

When it came time to pay for the lunch, each agreed to pay for their respective salads and drinks. Kambry then proposed splitting the cost of the pizza equally among the three (thus, each would pay $6.00 for the shared pizza). Under this proposal, the cost of lunch for each would be calculated as follows: $13.50 ($4.00 + $3.50 + $6.00) for Carsen, $10.50 ($3.00 + $1.50 + $6.00) for Joseph, and $8.00 ($2.00 + $6.00) for Kambry.

Joseph considered this proposal and then offered an alternative to Kambry's average costing approach. He proposed sharing the cost of the pizza in proportion to the cost of the salads as the salad choices reflected the differences in their appetites. Under this approach, Carsen would pay $8.00 for his pizza [(4/9) × $18], increasing his lunch cost to $15.50; Joseph would pay $6.00, leaving his lunch cost unchanged; and Kambry would pay $4.00, decreasing her lunch cost to $6.00.

Carsen considered both offers but expressed a different view. "Listen," he said, "I ate the lion's share of the pizza and therefore should pay the most." "I suggest that we pay in proportion to what we ate. There are 12 slices of pizza and that means each slice costs about $1.50. So I'll pay $12.00 for my share of the pizza, Kambry you will pay $1.50, and Joseph you will pay $4.50." Under the second proposal, the cost of the lunch for each would be $19.50 (Carsen), $9.00 (Joseph), and $3.50 (Kambry).

Joseph, a business major, learned several lessons about costing from this experience. First, he noted that the cost object is the lunch of each person. Second, some of the costs are exclusive to each person (the salads and drinks) and therefore are directly traceable and posed no controversy or problem. Third, the pizza cost (like overhead costs) is a shared cost and was the source of concern. He realized that shared costs are often allocated to units (e.g., number of lunches) based on average consumption and, thus, may not be related to the unit's consumption of the shared resource (like Kambry's proposal) or that they can be allocated using a measure that is correlated with consumption of the shared resource like the size of the salads. He concluded that Kambry's proposal would work well if they all ate about the same amount of pizza but that physical size diversity precluded this possibility. His proposal to use salad size (as measured by its cost) considered size diversity to some extent but failed to consider individual complexities (i.e., product complexity) such as Carsen's love of pizza and the need that he and Kambry had to monitor calories in order to maintain their wrestling weight classifications. Thus, Carsen's proposal to measure consumption by slices of pizza made more sense as it reflected both size diversity and product complexity and, thus, represented a more accurate and fair way of assigning this cost to each person.

CONCEPT CLIP

Exhibit 5.2   Product-Costing Data for Rio Novo's Porto Behlo Plant

	Activity Usage Measures			Activity Cost Data (Overhead Activities)	
	Deluxe	Regular	Total	Activity	Activity Cost
Units produced	10	100	110	Setting up equipment	$1,000
Prime costs	$800	$8,000	$8,800	Moving goods	1,000
Direct labor hours	20	80	100	Machining	1,500
Machine hours	10	40	50	Assembly	500
Setup hours	3	1	4	Total	$4,000
Number of moves	6	4	10		

From Exhibit 5.2, it can be seen that regular models, the high-volume product, use four times as many direct labor hours as deluxe models, the low-volume product (80 hours vs. 20 hours). Thus, if a plantwide rate is used, the regular models will be assigned four times more overhead cost than the deluxe models. But is this reasonable? Do unit-based drivers explain the consumption of all overhead activities? In particular, is it reasonable to assume that each product's consumption of overhead increases in direct proportion to the direct labor hours used? Now consider the four overhead activities to see if the unit-level drivers accurately reflect the demands of regular and deluxe model production.

Examination of the data in Exhibit 5.2 suggests that a significant portion of overhead costs is not driven or caused by direct labor hours. Each product's demands for setup and material-moving activities are more logically related to the setup hours and the number of moves, respectively. These nonunit activities represent 50% ($2,000/$4,000) of the total overhead costs—a significant percentage. Notice that the low-volume product, deluxe models, uses three times more setup hours than the regular models (3/1) and one and a half as many moves (6/4). However, using a plantwide rate based on direct labor hours, a unit-based activity driver assigns four times more setup and material-moving costs to the regular models than to the deluxe. Thus, product diversity exists, and we should expect product cost distortion because the quantity of unit-based overhead that each product consumes does not vary in direct proportion to the quantity consumed of nonunit-based overhead.

Here's **Why It's important**

Regardless of the nature of the product diversity, product cost will be distorted whenever the quantity of unit-based overhead that a product consumes does not vary in direct proportion to the quantity consumed of nonunit-based overhead. Logically, the cost of shared resources should be assigned in proportion to the amount of the resources consumed. Since activities represent bundles of resources consumed by products, it is reasonable to assign activity costs in proportion to the amount of activity consumed. Activity drivers measure activity output and thus can be used as measures of activity consumption. The proportion of each activity consumed by a product is defined as the **consumption ratio** and is calculated as:

$$\text{Consumption Ratio} = \frac{\text{Amount of Activity Driver per Product}}{\text{Total Driver Quantity}}$$

Example 5.1 illustrates how to calculate the consumption ratios for the two products.

The consumption ratios in Example 5.1 suggest that a plantwide rate based on direct labor hours will overcost the regular models and undercost the deluxe models.

EXAMPLE 5.1

How to Calculate Consumption Ratios

Refer to the activity usage information for Rio Novo's Porto Behlo plant in Exhibit 5.2 (p. 219).

Required:
Calculate the consumption ratios for each product.

Solution:
Step 1: Identify the activity driver for each activity.

Step 2: Divide the amount of driver used for each product by the total driver quantity.

EXAMPLE 5.1

(Continued)

	Consumption Ratios		
Overhead Activity	Deluxe Model	Regular Model	Activity Driver
Setting up equipment	0.75[a]	0.25[a]	Setup hours
Moving goods	0.60[b]	0.40[b]	Number of moves
Machining	0.20[c]	0.80[c]	Machine hours
Assembly	0.20[d]	0.80[d]	Direct labor hours

[a]3/4 (deluxe) and 1/4 (regular).
[b]6/10 (deluxe) and 4/10 (regular).
[c]10/50 (deluxe) and 40/50 (regular).
[d]20/100 (deluxe) and 80/100 (regular).

Solving the Problem of Cost Distortion This cost distortion can be solved using activity rates. Instead of assigning the overhead costs using a single, plantwide rate, a rate for each overhead activity can be calculated and used to assign overhead costs. An activity rate is the means by which activity costs are assigned to products. A rate for each activity is calculated by dividing the activity cost by an activity driver. A cause-and-effect relationship is the basis for choosing the activity driver used in the rate calculation.

Example 5.2 shows how to calculate activity rates.

Here's **Why It's important**

EXAMPLE 5.2

How to Calculate Activity Rates

Rio Novo's Porto Behlo plant activity cost and driver data follow:

Activity	Activity Cost ($)	Driver	Driver Quantity
Setting up equipment	1,000	Setup hours	4
Moving goods	1,000	Number of moves	10
Machining	1,500	Machine hours	50
Assembly	500	Direct labor hours	100

Required:
Calculate the activity rates.

Solution:
Divide the activity cost by the total driver quantity:

Setup rate:	$1,000/4 setup hours = $250 per setup hour
Materials handling rate:	$1,000/10 moves = $100 per move
Machining rate:	$1,500/50 machine hours = $30 per machine hour
Assembly rate:	$500/100 direct labor hours = $5 per direct labor hour

To increase the accuracy of overhead cost assignments, causal factors, called activity drivers, are chosen that measure the amount of activity consumed by a product. The activity rate multiplied by the amount used of each activity determines the amount of activity cost assigned to a particular product. The sum of all such assigned activity costs is the total amount of overhead consumed by a product. Overhead costs plus prime costs divided by units produced then yield the unit cost.

Example 5.3 shows how to calculate the unit cost for each product by using activity rates.

Here's **Why It's important**

EXAMPLE 5.3

How to Calculate Activity-Based Unit Costs

Rio Novo's Porto Behlo plant activity rate data for deluxe and regular models follow:

	Deluxe	Regular	Activity Rate
Units produced per year	10	100	
Prime costs	$800	$8,000	
Setup hours	3	1	$250
Number of moves	6	4	$100
Machine hours	10	40	$ 30
Direct labor hours	20	80	$ 5

Required:

Calculate the unit cost for deluxe and regular models.

Solution:

	Deluxe	Regular
Prime costs	$ 800	$ 8,000
Overhead costs:		
Setups:		
$250 × 3 setup hours	750	
$250 × 1 setup hour		250
Moving materials:		
$100 × 6 moves	600	
$100 × 4 moves		400
Machining:		
$30 × 10 machine hours	300	
$30 × 40 machine hours		1,200
Assembly:		
$5 × 20 direct labor hours	100	
$5 × 80 direct labor hours		400
Total manufacturing costs	$2,550	$10,250
Units produced	÷ 10	÷ 100
Unit cost (Total costs/Units)	$ 255	$102.50

Exhibit 5.3 visually summarizes the calculations in Examples 5.2 and 5.3.

Exhibit 5.3

Activity Rates and Activity-Based Unit Costs for Rio Novo's Porto Behlo Plant

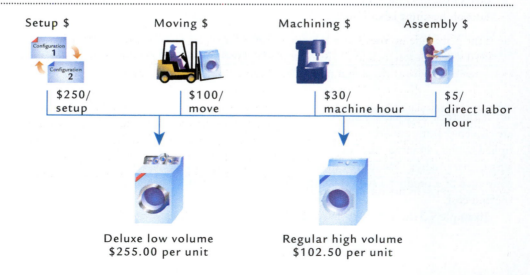

Setup $	Moving $	Machining $	Assembly $
$250/ setup	$100/ move	$30/ machine hour	$5/ direct labor hour

Deluxe low volume
$255.00 per unit

Regular high volume
$102.50 per unit

Comparison of Functional- and Activity-Based Product Costs A plantwide rate based on direct labor hours is calculated as follows:

$$\text{Overhead} = \frac{\text{Total Overhead Costs}}{\text{Total Direct Labor Hours}}$$

$4,000/100 = 40 per direct labor hour

The product cost for each product using this single unit-level overhead rate is calculated as follows:

	Deluxe	Regular
Prime costs	$ 800	$ 8,000
Overhead costs:		
$40 × 20	800	
$40 × 80		3,200
Total cost	$1,600	$11,200
Units produced	÷ 10	÷ 100
Unit cost	$ 160	$ 112

Now compare these product costs with the activity-based cost of Example 5.3. This comparison clearly illustrates the effects of using only unit-based activity drivers to assign overhead costs. The activity-based cost assignment reflects the pattern of overhead consumption and is, therefore, the most accurate. Activity-based product costing reveals that functional-based costing undercosts the low-volume deluxe models and overcosts the high-volume regular models. In fact, the ABC assignment increases the reported cost of the deluxe models by $95 per unit and decreases the reported cost of the regular models by $9.50 per unit—a movement in the right direction, given the pattern of overhead consumption.

Illustrating Relationships: Product Diversity and Product-Costing Accuracy

For unit-level overhead rates to fail, products must consume the nonunit-level activities in proportions significantly different than the unit-level activities. The greater the difference in this consumption pattern, the greater the potential product cost distortion. For example, the Regular model of Rio Novo consumes activities in the following proportions:

- 25% of the setup hours
- 40% of the number of moves
- 80% of the machine hours
- 80% of the direct labor hours

Since the plantwide overhead rate uses direct labor hours, a unit-level driver, 80% of the total overhead would be assigned to the Regular model. However, the Regular model consumes only an average of 32.5% of the nonunit-level overhead $[(0.25 + 0.40)/2]$ and so we would expect a significant cost distortion. Intuitively, if the *average* consumption ratio of the nonunit-level activities differs markedly from the unit-level consumption ratio, as 32.5% differs from 80%, then there is greater product diversity and greater product cost distortion. As expected, the distortion is significant because the plantwide rate assigns $3,200 of overhead while the ABC approach assigns only $2,250. Alternatively, if there is little or no product diversity, then products consume unit-level activities and nonunit-level activities in the same (or close to the same) proportion and a plantwide rate works well.

This diversity-accuracy relationship can be seen in the Rio Novo example in Examples 5.2 (p. 221) and 5.3 (p. 222), by allowing the average nonunit-level consumption ratio to vary. We see a special structure characterized by the following features:

- The Deluxe and Regular products have the same consumption ratios (0.20 and 0.80, respectively) for the unit-level activities (machining and assembly).
- The cost of the nonunit-level activities, setting up and moving, is the same ($1,000 for each activity).
- The total cost of the unit-level (nonunit-level) activities is $2,000.

This special structure means that the average consumption ratio for the two unit-level (nonunit-level) activities can be used to assign the activity costs to each product, achieving the same assignment as when done for each individual activity. This can be calculated as follows:

$$\text{Overhead Cost} = \text{Average Consumption Ratio} \times \text{Total Cost of Each Set of Activities}$$

The average consumption ratios for the Regular product are:

$$\text{Unit-Level Activities} = (0.80 + 0.80)/2$$
$$= 0.80$$
$$\text{Nonunit-Level Activities} = (0.25 + 0.40)/2$$
$$= 0.325$$

Thus, for the Regular product:

$$\text{Overhead Cost} = (0.80 \times \$2,000) + (0.325 \times \$2,000)$$
$$= \$1,600 + \$650$$
$$= \$2,250$$

This is the same as the assignments using individual activities and activity rates.

To explore the effect of product diversity on accuracy, hold the unit-level consumption ratios constant and allow the average nonunit-level consumption ratio to vary. This produces the following overhead cost assignment equation for the Regular product:

$$\text{Overhead Cost} = \$1,600 + (\text{Average Nonunit Consumption Ratio} \times \$2,000)$$

Using this equation, Exhibit 5.4 shows the overhead cost assigned to the Regular model as the average nonunit-level consumption ratio varies. The red line represents the average nonunit consumption ratio function. The blue horizontal line is the overhead cost assignment using the plantwide rate. Notice that when it intersects $3,200, the overhead cost assignment is the same for both ABC and plantwide assignments (the average consumption ratio is 0.80, which is the same as the consumption ratio for the plantwide rate). As the average consumption ratio decreases, the difference between the ABC and plantwide assignments increases. The vertical lines indicate the difference between the ABC and plantwide rate overhead assignments. Clearly, some values can occur that would produce little difference between the plantwide and ABC assignments; thus, it would be cheaper and simpler to use a single-rate costing system. For example, the vertical lines are small between 0.70 and 1.00, indicating that when the average nonunit consumption ratio is in this range, then a plantwide rate would provide good accuracy. The green vertical line represents the accuracy loss when the product diversity corresponds to the original example data.

The key message of the relationship analysis is that in a diverse product environment, activity-based costing promises greater accuracy. Given the importance of making decisions based on accurate facts, a detailed look at activity-based costing is certainly merited.

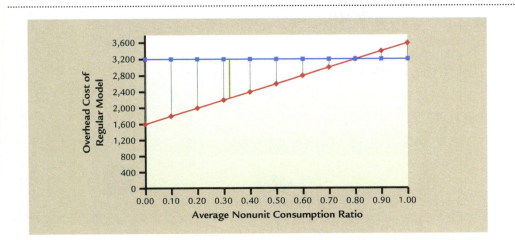

Exhibit 5.4

Diversity and Product-Costing Accuracy

Ethical Decisions

One of the ethical standards of the Institute of Management Accountants (IMA) requires that its members maintain professional expertise by continually developing knowledge and skills. An interesting issue is whether accounting professionals who resist learning different cost management methods are exhibiting ethical behavior. At the very least, cost accounting professionals should learn about different approaches and assess whether the benefit-cost trade-offs justify their use. ●

Check Point

1. **At Fitzgerald Inc., Department C inspects each product produced, and Department A inspects a small sample of each batch of products produced. Which inspection activity is unit-level, and which is nonunit-level?**

Answer:
A unit-level activity is performed each time a unit is produced, whereas a nonunit-level activity is performed at times that do not correspond to individual unit production. Thus, inspection is unit-level for Department C and nonunit-level for Department A.

2. **Suppose that the budgeted cost of the setup activity is $100,000 and that 4,000 setup hours are expected to be used. Furthermore, Product A uses 1,000 setup hours, and Product B uses 3,000 setup hours. How much setup cost will be assigned to each product?**

Answer:
First, calculate the activity rate: Setup Rate = $100,000/4,000 = $25 per setup hour. Next, multiply rate by hours used to get the desired result:
Product A: $25 × 1,000 = $25,000
Product B: $25 × 4,000 = $75,000

ACTIVITY-BASED PRODUCT COSTING

OBJECTIVE **2**

Explain how an activity-based costing system works for product costing.

Functional-based overhead costing involves two major stages:

1. Overhead costs are assigned to an organizational unit (plant or department).
2. Overhead costs are then assigned to cost objects.

As Exhibit 5.5 illustrates, an **activity-based costing (ABC) system** is also a two-stage process:

1. Trace costs to activities.
2. Trace activity costs to cost objects.

Exhibit 5.5

Activity-Based Costing:
Assigning Cost of Overhead

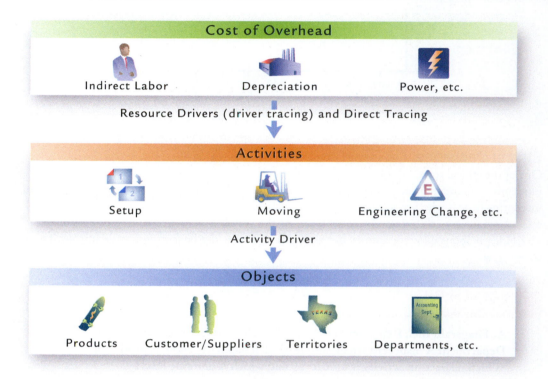

The underlying assumption is that activities consume resources, and cost objects, in turn, consume activities. An ABC system, however, emphasizes direct tracing and driver tracing (exploiting cause-and-effect relationships), while a unit-based costing system tends to be allocation-intensive (largely ignoring cause-and-effect relationships). Since the focus of ABC is activities, identifying activities must be the first step in designing an ABC system.

Identifying Activities and Their Attributes

An **activity** is action taken or work performed by equipment or people for other people. Identifying activities usually is accomplished by interviewing managers or representatives of functional work areas (departments). A set of key questions is asked in which answers provide much of the data needed for an ABC system.

Set of Key Questions   Interview questions can be used to identify activities and activity attributes needed for costing purposes. The information derived from these questions provides data helpful for assigning resource costs to individual activities. To prevent the number of activities from becoming unmanageably large, a common rule of thumb employed by the interviewer is to tell the interviewee to ignore activities that require less than 5% of an individual's time. Examples of questions that interviewers might ask to gather information include the following:

1. How many employees are in your department? (Activities consume labor.)
2. What do they do (please describe)? (Activities are people doing things for other people.)

3. Do customers outside your department use any equipment? (Activities also can be equipment working for other people. In other words, the equipment provides the service for someone by itself).
4. What resources are used by each activity (equipment, materials, energy)? (Activities consume resources in addition to labor.)
5. What are the outputs of each activity? (Helps to identify activity drivers.)
6. Who or what uses the activity output? (Identifies the cost object: products, other activities, customers, etc.)
7. How much time do workers spend on each activity? Time on each activity by equipment? (Information assigns the cost of labor and equipment to activities.)

Illustrative Example: Hemingway Bank Suppose that the manager of Hemingway Bank's credit card department is interviewed and presented with the seven questions just listed. Consider the purpose and response to each question in the order indicated.

- *Question 1 (labor resource):* There are five employees.
- *Question 2 (activity identification):* There are three major activities: processing credit card transactions, issuing customer statements, and answering customer questions.
- *Question 3 (activity identification):* Yes. Automatic bank tellers service customers who require cash advances.
- *Question 4 (resource identification):* Each employee has his or her own computer, printer, and desk. Paper and other supplies are needed to operate the printers. Each employee has a telephone as well.
- *Question 5 (potential activity drivers):* Processing transactions produces a posting for each transaction in our computer system and serves as a source for preparing the monthly statements. The number of monthly customer statements has to be the product for the issuing activity, and I suppose that customers served is the output for the answering activity. The number of cash advances measures the product of the automatic teller activity, although the teller really generates more transactions for other products such as checking accounts. So, perhaps the number of teller transactions is the real output.
- *Question 6 (potential cost objects identified):* We have three products: classic, gold, and platinum credit cards. Transactions are processed for these three types of cards, and statements are sent to clients holding these cards. Similarly, answers to questions are all directed to clients who hold these cards.
- *Question 7 (identifying resource drivers):* I just completed a work survey and have the percentage of time calculated for each worker. All five clerks work on each of the three departmental activities. About 40% of their time is spent processing transactions, with the rest of their time split evenly between preparing statements and answering questions. Phone time is used only for answering client questions, and computer time is 70% transaction processing, 20% statement preparation, and 10% answering questions.

Activity Dictionary These interview-derived data are used to prepare an *activity dictionary*. An **activity dictionary** lists the activities in an organization along with some critical activity attributes. Activity attributes are financial and nonfinancial information items that describe individual activities. What attributes are used depends on the purpose. Examples of activity attributes associated with a costing objective include the following:

- types of resources consumed
- amount (percentage) of time spent on an activity by workers
- cost objects that consume the activity output (reason for performing the activity)
- measure of the activity output (activity driver)
- activity name

Illustrative Example: Hemingway Bank Exhibit 5.6 illustrates the activity dictionary for Hemingway's credit card department. The three products, classic, gold, and platinum credit cards, in turn, consume the activities. It is not unusual for a typical organization to produce an activity dictionary containing 200 to 300 activities.

Exhibit 5.6

Activity Dictionary for Hemingway Bank's Credit Card Department

Activity Name	Activity Description	Cost Object(s)	Activity Driver
Processing	Sorting, keying, and transactions verifying	Credit cards	Number of transactions
Preparing statements	Reviewing, printing, stuffing, and mailing	Credit cards	Number of statements
Answering questions	Answering, logging, reviewing database, and making call backs	Credit cards	Number of cards
Providing automatic tellers	Accessing accounts, withdrawing funds	Credit cards, checking and savings accounts	Number of teller transactions

Assigning Costs to Activities

Here's **Why It's important**

Once activities are identified and described, the next task is to determine how much it costs to perform each activity. Activities consume resources such as labor, materials, energy, and capital. The cost of these resources is found in the general ledger, but the amount spent on each activity is not revealed. Thus, it becomes necessary to assign the resource costs to activities by using direct and driver tracing. When resources are exclusively used by an activity, direct tracing is used. For shared resources, driver tracing is used, and the drivers used to assign resource costs to activities are called *resource drivers*. **Resource drivers** are factors that measure the consumption of resources by activities.

Illustrative Example: Hemingway Bank For labor resources, a *work distribution matrix* often is used. A **work distribution matrix** identifies the amount of labor consumed by each activity and is derived from the interview process (or a written survey). If the time spent on an activity is 100%, then the direct labor cost is exclusive to the activity and direct tracing is used. Otherwise, driver tracing is used and the percentage of time spent on each activity is the consumption ratio. Exhibit 5.7 provides an example of a work distribution matrix supplied by the manager of Hemingway's credit card department for individual activities (refer to Question 7). Notice that for the Hemingway example, driver tracing would be used to assign the labor resource cost to each activity as the labor resources are shared by all three activities.

Exhibit 5.7

Work Distribution Matrix for Hemingway Bank's Credit Card Department

Activity	Percentage of Time per Activity
Processing transactions	40%
Preparing statements	30%
Answering questions	30%

Labor, of course, is not the only resource consumed by activities. Activities also consume materials, capital, and energy. The interview, for example, reveals that the activities within the credit card department use computers (capital), phones (capital), desks (capital), and paper (materials). The automatic teller activity uses the automatic teller (capital) and energy. The cost of these other resources must also be assigned to the various activities. They are assigned in the same way as was described for labor (using direct tracing and resource drivers). The cost of computers could be assigned by using driver tracing with hours of usage as the resource driver. **Example 5.4** illustrates how two types of resources (labor and capital) are assigned to activities.

Refer to the work distribution matrix for Hemingway Bank's credit card department in Exhibit 5.7. Assume that each clerk is paid a salary of $30,000 ($150,000 total clerical cost for five clerks). Furthermore, each clerk has a computer. The general ledger reveals that the cost per computer is $1,200 per year. Computer time is 70% transaction processing, 20% statement preparation, and 10% answering questions.

Required:

Assign the cost of labor and the cost of computers to each of the activities in the credit department. Is this assignment driver tracing or direct tracing?

Solution:

The amount of labor and computer cost assigned to each activity is given below.

Activity	Labor Cost	Computer Cost	Total
Processing transactions	$60,000 (0.40 × $150,000)	$4,200 (0.70 × $6,000)	$64,200
Preparing statements	$45,000 (0.30 × $150,000)	$1,200 (0.20 × $6,000)	$46,200
Answering questions	$45,000 (0.30 × $150,000)	$600 (0.10 × $6,000)	$45,600

Labor and computers are both shared resources, and their costs are assigned using a resource driver.

EXAMPLE 5.4

How to Assign Resource Costs to Activities by Using Direct Tracing and Resource Drivers

Labor and computer resources are not all the resources consumed by the activities associated with Hemingway's credit card department. Once the process described in Example 5.4 is applied for all resources, the total cost of each activity can be calculated. Exhibit 5.8 gives the cost of the activities associated with Hemingway's credit card department under the assumption that all resource costs have been assigned (these numbers are assumed because all resource data are not given for their calculation).

Processing transactions	$130,000
Preparing statements	102,000
Answering questions	92,400
Providing automatic tellers	250,000

Exhibit 5.8

Activity Costs for Hemingway Bank's Credit Card Department

Assigning Costs to Products

From Example 5.3 (p. 222), we know that activity costs are assigned to products by multiplying a predetermined activity rate by the usage of the activity, as measured by activity drivers. Exhibit 5.6 (p. 228) identified the activity drivers for each of the four credit card activities:

- number of transactions for processing transactions
- number of statements for preparing statements
- number of calls for answering questions
- number of teller transactions for the activity of providing automatic tellers

To calculate an activity rate, the practical capacity of each activity must be determined. To assign costs, the amount of each activity consumed by each product must also be known.

Illustrative Example: Hemingway Bank Assuming that the practical activity capacity is equal to the total activity usage by all products, the following actual data have been collected for Hemingway's credit card department:

	Classic Card	Gold Card	Platinum Card	Total
Number of cards	5,000	3,000	2,000	10,000
Transactions processed	600,000	300,000	100,000	1,000,000
Number of statements	60,000	36,000	24,000	120,000
Number of calls	10,000	12,000	8,000	30,000
Number of teller transactions*	15,000	3,000	2,000	20,000

*The number of teller transactions for the cards is 10% of the total transactions from all sources. Thus, teller transactions total 20,000 (0.10 × 200,000).

Applying Example 5.2 (p. 221) by using the data and costs from Exhibit 5.8, the activity rates are calculated as follows:

Rate calculations:	
Processing transactions:	$130,000/1,000,000 = $0.13 per transaction
Preparing statements:	$102,000/120,000 = $0.85 per statement
Answering questions:	$92,400/30,000 = $3.08 per call
Providing automatic tellers:	$250,000/200,000 = $1.25 per transaction

These rates provide the cost of each activity usage. Using these rates, costs are assigned as shown in Exhibit 5.9. However, we now know the whole story behind the development of the activity rates and usage measures. Furthermore, the banking example emphasizes the utility of ABC in service organizations.

Exhibit 5.9

Assigning Costs for Hemingway Bank's Credit Card Department

	Classic	Gold	Platinum
Processing transactions:			
$0.13 × 600,000	$ 78,000		
$0.13 × 300,000		$ 39,000	
$0.13 × 100,000			$13,000
Preparing statements:			
$0.85 × 60,000	51,000		
$0.85 × 36,000		30,600	
$0.85 × 24,000			20,400
Answering questions:			
$3.08 × 10,000	30,800		
$3.08 × 12,000		36,960	
$3.08 × 8,000			24,640
Providing automatic tellers:			
$1.25 × 15,000	18,750		
$1.25 × 3,000		3,750	
$1.25 × 2,000			2,500
Total costs	$178,550	$110,310	$60,540
Units	÷ 5,000	÷ 3,000	÷ 2,000
Unit cost	$ 35.71	$ 36.77	$ 30.27

Here's How It's Used: SUSTAINABILITY

Baxter International Inc. is a large health care company headquartered in Deerfield, Illinois. Baxter is well known for its environmental performance and reporting. Its annual sustainability report contains a fairly detailed environmental financial report. For many years, Baxter has followed an ecoefficiency paradigm, believing that environmental performance can be improved while simultaneously improving economic performance. The environmental financial report not only details environmental costs such as pollution controls, waste disposal, carbon taxes, and remediation, but it also discloses income, savings, and cost avoidance or environmental initiatives for the current year and the prior four years. For each year reported, it adds the cost avoidance from initiatives started in the prior six years and realized in the stated year. Using that total number, the income, savings, and cost avoidance for 2010 to 2014 ranged from $0.6 million (2014) to $100.4 million (2010), supporting the view that ecoefficiency really works for Baxter.*

While Baxter is at the forefront of disclosing environmental performance to outside parties, there is a real opportunity for Baxter and others to enhance their environmental performance capabilities by using activity-based costing to identify and break out environmental costs from overhead, a practice recommended by both the International Federation of Accountants and the United Nations Division for Sustainable Development.**

Assigning resource costs to environmental activities, identifying drivers, and then using these drivers to assign environmental costs to products can produce valuable managerial information. For example, ABC assignments may reveal that a particular product is responsible for much more toxic waste than other products. This information may then lead to a more efficient and environmentally friendly design for the product or its associated processes. It could also reveal that when the environmental costs are accurately assigned that the product is unprofitable and that improving environmental performance is obtained simply by dropping the product.

CONCEPT CLIP

*Baxter 2014 Sustainability Report.
**Mark Lemmon and Anthony Pembler, "Environmental Sustainability: Activity-Based Costing/Management," *Environmental Sustainability Guidance*, 2014: CPA, Canada.

Check Point

1. **What are some key differences between ABC and unit-based costing?**

Answer:
ABC uses cause-and-effect relationships to assign overhead costs. Unit-based costing uses drivers such as direct labor hours, which often have nothing to do with the actual overhead resources consumed by a product.

2. **What is the purpose of the interview questions?**

Answer:
The purpose is to identify activities, drivers, and other important attributes essential for ABC.

3. **Assume that a clerk spends 40% of her time counting parts and 60% of her time inspecting parts. Assuming her salary is $60,000, calculate the amount of resource cost assigned to each of the two activities.**

Answer:
Counting parts: $0.40 \times \$60,000 = \$24,000$
Inspecting parts: $0.60 \times \$60,000 = \$36,000$

ACTIVITY-BASED CUSTOMER COSTING AND ACTIVITY-BASED SUPPLIER COSTING

OBJECTIVE ▸ 3

Describe activity-based customer costing and activity-based supplier costing.

ABC systems originally became popular for their ability to improve product-costing accuracy by tracing activity costs to the products that consume the activities. However, since the beginning of the 21st century, the use of ABC has expanded into areas upstream (i.e., before the production section of the value chain—research and development, prototyping, etc.) and downstream (i.e., after the production section of the value chain—marketing, distribution, customer service, etc.) from production. Specifically, ABC often is used to more accurately determine the upstream costs of suppliers and the downstream costs of customers. Knowing the costs of suppliers and customers can be vital information for improving a company's profitability.

LSI Logic, a high-tech producer of semiconductors, implemented ABC customer costing and discovered that 10% of its customers were responsible for about 90% of its profits. LSI also discovered that it was actually losing money on about 50% of its customers. It worked to convert its unprofitable customers into profitable ones and invited those who would not provide a fair return to take their business elsewhere. As a consequence, LSI's sales decreased, but its profit tripled.[3] Exhibit 5.10 depicts this interesting yet common relationship between customers and their contribution to company profitability. Some managers refer to this graph as the "whale curve" of customer profitability, likely because of its resemblance to the shape of a whale cresting at the water's surface. The important observation from the curve is that the customers to the left of the hump, or peak, increase the company's profitability, while the customers to the right decrease the company's profitability. Therefore, activity-based customer costing is helpful in determining where each customer falls on the curve and, subsequently, how each customer should therefore be treated given its position on the curve. Of particular interest are those customers to the far right because they severely decrease the company's profitability and need to be terminated as unacceptably bad customers or altered in some way so as to become profitable customers for the company.

Exhibit 5.10

Whale Curve of Cumulative
Customer Profitability

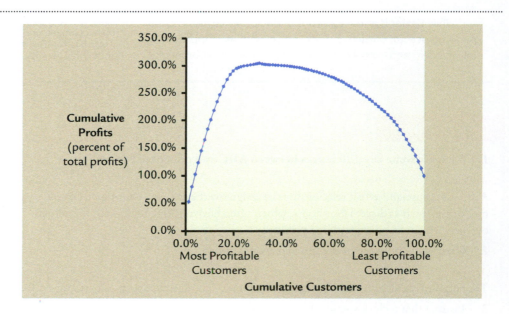

Activity-Based Customer Costing

Customers are cost objects of fundamental interest. As the LSI Logic experience illustrates, customer management can produce significant gains in profit. It is possible to have customer diversity, just as it is possible to have product diversity. Customers can consume customer-driven activities in different proportions. Sources of customer diversity include order frequency, delivery frequency, geographic distance, sales and promotional support, and engineering support requirements. Knowing how much it costs to service different customers can be vital information for the following purposes:

- setting pricing
- determining customer mix
- improving profitability

---

3   Gary Cokins, "Are All of Your Customers Profitable (To You)?" (June 14, 2001). www.bettermanagment.com/Library (accessed May 2010).

Furthermore, because of diversity of customers, multiple drivers are needed to trace costs accurately. This outcome means that ABC can be useful to organizations that have only one product, homogeneous products, or a just-in-time (JIT) structure where direct tracing diminishes the value of ABC for product costing.

Customer Costing versus Product Costing   Assigning the costs of customer service to customers is done in the same way that manufacturing costs are assigned to products. Customer-driven activities such as order entry, order picking, shipping, making sales calls, and evaluating a client's credit are identified and listed in an activity dictionary. The cost of the resources consumed is assigned to activities, and the cost of the activities is assigned to individual customers using activity drivers. Knowing the costs of individual customers or customer types can be helpful in setting prices, determining the best customer mix, and improving profitability.

Here's **Why It's important**

Example 5.5 illustrates how ABC assigns costs to customers.

EXAMPLE 5.5

How to Calculate Activity-Based Customer Costs

Milan Company produces precision parts for 11 major buyers. Of the 11 customers, one accounts for 50% of the sales, with the remaining 10 accounting for the rest of the sales. The 10 smaller customers purchase parts in roughly equal quantities. Orders placed by the smaller customers are about the same size. Data concerning Milan's customer activity follow:

	Large Customer	Ten Smaller Customers
Units purchased	500,000	500,000
Orders placed	2	200
Number of sales calls	10	210
Manufacturing costs	$3,000,000	$3,000,000
Order filling costs allocated*	$ 202,000	$ 202,000
Sales force costs allocated*	$ 110,000	$ 110,000

*Allocated based on sales volume.

Currently, customer-driven costs are assigned to customers based on units sold, a unit-level driver.

Required:
Assign costs to customers using an ABC approach.

Solution:
The appropriate drivers are orders placed and number of sales calls. The activity rates are:

$$\$404,000/202 \text{ orders} = \$2,000 \text{ per order}$$
$$\$220,000/220 \text{ calls} = \$1,000 \text{ per call}$$

Using this information, the customer-driven costs can be assigned to each group of customers as follows:

	Large Customer	Ten Smaller Customers
Order filling costs:		
($2,000 × 2)	$ 4,000	
($2,000 × 200)		$400,000
Sales force costs:		
($1,000 × 10)	10,000	
($1,000 × 210)		210,000
	$14,000	$610,000

Example 5.5 reveals that the activity-based cost assignments reveal a much different picture of the cost of servicing each type of customer. The smaller customers cost more due to their smaller, more frequent orders and the need of the sales force to engage in more negotiations to make a sale.

What does this analysis tell management that it didn't know before? First, the large customer costs much less to service than the smaller customers and perhaps should be charged less. Second, it raises some significant questions relative to the smaller customers. For example, is it possible to encourage larger, less frequent orders? Perhaps offering discounts for larger orders would be appropriate. Why is it more difficult to sell to the smaller customers? Why are more calls needed? Are they less informed than the larger customer about the products? Can we improve profits by influencing our customers to change their buying behavior?

Activity-Based Supplier Costing

ABC can also help managers identify the true cost of a firm's suppliers. The cost of a supplier is much more than the purchase price of the components or materials acquired. Just like customers, suppliers can affect many internal activities of a firm and significantly increase the cost of purchasing. A more correct view is one where the costs associated with quality, reliability, and late deliveries are added to the purchase costs. Managers are then required to evaluate suppliers based on total cost, not just purchase price. ABC is the key to tracing costs relating to these factors.

Here's How It's Used: **AT A SMALL CONSULTING FIRM**

Managing Customer Profitability

As a consultant, you recently implemented an activity-based customer-profitability system. In your written report to management, you classified the customers of the company into one of four categories based on current profitability and the potential for future profitability:[4]

> High Profitability, Substantial Future Potential
> Low Profitability, Substantial Future Potential
> High Profitability, Limited Future Potential
> Low Profitability, Limited Future Potential

After discussing the report with the CEO, he asks you to answer the following question:

How would you manage the customers in each of the four categories?

For highly profitable customers, and especially those with long-term potential, special efforts should be made to retain these customers as it is much more expensive to attract new customers. Offering these customers special discounts and new products and service lines coupled with managing their costs to serve to a lower level and improving business

processes are ways to increase customer satisfaction while at the same time maintaining or increasing profitability. For customers with low profitability but substantial potential, the goal is to move these customers up to a high profitability state. Pricing policies or initiatives related to both the order and the transactions caused by the order is one way to increase profitability (e.g., activity-based pricing is based on the costs to serve, something clearly revealed by the ABC customer model). Another way is to lower the costs to serve by improving activity efficiency and eliminating nonvalue-added activities. The final category of customers (low profitability and limited potential) is managed up or out—these customers need to be made profitable quickly or simply dropped.

Knowing customer profitability is important because not every revenue dollar contributes equally to overall profitability. Thus, it is critical for a manager to understand the net profit contribution that each customer makes to the company. Understanding individual customer profitability and the associated drivers allows managers to take actions to sustain and maintain profitable customers and transform unprofitable customers into profitable customers.[5]

CONCEPT CLIP

---

4 Based on a classification in Gary Cokins, *Performance Management: Finding the Missing Pieces (to Close the Intelligence Gap)* (Wiley and SAS Business Series, March 29, 2004).

5 Robert S. Kaplan and V. G. Narayanan, "Measuring and Managing Customer Profitability," *Journal of Cost Management* (September/October 2001): 5–15.

Supplier Costing Assigning the costs of supplier-related activities to suppliers follows the same pattern as ABC product and customer costing. Supplier-driven activities are identified and listed in an activity dictionary. Some examples of supplier-driven activities are purchasing, receiving, inspection of incoming components, reworking products (due to defective supplier components), expediting products (due to late deliveries of supplies), and warranty work (due to defective supplier components).

Here's **Why It's important**

The cost of the resources consumed is assigned to these activities, and then activity drivers assign the resulting activity cost to individual suppliers. These costs are then added to direct purchase costs. This outcome enables managers to improve their evaluation and selection of suppliers, with the objective of reducing total supplier costs.

Example 5.6 illustrates how to use ABC for supplier costing.

Assume that a purchasing manager uses two suppliers, Murray Inc. and Plata Associates, as the source of two machine parts: Part A1 and Part B2. Consider two activities: repairing products (under warranty) and expediting products. Repairing products occurs because of part failure (bought from suppliers). Expediting products occurs because suppliers are late in delivering needed parts. Activity cost information and other data needed for supplier costing follow:

EXAMPLE 5.6

How to Calculate Activity-Based Supplier Costs

I. Activity Costs Caused by Suppliers (e.g., failed parts or late delivery)

Activity	Costs
Repairing products	$800,000
Expediting products	$200,000

II. Supplier Data

	Murray Inc.		Plata Associates	
	Part A1	**Part B2**	**Part A1**	**Part B2**
Unit purchase price	$ 20	$ 52	$ 24	$ 56
Units purchased	80,000	40,000	10,000	10,000
Failed units	1,600	380	10	10
Late shipments	60	40	0	0

Required:
Determine the cost of each supplier by using ABC.

Solution:
Using the above data, the activity rates for assigning costs to suppliers are computed as follows:

Repair Rate = $800,000/2,000* units
= $400 per failed unit
*(1,600 + 380 + 10 + 10)

Expediting Rate = $200,000/100** late shipments
= $2,000 per late shipment
**(60 + 40)

Using these rates and the activity data, the total purchasing cost per unit of each component is computed:

(*Continued*)

EXAMPLE 5.6

(Continued)

	Murray Inc.		Plata Associates	
	Part A1	**Part B2**	**Part A1**	**Part B2**
Purchase cost:				
$20 × 80,000	$1,600,000			
$52 × 40,000		$2,080,000		
$24 × 10,000			$240,000	
$56 × 10,000				$560,000
Repairing products:				
$400 × 1,600	640,000			
$400 × 380		152,000		
$400 × 10			4,000	
$400 × 10				4,000
Expediting products:				
$2,000 × 60	120,000			
$2,000 × 40		80,000		
Total costs	$2,360,000	$2,312,000	$244,000	$564,000
Units	÷ 80,000	÷ 40,000	÷ 10,000	÷ 10,000
Total unit cost	$ 29.50	$ 57.80	$ 24.40	$ 56.40

The example in Example 5.6 shows that Murray, the "low-cost" supplier (as measured by the purchase price of the two parts), actually costs more when the supplier-related activities of repairing and expediting are considered. If all costs are considered, then the choice becomes clear: Plata Associates is the better supplier with a higher-quality product, more on-time deliveries, and, consequently, a lower overall cost per unit.

Check Point

1. **How are costs assigned to customers by using the ABC approach?**

   Answer:
   Costs are traced to activities and then assigned to customers based on their usage of these activities (as measured by activity drivers).

2. **How are costs assigned to suppliers by using the ABC approach?**

   Answer:
   Costs are traced to activities and then assigned to suppliers based on a cause-and-effect relationship (using activity drivers).

OBJECTIVE **4**

Explain how activity-based management can be used for cost reduction.

PROCESS-VALUE ANALYSIS

Process-value analysis is fundamental to *activity-based management*. **Activity-based management** is a system-wide, integrated approach that focuses management's attention on activities with the objective of improving customer value and profit achieved by providing this value. **Process-value analysis** focuses on cost reduction instead of cost assignment and emphasizes the maximization of systemwide performance. As Exhibit 5.11 illustrates, process-value analysis is concerned with:

- driver analysis
- activity analysis
- performance measurement

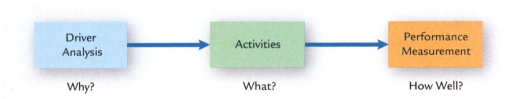

Exhibit 5.11

Process-Value Analysis Model

Driver Analysis: The Search for Root Causes

Managing activities requires an understanding of what causes activity costs. Every activity has inputs and outputs. **Activity inputs** are the resources consumed by the activity in producing its output. **Activity output** is the result or product of an activity. For example, if the activity is moving materials, the inputs would be such things as a forklift, a forklift driver, fuel (for the forklift), and crates. The output would be moved goods and materials. An **activity output measure** is the number of times the activity is performed. It is the quantifiable measure of the output. For example, the number of moves and distance moved are possible output measures for the material-moving activity.

The output measure effectively is a measure of the demands placed on an activity and is what we have been calling an *activity driver*. As the demands for an activity change, the cost of the activity can change. For example, as the number of programs written increases, the activity of writing programs may need to consume more inputs (labor, CD-ROMs, paper, and so on). However, output measures, such as the number of programs, may not (and usually do not) correspond to the root causes of activity costs. They are the consequences of the activity being performed. The purpose of driver analysis is to reveal root causes. Thus, **driver analysis** is the effort expended to identify those factors that are the root causes of activity costs. For example, an analysis may reveal that the root cause of the cost of moving materials is plant layout. Once the root cause is known, then action can be taken to improve the activity. Specifically, reorganizing plant layout can reduce the cost of moving materials.

Often, the root cause of the cost of an activity is also the root cause of other related activities. For example, the costs of inspecting purchased parts and reordering may both be caused by poor supplier quality. By working with suppliers to reduce the number of defective components supplied (or choosing suppliers that have fewer defects), the demand for both activities may then decrease, allowing the company to save money.

Activity Analysis: Identifying and Assessing Value Content

The heart of process-value analysis is activity analysis. **Activity analysis** is the process of identifying, describing, and evaluating the activities that an organization performs. Activity analysis produces four outcomes:

1. what activities are done
2. how many people perform the activities
3. the time and resources required to perform the activities
4. an assessment of the value of the activities to the organization, including a recommendation to select and keep only those that add value

Steps 1 through 3 have been described earlier and are common to the information needed for determining and assigning activity costs. Knowing how much an activity costs is clearly an important part of activity-based management. Step 4, determining the value-added content of activities, is concerned with cost reduction rather than cost assignment. Thus, some managerial accountants feel that this is the most important part of activity analysis. Activities can be classified as *value-added* or *nonvalue-added*.

Value-Added Activities Those activities necessary to remain in business are called **value-added activities**. Some activities—required activities—are necessary to comply with legal mandates. Activities needed to comply with the reporting requirements of the Securities and Exchange Commission (SEC) and the filing requirements of the Internal Revenue Service (IRS) are examples. These activities are value-added by *mandate*. The remaining activities in the firm are *discretionary*. A discretionary activity is classified as value-added, provided it simultaneously satisfies all of the following conditions:

- The activity produces a change of state.
- The change of state was not achievable by preceding activities.
- The activity enables other activities to be performed.

For example, consider the production of rods used in hydraulic cylinders. The first activity, cutting rods, cuts long rods into the correct lengths for the cylinders. Next, the cut rods are welded to cut plates. The cutting rods activity is value-added because:

- It causes a change of state—uncut rods become cut rods.
- No prior activity was supposed to create this change of state.
- It enables the welding activity to be performed.

Though the value-added properties are easy to see for an operational activity like cutting rods, what about a more general activity like supervising production workers? A managerial activity is specifically designed to manage other value-added activities—to ensure that they are performed in an efficient and timely manner. Supervision certainly satisfies the enabling condition. Is there a change in state? There are two ways of answering affirmatively:

- First, supervising can be viewed as an enabling resource that is consumed by the operational activities that do produce a change of state. Thus, supervising is a secondary activity that serves as an input that is needed to help bring about the change of state expected for value-added primary activities.
- Second, it could be argued that the supervision brings order by changing the state from uncoordinated activities to coordinated activities.

Once value-added activities are identified, we can define value-added costs. **Value-added costs** are the costs to perform value-added activities with perfect efficiency.

Nonvalue-Added Activities All activities other than those that are absolutely essential to remain in business, and therefore considered unnecessary, are referred to as **nonvalue-added activities**. A nonvalue-added activity can be identified by its failure to satisfy any one of the three previous defining conditions for adding value. Violation of the first two conditions is the usual case for nonvalue-added activities. Inspecting cut rods (for correct length), for example, is a nonvalue-added activity. Inspection is a state-detection activity, not a state-changing activity. (It tells us the state of the cut rod—whether it is the right length.) Thus, it fails the first condition (activity produced a change of state). Consider the activity of reworking goods or subassemblies. Rework is designed to bring a good from a nonconforming state to a conforming state. Thus, a change of state occurs. Yet the activity is nonvalue-added because it repeats work. It is doing something that should have been done by preceding activities. Condition 2 (change of state was not achievable by preceding activities) is violated.

Nonvalue-added costs are costs that are caused either by nonvalue-added activities or the inefficient performance of value-added activities. For nonvalue-added activities, the nonvalue-added cost is the cost of the activity itself. For inefficient value-added activities, the activity cost must be broken into its value- and nonvalue-added components. For example, if Receiving should use 10,000 receiving orders but uses 20,000, then half of the cost of Receiving is value-added and half is nonvalue-added. The value-added component is the waste-free component of the value-added activity and is, therefore, the *value-added standard*. Due to increased competition, many firms are attempting to eliminate nonvalue-added activities because they add unnecessary cost and impede performance. Firms are also striving to optimize value-added activities. Thus, activity analysis identifies and eventually eliminates all unnecessary activities and, simultaneously, increases the efficiency of necessary activities.

The theme of activity analysis is waste elimination. As waste is eliminated, costs are reduced. The cost reduction *follows* the elimination of waste. Note the value of managing the causes of the costs rather than the costs themselves. Though managing costs may increase the efficiency of an activity, if the activity is unnecessary, what does it matter if it is performed efficiently? An unnecessary activity is wasteful and should be eliminated. For example, moving raw materials and partially finished goods is often cited as a nonvalue-added activity. Installing an automated materials handling system may increase the efficiency of this activity, but changing to cellular manufacturing with on-site, just-in-time delivery of raw materials could virtually eliminate the activity. It's easy to see which is preferable.

Examples of Nonvalue-Added Activities Reordering parts, expediting production, and rework because of defective parts are all examples of nonvalue-added activities. Other examples include warranty work, handling customer complaints, and reporting defects. Nonvalue-added activities can exist anywhere in the organization. In the manufacturing operation, the following major activities are often cited as wasteful and unnecessary:

- *Scheduling:* An activity that uses time and resources to determine when different products have access to processes (or when and how many setups must be done) and how much will be produced.
- *Moving:* An activity that uses time and resources to move raw materials, work in process, and finished goods from one department to another.
- *Waiting:* An activity in which raw materials or work in process use time and resources by waiting on the next process.
- *Inspecting:* An activity in which time and resources are spent ensuring that the product meets specifications.
- *Storing:* An activity that uses time and resources while a good or raw material is held in inventory.

None of these activities adds any value for the customer. (Note that inspection would not be necessary if the product were produced correctly the first time and, therefore, adds no value for the customer.) The challenge of activity analysis is to find ways to produce the good without using any of these activities.

Cost Reduction Activity management carries with it the objective of cost reduction. Competitive conditions dictate that companies must deliver customer desired products on time and at the lowest possible cost. These conditions mean that an organization must continually strive for cost improvement. Activity management can reduce costs in four ways:[6]

- activity elimination
- activity selection
- activity reduction
- activity sharing

---

6 Peter B. B. Turney, "How Activity-Based Costing Helps Reduce Cost," *Journal of Cost Management* (Winter 1991): 29–35.

CONCEPT CLIP

For **Stillwater Designs**, warranty work is a significant cost. Warranty work associated with defective products is typically labeled a nonvalue-added cost. Stillwater Designs recognizes the nonvalue-added nature of this activity and takes measures to eliminate the causes of the defective units. The company tracks return failures (over time) and provides this information to its research and development (R&D) department. R&D then uses this information to make design improvements on existing models (running changes) as well as to change the design on future models. The objective of the design changes is to reduce the demand for the warranty activity, thus reducing warranty cost.

However, not all **Kicker** warranty costs can be classified as nonvalue-added. When products are returned, customer service decides whether or not the problem is covered under warranty.

Sometimes, problems are covered even though they are not attributable to a defective product. When the company decides to replace a nondefective product, it is making a conscious decision to increase customer satisfaction and brand loyalty. This part of the warranty cost is a "marketing warranty cost" and could be classified as a value-added cost. For example, customers sometimes buy amplifiers that are more powerful than the subwoofers can handle, resulting in burnt voice coils. By replacing the product (even though technically it's the customer's fault), the customer will be more likely to buy again and to provide good word-of-mouth advertising for Kicker products.

KICKER *Livin Loud*

Activity Elimination   **Activity elimination** focuses on nonvalue-added activities. Once activities that fail to add value are identified, measures must be taken to rid the organization of these activities. For example, the activity of inspecting incoming parts seems necessary to ensure that the product using the parts functions according to specifications. Use of a bad part can produce a bad final product. Yet this activity is necessary only because of the poor quality performance of the supplying firms. Selecting suppliers who are able to supply high-quality parts or who are willing to improve their quality performance to achieve this objective will eventually allow the elimination of incoming inspection. Cost reduction then follows.

Activity Selection   **Activity selection** involves choosing among different sets of activities that are caused by competing strategies. Different strategies cause different activities. Different product design strategies, for example, can require significantly different activities. Activities, in turn, cause costs. Each product design strategy has its own set of activities and associated costs. All other things being equal, the lowest-cost design strategy should be chosen. In a continual-improvement environment, redesign of existing products and processes can lead to a different, cheaper set of activities. Thus, activity selection can have a significant effect on cost reduction.

Activity Reduction   **Activity reduction** decreases the time and resources required by an activity. This approach to cost reduction should be primarily aimed at improving the efficiency of necessary activities or a short-term strategy for improving nonvalue-added activities until they can be eliminated. Setup activity is a necessary activity that is often cited as an example for which less time and fewer resources need to be used. Finding ways to reduce setup time—and thus lower the cost of setups—is another example of the concept of gradual reductions in activity costs.

Activity Sharing   **Activity sharing** increases the efficiency of necessary activities by using economies of scale. Specifically, the quantity of the cost driver is increased without increasing the total cost of the activity itself. This lowers the per-unit cost of the cost driver and the amount of cost traceable to the products that consume the activity. For example, a new product can be designed to use components already being used by other products. By using existing components, the activities associated with these components already exist, and the company avoids the creation of a whole new set of activities.

Here's **Why It's important**

Assessing Nonvalue-Added Costs   Nonvalue-added costs are caused either by nonvalue-added activities or value-added activities performed inefficiently. Determining the nonvalue-added cost is followed by a root-cause analysis and then by the selection of an approach to reduce the waste found in the activity. For example, defective products cause warranty work. Defective products, in turn, are caused by such factors as defective internal processes, poor product design, and defective supplier components. Correcting the causes will lead to the elimination of the warranty activity. Inefficient purchasing could be attributable to such root causes as poor product design (too many components), orders that are incorrectly filled out, and defective supplier components (producing additional orders). Correcting the causes will reduce the demand for the purchasing activity, and as the activity is reduced, cost reduction will follow.

Example 5.7 shows how to determine the nonvalue-added cost of activities.

EXAMPLE 5.7

How to Assess Nonvalue-Added Costs

Consider the following two activities: (1) Performing warranty work, cost: $120,000. The warranty cost of the most efficient competitor is $20,000. (2) Purchasing components, cost: $200,000 (10,000 purchase orders). A benchmarking study reveals that the most efficient level will use 5,000 purchase orders and entail a cost of $100,000.

Required:
Determine the nonvalue-added cost of each activity.

Solution:
Determine the value content of each activity: Is the activity nonvalue-added or value-added?

1. Performing warranty work is nonvalue-added; it is done to correct something that wasn't done right the first time. Thus, the nonvalue-added cost of performing warranty work is $120,000. The cost of the competitor has no bearing on the analysis. Root causes for warranty work are defective products.

2. Purchasing components is necessary so that materials are available to produce products and, thus, is value-added. However, the activity is not performed efficiently, as revealed by the benchmarking study. The cost per purchase order is $20 ($100,000/5,000). The nonvalue-added cost is calculated as:

$$(\text{Actual Quantity} - \text{Value-Added Quantity}) \times \text{Cost per Purchase Order}$$
$$(10,000 - 5,000) \times \$20 = \$100,000$$
$$(\text{or simply, } \$200,000 - \$100,000)$$

Activity Performance Measurement

Assessing how well activities (and processes) are performed is fundamental to management's efforts to improve profitability. Activity performance measures exist in both financial and nonfinancial forms. These measures are designed to assess how well an activity was performed and the results achieved. They are also designed to reveal if constant improvement is being realized. Measures of activity performance center on three major dimensions:

- efficiency
- time
- quality

Efficiency *Efficiency* focuses on the relationship of activity inputs to activity outputs. For example, one way to improve activity efficiency is to produce the same activity output with lower cost for the inputs used. Thus, cost and trends in cost become important measures of efficiency.

Time The *time* required to perform an activity is also critical. Longer times usually mean more resource consumption and less ability to respond to customer demands. Time measures of performance tend to be nonfinancial, whereas efficiency and quality measures are both financial and nonfinancial.

Cycle time and *velocity* are two operational measures of time-based performance that measure the time it takes for a firm to respond to such things as customer orders, customer complaints, and the development of new products. The objective is to reduce cycle time (increase velocity) and thus improve response time, making the firm more competitive. Cycle time can be applied to any activity or process that produces an output, and it measures how long it takes to produce an output from start to finish. In a manufacturing process, **cycle time** is the length of time that it takes to produce a unit of output from the time raw materials are received (starting point of the cycle) until the good is delivered to finished goods inventory (finishing point of the cycle). Thus, cycle time is the time required to produce one unit of a product:

$$\text{Cycle time} = \textit{Time/Units produced.}$$

Velocity is the number of units of output that can be produced in a given period of time:

$$\text{Velocity} = \textit{Units produced/Time.}$$

Notice that velocity is the reciprocal of cycle time.

Example 5.8 demonstrates how to compute cycle time and velocity.

EXAMPLE 5.8

How to Calculate Cycle Time and Velocity

Assume that Frost Company takes 10,000 hours to produce 20,000 units of a product.

Required:
What is the velocity in hours? Cycle time in hours? Cycle time in minutes?

Solution:
Velocity = 20,000/10,000 = 2 units per hour
Cycle Time = 10,000/20,000 = 1/2 hour = 30 minutes

Quality *Quality* is concerned with doing the activity right the first time it is performed. If the activity output is defective, then the activity may need to be repeated, causing unnecessary cost and reduction in efficiency. Quality cost management is a major topic and is discussed in more detail in Chapter 13.

Check Point

1. **What is the purpose of driver analysis?**

Answer:
The objective of driver analysis is to find the root causes of activity costs. By knowing root causes, costs can be managed effectively.

2. **What are the three dimensions of performance for activities? Explain why they are important.**

Answer:
Efficiency, time, and quality are the three performance dimensions. All three relate to the ability of a manager to reduce activity cost.

SUMMARY OF LEARNING OBJECTIVES

LO1. Explain why functional (or volume)-based costing approaches may produce distorted costs.
- Overhead costs have increased in significance over time and in many firms represent a much higher percentage of product costs than direct labor.
- Many overhead activities are unrelated to the units produced.
- Functional-based costing systems are not able to assign the costs of these nonunit-based overhead activities properly.
- Nonunit-based overhead activities often are consumed by products in different proportions than are unit-based overhead activities. Because of this nonproportionality, assigning overhead by using only unit-based drivers can distort product costs.
- If the nonunit-based overhead costs are a significant proportion of total overhead costs, the inaccuracy in cost assignments can be a serious matter.

LO2. Explain how an activity-based costing system works for product costing.
- Activities are identified and defined through the use of interviews and surveys. This information allows an activity dictionary to be constructed.
- The activity dictionary lists activities and potential activity drivers, classifies activities as primary or secondary, and provides any other attributes deemed to be important.
- Resource costs are assigned to activities by using direct tracing and resource drivers.
- The costs of secondary activities are ultimately assigned to primary activities by using activity drivers.
- Finally, the costs of primary activities are assigned to products, customers, and other cost objects.
- The cost assignment process is described by the following general steps: (1) identifying the major activities and building an activity dictionary, (2) determining the cost of those activities, (3) identifying a measure of consumption for activity costs (activity drivers), (4) calculating an activity rate, (5) measuring the demands placed on activities by each product, and (6) calculating product costs.

LO3. Describe activity-based customer costing and activity-based supplier costing.
- Tracing customer-driven costs to customers can provide significant information to managers.
- Accurate customer costs allow managers to make better pricing decisions, customer-mix decisions, and other customer-related decisions that improve profitability.
- Tracing supplier-driven costs to suppliers can enable managers to choose the true low-cost suppliers, producing a stronger competitive position and increased profitability.

LO4. Explain how activity-based management can be used for cost reduction.
- Assigning costs accurately is vital for good decision making.
- Assigning the costs of an activity accurately does not address the issue of whether or not the activity should be performed or whether it is being performed efficiently.
- Activity-based management focuses on process-value analysis.
- Process-value analysis has three components: driver analysis, activity analysis, and performance evaluation. These three steps determine what activities are being done, why they are being done, and how well they are done.
- Understanding the root causes of activities provides the opportunities to manage activities so that costs can be reduced.

SUMMARY OF IMPORTANT EQUATIONS

1. $\text{Consumption Ratio} = \dfrac{\text{Amount of Activity Driver per Product}}{\text{Total Driver Quantity}}$

2. $\text{Overhead} = \dfrac{\text{Total Overhead Costs}}{\text{Total Direct Labor Hours}}$

3. Cycle Time = Time/Units Produced

4. Velocity = Units Produced/Time

EXAMPLE 5.1   How to calculate consumption ratios, page 220

EXAMPLE 5.2   How to calculate activity rates, page 221

EXAMPLE 5.3   How to calculate activity-based unit costs, page 222

EXAMPLE 5.4   How to assign resource costs to activities by using direct tracing and resource drivers, page 229

EXAMPLE 5.5   How to calculate activity-based customer costs, page 233

EXAMPLE 5.6   How to calculate activity-based supplier costs, page 235

EXAMPLE 5.7   How to assess nonvalue-added costs, page 241

EXAMPLE 5.8   How to calculate cycle time and velocity, page 242

KEY TERMS

Activity, 226, action taken or work performed by equipment or people for other people.

Activity analysis, 237, the process of identifying, describing, and evaluating the activities an organization performs.

Activity-based costing (ABC) system, 226, a cost assignment approach that first uses direct and driver tracing to assign costs to activities and then uses drivers to assign costs to cost objects.

Activity-based management, 236, a systemwide, integrated approach that focuses management's attention on activities with the objective of improving customer value and the profit achieved by providing this value. It includes driver analysis, activity analysis, and performance evaluation, and draws on activity-based costing as a major source of information.

Activity dictionary, 227, a list of activities described by specific attributes such as name, definition, classification as primary or secondary, and activity driver.

Activity drivers, 218, factors that measure the consumption of activities by products and other cost objects.

Activity elimination, 240, the process of eliminating nonvalue-added activities.

Activity inputs, 237, the resources consumed by an activity in producing its output. (They are the factors that enable the activity to be performed.)

Activity output, 237, the result or product of an activity.

Activity output measure, 237, the number of times an activity is performed. It is the quantifiable measure of the output.

Activity reduction, 240, decreasing the time and resources required by an activity.

Activity selection, 240, the process of choosing among sets of activities caused by competing strategies.

Activity sharing, 240, increasing the efficiency of necessary activities by using economies of scale.

Consumption ratio, 220, the proportion of an overhead activity consumed by a product.

Cycle time, 242, the length of time required to produce one unit of a product.

Driver analysis, 237, the effort expended to identify those factors that are the root causes of activity costs.

Nonunit-level activity drivers, 218, factors that measure the consumption of nonunit-level activities by products and other cost objects.

Nonvalue-added activities, 238, all activities other than those that are absolutely essential to remain in business.

Nonvalue-added costs, 239, costs that are caused either by nonvalue-added activities or by the inefficient performance of value-added activities.

Process-value analysis, 236, an approach that focuses on processes and activities and emphasizes systemwide performance instead of individual performance.

Product diversity, 218, the situation present when products consume overhead in different proportions.

Resource drivers, 228, factors that measure the consumption of resources by activities.

Unit-level activities, 216, activities that are performed each time a unit is produced.

Unit-level activity drivers, 218, factors that measure the consumption of unit-level activities by products and other cost objects.

Value-added activities, 238, activities that are necessary for a business to achieve corporate objectives and remain in business.

Value-added costs, 238, costs caused by value-added activities.

Velocity, 242, the number of units that can be produced in a given period of time (e.g., output per hour).

Work distribution matrix, 228, identifies the amount of labor consumed by each activity and is derived from the interview process (or a written survey).

REVIEW PROBLEMS

I. Plantwide Rates

Gee Company produces two types of stereo units: deluxe and regular. For the most recent year, Gee reports the following data:

Budgeted overhead	$180,000
Expected activity (in direct labor hours)	50,000
Actual activity (in direct labor hours)	51,000
Actual overhead	$200,000

	Deluxe	Regular
Units produced	5,000	50,000
Prime costs	$40,000	$300,000
Direct labor hours	5,000	46,000

Required:

1. Calculate a predetermined overhead rate based on direct labor hours.
2. What is the applied overhead?
3. What is the under- or overapplied overhead?
4. Calculate the unit cost of each stereo unit.

(Continued)

Solution:

1. Rate = $180,000/50,000 = $3.60 per direct labor hour
2. Applied Overhead = $3.60 × 51,000 = $183,600
3. Overhead Variance = $200,000 − $183,600 = $16,400 underapplied
4. Unit cost:

	Deluxe	Regular
Prime costs	$ 40,000	$300,000
Overhead costs:		
$3.60 × 5,000	18,000	
$3.60 × 46,000		165,600
Total manufacturing costs	$ 58,000	$465,600
Units produced	÷ 5,000	÷ 50,000
Unit cost (Total costs/Units)	$ 11.60	$ 9.31*

*Rounded.

II. Departmental Rates

Gee Company gathers the following departmental data for a second year. Two types of stereo units are produced: deluxe and regular.

	Fabrication	Assembly
Budgeted overhead	$120,000	$60,000
Expected and actual usage (direct labor hours):		
Deluxe	3,000	2,000
Regular	3,000	43,000
	6,000	45,000
Expected and actual usage (machine hours):		
Deluxe	2,000	5,000
Regular	18,000	5,000
	20,000	10,000

In addition to the departmental data, the following information is provided:

	Deluxe	Regular
Units produced	5,000	50,000
Prime costs	$40,000	$300,000

Required:

1. Calculate departmental overhead rates by using machine hours for fabrication and direct labor hours for assembly.
2. Calculate the applied overhead by department.
3. Calculate the applied overhead by product.
4. Calculate unit costs.

Solution:

1. Departmental rates

   Fabrication: $120,000/20,000 machine hours = $6.00 per machine hour
   Assembly: $60,000/45,000 direct labor hours = $1.33* per direct labor hour
   *Rounded.

2. Applied overhead (by department):

   Fabrication: $6.00 × 20,000 = $120,000
   Assembly: $1.33 × 45,000 = $59,850

3. Applied overhead (by product):

   Deluxe: ($6.00 × 2,000) + ($1.33 × 2,000) = $14,660
   Regular: ($6.00 × 18,000) + ($1.33 × 43,000) = $165,190

4. Unit cost:

   Deluxe: ($40,000 + $14,660)/5,000 = $10.93*
   Regular: ($300,000 + $165,190)/50,000 = $9.30*

   *Rounded to nearest cent.

III. Activity-Based Rates

Gee Company produces two types of stereo units: deluxe and regular. Activity data follow:

Product-Costing Data

Activity Usage Measures	Deluxe	Regular	Total
Units produced per year	5,000	50,000	55,000
Prime costs	$39,000	$369,000	$408,000
Direct labor hours	5,000	45,000	50,000
Machine hours	10,000	90,000	100,000
Production runs	10	5	15
Number of moves	120	60	180

Activity Cost Data (Overhead Activities)

Activity	Cost
Setups	$ 60,000
Materials handling	30,000
Power	50,000
Testing	40,000
Total	$180,000

Required:

1. Calculate the consumption ratios for each activity.
2. Group activities based on the consumption ratios.
3. Calculate a rate for each pooled group of activities.
4. Using the pool rates, calculate unit product costs.

Solution:

1. Consumption ratios:

Overhead Activity	Deluxe	Regular	Activity Driver
Setups	0.67[a]	0.33[a]	Production runs
Materials handling	0.67[b]	0.33[b]	Number of moves
Power	0.10[c]	0.90[c]	Machine hours
Testing	0.10[d]	0.90[d]	Direct labor hours

[a] 10/15 (deluxe) and 5/15 (regular)
[b] 120/180 (deluxe) and 60/180 (regular)
[c] 10,000/100,000 (deluxe) and 90,000/100,000 (regular)
[d] 5,000/50,000 (deluxe) and 45,000/50,000 (regular)

2. Batch-level: Setups and Materials handling
   Unit-level: Power and Testing

(*Continued*)

3.

Batch-Level Pool		Unit-Level Pool	
Setups	$60,000	Power	$ 50,000
Materials handling	30,000	Testing	40,000
Total	$90,000	Total	$ 90,000
Runs	÷ 15	Machine hours	÷ 100,000
Pool rate	$ 6,000 per run	Pool rate	$ 0.90 per machine hour

4. Unit costs: Activity-based costing

	Deluxe	Regular
Prime costs	$ 39,000	$369,000
Overhead costs:		
Batch-level pool:		
($6,000 × 10)	60,000	
($6,000 × 5)		30,000
Unit-level pool:		
($0.90 × 10,000)	9,000	
($0.90 × 90,000)		81,000
Total manufacturing costs	$108,000	$480,000
Units produced	÷ 5,000	÷ 50,000
Unit cost (Total costs/Units)	$ 21.60	$ 9.60

DISCUSSION QUESTIONS

1. Describe the two-stage process associated with plantwide overhead rates.
2. Describe the two-stage process for departmental overhead rates.
3. What are nonunit-level overhead activities? Nonunit-based cost drivers? Give some examples.
4. What is product diversity?
5. What is an overhead consumption ratio?
6. What is activity-based product costing?
7. What is an activity dictionary?
8. Explain how costs are assigned to activities.
9. Describe the value of activity-based customer costing.
10. Explain how ABC can help a firm identify its true low-cost suppliers.
11. What is driver analysis? What role does it play in process-value analysis?
12. What are value-added activities? Value-added costs?
13. What are nonvalue-added activities? Nonvalue-added costs? Give an example of each.
14. Identify and define four different ways to manage activities so that costs can be reduced.
15. What is cycle time? Velocity?

MULTIPLE-CHOICE QUESTIONS

5-1   A batch-level driver is consumed by a product each and every time that

   a. a batch of products is produced.
   b. a unit is produced.
   c. a purchase order is issued.
   d. a customer complains.
   e. None of these.

5-2 Which of the following is a nonunit-level driver?

    a. Direct labor hours

    b. Machine hours

    c. Direct materials

    d. Setup hours

    e. Assembly hours

Use the following information for Multiple-Choice Questions 5-3 and 5-4:
Consider the information given on two products and their activity usage:

	Laser Printer	Inkjet Printer
Units produced	1,000	4,000
Setup hours	800	400
Inspection hours	500	500
Machine hours	200	1,000

5-3 Refer to the information above. The consumption ratios for the inspection activity for each product are

    a. 0.167; 0.833.

    b. 0.333; 0.667.

    c. 0.500; 0.500.

    d. 0.667; 0.333.

    e. None of these.

5-4 Refer to the information above. Suppose that machine hours are used to assign all overhead costs to the two products. Select the best answer from the following:

    a. Laser printers are overcosted, and inkjet printers are undercosted.

    b. Laser printers and inkjet printers are accurately costed.

    c. Laser printers are undercosted, and inkjet printers are overcosted.

    d. Using inspection hours to assign overhead costs is the most accurate approach.

    e. None of these.

5-5 The first stage of ABC entails the assignment of

    a. resource costs to departments.

    b. activity costs to products or customers.

    c. resource costs to a plantwide pool.

    d. resource costs to distribution channels.

    e. resource costs to individual activities.

5-6 The second stage of ABC entails the assignment of

    a. activity costs to products or customers.

    b. resource costs to departments.

    c. resource costs to a plantwide pool.

    d. resource costs to individual activities.

    e. resource costs to distribution channels.

5-7 Interview questions are asked to determine

    a. what activities are being performed.

    b. who performs the activities.

    c. the relative amount of time spent on each activity by individual workers.

    d. possible activity drivers for assigning costs to products.

    e. All of these.

5-8   The receiving department employs one worker who spends 25% of his time on the receiving activity and 75% of his time on inspecting products. His salary is $40,000. The amount of cost assigned to the receiving activity is

    a. $34,000.
    b. $40,000.
    c. $10,000.
    d. $30,000.
    e. None of these.

5-9   Assume that the moving activity has an expected cost of $80,000. Expected direct labor hours are 20,000, and expected number of moves is 40,000. The best activity rate for moving is

    a. $4 per move.
    b. $1.33 per hour-move.
    c. $4 per hour.
    d. $2 per move.
    e. None of these.

5-10   Which of the following is a true statement about activity-based customer costing?

    a. Customer diversity requires multiple drivers to trace costs accurately to customers.
    b. Customers consume customer-driven activities in the same proportions.
    c. It seldom produces changes in the company's customer mix.
    d. It never improves profitability.
    e. None of these.

5-11   Which of the following is a true statement about activity-based supplier costing?

    a. The cost of a supplier is the purchase price of the components or materials acquired.
    b. It encourages managers to increase the number of suppliers.
    c. It encourages managers to evaluate suppliers based on purchase cost.
    d. Suppliers can affect many internal activities of a firm and significantly increase the cost of purchasing.
    e. All of these.

5-12   This year, Lambert Company will ship 1,500,000 pounds of goods to customers at a cost of $1,200,000. If a customer orders 10,000 pounds and produces $200,000 of revenue (total revenue is $20 million), the amount of shipping cost assigned to the customer by using ABC would be

    a. unable to be determined.
    b. $8,000 ($0.80 per pound shipped).
    c. $24,000 (2% of the shipping cost).
    d. $12,000 (1% of the shipping cost).
    e. None of these.

[handwritten: 1200000 | 1500000 = .8]
[handwritten: 10,000 × .8 = $8000]

5-13   Lambert Company has two suppliers: Deming and Leming. The cost of warranty work due to defective components is $2,000,000. The total units repaired under warranty average 100,000, of which 90,000 have components from Deming and 10,000 have components from Leming. Select the items below that represent true statements.

    a. Components purchased from Leming cost $200,000 more than their purchase price.
    b. Components purchased from Deming cost $1,800,000 more than their purchase price.
    c. Components from Leming appear to be of higher quality.
    d. All of these.
    e. None of these.

5-14 A forklift and its driver used for moving materials are examples of

    a. activity inputs.
    b. activity output measures.
    c. resource drivers.
    d. activity outputs.
    e. root causes.

5-15 Which of the following are nonvalue-added activities?

    a. Moving goods
    b. Storing goods
    c. Inspecting finished goods
    d. Reworking a defective product
    e. All of these.

5-16 Suppose that a company is spending $60,000 per year for inspecting, $30,000 for purchasing, and $40,000 for reworking products. A good estimate of nonvalue-added costs would be

    a. $70,000.

    b. $130,000.

    c. $40,000.

    d. $90,000.

    e. $100,000.

5-17 The cost of inspecting incoming parts is most likely to be reduced by

    a. activity sharing.
    b. activity elimination.
    c. activity reduction.
    d. activity selection.
    e. None of these.

5-18 Thom Company produces 60 units in 10 hours. The cycle time for Thom

    a. is 6 units per hour.
    b. is 10 hours per unit.
    c. is 10 minutes per unit.
    d. is 6 minutes per unit.
    e. cannot be calculated.

5-19 Thom Company produces 60 units in 10 hours. The velocity for Thom

    a. is 6 units per hour.
    b. is 10 hours per unit.
    c. is 10 minutes per unit.
    d. is 6 minutes per unit.
    e. cannot be calculated.

5-20 Striving to produce the same activity output with lower costs for the input used is concerned with which of the following dimensions of activity performance?

    a. Quality
    b. Time
    c. Activity sharing
    d. Effectiveness
    e. Efficiency

BRIEF EXERCISES: SET A

> *Use the following information for Brief Exercises 5-21 and 5-22:*
> Zapato Company produces two types of boots: vaquero and vaquera. There are four activities associated with the two products. Drivers for the four activities are as follows:
>
> | | Vaquero | Vaquera |
> |---|---|---|
> | Cutting hours | 4,000 | 5,400 |
> | Assembly hours | 2,850 | 4,650 |
> | Inspection hours | 945 | 2,430 |
> | Rework hours | 150 | 450 |

OBJECTIVE 1
Example 5.1

Brief Exercise 5-21 Consumption Ratios

Refer to the information for Zapato Company given above.

Required:

1. Calculate the consumption ratios for the four drivers (round to two decimal places).
2. Is there evidence of product diversity? Explain.

OBJECTIVE 1
Example 5.2

Brief Exercise 5-22 Activity Rates

Refer to the information for Zapato Company given above. The following activity data have been collected:

Cutting	$225,600
Assembling	300,000
Inspecting	67,500
Reworking	45,000

Required:

Calculate the activity rates that would be used to assign costs to each product.

OBJECTIVE 1
Example 5.3

Brief Exercise 5-23 Calculating ABC Unit Costs

Perkins National Bank has collected the following information for four activities and two types of credit cards:

Activity	Driver	Classic	Gold	Activity Rate
Processing transactions	Transactions processed	12,000	7,200	$0.20
Preparing statements	Number of statements	12,000	7,200	0.95
Answering questions	Number of calls	24,000	36,000	4.00
Providing ATMs	ATM transactions	48,000	14,400	1.50

There are 7,500 holders of Classic cards and 30,000 holders of Gold cards.

Required:

Calculate the unit cost (rounded to the nearest cent) for Classic and Gold credit cards.

Brief Exercise 5-24 Assigning Costs to Activities

OBJECTIVE ▶2

Example 5.4

McCourt Company produces small engines for lawnmower producers. The accounts payable department at McCourt has 10 clerks who process and pay supplier invoices. The total cost of their salaries is $500,000. The work distribution for the activities that they perform is as follows:

Activity	Percentage of Time on Each Activity
Comparing source documents	25%
Resolving discrepancies	60
Processing payment	15

Required:

Assign the cost of labor to each of the three activities in the accounts payable department.

Brief Exercise 5-25 Activity-Based Customer Costing

OBJECTIVE ▶3

Example 5.5

Sleepeze Company produces mattresses for 20 retail outlets. Of the 20 retail outlets, 19 are small, separately owned furniture stores and one is a retail chain. The retail chain buys 60% of the mattresses produced. The 19 smaller customers purchase mattresses in approximately equal quantities, where the orders are about the same size. Data concerning Sleepeze's customer activity are as follows:

	Large Retailer	Smaller Retailers
Units purchased	108,000	72,000
Orders placed	36	3,600
Number of sales calls	18	882
Manufacturing costs	$43,200,000	$28,800,000
Order filling costs allocated*	$ 1,455,127	$ 970,085
Sales force costs allocated*	$ 719,820	$ 479,880

*Currently allocated on sales volume (units sold).

Currently, customer-driven costs are assigned to customers based on units sold, a unit-level driver.

Required:

Assign costs to customers by using an ABC approach. Round activity rates and activity costs to the nearest dollar.

Brief Exercise 5-26 Activity-Based Supplier Costing

OBJECTIVE ▶3

Example 5.6

Clearsound uses Alpha Electronics and La Paz Company to buy two electronic components used in the manufacture of its cell phones: Component 125X and Component 30Y. Consider two activities: testing components and reordering components. After the two components are inserted, testing is done to ensure that the two components in the phones are working properly. Reordering occurs because one or both of the components have failed the test and it is necessary to replenish component inventories. Activity cost information and other data needed for supplier costing are as follows:

I. Activity Costs Caused by Suppliers (testing failures and reordering as a result)

Activity	Costs
Testing components	$1,200,000
Reordering components	300,000

(*Continued*)

II. Supplier Data

	Alpha Electronics		La Paz Company	
	125X	30Y	125X	30Y
Unit purchase price	$10	$26	$12	$28
Units purchased	120,000	60,000	15,000	15,000
Failed tests	1,200	780	10	10
Number of reorders	60	40	0	0

Required:

Determine the cost of each supplier by using ABC. Round unit costs to two decimal places.

OBJECTIVE **4** ▶
Example 5.7

Brief Exercise 5-27 **Nonvalue-Added Costs**

Lemmons Inc. has the following two activities: (1) Retesting reworked products, cost: $720,000. The retesting cost of the most efficient competitor is $225,000. (2) Welding sub-assemblies, cost: $1,350,000 (67,500 welding hours). A benchmarking study reveals that the most efficient level for Lemmons would use 54,000 welding hours and entail a cost of $1,080,000.

Required:

Determine the nonvalue-added cost of each activity.

OBJECTIVE **4** ▶
Example 5.8

Brief Exercise 5-28 **Velocity and Cycle Time**

Kolby Company takes 36,000 hours to produce 144,000 units of a product.

Required:

What is the velocity? Cycle time?

BRIEF EXERCISES: SET B

Use the following information for Brief Exercises 5-29 and 5-30:
Cinturas Company produces two types of men's shirts: casual and formal. There are four activities associated with the two products. Drivers for the four activities are as follows:

	Casual	Formal
Cutting hours	12,000	18,000
Sewing hours	3,000	7,000
Inspection hours	2,000	4,000
Rework hours	400	600

OBJECTIVE **1** ▶
Example 5.1

Brief Exercise 5-29 **Consumption Ratios**

Refer to the information for Cinturas Company given above.

Required:

1. Calculate the consumption ratios for the four drivers.
2. Is there evidence of product diversity? Explain.

Brief Exercise 5-30 Activity Rates

OBJECTIVE 1
Example 5.2

Refer to the information above for Cinturas Company. The following activity data have been collected:

Cutting	$ 90,000
Sewing	100,000
Inspecting	36,000
Reworking	20,000

Required:

Calculate the activity rates that would be used to assign costs to each product.

Brief Exercise 5-31 Calculating ABC Unit Costs

OBJECTIVE 1
Example 5.3

Community Credit Union has collected the following information for four activities and two types of credit cards:

Activity	Driver	Silver	Premium	Activity Rate
Processing transactions	Transactions processed	20,000	12,000	$0.20
Preparing statements	Number of statements	20,000	12,000	0.85
Answering questions	Number of calls	40,000	60,000	2.00
Providing ATMs	ATM transactions	80,000	24,000	1.80

There are 12,500 holders of Silver cards and 50,000 holders of Premium cards.

Required:

Calculate the unit cost (rounded to the nearest cent) for Silver and Premium credit cards.

Brief Exercise 5-32 Assigning Costs to Activities

OBJECTIVE 2
Example 5.4

Craig Company produces electronic components for cell phone producers. The receiving department at Craig has eight clerks who process incoming goods. The total cost of their salaries is $440,000. The work distribution for the activities that they perform is as follows:

Activity	Percentage of Time on Each Activity
Unloading goods	25%
Counting goods	35
Inspecting goods	40

Required:

Assign the cost of labor to each of the three activities in the receiving department.

Brief Exercise 5-33 Activity-Based Customer Costing

OBJECTIVE 3
Example 5.5

Limpio Company produces dishwashers for 36 retail outlets. Of the 36 retail outlets, 34 are small, separately owned appliance stores and two are large retail chains. The two large retailers buy 80% of the dishwashers produced. The 34 smaller customers purchase dishwashers in approximately equal quantities, where the orders are about the same size. Data concerning Limpio's customer activity are as follows:

(Continued)

	Large Retailers	Smaller Retailers
Units purchased	60,000	15,000
Orders placed	20	1,500
Number of sales calls	8	816
Manufacturing costs	$4,500,000	$1,125,000
Order filling costs allocated*	$ 646,400	$ 161,600
Sales force costs allocated*	$ 320,000	$ 80,000

*Currently allocated on sales volume (units sold).

Currently, customer-driven costs are assigned to customers based on units sold, a unit-level driver.

Required:

Assign costs to customers by using an ABC approach. Round activity rates and activity costs to the nearest dollar.

Brief Exercise 5-34 **Activity-Based Supplier Costing**

Blackburn Inc. uses Otavalo Manufacturing and Piura Company to buy two precision-machined parts used in the manufacture of its permanent-magnet motors: Part #625 and Part #827. Consider two activities: testing parts and reordering parts. After the two parts are inserted, testing is done to ensure that the two parts work as intended. Reordering occurs because one or both of the parts have failed the test and it is necessary to replenish part inventories. Activity cost information and other data needed for supplier costing are as follows:

I. Activity Costs Caused by Suppliers (testing failures and reordering as a result)

Activity	Costs
Testing parts	$4,500,000
Reordering parts	1,125,000

II. Supplier Data

	Otavalo Manufacturing		Piura Company	
	Part #625	Part #827	Part #625	Part #827
Unit purchase price	$30	$78	$36	$84
Units purchased	450,000	225,000	56,250	56,250
Failed tests	4,500	2,925	39	36
Number of reorders	225	150	0	0

Required:

Determine the cost of each supplier by using ABC. Round unit costs to two decimal places.

Brief Exercise 5-35 **Nonvalue-Added Costs**

Evans Inc. has the following two activities: (1) Reworking products, cost: $740,000. The reworking cost of the most efficient similar-sized competitor is $200,000. (2) Purchasing parts, cost: $900,000 (45,000 purchasing hours). A benchmarking study reveals that the most efficient level for Evans would use 24,000 purchasing hours and entail a cost of $450,000.

Required:

Determine the nonvalue-added cost of each activity.

OBJECTIVE 4
Example 5.8

Brief Exercise 5-36 **Velocity and Cycle Time**

Tara Company takes 8,000 hours to produce 40,000 units of a product.

Required:

What is the velocity? Cycle time?

EXERCISES

OBJECTIVE ▸ 1

Exercise 5-37 Consumption Ratios; Activity Rates

Saludable Company produces two types of get-well cards: scented and regular. Drivers for the four activities are as follows:

	Scented Cards	Regular Cards
Inspection hours	1,080	720
Setup hours	420	180
Machine hours	960	2,880
Number of moves	2,880	720

The following activity data have been collected:

Inspecting products	$45,000
Setting up equipment	28,500
Machining	30,720
Moving materials	16,200

Required:

1. Calculate the consumption ratios for the four drivers (round to two decimal places).
2. **CONCEPTUAL CONNECTION** Is there evidence of product diversity? Explain the significance of product diversity for decision making if the company chooses to use machine hours to assign all overhead.
3. Calculate the activity rates that would be used to assign costs to each product (round to two decimal places).
4. Suppose that the activity rate for inspecting products is $20 per inspection hour. How many hours of inspection are expected for the coming year?

OBJECTIVE ▸ 2

Exercise 5-38 Activity Rates

Patten Company uses activity-based costing (ABC). Patten manufactures toy cars using two activities: plastic injection molding and decal application. Patten's 20X1 total budgeted overhead costs for these two activities are $675,000 (80% for injection molding and 20% for decal application). Molding overhead costs are driven by the number of pounds of plastic that are molded together. Decal application overhead costs are driven by the number of decals applied to toys. The budgeted activity data for 20X1 are as follows:

Pounds of plastic molded	3,000,000
Number of decals applied	375,000

Required:

1. Calculate the activity rate for the plastic injection molding activity (round to two decimal places).
2. Calculate the activity rate for the decal application activity (round to two decimal places).

OBJECTIVE ▸ 2

Exercise 5-39 Comparing ABC and Plantwide Overhead Cost Assignments

Wellington Chocolate Company uses activity-based costing (ABC). The controller identified two activities and their budgeted costs:

Setting up equipment	$ 432,000
Other overhead	1,440,000

Setting up equipment is based on setup hours, and other overhead is based on oven hours.

(Continued)

Wellington produces two products, Fudge and Cookies. Information on each product is as follows:

	Fudge	Cookies
Units produced	8,000	445,000
Setup hours	6,400	1,600
Oven hours	1,600	8,000

Required:

(*Note:* Round answers to two decimal places.)
1. Calculate the activity rate for (a) setting up equipment and (b) other overhead.
2. How much total overhead is assigned to Fudge using ABC?
3. What is the unit overhead assigned to Fudge using ABC?
4. Now, ignoring the ABC results, calculate the plantwide overhead rate, based on oven hours.
5. How much total overhead is assigned to Fudge using the plantwide overhead rate?
6. **CONCEPTUAL CONNECTION** Explain why the total overhead assigned to Fudge is different under the ABC system (i.e., using the activity rates) than under the non-ABC system (i.e., using the plantwide rate).

OBJECTIVE **1 ▶ 2** ▶   **Exercise 5-40 Activity-Based Product Costing**

EXCEL

Suppose that a surgical ward has gathered the following information for four nursing activities and two types of patients:

		Patient Category		
	Driver	Normal	Intensive	Activity Rate
Treating patients	Treatments	6,400	8,000	$4.00
Providing hygienic care	Hygienic hours	4,800	17,600	5.00
Responding to requests	Requests	32,000	80,000	2.00
Monitoring patients	Monitoring hours	6,000	72,000	3.00

Required:

1. Determine the total nursing costs assigned to each patient category.
2. Output is measured in patient days. Assuming that the normal patient category uses 8,000 patient days and the intensive patient category uses 6,400 patient days, calculate the nursing cost per patient day for each type of patient. (Round to two decimal places.)
3. **CONCEPTUAL CONNECTION** The supervisor of the surgical ward has suggested that patient days is the only driver needed to assign nursing costs to each type of patient. Calculate the charge per patient day (rounded to the nearest cent) using this approach and then explain to the supervisor why this would be a bad decision.

OBJECTIVE **2** ▶   **Exercise 5-41 Assigning Costs to Activities, Resource Drivers**

The receiving department has three activities: unloading, counting goods, and inspecting. Unloading uses a forklift that is leased for $15,000 per year. The forklift is used only for unloading. The fuel for the forklift is $3,600 per year. Other operating costs (maintenance) for the forklift total $1,500 per year. Inspection uses some special testing equipment that has depreciation of $1,200 per year and an operating cost of $750. Receiving has three employees who have an average salary of $50,000 per year. The work distribution matrix for the receiving personnel is as follows:

Activity	Percentage of Time on Each Activity
Unloading	40%
Counting	25
Inspecting	35

No other resources are used for these activities.

Required:

1. Calculate the cost of each activity.
2. **CONCEPTUAL CONNECTION** Explain the two methods used to assign costs to activities.

Exercise 5-42 Activity-Based Customer-Driven Costs

OBJECTIVE ◀ 2

EXCEL

Suppose that **Stillwater Designs** has two classes of distributors: JIT distributors and non-JIT distributors. The JIT distributor places small, frequent orders, and the non-JIT distributor tends to place larger, less frequent orders. Both types of distributors are buying the same product. Stillwater Designs provides the following information about customer-related activities and costs for the most recent quarter:

	JIT Distributors	Non-JIT Distributors
Sales orders	700	70
Sales calls	70	70
Service calls	350	175
Average order size	750	7,500
Manufacturing cost/unit	$125	$125
Customer costs:		
Processing sales orders	$3,080,000	
Selling goods	1,120,000	
Servicing goods	1,050,000	
Total	$5,250,000	

Required:

1. Calculate the total revenues per distributor category, and assign the customer costs to each distributor type by using revenues as the allocation base. Selling price for one unit is $150.
2. **CONCEPTUAL CONNECTION** Calculate the customer cost per distributor type using activity-based cost assignments. Discuss the merits of offering the non-JIT distributors a $2 price decrease (assume that they are agitating for a price concession).
3. **CONCEPTUAL CONNECTION** Assume that the JIT distributors are simply imposing the frequent orders on Stillwater Designs. No formal discussion has taken place between JIT customers and Stillwater Designs regarding the supply of goods on a JIT basis. The sales pattern has evolved over time. As an independent consultant, what would you suggest to Stillwater Designs' management?

Exercise 5-43 Activity-Based Supplier Costing

OBJECTIVE ◀ 3

EXCEL

Bowman Company manufactures cooling systems. Bowman produces all the parts necessary for its product except for one electronic component, which is purchased from two local suppliers: Manzer Inc. and Buckner Company. Both suppliers are reliable and seldom deliver late; however, Manzer sells the component for $89 per unit, while Buckner sells the same component for $86. Bowman purchases 80% of its components from Buckner because of its lower price. The total annual demand is 4,000,000 components.

To help assess the cost effect of the two components, the following data were collected for supplier-related activities and suppliers:

I. Activity Data

	Activity Cost
Inspecting components (sampling only)	$ 480,000
Reworking products (due to failed component)	6,084,000
Warranty work (due to failed component)	9,600,000

(Continued)

II. Supplier Data

	Manzer Inc.	Buckner Company
Unit purchase price	$89	$86
Units purchased	800,000	3,200,000
Sampling hours*	80	3,920
Rework hours	360	5,640
Warranty hours	800	15,200

*Sampling inspection for Manzer's product has been reduced because the reject rate is so low.

Required:

1. Calculate the cost per component for each supplier, taking into consideration the costs of the supplier-related activities and using the current prices and sales volume. (*Note*: Round the unit cost to two decimal places.)
2. Suppose that Bowman loses $4,000,000 in sales per year because it develops a poor reputation due to defective units attributable to failed components. Using warranty hours, assign the cost of lost sales to each supplier. By how much would this change the cost of each supplier's component? (Round to two decimal places.)
3. **CONCEPTUAL CONNECTION** Based on the analysis in Requirements 1 and 2, discuss the importance of activity-based supplier costing for internal decision making.

Use the following information for Exercises 5-44 through 5-46:
The following six situations at Diviney Manufacturing Inc. are independent.

a. A manual insertion process takes 30 minutes and 8 pounds of material to produce a product. Automating the insertion process requires 15 minutes of machine time and 7.5 pounds of material. The cost per labor hour is $12, the cost per machine hour is $8, and the cost per pound of materials is $10.

b. With its original design, a gear requires 8 hours of setup time. By redesigning the gear so that the number of different grooves needed is reduced by 50%, the setup time is reduced by 75%. The cost per setup hour is $50.

c. A product currently requires 6 moves. By redesigning the manufacturing layout, the number of moves can be reduced from 6 to 0. The cost per move is $20.

d. Inspection time for a plant is 16,000 hours per year. The cost of inspection consists of salaries of 8 inspectors, totaling $320,000. Inspection also uses supplies costing $5 per inspection hour. The company eliminated most defective components by eliminating low-quality suppliers. The number of production errors was reduced dramatically by installing a system of statistical process control. Further quality improvements were realized by redesigning the products, making them easier to manufacture. The net effect was to achieve a close to zero-defect state and eliminate the need for any inspection activity.

e. Each unit of a product requires 6 components. The average number of components is 6.5 due to component failure, requiring rework and extra components. Developing relations with the right suppliers and increasing the quality of the purchased component can reduce the average number of components to 6 components per unit. The cost per component is $500.

f. A plant produces 100 different electronic products. Each product requires an average of 8 components that are purchased externally. The components are different for each part. By redesigning the products, it is possible to produce the 100 products so that they all have 4 components in common. This will reduce the demand for purchasing, receiving, and paying bills. Estimated savings from the reduced demand are $900,000 per year.

Exercise 5-44 Nonvalue-Added Costs

OBJECTIVE ▶ 4

Refer to the information for Diviney Manufacturing on the previous page.

Required:

Estimate the nonvalue-added cost for each situation.

Exercise 5-45 Driver Analysis

OBJECTIVE ▶ 4

Refer to the information for Diviney Manufacturing on the previous page.

Required:

CONCEPTUAL CONNECTION For each situation, identify the possible root cause(s) of the activity cost (such as plant layout, process design, and product design).

Exercise 5-46 Type of Activity Management

OBJECTIVE ▶ 4

Refer to the information for Diviney Manufacturing on the previous page.

Required:

For each situation, identify the cost reduction measure: activity elimination, activity reduction, activity sharing, or activity selection.

Exercise 5-47 Cycle Time and Velocity

OBJECTIVE ▶ 1 ▶ 2 ▶ 3

In the first quarter of operations, a manufacturing cell produced 80,000 stereo speakers, using 20,000 production hours. In the second quarter, the cycle time was 10 minutes per unit with the same number of production hours as were used in the first quarter.

Required:

1. Compute the velocity (per hour) for the first quarter.
2. Compute the cycle time for the first quarter (minutes per unit produced).
3. How many units were produced in the second quarter?

Exercise 5-48 Product-Costing Accuracy, Consumption Ratios

OBJECTIVE ▶ 4

Plata Company produces two products: a mostly handcrafted soft leather briefcase sold under the label Maletin Elegant and a leather briefcase produced largely through automation and sold under the label Maletin Fina. The two products use two overhead activities, with the following costs:

Setting up equipment	$ 3,000
Machining	18,000

The controller has collected the expected annual prime costs for each briefcase, the machine hours, the setup hours, and the expected production.

	Elegant	Fina
Direct labor	$9,000	$3,000
Direct materials	$3,000	$3,000
Units	3,000	3,000
Machine hours	500	4,500
Setup hours	100	100

Required:

1. **CONCEPTUAL CONNECTION** Do you think that the direct labor costs and direct materials costs are accurately traced to each briefcase? Explain.
2. Calculate the consumption ratios for each activity. Round to two decimal places.

(Continued)

3. Calculate the overhead cost per unit for each briefcase by using a plantwide rate based on direct labor costs. Round rates to the nearest cent. Comment on this approach to assigning overhead.
4. **CONCEPTUAL CONNECTION** Calculate the overhead cost per unit for each briefcase by using overhead rates based on machine hours and setup hours. Explain why these assignments are more accurate than those using the direct labor costs.

OBJECTIVE 1 2

EXCEL

Exercise 5-49 Product-Costing Accuracy, Consumption Ratios, Activity Rates, Activity Costing

Tristar Manufacturing produces two types of battery-operated toy soldiers: infantry and special forces. The soldiers are produced by using one continuous process. Four activities have been identified: machining, setups, receiving, and packing. Resource drivers have been used to assign costs to each activity. The overhead activities, their costs, and the other related data are as follows:

Product	Machine Hours	Setups	Receiving Orders	Packing Orders
Infantry	20,000	300	900	1,600
Special forces	20,000	100	100	800
Costs	$80,000	$24,000	$18,000	$30,000

Required:

1. Calculate the total overhead assigned to each product by using only machine hours to calculate a plantwide rate.
2. Calculate consumption ratios for each activity. (Round to two decimal places.)
3. Calculate a rate for each activity by using the associated driver. (Round to two decimal places.)
4. Assign the overhead costs to each product by using the activity rates computed in Requirement 3.
5. **CONCEPTUAL CONNECTION** Comment on the difference between the assignment in Requirement 1 and the activity-based assignment.

OBJECTIVE 2

Exercise 5-50 Formation of an Activity Dictionary

A hospital is in the process of implementing an ABC system. A pilot study is being done to assess the effects of the costing changes on specific products. Of particular interest is the cost of caring for patients who receive in-patient recovery treatment for illness, surgery (noncardiac), and injury. These patients are housed on the third and fourth floors of the hospital. The floors are dedicated to patient care and have only nursing stations and patient rooms. A partial transcript of an interview with the hospital's nursing supervisor is as follows:

1. How many nurses are in the hospital?
   There are 101 nurses, including me.
2. Of these 100 nurses, how many are assigned to the third and fourth floors?
   Fifty nurses are assigned to these two floors.
3. What do these nurses do (please describe)?
   Provide nursing care for patients, which, as you know, means answering questions, changing bandages, administering medicine, changing clothes, etc.
4. And what do you do?
   I supervise and coordinate all the nursing activity in the hospital. This includes surgery, maternity, the emergency room, and the two floors you mentioned.
5. What other lodging and care activities are done for the third and fourth floors by persons other than the nurses?
   The patients must be fed. The hospital cafeteria delivers meals. The laundry department picks up dirty clothing and bedding once each shift. The floors also have a physical therapist assigned to provide care on a physician-directed basis.

6. Do patients use any equipment?
   Yes. Mostly monitoring equipment.
7. Who or what uses the activity output?
   Patients. But there are different kinds of patients. On these two floors, we classify patients into three categories according to severity: intensive care, intermediate care, and normal care. The more severe the illness, the more activity is used. Nurses spend much more time with intermediate care patients than with normal care. The more severe patients tend to use more of the laundry service as well. Their clothing and bedding need to be changed more frequently. On the other hand, severe patients use less food. They eat fewer meals. Typically, we measure each patient type by the number of days of hospital stay. And you have to realize that the same patient contributes to each type of product.

Required:

Prepare an activity dictionary with three categories: activity name, activity description, and activity driver.

Exercise 5-51 Activity Rates and Activity-Based Product Costing

OBJECTIVE ▶ 2

Hammer Company produces a variety of electronic equipment. One of its plants produces two laser printers: the deluxe and the regular. At the beginning of the year, the following data were prepared for this plant:

	Deluxe	Regular
Quantity	100,000	800,000
Selling price	$900	$750
Unit prime cost	$529	$483

In addition, the following information was provided so that overhead costs could be assigned to each product:

Activity Name	Activity Driver	Deluxe	Regular	Activity Cost
Setups	Number of setups	300	200	$ 2,000,000
Machining	Machine hours	100,000	300,000	80,000,000
Engineering	Engineering hours	50,000	100,000	6,000,000
Packing	Packing orders	100,000	400,000	100,000

Required:

1. Calculate the overhead rates for each activity. (Round to two decimal places.)
2. Calculate the per-unit product cost for each product. (Round to the nearest dollar.)

Exercise 5-52 Value- and Nonvalue-Added Costs

OBJECTIVE ▶ 4

Waterfun Technology produces engines for recreational boats. Because of competitive pressures, the company was making an effort to reduce costs. As part of this effort, management implemented an activity-based management system and began focusing its attention on processes and activities. Receiving was among the processes (activities) that were carefully studied. The study revealed that the number of receiving orders was a good driver for receiving costs. During the last year, the company incurred fixed receiving costs of $630,000 (salaries of 10 employees). These fixed costs provide a capacity of processing 72,000 receiving orders (7,200 per employee at practical capacity). Management decided that the efficient level for receiving should use 36,000 receiving orders.

Required:

1. **CONCEPTUAL CONNECTION** Explain why receiving would be viewed as a value-added activity. List all possible reasons. Also, list some possible reasons that explain why the demand for receiving is more than the efficient level of 36,000 orders.
2. Break the cost of receiving into its value-added and nonvalue-added components.

PROBLEMS

OBJECTIVE ▶ 1 ▶ 2

Problem 5-53 Functional-Based versus Activity-Based Costing

For years, Tamarindo Company produced only one product: backpacks. Recently, Tamarindo added a line of duffel bags. With this addition, the company began assigning overhead costs by using departmental rates. (Prior to this, the company used a predetermined plantwide rate based on units produced.) Surprisingly, after the addition of the duffel-bag line and the switch to departmental rates, the costs to produce the backpacks increased, and their profitability dropped.

Josie, the marketing manager, and Steve, the production manager, both complained about the increase in the production cost of backpacks. Josie was concerned because the increase in unit costs led to pressure to increase the unit price of backpacks. She was resisting this pressure because she was certain that the increase would harm the company's market share. Steve was receiving pressure to cut costs also, yet he was convinced that nothing different was being done in the way the backpacks were produced. After some discussion, the two managers decided that the problem had to be connected to the addition of the duffel-bag line.

Upon investigation, they were informed that the only real change in product-costing procedures was in the way overhead costs are assigned. A two-stage procedure was now in use. First, overhead costs are assigned to the two producing departments, Patterns and Finishing. Second, the costs accumulated in the producing departments are assigned to the two products by using direct labor hours as a driver (the rate in each department is based on direct labor hours). The managers were assured that great care was taken to associate overhead costs with individual products. So that they could construct their own example of overhead cost assignment, the controller provided them with the information necessary to show how accounting costs are assigned to products:

	Department		
	Patterns	Finishing	Total
Accounting cost	$30,000	$90,000	$120,000
Transactions processed	20,000	60,000	80,000
Total direct labor hours	15,000	30,000	45,000
Direct labor hours per backpack*	0.10	0.20	0.30
Direct labor hours per duffel bag*	0.20	0.40	0.60

*Hours required to produce one unit of each product.

The controller remarked that the cost of operating the accounting department had doubled with the addition of the new product line. The increase came because of the need to process additional transactions, which had also doubled in number.

During the first year of producing duffel bags, the company produced and sold 100,000 backpacks and 25,000 duffel bags. The 100,000 backpacks matched the prior year's output for that product.

Required:

(*Note:* Round rates and unit cost to the nearest cent.)

1. **CONCEPTUAL CONNECTION** Compute the amount of accounting cost assigned to a backpack before the duffel-bag line was added by using a plantwide rate approach based on units produced. Is this assignment accurate? Explain.
2. Suppose that the company decided to assign the accounting costs directly to the product lines by using the number of transactions as the activity driver. What is the accounting cost per unit of backpacks? Per unit of duffel bags?

3. Compute the amount of accounting cost assigned to each backpack and duffel bag by using departmental rates based on direct labor hours.

4. **CONCEPTUAL CONNECTION** Which way of assigning overhead does the best job—the functional-based approach by using departmental rates or the activity-based approach by using transactions processed for each product? Explain. Discuss the value of ABC before the duffel-bag line was added.

Problem 5-54 Plantwide versus Departmental Rates, Product-Costing Accuracy: Activity-Based Costing

OBJECTIVE ◀1 ◀2

EXCEL

Ramsey Company produces speakers (Model A and Model B). Both products pass through two producing departments. Model A's production is much more labor-intensive than that of Model B. Model B is also the more popular of the two speakers. The following data have been gathered for the two products:

	Product Data	
	Model A	**Model B**
Units produced per year	10,000	100,000
Prime costs	$150,000	$1,500,000
Direct labor hours	140,000	300,000
Machine hours	20,000	200,000
Production runs	40	60
Inspection hours	800	1,200
Maintenance hours	10,000	90,000
Overhead costs:		
Setup costs	$270,000	
Inspection costs	210,000	
Machining	240,000	
Maintenance	270,000	
Total	$990,000	

Required:

1. Compute the overhead cost per unit for each product by using a plantwide rate based on direct labor hours. (*Note:* Round to two decimal places.)

2. Compute the overhead cost per unit for each product by using ABC. (*Note:* Round rates and unit overhead cost to two decimal places.)

3. Suppose that Ramsey decides to use departmental overhead rates. There are two departments: Department 1 (machine intensive) with a rate of $3.50 per machine hour and Department 2 (labor intensive) with a rate of $0.90 per direct labor hour. The consumption of these two drivers is as follows:

	Department 1 Machine Hours	**Department 2** Direct Labor Hours
Model A	10,000	130,000
Model B	170,000	270,000

Compute the overhead cost per unit for each product by using departmental rates. (*Note:* Round to two decimal places.)

4. **CONCEPTUAL CONNECTION** Using the activity-based product costs as the standard, comment on the ability of departmental rates to improve the accuracy of product costing. Did the departmental rates do better than the plantwide rate?

OBJECTIVE **1** **2**

EXCEL

Problem 5-55 Production-Based Costing versus Activity-Based Costing, Assigning Costs to Activities, Resource Drivers

Willow Company produces lawnmowers. One of its plants produces two versions of mowers: a basic model and a deluxe model. The deluxe model has a sturdier frame, a higher horsepower engine, a wider blade, and mulching capability. At the beginning of the year, the following data were prepared for this plant:

	Basic Model	Deluxe Model
Expected quantity	40,000	20,000
Selling price	$180	$360
Prime costs	$80	$160
Machine hours	5,000	5,000
Direct labor hours	10,000	10,000
Engineering support (hours)	1,500	4,500
Receiving (orders processed)	250	500
Materials handling (number of moves)	1,200	4,800
Purchasing (number of requisitions)	100	200
Maintenance (hours used)	1,000	3,000
Paying suppliers (invoices processed)	250	500
Setting up equipment (number of setups)	16	64

Additionally, the following overhead activity costs are reported:

Maintaining equipment	$114,000
Engineering support	120,000
Materials handling	?
Setting up equipment	96,000
Purchasing materials	60,000
Receiving goods	40,000*
Paying suppliers	30,000
Providing space	20,000
Total	$?

*Receiving activity cost includes allocated share of forklift operators' salaries.

Facility-level costs are allocated in proportion to machine hours (provides a measure of time the facility is used by each product). Receiving and materials handling use three inputs: two forklifts, gasoline to operate the forklift, and three operators. The three operators are paid a salary of $40,000 each. The operators spend 25% of their time on the receiving activity and 75% on moving goods (materials handling). Gasoline costs $3 per move. Depreciation amounts to $8,000 per forklift per year.

Required:

(*Note:* Round answers to two decimal places.)
1. Calculate the cost of the materials handling activity. Label the cost assignments as driver tracing or direct tracing. Identify the resource drivers.
2. Calculate the cost per unit for each product by using direct labor hours to assign all overhead costs.
3. Calculate activity rates, and assign costs to each product. Calculate a unit cost for each product, and compare these costs with those calculated in Requirement 2.
4. Calculate consumption ratios for each activity.
5. **CONCEPTUAL CONNECTION** Explain how the consumption ratios calculated in Requirement 4 can be used to reduce the number of rates. Calculate the rates that would apply under this approach.

Problem 5-56 Activity Costing, Assigning Resource Costs, Primary and
Secondary Activities

Elmo Clinic has identified three activities for daily maternity care: occupancy and feeding, nursing, and nursing supervision. The nursing supervisor oversees 150 nurses, 25 of whom are maternity nurses (the other nurses are located in other care areas such as the emergency room and intensive care). The nursing supervisor has three assistants, a secretary, several offices, computers, phones, and furniture. The three assistants spend 75% of their time on the supervising activity and 25% of their time as surgical nurses. They each receive a salary of $60,000. The nursing supervisor has a salary of $80,000. She spends 100% of her time supervising. The secretary receives a salary of $35,000 per year. Other costs directly traceable to the supervisory activity (depreciation, utilities, phone, etc.) average $170,000 per year.

Daily care output is measured as "patient days." The clinic has traditionally assigned the cost of daily care by using a daily rate (a rate per patient day). Daily rates can differ between units, but within units the daily rates are the same for all patients. Under the traditional approach, the daily rate is computed by dividing the annual costs of occupancy and feeding, nursing, and a share of supervision by the unit's capacity expressed in patient days. The cost of supervision is assigned to each care area based on the number of nurses. A single driver (patient days) is used to assign the costs of daily care to each patient.

A pilot study has revealed that the demands for nursing care vary within the maternity unit, depending on the severity of a patient's case. Assume that the maternity unit has three levels of increasing severity: normal patients, cesarean patients, and patients with complications. The pilot study provided the following activity and cost information:

Activity	Annual Cost	Activity Driver	Annual Quantity
Occupancy and feeding	$1,500,000	Patient days	10,000
Nursing care (maternity)	1,200,000	Hours of nursing care	50,000
Nursing supervision	?	Number of nurses	150

The pilot study also revealed the following information concerning the three types of patients and their annual demands:

Patient Type	Patient Days Demanded	Nursing Hours Demanded
Normal	7,000	17,500
Cesarean	2,000	12,500
Complications	1,000	20,000
Total	10,000	50,000

Required:

1. Calculate the cost per patient day by using a functional-based approach.
2. Calculate the cost per patient day by using an activity-based approach. (Round rates and unit cost to two decimal places.)
3. **CONCEPTUAL CONNECTION** The hospital processes 1,250,000 pounds of laundry per year. The cost for the laundering activity is $600,000 per year. In a functional-based cost system, the cost of the laundry department is assigned to each user department in proportion to the pounds of laundry produced. Typically, maternity produces 240,000 pounds per year. How much would this change the cost per patient day calculated in Requirement 1? Now, describe what information you would need to modify the calculation made in Requirement 2. Under what conditions would this activity calculation provide a more accurate cost assignment?

OBJECTIVE  1 2 3

Problem 5-57 Customers as a Cost Object

Morrisom National Bank has requested an analysis of checking account profitability by customer type. Customers are categorized according to the size of their account: low balances, medium balances, and high balances. The activities associated with the three different customer categories and their associated annual costs are as follows:

Opening and closing accounts	$ 300,000
Issuing monthly statements	450,000
Processing transactions	3,075,000
Customer inquiries	600,000
Providing automatic teller machine (ATM) services	1,680,000
Total cost	$6,105,000

Additional data concerning the usage of the activities by the various customers are also provided:

	Account Balance		
	Low	**Medium**	**High**
Number of accounts opened/closed	22,500	4,500	3,000
Number of statements issued	675,000	150,000	75,000
Processing transactions	27,000,000	3,000,000	750,000
Number of telephone minutes	1,500,000	900,000	600,000
Number of ATM transactions	2,025,000	300,000	75,000
Number of checking accounts	57,000	12,000	6,000

Required:

(*Note:* Round answers to two decimal places.)

1. Calculate a cost per account per year by dividing the total cost of processing and maintaining checking accounts by the total number of accounts. What is the average fee per month that the bank should charge to cover the costs incurred because of checking accounts?
2. Calculate a cost per account by customer category by using activity rates.
3. Currently, the bank offers free checking to all of its customers. The interest revenues average $90 per account; however, the interest revenues earned per account by category are $80, $100, and $165 for the low-, medium-, and high-balance accounts, respectively. Calculate the average profit per account (average revenue minus average cost from Requirement 1). Then calculate the profit per account by using the revenue per customer type and the unit cost per customer type calculated in Requirement 2.
4. **CONCEPTUAL CONNECTION** After the analysis in Requirement 3, a vice president recommended eliminating the free checking feature for low-balance customers. The bank president expressed reluctance to do so, arguing that the low-balance customers more than made up for the loss through cross-sales. He presented a survey that showed that 50% of the customers would switch banks if a checking fee were imposed. Explain how you could verify the president's argument by using ABC.

OBJECTIVE  2 3

Problem 5-58 Activity-Based Costing and Customer-Driven Costs

Grundvig Manufacturing produces several types of bolts used in aircraft. The bolts are produced in batches and grouped into three product families. Because the product families are used in different kinds of aircraft, customers also can be grouped into three categories, corresponding to the product family that they purchase. The number of units sold to each customer class is the same. The selling prices for the three product families range from $0.50 to $0.80 per unit. Historically, the costs of order entry, processing, and handling were expensed and not traced to individual customer groups. These costs are not trivial and totaled $9,000,000 for the most recent year. Recently, the company started emphasizing a cost reduction strategy with an emphasis on creating a competitive advantage.

Upon investigation, management discovered that order-filling costs were driven by the number of customer orders processed with the following cost behavior:

Step-fixed cost component: $50,000 per step (2,000 orders define a step)*
Variable cost component: $20 per order

*Grundvig currently has sufficient steps to process 200,000 orders.

The expected customer orders for the year total 200,000. The expected usage of the order-filling activity and the average size of an order by customer category follow:

	Category I	Category II	Category III
Number of orders	100,000	60,000	40,000
Average order size	600	1,000	1,500

As a result of cost behavior analysis, the marketing manager recommended the imposition of a charge per customer order. The charge was implemented by adding the cost per order to the price of each order (computed by using the projected ordering costs and expected orders). This ordering cost was then reduced as the size of the order increased and was eliminated as the order size reached 2,000 units. Within a short period of communicating this new price information to customers, the average order size for all three product families increased to 2,000 units.

Required:

1. **CONCEPTUAL CONNECTION** Grundvig traditionally has expensed order-filling costs. What is the most likely reason for this practice?
2. Calculate the cost per order for each customer category. (*Note:* Round to two decimal places.)
3. **CONCEPTUAL CONNECTION** Calculate the reduction in order-filling costs produced by the change in pricing strategy (assuming that resource spending is reduced as much as possible and that the total units sold remain unchanged). Explain how exploiting customer activity information produced this cost reduction. Would any other internal activities benefit from this pricing strategy?

Problem 5-59 Activity-Based Supplier Costing

OBJECTIVE ▶ 2 ◀ 3

Levy Inc. manufactures tractors for agricultural usage. Levy purchases the engines needed for its tractors from two sources: Johnson Engines and Watson Company. The Johnson engine has a price of $1,000. The Watson engine is $900 per unit. Levy produces and sells 22,000 tractors. Of the 22,000 engines needed for the tractors, 4,000 are purchased from Johnson Engines, and 18,000 are purchased from Watson Company. The production manager, Jamie Murray, prefers the Johnson engine. However, Jan Booth, purchasing manager, maintains that the price difference is too great to buy more than the 4,000 units currently purchased. Booth also wants to maintain a significant connection with the Johnson source just in case the less expensive source cannot supply the needed quantities. Jamie, however, is convinced that the quality of the Johnson engine is worth the price difference.

Frank Wallace, the controller, has decided to use activity costing to resolve the issue. The following activity cost and supplier data have been collected:

(Continued)

Activity	Cost
Replacing engines[a]	$ 800,000
Expediting orders[b]	1,000,000
Repairing engines[c]	1,800,000

[a] All units are tested after assembly, and some are rejected because of engine failure. The failed engines are removed and replaced, with the supplier replacing any failed engine. The replaced engine is retested before being sold. Engine failure often causes collateral damage, and other parts often need to be replaced.
[b] Due to late or failed delivery of engines.
[c] Repair work is for units under warranty and almost invariably is due to engine failure. Repair usually means replacing the engine. This cost plus labor, transportation, and other costs make warranty work very expensive.

	Watson	Johnson
Engines replaced by source	1,980	20
Late or failed shipments	198	2
Warranty repairs (by source)	2,440	60

Required:

1. **CONCEPTUAL CONNECTION** Calculate the activity-based supplier cost per engine (acquisition cost plus supplier-related activity costs). (Round to the nearest cent.) Which of the two suppliers is the low-cost supplier? Explain why this is a better measure of engine cost than the usual purchase costs assigned to the engines.

2. **CONCEPTUAL CONNECTION** Consider the supplier cost information obtained in Requirement 1. Suppose further that Johnson can only supply a total of 20,000 units. What actions would you advise Levy to undertake with its suppliers?

OBJECTIVE ▶ 4 ▶   **Problem 5-60** Activity-Based Management, Nonvalue-Added Costs

Danna Martin, president of Mays Electronics, was concerned about the end-of-the year marketing report that she had just received. According to Larry Savage, marketing manager, a price decrease for the coming year was again needed to maintain the company's annual sales volume of integrated circuit boards (CBs). This would make a bad situation worse. The current selling price of $18 per unit was producing a $2-per-unit profit—half the customary $4-per-unit profit. Foreign competitors kept reducing their prices. To match the latest reduction would reduce the price from $18 to $14. This would put the price below the cost to produce and sell it. How could these firms sell for such a low price? Determined to find out if there were problems with the company's operations, Danna decided to hire a consultant to evaluate the way in which the CBs were produced and sold. After two weeks, the consultant had identified the following activities and costs:

Setting up equipment	$ 125,000
Materials handling	180,000
Inspecting products	122,000
Engineering support	120,000
Handling customer complaints	100,000
Filling warranties	170,000
Storing goods	80,000
Expediting goods	75,000
Using materials	500,000
Using power	48,000
Manual insertion labor[a]	250,000
Other direct labor	150,000
Total costs	$1,920,000[b]

[a] Diodes, resistors, and integrated circuits are inserted manually into the circuit board.
[b] This total cost produces a unit cost of $16 for last year's sales volume.

The consultant indicated that some preliminary activity analysis shows that per-unit costs can be reduced by at least $7. Since the marketing manager had indicated that the market share (sales volume) for the boards could be increased by 50% if the price could be reduced to $12, Danna became quite excited.

Required:

1. **CONCEPTUAL CONNECTION** What is activity-based management? What phases of activity analysis did the consultant provide? What else remains to be done?

2. **CONCEPTUAL CONNECTION** Identify as many nonvalue-added costs as possible. Compute the cost savings per unit that would be realized if these costs were eliminated. Was the consultant correct in the preliminary cost reduction assessment? Discuss actions that the company can take to reduce or eliminate the nonvalue-added activities.

3. Compute the unit cost required to maintain current market share, while earning a profit of $4 per unit. Now compute the unit cost required to expand sales by 50%, assuming a per-unit profit of $4. How much cost reduction would be required to achieve each unit cost?

4. Assume that further activity analysis revealed the following: switching to automated insertion would save $60,000 of engineering support and $90,000 of direct labor. Now, what is the total potential cost reduction per unit available from activity analysis? With these additional reductions, can Mays achieve the unit cost to maintain current sales? To increase it by 50%? What form of activity analysis is this: reduction, sharing, elimination, or selection?

5. **CONCEPTUAL CONNECTION** Calculate income based on current sales, prices, and costs. Then calculate the income by using a $14 price and a $12 price, assuming that the maximum cost reduction possible is achieved (including Requirement 4's reduction). What price should be selected?

Problem 5-61 Nonvalue-Added Costs, Activity Costs, Activity Cost Reduction

OBJECTIVE ▸ 3 ◂ 4

John Thomas, vice president of Mallett Company (a producer of a variety of plastic products), has been supervising the implementation of an ABC management system. John wants to improve process efficiency by improving the activities that define the processes. To illustrate the potential of the new system to the president, John has decided to focus on two processes: production and customer service.

Within each process, one activity will be selected for improvement: materials usage for production and sustaining engineering for customer service (sustaining engineers are responsible for redesigning products based on customer needs and feedback). Value-added standards are identified for each activity. For materials usage, the value-added standard calls for six pounds per unit of output (the products differ in shape and function, but their weight is uniform). The value-added standard is based on the elimination of all waste due to defective molds. The standard price of materials is $5 per pound. For sustaining engineering, the standard is 58% of current practical activity capacity. This standard is based on the fact that about 42% of the complaints have to do with design features that could have been avoided or anticipated by the company.

Current practical capacity (at the end of 20X1) is defined by the following requirements: 6,000 engineering hours for each product group that has been on the market or in development for 5 years or less and 2,400 hours per product group of more than 5 years. Four product groups have less than 5 years' experience, and 10 product groups have more. Each of the 24 engineers is paid a salary of $60,000. Each engineer can provide 2,000 hours of service per year. No other significant costs are incurred for the engineering activity.

Actual materials usage for 20X1 was 25% above the level called for by the value-added standard; engineering usage was 46,000 hours. A total of 80,000 units of output were produced.

(Continued)

John and the operational managers have selected some improvement measures that promise to reduce nonvalue-added activity usage by 40% in 20X2. Selected actual results achieved for 20X2 are as follows:

Units produced	80,000
Materials used	584,800
Engineering hours	35,400

The actual prices paid for materials and engineering hours are identical to the standard or budgeted prices.

Required:

1. For 20X1, calculate the nonvalue-added usage and costs for materials usage and sustaining engineering.
2. **CONCEPTUAL CONNECTION** Using the budgeted improvements, calculate the expected activity usage levels for 20X2. Now, compute the 20X2 usage variances (the difference between the expected and actual values), expressed in both physical and financial measures, for materials and engineering. Comment on the company's ability to achieve its targeted reductions. In particular, discuss what measures the company must take to capture any realized reductions in resource usage.

OBJECTIVE ▶ **4**   **Problem 5-62** Cycle Time, Velocity, Product Costing

Goldman Company has a JIT system in place. Each manufacturing cell is dedicated to the production of a single product or major subassembly. One cell, dedicated to the production of telescopes, has four operations: machining, finishing, assembly, and qualifying (testing).

For the coming year, the telescope cell has the following budgeted costs and cell time (both at theoretical capacity):

Budgeted conversion costs	$7,500,000
Budgeted raw materials	$9,000,000
Cell time	12,000 hours
Theoretical output	90,000 telescopes

During the year, the following actual results were obtained:

Actual conversion costs	$7,500,000
Actual materials	$7,800,000
Actual cell time	12,000 hours
Actual output	75,000 telescopes

Required:

(*Note:* Round answers to two decimal places.)

1. Compute the velocity (number of telescopes per hour) that the cell can theoretically achieve. Now, compute the theoretical cycle time (number of hours or minutes per telescope) that it takes to produce one telescope.
2. Compute the actual velocity and the actual cycle time.
3. **CONCEPTUAL CONNECTION** Compute the budgeted conversion costs per minute. Using this rate, compute the conversion costs per telescope if theoretical output is achieved. Using this measure, compute the conversion costs per telescope for actual output. Does this product-costing approach provide an incentive for the cell manager to reduce cycle time? Explain.

CASES

Case 5-63 Activity-Based Costing, Distorted Product Costs

OBJECTIVE 2 3 4

Sharp Paper Inc. has three paper mills, one of which is located in Memphis, Tennessee. The Memphis mill produces 300 different types of coated and uncoated specialty printing papers. Management was convinced that the value of the large variety of products more than offset the extra costs of the increased complexity.

During 20X1, the Memphis mill produced 120,000 tons of coated paper and 80,000 tons of uncoated paper. Of the 200,000 tons produced, 180,000 were sold. Sixty products account for 80% of the tons sold. Thus, 240 products are classified as low-volume products.

Lightweight lime hopsack in cartons (LLHC) is one of the low-volume products. LLHC is produced in rolls, converted into sheets of paper, and then sold in cartons. In 20X1, the cost to produce and sell one ton of LLHC was as follows:

Direct materials:		
Furnish (3 different pulps)	2,225 pounds	$ 450
Additives (11 different items)	200 pounds	500
Tub size	75 pounds	10
Recycled scrap paper	(296 pounds)	(20)
Total direct materials		$ 940
Direct labor		$ 450
Overhead:		
Paper machine ($100 per ton × 2,500 pounds)		$ 125
Finishing machine ($120 per ton × 2,500 pounds)		150
Total overhead		$ 275
Shipping and warehousing		$ 30
Total manufacturing and selling cost		$1,695

Overhead is applied by using a two-stage process. First, overhead is allocated to the paper and finishing machines by using the direct method of allocation with carefully selected cost drivers. Second, the overhead assigned to each machine is divided by the budgeted tons of output. These rates are then multiplied by the number of pounds required to produce one good ton.

In 20X1, LLHC sold for $2,400 per ton, making it one of the most profitable products. A similar examination of some of the other low-volume products revealed that they also had very respectable profit margins. Unfortunately, the performance of the high-volume products was less impressive, with many showing losses or very low profit margins. This situation led Ryan Chesser to call a meeting with his marketing vice president, Jennifer Woodruff, and his controller, Kaylin Penn.

Ryan: The above-average profitability of our low-volume specialty products and the poor profit performance of our high-volume products make me believe that we should switch our marketing emphasis to the low-volume line. Perhaps we should drop some of our high-volume products, particularly those showing a loss.

Jennifer: I'm not convinced that solution is the right one. I know our high-volume products are of high quality, and I'm convinced that we are as efficient in our production as other firms. I think that somehow our costs are not being assigned correctly. For example, the shipping and warehousing costs are assigned by dividing these costs by the total tons of paper sold. Yet ...

Kaylin: Jennifer, I hate to disagree, but the $30-per-ton charge for shipping and warehousing seems reasonable. I know that our method to assign these costs is identical to a number of other paper companies.

(Continued)

Jennifer: Well, that may be true, but do these other companies have the variety of products that we have? Our low-volume products require special handling and processing, but when we assign shipping and warehousing costs, we average these special costs across our entire product line. Every ton produced in our mill passes through our mill shipping department and is either sent directly to the customer or to our distribution center and then eventually to customers. My records indicate quite clearly that virtually all of the high-volume products are sent directly to customers, whereas most of the low-volume products are sent to the distribution center. Now, all of the products passing through the mill shipping department should receive a share of the $2,000,000 annual shipping costs. I'm not convinced, however, that all products should receive a share of the receiving and shipping costs of the distribution center as currently practiced.

Ryan: Kaylin, is this true? Does our system allocate our shipping and warehousing costs in this way?

Kaylin: Yes, I'm afraid it does. Jennifer may have a point. Perhaps we need to reevaluate our method to assign these costs to the product lines.

Ryan: Jennifer, do you have any suggestions concerning how the shipping and warehousing costs should be assigned?

Jennifer: It seems reasonable to make a distinction between products that spend time in the distribution center and those that do not. We should also distinguish between the receiving and shipping activities at the distribution center. All incoming shipments are packed on pallets and weigh one ton each. There are 14 cartons of paper per pallet. In 20X1, the receiving department processed 56,000 tons of paper. Receiving employs 15 people at an annual cost of $600,000. Other receiving costs total about $500,000. I would recommend that these costs be assigned by using tons processed.

Shipping, however, is different. There are two activities associated with shipping: picking the order from inventory and loading the paper. We employ 30 people for picking and 10 for loading, at an annual cost of $1,200,000. Other shipping costs total $1,100,000. Picking and loading are more concerned with the number of shipping items than with tonnage. That is, a shipping item may consist of two or three cartons instead of pallets. Accordingly, the shipping costs of the distribution center should be assigned by using the number of items shipped. In 20X1, for example, we handled 190,000 shipping items.

Ryan: These suggestions have merit. Kaylin, I would like to see what effect Jennifer's suggestions have on the per-unit assignment of shipping and warehousing for LLHC. If the effect is significant, then we will expand the analysis to include all products.

Kaylin: I'm willing to compute the effect, but I'd like to suggest one additional feature. Currently, we have a policy to carry about 25 tons of LLHC in inventory. Our current costing system totally ignores the cost of carrying this inventory. Since it costs us $1,665 to produce each ton of this product, we are tying up a lot of money in inventory—money that could be invested in other productive opportunities. In fact, the return lost is about 16% per year. This cost should also be assigned to the units sold.

Ryan: Kaylin, this also sounds good to me. Go ahead and include the carrying cost in your computation.

To help in the analysis, Kaylin gathered the following data for LLHC for 20X1:

Tons sold	10
Average cartons per shipment	2
Average shipments per ton	7

Required:

1. Identify the flaws associated with the current method of assigning shipping and warehousing costs to Sharp's products.
2. Compute the shipping and warehousing cost per ton of LLHC sold by using the new method suggested by Jennifer and Kaylin. Round rates and the cost per ton to two decimal places.

3. Using the new costs computed in Requirement 2, compute the profit per ton of LLHC. Compare this with the profit per ton computed by using the old method. Do you think that this same effect would be realized for other low-volume products? Explain.

4. Comment on Ryan's proposal to drop some high-volume products and place more emphasis on low-volume products. Discuss the role of the accounting system in supporting this type of decision making.

5. After receiving the analysis of LLHC, Ryan decided to expand the analysis to all products. He also had Kaylin reevaluate the way in which mill overhead was assigned to products. After the restructuring was completed, Ryan took the following actions: (a) the prices of most low-volume products were increased, (b) the prices of several high-volume products were decreased, and (c) some low-volume products were dropped. Explain why his strategy changed so dramatically.

Case 5-64 **Activity-Based Product Costing and Ethical Behavior**

OBJECTIVE ‹ **2** ‹ **3** ‹ **4**

Consider the following conversation between Leonard Bryner, president and manager of a firm engaged in job manufacturing, and Chuck Davis, certified management accountant, the firm's controller.

Leonard: Chuck, as you know, our firm has been losing market share over the past 3 years. We have been losing more and more bids, and I don't understand why. At first, I thought that other firms were undercutting simply to gain business, but after examining some of the public financial reports, I believe that they are making a reasonable rate of return. I am beginning to believe that our costs and costing methods are at fault.

Chuck: I can't agree with that. We have good control over our costs. Like most firms in our industry, we use a normal job-costing system. I really don't see any significant waste in the plant.

Leonard: After talking with some other managers at a recent industrial convention, I'm not so sure that waste by itself is the issue. They talked about activity-based management, activity-based costing, and continuous improvement. They mentioned the use of something called "activity drivers" to assign overhead. They claimed that these new procedures can help to produce more efficiency in manufacturing, better control of overhead, and more accurate product costing. A big deal was made of eliminating activities that added no value. Maybe our bids are too high because these other firms have found ways to decrease their overhead costs and to increase the accuracy of their product costing.

Chuck: I doubt it. For one thing, I don't see how we can increase product-costing accuracy. So many of our costs are indirect costs. Furthermore, everyone uses some measure of production activity to assign overhead costs. I imagine that what they are calling "activity drivers" is just some new buzzword for measures of production volume. Fads in costing come and go. I wouldn't worry about it. I'll bet that our problems with decreasing sales are temporary. You might recall that we experienced a similar problem about 12 years ago—it was 2 years before it straightened out.

Required:

1. Do you agree or disagree with Chuck Davis and the advice that he gave Leonard Bryner? Explain.

2. Was there anything wrong or unethical in the behavior that Chuck Davis displayed? Explain your reasoning.

3. Do you think that Chuck was well informed—that he was aware of the accounting implications of ABC and that he knew what was meant by cost drivers? Should he have been well informed? Review (in Chapter 1) the first category of the Statement of Ethical Professional Practice for management accountants. Do any of these standards apply in Chuck's case?

6

Process Costing

After studying Chapter 6, you should be able to:

1 ▸ Describe the basic characteristics and cost flows associated with process manufacturing.

2 ▸ Define *equivalent units* and explain their role in process costing. Explain the differences between the weighted average method and the FIFO method of accounting for process costs.

3 ▸ Prepare a departmental production report using the weighted average method.

4 ▸ Explain how nonuniform inputs and multiple processing departments affect process costing.

5 ▸ (*Appendix 6A*) Prepare a departmental production report using the FIFO method.

EXPERIENCE MANAGERIAL DECISIONS

with BP

The only consideration that most people give to gasoline is the price charged at the local pump. However, **BP**, one of the largest energy companies in the world, has been thinking about this issue and a lot more for quite a long time. BP was founded in 1901 after William D'Arcy obtained permission from the shah of Persia to dig for oil in what is now the Iranian desert. BP drastically expanded its reach and, as of the early 21st century, had active excavation and production occurring in 22 countries. BP runs its processes nonstop—24 hours a day, 365 days a year—to produce to full capacity, which represents 2.6 million barrels of oil each day or approximately 30 barrels every second. Producing that much of anything is mind boggling, which hints at the importance of BP's effective process-costing system in determining the costs associated with its numerous products, which include gasoline, heating fuel, greases, and asphalt.

In order to determine costs for a particular process, BP needs to know the total costs of production and the total number of units processed in a specified period of time. The costs include raw crude oil, which varies widely from sweet West Texas crude to heavier Canadian crude, plus labor and management overhead. Other costs include catalysts, which enhance the reactivity to make a molecule turn into something else, and chemicals, which become part of the final product. BP goes to a lot of trouble to combine its process-costing system outputs, current market prices, and a linear programming model in order to calculate the most profitable mix of products to produce from a given mix of raw crude materials. Determining the costs associated with running a refinery with a continuous production process is complex. However, by calculating process costs and carefully setting production levels and product mixes, BP is able to manage this complex process at its facilities around the globe, thereby providing significant profits for use in future energy discovery, distribution efforts, and unexpected and costly events such as the 2010 oil gusher in the Gulf of Mexico.

The 2010 oil rig explosion and subsequent oil gusher in the Gulf of Mexico have caused tremendous political and financial stress for BP and will continue to do so for some time. The costs associated with stopping the oil from gushing, subsequent cleanup, and ultimate reparations to businesses affected by the gusher are already huge and likely to continue increasing. The image and goodwill of BP have also been negatively impacted. The ultimate effect on BP is not yet known, but BP's ability to deal with these issues is certainly related to the company's significant profitability.

> "By calculating process costs and carefully setting production levels and product mixes, BP is able to manage this complex process at its facilities around the globe."

OBJECTIVE

Describe the basic characteristics and cost flows associated with process manufacturing.

CHARACTERISTICS OF PROCESS MANUFACTURING

As illustrated by **BP**, production processes help determine the best way of accounting for its costs. For example, BP's refinery in Whiting, Indiana, can process up to 400,000 barrels of crude oil per day. A barrel of crude oil is refined into a number of different products such as gasoline, heating oil, greases, and asphalts. In this setting, a large number of similar products pass through an identical set of processes. Since each product within a product line passing through the processes would receive similar "doses" of materials, labor, and overhead, there is no need to accumulate costs by batches (as a job-order costing system does). Instead, costs are accumulated by process. Process costing works well whenever relatively homogeneous products pass through a series of processes and receive similar amounts of manufacturing costs.

Consider the process-costing environment of Healthblend Nutritional Supplements, a company that manufactures minerals, herbs, and vitamins. Healthblend uses the following three processes:

- *Mixing or Picking:* In the mixing or picking department for a given product, the appropriate herbs, vitamins, minerals, and inert materials (typically some binder such as cornstarch) are selected, measured in the prescribed proportions, and then combined in a mixer to blend them thoroughly. When the mix is complete, the resulting mixture is sent to the encapsulation department.
- *Encapsulating:* In encapsulating, the vitamin, mineral, or herb blend is loaded into a machine that fills one-half of a gelatin capsule. The filled half is matched to another half of the capsule, and a safety seal is applied. This process is entirely mechanized. Overhead in this department consists of depreciation on machinery, maintenance of machinery, supervision, fringe benefits, lights, and power. Finally, the filled capsules are transferred to the bottling department.
- *Bottling:* In the bottling department, the capsules are loaded into a hopper and automatically counted into bottles, which are then mechanically capped. Workers manually pack the correct number of bottles into boxes to ship to retailers.

Types of Processes

Production at Healthblend is an example of sequential processing. **Sequential processing** requires that units pass through one process before they can be worked on in the next process in the sequence. Exhibit 6.1 shows the sequential pattern of the manufacture of Healthblend's minerals, herbs, and vitamins.

Exhibit 6.1

Sequential Processing Illustrated

Mixing   Encapsulating   Bottling   Finished Goods

Thus, in a process firm, units typically pass through a series of producing departments where each department or process brings a product one step closer to completion. In each department, materials, labor, and overhead may be needed. Upon completion of a particular process, the partially completed goods are transferred to the next department. After passing through the final department, the goods are completed and transferred to the warehouse.

Parallel processing is another processing pattern that requires two or more sequential processes to produce a finished good. Partially completed units (e.g., two subcomponents) can be worked on simultaneously in different processes and then brought together in a final process for completion. Consider, for example, the manufacture of hard disk drives for personal computers. In one series of processes, write heads and cartridge disk drives are produced, assembled, and tested. In a second series of processes, printed circuit boards are produced and tested. These two major subcomponents then come together for assembly in the final process. Exhibit 6.2 portrays this type of process pattern. Notice that the write head and drive processes can occur independently of (or parallel to) the circuit board production and testing processes.

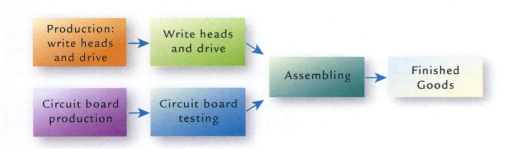

Exhibit 6.2

Parallel Processing Illustrated

Other forms of parallel processes also exist. However, regardless of which processing pattern exists within a firm, all units produced share a common property. Since units are homogeneous and subjected to the same operations for a given process, each unit produced in a period should receive the same unit cost. Understanding how unit costs are computed requires an understanding of the manufacturing cost flows that take place in a process-costing firm.

Here's How It's Used: IN YOUR LIFE

Example of Sequential and Parallel Process

The local chapter of Beta Alpha Psi has decided to have a bake sale to raise money for a homeless shelter. John Henderson, a member of the honor organization, agrees to bake two dozen cupcakes (for the first time in his life!). Because this is his first time, he searches the Internet for information about making cupcakes. He finds a good recipe on foodnetwork.com and realizes that there are three sequential processes to follow. First, there is a mixing process to create the batter. In this process, butter, sugar, eggs, flour, baking soda, baking powder, and vanilla extract are all blended (in the proper proportions) in a food processor. Next, while pulsing, milk is added down the funnel of the processor to create a smooth dropping consistency.

The second process is baking. For this process, two 12-bin muffin tins are lined with muffin papers. The oven is preheated to 400 degrees. Next, the batter from mixing is poured into the two muffin tins and baked for 15 to 20 minutes. The final

step in this process is cooling. First, John removes the muffin tins from the oven and allows them to cool on the rack for a few minutes. Then he removes the cupcakes from the tins and allows them to cool in their papers. The cupcakes are then ready for the final process: icing and boxing.

In this final process, icing is spread over each cupcake, and four iced cupcakes are placed in a small white box with a lid. The cupcakes will be sold for $2.50 per box at the bake sale.

However, while the cupcakes are baking, John discovers that he forgot to buy icing. He is relieved to find out that he can actually make the icing (using information from the same website that provided the cupcake recipe). It requires a fourth process that is independent of or parallel to baking. Thus, while the cupcakes are baking, John makes a white icing by whipping egg whites and confectioner's sugar and adding some lemon juice to create the right consistency. The icing becomes a material added at the beginning of the boxing process.

CONCEPT CLIP

How Costs Flow through the Accounts in Process Costing

The manufacturing cost flows for a process-costing system are generally the same as those for a job-order system. As raw materials are purchased, the cost of these materials flows into a raw materials inventory account. Similarly, raw materials, direct labor, and applied overhead costs flow into a work-in-process (WIP) account. When goods are completed, the cost of the completed goods is transferred from WIP to the finished goods account. Finally, as goods are sold, the cost of the finished goods is transferred to the cost of goods sold account. The journal entries generally parallel those described in a job-order costing system.

Although job-order and process cost flows are generally similar, some differences exist. In process costing, each producing department has its own WIP account. As goods are completed in one department, they are transferred to the next department. The costs attached to the goods transferred out are also transferred to the next department. Exhibit 6.3 illustrates this process for Healthblend. By the end of the process, all manufacturing costs end up in the final department (here, bottling) with the final product.

Exhibit 6.3

Flow of Manufacturing Costs through the Accounts of a Process-Costing Firm

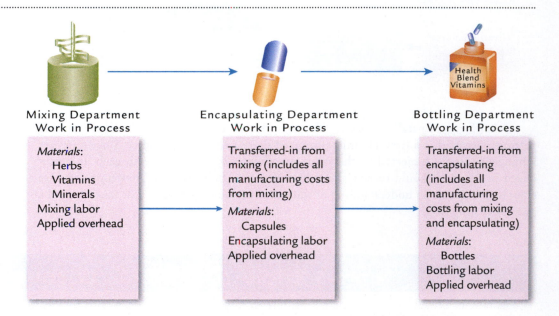

Mixing Department Work in Process	Encapsulating Department Work in Process	Bottling Department Work in Process
Materials: Herbs Vitamins Minerals Mixing labor Applied overhead	Transferred-in from mixing (includes all manufacturing costs from mixing) *Materials*: Capsules Encapsulating labor Applied overhead	Transferred-in from encapsulating (includes all manufacturing costs from mixing and encapsulating) *Materials*: Bottles Bottling labor Applied overhead

Here's **Why It's important**

In process costing, each department (process) accumulates its costs in a WIP account. When the work is finished in a process, the units and their associated costs are transferred to the next department by debiting the WIP account of the department receiving the units and crediting the WIP account of the transferring department.

Example 6.1 attaches costs to the various departments and shows how the costs flow from one department to the next.

EXAMPLE 6.1

How to Account for Cost Flows Without Work-in-Process Inventories

Suppose that Healthblend decides to produce 2,000 bottles of multivitamins with the following costs. There is no beginning or ending work in process for each department.

	Mixing Department	Encapsulating Department	Bottling Department
Direct materials	$1,700	$1,000	$800
Direct labor	50	60	300
Applied overhead	450	500	600

EXAMPLE 6.1

(*Continued*)

Required:

1. Calculate the costs transferred out of each department.
2. Prepare journal entries that reflect these cost transfers.

Solution:

1.

	Mixing Department	Encapsulating Department	Bottling Department
Direct materials	$1,700	$1,000	$ 800
Direct labor	50	60	300
Applied overhead	450	500	600
Costs added	$2,200	$1,560	$1,700
Costs transferred in	0	2,200	3,760
Costs transferred out	$2,200	$3,760	$5,460

2.

Work in Process (Encapsulating)	2,200	
Work in Process (Mixing)		2,200
Work in Process (Bottling)	3,760	
Work in Process (Encapsulating)		3,760
Finished Goods	5,460	
Work in Process (Bottling)		5,460

Example 6.1 shows that when the multivitamin mixture is transferred from the mixing department to the encapsulating department, it takes $2,200 of cost along with it. **Transferred-in costs** are costs transferred from a prior process to a subsequent process. For the subsequent process, transferred-in costs are a type of raw materials cost. The same relationship exists between the encapsulating and bottling departments. The completed bottles of multivitamins are transferred to the finished goods warehouse at a total cost of $5,460.

Accumulating Costs in the Production Report

In process costing, costs are accumulated by department for a period of time. The **production report** is the document that summarizes the manufacturing activity that takes place in a process department for a given period of time. A production report contains information on costs transferred in from prior departments as well as costs added in the department such as direct materials, direct labor, and overhead. Similar to the job-order cost sheet, it is subsidiary to the WIP account.

A production report provides information about the physical units processed in a department and their associated manufacturing costs. Thus, a production report is divided into the following sections and subdivisions:

- *Unit information section:* The unit information section has two major subdivisions:
  - units to account for
  - units accounted for

- *Cost information section:* The cost information section has two major subdivisions:
  - costs to account for
  - costs accounted for

A production report traces the flow of units through a department, identifies the costs charged to the department, shows the computation of unit costs, and reveals the disposition of the department's costs for the reporting period.

Service and Manufacturing Firms

Any product or service that is basically homogeneous and repetitively produced can take advantage of a process-costing approach. Let's look at three possibilities: services, manufacturing firms with a just-in-time (JIT) orientation, and traditional manufacturing firms.

Service Firms Check processing in a bank, teeth cleaning by a hygienist, air travel between Dallas and Los Angeles, and sorting mail by zip code are examples of homogeneous services that are repetitively produced. It is possible for firms engaged in service production to have WIP inventories. For example, a batch of tax returns can be partially completed at the end of a period. However, many services are provided so quickly that there are no WIP inventories. Teeth cleaning, funerals, surgical operations, and carpet cleaning are a few examples where WIP inventories virtually would be nonexistent. Therefore, process costing for services is relatively simple. The total costs for the period are divided by the number of services provided to compute unit cost:

> Unit Costs = Total Costs for the Period/Number of Services Provided

Manufacturing Firms Using JIT Manufacturing firms may also operate without significant WIP inventories. Specifically, firms that have adopted a JIT approach try to reduce WIP inventories to very low levels. Furthermore, JIT firms usually structure their manufacturing so that process costing can be used to determine product costs.

In many JIT firms, work cells are created that produce a product or subassembly from start to finish. Costs are collected by cell for a period of time, and output for the cell is measured for the same period. Unit cost is computed by dividing the costs of the period by output of the period:

> Unit Costs = Total Costs for the Period/Total Output of the Period

There is no ambiguity concerning what costs belong to the period and how output is measured. This simplification illustrates one of the significant benefits of JIT.

Traditional Manufacturing Firms On the other hand, traditional manufacturing firms may have significant beginning and ending WIP inventories. This causes complications in process costing due to several factors such as the presence of beginning and ending WIP inventories and different approaches to the treatment of beginning inventory cost. These complicating factors are discussed in the following sections.

THE IMPACT OF WORK-IN-PROCESS INVENTORIES ON PROCESS COSTING

The computation of unit cost for the work performed during a period is a key part of the production report. This unit cost is needed both to compute the cost of goods transferred out of a department and to value **ending work-in-process (EWIP)** inventory, the incomplete units on hand at the end of the period. Conceptually, calculating the unit cost is easy—just divide total cost by the number of units produced. However, the presence of WIP inventories causes two problems:

- Defining the units produced can be difficult, given that some units produced during a period are complete, while those in ending inventory are not. This is handled through the concept of equivalent units of production.
- How should the costs and work of **beginning work-in-process (BWIP)** inventory, incomplete units on hand at the beginning of the period, be treated? Should they be counted with the current-period work and costs or treated separately? Two methods have been developed to solve this problem: the weighted average method and the FIFO method.

Equivalent Units of Production

By definition, EWIP is not complete. Thus, a unit completed and transferred out during the period is not identical (or equivalent) to one in EWIP inventory, and the cost attached to the two units should not be the same. In computing the unit cost, the output of the period must be defined, a significant issue for process costing.

To illustrate, assume that Department A had the following data for October:

Units in BWIP	—
Units completed	1,000
Units in EWIP (25% complete)	600
Total manufacturing costs	$11,500

$\mathcal{H}ere's$ **Why It's important**

What is the output in October for this department? 1,000? 1,600? If the answer is 1,000 units, the effort expended on the units in EWIP is ignored. The manufacturing costs incurred in October belong to both the units completed and to the partially completed units in EWIP. Yet, if the answer is 1,600 units, the fact that the 600 units in EWIP are only partially completed is ignored. Therefore, output must be measured so that it reflects the effort expended on both completed and partially completed units. A measure that satisfies this objective is called *equivalent units of output*. **Equivalent units of output** are the complete units that could have been produced, given the total amount of manufacturing effort, as the following diagram illustrates:

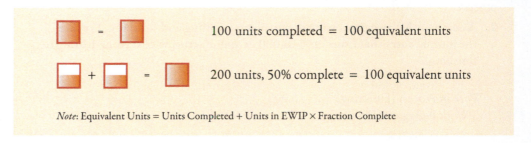

100 units completed = 100 equivalent units

200 units, 50% complete = 100 equivalent units

Note: Equivalent Units = Units Completed + Units in EWIP × Fraction Complete

Determining equivalent units of output for transferred-out units is easy. A unit would not be transferred out unless it was complete. Thus, every transferred-out unit is an equivalent unit. Units remaining in EWIP inventory, however, are not complete. Thus, someone in production must "eyeball" EWIP to estimate its degree of completion. **Example 6.2** illustrates how to calculate equivalent units of production.

EXAMPLE 6.2

How to Calculate Equivalent Units of Production with No Beginning Work in Process

Assume that a department has the following data for October: 1,000 units completed; 600 units, 25% complete

Required:
Calculate the equivalent units for October.

Solution:

1,000 units completed = 1,000 equivalent units

600 units × 0.25 = 150 equivalent units
October output = 1,150 equivalent units

$\mathcal{E}thics$ ### Ethical Decisions

Estimating the degree of completion is an act that requires judgment and ethical behavior. Overestimating the degree of completion will increase the equivalent units of output and decrease per-unit costs. This outcome, in turn, would cause an increase in both income (cost of goods sold will be less) and in assets (WIP cost will increase). Deliberately overestimating the degree of completion would clearly be in violation of ethical professional practice. ●

Knowing the output for a period and the manufacturing costs for the department for that period, a unit cost can be calculated as:

Unit Cost = Total Cost/Equivalent Units

$\mathcal{H}ere's$ **Why It's important**

Unit cost is calculated by dividing the cost of the period for a given process by the output of the period. The unit cost can then be used to determine the cost of units transferred out and

Here's How It's Used: IN YOUR LIFE

Equivalent Units of Homework

On Monday morning, Kelly Jackson received a homework assignment due on Friday. It consisted of completing 12 exercises in her calculus class, three exercises for each of four sections in the current chapter. Before working the exercises, she must first read and study the section material and then test her understanding by working the section's review exercises. She believes that the study time, the time for review exercises, and the time to work the assigned exercises are all about the same. Thus, once a section is read and studied, one-third of the labor input to produce a finished exercise is done. When the review exercise is complete, two-thirds of the labor input needed to produce a finished exercise is complete.

By Tuesday night, Kelly had read and studied the first two sections, worked the review exercises for those sections, and completed all the assigned exercises for section 1. By Wednesday night, she had read all four sections, worked all review exercises, and completed the assigned exercises for the first two sections.

Kelly wants to know her homework output for both Tuesday and Wednesday. She is convinced that it is more than simply the homework exercises actually completed. For Tuesday, her output (measured by equivalent units of assigned exercise) would be three completed exercises plus two [(2/3) × 3] equivalent exercises, for a total of five equivalent exercises. For Wednesday night, her homework output measure in equivalent units would be six completed units plus four equivalent exercises [(2/3) × 6], yielding a total of ten equivalent exercises. Unfortunately for Kelly, if she did no further work, the professor would only give her credit for the six fully completed exercises and not the 10 equivalent exercises! However, using equivalent units does help her measure and understand her degree of progress—and she only has two equivalent units of output to complete as of Wednesday night (that sounds a lot better than six more exercises). Moreover, a partially completed unit in the business world can't be sold until it's finished (just as homework can't be graded until it's finished!).

CONCEPT CLIP

---

the cost of the units in EWIP. The cost of goods (services) transferred out is the unit cost multiplied by the units completed. The cost of EWIP is the unit cost multiplied by the *equivalent units* in EWIP.

Example 6.3 shows how the calculations are done when there is no BWIP. In Example 6.3, the unit cost of $10 is used to assign a cost of $10,000 ($10 × 1,000) to the 1,000 units transferred out and a cost of $1,500 ($10 × 150) to the 600 units in EWIP. Notice that the cost of the EWIP is obtained by multiplying the unit cost by the *equivalent* units, not the actual number of partially completed units.

EXAMPLE 6.3

How to Measure Output and Assign Costs: No Beginning Work in Process

For the month of October, Department A incurred manufacturing costs of $11,500; units transferred out, 1,000; units in EWIP, 600 (25% complete).

Required:

1. Calculate the unit cost.
2. Calculate the cost of goods transferred out and the cost of EWIP.

Solution:

1.

Units completed	1,000
Units in EWIP × 25% (600 × 0.25)	150
Equivalent units	1,150

Cost per Equivalent Unit = Total Cost/Equivalent Units

Cost per Equivalent Unit = $11,500/1,150 units = $10

2. Cost of Goods Transferred Out = $10 per unit × 1,000 equivalent units = $10,000

Cost of EWIP = $10 per unit × 150 equivalent units = $1,500

Two Methods of Treating Beginning Work-in-Process Inventory

The calculations illustrated by Examples 6.2 and 6.3 become more complicated when there are BWIP inventories. The work done on these partially completed units represents prior-period work, and the costs assigned to them are prior-period costs. In computing a current-period unit cost for a department, two approaches have evolved for dealing with the prior-period output and prior-period costs found in BWIP:

- The **weighted average costing method** combines beginning inventory costs and work done with current-period costs and work to calculate this period's unit cost. In essence, the costs and work carried over from the prior period are counted as if they belong to the current period. Thus, beginning inventory work and costs are pooled with current work and costs, and an average unit cost is computed and applied to both units transferred out and units remaining in ending inventory.
- The **FIFO costing method** separates work and costs of the equivalent units in beginning inventory from work and costs of the equivalent units produced during the current period. Only current work and costs are used to calculate this period's unit cost. It is assumed that units from beginning inventory are completed first and transferred out. The costs of these units include the costs of the work done in the prior period as well as the current-period costs necessary to complete the units. Units started in the current period are divided into two categories: units started and completed and units started but not finished (EWIP). Units in both of these categories are valued using the current period's cost per equivalent unit.

If product costs do not change from period to period, or if there is no BWIP inventory, the FIFO and weighted average methods yield the same results. The weighted average method is discussed in more detail in the next section. Further discussion of the FIFO method is found in Appendix 6A.

Check Point

1. **Suppose that in July a company produced and transferred out 10,000 units and had 2,000 units in EWIP that are 70% complete. How many equivalent units were produced for July?**

   Answer:
   $10{,}000 + 0.70(2{,}000) = 11{,}400$

2. **What is the key difference between the FIFO and weighted average costing methods?**

   Answer:
   FIFO treats work and costs in BWIP separately from the work and costs of the current period. Weighted average rolls back and picks up the work and costs of BWIP and counts them as if they belong to the current period's work and costs.

OBJECTIVE

Prepare a departmental production report using the weighted average method.

WEIGHTED AVERAGE COSTING

The weighted average costing method treats beginning inventory costs and the accompanying equivalent output as if they belong to the current period. This is done for costs by adding the manufacturing costs in BWIP to the manufacturing costs incurred during the current period. The total cost is treated as if it were the current period's total manufacturing cost. Similarly, beginning inventory output and current-period output are merged in the calculation of equivalent units. Under the weighted average method, equivalent units of output are computed by adding units completed to equivalent units in EWIP. Notice that the equivalent units in BWIP are included in the computation. Consequently, these units are counted as part of the current period's equivalent units of output.

Overview of the Weighted Average Method

The weighted average method counts prior-period work and costs in BWIP as *if they belong* to the current period. Thus, equivalent units are the units completed in the period plus the equivalent units in EWIP. The unit cost is obtained by dividing the sum of the costs in BWIP and the current-period costs by the weighted average equivalent units. The resulting unit cost is a blend of the prior-period unit cost and the actual current-period unit cost. Under weighted average, valuation of goods transferred out is obtained by multiplying the unit cost by units transferred out and EWIP is valued by multiplying the unit cost by the equivalent units in EWIP.

Here's **Why It's important**

The essential conceptual and computational features of the weighted average method are illustrated in **Example 6.4**, which uses production data for Healthblend's mixing department for July. The objective is to calculate a unit cost for July and to use this unit cost to value goods transferred out and EWIP.

EXAMPLE 6.4

How to Measure Output and Assign Costs: Weighted Average Method

Heathblend's mixing department had the following data for the month of July:

Production:

Units in process, July 1, 75% complete	20,000 gallons
Units completed and transferred out	50,000 gallons
Units in process, July 31, 25% complete	10,000 gallons

Costs:

Work in process, July 1	$ 3,525
Costs added during July	$10,125

Required:

1. Calculate an output measure for July.

2. Assign costs to units transferred out and EWIP using the weighted average method.

Solution:

1. *Key:* □ = 10,000 units completed ☐ = 10,000 units, 25% complete

Output for July:

60,000 total units ⟶ Become 52,500 equivalent units

Units completed:
BWIP:

= 20,000

Units Started and Completed:

= 30,000   50,000

+ EWIP, 25% complete:

=   2,500

Equivalent Units   52,500

(Continued)

EXAMPLE 6.4

(Continued)

2.

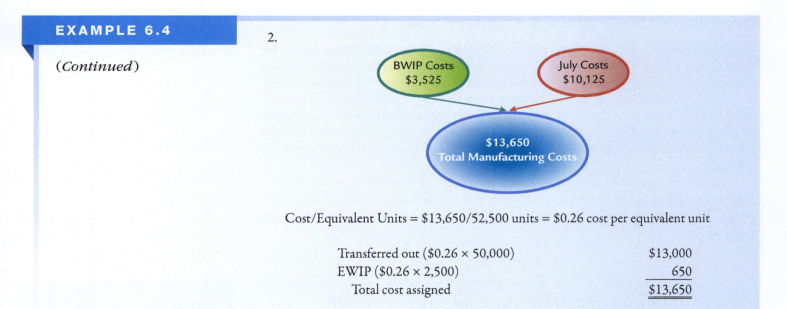

Cost/Equivalent Units = $13,650/52,500 units = $0.26 cost per equivalent unit

Transferred out ($0.26 × 50,000)	$13,000
EWIP ($0.26 × 2,500)	650
Total cost assigned	$13,650

Example 6.4 illustrates that costs from BWIP are pooled with costs added to production during July. These total pooled costs ($13,650) are divided by output to obtain a unit cost, which is then used to assign costs to units transferred out and to units in EWIP. On the output side, it is necessary to concentrate on the degree of completion of all units at the *end* of the period. There is no need to be concerned with the percentage of completion of BWIP inventory. The only issue is whether these units are complete or not by the end of July. Thus, equivalent units are computed by pooling manufacturing efforts from June and July.

Five Steps in Preparing a Production Report

The elements of Example 6.4 are used to prepare a production report. Recall that the production report summarizes cost and manufacturing activity for a producing department for a given period of time. The production report is subsidiary to the WIP account for a department. The following five steps describe the general pattern of a process-costing production report:

Step 1: Physical flow analysis
Step 2: Calculation of equivalent units
Step 3: Computation of unit cost
Step 4: Valuation of inventories (goods transferred out and EWIP)
Step 5: Cost reconciliation

These five steps provide structure to the method of accounting for process costs.

Here's **Why It's important**

Step 1: Physical Flow Analysis The **physical flow schedule** provides an analysis of the physical flow of units. The purpose of the schedule is to trace the physical units of production. Physical units are not equivalent units. They are units that may be in any stage of completion. The physical flow schedule traces the units in process regardless of their stage of completion. It has two parts: (1) units to account for and (2) units accounted for.

In the first part, the *units started* and *units in BWIP* are listed. In the second part, the units are accounted for by listing the *units completed and transferred out* and the *units started but not completed (EWIP)*. Clearly, the units to account for must equal the units accounted for. To construct the schedule from the information given, the following two relationships are often very helpful:

Units Started and Completed = Total Units Completed – Units in BWIP

Units Started = Units Started and Completed + Units in EWIP

Example 6.5 illustrates the preparation of a physical flow schedule.

EXAMPLE 6.5

**How to Prepare
a Physical Flow
Schedule**

Heathblend's mixing department had the following data for the month of July:

Production:

Units in process, July 1, 75% complete	20,000 gallons
Units completed and transferred out	50,000 gallons
Units in process, July 31, 25% complete	10,000 gallons

Required:
Prepare a physical flow schedule.

Solution:
Units Started and Completed = Units Completed – Units in BWIP = 50,000 – 20,000 = 30,000
Units Started = Units Started and Completed + Units in EWIP = 30,000 + 10,000 = 40,000

Physical flow schedule:

Units to account for:		
Units in BWIP (75% complete)		20,000
Units started during the period		40,000
Total units to account for		60,000
Units accounted for:		
Units completed and transferred out:		
Started and completed	30,000	
From beginning work in process	20,000	50,000
Units in EWIP (25% complete)		10,000
Total units accounted for		60,000

Notice from Example 6.5 that the "Total units to account for" must equal the "Total units accounted for." The physical flow schedule is important because it contains the information needed to calculate equivalent units (Step 2).

Step 2: Calculation of Equivalent Units Given the information in the physical flow schedule, the weighted average equivalent units for July can be calculated as follows:

Notice that July's output is measured as 52,500 units, 50,000 units completed and transferred out and 2,500 equivalent units from ending inventory (10,000 × 25%). What about beginning inventory? There were 20,000 units in beginning inventory, 75%

complete. These units are included in the 50,000 units completed and transferred out during the month. Thus, the weighted average method treats beginning inventory units as if they were started and completed during the current period. Because of this, the equivalent unit schedule shown in Step 2 shows only the total units completed. There is no need to show whether the units completed are from July or from BWIP, as was done by Example 6.4 (pp. 287–288).

Step 3: Computation of Unit Cost   In addition to July output, July manufacturing costs are needed to compute a unit cost. The weighted average method rolls back and includes the manufacturing costs associated with the units in BWIP and counts these costs as if they belong to July. Thus, as Example 6.4 illustrated, these costs are pooled to define total manufacturing costs for July:

$$\text{Total Manufacturing Costs for July} = \text{BWIP} + \text{Costs Added in July}$$
$$\$13,650 = \$3,525 + \$10,125$$

The manufacturing costs carried over from the prior period ($3,525) are treated as if they were current-period costs. The unit cost for July is computed as follows:

$$\text{Unit Cost} = \text{Total Costs/Equivalent Units for July}$$
$$\$0.26 = \$13,650/52,500$$

Step 4: Valuation of Inventories   Example 6.4 also showed how to value goods transferred out and EWIP. Using the unit cost of $0.26, we value the two inventories as follows:

- Cost of goods transferred to the encapsulating department is $13,000 (50,000 units × $0.26 per unit).
- Cost of EWIP is $650 (2,500 equivalent units × $0.26 per unit).

Units completed (from Step 1), equivalent units in EWIP (from Step 2), and the unit cost (from Step 3) are all needed to value both goods transferred out and EWIP.

Step 5: Cost Reconciliation   The total manufacturing costs assigned to inventories are as follows:

Goods transferred out	$13,000
Goods in EWIP	650
Total costs accounted for	$13,650

The manufacturing costs to account for are also $13,650.

BWIP	$ 3,525
Incurred during the period	10,125
Total costs to account for	$13,650

Thus, **cost reconciliation** checks to see if the costs to account for are exactly assigned to inventories. Remember, the total costs assigned to goods transferred out and to EWIP must agree with the total costs in BWIP and the manufacturing costs incurred during the current period.

Here's How It's Used: MANUFACTURING FIRM

Estimating the Degree of Completion

You are the cost accounting manager for a plant that produces riding lawnmowers. The plant manager receives a bonus at the end of each quarter if the plant's income meets or exceeds the quarter's budgeted income. The plant had no work in process at the beginning of the quarter; however, it had 2,500 partially completed units at the end of the quarter. During the quarter, 4,000 units were completed and sold. Manufacturing costs for the quarter totaled $2,750,000. The production line supervisors estimated that the units in process at the end of the quarter were 40% finished. Using this initial estimate, the income for the quarter was $190,000 less than the quarter's budgeted profit. After seeing this tentative result, the plant manager approaches you and argues that the degree of the completion is underestimated and that it should be 60% and not 40%. He explains that he personally examined the partially completed work and that 60% is his best guess. He would prefer that this new estimate be used.

What effect does the estimated degree of completion have on the quarter's income? Should you use the new estimate?

The two estimates produce significantly different unit costs, as illustrated below.

Measure	Equation	40% Degree of Completion	60% Degree of Completion
Total equivalent units	Equivalent Units = Units Completed + (Units in EWIP × Fraction Complete)	4,000 + (0.40 × 2,500) = 5,000 equivalent units	4,000 + (0.60 × 2,500) = 5,500 equivalent units
Unit cost	Unit Cost = Total Cost/Equivalent Units	$2,750,000/5,000 = $550	$2,750,000/5,500 = $500
Cost of goods sold	Cost of Goods Sold = Units Sold × Unit Cost	4,000 × $550 = $2,200,000	4,000 × $500 = $2,000,000

Compared to the 40% estimate, the 60% estimate increases income by $200,000.

Whether or not, as the cost accounting manager, you would feel comfortable using the new estimate depends on several factors. First, is the 60% estimate better than the 40% estimate? (Suppose the line supervisors insist that their estimate is correct.) Second, does the plant manager regularly participate in estimating degree of completion? If not, what are the motives for doing so this time? Answers to these questions are important. The estimate by the plant manager allows income to increase by a sufficient amount to qualify him for a bonus. If evidence favors the 40% estimate and the plant manager's motive is the bonus, then an ethical dilemma exists. In this case, you would need to follow the organization's established policies on the resolution of such conflicts.

Estimating the degree of completion is a vital and important part of process costing and needs to be done with care and honesty.

CONCEPT CLIP

Production Report

Steps 1 through 5 provide all of the information needed to prepare a production report for the mixing department for July. A production report has two sections: (1) a unit information section and (2) a cost information section. The unit information section presents the physical flow schedule and the equivalent units schedule. The cost information section also has two major subdivisions: (1) costs to account for and (2) costs accounted for. The first cost subdivision includes the calculation of the unit cost, and the second subdivision includes the valuation of goods transferred out and EWIP.

The method for preparing this report is shown in **Example 6.6**.

Here's **Why It's important**

EXAMPLE 6.6	
How to Prepare a Production Report: Weighted Average Method	Refer to Steps 1 to 5 of the Healthblend Company example.

Required:
Prepare a production report.

Solution:

Healthblend Company
Mixing Department
Production Report for July 20X1
(Weighted Average Method)

UNIT INFORMATION

Physical Flow

Units to account for:		Units accounted for:	
Units in beginning work in process	20,000	Units completed	50,000
Units started	40,000	Units in ending work in process	10,000
Total units to account for	60,000	Total units accounted for	60,000

Equivalent Units

Units completed	50,000
Units in ending work in process	2,500
Total equivalent units	52,500

COST INFORMATION

Costs to account for:	
Beginning work in process	$ 3,525
Incurred during the period	10,125
Total costs to account for	$13,650
Cost per equivalent unit	$ 0.26

Costs accounted for:	Transferred Out	Ending Work in Process	Total
Goods transferred out ($0.26 × 50,000)	$13,000	—	$13,000
Goods in ending work in process ($0.26 × 2,500)	—	$650	650
Total costs accounted for	$13,000	$650	$13,650

Evaluation of the Weighted Average Method

The major benefit of the weighted average method is simplicity. By treating units in BWIP as belonging to the current period, all equivalent units belong to the same category when it comes to calculating unit costs. Thus, unit cost computations are simplified. The main disadvantage of this method is reduced accuracy in computing unit costs for current-period output and for units in BWIP. If the unit cost in a process is relatively stable from one period to the next, the weighted average method is reasonably accurate. However, if the price of manufacturing inputs increases significantly from one period to the next, the unit cost of current output is understated, and the unit cost of BWIP units is overstated. If greater accuracy in computing unit costs is desired, a company should use the FIFO method to determine unit costs.

Check Point

1. **Suppose that for August the total units to account for are 20,000 and that there are 5,000 units in EWIP, 40% complete. How many units were completed and transferred out?**

Answer:
Units Completed = Units to Account For − Units, EWIP
= 20,000 − 5,000 = 15,000

2. **Refer to Question 1. Assume that there were 16,000 units started in August. How many units were in BWIP for August?**

Answer:
BWIP = Total Units to Account For − Units Started
= 20,000 − 16,000 = 4,000

3. **For August, there were 17,000 equivalent units produced. Costs in BWIP were $4,000, and costs added for August were $30,000. What is the cost per equivalent unit for August?**

Answer:
Unit Cost = ($4,000 + $30,000)/17,000 = $2.00

MULTIPLE INPUTS AND MULTIPLE DEPARTMENTS

OBJECTIVE **4**

Explain how nonuniform inputs and multiple processing departments affect process costing.

Accounting for production under process costing is complicated by nonuniform application of manufacturing inputs and the presence of multiple processing departments. How process-costing methods address these complications will now be discussed.

Nonuniform Application of Manufacturing Inputs

Up to this point, we have assumed that WIP being 60% complete meant that 60% of materials, labor, and overhead needed to complete the process have been used and that another 40% are needed to finish the units. In other words, we have assumed that manufacturing inputs are applied uniformly as the manufacturing process unfolds.

Assuming uniform application of conversion costs (direct labor and overhead) is not unreasonable. Direct labor input is usually needed throughout the process, and overhead is normally assigned on the basis of direct labor hours. Direct materials, on the other hand, are not as likely to be applied uniformly. In many instances, materials are added at either the beginning or the end of the process.

For example, look at the differences in Healthblend's three departments. In the mixing and encapsulating departments, all materials are added at the beginning of the process. However, in the bottling department, materials are added both at the beginning (filled capsules and bottles) and at the end (bottle caps and boxes). WIP in the mixing department that is 50% complete with respect to conversion inputs would be 100% complete with respect to the material inputs. But WIP in bottling that is 50% complete with respect to conversion would be 100% complete with respect to bottles and transferred-in capsules, but 0% complete with respect to bottle caps and boxes.

Different percentage completion figures for manufacturing inputs pose a problem for the calculation of equivalent units, unit cost, and valuation of EWIP (Steps 2–4). If materials are added at the beginning or end of a process, then there will be different completion percentages for materials and conversion costs. Typically, conversion costs are added uniformly and materials are added at discrete points in the production process. Assuming conversion is less than

Here's **Why It's important**

Here's How It's Used: AT KICKER

CONCEPT CLIP

Stillwater Designs builds a limited number of items on site. The manufacturing activities include designing and building prototypes and rebuilding of warranty returns (only of certain models such as the square L7s). Rebuilding of warranty returns follows a process manufacturing structure. All units are alike and go through the same steps.

- The woofers are removed from the cabinet, and the cabinet is stripped and cleaned.
- The speaker is torn down to its structures with all chemicals and glues removed.
- The speaker is passed through a demagnetizing process so that all metal pieces and shavings can be removed.
- The speaker is rebuilt using a recone kit to replace damaged and defective parts.

Once the cabinets and speakers are ready, they are assembled, tested, and boxed. Assembly involves placing the speakers in the cabinets and connecting the wire harnesses. There are two tests:

- In-phase test: The in-phase test is to make sure that the power is hooked up correctly.
- Air leak test: The product must be properly sealed because an air leak can damage the woofer.

Notice that the rebuilding and assembly processes are sequential. When finished, the rebuilt speakers and cabinets are transferred from the rebuilding process to the assembly process. Also, note that the cost of the final product is the cost of the materials transferred in from the rebuilding process, plus the cost of the other components and materials added, plus the assembly conversion cost. For example, at the end of the assembly process, the assembled product is packaged for delivery. In this simple process application, it is easy to see that some materials are added at the beginning of the assembly process (the cabinet and components) and some at the end of the process (packaging). The **Kicker** example also shows how process costing handles multiple departments.

100% at a given point in time, then materials added at the beginning are 100% complete, and materials added at the end are 0% complete. Accordingly, equivalent units are calculated for each type of input, and a unit cost is then calculated for each input. Calculating the unit cost for each category also requires that costs be accounted for by input category. The unit cost is the sum of the input category unit costs. Valuation of goods transferred out uses the unit cost, whereas valuation of EWIP uses input category unit costs.

Example 6.7 shows how to calculate Steps 2 through 4 with nonuniform inputs, using the weighted average method.

EXAMPLE 6.7	

How to Calculate Equivalent Units, Unit Costs, and Valuing Inventories with Nonuniform Inputs

The mixing department of Healthblend has the following data for September:

Production:

Units in process, September 1, 50% complete*	10,000
Units completed and transferred out	60,000
Units in process, September 30, 40% complete*	20,000

Costs:

WIP, September 1:	
Materials	$ 1,600
Conversion costs	200
Total	$ 1,800
Current costs:	
Materials	$12,000
Conversion costs	3,200
Total	$15,200

*With respect to conversion costs, all materials are added at the beginning of the process.

EXAMPLE 6.7

(Continued)

Required:
Calculate Steps 2 through 4 using the weighted average method.

Solution:

1. *Step 2:* Calculation of equivalent units, nonuniform application:

	Materials	Conversion
Units completed	60,000	60,000
Add: Units in Ending Work in Process × Fraction Complete:		
20,000 × 100%	20,000	—
20,000 × 40%	—	8,000
Equivalent units of output	80,000	68,000

2. *Step 3:* Calculation of unit costs:

Unit Materials Cost = ($1,600 + $12,000)/80,000 = $0.17
Unit Conversion Cost = ($200 + $3,200)/68,000 = $0.05
Total Unit Cost = Unit Materials Cost + Unit Conversion Cost
= $0.17 + $0.05
= $0.22 per completed unit

3. *Step 4:* Valuation of EWIP and goods transferred out:
The cost of EWIP is as follows:

Materials: $0.17 × 20,000	$3,400
Conversion: $0.05 × 8,000	400
Total cost	$3,800

Valuation of Goods Transferred Out:

Cost of Goods Transferred Out = $0.22 × 60,000 = $13,200

For illustrative purposes, a production report, based on Example 6.7, is shown in Exhibit 6.4 (p. 296). As the example shows, applying manufacturing inputs at different stages of a process poses no serious problems, though it requires more effort.

Multiple Departments

In process manufacturing, some departments receive partially completed goods from prior departments. In dealing with transferred-in goods, three important points should be remembered:

Here's **Why It's important**

- The cost of this material is the cost of the goods transferred out as computed in the prior department.
- The units started in the subsequent department correspond to the units transferred out from the prior department (assuming that there is a one-to-one relationship between the output measures of both departments).
- Goods transferred in from a prior department represent a material added at the beginning of the process for the department receiving the goods.
- Transferred-in material is treated as a separate material category for calculating equivalent units. Thus, the department receiving transferred-in goods would have three input categories:
  - one for the transferred-in materials
  - one for materials added
  - one for conversion costs

Exhibit 6.4

Production Report: Weighted Average Method

Healthblend Company
Mixing Department
Production Report for September 20X1
(Weighted Average Method)

UNIT INFORMATION

Units to account for:		Units accounted for:	
Units in beginning work in process	10,000	Units completed	60,000
Units started during the period	70,000	Units in ending work in process	20,000
Total units to account for	80,000	Total units accounted for	80,000

	Equivalent Units	
	Materials	Conversion
Units completed	60,000	60,000
Units in ending work in process	20,000	8,000
Total equivalent units	80,000	68,000

COST INFORMATION

	Materials	Conversion	Total
Costs to account for:			
Beginning work in process	$ 1,600	$ 200	$ 1,800
Incurred during the period	12,000	3,200	15,200
Total costs to account for	$13,600	$3,400	$17,000
Cost per equivalent unit	$ 0.17	$ 0.05	$ 0.22

	Transferred Out	Ending Work in Process	Total
Costs accounted for:			
Goods transferred out ($0.22 × 60,000)	$13,200	—	$13,200
Goods in ending work in process:			
Materials ($0.17 × 20,000)	—	$3,400	3,400
Conversion ($0.05 × 8,000)	—	400	400
Total costs to account for	$13,200	$3,800	$17,000

Example 6.8 shows how to calculate the first three process-costing steps when there are transferred-in goods, where Steps 2 and 3 are restricted to the transferred-in category.

EXAMPLE 6.8

How to Calculate the Physical Flow Schedule, Equivalent Units, and Unit Costs with Transferred-In Goods

For September, Healthblend's encapsulating department had 15,000 units in beginning inventory (with transferred-in costs of $3,000) and completed 70,000 units during the month. Further, the mixing department completed and transferred out 60,000 units at a cost of $13,200 in September.

Required:

1. Prepare a physical flow schedule with transferred-in goods.

2. Calculate equivalent units for the transferred-in category.

3. Calculate unit cost for the transferred-in category.

Solution:

1. In constructing a physical flow schedule for the encapsulating department, its dependence on the mixing department must be considered:

EXAMPLE 6.8

(*Continued*)

Units to account for:	
Units in BWIP	15,000
Units transferred in during September	60,000
Total units to account for	75,000
Units accounted for:	
Units completed and transferred out:	
Started and completed	55,000
From BWIP	15,000
Units in EWIP	5,000
Total units accounted for	75,000

2. Equivalent units for the transferred-in category only:

Transferred in:	
Units completed	70,000
Add: Units in EWIP × Fraction Complete (5,000 × 100%)*	5,000
Equivalent units of output	75,000

*Remember that the EWIP is 100% complete with respect to transferred-in costs, not to all costs of the encapsulating department.

3. To find the unit cost for the transferred-in category, we add the cost of the units transferred in from mixing in September to the transferred-in costs in BWIP and divide by transferred-in equivalent units:

$$\text{Unit Cost (Transferred-In Category)} = (\$13,200 + \$3,000)/75,000 \text{ units}$$
$$= \$16,200/75,000 \text{ units} = \$0.216$$

The only additional complication introduced in the analysis for a subsequent department is the presence of the transferred-in category. As shown, dealing with this category is similar to handling any other category. However, it must be remembered that the current cost of this special type of raw materials is the cost of the units transferred in from the prior process and that the units transferred in are the units started.

Check Point

1. **For BWIP, the cost of materials is $10,000; the conversion cost is $40,000. Costs added during December are $20,000 for materials and $80,000 for conversion. What is the cost per unit if the department has 20,000 equivalent units of materials and 40,000 units of conversion costs?**

Answer:
Unit Cost = Unit Materials Cost + Unit Conversion Cost
= [($10,000 + $20,000)/20,000] + [($40,000 + $80,000)/40,000]
= $1.50 + $3.00
= $4.50

2. **How are transferred-in goods viewed and treated by the receiving department?**

Answer:
Transferred-in goods are viewed as materials added at the beginning of the process. They are treated as a separate input category, and equivalent units and a unit cost are calculated for transferred-in materials.

OBJECTIVE

Prepare a departmental production
report using the FIFO method.

APPENDIX 6A: PRODUCTION REPORT—FIRST-IN, FIRST-OUT COSTING

Under the FIFO costing method, the equivalent units and manufacturing costs in BWIP are excluded from the current-period unit cost calculation. This method recognizes that the work and costs carried over from the prior period legitimately belong to that period.

Differences between the First-In, First-Out and Weighted Average Methods

If changes occur in the prices of the manufacturing inputs from one period to the next, then FIFO produces a more accurate (i.e., more current) unit cost than does the weighted average method. A more accurate unit cost means better cost control, better pricing decisions, and so on. Keep in mind that if the period is as short as a week or a month, however, the unit costs calculated under the two methods will not likely differ much. In that case, the FIFO method has little, if anything, to offer over the weighted average method. Perhaps for this reason, many firms use the weighted average method.

Since FIFO excludes prior-period work and costs, it is necessary to create two categories of completed units:

- BWIP units (FIFO assumes that units in BWIP are completed first, before any new units are started.)
- Units started and completed during the current period

For example, assume that a department had 20,000 units in BWIP and completed and transferred out a total of 50,000 units. Of the 50,000 completed units, 20,000 are the units initially found in WIP. The remaining 30,000 were started and completed during the current period.

Under FIFO, the equivalent units of work in BWIP from the prior period are not counted in calculating this period's equivalent units. Furthermore, the costs in BWIP from the prior period are excluded in calculating the unit cost. The unit cost is the costs of the period divided by the output of the period. *The cost of units transferred out is the sum of three different items:* (1) costs incurred in the prior period found in BWIP, (2) costs of completing the BWIP incurred this period, and (3) costs of the units started and completed this period. The cost of EWIP is the unit cost multiplied by the equivalent units in EWIP.

Example of the First-In, First-Out Method

Example 6.9 shows how FIFO handles output and cost calculations for the same Healthblend data used for the weighted average method (Example 6.4, p. 287) to highlight the differences between the two methods. It also shows that the equivalent unit calculation measures only the output for the current period.

EXAMPLE 6.9

How to Calculate Output and Cost Assignments: First-In, First-Out Method

In July, Healthblend had the following results:

Production:	
Units in process, July 1, 75% complete	20,000 gallons
Units completed and transferred out	50,000 gallons
Units in process, July 31, 25% complete	10,000 gallons
Costs:	
Work in process, July 1	$ 3,525
Costs added during July	$10,125

EXAMPLE 6.9

(*Continued*)

Required:

1. Calculate the output measure for July.
2. Assign costs to units transferred out and EWIP using the FIFO method.

Solution:

1. *Key:* ▪ = 10,000 units completed ▫ = 10,000 units, 25% complete

Output for July:
60,000 total units ⟶ Become 37,500 equivalent units
BWIP: To be completed (20,000 × 25%):

◫◫ = 5,000

+ Units started and completed:

▪▪▪ = 30,000

+ EWIP: Started but not completed
(10,000 × 0.25)

▫ = $\underline{2,500}$
= $\underline{\underline{37,500}}$

2. Costs for July:

Cost per unit = $10,125/37,500 units = $0.27

Transferred out:	
Cost from BWIP (prior-period carryover)	$ 3,525
To complete BWIP ($0.27 × 5,000)	1,350
Started and completed ($0.27 × 30,000)	8,100
Total	$12,975
EWIP ($0.27 × 2,500)	675
Total cost assigned	$13,650

Example 6.9 reveals that costs from the current period and costs carried over from June (beginning inventory costs) are not pooled to calculate July's unit cost. The unit cost calculation uses only July (current-period) costs. The five steps to cost out production follow.

Step 1: Physical Flow Analysis The purpose of Step 1 is to trace the physical units of production. As with the weighted average method, a physical flow schedule is prepared. This schedule is identical for both methods and is presented again in Exhibit 6.5. (See Example 6.5, p. 289, for details on how to prepare this schedule.)

Exhibit 6.5

Physical Flow Schedule

Units to account for:		
Units in beginning work in process (75% complete)		20,000
Units started during the period		40,000
Total units to account for		60,000
Units accounted for:		
Units completed:		
Started and completed	30,000	
From beginning work in process	20,000	50,000
Units in ending work in process (25% complete)		10,000
Total units accounted for		60,000

Step 2: Calculation of Equivalent Units From the equivalent unit computation, one difference between weighted average and FIFO becomes immediately apparent. Under FIFO, the equivalent units in BWIP (work done in the prior period) are not counted as part of the total equivalent work. Only the equivalent work to be completed this period is counted. The equivalent work to be completed for the units from the prior period is computed by multiplying the number of units in BWIP by the percentage of work remaining. Since in this example the percentage of work done in the prior period is 75%, the percentage left to be completed this period is 25%, or an equivalent of 5,000 additional units of work.

The effect of excluding prior-period effort is to produce the current-period equivalent output. Recall that under the weighted average method, 52,500 equivalent units were computed for this month. Under FIFO, only 37,500 units are calculated for the same month. These 37,500 units represent current-period output. The difference, of course, is explained by the fact that the weighted average method rolls back and counts the 15,000 equivalent units of prior-period work (20,000 units BWIP × 75%) as belonging to this period.

Step 3: Computation of Unit Cost The additional manufacturing costs incurred in the current period are $10,125. Thus, the current-period unit manufacturing cost is $10,125/37,500, or $0.27. Notice that the costs of beginning inventory are excluded from this calculation. Only current-period manufacturing costs are used.

Step 4: Valuation of Inventories Example 6.9 shows FIFO values for EWIP and goods transferred out. Since all equivalent units in ending work in process are current-period units, the cost of EWIP is simply $0.27 × 2,500, or $675, the same value that the weighted average method would produce. However, when it comes to valuing goods transferred out, a significant difference emerges between the weighted average method and FIFO.

Under weighted average, the cost of goods transferred out is simply the unit cost times the units completed. Under FIFO, however, there are two categories of completed units:

- Units started and completed (30,000)
- Units from beginning inventory (20,000)

The cost of each category must be calculated separately and then summed to obtain the total cost of goods transferred out. The cost of the first category is calculated as follows:

$$\text{Cost of Units Started and Completed} = \text{Unit Cost} \times \text{Units Started and Completed}$$
$$= \$0.27 \times 30,000$$
$$= \$8,100$$

For these units, the use of the current-period unit cost is entirely appropriate. However, the cost of BWIP units that were transferred out is another matter. These units started the period with $3,525 of manufacturing costs already incurred and 15,000 units of equivalent output already completed. To finish these units, the equivalent of 5,000 units was needed. Thus, the cost of these units being transferred out is calculated as follows:

Cost of Units in BWIP = Prior-Period Costs + (Unit Cost × Equivalent Units to Complete)

$$= \$3,525 + (\$0.27 \times 5,000)$$
$$= \$4,875$$

The unit cost of these 20,000 units, then, is about $0.244 ($4,875/20,000), a blend of prior-period and current manufacturing costs.

Step 5: Cost Reconciliation The total costs assigned to production are as follows:

Goods transferred out:	
Units in BWIP	$ 4,875
Units started and completed	8,100
Goods in EWIP	675
Total costs accounted for	$13,650

The total manufacturing costs to account for during the period are:

BWIP	$ 3,525
Incurred during the period	10,125
Total costs to account for	$13,650

The costs assigned, thus, equal the costs to account for.

With the completion of Step 5, the production report can be prepared. A production report has two sections: (1) a unit information section and (2) a cost information section. The unit information section presents the physical flow schedule and the equivalent units schedule. The cost information section has two major subdivisions: (1) costs to account for and (2) costs accounted for. The first cost subdivision includes the calculation of the unit cost, and the second subdivision includes the valuation of goods transferred out and EWIP

Example 6.10 shows how to prepare this report for FIFO.

Here's **Why It's important**

EXAMPLE 6.10

How to Prepare a Production Report: First-In, First-Out Method

Refer to the five steps for the Healthblend Company.

Required:
Prepare a production report for July 20X1 (FIFO method).

Solution:

> **Healthblend Company**
> **Mixing Department**
> **Production Report for July 20X1**
> **(FIFO Method)**
>
> **UNIT INFORMATION**

Units to account for:	
Units in beginning work in process	20,000
Units started during the period	40,000
Total units to account for	60,000

Units accounted for:	Physical Flow	Equivalent Units
Units started and completed	30,000	30,000
Units completed from beginning work in process	20,000	5,000
Units in ending work in process	10,000	2,500
Total units accounted for	60,000	37,500

(Continued)

EXAMPLE 6.10

(Continued)

COST INFORMATION			
Costs to account for:			
Beginning work in process		$ 3,525	
Incurred during the period		10,125	
Total costs to account for		$13,650	
Cost per equivalent unit		$ 0.27	

	Transferred Out	Ending Work in Process	Total
Costs accounted for:			
Units in beginning work in process:			
From prior period	$ 3,525	—	$ 3,525
From current period ($0.27 × 5,000)	1,350	—	1,350
Units started and completed ($0.27 × 30,000)	8,100	—	8,100
Goods in ending work in process ($0.27 × 2,500)	—	$675	675
Total costs accounted for	$12,975	$675	$13,650

Check Point

1. **The FIFO equivalent units for June are 10,000. The costs in BWIP are $2,500, and the costs added in June are $50,000. Calculate the unit cost under FIFO.**

Answer:
Unit Cost = $50,000/10,000 = $5.00

2. **The unit cost under FIFO is $5.00. The units started and completed are 9,000. At the beginning of the period, there are 1,000 units in BWIP, 60% complete. Costs in BWIP are $2,500. Calculate the cost of goods completed and transferred out.**

Answer:
Cost of Goods Transferred Out = $2,500 + [$5.00 × (0.40 × 1,000)] + ($5.00 × 9,000)
    = $49,500

SUMMARY OF LEARNING OBJECTIVES

LO1. Describe the basic characteristics and cost flows associated with process manufacturing.
- Cost flows under process costing are similar to those under job-order costing.
- Raw materials are purchased and debited to the raw materials account.
- Direct materials used in production, direct labor, and applied overhead are charged to the WIP account.
- In a production process with several processes, there is a WIP account for each department or process. Goods completed in one department are transferred out to the next department.
- When units are completed in the final department or process, their cost is credited to Work in Process and debited to Finished Goods.

LO2. Define *equivalent units* and explain their role in process costing. Explain the differences between the weighted average method and the FIFO method of accounting for process costs.

- Equivalent units of production are the complete units that could have been produced, given the total amount of manufacturing effort expended during the period.
- The number of physical units is multiplied by the percentage of completion to calculate equivalent units.
- The weighted average costing method combines beginning inventory costs to compute unit costs.
- The FIFO costing method separates units in beginning inventory from those produced during the current period.

LO3. Prepare a departmental production report using the weighted average method.

- The production report summarizes the manufacturing activity occurring in a department for a given period.
- It discloses information concerning the physical flow of units, equivalent units, and unit costs and the disposition of the manufacturing costs associated with the period.
- Five steps provide the needed information for a production report:
  - Physical flow analysis
  - Calculation of equivalent units
  - Computation of unit cost
  - Valuation of inventories
  - Cost reconciliation

LO4. Explain how nonuniform inputs and multiple processing departments affect process costing.

- Nonuniform inputs and multiple departments are easily handled by process-costing methods.
- When inputs are added nonuniformly, equivalent units and unit cost are calculated for each separate input category.
- The adjustment for multiple departments is also relatively simple.
- The goods transferred from a prior department to a subsequent department are treated as a material added at the beginning of the process. Thus, there is a separate transferred-in materials category, where the equivalent units and unit cost are calculated.

LO5. *(Appendix 6A)* Prepare a departmental production report using the FIFO method.

- A production report prepared according to the FIFO method separates the cost of BWIP from the cost of the current period.
- BWIP is assumed to be completed and transferred out first.
- Costs from BWIP are not pooled with the current-period costs in computing unit cost. Additionally, equivalent units of production exclude work done in the prior period.
- When calculating the cost of goods transferred out, the prior-period costs are added to the costs of completing the units in BWIP, and these costs are then added to the costs of units started and completed.

SUMMARY OF IMPORTANT EQUATIONS

1. Unit Cost = Total Cost/Equivalent Units
2. Units Started and Completed = Total Units Completed − Units in BWIP

    Units Started = Units Started and Completed + Units in EWIP

KEY TERMS

Beginning work-in-process (BWIP), 283, incomplete units on hand at the beginning of a period. Work done on these partially completed units represents prior-period work, with the costs assigned to them being prior-period costs.

Cost reconciliation, 290, the final section of the production report that compares costs to account for with the costs accounted for to ensure that they are equal.

Ending work-in-process (EWIP), 283, incomplete units on hand at the end of a period. The work and costs assigned to these partially completed units are carried over to the next period.

Equivalent units of output, 284, complete units that could have produced, given the total amount of manufacturing effort expended during the period.

FIFO costing method, 286, a process-costing method that separates units in beginning inventory from those produced during the current period. Unit costs include only current-period costs and production.

Parallel processing, 279, a processing pattern in which two or more sequential processes are required to produce a finished product.

Physical flow schedule, 288, a schedule that reconciles units to account for with units accounted for. The units are not adjusted for percent of completion.

Production report, 281, a document that summarizes the manufacturing activity that takes place in a process department for a given period of time.

Sequential processing, 278, a processing pattern in which units pass from one process to another in a set (sequential) order.

Transferred-in costs, 281, costs transferred from a prior process to a subsequent process.

Weighted average costing method, 286, a process-costing method that combines beginning inventory costs with current-period costs to compute unit costs. Costs and output from the current period and the prior period are averaged to compute unit costs.

REVIEW PROBLEMS

I. Process Costing

Springville Company, which uses the weighted average method, produces a product that passes through two departments: blending and cooking. In the blending department, all materials are added at the beginning of the process. All other manufacturing inputs are added uniformly. The following information pertains to the blending department for February:

a. BWIP, February 1: 100,000 pounds, 40% complete with respect to conversion costs. The costs assigned to this work are as follows:

Materials	$20,000
Labor	10,000
Overhead	30,000

b. EWIP, February 28: 50,000 pounds, 60% complete with respect to conversion costs.
c. Units completed and transferred out: 370,000 pounds. The following costs were added during the month:

Materials	$211,000
Labor	100,000
Overhead	270,000

Required:

1. Prepare a physical flow schedule.
2. Prepare a schedule of equivalent units.
3. Compute the cost per equivalent unit.
4. Compute the cost of goods transferred out and the cost of EWIP.
5. Prepare a cost reconciliation.

Solution:

1. Physical flow schedule:

Units to account for:		
Units in BWIP		100,000
Units started		320,000
Total units to account for		420,000
Units accounted for:		
Units completed and transferred out:		
Started and completed	270,000	
From BWIP	100,000	370,000
Units in EWIP		50,000
Total units accounted for		420,000

2. Schedule of equivalent units:

	Materials	Conversion
Units completed	370,000	370,000
Units in EWIP × Fraction complete:		
Materials (50,000 × 100%)	50,000	—
Conversion (50,000 × 60%)	—	30,000
Equivalent units of output	420,000	400,000

(*Continued*)

3. Cost per equivalent unit:

$$\text{Materials Unit Cost} = (\$20,000 + \$211,000)/420,000 \text{ units}$$
$$= \$0.550 \text{ per unit}$$
$$\text{Conversion Unit Cost} = (\$40,000 + \$370,000)/400,000 \text{ units}$$
$$= \$1.025$$
$$\text{Total Unit Cost} = \$1.575 \text{ per equivalent unit}$$

4. Cost of goods transferred out and cost of EWIP:

$$\text{Cost of Goods Transferred Out} = \$1.575 \times 370,000$$
$$= \$582,750$$
$$\text{Cost of EWIP} = (\$0.550 \times 50,000) + (\$1.025 \times 30,000)$$
$$= \$58,250$$

5. Cost reconciliation:

Costs to account for:	
BWIP	$ 60,000
Incurred during the period	581,000
Total costs to account for	$641,000
Costs accounted for:	
Goods transferred out	$582,750
WIP	58,250
Total costs accounted for	$641,000

II. Process Costing

Now suppose that Springville Company uses the FIFO method for inventory valuations. Springville produces a product that passes through two departments: blending and cooking. In the blending department, all materials are added at the beginning of the process. All other manufacturing inputs are added uniformly. The following information pertains to the blending department for February:

a. BWIP, February 1: 100,000 pounds, 40% complete with respect to conversion costs. The costs assigned to this work are as follows:

Materials	$20,000
Labor	10,000
Overhead	30,000

b. EWIP, February 28: 50,000 pounds, 60% complete with respect to conversion costs.
c. Units completed and transferred out: 370,000 pounds. The following costs were added during the month:

Materials	$211,000
Labor	100,000
Overhead	270,000

Required:

1. Prepare a physical flow schedule.
2. Prepare a schedule of equivalent units.
3. Compute the cost per equivalent unit.
4. Compute the cost of goods transferred out and the cost of EWIP.

Solution:

1. Physical flow schedule:

Units to account for:
Units in BWIP		100,000
Units started		320,000
Total units to account for		420,000

Units accounted for:
Units completed and transferred out:
Started and completed	270,000	
From BWIP	100,000	370,000
Units in EWIP		50,000
Total units accounted for		420,000

2. Schedule of equivalent units:

	Materials	Conversion
Units started and completed	270,000	270,000
Units, BWIP × Percentage complete	—	60,000
Units, EWIP × Percentage to complete:		
Direct materials (50,000 × 100%)	50,000	—
Conversion costs (50,000 × 60%)	—	30,000
Equivalent units of output	320,000	360,000

3. Cost per equivalent unit:

DM unit cost ($211,000/320,000 units)	$0.659*
CC unit cost ($370,000/360,000 units)	1.028
Total cost per equivalent unit	$1.687

*Rounded.

4. Cost of goods transferred out and cost of EWIP:

Cost of Goods Transferred Out = ($1.687 × 270,000) + ($1.028 × 60,000) + $60,000
= $577,170
Cost of EWIP = ($0.659 × 50,000) + ($1.028 × 30,000) = $63,790

DISCUSSION QUESTIONS

1. Describe the differences between process costing and job-order costing.
2. Distinguish between sequential processing and parallel processing.
3. What are the similarities in and differences between the manufacturing cost flows for job-order firms and process firms?
4. What journal entry would be made as goods are transferred out from one department to another department? From the final department to the warehouse?
5. How would process costing for services differ from process costing for manufactured goods?
6. How does the adoption of a JIT approach to manufacturing affect process costing?
7. What are equivalent units? Why are they needed in a process-costing system?
8. Under the weighted average method, how are prior-period costs and output treated? How are they treated under the FIFO method?
9. Under what conditions will the weighted average and FIFO methods give the same results?
10. Describe the five steps in accounting for the manufacturing activity of a processing department, and explain how they interrelate.
11. What is a production report? What purpose does this report serve?

12. How is the equivalent unit calculation affected when materials are added at the beginning or end of the process rather than uniformly throughout the process?

13. Explain why transferred-in costs are a special type of raw materials for the receiving department.

14. In assigning costs to goods transferred out, how do the weighted average and FIFO methods differ?

MULTIPLE-CHOICE QUESTIONS

6-1   Process costing works well whenever

   a. heterogeneous products pass through a series of processes and receive different doses of materials, labor, and overhead.
   b. material cost is accumulated by process and conversion cost is accumulated by process.
   c. homogeneous products pass through a series of processes and receive similar doses of conversion inputs and different doses of material inputs.
   d. homogeneous products pass through a series of processes and receive similar amounts of materials, labor, and overhead.
   e. None of these.

6-2   Job-order costing works well whenever

   a. homogeneous products pass through a series of processes and receive similar doses of conversion inputs and different doses of material inputs.
   b. homogeneous products pass through a series of processes and receive similar doses of materials, labor, and overhead.
   c. heterogeneous products pass through a series of processes and receive different doses of materials, labor, and overhead.
   d. material cost is accumulated by process and conversion cost is accumulated by process.

6-3   Sequential processing is characterized by

   a. a pattern where partially completed units are worked on simultaneously.
   b. a pattern where partially completed units must pass through one process before they can be worked on in later processes.
   c. a pattern where different partially completed units must pass through parallel processes before being brought together in a final process.
   d. a pattern where partially completed units must be purchased from outside suppliers and delivered to the final process in a sequential time mode.
   e. None of these.

6-4   To record the transfer of costs from a prior process to a subsequent process, the following entry would be made:

   a. debit Finished Goods and credit Work in Process.
   b. debit Work in Process (subsequent department) and credit Transferred-In Materials.
   c. debit Work in Process (prior department) and credit Work in Process (subsequent department).
   d. debit Work in Process (subsequent department) and credit Work in Process (prior department)
   e. None of these.

6-5   The costs transferred from a prior process to a subsequent process are

   a. treated as another type of materials cost for the receiving department.
   b. referred to as transferred-in costs (for the receiving department).
   c. referred to as the cost of goods transferred out (for the transferring department).
   d. All of these.
   e. None of these.

6-6 During the month of May, the grinding department produced and transferred out 2,300 units. EWIP had 500 units, 40% complete. There was no BWIP. The equivalent units of output for May are

a. 2,000.
b. 2,500.
c. 2,300.
d. 2,800.
e. None of these.

Use the following information for Multiple-Choice Questions 6-7 through 6-9:
The mixing department incurred $46,000 of manufacturing costs during the month of September. The department transferred out 2,300 units and had 500 units in EWIP, 40% complete. There was no BWIP.

6-7 The unit cost for the month of September is

a. $20.
b. $18.40.
c. $16.43.
d. $200.
e. $184.

6-8 The cost of goods transferred out is

a. $42,320.
b. $46,000.
c. $37,789.
d. $460,000.
e. None of these.

6-9 The cost of EWIP is

a. $9,200.
b. $10,000.
c. $3,680.
d. $3,286.
e. None of these.

6-10 During May, Kimbrell Manufacturing completed and transferred out 100,000 units. In EWIP, there were 25,000 units, 40% complete. Using the weighted average method, the equivalent units are

a. 100,000 units.
b. 125,000 units.
c. 105,000 units.
d. 110,000 units.
e. 120,000 units.

6-11 During June, Kimbrell Manufacturing completed and transferred out 100,000 units. In EWIP, there were 25,000 units, 80% complete. Using the weighted average method, the equivalent units are

a. 100,000 units.
b. 125,000 units.
c. 105,000 units.
d. 110,000 units.
e. 120,000 units.

6-12   For August, Kimbrell Manufacturing has costs in BWIP equal to $112,500. During August, the cost incurred was $450,000. Using the weighted average method, Kimbrell had 125,000 equivalent units for August. There were 100,000 units transferred out during the month. The cost of goods transferred out is

a. $500,000.
b. $400,000.
c. $450,000.
d. $360,000.
e. $50,000.

6-13   For September, Murphy Company has manufacturing costs in BWIP equal to $100,000. During September, the manufacturing costs incurred were $550,000. Using the weighted average method, Murphy had 100,000 equivalent units for September. The equivalent unit cost for September is

a. $1.00.
b. $7.50.
c. $6.50.
d. $6.00.
e. $6.62.

6-14   During June, Faust Manufacturing started and completed 80,000 units. In BWIP, there were 25,000 units, 80% complete. In EWIP, there were 25,000 units, 60% complete. Using FIFO, the equivalent units are

a. 80,000 units.
b. 95,000 units.
c. 85,000 units.
d. 115,000 units.
e. 100,000 units.

6-15   During July, Faust Manufacturing started and completed 80,000 units. In BWIP, there were 25,000 units, 20% complete. In EWIP, there were 25,000 units, 80% complete. Using FIFO, the equivalent units are

a. 80,000 units.
b. 120,000 units.
c. 65,000 units.
d. 85,000 units.
e. 100,000 units.

6-16   Assume for August that Faust Manufacturing has manufacturing costs in BWIP equal to $80,000. During August, the cost incurred was $720,000. Using the FIFO method, Faust had 120,000 equivalent units for August. The cost per equivalent unit for August is

a. $6.12.
b. $6.50.
c. $5.60.
d. $6.00.
e. $6.67.

6-17   For August, Lanny Company had 25,000 units in BWIP, 40% complete, with costs equal to $36,000. During August, the cost incurred was $450,000. Using the FIFO method, Lanny had 125,000 equivalent units for August. There were 100,000 units transferred out during the month. The cost of goods transferred out is

a. $500,000.
b. $360,000.
c. $450,000.
d. $400,000.
e. $50,000.

6-18 When materials are added either at the beginning or the end of the process, a unit cost should be calculated for the

    a. materials and conversion categories.
    b. materials category only.
    c. materials and labor categories.
    d. conversion category only.
    e. labor category only.

6-19 With nonuniform inputs, the cost of EWIP is calculated by

    a. adding the materials cost to the conversion cost.
    b. subtracting the cost of goods transferred out from the total cost of materials.
    c. multiplying the unit cost in each input category by the equivalent units of each input found in EWIP.
    d. multiplying the total unit cost by the units in EWIP.
    e. None of these.

6-20 Transferred-in goods are treated by the receiving department as

    a. units started for the period.
    b. a material added at the beginning of the process.
    c. a category of materials separate from conversion costs.
    d. All of these.
    e. None of these.

BRIEF EXERCISES: SET A

Brief Exercise 6-21 Basic Cost Flows

OBJECTIVE ‣ 1

Example 6.1

Gardner Company produces 18-ounce boxes of a wheat cereal in three departments: mixing, cooking, and packaging. During August, Gardner produced 250,000 boxes with the following costs:

	Mixing Department	Cooking Department	Packaging Department
Direct materials	$825,000	$379,500	$330,000
Direct labor	120,000	75,000	180,000
Applied overhead	225,000	82,500	332,500

Required:

1. Calculate the costs transferred out of each department.
2. Prepare journal entries that reflect these cost transfers.

Brief Exercise 6-22 Equivalent Units, No Beginning Work in Process

OBJECTIVE ‣ 2

Example 6.2

Frankle Manufacturing produces cylinders used in internal combustion engines. During June, Frankle's welding department had the following data:

Units in BWIP	—
Units completed	112,000
Units in EWIP (40% complete)	16,800

Required:

Calculate June's output for the welding department in equivalent units of production.

OBJECTIVE ▶ 2
Example 6.3

Brief Exercise 6-23 Unit Cost, Valuing Goods Transferred Out and EWIP

During April, the grinding department of Tranx Inc. completed and transferred out 315,000 units. At the end of April, there were 112,500 units in process, 60% complete. Tranx incurred manufacturing costs totaling $2,295,000.

Required:

1. Calculate the unit cost.
2. Calculate the cost of goods transferred out and the cost of EWIP.

OBJECTIVE ▶ 3
Example 6.4

Brief Exercise 6-24 Weighted Average Method, Unit Cost, Valuing Inventories

Applegate Enterprises produces premier raspberry jam. Output is measured in pints. Applegate uses the weighted average method. During January, Applegate had the following production data:

Units in process, January 1, 60% complete	108,000 pints
Units completed and transferred out	720,000 pints
Units in process, January 31, 40% complete	225,000 pints
Costs:	
Work in process, January 1	$ 162,000
Costs added during January	1,053,000

Required:

1. Using the weighted average method, calculate the equivalent units for January.
2. Calculate the unit cost for January.
3. Assign costs to units transferred out and EWIP.

OBJECTIVE ▶ 3
Example 6.5

Brief Exercise 6-25 Physical Flow Schedule

Golding Inc. just finished its second month of operations. Golding mass-produces integrated circuits. The following production information is provided for December:

Units in process, December 1, 80% complete	160,000
Units completed and transferred out	760,000
Units in process, December 31, 60% complete	120,000

Required:

Prepare a physical flow schedule.

OBJECTIVE ▶ 3
Example 6.6

Brief Exercise 6-26 Production Report, Weighted Average

Manzer Inc. manufactures bicycle frames in two departments: cutting and welding. Manzer uses the weighted average method. Manufacturing costs are added uniformly throughout the process. The following are cost and production data for the cutting department for October:

Production:	
Units in process, October 1, 40% complete	4,000
Units completed and transferred out	27,200
Units in process, October 31, 60% complete	8,000
Costs:	
WIP, October 1	$ 32,000
Costs added during October	608,000

Required:

Prepare a production report for the cutting department.

Brief Exercise 6-27 Nonuniform Inputs, Weighted Average

OBJECTIVE ▸ 4
Example 6.7

Carter Inc. had the following production and cost information for its fabrication department during April (with materials added at the beginning of the fabrication process):

Production:

Units in process, April 1, 50% complete with respect to conversion	10,000
Units completed	65,200
Units in process, April 30, 60% complete	12,000

Costs:

Work in process, April 1:	
Materials	$ 40,980
Conversion costs	28,920
Total	$ 69,900
Current costs:	
Materials	$125,000
Conversion costs	210,000
Total	$335,000

Carter uses the weighted average method.

Required:

1. Prepare an equivalent units schedule.
2. Calculate the unit cost. (*Note:* Round answers to two decimal places.)
3. Calculate the cost of units transferred out and the cost of EWIP.

Brief Exercise 6-28 Transferred-In Cost

OBJECTIVE ▸ 4
Example 6.8

Powers Inc. produces a protein drink. The product is sold by the gallon. The company has two departments: mixing and bottling. For August, the bottling department had 70,000 gallons in beginning inventory (with transferred-in costs of $283,000) and completed 262,500 gallons during the month. Further, the mixing department completed and transferred out 240,000 gallons at a cost of $957,000 in August.

Required:

1. Prepare a physical flow schedule for the bottling department.
2. Calculate equivalent units for the transferred-in category.
3. Calculate the unit cost for the transferred-in category.

Use the following information for Brief Exercises 6-29 and 6-30:
Aztec Inc. produces soft drinks. Mixing is the first department, and its output is measured in gallons. Aztec uses the FIFO method. All manufacturing costs are added uniformly. For July, the mixing department provided the following information:

Production:

Units in process, July 1, 80% complete	120,000 gallons
Units completed and transferred out	690,000 gallons
Units in process, July 31, 75% complete	80,000 gallons

Costs:

Work in process, July 1	$ 120,000
Costs added during July	1,471,500

OBJECTIVE **5**
Example 6.9

Brief Exercise 6-29 *(Appendix 6A)* **First-In, First-Out Method; Equivalent Units**

Refer to the information for Aztec Inc. on the previous page.

Required:

1. Calculate the equivalent units for July.
2. Calculate the unit cost. (*Note:* Round to two decimal places.)
3. Assign costs to units transferred out and EWIP using the FIFO method.

OBJECTIVE **5**
Example 6.10

Brief Exercise 6-30 *(Appendix 6A)* **FIFO; Production Report**

Refer to the information for Aztec Inc. on the previous page.

Required:

Prepare a production report.

BRIEF EXERCISES: SET B

OBJECTIVE **1**
Example 6.1

Brief Exercise 6-31 **Basic Cost Flows**

Hardy Company produces 18-ounce boxes of a rolled oat cereal in three departments: mixing, cooking, and packaging. During September, Hardy produced 200,000 boxes with the following costs:

	Mixing Department	Cooking Department	Packaging Department
Direct materials	$600,500	$285,500	$250,000
Direct labor	90,000	50,000	120,000
Applied overhead	117,000	65,000	156,000

Required:

1. Calculate the costs transferred out of each department.
2. Prepare journal entries that reflect these cost transfers.

OBJECTIVE **2**
Example 6.2

Brief Exercise 6-32 **Equivalent Units, No Beginning Work in Process**

Cardenas Pharmaceutical produces antibiotics. During April, Cardenas's tableting department had the following data:

Units in BWIP	—
Units completed	105,000
Units in EWIP (30% complete)	15,750

Required:

Calculate April's output for the tableting department in equivalent units of production.

OBJECTIVE **2**
Example 6.3

Brief Exercise 6-33 **Unit Cost, Valuing Goods Transferred Out and EWIP**

During August, the drilling department of Arenal Inc. completed and transferred out 190,000 units. At the end of August, there were 42,700 units in process, 70% complete. Arenal incurred manufacturing costs totaling $1,759,120.

Required:

1. Calculate the unit cost.
2. Calculate the cost of goods transferred out and the cost of EWIP.

Brief Exercise 6-34 Weighted Average Method, Unit Cost, Valuing Inventories

OBJECTIVE ▸ 3

Example 6.4

Polson Enterprises produces strawberry gelato. Output is measured in quarts. Polson uses the weighted average method. During July, Polson had the following production data:

Units in process, July 1, 60% complete	54,000 quarts
Units completed and transferred out	360,000 quarts
Units in process, July 31, 40% complete	112,500 quarts
Costs:	
Work in process, July 1	$ 81,000
Costs added during July	526,500

Required:

1. Using the weighted average method, calculate the equivalent units for July.
2. Calculate the unit cost for July.
3. Assign costs to units transferred out and EWIP.

Brief Exercise 6-35 Physical Flow Schedule

OBJECTIVE ▸ 3

Example 6.5

Craig Inc. just finished its third month of operations. Craig mass-produces carburetors used in motorcycle engines. The following production information is provided for December:

Units in process, December 1, 60% complete	60,000
Units completed and transferred out	245,000
Units in process, December 31, 80% complete	45,000

Required:

Prepare a physical flow schedule.

Brief Exercise 6-36 Production Report, Weighted Average

OBJECTIVE ▸ 3

Example 6.6

Washburn Inc. manufactures precision tools in two departments: molding and finishing. Washburn uses the weighted average method. Manufacturing costs are added uniformly throughout the process. The following are cost and production data for the molding department for June:

Production:	
Units in process, June 1, 50% complete	15,000
Units completed and transferred out	102,000
Units in process, June 30, 60% complete	30,000
Costs:	
WIP, June 1	$ 180,000
Costs added during June	3,420,000

Required:

Prepare a production report for the molding department.

Brief Exercise 6-37 Nonuniform Inputs, Weighted Average

OBJECTIVE ▸ 4

Example 6.7

Ming Inc. had the following production and cost information for its blending department during February (with materials added at the beginning of the process):

(Continued)

Production:

Units in process, February 1, 50% complete with respect to conversion	2,000
Units completed	13,040
Units in process, February 28, 60% complete	2,400

Costs:

Work in process, February1:	
Materials	$ 16,000
Conversion costs	12,000
Total	$ 28,000
Current costs:	
Materials	$ 50,000
Conversion costs	84,000
Total	$134,000

Ming uses the weighted average method.

Required:

1. Prepare an equivalent units schedule.
2. Calculate the unit cost. (*Note:* Round answers to two decimal places.)
3. Calculate the cost of units transferred out and the cost of EWIP.

OBJECTIVE 4

Example 6.8

Brief Exercise 6-38 Transferred-In Cost

Vigor Inc. produces an energy drink. The product is sold by the quart. The company has two departments: mixing and bottling. For May, the bottling department had 30,000 quarts in beginning inventory (with transferred-in costs of $63,000) and completed 140,000 quarts during the month. Further, the mixing department completed and transferred out 120,000 gallons at a cost of $237,000 in May.

Required:

1. Prepare a physical flow schedule for the bottling department.
2. Calculate equivalent units for the transferred-in category.
3. Calculate the unit cost for the transferred-in category.

Use the following information for Brief Exercises 6-39 and 6-40:
Saludable Inc. produces a freeze-dried kale powder. Drying is the first department, and its output is measured in pounds. Saludable uses the FIFO method. All manufacturing costs are added uniformly. For November, the drying department provided the following information:

Production:	
Units in process, November 1, 70% complete	6,000 pounds
Units completed and transferred out	34,500 pounds
Units in process, November 30, 60% complete	4,000 pounds
Costs:	
Work in process, November 1	$ 16,380
Costs added during November	130,800

OBJECTIVE 5

Example 6.9

Brief Exercise 6-39 *(Appendix 6A)* First-In, First-Out Method; Equivalent Units

Refer to the information for Saludable Inc. above.

Required:

1. Calculate the equivalent units for November.
2. Calculate the unit cost. (*Note:* Round to two decimal places.)
3. Assign costs to units transferred out and EWIP using the FIFO method.

Brief Exercise 6-40 *(Appendix 6A)* **FIFO; Production Report**

Refer to the information for Saludable Inc. on the previous page.

OBJECTIVE ▶ 5

Example 6.10

Required:

Prepare a production report.

EXERCISES

Exercise 6-41 **Basic Cost Flows**

Linsenmeyer Company produces a common machine component for industrial equipment in three departments: molding, grinding, and finishing. The following data are available for September:

OBJECTIVE ▶ 1

EXCEL

	Molding Department	Grinding Department	Finishing Department
Direct materials	$286,400	$ 30,400	$29,400
Direct labor	27,600	67,200	68,400
Applied overhead	35,000	272,000	57,000

During September, 18,000 components were completed. There is no beginning or ending WIP in any department.

Required:

1. Prepare a schedule showing, for each department, the cost of direct materials, direct labor, applied overhead, product transferred in from a prior department, and total manufacturing cost.
2. Calculate the unit cost. (*Note:* Round the unit cost to two decimal places.)

Exercise 6-42 **Journal Entries, Basic Cost Flows**

In December, Davis Company had the following cost flows:

OBJECTIVE ▶ 1

	Molding Department	Grinding Department	Finishing Department
Direct materials	$111,600	$ 30,000	$ 17,200
Direct labor	8,000	13,600	11,600
Applied overhead	8,400	60,400	11,200
Transferred-in cost:			
From Molding		128,000	
From Grinding			232,000
Total cost	$128,000	$232,000	$272,000

Required:

1. Prepare the journal entries to transfer costs from (a) Molding to Grinding, (b) Grinding to Finishing, and (c) Finishing to Finished Goods.
2. **CONCEPTUAL CONNECTION** Explain how the journal entries differ from a job-order cost system.

OBJECTIVE **2**

EXCEL

Exercise 6-43 Equivalent Units, Unit Cost, Valuation of Goods Transferred Out and Ending Work in Process

The blending department had the following data for the month of March:

Units in BWIP	—
Units completed	21,600
Units in EWIP (60% complete)	2,250
Total manufacturing costs	$82,620

Required:

1. What is the output in equivalent units for March?
2. What is the unit manufacturing cost for March?
3. Compute the cost of goods transferred out for March.
4. Calculate the value of March's EWIP.

OBJECTIVE **3**

Exercise 6-44 Weighted Average Method, Equivalent Units

Goforth Company produces a product where all manufacturing inputs are applied uniformly. Goforth produced the following physical flow schedule for April:

Units to account for:	
Units in BWIP (40% complete)	180,000
Units started	420,000
Total units to account for	600,000
Units accounted for:	
Units completed:	
From BWIP	180,000
Started and completed	324,000
	504,000
Units in EWIP (75% complete)	96,000
Total units accounted for	600,000

Required:

Prepare a schedule of equivalent units using the weighted average method.

OBJECTIVE **3**

Exercise 6-45 Weighted Average Method, Unit Cost, Valuing Inventories

Cassien Inc. manufactures products that pass through two or more processes. During June, equivalent units were computed using the weighted average method:

Units completed	53,400
Units in EWIP × Fraction complete (36,000 × 60%)	21,600
Equivalent units of output	75,000
June's costs to account for are as follows:	
BWIP (10,000 units, 80% complete)	$ 50,000
Materials	90,000
Conversion costs	34,000
Total	$174,000

Required:

1. Calculate the unit cost for June using the weighted average method.
2. Using the weighted average method, determine the cost of EWIP and the cost of the goods transferred out.

3. **CONCEPTUAL CONNECTION** Cassien had just finished implementing a series of measures designed to reduce the unit cost to $2.00 and was assured that this had been achieved and should be realized for June's production. Yet, upon seeing the unit cost for June, the president of the company was disappointed. Can you explain why the full effect of the cost reductions may not show up in June? What can you suggest to overcome this problem?

Exercise 6-46 Weighted Average Method, Unit Costs, Valuing Inventories

OBJECTIVE ▶ 3

Byford Inc. produces a product that passes through two processes. During November, equivalent units were calculated using the weighted average method:

Units completed	196,000
Add: Units in EWIP × Fraction complete (60,000 × 40%)	24,000
Equivalent units of output (weighted average)	220,000
Less: Units in BWIP × Fraction complete (50,000 × 70%)	35,000
Equivalent units of output (FIFO)	185,000

The costs that Byford had to account for during the month of November were as follows:

BWIP	$ 107 000
Costs added	993,000
Total	$1,100,000

Required:

1. Using the weighted average method, determine unit cost.
2. Under the weighted average method, what is the total cost of units transferred out? What is the cost assigned to units in ending inventory?
3. **CONCEPTUAL CONNECTION** Bill Johnson, the manager of Byford, is considering switching from weighted average to FIFO. Explain the key differences between the two approaches and make a recommendation to Bill about which method should be used.

Exercise 6-47 Physical Flow Schedule

OBJECTIVE ▶ 3

EXCEL

The following information was obtained for the grinding department of Harlan Company for May:

a. BWIP had 91,500 units, 30% complete with respect to manufacturing costs.
b. EWIP had 25,200 units, 25% complete with respect to manufacturing costs.
c. Started 99,000 units in May.

Required:
Prepare a physical flow schedule.

Exercise 6-48 Physical Flow Schedule

OBJECTIVE ▶ 3

Nelrok Company manufactures fertilizer. Department 1 mixes the chemicals required for the fertilizer. The following data are for the year:

BWIP (40% complete)	25,000
Units started	142,500
Units in EWIP (60% complete)	35,000

Required:
Prepare a physical flow schedule.

OBJECTIVE **3**

EXCEL

Exercise 6-49 Production Report, Weighted Average

Mino Inc. manufactures chocolate syrup in three departments: cooking, mixing, and bottling. Mino uses the weighted average method. The following are cost and production data for the cooking department for April (*Note:* Assume that units are measured in gallons.):

Production:

Units in process, April 1 (60% complete)	20,000
Units completed and transferred out	50,000
Units in process, April 30 (20% complete)	10,000

Costs:

WIP, April 1	$ 93,600
Costs added during April	314,600

Required:

Prepare a production report for the cooking department.

OBJECTIVE **4**

Exercise 6-50 Nonuniform Inputs, Equivalent Units

Terry Linens Inc. manufactures bed and bath linens. The bath linens department sews terry cloth into towels of various sizes. Terry uses the weighted average method. All materials are added at the beginning of the process. The following data are for the bath linens department for August:

Production:

Units in process, August 1, 25% complete*	10,000
Units completed and transferred out	60,000
Units in process, August 31, 60% complete*	20,000

*With respect to conversion costs.

Required:

Calculate equivalent units of production for the bath linens department for August.

OBJECTIVE **4**

Exercise 6-51 Unit Cost and Cost Assignment, Nonuniform Inputs

Loran Inc. had the following equivalent units schedule and cost for its fabrication department during September:

	Materials	Conversion
Units completed	180,000	180,000
Add: Units in ending WIP × Fraction complete (60,000 × 60%)	60,000	36,000
Equivalent units of output	240,000	216,000
Costs:		
Work in process, September 1:		
Materials	$ 147,000	
Conversion costs	7,875	
Total	$ 154,875	
Current costs:		
Materials	$1,053,000	
Conversion costs	236,205	
Total	$1,289,205	

Required:

1. Calculate the unit cost for materials, for conversion, and in total for the fabrication department for September.
2. Calculate the cost of units transferred out and the cost of EWIP.

Exercise 6-52 Nonuniform Inputs, Transferred-In Cost

OBJECTIVE ▶ 4

Drysdale Dairy produces a variety of dairy products. In Department 12, cream (transferred in from Department 6) and other materials (sugar and flavorings) are mixed at the beginning of the process and churned to make ice cream. The following data are for Department 12 for August:

Production:

Units in process, August 1, 25% complete*	40,000
Units completed and transferred out	120,000
Units in process, August 31, 60% complete*	30,000

*With respect to conversion costs.

Required:

1. Prepare a physical flow schedule for the month.
2. Using the weighted average method, calculate equivalent units for the following categories: transferred-in, materials, and conversion.

Exercise 6-53 Transferred-In Cost

OBJECTIVE ▶ 4

Golding's finishing department had the following data for July:

	Transferred-In	Materials	Conversion
Units transferred out	60,000	60,000	60,000
Units in EWIP	15,000	15,000	9,000
Equivalent units	75,000	75,000	69,000

Costs:

Work in process, July 1:	
Transferred in from fabricating	$ 2,100
Materials	1,500
Conversion costs	3,000
Total	$ 6,600
Current costs:	
Transferred in from fabricating	$30,900
Materials	22,500
Conversion costs	45,300
Total	$98,700

Required:

1. Calculate unit costs for the following categories: transferred-in, materials, and conversion.
2. Calculate total unit cost.

Exercise 6-54 (Appendix 6A) First-In, First-Out Method; Equivalent Units

OBJECTIVE ▶ 5

Lawson Company produces a product where all manufacturing inputs are applied uniformly. Lawson produced the following physical flow schedule for March:

Units to account for:	
Units in BWIP (40% complete)	15,000
Units started	35,000
Total units to account for	50,000
Units accounted for:	
Units completed:	
From BWIP	15,000
Started and completed	27,000
	42,000
Units in EWIP (75% complete)	8,000
Total units accounted for	50,000

(Continued)

Required:

Prepare a schedule of equivalent units using the FIFO method.

OBJECTIVE 5

Exercise 6-55 *(Appendix 6A)* First-In, First-Out Method; Unit Cost; Valuing Inventories

Loren Inc. manufactures products that pass through two or more processes. During April, equivalent units were computed using the FIFO method:

Units started and completed	4,600
Units in BWIP × Fraction to complete (60%)	840
Units in EWIP × Fraction complete (4,000 × 60%)	2,400
Equivalent units of output (FIFO)	7,840
April's costs to account for are as follows:	
BWIP (40% complete)	$ 1,120
Materials	10,000
Conversion cost	4,000
Total	$15,120

Required:

1. Calculate the unit cost for April using the FIFO method. (*Note:* Round to two decimal places.)
2. Using the FIFO method, determine the cost of EWIP and the cost of the goods transferred out.

PROBLEMS

OBJECTIVE 1 2

Problem 6-56 Basic Flows, Equivalent Units

Thayn Company produces an arthritis medication that passes through two departments: mixing and tableting. Thayn uses the weighted average method. Data for February for mixing are as follows: BWIP was zero; EWIP had 36,000 units, 50% complete; and 420,000 units were started. Tableting's data for February are as follows: BWIP was 24,000 units, 20% complete; and 12,000 units were in EWIP, 40% complete.

Required:

1. For mixing, calculate the (a) number of units transferred to tableting and (b) equivalent units of production.
2. For tableting, calculate the number of units transferred out to Finished Goods.
3. **CONCEPTUAL CONNECTION** Suppose that the units in the mixing department are measured in ounces, while the units in tableting are measured in bottles of 100 tablets, with a total weight of eight ounces (excluding the bottle). Decide how you would treat units that are measured differently and then repeat Requirement 2 using this approach.

OBJECTIVE 1 2 3 4

Problem 6-57 Steps in Preparing a Production Report

Recently, **Stillwater Designs** expanded its market by becoming an original equipment supplier to **Jeep Wrangler**. Stillwater Designs produces factory upgraded speakers specifically for Jeep Wrangler. The Kicker components and speaker cabinets are outsourced with assembly remaining in house. Stillwater Designs assembles the product by placing the speakers and other components in cabinets that define an audio package upgrade and that can be placed into the Jeep Wrangler, producing the desired factory-installed appearance. Speaker cabinets and associated Kicker components are added at the beginning of the assembly process.

Assume that Stillwater Designs uses the weighted average method to cost out the audio package. The following are cost and production data for the assembly process for April:

Production:	
Units in process, April 1, 60% complete	60,000
Units completed and transferred out	150,000
Units in process, April 30, 20% complete	30,000
Costs:	
WIP, April 1:	
Cabinets	$ 1,200,000
Kicker components	12,600,000
Conversion costs	5,400,000
Costs added during April:	
Cabinets	$ 2,400,000
Kicker components	25,200,000
Conversion costs	8,640,000

Required:

1. Prepare a physical flow analysis for the assembly department for the month of April.
2. Calculate equivalent units of production for the assembly department for the month of April.
3. Calculate unit cost for the assembly department for the month of April.
4. Calculate the cost of units transferred out and the cost of EWIP inventory.
5. Prepare a cost reconciliation for the assembly department for the month of April.

Problem 6-58 **Steps for a Production Report**

Refer to the data of Problem 6-57.

OBJECTIVE 1 3

Required:

1. Prepare a production report for the assembly department for the month of April.
2. **CONCEPTUAL CONNECTION** Write a one-page report that compares the purpose and content of the production report with the job-order cost sheet.

Use the following information for Problems 6-59 and 6-60:
Alfombra Inc. manufactures throw rugs. The throw rug department weaves cloth and yarn into throw rugs of various sizes. Alfombra uses the weighted average method. Materials are added uniformly throughout the weaving process. In August, Alfombra switched from FIFO to the weighted average method. The following data are for the throw rug department for August:

Production:	
Units in process, August 1, 60% complete	40,000
Units completed and transferred out	120,000
Units in process, August 31, 60% complete	40,000
Costs:	
WIP, August 1	$144,000
Current costs	604,800
Total	$748,800

OBJECTIVE  1 ▸ 2 ▸ 3 ▸ 4

Problem 6-59 Equivalent Units, Unit Cost, Weighted Average

Refer to the information for Alfombra Inc. on the previous page.

Required:

1. Prepare a physical flow analysis for the throw rug department for August.
2. Calculate equivalent units of production for the throw rug department for August.
3. Calculate the unit cost for the throw rug department for August.
4. Show that the cost per unit calculated in Requirement 3 is a weighted average of the FIFO cost per equivalent unit in BWIP and the FIFO cost per equivalent unit for August. (*Hint:* The weights are in proportion to the number of units from each source.)

OBJECTIVE 3

EXCEL

Problem 6-60 Production Report

Refer to the information for Alfombra Inc. on the previous page. The owner of Alfombra insisted on a formal report that provided all the details of the weighted average method. In the manufacturing process, all materials are added uniformly throughout the process.

Required:

Prepare a production report for the throw rug department for August using the weighted average method.

OBJECTIVE  1 ▸ 2 ▸ 3

Problem 6-61 Weighted Average Method, Physical Flow, Equivalent Units, Unit Costs, Cost Assignment

Mimasca Inc. manufactures various holiday masks. Each mask is shaped from a piece of rubber in the molding department. The masks are then transferred to the finishing department, where they are painted and have elastic bands attached. Mimasca uses the weighted average method. In May, the molding department reported the following data:

a. BWIP consisted of 15,000 units, 20% complete. Cost in beginning inventory totaled $1,656.
b. Costs added to production during the month were $26,094.
c. At the end of the month, 45,000 units were transferred out to finishing. Then, 5,000 units remained in EWIP, 25% complete.

Required:

1. Prepare a physical flow schedule.
2. Calculate equivalent units of production.
3. Compute unit cost.
4. Calculate the cost of goods transferred to finishing at the end of the month. Calculate the cost of ending inventory.
5. **CONCEPTUAL CONNECTION** Assume that the masks are inspected at the end of the molding process. Of the 45,000 units inspected, 2,500 are rejected as faulty and are discarded. Thus, only 42,500 units are transferred to the finishing department. The manager of Mimasca considers all such spoilage as abnormal and does not want to assign any of this cost to the 42,500 good units produced and transferred to finishing. Your task is to determine the cost of this spoilage of 2,500 units and then to discuss how you would account for this spoilage cost. Now suppose that the manager feels that this spoilage cost is just part of the cost of producing the good units transferred out. Therefore, he wants to assign this cost to the good production. Explain how this would be handled. (*Hint:* Spoiled units are a type of output, and equivalent units of spoilage can be calculated.)

Use the following information for Problems 6-62 and 6-63:

Millie Company produces a product that passes through an assembly process and a finishing process. All manufacturing costs are added uniformly for both processes. The following information was obtained for the assembly department for June:

a. WIP, June 1, had 24,000 units (60% completed) and the following costs:

Direct materials	$186,256
Direct labor	64,864
Overhead applied	34,400

b. During June, 70,000 units were completed and transferred to the finishing department, and the following costs were added to production:

Direct materials	$267,880
Direct labor	253,000
Overhead applied	117,600

c. On June 30, there were 10,000 partially completed units in process. These units were 70% complete.

Problem 6-62 Weighted Average Method, Single-Department Analysis

OBJECTIVE ▸ 1 ▸ 2 ▸ 3

Refer to the information for Millie Company above.

Required:

Prepare a production report for the assembly department for June using the weighted average method of costing. The report should disclose the physical flow of units, equivalent units, and unit costs and should track the disposition of manufacturing costs.

Problem 6-63 (Appendix 6A) First-In, First-Out Method; Single-Department Analysis; One Cost Category

OBJECTIVE ▸ 5

EXCEL

Refer to the information for Millie Company above.

Required:

Prepare a production report for the assembly department for June using the FIFO method of costing. The report should disclose the physical flow of units, equivalent units, and unit costs and should track the disposition of manufacturing costs. (*Note:* Carry the unit cost computation to four decimal places.)

Problem 6-64 Weighted Average Method, Separate Materials Cost

OBJECTIVE ▸ 1 ▸ 2 ▸ 3

Janbo Company produces a variety of stationery products. One product, sealing wax sticks, passes through two processes: blending and molding. The weighted average method is used to account for the costs of production. After blending, the resulting product is sent to the molding department, where it is poured into molds and cooled. The following information relates to the blending process for August:

a. WIP, August 1, had 30,000 pounds, 20% complete. Costs associated with partially completed units were:

Materials	$220,000
Direct labor	30,000
Overhead applied	20,000

b. WIP, August 31, had 50,000 pounds, 40% complete.
c. Units completed and transferred out totaled 480,000 pounds. Costs added during the month were (all inputs are added uniformly):

(Continued)

Materials	$5,800,000
Direct labor	4,250,000
Overhead applied	1,292,500

Required:

1. Prepare (a) a physical flow schedule and (b) an equivalent unit schedule.
2. Calculate the unit cost. (*Note:* Round to three decimal places.)
3. Compute the cost of EWIP and the cost of goods transferred out.
4. Prepare a cost reconciliation.
5. Suppose that the materials added uniformly in blending are paraffin and pigment and that the manager of the company wants to know how much each of these materials costs per equivalent unit produced. The costs of the materials in BWIP are as follows:

Paraffin	$120,000
Pigment	100,000

The costs of the materials added during the month are also given:

Paraffin	$3,250,000
Pigment	2,550,000

Prepare an equivalent unit schedule with cost categories for each material. Calculate the cost per unit for each type of material.

OBJECTIVE

Problem 6-65 Weighted Average Method, Journal Entries

Seacrest Company uses a process-costing system. The company manufactures a product that is processed in two departments: A and B. As work is completed, it is transferred out. All inputs are added uniformly in Department A. The following summarizes the production activity and costs for November:

	Department A	Department B
Beginning inventories:		
Physical units	5,000	8,000
Costs:		
Transferred in	—	$ 45,320
Direct materials	$10,000	—
Conversion costs	$ 6,900	$ 16,800
Current production:		
Units started	25,000	?
Units transferred out	28,000	33,000
Costs:		
Transferred in	—	?
Direct materials	$57,800	$ 37,950
Conversion costs	$95,220	$128,100
Percentage completion:		
Beginning inventory	40%	50%
Ending inventory	80%	50%

Required:

1. Using the weighted average method, prepare the following for Department A: (a) a physical flow schedule, (b) an equivalent unit calculation, (c) calculation of unit costs (*Note:* Round to four decimal places.), (d) cost of EWIP and cost of goods transferred out, and (e) a cost reconciliation.

2. **CONCEPTUAL CONNECTION** Prepare journal entries that show the flow of manufacturing costs for Department A. Use a conversion cost control account for conversion costs. Many firms are now combining direct labor and overhead costs into one category. They are not tracking direct labor separately. Offer some reasons for this practice.

Problem 6-66 *(Appendix 6A)* First-In, First-Out Method; Journal Entries

OBJECTIVE ◄ 5

Refer to **Problem 6-65.**

Required:

1. Using the FIFO method, prepare the following for Department A: (a) a physical flow schedule, (b) an equivalent unit calculation, (c) calculation of unit costs (*Note:* Round to three decimal places.), (d) cost of EWIP and cost of goods transferred out, and (e) a cost reconciliation.
2. **CONCEPTUAL CONNECTION** Prepare journal entries that show the flow of manufacturing costs for Department A. Use a conversion cost control account for conversion costs. Many firms are now combining direct labor and overhead costs into one category. They are not tracking direct labor separately. Offer some reasons for this practice.

Problem 6-67 Weighted Average Method, Nonuniform Inputs, Multiple Departments

OBJECTIVE ◄ 1 ◄ 2 ◄ 4 ◄ 5

Benson Pharmaceuticals uses a process-costing system to compute the unit costs of the over-the-counter cold remedies that it produces. It has three departments: mixing, encapsulating, and bottling. In mixing, the ingredients for the cold capsules are measured, sifted, and blended (with materials assumed to be uniformly added throughout the process). The mix is transferred out in gallon containers. The encapsulating department takes the powdered mix and places it in capsules (which are necessarily added at the beginning of the process). One gallon of powdered mix converts into 1,500 capsules. After the capsules are filled and polished, they are transferred to bottling, where they are placed in bottles that are then affixed with a safety seal, lid, and label. Each bottle receives 50 capsules.

During March, the following results are available for the first two departments:

	Mixing	Encapsulating
Beginning inventories:		
Physical units	10 gallons	4,000
Costs:		
Materials	$252	$32
Labor	$282	$20
Overhead	?	?
Transferred in		$140
Current production:		
Transferred out	140 gallons	208,000
Ending inventory	20 gallons	6,000
Costs:		
Materials	$3,636	$1,573
Transferred in	—	?
Labor	$4,618	$1,944
Overhead	?	?
Percentage of completion:		
Beginning inventory	40%	50%
Ending inventory	50%	40%

(Continued)

Overhead in both departments is applied as a percentage of direct labor costs. In the mixing department, overhead is 200% of direct labor. In the encapsulating department, the overhead rate is 150% of direct labor.

Required:

1. Prepare a production report for the mixing department using the weighted average method. Follow the five steps outlined in the chapter. (*Note:* Round to two decimal places for the unit cost.)
2. Prepare a production report for the encapsulating department using the weighted average method. Follow the five steps outlined in the chapter. (*Note:* Round to four decimal places for the unit cost.)
3. **CONCEPTUAL CONNECTION** Explain why the weighted average method is easier to use than FIFO. Explain when weighted average will give about the same results as FIFO.

OBJECTIVE ▶ **5**

Problem 6-68 *(Appendix 6A)* **First-In, First-Out Method**

Refer to **Problem 6-67**.

Required:

Prepare a production report for the mixing and encapsulating departments using the FIFO method. (*Note:* Round the unit cost to four decimal places.) (*Hint:* For the second department, you must convert gallons to capsules.)

CASES

OBJECTIVE ▶ **1** ▶ **2** ▶ **3** ▶ **4**

Case 6-69 Process Costing versus Alternative Costing Methods, Impact on Resource Allocation Decision

Golding Manufacturing, a division of Farnsworth Sporting Inc., produces two different models of bows and eight models of knives. The bow-manufacturing process involves the production of two major subassemblies: the limbs and the handles. The limbs pass through four sequential processes before reaching final assembly: layup, molding, fabricating, and finishing. In the layup department, limbs are created by laminating layers of wood. In the molding department, the limbs are heat-treated, under pressure, to form strong resilient limbs. In the fabricating department, any protruding glue or other processing residue is removed. Finally, in the finishing department, the limbs are cleaned with acetone, dried, and sprayed with the final finishes.

The handles pass through two processes before reaching final assembly: pattern and finishing. In the pattern department, blocks of wood are fed into a machine that is set to shape the handles. Different patterns are possible, depending on the machine's setting. After coming out of the machine, the handles are cleaned and smoothed. They then pass to the finishing department, where they are sprayed with the final finishes. In final assembly, the limbs and handles are assembled into different models using purchased parts such as pulley assemblies, weight-adjustment bolts, side plates, and string.

Golding, since its inception, has been using process costing to assign product costs. A predetermined overhead rate is used based on direct labor dollars (80% of direct labor dollars). Recently, Golding has hired a new controller, Karen Jenkins. After reviewing the product-costing procedures, Karen requested a meeting with the divisional manager, Aaron Suhr. The following is a transcript of their conversation:

Karen: Aaron, I have some concerns about our cost accounting system. We make two different models of bows and are treating them as if they were the same product. Now I know that the only real difference between the models is the handle. The processing of the handles is the same, but the handles differ significantly in the amount and quality of wood used. Our current costing does not reflect this difference in material input.

Aaron: Your predecessor is responsible. He believed that tracking the difference in material cost wasn't worth the effort. He simply didn't believe that it would make much difference in the unit cost of either model.

Karen: Well, he may have been right, but I have my doubts. If there is a significant difference, it could affect our views of which model is more important to the company. The additional bookkeeping isn't very stringent. All we have to worry about is the pattern department. The other departments fit what I view as a process-costing pattern.

Aaron: Why don't you look into it? If there is a significant difference, go ahead and adjust the costing system.

After the meeting, Karen decided to collect cost data on the two models: the Deluxe model and the Econo model. She decided to track the costs for one week. At the end of the week, she had collected the following data from the pattern department:

a. There were a total of 2,500 bows completed: 1,000 Deluxe models and 1,500 Econo models.
b. There was no BWIP; however, there were 300 units in EWIP: 200 Deluxe and 100 Econo models. Both models were 80% complete with respect to conversion costs and 100% complete with respect to materials.
c. The pattern department experienced the following costs:

Direct materials	$114,000
Direct labor	45,667

d. On an experimental basis, the requisition forms for materials were modified to identify the dollar value of the materials used by the Econo and Deluxe models:

Econo model	$30,000
Deluxe model	84,000

Required:

1. Compute the unit cost for the handles produced by the pattern department, assuming that process costing is totally appropriate. Round unit cost to two decimal places.
2. Compute the unit cost of each handle, using the separate cost information provided on materials. Round unit cost to two decimal places.
3. Compare the unit costs computed in Requirements 1 and 2. Is Karen justified in her belief that a pure process-costing relationship is not appropriate? Describe the costing system that you would recommend.
4. In the past, the marketing manager has requested more money for advertising the Econo line. Aaron has repeatedly refused to grant any increase in this product's advertising budget because its per-unit profit (selling price minus manufacturing cost) is so low. Given the results in Requirements 1 through 3, was Aaron justified in his position?

Case 6-70 (Appendix 6A) Equivalent Units; Valuation of Work-in-Process Inventories; First-In, First-Out versus Weighted Average

OBJECTIVE ▸1 ▸2 ▸3 ▸4 ▸5

AKL Foundry manufactures metal components for different kinds of equipment used by the aerospace, commercial aircraft, medical equipment, and electronic industries. The company uses investment casting to produce the required components. Investment casting consists of creating, in wax, a replica of the final product and pouring a hard shell around it. After removing the wax, molten metal is poured into the resulting cavity. What remains after the shell is broken is the desired metal object ready to be put to its designated use.

Metal components pass through eight processes: gating, shell creating, foundry work, cut-off, grinding, finishing, welding, and strengthening. Gating creates the wax mold and clusters the wax pattern around a sprue (a hole through which the molten metal will be poured through

(Continued)

the gates into the mold in the foundry process), which is joined and supported by gates (flow channels) to form a tree of patterns. In the shell-creating process, the wax molds are alternately dipped in a ceramic slurry and a fluidized bed of progressively coarser refractory grain until a sufficiently thick shell (or mold) completely encases the wax pattern. After drying, the mold is sent to the foundry process. Here, the wax is melted out of the mold, and the shell is fired, strengthened, and brought to the proper temperature. Molten metal is then poured into the de-waxed shell. Finally, the ceramic shell is removed, and the finished product is sent to the cutoff process, where the parts are separated from the tree by the use of a band saw. The parts are then sent to the grinding process, where the gates that allowed the molten metal to flow into the ceramic cavities are ground off using large abrasive grinders. In the finishing process, rough edges caused by the grinders are removed by small handheld pneumatic tools. Parts that are flawed at this point are sent to welding for corrective treatment. The last process uses heat to treat the parts to bring them to the desired strength.

In 20X1, the two partners who owned AKL Foundry decided to split up and divide the business. In dissolving their business relationship, they were faced with the problem of dividing the business assets equitably. Since the company had two plants—one in Arizona and one in New Mexico—a suggestion was made to split the business on the basis of geographic location. One partner would assume ownership of the plant in New Mexico, and the other would assume ownership of the plant in Arizona. However, this arrangement had one major complication: the amount of WIP inventory located in the Arizona plant.

The Arizona facilities had been in operation for more than a decade and were full of WIP. The New Mexico facility had been operational for only 2 years and had much smaller WIP inventories. The partner located in New Mexico argued that to disregard the unequal value of the WIP inventories would be grossly unfair.

Unfortunately, during the entire business history of AKL Foundry, WIP inventories had never been assigned any value. In computing the cost of goods sold each year, the company had followed the policy of adding depreciation to the out-of-pocket costs of direct labor, direct materials, and overhead. Accruals for the company are nearly nonexistent, and there are hardly ever any ending inventories of materials.

During 20X1, the Arizona plant had sales of $2,028,670. The cost of goods sold is itemized as follows:

Direct materials	$378,000
Direct labor	530,300
Overhead	643,518

Upon request, the owners of AKL provided the following supplementary information (percentages are cumulative):

Costs Used by Each Process as a Percentage of Total Cost

	Direct Materials (%)	Direct Total Labor Cost (%)
Gating	23	35
Shell creating	70	50
Foundry work	100	70
Cutoff	100	72
Grinding	100	80
Finishing	100	90
Welding	100	93
Strengthening	100	100

Gating had 10,000 units in BWIP, 60% complete. Assume that all materials are added at the beginning of each process. During the year, 50,000 units were completed and transferred out. The ending inventory had 11,000 unfinished units, 60% complete.

Required:

1. The partners of AKL want a reasonable estimate of the cost of WIP inventories. Using the gating department's inventory as an example, prepare an estimate of the cost of the EWIP. What assumptions did you make? Did you use the FIFO or weighted average method? Why? (*Note*: Round unit cost to two decimal places.)

2. Assume that the shell-creating process has 8,000 units in BWIP, 20% complete. During the year, 50,000 units were completed and transferred out. (*Note:* All 50,000 units were sold; no other units were sold.) The EWIP inventory had 8,000 units, 30% complete. Compute the value of the shell-creating department's EWIP. What additional assumptions had to be made?

Case 6-71 Production Report, Ethical Behavior

OBJECTIVE ▶ 3

Consider the following conversation between Gary Means, manager of a division that produces industrial machinery, and his controller, Donna Simpson, a certified management accountant and certified public accountant:

Gary: Donna, we have a real problem. Our operating cash is too low, and we are in desperate need of a loan. As you know, our financial position is marginal, and we need to show as much income as possible—and our assets need bolstering as well.

Donna: I understand the problem, but I don't see what can be done at this point. This is the last week of the fiscal year, and it looks like we'll report income just slightly above breakeven.

Gary: I know all this. What we need is some creative accounting. I have an idea that might help us, and I wanted to see if you would go along with it. We have 200 partially finished machines in process, about 20% complete. That compares with the 1,000 units that we completed and sold during the year. When you computed the per-unit cost, you used 1,040 equivalent units, giving us a manufacturing cost of $1,500 per unit. That per-unit cost gives us cost of goods sold equal to $1.5 million and ending work in process worth $60,000. The presence of the work in process gives us a chance to improve our financial position. If we report the units in work in process as 80% complete, this will increase our equivalent units to 1,160. This, in turn, will decrease our unit cost to about $1,345 and cost of goods sold to $1.345 million. The value of our work in process will increase to $215,200. With those financial stats, the loan would be a cinch.

Donna: Gary, I don't know. What you're suggesting is risky. It wouldn't take much auditing skill to catch this one.

Gary: You don't have to worry about that. The auditors won't be here for at least 6 to 8 more weeks. By that time, we can have those partially completed units completed and sold. I can bury the labor cost by having some of our more loyal workers work overtime for some bonuses. The overtime will never be reported. And, as you know, bonuses come out of the corporate budget and are assigned to overhead—next year's overhead. Donna, this will work. If we look good and get the loan to boot, corporate headquarters will treat us well. If we don't do this, we could lose our jobs.

Required:

1. Should Donna agree to Gary's proposal? Why or why not? To assist in deciding, review the corporate code of ethics standards described in Chapter 1. Do any apply?

2. Assume that Donna refuses to cooperate and that Gary accepts this decision and drops the matter. Does Donna have any obligation to report the divisional manager's behavior to a superior? Explain.

3. Assume that Donna refuses to cooperate; however, Gary insists that the changes be made. Now what should she do? What would you do?

4. Suppose that Donna is 63 and that the prospects for employment elsewhere are bleak. Assume again that Gary insists that the changes be made. Donna also knows that his supervisor, the owner of the company, is his father-in-law. Under these circumstances, would your recommendations for Donna differ?

7 Cost-Volume-Profit Analysis

After studying Chapter 7, you should be able to:

1 ▶ Determine the break-even point in number of units and in total sales dollars.

2 ▶ Determine the number of units that must be sold, and the amount of revenue required, to earn a targeted profit.

3 ▶ Prepare a cost-volume-profit graph, and explain its meaning.

4 ▶ Apply cost-volume-profit analysis in a multiple-product setting.

5 ▶ Explain the impact of risk, uncertainty, and changing variables on cost-volume-profit analysis.

Paul Burns/Fancy/Jupiterimages

EXPERIENCE MANAGERIAL DECISIONS

with Boyne Resorts

Boyne USA Resorts has ski resorts in British Columbia, Washington, Montana, and Michigan. Boyne earns much of its revenue from winter skiing. However, ski volume depends heavily on natural snowfall, which varies greatly from year to year. As a result, Boyne uses creative thinking along with cost-volume-profit (CVP) analyses to develop activities that yield additional profit. Consider ski lifts at Boyne Highlands, an important revenue source for the company. What other revenue-generating activities might Boyne develop that use such ski lifts? What fixed and variable costs are associated with these activities, and what might the profit be?

Boyne's various lift ticket packages accommodate as many snow skiers and snow boarders as possible. Lift tickets are interchangeable between multiple Boyne properties and can be used during night skiing in certain areas. Like many ski resorts, Boyne markets spring, summer, and fall activities as well. For instance, many resorts promote mountain biking and hiking where participants purchase lift tickets for gondolas (enclosed lifts) that carry them and their gear to the top of the mountain to begin their descent. Other ski resorts, such as Aspen, build elaborate children's playgrounds and bungee trampolines at the top of the lifts to generate summer business in ski areas that might otherwise be dormant during the off-season. Still other resorts build elaborate mountaintop restaurants and entertainment areas that can be reached only via ski lifts or gondolas, thereby increasing revenues and profits. Using CVP equations and contribution margin formulas, as well as cost-volume-profit graphs, Boyne spends considerable effort analyzing the revenue, cost, volume, and profit implications of these varied activities. With careful CVP analysis and sound judgment, Boyne attempts to make the best decisions possible to continue its profitability and reputation for fun.

> "Other ski resorts, such as Aspen, build elaborate children's playgrounds and bungee trampolines at the top of the lifts to generate summer business in ski areas that might otherwise be dormant during the off-season."

BREAK-EVEN POINT IN UNITS AND IN SALES DOLLARS

Here's **Why It's important**

Cost-volume-profit (CVP) analysis estimates how changes in costs (both variable and fixed), sales volume, and price affect a company's profit. CVP is a powerful tool for planning and decision making. In fact, CVP is one of the most versatile and widely applicable tools used by managerial accountants to help managers make better decisions.

Companies use CVP analysis to reach important benchmarks, such as their break-even point. The **break-even point** is the point where total revenue equals total cost (i.e., the point of zero profit). New companies typically experience losses (negative operating income) initially and view their first break-even period as a significant milestone. For example, online retail pioneer **Amazon.com** was founded in 1994 but did not break even until the fourth quarter of 2001. Also, managers become very interested in CVP analysis during times of economic trouble. For example, to the dismay of many of its shareholders, **SiriusXM Radio** signed shock-jock Howard Stern to a 5-year, $500 million employment contract for joining the young company. As a result of Stern's huge contract cost, some analysts estimated that Sirius would need an additional 2.4 million subscribers (i.e., customers) to reach break-even. Therefore, CVP analysis helps managers pinpoint problems and find solutions.

CVP analysis can address many other issues as well, including:

- the number of units that must be sold to break even
- the impact of a given reduction in fixed costs on the break-even point
- the impact of an increase in price on profit

Additionally, CVP analysis allows managers to do sensitivity analysis by examining the impact of various price or cost levels on profit.

Since CVP analysis shows how revenues, expenses, and profits behave as volume changes, it is natural to begin by finding the firm's break-even point in units sold.

In this section, we will introduce the basics of CVP analysis by looking at:

- the contribution margin income statement
- calculating the break-even point in units
- calculating the contribution margin ratio and the variable cost ratio
- calculating the break-even point in sales dollars

Using Operating Income in Cost-Volume-Profit Analysis

In CVP analysis, the terms "cost" and "expense" are often used interchangeably. This is because the conceptual foundation of CVP analysis is the economics of break-even analysis in the short run. For this, it is assumed that all units produced are sold. Therefore, all product and period costs do end up as expenses on the income statement. We will look more closely at the

Here's How It's Used: **IN YOUR LIFE**

Carson just graduated from State U with a major in accounting. He needs a reliable car for work and is considering a fairly basic sedan, like a **Toyota** Camry. Carson likes the idea of a hybrid vehicle and its benefits for the environment. He wonders if the extra cost is worth it in terms of gasoline cost saved. Carson looked at the difference in price between the basic Camry and the hybrid and found that it was close to $3,500. He thinks he'll drive approximately 12,000 miles per year and that gasoline will average $2.50 per gallon—Carson's an optimist! With

those numbers and the mileage advantage of the hybrid over a regular gasoline engine, Carson found that he will save $300 a year in fuel costs and that it will take over 11.5 years to break even. If gas prices average $3.50 per gallon, it will take about 8.3 years to break even. Is it worth it? Carson has some hard thinking to do. He'll think about his financial situation as well as his belief in the environmental benefits of the hybrid. He'll also examine his assumptions about future gas prices. Clearly, the higher the price of gas, the lower the break-even point.

assumptions of CVP later in this chapter. Remember from Chapter 2 that operating income is total revenue minus total expense:

$$\text{Operating Income} = \text{Total Revenue} - \text{Total Expense}$$

For the income statement, expenses are classified according to function; that is, the manufacturing (or service provision) function, the selling function, and the administrative function. For CVP analysis, however, it is much more useful to organize costs into fixed and variable components. The focus is on the firm as a whole. Therefore, the costs refer to all costs of the company—production, selling, and administration. Recall that **Boyne** separates costs into fixed and variable categories. Fixed costs include taxes, the cost of snow-making machinery, and advertising. Variable costs include wages of temporary workers hired during the height of ski season, power to run the lifts, and food and drink for restaurants.

In general, variable costs are all costs that increase as more units are sold, including:

- direct materials
- direct labor
- variable overhead
- variable selling expenses

Similarly, fixed costs include:

- fixed overhead
- fixed selling and administrative expenses

The income statement format that is based on the separation of costs into fixed and variable components is called the **contribution margin income statement**. Exhibit 7.1 shows the format for the contribution margin income statement.

Sales	$ XXX
Total variable cost	(XXX)
Total contribution margin	$ XXX
Total fixed cost	(XXX)
Operating income	$ XXX

Exhibit 7.1

The Contribution Margin Income Statement

Contribution margin is the difference between sales and variable expense. It is the amount of sales revenue left over after all the variable expenses are covered that can be used to contribute to fixed expense and operating income. By separating expenses into fixed and variable

Here's How It's Used: AT KICKER

Kicker separates cost into fixed and variable parts by using judgment. Because most of the manufacturing is outsourced, the cost of a set of speakers starts with the purchase price from the manufacturer. This cost is strictly variable. Additional variable costs include duty (ranging from 9 to 30%, electronics are at the high end) and freight as all units are shipped to Stillwater, Oklahoma, for distribution. In-house labor may be needed at Kicker's Stillwater facilities, and that cost has both fixed (salaried workers) and variable (temporary workers) components.

Stillwater's salaried staff, research and development, depreciation on property, plant, and equipment, utilities, and so on, are all fixed.

These fixed and variable costs are used in monthly cost-volume-profit analysis and in management decision making. For example, the monthly cost-volume-profit figures can be used for control by monitoring the effect of changing volume on profit and spotlighting increases in fixed and variable costs. If costs are going up, management discovers the problem early and can make adjustments.

components, it is easy for managers to see the impact of higher or lower sales on profit. The contribution margin can be calculated in total (as it was in Exhibit 7.1) or per unit.

$$\text{Unit Contribution Margin} = \text{Price} - \text{Unit Variable Cost}$$

$$\text{Total Contribution Margin} = \text{Sales} - \text{Total Variable Cost}$$

Let's use Whittier Company, a manufacturer of mulching lawnmowers, as an example. **Example 7.1** illustrates how to calculate the variable and fixed expenses and prepare the contribution margin statement for Whittier.

Notice that the contribution margin income statement in Example 7.1 shows a total contribution margin of $75,000. The per-unit contribution margin is $75 ($400 − $325). That is, every mower sold contributes $75 toward fixed expense and operating income.

EXAMPLE 7.1

How to Prepare a Contribution Margin Income Statement

Whittier Company plans to sell 1,000 mowers at $400 each in the coming year. Product costs include:

Direct materials per mower	$ 180
Direct labor per mower	100
Variable factory overhead per mower	25
Total fixed factory overhead	15,000

Variable selling expense is a commission of $20 per mower; fixed selling and administrative expense totals $30,000.

Required:

1. Calculate the total variable expense per unit.
2. Calculate the total fixed expense for the year.
3. Calculate the unit contribution margin.
4. Prepare a contribution margin income statement for Whittier for the coming year.

Solution:

1. Total variable expense per unit:

$$\text{Total Variable Expense per Unit} = \text{Direct Materials} + \text{Direct Labor} + \text{Variable Overhead} + \text{Variable Selling Expense}$$
$$= \$180 + \$100 + \$25 + \$20$$
$$= \$325$$

2. Total Fixed Expense = Fixed Factory Overhead + Fixed Selling and Administrative Expense
$$= \$15,000 + \$30,000 = \$45,000$$

3. Unit Contribution Margin = Price − Unit Variable Cost
$$= \$400 - \$325 = \$75$$

4.

Whittier Company
Contribution Margin Income Statement For the Coming Year

	Total	Per Unit
Sales ($400 × 1,000 mowers)	$400,000	$400
Total variable expense ($325 × 1,000)	325,000	325
Total contribution margin	$ 75,000	$ 75
Total fixed expense	45,000	
Operating income	$ 30,000	

What does Whittier's contribution margin income statement show? First, we see that Whittier will more than break even at sales of 1,000 mowers, since operating income is $30,000. Clearly, Whittier would just break even if total contribution margin equaled the total fixed cost. Exhibit 7.2 illustrates this important observation.

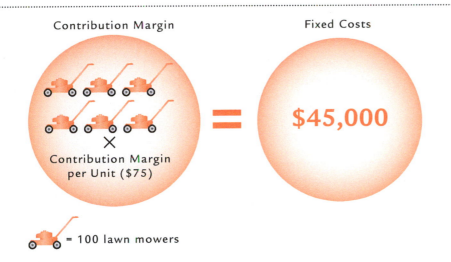

Exhibit 7.2

Contribution Margin and Fixed Cost at Break-Even for Whittier Company

Break-Even Point in Units

If the contribution margin income statement is recast as an equation, it becomes more useful for solving CVP problems. The operating income equation is:

Operating Income = Sales – Total Variable Expenses – Total Fixed Expenses

Notice that all we have done is remove the total contribution margin line from Exhibit 7.1 (p. 335), since it is identical to sales minus total variable expense. This equation is the basis of all the coming work on CVP. We can think of it as the basic CVP equation.

We can expand the operating income equation by expressing sales revenues and variable expenses in terms of unit dollar amounts and the number of units sold. Specifically, sales revenue equals the unit selling price times the number of units sold, and total variable costs equal the unit variable cost times the number of units sold. With these expressions, the operating income equation becomes:

Operating Income = (Price × Number of Units Sold) – (Variable Cost per Unit × Number of Units Sold) – Total Fixed Cost

At the break-even point, operating income equals $0. The break-even point tells managers how many units must be sold to cover all costs. Once more than the break-even units are sold, the company begins to earn a profit. So to get the break-even units using the operating income statement, we set operating income to zero, and then solve for the number of units. Doing this leads to the following equation:

Break-Even Units = Total Fixed Cost/(Price – Variable Cost per Unit)

Note that the denominator, price minus variable cost per unit, is equal to the unit contribution margin. The operating income equation can be rearranged as follows to show the number of units at break-even:

$$\text{Break-Even Units} = \frac{\text{Total Fixed Cost}}{\text{Unit Contribution Margin}}$$

Using this equation is the contribution margin approach, and we see that the break-even units are equal to the fixed cost divided by the contribution margin per unit. So, if a company sells enough units for the contribution margin to just cover fixed costs, it will earn zero operating income: it will break even. It is quicker to solve break-even problems using the contribution margin equation than it is using the original operating income equation. **Example 7.2** shows how to find the break-even units for Whittier Company using both the operating income equation and the contribution margin equation.

EXAMPLE 7.2	
How to Calculate the Break-Even Point in Units	

Refer to the Whittier Company information in Example 7.1. Recall that mowers sell for $400 each, and variable cost per mower is $325. Total fixed cost equals $45,000.

Required:

1. Calculate the number of mowers that Whittier must sell to break even, using the operating income equation.

2. Calculate the number of mowers that Whittier must sell to break even, using the contribution margin equation.

3. Check your answer by preparing a contribution margin income statement based on the break-even point.

Solution:

1. Operating Income = (Price × Units) − (Variable Cost × Units) − Total Fixed Cost

$$0 = (\$400 \times \text{Units}) - (\$325 \times \text{Units}) - \$45,000$$

$$\text{Units} = \$45,000/(\$400 - \$325)$$

$$= 600$$

2. Break-Even Number of Mowers = Total Fixed Cost/Unit Contribution Margin

$$= \$45,000/\$75 = 600$$

3. Contribution margin income statement based on 600 mowers.

Sales ($400 × 600 mowers)	$240,000
Total variable expense ($325 × 600)	195,000
Total contribution margin	$ 45,000
Total fixed expense	45,000
Operating income	$ 0

Indeed, selling 600 units does yield a zero profit.

Break-Even Point in Sales Dollars

Sometimes, managers using CVP analysis may prefer to use sales revenue as the measure of sales activity instead of units sold. A units sold measure can be converted to a sales revenue measure by multiplying the unit selling price by the units sold:

$$\text{Sales Revenue} = \text{Price} \times \text{Units Sold}$$

For example, the break-even point for Whittier is 600 mulching mowers. Since the selling price for each mower is $400, the break-even volume in sales revenue is $240,000 ($400 × 600).

Any answer expressed in units sold can be easily converted to one expressed in sales revenues, but the answer can be computed more directly by developing a separate formula for the sales revenue case. Here, the important variable is sales dollars, so both the revenue and the variable costs must be expressed in dollars instead of units. Since sales revenue is always expressed in dollars, measuring that variable is no problem. Let's look more closely at variable costs and see how they can be expressed in terms of sales dollars.

Variable Cost Ratio To calculate the break-even point in sales dollars, total variable costs are defined as a percentage of sales rather than as an amount per unit sold. Suppose that a company sells a product for $10 per unit and incurs a variable cost of $6 per unit. The contribution margin would be $4:

$$\text{Price} - \text{Variable Cost per Unit} = \$10 - \$6 = \$4$$

If 10 units are sold, total variable costs are $60:

$$\text{Variable Cost} \times \text{Units Sold} = \$6 \times 10 \text{ units} = \$60$$

Alternatively, since each unit sold earns $10 of revenue and has $6 of variable cost, one could say that 60% of each dollar of revenue earned is attributable to variable cost:

$$\frac{\text{Variable Cost per Unit}}{\text{Price}} = \frac{\$6}{\$10} = 60\%$$

Thus, sales revenues of $100 would result in total variable costs of $60 (0.60 × $100). This 60% is the variable cost ratio.

The **variable cost ratio** is the proportion of each sales dollar that must be used to cover variable costs. The variable cost ratio can be computed using either total data or unit data.

$$\text{Variable Cost Ratio} = \frac{\text{Total Variable Cost}}{\text{Sales}}$$

OR

$$\text{Variable Cost Ratio} = \frac{\text{Unit Variable Cost}}{\text{Price}}$$

Contribution Margin Ratio The percentage of sales dollars remaining after variable costs are covered is the contribution margin ratio. The **contribution margin ratio** is the proportion of each sales dollar available to cover fixed costs and provide for profit. For Whittier, if the variable cost ratio is 60% of sales, then the contribution margin ratio must be the remaining 40% of sales. It makes sense that the complement of the variable cost ratio is the contribution margin ratio. After all, total variable costs and total contribution margin sum to sales revenue.

$$\text{Contribution Margin Ratio} = \frac{\text{Total Contribution Margin}}{\text{Sales}}$$

$$\text{Contribution Margin Ratio} = \frac{\text{Unit Contribution Margin}}{\text{Price}}$$

Just as the variable cost ratio can be computed using total or unit figures, the contribution margin ratio, 40% in our example, can also be computed in these two ways. So, one can divide the total contribution margin by total sales:

$$\frac{\text{Total Contribution Margin}}{\text{Total Sales}} = \frac{\$40}{\$100} = 40\%$$

Alternatively, one can use the unit contribution margin divided by price:

$$\frac{\text{Contribution Margin per Unit}}{\text{Price}} = \frac{\$4}{\$10} = 40\%$$

Naturally, if the variable cost ratio is known, it can be subtracted from 1 to yield the contribution margin ratio:

$$1 - \text{Variable Cost Ratio} = \text{Contribution Margin Ratio}$$
$$1 - 0.60 = 0.40$$

Example 7.3 shows how the income statement can be expanded to yield the variable cost ratio and the contribution margin ratio.

EXAMPLE 7.3

How to Calculate the Variable Cost Ratio and the Contribution Margin Ratio

Whittier Company plans to sell 1,000 mowers at $400 each in the coming year. Variable cost per unit is $325. Total fixed cost is $45,000.

Required:

1. Calculate the variable cost ratio.

2. Calculate the contribution margin ratio using unit figures.

3. Prepare a contribution margin income statement based on the budgeted figures for next year. In a column next to the income statement, show the percentages based on sales for sales, total variable expense, and total contribution margin.

Solution:

1. $\text{Variable Cost Ratio} = \dfrac{\text{Variable Cost per Unit}}{\text{Price}}$

   $= \dfrac{\$325}{\$400} = 0.8125, \text{ or } 81.25\%$

2. Contribution Margin per Unit = Price − Variable Cost per Unit
   = $400 − $325 = $75

   $\text{Contribution Margin Ratio} = \dfrac{\text{Contribution Margin per Unit}}{\text{Price}}$

   $= \dfrac{\$75}{\$400} = 0.1875, \text{ or } 18.75\%$

3. Contribution margin income statement based on budgeted figures:

		Percent of Sales
Sales ($400 × 1,000 mowers)	$400,000	100.00
Total variable expense (0.8125 × $400,000)	325,000	81.25
Total contribution margin	$ 75,000	18.75
Total fixed expense	45,000	
Operating income	$ 30,000	

Notice in Example 7.3, Requirement 3, that sales revenue, variable costs, and contribution margin have been expressed as a percent of sales. The variable cost ratio is 0.8125 ($325,000/$400,000); the contribution margin ratio is 0.1875 (computed either as 1 − 0.8125, or $75,000/$400,000).

How do fixed costs relate to the variable cost ratio and contribution margin ratio? Since the total contribution margin is the revenue remaining after total variable costs are covered, it must be the revenue available to cover fixed costs and contribute to profit. How does the relationship of fixed cost to contribution margin affect operating income? There are three possibilities:

- Fixed cost equals contribution margin; operating income is zero; the company breaks even.
- Fixed cost is less than contribution margin; operating income is greater than zero; the company makes a profit.
- Fixed cost is greater than contribution margin; operating income is less than zero; the company incurs a loss.

Calculating Break-Even Point in Sales Dollars Now, let's turn to the equation for calculating the break-even point in sales dollars. One way of calculating break-even sales revenue is to multiply the break-even units by the price. However, often the company is a multiple-product firm, and it can be difficult to figure the break-even point for each product sold.

The break-even point in sales dollars makes it easy for managers to see instantly how close they are to breaking even using only sales revenue data. Since sales are typically recorded immediately, the manager does not have to wait to have an income statement prepared in order to see how close the company is to breaking even.

Here's **Why It's important**

Just as it was quicker to use an equation to calculate the break-even units directly, it is helpful to have an equation to figure the break-even sales dollars. This equation is:

$$\text{Break-Even Sales} = \frac{\text{Total Fixed Expenses}}{\text{Contribution Margin Ratio}}$$

Example 7.4 shows how to obtain the break-even point in sales dollars for Whittier Company.

EXAMPLE 7.4

How to Calculate the Break-Even Point in Sales Dollars

Whittier Company plans to sell 1,000 mowers at $400 each in the coming year. Total variable expense per unit is $325. Total fixed expense is $45,000.

Required:

1. Calculate the contribution margin ratio.
2. Calculate the sales revenue that Whittier must make to break even by using the break-even point in sales equation.
3. Check your answer by preparing a contribution margin income statement based on the break-even point in sales dollars.

Solution:

1. Contribution Margin per Unit = Price – Variable Cost per Unit
   = $400 – $325 = $75

$$\text{Contribution Margin Ratio} = \frac{\text{Contribution Margin per Unit}}{\text{Price}}$$

$$= \frac{\$75}{\$400} = 0.1875, \text{ or } 18.75\%$$

[*Hint:* The contribution margin ratio comes out cleanly to four decimal places. Don't round it, and your break-even point in sales dollars will yield an operating income of $0 (rather than being a few dollars off due to rounding).]

Notice that the variable cost ratio equals 0.8125, or the difference between 1.0000 and the contribution margin ratio.

(Continued)

EXAMPLE 7.4

(Continued)

2. Calculate the break-even point in sales dollars:

$$\text{Break-Even Sales Dollars} = \frac{\text{Total Fixed Cost}}{\text{Contribution Margin Ratio}} = \frac{\$45,000}{0.1875} = \$240,000$$

3. Contribution margin income statement based on sales of $240,000:

Sales	$240,000
Total variable expense (0.8125 × $240,000)	195,000
Total contribution margin	$ 45,000
Total fixed expense	45,000
Operating income	$ 0

Indeed, sales equal to $240,000 does yield a zero profit.

Accountants for the snowsports division of **Boyne USA Resorts** analyze their fixed and variable costs each month as they work to anticipate their break-even point and potential operating income. The contribution margin income statement is a powerful tool to help them with this. They pay close attention to the week between Christmas and New Years, as this is their peak revenue opportunity. Depending on what occurs that week, pricing and cost management for the rest of the season are adjusted. This is an excellent example of the use of CVP in control.

Here's How It's Used: SUSTAINABILITY

Many cities and counties encourage residents to recycle waste materials, including glass, paper, cardboard, cans, and plastic. Traditionally, cities had residents set out two blue recycling bins each week to be collected in special trash pickups. This is dual-stream recycling, in which paper and cardboard are separated from glass, cans, and plastics. The separation makes it easier for the recycling plant to use the higher value paper and cardboard with less chance of contamination (which occurs when residents toss trash, such as banana peels, in the recycling bin). Cities had actually been making money from the sale of paper and cardboard to recycling centers. In a true win-win, the recycling led not only to dollar payments but also to less trash in local landfills and fewer trees needed for paper manufacturing.

Recently, many cities, such as the District of Columbia, have gone to single-stream recycling in which all recyclable wastes are put into one bin. The advantage is that it is easier for residents to set out the one bin and avoid the sorting chore. The downside is that many residents also add non-acceptable waste to the bins—essentially using them as trash cans. This contamination makes the resulting waste less valuable. Coupled with the falling market price for plastic and aluminum, this has led to less profitability—or even losses on recycling. For example, Fairfax County in Virginia made $16 per ton of recyclables in 2011, but paid about $38 per ton in 2015. The increased cost of waste disposal has led county officials to reconsider the single-stream recycling process. That reconsideration surely uses the concepts of variable cost of collection and disposal along with the falling price of the recycled material. Cities can then compare the break-even point for the single-stream versus the dual-stream process.

Sensitivity analysis is used as cities consider the volatile price for the various recyclables. The price paid for paper depends crucially on the amount of contaminant included. Cities that have gone to single-stream recycling have much more contaminant and many have found that no one will purchase the paper; it must be buried in landfills or cities must pay to have it carted away.

The concepts of variable cost, price, and fixed cost help cities determine to what extent recycling is profitable or not, and whether or not the community can afford the extra costs.

Check Point

1. **If the contribution margin ratio is 30%, what is the variable cost ratio? If the variable cost ratio is 77%, what is the contribution margin ratio?**

Answer:

Variable Cost Ratio = 1.00 − 0.30 = 0.70, or 70%

Contribution Margin Ratio = 1.00 − 0.77 = 0.23, or 23%

2. **Explain why the contribution margin ratio and the variable cost ratio always total 100%.**

Answer:

The contribution margin ratio and the variable cost ratio always equal 100% of sales revenue. By definition, total variable cost and total contribution margin sum to sales revenue.

UNITS AND SALES DOLLARS NEEDED TO ACHIEVE A TARGET INCOME

OBJECTIVE ◀ 2

Determine the number of units that must be sold, and the amount of revenue required, to earn a targeted profit.

While the break-even point is useful information and an important benchmark for relatively young companies, most companies would like to earn operating income greater than $0. CVP analysis gives us a way to determine how many units must be sold, or how much sales revenue must be generated, to earn a particular target income. By looking at the number of units or sales dollars needed to earn a target operating income, managers turn their focus away from a point of zero profit and can aim toward making a particular positive profit. Managers can easily compare, at any point in time, the actual sales revenue made with the sales revenue needed to earn a particular profit objective.

Here's **Why It's important**

In this section, we will look at:

- the number of units that must be sold to earn a targeted operating income
- the sales dollars needed to earn a targeted operating income

Units to Be Sold to Achieve a Target Income

Remember that at the break-even point, operating income is $0. How can the equations used in our earlier break-even analyses be adjusted to find the number of units that must be sold to earn a target income? The answer is to add the target income amount to the fixed costs. Let's try it two different ways—with the operating income equation and with the basic break-even equation.

Remember that the equation for the operating income is:

Operating Income = (Price × Units Sold) − (Unit Variable Cost × Units Sold) − Fixed Cost

To solve for positive operating income, replace the operating income term with the target income. Recall that Whittier sells mowers at $400 each, incurs variable cost per unit of $325, and has total fixed expense of $45,000. Suppose that Whittier wants to make a target operating income of $37,500. The number of units that must be sold to achieve that target income is calculated as follows:

$$\$37,500 = (\$400 \times \text{Number of Units}) - (\$325 \times \text{Number of Units}) - \$45,000$$

$$\text{Number of Units} = \frac{\$37,500 + \$45,000}{\$400 - \$325} = 1,100$$

Does the sale of 1,100 units really result in operating income of $37,500? The contribution margin income statement provides a good check.

Sales ($400 × 1,100)	$440,000
Total variable expense ($325 × 1,100)	357,500
Total contribution margin	$ 82,500
Total fixed expense	45,000
Operating income	$ 37,500

Indeed, selling 1,100 units does yield operating income of $37,500.

The operating income equation can be used to find the number of units to sell to earn a targeted income. However, it is quicker to adjust the break-even units equation by adding target income to the fixed cost. This adjustment results in the following equation:

$$\text{Number of Units to Earn Target Income} = \frac{\text{Total Fixed Cost} + \text{Target Income}}{\text{Contribution Margin per Unit}}$$

This equation was used when calculating the 1,100 units needed to earn operating income of $37,500. **Example 7.5** shows how Whittier Company can use this approach.

EXAMPLE 7.5

How to Calculate the Number of Units to Be Sold to Earn a Target Operating Income

Whittier Company sells mowers at $400 each. Variable cost per unit is $325, and total fixed cost is $45,000.

Required:

1. Calculate the number of units that Whittier must sell to earn operating income of $37,500.

2. Check your answer by preparing a contribution margin income statement based on the number of units calculated.

Solution:

1. $\text{Number of Units} = \dfrac{\text{Target Income} + \text{Total Fixed Cost}}{\text{Unit Contribution Margin}}$

   $= \dfrac{\$37,500 + \$45,000}{\$75} = 1,100$

2. Contribution margin income statement based on sales of 1,100 units:

Sales ($400 × 1,100)	$440,000
Total variable expense ($325 × 1,100)	357,500
Total contribution margin	$ 82,500
Total fixed expense	45,000
Operating income	$ 37,500

Indeed, selling 1,100 units does yield operating income of $37,500.

Another way to check the number of units to be sold to yield a target operating income is to use the break-even point. As shown in Example 7.5, Whittier must sell 1,100 mowers, or 500 more than the break-even volume of 600 units, to earn a profit of $37,500. The contribution margin per mower is $75. Multiplying $75 by the 500 mowers above break-even produces the operating income of $37,500 ($75 × 500). This outcome demonstrates that contribution margin per unit for each unit above break-even is equivalent to operating income per unit. Since the break-even point had already been computed, the number of mowers to be sold to yield a $37,500 operating income could have been calculated by dividing the unit contribution margin into the target income and adding the resulting amount to the break-even volume:

$$\text{Units for Income} = \frac{\text{Target Income}}{\text{Unit Contribution Margin}} + \text{Break-Even Volume}$$

In general, assuming that fixed costs remain the same, the impact on a firm's income resulting from a change in the number of units sold can be assessed by multiplying the unit contribution margin by the change in units sold:

$$\text{Change in Operating Income} = \text{Unit Contribution Margin} \times \text{Change in Units Sold}$$

For example, if 1,400 mowers instead of 1,100 are sold, how much more operating income will be earned? The change in units sold is an increase of 300 mowers, and the unit contribution margin is $75. Thus, operating income will increase by $22,500 ($75 × 300) over the $37,500 initially calculated, and total operating income will be $60,000.

Sales Revenue to Achieve a Target Income

Consider the following question: How much sales revenue must Whittier generate to earn an operating income of $37,500? This question is similar to the one we asked earlier in terms of units but phrases the question directly in terms of sales revenue. To answer the question, add the targeted operating income of $37,500 to the $45,000 of fixed cost and divide by the contribution margin ratio. This equation is:

$$\text{Sales Dollars to Earn Target Income} = \frac{\text{Total Fixed Cost} + \text{Target Income}}{\text{Contribution Margin Ratio}}$$

Example 7.6 shows how to calculate the sales revenue needed to earn a target operating income of $37,500.

EXAMPLE 7.6

How to Calculate Sales Needed to Earn a Target Operating Income

Whittier Company sells mowers at $400 each. Variable cost per unit is $325, and total fixed cost is $45,000.

Required:

1. Calculate the contribution margin ratio.
2. Calculate the sales that Whittier must make to earn an operating income of $37,500.
3. Check your answer by preparing a contribution margin income statement based on the sales dollars calculated.

Solution:

1. $\text{Contribution Margin Ratio} = \dfrac{\$400 - \$325}{\$400} = 0.1875$

2. $\text{Sales Dollars} = \dfrac{\text{Target Income} + \text{Total Fixed Cost}}{\text{Contribution Margin Ratio}}$

   $= \dfrac{\$37,500 + \$45,000}{0.1875} = \$440,000$

(Continued)

EXAMPLE 7.6

(Continued)

3. Contribution margin income statement based on sales revenue of $440,000:

Sales	$440,000
Total variable expense (0.8125 × $440,000)	357,500
Total contribution margin	$ 82,500
Total fixed expense	45,000
Operating income	$ 37,500

Indeed, sales revenue of $440,000 does yield operating income of $37,500.

Whittier must earn revenues equal to $440,000 to achieve a profit target of $37,500. Since break-even sales equals $240,000, additional sales of $200,000 ($440,000 − $240,000) must be earned above break-even. Notice that multiplying the contribution margin ratio by revenues above break-even yields the profit of $37,500 (0.1875 × $200,000). Above break even, the contribution margin ratio is a profit ratio; therefore, it represents the proportion of each sales dollar attributable to profit. For Whittier, every sales dollar earned above break-even increases profits by $0.1875.

In general, assuming that fixed costs remain unchanged, the contribution margin ratio can be used to find the profit impact of a change in sales revenue. To obtain the total change in profits from a change in revenues, multiply the contribution margin ratio by the change in sales:

$$\text{Change in Profits} = \text{Contribution Margin Ratio} \times \text{Change in Sales}$$

For example, if sales revenues are $400,000 instead of $440,000, how will profit be affected? A $40,000 decrease in sales revenues will decrease profits by $7,500 (0.1875 × $40,000).

Check Point

1. **Lorna makes and sells decorative candles through gift shops. She knows she must sell 200 candles a month to break even. Every candle has a contribution margin of $1.50. So far this month, Lorna has sold 320 candles. How much has Lorna earned so far this month in operating income?**

    Answer:
    320 Candles Sold − 200 Candles at Break-even = 120 Candles Sold above Break-even
    120 additional candles × $1.50 = $180
    Lorna has earned operating income of $180 so far during the month.

2. **If Lorna sells 10 more candles, by how much will income increase?**

    Answer:
    An additional 10 candles contribute $15 to operating income ($1.50 × 10). Lorna's new operating income is $195 ($180 + $15).

OBJECTIVE ▸ **3**
Prepare a cost-volume-profit graph, and explain its meaning.

Here's **Why It's important**

GRAPHS OF COST-VOLUME-PROFIT RELATIONSHIPS

We can plot the relationship between units and costs and revenues on a graph. Graphing sales revenue and total costs against units sold helps managers clearly see the difference between variable cost and revenue. It may also help them understand quickly what impact an increase or decrease in sales will have on the break-even point. In this section, we will:

- prepare a cost-volume-profit graph
- review the assumptions of CVP analysis
- use the cost-volume-profit graph to show how changes in one variable can affect costs and profit

The Cost-Volume-Profit Graph

The **cost-volume-profit graph** depicts the relationships among cost, volume, and profits (operating income) by plotting the total revenue line and the total cost line on a graph. To obtain the more detailed relationships, it is necessary to graph two separate lines—the total revenue line and the total cost line. These two lines are represented by the following two equations:

$$\text{Revenue} = \text{Price} \times \text{Units}$$
$$\text{Total Cost} = (\text{Unit Variable Cost} \times \text{Units}) + \text{Fixed Cost}$$

Suppose that Tyson Company produces a single product with total fixed costs of $100, unit variable cost of $5, and a selling price of $10 per unit. The revenue and cost equations are:

$$\text{Revenue} = \$10 \times \text{Units}$$
$$\text{Total Cost} = (\$5 \times \text{Units}) + \$100$$

To portray both equations in the same graph, the vertical axis is measured in dollars, and the horizontal axis is measured in units sold.

Two points are needed to graph each equation. For the revenue equation, setting number of units equal to 0 results in revenue of $0, and setting number of units equal to 20 results in revenue of $200. Therefore, the two points for the revenue equation are (0, $0) and (20, $200). For the cost equation, units sold of 0 and units sold of 20 produce the points (0, $100) and (20, $200). The graph of each equation appears in Exhibit 7.3.

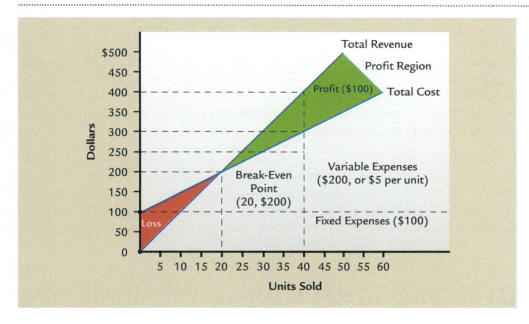

Exhibit 7.3

Cost-Volume-Profit Graph

Notice that the total revenue line begins at the origin and rises with a slope equal to the selling price per unit (a slope of 10). The total cost line intercepts the vertical axis at a point equal to total fixed costs and rises with a slope equal to the variable cost per unit (a slope of 5). When the total revenue line lies below the total cost line, a loss region is defined. Similarly, when the total revenue line lies above the total cost line, a profit region is defined. The point where the total revenue line and the total cost line intersect is the break-even point. To break even, Tyson must sell 20 units and, thus, receive $200 in total revenues.

Let's look more closely at the CVP graph. Consider the sale of 40 units. We can see that producing and selling 40 units yields revenue of $400 with total costs of $300, so that profit is $100. Furthermore, the total costs can be broken down into fixed costs of $100 and variable costs of $200. The CVP graph provides a rich view of revenue and cost information.

Assumptions of Cost-Volume-Profit Analysis

The cost-volume-profit graph relies on important assumptions. Some of these assumptions are as follows:

- There are identifiable linear revenue and linear cost functions that remain constant over the relevant range.
- Selling prices and costs are known with certainty.
- Units produced are sold—there are no finished goods inventories.
- Sales mix is known with certainty for multiple-product break-even settings (explained later in this chapter).

Linear Cost and Revenue Functions   CVP assumes that cost and revenue functions are linear; that is, they are straight lines. But, as was discussed in Chapter 3 on cost behavior, these functions are often not linear. They may be curved or step functions. Fortunately, it is not necessary to consider all possible ranges of production and sales for a firm. Remember that CVP analysis is a short-run decision-making tool. (We know that it is short run in orientation because some costs are fixed.) It is only necessary for us to determine the current operating range, or relevant range, for which the linear cost and revenue relationships are valid. Once a relevant range has been identified, then the cost and price relationships are assumed to be known and constant.

Prices and Costs Known with Certainty   In reality, firms seldom know prices, variable costs, and fixed costs with certainty. A change in one variable usually affects the value of others. Often, there is a probability distribution to consider. There are formal ways of explicitly building uncertainty into the CVP model. These issues are explored in the section on incorporating risk and uncertainty into CVP analysis.

Production Equal to Sales   CVP assumes that all units produced are sold. There is no change in inventory over the period. The idea that inventory has no impact on break-even analysis makes sense. Break-even analysis is a short-run decision-making technique, so we are looking to cover all costs of a particular period of time. Inventory embodies costs of a previous period and is not considered in CVP analyses.

Constant Sales Mix   In single-product analysis, the sales mix is obviously constant—the one product accounts for 100% of sales. Multiple-product break-even analysis requires a constant sales mix. However, it is virtually impossible to predict with certainty the sales mix. Typically, this constraint is handled in practice through sensitivity analysis. By using the capabilities of spreadsheet analysis, the sensitivity of variables to a variety of sales mixes can be readily assessed.

ILLUSTRATING RELATIONSHIPS AMONG CVP VARIABLES

It is critically important to understand the relationships among the CVP variables of price, unit variable cost, and total fixed costs. Consider Lott Company, which produces and sells a product with the following costs.

Unit sales price	$	10
Unit costs		5
Fixed costs		10,000

Contribution Margin = $10 – $5 = $5
Break-Even Units = $10,000/($10 – $5) = 2,000

This is illustrated in Panel A of Exhibit 7.4. The total revenue line has a slope of 10 and the total cost line has a slope of 5. The point of intersection is 2,000 units, which is the break-even point. Units sold above break-even yield a profit; units sold below break-even result in a loss. What happens if changes occur in the price, unit variable cost, and fixed costs?

Exhibit 7.4 Cost-Volume-Profit Relationships

Panel A.

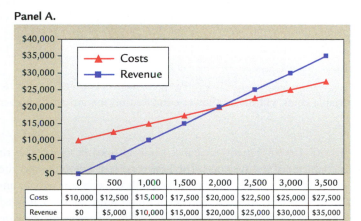

	0	500	1,000	1,500	2,000	2,500	3,000	3,500
Costs	$10,000	$12,500	$15,000	$17,500	$20,000	$22,500	$25,000	$27,500
Revenue	$0	$5,000	$10,000	$15,000	$20,000	$25,000	$30,000	$35,000

Unit sales price	$10.00
Cost per unit	$5.00
Fixed costs	$10,000
Break-even point (in units)	2,000 units

Panel B.

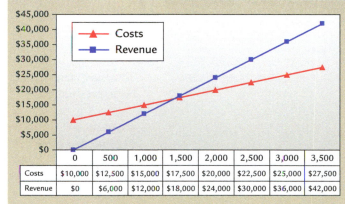

	0	500	1,000	1,500	2,000	2,500	3,000	3,500
Costs	$10,000	$12,500	$15,000	$17,500	$20,000	$22,500	$25,000	$27,500
Revenue	$0	$6,000	$12,000	$18,000	$24,000	$30,000	$36,000	$42,000

Unit sales price	$12.00
Cost per unit	$5.00
Fixed costs	$10,000
Break-even point (in units)	1,429 units (rounded)

Panel C.

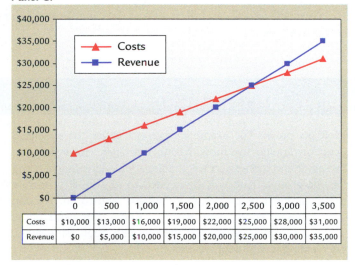

	0	500	1,000	1,500	2,000	2,500	3,000	3,500
Costs	$10,000	$13,000	$16,000	$19,000	$22,000	$25,000	$28,000	$31,000
Revenue	$0	$5,000	$10,000	$15,000	$20,000	$25,000	$30,000	$35,000

Unit sales price	$10.00
Cost per unit	$6.00
Fixed costs	$10,000
Break-even point (in units)	2,500 units

Panel D.

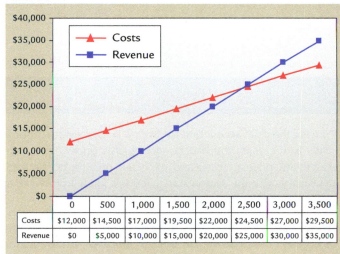

	0	500	1,000	1,500	2,000	2,500	3,000	3,500
Costs	$12,000	$14,500	$17,000	$19,500	$22,000	$24,500	$27,000	$29,500
Revenue	$0	$5,000	$10,000	$15,000	$20,000	$25,000	$30,000	$35,000

Unit sales price	$10.00
Cost per unit	$5.00
Fixed costs	$12,000
Break-even point (in units)	2,400 units

Impact of Changing Sales Price In Panel B, price increases to $12, but unit variable cost and total fixed cost are the same. The new unit contribution margin is $7 ($12 − $5). Compare the new, steeper revenue, with a slope of 12, to the original revenue line shown in Panel A. The total cost line remains unchanged. The intersection of the revenue and total cost lines has moved toward the left, resulting in a new, lower break-even point of 1,429 units (rounded).

$$\text{Break-Even Units} = \frac{\$10,000}{\$12 - \$5} = 1,429 \text{ (rounded)}$$

Any increase in price will mean a higher contribution margin and, thus, a lower break-even point.

Impact of Changing Unit Variable Costs In Panel C, unit variable cost increases to $6, but price and total fixed costs are the same. The new contribution margin is lower at $4 ($10 − $6). The total revenue line is the same as in Panel A. However, the total cost line has a steeper slope of 6, and it intersects the total revenue line further out to the right, resulting in a higher break-even point. Compare the new total cost line to the original line shown in Panel A.

$$\text{Break-Even Units} = \frac{\$10,000}{\$10 - \$6} = 2,500$$

Thus, any increase in unit variable costs will mean a lower contribution margin and a higher break-even point.

Impact of Changing Fixed Costs Finally, in Panel D, total fixed costs increase to $12,000, but price and unit variable cost are the same. The new total cost line intersects the vertical axis at $12,000, not the original $10,000. Since price and unit variable cost remain unchanged, the contribution margin stays at $5 per unit and the total revenue line is unchanged from Panel A. However, the total cost line has shifted upward by $2,000, reflecting the increase in fixed costs. The new break-even point occurs farther out to the right from what it was in Panel A and shows break-even units of 2,400.

$$\text{Break-Even Units} = \frac{\$12,000}{\$10 - \$5} = 2,400$$

Thus, any increase in fixed costs will mean a higher break-even point.

Of course, many changes can be made to this simple data set for Lott Company to see how the contribution margin and break-even point are affected.

Here's How It's Used: AT BOYNE RESORTS

You are the chief accountant for **Boyne Resorts** winter sports. Early in the year, you had budgeted sales prices (lift tickets, restaurant prices), costs, and expected quantity to be sold. However, once the season starts, you will know from week to week more about the actual weather conditions.

How can you use this information about current weather conditions to better predict budgets for Boyne?

You can recast the budgeted statements according to how the weather will affect skiing. If the snow is good, some costs will go down. For example, you will lower the predicted cost of running the snow-making machines. However, good weather and more skiers will require additional seasonal hiring as more direct labor will be needed to run the lifts, operate ski equipment rental shops, restaurants, and so on. You can put together contribution margin income statements under various scenarios, increasing volume with good ski weather, decreasing it with poor weather.

Having the ability to recast budgets will help managers respond quickly to the changing conditions and be able to raise or lower some prices as needed.

Check Point

1. **Suppose that the revenue line in Exhibit 7.3 had a steeper slope due to a higher price. What would that imply for the break-even point? For the amount of operating income (profit) for units sold above break-even?**

Answer:

A steeper revenue line would intersect the total cost line sooner. Thus, the break-even point would be lower; operating income above break-even would be higher. (*Hint:* Draw a steeper total revenue line on Exhibit 7.4 to check this reasoning. Remember, revenue still starts at the origin; zero units sold means zero total revenue.) Increased variable cost per unit means a steep slope for the total cost line. Thus, the break-even point would be higher, and the operating income above break-even would be lower.

2. **Now suppose that the revenue line remains unchanged, but that variable cost per unit increases. How would this increase affect the total cost line? What would this increase imply for the break-even point? For the amount of operating income (profit) for units sold above break-even?**

Answer:

Increased variable cost per unit means a steep slope for the total cost line. Thus, the break-even point would be higher, and the operating income above break-even would be lower.

MULTIPLE-PRODUCT ANALYSIS

OBJECTIVE 4

Apply cost-volume-profit analysis in a multiple-product setting.

Cost-volume-profit analysis is fairly simple in the single-product setting. However, most firms produce and sell a number of products or services. Even though CVP analysis becomes more complex with multiple products, the operation is reasonably straightforward. When managers calculate the break-even point for individual products, they can see the contribution each makes to profit and can tell at any point in time how close a product is to breaking even. In this section, we will:

Here's **Why It's important**

- prepare an income statement segmented by product line
- calculate the break-even point in units for each product
- calculate the break-even point in sales dollars for the multiple-product firm

Let's expand the Whittier example to a multiple-product setting. Whittier has decided to offer two models of mowers: a mulching mower that sells for $400 and a riding mower that sells for $800. The marketing department is convinced that 1,200 mulching mowers and 800 riding mowers can be sold during the coming year. The controller has prepared the following projected income statement, segmented by product line, based on the sales forecast:

	Mulching Mower	Riding Mower	Total
Sales	$480,000	$640,000	$1,120,000
Total variable cost	390,000	480,000	870,000
Contribution margin	$ 90,000	$160,000	$ 250,000
Direct fixed cost	30,000	40,000	70,000
Product margin	$ 60,000	$120,000	$ 180,000
Common fixed cost			26,250
Operating income			$ 153,750

Note that the controller has separated *direct fixed expenses* from *common fixed expenses*. The **direct fixed expenses** are those fixed costs that can be traced to each segment and would be avoided if the segment did not exist. The **common fixed expenses** are the fixed costs that are not traceable to the segments and would remain even if one of the segments was eliminated.

Break-Even Point in Units

The owner of Whittier is a bit concerned about adding a new product line and wants to know how many units of each model must be sold to break even. If you were responsible for answering this question, how would you respond? One possibility is to use the equation developed earlier in which fixed costs were divided by the contribution margin. However, this equation was developed for single-product analysis. For two products, there are two variable costs per unit and two contribution margins per unit, calculated as follows:

	Mulching Mower	Riding Mower
Variable cost per unit	$\dfrac{\$390,000}{1,200} = \$325$	$\dfrac{\$480,000}{800} = \$600$
Contribution margin per unit	$400 - $325 = $75	$800 - $600 = $200

One possible solution is to apply the analysis separately to each product line. It is possible to obtain individual break-even points when income is defined as product margin. Break-even for the mulching mower is as follows:

$$\text{Mulching Mower Break-Even Units} = \frac{\text{Fixed Cost}}{\text{Price} - \text{Unit Variable Cost}}$$

$$= \frac{\$30,000}{\$75}$$

$$= 400 \text{ units}$$

Break-even for the riding mower can be computed as well:

$$\text{Riding Mower Break-Even Units} = \frac{\text{Fixed Cost}}{\text{Price} - \text{Unit Variable Cost}}$$

$$= \frac{\$40,000}{\$200}$$

$$= 200 \text{ units}$$

Thus, 400 mulching mowers and 200 riding mowers must be sold to achieve a break-even product margin. But a break-even product margin covers only direct fixed costs; the common fixed costs remain to be covered. Selling these numbers of mowers would result in a loss equal to the common fixed costs. This level of sales is not the break-even point for the firm as a whole. Somehow the common fixed costs must be factored into the analysis.

We could allocate the common fixed costs to each product line before computing a break-even point. However, the allocation of the common fixed costs is arbitrary. Thus, no meaningful break-even volume is readily apparent.

Another possible solution is to convert the multiple-product problem into a single-product problem. If this can be done, then all of the single-product CVP methodology can be applied directly. The key to this conversion is to identify the expected sales mix, in units, of the products being marketed. **Sales mix** is the relative combination of products being sold by a firm.

Determining the Sales Mix   The sales mix is measured in units sold. For example, if Whittier plans to sell 1,200 mulching mowers and 800 riding mowers, then the sales mix in units is 1,200:800. Usually, the sales mix is reduced to the smallest possible whole numbers. Thus, the relative mix, 1,200:800, can be reduced to 12:8, and further reduced to 3:2. That is, Whittier expects that for every three mulching mowers sold, two riding mowers will be sold.

An endless number of different sales mixes can be used to define the break-even volume in a multiple-product setting. For example, a sales mix of 2:1 will define a break-even point of 550 mulching mowers and 275 riding mowers. The total contribution margin produced by this mix is $96,250:

$$(\text{Mulching Mower Price} \times \text{Break-Even Quantity}) + (\text{Riding Mower Price} \times \text{Break-Even Quantity})$$

$$(\$75 \times 550) + (\$200 \times 275)$$

Similarly, if 350 mulching mowers and 350 riding mowers are sold (corresponding to a 1:1 sales mix), then the total contribution margin is also $96,250:

$$(\$75 \times 350) + (\$200 \times 350)$$

Since total fixed costs are $96,250, both sales mixes define break-even points. Fortunately, every sales mix need not be considered. According to Whittier's marketing study, a sales mix of 3:2 can be expected. This is the ratio that should be used; all others can be ignored. The sales mix that is expected to prevail should be used for CVP analysis.

Sales Mix and Cost-Volume-Profit Analysis Defining a particular sales mix allows the conversion of a multiple-product problem into a single-product CVP format. Since Whittier expects to sell three mulching mowers for every two riding mowers, it can define the single product it sells as a package containing three mulching mowers and two riding mowers. By defining the product as a package, the multiple-product problem is converted into a single-product one. To use the approach of break-even point in units, the package selling price and the variable cost per package must be known. To compute these package values, the sales mix, individual product prices, and individual variable costs are needed. **Example 7.7** shows how to determine the overall break-even point for each product.

EXAMPLE 7.7

How to Calculate the Break-Even Units for a Multiple-Product Firm

Recall that Whittier sells two products: mulching mowers priced at $400 and riding mowers priced at $800. The variable cost per unit is $325 per mulching mower and $600 per riding mower. Total fixed cost is $96,250. Whittier's expected sales mix is three mulching mowers to two riding mowers.

Required:

1. Form a package of mulching and riding mowers based on the sales mix and calculate the package contribution margin.

2. Calculate the break-even point in units for mulching mowers and for riding mowers.

3. Check your answers by preparing a contribution margin income statement.

Solution:

1. Each package consists of three mulching mowers and two riding mowers:

Product	Price	Unit Variable Cost	Unit Contribution Margin	Sales Mix	Package Contribution Margin
Mulching	$400	$325	$ 75	3	$ 225
Riding	800	600	200	2	400
Package total					$ 625

The three mulching mowers in the package yield $225 (3 × $75) in contribution margin. The two riding mowers in the package yield $400 (2 × $200) in contribution margin. Thus, a package of five mowers (three mulching and two riding) has a total contribution margin of $625.

2. Break-Even Packages = $\dfrac{\text{Total Fixed Cost}}{\text{Package Contribution Margin}}$

$$= \frac{\$96,250}{\$625}$$

$$= 154 \text{ packages}$$

Mulching Mower Break-Even Units = 154 × 3 = 462
Riding Mower Break-Even Units = 154 × 2 = 308

(Continued)

EXAMPLE 7.7

(Continued)

3. Income statement—break-even solution:

	Mulching Mower	**Riding Mower**	**Total**
Sales	$184,800	$246,400	$431,200
Total variable cost	150,150	184,800	334,950
Contribution margin	$ 34,650	$ 61,600	$ 96,250
Total fixed cost			96,250
Operating income			$ 0

The complexity of determining the break-even point in units increases dramatically as the number of products increases. Imagine performing this analysis for a firm with several hundred products. Luckily, computers can easily handle a problem with so much data. Furthermore, many firms simplify the problem by analyzing product groups rather than individual products. Another way to handle the increased complexity is to switch from the units sold to the sales revenue approach. This approach can accomplish a multiple-product CVP analysis using only the summary data found in an organization's income statement. **Boyne** can take this approach to determine an overall break-even point for the company as it combines the sales, variable costs and fixed costs across all of its lines of business, including lift tickets, equipment rental, restaurant and gift shop sales, and so on.

Break-Even Point in Sales Dollars

To illustrate the break-even point in sales dollars, the same examples will be used. However, the only information needed is the projected income statement for Whittier Company as a whole.

Sales	$1,120,000
Total variable cost	870,000
Contribution margin	$ 250,000
Total fixed cost	96,250
Operating income	$ 153,750

Notice that this income statement corresponds to the total column of the more detailed income statement examined previously. The projected income statement rests on the assumption that 1,200 mulching mowers and 800 riding mowers will be sold (a 3:2 sales mix). The break-even point in sales revenue also rests on the expected sales mix. (As with the units sold approach, different sales mixes will produce different results.)

With the income statement, the usual CVP questions can be addressed. For example, how much sales revenue must be earned to break even? **Example 7.8** shows how to calculate the break-even point in sales dollars for a multiple-product firm.

EXAMPLE 7.8

How to Calculate the Break-Even Sales Dollars for a Multiple-Product Firm

Recall that Whittier Company sells two products that are expected to produce total revenue next year of $1,120,000 and total variable cost of $870,000. Total fixed cost is expected to equal $96,250.

Required:

1. Calculate the break-even point in sales dollars for Whittier.

2. Check your answer by preparing a contribution margin income statement.

EXAMPLE 7.8

(*Continued*)

Solution:

1. Contribution Margin Ratio $= \dfrac{\$250,000}{\$1,120,000}$

    $= 0.2232$

    Break-Even Sales $= \dfrac{\text{Fixed Cost}}{\text{Contribution Margin Ratio}}$

    $= \dfrac{\$96,250}{0.2232}$

    $= \$431,228$

    [*Note:* Total break-even sales differ slightly between Examples 7.7 and 7.8 ($431,200 vs. $431,228) due to the rounding of the contribution margin ratio to only four decimal places (0.2232).]

2. Income statement—break-even solution:

Sales	$431,228
Total variable cost (0.7768 × $431,228)	334,978
Contribution margin	$ 96,250
Total fixed cost	96,250
Operating income	$ 0

The break-even point in sales dollars implicitly uses the assumed sales mix but avoids the requirement of building a package contribution margin. No knowledge of individual product data is needed. The computational effort is similar to that used in the single-product setting. Unlike the break-even point in units, the answer to CVP questions using sales dollars is still expressed in a single summary measure. The sales revenue approach, however, does sacrifice information concerning individual product performance.

Here's How It's Used: BY A NEW BUSINESS

You are an accountant in private practice. A friend of yours, Linda, recently started a novelty greeting card business. Linda designs greeting cards that allow the sender to write in his or her own message. She uses heavy card stock, cut to size, and decorates the front of each card with bits of fabric, lace, and ribbon in seasonal motifs (e.g., a heart for Valentine's Day, a pine tree for Christmas). Linda hired several friends to make the cards, according to Linda's instructions, on a piece-work basis. (In piece work, the worker is paid on the basis of number of units produced.) The workers could make the cards at their homes, meaning that no factory facilities were involved. Linda designs the cards and travels around her four-state region to sell the completed cards on consignment. For the few months the company has been in existence, the cards have been selling well, but Linda is operating at a loss.

What types of information do you need to find the break-even point? How can the business owner use this information to make decisions?

In order to determine the break-even point, you need to determine the prices and variable costs for the cards. Since creating a multiple-product break-even analysis could be complex, it may be easier to determine the average price and the average variable cost for the cards, then find the total fixed cost, and tell Linda how many cards she would need to sell to break even.

Suppose that the break-even number of cards is 250 per month, and that the average contribution margin per card is $0.80. Then, as soon as Linda sells the 250th card, she knows she is in the black. From then on, every card sold adds $0.80 to her profit. This was very important information for Linda—whose business losses are coming right out of her family's checking account. Not only does Linda have a sales goal for each month, but she also knows at any point in time how much income she has made.

Owners of small businesses find break-even analysis and concepts to be very helpful. A knowledge of contribution margin helps owners exercise control by knowing how they are doing at any point in time.

1. **Suppose a men's clothing store sells two brands of suits: designer suits with a contribution margin of $600 each and regular suits with a contribution margin of $500 each. At break-even, the store must sell a total of 100 suits a month. Last month, the store sold 100 suits in total but incurred an operating loss. There was no change in fixed cost, variable cost, or price. What happened?**

   Answer:

   Probably, the sales mix shifted toward the relatively lower contribution margin suits. For example, suppose that the break-even point for regular suits was 80, and the break-even point for designer suits was 20. If the mix shifted to 90 regular and 10 designer, it is easy to see that less total contribution margin (and, hence, operating income) would be realized.

2. **A company sells two products. Product A has a contribution margin of $10, and Product B has a contribution margin of $15. The break-even point is 1,000 units of Product A and 500 units of Product B. Then total fixed costs increase. What will happen to the break-even points of Products A and B?**

   Answer:

   Since the contribution margins of the two products remain the same, as does the sales mix, the total break-even packages will increase (greater fixed costs) and this will mean more units of both products must be sold to break even.

OBJECTIVE ▶ **5**

Explain the impact of risk, uncertainty, and changing variables on cost-volume-profit analysis.

Here's **Why It's important**

COST-VOLUME-PROFIT ANALYSIS AND RISK AND UNCERTAINTY

The CVP assumptions include costs and prices known with certainty. However, this does not happen in the real world. Because firms operate in a dynamic environment, they must be aware of changes in prices, variable costs, and fixed costs. They must also account for the effect of risk and uncertainty. The break-even point can be affected by changes in price, unit variable cost, and fixed cost. Managers can use CVP analysis to handle risk and uncertainty.

For example, France-based **Airbus** reported its first ever loss in 2006. The loss resulted from a decreased sales volume and costly production delays in the redesign of its "extra wide-body" passenger jet to compete with **Boeing's** 787 Dreamliner. In response to this loss, Airbus used CVP analysis to estimate how a $2.6 billion reduction in its annual variable and fixed costs, as well as various reductions in its $144 million unit jet price, would affect its annual profit.[1] Shipping giant **Maersk** added capacity just before the recession of 2008 hit. As a result, shipping rates were so low that Maersk had a more than $2 billion loss in 2009. Improved economic conditions and an increase in demand above that originally predicted allowed the company to announce that it would break even in 2010.[2]

For a given sales mix, CVP analysis can be used as if the firm were selling a single product. However, when the prices of individual products change, the sales mix can be affected because consumers may buy relatively more or less of the product. Keep in mind that a new sales mix will affect the units of each product that need to be sold in order to achieve a desired profit target. If

---

1 "Planemaker Airbus to Report Its First Annual Loss," *USA Today* (January 18, 2007): 3B.

2 Peter T. Leach, "Maersk Line Close to Break Even, CEO Says," *The Journal of Commerce Online* (March 29, 2010). Taken from www.joc.com/maritime/maersk-line-close-break-even-says-ceo.

the sales mix for the coming period is uncertain, it may be necessary to look at several different mixes. In this way, a manager gains insight into the possible outcomes facing the firm.

Suppose that Whittier recently conducted a market study of the mulching mower that revealed three different alternatives:

- *Alternative 1:* If advertising expenditures increase by $8,000, then sales will increase from 1,600 units to 1,725 units.
- *Alternative 2:* A price decrease from $400 to $375 per mower will increase sales from 1,600 units to 1,900 units.
- *Alternative 3:* Decreasing price to $375 *and* increasing advertising expenditures by $8,000 will increase sales from 1,600 units to 2,600 units.

Should Whittier maintain its current price and advertising policies, or should it select one of the three alternatives described by the marketing study?

The first alternative, increasing advertising costs by $8,000 with a resulting sales increase of 125 units, is summarized in Exhibit 7.5. This alternative can be analyzed by using the contribution margin per unit of $75. Since units sold increase by 125, the increase in total contribution margin is $9,375 ($75 × 125 units). However, since fixed costs increase by $8,000, profits only increase by $1,375 ($9,375 − $8,000). Notice that we need to look only at the incremental increase in total contribution margin and fixed expenses to compute the increase in total operating income.

	Before the Increased Advertising	With the Increased Advertising
Units sold	1,600	1,725
Unit contribution margin	× $75	× $75
Total contribution margin	$120,000	$129,375
Less: Fixed expenses	45,000	53,000
Operating income	$ 75,000	$ 76,375

	Difference in Profit
Change in sales volume	125
Unit contribution margin	× $75
Change in contribution margin	$9,375
Less: Change in fixed expenses	8,000
Increase in operating income	$1,375

Exhibit 7.5

Summary of the Effects of Alternative 1

For the second alternative, the price is dropped to $375 (from $400), and the units sold increase to 1,900 (from 1,600). The effects of this alternative are summarized in Exhibit 7.6 (p. 358). Here, fixed expenses do not change, so only the change in total contribution margin is relevant. For the current price of $400, the contribution margin per unit is $75 ($400 − $325), and the total contribution margin is $120,000 ($75 × 1,600). For the new price, the contribution margin drops to $50 per unit ($375 − $325). If 1,900 units are sold at the new price, then the new total contribution margin is $95,000 ($50 × 1,900). Dropping the price results in a profit decline of $25,000 ($120,000 − $95,000).

The third alternative calls for a decrease in the unit selling price and an increase in advertising costs. Like the first alternative, the profit impact can be assessed by looking at the incremental effects on contribution margin and fixed expenses. The incremental profit change can be found by:

1. computing the incremental change in total contribution margin
2. computing the incremental change in fixed expenses
3. adding the two results

Exhibit 7.6

Summary of the Effects of Alternative 2

	Before the Proposed Price Decrease	With the Proposed Price Decrease
Units sold	1,600	1,900
Unit contribution margin	× $75	× $50
Total contribution margin	$120,000	$95,000
Less: Fixed expenses	45,000	45,000
Operating income	$ 75,000	$50,000
		Difference in Profit
Change in contribution margin ($95,000 − $120,000)		$(25,000)
Less: Change in fixed expenses		—
Decrease in operating income		$(25,000)

As shown in Exhibit 7.7, the current total contribution margin (for 1,600 units sold) is $120,000. Since the new unit contribution margin is $50, the new total contribution margin is $130,000 ($50 × 2,600 units). Thus, the incremental increase in total contribution margin is $10,000 ($130,000 − $120,000). However, to achieve this incremental increase in contribution margin, an incremental increase of $8,000 in fixed costs is needed. The net effect is an incremental increase in operating income of $2,000.

Exhibit 7.7

Summary of the Effects of Alternative 3

	Before the Proposed Price and Advertising Changes	With the Proposed Price Decrease and Advertising Increase
Units sold	1,600	2,600
Unit contribution margin	× $75	× $50
Total contribution margin	$120,000	$130,000
Less: Fixed expenses	45,000	53,000
Profit	$ 75,000	$ 77,000
		Difference in Profit
Change in contribution margin ($130,000 − $120,000)		$10,000
Less: Change in fixed expenses ($53,000 − $45,000)		8,000
Increase in profit		$ 2,000

Of the three alternatives identified by the marketing study, the third alternative promises the most benefit. It increases total operating income by $2,000. The first alternative increases operating income by only $1,375, and the second *decreases* operating income by $25,000.

These examples are all based on a units sold approach. However, we could just as easily have applied a sales revenue approach. The answers would be the same.

Introducing Risk and Uncertainty

An important assumption of CVP analysis is that prices and costs are known with certainty. This assumption is seldom accurate. Risk and uncertainty are a part of business decision making and must be dealt with somehow. **Boyne**, for example, can run CVP analysis under various weather assumptions. A good year of snow requires less snow making, lowering costs and leading to increased skiing and revenue. Formally, risk differs from uncertainty in that under risk, the probability distributions of the variables are known; under uncertainty, they are not known. For purposes of CVP analysis, however, the terms will be used interchangeably.

How do managers deal with risk and uncertainty? There are a variety of methods.

- First, of course, is that management must realize the uncertain nature of future prices, costs, and quantities.
- Next, managers move from consideration of a break-even point to what might be called a "break-even band." In other words, given the uncertain nature of the data, perhaps a firm might break even when 1,800 to 2,000 units are sold instead of at the point estimate of 1,900 units.
- Further, managers may engage in sensitivity or what-if analysis. In this instance, a computer spreadsheet is helpful because managers can set up the break-even (or targeted profit) relationships and then check to see the impact that varying costs and prices have on quantity sold.

Two concepts useful to management are *margin of safety* and *operating leverage*. Both of these concepts may be considered measures of risk. Each requires knowledge of fixed and variable costs.

Margin of Safety The **margin of safety** is the units sold or the revenue earned above the break-even volume. It is calculated as follows:

$$\text{Margin of Safety} = \text{Sales} - \text{Break-Even Sales}$$

For example, if the break-even volume for a company is 200 units and the company is currently selling 500 units, then the margin of safety is 300 units:

$$\text{Sales} - \text{Break-Even Units} = 500 - 200$$

The margin of safety can be expressed in sales revenue as well. If the break-even volume is $200,000 and current revenues are $500,000, then the margin of safety is $300,000:

$$\text{Revenues} - \text{Margin of Safety} = \$500,000 - \$200,000$$

In addition, margin of safety sales revenue can be expressed as a percentage of total sales dollars, which some managers refer to as the margin of safety ratio. In this example, the margin of safety ratio would be 60%:

$$\frac{\text{Margin of Safety}}{\text{Revenues}} = \frac{\$300,000}{\$500,000}$$

Exhibit 7.8 illustrates the margin of safety.

Exhibit 7.8

Margin of Safety

Example 7.9 shows the expected margin of safety for Whittier.

<table>
<tr><td>

EXAMPLE 7.9

How to Calculate the Margin of Safety

</td><td>

Recall that Whittier plans to sell 1,000 mowers at $400 each in the coming year. Whittier has unit variable cost of $325 and total fixed cost of $45,000. Break-even units were previously calculated as 600.

Required:

1. Calculate the margin of safety for Whittier in terms of the number of units.

2. Calculate the margin of safety for Whittier in terms of sales revenue.

Solution:

1. Margin of Safety in Units = 1,000 − 600 = 400

2. Margin of Safety in Sales Revenue = $400(1,000) − $400(600) = $160,000

</td></tr>
</table>

The margin of safety can be viewed as a crude measure of risk. There are always events, unknown when plans are made, that can lower sales below the original expected level. In the event that sales take a downward turn, the risk of suffering losses is less if a firm's expected margin of safety is large than if the margin of safety is small. Managers who face a low margin of safety may wish to consider actions to increase sales or decrease costs. These steps will increase the margin of safety and lower the risk of incurring losses.

Operating Leverage   In physics, a lever is a simple machine used to multiply force. Basically, the lever multiplies the effort applied to create more work. The larger the load moved by a given amount of effort, the greater is the mechanical advantage. In financial terms, operating leverage is concerned with the relative mix of fixed costs and variable costs in an organization. Sometimes fixed costs can be traded off for variable costs. As variable costs decrease, the unit contribution margin increases, making the contribution of each unit sold that much greater. In such a case, fluctuations in sales have an increased effect on profitability. Thus, firms that have realized lower variable costs by increasing the proportion of fixed costs will benefit with greater increases in profits as sales increase than will firms with a lower proportion of fixed costs. Fixed costs are being used as leverage to increase profits. Unfortunately, it is also true that firms with a higher operating leverage will experience greater reductions in profits as sales decrease. **Operating leverage** is the use of fixed costs to extract higher percentage changes in profits as sales activity changes.

The **degree of operating leverage (DOL)** can be measured for a given level of sales by taking the ratio of contribution margin to operating income, as follows:

$$\text{Degree of Operating Leverage} = \frac{\text{Total Contribution Margin}}{\text{Operating Income}}$$

If fixed costs are used to lower variable costs such that contribution margin increases and operating income decreases, then the degree of operating leverage increases—signaling an increase in risk. **Example 7.10**, on the next page, shows how to compute the degree of operating leverage for Whittier.

EXAMPLE 7.10

How to Calculate the Degree of Operating Leverage

Recall that Whittier plans to sell 1,000 mowers at $400 each in the coming year. Whittier has unit variable cost per unit of $325 and total fixed cost of $45,000. Operating income at that level of sales was previously computed as $30,000.

Required:
Calculate the degree of operating leverage for Whittier.

Solution:

$$\text{Degree of Operating Leverage} = \frac{\text{Total Contribution Margin}}{\text{Operating Income}}$$

$$= \frac{(\$400 - \$325)(1{,}000 \text{ units})}{\$30{,}000}$$

$$= 2.5$$

The greater the degree of operating leverage, the more that changes in sales will affect operating income. Because of this phenomenon, the mix of costs that an organization chooses influences its operating risk and profit level. A company's mix of fixed costs relative to variable costs is referred to as its **cost structure**. Often, a company changes its cost structure by taking on more of one type of cost in exchange for reducing its amount of the other type of cost. For example, as U.S. companies try to compete more effectively with foreign competitors' significantly lower hourly labor costs (a variable cost), many are altering their cost structures by taking on more plant machine automation (a fixed cost) in exchange for using less labor.

To illustrate the impact of these concepts on management decision making, consider a firm that is planning to add a new product line. In adding the line, the firm can choose to rely heavily on automation or on labor. If the firm chooses to emphasize automation rather than labor, fixed costs will be higher, and unit variable costs will be lower. Relevant data for a sales level of 10,000 units follow:

	Automated System	Manual System
Sales	$1,000,000	$1,000,000
Total variable cost	500,000	800,000
Contribution margin	$ 500,000	$ 200,000
Total fixed cost	375,000	100,000
Operating income	$ 125,000	$ 100,000
Unit selling price	$ 100	$ 100
Unit variable cost	50	80
Unit contribution margin	50	20

The degree of operating leverage for the automated system is 4.0 ($500,000/$125,000). The degree of operating leverage for the manual system is 2.0 ($200,000/$100,000). What happens to profit in each system if sales increase by 40%? We can generate the following income statements:

	Automated System	Manual System
Sales	$1,400,000	$1,400,000
Total variable cost	700,000	1,120,000
Contribution margin	$ 700,000	$ 280,000
Total fixed cost	375,000	100,000
Operating income	$ 325,000	$ 180,000

Profits for the automated system would increase by $200,000 ($325,000 − $125,000) for a 160% increase. In the manual system, profits increase by only $80,000 ($180,000 − $100,000) for an 80% increase. The automated system has a greater percentage increase because it has a higher degree of operating leverage.

The degree of operating leverage can be used directly to calculate the change in operating income that would result from a given percentage change in sales.

> Percentage Change in Profits = Degree of Operating Leverage × Percent Change in Sales

Since sales are predicted to increase by 40% and the DOL for the automated system is 4.0, operating income increases by 160%. Since operating income based on the original sales level is $125,000, the operating income based on the increased sales level would be $325,000:

$$\text{Operating Income} + (\text{Operating Income} \times \text{Percent Change in Sales})$$
$$= \$125,000 + (\$125,000 \times 1.6)$$

Similarly, for the manual system, increased sales of 40% and DOL of 2.0 imply increased operating income of 80%. Therefore, operating income based on the increased sales level would be $180,000:

$$\$100,000 + (\$100,000 \times 0.8)$$

Example 7.11 illustrates the impact of increased sales on operating income using the degree of operating leverage.

EXAMPLE 7.11

How to Calculate the Impact of Increased Sales on Operating Income Using the Degree of Operating Leverage

Recall that Whittier had expected to sell 1,000 mowers and earn operating income equal to $30,000 next year. Whittier's degree of operating leverage is equal to 2.5. The company plans to increase sales by 20% next year.

Required:

1. Calculate the percent change in operating income expected by Whittier for next year using the degree of operating leverage.
2. Calculate the operating income expected by Whittier next year using the percent change in operating income calculated in Requirement 1.

Solution:

1. Percent Change in Operating Income = DOL × Percent Change in Sales

   $$= 2.5 \times 20\% = 50\%$$

2. Expected Operating Income = $30,000 + (0.5 × $30,000) = $45,000

In choosing between the two systems, the effect of operating leverage is a valuable piece of information. Higher operating leverage multiplies the impact of increased sales on income. However, the effect is a two-edged sword. As sales decrease, the automated system will also show much higher percentage decreases. The increased operating leverage is available under the automated system because of the presence of increased fixed costs. The break-even point for the automated system is 7,500 units ($375,000/$50), whereas the break-even point for the manual system is 5,000 units ($100,000/$20). Thus, the automated system has greater operating risk.

The increased risk, of course, provides a potentially higher profit level as long as units sold exceed 9,167. Why 9,167? Because that is the quantity for which the operating income for the automated system equals the operating income for the manual system. The quantity at which two systems produce the same operating income is referred to as the **indifference point**. This number of units is computed by setting the operating income equations of the two systems equal and solving for number of units:

$$\$50(\text{Units}) - \$375,000 = \$20(\text{Units}) - \$100,000$$
$$\text{Units} = 9,167$$

In choosing between the automated and manual systems, the manager must consider the likelihood that sales will exceed 9,167 units. If there is a strong belief that sales will easily exceed this level, then the choice is obviously the automated system. On the other hand, if sales are unlikely to exceed 9,167 units, then the manual system is preferable. Exhibit 7.9 summarizes the relative differences between the manual and automated systems in terms of some of the CVP concepts.

	Manual System	**Automated System**
Price	Same	Same
Variable cost	▲ Relatively higher	▼ Relatively lower
Fixed cost	▼ Relatively lower	▲ Relatively higher
Contribution margin	▼ Relatively lower	▲ Relatively higher
Break-even point	▼ Relatively lower	▲ Relatively higher
Margin of safety	▲ Relatively higher	▼ Relatively lower
Degree of operating leverage	▼ Relatively lower	▲ Relatively higher
Down-side risk	▼ Relatively lower	▲ Relatively higher
Up-side potential	▼ Relatively lower	▲ Relatively higher

Exhibit 7.9

Differences between a Manual and an Automated System

Sensitivity Analysis and Cost-Volume-Profit

The widespread use of personal computers and spreadsheets has placed sensitivity analysis within reach of most managers. An important tool, **sensitivity analysis** is a "what-if" technique that examines the impact of changes in underlying assumptions on an answer. It is relatively simple to input data on prices, variable costs, fixed costs, and sales mix and to set up formulas to calculate break-even points and expected profits. Then, the data can be varied as desired to see how changes impact the expected profit.

In the example on operating leverage, a company analyzed the impact on profit of using an automated versus a manual system. The computations were essentially done by hand, and too much variation is cumbersome. Using the power of a computer, it would be an easy matter to

Here's How It's Used: IN YOUR LIFE

You may face decisions that use sensitivity analysis in deciding which product or service to use. For example, Lacy Daniels just graduated with a degree in accounting and now works for a national accounting firm as an entry-level auditor. Lacy travels frequently for her work but wants to stay in shape and exercise while she's in her home town. A local gym offers a rate of $12 for a day visit or $90 for a month membership. Which should Lacy choose? The answer depends on Lacy's expected use of the gym. If she thinks she can only go four times a month, the day visit rate is clearly better since it will cost $48 for a month ($12 × 4 visits) rather than $90. However, if Lacy thinks she can go an average of about 10 times a month, then the monthly membership is better since it is less than $120 ($12 × 10 visits). The break-even point between the two rates is 7.5 ($90/$12), meaning that at fewer than eight times a month, the day rate is the better choice.

change the sales price in $1 increments between $75 and $125, with related assumptions about quantity sold. At the same time, variable and fixed costs could be adjusted. For example, suppose that the automated system has fixed costs of $375,000 but that those costs could easily double in the first year and come back down in the second and third years as bugs are worked out of the system and workers learn to use it. Again, the spreadsheet can effortlessly handle the many computations.

A spreadsheet, while wonderful for cranking out numerical answers, cannot do the most difficult job in CVP analysis. That job is determining the data to be entered in the first place. The managerial accountant must be aware of the cost and price distributions of the firm as well as of the impact of changing economic conditions on these variables. The fact that variables are seldom known with certainty is no excuse for ignoring the impact of uncertainty on CVP analysis. Fortunately, sensitivity analysis can also give managers a feel for the degree to which a poorly forecast variable will affect an answer. That is also an advantage.

Ethical Decisions

It is important to note that the CVP results are only one input into business decisions. Many other factors may bear on decisions to choose one type of process over another, for example, or whether or not to delete certain costs. Businesses and nonprofit entities often face trade-offs involving safety. Ethical concerns also have an important place in CVP analysis. When one company buys another one, it bases its decision in part on the information presented by the to-be-acquired firm. For example, China's **Geely** purchased **Volvo** from **Ford** in 2010. As the head of Geely stated, "As far as I know, Volvo is in good operating condition and it's possible it could break even in the fourth quarter of this year."[3] Often, however, the costs and probabilities are not known with sufficient certainty. In that case, these factors are included in the ultimate decision-making process. Chapter 8, on short-run decision making, covers this topic in more detail. ●

Despite the fact that future conditions cannot be known with certainty, there are various ways of incorporating risk and uncertainty into the analysis. One possibility is that cost of potential problems can be estimated and included in the CVP results. Another is that various scenarios can be considered by running sensitivity analysis—varying costs and prices to see what happens.

Check Point

1. **Two companies have identical sales revenue of $15 million. Is it true that both have the same operating income and the same margin of safety? Is it possible that one company has a higher margin of safety?**

   Answer:
   It is not necessarily true that the two companies make the same operating income. If one company has lower variable costs per unit and/or a lower total fixed cost, then its operating income would be higher. The differences in variable cost per unit and total fixed cost would lead to different break-even revenues. Of course, the company with the lower break-even sales would have a higher margin of safety.

2. **A company's margin of safety is $30,000. For the coming year, sales are expected to decrease by $14,000. What is the impact on the margin of safety?**

   Answer:
   The new margin of safety is $16,000. That is, break-even sales are unchanged, but expected sales are $14,000 lower, so the new margin of safety is $30,000 − $14,000 = $16,000.

---

3   Drew Johnson, "Geely: Volvo Could Break Even by Year's End," *Left Lane News* (April 13, 2010). Taken from www. leftlanenews.com/geely-volvo-could-break-even-by-years-end.html.

SUMMARY OF LEARNING OBJECTIVES

LO1. Determine the break-even point in number of units and in total sales dollars.
- At break-even, total costs (variable and fixed) equal total sales revenue.
- Break-even units equal total fixed costs divided by the contribution margin (price minus variable cost per unit).
- Break-even revenue equals total fixed costs divided by the contribution margin ratio.

LO2. Determine the number of units that must be sold, and the amount of revenue required, to earn a targeted profit.
- To earn a target (desired) profit, total costs (variable and fixed) plus the amount of target profit must equal total sales revenue.
- Units to earn target profit equal total fixed costs plus target profit divided by the contribution margin.
- Sales revenue to earn target profit equals total fixed costs plus target profit divided by the contribution margin ratio.

LO3. Prepare a cost-volume-profit graph, and explain its meaning.
- CVP assumes linear revenue and cost functions, no finished goods ending inventories, constant sales mix, and selling prices and fixed and variable costs that are known with certainty.
- CVP graphs plot a line for total costs and a line for total sales revenue. The intersection of these two lines is the break-even point in units.

LO4. Apply cost-volume-profit analysis in a multiple-product setting.
- Multiple-product analysis requires the expected sales mix.
- Break-even units for each product will change as the sales mix changes.
- Increased sales of high contribution margin products decrease the break-even point.
- Increased sales of low contribution margin products increase the break-even point.

LO5. Explain the impact of risk, uncertainty, and changing variables on cost-volume-profit analysis.
- Uncertainty regarding costs, prices, and sales mix affects the break-even point.
- Sensitivity analysis allows managers to vary costs, prices, and sales mix to show various possible break-even points.
- Margin of safety shows how far the company's actual sales and/or units are above or below the break-even point.
- Operating leverage is the use of fixed costs to increase the percentage changes in profits as sales activity changes.

SUMMARY OF IMPORTANT EQUATIONS

1. Unit Contribution Margin = Price − Unit Variable Cost
   Total Contribution Margin = Sales − Total Variable Cost

2. Operating Income = (Price × Number of Units Sold) − (Variable Cost per Unit × Number of Units Sold) − Total Fixed Cost

3. Break-Even Units = Total Fixed Cost/Unit Contribution Margin

4. Sales Revenue = Price × Units Sold

5. Variable Cost Ratio = Total Variable Cost/Sales

6. Variable Cost Ratio = Unit Variable Cost/Price

7. Contribution Margin Ratio = Total Contribution Margin/Sales

8. Contribution Margin Ratio = Unit Contribution Margin/Price

9. Break-Even Sales = Total Fixed Expenses/Contribution Margin Ratio

10. Margin of Safety = Sales – Break-Even Sales

11. Degree of Operating Leverage = Total Contribution Margin/Operating Income

12. Percentage Change in Profits = Degree of Operating Leverage × Percent Change in Sales

EXAMPLE 7.1 How to prepare a contribution margin income statement, page 336

EXAMPLE 7.2 How to calculate the break-even point in units, page 338

EXAMPLE 7.3 How to calculate the variable cost ratio and the contribution margin ratio, page 340

EXAMPLE 7.4 How to calculate the break-even point in sales dollars, page 341

EXAMPLE 7.5 How to calculate the number of units to be sold to earn a target operating income, page 344

EXAMPLE 7.6 How to calculate sales needed to earn a target operating income, page 345

EXAMPLE 7.7 How to calculate the break-even units for a multiple-product firm, page 353

EXAMPLE 7.8 How to calculate the break-even sales dollars for a multiple-product firm, page 354

EXAMPLE 7.9 How to calculate the margin of safety, page 360

EXAMPLE 7.10 How to calculate the degree of operating leverage, page 361

EXAMPLE 7.11 How to calculate the impact of increased sales on operating income using the degree of operating leverage, page 362

KEY TERMS

Break-even point, 334, the point at which total revenue equals total cost (both fixed and variable cost). At break-even, profit is zero.

Common fixed expenses, 351, fixed expenses that cannot be traced to individual segments or products. They will continue to exist even if one segment or product is eliminated.

Contribution margin, 335, the difference between total sales and total variable costs on a total basis, or price minus unit variable cost on a per-unit basis. Total contribution margin is the amount left over from sales to contribute to covering fixed costs and profit.

Contribution margin income statement, 335, the cost behavior-based income statement. Costs are separated into fixed and variable categories. First, total variable cost is subtracted from sales to get the contribution margin. Next, total fixed expenses are subtracted to get operating income (profit).

Contribution margin ratio, 339, the ratio of total contribution margin to sales or of unit contribution to price. Contribution margin ratio is also computed as 1 (100%) minus the variable cost ratio. It represents the percentage of each sales dollar available to contribute to fixed cost and profit.

Cost structure, 361, the company's relative mix of fixed to variable costs. It is useful in determining operating leverage.

Cost-volume-profit (CVP) analysis, 334, estimates how changes in costs (both variable and fixed), sales volume, and price affect profit.

Cost-volume-profit graph, 347, a graph showing the relationships among cost, volume (units sold), and profit using a total cost line and a total revenue line. The intersection of the total cost line with the total revenue line is the break-even point.

Degree of operating leverage (DOL), 360, shows the degree to which fixed costs are used to obtain a higher percent change in profits as sales change. DOL is equal to the total contribution margin divided by operating income.

Direct fixed expenses, 351, fixed costs that are directly traceable to a given segment and, consequently, disappear if the segment is eliminated.

Indifference point, 363, the point at which two different operating systems produce the same income.

Margin of safety, 359, the number of units sold or the amount of sales revenue earned above the break-even point.

Operating leverage, 360, occurs when fixed costs are used to obtain higher change in profits as sales change.

Sales mix, 352, the relative combination of products sold by a company. Sales mix is usually expressed in the lowest whole units. For example, a sales mix of 3:2 means that for every 3 units of Product A sold, 2 units of Product B are sold.

Sensitivity analysis, 363, a "what-if" technique used to see what impact a change in an underlying variable has on the answer.

Variable cost ratio, 339, the ratio of total variable cost to sales or of unit variable cost to price. Variable cost ratio is also computed as 1 (100%) minus the contribution margin ratio. It represents the percentage of each sales dollar used to cover variable cost.

REVIEW PROBLEMS

I. Single-Product Cost-Volume-Profit Analysis

Cutlass Company's projected profit for the coming year is as follows:

	Total	Per Unit
Sales	$200,000	$20
Total variable cost	120,000	12
Contribution margin	$ 80,000	$ 8
Total fixed cost	64,000	
Operating income	$ 16,000	

Required:

1. Compute the variable cost ratio. Compute the contribution margin ratio.
2. Compute the break-even point in units.
3. Compute the break-even point in sales dollars.
4. How many units must be sold to earn a profit of $30,000?
5. Using the contribution margin ratio computed in Requirement 1, compute the additional profit that Cutlass would earn if sales were $25,000 more than expected.
6. For the projected level of sales, compute the margin of safety in units and in sales dollars.
7. Calculate the degree of operating leverage. Now suppose that Cutlass revises the forecast to show a 30% increase in sales over the original forecast. What is the percent change in

(Continued)

operating income expected for the revised forecast? What is the total operating income expected by Cutlass after revising the sales forecast?

Solution:

1. Variable Cost Ratio $= \dfrac{\text{Total Variable Cost}}{\text{Sales}}$

$$= \dfrac{\$120,000}{\$200,000}$$

$$= 0.60, \text{ or } 60\%$$

Contribution Margin Ratio $= \dfrac{\text{Total Contribution Margin}}{\text{Sales}}$

$$= \dfrac{\$80,000}{\$200,000}$$

$$= 0.40, \text{ or } 40\%$$

2. The break-even point is computed as follows:

$$\text{Units} = \dfrac{\text{Total Fixed Cost}}{(\text{Price} - \text{Variable Cost per Unit})}$$

$$= \dfrac{\$64,000}{(\$20 - \$12)}$$

$$= \dfrac{\$64,000}{\$8} = 8,000$$

3. The break-even point in sales dollars is computed as follows:

$$\text{Break-Even Sales Dollars} = \dfrac{\text{Total Fixed Cost}}{\text{Contribution Margin Ratio}}$$

$$= \dfrac{\$64,000}{0.40}$$

$$= \$160,000$$

4. The number of units that must be sold to earn a profit of $30,000 is calculated as follows:

$$\text{Units} = \dfrac{(\$64,000 + \$30,000)}{\$8}$$

$$= \dfrac{\$94,000}{\$8}$$

$$= 11,750$$

5. The additional contribution margin on additional sales of $25,000 would be $0.40 \times \$25,000 = \$10,000$.

6. Margin of Safety in Units = Projected Units − Break-Even Units

$$= 10,000 - 8,000 = 2,000$$

Margin of Safety in Sales Dollars = $200,000 − $160,000 = $40,000

7. Degree of Operating Leverage $= \dfrac{\text{Total Contribution Margin}}{\text{Operating Income}}$

$$= \dfrac{\$80,000}{\$16,000} = 5.0$$

Percentage Change in Operating Income = Degree of Operating Leverage

$$\times \text{Percent Change in Sales}$$

$$= 5.0 \times 30\%$$

$$= 150\%$$

Expected Operating Income = $16,000 + (1.5 \times \$16,000)$

$$= \$40,000$$

II. Multiple-Product Cost-Volume-Profit Analysis

Alpha Company produces and sells two products: Alpha-Basic and Alpha-Deluxe. In the coming year, Alpha expects to sell 3,000 units of Alpha-Basic and 1,500 units of Alpha-Deluxe. Information on the two products is as follows:

	Alpha-Basic	Alpha-Deluxe
Price	$120	$200
Variable cost per unit	40	80

Total fixed cost is $140,000.

Required:

1. What is the sales mix of Alpha-Basic to Alpha-Deluxe?
2. Compute the break-even quantity of each product.

Solution:

1. The sales mix of Alpha-Basic to Alpha-Deluxe is 3,000:1,500 or 2:1.
2. Each package consists of two Alpha-Basic and one Alpha-Deluxe:

Product	Price	Unit Variable Cost	Unit Contribution Margin	Sales Mix	Package Unit Contribution Margin
Alpha-Basic	$120	$40	$ 80	2	$160
Alpha-Deluxe	200	80	120	1	120
Package total					$280

$$\text{Break-Even Packages} = \frac{\text{Total Fixed Cost}}{\text{Package Contribution Margin}}$$

$$= \frac{\$140,000}{\$280}$$

$$= 500$$

1. Alpha-Basic break-even units = 500 × 2 = 1,000
2. Alpha-Deluxe break-even units = 500 × 1 = 500

DISCUSSION QUESTIONS

1. Explain how CVP analysis can be used for managerial planning.
2. Describe the difference between the units sold approach to CVP analysis and the sales revenue approach.
3. Define the term *break-even point*.
4. Explain why contribution margin per unit becomes profit per unit above the break-even point.
5. What is the variable cost ratio? The contribution margin ratio? How are the two ratios related?
6. Suppose a firm with a contribution margin ratio of 0.3 increased its advertising expenses by $10,000 and found that sales increased by $30,000. Was it a good decision to increase advertising expenses? Suppose that the contribution margin ratio is now 0.4. Would it be a good decision to increase advertising expenses?
7. Define the term *sales mix*. Give an example to support your definition.
8. Explain how CVP analysis developed for single products can be used in a multiple-product setting.
9. Since break-even analysis focuses on making zero profit, it is of no value in determining the units a firm must sell to earn a targeted profit. Do you agree or disagree with this statement? Why?

10. How does targeted profit enter into the break-even units equation?

11. Explain how a change in sales mix can change a company's break-even point.

12. Define the term *margin of safety*. Explain how it can be used as a crude measure of operating risk.

13. Explain what is meant by the term *operating leverage*. What impact does increased leverage have on risk?

14. How can sensitivity analysis be used in conjunction with CVP analysis?

15. Why is a declining margin of safety over a period of time an issue of concern to managers?

MULTIPLE-CHOICE QUESTIONS

7-1   If the variable cost per unit goes down,

Contribution margin	**Break-even point**
a. increases	increases.
b. increases	decreases.
c. decreases	decreases.
d. decreases	increases.
e. decreases	remains unchanged.

7-2   The amount of revenue required to earn a targeted profit is equal to

a. total fixed cost divided by contribution margin.
b. total fixed cost divided by the contribution margin ratio.
c. targeted profit divided by the contribution margin ratio.
d. total fixed cost plus targeted profit divided by contribution margin ratio.
e. targeted profit divided by the variable cost ratio.

7-3   Break-even revenue for the multiple-product firm can

a. be calculated by dividing total fixed cost by the overall contribution margin ratio.
b. be calculated by dividing segment fixed cost by the overall contribution margin ratio.
c. be calculated by dividing total fixed cost by the overall variable cost ratio.
d. be calculated by multiplying total fixed cost by the contribution margin ratio.
e. not be calculated; break-even revenue can only be computed for a single-product firm.

7-4   In the cost-volume-profit graph,

a. the break-even point is found where the total revenue curve crosses the *x*-axis.
b. the area of profit is to the left of the break-even point.
c. the area of loss cannot be determined.
d. both the total revenue curve and the total cost curve appear.
e. neither the total revenue curve nor the total cost curve appear.

7-5   An important assumption of cost-volume-profit analysis is that

a. both costs and revenues are linear functions.
b. all cost and revenue relationships are analyzed within the relevant range.
c. there is no change in inventories.
d. the sales mix remains constant.
e. All of these.

7-6   The use of fixed costs to extract higher percentage changes in profits as sales activity changes involves

a. margin of safety.
b. unit contribution margin.
c. degree of operating leverage.
d. sensitivity analysis.
e. variable cost reduction.

7-7   If the margin of safety is 0, then
  a. the company is precisely breaking even.
  b. the company is operating at a loss.
  c. the company is earning a small profit.
  d. the margin of safety cannot be less than or equal to 0; it must be positive.
  e. None of these.

7-8   The contribution margin is the
  a. amount by which sales exceed total fixed cost.
  b. difference between sales and total cost.
  c. difference between sales and operating income.
  d. difference between sales and total variable cost.
  e. difference between variable cost and fixed cost.

Use the following information for Multiple-Choice Questions 7-9 and 7-10:
Dartmouth Company produces a single product with a price of $12, variable cost per unit of $3, and total fixed cost of $7,200.

7-9   Refer to the information for Dartmouth above. Dartmouth's break-even point in units

  a. is 600.
  b. is 480.
  c. is 1,000.
  d. is 800.
  e. cannot be determined from the information given.

7-10   Refer to the information for Dartmouth above. The variable cost ratio and the contribution margin ratio for Dartmouth are

	Variable cost ratio	Contribution margin ratio
a.	80%	80%.
b.	20%	80%.
c.	25%	75%.
d.	75%	25%.
e.	The contribution margin ratio cannot be determined from the information given.	

7-11   If a company's total fixed cost decreases by $10,000, which of the following will be true?

  a. The break-even point will increase.
  b. The variable cost ratio will increase.
  c. The break-even point will be unchanged.
  d. The variable cost ratio will be unchanged.
  e. The contribution margin ratio will increase.

7-12   Solemon Company has total fixed cost of $15,000, variable cost per unit of $6, and a price of $8. If Solemon wants to earn a targeted profit of $3,600, how many units must be sold?

  a. 2,500
  b. 7,500
  c. 9,300
  d. 18,600
  e. 18,750

BRIEF EXERCISES: SET A

OBJECTIVE ▸ 1

Example 7.1

Brief Exercise 7-13 Variable Cost, Fixed Cost, Contribution Margin Income Statement

Head-First Company plans to sell 5,000 bicycle helmets at $75 each in the coming year. Product costs include:

Direct materials per helmet	$ 30
Direct labor per helmet	8
Variable factory overhead per helmet	4
Total fixed factory overhead	20,000

Variable selling expense is a commission of $3 per helmet; fixed selling and administrative expense totals $29,500.

Required:

1. Calculate the total variable cost per unit.
2. Calculate the total fixed expense for the year.
3. Prepare a contribution margin income statement for Head-First Company for the coming year.

OBJECTIVE ▸ 1

Example 7.2

Brief Exercise 7-14 Break-Even Point in Units

Head-First Company plans to sell 5,000 bicycle helmets at $75 each in the coming year. Unit variable cost is $45 (includes direct materials, direct labor, variable factory overhead, and variable selling expense). Total fixed cost equals $49,500 (includes fixed factory overhead and fixed selling and administrative expense).

Required:

1. Calculate the break-even number of helmets.
2. Check your answer by preparing a contribution margin income statement based on the break-even units.

OBJECTIVE ▸ 1

Example 7.3

Brief Exercise 7-15 Variable Cost Ratio, Contribution Margin Ratio

Head-First Company plans to sell 5,000 bicycle helmets at $75 each in the coming year. Unit variable cost is $45 (includes direct materials, direct labor, variable factory overhead, and variable selling expense). Fixed factory overhead is $20,000, and fixed selling and administrative expense is $29,500.

Required:

1. Calculate the variable cost ratio.
2. Calculate the contribution margin ratio.
3. Prepare a contribution margin income statement based on the budgeted figures for next year. In a column next to the income statement, show the percentages based on sales for sales, total variable cost, and total contribution margin.

OBJECTIVE ▸ 1

Example 7.4

Brief Exercise 7-16 Break-Even Point in Sales Dollars

Head-First Company plans to sell 5,000 bicycle helmets at $75 each in the coming year. Variable cost is 60% of the sales price; contribution margin is 40% of the sales price. Total fixed cost equals $49,500 (includes fixed factory overhead and fixed selling and administrative expense).

Required:

1. Calculate the sales revenue that Head-First must make to break even by using the break-even point in sales equation.
2. Check your answer by preparing a contribution margin income statement based on the break-even point in sales dollars.

Brief Exercise 7-17 Units to Earn Target Income

OBJECTIVE ◀ 2

Example 7.5

Head-First Company plans to sell 5,000 bicycle helmets at $75 each in the coming year. Unit variable cost is $45 (includes direct materials, direct labor, variable factory overhead, and variable selling expense). Total fixed cost equals $49,500 (includes fixed factory overhead and fixed selling and administrative expense).

Required:

1. Calculate the number of helmets Head-First must sell to earn operating income of $81,900.
2. Check your answer by preparing a contribution margin income statement based on the number of units calculated.

Brief Exercise 7-18 Sales Needed to Earn Target Income

OBJECTIVE ◀ 2

Example 7.6

Head-First Company plans to sell 5,000 bicycle helmets at $75 each in the coming year. Variable cost is 60% of the sales price; contribution margin is 40% of the sales price. Total fixed cost equals $49,500 (includes fixed factory overhead and fixed selling and administrative expense).

Required:

1. Calculate the sales revenue that Head-First must make to earn operating income of $81,900 by using the point in sales equation.
2. Check your answer by preparing a contribution margin income statement based on the sales dollars calculated in Requirement 1.

Brief Exercise 7-19 Break-Even Point in Units for a Multiple-Product Firm

OBJECTIVE ◀ 4

Example 7.7

Suppose that Head-First Company now sells both bicycle helmets and motorcycle helmets. The bicycle helmets are priced at $75 and have variable costs of $45 each. The motorcycle helmets are priced at $220 and have variable costs of $140 each. Total fixed cost for Head-First as a whole equals $58,900 (includes all fixed factory overhead and fixed selling and administrative expense). Next year, Head-First expects to sell 5,000 bicycle helmets and 2,000 motorcycle helmets.

Required:

1. Form a package of bicycle and motorcycle helmets based on the sales mix expected for the coming year.
2. Calculate the break-even point in units for bicycle helmets and for motorcycle helmets.
3. Check your answer by preparing a contribution margin income statement.

Brief Exercise 7-20 Break-Even Sales Dollars for a Multiple-Product Firm

OBJECTIVE ◀ 4

Example 7.8

Head-First Company now sells both bicycle helmets and motorcycle helmets. Next year, Head-First expects to produce total revenue of $570,000 and incur total variable cost of $388,000. Total fixed cost is expected to be $58,900.

Required:

1. Calculate the break-even point in sales dollars for Head-First. (*Note:* Round the contribution margin ratio to four decimal places and sales to the nearest dollar.)
2. Check your answer by preparing a contribution margin income statement.

OBJECTIVE **5**
Example 7.9

Brief Exercise 7-21 **Margin of Safety**

Head-First Company plans to sell 5,000 bicycle helmets at $75 each in the coming year. Unit variable cost is $45 (includes direct materials, direct labor, variable factory overhead, and variable selling expense). Total fixed cost equals $49,500 (includes fixed factory overhead and fixed selling and administrative expense). Break-even units equal 1,650.

Required:

1. Calculate the margin of safety in terms of the number of units.
2. Calculate the margin of safety in terms of sales revenue.

OBJECTIVE **5**
Example 7.10

Brief Exercise 7-22 **Degree of Operating Leverage**

Head-First Company plans to sell 5,000 bicycle helmets at $75 each in the coming year. Unit variable cost is $45 (includes direct materials, direct labor, variable factory overhead, and variable selling expense). Total fixed cost equals $49,500 (includes fixed factory overhead and fixed selling and administrative expense). Operating income at 5,000 units sold is $100,500.

Required:

Calculate the degree of operating leverage. (*Note:* Round answer to the nearest tenth.)

OBJECTIVE **5**
Example 7.11

Brief Exercise 7-23 **Impact of Increased Sales on Operating Income Using the Degree of Operating Leverage**

Head-First Company had planned to sell 5,000 bicycle helmets at $75 each in the coming year. Unit variable cost is $45 (includes direct materials, direct labor, variable factory overhead, and variable selling expense). Total fixed cost equals $49,500 (includes fixed factory overhead and fixed selling and administrative expense). Operating income at 5,000 units sold is $100,500. The degree of operating leverage is 1.5. Now Head-First expects to increase sales by 10% next year.

Required:

1. Calculate the percent change in operating income expected.
2. Calculate the operating income expected next year using the percent change in operating income calculated in Requirement 1.

BRIEF EXERCISES: SET B

OBJECTIVE **1**
Example 7.1

Brief Exercise 7-24 **Variable Cost, Fixed Cost, Contribution Margin Income Statement**

Chillmax Company plans to sell 3,500 pairs of casual shoes at $60 each in the coming year. Product costs include:

Direct materials per pair	$ 12
Direct labor per pair	4
Variable factory overhead per pair	2
Total fixed factory overhead	30,000

Variable selling expense is a commission of $3 per pair; fixed selling and administrative expense totals $48,000.

Required:

1. Calculate the total variable cost per unit.
2. Calculate the total fixed expense for the year.
3. Prepare a contribution margin income statement for Chillmax Company for the coming year.

Brief Exercise 7-25 Break-Even Point in Units

OBJECTIVE ◀ 1

Example 7.2

Chillmax Company plans to sell 3,500 pairs of shoes at $60 each in the coming year. Unit variable cost is $21 (includes direct materials, direct labor, variable factory overhead, and variable selling expense). Total fixed cost equals $78,000 (includes fixed factory overhead and fixed selling and administrative expense).

Required:

1. Calculate the break-even pairs of shoes.
2. Check your answer by preparing a contribution margin income statement based on the break-even units.

Brief Exercise 7-26 Variable Cost Ratio, Contribution Margin Ratio

OBJECTIVE ◀ 1

Example 7.3

Chillmax Company plans to sell 3,500 pairs of shoes at $60 each in the coming year. Unit variable cost is $21 (includes direct materials, direct labor, variable factory overhead, and variable selling expense). Fixed factory overhead is $30,000 and fixed selling and administrative expense is $48,000.

Required:

1. Calculate the variable cost ratio.
2. Calculate the contribution margin ratio.
3. Prepare a contribution margin income statement based on the budgeted figures for next year. In a column next to the income statement, show the percentages based on sales for sales, total variable cost, and total contribution margin.

Brief Exercise 7-27 Break-Even Point in Sales Dollars

OBJECTIVE ◀ 1

Example 7.4

Chillmax Company plans to sell 3,500 pairs of shoes at $60 each in the coming year. Variable cost is 35% of the sales price; contribution margin is 65% of the sales price. Total fixed cost equals $78,000 (includes fixed factory overhead and fixed selling and administrative expense).

Required:

1. Calculate the sales revenue that Chillmax must make to break even by using the break-even point in sales equation.
2. Check your answer by preparing a contribution margin income statement based on the break-even point in sales dollars.

Brief Exercise 7-28 Units to Earn Target Income

OBJECTIVE ◀ 2

Example 7.5

Chillmax Company plans to sell 3,500 pairs of shoes at $60 each in the coming year. Unit variable cost is $21 (includes direct materials, direct labor, variable factory overhead, and variable selling expense). Total fixed cost equals $78,000 (includes fixed factory overhead and fixed selling and administrative expense).

Required:

1. Calculate the number of pairs of shoes Chillmax must sell to earn operating income of $81,900.
2. Check your answer by preparing a contribution margin income statement based on the number of units calculated.

Brief Exercise 7-29 Sales Needed to Earn Target Income

OBJECTIVE ◀ 2

Example 7.6

Chillmax Company plans to sell 3,500 pairs of shoes at $60 each in the coming year. Variable cost is 35% of the sales price; contribution margin is 65% of the sales price. Total fixed cost equals $78,000 (includes fixed factory overhead and fixed selling and administrative expense).

(*Continued*)

Required:

1. Calculate the sales revenue that Chillmax must make to earn operating income of $81,900 by using the point in sales equation.
2. Check your answer by preparing a contribution margin income statement based on the sales dollars calculated in Requirement 1.

OBJECTIVE ▶ 4
Example 7.7

Brief Exercise 7-30 Break-Even Point in Units for a Multiple-Product Firm

Suppose that Chillmax Company now sells both pairs of shoes and fabric carryalls. The pairs of shoes are priced at $60 and have variable costs of $21 each. The carryalls are priced at $36 and have variable costs of $9 each. Total fixed cost for Chillmax as a whole equals $91,500 (includes all fixed factory overhead and fixed selling and administrative expense). Next year, Chillmax expects to sell 3,500 pairs of shoes and 875 carryalls.

Required:

1. Form a package of shoes and carryalls based on the sales mix expected for the coming year.
2. Calculate the break-even point in units for pairs of shoes and for carryalls.
3. Check your answer by preparing a contribution margin income statement.

OBJECTIVE ▶ 4
Example 7.8

Brief Exercise 7-31 Break-Even Sales Dollars for a Multiple-Product Firm

Chillmax Company now sells both pairs of shoes and carryalls. Next year, Chillmax expects to produce total revenue of $210,000 and incur total variable cost of $81,375. Total fixed cost is expected to be $91,500.

Required:

1. Calculate the break-even point in sales dollars for Chillmax. (*Note:* Round the contribution margin ratio to four decimal places and sales to the nearest dollar.)
2. Check your answer by preparing a contribution margin income statement.

OBJECTIVE ▶ 5
Example 7.9

Brief Exercise 7-32 Margin of Safety

Chillmax Company plans to sell 3,500 pairs of shoes at $60 each in the coming year. Unit variable cost is $21 (includes direct materials, direct labor, variable factory overhead, and variable selling expense). Total fixed cost equals $78,000 (includes fixed factory overhead and fixed selling and administrative expense). Break-even units equal 2,000.

Required:

1. Calculate the margin of safety in terms of the number of units.
2. Calculate the margin of safety in terms of sales revenue.

OBJECTIVE ▶ 5
Example 7.10

Brief Exercise 7-33 Degree of Operating Leverage

Chillmax Company plans to sell 3,500 pairs of shoes at $60 each in the coming year. Unit variable cost is $21 (includes direct materials, direct labor, variable factory overhead, and variable selling expense). Total fixed cost equals $78,000 (includes fixed factory overhead and fixed selling and administrative expense). Operating income at 3,500 units sold is $58,500.

Required:

Calculate the degree of operating leverage. (*Note:* Round answer to the nearest tenth.)

OBJECTIVE ▶ 5
Example 7.11

Brief Exercise 7-34 Impact of Increased Sales on Operating Income Using the Degree of Operating Leverage

Chillmax Company had planned to sell 3,500 pairs of shoes at $60 each in the coming year. Unit variable cost is $21 (includes direct materials, direct labor, variable factory overhead, and variable selling expense). Total fixed cost equals $78,000 (includes fixed factory overhead and fixed selling and administrative expense). Operating income at 3,500 units sold is $58,500. The degree of operating leverage is 2.3. Now Chillmax expects to increase sales by 10% next year.

Required:

1. Calculate the percent change in operating income expected.
2. Calculate the operating income expected next year using the percent change in operating income calculated in Requirement 1.

EXERCISES

Exercise 7-35 Basic Break-Even Calculations

OBJECTIVE ▸ 1

Suppose that Larimer Company sells a product for $24. Unit costs are as follows:

Direct materials	$4.98
Direct labor	2.10
Variable factory overhead	1.00
Variable selling and administrative expense	2.00

Total fixed factory overhead is $26,500 per year, and total fixed selling and administrative expense is $15,260.

Required:

1. Calculate the variable cost per unit and the contribution margin per unit.
2. Calculate the contribution margin ratio and the variable cost ratio.
3. Calculate the break-even units.
4. Prepare a contribution margin income statement at the break-even number of units.

Exercise 7-36 Price, Variable Cost per Unit, Contribution Margin, Contribution Margin Ratio, Fixed Expense

OBJECTIVE ▸ 1

For each of the following independent situations, calculate the amount(s) required.

Required:

1. At the break-even point, Jefferson Company sells 115,000 units and has fixed cost of $349,600. The variable cost per unit is $4.56. What price does Jefferson charge per unit?
2. Sooner Industries charges a price of $120 and has fixed cost of $458,000. Next year, Sooner expects to sell 15,600 units and make operating income of $166,000. What is the variable cost per unit? What is the contribution margin ratio? (*Note:* Round answer to four decimal places.)
3. Last year, Jasper Company earned operating income of $22,500 with a contribution margin ratio of 0.25. Actual revenue was $235,000. Calculate the total fixed cost.
4. Laramie Company has a variable cost ratio of 0.56. The fixed cost is $103,840 and 23,600 units are sold at break-even. What is the price? What is the variable cost per unit? The contribution margin per unit?

Exercise 7-37 Contribution Margin Ratio, Variable Cost Ratio, Break-Even Sales Revenue

OBJECTIVE ▸ 1

The controller of Ashton Company prepared the following projected income statement:

Sales	$88,000
Total variable cost	23,760
Contribution margin	$64,240
Total fixed cost	43,800
Operating income	$20,440

(Continued)

Required:

1. Calculate the contribution margin ratio.
2. Calculate the variable cost ratio.
3. Calculate the break-even sales revenue for Ashton.
4. **CONCEPTUAL CONNECTION** How could Ashton increase projected operating income without increasing the total sales revenue?

OBJECTIVE 2

Exercise 7-38 Income Statement, Break-Even Units, Units to Earn Target Income

Khaling Company sold 19,000 units last year at $18.00 each. Variable cost was $14.60, and total fixed cost was $68,000.

Required:

1. Prepare an income statement for Khaling for last year.
2. Calculate the break-even point in units.
3. Calculate the units that Khaling must sell to earn operating income of $20,400 this year.

OBJECTIVE 1

Exercise 7-39 Units Sold to Break Even, Unit Variable Cost, Unit Manufacturing Cost, Units to Earn Target Income

Werner Company produces and sells disposable foil baking pans to retailers for $2.75 per pan. The variable cost per pan is as follows:

Direct materials	$0.37
Direct labor	0.63
Variable factory overhead	0.53
Variable selling expense	0.12

Fixed manufacturing cost totals $111,425 per year. Administrative cost (all fixed) totals $48,350.

Required:

1. Compute the number of pans that must be sold for Werner to break even.
2. **CONCEPTUAL CONNECTION** What is the unit variable cost? What is the unit variable manufacturing cost? Which is used in cost-volume-profit analysis and why?
3. How many pans must be sold for Werner to earn operating income of $13,530?
4. How much sales revenue must Werner have to earn operating income of $13,530?

OBJECTIVE 5

Exercise 7-40 Margin of Safety

Comer Company produces and sells strings of colorful indoor/outdoor lights for holiday display to retailers for $8.12 per string. The variable costs per string are as follows:

Direct materials	$1.87
Direct labor	1.70
Variable factory overhead	0.57
Variable selling expense	0.42

Fixed manufacturing cost totals $245,650 per year. Administrative cost (all fixed) totals $297,606. Comer expects to sell 225,000 strings of lights next year.

Required:

1. Calculate the break-even point in units.
2. Calculate the margin of safety in units.
3. Calculate the margin of safety in dollars.

4. **CONCEPTUAL CONNECTION** Suppose Comer actually experiences a price decrease next year, while all other costs and the number of units sold remain the same. Would this increase or decrease risk for the company? (*Hint*: Consider what would happen to the number of break-even units and to the margin of safety.)

OBJECTIVE ◂ **1**

Exercise 7-41 Contribution Margin, Unit Amounts, Break-Even Units

Information on four independent companies follows. Calculate the correct amount for each question mark. (*Note*: Round unit dollar amounts and ratios to two decimal places; round break-even units to the nearest whole unit.)

EXCEL

	Laertes	Ophelia	Fortinbras	Claudius
Sales	$15,000	$?	$?	$10,600
Total variable cost	5,000	11,700	9,750	?
Total contribution margin	$10,000	$ 3,900	$?	$?
Total fixed cost	?	4,000	?	4,452
Operating income (loss)	$ 500	$?	$ 364	$ 848
Units sold	?	1,300	125	1,000
Price per unit	$ 5.00	?	$130.00	?
Variable cost per unit	$?	$ 9.00	$?	$?
Contribution margin per unit	$?	$ 3.00	$?	$?
Contribution margin ratio	?	?	40%	?
Break-even units	?	?	?	?

Exercise 7-42 Sales Revenue Approach, Variable Cost Ratio, Contribution Margin Ratio

OBJECTIVE ◂ **1** ◂ **2** ◂ **5**

Arberg Company's controller prepared the following budgeted income statement for the coming year:

Sales	$415,000
Total variable cost	302,950
Contribution margin	$112,050
Total fixed cost	64,800
Operating income	$ 47,250

Required:

1. What is Arberg's variable cost ratio? What is its contribution margin ratio?
2. Suppose Arberg's actual revenues are $30,000 more than budgeted. By how much will operating income increase? Give the answer without preparing a new income statement.
3. How much sales revenue must Arberg earn to break even? Prepare a contribution margin income statement to verify the accuracy of your answer.
4. What is Arberg's expected margin of safety?
5. What is Arberg's margin of safety if sales revenue is $380,000?

Use the following information for Exercises 7-43 and 7-44:
Cherry Blossom Products Inc. produces and sells yoga-training products: how-to DVDs and a basic equipment set (blocks, strap, and small pillows). Last year, Cherry Blossom Products sold 13,500 DVDs and 4,500 equipment sets. Information on the two products is as follows:

	DVDs	Equipment Sets
Price	$8	$25
Variable cost per unit	4	15

Total fixed cost is $84,920.

OBJECTIVE 4

EXCEL

Exercise 7-43 Multiple-Product Break-even

Refer to the information for Cherry Blossom Products on the previous page.

Required:

1. What is the sales mix of DVDs and equipment sets?
2. Compute the break-even quantity of each product.

OBJECTIVE 1 ▶ 5

EXCEL

Exercise 7-44 Multiple-Product Break-even, Break-Even Sales Revenue

Refer to the information for Cherry Blossom Products on the previous page. Suppose that in the coming year, the company plans to produce an extra-thick yoga mat for sale to health clubs. The company estimates that 9,000 mats can be sold at a price of $15 and a variable cost per unit of $9. Total fixed cost must be increased by $28,980 (making total fixed cost $113,900). Assume that anticipated sales of the other products, as well as their prices and variable costs, remain the same.

Required:

1. What is the sales mix of DVDs, equipment sets, and yoga mats?
2. Compute the break-even quantity of each product.
3. Prepare an income statement for Cherry Blossom Products for the coming year. What is the overall contribution margin ratio? Use the contribution margin ratio to compute overall break-even sales revenue. (*Note*: Round the contribution margin ratio to four decimal places; round the break-even sales revenue to the nearest dollar.)
4. Compute the margin of safety for the coming year in sales dollars.

OBJECTIVE 1 ▶ 4 ▶ 5

EXCEL

Exercise 7-45 Contribution Margin Ratio, Break-Even Sales Revenue, and Margin of Safety for Multiple-Product Firm

Texas-Q Company produces and sells barbeque grills. Texas-Q sells three models: a small portable gas grill, a larger stationary gas grill, and the specialty smoker. In the coming year, Texas-Q expects to sell 20,000 portable grills, 50,000 stationary grills, and 5,000 smokers. Information on the three models is as follows:

	Portable	Stationary	Smokers
Price	$90	$200	$250
Variable cost per unit	45	130	140

Total fixed cost is $2,128,500.

Required:

1. What is the sales mix of portable grills to stationary grills to smokers?
2. Compute the break-even quantity of each product.
3. Prepare an income statement for Texas-Q for the coming year. What is the overall contribution margin ratio? Use the contribution margin ratio to compute overall break-even sales revenue. (*Note*: Round the contribution margin ratio to four decimal places; round the break-even sales revenue to the nearest dollar.)
4. Compute the margin of safety for the coming year.

OBJECTIVE 3

Exercise 7-46 Cost-Volume-Profit Graphs

Lotts Company produces and sells one product. The selling price is $10, and the unit variable cost is $6. Total fixed cost is $10,000.

Required:

1. Prepare a CVP graph with "Units Sold" as the horizontal axis and "Dollars" as the vertical axis. Label the break-even point on the horizontal axis.
2. Prepare CVP graphs for each of the following independent scenarios: (a) Fixed cost increases by $5,000, (b) Unit variable cost increases to $7, (c) Unit selling price increases to $12, and (d) Fixed cost increases by $5,000 and unit variable cost is $7.

Exercise 7-47 Basic Cost-Volume-Profit Concepts

OBJECTIVE ◀ 1

Klamath Company produces a single product. The projected income statement for the coming year is as follows:

Sales (54,600 units @ $34)	$1,856,400
Total variable cost	1,064,700
Contribution margin	$ 791,700
Total fixed cost	801,850
Operating income	$ (10,150)

Required:

1. Compute the unit contribution margin and the units that must be sold to break even.
2. Suppose 10,000 units are sold above break-even. What is the operating income?
3. Compute the contribution margin ratio. Use the contribution margin ratio to compute the break-even point in sales revenue. (*Note:* Round the contribution margin ratio to four decimal places, and round the sales revenue to the nearest dollar.) Suppose that revenues are $200,000 more than expected *for the coming year.* What would the total operating income be?

Exercise 7-48 Margin of Safety and Operating Leverage

OBJECTIVE ◀ 1 ◀ 5

Medina Company produces a single product. The projected income statement for the coming year is as follows:

Sales (40,000 units @ $45)	$1,800,000
Total variable cost	1,044,000
Contribution margin	$ 756,000
Total fixed cost	733,320
Operating income	$ 22,680

(*Note*: Round all dollar answers to the nearest dollar. Round contribution margin ratio and degree of operating leverage to two decimal places.)

Required:

1. Compute the break-even sales dollars.
2. Compute the margin of safety in sales dollars.
3. Compute the degree of operating leverage. (*Note:* Round answer to two decimal places.)
4. Compute the new operating income if sales are 20% higher than expected. (*Note*: Round answer to the nearest dollar.)

Exercise 7-49 Multiple-Product Break-even

OBJECTIVE ◀ 1 ◀ 4

Parker Pottery produces a line of vases and a line of ceramic figurines. Each line uses the same equipment and labor; hence, there are no traceable fixed costs. Common fixed cost equals $30,000. Parker's accountant has begun to assess the profitability of the two lines and has gathered the following data for last year:

(*Continued*)

	Vases	Figurines
Price	$ 40	$ 70
Variable cost	30	42
Contribution margin	$ 10	$ 28
Number of units	1,000	500

Required:

1. Compute the number of vases and the number of figurines that must be sold for the company to break even.
2. Parker Pottery is considering upgrading its factory to improve the quality of its products. The upgrade will add $5,260 per year to total fixed cost. If the upgrade is successful, the projected sales of vases will be 1,500, and figurine sales will increase to 1,000 units. What is the new break-even point in units for each of the products?

OBJECTIVE `1` `2` `4` `5`

Exercise 7-50 Break-Even Units, Contribution Margin Ratio, Multiple-Product Break-even, Margin of Safety, Degree of Operating Leverage

Jellico Inc.'s projected operating income (based on sales of 450,000 units) for the coming year is as follows:

	Total
Sales	$11,700,000
Total variable cost	8,190,000
Contribution margin	$ 3,510,000
Total fixed cost	2,254,200
Operating income	$ 1,255,800

Required:

1. Compute: (a) variable cost per unit, (b) contribution margin per unit, (c) contribution margin ratio, (d) break-even point in units, and (e) break-even point in sales dollars.
2. How many units must be sold to earn operating income of $296,400?
3. Compute the additional operating income that Jellico would earn if sales were $50,000 more than expected.
4. For the projected level of sales, compute the margin of safety in units, and then in sales dollars.
5. Compute the degree of operating leverage. (*Note*: Round answer to two decimal places.)
6. Compute the new operating income if sales are 10% higher than expected.

PROBLEMS

OBJECTIVE `1` `2` `5`

Problem 7-51 Break-Even Units, Contribution Margin Ratio, Margin of Safety

Khumbu Company's projected profit for the coming year is as follows:

	Total	Per Unit
Sales	$2,040,000	$24
Total variable cost	1,530,000	18
Contribution margin	$ 510,000	$ 6
Total fixed cost	380,400	
Operating income	$ 129,600	

Required:

1. Compute the break-even point in units.
2. How many units must be sold to earn a profit of $240,000?
3. Compute the contribution margin ratio. Using that ratio, compute the additional profit that Khumbu would earn if sales were $160,000 more than expected.
4. For the projected level of sales, compute the margin of safety in units.

Problem 7-52 Break-Even Units, Operating Income, Margin of Safety OBJECTIVE ◀ 1 ◀ 5

Kallard Manufacturing Company produces t-shirts screen-printed with the logos of various sports teams. Each shirt is priced at $13.50 and has a unit variable cost of $9.85. Total fixed cost is $197,600.

Required:

1. Compute the break-even point in units. (*Note*: Round answer to the nearest whole unit.)
2. Suppose that Kallard could reduce its fixed costs by $23,500 by reducing the amount of setup and engineering time needed. How many units must be sold to break even in this case? (*Note*: Round answer to the nearest whole unit.)
3. **CONCEPTUAL CONNECTION** How does the reduction in fixed cost affect the break-even point? Operating income? Margin of safety?

Problem 7-53 Contribution Margin, Break-Even Units, Break-Even Sales, Margin of Safety, Degree of Operating Leverage OBJECTIVE ◀ 1 ◀ 2 ◀ 5

Aldovar Company produces a variety of chemicals. One division makes reagents for laboratories. The division's projected income statement for the coming year is:

Sales (203,000 units @ $70)	$14,210,000
Total variable cost	8,120,000
Contribution margin	$ 6,090,000
Total fixed cost	4,945,500
Operating income	$ 1,144,500

Required:

1. Compute the contribution margin per unit, and calculate the break-even point in units. (*Note*: Round answer to the nearest unit.) Calculate the contribution margin ratio and use it to calculate the break-even sales revenue. (*Note*: Round contribution margin ratio to four decimal places, and round the break-even sales revenue to the nearest dollar.)
2. The divisional manager has decided to increase the advertising budget by $250,000. This will increase sales revenues by $1 million. By how much will operating income increase or decrease as a result of this action?
3. Suppose sales revenues exceed the estimated amount on the income statement by $1,500,000. Without preparing a new income statement, by how much are profits underestimated?
4. Compute the margin of safety based on the original income statement.
5. Compute the degree of operating leverage based on the original income statement. If sales revenues are 8% greater than expected, what is the percentage increase in operating income? (*Note*: Round operating leverage to two decimal places.)

Problem 7-54 Multiple-Product Analysis, Changes in Sales Mix, Sales to Earn Target Operating Income OBJECTIVE ◀ 2 ◀ 4

Basu Company produces two types of sleds for playing in the snow: basic sled and aerosled. The projected income for the coming year, segmented by product line, follows:

EXCEL

(*Continued*)

	Basic Sled	Aerosled	Total
Sales	$3,000,000	$2,400,000	$5,400,000
Total variable cost	1,000,000	1,000,000	2,000,000
Contribution margin	$2,000,000	$1,400,000	$3,400,000
Direct fixed cost	778,000	650,000	1,428,000
Product margin	$1,222,000	$ 750,000	$1,972,000
Common fixed cost			198,900
Operating income			$1,773,100

The selling prices are $30 for the basic sled and $60 for the aerosled. (Round break-even packages and break-even units to the nearest whole unit.)

Required:

1. Compute the number of units of each product that must be sold for Basu to break even.
2. Assume that the marketing manager changes the sales mix of the two products so that the ratio is five basic sleds to three aerosleds. Repeat Requirement 1.
3. **CONCEPTUAL CONNECTION** Refer to the original data. Suppose that Basu can increase the sales of aerosleds with increased advertising. The extra advertising would cost an additional $195,000, and some of the potential purchasers of basic sleds would switch to aerosleds. In total, sales of aerosleds would increase by 12,000 units, and sales of basic sleds would decrease by 5,000 units. Would Basu be better off with this strategy?

OBJECTIVE 1 ▶ 2 ▶ 3 ▶ 5   **Problem 7-55 Cost-Volume-Profit Equation, Basic Concepts, Solving for Unknowns**

Legrand Company produces hand cream in plastic jars. Each jar sells for $3.40. The variable cost for each jar (materials, labor, and overhead) totals $2.55. The total fixed cost is $58,140. During the most recent year, 81,600 jars were sold.

Required:

1. What is the break-even point in units for Legrand? What is the margin of safety in units for the most recent year?
2. Prepare an income statement for Legrand's most recent year.
3. How many units must be sold for Legrand to earn a profit of $25,500?
4. What is the level of sales dollars needed for Legrand to earn operating income of 10% of sales?

OBJECTIVE 1 ▶ 5   **Problem 7-56 Contribution Margin Ratio, Break-Even Sales, Operating Leverage**

Elgart Company produces plastic mailboxes. The projected income statement for the coming year follows:

Sales	$460,300
Total variable cost	165,708
Contribution margin	$294,592
Total fixed cost	150,000
Operating income	$144,592

Required:

1. Compute the contribution margin ratio for the mailboxes.
2. How much revenue must Elgart earn in order to break even?
3. What is the effect on the contribution margin ratio if the unit selling price and unit variable cost each increase by 15%?
4. **CONCEPTUAL CONNECTION** Suppose that management has decided to give a 4% commission on all sales. The projected income statement does not reflect this commission. Recompute the contribution margin ratio, assuming that the commission will be paid. What effect does this have on the break-even point?

5. **CONCEPTUAL CONNECTION** If the commission is paid as described in Requirement 4, management expects sales revenues to increase by $80,000. How will this affect operating leverage? Is it a sound decision to implement the commission? Support your answer with appropriate computations.

Problem 7-57 **Multiple Products, Break-Even Analysis, Operating Leverage**

OBJECTIVE ◀ 4 ◀ 5

Carlyle Lighting Products produces two different types of lamps: a floor lamp and a desk lamp. Floor lamps sell for $30, and desk lamps sell for $20. The projected income statement for the coming year follows:

Sales	$600,000
Total variable cost	400,000
Contribution margin	$200,000
Total fixed cost	150,000
Operating income	$ 50,000

The owner of Carlyle estimates that 60% of the sales revenues will be produced by floor lamps and the remaining 40% by desk lamps. Floor lamps are also responsible for 60% of the variable cost. Of the fixed cost, one-third is common to both products, and one-half is directly traceable to the floor lamp product line.

Required:

1. Compute the sales revenue that must be earned for Carlyle to break even. (Round the contribution margin ratio to six digits and sales revenue to the nearest dollar.)
2. Compute the number of floor lamps and desk lamps that must be sold for Carlyle to break even.
3. Compute the degree of operating leverage for Carlyle. Now assume that the actual revenues will be 40% higher than the projected revenues. By what percentage will profits increase with this change in sales volume?

Problem 7-58 **Multiple-Product Break-even**

OBJECTIVE ◀ 1 ◀ 4

Polaris Inc. manufactures two types of metal stampings for the automobile industry: door handles and trim kits. Fixed cost equals $146,000. Each door handle sells for $12 and has variable cost of $9; each trim kit sells for $8 and has variable cost of $5.

Required:

1. What are the contribution margin per unit and the contribution margin ratio for door handles and for trim kits?
2. If Polaris sells 20,000 door handles and 40,000 trim kits, what is the operating income?
3. How many door handles and how many trim kits must be sold for Polaris to break even?
4. **CONCEPTUAL CONNECTION** Assume that Polaris has the opportunity to rearrange its plant to produce only trim kits. If this is done, fixed costs will decrease by $35,000, and 70,000 trim kits can be produced and sold. Is this a good idea? Explain.

Problem 7-59 **Cost-Volume-Profit, Margin of Safety**

OBJECTIVE ◀ 1 ◀ 5

Victoria Company produces a single product. Last year's income statement is as follows:

Sales (29,000 units)	$1,218,000
Total variable cost	812,000
Contribution margin	$ 406,000
Total fixed cost	300,000
Operating income	$ 106,000

(Continued)

Required:

1. Compute the break-even point in units and sales dollars calculated using the break-even units.
2. What was the margin of safety for Victoria last year in sales dollars?
3. Suppose that Victoria is considering an investment in new technology that will increase fixed cost by $250,000 per year but will lower variable costs to 45% of sales. Units sold will remain unchanged. Prepare a budgeted income statement assuming that Victoria makes this investment. What is the new break-even point in sales dollars, assuming that the investment is made?

OBJECTIVE **1 ▶ 5**

Problem 7-60   Cost-Volume-Profit, Margin of Safety

Abraham Company had revenues of $830,000 last year with total variable costs of $647,400 and fixed costs of $110,000.

Required:

1. What is the variable cost ratio for Abraham? What is the contribution margin ratio?
2. What is the break-even point in sales revenue?
3. What was the margin of safety for Abraham last year?
4. **CONCEPTUAL CONNECTION** Abraham is considering starting a multimedia advertising campaign that is supposed to increase sales by $12,000 per year. The campaign will cost $4,500. Is the advertising campaign a good idea? Explain.

OBJECTIVE **1 ▶**

Problem 7-61   Using the Break-Even Equations to Solve for Price and Variable Cost per Unit

Solve the following independent problems.

Required:

1. Andromeda Company's break-even point is 2,400 units. Variable cost per unit is $42; total fixed costs are $67,200 per year. What price does Andromeda charge?
2. Immelt Company charges a price of $6.50; total fixed cost is $314,400 per year, and the break-even point is 131,000 units. What is the variable cost per unit?

OBJECTIVE **1 ▶ 2 ▶ 5**

Problem 7-62   Contribution Margin, Cost-Volume-Profit, Margin of Safety

Candyland Inc. produces a particularly rich praline fudge. Each 10-ounce box sells for $5.60. Variable unit costs are as follows:

Pecans	$0.70
Sugar	0.35
Butter	1.85
Other ingredients	0.34
Box, packing material	0.76
Selling commission	0.20

Fixed overhead cost is $32,300 per year. Fixed selling and administrative costs are $12,500 per year. Candyland sold 35,000 boxes last year.

Required:

1. What is the contribution margin per unit for a box of praline fudge? What is the contribution margin ratio?
2. How many boxes must be sold to break even? What is the break-even sales revenue?
3. What was Candyland's operating income last year?
4. What was the margin of safety in sales dollars?

5. **CONCEPTUAL CONNECTION** Suppose that Candyland Inc. raises the price to $6.20 per box but anticipates a sales drop to 31,500 boxes. What will be the new break-even point in units? Should Candyland raise the price? Explain.

Problem 7-63 Break-Even Sales, Operating Leverage, Change in Income

OBJECTIVE ◀ 1 ◀ 5

Income statements for two different companies in the same industry are as follows:

	Duncan	Macduff
Sales	$375,000	$375,000
Total variable cost	300,000	150,000
Contribution margin	$ 75,000	$225,000
Total fixed cost	50,000	200,000
Operating income	$ 25,000	$ 25,000

Required:

1. Compute the degree of operating leverage for each company.
2. **CONCEPTUAL CONNECTION** Compute the break-even point in dollars for each company. Explain why the break-even point for Macduff is higher.
3. **CONCEPTUAL CONNECTION** Suppose that both companies experience a 30% increase in revenues. Compute the percentage change in profits for each company. Explain why the percentage increase in Macduff's profits is so much larger than that of Duncan.

Problem 7-64 Contribution Margin, Break-Even Sales, Margin of Safety

OBJECTIVE ◀ 1 ◀ 5

Suppose that **Kicker** had the following sales and cost experience (in thousands of dollars) for May of the current year and for May of the prior year:

EXCEL

	May, Current Year	May, Prior Year
Total sales	$ 43,560	$ 41,700
Materials	(17,000)	(16,000)
Labor and supplies	(1,400)	(1,200)
Commissions	(1,250)	(1,100)
Contribution margin	$ 23,910	$ 23,400
Fixed warehouse cost	(680)	(500)
Fixed administrative cost	(4,300)	(4,300)
Fixed selling cost	(5,600)	(5,000)
Research and development	(9,750)	(4,000)
Operating income	$ 3,580	$ 9,600

In May of the prior year, Kicker started an intensive quality program designed to enable it to build original equipment manufacture (OEM) speaker systems for a major automobile company. The program was housed in research and development. In the beginning of the current year, Kicker's accounting department exercised tighter control over sales commissions, ensuring that no dubious (e.g., double) payments were made. The increased sales in the current year required additional warehouse space that Kicker rented in town. (Round ratios to four decimal places. Round sales dollars computations to the nearest dollar.)

Required:

1. Calculate the contribution margin ratio for May of both years.
2. Calculate the break-even point in sales dollars for both years.
3. Calculate the margin of safety in sales dollars for both years.
4. **CONCEPTUAL CONNECTION** Analyze the differences shown by your calculations in Requirements 1, 2, and 3.

CASES

Case 7-65 Cost-Volume-Profit with Multiple Products, Sales Mix Changes, Changes in Fixed and Variable Costs

Artistic Woodcrafting Inc. began several years ago as a one-person, cabinet-making operation. Employees were added as the business expanded. Last year, sales volume totaled $850,000. Volume for the first five months of the current year totaled $600,000, and sales were expected to be $1.6 million for the entire year. Unfortunately, the cabinet business in the region where Artistic is located is highly competitive. More than 200 cabinet shops are all competing for the same business.

Artistic currently offers two different quality grades of cabinets: Grade I and Grade II, with Grade I being the higher quality. The average unit selling prices, unit variable costs, and direct fixed costs are as follows:

	Unit Price	Unit Variable Cost	Direct Fixed Cost
Grade I	$3,400	$2,686	$95,000
Grade II	1,600	1,328	95,000

Common fixed costs (fixed costs not traceable to either cabinet) are $35,000. Currently, for every three Grade I cabinets sold, seven Grade II cabinets are sold.

Required:

1. Calculate the number of Grade I and Grade II cabinets that are expected to be sold during the current year.
2. Calculate the number of Grade I and Grade II cabinets that must be sold for Artistic to break even.
3. Artistic can buy computer-controlled machines that will make doors, drawers, and frames. If the machines are purchased, the variable costs for each type of cabinet will decrease by 9%, but common fixed cost will increase by $44,000. Compute the effect on operating income, and also calculate the new break-even point. Assume the machines are purchased at the beginning of the sixth month. Fixed costs for the company are incurred uniformly throughout the year.
4. Refer to the original data. Artistic is considering adding a retail outlet. This will increase common fixed cost by $70,000 per year. As a result of adding the retail outlet, the additional publicity and emphasis on quality will allow the firm to change the sales mix to 1:1. The retail outlet is also expected to increase sales by 30%. Assume that the outlet is opened at the beginning of the sixth month. Calculate the effect on the company's expected profits for the current year, and calculate the new break-even point. Assume that fixed costs are incurred uniformly throughout the year.

Case 7-66 Ethics and a Cost-Volume-Profit Application

Danna Lumus, the marketing manager for a division that produces a variety of paper products, is considering the divisional manager's request for a sales forecast for a new line of paper napkins. The divisional manager has been gathering data so that he can choose between two different production processes. The first process would have a variable cost of $10 per case produced and total fixed cost of $100,000. The second process would have a variable cost of $6 per case and total fixed cost of $200,000. The selling price would be $30 per case. Danna had just completed a marketing analysis that projects annual sales of 30,000 cases.

Danna is reluctant to report the 30,000 forecast to the divisional manager. She knows that the first process would be labor intensive, whereas the second would be largely automated with little labor and no requirement for an additional production supervisor. If the first process is chosen, Jerry Johnson, a good friend, will be appointed as the line supervisor. If the second process is chosen, Jerry and an entire line of laborers will be laid off. After some consideration, Danna revises the projected sales downward to 22,000 cases.

She believes that the revision downward is justified. Since it will lead the divisional manager to choose the manual system, it shows a sensitivity to the needs of current employees—a sensitivity that she is afraid her divisional manager does not possess. He is too focused on quantitative factors in his decision making and usually ignores the qualitative aspects.

Required:

1. Compute the break-even point in units for each process.
2. Compute the sales volume for which the two processes are equally profitable. Identify the range of sales for which the manual process is more profitable than the automated process. Identify the range of sales for which the automated process is more profitable than the manual process. Why does the divisional manager want the sales forecast?
3. Discuss Danna's decision to alter the sales forecast. Do you agree with it? Is she acting ethically? Is her decision justified since it helps a number of employees retain their employment? Should the impact on employees be factored into decisions? In fact, is it unethical not to consider the impact of decisions on employees?

Making the Connection

Cost Behavior and Cost-Volume-Profit Analysis for Many Glacier Hotel

Chapters	Objectives	Examples
2	2-2	3-2
3	3-3	7-2
7	7-1	7-5
	7-2	7-7
	7-4	7-9
	7-5	

The purpose of this integrated exercise is to demonstrate the interrelationship between cost estimation techniques and subsequent uses of cost information. In particular, this exercise illustrates how the variable and fixed cost information estimated from a high-low analysis can be used in a single- and multiple-product CVP analysis.

Using the High-Low Method to Estimate Variable and Fixed Costs

Located on Swiftcurrent Lake in Glacier National Park, **Many Glacier Hotel** was built in 1915 by the Great Northern Railway. In an effort to supplement its lodging revenue, the hotel decided in 20X1 to begin manufacturing and selling small wooden canoes decorated with symbols hand painted by Native Americans living near the park. Due to the great success of the canoes, the hotel began manufacturing and selling paddles as well in 20X3. Many hotel guests purchase a canoe and paddles for use in self-guided tours of Swiftcurrent Lake. Because production of the two products began in different years, the canoes and paddles are produced in separate production facilities and employ different laborers. Each canoe sells for $500, and each paddle sells for $50. A 20X3 fire destroyed the hotel's accounting records. However, a new system put into place before the 20X4 season provides the following aggregated data for the hotel's canoe and paddle manufacturing and marketing activities:

Manufacturing Data:

Year	Number of Canoes Manufactured	Total Canoe Manufacturing Costs	Year	Number of Paddles Manufactured	Total Paddle Manufacturing Costs
20X9	250	$103,000	20X9	900	$38,500
20X8	275	128,000	20X8	1,200	49,000
20X7	240	108,000	20X7	1,000	44,000
20X6	310	114,000	20X6	1,100	45,500
20X5	350	141,500	20X5	1,400	52,000
20X4	400	140,000	20X4	1,700	66,500

Marketing Data:

Year	Number of Canoes Sold	Total Canoe Marketing Costs	Year	Number of Paddles Sold	Total Paddle Marketing Costs
20X9	250	$45,000	20X9	900	$ 7,500
20X8	275	43,000	20X8	1,200	9,000
20X7	240	44,000	20X7	1,000	8,000
20X6	310	51,000	20X6	1,100	8,500
20X5	350	62,000	20X5	1,400	10,000
20X4	400	60,000	20X4	1,700	11,500

Required:

1. High-Low Cost Estimation Method

   a. Use the high-low method to estimate the per-unit variable costs and total fixed costs for the *canoe* product line.
   b. Use the high-low method to estimate the per-unit variable costs and total fixed costs for the *paddle* product line.

2. Cost-Volume-Profit Analysis, Single-Product Setting

   Use CVP analysis to calculate the break-even point in units for
   a. The *canoe* product line *only* (i.e., single-product setting)
   b. The *paddle* product line *only* (i.e., single-product setting)

3. Cost-Volume-Profit Analysis, Multiple-Product Setting

   The hotel's accounting system data show an average sales mix of approximately 300 canoes and 1,200 paddles each season. Significantly more paddles are sold relative to canoes because some inexperienced canoe guests accidentally break one or more paddles, while other guests purchase additional paddles as presents for friends and relatives. In addition, for this multiple-product CVP analysis, assume the existence of an additional $30,000 of common fixed costs for a customer service hotline used for both canoe and paddle customers. Use CVP analysis to calculate the break-even point in units for both the canoe and paddle product lines combined (i.e., the multiple-product setting).

4. Cost Classification

   a. Classify the manufacturing costs, marketing costs, and customer service hotline costs either as production costs or period costs.
   b. For the period costs, further classify them into either selling expenses or general and administrative expenses.

5. Sensitivity Cost-Volume-Profit Analysis and Production Versus Period Costs, Multiple-Product Setting

   If both the variable and fixed *production* costs (refer to your answer to Requirement 1) associated with the *canoe* product line increased by 5% (beyond the estimate from the high-low analysis), how many canoes and paddles would need to be sold in order to earn a target income of $96,000? Assume the same sales mix and additional fixed costs as in Requirement 3.

6. Margin of Safety

   Calculate the hotel's margin of safety (both in units and in sales dollars) for Many Glacier Hotel, assuming the same facts as in Requirement 3, and assuming that it sells 700 canoes and 2,500 paddles next year.

8

Tactical Decision Making and Relevant Analysis

After studying Chapter 8, you should be able to:

1 Describe the short-run decision-making model, and explain how cost behavior affects the information used to make decisions.

2 Apply relevant costing and decision-making concepts in a variety of business situations.

3 Choose the optimal product mix when faced with one constrained resource.

4 Explain the impact of cost on pricing decisions.

Dave Martin/Getty Images Sport/Getty Images

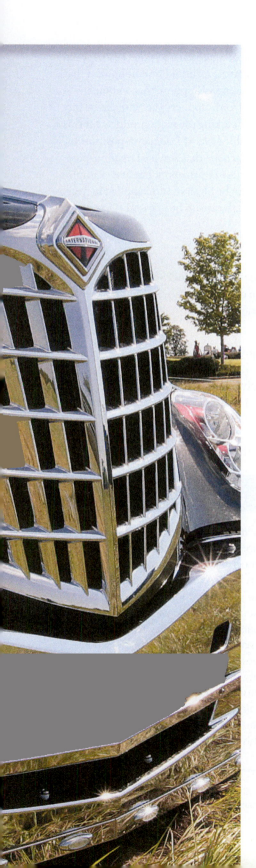

EXPERIENCE MANAGERIAL DECISIONS

with Navistar, Inc.

Relevant decision analysis represents one of the most exciting and widely applicable managerial accounting tools in existence. One big proponent of relevant analysis is **Navistar, Inc.**, a multibillion Fortune 300 company founded in 1902. More than 100 years later, the company has grown to manufacture components and electronics for a wide variety of vehicles, including buses, tractor trailers, military vehicles, and trucks, for its diverse customers all around the world.

Faced with important, long-term growth issues, Navistar used relevant analysis to decide whether to expand axle production at its truck assembly plant in Ontario or to outsource its extra axle production requirements to an outside supplier company. Before the analysis could be conducted, Navistar's managerial accountants first had to identify all relevant factors, both quantitative and qualitative, as well as the short- and long-term impacts of these factors. Some factors were relatively easy to identify and measure, such as the labor cost that would be required if the additional axles were made in-house or the cost of acquiring the extra factory space needed to produce the additional axles in-house. However, other factors, such as the need to eliminate bottlenecks that would be created from producing the additional axles in-house, complicated the in-house analysis.

> "Faced with important, long-term growth issues, Navistar used relevant analysis to decide whether to expand axle production at its truck assembly plant in Ontario."

In addition, if Navistar decided to make the additional axles in-house, it would require significant capacity-related capital expenditures. That carried a risk associated with the possibility that the current demand for additional axles might not persist in the long term. In this case, Navistar would be stuck with the cost of the additional capacity without the business to generate additional revenues to cover those costs. On the other hand, if the additional axle production were outsourced, Navistar would have to ensure that its new axle supplier partnered with the Canadian Auto Workers union to minimize the outsourcing effect on Navistar's existing workforce labor agreements. Furthermore, suppliers would have to be trained to deliver parts and subassemblies in sequence with Navistar's demanding schedule. This training represented a considerable outsourcing cost to Navistar.

In the end, the relevant costing analysis helped Navistar's executives decide to outsource its additional axle production. As a result, Navistar's Ontario plant has enjoyed annual cost savings of over $3 million! A careful analysis of all relevant factors helped the company make the right decision and avoid being burdened in the long run by the costs of excess capacity that occur in the always cyclical truck assembly business.

CONCEPT CLIP

SHORT-RUN DECISION MAKING

Short-run decision making consists of choosing among alternatives with an immediate or limited end in view. Short-term decisions sometimes are referred to as tactical, or relevant, decisions because they involve choosing between alternatives with an immediate or limited time frame in mind. Strategic decisions, on the other hand, usually are long term in nature because they involve choosing between different strategies that attempt to provide a competitive advantage over a long time frame. Accepting a special order for less than the normal selling price to utilize idle excess capacity and to increase this year's profits is an example of a tactical decision (i.e., a special sales decision). While such decisions tend to be *short run* in nature, it should be emphasized that they often have long-run consequences. Consider a second example. Suppose that a company is thinking about producing a component instead of buying it from suppliers (i.e., a make-or-buy decision). The immediate objective may be to lower the cost of making the main product. Yet this decision may be a small part of the overall strategy of establishing a cost leadership position for the firm. Therefore, short-run decisions often are *small-scale actions* that serve a larger purpose. Students find tactical decision making an especially exciting issue to learn about because examples of make-or-buy, special sales, and segment analysis decisions can be observed and applied in nearly every community, involving both large corporations and local start-up businesses!

The Decision-Making Model

Here's **Why It's important**

How does a company go about making good short-run decisions? A **decision model**, such as the one below, is a specific set of procedures that produces a decision. It can be used to structure the decision maker's thinking and to organize the information.

Step 1. Recognize and define the problem.

Step 2. Identify alternatives as possible solutions to the problem. Eliminate alternatives that clearly are not feasible.

Step 3. Identify the costs and benefits associated with each feasible alternative. Classify costs and benefits as relevant or irrelevant, and eliminate irrelevant ones from consideration.

Step 4. Estimate the relevant costs and benefits for each feasible alternative.

Step 5. Assess qualitative factors.

Step 6. Make the decision by selecting the alternative with the greatest overall net benefit.

Here's How It's Used: IN YOUR COLLEGE TOWN

As an inquisitive undergraduate business major, Jack wondered if the relevant decisions mentioned in his managerial accounting class could actually be observed in his college town. He quickly identified a number of exciting relevant decisions at work in the uptown businesses he frequented near campus. For instance, Jack noticed numerous product-line additions (i.e., *keep-or-drop decisions*), including the unveiling of two additional **Starbucks** cafes, **Chipotle**'s initial entry into town, and even the arrival of an **Apple Store**! He also noticed that the **Target** pharmacy where he used to fill all of his prescriptions had been converted into a **CVS Pharmacy**, even though it was still located within the Target store![1] Examples of relevant decisions also cropped up on campus. When Jack's senior pre-med roommate, Daniel, registered for his capstone course, he was told that it had been

outsourced (i.e., *make-or-buy decisions*) to an online university that specialized in certain senior-level medical courses. The dean informed Daniel that it was much cheaper for the university to allow its few pre-med students to take the course from another university rather than hire the specialized instructors necessary to teach the course in-house. Finally, Jack was disappointed when his intramural basketball tournament was moved away from the university arena to make way for the local high school graduation. After some investigation, he learned that the university often rented out its high-end capacity assets (e.g., auditorium, sports arenas, business school atrium) to outside organizations (i.e., *special sales decisions*). To Jack's surprise, relevant decisions were quite common in his college town, which excited him to study this useful topic!

---

1 "Target Pharmacy and Clinic Conversions to CVS Pharmacy and Minute Clinic Underway." Taken from https://corporate.target.com/article/2016/02/cvs-target-pharmacy-clinic-conversion.

The decision-making model just described has six steps. Nothing is special about this particular listing. You may find it more useful to break the steps into 8 or 10 segments. Alternatively, you may find it useful to aggregate them into a shorter list. For example, you could use a three-step model:

Step 1. Identify the decision.
Step 2. Identify alternatives and their associated relevant costs.
Step 3. Make the decision.

The key point is to find a comfortable way for you to remember the important steps in the decision-making model. The following discussion presents a decision model that builds toward a definition of relevance that can be applied to potentially important financial items, such as costs and revenues, to make effective tactical business decisions.

To illustrate the decision-making model, consider Audio-Blast Inc., a company that manufactures speaker systems for new automobiles. Recently, Audio-Blast was approached by a major automobile manufacturer about the possibility of installing Audio-Blast's main product—the mega-blast speaker system—into its new sports car. Audio-Blast speakers would be installed at the factory. Suppose that Audio-Blast decides to pursue the speaker order from the automobile manufacturer. Currently, the company does not have sufficient productive and storage capacity to fulfill the order. How might the decision-making model help Audio-Blast find the best way of obtaining that capacity?

Step 1: Recognize and Define the Problem

The first step is to recognize and define a specific problem. For example, the members of Audio-Blast's management team recognized the need for additional productive capacity as well as increased space for raw materials and finished goods inventories. The number of workers and the amount of space needed, the reasons for the need, and how the additional space would be used are all important dimensions of the problem. However, the central question is *how* to acquire the additional capacity.

Step 2: Identify the Alternatives as Possible Solutions

The second step is to list and consider possible solutions. Suppose that the production head and the consulting engineer identified the following possible solutions:

1. Build a new factory with sufficient capacity to handle current and foreseeable needs.
2. Lease a larger facility, and sublease its current facility.
3. Lease an additional, similar facility.
4. Institute a second shift in the main factory, and lease an additional building that would be used for storage of raw materials and finished goods inventories only, thereby freeing up space for expanded production.
5. Outsource production to another company, and resell the speakers to the auto manufacturer.

As part of this step, Audio-Blast's upper management team met to discuss and eliminate alternatives that clearly were not feasible. The first alternative was eliminated because it carried too much risk for the company. The order had not even been secured, and the popularity of the new sports car model was not proven. The second alternative was rejected because the economy in Audio-Blast's small town was such that subleasing a facility of its size was not possible. The third alternative was eliminated because it went too far in solving the space problem and, presumably, was too expensive. The fourth and fifth alternatives were feasible; they were within the cost and risk constraints and solved the needs of the company. Notice that the president linked the short-run decision (increase productive capacity) to the company's overall growth strategy by rejecting alternatives that involved too much risk at this stage of the company's development.

Step 3: Identify the Costs and Benefits Associated with Each Feasible Alternative

In the third step, the costs and benefits associated with each feasible alternative are identified. At this point, clearly irrelevant costs can be eliminated from consideration. (It is fine to include irrelevant costs and benefits in the analysis as long as they are included for *all* alternatives. We usually do not include them because focusing only on the relevant costs and benefits reduces the amount of data to be collected.) Typically, the controller's department is responsible for gathering necessary data.

Assume that Audio-Blast determines that the costs of making 20,000 speakers include the following:

$$\text{Direct Materials } (\$60,000) + \text{Direct Labor } (\$110,000) + \text{Variable Overhead } (\$10,000)$$
$$= \text{Total Variable Production Cost } (\underline{\$180,000})$$

In addition, a second shift must be put in place and a warehouse must be leased to store raw materials and finished goods inventories if Audio-Blast continues to manufacture the speakers internally. Additional costs of the second shift, including a production supervisor and part-time maintenance and engineering, amount to $90,000 per year. A building that could serve as a warehouse is sitting empty across the street and can be rented for $20,000 per year. Costs of operating the building for inventory storage, including telephone and Internet access as well as salaries of materials handlers, would amount to $80,000 per year. The second alternative is to purchase the speakers externally and use the freed-up production space for inventory. An outside supplier has offered to supply sufficient volume for $360,000 per year.

Note that when the cash flow patterns become complicated for competing alternatives, it is difficult to produce a stream of equal cash flows for each alternative. In such a case, more sophisticated procedures can and should be used for the analysis. These procedures are discussed in Chapter 12, which deals with the long-run investment decisions referred to as *capital expenditure decisions*.

Step 4: Estimate the Relevant Costs and Benefits for Each Feasible Alternative

We now see that the fourth alternative—continuing to produce internally and leasing more space—costs $370,000. The fifth alternative—purchasing outside and using internal space—costs $360,000. The comparison follows:

Alternative 4		Alternative 5	
Variable cost of production	$180,000	Purchase price	$360,000
Added second shift costs	90,000		
Building lease and operating costs	100,000		
Total	$370,000		

The **differential cost** is the difference between the summed costs of two alternatives in a decision. Notice that the differential cost is $10,000 in favor of the fifth alternative. Typically, a differential cost compares the sum of each alternative's *relevant* costs only, as in the differential cost comparison of Alternatives 4 and 5. Emphasis on differential cost allows decision makers to include irrelevant costs in the alternatives if they choose to do so. However, the inclusion of irrelevant costs is acceptable *only if all irrelevant costs are included for each alternative*. For example, suppose that the controller had included fixed manufacturing cost that must be paid whether or not the speakers are made internally or externally. Then, the total cost of each alternative would increase, but the differential cost would still be $10,000. Again, as noted earlier in the chapter, it is recommended to compare only relevant costs because the inclusion of irrelevant costs often adds unnecessary data collection expenses and confusion in communicating additional information that is not relevant to the given analysis.

Step 5: Assess Qualitative Factors

While the costs and revenues associated with the alternatives are important, they do not tell the whole story. Qualitative factors can significantly affect the manager's decision. Qualitative factors simply are those factors that are hard to quantify in financial terms, including things like political pressure and product safety.

- *Political Pressure*: Companies like **Levi's** that relocate some or all of their U.S. manufacturing facilities to countries outside of the United States with cheaper labor or lower water costs often face stiff political pressure in the United States as a result of such offshoring decisions. Some managers worry that such political pressure from customers can have long-term negative effects on sales that more than offset the labor cost savings that spurred the decision to offshore.
- *Product Safety*: Product safety represents another key qualitative factor for outsourcing organizations, as illustrated by the trouble **Toyota** faced when it appeared to let its product quality slip by postponing safety recalls to save money in the short term. **Mattel** also discovered the importance of safety as a key qualitative factor when it discovered that its Chinese suppliers used illegal lead paint on thousands of its toys, which led to an onslaught of toy recalls and a decrease in parents' trust of Mattel's products.

Returning to Audio-Blast, its president likely would be concerned with qualitative considerations such as the quality of the speakers purchased externally, the reliability of supply sources, the expected stability of prices over the next several years, labor relations, community image, and so on. To illustrate the possible impact of qualitative factors on Audio-Blast's decision, consider the first two factors, quality and reliability of supply:

- *Quality:* If the quality of speakers is significantly less when purchased externally from what is available internally, then the quantitative advantage from purchasing may be more fictitious than real. Reselling lower-quality speakers to such a high-profile buyer could permanently damage Audio-Blast's reputation. Because of this possibility, Audio-Blast may choose to continue to produce the speakers internally. For example, poor quality led U.S. safety regulators to recall over 70 million **Takata** air bag inflators from various automobiles. This costly recall was the largest in U.S. history.
- *Reliability of Supply:* If supply sources are not reliable, production schedules could be interrupted, and customer orders could arrive late. For example, the tsunami off the coast of Japan significantly disrupted supply chains across the globe for numerous companies from **Sony** to **Honda** to **Apple**. The eruption of an Icelandic volcano also posed tremendous business interruption challenges.[2] In addition, increasingly common and costly customer information breaches at many organizations, such as **Target**, force managers to include data integrity as an important qualitative factor to consider when making tactical decisions regarding supplier selection.[3] These factors can increase labor costs and overhead and hurt sales. Again, depending on the perceived trade-offs, Audio-Blast may decide that producing the speakers internally is better than purchasing them, even if relevant cost analysis gives the initial advantage to purchasing.

How should qualitative factors be handled in the decision-making process? First, they must be identified. Secondly, the decision maker should try to quantify them. Often, qualitative factors are difficult, but not impossible, to quantify. For example, possible unreliability of the outside supplier might be quantified as the probable number of late delivery days multiplied by the penalty Audio-Blast would be charged by the auto manufacturer for later delivery.

More difficult measurement challenges exist. For example, **Mobil Corporation** decided to implement a strategic change of focusing on a new target audience, including "road warriors"

---

2   Dave Lenckus, "Coverage Trends in Manufacturing's 'Big 3' Risks: Workers' Comp, Product Recall, and Supply Chains," *Life Health Pro* (February 9, 2012). Taken from www.lifehealthpro.com/2012/02/09/coverage-trends-in-manufacturings-big-3-risks-work.

3   Tom Webb, "Analyst Sees Target Data Breach Costs Topping $1 Billion," *Pioneer Press* (January 30, 2014). Taken from www.twincities.com/business/ci_25029900/analyst-sees-target-data-breach-costs-topping-1.

Here's How It's Used: AT KICKER

Two years ago, the loan officer at **Kicker**'s bank left for another job out of state. This departure was an excellent time for Kicker to reevaluate its banking relationship. The company took a number of bids from the four major banks in town. In the process, Kicker executives learned a great deal about various banking services and the way that banks charged for them. Some examples include Internet service, loan rates, credit card transactions, returned check fees, and wire fees. Qualitative factors played a role in the ultimate decision. For example, how quickly does the bank respond? Does Kicker feel comfortable with its banking officer (is she or he knowledgeable about the speaker and electronics industry and attuned to Kicker's special needs)? After weighing both the monetary and nonmonetary factors, Kicker switched banks.

(employees who drive a lot), "true blues" (affluent, loyal customers), and generation F3 (yuppies on the go who want fuel, want food, and want them fast).[4] However, successful implementation required that the company find a way to measure the experience of new target customers at newly designed Mobil gas pumps and convenience stores. After considerable thought, an innovative manager developed one of the first recognized "secret shopper" programs in which Mobil employees secretly dressed as customers in order to live the Mobil gas station "experience." These secret shoppers then recorded numerous aspects of their experience on quantitative scales for feedback to station managers. Without such evaluative data, it would have been extremely difficult for Mobil managers to assess the causes of success or failure of the new strategy implementation. Finally, truly qualitative factors, such as the impact of late orders on customer relations, must be taken into consideration in the final step of the decision-making model—the selection of the alternative with the greatest overall benefit.

Step 6: Make the Decision

Once all relevant costs and benefits for each alternative have been assessed and the qualitative factors weighed, a decision can be made.

The most challenging step of this decision-making model is Step 4, because it involves estimating the relevant cost and relevant revenues for each decision alternative under consideration. However, in order to estimate these relevant financial items, managers must clearly understand what it means for a financial item to be relevant. Without a useful definition of relevance, managers include unnecessary information that is costly to collect, verify, and explain to other interested parties affected by the given decision. As demonstrated throughout this chapter, understanding which costs and revenues are relevant helps managers to make more effective tactical decisions, including make-or-buy, special sales, product/service line, keep-or-drop, further processing, and product mix. Therefore, this section concludes by defining relevance.

Here's **Why It's important**

Ethical Decisions

Ethics

Ethical concerns revolve around the way in which decisions are implemented and the possible sacrifice of long-run objectives for short-run gain. Relevant costs are used in making short-run decisions. However, decision makers should always maintain an ethical framework. Reaching objectives is important, but how you get there is perhaps more important. Unfortunately, many managers have the opposite view. Part of the reason for the problem is the extreme pressure to perform that many managers face. Often, the individual who is not a top performer may be laid

---

4   Marc Epstein and Bill Birchard, *Counting What Counts: Turning Corporate Accountability to Competitive Advantage* (New York, NY: Perseus Books, 2000).

off or demoted. Under such conditions, there is great temptation to engage in questionable behavior today and to let the future take care of itself. Unfortunately, as the historic banking regulatory upheaval of the late 2000s demonstrates, many financial services institutions in the mid-2000s yielded to unethical temptations to lend excessive amounts of money to prospective homeowners who in the end could not afford such loans. Whenever relevant costing is used, it is important to include all costs that are relevant—including those involving ethical ramifications. ●

Relevant Costs Defined

The decision-making approach just described emphasized the importance of identifying and using *relevant* financial items. While costs comprise the majority of important financial items in relevant decision analyses, revenues can play an important role as well and, as such, the following definition of relevance applies to both costs and revenues. **Relevant costs** (and revenues) possess two characteristics: (1) they are *future* items AND (2) they *differ* across alternatives. All pending decisions relate to the future. Accordingly, only future costs and future revenues can be relevant to decisions. However, to be relevant, a cost or revenue must not only be a future item but must also differ from one alternative to another. If a future cost or revenue is the same for more than one alternative, then it has no effect on the decision. Such an item is *irrelevant*. The ability to identify relevant and irrelevant costs (and revenues) is a very important decision-making skill.

Here's **Why It's important**

CONCEPT CLIP

Relevant Costs Illustrated   Consider Audio-Blast's make-or-buy alternatives. The cost of direct labor to produce the additional 20,000 speakers is $110,000. In order to determine if this $110,000 is a relevant cost, we need to ask the following:

1. *Is the direct labor cost a future cost?*
    It is certainly a future cost. Producing the speakers for the auto manufacturer requires the services of direct laborers who must be paid.
2. *Does it differ across the two alternatives?*
    If the speakers are purchased from an external supplier, then a second shift, with its direct labor, will not be needed. Thus, the cost of direct labor *differs* across alternatives ($110,000 for the make alternative, and $0 for the buy alternative).

Therefore, it is a relevant cost.

   Implicit in this analysis is the use of a past cost to estimate a future cost. The most recent cost of direct labor has averaged $5.50 per speaker; for 20,000 speakers, the direct labor will cost $110,000. This past cost was used as the estimate of next year's cost. Although past costs are not relevant, they often are used to predict what future costs will be.

Opportunity Costs   Another type of relevant cost is opportunity cost. **Opportunity cost** is the benefit sacrificed or forgone when one alternative is chosen over another. Therefore, an opportunity cost is relevant because it is both a future cost and one that differs across alternatives. While an opportunity cost is not an accounting cost, because accountants do not record the cost of what might happen in the future (i.e., they do not appear in financial statements), it is an important consideration in relevant decision making.

   For example, if you are deciding whether to work full time or to go to school full time, the opportunity cost of going to school would be the wages you give up by not working. Companies also include opportunity costs in many of their decision analyses. When international accounting firm **EY** estimates the net benefit of sending thousands of its accountants to week-long training courses, it includes the opportunity cost of the tens of millions of dollars in lost revenue that it forgoes by not being able to bill clients for the time accountants spend in training. Oftentimes, opportunity costs are quite challenging to estimate. However, their inclusion can change the

Here's How It's Used: IN YOUR LIFE

Finding ways to generate extra cash appeals to almost everyone, especially college students. At the end of each semester, Allyson has to make an important decision regarding what to do with her textbooks—either keep them *or* sell them back to the university bookstore. After taking her last exam, she ran to the bookstore and learned that each of her five textbooks could be sold for $25 per book. She quickly calculated that the opportunity cost of her keeping the books (i.e., not selling them back to the bookstore) was $125, which would go a long way for some end-of-the-semester beverages or Christmas presents for friends and family. However, as she placed her books upon the buyback counter, she quickly wondered if there was an opportunity cost of *selling* (i.e., not keeping) them that she should estimate before collecting her cash. And if there was an opportunity cost of selling the books, how would she estimate this cost? Allyson will need

to determine the likelihood that she will want to access any of the information in the books during her remaining courses or upcoming professional internship. If so, she also will need to estimate the amount of time she would need to spend finding such information when she no longer has access to her old textbooks, plus the monetary value she places on her time spent searching for this needed information. For example, Allyson believes that her roommate asked to borrow one of her textbooks while on an **Apple** internship this semester to help prepare geographically segmented income statements. Suddenly, Allyson wasn't so sure that the opportunity cost of selling back her textbooks was $0. Increasingly, she wondered whether she might even be better off financially by *keeping* her textbooks this semester because the opportunity cost of selling them back to the bookstore could actually be *higher* than the opportunity cost of keeping them!

final result of the analysis, such as whether to accept or reject a special sales opportunity or to outsource a product rather than make it in-house. Therefore, managerial accountants have the ability to add significant value to relevant decision making by finding ways to measure particularly challenging opportunity costs.

Irrelevant Past Cost Illustrated   Audio-Blast uses large power saws to cut the lumber that forms the housings for speakers. These saws were purchased 3 years ago and are being depreciated at an annual rate of $25,000. In order to determine if this $25,000 is a relevant cost, we need to ask the following:

1. *Is the depreciation cost a future cost?*
    Depreciation represents an allocation of a cost already incurred. It is a **sunk cost**, a cost that cannot be affected by any future action. Although we allocate this sunk cost to future periods and call that allocation depreciation, none of the original cost is avoidable.
2. *Does it differ across the two alternatives?*
    Sunk costs are always the same across alternatives and, therefore, always irrelevant.

Thus, depreciation costs, like all sunk costs, fail to possess the two characteristics required of relevant costs and, therefore, always are irrelevant.

In choosing between the two alternatives, the original cost of the power saws and their associated depreciation are not relevant factors. However, it should be noted that salvage value of the machinery is a relevant cost for certain decisions. For example, if Audio-Blast decides to transform itself into a distributor, not a producer, of speakers, the amount that can be realized from the sale of the power equipment will be relevant and will be included as a benefit of the switch to distributor status.

Sunk costs   It is important to note the psychology behind managers' treatment of sunk costs. Although managers *should ignore* sunk costs for relevant decisions, such as whether or not to continue funding a particular product in the future, it unfortunately is human nature to allow sunk costs to affect these decisions. For example, **Toshiba** and its HD DVD product team engaged in a fierce, multiyear battle with **Sony** and its Blu-ray product team for recognition as the universally accepted format in the growing next-generation high-definition DVD market. Throughout the battle, both sides spent millions of dollars developing, manufacturing, and advertising their own format. However, Sony's Blu-ray sales trounced Toshiba's HD DVD sales one Christmas shopping season, which prompted Hollywood giant **Warner Bros.** to decide to release its films only on Sony's Blu-ray format, rather than on both formats as it had done previously. (The other major production companies had already sided with Sony as well.) Around the same time, some retailers announced they would only carry DVDs with the Blu-ray format. To objective entertainment business experts outside of Toshiba, this decision by Warner Bros. was the final blow to Toshiba's format and it was obvious that the HD DVD product line should be discontinued immediately to cut its losses and stop the financial bleeding. However, rather than ignore its significant sunk costs by cutting its future losses, Toshiba announced that it was "unwilling to concede defeat in the next-generation-DVD battle" and decided to launch an "aggressive advertising campaign to promote its [Toshiba's] HD DVD players and slash prices about 50%."[5] Therefore, not only did Toshiba continue to spend money developing, manufacturing, and marketing its failed product, it expected to earn only about half of the regular sales revenue per unit sold. Eventually, even Toshiba recognized the handwriting on the wall and dropped its HD DVD format, but only after throwing away a considerable amount of money on a product that most experts believed should have been dropped much earlier.

Another classic example of inappropriately honoring sunk costs is **Coca-Cola**'s New Coke debacle in the mid-1980s. The development and launching of New Coke was very costly and also an undeniably huge failure. However, Coca-Cola unwisely elected to continue to spend money to advertise and maintain its failed new product simply because it had already spent so much money on the product in the past. As business experts repeatedly noted, no amount of advertising cost was going to change the company's past expenditures to develop and launch New Coke and the company would have been far better off to scrap New Coke as soon as its failure was apparent.

The **XFL** football league and the **Concorde** supersonic jet over a period of 20 years are additional examples of companies that failed to cut their losses and drop their product or service and instead continued to pour money into past failed ideas because of their large associated sunk costs. Inappropriately honoring sunk costs poses challenges for lawmakers as well. For example, Boston's "Big Dig" and Seattle's "Bertha" tunneling projects faced massive cost overruns and long delays. While some lawmakers correctly noted that the government should recognize the cost overruns, design flaws, and other problems by no longer "throwing good money out for bad," other lawmakers succumbed to the allure of sunk costs and doubled down by reiterating "our focus and commitment now, as it was then [when the project began six years earlier], is on delivering this critical safety project to the people of Washington."[6]

Irrelevant Future Cost Illustrated Suppose that Audio-Blast currently pays an Internet provider $5,000 per year to store its website on the server. Since Audio-Blast intends to keep the web page no matter what is decided regarding the potential speaker order, that cost is not relevant to the decision.

The same concepts apply to benefits. One alternative may produce an amount of future benefits different from another alternative (e.g., differences in future revenues). If future benefits differ across alternatives, then they are relevant and should be included in the analysis.

Cost Behavior and Relevant Costs

Most short-run decisions require extensive consideration of cost behavior. It is easy to fall into the trap of believing that variable costs are relevant and fixed costs are not. But this assumption is not true. For example, the variable costs of production were relevant to Audio-Blast's decision. The fixed costs associated with the existing factory were not relevant. However, the additional fixed cost of the supervisor for a second shift was relevant to the decision.

---

5 Michelle Kessler, "Toshiba Turns Up Heat in DVD War," *USA Today* (January 15, 2008): 4B.

6 Victoria Cavaliere, "Washington State Bill Would Scrap Delayed Seattle Tunnel Project," *Reuters* (January 27, 2015). Taken from http://www.reuters.com/article/us-usa-seattle-tunnel-idUSKBN0L02NM20150127.

The key point is that changes in supply and demand for resources must be considered when assessing relevance. If changes in demand and supply for resources across alternatives bring about changes in spending, then the changes in resource spending are the relevant costs that should be used in assessing the relative desirability of the two alternatives.

Flexible resources can be easily purchased in the amount needed and at the time of use. For example, electricity used to run stoves that boil fruit in the production of jelly is a resource that can be acquired and used as needed. Thus, if the jelly manufacturer wants to increase production of jelly, electricity will increase just enough to satisfy that demand. This type of resource is typically referred to as a strictly variable cost.

Some resources are purchased before they are used. Clearly, investment in a factory of a particular size falls into this category; so does a year-to-year lease of office space or equipment. These costs usually are treated as fixed costs. If the decision covers a situation shorter than the time period for which the resource is fixed, then this cost usually is irrelevant.

Still other resources are acquired in advance of usage through implicit contracting; they are usually acquired in lumpy amounts. In Chapter 3, these costs were shown as step costs. This category might include an organization's salaried and hourly employees. The implicit understanding is that the organization will maintain employment levels even though there may be temporary downturns in the quantity of an activity used. This understanding means that an activity may have unused capacity available. Recall that the relevant range is important in considering step costs. As long as a company remains within the relevant range, it will not go up or down a step, so the cost is fixed for all intents and purposes.

For example, assume that a company has three purchasing agents, each of whom can process 15,000 purchase orders a year. This assumption means that the existing staff can handle 45,000 purchase orders a year. If the company is processing only 40,000 purchase orders, then there is some unused capacity in purchasing. If the company is considering a special order that will require an additional 2,000 purchase orders, then there is no increased cost to purchasing. However, if the company considers an expansion that will require an additional 8,000 purchase orders per year, then an additional staffing cost will need to be incurred in purchasing.

Check Point

1. **Apply the decision-making model outlined in this section to a problem you have faced. For example, the problem might be whether or not to go to college or which car to buy. Include all of the steps. Will the application of the decision-making model help you to make the decision? Why or why not?**

   Answer:
   Answers will vary.

2. **List the six steps of the decision-making model, and briefly explain how each one applies to your decision.**

   Answer:
   Answers will vary.

OBJECTIVE **2**

Apply relevant costing and decision-making concepts in a variety of business situations.

SOME COMMON RELEVANT COST APPLICATIONS

Relevant costing is of value in solving many different types of problems. Traditionally, these applications include decisions:

- to make or buy a component.
- to accept a special order at less than the usual price.

- to keep or drop a segment or product or service line.
- to further process joint products or sell them at the split-off point.

Though by no means an exhaustive list, many of the same decision-making principles apply to a variety of problems.

Make-or-Buy Decisions

Managers often face the decision of whether to make a particular product (or provide a service) or to purchase it from an outside supplier. A manufacturer may need to consider whether to make or buy components used in manufacturing. A manager of a service firm may need to decide whether to provide a service in-house or to outsource it. For example, many large accounting firms increasingly are sending certain accounting service tasks overseas in an effort to reduce their U.S. staff accountant labor costs, as well as to free up U.S. staff accountants' time for more challenging, value-adding service tasks. **Make-or-buy decisions** are those decisions involving a choice between internal and external production. Exhibit 8.1 illustrates the make-or-buy decision.

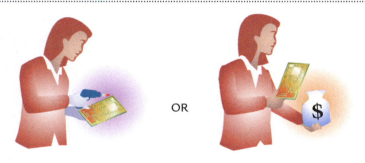

OR

Exhibit 8.1
Make-or-Buy Decisions

Assume that Swasey Manufacturing currently produces an electronic component used in one of its printers. In one year, Swasey will switch production to another type of printer, and the electronic component will not be used. However, for the coming year, Swasey must produce 10,000 of these parts to support the production requirements for the old printer.

A potential supplier has approached Swasey about the component. The supplier will build the electronic component to Swasey's specifications for $4.75 per unit. The offer sounds very attractive, since the full manufacturing cost per unit is $8.20. Should Swasey Manufacturing make or buy the component?

Here's How It's Used: AT NAVISTAR, INC.

Let's return briefly to **Navistar, Inc.**'s use of relevant analysis in making the make-or-buy decision for its additional axle needs. In question was whether it should manufacture (i.e., "make") the additional axles it needed or purchase (i.e., "buy") them from an external vendor. After a careful discussion with a cross-functional team representing personnel from Human Resources, Accounting, Purchasing, and Finance, managers decided that the key costs on the "make" side included one-time capital and start-up expenditures on machines and ongoing expenditures for labor, repairs and maintenance, utilities, depreciation, and insurance. Key costs on the "buy" side included one-time vendor tooling expenditures and ongoing expenditures for freight, logistics, inventory storage and movement, and training. In addition, managers considered important qualitative characteristics such as ensuring high quality, which was particularly relevant for the training costs because Navistar wanted to be sure that any purchased axles were of a high quality and delivered to the right place at the appropriate time. After these relevant costs were identified, quantified, and analyzed, Navistar confidently elected to outsource its additional axle production.

Recall the steps involved in short-run decision making (p. 394). The problem (Step 1) and the feasible alternatives (Step 2) are both readily identifiable. Since the horizon for the decision is only one period, there is no need to be concerned about periodically recurring costs (Step 3). Relevant costing is particularly useful for short-run analysis. We simply need to identify the relevant costs (Step 4), total them, and make a choice (Step 6) [assuming no overriding qualitative concerns (Step 5)].

The full absorption cost of the component is computed as follows:

	Total Cost	Unit Cost
Direct materials	$10,000	$1.00
Direct labor	20,000	2.00
Variable overhead	8,000	0.80
Fixed overhead	44,000	4.40
Total	$82,000	$8.20

Fixed overhead consists of common factory costs that are allocated to each product line. No matter what happens to the component line, overall fixed overhead will not be affected. As a result, the fixed overhead is irrelevant; it can be ignored in structuring the problem.

All other costs in this example are relevant. The costs of direct materials and direct labor are relevant because they will not be needed if the part is purchased externally. Similarly, variable overhead is relevant, because its cost would not be incurred if the component were purchased externally.

Now, what about the purchase of the component? Of course, the purchase price is relevant. If the component were made, this cost would not be incurred. Are there any other costs associated with an outside purchase? A check with the purchasing department and receiving dock confirmed that there was sufficient slack in the system to easily handle the additional purchase, suggesting that there are no additional relevant costs of purchasing the component.

Here's **Why It's important**

The make-or-buy decision situation requires the company to focus on the relevant items (usually costs) associated with either making or purchasing a given product. Typically, the alternative (make or buy) with the lower relevant costs represents the best decision for the company. **Example 8.1** shows how to structure this make-or-buy problem.

Be sure to read the analysis in Example 8.1 carefully. At first, the fixed overhead remains whether or not the component is made internally. In this case, fixed overhead is not relevant, and making the product is $9,500 cheaper than buying it. Later, in Requirement 4, part of the

---

Here's How It's Used: **SUSTAINABILITY AT HEWLETT-PACKARD**

One type of relevant cost that is becoming increasingly large due to globalization and the green environmental movement concerns the disposal costs associated with electronic waste (or e-waste). Increasingly, government agencies are assessing manufacturers of computers, televisions, digital music devices, etc., a costly fee at production to cover product disposal costs that public landfills eventually incur once the products reach the end of their life cycle, become obsolete, and are thrown out to pollute the environment. **Hewlett-Packard Co.** has taken a strategic leadership position by recycling approximately 10% of its sales as a more cost-effective means than incurring the aforementioned governmental fees at production. Some experts estimate annual global e-waste at approximately 50 million tons. Not all companies are as business savvy or environmentally responsible as Hewlett-Packard, as evidenced by the $19 billion estimated value of illegally traded and dumped e-waste.[7] The failure to properly forecast e-waste levels and consider their relevant life cycle costs can cause the make side of the make-or-buy analysis to appear more attractive (i.e., less costly) than it is in reality.

---

7 Shereen Zorba, "Illegally Traded and Dumped E-Waste Worth Up to $19 Billion Annually Poses Risks to Health, Deprives Countries of Resources, Says UNEP Report," *UNEP News Centre* (May 12 2015). Taken from http://www. unep.org/newscentre/default.aspx?DocumentID=26816&ArticleID=35021.

Swasey Manufacturing needed to determine if it would be cheaper to make 10,000 units of a component in-house or to purchase them from an outside supplier for $4.75 each. Cost information on internal production includes the following:

	Total Cost	Unit Cost
Direct materials	$10,000	$1.00
Direct labor	20,000	2.00
Variable overhead	8,000	0.80
Fixed overhead	44,000	4.40
Total	$82,000	$8.20

EXAMPLE 8.1

How to Structure a Make-or-Buy Problem

Fixed overhead will continue whether the component is produced internally or externally. No additional costs of purchasing will be incurred beyond the purchase price.

Required:

1. What are the alternatives for Swasey Manufacturing?

2. List the relevant cost(s) of internal production and of external purchase.

3. Which alternative is more cost effective and by how much?

4. Now assume that the fixed overhead includes $10,000 of cost that can be avoided if the component is purchased externally. Which alternative is more cost effective and by how much?

Solution:

1. There are two alternatives: make the component in-house or purchase it externally.

2. Relevant costs of making the component in-house include direct materials, direct labor, and variable overhead. Relevant costs of purchasing the component externally include the purchase price.

	Alternatives		Differential
	Make	Buy	Cost to Make
Direct materials	$10 000	—	$ 10,000
Direct labor	20,000	—	20,000
Variable overhead	8,000	—	8,000
Purchase cost	—	$47,500	(47,500)
Total relevant cost	$38,000	$47,500	$ (9,500)

3. It is cheaper (by $9,500) to make the component in-house.

4.

	Alternatives		Differential
	Make	Buy	Cost to Make
Direct materials	$10 000	—	$ 10,000
Direct labor	20,000	—	20,000
Variable overhead	8,000	—	8,000
Avoidable fixed overhead	10,000	—	10,000
Purchase cost	—	$47,500	(47,500)
Total relevant cost	$48,000	$47,500	$ 500

Now it is cheaper (by $500) to purchase the component.

fixed overhead is avoidable. This condition means that purchasing the component externally will save $10,000 in fixed cost (i.e., Swasey can avoid $10,000 of fixed overhead if it buys the component). Now, the $10,000 of fixed cost is relevant—it is a future cost and it differs between the two alternatives—and the offer of the supplier should be accepted; it is $500 cheaper to buy the component.

The same analysis can be performed on a unit-cost basis. Once the relevant costs are identified, relevant unit costs can be compared. For this example, these costs are $3.80 ($38,000/10,000) for the "make" alternative and $4.75 ($47,500/10,000) for the "buy" alternative.

CONCEPT CLIP

Special-Order Decisions

From time to time, a company may consider offering a product or service at a price different from the usual price. Prices can vary to customers in the same market, and firms often have the opportunity to consider special orders from potential customers in markets not ordinarily served. For example, **General Motors** contracted with the Pentagon to use excess production capacity to manufacture its popular 4-wheel drive pickup truck for use by U.S. troops in desert combat situations, except that these trucks were altered to include bulletproof windows, mounts for machine guns, and night vision capability. A potentially important qualitative factor in this example is that certain customer segments might hold strong opinions about General Motors' association with combat activities. Such opinions might help or hurt regular sales, but their effect should be estimated and included in the relevant analysis if they are deemed to be significant. **Special-order decisions** focus on whether a specially priced order should be accepted or rejected. These orders often can be attractive, especially when the firm is operating below its maximum productive capacity. Exhibit 8.2 illustrates the special-order decision.

Exhibit 8.2

Accept or Reject a Special Order

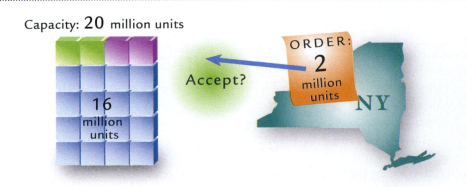

Another interesting example of special-order sales decisions involves airlines (e.g., **American Airlines**) and hotels (e.g., **Westin Hotels**), when management must estimate the relevant costs associated with filling an otherwise empty airline seat or hotel room as the date of the flight or hotel weekend draws near. After the relevant costs are determined, management can then decide the price that it is willing to accept in these common short-term unused capacity scenarios.

Suppose that an ice cream company produces only premium ice cream. Its factory has a capacity of 20 million half-gallon units but only plans to produce 16 million units. The total costs associated with producing and selling 16 million units are as follows (in thousands of dollars):

	Total	Unit Cost
Variable costs:		
Ingredients	$15,200	$0.95
Packaging	3,200	0.20
Direct labor	4,000	0.25
Variable overhead	1,280	0.08
Selling commission	320	0.02
Total variable costs	$24,000	$1.50
Total fixed costs	1,552	0.097
Total costs	$25,552	$1.597
Selling price		$2.00

An ice cream distributor from a geographic region not normally served by the company has offered to buy 2 million units at $1.55 per unit, provided its own label can be attached to the product. Since the distributor approached the company directly, there is no sales commission. As the manager of the ice cream company, would you accept or reject this order?

The offer of $1.55 is well below the normal selling price of $2.00; in fact, it is even below the total unit cost. Even so, accepting the order may be profitable. The company has idle capacity, and the order will not replace, or cannibalize, other units being produced to sell at the normal price. Additionally, many of the costs are not relevant. Fixed costs will continue regardless of whether the order is accepted or rejected.

If the order is accepted, a benefit of $1.55 per unit will be realized that otherwise wouldn't be. However, all of the variable costs except for commissions ($0.02) also will be incurred, producing a cost of $1.48 per unit. The net benefit is $0.07 ($1.55 − $1.48) per unit. The relevant cost analysis can be summarized as follows:

	Accept	Reject	Differential Benefit to Accept
Revenues	$ 3,100,000	$—	$ 3,100,000
Ingredients	(1,900,000)	—	(1,900,000)
Packaging	(400,000)	—	(400,000)
Direct labor	(500,000)	—	(500,000)
Variable overhead	(160,000)	—	(160,000)
Profit	$ 140,000	$ 0	$ 140,000

We see that for this company, accepting the special order will increase profits by $140,000 ($0.07 × 2,000,000).

A special order occurs when a company uses its excess capacity to produce a "one-time" order for another company. The challenge in a special-order analysis is to estimate the relevant costs and benefits associated with the order because many of the company's costs will be unaffected (and therefore irrelevant) by whether the order is accepted or rejected. **Example 8.2** shows how to apply relevant costing to a special-order problem.

Here's **Why It's important**

EXAMPLE 8.2

Leibnitz Company has been approached by a new customer with an offer to purchase 20,000 units of model TR8 at a price of $9 each. The new customer is geographically separated from the company's other customers, and existing sales would not be affected. Leibnitz normally produces 100,000 units of TR8 per year, but only plans to produce and sell 75,000 in the

How to Structure a Special-Order Problem

(Continued)

EXAMPLE 8.2

(Continued)

coming year. The normal sales price is $14 per unit. Unit cost information for the normal level of activity is as follows:

Direct materials	$3.00
Direct labor	2.80
Variable overhead	1.50
Fixed overhead	2.00
Total	$9.30

Fixed overhead will not be affected by whether or not the special order is accepted.

Required:

1. What are the relevant costs and benefits of the two alternatives (accept or reject the special order)?

2. By how much will operating income increase or decrease if the order is accepted?

Solution:

1. Relevant costs and benefits of accepting the special order include the sales price of $9, direct materials, direct labor, and variable overhead. No relevant costs or benefits are attached to rejecting the order.

2. If the problem is analyzed on a unit basis:

	Accept	Reject	Differential Benefit to Accept
Price	$ 9.00	$—	$ 9.00
Direct materials	(3.00)	—	(3.00)
Direct labor	(2.80)	—	(2.80)
Variable overhead	(1.50)	—	(1.50)
Increase in operating income	$ 1.70	$ 0	$ 1.70

Operating income will increase by $34,000 ($1.70 × 20,000 units) if the special order is accepted.

Keep-or-Drop Decisions

CONCEPT CLIP

Often, a manager needs to determine whether a segment, such as a particular product or service line or a geographic sales region, should be kept or dropped. Keep-or-drop decisions can be relatively small scale in nature, such as when **Nike** decides what to do with particular existing celebrity- and athlete-sponsored clothing or equipment lines, or **Lay's** introduces a new product like its chocolate-covered potato chips aimed at millennial women.[8] On the other hand, these decisions can be very large scale in nature, such as when **Ford Motor Company** contemplated the sale of its luxury Jaguar and Land Rover automobile lines to Indian automaker **Tata Motors**. Such decisions also can involve large physical assets, such as when **MGM Resorts International** in Las Vegas contemplated whether or not to raze its luxury hotel (the Harmon) before it even opened as a result of alleged construction and engineering problems.[9] In addition, **Starbucks** spent years studying market conditions,

---

8 Vanessa Wong, "Lay's New Chocolate-Covered Potato Chips: For Women, of Course," *Bloomberg Businessweek* (November 4, 2013).

9 Alexandra Berzon, "MGM Folds Vegas Tower," *The Wall Street Journal* (August 16, 2011): B1.

opportunities, and risks before it finally opened its first stores in large new markets with distinctly different challenges—the predominantly tea-drinking Indian market and, conversely, the proud and historic coffee culture of the Italian market considered by many connoisseurs to be the "standard against which all coffee should be measured."[10] As an example of a major product drop decision, **CVS** elected to stop selling cigarettes at its 7,600 U.S. store locations. CVS made this decision to more closely align its product and service offerings with its strategic aspirations to become a major health care provider for customers. However, the decision cost CVS an estimated $2 billion annually in lost sales revenue from tobacco and related sundries sales.[11]

As these examples suggest, making effective **keep-or-drop decisions** requires that managers identify and consider only the relevant information of the business segment in question. A **segment** is a subunit of a company of sufficient importance to warrant the production of performance reports. Segments can be divisions, departments, product lines, customer classes, and so on. Segmented reports prepared on a variable-costing basis are important because they provide managers with this valuable information. For example, both the contribution margin and the segment margin shown on a segmented income statement are useful in evaluating the performance of segments and, in particular, identifying the relevant information necessary for making effective keep-or-drop decisions. Therefore, before discussing the specifics of keep-or-drop decisions, it is important first to understand how to prepare and interpret segmented income statements using variable costing.

Segmented Income Statements Using Variable Costing   Variable costing is useful in preparing segmented income statements because it presents the segment's variable expenses (which typically are relevant unless additional insights suggest otherwise) separate from its fixed expenses, which are further separated into *direct fixed expenses* (all—or a portion—of which typically are relevant) and *common fixed expenses* (which are irrelevant). This subdivision of fixed costs into direct and common helps managers' ability to evaluate each segment's contribution to overall firm performance and determine the relevant items to consider in the keep-or-drop decision.

Here's Why It's important

Direct Fixed Expenses   **Direct fixed expenses** are fixed expenses that are directly traceable to a segment. These sometimes are referred to as *avoidable fixed expenses* or *traceable fixed expenses* because they vanish if the segment is eliminated—in other words, they are relevant to the keep-or-drop decision. For example, if the segments were sales regions, a direct fixed expense for each region would be the rent for the sales office, salary of the sales manager of each region, and so on. If one region were to be eliminated, then those fixed expenses would disappear. **Zingerman's**, from the opening scenario of Chapter 3, bakes and sells cakes and pastries in its Bakehouse. The ovens and cooking equipment are direct fixed costs for the Bakehouse. If the Bakehouse were eliminated, those costs would disappear.

Common Fixed Expenses   **Common fixed expenses** are jointly caused by two or more segments. These expenses persist even if one of the segments to which they are common is eliminated—in other words, they are *not* relevant to the keep-or-drop decision. For example, depreciation on the corporate headquarters building, the salary of the CEO, and the cost of printing and distributing the annual report to shareholders are common fixed expenses for **Walt Disney Company**. If Walt Disney Company were to sell a theme park or open a new one, those common expenses would not be affected. In addition, ZingNet (again from the opening scenario of

---

10 Manuela Saragosa, "Coffee: Do Italians Do It Better?" *BBC News* (August 13, 2015). http://www.bbc.com/news/business-33527053 (accessed March 20, 2016).

11 Phil Wahba, "How CVS Plans to Replace $2 Billion in Lost Tobacco Sales," *Fortune* (June 22, 2015). http://fortune.com/2015/06/22/cvs-retail-strategy-without-tobacco/ (accessed March 26, 2016).

Chapter 3) is a support service used by all of **Zingerman's** business segments. If one segment, say the Bakehouse, were eliminated, the costs of ZingNet would be unaffected. These are common fixed costs of the company.

Here's **Why It's important**

Preparing Segmented Income Statements Segmented income statements allow managers to see the profitability of individual segments of the company, which is helpful when making add-or-drop decisions. **Example 8.3** shows how to prepare a segmented income statement where the segments are product lines.

EXAMPLE 8.3

How to Prepare a Segmented Income Statement

Audiomatronics Inc. produces MP3 players and smartphones in a single factory. The following information was provided for the coming year:

	MP3 Players	Smartphones
Sales	$400,000	$290,000
Variable cost of goods sold	200,000	150,000
Direct fixed overhead	30,000	20,000

A 5% sales commission is paid for each of the product lines. Direct fixed selling and administrative expense was estimated to be $10,000 for the MP3 line and $15,000 for the smartphone line. Common fixed overhead for the factory was estimated to be $100,000; common selling and administrative expense was estimated to be $20,000.

Required:

Prepare a segmented income statement for Audiomatronics Inc. for the coming year, using variable costing.

Solution:

Audiomatronics Inc.
Segmented Income Statement
For the Coming Year

	MP3 Players	Smartphones	Total
Sales	$400,000	$290,000	$690,000
Less variable expenses:			
Variable cost of goods sold	200,000	150,000	350,000
Variable selling expense*	20,000	14,500	34,500
Contribution margin	$180,000	$125,500	$305,500
Less direct fixed expenses:			
Direct fixed overhead	30,000	20,000	50,000
Direct selling and administrative	10,000	15,000	25,000
Segment margin	$140,000	$ 90,500	$230,500
Less common fixed expenses:			
Common fixed overhead			100,000
Common selling and administrative			20,000
Operating income			$110,500

*Variable Selling Expense for MP3 Players = 0.05 × Sales = 0.05 × $400,000 = $20,000
Variable Selling Expense for Smartphones = 0.05 × Sales = 0.05 × $290,000 = $14,500

Notice that Example 8.3 shows that both products have large positive contribution margins ($180,000 for MP3 players and $125,500 for smartphones). Both products are providing revenue above variable costs that can be used to help cover the firm's fixed costs. However, some of the firm's fixed costs are caused by the segments themselves. Thus, the real measure of the profit contribution of each segment is what is left over after these direct fixed costs are covered (i.e., $140,000 and $90,500 for MP3 and smartphones, respectively).

The profit contribution each segment makes toward covering a firm's common fixed costs is called the **segment margin**. A segment should at least be able to cover both its own variable costs and direct fixed costs. A negative segment margin drags down the firm's total profit, making it time to consider dropping the product. Ignoring any effect a segment may have on the sales of other segments, the segment margin measures the change in a firm's profits that would occur if the segment were eliminated.

Here's How It's Used: AT FOLSOM MANUFACTURING

You are the financial vice president for Folsom Company, which sells three products, Alpha, Beta, and Gamma. You have just received the income statement shown in Panel A of Exhibit 8.3. Clearly, Gamma is unprofitable. In fact, the company is losing $13,740 a year on Gamma.

Should you drop Gamma? Will income go up if you do?

Take a closer look at the income statement. Observe that both the direct fixed costs and the allocated common fixed costs are subtracted from each segment's contribution margin. This observation is misleading; it seems that dropping any segment would result in losing the operating income associated with the

segment. However, if one segment is dropped, the allocated common fixed costs will remain.

A more useful income statement—one that is *segmented*—is presented in Panel B of Exhibit 8.3. Here, the segment margin for all three products is positive, as is overall income. While Gamma is not as profitable as Alpha and Beta, it is profitable. Dropping Gamma will result in a decrease in operating income of $12,000, the amount of the segment margin.

Separating the direct fixed costs from the common fixed costs, and focusing on the segment margin, will give a truer picture of a segment's profitability.

Exhibit 8.3 Comparison of Segmented Income Statement With and Without Allocated Common Fixed Expense

Folsom Company information for last year:

	Alpha	Beta	Gamma
Units produced and sold	10,000	30,000	26,000
Price	$30	$25	$14
Variable cost per unit	$20	$18	$12
Direct fixed expense	$35,000	$38,000	$40,000

	A. Segmented Income Statement with Allocation of Common Fixed Expense				B. Segmented Income Statement without Allocation of Common Fixed Expense			
	Alpha	Beta	Gamma	Total	Alpha	Beta	Gamma	Total
Sales	$300,000	$750,000	$364,000	$1,414,000	$300,000	$750,000	$364,000	$1,414,000
Less: Variable cost	200,000	540,000	312,000	1,052,000	200,000	540,000	312,000	1,052,000
Contribution margin	$100,000	$210,000	$ 52,000	$ 362,000	$100,000	$210,000	$ 52,000	$ 362,000
Less: Direct fixed cost	35,000	38,000	40,000	113,000	35,000	38,000	40,000	113,000
Segment margin	$ 65,000	$172,000	$ 12,000	$ 249,000	$ 65,000	$172,000	$ 12,000	$ 249,000
Less: Allocated common cost	21,220	53,040	25,740	100,000				100,000
Operating income	$ 43,780	$118,960	$ (13,740)	$ 149,000				$ 149,000

As mentioned earlier, formal segmented income statements play a critical role in helping to determine exactly what information is relevant to the keep-or-drop decision. Consider Norton Materials Inc., which produces concrete blocks, bricks, and roofing tile. The controller has prepared the following estimated segment income statement for next year (in thousands of dollars):

	Blocks	Bricks	Tile	Total
Sales revenue	$500	$800	$150	$1,450
Less: Variable expenses	250	480	140	870
Contribution margin	$250	$320	$ 10	$ 580
Less direct fixed expenses:				
Advertising	(10)	(10)	(10)	(30)
Salaries	(37)	(40)	(35)	(112)
Depreciation	(53)	(40)	(10)	(103)
Segment margin	$150	$230	$(45)	$ 335

The projected performance of the roofing tile line shows a negative segment margin. This occurrence would be the third consecutive year of poor performance for that line. The president of Norton Materials, Tom Blackburn—concerned about this poor performance—is trying to decide whether to keep or drop the roofing tile line.

His first reaction is to try to increase the sales revenue of roofing tiles, possibly through an aggressive sales promotion coupled with an increase in the selling price. The marketing manager thinks that this approach would be fruitless, however. The market is saturated, and the level of competition is too keen to hold out any hope for increasing the firm's market share.

Increasing the product line's profits through cost cutting is not feasible either. Costs were cut the past 2 years to reduce the loss to its present anticipated level. Any further reductions would lower the quality of the product and adversely affect sales.

With no hope for improving the profit performance of the line beyond its projected level, Tom has decided to drop it. He reasons that the firm will lose a total of $10,000 in contribution margin but will save $45,000 by dismissing the line's supervisor and eliminating its advertising budget. (The depreciation cost of $10,000 is not relevant because it represents an allocation of a sunk cost.) Thus, dropping the tile product line has a $35,000 advantage over keeping it. **Example 8.4** shows how to structure this information as a keep-or-drop product-line problem.

Here's **Why It's important**

Companies often must consider whether a segment or product line should remain. The most important aspect of this analysis is determining which costs will be eliminated (i.e., be relevant) and which costs will remain (i.e., be irrelevant) regardless of whether or not the segment or product is dropped.

EXAMPLE 8.4	Shown below is a segmented income statement for Norton Materials Inc.'s three product lines:

How to Structure a Keep-or-Drop Product-Line Problem

	Blocks	Bricks	Tile	Total
Sales revenue	$500,000	$800,000	$150,000	$1,450,000
Less: Variable expenses	250,000	480,000	140,000	870,000
Contribution margin	$250,000	$320,000	$ 10,000	$ 580,000
Less direct fixed expenses:				
Advertising	(10,000)	(10,000)	(10,000)	(30,000)
Supervision salaries	(37,000)	(40,000)	(35,000)	(112,000)
Depreciation	(53,000)	(40,000)	(10,000)	(103,000)
Segment margin	$150,000	$230,000	$(45,000)	$ 335,000

EXAMPLE 8.4

(*Continued*)

The roofing tile line has a contribution margin of $10,000 (sales of $150,000 minus total variable costs of $140,000). All variable costs are relevant. Relevant fixed costs associated with this line include $10,000 in advertising and $35,000 in supervision salaries.

Required:

1. List the alternatives being considered with respect to the roofing tile line.

2. List the relevant benefits and costs for each alternative.

3. Which alternative is more cost effective and by how much?

Solution:

1. The two alternatives are to keep the roofing tile line or to drop it.

2. The relevant benefits and costs of keeping the roofing tile line include sales of $150,000, variable costs of $140,000, advertising cost of $10,000, and supervision cost of $35,000. None of the relevant benefits and costs of keeping the roofing tile line would occur under the drop alternative.

3.

	Keep	Drop	Differential Amount to Keep
Sales	$150,000	$—	$150,000
Less: Variable expenses	140,000	—	140,000
Contribution margin	$ 10,000	$—	$ 10,000
Less: Advertising	(10,000)	—	(10,000)
Cost of supervision	(35,000)	—	(35,000)
Total relevant benefit (loss)	$(35,000)	$ 0	$ (35,000)

The difference is $35,000 in favor of dropping the roofing tile line.

A merger between companies is another type of keep-or-drop decision that requires managerial accountants to estimate relevant costs, such as which costs would go away when two companies merge and which costs would remain. For example, when **XM Satellite Radio** and **Sirius Satellite Radio** first considered merging into one giant satellite radio company, proponents argued that the merger would create significant cost savings to the new company that could be passed along to consumers in the form of lower prices. They reasoned that many of the costs that XM and Sirius incurred as separate companies would either decrease or be eliminated because the new combined company would need only one research and development group, one marketing department, etc. Any costs that would decrease or go away after the merger would be relevant costs for the merger analysis, while any costs that would remain unchanged after the merger would be irrelevant.

Keep or Drop with Complementary Effects A potential complication of a keep-or-drop analysis is the implication such a decision might have on other aspects of the business. Such implications must be included in the analysis before making a final decision. For example, suppose that dropping Norton's roofing tile line would lower sales of blocks by 10% and bricks by 8%, as many customers buy roofing tile at the same time that they purchase blocks or bricks. Some customers will go elsewhere if they cannot buy both products at the same location. How does this information affect the keep-or-drop decision? **Example 8.5** shows the impact on all product lines.

The example provides some insights beyond the simple application of the decision model. The initial analysis, which focused on two feasible alternatives, led to a tentative decision to drop the product line. Additional information provided by the marketing manager led to a reversal of

Here's **Why It's important**

EXAMPLE 8.5

How to Structure a Keep-or-Drop Product-Line Problem with Complementary Effects

Refer to Norton Materials' segmented income statement in Example 8.4 (p. 412). Assume that dropping the product line reduces sales of blocks by 10% and sales of bricks by 8%. All other information remains the same.

Required:

1. If the roofing tile line is dropped, what is the contribution margin for the block line? For the brick line?

2. Which alternative (keep or drop the roofing tile line) is now more cost effective and by how much?

Solution:

1. Previous contribution margin of blocks was $250,000. A 10% decrease in sales implies a 10% decrease in total variable costs, so the contribution margin decreases by 10%.

   New Contribution Margin for Blocks = $250,000 − 0.10($250,000) = $225,000

   The reasoning is the same for the brick line, but the decrease is 8%.

   New Contribution Margin for Bricks = $320,000 − 0.08($320,000) = $294,400

   Therefore, if the roofing tile product line were dropped, the resulting total contribution margin for Norton Materials would equal $519,400 ($225,000 + $294,400).

2.

	Keep	Drop	Differential Amount to Keep
Contribution margin	$ 580,000	$519,400	$ 60,600
Less: Advertising	(30,000)	(20,000)	(10,000)
Cost of supervision	(112,000)	(77,000)	(35,000)
Total	$ 438,000	$422,400	$ 15,600

Notice that the contribution margin for the drop alternative equals the new contribution margins of the block and brick lines ($225,000 + $294,400). Also, advertising and supervision remain relevant across these alternatives.

Now the analysis favors keeping the roofing tile line. In fact, company income will be $15,600 higher if all three lines are kept as opposed to dropping the roofing tile line.

the first decision. Perhaps other feasible alternatives exist as well. These additional alternatives would require still more analyses.

Further Processing of Joint Products

Joint products have common processes and costs of production up to a split-off point. At that point, they become distinguishable as separately identifiable products. For example, certain minerals such as copper and gold may both be found in a given ore. The ore must be mined, crushed, and treated before the copper and gold are separated. The point of separation is called the **split-off point**. The costs of mining, crushing, and treatment are common to both products and, therefore, are incurred regardless of whether the ore is sold at the split-off point or further processed into copper, gold, and any other substances that exist in the ore. As a result, joint costs are irrelevant to the decision of whether to sell at the split-off point or to process further.

Many joint products are sold at the split-off point. However, sometimes it is more profitable to process a joint product further, beyond the split-off point, prior to selling it. A **sell-or-process-further decision** is an important relevant decision that a manager must make.

Here's How It's Used: DATA ANALYTICS AND YANKEE STADIUM

You are an elected official in a major city that is considering whether or not to move forward with a proposed plan to demolish the city's existing professional sports stadium and build an elaborate new stadium. One of the most difficult aspects of this decision is estimating the new stadium's incremental revenues and costs that would result if it were built.

What specific types of relevant revenues and relevant costs would you consider in making this important decision?

There are many stadium events for which the associated relevant revenues and relevant costs must be estimated accurately if the correct decision is to be made. These stadium events (and their relevant revenues and costs) include:

- Main attraction sporting events (e.g., ticket revenues from baseball, basketball, and/or football games for which the stadium would be built; additional staffing, cleanup, and insurance costs)
- Concessions and other sales (e.g., contribution margins or fees earned from product and service sales—most new stadiums boast as many high-end shopping opportunities as an upscale mall!)
- Television contract terms (e.g., the amount and percentage of revenue brought in by *additional* games being televised in the new stadium, perhaps in primetime slots)
- Offseason events (e.g., the ticket revenue from boxing matches, music concerts, etc.)

For this relevant stadium decision, estimating the relevant revenues might be even more difficult than estimating the relevant costs. For instance, projecting how many *more* people will want to attend games in a new stadium can be unclear, as well as how much money they would be willing to spend for various seats located around the stadium. Increasingly, all parties involved in these high-priced stadium deals rely on data analytics to estimate the relevant revenues and costs as accurately as possible.

Several New York City area stadiums experienced difficulty in accurately estimating these relevant financial items. For example, the **New York Yankees** and **New York Mets** organizations built new stadiums with price tags of over $1.2 billion and $800 million, respectively! However, in the new Yankee stadium, many of the more expensive seats—the ones behind the batter and, thus, most visible on television—remained empty because of their hefty $2,500 per seat price tag. In fact, the Yankee organization decreased some of its highest ticket prices by 50% during the stadium's first season in an attempt to fill these high profile empty seats. In other words, decision makers struggled to estimate the amount of incremental revenue that would result from some of the more important seats in a new Yankee stadium. Undaunted by such challenging relevant analyses, however, the New York area also built a $1.6 billion new Meadowlands Stadium to be shared by the **New York Jets** and **New York Giants**.

In addition to the previously mentioned relevant items, some citizens raise objections to such large amounts of money being spent on replacing existing fully functional sporting facilities with gargantuan sports palaces. They argue that $1 billion could be better spent on different causes. Such sentiments, whether you agree or disagree with them, represent potentially important qualitative factors that effective managerial accountants should take into account when performing relevant analyses for proposed new stadiums, especially when these citizens represent taxpayers or potential fans the stadium builders count on for purchasing expensive tickets in the future.

Data analytics are very helpful in estimating the relevant costs and revenues for such stadiums, including offseason events, as well as additional qualitative factors like citizen sentiment toward the team and the local community.

Consider Appletime Corporation, a large corporate farm that specializes in growing apples. Each plot produces approximately one ton of apples. The trees in each plot must be sprayed, fertilized, watered, and pruned. When the apples are ripened, workers are hired to pick them. The apples are then transported to a warehouse, where they are washed and sorted. The approximate cost of all these activities (including processing) is $300 per ton per year.

Apples are sorted into three grades (A, B, and C), determined by size and blemishes. Large apples without blemishes (bruises, cuts, wormholes, and so on) are sorted into one bin and classified as Grade A. Small apples without blemishes are sorted into a second bin and classified as Grade B. All remaining apples are placed in a third bin and classified as Grade C. Every ton of apples produces 800 pounds of Grade A, 600 pounds of Grade B, and 600 pounds of Grade C apples.

Grade A apples are sold to large supermarkets for $0.40 per pound. Grade B apples are packaged in five-pound bags and sold to supermarkets for $1.30 per bag. (The cost of each bag is $0.05.) Grade C apples are processed further and made into applesauce. The sauce is sold in

16-ounce cans for $0.75 each. The cost of processing is $0.10 per pound of apples. The final output is 500 sixteen-ounce cans.

A large supermarket chain recently requested that Appletime supply 16-ounce cans of apple pie filling, for which the chain is willing to pay $0.90 per can. Appletime determined that the Grade B apples would be suitable for this purpose and estimated that it would cost $0.24 per pound to process the apples into pie filling. The output would be 500 cans. Exhibit 8.4 illustrates the decision to sell Grade B apples at the split-off point or to process them further into pie filling.

Exhibit 8.4

Further Processing of Joint Products

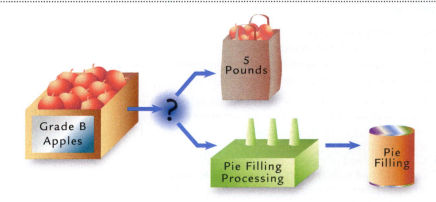

In deciding whether to sell Grade B apples at split-off or to process them further and sell them as pie filling, the common costs of spraying, pruning, and so on, are not relevant. The company must pay the $300 per ton for these activities regardless of whether it sells at split-off or processes further. However, the revenues earned at split-off are likely to differ from the revenues that would be received if the Grade B apples were further processed and sold as pie filling. Therefore, revenues are a relevant consideration. Similarly, the processing costs occur only if further processing takes place. Hence, processing costs are relevant.

Here's **Why It's important**

Because joint costs are incurred prior to the split-off point, they are sunk costs in determining whether to sell a product at split-off or process it further. Only the sales value at split-off, the further processing costs, and the eventual sales value are relevant to this decision. **Example 8.6** shows how to structure the sell-or-process-further decision for the Grade B apples.

EXAMPLE 8.6

How to Structure the Sell-or-Process-Further Decision

Appletime grows apples and then sorts them into one of three grades, A, B, or C, based on their condition. Appletime must decide whether to sell the Grade B apples at split-off or to process them into apple pie filling. The company normally sells the Grade B apples in 120 five-pound bags at a per-unit price of $1.25. If the apples are processed into pie filling, the result will be 500 cans of filling with additional costs of $0.24 per can. The buyer will pay $0.90 per can.

Required:

1. What is the contribution to income from selling the Grade B apples in five-pound bags?

2. What is the contribution to income from processing the Grade B apples into pie filling?

3. Should Appletime continue to sell the Grade B apples in bags or process them further into pie filling?

EXAMPLE 8.6

(Continued)

Solution:

1. Revenue from Apples in Bags = $1.25 × 120 = $150

2. Revenue from Further Processing = $0.90 × 500 = $450
   Further Processing Cost = $0.24 × 500 = $120
   Income from Further Processing = $450 – $120 = $330

3. Appletime should process the Grade B apples into pie filling because the company will make $330 versus the $150 it would make by selling the apples in bags.

Check Point

1. **You also deal with make-or-buy decisions. For example, do you change the oil in your car yourself, or do you take it to the shop? Choose one or the other options, and explain why you have chosen to "make it" or "buy it." What factors could influence you to change your mind?**

Answer:
Suppose that you choose the oil-change decision. You might decide to change it yourself because (1) you know how to do it, (2) you have the appropriate tools to do the job, (3) you have the time, and (4) you don't mind messing around under the hood. Alternatively, you might decide to have it done because (1) you don't have confidence in your ability to do it, (2) you don't own the equipment (nozzle, pan to hold oil), (3) you are unsure which oil to choose, or (4) you don't want to do the job. A factor that could influence your decision between changing your own oil or taking your car to a shop might be that, after graduation, you will be working full time and will want to use your free time for other things.

2. **Suppose that a department store decides to drop a department, such as the furniture department.**
    (a) What are the direct fixed costs involved?
    (b) What are the common fixed costs that would not be reduced if the department is dropped?

Answer:
(a) The direct fixed costs of the furniture department include the wages of the clerks working in that department, the special fixtures that might be required to display some items (e.g., bedding), and the cost of display samples.
(b) The common fixed costs include utilities for the store as a whole, the cost of advertising special sales events, and the cost of the overall store manager.

PRODUCT MIX DECISIONS

OBJECTIVE ‹ 3
Choose the optimal product mix when faced with one constrained resource.

Most of the time, organizations have wide flexibility in choosing their product mix. Product mix refers to the relative amount of each product manufactured (or service provided) by a company. Decisions about product mix can have a significant impact on an organization's profitability.

Each mix represents an alternative that carries with it an associated profit level. A manager should choose the alternative that maximizes total profits. Since fixed costs do not vary with activity level, the total fixed costs of a firm will be the same for all possible mixes and, therefore, are not relevant to the decision. Thus, a manager needs to choose the alternative that maximizes total contribution margin.

Assume that Jorgenson Company produces two types of gears: X and Y, with unit contribution margins of $25 and $10, respectively. If the firm possesses unlimited resources and the demand for each product is unlimited, then the product mix decision is simple—produce an infinite number of each product. Unfortunately, every firm faces limited resources and limited demand for each product. These limitations are called **constraints**. A manager must choose the optimal mix, given the constraints found within the firm.

Assuming that Jorgenson can sell all that is produced, some individuals might argue that only Gear X should be produced and sold—it has the larger contribution margin. However, this solution is not necessarily the best choice. The selection of the optimal mix can be significantly affected by the relationships of the constrained, or scarce, resources to the individual products. These relationships affect the quantity of each product that can be produced and, consequently, the total contribution margin that can be earned. This point is most vividly illustrated when faced with one resource constraint.

Here's **Why It's important**

A company often faces a situation where one of its processes (or resources) cannot handle all of the demands placed on it. Therefore, a company must decide how best to allocate this scarce resource to production operations in order to maximize company profit. **Example 8.7** shows how to determine the optimal product mix with one constrained resource.

EXAMPLE 8.7

How to Determine the Optimal Product Mix with One Constrained Resource

Jorgenson Company produces two types of gears, X and Y, with unit contribution margins of $25 and $10, respectively. Each gear must be notched by a special machine. The firm owns eight machines that together provide 40,000 hours of machine time per year. Gear X requires 2 hours of machine time, and Gear Y requires 0.5 hour of machine time. There are no other constraints.

Required:

1. What is the contribution margin per hour of machine time for each gear?

2. What is the optimal mix of gears?

3. What is the total contribution margin earned for the optimal mix?

Solution:

1.

	Gear X	Gear Y
Contribution margin per unit	$25.00	$10.00
Required machine time per unit	÷2	÷0.5
Contribution margin per hour of machine time	$12.50	$20.00

2. Since Gear Y yields $20 of contribution margin per hour of machine time, all machine time should be devoted to the production of Gear Y.
   Units Gear Y = 40,000 total hours/0.5 hour per Gear Y = 80,000 units
   The optimal mix is Gear Y = 80,000 units and Gear X = 0 units.

3. Total Contribution Margin of Optimal Mix = (80,000 units Gear Y) × $10 = $800,000

Example 8.7 clearly illustrates a fundamentally important point involving relevant decision making with a constrained resource. This point is that the contribution margin *per unit* of each product is not the critical concern when deciding how much of each product type to produce and sell. Instead, the contribution margin *per unit of the scarce resource* is the deciding factor, which means that the product yielding the highest contribution margin per unit of the scarce resource should be selected. Returning to Example 8.7, Gear X earns a contribution margin per unit of $25, which is 2.5 times greater than the $10 contribution margin per unit earned by Gear Y. However, each Gear X unit requires *more* than 2.5 times as much machine time (the constrained factor) to produce than does each Gear Y unit, thereby making Gear Y more attractive financially than Gear X. Specifically, Gear X earns $12.50 of contribution margin per machine hour ($25/2), but Gear Y earns $20 of contribution margin per machine hour ($10/0.5). Thus, Gear Y is the more attractive product, and the optimal mix is 80,000 units of Gear Y and no units of Gear X.

> Contribution Margin per Unit of Scarce Resource = (Selling Price per Unit – Variable Cost per Unit)/Required Amount of Scarce Resource per Unit

Suppose, however, that there is also a demand constraint. Only 60,000 units of Gear Y can be sold. A complication of the scarce resource question arises when there also is a sales constraint that indicates the maximum sales that can be achieved. Keeping both the constrained resource and the sales constraint in mind is essential if the best decision is to be made. **Example 8.8** shows how to incorporate this additional constraint.

Here's **Why It's important**

EXAMPLE 8.8

How to Determine the Optimal Product Mix with One Constrained Resource and a Sales Constraint

Jorgenson Company produces two types of gears, X and Y, with unit contribution margins of $25 and $10, respectively. Each gear must be notched by a special machine. The firm owns eight machines that together provide 40,000 hours of machine time per year. Gear X requires 2 hours of machine time, and Gear Y requires 0.5 hour of machine time. A maximum of 60,000 units of each gear can be sold.

Required:

1. What is the contribution margin per hour of machine time for each gear?
2. What is the optimal mix of gears?
3. What is the total contribution margin earned for the optimal mix?

Solution:

1.

	Gear X	Gear Y
Contribution margin per unit	$25.00	$10.00
Required machine time per unit	÷2	÷0.5
Contribution margin per hour of machine time	$12.50	$20.00

2. Since Gear Y yields $20 of contribution margin per hour of machine time, the first priority is to produce all of Gear Y that the market will take (i.e., demands).

Machine Time Required for Maximum Amount of Gear Y = 60,000 units × 0.5 machine hour required for each Gear Y unit = 30,000 hours needed to manufacture 60,000 Gear Y units

Remaining Machine Time for Gear X = 40,000 – 30,000 hours = 10,000 hours

Units of Gear X to Be Produced in Remaining 10,000 Hours = 10,000 hours/2 hours per Gear X unit = 5,000 Gear X units

(Continued)

EXAMPLE 8.8

(Continued)

Now the optimal mix is 60,000 units of Gear Y and 5,000 units of Gear X. This mix will precisely exhaust the machine time available.

3. Total Contribution Margin of Optimal Mix = (60,000 units Gear Y × $10)
                                             + (5,000 units Gear X × $25)
                                             = $725,000

Coffee chain **Caribou Coffee** as well as other retail businesses pay careful attention to profitability and sales per square foot of floor space, which often is the most important constrained resource. The importance of this metric explains why fast-food restaurants like **McDonald's** push their drive-through service—customers using the drive-through option do not require any internal store floor space. In fact, some restaurants generate more than 80% of sales from this service.

Multiple Constrained Resources

The presence of only one constrained resource might not be realistic. Organizations often face multiple constraints: limitations of raw materials, limitations of skilled labor, limited demand for each product, and so on. The solution of the product mix problem in the presence of multiple constraints is considerably more complicated and requires the use of a specialized mathematical technique known as *linear programming*, which is reserved for advanced cost management courses.

Check Point

Consider your, or a friend's, cell phone plan. Often, there are different types of minutes—priced at different levels. For example, a plan might include 300 "anytime" minutes and 1,000 "night and weekend minutes." Discuss these different types of minutes as constraints. What do they constrain? Do these constraints affect the decision to call a friend?

Answer:

They constrain the amount of time that you can talk per month. Early in the month, you might phone friends regularly. Later in the month, you might try to figure out how many minutes you have left and try harder to time your calls. For example, calls that must be made at a particular time may use "anytime minutes" (e.g., to set up a job interview appointment between 9 A.M. and 5 P.M.). Calls to friends and family might be postponed to the evening or the weekend.

OBJECTIVE 4

Explain the impact of cost on pricing decisions.

THE USE OF COSTS IN PRICING DECISIONS

One of the more difficult decisions faced by a company is pricing. This section examines the impact of cost on price and the role of the accountant in gathering the needed information.

Cost-Based Pricing

Demand is one side of the pricing equation; supply is the other side. Since revenue must cover all costs for the firm to make a profit, many companies start with cost to determine price. That is, they calculate product (or service) cost and add the desired profit. The mechanics of this approach involve a cost base and a markup. The **markup** is a percentage applied to the base cost and is calculated as follows:

Price Using Markup = Cost per Unit + (Cost per Unit × Markup Percentage)

CONCEPT CLIP

The markup includes desired profit and any costs not included in the base cost. Companies that bid for jobs routinely base bid price on cost. Law firms and public accounting firms are service organizations that use cost-plus pricing to bid for clients. Other popular service firms, such as **Netflix** and **DIRECTV** also must carefully consider both the costs to deliver their entertainment services, as well as customer demand for their services (i.e., how much customers are willing to pay for packages such as NFL Sunday Ticket, etc.), when using cost-based pricing.

The challenges of cost-based pricing include accurately estimating the appropriate product or service costs to be marked up and selecting an appropriate markup percentage. For example, setting the markup percentage too high can lead to fewer customer sales and new competitors entering the market because they believe they can offer the same product or service but at a lower price. Setting the markup percentage too low can lead to the organization making less profit—or even a loss if total revenues are lower than total costs—than if the markup percentage were set more appropriately. **Example 8.9** shows how to apply a markup percentage to cost to obtain price.

$Here's$ **Why It's important**

EXAMPLE 8.9

How to Calculate Price by Applying a Markup Percentage to Cost

Elvin Company assembles and installs computers to customer specifications. Elvin has decided to price its jobs at the cost of direct materials and direct labor plus 20%. The job for a local vocational-technical school included the following costs:

Direct materials	$65,000
Direct labor (assembly and installation)	4,000

Required:
Calculate the price charged by Elvin Company to the vocational-technical school.

Solution:

$$\text{Price} = \text{Cost} + (\text{Markup Percentage} \times \text{Cost})$$
$$= \$69,000 + 0.20(\$69,000)$$
$$= \$69,000 + \$13,800$$
$$= \$82,800$$

Notice in Example 8.9 that the markup of 20% is not pure profit. Instead, it includes other costs not specified, such as overhead (including Elvin's offices and management salaries) as well as any marketing and administrative expenses. The markup percentage can be calculated using a variety of bases.

Retail stores often use markup pricing, and typical markup is 100% of cost. Thus, if Graham Department Store purchases a sweater for $24, the retail price marked is $48 [$24 + (1.00 × $24)]. Again, the 100% markup is not pure profit—it goes toward the salaries of the clerks, payment for space and equipment (cash registers, furniture, and fixtures), utilities, advertising, and so on. A major advantage of markup pricing is that standard markups are easy to apply. Consider the difficulty of setting a price for every piece of merchandise in a hardware or department store. It is much simpler to apply a uniform markup to cost and then to adjust prices upward (downward) if demand is more (less) than anticipated.

Several important observations concerning the relationship between the base cost, the markup percentage, and the firm's cost system are in order at this point. First, when the firm includes relatively few costs in the base cost (rather than a large number of costs), it usually becomes very important that the firm selects a large enough markup percentage to ensure that the markup covers all of the remaining costs not included in the base cost. Determining a price that is large enough to cover significant other costs with the markup requires considerable judgment and cost estimation. Second, on a related note, the effectiveness of cost-plus pricing relies heavily on the accuracy of the cost system and managers' understanding of the firm's cost structure. For example, assume that a firm marks up only its direct manufacturing costs and does not understand well the behavior of its indirect manufacturing costs or its nonmanufacturing costs (e.g., research and development costs, distribution costs, customer service costs, etc.). In this case, it is likely that the firm will encounter problems in setting prices either too high—and will be undercut by competitors with more appropriate lower prices—or too low—and will not cover all costs, thereby resulting in a net loss.

Target Costing and Pricing

Many American and European firms set the price of a new product as the sum of the costs and the desired profit. The rationale is that the company must earn sufficient revenues to cover all costs and yield a profit. Peter Drucker writes, "This is true but irrelevant: Customers do not see it as their job to ensure manufacturers a profit. The only sound way to price is to start out with what the market is willing to pay."[12]

Target costing is a method of determining the cost of a product or service based on the price (target price) that customers are willing to pay. The marketing department determines what characteristics and price for a product are most demanded by consumers. The company's engineers must then design and develop the product such that cost and profit can be covered by that price. Japanese firms have practiced this approach for years; American companies increasingly use target costing. For example, **Olympus**, **Toyota**, **Boeing**, **Nissan**, and **Caterpillar** have used a value chain perspective to implement target costing. Target costing recognizes that between 75 and 90% of a product's cost becomes "committed" or "locked into" by the time it finishes the design stage. Therefore, it is most effective to make such large changes in the design and development stage of the product life cycle because at this point the features of the product, as well as its costs, still are fairly easy to adjust. Typical target costing efforts to reduce costs focus on redesigning the product to require fewer or less costly materials, labor, and processes during production, delivery and customer service. **Mercedes**, for instance, used target costing extensively in the design of its popular M-class sports utility vehicle series, which made its public debut in the blockbuster movie *Jurassic Park*.

Consider the target costing experience used by Digitime Company in developing a wristwatch that incorporates a PDA (personal digital assistant). The "cool factor" on this item is high, but actually inputting data on the watch is difficult. So, the company expects to be able to charge a premium price to a relatively small number of early adopters. The marketing vice president's price estimate is $200. Digitime's management requires a 15% profit on new products. Therefore, **target cost** is calculated using the following equation:

$$\text{Target Cost} = \text{Target Price} - \text{Desired Profit}$$

Here's **Why It's important**

When prices are set by the market, a company might use target costing to determine the cost at which it must be able to produce and sell its product in order to achieve its desired profit margin given the market determined price. **Example 8.10** shows how to calculate a target cost.

---

12 Peter Drucker, "The Five Deadly Business Sins," *The Wall Street Journal* (October 21, 1993): A22.

EXAMPLE 8.10

How to Calculate a Target Cost

Digitime manufactures wristwatches and is designing a new watch model that incorporates a PDA, which Digitime hopes consumers will view as a fun and valuable design feature. As such, the new PDA watch has a target price of $200. Management requires a 15% profit on new product revenues.

Required:

1. Calculate the amount of desired profit.
2. Calculate the target cost.

Solution:

1. Desired Profit = 0.15 × Target Price
   = 0.15 × $200
   = $30

2. Target Cost = Target Price − Desired Profit
   = $200 − $30
   = $170

Target costing involves much more up-front work than cost-based pricing. If Digitime can't make the watch for $170, then the engineers and designers will have to go back to the drawing board and find a way to get it done on budget. However, let's not forget the additional work that must be done if the cost-based price turns out to be higher than what customers will accept. Then, the arduous task of bringing costs into line to support a lower price, or the opportunity cost of missing the market altogether, begins. For example, in the 1980s, the U.S. consumer electronics market became virtually nonexistent because cost-based pricing led to increasingly higher prices. Japanese (and later Korean) firms practicing target costing offered lower prices and just the features wanted by consumers to win the market.

Target costing can be used most effectively in the design and development stage of the product life cycle. At that point, the features of the product, as well as its costs, still are relatively easy to adjust.

Check Point

Consider a situation in which you want to buy something, but it is quite expensive. Suppose the salesperson says that the price of the item is high because the cost to the store is high (i.e., price is related to cost). Suppose, on the other hand, that the salesperson says the price is high because the demand for the item is strong (i.e., price is not related to cost). Which explanation would make you happier to buy the item?

Answer:
You would probably be more likely to buy the item when the reason for the high price is high cost to the store. This situation makes the high price seem "fairer" to you, since the store is not gouging you but simply is trying to make a normal profit.

SUMMARY OF LEARNING OBJECTIVES

LO1. Describe the short-run decision-making model, and explain how cost behavior affects the information used to make decisions.
- The six steps of the decision-making model are:
  - Recognize and define the problem.
  - Identify feasible alternatives.
  - Identify costs and benefits with each feasible alternative.

- Estimate the relevant costs and benefits for each feasible alternative.
- Assess qualitative factors.
- Make the decision by selecting the alternative with the greatest overall net benefit.
  - Relevant costs:
    - These are future costs that differ across alternatives.
    - They frequently are variable costs—called flexible resources.

LO2. Apply relevant costing and decision-making concepts in a variety of business situations.
- Make-or-buy decision
- Special-order decision
- Keep-or-drop decision
  - Segmented income statements
  - Complementary effects
- Further processing of joint products

LO3. Choose the optimal product mix when faced with one constrained resource.
- Single constraint leads to production of product with the greatest contribution margin per unit of scarce resource.
- Multiple constraints require linear programming.

LO4. Explain the impact of cost on pricing decisions.
- Markup costing applies markup to cost to determine price.
- Target costing works backward from desired price to find allowable cost.

SUMMARY OF IMPORTANT EQUATIONS

1. Contribution Margin per Unit of Scarce Resource =
   (Selling Price per Unit − Variable Cost per Unit)/Required Amount of Scarce Resource per Unit

2. Price Using Markup = Cost per Unit + (Cost per Unit × Markup Percentage)

3. Target Cost = Target Price − Desired Profit

EXAMPLE 8.1	How to structure a make-or-buy problem, page 405
EXAMPLE 8.2	How to structure a special-order problem, page 407
EXAMPLE 8.3	How to prepare a segmented income statement, page 410
EXAMPLE 8.4	How to structure a keep-or-drop product-line problem, page 412
EXAMPLE 8.5	How to structure a keep-or-drop product-line problem with complementary effects, page 414
EXAMPLE 8.6	How to structure the sell-or-process-further decision, page 416
EXAMPLE 8.7	How to determine the optimal product mix with one constrained resource, page 418
EXAMPLE 8.8	How to determine the optimal product mix with one constrained resource and a sales constraint, page 419
EXAMPLE 8.9	How to calculate price by applying a markup percentage to cost, page 421
EXAMPLE 8.10	How to calculate a target cost, page 423

KEY TERMS

Common fixed expenses, 409, fixed expenses that cannot be directly traced to individual segments and that are unaffected by the elimination of any one segment.

Constraints, 418, mathematical expressions that express resource limitations.

Decision model, 394, a specific set of procedures that, when followed, produces a decision.

Differential cost, 396, the difference in total cost between the alternatives in a decision.

Direct fixed expenses, 409, fixed costs that are directly traceable to a given segment and, consequently, disappear if the segment is eliminated.

Joint products, 414, products that are inseparable prior to a split-off point. All manufacturing costs up to the split-off point are joint costs.

Keep-or-drop decisions, 409, relevant costing analyses that focus on keeping or dropping a segment of a business.

Make-or-buy decisions, 403, relevant costing analyses that focus on whether a component should be made internally or purchased externally.

Markup, 421, the percentage applied to a base cost; it includes desired profit and any costs not included in the base cost.

Opportunity cost, 399, the benefit given up or sacrificed when one alternative is chosen over another.

Relevant costs, 399, future costs that change across alternatives.

Segment, 409, a subunit of a company of sufficient importance to warrant the production of performance reports.

Segment margin, 411, the contribution a segment makes to cover common fixed costs and provide for profit after direct fixed costs and variable costs are deducted from the segment's sales revenue.

Sell-or-process-further decision, 414, relevant costing analysis that focuses on whether a product should be processed beyond the split-off point.

Special-order decisions, 406, relevant costing analyses that focus on whether a specially priced order should be accepted or rejected.

Split-off point, 414, the point at which products become distinguishable after passing through a common process.

Sunk cost, 400, costs for which the outlay has already been made and that cannot be affected by a future decision.

Target cost, 422, the difference between the sales price needed to achieve a projected market share and the desired per-unit profit.

Target costing, 422, a method of determining the cost of a product or service based on the price (target price) that customers are willing to pay.

REVIEW PROBLEMS

I. Special-Order Decision

Pastin Company produces a light-weight travel raincoat with the following unit cost:

Direct materials	$4.00
Direct labor	1.00
Variable overhead	1.75
Fixed overhead	2.00
Unit cost	$8.75

(Continued)

While production capacity is 200,000 units per year, Pastin expects to produce only 170,000 raincoats for the coming year. The fixed selling costs total $85,000 per year, and variable selling costs are $0.50 per unit sold. The raincoats normally sell for $12 each.

At the beginning of the year, a customer from a geographic region outside the area normally served by the company offered to buy 20,000 raincoats for $8 each. The customer would pay all transportation costs, and there would be no variable selling costs.

Required:

1. Should the company accept the order? Provide both qualitative and quantitative justification for your decision. Assume that no other orders are expected beyond the regular business and the special order.

Solution:

1. The company expects idle capacity. Accepting the special order would bring production up to near capacity. The two options are to accept or reject the order. If the order is accepted, then the company could avoid laying off employees and would enhance and maintain its community image. However, the order is considerably below the normal selling price of $12. Because the price is so low, the company needs to assess the potential impact of the sale on its regular customers and on the profitability of the firm. Considering the fact that the customer is located in a region not usually served by the company, the likelihood of an adverse impact on regular business is not high. Thus, the qualitative factors seem to favor acceptance.

To assess profitability, the firm should identify the relevant costs and benefits of each alternative. This analysis is as follows:

	Accept	Reject
Revenues	$160,000	$—
Direct materials	(80,000)	—
Direct labor	(20,000)	—
Variable overhead	(35,000)	—
Total benefits	$ 25,000	$ 0

Accepting the order would increase profits by $25,000. (The fixed overhead and selling costs are all irrelevant because they are the same across both alternatives.) *Conclusion:* The order should be accepted because both qualitative and quantitative factors favor it.

II. Optimal Mix

Two types of gears are produced: A and B. Gear A has a unit contribution margin of $200, and Gear B has a unit contribution margin of $400. Gear A uses 2 hours of grinding time, and Gear B uses 5 hours of grinding time. There are 200 hours of grinding time available per week. This is the only constraint.

Required:

1. Is the grinding constraint an internal constraint or an external constraint?
2. Determine the optimal mix. What is the total contribution margin?
3. Suppose that there is an additional demand constraint: Market conditions will allow the sale of only 80 units of each gear. Now, what is the optimal mix? Total contribution margin per week?

Solution:

1. It's an internal constraint.
2. Gear A: $200/2 = $100 per grinding hour
   Gear B: $400/5 = $80 per grinding hour
   Since Gear A earns more contribution margin per unit of scarce resource than Gear B, only Gear A should be produced and sold. This is based on the fact that we can sell all we want of each product.
   Optimal mix: Gear A = 100 units* and Gear B = 0
   Total Contribution Margin = $200 × 100 = $20,000 per week
   *200 hours/2 hours per unit = 100 units of A can be produced per week
3. Now, we should sell 80 units of Gear A using 160 hours (2 × 80) and 8 units of Gear B (40 hours/5 hours per unit).
   Total Contribution Margin = (80 × $200) + (8 × $400) = $19,200 per week

DISCUSSION QUESTIONS

1. What is the difference between tactical and strategic decisions?
2. What are some ways that a manager can identify a feasible set of decision alternatives?
3. What role do past costs play in relevant costing decisions?
4. Explain why depreciation on an existing asset is always irrelevant.
5. Give an example of a future cost that is not relevant.
6. Can direct materials ever be irrelevant in a make-or-buy decision? Explain.
7. Why would a firm ever offer a price on a product that is below its full cost?
8. What is a segment?
9. What is the difference between contribution margin and segment margin?
10. Discuss the importance of complementary effects in a keep-or-drop decision.
11. Should joint costs be considered in a sell-or-process-further decision? Explain.
12. Suppose that a product can be sold at split-off for $5,000 or processed further at a cost of $1,000 and then sold for $6,400. Should the product be processed further?
13. Suppose that a firm produces two products. Should the firm always place the most emphasis on the product with the largest contribution margin per unit? Explain.

MULTIPLE-CHOICE QUESTIONS

8-1 Which of the following is *not* a step in the short-run decision-making model?
   a. Defining the problem.
   b. Identifying alternatives.
   c. Identifying the costs and benefits of feasible alternatives.
   d. Assessing qualitative factors.
   e. All of these.

8-2 Costs that *cannot* be affected by any future action are called
   a. differential costs.
   b. sunk costs.
   c. inventory costs.
   d. relevant costs.
   e. joint costs.

> *Use the following information for Multiple-Choice Questions 8-3 through* 8-5:
> Sandy is considering moving from her apartment into a small house with a fenced yard. The apartment is noisy, and she has difficulty studying. In addition, the fenced yard would be great for her dog. The distance from school is about the same from the house and from the apartment. The apartment costs $750 per month, and she has 2 months remaining on her lease. The lease cannot be broken, so Sandy must pay the last 2 months of rent whether she lives there or not. The rent for the house is $450 per month, plus utilities, which should average $100 per month. The apartment is furnished; the house is not. If Sandy moves into the house, she will need to buy a bed, dresser, desk, and chair immediately. She thinks that she can pick up some used furniture for a good price.

8-3   Refer to the information for Sandy above. Which of the following costs is irrelevant to Sandy's decision to stay in the apartment or move to the house?

   a. House rent of $450 per month
   b. Utilities for the house of $100 per month
   c. The noise in the apartment house
   d. The cost of the used furniture
   e. The last 2 months of rent in the apartment

8-4   Refer to the information for Sandy above. Which of the following is a qualitative factor?

   a. House rent of $450 per month
   b. Utilities for the house of $100 per month
   c. The noise in the apartment house
   d. The cost of the used furniture
   e. The last 2 months of rent in the apartment

8-5   Refer to the information for Sandy above. Suppose that the apartment building was within walking distance to campus and the house was five miles away. Sandy does not own a car. How would that affect her decision?

   a. It would make the house more desirable.
   b. It would make the apartment more desirable.
   c. It would make both choices less desirable.
   d. It would make both choices more desirable.
   e. It would have no effect on the decision; buying or not buying a car is a separate decision.

8-6   Which of the following statements is false?

   a. Fixed costs are never relevant.
   b. Variable costs are never relevant.
   c. Usually, variable costs are irrelevant.
   d. Step costs are irrelevant when a decision alternative requires moving outside of the existing relevant range.
   e. All of these.

8-7   In a segmented income statement, which of the following statements is true?

   a. Segment margin is greater than contribution margin.
   b. Common fixed expenses must be allocated to each segment.
   c. Contribution margin is equal to sales less all variable and direct fixed expenses of a segment.
   d. Segment margin is equal to contribution margin less direct and common fixed expenses.
   e. Segment margin is equal to contribution margin less direct fixed expenses.

8-8   In a make-or-buy decision,

   a. the company must choose between expanding or dropping a product line.
   b. the company must choose between accepting or rejecting a special order.
   c. the company would consider the purchase price of the externally provided good to be relevant.
   d. the company would consider all fixed overhead to be irrelevant.
   e. None of these.

8-9   Carroll Company, a manufacturer of vitamins and minerals, has been asked by a large drugstore chain to provide bottles of vitamin E. The bottles would be labeled with the name of the drugstore chain, and the chain would pay Carroll $2.30 per bottle rather than the $3.00 regular price. Which type of a decision is this?

   a. Make-or-buy
   b. Special-order
   c. Keep-or-drop
   d. Economic order quantity
   e. Markup pricing

8-10 A segment could be which of the following?

   a. Product
   b. Customer type
   c. Geographic region
   d. All of these.
   e. None of these.

8-11 Garrett Company provided the following information:

	Product 1	Product 2
Units sold	10,000	20,000
Price	$20	$15
Variable cost per unit	$10	$10
Direct fixed cost	$35,000	$75,000

Common fixed cost totaled $46,000. Garrett allocates common fixed cost to Product 1 and Product 2 on the basis of sales. If Product 2 is dropped, which of the following is true?

   a. Sales will increase by $300,000.
   b. Overall operating income will increase by $2,600.
   c. Overall operating income will decrease by $25,000.
   d. Overall operating income will not change.
   e. Common fixed cost will decrease by $27,600.

8-12 Jennings Hardware Store marks up its merchandise by 30%. If a part costs $25.00, which of the following is true?

   a. The price is $7.50.
   b. The markup is $32.50.
   c. The price is $32.50.
   d. The markup is pure profit.
   e. All of these.

8-13 When a company faces a production constraint or scarce resource (e.g., only a certain number of machine hours are available), it is important to

   a. produce the product with the highest contribution margin in total.
   b. produce the product with the lowest full manufacturing cost.
   c. produce the product with the highest contribution margin per unit of scarce resource.
   d. produce the product with the highest contribution margin per unit.
   e. The constraint is not relevant to the production problem.

8-14 In the keep-or-drop decision, the company will find which of the following income statement formats most useful?

    a. A segmented income statement in the contribution margin format

    b. A segmented income statement in the full costing format that is used for financial reporting

    c. An overall income statement in the contribution margin format

    d. An overall income statement in the full costing format that is used for financial reporting

    e. Income statements are of no use in making this type of decision.

8-15 In the sell-or-process-further decision,

    a. joint costs are always relevant.

    b. total costs of joint processing and further processing are relevant.

    c. all costs incurred prior to the split-off point are relevant.

    d. the most profitable outcome may be to further process some separately identifiable products beyond the split-off point, but sell others at the split-off point.

    e. None of these.

BRIEF EXERCISES: SET A

OBJECTIVE **2**
Example 8.1

Brief Exercise 8-16 Structuring a Make-or-Buy Problem

Fresh Foods, a large restaurant chain, needs to determine if it would be cheaper to produce 5,000 units of its main food ingredient for use in its restaurants or to purchase them from an outside supplier for $12 each. Cost information on internal production includes the following:

	Total Cost	Unit Cost
Direct materials	$25,000	$ 5.00
Direct labor	15,000	3.00
Variable manufacturing overhead	7,500	1.50
Variable marketing overhead	10,000	2.00
Fixed plant overhead	30,000	6.00
Total	$87,500	$17.50

Fixed overhead will continue whether the ingredient is produced internally or externally. No additional costs of purchasing will be incurred beyond the purchase price.

Required:

1. What are the alternatives for Fresh Foods?
2. List the relevant cost(s) of internal production and of external purchase.
3. Which alternative is more cost effective and by how much?
4. Now assume that 20% of the fixed overhead can be avoided if the ingredient is purchased externally. Which alternative is more cost effective and by how much?

OBJECTIVE **2**
Example 8.2

Brief Exercise 8-17 Structuring a Special-Order Problem

Harrison Ford Company has been approached by a new customer with an offer to purchase 10,000 units of its model IJ5 at a price of $5 each. The new customer is geographically separated from the company's other customers, and existing sales would not be affected. Harrison normally produces 75,000 units of IJ5 per year but only plans to produce and sell 60,000 in the coming year. The normal sales price is $12 per unit. Unit cost information for the normal level of activity is as follows:

Direct materials	$1.75
Direct labor	2.50
Variable overhead	1.50
Fixed overhead	3.25
Total	$9.00

Fixed overhead will not be affected by whether or not the special order is accepted.

Required:

1. What are the relevant costs and benefits of the two alternatives (accept or reject the special order)?
2. By how much will operating income increase or decrease if the order is accepted?

Brief Exercise 8-18 Segmented Income Statement

OBJECTIVE ▸ 2
Example 8.3

Gorman Nurseries Inc. grows poinsettias and fruit trees in a green house/nursery operation. The following information was provided for the coming year.

	Poinsettias	Fruit Trees
Sales	$970,000	$3,100,000
Variable cost of goods sold	460,000	1,630,000
Direct fixed overhead	160,000	200,000

A sales commission of 4% of sales is paid for each of the two product lines. Direct fixed selling and administrative expense was estimated to be $146,000 for the poinsettia line and $87,000 for the fruit tree line.

Common fixed overhead for the nursery operation was estimated to be $800,000; common selling and administrative expense was estimated to be $450,000.

Required:

Prepare a segmented income statement for Gorman Nurseries for the coming year, using variable costing.

Use the following information for Brief Exercises 8-19 and 8-20:
Shown below is a segmented income statement for Hickory Company's three wooden flooring product lines:

	Strip	Plank	Parquet	Total
Sales revenue	$400,000	$200,000	$300,000	$900,000
Less: Variable expenses	225,000	120,000	250,000	595,000
Contribution margin	$175,000	$ 80,000	$ 50,000	$305,000
Less direct fixed expenses:				
Machine rent	(5,000)	(20,000)	(50,000)	(75,000)
Supervision	(15,000)	(10,000)	(20,000)	(45,000)
Depreciation	(35,000)	(10,000)	(25,000)	(70,000)
Segment margin	$120,000	$ 40,000	$(45,000)	$115,000

Brief Exercise 8-19 Structuring a Keep-or-Drop Product-Line Problem

OBJECTIVE ▸ 2
Example 8.4

Refer to the information for Hickory Company above. Hickory's management is deciding whether to keep or drop the parquet product line. Hickory's parquet flooring product line has a contribution margin of $50,000 (sales of $300,000 less total variable costs of $250,000). All variable costs are relevant. Relevant fixed costs associated with this line include 80% of parquet's machine rent and all of parquet's supervision salaries.

(Continued)

Required:

1. List the alternatives being considered with respect to the parquet flooring line.
2. List the relevant benefits and costs for each alternative.
3. Which alternative is more cost effective and by how much?

OBJECTIVE **2**
Example 8.5

Brief Exercise 8-20 Structuring a Keep-or-Drop Product-Line Problem with Complementary Effects

Refer to the information for Hickory Company on the previous page. Relevant fixed costs associated with this line include 80% of parquet's machine rent and all of parquet's supervision salaries. In addition, assume that dropping the parquet product line would reduce sales of the strip line by 10% and sales of the plank line by 5%. All other information remains the same.

Required:

1. If the parquet product line is dropped, what is the contribution margin for the strip line? For the plank line?
2. Which alternative (keep or drop the parquet product line) is now more cost effective and by how much?

OBJECTIVE **2**
Example 8.6

Brief Exercise 8-21 Structuring the Sell-or-Process-Further Decision

Jack's Lumber Yard receives 8,000 large trees each period that it subsequently processes into rough logs by stripping off the tree bark and leaves (i.e., one tree equals one log). Jack's then must decide whether to sell its rough logs (for use in log cabin construction) at split-off or to process them further into refined lumber (for use in regular construction framing). Jack's normally sells logs for a per-unit price of $495. Alternately, each log can be processed further into 800 board feet of lumber at an additional cost of $0.15 per board foot. Also, lumber can be sold for $0.75 per board foot.

Required:

1. What is the contribution to income from selling the logs for log cabin construction?
2. What is the contribution to income from processing the logs into lumber?
3. Should Jack's continue to sell the logs or process them further into lumber?

Use the following information for Brief Exercises 8-22 and 8-23:
Comfy Fit Company manufactures two types of university sweatshirts, the Swoop and the Rufus, with unit contribution margins of $5 and $15, respectively. Regardless of type, each sweatshirt must be fed through a stitching machine to affix the appropriate university logo. The firm leases seven machines that each provides 1,000 hours of machine time per year. Each Swoop sweatshirt requires 6 minutes of machine time, and each Rufus sweatshirt requires 20 minutes of machine time. [*Note:* For all answers that are less than 1.0, round the answer to two decimal places. For all unit answers (e.g., the answer is greater than 1.0), round the answer to the nearest whole number.]

OBJECTIVE **3**
Example 8.7

Brief Exercise 8-22 Determining the Optimal Product Mix with One Constrained Resource

Refer to the information for Comfy Fit Company above. Assume that there are no other constraints.

Required:

1. What is the contribution margin per hour of machine time for each type of sweatshirt?
2. What is the optimal mix of sweatshirts?
3. What is the total contribution margin earned for the optimal mix?

Brief Exercise 8-23 Determining the Optimal Product Mix with One Constrained Resource and a Sales Constraint

OBJECTIVE ◄ 3

Example 8.8

Refer to the information for Comfy Fit Company on the previous page. Assume that a maximum of 40,000 units of each sweatshirt can be sold.

Required:

1. What is the contribution margin per hour of machine time for each type of sweatshirt?
2. What is the optimal mix of sweatshirts?
3. What is the total contribution margin earned for the optimal mix?

Brief Exercise 8-24 Calculating Price by Applying a Markup Percentage to Cost

OBJECTIVE ◄ 4

Example 8.9

Integrity Accounting Firm provides various financial services to organizations. Integrity has decided to price its jobs at the total variable costs of the job plus 15%. The job for a medium-sized dance club client included the following costs:

Direct materials	$ 20,000
Direct labor (partners and staff accountants)	150,000
Depreciation (using straight-line method) on Integrity's office building	50,000

Required:

Calculate the price charged by Integrity Accounting to the dance club.

Brief Exercise 8-25 Calculating a Target Cost

OBJECTIVE ◄ 4

Example 8.10

Yuhu manufactures cell phones and is developing a new model with a feature (aptly named Don't Drink and Dial) that prevents the phone from dialing an owner-defined list of phone numbers between the hours of midnight and 6:00 A.M. The new phone model has a target price of $380. Management requires a 25% profit on new product revenues.

Required:

1. Calculate the amount of desired profit.
2. Calculate the target cost.

BRIEF EXERCISES: SET B

Brief Exercise 8-26 Structuring a Make-or-Buy Problem

OBJECTIVE ◄ 2

Example 8.1

Coed Scents, a national producer of young adult perfumes and colognes, needs to determine if it would be cheaper to produce 100,000 bottles of its most popular perfume, Two AM, for sale in its college town shops or to purchase them from an outside supplier for $25 each. Cost information on internal production includes the following:

	Total Cost	Unit Cost
Direct materials	$2,000,000	$20.00
Direct labor	350,000	3.50
Variable manufacturing overhead	150,000	1.50
Variable marketing overhead	250,000	2.50
Fixed plant overhead	300,000	3.00
Total	$3,050,000	$30.50

Fixed overhead will continue whether Two AM is produced internally or externally. No additional costs of purchasing will be incurred beyond the purchase price.

(Continued)

Required:

1. What are the alternatives for Coed Scents?
2. List the relevant cost(s) of internal production and of external purchase.
3. Which alternative is more cost effective and by how much?
4. Now assume that Coed Scents' internal audit team learned through a special data analytics project that intellectual property theft is a significant threat for outsourced production. The team estimates that if Coed Scents outsources its production, it will need to spend $350,000 to manage intellectual property theft of its Two AM brand by competitors operating in the country where the outsourced production occurs. Which alternative is more cost effective and by how much?

OBJECTIVE 2
Example 8.2

Brief Exercise 8-27 Structuring a Special-Order Problem

Rabbit Foot Motors has been approached by a new customer with an offer to purchase 5,000 units of its hands-free, Wi-Fi-enabled automotive model—the SMAK—at a price of $18,000 per automobile. Rabbit Foot's other sales would not be affected by this new customer offer. Rabbit Foot normally produces 100,000 units of its SMAK model per year but only plans to produce and sell 90,000 in the coming year. The normal sales price is $35,000 per SMAK. Unit cost information for the normal level of activity is as follows:

Direct materials	$10,000
Direct labor	2,000
Variable overhead	4,000
Fixed overhead	8,000
Total	$24,000

Fixed overhead will not be affected by whether or not the special order is accepted.

Required:

1. What are the relevant costs and benefits of the two alternatives (accept or reject the special order)?
2. By how much will operating income increase or decrease if the order is accepted?

OBJECTIVE 2
Example 8.3

Brief Exercise 8-28 Segmented Income Statement

Kraft Bowlen owns two sports franchises—the Bladers (a hockey team) and the Ballers (a basketball team). The following information was provided for the coming year.

	Bladers	Ballers
Sales	$80,000,000	$180,000,000
Variable cost of goods sold	10,000,000	30,000,000
Direct fixed overhead	20,000,000	100,000,000

A sales commission of 5% of sales revenue is paid for each of the two sports franchises. Direct fixed selling and administrative expense was estimated to be $4,000,000 for the Bladers franchise and $10,000,000 for the Ballers franchise.

Common fixed overhead associated with owning the franchises was estimated to be $18,000,000; common selling and administrative expense was estimated to be $8,000,000.

Required:

Prepare a segmented income statement for Kraft Bowlen for the coming year, using variable costing.

Use the following information for Brief Exercises 8-29 and 8-30:

Shown below is a segmented income statement for Mullett Marina's three main boating service lines:

	Winter Storage	Boat Fuel & Concessions	Boat Maintenance	Total
Sales revenue	$4,000,000	$1,000,000	$5,000,000	$10,000,000
Less: Variable expenses	2,000,000	200,000	4,900,000	7,100,000
Contribution margin	$2,000,000	$ 800,000	$ 100,000	$ 2,900,000
Less direct fixed expenses:				
Garage/warehouse rent	(700,000)	(55,000)	(350,000)	(1,105,000)
Supervision	(50,000)	(70,000)	(150,000)	(270,000)
Equipment depreciation	(250,000)	(75,000)	(100,000)	(425,000)
Segment margin	$1,000,000	$ 600,000	$ (500,000)	$ 1,100,000

Brief Exercise 8-29 Structuring a Keep-or-Drop Product-Line Problem

OBJECTIVE ▶ 2

Example 8.4

Refer to the information for Mullett Marina above. Mullett's management is deciding whether to keep or drop the Boat Maintenance service line. Mullett's Boat Maintenance service line has a contribution margin of $100,000 (sales of $5,000,000 less total variable costs of $4,900,000). All variable costs are relevant. Relevant fixed costs associated with this line include 60% of Boat Maintenance's garage/warehouse rent and 50% of Boat Maintenance's supervision salaries.

Required:

1. List the alternatives being considered with respect to the Boat Maintenance service line.
2. List the relevant benefits and costs for each alternative.
3. Which alternative is more cost effective and by how much?

Brief Exercise 8-30 Structuring a Keep-or-Drop Product-Line Problem with Complementary Effects

OBJECTIVE ▶ 2

Example 8.5

Refer to the information for Mullett Marina above. Relevant fixed costs associated with this line include 60% of Boat Maintenance's garage/warehouse rent and 50% of Boat Maintenance's supervision salaries. In addition, assume that dropping the Boat Maintenance service line would reduce sales of the Winter Storage line by 20% and sales of the Boat Fuel & Concessions line by 10%. All other information remains the same.

Required:

1. If the Boat Maintenance service line is dropped, what is the contribution margin for the Boat Fuel & Concessions line? For the Winter Storage line?
2. Which alternative (keep or drop the Boat Maintenance line) is now more cost effective and by how much?

Brief Exercise 8-31 Structuring the Sell-or-Process-Further Decision

OBJECTIVE ▶ 2

Example 8.6

Bart's Butters receives 1,000,000 containers of raw milk each period that it subsequently processes into consumable milk by adjusting the fat content, adding vitamins, and destroying any potentially harmful bacteria. For Bart's, one container equals one gallon of consumable milk. Bart's then must decide whether to sell its consumable milk at split-off or to process it further into butter. Bart's normally sells consumable milk for a per-gallon price of $3. Alternately, each gallon of milk can be processed further into one-half tub of butter (i.e., one gallon of milk equals 0.5 gallon of butter) at an additional cost of $1.50 per tub of butter. Also, butter can be sold for $6.00 per tub.

(Continued)

Required:

1. What is the contribution to income from selling the consumable milk?
2. What is the contribution to income from processing the consumable milk into butter?
3. Should Bart's continue to sell the consumable milk or process it further into butter?

> *Use the following information for Brief Exercises 8-32 and 8-33:*
> Relax Spas provides two types of massage services, the Full Body and the Trouble Spots, with unit contribution margins of $198 and $90, respectively. Regardless of type, each massage requires the use of a certified masseuse. Relax Spas has four masseuses on staff who each work 1,500 hours per year. Each Full Body massage uses 90 minutes of masseuse time, and each Trouble Spot massage uses 30 minutes of masseuse time. [*Note:* For all answers that are less than 1.0, round the answer to two decimal places. For all unit answers (e.g., the answer is greater than 1.0), round the answer to the nearest whole number.]

OBJECTIVE 3
Example 8.7

Brief Exercise 8-32 Determining the Optimal Product Mix with One Constrained Resource

Refer to the information for Relax Spas above. Assume that there are no other constraints.

Required:

1. What is the contribution margin per hour of masseuse time for each type of massage?
2. What is the optimal mix of massages?
3. What is the total contribution margin earned for the optimal mix?

OBJECTIVE 3
Example 8.8

Brief Exercise 8-33 Determining the Optimal Product Mix with One Constrained Resource and a Sales Constraint

Refer to the information for Relax Spas above. Assume that a maximum of 8,000 massages of each type can be sold.

Required:

1. What is the contribution margin per hour of masseuse time for each type of massage?
2. What is the optimal mix of massages?
3. What is the total contribution margin earned for the optimal mix?

OBJECTIVE 4
Example 8.9

Brief Exercise 8-34 Calculating Price by Applying a Markup Percentage to Cost

Enviro Consulting Firm provides various environmental consulting services to organizations. Enviro has decided to price its jobs at the total direct variable costs of the job plus 10%. The job for a new client included the following costs:

Direct materials	$500,000
Direct labor (partners and staff accountants)	250,000
Depreciation (using straight-line method) on Enviro's office building	300,000

Required:

Calculate the price charged by Enviro Consulting Firm to its new client.

OBJECTIVE 4
Example 8.10

Brief Exercise 8-35 Calculating a Target Cost

Sisters, Inc. manufactures professional-level printers that perform multiple features, such as high-resolution color scanning, printing, faxing, and copying. The new printer model has a target price of $600. Management requires a 20% profit on new product revenues.

Required:

1. Calculate the amount of desired profit.
2. Calculate the target cost.

EXERCISES

Exercise 8-36 Model for Making Tactical Decisions

OBJECTIVE ◀ 1

The model for making tactical decisions described in the text has six steps. These steps are listed, out of order, below.

Required:

Put the steps in the correct order, starting with the step that should be taken first.
1. Select the alternative with the greatest overall benefit.
2. Identify the costs and benefits associated with each feasible alternative.
3. Assess qualitative factors.
4. Recognize and define the problem.
5. Identify alternatives as possible solutions to the problem.
6. Total the relevant costs and benefits for each alternative.

Exercise 8-37 Model for Making Tactical Decisions

OBJECTIVE ◀ 1

Austin Porter is a sophomore at a small Midwestern university (SMWU). He is considering whether to continue at this university or to transfer to one with a nationally recognized engineering program. Austin's decision-making process included the following:
a. He surfed the web to check out the sites of a number of colleges and universities with engineering programs.
b. Austin wrote to five of the universities to obtain information on their engineering colleges, tuition and room and board costs, the likelihood of being accepted, and so on.
c. Austin compared costs of the five other schools with the cost of his present school. He totaled the balance in his checking and savings accounts, estimated the earnings from his work-study job, and asked his parents whether or not they would be able to help him out.
d. Austin's high-school sweetheart had a long heart-to-heart talk with him about their future—specifically, that there might be no future if he left town.
e. Austin thought that while he enjoyed his present college, its engineering program did not have the national reputation that would enable him to get a good job on either the East or West Coast. Working for a large company on the coast was an important dream of his.
f. Austin's major advisor agreed that a school with a national reputation would make job hunting easier. However, he reminded Austin that small college graduates had occasionally gotten the kind of jobs that Austin wanted.
g. Austin had a number of good friends at SMWU, and they were encouraging him to stay.
h. A friend of Austin's from high school returned home for a long weekend. She attends a prestigious university and told Austin of the fun and opportunities available at her school. She encouraged Austin to check out the possibilities elsewhere.
i. A friendly professor outside of Austin's major area ran into him at the student union. She listened to his thinking and reminded him that a degree from SMWU would easily get him into a good graduate program. Perhaps he should consider postponing the job hunt until he had his master's degree in hand.
j. Two of the three prestigious universities accepted Austin and offered financial aid. The third one rejected his application.
k. Austin made his decision.

Required:

Classify the Events a through k under one of the six steps of the model for making tactical decisions described in your text.

Use the following information for Exercises 8-38 and 8-39:

Zion Manufacturing had always made its components in-house. However, Bryce Component Works had recently offered to supply one component, K2, at a price of $25 each. Zion uses 10,000 units of Component K2 each year. The cost per unit of this component is as follows:

Direct materials	$12.00
Direct labor	8.25
Variable overhead	4.50
Fixed overhead	2.00
Total	$26.75

OBJECTIVE 1 2

Exercise 8-38 **Make-or-Buy Decision**

Refer to the information for Zion Manufacturing above. The fixed overhead is an allocated expense; none of it would be eliminated if production of Component K2 stopped.

Required:

1. What are the alternatives facing Zion Manufacturing with respect to production of Component K2?
2. List the relevant costs for each alternative. If Zion decides to purchase the component from Bryce, by how much will operating income increase or decrease?
3. **CONCEPTUAL CONNECTION** Which alternative is better?

OBJECTIVE 2

Exercise 8-39 **Make-or-Buy Decision**

Refer to the information for Zion Manufacturing above. Assume that 75% of Zion Manufacturing's fixed overhead for Component K2 would be eliminated if that component were no longer produced.

Required:

1. **CONCEPTUAL CONNECTION** If Zion decides to purchase the component from Bryce, by how much will operating income increase or decrease? Which alternative is better?
2. **CONCEPTUAL CONNECTION** Briefly explain how increasing or decreasing the 75% figure affects Zion's final decision to make or purchase the component.
3. **CONCEPTUAL CONNECTION** By how much would the per-unit relevant fixed cost have to decrease before Zion would be indifferent (i.e., incur the same cost) between "making" versus "purchasing" the component? Show and briefly explain your calculations.

Use the following information for Exercises 8-40 and 8-41:

Smooth Move Company manufactures professional paperweights and has been approached by a new customer with an offer to purchase 15,000 units at a per-unit price of $7.00. The new customer is geographically separated from Smooth Move's other customers, and existing sales will not be affected. Smooth Move normally produces 82,000 units but plans to produce and sell only 65,000 in the coming year. The normal sales price is $12 per unit. Unit cost information is as follows:

Direct materials	$3.10
Direct labor	2.25
Variable overhead	1.15
Fixed overhead	1.80
Total	$8.30

Exercise 8-40 Special-Order Decision

OBJECTIVE 2

EXCEL

Refer to the information for Smooth Move Company on the previous page. If Smooth Move accepts the order, no fixed manufacturing activities will be affected because there is sufficient excess capacity.

Required:

1. What are the alternatives for Smooth Move?
2. **CONCEPTUAL CONNECTION** Should Smooth Move accept the special order? By how much will profit increase or decrease if the order is accepted?
3. **CONCEPTUAL CONNECTION** Briefly explain the significance of the statement in the exercise that "existing sales will not be affected" (by the special sale).

Exercise 8-41 Special Order

OBJECTIVE 2

EXCEL

Refer to the information for Smooth Move Company on the previous page. Suppose a customer wants to have its company logo affixed to each paperweight using a label. Smooth Move would have to purchase a special logo labeling machine that will cost $12,000. The machine will be able to label the 15,000 units and then it will be scrapped (with no further value). No other fixed overhead activities will be incurred. In addition, each special logo requires additional direct materials of $0.20.

Required:

CONCEPTUAL CONNECTION Should Smooth Move accept the special order? By how much will profit increase or decrease if the order is accepted?

Exercise 8-42 Segmented Income Statement

OBJECTIVE 2

Knitline Inc. produces high-end sweaters and jackets in a single factory. The following information was provided for the coming year.

	Sweaters	Jackets
Sales	$210,000	$450,000
Variable cost of goods sold	145,000	196,000
Direct fixed overhead	25,000	47,000

A sales commission of 5% of sales is paid for each of the two product lines. Direct fixed selling and administrative expense was estimated to be $20,000 for the sweater line and $50,000 for the jacket line.

Common fixed overhead for the factory was estimated to be $45,000. Common selling and administrative expense was estimated to be $15,000.

Required:

1. Prepare a segmented income statement for Knitline for the coming year, using variable costing.
2. **CONCEPTUAL CONNECTION** Suppose that next year, all revenues and costs are expected to remain the same except for direct fixed overhead expense, which will go up by $10,000 for one of the product lines due to costs related to new equipment. Does it matter which line (sweaters or jackets) requires the new equipment? Why?

Use the following information for Exercises 8-43 through 8-45:
Petoskey Company produces three products: Alanson, Boyne, and Conway. A segmented income statement, with amounts given in thousands, follows:

	Alanson	Boyne	Conway	Total
Sales revenue	$1,280	$185	$300	$1,765
Less: Variable expenses	1,115	45	225	1,385
Contribution margin	$ 165	$140	$ 75	$ 380
Less direct fixed expenses:				
Depreciation	50	15	10	75
Salaries	95	85	80	260
Segment margin	$ 20	$ 40	$ (15)	$ 45

Direct fixed expenses consist of depreciation and plant supervisory salaries. All depreciation on the equipment is dedicated to the product lines. None of the equipment can be sold.

OBJECTIVE 2

Exercise 8-43 Keep-or-Drop Decision

Refer to the information for Petoskey Company above. Assume that each of the three products has a different supervisor whose position would *remain* if the associated product were dropped.

Required:

CONCEPTUAL CONNECTION Estimate the impact on profit that would result from dropping Conway. Explain why Petoskey should keep or drop Conway.

OBJECTIVE 2

Exercise 8-44 Keep-or-Drop Decision

Refer to the information for Petoskey Company above. Assume that each of the three products has a different supervisor whose position would *be eliminated* if the associated product were dropped.

Required:

CONCEPTUAL CONNECTION Estimate the impact on profit that would result from dropping Conway. Explain why Petoskey should keep or drop Conway.

OBJECTIVE 2

Exercise 8-45 Keep-or-Drop Decision

Refer to the information for Petoskey Company from **Exercise 8-44**. Assume that 20% of the Alanson customers choose to buy from Petoskey because it offers a full range of products, including Conway. If Conway were no longer available from Petoskey, these customers would go elsewhere to purchase Alanson.

Required:

CONCEPTUAL CONNECTION Estimate the impact on profit that would result from dropping Conway. Explain why Petoskey should keep or drop Conway.

OBJECTIVE 2

Exercise 8-46 Sell at Split-Off or Process Further

Bozo Inc. manufactures two products from a joint production process. The joint process costs $110,000 and yields 6,000 pounds of LTE compound and 14,000 pounds of HS compound. LTE can be sold at split-off for $55 per pound. HS can be sold at split-off for $9 per pound. A buyer of HS asked Bozo to process HS further into CS compound. If HS were processed further, it would cost $34,000 to turn 14,000 pounds of HS into 4,000 pounds of CS. The CS would sell for $45 per pound.

Required:

1. What is the contribution to income from selling the 14,000 pounds of HS at split-off?
2. **CONCEPTUAL CONNECTION** What is the contribution to income from processing the 14,000 pounds of HS into 4,000 pounds of CS? Should Bozo continue to sell the HS at split-off or process it further into CS?

Use the following information for Exercises 8-47 and 8-48:
Billings Company produces two products, Product Reno and Product Tahoe. Each product goes through its own assembly and finishing departments. However, both of them must go through the painting department. The painting department has capacity of 2,460 hours per year. Product Reno has a unit contribution margin of $120 and requires 5 hours of painting department time. Product Tahoe has a unit contribution margin of $75 and requires 3 hours of painting department time. There are no other constraints.

Exercise 8-47 Choosing the Optimal Product Mix with One Constrained Resource

OBJECTIVE ▶ 3

Refer to the information for Billings Company above.

Required:

1. What is the contribution margin per hour of painting department time for each product?
2. What is the optimal mix of products?
3. What is the total contribution margin earned for the optimal mix?

Exercise 8-48 Choosing the Optimal Product Mix with a Constrained Resource and a Demand Constraint

OBJECTIVE ▶ 3

Refer to the information for Billings Company above. Assume that only 500 units of each product can be sold.

Required:

1. What is the optimal mix of products?
2. What is the total contribution margin earned for the optimal mix?

Exercise 8-49 Calculating Price Using a Markup Percentage of Cost

OBJECTIVE ▶ 4

Lake McDonald Gift Shop has decided to price the National Parks Memory Card Game that it sells at cost plus 65%. The National Parks Memory Card Game costs $20 each, and another one, the Guess This Animal Track Game, costs $40 each.

Required:

1. What price will Lake McDonald Gift Shop charge for each National Parks Memory Card Game?
2. What price will Lake McDonald Gift Shop charge for each Guess This Animal Track Game?
3. **CONCEPTUAL CONNECTION** Briefly explain two specific challenges that the financial manager of Lake McDonald Gift Shop might encounter in employing this cost-plus pricing approach.

Exercise 8-50 Target Costing

OBJECTIVE ▶ 4

EXCEL

H. Banks Company would like to design, produce, and sell versatile toasters for the home kitchen market. The toaster will have four slots that adjust in thickness to accommodate both slim slices of bread and oversized bagels. The target price is $60. Banks requires that new products be priced such that 20% of the price is profit.

(Continued)

Required:

1. Calculate the amount of desired profit per unit of the new toaster.
2. Calculate the target cost per unit of the new toaster.

OBJECTIVE **1** **2**

Exercise 8-51 Keep or Buy, Sunk Costs

Heather Alburty purchased a previously owned, 2004 Grand Am for $8,900. Since purchasing the car, she has spent the following amounts on parts and labor:

New stereo system	$1,200
Trick paint	400
New wide racing tires	800
Total	$2,400

Unfortunately, the new stereo doesn't completely drown out the sounds of a grinding transmission. Apparently, the Grand Am needs a considerable amount of work to make it reliable transportation. Heather estimates that the needed repairs include the following:

Transmission overhaul	$2,000
Water pump	400
Master cylinder work	1,100
Total	$3,500

In a visit to a used car dealer, Heather has found a 2005 Neon in mint condition for $9,400. Heather has advertised and found that she can sell the Grand Am for only $6,400. If she buys the Neon, she will pay cash, but she would need to sell the Grand Am.

Required:

1. **CONCEPTUAL CONNECTION** In trying to decide whether to restore the Grand Am or to buy the Neon, Heather is distressed because she already has spent $11,300 on the Grand Am. The investment seems too much to give up. How would you react to her concern?
2. **CONCEPTUAL CONNECTION** Assuming that Heather would be equally happy with the Grand Am or the Neon, should she buy the Neon, or should she restore the Grand Am?

Use the following information for Exercises 8-52 and 8-53:
Blasingham Company is currently manufacturing Part Q108, producing 35,000 units annually. The part is used in the production of several products made by Blasingham. The cost per unit for Q108 is as follows:

Direct materials	$ 6.00
Direct labor	2.00
Variable overhead	1.50
Fixed overhead	3.50
Total	$13.00

OBJECTIVE **2**

Exercise 8-52 Make or Buy

Refer to the information for Blasingham Company above. Of the total fixed overhead assigned to Q108, $77,000 is direct fixed overhead (the lease of production machinery and salary of a production line supervisor—neither of which will be needed if the line is dropped). The remaining fixed overhead is common fixed overhead. An outside supplier has offered to sell the part to Blasingham for $11. There is no alternative use for the facilities currently used to produce the part.

Required:

1. **CONCEPTUAL CONNECTION** Should Blasingham Company make or buy Part Q108?
2. What is the most that Blasingham would be willing to pay an outside supplier?
3. If Blasingham buys the part, by how much will income increase or decrease?

Exercise 8-53 Make or Buy

OBJECTIVE 1 2

Refer to the information for Blasingham Company on the previous page. All of the fixed overhead is common fixed overhead. An outside supplier has offered to sell the part to Blasingham for $11. There is no alternative use for the facilities currently used to produce the part.

Required:

1. **CONCEPTUAL CONNECTION** Should Blasingham Company make or buy Part Q108?
2. What is the most Blasingham would be willing to pay an outside supplier?
3. If Blasingham buys the part, by how much will income increase or decrease?

PROBLEMS

Problem 8-54 Special-Order Decision

OBJECTIVE 1 2

Rianne Company produces a light fixture with the following unit cost:

Direct materials	$2
Direct labor	1
Variable overhead	3
Fixed overhead	2
Unit cost	$8

The production capacity is 300,000 units per year. Because of a depressed housing market, the company expects to produce only 180,000 fixtures for the coming year. The company also has fixed selling costs totaling $500,000 per year and variable selling costs of $1 per unit sold. The fixtures normally sell for $12 each.

At the beginning of the year, a customer from a geographic region outside the area normally served by the company offered to buy 100,000 fixtures for $7 each. The customer also offered to pay all transportation costs. Since there would be no sales commissions involved, this order would not have any variable selling costs.

Required:

1. **CONCEPTUAL CONNECTION** Based on a quantitative (numerical) analysis, should the company accept the order?
2. **CONCEPTUAL CONNECTION** What qualitative factors might impact the decision? Assume that no other orders are expected beyond the regular business and the special order.

Problem 8-55 Segmented Income Statements, Product-Line Analysis

OBJECTIVE 2

EXCEL

Alard Company produces blenders and coffee makers. During the past year, the company produced and sold 65,000 blenders and 75,000 coffee makers. Fixed costs for Alard totaled $340,000, of which $184,000 can be avoided if the blenders are not produced and $142,500 can be avoided if the coffee makers are not produced. Revenue and variable cost information follows:

	Blenders	Coffee Makers
Selling price per appliance	$24	$29
Variable expenses per appliance	18	27

(Continued)

Required:

1. Prepare segmented income statements. Separate direct and common fixed costs.
2. What would the effect be on Alard's profit if the coffee maker line is dropped? The blender line?
3. What would the effect be on firm profits if an additional 10,000 blenders could be produced (using existing capacity) and sold for $21.50 on a special-order basis? Existing sales would be unaffected by the special order.

OBJECTIVE ▶2▶ **Problem 8-56** Segmented Income Statement, Management Decision Making

FunTime Company produces three lines of greeting cards: scented, musical, and regular. Segmented income statements for the past year are as follows:

	Scented	Musical	Regular	Total
Sales	$10,000	$15,000	$25,000	$50,000
Less: Variable expenses	7,000	12,000	12,500	31,500
Contribution margin	$ 3,000	$ 3,000	$12,500	$18,500
Less: Direct fixed expenses	4,000	5,000	3,000	12,000
Segment margin	$ (1,000)	$ (2,000)	$ 9,500	$ 6,500
Less: Common fixed expenses				7,500
Operating income (loss)				$(1,000)

Kathy Bunker, president of FunTime, is concerned about the financial performance of her firm and is seriously considering dropping both the scented and musical product lines. However, before making a final decision, she consults Jim Dorn, FunTime's vice president of marketing.

Required:

1. **CONCEPTUAL CONNECTION** Jim believes that by increasing advertising by $1,000 ($250 for the scented line and $750 for the musical line), sales of those two lines would increase by 30%. If you were Kathy, how would you react to this information?
2. **CONCEPTUAL CONNECTION** Jim warns Kathy that eliminating the scented and musical lines would lower the sales of the regular line by 20%. Given this information, would it be profitable to eliminate the scented and musical lines?
3. **CONCEPTUAL CONNECTION** Suppose that eliminating either line reduces sales of the regular cards by 10%. Would a combination of increased advertising (the option described in Requirement 1) and eliminating one of the lines be beneficial? Identify the best combination for the firm.

OBJECTIVE ▶1▶ 2▶ **Problem 8-57** Make or Buy, Qualitative Considerations

Hetrick Dentistry Services operates in a large metropolitan area. Currently, Hetrick has its own dental laboratory to produce porcelain and gold crowns. The unit costs to produce the crowns are as follows:

	Porcelain	Gold
Raw materials	$ 70	$130
Direct labor	27	27
Variable overhead	8	8
Fixed overhead	22	22
Total	$127	$187

Fixed overhead is detailed as follows:

Salary (supervisor)	$26,000
Depreciation	5,000
Rent (lab facility)	32,000

Overhead is applied on the basis of direct labor hours. These rates were computed by using 5,500 direct labor hours.

A local dental laboratory has offered to supply Hetrick all the crowns it needs. Its price is $125 for porcelain crowns and $150 for gold crowns; however, the offer is conditional on supplying both types of crowns—it will not supply just one type for the price indicated. If the offer is accepted, the equipment used by Hetrick's laboratory would be scrapped (it is old and has no market value), and the lab facility would be closed. Hetrick uses 2,000 porcelain crowns and 600 gold crowns per year.

Required:

1. **CONCEPTUAL CONNECTION** Should Hetrick continue to make its own crowns, or should they be purchased from the external supplier? What is the dollar effect of purchasing?
2. **CONCEPTUAL CONNECTION** What qualitative factors should Hetrick consider in making this decision?
3. **CONCEPTUAL CONNECTION** Suppose that the lab facility is owned rather than rented and that the $32,000 is depreciation rather than rent. What effect does this have on the analysis in Requirement 1?
4. **CONCEPTUAL CONNECTION** Refer to the original data. Assume that the volume of crowns used is 4,200 porcelain and 600 gold. Should Hetrick make or buy the crowns? Explain the outcome.

Problem 8-58 Sell or Process Further

OBJECTIVE  1 2

EXCEL

Zanda Drug Corporation buys three chemicals that are processed to produce two types of analgesics used as ingredients for popular over-the-counter drugs. The purchased chemicals are blended for 2 to 3 hours and then heated for 15 minutes. The results of the process are two separate analgesics, depryl and pencol, which are sent to a drying room until their moisture content is reduced to 6 to 8%. For every 1,300 pounds of chemicals used, 600 pounds of depryl and 600 pounds of pencol are produced. After drying, depryl and pencol are sold to companies that process them into their final form. The selling prices are $12 per pound for depryl and $30 per pound for pencol. The costs to produce 600 pounds of each analgesic are as follows:

Chemicals	$8,500
Direct labor	6,735
Overhead	9,900

The analgesics are packaged in 20-pound bags and shipped. The cost of each bag is $1.30. Shipping costs $0.10 per pound.

Zanda could process depryl further by grinding it into a fine powder and then molding the powder into tablets. The tablets can be sold directly to retail drug stores as a generic brand. If this route were taken, the revenue received per bottle of tablets would be $4.00, with 10 bottles produced by every pound of depryl. The costs of grinding and tableting total $2.50 per pound of depryl. Bottles cost $0.40 each. Bottles are shipped in boxes that hold 25 bottles at a shipping cost of $1.60 per box.

Required:

1. **CONCEPTUAL CONNECTION** Should Zanda sell depryl at split-off, or should depryl be processed and sold as tablets?
2. If Zanda normally sells 265,000 pounds of depryl per year, what will be the difference in profits if depryl is processed further?

OBJECTIVE 1 2

Problem 8-59 Keep or Drop

AudioMart is a retailer of radios, stereos, and televisions. The store carries two portable sound systems that have radios, tape players, and speakers. System A, of slightly higher quality than System B, costs $20 more. With rare exceptions, the store also sells a headset when a system is sold. The headset can be used with either system. Variable-costing income statements for the three products follow:

	System A	System B	Headset
Sales	$45,000	$ 32,500	$8,000
Less: Variable expenses	20,000	25,500	3,200
Contribution margin	$25,000	$ 7,000	$4,800
Less: Fixed costs*	10,000	18,000	2,700
Operating income	$15,000	$(11,000)	$2,100

*This includes common fixed costs totaling $18,000, allocated to each product in proportion to its revenues.

The owner of the store is concerned about the profit performance of System B and is considering dropping it. If the product is dropped, sales of System A will increase by 30%, and sales of headsets will drop by 25%. (*Note:* Round all answers to the nearest whole number.)

Required:

1. Prepare segmented income statements for the three products, using a better format.
2. **CONCEPTUAL CONNECTION** Prepare segmented income statements for System A and the headsets assuming that System B is dropped. Should B be dropped?
3. **CONCEPTUAL CONNECTION** Suppose that a third system, System C, with a similar quality to System B, could be acquired. Assume that with C the sales of A would remain unchanged; however, C would produce only 80% of the revenues of B, and sales of the headsets would drop by 10%. The contribution margin ratio of C is 50%, and its direct fixed costs would be identical to those of B. Should System B be dropped and replaced with System C?

OBJECTIVE 1 2

Problem 8-60 Accept or Reject a Special Order

Steve Murningham, manager of an electronics division, was considering an offer by Pat Sellers, manager of a sister division. Pat's division was operating below capacity and had just been given an opportunity to produce 8,000 units of one of its products for a customer in a market not normally served. The opportunity involves a product that uses an electrical component produced by Steve's division. Each unit that Pat's division produces requires two of the components. However, the price that the customer is willing to pay is well below the price that is usually charged. To make a reasonable profit on the order, Pat needs a price concession from Steve's division. Pat had offered to pay full manufacturing cost for the parts. So Steve would know that everything was above board, Pat supplied the following unit cost and price information concerning the special order, excluding the cost of the electrical component:

Selling price	$32
Less costs:	
Direct materials	17
Direct labor	7
Variable overhead	2
Fixed overhead	3
Operating profit	$ 3

The normal selling price of the electrical component is $2.30 per unit. Its full manufacturing cost is $1.85 ($1.05 variable and $0.80 fixed). Pat argued that paying $2.30 per component would wipe out the operating profit and result in her division showing a loss. Steve was interested in the offer because his division was also operating below capacity. (The order would not use all the excess capacity.)

Required:

1. **CONCEPTUAL CONNECTION** Should Steve accept the order at a selling price of $1.85 per unit? By how much will his division's profits be changed if the order is accepted? By how much will the profits of Pat's division change if Steve agrees to supply the part at full cost?
2. **CONCEPTUAL CONNECTION** Suppose that Steve offers to supply the component at $2. In offering this price, Steve says that it is a firm offer, not subject to negotiation. Should Pat accept this price and produce the special order? If Pat accepts the price, what is the change in profits for Steve's division?
3. **CONCEPTUAL CONNECTION** Assume that Steve's division is operating at full capacity and that Steve refuses to supply the part for less than the full price. Should Pat still accept the special order? Explain.

Problem 8-61 Cost-Based Pricing Decision

OBJECTIVE ◀ 4

Jeremy Costa, owner of Costa Cabinets Inc., is preparing a bid on a job that requires $1,800 of direct materials, $1,600 of direct labor, and $800 of overhead. Jeremy normally applies a standard markup based on cost of goods sold to arrive at an initial bid price. He then adjusts the price as necessary in light of other factors (e.g., competitive pressure). Last year's income statement is as follows:

Sales	$130,000
Cost of goods sold	48,100
Gross margin	$ 81,900
Selling and administrative expenses	46,300
Operating income	$ 35,600

Required:

1. Calculate the markup that Jeremy will use.
2. What is Jeremy's initial bid price?

Problem 8-62 Product Mix Decision, Single Constraint

OBJECTIVE ◀ 3

Sealing Company manufactures three types of DVD storage units. Each of the three types requires the use of a special machine that has a total operating capacity of 15,000 hours per year. Information on the three types of storage units is as follows:

	Basic	Standard	Deluxe
Selling price	$9.00	$30.00	$35.00
Variable cost	$6.00	$20.00	$10.00
Machine hours required	0.10	0.50	0.75

Sealing's marketing director has assessed demand for the three types of storage units and believes that the firm can sell as many units as it can produce.

Required:

1. How many of each type of unit should be produced and sold to maximize the company's contribution margin? What is the total contribution margin for your selection?
2. Now suppose that Sealing Company believes that it can sell no more than 12,000 of the deluxe model but up to 50,000 each of the basic and standard models at the selling prices estimated. What product mix would you recommend, and what would be the total contribution margin?

OBJECTIVE **1** ▶ **2**

Problem 8-63 Special-Order Decision, Qualitative Aspects

Randy Stone, manager of Specialty Paper Products Company, was agonizing over an offer for an order requesting 5,000 boxes of calendars. Specialty Paper Products was operating at 70% of its capacity and could use the extra business. Unfortunately, the order's offering price of $4.20 per box was below the cost to produce the calendars. The controller, Louis Barns, was opposed to taking a loss on the deal. However, the personnel manager, Yatika Blaine, argued in favor of accepting the order even though a loss would be incurred. It would avoid the problem of layoffs and would help to maintain the company's community image. The full cost to produce a box of calendars follows:

Direct materials	$1.15
Direct labor	2.00
Variable overhead	1.10
Fixed overhead	1.00
Total	$5.25

Later that day, Louis and Yatika met over coffee. Louis sympathized with Yatika's concerns and suggested that the two of them rethink the special-order decision. He offered to determine relevant costs if Yatika would list the activities that would be affected by a layoff. Yatika eagerly agreed and came up with the following activities: an increase in the state unemployment insurance rate from 1% to 2% of total payroll, notification costs to lay off approximately 20 employees, and increased costs of rehiring and retraining workers when the downturn was over. Louis determined that these activities would cost the following amounts:

- Total payroll is $1,460,000 per year.
- Layoff paperwork is $25 per laid-off employee.
- Rehiring and retraining is $150 per new employee.

Required:

1. **CONCEPTUAL CONNECTION** Assume that the company will accept the order only if it increases total profits (without taking the potential layoffs into consideration). Should the company accept or reject the order? Provide supporting computations.
2. **CONCEPTUAL CONNECTION** Consider the new information on activity costs associated with the layoff. Should the company accept or reject the order? Provide supporting computations.

OBJECTIVE **1** ▶ **2**

Problem 8-64 Sell or Process Further, Basic Analysis

Shenista Inc. produces four products (Alpha, Beta, Gamma, and Delta) from a common input. The joint costs for a typical quarter follow:

Direct materials	$95,000
Direct labor	43,000
Overhead	85,000

The revenues from each product are as follows: Alpha, $100,000; Beta, $93,000; Gamma, $30,000; and Delta, $40,000.

Management is considering processing Delta beyond the split-off point, which would increase the sales value of Delta to $75,000. However, to process Delta further means that the company must rent some special equipment that costs $15,400 per quarter. Additional materials and labor also needed will cost $8,500 per quarter.

Required:

1. What is the operating profit earned by the four products for one quarter?
2. **CONCEPTUAL CONNECTION** Should the division process Delta further or sell it at split-off? What is the effect of the decision on quarterly operating profit?

OBJECTIVE ▶ 3

Problem 8-65 Product Mix Decision, Single Constraint

Norton Company produces two products (Juno and Hera) that use the same material input. Juno uses two pounds of the material for every unit produced, and Hera uses five pounds. Currently, Norton has 16,000 pounds of the material in inventory. All of the material is imported. For the coming year, Norton plans to import an additional 8,000 pounds to produce 2,000 units of Juno and 4,000 units of Hera. The unit contribution margin is $30 for Juno and $60 for Hera. Also, assume that Norton's marketing department estimates that the company can sell a maximum of 2,000 units of Juno and 4,000 units of Hera.

Norton has received word that the source of the material has been shut down by embargo. Consequently, the company will not be able to import the 8,000 pounds it planned to use in the coming year's production. There is no other source of the material.

Required:

1. Compute the total contribution margin that the company would earn if it could manufacture 2,000 units of Juno and 4,000 units of Hera.
2. Determine the optimal usage of the company's inventory of 16,000 pounds of the material. Compute the total contribution margin for the product mix that you recommend.

OBJECTIVE ◀ 2

Problem 8-66 Sell at Split-Off or Process Further

Eunice Company produces two products from a joint process. Joint costs are $70,000 for one batch, which yields 1,000 liters of germain and 4,000 liters of hastain. Germain can be sold at the split-off point for $24 or be processed further, into geraiten, at a manufacturing cost of $4,100 (for the 1,000 liters) and sold for $33 per liter.

If geraiten is sold, additional distribution costs of $0.80 per liter and sales commissions of 10% of sales will be incurred. In addition, Eunice's legal department is concerned about potential liability issues with geraiten—issues that do not arise with germain.

Required:

1. **CONCEPTUAL CONNECTION** Considering only gross profit, should germain be sold at the split-off point or processed further?
2. **CONCEPTUAL CONNECTION** Taking a value-chain approach (by considering distribution, marketing, and after-the-sale costs), determine whether or not germain should be processed into geraiten.

OBJECTIVE ◀ 1 2

Problem 8-67 Differential Costing

As pointed out earlier in "Here's the Real Kicker," **Kicker** changed banks a couple of years ago because the loan officer at its bank moved out of state. Kicker saw that as an opportunity to take bids for its banking business and to fine-tune the banking services it was using. This problem uses that situation as the underlying scenario but uses three banks: FirstBank, Community Bank, and RegionalOne Bank. A set of representative data was presented to each bank for the purpose of preparing a bid. The data are as follows:

Checking accounts needed: 6
Checks per month:* 2,000
Foreign debits/credits on checking accounts per month: 200
Deposits per month:* 300
Returned checks:* 25 per month
Credit card charges per month: 4,000
Wire transfers per month: 100, of which 60 are to foreign bank accounts
Monthly credit needs (line of credit availability and cost): $100,000 average monthly usage

*These are overall totals for the six accounts during a month.

Internet banking services?
Knowledgeable loan officer?
Responsiveness of bank?

(Continued)

FirstBank Bid:

Checking accounts:	$5 monthly maintenance fee per account
	$0.10 foreign debit/credit
	$0.50 earned for each deposit
	$3 per returned check

Credit card fees: $0.50 per item
Wire transfers: $15 to domestic bank accounts, $50 to foreign bank accounts

Line of credit:	Yes, this amount is available,
	interest charged at prime plus 2%,
	subject to a 6% minimum interest rate

Internet banking services?	Yes, full online banking available:
	$15 one-time setup fee for each account
	$20 monthly fee for software module

The loan officer assigned to the potential **Kicker** account had 10 years of experience with medium to large business banking and showed an understanding of the audio industry.

Community Bank Bid:

Checking accounts:	No fees for the accounts, and no credits earned on deposits
	$2.00 per returned check
Credit card fees:	$0.50 per item,
	$7 per batch processed. Only manual processing was available, and
	Kicker estimated 20 batches per month

Wire transfers: $30 per wire transfer

Line of credit:	Yes, this amount is available:
	interest charged at prime plus 2%
	subject to a 7% minimum interest rate

Internet banking services? Not currently, but within the next 6 months
The loan officer assigned to the potential **Kicker** account had 4 years of experience with medium to large business banking, none of which pertained to the audio industry.

RegionalOne Bank Bid:

Checking accounts:	$5 monthly maintenance fee per account to be waived for Kicker
	$0.20 foreign debit/credit
	$0.30 earned for each deposit
	$3.80 per returned check

Credit card fees: $0.50 per item
Wire transfers: $10 to domestic bank accounts, $55 to foreign bank accounts

Line of credit:	Yes, this amount is available:
	interest charged at prime plus 2%
	subject to a 6.5% minimum interest rate
Internet banking services?	Yes, full online banking available:
	one-time setup fee for each account waived for Kicker
	$20 monthly fee for software module

The loan officer assigned to the potential **Kicker** account had 2 years of experience with large business banking. Another branch of the bank had expertise in the audio industry and would be willing to help as needed. This bank was the first one to submit a bid.

Required:

1. Calculate the predicted monthly cost of banking with each bank. Round answers to the nearest dollar.

2. **CONCEPTUAL CONNECTION** Suppose **Kicker** felt that full online Internet banking was critical. How would that affect your analysis from Requirement 1? How would you incorporate the subjective factors (e.g., experience, access to expertise)?

CASES

Case 8-68 Make or Buy: Ethical Considerations

OBJECTIVE ◀1 ◀2

Pamela McDonald, chief management accountant and controller for Murray Manufacturing Inc., was having lunch with Roger Branch, manager of the company's power department. Over the past 6 months, Pamela and Roger had developed a romantic relationship and were making plans for marriage. To keep company gossip at a minimum, Pamela and Roger had kept the relationship very quiet, and no one in the company was aware of it. The topic of the luncheon conversation centered on a decision concerning the company's power department that Larry Johnson, president of the company, was about to make.

Pamela: Roger, in our last executive meeting, we were told that a local utility company offered to supply power and quoted a price per kilowatt-hour that they said would hold for the next 3 years. They even offered to enter into a contractual agreement with us.

Roger: This is news to me. Is the bid price a threat to my area? Can they sell us power cheaper than we make it? And why wasn't I informed about this matter? I should have some input. This burns me. I think I should give Larry a call this afternoon and lodge a strong complaint.

Pamela: Calm down, Roger. The last thing I want you to do is call Larry. Larry made us all promise to keep this whole deal quiet until a decision had been made. He did not want you involved because he wanted to make an unbiased decision. You know that the company is struggling somewhat, and they are looking for ways to save money.

Roger: Yeah, but at my expense? And at the expense of my department's workers? At my age, I doubt that I could find a job that pays as well and has the same benefits. How much of a threat is this offer?

Pamela: Jack Lacy, my assistant controller, prepared an analysis while I was on vacation. It showed that internal production is cheaper than buying, but not by much. Larry asked me to review the findings and submit a final recommendation for next Wednesday's meeting. I've reviewed Jack's analysis, and it's faulty. He overlooked the interactions of your department with other service departments. When these are considered, the analysis is overwhelmingly in favor of purchasing the power. The savings are about $300,000 per year.

Roger: If Larry hears that, my department's gone. Pam, you can't let this happen. I'm 3 years away from having a vested retirement. And my workers—they have home mortgages, kids in college, families to support. No, it's not right. Pam, just tell him that your assistant's analysis is on target. He'll never know the difference.

Pamela: Roger, what you're suggesting doesn't sound right either. Would it be ethical for me to fail to disclose this information?

Roger: Ethical? Do you think it's right to lay off employees that have been loyal, faithful workers simply to fatten the pockets of the owners of this company? The Murrays already are so rich that they don't know what to do with their money. I think that it's even more unethical to penalize me and my workers. Why should we have to bear the consequences of some bad marketing decisions? Anyway, the effects of those decisions are about gone, and the company should be back to normal within a year or so.

Pamela: You may be right. Perhaps the well-being of you and your workers is more important than saving $300,000 for the Murrays.

(Continued)

Required:

1. Should Pamela have told Roger about the impending decision concerning the power department? What do you think most corporate codes of ethics would say about this?
2. Should Pamela provide Larry with the correct data concerning the power department? Or should she protect its workers? What would you do if you were Pamela?

OBJECTIVE **1 ▶ 2 ▶**   **Case 8-69** **Keep or Drop a Division**

Jan Shumard, president and general manager of Danbury Company, was concerned about the future of one of the company's largest divisions. The division's most recent quarterly income statement follows:

Sales	$3,751,500
Less: Cost of goods sold	2,722,400
Gross profit	$1,029,100
Less: Selling and administrative expenses	1,100,000
Operating (loss)	$ (70,900)

Jan is giving serious consideration to shutting down the division because this is the ninth consecutive quarter that it has shown a loss. To help him in his decision, the following additional information has been gathered:

- The division produces one product at a selling price of $100 to outside parties. The division sells 50% of its output to another division within the company for $83 per unit (full manufacturing cost plus 25%). The internal price is set by company policy. If the division is shut down, the user division will buy the part externally for $100 per unit.
- The fixed overhead assigned per unit is $20.
- There is no alternative use for the facilities if shut down. The facilities and equipment will be sold and the proceeds invested to produce an annuity of $100,000 per year. Of the fixed selling and administrative expenses, 30% represent allocated expenses from corporate headquarters. Variable selling expenses are $5 per unit sold for units sold externally. These expenses are avoided for internal sales. No variable administrative expenses are incurred.

Required:

1. Prepare an income statement that more accurately reflects the division's profit performance.
2. Should the president shut down the division? What will be the effect on the company's profits if the division is closed?

OBJECTIVE **1 ▶ 2 ▶**   **Case 8-70** **Internet Research, Group Case**

Often, websites for major airlines contain news of current special fares and flights. A decision to run a brief "fare special" is an example of a tactical decision. Form a group with one to three other students. Have each member of the group choose one or two airlines and check their websites for recent examples of fare specials. Have the group collaborate in preparing a presentation to the class discussing the types of cost and revenue information that would go into making this type of tactical decision.

9

Profit Planning and Flexible Budgets

After studying Chapter 9, you should be able to:

1 ▸ Define budgeting and discuss its role in planning, control, and decision making.

2 ▸ Define and prepare the operating budget, identify its major components, and explain the interrelationships of its various components.

3 ▸ Define and prepare the financial budget, identify its major components, and explain the interrelationships of its various components.

4 ▸ Prepare a flexible budget, and use it for planning and for performance reporting.

5 ▸ Describe the behavioral dimension of budgeting.

moodboard/Jupiter Images

EXPERIENCE MANAGERIAL DECISIONS

with The Second City

The Second City has been North America's premiere live improvisational and sketch comedy theater company for the past 50 years. Many famous stars began their careers at The Second City, including John Candy, Tina Fey, Mike Myers, Eugene Levy, and Bill Murray. More than just The Second City Television (SCTV), The Second City includes training centers, national touring companies, media and entertainment offshoots, and a corporate communication division. The Second City is an entrepreneurial organization, as evidenced most recently by its decision to provide comedy theater aboard **Norwegian Cruise Line** ships.

Given the nature of its businesses, The Second City spends a significant amount each year on overhead costs. These overhead costs must be allocated to each business unit to create accurate budgets. Its fixed overhead costs are associated with capacity and relate primarily to its home and resident stages in Chicago, Toronto, Las Vegas, Denver, and Detroit, rather than to its traveling shows. Examples of The Second City's fixed overhead costs include salaries, stage and other facilities rent, facilities maintenance, depreciation, taxes, and insurance. These overhead costs then are assigned to individual business budgets by using allocation bases such as square footage, number of employees, and percentage of earnings. The Second City then uses flexible budgets to compare with actual overhead cost variances to "red flag" potential problems that might need managerial attention.

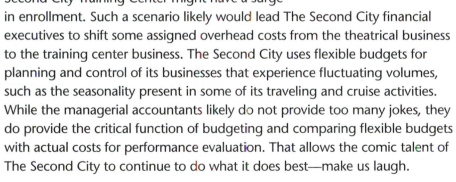

"Examples of The Second City's fixed overhead costs include salaries, stage and other facilities rent, facilities maintenance, depreciation, taxes, and insurance. These overhead costs then are assigned to individual business budgets by using allocation bases such as square footage, number of employees, and percentage of earnings. The Second City then uses flexible budgets to compare with actual overhead cost variances to 'red flag' potential problems that might need managerial attention."

For example, The Second City Theatricals might have a slow year because the producers are too busy with other ventures to mount a new production, while at the same time, The Second City Training Center might have a surge in enrollment. Such a scenario likely would lead The Second City financial executives to shift some assigned overhead costs from the theatrical business to the training center business. The Second City uses flexible budgets for planning and control of its businesses that experience fluctuating volumes, such as the seasonality present in some of its traveling and cruise activities. While the managerial accountants likely do not provide too many jokes, they do provide the critical function of budgeting and comparing flexible budgets with actual costs for performance evaluation. That allows the comic talent of The Second City to continue to do what it does best—make us laugh.

OBJECTIVE **1**
Define budgeting and discuss its role in planning, control, and decision making.

Here's **Why It's important**

DESCRIPTION OF BUDGETING

All businesses should prepare budgets. Budgets help business owners and managers to plan ahead, and later, exercise control by comparing what actually happened to what was expected in the budget. Budgets formalize managers' expectations regarding sales, prices, and costs. Even small businesses and nonprofit entities can benefit from the planning and control provided by budgets.

Budgeting and Planning and Control

Planning and control are linked. *Planning* is looking ahead to see what actions should be taken to realize particular goals. *Control* is looking backward, determining what actually happened and comparing it with the previously planned outcomes. This comparison can then be used to adjust the budget, looking forward once more. Exhibit 9.1 illustrates the cycle of planning and control using budgets.

Exhibit 9.1

Planning, Control, and Budgets

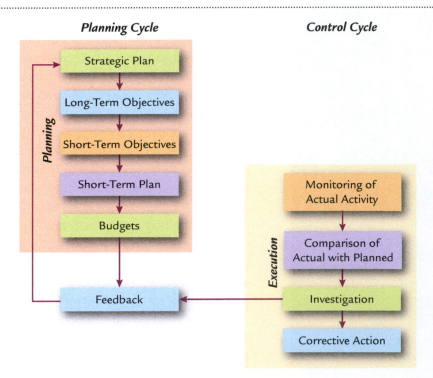

Planning Cycle   *Control Cycle*

Budgets are financial plans for the future and are a key component of planning. They identify objectives and the actions needed to achieve them. Before preparing a budget, an organization should develop a strategic plan. The **strategic plan** plots a direction for an organization's future activities and operations; it generally covers at least 5 years. The overall strategy is then translated into the long- and short-term objectives that form the basis of the budget. The budget and the strategic plan should be tightly linked. Since budgets, especially 1-year plans, are short run in nature, this linkage is important because it helps management to ensure that not all attention is focused on the short run. For example, in early 2009, **Home Depot Inc.** planned to open 12 new stores in that year. By November, however, the economic situation had deteriorated badly. The number of transactions was down as was the size of the average sale. Home Depot slashed its capital expenditure by 52% and its administrative expenses by 8.4%. The company, then, was better positioned to return to the earlier budgeted amounts if the economic situation improved or strategic objectives changed.[1]

---

1 Chris Burritt, "Home Depot Says Profit Fell as Shoppers Spent Less," *Bloomberg.com* (November 17, 2009).

Advantages of Budgeting

A budgetary system gives an organization several advantages.

Planning Budgeting forces management to plan for the future. It encourages managers to develop an overall direction for the organization, foresee problems, and develop future policies.

Information for Decision Making Budgets improve decision making. For example, a restaurant owner who knows the expected revenues and the costs of meat, vegetables, cheeses, and so on, might make menu changes that play up the less expensive items and reduce the use of more expensive ingredients. These better decisions, in turn, may keep customers happy while still providing a profitable living for the chefs, waiters, and others who work at the restaurant.

Standards for Performance Evaluation Budgets set standards that can control the use of a company's resources and motivate employees. A vital part of the budgetary system, control is achieved by comparing actual results with budgeted results on a periodic basis (e.g., monthly). A large difference between actual and planned results is feedback that prompts managers to take corrective action. For example, High Sierra, Inc. saw that sales of certain items were not meeting the budgeted amounts. Further market research showed that few customers needed the features of those particular products. As a result, the company could reduce its budgeted production in units and phase out the products.

Improved Communication and Coordination Budgets also serve to communicate and coordinate the plans of the organization to each employee. Accordingly, employees can be aware of their particular role in achieving those objectives. Since budgets for the various areas and activities of the organization must all work together to achieve organizational objectives, coordination is promoted. Managers can see the needs of other areas and are encouraged to subordinate their individual interests to those of the organization. The role of communication and coordination becomes even more important as an organization grows.

The Master Budget

The **master budget** is the comprehensive financial plan for the organization as a whole. Typically, the master budget is for a 1-year period, corresponding to the fiscal year of the company. Yearly budgets are broken down into quarterly and monthly budgets. The use of smaller time periods allows managers to compare actual data with budgeted data more frequently, so problems may be noticed and resolved sooner.

Some organizations have developed a continuous budgeting philosophy. A **continuous budget** is a moving 12-month budget. As a month expires in the budget, an additional month in the future is added so that the company always has a 12-month plan on hand. Proponents of continuous budgeting maintain that it forces managers to plan ahead constantly.

Here's How It's Used: IN YOUR LIFE

The budgets in this chapter can be used in one's everyday life in a number of ways. For example, every time you go to the grocery store, you are implicitly making up a purchases budget. You decide how much you need of each item and whether or not you want any extra to have on hand (desired ending inventory), and then you subtract any units you already have on hand (beginning inventory).

Most of us use a cash budget for our monthly or yearly budgeting, since we typically only deal in cash. Then, we can just use the basic cash budget setup—amount of cash expected less cash to be spent—to figure out our cash needs each month. Some months have higher anticipated expenses (e.g., December for Christmas presents); others may have less. A cash budget helps us see what's available so that we aren't blindsided by a car insurance payment, for example.

Directing and Coordinating Most organizations prepare the master budget for the coming year during the last 4 or 5 months of the current year. The **budget committee** reviews the budget, provides policy guidelines and budgetary goals, resolves differences that arise as the budget is prepared, approves the final budget, and monitors the actual performance of the organization as the year unfolds. The president of the organization appoints the members of the committee, who are usually the president, vice president of marketing, vice president of manufacturing, other vice presidents, and the controller. The controller usually serves as the **budget director**, the person responsible for directing and coordinating the organization's overall budgeting process.

Major Components of the Master Budget A master budget can be divided into operating and financial budgets:

- **Operating budgets** describe the income-generating activities of a firm: sales, production, and finished goods inventories. The ultimate outcome of the operating budgets is a pro forma or budgeted income statement.
- **Financial budgets** detail the inflows and outflows of cash and the overall financial position. Planned cash inflows and outflows appear in the cash budget. The expected financial position at the end of the budget period is shown in a budgeted, or pro forma, balance sheet.

Since many of the financing activities are not known until the operating budgets are known, the operating budget is prepared first. Describing and illustrating the individual budgets that make up the master budget will reveal the interdependencies of the component budgets. A diagram displaying these interrelationships is shown in Exhibit 9.2. Details of the capital budget are covered in a separate chapter.

Exhibit 9.2

The Master Budget and Its Interrelationships

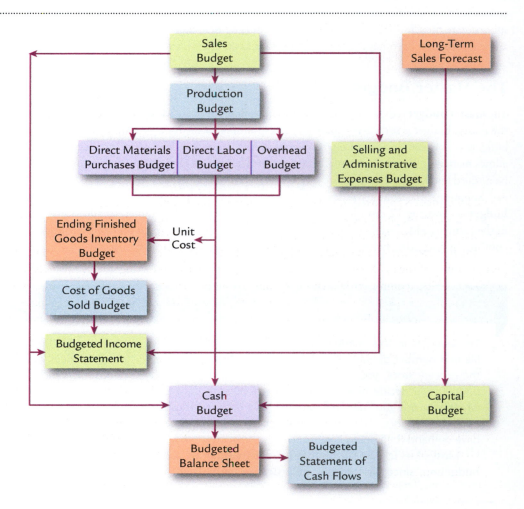

1. How can a budget help in planning and control?

Answer:

A budget requires a plan. It also sets benchmarks that can be used to evaluate performance.

2. What is the main objective of continuous budgeting?

Answer:

It forces managers to plan ahead constantly—something especially needed when firms operate in rapidly changing environments.

PREPARING THE OPERATING BUDGET

The operating budget consists of a budgeted income statement accompanied by the following supporting schedules:

- sales budget
- production budget
- direct materials purchases budget
- direct labor budget
- overhead budget
- selling and administrative expenses budget
- ending finished goods inventory budget
- cost of goods sold budget

OBJECTIVE 2
Define and prepare the operating budget, identify its major components, and explain the interrelationships of its various components.

We illustrate the master budgeting process with an example based on the activities of Texas Rex Inc., a trendy restaurant in the Southwest that sells T-shirts with the Texas Rex logo (a dinosaur that engages in a variety of adventures while eating the Mexican food for which the restaurant is known). The example focuses on the Texas Rex clothing manufacturing plant.

Sales Budget

The **sales budget** is approved by the budget committee and describes expected sales in units and dollars. Because the sales budget is the basis for all of the other operating budgets and most of the financial budgets, it is important that it be as accurate as possible.

The first step in creating a sales budget is to develop the sales forecast. This is usually the responsibility of the marketing department. One approach to forecasting sales is the *bottom-up approach*, which requires individual salespeople to submit sales predictions. These are aggregated to form a total sales forecast. The accuracy of this sales forecast may be improved by considering other factors such as the general economic climate, competition, advertising, pricing policies, and so on. Some companies use more formal approaches, such as time-series analysis, correlation analysis, and econometric modeling. For example, the regression technique studied in Appendix 3A can be applied to forecasting sales, in addition to costs.

The sales forecast is just the initial estimate, and it is often adjusted by the budget committee. The budget committee may decide that the forecast is too pessimistic or too optimistic and revise it appropriately. For example, **Nintendo** set very conservative sales estimates for 2008 and later had to increase its sales forecast. Wii hardware sales alone were so robust that sales were expected to increase by 1 million units more than the company's original forecast.[2]

2 Pulkit Chandna, "Pachter Finds Nintendo's Sales Forecast Too Humble" (January 31, 2008). www.gamertell.com/gaming/comment/analyst-nintendos-forecasts-remain-too-low/ (accessed January 31, 2008).

Stillwater Designs has 14 departments. Each department is given a budget for the coming fiscal year. The budgeting process begins with a sales forecast prepared by the president and vice presidents. The fiscal year for the company is October 1 through September 30, which is driven by the seasonal nature of the business. In January of each year, there is a consumer electronics show in Las Vegas, Nevada. New products are introduced, and initial orders from distributors are taken. The sales season starts in earnest in March, reaches its peak in June or July, and drops to its lowest level in the fall. The sales season is driven by the anticipation of warm weather. The young men buying the **Kicker** speakers and amplifiers want to drive with windows down—with the apparent hope of impressing young women. The budget is therefore prepared during August and September, the last 2 months of the fiscal year.

Each department is given a percentage of sales as its budget. The amount ultimately decided upon is not simply a top-down decision. Department managers submit a request for their desired budget. Negotiation takes place between the department managers and their associated vice presidents. (Each departmental manager is answerable to a specific vice president.) Whether or not the desired levels are provided depends on how well the departmental manager can justify the expenditures. An important criterion is the notion that resources are expended to make profits.

The budget is reviewed monthly. Any large deviations from the budget (usually more than a 10% deviation) are investigated. However, no formal incentive system is tied to budgetary performance. The budget is viewed as a guideline. If more resources are needed, then they can be obtained provided the request is backed up with a good idea and a promising payout.

Example 9.1 shows how to prepare the sales budget for Texas Rex's standard T-shirt line. For simplicity, assume that Texas Rex has only one product: a standard short-sleeved T-shirt with the Texas Rex logo screen printed on the back. (For a multiple-product firm, the sales budget reflects sales for each product in units and sales dollars.)

EXAMPLE 9.1

How to Prepare a Sales Budget

Budgeted units to be sold for each quarter of the coming year: 1,000, 1,200, 1,500, and 2,000. Selling price is $10 per T-shirt.

Required:
Prepare a sales budget for each quarter and for the year.

Solution:

Texas Rex Inc.
Sales Budget
For the Coming Year

	Quarter 1	2	3	4	Year
Units	1,000	1,200	1,500	2,000	5,700
Unit selling price	× $10	× $10	× $10	× $10	× $10
Budgeted sales	$10,000	$12,000	$15,000	$20,000	$57,000

Notice that the sales budget in Example 9.1 reveals that Texas Rex's sales fluctuate seasonally. Most sales take place in the summer and fall quarters. This is due to the popularity of the T-shirts in the summer and the sales promotions that Texas Rex puts on for "back to school" and Christmas.

Here's How It's Used: BUDGETING IN A REGIONAL MEDICAL CENTER

You are the controller for a large, regional medical center. The chief of cardiology has been pushing to have a free-standing heart hospital built on the medical center campus. However, you are concerned that taking the heart cases away from the main hospital will hurt its bottom line. While the medical center is nonprofit, it does need to cover all of its costs to stay in business. You also wonder whether the heart hospital will break even.

What information do you need to forecast revenues and costs of the heart hospital?

This is a two-part problem. The first question, what impact will the heart hospital have on the main hospital's revenues, requires knowledge of the number and types of heart cases seen at the main hospital each year. This information could come from the sales revenue budget from the previous year,

assuming that the total number of patient days and procedures are broken out by type of case and procedure. Since so many of the costs of a hospital are fixed, there will probably be little decrease in costs as those heart patients leave for the free-standing heart hospital. The second question requires a forecast of the number of patients and probable reimbursement rates expected for procedures to be performed by the heart hospital. This information can be compared with budgeted operating costs to see if the heart hospital's revenues can cover its costs.

Forecasts of sales revenues and costs are dependent on detailed information provided by sources like the marketing or sales department and past accounting information and need to be revised and updated as new information or circumstances dictate. Clearly, service industries need the same kind of detailed information on prospective sales (quantity times price) that manufacturing or retail industries do.

Production Budget

The **production budget** tells how many units must be produced to meet sales needs and to satisfy ending inventory requirements. The Texas Rex production budget would show how many T-shirts are needed to satisfy sales demand for each quarter and for the year. If there were no beginning or ending inventories, the T-shirts to be produced would exactly equal the units to be sold. This would be the case in a just-in-time (JIT) firm. However, many firms use inventories as a buffer against uncertainties in demand or production. Thus, they need to plan for inventory levels as well as sales.

CONCEPT CLIP

To compute the units to be produced, both unit sales and units of beginning and ending finished goods inventory are needed:

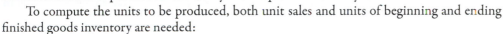

Units to Be Produced = Expected Unit Sales + Units in Desired Ending
Inventory (EI) − Units in Beginning Inventory (BI)

Example 9.2 shows how to prepare a production budget using this formula. Consider the first column (Quarter 1) of the budget in Example 9.2. Texas Rex anticipates sales of 1,000 T-shirts. In addition, the company wants 240 T-shirts in ending inventory at the end of the first quarter (0.20 × 1,200). Thus, 1,240 T-shirts are needed during the first quarter. Where will these 1,240 T-shirts come from? Beginning inventory can provide 180 of them, leaving 1,060 to be produced during the quarter. Notice that the production budget is expressed in terms of units.

EXAMPLE 9.2

How to Prepare a Production Budget

Budgeted units to be sold for each quarter: 1,000, 1,200, 1,500, and 2,000. Assume that company policy requires 20% of the next quarter's sales in ending inventory and that beginning inventory of T-shirts for the first quarter of the year was 180. Assume also that sales for the first quarter of the year after the budget year are estimated at 1,000 units.

Required:

1. Calculate the desired ending inventory in units for each quarter of the year. What is the ending inventory in units for the year?

2. Prepare a production budget for each quarter and for the year.

(Continued)

EXAMPLE 9.2

(Continued)

Solution:

1. Ending inventory, Quarter 1 = 0.20 × 1,200 units = 240
   Ending inventory, Quarter 2 = 0.20 × 1,500 units = 300
   Ending inventory, Quarter 3 = 0.20 × 2,000 units = 400
   Ending inventory, Quarter 4 = 0.20 × 1,000 units = 200
   Ending Inventory for the Year = Ending Inventory for Quarter 4 = 200 units

2.

Texas Rex Inc.
Production Budget
For the Coming Year

	1	2	3	4	Year
	Quarter				
Sales in units	1,000	1,200	1,500	2,000	5,700
Desired ending inventory	240	300	400	200	200
Total needs	1,240	1,500	1,900	2,200	5,900
Less: Beginning inventory*	(180)	(240)	(300)	(400)	(180)
Units to be produced	1,060	1,260	1,600	1,800	5,720

*Beginning inventory for Quarter 1 is given. Beginning inventory for the remaining quarters is equal to ending inventory for the previous quarter.

Two important points regarding Example 9.2 should be emphasized:

- The beginning inventory for one quarter is always equal to the ending inventory of the previous quarter. For Quarter 2, the beginning inventory is 240 T-shirts, which is identical to the desired ending inventory for Quarter 1.
- The column for the year is not simply the addition of the amounts for the four quarters. Notice that the desired ending inventory for the year is 200 T-shirts, which is, of course, equal to the desired ending inventory for the fourth quarter.

Direct Materials Purchases Budget

After the production budget is completed, the budgets for direct materials, direct labor, and overhead can be prepared. The **direct materials purchases budget** tells the amount and cost of raw materials to be purchased in each time period. It depends on the expected use of materials in production and the raw materials inventory needs of the firm. The company needs to prepare a separate direct materials purchases budget for every type of raw material used. The formula used for calculating purchases is as follows:

> Purchases = Direct Materials Needed for Production
> + Direct Materials in Desired Ending Inventory
> − Direct Materials in Beginning Inventory

The quantity of direct materials in inventory is determined by the firm's inventory policy. Texas Rex uses two types of raw materials: plain T-shirts and ink. The direct materials purchases budgets for these two materials are presented in **Example 9.3**.

Budgeted units to be produced for each quarter: 1,060, 1,260, 1,600, and 1,800. Plain T-shirts cost $3 each, and ink (for the screen printing) costs $0.20 per ounce. On a per-unit basis, the factory needs one plain T-shirt and 5 ounces of ink for each logoed T-shirt that it produces. Texas Rex's policy is to have 10% of the following quarter's production needs in ending inventory. The factory has 58 plain T-shirts and 390 ounces of ink on hand on January 1. On December 31, the desired ending inventory is 106 plain T-shirts and 530 ounces of ink.

Required:

1. Calculate the ending inventory of plain T-shirts and of ink for Quarters 1, 2, and 3.

2. Prepare a direct materials purchases budget for plain T-shirts and one for ink.

Solution:

1. Ending inventory plain T-shirts, Quarter 1 = 0.10 × (1,260 units × 1 T-shirt) = 126
   Ending inventory plain T-shirts, Quarter 2 = 0.10 × (1,600 units × 1 T-shirt) = 160
   Ending inventory plain T-shirts, Quarter 3 = 0.10 × (1,800 units × 1 T-shirt) = 180
   Ending inventory ink, Quarter 1 = 0.10 × (1,260 units × 5 ounces) = 630
   Ending inventory ink, Quarter 2 = 0.10 × (1,600 units × 5 ounces) = 800
   Ending inventory ink, Quarter 3 = 0.10 × (1,800 units × 5 ounces) = 900

2.

Texas Rex Inc.
Direct Materials Purchases Budget
For the Coming Year

Plain T-shirts	Quarter				
	1	2	3	4	Year
Units to be produced	1,060	1,260	1,600	1,800	5,720
Direct materials per unit	× 1	× 1	× 1	× 1	× 1
Production needs	1,060	1,260	1,600	1,800	5,720
Desired ending inventory	126	160	180	106	106
Total needs	1,186	1,420	1,780	1,906	5,826
Less: Beginning inventory	(58)	(126)	(160)	(180)	(58)
Direct materials to be purchased	1,128	1,294	1,620	1,726	5,768
Cost per T-shirt	× $3	× $3	× $3	× $3	× $3
Total purchase cost plain T-shirts	$3,384	$3,882	$4,860	$5,178	$17,304

Ink					
Units to be produced	1,060	1,260	1,600	1,800	5,720
Direct materials per unit	× 5	× 5	× 5	× 5	× 5
Production needs	5,300	6,300	8,000	9,000	28,600
Desired ending inventory	630	800	900	530	530
Total needs	5,930	7,100	8,900	9,530	29,130
Less: Beginning inventory	(390)	(630)	(800)	(900)	(390)
Direct materials to be purchased	5,540	6,470	8,100	8,630	28,740
Cost per ounce	×$0.20	×$0.20	×$0.20	×$0.20	× $0.20
Total purchase cost of ink	$1,108	$1,294	$1,620	$1,726	$5,748
Total direct materials purchase cost	$4,492	$5,176	$6,480	$6,904	$23,052

CONCEPT CLIP

Notice how similar the direct materials purchases budget is to the production budget. Consider the first quarter, starting with the plain T-shirts. It takes one plain T-shirt for every logo T-shirt, so the 1,060 logo T-shirts to be produced are multiplied by 1 to obtain the number of plain T-shirts needed for production. Next, the desired ending inventory of 126 (10% of the next quarter's production needs) is added. Thus, 1,186 plain T-shirts are needed during the first quarter. Of this total, 58 are already in beginning inventory, meaning that the remaining 1,128 must be purchased. Multiplying the 1,128 plain T-shirts by the cost of $3 each gives Texas Rex the $3,384 expected cost of plain T-shirt purchases for the first quarter of the year. The direct materials purchases budget for ink is done in the same way as T-shirts, except that each unit produced requires 5 ounces of ink. So the total units to be produced must be multiplied by 5 to get the production needs of ink.

Direct Labor Budget

The **direct labor budget** shows the total direct labor hours and the direct labor cost needed for the number of units in the production budget. As with direct materials, the budgeted hours of direct labor are determined by the relationship between labor and output. The direct labor budget for Texas Rex is shown in **Example 9.4**.

<table>
<tr><td>EXAMPLE 9.4</td></tr>
<tr><td>How to Prepare a Direct Labor Budget</td></tr>
</table>

Recall from Example 9.2 (p. 461) that budgeted units to be produced for each quarter are: 1,060, 1,260, 1,600, and 1,800. It takes 0.12 hour to produce one T-shirt. The average wage cost per hour is $10.

Required:
Prepare a direct labor budget.

Solution:

Texas Rex Inc.
Direct Labor Budget
For the Coming Year

	Quarter				
	1	2	3	4	Year
Units to be produced	1,060	1,260	1,600	1,800	5,720
Direct labor time per unit in hours	× 0.12	× 0.12	× 0.12	× 0.12	× 0.12
Total hours needed	127.2	151.2	192.0	216.0	686.4
Average wage per hour	× $10	× $10	× $10	× $10	× $10
Total direct labor cost	$1,272	$1,512	$1,920	$2,160	$6,864

Overhead Budget

The **overhead budget** shows the expected cost of all production costs other than direct materials and direct labor. Many companies use direct labor hours as the driver for overhead. Then costs that vary with direct labor hours are pooled and called variable overhead. The remaining overhead items are pooled into fixed overhead. The method for preparing an overhead budget using this approach to cost behavior is shown in **Example 9.5**.

<table>
<tr><td>EXAMPLE 9.5</td></tr>
<tr><td>How to Prepare an Overhead Budget</td></tr>
</table>

Refer to Example 9.4 for the direct labor budget. The variable overhead rate is $5 per direct labor hour. Fixed overhead is budgeted at $1,645 per quarter (this amount includes $540 per quarter for depreciation).

Required:
Prepare an overhead budget.

EXAMPLE 9.5

(Continued)

Solution:

Texas Rex Inc.
Overhead Budget
For the Coming Year

| | \multicolumn{4}{c}{Quarter} | | | | |
	1	2	3	4	Year
Budgeted direct labor hours	127.2	151.2	192.0	216.0	686.4
Variable overhead rate	× $5	× $5	× $5	× $5	× $5
Budgeted variable overhead	$ 636	$ 756	$ 960	$1,080	$ 3,432
Budgeted fixed overhead*	1,645	1,645	1,645	1,645	6,580
Total overhead	$2,281	$2,401	$2,605	$2,725	$10,012

*Includes $540 of depreciation in each quarter.

Ending Finished Goods Inventory Budget

The **ending finished goods inventory budget** supplies information needed for the balance sheet and also serves as an important input for the preparation of the cost of goods sold budget. To prepare this budget, the unit cost of producing each T-shirt must be calculated by using information from the direct materials, direct labor, and overhead budgets. The way to calculate the unit cost of a T-shirt and the cost of the planned ending inventory is shown in **Example 9.6**.

EXAMPLE 9.6

How to Prepare an Ending Finished Goods Inventory Budget

Refer to Examples 9.3 (p. 463), 9.4 (p. 464), and 9.5 (p. 464) for the direct materials, direct labor, and overhead budgets.

Required:

1. Calculate the unit product cost.

2. Prepare an ending finished goods inventory budget.

Solution:

1. Direct materials:

Plain T-shirt	$3	
Ink (5 oz. @ $0.20)	1	$4.00
Direct labor (0.12 hr. @ $10)		1.20
Overhead:		
Variable (0.12 hr. @ $5)		0.60
Fixed (0.12 hr. @ $9.59*)		1.15**
Total unit cost		$6.95

*Budgeted Fixed Overhead/Budgeted Direct Labor Hours = $6,580/686.4 = $9.59
**Rounded

2.
Texas Rex Inc.
Ending Finished Goods Inventory Budget
For the Coming Year

Logo T-shirts	200
Unit cost	×$6.95
Total ending inventory	$ 1,390

Notice that the ending finished goods inventory budget brings together information from the production, direct labor, and overhead budgets to compute the unit product cost for the year.

Cost of Goods Sold Budget

Assuming that the beginning finished goods inventory is valued at $1,251, the budgeted cost of goods sold schedule can be prepared using information from Examples 9.3 to 9.6. The **cost of goods sold budget** reveals the expected cost of the goods to be sold and is shown in **Example 9.7**.

EXAMPLE 9.7

How to Prepare a Cost of Goods Sold Budget

Refer to Examples 9.3 through 9.6 (beginning p. 463) for the direct materials, direct labor, overhead, and ending finished goods budgets. The cost of beginning finished goods inventory is $1,251.

Required:
Prepare a cost of goods sold budget.

Solution:

Texas Rex Inc.
Cost of Goods Sold Budget
For the Coming Year

Direct materials used (Example 9.3)*	$22,880
Direct labor used (Example 9.4)	6,864
Overhead (Example 9.5)	10,012
Budgeted manufacturing costs	$39,756
Beginning finished goods	1,251
Cost of goods available for sale	$41,007
Less: Ending finished goods (Example 9.6)	(1,390)
Budgeted cost of goods sold	$39,617

*Production Needs = (5,720 plain T-shirts × $3) + (28,600 oz. ink × $0.20)

The budgeted cost of goods sold will appear in the budgeted income statement.

Selling and Administrative Expenses Budget

The next budget to be prepared, the **selling and administrative expenses budget**, outlines planned expenditures for nonmanufacturing activities. As with overhead, selling and administrative expenses can be broken down into fixed and variable components. Such items as sales commissions, freight, and supplies vary with sales activity. The selling and administrative expenses budget is illustrated in **Example 9.8**.

EXAMPLE 9.8

How to Prepare a Selling and Administrative Expenses Budget

Refer to Example 9.1 (p. 460) for the sales budget. Variable expenses are $0.10 per unit sold. Salaries average $1,420 per quarter; utilities, $50 per quarter; and depreciation, $150 per quarter. Advertising for Quarters 1 through 4 is $100, $200, $800, and $500, respectively.

Required:
Prepare a selling and administrative expenses budget.

Solution:

Texas Rex Inc.
Selling and Administrative Expenses Budget
For the Coming Year

	Quarter				
	1	**2**	**3**	**4**	**Year**
Planned sales in units (Example 9.1)	1,000	1,200	1,500	2,000	5,700
Variable selling and administrative expenses per unit	×$0.10	×$0.10	×$0.10	×$0.10	×$0.10
Total variable expenses	$ 100	$ 120	$ 150	$ 200	$ 570
Fixed selling and administrative expenses:					
Salaries	$1,420	$1,420	$1,420	$1,420	$5,680
Utilities	50	50	50	50	200
Advertising	100	200	800	500	1,600
Depreciation	150	150	150	150	600
Total fixed expenses	$1,720	$1,820	$2,420	$2,120	$8,080
Total selling and administrative expenses	$1,820	$1,940	$2,570	$2,320	$8,650

Notice how the selling and administrative expenses budget follows a very similar format as that of the overhead budget. In both cases, variable and fixed expenses are calculated. Notice also that depreciation, a noncash expense, is shown separately. This will be important later on when the company prepares the cash budget.

Budgeted Income Statement

With the completion of the budgeted cost of goods sold and the budgeted selling and administrative expenses budget, Texas Rex has all the operating budgets needed to prepare an estimate of *operating* income. The way to prepare this budgeted income statement is shown in **Example 9.9**. The eight budgets already prepared, along with the budgeted operating income statement, define the operating budget for Texas Rex.

EXAMPLE 9.9

How to Prepare a Budgeted Income Statement

Refer to Examples 9.1 (p. 460), 9.7 (p. 466), 9.8 (p. 467), and 9.12 (p. 472) for the sales budget, the cost of goods sold budget, the selling and administrative expenses budget, and the cash budget. Assume that the tax rate is 40%.

Required:
Prepare a budgeted income statement.

(*Continued*)

EXAMPLE 9.9

(Continued)

Solution:

Texas Rex Inc.
Budgeted Income Statement
For the Coming Year

Sales (Example 9.1)	$ 57,000
Less: Cost of goods sold (Example 9.7)	(39,617)
Gross margin	$ 17,383
Less: Selling and administrative expenses (Example 9.8)	(8,650)
Operating income	$ 8,733
Less: Interest expense (Example 9.12)	(60)
Income before income taxes	$ 8,673
Less: Income taxes (0.40 × $8,673)	(3,469)*
Net income	$ 5,204

*Rounded

Operating income is *not* equivalent to the net income of a firm. To yield net income, interest expense and taxes must be subtracted from operating income. The interest expense deduction is taken from the cash budget for Texas Rex (Example 9.12, p. 472), a budget discussed in the section on financial budgets. The taxes owed depend on the current federal and state tax laws. For simplicity, a combined rate of 40% is assumed.

Check Point

1. **Why is the sales budget not necessarily the same as the sales forecast?**

Answer:
The sales forecast is a starting point and an important input to the budgetary process. However, it is usually adjusted up or down, depending on the strategic objectives and plans of management.

2. **Loring Company expects to produce 1,000 units of product next month, based on an ending inventory policy of 20% of the following month's sales. Now suppose that Loring adjusts the ending inventory policy to 10% of sales. What is the impact of budgeted units produced?**

Answer:
Expected or budgeted units produced will decrease, since the need for units in ending inventory has decreased.

3. **What operating budgets are needed to calculate a budgeted unit cost?**

Answer:
Materials, labor, and overhead budgets. It could be argued that sales and production budgets are needed also because the three budgets listed cannot be developed until the sales and production budgets are known.

4. **Why is it not possible to prepare a budgeted income statement by using only operating budgets?**

Answer:
Interest expense comes from the financial budgets. Only operating income can be computed by using operating budgets.

PREPARING THE FINANCIAL BUDGET

OBJECTIVE ▶ **3**

Define and prepare the financial budget, identify its major components, and explain the interrelationships of its various components.

The remaining budgets found in the master budget are the financial budgets. The usual financial budgets prepared are:

- cash budget
- budgeted balance sheet
- budget for capital expenditures

The master budget also contains a plan for acquiring long-term assets—assets that have a time horizon that extends beyond the 1-year operating period. Some of these assets may be purchased during the coming year. Plans to purchase others may be detailed for future periods. This part of the master budget is typically referred to as the *capital budget*. Decision making for capital expenditures is considered in Chapter 12. Accordingly, only the cash budget and the budgeted balance sheet will be illustrated here.

Cash Budget

Understanding cash flows is critical in managing a business. Often, a business successfully produces and sells products but fails because of timing problems associated with cash inflows and outflows. Examples include the smallest entrepreneurs, who are required by suppliers to pay cash up front but must sell to their customers on credit, as well as large corporations like **Sears**. In early 2008, Sears acknowledged that available cash had dropped by nearly 60% over 2007. A cash crunch was leading Sears to consider selling assets.[3] By the end of 2009, Sears had closed more than 60 stores, liquidating inventory and realizing cash from the closings.[4]

By knowing when cash inflows and outflows are likely to occur, a manager can plan to borrow cash when needed and to repay the loans during periods of excess cash. Because cash flow is the lifeblood of an organization, the cash budget is one of the most important budgets in the master budget. The basic structure of a **cash budget** includes cash receipts, disbursements, any excess or deficiency of cash, and financing. At its simplest, a cash budget is cash inflows minus cash outflows. Suppose, for example, that a company expects $3,000 in the cash account on June 1. During June, cash sales of $45,000 are predicted, as are cash disbursements of $39,000. The company wants to have a $2,500 minimum cash balance. The resulting cash budget for June is illustrated in Exhibit 9.3.

Here's **Why It's important**

Expected beginning balance	$ 3,000
Add cash receipts	45,000
Cash available	$48,000
Less disbursements	39,000
Expected ending balance	$ 9,000

Exhibit 9.3
The Cash Budget

Cash Available   Cash available consists of the beginning cash balance and the expected cash receipts.

> Cash Available = Beginning Cash Balance + Expected Cash Receipts

Expected cash receipts include all sources of cash for the period being considered. The principal source of cash is from sales. Since a large proportion of sales is usually on account, a major task of an organization is to determine the pattern of collection for its accounts receivable. If a company has been in business for a while, it can use past experience to determine what

---

3   Gary McWilliams, "Profit Down, Sears May Hold Yard Sale," *The Wall Street Journal* (February 29, 2008): A13.
4   Edward S. Lampert Chairman's Letter, February 23, 2010. Taken from www.searsholdings.com/invest/.

percentage of credit sales are paid in the month of and months following sales. This is used to create a schedule of cash collections on accounts receivable. **Example 9.10** shows how to create a schedule for cash collections on accounts receivable for Texas Rex.

EXAMPLE 9.10	From past experience, Texas Rex expects that, on average, 25% of total sales are cash and 75% of total sales are on credit. Of the credit sales, Texas Rex expects that 90% will be paid in cash during the quarter of sale, and the remaining 10% will be paid in the following quarter. Recall from Example 9.1 (p. 460) that Texas Rex expects the following total sales:

How to Prepare a Schedule for Cash Collections on Accounts Receivable

Quarter 1	$10,000
Quarter 2	$12,000
Quarter 3	$15,000
Quarter 4	$20,000

The balance in Accounts Receivable as of the last quarter of the prior year was $1,350. This will be collected in cash during the first quarter of the coming year.

Required:

1. Calculate cash sales expected in each quarter of the coming year.

2. Prepare a schedule showing cash receipts from sales expected in each quarter of the coming year.

Solution:

1. Cash sales expected in Quarter 1 = $10,000 × 0.25 = $2,500
   Cash sales expected in Quarter 2 = $12,000 × 0.25 = $3,000
   Cash sales expected in Quarter 3 = $15,000 × 0.25 = $3,750
   Cash sales expected in Quarter 4 = $20,000 × 0.25 = $5,000

2.

	Quarter			
Source	1	2	3	4
Cash sales	$ 2,500	$ 3,000	$ 3,750	$ 5,000
Received on account from:				
Quarter 4, prior year	1,350			
Quarter 1	6,750[a]	750[b]		
Quarter 2		8,100[c]	900[d]	
Quarter 3			10,125[e]	1,125[f]
Quarter 4				13,500[g]
Total cash receipts	$10,600	$11,850	$14,775	$19,625

[a] ($10,000 × 0.75)(0.9)
[b] ($10,000 × 0.75)(0.1)
[c] ($12,000 × 0.75)(0.9)
[d] ($12,000 × 0.75)(0.1)
[e] ($15,000 × 0.75)(0.9)
[f] ($15,000 × 0.75)(0.1)
[g] ($20,000 × 0.75)(0.9)

While Texas Rex expects no bad debts expense, that may not be the case for all firms. If a firm expects less than 100% of the credit sales to be received in cash, then it expects some bad debts. For example, if a firm expected to be repaid 98% of credit sales, then it expects 2% bad debts. In other words, not everyone pays for their credit sales. This 2% is ignored for purposes of cash budgeting since it will not be received in cash. Different firms have different accounts receivable repayment experiences.

Cash Disbursements The cash disbursements section lists all planned cash outlays for the period. All expenses that do not require a cash outlay are *excluded* from the list (e.g., depreciation). Just as sources of cash may require a schedule of cash collections on accounts receivable to calculate cash expected from credit sales, the disbursements section may require care in handling payments on account. **Example 9.11** shows how to handle timing differences arising from paying for items on account.

CONCEPT CLIP

EXAMPLE 9.11

How to Determine Cash Payments on Accounts Payable

Texas Rex purchases all raw materials on account. Eighty percent of purchases are paid for in the quarter of purchase; the remaining 20% are paid for in the following quarter. The purchases for the fourth quarter of the prior year were $5,000. Recall from Example 9.3 (p. 463) that Texas Rex expects the following purchases of raw materials:

Quarter 1	$4,492
Quarter 2	$5,176
Quarter 3	$6,480
Quarter 4	$6,904

Required:
Prepare a schedule showing anticipated payments for accounts payable for materials.

Solution:
Cash needed for payments on account:

	Quarter			
Source	1	2	3	4
Quarter 4, prior year	$1,000[a]			
Quarter 1	3,594[b]	$ 898[c]		
Quarter 2		4,141[d]	$1,035[e]	
Quarter 3			5,184[f]	$1,296[g]
Quarter 4				5,523[h]
Total cash needed	$4,594	$5,039	$6,219	$6,819

(*Note*: All footnote calculations are rounded.)
[a] $5,000 × 0.20)   [e] ($5,176 × 0.20)
[b] ($4,492 × 0.80)   [f] ($6,480 × 0.80)
[c] ($4,492 × 0.20)   [g] ($6,480 × 0.20)
[d] ($5,176 × 0.80)   [h] ($6,904 × 0.80)

Note that Example 9.11 does not allow for less than 100% repayment of accounts payable. The ethical firm always intends to repay its debts.

A disbursement that is typically not included in the disbursements section is interest on short-term borrowing. This interest expenditure is reserved for the section on loan repayments.

Cash Excess or Deficiency The cash budget shown in Exhibit 9.3 (p. 469) is a very simple one. Sometimes companies expand this format, as is done for the cash budget for Texas Rex in Example 9.12, by adding lines to show any borrowing or repayment necessary to achieve a minimum desired cash amount. When this is done, the preliminary ending cash balance is called *cash excess* or *cash deficiency*. The cash excess or deficiency line is compared to the minimum cash balance required by company policy. The minimum cash balance is simply the lowest amount of cash on hand that the firm finds acceptable. Consider your own checking account. You probably try to keep at least some cash in the account, perhaps because by having a minimum balance you avoid service charges, or because a minimum balance allows you to make an unplanned purchase. Similarly, companies also require minimum cash balances. The amount varies from firm to firm and is determined by each company's particular needs and policies. If there is a cash deficiency, then the cash on hand is less than the cash needed. In such a case, a short-term loan will be needed. On the other hand, with a cash excess (cash available is greater than the firm's cash needs), the firm has the ability to repay loans and perhaps to make some temporary investments. For example, in mid-2010, **Target** raised its dividend from $0.17 to $0.25, reasoning that its surplus of cash was above what was needed for reinvestment in its core business. **Pep Boys** (automotive parts supplier) announced that its cash balance was up by four times what it had been the year before and was considering additional capital investment.[5]

Borrowings and Repayments If a company converts its preliminary cash balance line to a cash excess (deficiency) line, it may be borrowing or repaying money. If there is a deficiency, this section shows the necessary amount to be borrowed. When excess cash is available, this section shows planned repayments, including interest expense.

Ending Cash Balance The last line of the cash budget is the ending cash balance. This is the planned amount of cash to be on hand at the end of the period after all receipts and disbursements, as well as borrowings and repayments, are considered.

Ending Cash Balance = Cash Available – Expected Cash Disbursements

Preparing a Cash Budget The way to prepare a cash budget is illustrated in **Example 9.12**. Much of the information needed to prepare the cash budget comes from the operating budgets and from the schedules for cash receipts on accounts receivable and cash payments on accounts

---

EXAMPLE 9.12

How to Prepare a Cash Budget

Refer to Examples 9.4 (p. 464), 9.5 (p. 464), 9.8 (p. 467), 9.9 (p. 467), 9.10 (p. 470), and 9.11 (p. 471) as well as the following details:

a. A $1,000 minimum cash balance is required for the end of each quarter. Money can be borrowed and repaid in multiples of $1,000. Interest is 12% per year. Interest payments are made only for the amount of the principal being repaid. All borrowing takes place at the beginning of a quarter, and all repayment takes place at the end of a quarter.

b. Budgeted depreciation is $540 per quarter for overhead and $150 per quarter for selling and administrative expenses (Examples 9.5 and 9.8).

c. The capital budget for the coming year revealed plans to purchase additional screen printing equipment. The cash outlay for the equipment, $6,500, will take place in the first quarter. The company plans to finance the acquisition of the equipment with operating cash, supplementing it with short-term loans as necessary.

d. Corporate income taxes are approximately $3,469 and will be paid at the end of the fourth quarter (Example 9.9).

e. Beginning cash balance equals $5,200.

f. All amounts in the budget are rounded to the nearest dollar.

Required:
Prepare a cash budget for Texas Rex.

---

5 Justin Lahart, "U.S. Firms Build Up Record Cash Piles," *The Wall Street Journal* (June 10, 2010). Taken from http://online. wsj.com/article/SB10001424052748704312104575298652567988246.html?mod=djem_jiewr_AC_domainid.

Solution:

EXAMPLE 9.12

Texas Rex Inc.
Cash Budget
For the Coming Year Quarter

(Continued)

	1	2	3	4	Year	Source*
Beginning cash balance	$ 5,200	$ 1,023	$ 1,611	$ 3,762	$ 5,200	e
Cash sales and collections on account:	10,600	11,850	14,775	19,625	56,850	10
Total cash available	$ 15,800	$ 12,873	$ 16,386	$ 23,387	$ 62,050	
Less disbursements:						
Payments for:						
Raw materials	$ (4,594)	$ (5,039)	$ (6,219)	$ (6,819)	$(22,671)	11
Direct labor	(1,272)	(1,512)	(1,920)	(2,160)	(6,864)	4
Overhead	(1,741)	(1,861)	(2,065)	(2,185)	(7,852)	b,5
Selling and administrative expenses	(1,670)	(1,790)	(2,420)	(2,170)	(8,050)	b,8
Income taxes	—	—	—	(3,469)	(3,469)	d,9
Equipment	(6,500)	—	—	—	(6,500)	c
Total disbursements	$(15,777)	$(10,202)	$(12,624)	$(16,803)	$(55,406)	
Excess (deficiency) of cash available over needs	$ 23	$ 2,671	$ 3,762	$ 6,584	$ 6,644	
Financing:						
Borrowings	1,000	—	—	—	1,000	a
Repayments	—	(1,000)	—	—	(1,000)	a
Interest**	—	(60)	—	—	(60)	a
Total financing	$ 1,000	$ (1,060)	—	—	$ (60)	
Ending cash balance***	$ 1,023	$ 1,611	$ 3,762	$ 6,584	$ 6,584	

*Letters refer to the detailed information above. Numbers refer to Example schedules.
**Interest payment is 6/12 × 0.12 × $1,000. Since borrowings occur at the beginning of the quarter and repayments at the end of the quarter, the principal repayment takes place after 6 months.
***Total cash available minus total disbursements plus (or minus) total financing.

payable. It is important to recall that only cash expenditures are included in the cash budget. The operating budgets for overhead and selling and administrative expenses included depreciation expense, which is a noncash expense. Therefore, depreciation expense was subtracted from the totals to yield the cash expenditures for overhead and for selling and administrative expenses.

The cash budget underscores the importance of breaking down the annual budget into smaller time periods. The cash budget for the year gives the impression that sufficient operating cash will be available to finance the acquisition of the new equipment. Quarterly information, however, shows the need for short-term borrowing ($1,000) because of both the acquisition of the new equipment and the timing of the firm's cash flows. Most firms prepare monthly cash budgets, and some even prepare weekly and daily budgets.

Texas Rex's cash budget provides another piece of useful information. By the end of the third quarter, the firm has more cash ($3,762) than needed to meet operating needs. Management should consider investing the excess cash in an interest-bearing account. Once plans are finalized for use of the excess cash, the cash budget should be revised to reflect those plans. Budgeting is a dynamic process. As the budget is developed, new information becomes available, and better plans can be formulated.

Budgeted Balance Sheet

The budgeted balance sheet depends on information contained in the current balance sheet and in the other budgets in the master budget. Exhibit 9.4 shows the budgeted balance sheets as of December 31, 20X0, the prior year, and December 31, 20X1, the coming year. Explanations for the budgeted figures are provided in the footnotes.

Exhibit 9.4

Budgeted Balance Sheet

Texas Rex Inc. Balance Sheet December 31, 20X0		
Assets		
Current assets:		
Cash	$ 5,200	
Accounts receivable	1,350	
Raw materials inventory	252	
Finished goods inventory	1,251	
Total current assets		$ 8,053
Property, plant, and equipment (PP&E):		
Land	$ 1,100	
Building and equipment	30,000	
Accumulated depreciation	(5,000)	
Total PP&E		26,100
Total assets		$34,153
Liabilities and Owner's Equity		
Current liabilities:		
Accounts payable		$ 1,000
Owner's equity:		
Retained earnings		33,153
Total liabilities and owner's equity		$34,153

Texas Rex Inc. Budgeted Balance Sheet December 31, 20X1		
Assets		
Current assets:		
Cash	$ 6,584[a]	
Accounts receivable	1,500[b]	
Raw materials inventory	424[c]	
Finished goods inventory	1,390[d]	
Total current assets		$ 9,898
Property, plant, and equipment (PP&E):		
Land	$ 1,100[e]	
Building and equipment	36,500[f]	
Accumulated depreciation	(7,760)[g]	
Total PP&E		29,840
Total assets		$39,738
Liabilities and Owner's Equity		
Current liabilities:		
Accounts payable		$ 1,381[h]
Owner's equity:		
Retained earnings		38,357[i]
Total liabilities and owner's equity		$39,738

a Ending balance from Example 9.12.
b Ten percent of fourth-quarter credit sales (0.75 × $20,000)—see Example 9.1 and 9.12.
c From Example 9.3 [(106 × $3) + (530 × $0.20)].
d From Example 9.6.
e From the December 31, 20X0, balance sheet.
f December 31, 20X0, balance ($30,000) plus new equipment acquisition of $6,500 (see the 20X0 ending balance sheet and Example 9.12).
g From the December 31, 20X0, balance sheet, Example 9.5, and Example 9.8 ($5,000 + $2,160 + $600).
h Twenty percent of fourth-quarter purchases (0.20 × $6,904)—see Examples 9.3 and 9.12.
i $33,153 + $5,204 (December 31, 20X0, balance plus net income from Example 9.9).

Here's How It's Used: IN A SMALL PAINTING COMPANY

You are the accountant for a number of small businesses in your town, one of which is Ramon's Paint and Plaster. Ramon has been through a tough year as construction in the town has been down. However, new home construction is picking up and Ramon has been asked to bid on twice as many jobs in the past month as he was last year at this time. Ramon needs to know what his cash flow will be for the coming year. You are starting to amass information to help you forecast monthly cash inflows and outflows for the next 6 months.

What information do you need to forecast cash inflows and outflows for the paint and plaster business for the next 6 months?

This is a two-part problem. The first question, what inflows of cash are expected, depends on the number and size of the jobs Ramon can successfully bid on. Ramon's business has been primarily residential, so you'll need to know the number of housing starts (or the number of building permits applied for) and the number of remodeling jobs expected. You will also need to consider the price Ramon charges as well as the

probability of prompt payment. Some builders have a good reputation for paying promptly in the first 10 days of the month following work by Ramon's crew. Others lag behind. While you can encourage Ramon to work primarily with the better builders, he may be forced to accept some jobs with contractors who frequently pay later.

The second question requires a forecast of the potential cash outflows. Ramon has a crew of six workers and the hourly rate is known. He also can figure out the cost of the paint and plaster materials fairly accurately, once the size of the job is known. It will be difficult to forecast the cash inflows and outflows too far in advance. As a result, you will probably want to set up the cash budget for 1 to 3 months in advance and then update the forecasted numbers as the year progresses.

Forecasts of cash inflows and outflows depend on the economic conditions, the reputation of the payment patterns of the customers, and the prices charged both for the jobs obtained as well as for the supplies used. Information from the past year can be used as a baseline; however, changing economic conditions will affect future amounts.

Check Point

1. **Sales for a month totaled $10,000. Cash receipts for the same month were $15,000. How is it possible for cash receipts to be more than sales?**

Answer:
Money can be collected from credit sales of the prior month(s).

2. **Why would a company want a minimum cash balance? Suppose that the minimum cash balance is $1,000 and that the projected cash surplus is $500. What would a company have to do to achieve the desired minimum?**

Answer:
A minimum cash balance is needed to reduce the risk of insufficient funds and satisfy account agreements with the banks. In the event of a shortage, it is necessary to borrow the difference.

USING FLEXIBLE BUDGETS FOR PLANNING AND PERFORMANCE REPORTING

Budgets are useful for both planning and control, where they are used as benchmarks for performance evaluation. The flexible budget serves both planning and control needs.

Flexible Budgets   A **flexible (variable) budget** enables a firm to compute expected costs for a range of activity levels. The key to flexible budgeting is knowledge of fixed and variable costs. The two types of flexible budgets are:

- before-the-fact, in which the budget gives expected outcomes for a range of activity levels and provides useful information for planning and decision making.
- after-the-fact, in which a budget is based on the actual level of activity. It is useful for control.

OBJECTIVE 4

Prepare a flexible budget, and use it for planning and for performance reporting.

CONCEPT CLIP

A before-the-fact flexible budget allows managers to develop financial results for a number of potential scenarios. The after-the-fact flexible budget is used to compute what costs should have been for the actual level of activity. Those expected costs are then compared with the actual costs in order to assess performance. Flexible budgeting is the key to providing the frequent feedback that managers need to exercise control and effectively carry out the plans of an organization.

To illustrate a before-the-fact flexible budget, suppose that the management of Cool-U, a maker of screen-printed T-shirts, wants to know the cost of producing 1,000 T-shirts, 1,200 T-shirts, and 1,400 T-shirts. To compute the expected cost for these different levels of output, managers need to know the cost behavior pattern of each item in the budget. Knowing the variable cost per unit and the total fixed costs allows the calculation of the expected costs for any level of activity within the relevant range. Example 9.13 shows how budgets can be prepared for different levels of activity, using cost formulas for each item.

EXAMPLE 9.13

How to Prepare a Before-the-Fact Flexible Budget

Levels of output: 1,000, 1,200, and 1,400.
Materials:
　1 plain T-shirt @ $3.00
　5 ounces of ink @ $0.20 per oz.
Labor:
　0.12 hr. @ $10.00
Variable overhead (VOH):
　Maintenance: 0.12 hr. @ $3.75
　Power: 0.12 hr. @ $1.25
Fixed overhead (FOH):
　Grounds keeping: $1,200 per quarter
　Depreciation: $600 per quarter

Required:
Prepare a budget for three levels of output: 1,000, 1,200, and 1,400 units.

Solution:

Production Costs	Variable Cost per Unit	Range of Production (units) 1,000	1,200	1,400
Variable:				
Direct materials	$ 4.00[a]	$ 4,000[b]	$4,800	$5,600
Direct labor	1.20[c]	1,200[d]	1,440	1,680
VOH:				
Maintenance	0.45[e]	450[f]	540	630
Power	0.15[g]	150[h]	180	210
Total variable costs	$ 5.80	$ 5,800	$6,960	$8,120
FOH:				
Grounds keeping		$ 1,200	$1,200	$1,200
Depreciation		600	600	600
Total fixed costs		$ 1,800	$1,800	$1,800
Total production costs		$ 7,600	$8,760	$9,920

[a] T-shirt Cost + Ink Cost = [($3.00 × 1 T-shirt) × ($0.20 × 5 oz.)]
[b] ($4 × 1,000 units)
[c] ($10.00 per direct labor hour × 0.12 direct labor hour per unit)
[d] ($1.20 × 1,000 units)
[e] ($3.75 per direct labor hour × 0.12 direct labor hour per unit)
[f] ($0.45 × 1,000 units)
[g] ($1.25 per direct labor hour × 0.12 direct labor hour per unit)
[h] ($0.15 × 1,000 units)

Example 9.13 shows that total budgeted production costs increase as the production level increases. Budgeted costs change because total variable costs go up as output increases. Because of this, flexible budgets are sometimes referred to as variable budgets. Since Cool-U has a mix of variable and fixed costs, the overall average cost of producing one T-shirt goes *down* as production goes *up*. This makes sense. As production increases, there are more units over which to spread the fixed production costs.

Often, the flexible budget formulas are based on direct labor hours instead of units. This can be done because direct labor hours are correlated with units produced. For example, the variable cost formulas for VOH are $3.75 and $1.25 per direct labor hour ($5.00 per direct labor hour in total) for maintenance and power, respectively. When standard hours are used, we need to convert units into direct labor hours. For Cool-U, the production of 1,000 budgeted units means that 120 direct labor hours will be needed (0.12 direct labor hour per unit × 1,000 budgeted units).

An after-the-fact flexible budget allows management to compute what the costs should be for the level of *output that actually occurred*. Suppose that Cool-U thought that 1,060 units would be produced and budgeted for that amount in the master budget. However, actual production was 1,200 units. Many managers would compare the budgeted costs from the master budget for 1,060 units (computed using the cost formulas from Example 9.13) with actual costs as shown in Exhibit 9.5 below.

	Actual	**Budgeted**	**Variance**
Units produced	1,200	1,060	140 F
Direct materials cost	$4,830	$4,240	$590 U
Direct labor cost	1,500	1,272	228 U
Variable overhead:			
Maintenance	535	477	58 U
Power	170	159	11 U
Fixed overhead:			
Grounds keeping	1,050	1,200	(150) F
Depreciation	600	600	0
Total	$8,685	$7,948	$737 U

Exhibit 9.5

Performance Report Comparing Actual Costs to the Static Budget

This is an example of comparing actual costs to the static budget. A **static budget** is a budget created in advance that is based on a particular level of activity. The master budget is generally created for a particular level of activity. Thus, one way to prepare a performance report is to compare the actual costs with the budgeted costs from the master budget. However, it does not make sense to compare the actual costs for 1,200 T-shirts to the budgeted costs for 1,060 T-shirts. Management needs a performance report that compares actual and budgeted costs for the actual level of activity. This is the second type of flexible budget, and preparation of this report is shown in Example 9.14.

According to Exhibit 9.5, there were unfavorable variances for direct materials, direct labor, maintenance, and power. However, actual costs for production of 1,200 T-shirts are being compared with planned costs for production of 1,060. Because direct materials, direct labor, and VOH are variable costs, they should be higher at higher production levels. Thus, even if cost control were perfect for the production of 1,200 units, unfavorable variances would be produced for at least some of the variable costs. To create a meaningful **performance report**, actual costs and expected costs must be compared at the *same* level of activity. Since actual output often differs from planned output, a method is needed to compute what the costs should have been for the actual output level.

The revised performance report in Example 9.14 paints a much different picture than the one in Exhibit 9.5. All of the variances are fairly small. Had they been larger, management should search for the cause and try to correct the problems.

EXAMPLE 9.14

How to Prepare a Performance Report Using a Flexible Budget

From Example 9.13 and the actual costs for 1,200 units shown in Exhibit 9.5, the actual and budgeted costs for the actual level of activity are as follows:

	Actual Costs	Budgeted Costs
Units produced	1,200	1,200
Direct materials cost	$4,830	$4,800
Direct labor cost	1,500	1,440
VOH:		
Maintenance	535	540
Power	170	180
FOH:		
Grounds keeping	1,050	1,200
Depreciation	600	600

Required:

Prepare a performance report using budgeted costs for the actual level of activity.

Solution:

	Actual Costs	Budget	Variance
Units produced	1,200	1,200	—
Production costs:			
Direct materials	$4,830	$4,800	$ 30 U
Direct labor	1,500	1,440	60 U
VOH:			
Maintenance	535	540	(5) F
Power	170	180	(10) F
Total variable costs	$7,035	$6,960	$ 75 U
FOH:			
Grounds keeping	$1,050	$1,200	$(150) F
Depreciation	600	600	(0)
Total fixed costs	$1,650	$1,800	$(150) F
Total production costs	$8,685	$8,760	$ (75) F

A difference between the actual amount and the flexible budget amount is the **flexible budget variance**. The flexible budget provides a measure of the efficiency of a manager. That is, how well did the manager control costs for the actual level of production? To measure whether or not a manager accomplishes his or her goals, the static budget is used. The static budget represents certain goals that the firm wants to achieve. A manager is effective if the goals described by the static budget are achieved or exceeded. In the Cool-U example, production volume was 140 units greater than the original budgeted amount. The manager exceeded the original budgeted goal. As long as the extra units can be sold, the effectiveness of the manager is not in question.

Ethical Decisions

Companies that use static budgets as the benchmark for performance evaluation invite potential abuse by managers. Although unethical, a manager could deliberately produce less than the planned output—producing, for example, 1,000 T-shirts instead of the planned 1,060. By producing less, the actual costs will be less than the budgeted amounts, creating a favorable performance outcome. Using flexible budgeting allows the benchmark to be adjusted to reflect the expected costs for the actual level of output. ●

Here's How It's Used: AT THE SECOND CITY

Suppose you are the chief accountant for **The Second City**, the company described in the chapter opener. Your job includes budgeting for the live performances, including the national touring companies and the customized comedy shows put on by the company. (See www.secondcity.com/ for examples of the live performances.) At the beginning of each year, you must put together budgets for these performances based on projected demand for the shows and projected costs. As the year unfolds, you want to update the budgets in accordance with new information and create performance reports that compare the actual costs with projected costs.

What information will you need to create both the master budget and flexible budgets for the live performances?

You will need to consider the fixed and variable costs associated with putting on live performances away from The Second City's Chicago base. The variable costs will include travel and salary costs for the performers, stage and facilities rent for each venue, and other variable costs associated with the shows (e.g., costs of hiring ticket sellers and ushers, supplies such as programs and tickets). Clearly, the variable costs will increase with an increase in the number of shows and venues. Some fixed costs must also be determined. These include the salaries of the writers, insurance, costs of props and costumes, and costs of marketing the shows to prospective customers including corporations and regional theaters.

Knowing the difference between the fixed and variable costs will enable you to create budgets that are useful to management in planning for the year ahead, as well as controlling costs as the year unfolds.

Check Point

1. **Why are static budgets usually not a good choice for benchmarks in preparing a performance report?**

Answer:
The actual output may differ from the budgeted output, thus causing significant differences in cost. Comparing planned costs for one level of activity with the actual costs of a different level of activity does not provide good control information.

2. **The flexible budget for 2,000 units shows a unit cost of $4.60. The unit cost for 3,000 units is $4.20. Why is the unit cost less for more units?**

Answer:
The unit cost is less for a greater number of units because there must be fixed costs involved. As production goes up, the unit cost goes down as there are more units over which to spread the same total fixed cost.

USING BUDGETS FOR PERFORMANCE EVALUATION

OBJECTIVE ▶ 5
Describe the behavioral dimension of budgeting.

 Here's **Why It's important**

Budgets are often used to judge the performance of managers. Bonuses, salary increases, and promotions are all affected by a manager's ability to achieve or beat budgeted goals. Since a manager's financial status and career can be affected, budgets can have a significant behavioral effect. Whether that effect is positive or negative depends in large part on how budgets are used.

Positive effects occur when the goals of each manager are aligned with the goals of the organization. The alignment of managerial and organizational goals is often referred to as **goal congruence**. If the budget is improperly administered, subordinate managers may subvert the organization's goals. **Dysfunctional behavior** is individual behavior that conflicts with the goals of the organization.

An ideal budgetary system achieves complete goal congruence and, simultaneously, creates a drive in managers to achieve the organization's goals in an ethical manner. While an ideal budgetary system probably does not exist, research and practice have identified some key features that promote a reasonable degree of positive behavior. These features include:

- frequent feedback on performance
- monetary and nonmonetary incentives
- participative budgeting
- realistic standards
- controllability of costs
- multiple measures of performance

Frequent Feedback on Performance

Managers need to know how they are doing as the year progresses. Frequent, timely performance reports allow managers to know how successful their efforts have been, to take corrective actions, and to change plans as necessary.

Monetary and Nonmonetary Incentives

A sound budgetary system encourages goal-congruent behavior. Incentives are the means an organization uses to influence a manager to work to achieve its goals. Traditional organizational theory assumes that employees are primarily motivated by monetary rewards, they resist work, and they are inefficient and wasteful. Thus, **monetary incentives** are used to control a manager's tendency to shirk and waste resources by relating budgetary performance to salary increases, bonuses, and promotions. The threat of dismissal is the ultimate economic sanction for poor performance. In reality, employees are motivated by more than economic factors. Employees are also motivated by intrinsic psychological and social factors, such as the satisfaction of a job well done, recognition, responsibility, self-esteem, and the nature of the work itself. Thus **nonmonetary incentives**, including job enrichment, increased responsibility and autonomy, recognition programs, and so on, can be used to enhance a budgetary control system.

Participative Budgeting

Rather than imposing budgets on subordinate managers, **participative budgeting** allows subordinate managers considerable say in how the budgets are established. Typically, overall objectives are shared with the manager, who helps develop a budget that will accomplish these objectives. Participative budgeting fosters a sense of responsibility and encourages creativity. Since the subordinate manager creates the budget, the budget's goals will more likely become the manager's personal goals, resulting in greater goal congruence. The increased responsibility and challenge inherent in the process are nonmonetary incentives that lead to a higher level of performance.

Participative budgeting has three potential problems:

- setting standards that are either too high or too low
- building slack into the budget (often referred to as padding the budget)
- pseudoparticipation

Standard Setting   Some managers may tend to set the budget either too loose or too tight. Since budgeted goals become the manager's goals when participation is allowed, making this mistake in setting the budget can result in decreased performance levels. If goals are too easily achieved, a manager may lose interest, and performance may actually drop. Feeling challenged is important to aggressive and creative individuals. Similarly, setting the budget too tight ensures failure to achieve the standards and frustrates managers. This frustration, too, can lead to poorer performance (see Exhibit 9.6). The trick is to get managers to set high but achievable goals.

Standard Set Too Loose
Goals Too Easily Achieved

Standard Set Too Tight
Frustration

Exhibit 9.6
The Art of Standard Setting

Budgetary Slack The second problem with participative budgeting is the opportunity to build slack into the budget. **Budgetary slack** (or *padding the budget*) exists when a manager deliberately underestimates revenues or overestimates costs in an effort to make the future period appear less attractive in the budget than they think it will really be. These approaches increase the likelihood that the manager will achieve the budget and consequently reduce the risk that the manager faces. Top management should carefully review budgets proposed by subordinate managers to decrease the effects of building slack into the budget.

Ethical Decisions

The act of padding the budget is questionable when considering what is viewed as ethical professional practice. Padding the budget is a deliberate misrepresentation of costs and/or revenues. It is certainly not communicating information fairly and objectively and constitutes a violation of the credibility standard. The motive for such behavior is also not consistent with the professional responsibility to exhibit integrity. While it might be useful to estimate some costs at a little higher amount than expected to factor in uncertainty, excessive padding is misrepresentation and can lead to failure to spend resources in other areas that may need them. ●

Pseudoparticipation The third problem with participation occurs when top management assumes total control of the budgeting process, seeking only superficial participation from lower-level managers. This practice is termed **pseudoparticipation**. Top management is simply obtaining formal acceptance of the budget from subordinate managers, not seeking real input. Accordingly, none of the behavioral benefits of participation will be realized.

Realistic Standards

Since budgeted objectives are used to gauge performance, they should reflect operating realities, including the following:

- *Actual Levels of Activity:* Flexible budgets are used to ensure that budgeted costs can be realistically compared with costs for actual levels of activity.
- *Seasonal Variations:* Interim budgets should reflect seasonal effects. **Toys "R" Us**, for example, would expect much higher sales in the quarter that includes Christmas than in other quarters.

- *Efficiencies:* Budgetary cuts should be based on *planned* increases in efficiency and not simply arbitrary across-the-board reductions. Across-the-board cuts without any formal evaluation may impair the ability of some units to carry out their missions.
- *General Economic Trends:* General economic conditions also need to be considered. Budgeting for a significant increase in sales when a recession is projected is not only foolish but also potentially dangerous.

Controllability of Costs

Ideally, managers are held accountable only for costs that they can control. **Controllable costs** are costs whose level a manager can influence. For example, divisional managers have no power to authorize such corporate-level costs as research and development and salaries of top managers. Therefore, they should not be held accountable for the incurrence of those costs. If noncontrollable costs are put in the budgets of subordinate managers to help them understand that these costs also need to be covered, then they should be separated from controllable costs and labeled as *noncontrollable*.

Multiple Measures of Performance

Some organizations make the mistake of using budgets as their only measure of managerial performance. While financial measures of performance are important, overemphasis can lead to a form of dysfunctional behavior called *milking the firm* or *myopia*. **Myopic behavior** occurs when a manager takes actions that improve budgetary performance in the short run but bring long-run harm to the firm. For example, to meet budgeted cost objectives or profits, managers can delay promoting deserving employees or reducing expenditures for preventive maintenance, advertising, and new product development. Using measures that are both financial and nonfinancial and that are long and short term can alleviate this problem. For example, Starwood Hotels incurs considerable costs every year to research consumer trends and to train its hotel staff members to help ensure sustainable growth in room revenue for its luxury St. Regis brand. Budgetary measures alone cannot prevent myopic behavior.

Here's How It's Used: AT HIGH SIERRA SPORTS

High Sierra Sports, a division of Samsonite Corp., produces a variety of quality outdoor and foul weather gear, including backpacks, duffel bags, book bags, and other adventure travel gear. The company successfully uses budgeting for both planning and control to allow for the right balance of variance in the product mix as well as expansion within product lines. Based on the master budget, High Sierra expanded its high-performing Adventure travel lines and also introduced new day packs and wheeled book bags. Both moves enhanced its reputation for adventure lifestyle gear.

When planning, High Sierra uses the 80-20 rule to evaluate accounts and determine where significant forecasting effort is needed. The 80-20 rule, or Pareto Principle, states that 80% of the results come from 20% of the causes. For High Sierra, about 20% of the accounts, the largest ones, account for roughly 80% of sales. The senior vice president of sales and operations reviews the forecasted sales for each of these significant accounts with that account's sales manager to understand the reasoning behind the forecasted numbers and to make any necessary adjustments. Remaining smaller accounts are adjusted using a rule of thumb (e.g., perhaps a 10% growth rate in sales).

As the year unfolds, the company uses continuous budgeting for control as it compares actual results with budgeted results. For example, if sales are not meeting budget targets, managers must look into areas where expenses can be decreased to maintain an appropriate EBITA (earnings before interest, taxes, and amortization). On the other hand, if sales are higher than expected, managers must adapt by increasing related expenses, such as personnel and travel cost.

1. **In the last quarter of the fiscal year, a divisional manager chose to delay budgeted preventive maintenance expenditures so that the budgeted income goals could be achieved. Is this an example of goal congruent behavior or dysfunctional behavior?**

Answer:
Assuming that the budgeted maintenance expenditures were well specified, the manager is sacrificing the long-run well-being of the division to achieve a short-run benefit (dysfunctional behavior).

2. **Assume that a company evaluates and rewards its managers based on their ability to achieve budgeted goals. Why would the same company ask its managers to participate in setting their budgeted standards?**

Answer:
Participation encourages managers to internalize the goals and make them their own, leading to improved performance.

SUMMARY OF LEARNING OBJECTIVES

LO1. Define budgeting and discuss its role in planning, control, and decision making.
- Budgeting is the creation of a plan of action expressed in financial terms.
- Budgeting plays a key role in planning, control, and decision making.
- Budgets serve to improve communication and coordination, a role that becomes increasingly important as organizations grow in size.
- The master budget, which is the comprehensive financial plan of an organization, is made up of the operating and financial budgets.

LO2. Define and prepare the operating budget, identify its major components, and explain the interrelationships of its various components.
- The operating budget is the budgeted income statement and all supporting budgets.
- The sales budget consists of the anticipated quantity and price of all products to be sold. It is done first, and the results feed directly into the production budget.
- The production budget gives the expected production in units to meet forecasted sales and desired ending inventory goals. Expected production is supplemented by beginning inventory. The results of the production budget are needed for the direct materials purchases budget and the direct labor budget.
- The direct materials purchases budget gives the necessary purchases during the year for every type of raw material to meet production and desired ending inventory goals.
- The direct labor budget shows the number of direct labor hours, and the direct labor cost needed to support production. The resulting direct labor hours are needed to prepare the overhead budget.
- The overhead budget may be broken down into fixed and variable components to facilitate preparation of the budget.
- The selling and administrative expenses budget gives the forecasted costs for these functions.

- The finished goods inventory budget and the cost of goods sold budget detail production costs for the expected ending inventory and the units sold, respectively.
- The budgeted income statement outlines the net income to be realized if budgeted plans come to fruition.

LO3. Define and prepare the financial budget, identify its major components, and explain the interrelationships of its various components.
- The financial budget includes the cash budget, the capital expenditures budget, and the budgeted balance sheet.
- The cash budget is the beginning balance in the cash account, plus anticipated receipts, minus anticipated disbursements, plus or minus any necessary borrowing.
- The budgeted (or pro forma) balance sheet gives the anticipated ending balances of the asset, liability, and equity accounts if budgeted plans hold.

LO4. Prepare a flexible budget, and use it for planning and for performance reporting.
- Static budgets provide expected cost for a given level of activity. If the actual level of activity differs from the static budget level, then comparing actual costs with budgeted costs does not make sense. The solution is flexible budgeting.
- Flexible budgets divide costs into those that vary with units of production (or direct labor hours) and those that are fixed with respect to unit-level drivers. These relationships allow the identification of a cost formula for each item in the budget.
- Cost formulas calculate expected costs for various levels of activity. There are two applications of flexible budgets: before-the-fact and after-the-fact.
- Before-the-fact applications allow managers to see what costs will be for different levels of activity, thus helping in planning.
- After-the-fact applications allow managers to see what the cost should have been for the actual level of activity. Knowing these after-the-fact expected or budgeted costs provides the opportunity to evaluate efficiency by comparing actual costs with budgeted costs.

LO5. Describe the behavioral dimension of budgeting.
- The success of a budgetary system depends on how seriously human factors are considered.
- To discourage dysfunctional behavior, organizations should avoid overemphasizing budgets as a control mechanism.
- Budgets can be improved as performance measures by using participative budgeting and other nonmonetary incentives, providing frequent feedback on performance, using flexible budgeting, ensuring that the budgetary objectives reflect reality, and holding managers accountable for only controllable costs.

SUMMARY OF IMPORTANT EQUATIONS

1. Units to Be Produced = Expected Unit Sales + Units in Desired Ending Inventory (EI)
   – Units in Beginning Inventory (BI)

2. Purchases = Direct Materials Needed for Production
   + Direct Materials in Desired Ending Inventory
   – Direct Materials in Beginning Inventory

3. Cash Available = Beginning Cash Balance + Expected Cash Receipts

4. Ending Cash Balance = Cash Available – Expected Cash Disbursements

KEY TERMS

Budget committee, 458, the group that reviews the budget, provides policy guidelines and policy goals, resolves differences that arise as the budget is prepared, approves the final budget, and monitors the actual performance of the organization as the year unfolds.

Budget director, 458, typically the controller, this is the person responsible for directing and coordinating the organization's overall budgeting process.

Budgetary slack, 481, padding the budget, which occurs when a manager deliberately underestimates revenues or overestimates costs in order to make budgeted expectations more easily achievable in the future.

Budgets, 456, financial plans for the future.

Cash budget, 469, a budget that shows budgeted cash inflows and outflows for the time period so that managers can determine any expected cash excess or deficiency.

Continuous budget, 457, a moving 12-month budget. As one month expires, another month in the future is added.

Controllable costs, 482, costs whose level a manager can influence or control.

Cost of goods sold budget, 466, a budget that shows the expected production cost of the units budgeted to be sold during the period.

Direct labor budget, 464, the budget showing the expected number of direct labor hours to be worked and the total cost of direct labor for the budget period.

Direct materials purchases budget, 462, a budget that shows the amount and cost of every type of raw material to be purchased in each time period.

Dysfunctional behavior, 479, individual behavior that is in basic conflict with the goals of the organization.

Ending finished goods inventory budget, 465, budget that shows the cost of units budgeted to be in ending finished goods inventory.

Financial budgets, 458, budgets that detail the inflows and outflows of cash and the overall financial position of the firm.

Flexible (variable) budget, 475, budget that shows expected costs for a particular activity level. A before-the-fact flexible budget gives expected costs for a range of activity levels. An after-the-fact flexible budget gives expected costs for the actual level of activity.

Flexible budget variance, 478, the difference between the budgeted costs and actual costs for the chosen level of activity.

Goal congruence, 479, the alignment of managerial and organizational goals.

Master budget, 457, the comprehensive financial plan for the organization as a whole. It covers a fiscal year.

Monetary incentives, 480, monetary rewards used to control a manager's tendency to shirk and waste resources by tying budgetary performance to salary increases, bonuses, and promotions.

Myopic behavior, 482, when a manager takes actions that improve budgetary performance in the short run but bring long-run harm to the firm.

Nonmonetary incentives, 480, rewards that include job enrichment, increased responsibility and autonomy, and recognition programs.

Operating budgets, 458, budgets that describe the income-generating activities of a firm, sales, production, and finished goods inventories, ending with the budgeted income statement.

Overhead budget, 464, a budget that shows the expected cost of all production costs other than direct materials and direct labor.

Participative budgeting, 480, type of budgeting that allows subordinate managers considerable say in how the budgets are established.

Performance report, 477, a form that compares actual costs with budgeted costs.

Production budget, 461, a budget that details the number of units of each product to be produced in the coming year, in order to satisfy sales and desired ending inventory needs.

Pseudoparticipation, 481, when top management has total control of the budgeting process, allowing only superficial participation from lower-level managers.

Sales budget, 459, a budget that describes expected sales in units and dollars for every product or service sold.

Selling and administrative expenses budget, 466, a budget that shows the expected costs for nonmanufacturing costs of selling and administration.

Static budget, 477, a budget created in advance for a particular level of activity.

Strategic plan, 456, a plan that plots a direction for an organization's future activities and operations; it generally covers at least 5 years. The overall strategy is then translated into the long- and short-term objectives that form the basis of the budget.

REVIEW PROBLEMS

I. Select Operational Budgets

Joven Products produces coat racks. The projected sales for the first quarter of the coming year and the beginning and ending inventory data are as follows:

Unit sales	100,000
Unit price	$15
Units in beginning inventory	8,000
Units in targeted ending inventory	12,000

The coat racks are molded and then painted. Each rack requires 4 pounds of metal, which costs $2.50 per pound. The beginning inventory of materials is 4,000 pounds. Joven Products wants to have 6,000 pounds of metal in inventory at the end of the quarter. Each rack produced requires 30 minutes of direct labor time, which is billed at $14 per hour.

Required:

1. Prepare a sales budget for the first quarter.
2. Prepare a production budget for the first quarter.
3. Prepare a direct materials purchases budget for the first quarter.
4. Prepare a direct labor budget for the first quarter.

Solution:

1.

Joven Products
Sales Budget
For the First Quarter

Units	100,000
Unit price	× $15
Sales	$1,500,000

2.

Joven Products
Production Budget
For the First Quarter

Sales (in units)	100,000
Desired ending inventory	12,000
Total needs	112,000
Less: Beginning inventory	8,000
Units to be produced	104,000

3.

Joven Products
Direct Materials Purchases Budget
For the First Quarter

Units to be produced	104,000
Direct materials per unit (lb.)	× 4
Production needs (lb.)	416,000
Desired ending inventory (lb.)	6,000
Total needs (lb.)	422,000
Less: Beginning inventory (lb.)	4,000
Materials to be purchased (lb.)	418,000
Cost per pound	× $2.50
Total purchase cost	$1,045,000

(Continued)

4.

Joven Products
Direct Labor Budget
For the First Quarter

Units to be produced	104,000
Labor hours per unit	× 0.5
Total hours needed	52,000
Cost per hour	× $14
Total direct labor cost	$728,000

II. Cash Budgeting

Kylles Inc. expects to receive cash from sales of $45,000 in March. In addition, Kylles expects to sell property worth $3,500. Payments for materials and supplies are expected to total $10,000, direct labor payroll will be $12,500, and other expenditures are budgeted at $14,900. On March 1, the cash account balance is $1,230.

Required:

1. Prepare a cash budget for Kylles Inc. for the month of March.
2. Assume that Kylles Inc. wanted a minimum cash balance of $15,000 and that it could borrow from the bank in multiples of $1,000 at an interest rate of 12% per year. What would the adjusted ending balance for March be for Kylles? How much interest would Kylles owe in April, assuming that the entire amount borrowed in March would be paid back?

Solution:

1.

Kylles Inc.
Cash Budget for the Month of March

Beginning cash balance	$ 1,230
Cash sales	45,000
Sale of property	3,500
Total cash available	$49,730
Less disbursements:	
Materials and supplies	$10,000
Direct labor payroll	12,500
Other expenditures	14,900
Total disbursements	$37,400
Ending cash balance	$12,330

2.

Unadjusted ending balance	$12,330
Plus borrowing	3,000
Adjusted ending balance	$15,330

In April, interest owed would be $(1/12 \times 0.12 \times \$3,000) = \$30$.

III. Flexible Budgeting

Trina Hoyt, controller of Ferrel Company, wants to prepare a quarterly budget for three different levels of output (measured in units): 2,000, 2,500, and 3,000.

The product uses the following inputs:

Materials:

      3 pounds of plastic @ $6.00

      4 ounces of metal @ $2.00

Labor:

      0.5 hr. @ $10.00

VOH:

      Inspection: 0.2 hr. @ $10

      Machining: 0.3 hr. @ $5

FOH:

      Rent: $15,000 per quarter

      Utilities: $3,000 per quarter

Required:

Prepare a budget for three levels of output: 2,000, 2,500, and 3,000 units.

Solution:

Production Costs	Variable Cost per Unit	Range of Production (units) 2,000	2,500	3,000
Variable:				
Direct materials	$26.00[a]	$52,000[b]	$ 65,000	$ 78,000
Direct labor	5.00[c]	10,000[d]	12,500	15,000
VOH:				
Inspection	2.00[e]	4,000[f]	5,000	6,000
Machining	1.50[g]	3,000[h]	3,750	4,500
Total variable costs	$34.50	$69,000	$ 86,250	$103,500
FOH:				
Rent		$15,000	$ 15,000	$ 15,000
Utilities		3,000	3,000	3,000
Total fixed costs		$18,000	$ 18,000	$ 18,000
Total production costs		$87,000	$104,250	$121,500

[a] $(3 \times \$6.00) + (4 \times \$2.00)$
[b] $(\$26 \times 2,000)$
[c] $(0.5 \times \$10.00)$
[d] $(\$5 \times 2,000)$
[e] $(0.2 \times \$10)$
[f] $(\$2 \times 2,000)$
[g] $(0.3 \times \$5.00)$
[h] $(\$1.50 \times 2,000)$

DISCUSSION QUESTIONS

1. Define the term *budget*. How are budgets used in planning?
2. Define *control*. How are budgets used to control?
3. Explain how both small and large organizations can benefit from budgeting.
4. Discuss some reasons for budgeting.
5. What is a master budget? An operating budget? A financial budget?
6. Explain the role of a sales forecast in budgeting. What is the difference between a sales forecast and a sales budget?
7. All budgets depend on the sales budget. Is this true? Explain.
8. Why is goal congruence important?
9. Why is it important for a manager to receive frequent feedback on his or her performance?

10. What is participative budgeting? Discuss some of its advantages.
11. A budget too easily achieved will lead to diminished performance. Do you agree? Explain.
12. Explain why a manager has an incentive to build slack into the budget.
13. Discuss the differences between static and flexible budgets.
14. Explain why mixed costs must be broken down into their fixed and variable components before a flexible budget can be developed.
15. What is the purpose of a before-the-fact flexible budget? What is the purpose of an after-the-fact flexible budget?

MULTIPLE-CHOICE QUESTIONS

9-1　A budget

    a. is a long-term plan.
    b. covers at least 2 years.
    c. is only a control tool.
    d. is a short-term financial plan.
    e. is necessary only for large firms.

9-2　Which of the following is part of the control process?

    a. Monitoring of actual activity
    b. Comparison of actual with planned activity
    c. Investigating
    d. Taking corrective action
    e. All of these.

9-3　Which of the following is *not* an advantage of budgeting?

    a. It forces managers to plan.
    b. It provides information for decision making.
    c. It guarantees an improvement in organizational efficiency.
    d. It provides a standard for performance evaluation.
    e. It improves communication and coordination.

9-4　The budget committee

    a. reviews the budget.
    b. resolves differences that arise as the budget is prepared.
    c. approves the final budget.
    d. is directed (typically) by the controller.
    e. All of these.

9-5　A moving, 12-month budget that is updated monthly is

    a. not used by manufacturing firms.
    b. a waste of time and effort.
    c. a master budget.
    d. a continuous budget.
    e. always used by firms that prepare a master budget.

9-6　Which of the following is *not* part of the operating budget?

    a. The direct labor budget
    b. The cost of goods sold budget
    c. The production budget
    d. The capital budget
    e. The selling and administrative expenses budget

9-7 Before a direct materials purchases budget can be prepared, you should first

    a. prepare a sales budget.

    b. prepare a production budget.

    c. decide on the desired ending inventory of materials.

    d. obtain the expected price of each type of material.

    e. All of these.

9-8 The first step in preparing the sales budget is to

    a. prepare a sales forecast.

    b. review the production budget carefully.

    c. assess the desired ending inventory of finished goods.

    d. talk with past customers.

    e. increase sales beyond the forecast level.

9-9 Which of the following is needed to prepare the production budget?

    a. Direct materials needed for production

    b. Direct labor needed for production

    c. Expected unit sales

    d. Units of materials in ending inventory

    e. None of these.

9-10 A company requires 100 pounds of plastic to meet the production needs of a small toy. It currently has 10 pounds of plastic inventory. The desired ending inventory of plastic is 30 pounds. How many pounds of plastic should be budgeted for purchasing during the coming period?

    a. 80 pounds

    b. 110 pounds

    c. 120 pounds

    d. 130 pounds

    e. None of these.

9-11 A company plans to sell 220 units. The selling price per unit is $24. There are 50 units in beginning inventory, and the company would like to have 20 units in ending inventory. How many units should be produced for the coming period?

    a. 250

    b. 200

    c. 230

    d. 220

    e. None of these.

9-12 Select the one budget below that is *not* an operating budget.

    a. Cost of goods sold budget

    b. Cash budget

    c. Production budget

    d. Overhead budget

    e. All of these.

9-13 A company has the following collection pattern: month of sale, 40%; month following sale, 60%.

If credit sales for January and February are $100,000 and $200,000, respectively, the cash collections for February are

    a. $140,000.

    b. $300,000.

    c. $120,000.

    d. $160,000.

    e. $80,000.

9-14 The percentage of accounts receivable that is uncollectible can be ignored for cash budgeting because

    a. no cash is received from an account that defaults.

    b. it is included in cash sales.

    c. it appears on the budgeted income statement.

    d. for most companies, it is not a material amount.

    e. None of these.

9-15 Which of the following is *not* an advantage of participative budgeting?

    a. It encourages budgetary slack.

    b. It tends to lead to a higher level of performance.

    c. It fosters a sense of responsibility.

    d. It encourages greater goal congruence.

    e. It fosters a sense of creativity in managers.

9-16 Which of the following items is a possible example of myopic behavior?

    a. Failure to promote deserving employees

    b. Reducing expenditures on preventive maintenance

    c. Cutting back on new product development

    d. Buying cheaper, lower-quality materials so that the company does not exceed the materials purchases budget

    e. All of these.

9-17 For performance reporting, it is best to compare actual costs with budgeted costs using

    a. short-term budgets.

    b. static budgets.

    c. flexible budgets.

    d. master budgets.

    e. None of these.

9-18 To create a meaningful performance report, actual costs and expected costs should be compared

    a. at the actual level of activity.

    b. weekly.

    c. at the budgeted level of activity.

    d. at the average level of activity.

    e. hourly.

9-19 To help assess performance, managers should use a

    a. static budget.

    b. master budget.

    c. continuous budget.

    d. before-the-fact flexible budget.

    e. None of these.

9-20 A firm comparing the actual variable costs of producing 10,000 units with the total variable costs of a static budget based on 9,000 units would probably see

    a. no variances.

    b. small favorable variances.

    c. large unfavorable variances.

    d. large favorable variances.

    e. small unfavorable variances.

BRIEF EXERCISES: SET A

Brief Exercise 9-21 Preparing a Sales Budget

OBJECTIVE ▸ 2
Example 9.1

Patrick Inc. sells industrial solvents in 5-gallon drums. Patrick expects the following units to be sold in the first 3 months of the coming year:

January	41,000
February	38,000
March	50,000

The average price for a drum is $35.

Required:

Prepare a sales budget for the first 3 months of the coming year, showing units and sales revenue by month and in total for the quarter.

Brief Exercise 9-22 Preparing a Production Budget

OBJECTIVE ▸ 2
Example 9.2

Patrick Inc. makes industrial solvents. In the first 4 months of the coming year, Patrick expects the following unit sales:

January	41,000
February	38,000
March	50,000
April	51,000

Patrick's policy is to have 25% of next month's sales in ending inventory. On January 1, it is expected that there will be 6,700 drums of solvent on hand.

Required:

Prepare a production budget for the first quarter of the year. Show the number of drums that should be produced each month as well as for the quarter in total.

Brief Exercise 9-23 Preparing a Direct Materials Purchases Budget

OBJECTIVE ▸ 2
Example 9.3

Patrick Inc. makes industrial solvents sold in 5-gallon drums. Planned production in units for the first 3 months of the coming year is:

January	43,800
February	41,000
March	50,250

Each drum requires 5.5 gallons of chemicals and one plastic drum. Company policy requires that ending inventories of raw materials for each month be 15% of the next month's production needs. That policy was met for the ending inventory of December in the prior year. The cost of one gallon of chemicals is $2.00. The cost of one drum is $1.60. (*Note:* Round all unit amounts to the nearest unit. Round all dollar amounts to the nearest dollar.)

Required:

1. Calculate the ending inventory of chemicals in gallons for December of the prior year and for January and February. What is the beginning inventory of chemicals for January?
2. Prepare a direct materials purchases budget for chemicals for the months of January and February.
3. Calculate the ending inventory of drums for December of the prior year and for January and February.
4. Prepare a direct materials purchases budget for drums for the months of January and February.

OBJECTIVE ▶2▶
Example 9.4

Brief Exercise 9-24 **Preparing a Direct Labor Budget**

Patrick Inc. makes industrial solvents. Planned production in units for the first 3 months of the coming year is:

January	43,800
February	41,000
March	50,250

Each drum of industrial solvent takes 0.3 direct labor hour. The average wage is $18 per hour.

Required:

Prepare a direct labor budget for the months of January, February, and March, as well as the total for the first quarter.

OBJECTIVE ▶2▶
Example 9.5

Brief Exercise 9-25 **Preparing an Overhead Budget**

Patrick Inc. makes industrial solvents. Budgeted direct labor hours for the first 3 months of the coming year are:

January	13,140
February	12,300
March	15,075

The variable overhead rate is $0.70 per direct labor hour. Fixed overhead is budgeted at $2,750 per month.

Required:

Prepare an overhead budget for the months of January, February, and March, as well as the total for the first quarter. (*Note*: Round all dollar amounts to the nearest dollar.)

OBJECTIVE ▶2▶
Example 9.6

Brief Exercise 9-26 **Preparing an Ending Finished Goods Inventory Budget**

Andrews Company manufactures a line of office chairs. Each chair takes $14 of direct materials and uses 1.9 direct labor hours at $16 per direct labor hour. The variable overhead rate is $1.20 per direct labor hour, and the fixed overhead rate is $1.60 per direct labor hour. Andrews expects to have 675 chairs in ending inventory. There is no beginning inventory of office chairs.

Required:

1. Calculate the unit product cost. (*Note:* Round to the nearest cent.)
2. Calculate the cost of budgeted ending inventory. (*Note:* Round to the nearest dollar.)

OBJECTIVE ▶2▶
Example 9.7

Brief Exercise 9-27 **Preparing a Cost of Goods Sold Budget**

Andrews Company manufactures a line of office chairs. Each chair takes $14 of direct materials and uses 1.9 direct labor hours at $16 per direct labor hour. The variable overhead rate is $1.20 per direct labor hour, and the fixed overhead rate is $1.60 per direct labor hour. Andrews expects to produce 20,000 chairs next year and expects to have 675 chairs in ending inventory. There is no beginning inventory of office chairs.

Required:

Prepare a cost of goods sold budget for Andrews Company.

OBJECTIVE ▶2▶
Example 9.8

Brief Exercise 9-28 **Preparing a Selling and Administrative Expenses Budget**

Fazel Company makes and sells paper products. In the coming year, Fazel expects total sales of $19,730,000. There is a 3% commission on sales. In addition, fixed expenses of the sales and administrative offices include the following:

Salaries	$ 960,000
Utilities	365,000
Office space	230,000
Advertising	1,200,000

Required:

Prepare a selling and administrative expenses budget for Fazel Company for the coming year.

Brief Exercise 9-29 Preparing a Budgeted Income Statement

OBJECTIVE ▶ 2

Example 9.9

Oliver Company provided the following information for the coming year:

Units produced and sold	160,000
Cost of goods sold per unit	$6.30
Selling price	$10.80
Variable selling and administrative expenses per unit	$1.10
Fixed selling and administrative expenses	$423,000
Tax rate	35%

Required:

Prepare a budgeted income statement for Oliver Company for the coming year. (*Note:* Round all income statement amounts to the nearest dollar.)

Brief Exercise 9-30 Preparing a Schedule of Cash Collections on Accounts Receivable

OBJECTIVE ▶ 3

Example 9.10

Kailua and Company is a legal services firm. All sales of legal services are billed to the client (there are no cash sales). Kailua expects that, on average, 20% will be paid in the month of billing, 50% will be paid in the month following billing, and 25% will be paid in the second month following billing. For the next 5 months, the following sales billings are expected:

May	$ 84,000
June	100,800
July	77,000
August	86,800
September	91,000

Required:

Prepare a schedule showing the cash expected in payments on accounts receivable in August and in September.

Brief Exercise 9-31 Preparing an Accounts Payable Schedule

OBJECTIVE ▶ 3

Example 9.11

Wight Inc. purchases raw materials on account for use in production. The direct materials purchases budget shows the following expected purchases on account:

April	$374,400
May	411,200
June	416,000

Wight typically pays 20% on account in the month of billing and 80% the next month.

Required:

1. How much cash is required for payments on account in May?
2. How much cash is expected for payments on account in June?

OBJECTIVE 3
Example 9.12

Brief Exercise 9-32 Preparing a Cash Budget

La Famiglia Pizzeria provided the following information for the month of October:

a. Sales are budgeted to be $157,000. About 85% of sales is cash; the remainder is on account.

b. La Famiglia expects that, on average, 70% of credit sales will be paid in the month of sale, and 28% will be paid in the following month.

c. Food and supplies purchases, all on account, are expected to be $116,000. La Famiglia pays 25% in the month of purchase and 75% in the month following purchase.

d. Most of the work is done by the owners, who typically withdraw $6,000 a month from the business as their salary. (*Note:* The $6,000 is a payment in total to the two owners, not per person.) Various part-time workers cost $7,300 per month. They are paid for their work weekly, so on average 90% of their wages is paid in the month incurred and the remaining 10% in the next month.

e. Utilities average $5,950 per month. Rent on the building is $4,100 per month.

f. Insurance is paid quarterly; the next payment of $1,200 is due in October.

g. September sales were $181,500 and purchases of food and supplies in September equaled $130,000.

h. The cash balance on October 1 is $2,147.

Required:

1. Calculate the cash receipts expected in October. (*Hint:* Remember to include both cash sales and payments from credit sales.)

2. Calculate the cash needed in October to pay for food purchases.

3. Prepare a cash budget for the month of October.

OBJECTIVE 4
Example 9.13

Brief Exercise 9-33 Flexible Budget with Different Levels of Production

Bowling Company budgeted the following amounts:

Variable costs of production:	
Direct materials	3 pounds @ $0.60 per pound
Direct labor	0.5 hr. @ $16.00 per hour
VOH	0.5 hr. @ $2.20
FOH:	
Materials handling	$6,200
Depreciation	$2,600

Required:

Prepare a flexible budget for 2,500 units, 3,000 units, and 3,500 units.

OBJECTIVE 4
Example 9.14

Brief Exercise 9-34 Performance Report Based on Budgeted and Actual Levels of Production

Bowling Company budgeted the following amounts:

Variable costs of production:	
Direct materials	3 pounds @ $0.60 per pound
Direct labor	0.5 hr. @ $16.00 per hour
VOH	0.5 hr. @ $2.20
FOH:	
Materials handling	$6,200
Depreciation	$2,600

At the end of the year, Bowling had the following actual costs for production of 3,800 units:

Direct materials	$ 6,800
Direct labor	30,500
VOH	4,200
FOH:	
Materials handling	6,300
Depreciation	2,600

Required:

1. Calculate the budgeted amounts for each cost category listed above for the 4,000 budgeted units.
2. Prepare a performance report using a budget based on expected production of 4,000 units.
3. Prepare a performance report using a budget based on the actual level of production of 3,800 units.

BRIEF EXERCISES: SET B

Brief Exercise 9-35 Preparing a Sales Budget

OBJECTIVE ▶ 2
Example 9.1

Tulum Inc. sells powdered Mexican chocolate to restaurants. Its basic unit is a 4-pound box of the spiced chocolate mixture. Tulum expects the following units to be sold in the first 3 months of the coming year:

January	22,000
February	20,000
March	30,000

The average price for a box is $20.

Required:

Prepare a sales budget for the first 3 months of the coming year, showing units and sales revenue by month and in total for the quarter.

Brief Exercise 9-36 Preparing a Production Budget

OBJECTIVE ▶ 2
Example 9.2

Tulum Inc. makes a Mexican chocolate mix. In the first 4 months of the coming year, Tulum expects the following unit sales:

January	22,000
February	20,000
March	30,000
April	31,000

Tulum's policy is to have 20% of next month's sales in ending inventory. On January 1, it is expected that there will be 1,300 boxes of the chocolate mixture on hand.

Required:

Prepare a production budget for the first quarter of the year. Show the boxes that should be produced each month as well as for the quarter in total.

OBJECTIVE ▶ 2
Example 9.3

Brief Exercise 9-37 Preparing a Direct Materials Purchases Budget

Tulum Inc. makes a Mexican chocolate mix sold in 4-pound boxes. Planned production in units for the first 3 months of the coming year is:

January	24,700
February	22,000
March	30,200

Each box requires 4.2 pounds of chocolate mix and one box. Company policy requires that ending inventories of raw materials for each month be 10% of the next month's production needs. That policy was met for the ending inventory of December in the prior year. The cost of 1 pound of chocolate mix is $1.50. The cost of one box is $0.10. (*Note:* Round all unit amounts to the nearest unit. Round all dollar amounts to the nearest dollar.)

Required:

1. Calculate the ending inventory of chocolate mix in pounds for December of the prior year and for January and February. What is the beginning inventory of chocolate mix for January?
2. Prepare a direct materials purchases budget for chocolate mix for the months of January and February.
3. Calculate the ending inventory of boxes for December of the prior year and for January and February.
4. Prepare a direct materials purchases budget for boxes for the months of January and February.

OBJECTIVE ▶ 2
Example 9.4

Brief Exercise 9-38 Preparing a Direct Labor Budget

Tulum Inc. makes a Mexican chocolate mix. Planned production in units for the first 3 months of the coming year is:

January	24,700
February	22,000
March	30,200

Each box of chocolate mix takes 0.4 direct labor hour. The average wage is $17 per hour.

Required:

Prepare a direct labor budget for the months of January, February, and March, as well as the total for the first quarter.

OBJECTIVE ▶ 2
Example 9.5

Brief Exercise 9-39 Preparing an Overhead Budget

Tulum Inc. makes a Mexican chocolate mix. Budgeted direct labor hours for the first 3 months of the coming year are:

January	9,880
February	8,800
March	12,200

The variable overhead rate is $0.50 per direct labor hour. Fixed overhead is budgeted at $3,140 per month.

Required:

Prepare an overhead budget for the months of January, February, and March, as well as the total for the first quarter. (*Note*: Round all dollar amounts to the nearest dollar.)

Brief Exercise 9-40 Preparing an Ending Finished Goods Inventory Budget

OBJECTIVE ▸ 2
Example 9.6

Lazlo Company manufactures a line of table lamps. Each lamp takes $5 of direct materials and uses 0.9 direct labor hour at $18 per direct labor hour. The variable overhead rate is $1.00 per direct labor hour, and the fixed overhead rate is $2.00 per direct labor hour. Lazlo expects to have 830 lamps in ending inventory. There is no beginning inventory of table lamps.

Required:

1. Calculate the unit product cost. (*Note:* Round to the nearest cent.)
2. Calculate the cost of budgeted ending inventory. (*Note:* Round to the nearest dollar.)

Brief Exercise 9-41 Preparing a Cost of Goods Sold Budget

OBJECTIVE ▸ 2
Example 9.7

Lazlo Company manufactures a line of table lamps. Each lamp takes $5.00 of direct materials and uses 0.9 direct labor hour at $18.00 per direct labor hour. The variable overhead rate is $1.00 per direct labor hour and the fixed overhead rate is $2.00 per direct labor hour. Lazlo expects to produce 16,000 lamps next year and expects to have 830 lamps in ending inventory. There is no beginning inventory of table lamps.

Required:

Prepare a cost of goods sold budget for Lazlo Company.

Brief Exercise 9-42 Preparing a Selling and Administrative Expenses Budget

OBJECTIVE ▸ 2
Example 9.8

Elwood Company makes and sells plastic trash bags. In the coming year, Elwood expects total sales of $18,620,000. There is a 4% commission on sales. In addition, fixed expenses of the sales and administrative offices include the following:

Salaries	$ 796,000
Utilities	173,000
Office space	312,000
Advertising	1,100,000

Required:

Prepare a selling and administrative expenses budget for Elwood Company for the coming year.

Brief Exercise 9-43 Preparing a Budgeted Income Statement

OBJECTIVE ▸ 2
Example 9.9

Jameson Company provided the following information for the coming year:

Units produced and sold	230,000
Cost of goods sold per unit	$5.30
Selling price	$9.70
Variable selling and administrative expenses per unit	$1.60
Fixed selling and administrative expenses	$387,000
Tax rate	35%

Required:

Prepare a budgeted income statement for Jameson Company for the coming year. (*Note:* Round all income statement amounts to the nearest dollar.)

Brief Exercise 9-44 Preparing a Schedule of Cash Collections on Accounts Receivable

OBJECTIVE ▸ 3
Example 9.10

Weiland and Company is a medical billing services firm. All sales of billing services are billed to the client (there are no cash sales). Weiland expects that, on average, 15% will be paid in the

(Continued)

month of billing, 40% will be paid in the month following billing, and 42% will be paid in the second month following billing. For the next 5 months, the following sales billings are expected:

May	$184,000
June	192,000
July	207,000
August	175,000
September	164,000

Required:

Prepare a schedule showing the cash expected in payments on accounts receivable in August and in September.

OBJECTIVE 3
Example 9.11

Brief Exercise 9-45 Preparing an Accounts Payable Schedule

Pilsner Inc. purchases raw materials on account for use in production. The direct materials purchases budget shows the following expected purchases on account:

April	$374,400
May	411,200
June	416,000

Pilsner typically pays 25% on account in the month of billing and 75% the next month.

Required:

1. How much cash is required for payments on account in May?
2. How much cash is expected for payments on account in June?

OBJECTIVE 3
Example 9.12

Brief Exercise 9-46 Preparing a Cash Budget

Oliver's Bistro provided the following information for the month of October:
a. Sales are budgeted to be $395,000. About 80% of sales is cash; the remainder is on account.
b. Oliver's Bistro expects that, on average, 70% of credit sales will be paid in the month of sale, and 28% will be paid in the following month.
c. Food and supplies purchases, all on account, are expected to be $285,000. Oliver pays 35% in the month of purchase and 65% in the month following purchase.
d. Most of the work is done by Oliver and his wife, who typically withdraw $18,500 a month from the business as their salary. (*Note:* The $18,500 is a payment in total to the two owners, not per person.) Various part-time workers cost $29,300 per month. They are paid for their work weekly, so on average 90% of their wages is paid in the month incurred and the remaining 10% in the next month.
e. Utilities and insurance average $8,750 per month. Rent on the building is $14,000 per month.
f. In September, a freezer had to be replaced for $39,000. That amount is due in total in October.
g. September sales were $390,000, and purchases of food and supplies in September equaled $275,000.
h. The cash balance on October 1 is $1,916.

Required:

1. Calculate the cash receipts expected in October. (*Hint*: Remember to include both cash sales and payments from credit sales.)
2. Calculate the cash needed in October to pay for food purchases.
3. Prepare a cash budget for the month of October.

Brief Exercise 9-47 Flexible Budget with Different Levels of Production

Balboa Company budgeted the following amounts:

Variable costs of production:	
Direct materials	3 pounds @ $1.30 per pound
Direct labor	0.5 hr. @ $18.00 per hour
VOH	0.5 hr. @ $3.40
FOH:	
Materials handling	$8,600
Depreciation	$4,350

Required:

Prepare a flexible budget for 4,000 units, 4,500 units, and 5,000 units.

Brief Exercise 9-48 Performance Report Based on Budgeted and Actual Levels of Production

Balboa Company budgeted production of 4,500 units with the following amounts:

Variable costs of production:	
Direct materials	3 pounds @ $1.30 per pound
Direct labor	0.5 hr. @ $18.00 per hour
VOH	0.5 hr. @ $3.40
FOH:	
Materials handling	$6,200
Depreciation	$2,600

At the end of the year, Balboa had the following actual costs for production of 4,700 units:

Direct materials	$18,320
Direct labor	42,400
VOH	7,900
FOH:	
Materials handling	8,800
Depreciation	4,350

Required:

1. Calculate the budgeted amounts for each cost category listed above for the 4,500 budgeted units.
2. Prepare a performance report using a budget based on expected (budgeted) production of 4,500 units.
3. Prepare a performance report using a budget based on the actual level of production of 4,700 units.

EXERCISES

Exercise 9-49 Planning and Control

a. Dr. Jones, a dentist, wants to increase the size and profitability of his business by building a reputation for quality and timely service.
b. To achieve this, he plans on adding a dental laboratory to his building so that crowns, bridges, and dentures can be made in-house.

(Continued)

c. To add the laboratory, he needs additional money, which he decides must be obtained by increasing revenues. After some careful calculation, Dr. Jones concludes that annual revenues must be increased by 10%.

d. Dr. Jones finds that his fees for fillings and crowns are below the average in his community and decides that the 10% increase can be achieved by increasing these fees.

e. He then identifies the quantity of fillings and crowns expected for the coming year, the new per-unit fee, and the total fees expected.

f. As the year unfolds (on a month-by-month basis), Dr. Jones compares the actual revenues received with the budgeted revenues. For the first 3 months, actual revenues were less than planned.

g. Upon investigating, he discovered that he had some reduction in the number of patients because he had also changed his available hours of operation.

h. He returned to his old schedule and found out that the number of patients was restored to the original expected levels.

i. However, to make up the shortfall, he also increased the price of some of his other services.

Required:

Match each statement with the following planning and control elements. (*Note:* A letter may be matched to more than one item.)

1. Corrective action
2. Budgets
3. Feedback
4. Investigation
5. Short-term plan
6. Comparison of actual with planned
7. Monitoring of actual activity
8. Strategic plan
9. Short-term objectives
10. Long-term objectives

Use the following information for Exercises 9-50 and 9-51:
Assume that **Stillwater Designs** produces two automotive subwoofers: S12L7 and S12L5. The S12L7 sells for $475, and the S12L5 sells for $300. Projected sales (number of speakers) for the coming 5 quarters are as follows:

	S12L7	S12L5
First quarter, 20X1	800	1,300
Second quarter, 20X1	2,200	1,400
Third quarter, 20X1	5,600	5,300
Fourth quarter, 20X1	4,600	3,900
First quarter, 20X2	900	1,200

The vice president of sales believes that the projected sales are realistic and can be achieved by the company.

OBJECTIVE 1 ▶ 2

Exercise 9-50 Sales Budget

Refer to the information regarding **Stillwater Designs** above.

Required:

1. Prepare a sales budget for each quarter of 20X1 and for the year in total. Show sales by product and in total for each time period.

2. **CONCEPTUAL CONNECTION** How will Stillwater Designs use this sales budget?

Exercise 9-51 Production Budget

OBJECTIVE 2

Refer to the information regarding **Stillwater Designs** on the previous page. Stillwater Designs needs a production budget for each product (representing the amount that must be outsourced to manufacturers located in Asia). Beginning inventory of S12L7 for the first quarter of 20X1 was 340 boxes. The company's policy is to have 20% of the next quarter's sales of S12L7 in ending inventory. Beginning inventory of S12L5 was 170 boxes. The company's policy is to have 30% of the next quarter's sales of S12L5 in ending inventory.

Required:

Prepare a production budget for each quarter for 20X1 and for the year in total.

Exercise 9-52 Production Budget and Direct Materials Purchases Budgets

OBJECTIVE 2

EXCEL

Peanut Land Inc. produces all-natural organic peanut butter. The peanut butter is sold in 12-ounce jars. The sales budget for the first 4 months of the year is as follows:

	Unit Sales	Dollar Sales ($)
January	36,000	108,000
February	38,000	114,000
March	41,000	123,000
April	43,000	129,000

Company policy requires that ending inventories for each month be 25% of next month's sales. At the beginning of January, the inventory of peanut butter is 9,300 jars.

Each jar of peanut butter needs two raw materials: 24 ounces of peanuts and one jar set (a glass jar and lid). Company policy requires that ending inventories of raw materials for each month be 10% of the next month's production needs. That policy was met on January 1.

Required:

1. Prepare a production budget for the first quarter of the year. Show the number of jars that should be produced each month as well as for the quarter in total.
2. Prepare separate direct materials purchases budgets for jars and for peanuts for the months of January and February.

Exercise 9-53 Production Budget

OBJECTIVE 2

Aqua-Pro Inc. produces submersible water pumps for ponds and cisterns. The unit sales for selected months of the year are as follows:

	Unit Sales
April	180,000
May	220,000
June	200,000
July	240,000

Company policy requires that ending inventories for each month be 25% of next month's sales. However, at the beginning of April, due to greater sales in March than anticipated, the beginning inventory of water pumps is only 21,000.

Required:

Prepare a production budget for the second quarter of the year. Show the number of units that should be produced each month as well as for the quarter in total.

OBJECTIVE **2**

EXCEL

Exercise 9-54 Direct Materials Purchases Budget

Langer Company produces plastic items, including plastic housings for humidifiers. Each housing requires about 15 ounces of plastic costing $0.08 per ounce. Langer molds the plastic into the proper shape. Langer has budgeted production of the housings for the next 4 months as follows:

	Units
July	3,500
August	4,400
September	4,900
October	6,300

Inventory policy requires that sufficient plastic be in ending monthly inventory to satisfy 20% of the following month's production needs. The inventory of plastic at the beginning of July equals exactly the amount needed to satisfy the inventory policy.

Required:

Prepare a direct materials purchases budget for July, August, and September, showing purchases in units and in dollars for each month and in total.

OBJECTIVE **2**

Exercise 9-55 Direct Labor Budget

Evans Company produces asphalt roofing materials. The production budget in bundles for Evans' most popular weight of asphalt shingle is shown for the following months:

	Units
March	4,000
April	13,000
May	14,400
June	17,000

Each bundle produced requires (on average) 0.40 direct labor hour. The average cost of direct labor is $20 per hour.

Required:

Prepare a direct labor budget for March, April, and May, showing the hours needed and the direct labor cost for each month and in total.

OBJECTIVE **2**

Exercise 9-56 Sales Budget

Alger Inc. manufactures six models of leaf blowers and weed eaters. Alger's budgeting team is finalizing the sales budget for the coming year. Sales in units and dollars for last year follow:

Product	Number Sold	Price ($)	Revenue
LB-1	14,700	32.00	$ 470,400
LB-2	18,000	20.00	360,000
WE-6	25,200	15.00	378,000
WE-7	16,200	10.00	162,000
WE-8	6,900	18.00	124,200
WE-9	4,000	22.00	88,000
Total			$1,582,600

In looking over the previous year's sales figures, Alger's sales budgeting team recalled the following:

a. Model LB-1 is a newer version of the leaf blower with a gasoline engine. The LB-1 is mounted on wheels instead of being carried. This model is designed for the commercial market and did better than expected in its first year. As a result, the number of units of Model LB-1 to be sold was forecast at 250% of the previous year's units.

b. Models WE-8 and WE-9 were introduced on July 1 of last year. They are lighter versions of the traditional weed eater and are designed for smaller households or condo units. Alger estimates that demand for both models will continue at the previous year's rate.

c. A competitor has announced plans to introduce an improved version of model WE-6, Alger's traditional weed eater. Alger believes that the model WE-6 price must be cut 30% to maintain unit sales at the previous year's level.

d. It was assumed that unit sales of all other models would increase by 5%, prices remaining constant.

Required:

Prepare a sales budget by product and in total for Alger Inc. for the coming year.

Exercise 9-57 Production Budget and Direct Materials Purchases Budget   OBJECTIVE ▶ 2

Jani Subramanian, owner of Jani's Flowers and Gifts, produces gift baskets for various special occasions. Each gift basket includes fruit or assorted small gifts (e.g., a coffee mug, deck of cards, novelty cocoa mixes, scented soap) in a basket that is wrapped in colorful cellophane. Jani has estimated the following unit sales of the standard gift basket for the rest of the year and for January of next year.

September	250
October	200
November	230
December	380
January	100

Jani likes to have 5% of the next month's sales needs on hand at the end of each month. This requirement was met on August 31.

Two materials are needed for each fruit basket:

Fruit	1 pound
Small gifts	6 items

The materials inventory policy is to have 5% of the next month's fruit needs on hand and 30% of the next month's production needs of small gifts. (The relatively low inventory amount for fruit is designed to prevent spoilage.) Materials inventory on August 31 met this company policy.

Required:

1. Prepare a production budget for September, October, November, and December for gift baskets. (*Note:* Round all answers to the nearest whole unit.)

2. Prepare a direct materials purchases budget for the two types of materials used in the production of gift baskets for the months of September, October, and November. (*Note:* Round answers to the nearest whole unit.)

3. **CONCEPTUAL CONNECTION** Why do you think there is such a big difference in budgeted units from November to December? Why did Jani budget fewer units in January than in December?

Exercise 9-58 Schedule of Cash Collections on Accounts Receivable and   OBJECTIVE ▶ 3
Cash Budget

Bennett Inc. found that about 15% of its sales during the month were for cash. Bennett has the following accounts receivable collection experience:

(*Continued*)

Percent collected in the month of sale	25
Percent collected in the month after the sale	68
Percent collected in the second month after the sale	5

Bennett's anticipated sales for the next few months are as follows:

April	$250,000
May	290,000
June	280,000
July	295,000
August	300,000

(*Note:* Round all amounts to the nearest dollar.)

Required:

1. Calculate credit sales for May, June, July, and August.
2. Prepare a schedule of cash receipts for July and August.

OBJECTIVE ▶ **3** ▶

Exercise 9-59 Schedule of Cash Collections on Accounts Receivable and Cash Budget

Roybal Inc. sells all of its product on account. Roybal has the following accounts receivable collection experience:

Percent collected in the month of sale	20
Percent collected in the month after the sale	55
Percent collected in the second month after the sale	23

To encourage payment in the month of sale, Roybal gives a 2% cash discount. Roybal's anticipated sales for the next few months are as follows:

April	$190,000
May	248,000
June	260,000
July	240,000
August	300,000

Required:

1. Prepare a schedule of cash receipts for July.
2. Prepare a schedule of cash receipts for August.

OBJECTIVE ▶ **3** ▶

Exercise 9-60 Cash Payments Schedule

Fein Company provided the following information relating to cash payments:

a. Fein purchased direct materials on account in the following amounts:

June	$68,000
July	77,000
August	73,000

b. Fein pays 20% of accounts payable in the month of purchase and the remaining 80% in the following month.
c. In July, direct labor cost was $32,300. August direct labor cost was $35,400. The company finds that typically 90% of direct labor cost is paid in cash during the month, with the remainder paid in the following month.
d. August overhead amounted to $71,200, including $6,350 of depreciation.

e. Fein had taken out a 4-month loan of $15,000 on May 1. Interest, due with payment of principal, accrued at the rate of 9% per year. The loan and all interest were repaid on August 31. (*Note:* Use whole months to compute interest payment.)

Required:

Prepare a schedule of cash payments for Fein Company for the month of August.

Exercise 9-61 Cash Budget   OBJECTIVE ▶ **3**

The owner of a building supply company has requested a cash budget for June. After examining the records of the company, you find the following:

a. Cash balance on June 1 is $736.
b. Actual sales for April and May are as follows:

	April	May
Cash sales	$10,000	$18,000
Credit sales	28,900	35,000
Total sales	$38,900	$53,000

c. Credit sales are collected over a 3-month period: 40% in the month of sale, 30% in the second month, and 20% in the third month. The sales collected in the third month are subject to a 2% late fee, which is paid by those customers in addition to what they owe. The remaining sales are uncollectible.
d. Inventory purchases average 64% of a month's total sales. Of those purchases, 20% are paid for in the month of purchase. The remaining 80% are paid for in the following month.
e. Salaries and wages total $11,750 per month, including a $4,500 salary paid to the owner.
f. Rent is $4,100 per month.
g. Taxes to be paid in June are $6,780.
    The owner also tells you that he expects cash sales of $18,600 and credit sales of $54,000 for June. No minimum cash balance is required. The owner of the company doesn't have access to short-term loans.

Required:

1. Prepare a cash budget for June. Include supporting schedules for cash collections and cash payments. (Round all amounts to the nearest dollar.)
2. **CONCEPTUAL CONNECTION** Did the business show a negative cash balance for June? Suppose that the owner has no hope of establishing a line of credit for the business, what recommendations would you give the owner for dealing with a negative cash balance?

Exercise 9-62 Flexible Budget for Various Levels of Production   OBJECTIVE ▶ **1**

Budgeted amounts for the year:

EXCEL

Materials	2 leather strips @ $7.00
Labor	1.5 hr. @ $18.00
VOH	1.5 hr. @ $1.20
FOH	$6,800

Required:

1. Prepare a flexible budget for 3,500, 4,000, and 4,500 units.
2. **CONCEPTUAL CONNECTION** Calculate the unit cost at 3,500, 4,000, and 4,500 units. (*Note:* Round unit costs to the nearest cent.) What happens to unit cost as the number of units produced increases?

Use the following information for Exercises 9-63 and 9-64:

Palladium Inc. produces a variety of household cleaning products. Palladium's controller has developed standard costs for the following four overhead items:

Overhead Item	Total Fixed Cost	Variable Rate per Direct Labor Hour
Maintenance	$ 86,000	$0.20
Power		0.45
Indirect labor	140,000	2.10
Rent	35,000	

Next year, Palladium expects production to require 90,000 direct labor hours.

OBJECTIVE 1

Exercise 9-63 Flexible Budget for Various Levels of Activity

Refer to the information for Palladium Inc. above.

Required:

1. Prepare an overhead budget for the expected level of direct labor hours for the coming year.
2. Prepare an overhead budget that reflects production that is 15% higher than expected and for production that is 15% lower than expected.

OBJECTIVE 1

Exercise 9-64 Performance Report Based on Actual Production

Refer to the information for Palladium Inc. above. Assume that actual production required 93,000 direct labor hours at standard. The actual overhead costs incurred were as follows:

Maintenance	$107,000	Indirect labor	$336,000
Power	41,200	Rent	35,000

Required:

Prepare a performance report for the period based on actual production.

PROBLEMS

OBJECTIVE 3

Problem 9-65 Cash Budget

Aragon and Associates has found from past experience that 25% of its services are for cash. The remaining 75% are on credit. An aging schedule for accounts receivable reveals the following pattern:

a. Ten percent of fees on credit are collected in the month that service is rendered.
b. Sixty percent of fees on credit are collected in the month following service.
c. Twenty-six percent of fees on credit are collected in the second month following service.
d. Four percent of fees on credit are never collected.

Fees (on credit) that have not been paid until the second month following performance of the legal service are considered overdue and are subject to a 3% late charge.

Aragon has developed the following forecast of fees:

May	$180,000
June	200,000
July	190,000
August	194,000
September	240,000

(*Note:* Round all amounts to the nearest dollar.)

Required:

Prepare a schedule of cash receipts for August and September.

Problem 9-66 Operating Budget, Comprehensive Analysis

OBJECTIVE 1 2 3 4

EXCEL

Allison Manufacturing produces a subassembly used in the production of jet aircraft engines. The assembly is sold to engine manufacturers and aircraft maintenance facilities. Projected sales in units for the coming 5 months follow:

January	40,000
February	50,000
March	60,000
April	60,000
May	62,000

The following data pertain to production policies and manufacturing specifications followed by Allison Manufacturing:

a. Finished goods inventory on January 1 is 32,000 units, each costing $166.06. The desired ending inventory for each month is 80% of the next month's sales.

b. The data on materials used are as follows:

Direct Material	Per-Unit Usage	DM Unit Cost
Metal	10 lbs.	$8
Components	6	5

Inventory policy dictates that sufficient materials be on hand at the end of the month to produce 50% of the next month's production needs. This is exactly the amount of material on hand on December 31 of the prior year.

c. The direct labor used per unit of output is 3 hours. The average direct labor cost per hour is $14.25.

d. Overhead each month is estimated using a flexible budget formula. (*Note:* Activity is measured in direct labor hours.)

	Fixed-Cost Component	Variable-Cost Component
Supplies	—	$1.00
Power	—	0.50
Maintenance	$ 30,000	0.40
Supervision	16,000	—
Depreciation	200,000	—
Taxes	12,000	—
Other	80,000	0.50

e. Monthly selling and administrative expenses are also estimated using a flexible budgeting formula. (*Note:* Activity is measured in units sold.)

	Fixed Costs	Variable Costs
Salaries	$50,000	—
Commissions	—	$2.00
Depreciation	40,000	—
Shipping	—	1.00
Other	20,000	0.60

f. The unit selling price of the subassembly is $205.

g. All sales and purchases are for cash. The cash balance on January 1 equals $400,000. The firm requires a minimum ending balance of $50,000. If the firm develops a cash shortage

(*Continued*)

by the end of the month, sufficient cash is borrowed to cover the shortage. Any cash borrowed is repaid at the end of the quarter, as is the interest due (cash borrowed at the end of the quarter is repaid at the end of the following quarter). The interest rate is 12% per annum. No money is owed at the beginning of January.

Required:

1. Prepare a monthly operating budget for the first quarter with the following schedules. (*Note*: Assume that there is no change in work-in-process inventories.)

   a. Sales budget
   b. Production budget
   c. Direct materials purchases budget
   d. Direct labor budget
   e. Overhead budget
   f. Selling and administrative expenses budget
   g. Ending finished goods inventory budget
   h. Cost of goods sold budget
   i. Budgeted income statement
   j. Cash budget

2. **CONCEPTUAL CONNECTION** Form a group with two or three other students. Locate a manufacturing plant in your community that has headquarters elsewhere. Interview the controller for the plant regarding the master budgeting process. Ask when the process starts each year, what schedules and budgets are prepared at the plant level, how the controller forecasts the amounts, and how those schedules and budgets fit in with the overall corporate budget. Is the budgetary process participative? Also, find out how budgets are used for performance analysis. Write a summary of the interview.

Use the following information for Problems 9-67 through 9-69:
Ladan Suriman, controller for Healthy Pet Company, has been instructed to develop a flexible budget for overhead costs. The company produces two types of dog food. BasicDiet is a standard mixture for healthy dogs. SpecialDiet is a reduced protein formulation for older dogs with health problems. The two dog foods use common raw materials in different proportions. The company expects to produce 80,000 bags of each product during the coming year. BasicDiet requires 0.20 direct labor hour per bag, and SpecialDiet requires 0.30 direct labor hour per bag. Ladan has developed the following fixed and variable costs for each of the four overhead items:

Overhead Item	Fixed Cost	Variable Rate per Direct Labor Hour
Maintenance	$57,250	$0.50
Power		0.40
Indirect labor	43,500	2.10
Rent	39,000	

OBJECTIVE 1

EXCEL

Problem 9-67 Overhead Budget for a Particular Level of Activity

Refer to the information for Healthy Pet Company above.

Required:

1. Calculate the total direct labor hours required for the production of 80,000 bags of BasicDiet and 80,000 bags of SpecialDiet.
2. Prepare an overhead budget for the expected activity level (calculated in Requirement 1) for the coming year.

Problem 9-68 Flexible Budget for Various Production Levels

OBJECTIVE ▶ 1

Refer to the information for Healthy Pet Company on the previous page.

Required:

1. Calculate the direct labor hours required for production that is 10% higher than expected. Calculate the direct labor hours required for production that is 20% lower than expected.
2. Prepare an overhead budget that reflects production that is 10% higher than expected and for production that is 20% lower than expected. (*Hint*: Use total direct labor hours calculated in Requirement 1.)

Problem 9-69 Performance Report Based on Actual Production

OBJECTIVE ▶ 1

Refer to the information for Healthy Pet Company on the previous page. Assume that Healthy Pet actually produced 100,000 bags of BasicDiet and 90,000 bags of SpecialDiet. The actual overhead costs incurred were as follows:

Maintenance	$81,300	Indirect labor	$143,600
Power	18,700	Rent	39,000

Required:

1. Calculate the number of direct labor hours budgeted for actual production of the two products.
2. Prepare a performance report for the period based on actual production.
3. **CONCEPTUAL CONNECTION** Based on the report, would you judge any of the variances to be significant? Can you think of some possible reasons for the variances?

Problem 9-70 Understanding Relationships, Cash Budget, Pro Forma Balance Sheet

OBJECTIVE ▶ 3

Ryan Richards, controller for Grange Retailers, has assembled the following data to assist in the preparation of a cash budget for the third quarter of the year:

a. Sales:

May (actual)	$100,000
June (actual)	120,000
July (estimated)	90,000
August (estimated)	100,000
September (estimated)	135,000
October (estimated)	110,000

b. Each month, 30% of sales are for cash and 70% are on credit. The collection pattern for credit sales is 20% in the month of sale, 50% in the following month, and 30% in the second month following the sale.
c. Each month, the ending inventory exactly equals 50% of the cost of next month's sales. The markup on goods is 25% of cost.
d. Inventory purchases are paid for in the month following the purchase.
e. Recurring monthly expenses are as follows:

Salaries and wages	$10,000
Depreciation on plant and equipment	4,000
Utilities	1,000
Other	1,700

f. Property taxes of $15,000 are due and payable on July 15.

(Continued)

g. Advertising fees of $6,000 must be paid on August 20.

h. A lease on a new storage facility is scheduled to begin on September 2. Monthly payments are $5,000.

i. The company has a policy to maintain a minimum cash balance of $10,000. If necessary, it will borrow to meet its short-term needs. All borrowing is done at the beginning of the month. All payments on principal and interest are made at the end of a month. The annual interest rate is 9%. The company must borrow in multiples of $1,000.

j. A partially completed balance sheet as of June 30 follows. (*Note:* Accounts payable is for inventory purchases only.)

Cash	$?	
Accounts receivable	?	
Inventory	?	
Plant and equipment, net	425,000	
Accounts payable		$?
Common stock		210,000
Retained earnings		268,750
Total	$?	$?

Required:

1. Complete the balance sheet given in Item j.
2. Prepare a cash budget for each month in the third quarter and for the quarter in total (the third quarter begins on July 1). Prepare a supporting schedule of cash collections.
3. Prepare a pro forma balance sheet as of September 30.
4. **CONCEPTUAL CONNECTION** Form a group with two or three other students. Discuss why a bank might require a cash budget for businesses that are seeking short-term loans. Determine what other financial reports might be useful for a loan decision. Also, discuss how the reliability of cash budgets and other financial information can be determined.

OBJECTIVE **1** ▶ **4** ▶

Problem 9-71 Participative Budgeting, Not-for-Profit Setting

Dwight D. Eisenhower was the 34th president of the United States and the Supreme Commander of the Allied Forces during World War II. Much of his army career was spent in planning. He once said that "planning is everything; the plan is nothing."

Required:

CONCEPTUAL CONNECTION What do you think he meant by this? Consider his comment with respect to the master budget. Do you agree or disagree? Be sure to include the impact of the master budget on planning and control.

OBJECTIVE **3** ▶

Problem 9-72 Cash Budget

EXCEL

The controller of Feinberg Company is gathering data to prepare the cash budget for July. He plans to develop the budget from the following information:

a. Of all sales, 40% are cash sales.

b. Of credit sales, 45% are collected within the month of sale. Half of the credit sales collected within the month receive a 2% cash discount (for accounts paid within 10 days). Thirty percent of credit sales are collected in the following month; remaining credit sales are collected the month thereafter. There are virtually no bad debts.

c. Sales for the second two quarters of the year follow. (*Note:* The first 3 months are actual sales, and the last 3 months are estimated sales.)

	Sales
April	$ 450,000
May	580,000
June	900,000
July	1,140,000
August	1,200,000
September	1,134,000

d. The company sells all that it produces each month. The cost of raw materials equals 26% of each sales dollar. The company requires a monthly ending inventory of raw materials equal to the coming month's production requirements. Of raw materials purchases, 50% is paid for in the month of purchase. The remaining 50% is paid for in the following month.

e. Wages total $105,000 each month and are paid in the month incurred.

f. Budgeted monthly operating expenses total $376,000, of which $45,000 is depreciation and $6,000 is expiration of prepaid insurance (the annual premium of $72,000 is paid on January 1).

g. Dividends of $130,000, declared on June 30, will be paid on July 15.

h. Old equipment will be sold for $25,200 on July 4.

i. On July 13, new equipment will be purchased for $173,000.

j. The company maintains a minimum cash balance of $20,000.

k. The cash balance on July 1 is $27,000.

Required:

Prepare a cash budget for July. Give a supporting schedule that details the cash collections from sales.

Problem 9-73 Understanding Relationships, Master Budget, Comprehensive Review

OBJECTIVE 1 2 3

Optima Company is a high-technology organization that produces a mass-storage system. The design of Optima's system is unique and represents a breakthrough in the industry. The units Optima produces combine positive features of both compact and hard disks. The company is completing its fifth year of operations and is preparing to build its master budget for the coming year (20X1). The budget will detail each quarter's activity and the activity for the year in total. The master budget will be based on the following information:

a. Fourth-quarter sales for 20X0 are 55,000 units.

b. Unit sales by quarter (for 20X1) are projected as follows:

First quarter	65,000
Second quarter	70,000
Third quarter	75,000
Fourth quarter	90,000

The selling price is $400 per unit. All sales are credit sales. Optima collects 85% of all sales within the quarter in which they are realized; the other 15% is collected in the following quarter. There are no bad debts.

c. There is no beginning inventory of finished goods. Optima is planning the following ending finished goods inventories for each quarter:

First quarter	13,000 units
Second quarter	15,000 units
Third quarter	20,000 units
Fourth quarter	10,000 units

(Continued)

d. Each mass-storage unit uses 5 hours of direct labor and three units of direct materials. Laborers are paid $10 per hour, and one unit of direct materials costs $80.

e. There are 65,700 units of direct materials in beginning inventory as of January 1, 20X1. At the end of each quarter, Optima plans to have 30% of the direct materials needed for next quarter's unit sales. Optima will end the year with the same amount of direct materials found in this year's beginning inventory.

f. Optima buys direct materials on account. Half of the purchases are paid for in the quarter of acquisition, and the remaining half are paid for in the following quarter. Wages and salaries are paid on the 15th and 30th of each month.

g. Fixed overhead totals $1 million each quarter. Of this total, $350,000 represents depreciation. All other fixed expenses are paid for in cash in the quarter incurred. The fixed overhead rate is computed by dividing the year's total fixed overhead by the year's budgeted production in units.

h. Variable overhead is budgeted at $6 per direct labor hour. All variable overhead expenses are paid for in the quarter incurred.

i. Fixed selling and administrative expenses total $250,000 per quarter, including $50,000 depreciation.

j. Variable selling and administrative expenses are budgeted at $10 per unit sold. All selling and administrative expenses are paid for in the quarter incurred.

k. The balance sheet as of December 31, 20X0, is as follows:

Assets

Cash	$ 250,000
Direct materials inventory	5,256,000
Accounts receivable	3,300,000
Plant and equipment, net	33,500,000
Total assets	$42,306,000

Liabilities and Stockholders' Equity

Accounts payable	$ 7,248,000*
Capital stock	27,000,000
Retained earnings	8,058,000
Total liabilities and stockholders' equity	$42,306,000

*For purchase of direct materials only.

l. Optima will pay quarterly dividends of $300,000. At the end of the fourth quarter, $2 million of equipment will be purchased.

Required:

Prepare a master budget for Optima Company for each quarter of 20X1 and for the year in total. The following component budgets must be included:

1. Sales budget
2. Production budget
3. Direct materials purchases budget
4. Direct labor budget
5. Overhead budget
6. Selling and administrative expenses budget
7. Ending finished goods inventory budget
8. Cost of goods sold budget (*Note:* Assume that there is no change in work-in-process inventories.)
9. Cash budget
10. Pro forma income statement (using absorption costing) (*Note:* Ignore income taxes.)
11. Pro forma balance sheet (*Note:* Ignore income taxes.)

Problem 9-74 Direct Materials and Direct Labor Budgets

OBJECTIVE 2

EXCEL

Willison Company produces stuffed toy animals; one of these is Betty Rabbit. Each rabbit takes 0.2 yard of fabric and 6 ounces of polyfiberfill. Fabric costs $3.50 per yard, and polyfiberfill is $0.05 per ounce. Willison has budgeted production of stuffed rabbits for the next 4 months as follows:

	Units
October	20,000
November	40,000
December	25,000
January	30,000

Inventory policy requires that sufficient fabric be in ending monthly inventory to satisfy 15% of the following month's production needs and sufficient polyfiberfill be in inventory to satisfy 30% of the following month's production needs. Inventory of fabric and polyfiberfill at the beginning of October equals exactly the amount needed to satisfy the inventory policy.

Each rabbit produced requires (on average) 0.10 direct labor per hour. The average cost of direct labor is $15.50 per hour.

Required:

1. Prepare a direct materials purchases budget of fabric for the last quarter of the year, showing purchases in units and in dollars for each month and for the quarter in total.
2. Prepare a direct materials purchases budget of polyfiberfill for the last quarter of the year, showing purchases in units and in dollars for each month and for the quarter in total.
3. Prepare a direct labor budget for the last quarter of the year, showing the hours needed and the direct labor cost for each month and for the quarter in total.

Problem 9-75 Cash Budgeting

OBJECTIVE 3

Jordana Krull owns The Eatery in Miami, Florida. The Eatery is an affordable restaurant located near tourist attractions. Jordana accepts cash and checks. Checks are deposited immediately. The bank charges $0.50 per check; the amount per check averages $65. Bad checks that Jordana cannot collect make up 2% of check revenue.

During a typical month, The Eatery has sales of $75,000. About 75% are cash sales. Estimated sales for the next 3 months are as follows:

July	$60,000
August	75,000
September	80,000

Jordana thinks that it may be time to refuse to accept checks and to start accepting credit cards. She is negotiating with a credit card processing service that will allow her to accept all major credit cards. She would start the new policy on July 1. Jordana estimates that with the drop in sales from the no-checks policy and the increase in sales from the acceptance of credit cards, the net increase in sales will be 20%. The credit card processing service will charge no setup fee; however, the following fees and conditions apply:

- Monthly gateway and statement fee totaling $19, paid on the first day of the month.
- Discount fee of 2% of the total sale. This is not paid separately; instead, the amount that Jordana receives from each credit sale is reduced by 2%. For example, on a credit card sale of $150, the processing company would take $3 and remit a net amount of $147 to Jordana's account.
- Transaction fee of $0.25 per transaction paid at the time of the transaction.

There will be a 2-day delay between the date of the transaction and the date on which the net amount will be deposited into Jordana's account. On average, 94% of a month's net credit

(Continued)

card sales will be deposited into her account that month. The remaining 6% will be deposited the next month.

If Jordana adds credit cards, she believes that cash sales will average just 5% of total sales, and that the average credit card transaction will be $50.

Required:

1. Prepare a schedule of cash receipts for August and September under the current policy of accepting checks.
2. Assuming that Jordana decides to accept credit cards:
   a. Calculate revised total sales, cash sales, and credit card sales by month for August and September.
   b. Calculate the total estimated credit card transactions for August and September.
3. Prepare a schedule of cash receipts for August and September that incorporates the changes in policy.

CASES

OBJECTIVE 1 2

Case 9-76 Budgeting in the Government Sector, Internet Research

Similar to companies, the U.S. government must prepare a budget each year. However, unlike private, for-profit companies, the budget and its details are available to the public. The entire budgetary process is established by law. The government makes available a considerable amount of information concerning the federal budget. Most of this information can be found on the Internet. Using Internet resources (e.g., consider accessing the Office of Management and Budget at www.whitehouse.gov/omb), answer the following questions:

Required:

1. When is the federal budget prepared?
2. Who is responsible for preparing the federal budget?
3. How is the final federal budget determined? Explain in detail how the government creates its budget.
4. What percentage of the gross domestic product (GDP) is represented by the federal budget?
5. What are the revenue sources for the federal budget? Indicate the percentage contribution of each of the major sources.
6. How does U.S. spending as a percentage of GDP compare with spending of other countries?
7. How are deficits financed?

OBJECTIVE 1 3 4

Case 9-77 Cash Budget

Dr. Roger Jones is a successful dentist but is experiencing recurring financial difficulties. For example, Dr. Jones owns his office building, which he leased to the professional corporation that housed his dental practice. (He owns all shares in the corporation.) After the corporation's failure to pay payroll taxes for the past 6 months, however, the Internal Revenue Service is threatening to impound the business and sell its assets. Also, the corporation has had difficulty paying its suppliers, owing one of them over $200,000 plus interest. In the past, Dr. Jones had borrowed money on the equity in either his personal residence or his office building, but he has grown weary of these recurring problems and has hired a local consultant for advice.

According to the consultant, the financial difficulties facing Dr. Jones have been caused by the absence of proper planning and control. Budgetary control is sorely needed. The following financial information is available for a typical month:

Revenues

	Average Fee ($)	Quantity
Fillings	50	90
Crowns	300	19
Root canals	170	8
Bridges	500	7
Extractions	45	30
Cleaning	25	108
X-rays	15	150

Costs

Salaries:		
Two dental assistants	$1,900	
Receptionist/bookkeeper	1,500	
Hygienist	1,800	
Public relations (Mrs. Jones)	1,000	
Personal salary	6,500	
Total salaries		$12,700
Benefits		1,344
Building lease		1,500
Dental supplies		1,200
Janitorial		300
Utilities		400
Phone		150
Office supplies		100
Lab fees		5,000
Loan payments		570
Interest payments		500
Miscellaneous		200
Depreciation		700
Total costs		$24,664

Benefits include Dr. Jones's share of social security and a health insurance premium for all employees. Although all revenues billed in a month are not collected, the cash flowing into the business is approximately equal to the month's billings because of collections from prior months. The office is open Monday through Thursday from 9:00 A.M. to 4:00 P.M. and on Friday from 9:00 A.M. to 12:30 P.M. A total of 32 hours are worked each week. Additional hours could be worked, but Dr. Jones is reluctant to do so because of other personal endeavors that he enjoys.

Dr. Jones has noted that the two dental assistants and receptionist are not fully utilized. He estimates that they are busy about 65 to 70% of the time. His wife spends about 5 hours each week on a monthly newsletter that is sent to all patients. She also maintains a birthday list and sends cards to patients on their birthdays.

Dr. Jones recently attended an informational seminar designed to teach dentists how to increase their revenues. An idea from that seminar persuaded him to invest in promotion and public relations (the newsletter and the birthday list).

Required:

1. Prepare a monthly cash budget for Dr. Jones.
2. Using the cash budget prepared in Requirement 1 and the information given in the case, recommend actions to solve Dr. Jones's financial problems. Prepare a cash budget

(Continued)

that reflects these recommendations and demonstrates to him that the problems can be corrected. Do you think that he will accept your recommendations? Do any of the behavioral principles discussed in the chapter have a role in this type of setting? Explain.

OBJECTIVE ▶ 1 ▶ 4 ▶

Case 9-78 Budgetary Performance, Rewards, Ethical Behavior

Linda Ellis, division manager, is evaluated and rewarded on the basis of budgetary performance. Linda, her assistants, and the plant managers are all eligible to receive a bonus if actual divisional profits are between budgeted profits and 120% of budgeted profits. The bonuses are based on a fixed percentage of actual profits. Profits above 120% of budgeted profits earn a bonus at the 120% level (in other words, there is an upper limit on possible bonus payments). If the actual profits are less than budgeted profits, no bonuses are awarded. Consider the following actions taken by Linda:

a. Linda tends to overestimate expenses and underestimate revenues. This approach facilitates the ability of the division to attain budgeted profits. Linda believes that the action is justified because it increases the likelihood of receiving bonuses and helps to keep the morale of the managers high.

b. Suppose that toward the end of the fiscal year, Linda saw that the division would not achieve budgeted profits. Accordingly, she instructed the sales department to defer the closing of a number of sales agreements to the following fiscal year. She also decided to write off some inventory that was nearly worthless. Deferring revenues to next year and writing off the inventory in a no-bonus year increased the chances of a bonus for next year.

c. Assume that toward the end of the year, Linda saw that actual profits would likely exceed the 120% limit and that she took actions similar to those described in Item b.

Required:

1. Comment on the ethics of Linda's behavior. Are her actions right or wrong? What role does the company play in encouraging her actions?
2. Suppose that you are the marketing manager for the division, and you receive instructions to defer the closing of sales until the next fiscal year. What would you do?
3. Suppose that you are a plant manager, and you know that your budget has been padded by the division manager. Further, suppose that the padding is common knowledge among the plant managers, who support it because it increases the ability to achieve the budget and receive a bonus. What would you do?
4. Suppose that you are the division controller, and you receive instructions from the division manager to accelerate the recognition of some expenses that legitimately belong to a future period. What would you do?

10

Standard Costing and Variance Analysis

After studying Chapter 10, you should be able to:

1 Explain how unit standards are set, explain why standard cost systems are adopted, and describe the purpose of a standard cost sheet.

2 Describe the basic concepts underlying variance analysis, and explain when variances should be investigated.

3 Compute the materials and labor variances, and explain how they are used for control.

4 Compute the overhead variances, and explain how they are used for control.

5 *(Appendix 10A)* Prepare journal entries for materials and labor variances.

EXPERIENCE MANAGERIAL DECISIONS

with Navistar, Inc.

Understanding an income statement is a relatively easy task. However, understanding the causes underlying net income represents a far more challenging task, especially for Fortune 300 companies like **Navistar, Inc.**, whose annual net income typically falls in the neighborhood of several hundred million dollars. Navistar, Inc. uses variance analysis to learn which parts of the company are contributing to net income as expected and which parts are not contributing to net income as expected and, as such, will require careful attention to improve in the future.

For example, Navistar, Inc. recently reported that its monthly production cost was $48 million to manufacture 1,228 actual units—considerably higher than its budgeted production cost of only $41 million to produce 883 expected units. If you were the manager in charge of Navistar, Inc.'s production, what would you do after receiving the news that actual costs were $7 million greater than expected (or approximately 17% more than the budgeted total production cost)?

Before Navistar, Inc.'s management took any rash actions, it performed an in-depth variance analysis on all of its key production factors to try and understand what had caused the unfavorable static budget variance between its actual costs at month-end and its budgeted costs at the beginning of the month. These key production factors included direct and indirect materials, direct and indirect labor, benefits, utilities, depreciation, and information technology expense.

> "Navistar, Inc.'s managers were happy to learn that when adjusting the total budgeted costs for the higher production volume, total production costs should have increased by over $11 million, much more than the actual cost increase of $7 million."

Variance analysis revealed that the $7 million unfavorable static budget variance was comprised of numerous smaller variances, some favorable and others unfavorable, involving many of Navistar, Inc.'s key production factors. Most importantly, Navistar, Inc.'s managers were happy to learn that when adjusting the total budgeted costs for the higher production volume, total production costs should have increased by over $11 million, much more than the actual cost increase of $7 million. In fact, effective management of labor and materials purchasing—both of which had large favorable flexible budget variances—actually helped Navistar, Inc. to save $4 million. Without variance analysis, Navistar, Inc. would have a much harder time understanding the causes of its net income and taking the appropriate action when components of income are different than expected.

OBJECTIVE

Explain how unit standards are set, explain why standard cost systems are adopted, and describe the purpose of a standard cost sheet.

UNIT STANDARDS AND BASIC CONCEPTS OF STANDARD COSTING

Most operating managers recognize the need to control costs. Cost control often means the difference between success and failure or between above-average profits and lesser profits. For example, **Navistar, Inc.** had a specific plan to produce 883 trucks for a given month at a cost of $41 million. In reality, it produced 1,228 units at a cost of $48 million. Clearly, in total it spent more than planned but also produced more than it planned. The key question is whether the $48 million associated with the 1,228 trucks was consistent with the original plan or not. Were production costs in control or not? Did the manager do well or not?

In order to answer these questions, information about the budgeted and actual costs must be compared. The total cost per unit is computed as follows:

$$\text{Cost per Unit} = \text{Total Cost/Total Units}$$

Therefore, cost per unit for both scenarios can be calculated as follows:

	Budgeted	**Actual**
Cost per Unit =	$46,433 cost per unit =	$39,088 per unit =
Total Cost/Total Units	($41 million/883 units)	($48 million/1,228 units)

Comparing the actual cost per vehicle with the standard cost produces a favorable variance of $7,345 per truck ($46,433 − $39,088), about a 16% savings. This outcome reveals that the **Navistar, Inc.** managers were cost conscious and able to increase overall production efficiency.

In Chapter 9, we learned that budgets set standards that are used to control and evaluate managerial performance. However, budgets are aggregate measures of performance. They identify the revenues and costs in total that an organization should experience if plans are executed as expected. By comparing the actual costs and actual revenues with the corresponding budgeted amounts at the same level of activity, a measure of managerial efficiency emerges.

Although this process provides significant information for control, developing standards for unit amounts, as well as for total amounts, can further enhance control.

To determine the unit standard cost for a particular input, two decisions must be made:

- *The quantity decision*: The amount of input that *should be used* per unit of output
- *The pricing decision*: The amount that *should be paid* per unit of the input to be used

The quantity decision produces **quantity standards**, and the pricing decision produces **price standards**. The unit standard cost can be computed by multiplying these two standards:

$$\text{Standard Cost per Unit} = \text{Quantity Standard} \times \text{Price Standard}$$

For example, a soft-drink bottling company may decide that 5 ounces of fructose should be used for every 16-ounce bottle of cola (the quantity standard), and the price of the fructose should be $0.05 per ounce (the price standard). The standard cost of the fructose per bottle of cola would be:

$$\$0.25 = 5 \times \$0.05$$

The standard cost per unit of fructose can be used to predict what the total cost of fructose should be as the activity level varies; thus, it becomes a flexible budget formula. If 10,000 bottles of cola are produced, then the total expected cost of fructose is $2,500 ($0.25 × 10,000); if 15,000 bottles are produced, then the total expected cost of fructose is $3,750 ($0.25 × 15,000).

How Standards Are Developed

Three potential sources of quantitative standards are as follows:

- Historical experience: Historical experience can provide an initial guideline for setting standards, but should be used with caution because it can perpetuate existing inefficiencies.
- Engineering studies: Engineering studies can identify efficient approaches and can provide rigorous guidelines, but engineered standards often are too rigorous.
- Input from *operating personnel*: Since operating personnel are accountable for meeting standards, they should have significant input in setting standards.

Price standards are the joint responsibility of operations, purchasing, personnel, and accounting. Operating personnel determine the quality of the inputs required. Personnel and purchasing have the responsibility of acquiring the labor and materials quality requested at the lowest price. Market forces limit the range of choices for price standards. In setting price standards, purchasing must consider discounts, freight, and quality. Personnel, on the other hand, must consider payroll taxes, fringe benefits, and qualifications. Accounting is responsible for recording the price standards as well as for preparing reports that compare actual performance with the standard.

Types of Standards

Standards are generally classified as either ideal or currently attainable.

- *Ideal standards* demand maximum efficiency and can be achieved only if everything operates perfectly. No machine breakdowns, slack, or lack of skill (even momentarily) are allowed.
- *Currently attainable standards* can be achieved under efficient operating conditions. Allowance is made for normal breakdowns, interruptions, less than perfect skill, and so on. These standards are demanding but achievable.

Exhibit 10.1 provides a visual and conceptual portrayal of the two standards.

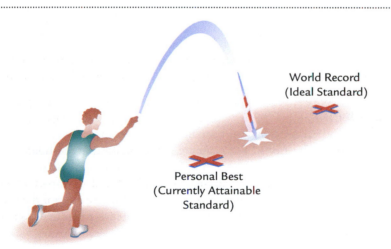

Exhibit 10.1

Types of Standards

World Record
(Ideal Standard)

Personal Best
(Currently Attainable
Standard)

Of the two types, currently attainable standards offer the most behavioral benefits. If standards are too tight and never achievable, workers become frustrated and performance levels decline. However, challenging but achievable standards tend to extract higher performance levels—particularly when the individuals subject to the standards have participated in their creation.

Why Standard Cost Systems Are Adopted

Two reasons for adopting a standard cost system are frequently mentioned: to improve planning and control and to facilitate product costing.

Planning and Control   Standard costing systems enhance planning and control and improve performance measurement. A flexible budgeting system is a key feature of standard costing systems. Comparing actual costs with budgeted costs identifies *variances,* the difference between the actual and planned costs for the actual level of activity. Overall variances can be further broken down into a price variance or a usage or efficiency variance if unit price or quantity standards have been developed. This additional information is very helpful for managers. For example, if the variance is unfavorable, this decomposition can inform a manager whether it is attributable to discrepancies between planned prices and actual prices, to discrepancies between planned usage and actual usage, or to both. Since managers have more control over the usage of inputs than over their prices, efficiency variances provide specific signals regarding the need for corrective action and where that action should be focused. Thus, in principle, the use of efficiency variances enhances operational control. Additionally, by breaking out the price variance, over which managers potentially have less control, the system provides an improved measure of managerial efficiency.

The benefits of operational control, however, may not extend to the manufacturing environments that are emphasizing continuous improvement and just-in-time (JIT) purchasing and manufacturing. The use of a standard cost system for operational control in these settings can produce dysfunctional behavior. For example, materials price variance reporting may encourage the purchasing department to buy in large quantities in order to take advantage of discounts. Yet this practice might lead to holding significant inventories, something not desired by JIT firms. Therefore, the detailed computation of variances—at least at the operational level—is discouraged for JIT firms. Nonetheless, standards in this newer manufacturing environment are still useful for planning, such as in the creation of bids. Also, variances may still be computed and presented in reports to higher-level managers so that the financial dimension can be monitored. In addition, other incentives, such as a fee charged to managers for holding excessive inventories, can be created to discourage managers from allowing inventories to grow beyond the level desired by JIT systems.

Finally, many U.S. firms operate with conventional product-costing systems (about 76% of those surveyed).[1] Surveys in countries such as Dubai and Malaysia also indicate that standard costing systems specifically continue to be used by well over 70% of the firms responding.[2] Thus, there is evidence that standard costing continues to be an important management accounting tool.

Ethical Decisions

Standard costing and variance analysis for controlling cost and evaluating performance can have strong ethical implications.[3] For example, standard costing methods have been proposed for medicine as a means for controlling costs and enhancing performance. Research has revealed wide variations in how physicians diagnose and treat patients with similar conditions. Some of these clinical variations are attributable to unwarranted tests and treatments stemming from the perceived need to practice defensive medicine against malpractice lawsuits. Others may be motivated by the desire to increase revenues.

1   Ashish Garg, Debashis Ghosh, James Hudick, and Chuen Nowacki, "Roles and Practices in Management Accounting Today," *Strategic Finance* (July 2003): 30–35.

2   Atiea Marie and Ananth Rao, "Is Standard Costing Still Relevant?" "Is Standard Costing Obsolete? Evidence from Dubai," *Management Accounting Quarterly,* Vol. 11, Iss. 2 (Winter 2010): 1–11; Maliah Sulaiman, Nik Nazli Nik Ahmad, and Norhayati Mohd Alwi, "Is Standard Costing Obsolete? Empirical Evidence from Malaysia," *Managerial Auditing Journal,* Vol. 20, Iss. 2 (2005): 109–124.

3   This ethical decision context is based largely on the following article: Greg M. Thebadouix, Marsha Sheidt, and Elizabeth Luckey, "Accounting and Medicine: An Exploratory Investigation into Physician's Attitudes, Toward the Use of Standard Cost-Accounting Methods in Medicine," *Journal of Business Ethics* (2007): 75:137–149.

Standardization of medicine, called evidence-based best practices (EBBP), is one approach being considered to reduce this variation. EBBP specifies the diagnosis and treatment approach for a disease including the best tests and treatment regimens. The next step is to tie the EBBP to standardized costs. There is concern among physicians that this is a cook-book approach laden with ethical dilemmas. For example, one physician noted that the interpretation of a favorable variance may be difficult because it either reflects inadequate treatment or compliance to guide-lines. A neonatal doctor expressed concerns that cost data would affect her clinical decisions relating to babies with low survival odds. ●

Product Costing   In a *standard* costing system, costs are assigned to products using quantity and price standards for all three manufacturing costs: direct materials, direct labor, and over-head. At the other end of the cost assignment spectrum, an *actual* costing system assigns the actual costs of all three manufacturing inputs to products. In the middle of this spectrum is a *normal* costing system, which predetermines overhead costs for the purpose of product costing but assigns direct materials and direct labor to products by using actual costs. Thus, a normal costing system assigns actual direct costs to products but allocates budgeted indirect costs to products using a budgeted rate and actual activity. Exhibit 10.2 summarizes these three cost assignment approaches.

	Standard Costing System	Normal Costing System	Actual Costing System
Direct materials	Standard	Actual	Actual
Direct labor	Standard	Actual	Actual
Overhead	Standard	Budgeted	Actual

Exhibit 10.2

Cost Assignment Approaches

Standard product costing has several advantages over normal costing and actual costing. One, of course, is the greater capacity for control. Standard costing systems also provide readily available unit cost information that can be used for pricing decisions at any time throughout the period because actual costs (either direct or indirect) do not need to be known. . Other simplifi-cations also are possible. For example, if a process-costing system uses standard costing to assign product costs, there is no need to compute a unit cost for each equivalent unit cost category. A standard unit cost would exist for each category. Additionally, there is no need to distinguish between the first-in, first-out (FIFO) and weighted average methods of accounting for begin-ning inventory costs. Usually, a standard process-costing system will follow the equivalent unit calculation of the FIFO approach. That is, current equivalent units of work are calculated. By calculating current equivalent work, current actual production costs can be compared with stan-dard costs for control purposes.

In manufacturing firms, standard costs are developed for direct materials, direct labor, and overhead. Using these costs, the **standard cost per unit** is computed. The **standard cost sheet** provides the production data needed to calculate the standard unit cost. To illustrate, a standard cost sheet will be developed for a 16-ounce bag of corn chips produced by Crunchy Chips Inc. The production of corn chips begins by steaming and soaking corn kernels overnight in a lime solution. This process softens the kernels so that they can be shaped into a sheet of dough. The dough is then cut into small triangular chips. Next, the chips are toasted in an oven and dropped into a deep fry-er. After cooking, the chips pass under a salting device and are inspected for quality. Substandard chips are sorted and discarded, and the chips that pass inspection are bagged by a packaging ma-chine. The bagged chips are manually packed into boxes for shipping.

Four materials are used to process corn chips: yellow corn, cooking oil, salt, and lime. The package in which the chips are placed is also classified as a direct material. Crunchy Chips has two types of direct laborers: machine operators and inspectors (or sorters). Variable overhead is made up of three costs: gas, electricity, and water. Both variable and fixed overhead are applied by using direct labor hours. The standard cost sheet is given in Exhibit 10.3.

Exhibit 10.3

Standard Cost Sheet for
Corn Chips

Description	Standard Price	Standard Usage	Standard Cost*	Subtotal
Direct materials:				
Yellow corn	$ 0.01	18 oz.	$0.18	
Cooking oil	0.03	2 oz.	0.06	
Salt	0.01	1 oz.	0.01	
Lime	0.50	0.04 oz.	0.02	
Bags	0.05	1 bag	0.05	
Total direct materials				$0.32
Direct labor:				
Inspection	8.00	0.01 hr.	$0.08	
Machine operators	10.00	0.01 hr.	0.10	
Total direct labor				0.18
Overhead:				
Variable overhead	4.00	0.02 hr.	$0.08	
Fixed overhead	15.00	0.02 hr.	0.30	
Total overhead				0.38
Total standard unit cost				$0.88

*Calculated by multiplying price by usage.

Exhibit 10.3 shows the company should use 18 ounces of corn to produce a 16-ounce package of chips. There are two reasons for this 2-ounce difference:

- *Waste*: Some chips are discarded during the inspection process. The company plans on a normal amount of waste.
- *Packaging*: The company wants to have more than 16 ounces in each package to increase customer satisfaction with its product and to avoid any problems with fair packaging laws.

Exhibit 10.3 also reveals that the standard usage for variable and fixed overhead is tied to the direct labor standards. For variable overhead, the rate is $4.00 per direct labor hour. Since one package of corn chips should use 0.02 hour of direct labor per unit, the variable overhead cost assigned to a package of corn chips is $0.08 ($4.00 × 0.02). For fixed overhead, the rate is $15.00 per direct labor hour, making the fixed overhead cost per package of corn chips $0.30 ($15.00 × 0.02). About one-third of the cost of production is fixed, indicating a capital-intensive production effort. Indeed, much of the operation is mechanized.

Here's **Why It's important**

The standard cost sheet also shows the quantity of each input that should be used to produce one unit of output. The unit quantity standards can be used to compute the total amount of inputs allowed for the actual output. This computation is an essential component in computing efficiency variances. A manager should be able to compute the **standard quantity of materials allowed (SQ)** and the **standard hours allowed (SH)** for the actual output, where

$$SQ = \text{Unit Quantity Standard} \times \text{Actual Output}$$

and

$$SH = \text{Unit Labor Standard} \times \text{Actual Output}$$

This computation must be done for every class of direct material and every class of direct labor. Managers can use the standard quantities allowed for planning (e.g., to determine how much will be required for planned production) or for control by comparing the allowed inputs with actual inputs used.

Example 10.1 shows how to compute these quantities by using one type of material and one class of labor.

How to Compute Standard Quantities Allowed (*SQ* and *SH*)

Assume that 100,000 packages of corn chips are produced during the first week of March. Recall from Exhibit 10.3 that the unit quantity standard is 18 ounces of yellow corn per package, and the unit quantity standard for machine operators is 0.01 hour per package produced.

Required:
How much yellow corn and how many operator hours should be used for the actual output of 100,000 packages?

Solution:
Corn allowed:

SQ = Unit Quantity Standard × Actual Output
   = 18 × 100,000
   = 1,800,000 ounces

Operator hours allowed:

SH = Unit Labor Standard × Actual Output
   = 0.01 × 100,000
   = 1,000 direct labor hours

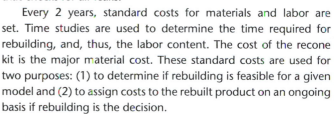

Here's How It's Used: AT KICKER

About 15% of the defective **Kicker** speakers returned to **Stillwater Designs** can be rebuilt. The other 85% are sold as metal scrap. Speakers are candidates for rebuilding if the cost of direct materials and labor is less than the sum of the speaker's purchase cost, shipping cost, and duty. (The production of Kicker speakers is outsourced to mostly Asian producers.) This is true, for example, of the square S12L7 speakers.

To rebuild a square S12L7, the returned speaker is torn down to its basic structures, chemical and glue residues are removed, and the speaker is demagnetized in order to get rid of metal shavings and pieces. After this preparatory work, recone kits are used to replace the stripped-out components. The rebuilt woofer is then placed in a cabinet and sealed. The completed unit undergoes two tests—one to ensure that the power is hooked up correctly and a second that checks for air leaks.

Every 2 years, standard costs for materials and labor are set. Time studies are used to determine the time required for rebuilding, and, thus, the labor content. The cost of the recone kit is the major material cost. These standard costs are used for two purposes: (1) to determine if rebuilding is feasible for a given model and (2) to assign costs to the rebuilt product on an ongoing basis if rebuilding is the decision.

Check Point

1. **What is the difference between an ideal standard and a currently attainable standard?**

Answer:
An ideal standard is a standard of perfection—absolute efficiency is required. A currently attainable standard is rigorous but achievable and reflects a reasonable level of efficiency.

(Continued)

2. Why would a firm adopt a standard costing system?

Answer:

Standard costing enhances planning and control and improves performance evaluation. It also simplifies product costing. Having a readily available product cost facilitates pricing decisions.

3. Refer to Exhibit 10.3 (p. 526). Assume that 5,000 packages of corn chips are produced on the first day of April. How much cooking oil and how many inspection hours should be used for the actual output of 5,000 packages?

Answer:

Oil allowed:

$SQ = 2 \times 5{,}000 = 10{,}000$ ounces

Inspection hours allowed:

$SH = 0.01 \times 5{,}000 = 50$ inspection hours

OBJECTIVE 2

Describe the basic concepts underlying variance analysis, and explain when variances should be investigated.

VARIANCE ANALYSIS: GENERAL DESCRIPTION

Actual input cost can be calculated as:

$$\text{Actual Cost} = AP \times AQ$$

where

AP = Actual Price per Unit
AQ = Actual Quantity of Input Used

It is also possible to calculate the costs that should have been incurred for the actual level of activity. This figure is obtained by multiplying the amount of input allowed (either materials or labor) for the actual output by the standard price of the input, as follows:

$$\text{Planned Cost} = SP \times SQ$$

where

SP = Standard Price per Unit
SQ = Standard Quantity of Input Allowed for the Actual Output

The **total budget variance** is the difference between the actual cost of the input and its planned cost:

$$\text{Total Variance} = \text{Actual Cost} - \text{Planned Cost}$$
$$= (AP \times AQ) - (SP \times SQ)$$

For convenience, the total budget variance will simply be called the *total variance*.

Because responsibility for deviations from planned prices tends to be located in the purchasing or personnel department and responsibility for deviations from planned usage of inputs tends to be located in the production department, it is important to separate the total variance into price and usage (quantity) variances.

Price and Usage Variances

Exhibit 10.4 provides a general model for calculating price and quantity variances for materials and labor. For labor, the price variance is usually called a *rate variance*. **Price (rate) variance** is the difference between the actual and standard unit price of an input multiplied by the number of inputs used:

$$\text{Price Variance} = (AP - SP) \times AQ$$

The usage (quantity) variance is called an *efficiency variance*. **Usage (efficiency) variance** is the difference between the actual and standard quantity of inputs multiplied by the standard unit price of the input:

$$\text{Usage Variance} = (AQ - SQ) \times SP$$

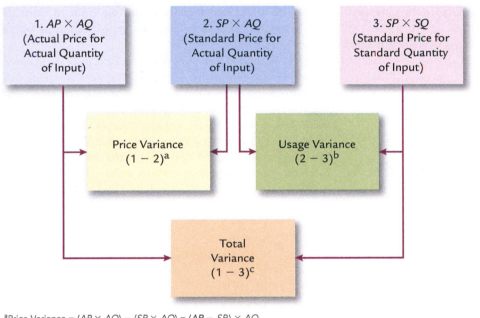

Exhibit 10.4

Variance Analysis: General Description

[a]Price Variance = $(AP \times AQ) - (SP \times AQ) = (AP - SP) \times AQ$
[b]Usage Variance = $(SP \times AQ) - (SP \times SQ) = (AQ - SQ) \times SP$
[c]Total Variance = $(AP \times AQ) - (SP \times SQ)$

    Unfavorable (U) variances occur whenever actual prices or actual usage of inputs are greater than standard prices or standard usage. When the opposite occurs, **favorable (F) variances** are obtained. Favorable and unfavorable variances are not equivalent to good and bad variances. The terms merely indicate the relationship of the actual prices (or quantities) to the standard prices (or quantities). Whether or not the variances are good or bad depends on why they occurred. Determining the cause of a variance requires managers to do some investigation.

The Decision to Investigate

Rarely will actual performance exactly meet the established standards, and management does not expect it to do so. Instead, it is important to understand when further investigation is necessary. Investigating the cause of variances and taking corrective action, like all activities, have a cost associated with them. As a general principle, an investigation should be undertaken only if the expected benefits are greater than the expected costs. Assessing the costs and benefits of a variance investigation is not an easy task, however. A manager must consider whether a variance will recur. If so, the process may be permanently out of control, meaning that periodic savings may be achieved if corrective action is taken. But how is it possible to know if the variance is going to recur unless an investigation is conducted? And how is it possible to know the cost of corrective action unless the cause of the variance is known?

    Because it is difficult to assess the costs and benefits of variance analysis on a case-by-case basis, many firms adopt the general guideline of investigating variances only if they fall outside of an acceptable range. They are not investigated unless they are large enough to be of concern.

Here's How It's Used: IN YOUR LIFE

Kylee Hepworth had just been hired as a tutor by Lisa Gardner. Kylee was in her last semester of a Masters of Accounting program. Lisa, on the other hand, was just beginning her study of accounting and although she had done very well in the financial accounting course (she had earned an A), managerial accounting was proving to be more challenging for her. Yet she was determined to do well and so had acted on a recommendation of an advisor to hire a tutor. For her first, lesson, Lisa had asked Kylee to explain variances in standard costing.

Kylee drew the following diagram on the white board and then explained it as follows:

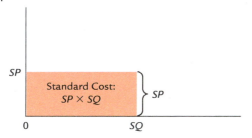

"Notice that the length of the rectangle is SP and the width is SQ. Thus, SP × SQ is the standard cost and is represented by the area of the rectangle, shaded in orange."

"Now suppose that actual price of the input is AP and the actual quantity is AQ, where AP and AQ are both more than SP and SQ."

Kylee then drew another diagram and continued with her explanation.

"The area of the large rectangle is AQ × AP, which is the actual cost of the input and is the sum of the green and orange areas. The difference between the total actual cost AQ × AP (green + orange areas) and the orange area is the green area [(AQ × AP) − (SP × SQ)] and is the total variance. Lisa, do you have any questions?"

Lisa responded: "Not about the total variance. In this case, I can see that it is caused by the actual price being more than the standard price and the actual usage of the input being more than the amount allowed. But we have to calculate both price and usage variances. Can you explain those with a diagram like this?"

"Absolutely, and it involves one more step. Just extend the SP line all the way over to the AQ axis and it divides the green area into two pieces: one for the price variance (colored yellow) and one for the quantity variance (colored blue). The length of the yellow rectangle is (AP − SP) and its width is AQ. Thus, the yellow area is the price variance (PV) and is equal to (AP − SP) × AQ. For the quantity variance, the length of the blue rectangle is SP and the width is (AQ − SQ); thus, the area is (AQ − SQ) × SP and that gives the quantity variance."

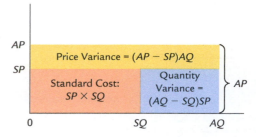

"Lisa, in concluding, there are two points I want to make. First, the sum of the price variance and the quantity variance is the total variance for the input (yellow + blue = green). Second, once you know the price and quantity variance formulas they are essentially the same for labor and material inputs. So, in reality, you only have to remember these two formulas instead of four. I'll explain this last point more thoroughly in our next session."

Here's Why It's important

They must be large enough to be caused by something other than random factors and large enough (on average) to justify the costs of investigating and taking corrective action.

How do managers determine whether variances are significant? How is the acceptable range established? Because of random variations around the standard, actual costs rarely equal standard costs. When variances are in an acceptance range of performance, they are assumed to be caused by random factors. The acceptable range is the standard, plus or minus an allowable deviation. The top and bottom measures of the allowable range are called the **control limits**. Control limits are used as a means to tell managers when variances fall outside an acceptable range and thus should be investigated so that corrective action can be taken. The upper control limit is the standard plus the allowable deviation, and the lower control limit is the standard minus the allowable deviation. Current practice sets the control limits subjectively: Based on past experience, intuition, and judgment, management determines the allowable deviation from standard.[4] The actual deviations from standard often are plotted over time against the upper and lower limits to allow managers to see the significance of the variance. **Example 10.2** shows how control limits are used to trigger an investigation.

EXAMPLE 10.2

How to Use Control Limits to Trigger a Variance Investigation

Standard cost: $100,000; allowable deviation: ± $10,000. Actual costs for 6 months are:

June	$ 97,500	September	$102,500
July	105,000	October	107,500
August	95,000	November	112,500

Required:
Plot the actual costs over time against the upper and lower control limits. Determine when a variance should be investigated.

Solution:

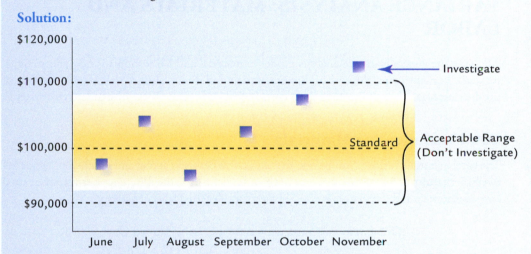

The control chart reveals that the last variance should be investigated. The chart also reveals a short-term increasing trend that suggests the process is moving out of control. A nongraphical approach is to calculate the difference between the actual cost and the upper or lower limit and see if it exceeds $10,000.

The control chart in **Example 10.2** graphically illustrates the concept of control limits. The assumed standard is $100,000, and the allowable deviation is plus or minus $10,000. The upper limit is $110,000, and the lower limit is $90,000. Investigation occurs whenever an observation falls outside of these limits (as would be the case for the sixth observation). Trends can also be important.

The control limits often are expressed both as a percentage of the standard and as an absolute dollar amount. For example, the allowable deviation may be expressed as the lesser of 10% of the standard amount, or $10,000. In other words, management will not accept a deviation of more than $10,000 even if that deviation is less than 10% of the standard. Alternatively, even if the dollar amount is less than $10,000, an investigation is required if the deviation is more than 10% of the standard amount.

---

4 Gaumnitz and Kollaritsch, "Manufacturing Variances: Current Practices and Trends," reports that about 45 to 47% of the firms use dollar or percentage control limits. Most of the remaining firms use judgment rather than any formal identification of limits.

OBJECTIVE 3

Compute the materials and labor variances, and explain how they are used for control.

VARIANCE ANALYSIS: MATERIALS AND LABOR

Applying the general variance analysis model to material and labor inputs is easy and straightforward. In many firms, the cost of direct materials and direct labor represents the majority of production costs; thus, controlling these costs is vital and a major focus of standard cost systems.

Total Variance for Materials

 Why It's important

The total materials variance can be due to a difference between actual and planned prices or between actual and standard quantities or both and is defined as the difference between the actual cost of materials and the materials cost allowed for the actual level of activity:

$$\text{Total Materials Variance} = \text{Actual Cost} - \text{Planned Cost}$$
$$= (AP \times AQ) - (SP \times SQ)$$

Example 10.3 illustrates how to calculate the total variance for materials by using selected data from Crunchy Chips for the first week of March. To keep the example simple, only one material (corn) is illustrated.

EXAMPLE 10.3

How to Calculate the Total Variance for Materials

Refer to the unit standards from Exhibit 10.3 (p. 526). The actual results for the first week in March are:

Actual production	48,500 bags of corn chips
Actual cost of corn	780,000 ounces at $0.015 = $11,700
Actual cost of inspection labor	360 hours at $8.35 = $3,006

Required:
Calculate the total variance for corn for the first week in March.

EXAMPLE 10.3

(Continued)

Solution:

	Actual Costs	**Budgeted Costs***	**Total Variance**
	$AP \times AQ$	$SP \times SQ$	$(AP \times AQ) - (SP \times SQ)$
Corn	$11,700	$8,730	$2,970 *U*

*The standard quantities for materials and labor are computed as unit quantity standards from Exhibit 10.3:

Corn: $SQ = 18 \times 48,500 = 873,000$ ounces.

Multiplying these standard quantities by the unit standard prices given in Exhibit 10.3 produces the budgeted amounts appearing in this column:

Corn: $0.01 \times 873,000 = $8,730$

Direct Materials Variances

Computing the direct materials price variance (*MPV*) and the direct materials usage variance (*MUV*) tells managers how much of the total direct materials variance is due to price and how much is due to usage. The more detailed information then enables a manager to exercise better control over this input. However, the sum of the price and usage variances will add up to the total materials variance calculated in **Example 10.3** *only if the materials purchased equal the materials used*. The materials price variance is computed by using the actual quantity of materials purchased, and the materials usage variance is computed by using the actual quantity of materials used, calculated as:

$$MPV = (AP - SP) \times AQ$$
$$MUV = (AQ - SQ) \times SP$$

Since it is better to have information on variances earlier rather than later, the materials price variance uses the actual quantity of materials purchased rather than the actual quantity of materials used. Old information often is useless information. Materials may sit in inventory for weeks or months before they are needed in production. By the time the materials price variance is computed, signaling a problem, it may be too late to take corrective action. Or, even if corrective action is still possible, the delay may cost the company thousands of dollars. For example, suppose a new purchasing agent is unaware of the availability of a quantity discount on a raw material. If the materials price variance that ignores the discount is computed when a new purchase is made, the resulting unfavorable signal would lead to quick corrective action. (In this case, the action would be to use the discount for future purchases.) If the materials price variance is not computed until the material is issued to production, it may be several weeks or even months before the problem is discovered. The more timely the information, the more likely that proper managerial action can be taken.

Materials price and usage variances normally should be calculated using variance formulas. However, the 3-pronged (columnar) approach is used when the materials purchased equal the materials used. **Example 10.4** shows how to calculate the materials price and usage variances using either a columnar approach or a formula approach for the Crunchy Chips example (for corn only).

Here's **Why It's important**

EXAMPLE 10.4

How to Calculate Materials Variances: Formula and Columnar Approaches

Refer to the unit standards from Exhibit 10.3 (p. 526). The actual results for the first week in March are:

Actual production	48,500 bags of corn chips
Actual cost of corn	780,000 ounces @ $0.015

Required:

Calculate the materials price and usage variances by using the 3-pronged (columnar) and formula approaches.

Solution:

1. Columnar (this approach is possible only if the materials purchased equal materials used):

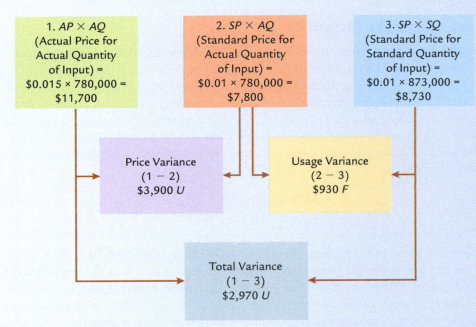

2. Formulas (recommended approach for materials variances because materials purchased may differ from materials used):

$$MPV = (AP - SP) \times AQ$$
$$= (\$0.015 - \$0.01) \times 780,000$$
$$= \$3,900 \; U$$

$$MUV = (AQ - SQ) \times SP$$
$$= (780,000 - 873,000) \times \$0.01$$
$$= \$930 \; F$$

The **materials price variance (MPV)** measures the difference between what should have been paid for raw materials and what was actually paid and is calculated as:

$$MPV = (AP \times AQ) - (SP \times AQ)$$

or, factoring, we have:

$$MPV = (AP - SP) \times AQ$$

where

AP = Actual Price per Unit

SP = Standard Price per Unit

AQ = Actual Quantity of Material Purchased

It should be noted that the *MPV* formula uses the *actual* quantity purchased, rather than the standard amount that should have been purchased, because purchasing managers typically influence the amount of materials actually purchased. Likewise, the *MPV* uses material *purchased*, rather than used, because purchasing managers typically do not control the amount of material actually used in production. Thus, the *MPV* contains items over which purchasing managers likely have control, which is helpful given that their bonuses often are affected by the *MPV*.

The **materials usage variance (*MUV*)** measures the difference between the direct materials actually used and the direct materials that should have been used for the actual output. The formula for computing this variance is:

$$MUV = (SP \times AQ) - (SP \times SQ)$$

or, factoring:

$$MUV = (AQ - SQ) \times SP$$

where

AQ = Actual Quantity of Materials Used

SQ = Standard Quantity of Materials Allowed for the Actual Output

SP = Standard Price per Unit

The *MUV* formula uses the *standard* price that should have been paid, rather than the actual price that was paid, because production managers typically do not influence the actual price paid for materials. Using the standard price in the *MUV*—a variance for which production managers typically are held accountable—prevents them from unfairly being affected by the actual price.

Using Materials Variance Information

Calculating materials variances is only the first step. Using the variance information to exercise control is fundamental to a standard cost system. Responsibility must be assigned, variance significance must be assessed, and the variances must be accounted for and disposed of at the end of the year.

Responsibility for the Materials Price Variance The responsibility for controlling the materials price variance usually belongs to the purchasing agent. Admittedly, the price of materials is largely beyond the agent's control; however, the price variance can be influenced by such factors as quality, quantity discounts, distance of the source from the plant, and so on. These factors often are under the control of the agent.

Using the price variance to evaluate the performance of purchasing has some limitations. Emphasis on meeting or beating the standard can produce some undesirable outcomes. For example, if the purchasing agent feels pressured to produce favorable variances, materials of lower quality than desired may be purchased or too much inventory may be acquired to take advantage of quantity discounts.

Analysis of the Materials Price Variance The first step in variance analysis is deciding whether or not the variance is significant. If it is judged insignificant, no further steps are needed. The materials price variance is $3,900 unfavorable, which is about 45% of standard cost ($3,900/$8,730). Most managers would judge this variance to be significant. The next step is to find out why it occurred.

For Crunchy Chips, the investigation revealed that a higher-quality corn was purchased because of a shortage of the usual grade in the market. Once the reason is known, corrective action can be taken if necessary—and if possible. In this case, no corrective action is needed. The firm has no control over the supply shortage. It will simply have to wait until market conditions improve.

Responsibility for the Materials Usage Variance The production manager is generally responsible for materials usage. Minimizing scrap, waste, and rework are all ways in which the manager can ensure that the standard is met. However, at times, the cause of the variance is attributable to others outside of the production area, as the next section shows.

As with the price variance, using the usage variance to evaluate performance can lead to undesirable behavior. For example, a production manager feeling pressure to produce a favorable variance might allow a defective unit to be transferred to finished goods. While this transfer avoids the problem of wasted materials, it may create customer relation problems.

Analysis of the Materials Usage Variance The materials usage variance is approximately 11% of standard cost ($930/$8,730). A deviation greater than 10% likely is to be judged significant. Thus, investigation is needed. Investigation revealed that the favorable materials usage variance was the result of the higher-quality corn acquired by the purchasing department. In this case, the favorable variance is essentially assignable to purchasing. Since the materials usage variance is favorable—but smaller than the unfavorable price variance—the overall result of the change in purchasing is unfavorable. In the future, management should try to resume purchasing the normal-quality corn.

If the overall variance had been favorable, a different response would be expected. If the favorable variance were expected to persist, the higher-quality corn should be purchased regularly and the price and quantity standards revised to reflect it. In other words, standards are not static. As improvements in production take place and conditions change, standards may need to be revised to reflect the new operating environment. The importance of evaluating current business conditions and updating standards to reflect any changes in these conditions cannot be overemphasized.

Accounting and Disposition of Materials Variances Recognizing the price variance for materials at the point of purchase also means that the raw materials inventory is carried at standard cost. In general, materials variances are not inventoried. Typically, materials variances are added to cost of goods sold if unfavorable and are subtracted from cost of goods sold if favorable. The journal entries associated with the purchase and usage of raw materials for a standard cost system are illustrated in Appendix 10A.

Total Variance Analysis: Direct Labor

Here's **Why It's important**

The total direct labor variance can be due to a difference between actual and planned wage rates, or between actual hours worked, or a combination of both. The total labor variance measures the difference between the actual costs of labor and the costs allowed for the actual level of activity:

$$\text{Total Labor Variance} = (AR \times AH) - (SR \times SH)$$

where

AH = Actual Direct Labor Hours Used

SH = Standard Hours Allowed

AR = Actual Hourly Wage Rate

SR = Standard Hourly Wage Rate

Here's How It's Used: IN YOUR LIFE

Lisa Gardner was meeting for a second time with her tutor, Kylee Hepworth. In this tutoring session, Lisa wanted help with the materials and labor variances. Kylee began her instruction by putting the formulas on the white board and then made the following statement:

"Lisa, to help you understand how labor and materials variances work, let me give you an example from my own life. Recently, Beta Alpha Psi had a bake sale and I committed to making 5 dozen cupcakes. However, I didn't have time to do this, so I hired my younger sister to make the cupcakes. I agreed to pay her $10 per hour for making them. Thus, the standard rate of labor is $10 per hour ($SR = \$10$). Following my chosen recipe, it takes two batches to make 60 cupcakes, and each batch should take 2 hours of labor from start to finish (mixing, baking, and frosting the cupcakes). Thus, the hours allowed or the standard quantity of labor would be 4 hours ($SH = 4$ hours).

To illustrate the standards for materials, I will only use the ingredient of butter. I had all the needed ingredients on hand except for butter. The recipe called for 2 sticks of butter per batch. Thus, for two batches, the butter allowed is 4 sticks ($SQ = 4$). I gave my sister $4.80 to buy a pound of butter (buying my preferred brand). Since there are 4 sticks of butter in a pound, the standard price per stick of butter was $1.20 ($SP = \$1.20$).

Now we need the actual outcomes. As it turned out, my sister brought our little brother with her. And just as she finished mixing the first batch, he reached into the bowl to grab a lick of the dough and knocked the bowl to the floor,

breaking it and losing all the mix. My sister then had to go to the store and buy another pound of butter (also costing $4.80 or $1.20 per stick). She ended up actually using 6 sticks of butter, 4 from the original package and 2 from the second package ($AQ = 6$). Because of having to redo a batch and make a special trip to the store, the actual time for producing two good batches was 5.5 hours ($AH = 5.5$).

I expected to pay $10 per hour for labor and I did. Thus,

$$LRV = (AR - SR)AH$$
$$= (\$10 - \$10)5.5 = 0$$

I also expected to pay $1.20 per stick of butter and I did; thus,

$$MPV = (AP - SP)AQ$$
$$= (\$1.20 - \$1.20)6 = 0$$

However, I didn't do so well when it came to the usage of labor and materials. I expected to pay for 4 hours of work from my sister but I paid for 5.5 hours; thus, the labor usage (efficiency) variance for me was $15:

$$LEV = (AH - SH)SR = (5.5 - 4.0)\$10 = \$15 \ U$$

Similarly for butter, 6 sticks were used instead of 4, costing me $2.40 more than expected:

$$MUV = (AQ - SQ)SR$$
$$= (6 - 4)\$1.20 = \$2.40 \ U$$

Notice I have labeled these variances unfavorable because I paid more than I should have.

Example 10.5 illustrates how to calculate the total variance for labor by using selected data from Crunchy Chips for the first week of March. To keep the example simple, only inspection labor is illustrated.

Refer to the unit standards from Exhibit 10.3 (p. 526). The actual results for the first week in March are:

Actual production	48,500 bags of corn chips
Actual cost of inspection labor	360 hours @ $8.35 = $3,006

Required:

Calculate the total labor variance for inspection labor for the first week in March.

EXAMPLE 10.5

How to Calculate the Total Variance for Labor

(*Continued*)

EXAMPLE 10.5

(Continued)

Solution:

	Actual Costs	**Budgeted Costs***	**Total Variance**
	$AR \times AH$	$SR \times SH$	$(AR \times AH) - (SR \times SH)$
Inspection labor	$3,006	$3,880	$874 F

*The standard quantities for inspection labor are computed as unit quantity standards from Exhibit 10.3:

Labor: $SH = 0.01 \times 48{,}500 = 485$ hours

Multiplying these standard quantities by the unit standard prices given in Exhibit 10.3 produces the budgeted amounts appearing in this column:

Labor: $8.00 \times 485 = $3{,}880

Direct Labor Variances

Here's **Why It's important**

Computing the direct labor rate variance (*LRV*) and the direct labor efficiency variance (*LEV*) tells managers how much of the total labor variance is due to differences in wage rates and how much is due to differences in hours worked. This more detailed information allows a manager to exercise better control over the labor input. Labor hours cannot be purchased and stored for future use as can be done with materials (i.e., there can be no difference between the amount of labor purchased and the amount of labor used). Therefore, unlike the total materials variance, the labor rate and labor efficiency variances always will add up to the total labor variance, as calculated in **Example 10.5**:

Total Labor Variance = Labor Rate Variance + Labor Efficiency Variance

Thus, the rate (price) and efficiency (usage) variances for labor can be calculated by using either the columnar approach or the associated formulas. Which technique to use is a matter of preference. The formulas are adapted to reflect the specific terms used for labor prices (rates) and usage (efficiency).

The **labor rate variance (*LRV*)** computes the difference between what was paid to direct laborers and what should have been paid:

$$LRV = (AR \times AH) - (SR \times AH)$$

or, factoring:

$$LRV = (AR - SR) \times AH$$

The **labor efficiency variance (*LEV*)** measures the difference between the labor hours that were actually used and the labor hours that should have been used:

$$LEV = (SR \times AH) - (SR \times SH)$$

or, factoring:

$$LEV = (AH - SH) \times SR$$

Example 10.6 shows how to calculate the labor rate and efficiency variances for Crunchy Chips (for inspection labor only) using either a columnar approach or a formula approach.

Refer to the unit standards from Exhibit 10.3 (p. 526). The actual results for the first week in March are:

| Actual production | 48,500 bags of corn chips |
| Actual cost of inspection labor | 360 hours @ $8.35 |

Required:

Calculate the labor rate and efficiency variances by using the 3-pronged (columnar) and formula approaches.

Solution:

Columnar:

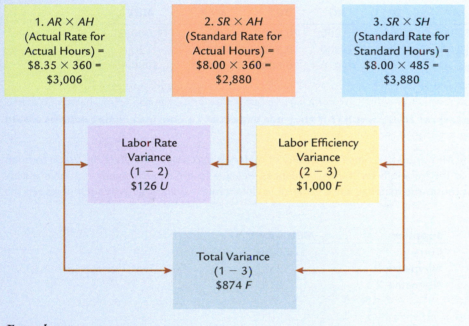

Formulas:

$LRV = (AR - SR) \times AH$
$= (\$8.35 - \$8.00) \times 360$
$= \$126\ U$

$LEV = (AH - SH) \times SR$
$= (360 - 485) \times \$8.00$
$= \$1,000\ F$

Using Labor Variance Information

As with materials variances, calculating labor variances initiates the feedback process. Using the labor variance information to exercise control is fundamental. Responsibility must be assigned, variance significance must be assessed, and the variances must be accounted for and disposed of at the end of the year.

Responsibility for the Labor Rate Variance Labor rates are largely determined by such external forces as labor markets and union contracts. The actual wage rate rarely departs from the standard rate. When labor rate variances do occur, they usually do so because an average wage rate is used for the rate standard and because more skilled and more highly paid laborers are used for less skilled tasks. Unexpected overtime also can be the cause of a labor rate variance.

Here's How It's Used: SMALL MANUFACTURING FIRM

As plant manager, you have been approached by the purchasing manager and the production manager and provided the following input. Kent Bowman, the purchasing manager, is unhappy with the quality of the electronic components being purchased. He claims that the quality of the component from the current supplier makes it impossible to meet the materials usage standard of 1.05 components per unit produced. (One component out of every hundred must be replaced before a good product is obtained.) Laura Shorts, the purchasing agent, on the other hand, claims that the current supplier is the only supplier available that will sell the needed component for $2.00, which exactly meets the current price standard. There are two alternative suppliers that sell higher quality components, but the prices are higher.

To obtain more information, you ask Laura to buy the component from each of the alternative suppliers. That way, the MPV and MUV can be compared for all three suppliers. Laura provides the following results. (There are no beginning or ending inventories of the component for any of the three suppliers.)

Supplier	AP	SP	AQ	SQ*	MPV	MUV
Current	$2.00	$2.00	11,000	10,500	$0	$1,000 U
Alternative 1	$2.05	$2.00	10,500	10,500	$525 U	$0
Alternative 2	$2.10	$2.00	10,010	10,500	$1,001 U	$980 F

*1.05 × 10,000.

As plant manager, how would you interpret these results? If they are expected to continue, what actions would you take?

There is a definite relationship between the MPV and MUV. Since the quality of materials purchased can affect the usage through rejects and waste, it is important to look at the trade-offs for the two variances. Relative to the current standard, higher quality improves the materials usage variance but causes the materials price variance to deteriorate. Adding the two together reveals the best outcome for the company:

Supplier	MPV + MUV
Current	$1,000 U
Alternative 1	525 U
Alternative 2	21 U

The best outcome is for the Alternative 2 supplier. Thus, the purchasing manager should be instructed to buy from this supplier, and the price standard should be changed to $2.10 and the unit materials standard to 1.001.

Managers often have to consider the perspectives of both the purchasing and production departments. It's important to understand how each department measures success (MPV versus MUV) in order to make the best decision for the company.

Wage rates for a particular labor activity often differ among workers because of differing levels of seniority. Rather than selecting labor rate standards reflecting those different levels, an average wage rate often is chosen. As the seniority mix of workers changes, the average rate changes. This rate change will give rise to a labor rate variance. It also calls for a new standard to reflect the new seniority mix. Controllability is not assignable for this cause of a labor rate variance.

However, the use of labor is controllable by the production manager. The use of more skilled workers to perform less skilled tasks (or vice versa) is a decision that a production manager consciously makes. For this reason, responsibility for the labor rate variance generally is assigned to the individuals who decide how labor will be used.

Analysis of the Labor Rate Variance The labor rate variance for Crunchy Chips is only 3% of the standard cost ($126/$3,880). Although a 3% variance is not likely to be judged significant, for illustrative purposes, assume that an investigation is conducted. The cause of the variance is found to be the use of more highly paid and skilled machine operators as inspectors, which occurred because two inspectors quit without formal notice. The corrective action is to hire and train two new inspectors.

Responsibility for the Labor Efficiency Variance Generally speaking, production managers are responsible for the productive use of direct labor. However, as is true of all variances, once the cause is discovered, responsibility may be assigned elsewhere. For example, frequent breakdowns of machinery may cause interruptions and nonproductive use of labor. But the responsibility for these breakdowns may be faulty maintenance. If so, the maintenance manager should be charged with the unfavorable labor efficiency variance.

Production managers may be tempted to engage in dysfunctional behavior if too much emphasis is placed on the labor efficiency variance. For example, to avoid losing hours or using additional hours because of possible rework, a production manager could deliberately transfer defective units to finished goods.

Analysis of the Labor Efficiency Variance The labor efficiency variance for Crunchy Chips is 26% of standard cost ($1,000/$3,880). This favorable variance is significant, so an investigation was undertaken. Investigation revealed that inspections flowed more smoothly because of the higher quality of materials. This additional benefit of the higher-quality materials should be factored into whether Crunchy should return to purchasing the normal-quality corn when it becomes available or whether the higher-quality material should again be purchased. In this case, even with this additional benefit, the materials price variance is so large that the correct action is to acquire the normal-quality material when it again becomes available.

Additional Cost Management Practices

In addition to standard costing, some companies choose to employ other cost management practices, such as kaizen costing and target costing to control production costs.

Kaizen Costing Kaizen costing focuses on the continuous reduction of the *manufacturing* costs of existing products and processes. *Kaizen* is a Japanese word meaning continuous improvement. The philosophy in a standard costing system is that the budgeted expectation, or standard, should be met each period. However, as the phrase "continuous improvement" suggests, the philosophy in a kaizen costing system is that the budgeted expectation, or kaizen standard, of the current period should exceed the improvement accomplished the previous period. Using this philosophy, each period's kaizen standard is set based on prior periods' improvements, thereby locking in these improvements to push for even greater improvements in the future. Typically, continuous cost improvements are achieved by identifying a large number of relatively small cost-reducing opportunities (e.g., repositioning factory work space, placing or transporting work-in-process inventory in such a way that the next worker can immediately access the inventory and begin working on it, etc.). For example, Honda uses kaizen costing practices to help its engineers implement the product design improvements identified by its shop floor workers.

Target Costing Target costing focuses on the reduction of the *design* costs of existing and future products and processes. Increasingly, companies such as Toyota, Boeing, and Olympus are emphasizing cost management in the design stage as they begin to recognize that an astonishingly large percentage (somewhere between 75 to 90%) of a product's total costs are "locked in" or "committed to" by the time it finishes the design stage and moves into the manufacturing stage.[5] A **target cost** is the difference between the sales price needed to capture a predetermined market share and the desired per-unit profit:

> Target Cost per Unit = Expected Sales Price per Unit – Desired Profit per Unit

The sales price reflects the product specifications or functions valued by the customer. If the target cost is *less* than the current actual cost, then management must find cost reductions that decrease the actual cost to the target cost. Some managers refer to this process as closing the cost gap, which is the difference between current actual cost and the necessary target cost.

Closing this cost gap is the principal challenge of target costing and usually requires the participation of suppliers and other business partners outside of the company over a period of several years. If this cost gap is not closed to zero (i.e., the actual cost is not reduced to the target cost) by the date the new product is planned to launch, then most target costing proponents will follow the cardinal rule of target costing and delay the product launch date until the gap is closed. The reason for the delay is that many managers feel that once the product launches, the incentive to reduce the actual cost falls significantly and, thus, the likelihood of the actual cost eventually decreasing to the target cost level necessary to generate the desired profit margin becomes unacceptably small. **Caterpillar** is famous for adhering to this rule, even though the launch delay means that the company must forgo significant sales revenues during the delay period.

As you might have noticed, target costing is more than just cost control, because it includes expected sales revenues and desired profit margins in the calculation of the target cost. For this reason, target costing often is referred to as a profit planning technique. In addition, target costing is more of a long-term approach to cost reduction, whereas kaizen costing is more of a continuous, short-term approach to cost reduction. Finally, given that target and kaizen costing practices focus on different segments of the value chain, they can serve as effective complements as an organization strives to reduce its costs along the entire value chain.

Check Point

1. **When is the total materials variance the sum of the price variance and the usage variance?**

Answer:
When the materials purchased equal the materials used

2. **If the actual price of cooking oil is $0.035 per ounce and the standard price is $0.03 per ounce, what is the materials price variance if 10,000 ounces of oil are purchased?**

Answer:
$MPV = (AP - SP)AQ = (\$0.035 - \$0.03)10,000 = \$50\ U$

3. **If the standard labor rate is 2 hours per unit and the standard rate is $15 per hour, what is the labor efficiency variance if 18,000 actual hours are used to produce 10,000 units of product?**

Answer:
$LEV = (AH - SH)SR = (18,000 - 20,000)\$15 = \$30,000\ F$

---

5 Julie H. Hertenstein and Marjorie B. Platt, *Management Accounting*, Vol. 79, Iss. 10 (April 1998); 6 pages.

OVERHEAD ANALYSIS

OBJECTIVE ◀ **4**

Compute the overhead variances, and explain how they are used for control.

Total variances for direct materials and direct labor were broken down into price and efficiency variances. In a similar way, the total overhead variance, or the difference between applied and actual overhead, is also broken down into component variances. Although there are several methods of overhead variance analysis, only the 4-variance method is presented. The 4-variance method divides overhead into fixed and variable categories. Next, two variances are calculated for each category.

- Variable overhead variances
  - Variable overhead spending variance
  - Variable overhead efficiency variance
- Fixed overhead variances
  - Fixed overhead spending variance
  - Fixed overhead volume variance

Total Variable Overhead Variance

The total variable overhead variance is simply the difference between the *actual variable overhead and applied variable overhead. VOH* is applied by using hours allowed in a standard cost system:

$$\text{Total } VOH \text{ Variance} = \text{Actual } VOH - SVOR \times SH$$

where

VOH = Variable Overhead

$SVOR$ = Standard Variable Overhead Rate

The total *VOH* variance combines the effect of differences in the prices of overhead items and in the use of direct labor hours which are typically used to apply overhead. The total variable overhead variance can be divided into spending and efficiency variances. Variable overhead spending and efficiency variances can be calculated by using either the 3-pronged (columnar) approach or formulas. The best approach is a matter of preference. However, the formulas first need to be expressed specifically for *VOH*.

Here's **Why It's important**

Example 10.7 illustrates how to calculate the total variable overhead variance using Crunchy Chips' standard cost system (see Exhibit 10.3, p. 526).

EXAMPLE 10.7

How to Calculate the Total Variable Overhead Variance

Assume that Crunchy Chips had the following data for the first quarter (ending March 31):

Standard variable overhead rate (*SVOR*)	$4.00 per direct labor hour
Actual variable overhead costs (*AH*)	$38,750
Standard hours allowed per unit	0.02 hour
Actual direct labor hours worked (*AH*)	10,500 hours
Actual production (packages)	500,000 units

Required:

Calculate (1) the standard direct labor hours for actual production and (2) the total variable overhead variance.

(Continued)

EXAMPLE 10.7

(Continued)

Solution:

1. Standard direct labor hours = 0.02 × 500,000 units

   = 10,000 direct labor hours

2. Actual variable overhead $38,750
   Applied variable overhead ($SH \times SVOR$)   40,000
   Total variable overhead variance $(1,250)$ *F*

Variable Overhead Variances

The total variable overhead variance can be broken down into the variable overhead spending and efficiency variances. These variances give managers a better understanding of the underlying causes of the overall variance, and this provides information that allows better control of variable overhead.

Variable Overhead Spending Variance   The **variable overhead spending variance** measures the aggregate effect of differences between the actual variable overhead and the standard variable overhead rate ($SVOR$) multiplied by the actual direct labor hours worked. The formula for computing the variable overhead spending variance is:

$$VOH \text{ Spending Variance} = \text{Actual } VOH - (AH \times SVOR)$$

Variable Overhead Efficiency Variance VOH is assumed to vary in proportion to changes in the direct labor hours used. The **variable overhead efficiency variance** measures the change in the actual variable overhead cost (VOH) that occurs because of efficient (or inefficient) use of direct labor. The variable overhead efficiency variance is computed by using the following formula:

$$VOH \text{ Efficiency Variance} = (AH - SH) \times SVOR$$

Example 10.8 shows how to calculate the variable overhead variances for Crunchy Chips using both a columnar and a formula approach.

EXAMPLE 10.8

How to Calculate Variable Overhead Spending and Efficiency Variances: Columnar and Formula Approaches

Assume that Crunchy Chips had the following data:

Standard variable overhead rate ($SVOR$)	$4.00 per direct labor hour
Actual variable overhead	$38,750
Actual hours worked (AH)	10,500 hours
Number of 16-oz. packages produced	500,000 units
Hours allowed for production (SH)	10,000 hours*

*0.02 × 500,000.

Required:

Calculate the variable overhead spending and efficiency variances.

EXAMPLE 10.8

(*Continued*)

Solution:

Columnar:

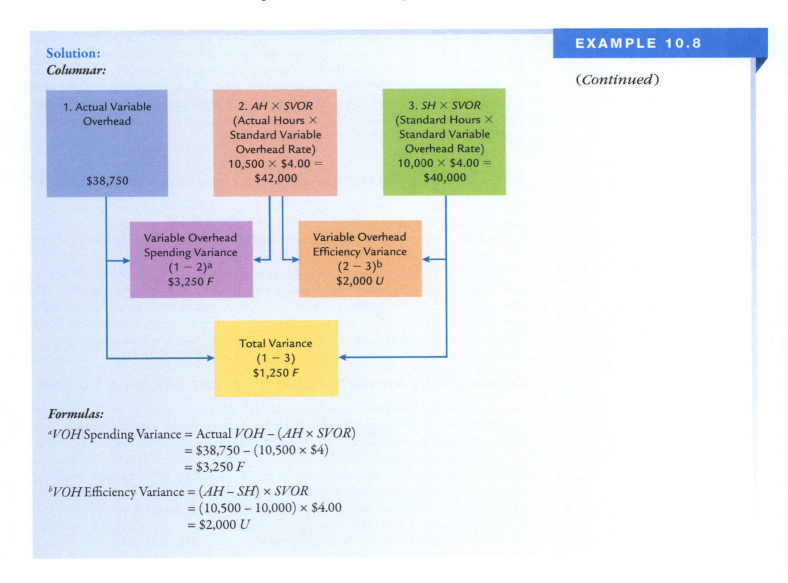

Formulas:

[a]*VOH* Spending Variance = Actual *VOH* − (*AH* × *SVOR*)

$$= \$38{,}750 - (10{,}500 \times \$4)$$

$$= \$3{,}250\ F$$

[b]*VOH* Efficiency Variance = (*AH* − *SH*) × *SVOR*

$$= (10{,}500 - 10{,}000) \times \$4.00$$

$$= \$2{,}000\ U$$

Comparison of the Variable Overhead Spending Variance with the Price Variances of Materials and Labor

While the variable overhead spending variance is similar to the price variances of materials and labor, there are some conceptual differences. *VOH* is not a single input—it is made up of a large number of individual items, such as indirect materials, indirect labor, electricity, maintenance, and so on. The standard variable overhead rate represents the weighted cost per direct labor hour that should be incurred for all variable overhead items. The difference between what should have been spent for actual direct labor hours worked and what actually was spent is a type of price variance.

One reason that a variable overhead spending variance can arise is that prices for individual variable overhead items have increased or decreased. Assume that the price changes of individual overhead items are the only cause of the spending variance. If the spending variance is unfavorable, price increases for individual variable overhead items are the cause. If the spending variance is favorable, price decreases are dominating.

The second reason for a variable overhead spending variance is the use of the items that comprise variable overhead. Waste or inefficiency in the use of *VOH* increases the actual variable overhead cost. Thus, even if the actual prices of the individual overhead items were equal to the budgeted or standard prices, an unfavorable variable overhead spending variance could still take place. For example, more kilowatt-hours of power may be used than should be, yet this is not captured by any change in direct labor hours. However, the effect is reflected by an increase in the total cost of power and, thus, the total cost of *VOH*. Similarly, efficiency can decrease the actual variable overhead cost. Efficient use of variable overhead items contributes to a favorable spending variance. If the waste effect dominates, then the net contribution will be unfavorable. If efficiency dominates, then the net contribution is favorable. Therefore, the variable overhead spending variance is the result of both price and efficiency.

Responsibility for the Variable Overhead Spending Variance

Variable overhead items may be affected by several responsibility centers. For example, utilities are a joint cost. To the extent that consumption of *VOH* can be traced to a responsibility center, responsibility can be assigned. Consumption of indirect materials is an example of a traceable variable overhead cost.

Controllability is a prerequisite for assigning responsibility. Price changes of variable overhead items are essentially beyond the control of supervisors. If price changes are small (as they often are), then the spending variance is primarily a matter of the efficient use of overhead in production. This is controllable by production supervisors. Accordingly, responsibility for the variable overhead spending variance is generally assigned to production departments.

Responsibility for the Variable Overhead Efficiency Variance

The variable overhead efficiency variance is directly related to the direct labor efficiency or usage variance. If *VOH* is truly proportional to direct labor consumption, then like the labor usage variance, the variable overhead efficiency variance is caused by efficient or inefficient use of direct labor. If more (or fewer) direct labor hours are used than the standard calls for, then the total variable overhead cost will increase (or decrease). The validity of the measure depends on the validity of the relationship between variable overhead costs and direct labor hours. In other words, do variable overhead costs really change in proportion to changes in direct labor hours? If so, responsibility for the variable overhead efficiency variance should be assigned to the individual who has responsibility for the use of direct labor: the production manager.

A Performance Report for the Variable Overhead Spending and Efficiency Variances

Here's **Why It's important**

Example 10.8 (p. 544) showed a favorable $3,250 variable overhead spending variance and an unfavorable $2,000 variable overhead efficiency variance. The $3,250 favorable spending variance means that overall Crunchy Chips spent less than expected on variable overhead. The reasons for the $2,000 unfavorable variable overhead efficiency variance are the same as those offered for an unfavorable labor usage variance. An unfavorable variance means that more hours were used than called for by the standard. Even if the total variable overhead spending and efficiency variances are insignificant, they reveal nothing about how well costs of *individual* variable overhead items were controlled. It is possible for two large variances of opposite sign to cancel each other out. Control of *VOH* requires line-by-line analysis for each item.

Example 10.9 shows how to prepare a performance report that supplies the line-by-line information essential for detailed analysis of the variable overhead variances.

Crunchy Chips had the following data for the first quarter (ending March 31):

Standard variable overhead rate (*SVOR*)	$4.00 per direct labor hour
Actual costs:	
Maintenance	$26,875
Power	$11,875
Actual hours worked (*AH*)	10,500 hours
Number of packages produced	500,000 units
Hours allowed for production (*SH*)	10,000 hours*
Variable overhead (*VOH*):	
Maintenance	0.02 hr. @ $2.75
Power	0.02 hr. @ $1.25

*0.02 × 500,000.

Required:
Prepare a performance report that shows the variances on an item-by-item basis.

Solution:

Performance Report for the Quarter Ended March 31, 20XX

Cost	Cost Formula[a]	Actual Costs	Budget for Actual Hours[b]	Spending Variance[c]	Budget for Standard Hours[d]	Efficiency Variance[e]
Maintenance	$2.75	$26,875	$28,875	$2,000 *F*	$27,500	$1,375 *U*
Power	1.25	11,875	13,125	1,250 *F*	12,500	625 *U*
Total	$4.00	$38,750	$42,000	$3,250 *F*	$40,000	$2,000 *U*

[a] Per direct labor hour.
[b] Computed using the cost formula and 10,500 actual hours.
[c] Spending Variance = Actual Costs − Budget for Actual Hours.
[d] Computed using the cost formula and an activity level of 10,000 standard hours.
[e] Efficiency Variance = Budget for Actual Hours − Budget for Standard Hours.

The analysis on a line-by-line basis reveals no unusual problems, such as two large individual item variances with opposite signs. No individual item variance is more than 10% of its budgeted amount. Thus, no single variance appears large enough to be of concern.

Fixed Overhead Analysis

Fixed overhead costs are capacity costs acquired in advance of usage. For example, Navistar, Inc., described in the chapter opener, has fixed overhead costs that include salaries, plant and equipment, lease payments, depreciation, and taxes. Recall from Chapter 4 that the predetermined overhead rate is calculated at the beginning of the year by dividing budgeted overhead by the budgeted amount of the base (e.g., direct labor hours). Now, however, we need to divide that predetermined overhead rate into variable and fixed overhead rates. It is easy to find the variable overhead rate, since that rate is unchanged, even though direct labor hours vary as production output changes. However, the fixed overhead rate changes as the underlying production level changes. To keep a stable fixed overhead rate throughout the year, companies often use practical capacity to determine the number of direct labor hours to use in the denominator of the fixed overhead rate calculation.

Suppose that Crunchy Chips can produce 525,000 packages of corn chips per quarter under efficient operating conditions. Practical capacity measured in standard hours (SH_p) is calculated by the following formula:

$$\text{Practical Capacity at Standard} = SH_p$$
$$= 0.02 \times 525{,}000$$
$$= 10{,}500 \text{ hours}$$

Crunchy Chips' budgeted fixed overhead costs per quarter total $157,500. The standard fixed overhead rate ($SFOR$) is calculated as follows:

$$SFOR = \text{Budgeted FOH}/SH_p$$

where

$$FOH = \text{Fixed Overhead}$$

Thus, for Crunchy Chips,

$$SFOR = \$157{,}500/10{,}500$$
$$= \$15 \text{ per direct labor hour}$$

Some firms use normal (average) or expected capacity instead of practical capacity to calculate fixed overhead rates. In this case, the standard hours used to calculate the fixed overhead rate typically will be less than the standard direct labor hours at practical capacity.

Total Fixed Overhead Variance

The total fixed overhead variance is the difference between actual fixed overhead and applied fixed overhead, where applied fixed overhead is obtained by multiplying the standard fixed overhead rate ($SFOR$) times the standard hours allowed for the actual output (SH). Thus, the applied fixed overhead is:

$$\text{Applied FOH} = SH \times SFOR$$

The total fixed overhead variance is the difference between the actual fixed overhead and the applied fixed overhead:

$$\text{Total FOH Variance} = \text{Actual FOH} - \text{Applied FOH}$$

Example 10.10 illustrates how to calculate the total fixed overhead variance for Crunchy Chips.

EXAMPLE 10.10

How to Calculate the Total Fixed Overhead Variance

Standard fixed overhead rate ($SFOR$)	$15.00 per direct labor hour
Actual FOH	$160,000
Standard hours allowed per unit	0.02 hour
Actual production	500,000 units

Required:
Calculate the (1) standard hours for actual units produced, (2) total applied FOH, and (3) total FOH variance.

EXAMPLE 10.10

(*Continued*)

Solution:

1. SH = Actual Units × Standard Hours Allowed per Unit
   = 500,000 units × 0.02 hour
   = 10,000 hours

2. Applied $FOH = SH \times SFOR$
   = 10,000 × $15
   = $150,000

3. Actual fixed overhead cost $160,000
   Applied fixed overhead   150,000
   Total variance $ 10,000 U

Fixed Overhead Variances

The total fixed overhead variance can be divided into spending and volume variances. Spending and volume variances can be calculated by using either the 3-pronged (columnar) approach or formulas. The best approach to use is a matter of preference. However, the formulas first need to be expressed specifically for FOH.

Fixed Overhead Spending Variance The **fixed overhead spending variance** is defined as the difference between the actual fixed overhead ($AFOH$) and the budgeted fixed overhead ($BFOH$):

$$FOH \text{ Spending Variance} = AFOH - BFOH$$

Fixed Overhead Volume Variance The **fixed overhead volume variance** is the difference between budgeted fixed overhead ($BFOH$) and applied fixed overhead:

$$\text{Volume Variance} = \text{Budgeted } FOH - \text{Applied } FOH$$
$$= BFOH - (SH \times SFOR)$$

The volume variance measures the effect of the actual output differing from the output used at the beginning of the year to compute the predetermined standard fixed overhead rate. If you think of the output used to calculate the fixed overhead rate as the capacity acquired (practical capacity) and the actual output as the capacity used, then the volume variance is the cost of unused capacity. **Example 10.11** illustrates how to calculate the fixed overhead variances using either a columnar or a formula approach.

Actual fixed overhead (AH)	$160,000
Standard fixed overhead rate ($SFOR$)	$15.00 per direct labor hour
Budgeted fixed overhead ($BFOH$)	$157,500
Number of packages produced	500,000 units
Hours allowed for production (SH)	10,000 hours*

*0.02 × 500,000.

EXAMPLE 10.11

How to Calculate Fixed Overhead Variances: Columnar and Formula Approaches

(*Continued*)

EXAMPLE 10.11

(Continued)

Required:

Calculate the fixed overhead spending and volume variances.

Solution:
Columnar:

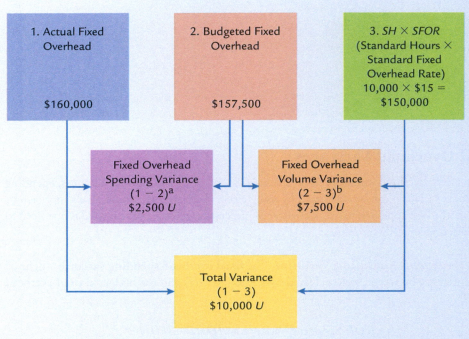

Formulas:

[a]*FOH* Spending Variance = Actual *FOH* – *BFOH*
$$= \$160,000 - \$157,500$$
$$= \$2,500 \text{ U}$$

[b]*FOH* Volume Variance = *BFOH* – Applied *FOH*
$$= BFOH - (SH \times SFOR)$$
$$= \$157,500 - (10,000 \times \$15)$$
$$= \$157,500 - \$150,000$$
$$= \$7,500 \text{ U}$$

Responsibility for the Fixed Overhead Spending Variance

FOH is made up of items such as salaries, depreciation, taxes, and insurance. Many fixed overhead items—long-run investments, for instance—cannot be changed in the short run. Consequently, fixed overhead costs are often beyond the immediate control of management. Since many fixed overhead costs are affected primarily by long-run decisions, and not by changes in production levels, the budget variance is usually small. For example, actual depreciation, salaries, taxes, and insurance costs are not likely to be much different from planned costs.

Analysis of the Fixed Overhead Spending Variance

As with *VOH*, *FOH* is made up of many individual items and a line-by-line comparison of budgeted costs with actual costs provides more information concerning the causes of the spending variance. Thus, items like grounds upkeep, insurance, and salaries of line supervisors would be

Here's How It's Used: SMALL MANUFACTURING FIRM

Brandt Gardner, the owner-manager of a small firm that manufactures feed processing equipment and round-hay bailers, is unhappy with the latest report on financial performance in the Kansas City, Missouri, plant. The company had recently installed a standard cost system in the Kansas City plant with the objective of controlling manufacturing costs. The performance report for the year ended revealed that the variances for materials, labor, and variable overhead were all within the desired ranges, but the fixed overhead spending and volume variances were both significantly unfavorable. Brandt wanted an explanation of the fixed overhead variances and a recommendation for improving fixed overhead cost performance. The following is extracted from a memo sent by the controller of the Kansas City plant:

Spending Variance Analysis Fixed overhead is made up of both committed and discretionary costs. The committed costs are fixed in level and span multiple years, and the actual costs incurred typically correspond to the budgeted costs. Examples include lease payments, rent, depreciation, and union contracts. This year, however, two of these items caused an unfavorable spending variance. We renewed the lease for our forklifts and the lease cost was higher than expected. The largest departure from budget though came from the new 3-year union contract. The agreed-upon settlement produced labor costs much higher than anticipated. Discretionary fixed costs are another matter. The agreed-upon amounts are short term and can vary more from year to year. They are primarily salaries paid to line supervisors, purchasing agents, personnel employees, etc.

Interestingly, the only variance for the discretionary items came in the purchasing area. This is attributable to the unexpected resignation of the purchasing department manager. We had to pay a higher salary for his replacement. Based on the nature of the variances, I see no need to take any immediate actions. Perhaps we need to consider how to develop a stronger negotiating position for future contract renewals.

Volume Variance Analysis We use practical capacity for calculating the $SFOR$. Since practical capacity is the most we can produce if we operate efficiently, we will usually have an unfavorable volume variance. This is shown by expressing the formula in the following way:

$$Volume\ Variance = BFOH - SFOH$$
$$= (SFOR \times SH_p) - (SFOR \times SH)$$
$$= (SH_p - SH)SFOR$$

Since the hours allowed for practical volume (SH_p) are always greater than or equal to the hours allowed for the actual volume (SH), then the variance is usually unfavorable. The volume variance is therefore a measure of unused capacity. The large unfavorable volume variance is because we operated at about 60% of capacity ($SH = 0.60SH_p$). The solution is to increase sales and thus increase production. Much of the unused capacity was caused by a drop in demand because of drought conditions which depressed agricultural production and decreased demand for our product. Once the climate is back to normal, much of the problem will be reversed.

listed, and the budgeted cost of each item would be compared with its actual cost. Suppose, for example, that the budget for grounds upkeep was $15,000 and only $13,000 was spent. Less was spent on grounds upkeep than expected ($2,000 favorable variance). Since the amount is more than 10% of its budget, it merits investigation. An investigation, for example, might reveal that the weather was especially wet and thus reduced the cost of watering for the period involved. In this case, no action is needed, as a natural correction would be forthcoming. A similar analysis would be done for each item in the fixed overhead budget.

Responsibility for the Fixed Overhead Volume Variance

Assuming that volume variance measures capacity utilization implies that the general responsibility for this variance should be assigned to the production department. At times, however, a significant volume variance may be due to factors beyond the control of production. For example, if the purchasing department buys lower-quality raw materials than usual, significant rework time may result. This will cause lower production and an unfavorable volume variance. In this case, responsibility for the variance rests with purchasing, not production.

Analysis of the Volume Variance

The $7,500 unfavorable volume variance (**Example 10.11**, p. 549) occurs because the production capacity is 10,500 hours and only 10,000 hours were allowed for the actual production. Why the company failed to use all of its capacity is not known. Given that unused capacity is less than 10% of the total, no investigation is merited. Exhibit 10.5 graphically illustrates the volume variance. Notice that the volume variance occurs because fixed overhead is treated as if it were a variable cost. In reality, fixed costs do not change as activity changes, as a predetermined fixed overhead rate allows.

Exhibit 10.5

Graphical Analysis of the Volume Variance

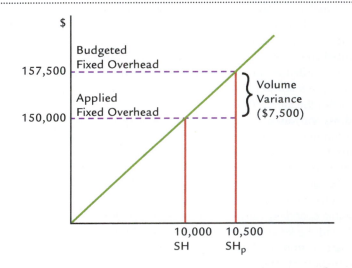

Check Point

1. **How does the variable overhead spending variance differ from the materials and labor price variances?**

   Answer:
   The variable overhead spending variance is affected by price changes of individual items as well as efficiency issues.

2. **Why are the labor efficiency and variable overhead efficiency variances similar in nature?**

   Answer:
   Both depend on the difference between actual and standard direct labor hours.

3. **Assume that *SFOR* = $10 and SH_p = 5,000 hours. What is the budgeted *FOH*?**

   Answer:
   $SFOR = BFOH/SH_p$
   Thus, $BFOH = SFOR \times SH_p$
   $= \$10 \times 5{,}000 = \$50{,}000$

OBJECTIVE 5

Prepare journal entries for materials and labor variances.

APPENDIX 10A: ACCOUNTING FOR VARIANCES

To illustrate recording variances, we will assume that the materials price variance is computed at the time materials are purchased. With this assumption, we can state a general rule for a firm's inventory accounts: All inventories are carried at standard cost. As a result, actual costs are not entered into an inventory account. Instead, applied standard costs flow through inventory and eventually to cost of goods sold. As illustrated in this appendix, the accounts containing the variances between applied standard costs and actual costs are closed, which allows the amount of actual costs to ultimately impact the final cost of goods sold number that appears in the financial statements. In recording variances, unfavorable variances always are debits, and favorable variances always are credits.

Entries for Direct Materials Variances

Materials Price Variance   The entry to record the purchase of materials follows (assuming an unfavorable *MPV* and that *AQ* is materials purchased):

Materials	$SP \times AQ$	
Materials Price Variance	$(AP - SP) \times AQ$	
Accounts Payable		$AP \times AQ$

For example, if *AP* is $0.0069 per ounce of corn, *SP* is $0.0060 per ounce, and 780,000 ounces of corn are purchased, the entry would be:

Materials	4,680	
Materials Price Variance	702	
Accounts Payable		5,382

Notice that the raw materials are carried in the inventory account at standard cost.

Materials Usage Variance   The general form for the entry to record the issuance and usage of materials, assuming a favorable *MUV*, is as follows:

Work in Process	$SP \times SQ$	
Materials Usage Variance		$(AQ - SQ) \times SP$
Materials		$SP \times AQ$

Here, *AQ* is the materials issued and used, not necessarily equal to the materials purchased. Notice that only standard quantities and standard prices are used to assign costs to Work in Process. No actual costs enter this account.

For example, if *AQ* is 780,000 ounces of corn, *SQ* is 873,000 ounces, and *SP* is $0.006, then the entry would be:

Work in Process	5,238	
Materials Usage Variance		558
Materials		4,680

Notice that the favorable usage variance appears as a credit entry.

Entries for Direct Labor Variances

Unlike the materials variances, the entry to record both types of labor variances is made simultaneously. The general form of this entry follows (assuming an unfavorable labor rate variance and an unfavorable labor efficiency variance).

Work in Process	$SR \times SH$	
Labor Efficiency Variance	$(AH - SH) \times SR$	
Labor Rate Variance	$(AR - SR) \times AH$	
Accrued Payroll		$AR \times AH$

Again, notice that only standard hours and standard rates are used to assign costs to Work in Process. Actual prices or quantities are not used.

To give a specific example, assume that *AR* is $7.35 per hour, *SR* is $7.00 per hour, *AH* is 360 hours of inspection, and *SH* is 339.5 hours. The following journal entry would be made:

Work in Process	2,376.50	
Labor Efficiency Variance	143.50	
Labor Rate Variance	126.00	
Accrued Payroll		2,646.00

Disposition of Materials and Labor Variances

At the end of the year, the variances for materials and labor usually are closed to Cost of Goods Sold. (This practice is acceptable, provided that variances are not material in amount.) Using the previous data, the entries would take the following form:

Cost of Goods Sold	971.50	
Materials Price Variance		702.00
Labor Efficiency Variance		143.50
Labor Rate Variance		126.00
Materials Usage Variance	558.00	
Cost of Goods Sold		558.00

If the variances are material, they must be prorated among various accounts. For the materials price variance, it is prorated among Materials Inventory, Work in Process, Finished Goods, and Cost of Goods Sold. The remaining materials and labor variances are prorated among Work in Process, Finished Goods, and Cost of Goods Sold. Typically, materials variances are prorated on the basis of the materials balances in each of these accounts and the labor variances on the basis of the labor balances in the accounts.

Check Point

1. **If a company bought 100 pounds of material for $5 per pound and the standard price is $4.00 per pound, what amount would be debited to the materials inventory account?**

   Answer:
   Inventories are carried at standard and so the amount that would be debited is $4.00 × 100 = $400.

2. **How are the materials and labor variances treated at the end of the year if they are not material?**

   Answer:
   The variances are closed to Cost of Goods Sold. Unfavorable variances are cleared by debiting Cost of Goods Sold and crediting the associated material or labor variance account, and favorable variances are cleared by debiting the materials or labor variance account and crediting the cost of goods sold account.

SUMMARY OF LEARNING OBJECTIVES

LO1. Explain how unit standards are set, explain why standard cost systems are adopted, and describe the purpose of a standard cost sheet.
- A standard cost system budgets quantities and costs on a unit basis. These unit budgets are for labor, materials, and overhead. Standard costs, therefore, are the amount that should be expended to produce a product or service.
- Standards are set by using historical experience, engineering studies, and input from operating personnel, marketing, and accounting.
- Currently attainable standards are those that can be achieved under efficient operating conditions.
- Ideal standards are those achievable under maximum efficiency, or ideal operating conditions.
- Standard cost systems are adopted to improve planning and control and to facilitate product costing. By comparing actual outcomes with standards and breaking the variance into price and quantity components, detailed feedback is provided to managers. This information allows managers to exercise a greater degree of cost control than that found in a normal or actual cost system.
- The standard cost sheet provides the details for computing the standard cost per unit. It shows the standard costs for materials, labor, and variable and fixed overhead.
- The standard cost sheet reveals the quantity of each input that should be used to produce one unit of output. By using these unit quantity standards, the standard quantity of materials allowed and the standard hours allowed can be computed for the actual output.

LO2. Describe the basic concepts underlying variance analysis, and explain when variances should be investigated.
- The total variance is the difference between actual costs and planned costs.
- In a standard costing system, the total variance is broken down into price and usage variances. By breaking the total variances into price and usage variances, managers are better able to analyze and control the total variance.
- Variances should be investigated if they are material (i.e., significant) and if the benefits of corrective action are greater than the costs of investigation. Because of the difficulty of assessing cost and benefits on a case-by-case basis, many firms set up formal control limits—either a dollar amount, a percentage, or both. Other firms use judgment to assess the need to investigate.

LO3. Compute the materials and labor variances, and explain how they are used for control.
- The materials price and usage variances are computed by using either a 3-pronged (columnar) approach or formulas.
- The materials price variance is the difference between what was actually paid for materials (generally associated with the purchasing activity) and what should have been paid.
- The materials usage variance is the difference between the actual amount of materials used (generally associated with the production activity) and the amount of materials that should have been used.
- When a significant variance is signaled, an investigation is undertaken to find the cause. Corrective action is taken, if possible, to put the system back in control.
- The labor variances are computed by using either a 3-pronged approach or formulas.
- The labor rate variance is caused by the actual wage rate differing from the standard wage rate. It is the difference between the wages that were paid and those that should have been paid.
- The labor efficiency variance is the difference between the actual amount of labor that was used and the amount of labor that should have been used.

- When a significant variance is signaled, investigation is called for, and corrective action should be taken, if possible, to put the system back in control.
- Kaizen costing focuses on continuous short-term improvements in manufacturing costs, while target costing focuses on long-term improvements in design costs. Target cost is the difference between the targeted revenue and the targeted profit.

LO4. Compute the overhead variances, and explain how they are used for control.
- Comparing actual variable and fixed overhead costs with applied overhead costs yields a total overhead variance.
- In a standard cost system, it is possible to break down overhead variances into component variances.
- For variable overhead, the two component variances are the spending variance and the efficiency variance.
- The spending variance is the result of comparing the actual costs with budgeted costs.
- The variable overhead efficiency variance is the result of efficient or inefficient use of labor because variable overhead is assumed to vary with direct labor hours.
- For fixed overhead, the two component variances are the spending variance and the volume variance.
- The spending variance is the result of comparing the actual costs with budgeted costs.
- The fixed overhead volume variance is the result of producing a level different than that used to calculate the predetermined fixed overhead rate. It can be interpreted as a measure of capacity utilization.

LO5. *(Appendix 10A)* Prepare journal entries for materials and labor variances.
- Assuming that the materials price variance is computed at the point of purchase, all inventories are carried at standard cost.
- Actual costs are not entered into an inventory account. Instead, standard costs are applied to inventory and eventually flow through to cost of goods sold.
- Accounts are created for materials price and usage variances and for labor rate and efficiency variances.
- Unfavorable variances are always debits; favorable variances are always credits.
- The closing of the variance accounts, which contain the difference between applied standard costs and actual costs, results in the amount of actual costs ultimately impacting cost of goods sold.

SUMMARY OF IMPORTANT EQUATIONS

Abbreviations:

FOH = Fixed Overhead
VOH = Variable Overhead
$BFOH$ = Budgeted FOH
AH = Actual Direct Labor Hours
SH = Direct Labor Hours That *Should Have Been Worked* for Actual Units Produced
SQ = Quantity of Materials That *Should Have Been Used* for Actual Units Produced
AP = Actual Price per Unit
SP = Standard Price per Unit
$SFOR$ = Standard Fixed Overhead Rate
$SVOR$ = Standard Variable Overhead Rate

1. Cost per Unit = Total Cost/Total Units

2. Standard Cost per Unit = Quantity Standard × Price Standard

3. SQ = Unit Quantity Standard × Actual Output

4. SH = Unit Labor Standard × Actual Output

5. Total Variance = Actual Cost – Planned Cost = $(AP \times AQ) - (SP \times SQ)$

6. Total Materials Variance = Actual Cost – Planned Cost = $(AP \times AQ) - (SP \times SQ)$

7. $MPV = (AP - SP) \times AQ$

8. $MUV = (AQ - SQ) \times SP$

9. $MPV = (AP \times AQ) - (SP \times AQ)$

10. $MUV = (SP \times AQ) - (SP \times SQ)$

11. Total Labor Variance = $(AR \times AH) - (SR \times SH)$

12. Total Labor Variance = Labor Rate Variance + Labor Efficiency Variance

13. $LRV = (AR \times AH) - (SR \times AH)$

14. $LRV = (AR - SR) \times AH$

15. $LEV = (SR \times AH) - (SR \times SH)$

16. $LEV = (AH - SH) \times SR$

17. Target Cost per Unit = Expected Sales Price per Unit – Desired Profit per Unit

18. VOH Spending Variance = Actual VOH – $(AH \times SVOR)$

19. VOH Efficiency Variance = $(AH - SH) \times SVOR$

20. Practical Capacity at Standard = SH_p

21. $SFOR = BFOH/SH_p$

22. Applied $FOH = SH \times SFOR$

23. Total FOH Variance = Actual FOH – Applied FOH

24. FOH Spending Variance = $AFOH - BFOH$

25. Volume Variance = $BFOH$ – Applied FOH
$$= BFOH - (SH \times SFOR)$$

EXAMPLE 10.1	How to compute standard quantities allowed (SQ and SH), page 527
EXAMPLE 10.2	How to use control limits to trigger a variance investigation, page 531
EXAMPLE 10.3	How to calculate the total variance for materials, page 532
EXAMPLE 10.4	How to calculate materials variances: formula and columnar approaches, page 534
EXAMPLE 10.5	How to calculate the total variance for labor, page 537
EXAMPLE 10.6	How to calculate labor variances: formula and columnar approaches, page 539
EXAMPLE 10.7	How to calculate the total variable overhead variance, page 543
EXAMPLE 10.8	How to calculate variable overhead spending and efficiency variances: columnar and formula approaches, page 544
EXAMPLE 10.9	How to prepare a performance report for the variable overhead variances, page 547
EXAMPLE 10.10	How to calculate the total fixed overhead variance, page 548
EXAMPLE 10.11	How to calculate fixed overhead variances: columnar and formula approaches, page 549

KEY TERMS

Control limits, 530, the maximum allowable deviation from a standard.

Favorable (*F*) variances, 529, variances produced whenever the actual amounts are less than the budgeted or standard allowances.

Fixed overhead spending variance, 549, the difference between the actual fixed overhead (AFOH) and the budgeted fixed overhead (BFOH).

Fixed overhead volume variance, 549, the difference between budgeted fixed overhead (BFOH) and applied fixed overhead.

Labor efficiency variance (*LEV*), 538, the difference between the actual direct labor hours used and the standard direct labor hours allowed multiplied by the standard hourly wage rate.

Labor rate variance (*LRV*), 538, the difference between the actual hourly rate paid and the standard hourly rate multiplied by the actual hours worked,

Materials price variance (*MPV*), 534, the difference between the actual price paid per unit of materials and the standard price allowed per unit multiplied by the actual quantity of materials purchased.

Materials usage variance (*MUV*), 535, the difference between the direct materials actually used and the direct materials allowed for the actual output multiplied by the standard price.

Price (rate) variance, 528, the difference between the actual and standard unit price of an input multiplied by the number of inputs used.

Price standards, 522, the amount that *should be paid* per unit of the input to be used.

Quantity standards, 522, the amount of input that *should be used* per unit of output.

Standard cost per unit, 525, the per-unit cost that should be achieved, given materials, labor, and overhead standards.

Standard cost sheet, 525, a listing of the standard costs and standard quantities of direct materials, direct labor, and overhead that should apply to a single product.

Standard hours allowed (*SH*), 526, the direct labor hours that should have been used to produce the actual output (Unit labor standard × Actual output).

Standard quantity of materials allowed (*SQ*), 526, the quantity of materials that should have been used to produce the actual output (Unit materials standard × Actual output).

Target cost, 542, the difference between the sales price needed to achieve a projected market share and the desired per-unit profit.

Total budget variance, 528, the difference between the actual cost of an input and its planned cost.

Unfavorable (*U*) variances, 529, variances produced whenever the actual input amounts are greater than the budgeted or standard allowances.

Usage (efficiency) variance, 529, the difference between standard quantities and actual quantities multiplied by standard price.

Variable overhead efficiency variance, 544, the difference between the actual direct labor hours used and the standard hours allowed multiplied by the standard variable overhead rate.

Variable overhead spending variance, 544, the difference between the actual variable overhead and the budgeted variable overhead based on actual hours used to produce the actual output.

REVIEW PROBLEM

I. Materials, Labor, and Overhead Variances

Willhelm Manufacturing has the following standards for one of its products:

Direct materials (2 ft. @ $5)	$10
Direct labor (0.5 hr. @ $10)	5

During the most recent year, the following actual results were recorded:

Production	6,000 units
Direct materials (11,750 ft. purchased and used)	$61,100
Direct labor (2,900 hrs.)	29,580

Required:

Compute the following variances:

1. Materials price and usage variances.
2. Labor rate and efficiency variances.

Solution:

1. Materials variances:

$$MPV = (AP - SP) \times AQ$$
$$= (\$5.20 - \$5.00) \times 11{,}750 = \$2{,}350 \; U$$
$$MUV = (AQ - SQ) \times SP$$
$$= (11{,}750 - 12{,}000) \times \$5.00 = \$1{,}250 \; F$$

2. Labor variances:

$$LRV = (AR - SR) \times AH$$
$$= (\$10.20 - \$10.00) \times 2{,}900 = \$580 \; U$$
$$LEV = (AH - SH) \times SR$$
$$= (2{,}900 - 3{,}000) \times \$10.00 = \$1{,}000 \; F$$

DISCUSSION QUESTIONS

1. Discuss the difference between budgets and standard costs.
2. Describe the relationship that unit standards have with flexible budgeting.
3. Why is historical experience often a poor basis for establishing standards?
4. What are ideal standards? Currently attainable standards? Of the two, which is usually adopted? Why?
5. Explain why standard costing systems are adopted.
6. How does standard costing improve the control function?
7. Discuss the differences among actual costing, normal costing, and standard costing.
8. What is the purpose of a standard cost sheet?
9. The budget variance for variable production costs is broken down into quantity and price variances. Explain why the quantity variance is more useful for control purposes than the price variance.
10. When should a standard cost variance be investigated?
11. What are control limits, and how are they set?
12. Explain why the materials price variance is often computed at the point of purchase rather than at the point of issuance.
13. The materials usage variance is always the responsibility of the production supervisor. Do you agree or disagree? Why?

14. The labor rate variance is never controllable. Do you agree or disagree? Why?
15. Suggest some possible causes of an unfavorable labor efficiency variance.
16. What is kaizen costing? On which part of the value chain does kaizen costing focus?
17. What is target costing? Describe how costs are reduced so that the target cost can be met.
18. Explain why the variable overhead spending variance is not a pure price variance.
19. The variable overhead efficiency variance has nothing to do with efficient use of variable overhead. Do you agree or disagree? Why?
20. Describe the difference between the variable overhead efficiency variance and the labor efficiency variance.
21. What is the cause of an unfavorable volume variance?
22. Does the volume variance convey any meaningful information to managers?
23. Which do you think is more important for control of fixed overhead costs: the spending variance or the volume variance? Explain.

MULTIPLE-CHOICE QUESTIONS

10-1   Standards set by engineering studies

   a. can determine the most efficient way of operating.
   b. can provide rigorous guidelines.
   c. may not be achievable by operating personnel.
   d. often do not allow operating personnel to have much input.
   e. All of these.

10-2   A currently attainable standard is one that

   a. relies on maximum efficiency.
   b. uses only historical experience.
   c. is based on ideal operating conditions.
   d. can be easily achieved.
   e. None of these.

10-3   An ideal standard is one that

   a. uses only historical experience.
   b. relies on maximum efficiency.
   c. can be achieved under efficient operating conditions.
   d. makes allowances for normal breakdowns, interruptions, less than perfect skill, and so on.
   e. None of these.

10-4   The underlying details for the standard cost per unit are provided in

   a. the standard work-in-process account.
   b. the standard production budget.
   c. the standard cost sheet.
   d. the balance sheet.
   e. None of these.

10-5   The standard quantity of materials allowed is computed as

   a. Unit Quantity Standard × Standard Output.
   b. Unit Quantity Standard × Normal Output.
   c. Unit Quantity Standard × Practical Output.
   d. Unit Quantity Standard × Actual Output.
   e. None of these.

10-6 The standard direct labor hours allowed is computed as

    a. Unit Labor Standard × Actual Output.
    b. Unit Labor Standard × Practical Output.
    c. Unit Labor Standard × Standard Output.
    d. Unit Labor Standard × Normal Output.
    e. Unit Labor Standard × Theoretical Output.

10-7 Investigating variances from standard is

    a. always done.
    b. done if the variance is inside an acceptable range.
    c. not done if the variance is expected to recur.
    d. done if the variance is outside the control limits.
    e. None of these.

10-8 Responsibility for the materials price variance typically belongs to

    a. production.
    b. purchasing.
    c. marketing.
    d. personnel.
    e. the chief executive officer (CEO).

10-9 The materials price variance is usually computed

    a. when goods are finished.
    b. when materials are issued to production.
    c. when materials are purchased.
    d. after suppliers are paid.
    e. None of these.

10-10 Responsibility for the materials usage variance is usually assigned to

    a. the chief executive officer (CEO).
    b. marketing.
    c. purchasing.
    d. personnel.
    e. production.

10-11 Responsibility for the labor rate variance typically is assigned to

    a. production.
    b. labor markets.
    c. personnel.
    d. labor unions.
    e. engineering.

10-12 Responsibility for the labor efficiency variance typically is assigned to

    a. labor unions.
    b. personnel.
    c. engineering.
    d. production.
    e. outside trainers.

10-13 (*Appendix 10A*) Which of the following items describes practices surrounding the recording of variances?

    a. All inventories are typically carried at standard.
    b. Unfavorable variances appear as debits.
    c. Favorable variances appear as credits.
    d. Immaterial variances are typically closed to Cost of Goods Sold.
    e. All of these.

10-14 *(Appendix 10A)* Which of the following is true concerning labor variances that are not material in amount?

    a. They are closed to Cost of Goods Sold.

    b. They are prorated among Work in Process, Finished Goods, and Cost of Goods Sold.

    c. They are prorated among Materials, Work in Process, Finished Goods, and Cost of Goods Sold.

    d. They are reported on the balance sheet at the end of the year.

    e. All of these.

10-15 The total variable overhead variance is the difference between

    a. the budgeted variable overhead and the actual variable overhead.

    b. the actual variable overhead and the applied variable overhead.

    c. the budgeted variable overhead and the applied variable overhead.

    d. the applied variable overhead and the budgeted total overhead.

    e. None of these.

10-16 A variable overhead spending variance can occur because

    a. prices for individual overhead items have increased.

    b. prices for individual overhead items have decreased.

    c. more of an individual overhead item was used than expected.

    d. less of an individual overhead item was used than expected.

    e. All of these.

10-17 The total variable overhead variance can be expressed as the sum of

    a. the underapplied variable overhead and the spending variance.

    b. the efficiency variance and the overapplied variable overhead.

    c. the spending, efficiency, and volume variances.

    d. the spending and efficiency variances.

    e. None of these.

10-18 The total fixed overhead variance is

    a. the difference between actual and applied fixed overhead costs.

    b. the difference between budgeted and applied fixed overhead costs.

    c. the difference between budgeted fixed and variable overhead costs.

    d. the difference between actual and budgeted fixed overhead costs.

    e. None of these.

10-19 The total fixed overhead variance can be expressed as the sum of

    a. the spending and efficiency variances.

    b. the efficiency and volume variances.

    c. the spending and volume variances.

    d. the flexible budget and the volume variances.

    e. None of these.

10-20 An unfavorable volume variance can occur because

    a. too much finished goods inventory was held.

    b. the company overproduced.

    c. the actual output was less than expected or practical capacity.

    d. the actual output was greater than expected or practical capacity.

    e. All of these.

BRIEF EXERCISES: SET A

Brief Exercise 10-21 Standard Quantities Allowed of Labor and Materials

OBJECTIVE ◄ 1
Example 10.1

Miel Company produces ready-to-cook oatmeal. Each carton of oatmeal requires 16 ounces of rolled oats per carton (the unit quantity standard) and 0.04 labor hour (the unit labor standard). During the year, 960,000 cartons of oatmeal were produced.

Required:

1. Calculate the total amount of oats allowed for the actual output.
2. Calculate the total amount of labor hours allowed for the actual output.

Brief Exercise 10-22 Control Limits

OBJECTIVE ◄ 2
Example 10.2

During the last 6 weeks, the actual costs of materials for Brennen Company were as follows:

Week 1	$57,600	Week 4	$68,400
Week 2	$60,000	Week 5	$69,000
Week 3	$63,000	Week 6	$69,500

The standard materials cost for each week was $60,000 with an allowable deviation of ±6,000.

Required:

Plot the actual costs over time against the upper and lower limits. Comment on whether or not there is a need to investigate any of the variances.

> *Use the following information to complete Brief Exercises 10-23 and 10-24:*
> Krumple Inc. produces aluminum cans. Production of 12-ounce cans has a standard unit quantity of 4.7 ounces of aluminum per can. During the month of April, 450,000 cans were produced using 1,875,000 ounces of aluminum. The actual cost of aluminum was $0.10 per ounce and the standard price was $0.08 per ounce. There are no beginning or ending inventories of aluminum.

Brief Exercise 10-23 Total Materials Variance

OBJECTIVE ◄ 3
Example 10.3

Refer to the information for Krumple Inc. above.

Required:

Calculate the total variance for aluminum for the month of April.

Brief Exercise 10-24 Materials Variances

OBJECTIVE ◄ 3
Example 10.4

Refer to the information for Krumple Inc. above.

Required:

Calculate the materials price and usage variances using the columnar and formula approaches.

> *Use the following information to complete Brief Exercises 10-25 and 10-26:*
> Tico Inc. produces plastic bottles. Each bottle has a standard labor requirement of 0.03 hour. During the month of April, 900,000 bottles were produced using 25,200 labor hours @ $15.00. The standard wage rate is $13.50 per hour.

OBJECTIVE ▶3
Example 10.5

Brief Exercise 10-25 Total Labor Variance

Refer to the information for Tico Inc. on the previous page.

Required:

Calculate the total variance for production labor for the month of April.

OBJECTIVE ▶3
Example 10.6

Brief Exercise 10-26 Labor Rate and Efficiency Variances

Refer to the information above for Tico Inc. on the previous page

Required:

Calculate the labor rate and efficiency variances using the columnar and formula approaches.

OBJECTIVE ▶4
Example 10.4

Brief Exercise 10-27 Total Variable Overhead Variance

Rath Company showed the following information for the year:

Standard variable overhead rate (*SVOR*) per direct labor hour	$3.75
Standard hours (*SH*) allowed per unit	4
Actual production in units	15,000
Actual variable overhead costs	$222,816
Actual direct labor hours	57,200

Required:

1. Calculate the standard direct labor hours for actual production.
2. Calculate the applied variable overhead.
3. Calculate the total variable overhead variance.

OBJECTIVE ▶4
Example 10.5

Brief Exercise 10-28 Variable Overhead Spending and Efficiency Variances, Columnar and Formula Approaches

Rath Company provided the following information:

Standard variable overhead rate (*SVOR*) per direct labor hour	$3.75
Actual variable overhead costs	$222,816
Actual direct labor hours worked (*AH*)	57,200
Actual production in units	15,000
Standard hours (*SH*) allowed for actual units produced	60,000

Required:

1. Using the columnar approach, calculate the variable overhead spending and efficiency variances.
2. Using the formula approach, calculate the variable overhead spending variance.
3. Using the formula approach, calculate the variable overhead efficiency variance.
4. Calculate the total variable overhead variance.

OBJECTIVE ▶4
Example 10.6

Brief Exercise 10-29 Performance Report for Variable Variances

Humo Company provided the following information:

Standard variable overhead rate (*SVOR*) per direct labor hour	$4.07
Actual variable overhead costs:	
Inspection	$123,300
Power	$104,600
Actual direct labor hours worked (*AH*)	61,200

Actual production in units	15,000
Standard hours (*SH*) allowed for actual units produced	61,000
VOH:	
Inspection	4 hours @ $2.20
Power	4 hours @ $1.87

Required:

Prepare a performance report that shows the variances for each variable overhead item (inspection and power).

Brief Exercise 10-30 Total Fixed Overhead Variance

OBJECTIVE 4
Example 10.7

Bradshaw Company provided the following data:

Standard fixed overhead rate (*SFOR*)	$5 per direct labor hour
Actual fixed overhead costs	$301,680
Standard hours allowed per unit	4 hours
Actual production	15,000 units

Required:

1. Calculate the standard hours allowed for actual production.
2. Calculate the applied fixed overhead.
3. Calculate the total fixed overhead variance.

Brief Exercise 10-31 Fixed Overhead Spending and Volume Variances, Columnar and Formula Approaches

OBJECTIVE 4
Example 10.8

Branch Company provided the following information:

Standard fixed overhead rate (*SFOR*) per direct labor hour	$5.00
Actual fixed overhead	$305,000
BFOH	$300,000
Actual production in units	16,000
Standard hours allowed for actual units produced (*SH*)	64,000

Required:

1. Using the columnar approach, calculate the fixed overhead spending and volume variances.
2. Using the formula approach, calculate the fixed overhead spending variance.
3. Using the formula approach, calculate the fixed overhead volume variance.
4. Calculate the total fixed overhead variance.

BRIEF EXERCISES: SET B

Brief Exercise 10-32 Standard Quantities Allowed of Labor and Materials

OBJECTIVE 1
Example 10.1

Dulce Company produces chocolate. Each pound of chocolate requires 400 cocoa beans (the unit quantity standard) and 0.15 labor hour (the unit labor standard). During the year, 480,000 pounds of chocolate were produced.

Required:

1. Calculate the number of cocoa beans allowed for the actual output.
2. Calculate the total amount of labor hours allowed for the actual output.

OBJECTIVE **2**
Example 10.2

Brief Exercise 10-33 Control Limits

During the last 6 weeks, the actual costs of labor for Solsana Company were as follows:

Week 1	$38,500	Week 4	$45,600
Week 2	$40,000	Week 5	$48,000
Week 3	$42,000	Week 6	$51,000

The standard materials cost for each week was $40,000 with an allowable deviation of ±5,000.

Required:

Plot the actual costs over time against the upper and lower limits. Comment on whether or not there is a need to investigate any of the variances.

Use the following information to complete Brief Exercises 10-34 and 10-35:
Young Inc. produces plastic bottles. Production of 16-ounce bottles has a standard unit quantity of 0.45 ounce of plastic per bottle. During the month of June, 240,000 bottles were produced using 110,000 ounces of plastic. The actual cost of plastic was $0.042 per ounce, and the standard price was $0.045 per ounce. There is no beginning or ending inventories of plastic.

OBJECTIVE **3**
Example 10.3

Brief Exercise 10-34 Total Materials Variance

Refer to the information for Young Inc. above.

Required:

Calculate the total variance for plastic for the month of June

OBJECTIVE **3**
Example 10.4

Brief Exercise 10-35 Materials Variances

Refer to the information for Young Inc. above.

Required:

Calculate the materials price and usage variances using the columnar and formula approaches.

Use the following information to complete Brief Exercises 10-36 and 10-37:
Ambient Inc. produces aluminum cans. Each can has a standard labor requirement of 0.03 hour. During the month of May, 500,000 cans were produced using 14,000 labor hours @ $15.00. The standard wage rate is $14.50 per hour.

OBJECTIVE **3**
Example 10.5

Brief Exercise 10-36 Total Labor Variance

Refer to the information for Ambient Inc. above.

Required:

Calculate the total variance for production labor for the month of May.

OBJECTIVE **3**
Example 10.6

Brief Exercise 10-37 Labor Rate and Efficiency Variances

Refer to the information for Ambient Inc. above.

Required:

Calculate the labor rate and efficiency variances using the columnar and formula approaches.

Brief Exercise 10-38 Total Variable Overhead Variance

OBJECTIVE ▶ 4
Example 11.4

Mulliner Company showed the following information for the year:

Standard variable overhead rate (*SVOR*) per direct labor hour	$3.50
Standard hours (*SH*) allowed per unit	3
Actual production in units	20,000
Actual variable overhead costs	$220,500
Actual direct labor hours	61,200

Required:

1. Calculate the standard direct labor hours for actual production.
2. Calculate the applied variable overhead.
3. Calculate the total variable overhead variance.

Brief Exercise 10-39 Variable Overhead Spending and Efficiency Variances, Columnar and Formula Approaches

OBJECTIVE ▶ 4
Example 11.5

Aretha Company provided the following information:

Standard variable overhead rate (*SVOR*) per direct labor hour	$4.70
Actual variable overhead costs	$335,750
Actual direct labor hours worked (*AH*)	69,200
Actual production in units	14,000
Standard hours (*SH*) allowed for actual units produced	70,000

Required:

1. Using the columnar approach, calculate the variable overhead spending and efficiency variances.
2. Using the formula approach, calculate the variable overhead spending variance.
3. Using the formula approach, calculate the variable overhead efficiency variance.
4. Calculate the total variable overhead variance.

Brief Exercise 10-40 Performance Report for Variable Variances

OBJECTIVE ▶ 4
Example 11.6

Potter Company provided the following information:

Standard variable overhead rate (*SVOR*) per direct labor hour	$5.00
Actual variable overhead costs:	
Inspection	$162,000
Power	$220,600
Actual direct labor hours worked (*AH*)	77,000
Actual production in units	25,000
Standard hours (*SH*) allowed for actual units produced	75,000
VOH:	
Inspection	3 hours @ $2.00
Power	3 hours @ $3.00

Required:

Prepare a performance report that shows the variances for each variable overhead item (inspection and power).

OBJECTIVE ▶ 4
Example 11.7

Brief Exercise 10-41 Total Fixed Overhead Variance

Bulger Company provided the following data:

Standard fixed overhead rate (*SFOR*)	$8 per direct labor hour
Actual fixed overhead costs	$985,300
Standard hours allowed per unit	6 hours
Actual production	20,000 units

Required:

1. Calculate the standard hours allowed for actual production.
2. Calculate the applied fixed overhead.
3. Calculate the total fixed overhead variance.

OBJECTIVE ▶ 4
Example 11.8

Brief Exercise 10-42 Fixed Overhead Spending and Volume Variances, Columnar and Formula Approaches

Corey Company provided the following information:

Standard fixed overhead rate (*SFOR*) per direct labor hour	$10.00
Actual fixed overhead	$425,000
Budgeted fixed overhead	$500,000
Actual production in units	8,500
Standard hours allowed for actual units produced (*SH*)	42,500

Required:

1. Using the columnar approach, calculate the fixed overhead spending and volume variances.
2. Using the formula approach, calculate the fixed overhead spending variance.
3. Using the formula approach, calculate the fixed overhead volume variance.
4. Calculate the total fixed overhead variance.

EXERCISES

OBJECTIVE ▶ 1

Exercise 10-43 Standard Quantities of Labor and Materials

Stillwater Designs rebuilds defective units of its S12L7 **Kicker** speaker model. During the year, Stillwater rebuilt 15,000 units. Materials and labor standards for performing the repairs are as follows:

Direct materials (1 recon kit @ $160)	$160.00
Direct materials (1 cabinet @ $55)	55.00
Direct labor (5 hrs. @ $15)	75.00

Required:

1. Compute the standard hours allowed for a volume of 15,000 rebuilt units.
2. Compute the standard number of kits and cabinets allowed for a volume of 15,000 rebuilt units.
3. Suppose that during the first month of the year, 15,000 standard hours were allowed for the units rebuilt. How many units were rebuilt during the first month?

Exercise 10-44 Investigation of Variances

OBJECTIVE ▶ 2

Sommers Company uses the following rule to determine whether materials usage variances should be investigated: A materials usage variance will be investigated anytime the amount exceeds the lesser of $12,000 or 10% of the standard cost. Reports for the past 5 weeks provided the following information:

Week	MUV	Standard Materials Cost
1	$10,500 F	$120,000
2	10,700 F	100,500
3	9,000 U	120,000
4	13,500 U	127,500
5	10,500 U	103,500

Required:

1. Using the rule provided, identify the cases that will be investigated.
2. **CONCEPTUAL CONNECTION** Suppose investigation reveals that the cause of an unfavorable materials usage variance is the use of lower-quality materials than are normally used. Who is responsible? What corrective action would likely be taken?
3. **CONCEPTUAL CONNECTION** Suppose investigation reveals that the cause of a significant unfavorable materials usage variance is attributable to a new approach to manufacturing that takes less labor time but causes more material waste. Examination of the labor efficiency variance reveals that it is favorable and larger than the unfavorable materials usage variance. Who is responsible? What action should be taken?

> *Use the following information for Exercises 10-45 through 10-47:*
> Cinturon Corporation produces high-quality leather belts. The company's plant in Boise uses a standard costing system and has set the following standards for materials and labor:
>
> | | |
> |---|---|
> | Leather (3 strips @ $4) | $12.00 |
> | Direct labor (0.75 hr. @ $12) | 9.00 |
> | Total prime cost | $21.00 |
>
> During the first month of the year, the Boise plant produced 92,000 belts. Actual leather purchased was 287,500 strips at $3.60 per strip. There was no beginning or ending inventories of leather. Actual direct labor was 78,200 hours at $12.50 per hour.

Exercise 10-45 Budget Variances, Materials and Labor

OBJECTIVE ▶ 3

Refer to the information for Cinturon Corporation above.

Required:

1. Compute the costs of leather and direct labor that should be incurred for the production of 92,000 leather belts.
2. Compute the total budget variances for materials and labor.
3. **CONCEPTUAL CONNECTION** Would you consider these variances material with a need for investigation? Explain.

Exercise 10-46 Materials Variances

Refer to the information for Cinturon Corporation on the previous page.

EXCEL

Required:

1. Break down the total variance for materials into a price variance and a usage variance using the columnar and formula approaches.
2. **CONCEPTUAL CONNECTION** Suppose the Boise plant manager investigates the materials variances and is told by the purchasing manager that a cheaper source of leather strips had been discovered and that this is the reason for the favorable materials price variance. Quite pleased, the purchasing manager suggests that the materials price standard be updated to reflect this new, less expensive source of leather strips. Should the plant manager update the materials price standard as suggested? Why or why not?

Exercise 10-47 Labor Variances

Refer to the information for Cinturon Corporation on the previous page.

Required:

1. Break down the total variance for labor into a rate variance and an efficiency variance using the columnar and formula approaches.
2. **CONCEPTUAL CONNECTION** As part of the investigation of the unfavorable variances, the plant manager interviews the production manager. The production manager complains strongly about the quality of the leather strips. He indicates that the strips are of lower quality than usual and that workers have to be more careful to avoid a belt with cracks and more time is required. Also, even with extra care, many belts have to be discarded and new ones produced to replace the rejects. This replacement work has also produced some overtime demands. What corrective action should the plant manager take?

Exercise 10-48 Materials Variances

Manzana Company produces apple juice sold in gallons. Recently, the company adopted the following material standard for 1 gallon of its apple juice:

Direct materials 128 oz. @ $0.05 = $6.40

During the first week of operation, the company experienced the following results:

a. Gallon units produced: 20,000.
b. Ounces of materials purchased and used: 2,650,000 ounces at $0.045.
c. No beginning or ending inventories of raw materials.

Required:

1. Compute the materials price variance.
2. Compute the materials usage variance.
3. During the second week, the materials usage variance was $4,000 unfavorable and the materials price variance was $20,000 unfavorable. The company purchased and used 2,000,000 ounces of material during this week. How many gallons of juice were produced, and what was the actual price paid per ounce of materials?

Exercise 10-49 Labor Variances

Verde Company produces wheels for bicycles. During the year, 660,000 wheels were produced. The actual labor used was 360,000 hours at $9.50 per hour. Verde has the following labor standard: 0.5 hour at $10.00.

Required:

1. Compute the labor rate variance.
2. Compute the labor efficiency variance.

Exercise 10-50 Materials and Labor Variances

OBJECTIVE ▶ 3

At the beginning of the year, Craig Company had the following standard cost sheet for one of its plastic products:

Direct materials (5 lbs. @ $4.00)	$20.00
Direct labor (2 hrs. @ $15.00)	30.00
Standard prime cost per unit	$50.00

The actual results for the year are as follows:

a. Units produced: 400,000.
b. Materials purchased: 2,060,000 pounds @ $3.95.
c. Materials used: 2,100,000 pounds.
d. Direct labor: 825,000 hours @ $14.85.

Required:

1. Compute price and usage variances for materials.
2. Compute the labor rate and labor efficiency variances, using both the formula and columnar approaches.

Exercise 10-51 Variances, Evaluation, and Behavior

OBJECTIVE ▶ 1

Jackie Iverson was furious. She was about ready to fire Tom Rich, her purchasing agent. Just a month ago, she had given him a salary increase and a bonus for his performance. She had been especially pleased with his ability to meet or beat the price standards. But now, she found out that it was because of a huge purchase of raw materials. It would take months to use that inventory, and there was hardly space to store it. In the meantime, space had to be found for the other materials supplies that would be ordered and processed on a regular basis. Additionally, it was a lot of capital to tie up in inventory—money that could have been used to help finance the cash needs of the new product just coming online.

Her interview with Tom was frustrating. He was defensive, arguing that he thought she wanted those standards met and that the means were not that important. He also pointed out that quantity purchases were the only way to meet the price standards. Otherwise, an unfavorable variance would have been realized.

Required:

1. **CONCEPTUAL CONNECTION** Why did Tom Rich purchase the large quantity of raw materials? Do you think that this behavior was the objective of the price standard? If not, what is the objective(s)?
2. **CONCEPTUAL CONNECTION** Suppose that Tom is right and that the only way to meet the price standards is through the use of quantity discounts. Also, assume that using quantity discounts is not a desirable practice for this company. What would you do to solve this dilemma?
3. **CONCEPTUAL CONNECTION** Should Tom be fired? Explain.

> *Use the following information for Exercises 10-52 and 10-53:*
> Deporte Company produces single-colored T-shirts. Materials for the shirts are dyed in large vats. After dying the materials for a given color, the vats must be cleaned and prepared for the next batch of materials to be colored. The following standards for changeover for a given batch have been established:
>
> | | |
> |---|---:|
> | Direct materials (2.4 lbs. @ $0.95) | $2.28 |
> | Direct labor (0.75 hr. @ $7.40) | 5.55 |
> | Standard prime cost | $7.83 |
>
> During the year, 79,500 pounds of material were purchased and used for the changeover activity. There were 30,000 batches produced, with the following actual prime costs:
>
> | | |
> |---|---|
> | Direct materials | $ 63,000 |
> | Direct labor | $163,385 (for 22,450 hrs.) |

OBJECTIVE ▶ 3

Exercise 10-52 Materials and Labor Variances

Refer to the information for Deporte Company above.

Required:

Compute the materials and labor variances associated with the changeover activity, labeling each variance as favorable or unfavorable.

OBJECTIVE ▶ 5

Exercise 10-53 *(Appendix 10A)* Journal Entries

Refer to the information for Deporte Company above.

Required:

1. Prepare a journal entry for the purchase of raw materials.
2. Prepare a journal entry for the issuance of raw materials.
3. Prepare a journal entry for the addition of labor to Work in Process.
4. Prepare a journal entry for the closing of variances to Cost of Goods Sold.

OBJECTIVE ▶ 3 ▶ 5

Exercise 10-54 *(Appendix 10A)* Materials Variances, Journal Entries

Esteban Products produces instructional aids, including white boards, which use colored markers instead of chalk. These are particularly popular for conference rooms in educational institutions and executive offices of large corporations. The standard cost of materials for this product is 12 pounds at $8.25 per pound.

During the first month of the year, 3,200 boards were produced. Information concerning actual costs and usage of materials follows:

Materials purchased	38,000 lbs. @ $8.35
Materials used	37,500 lbs.

Required:

1. Compute the materials price and usage variances.
2. Prepare journal entries for all activities relating to materials.

Exercise 10-55 *(Appendix 10A)* Labor Variances, Journal Entries

OBJECTIVE ▸ 3 ▸ 5

Escuchar Products, a producer of DVD players, has established a labor standard for its product—direct labor: 2 hrs at $9.65 per hour. During January, Escuchar produced 12,800 DVD players. The actual direct labor used was 25,040 hours at a total cost of $245,392.

Required:

1. Compute the labor rate and efficiency variances.
2. Prepare journal entries for all activities relating to labor.

Use the following information for Exercises 10-56 and 10-57:

Rostand Inc. operates a delivery service for over 70 restaurants. The corporation has a fleet of vehicles and has invested in a sophisticated, computerized communications system to coordinate its deliveries. Rostand has gathered the following actual data on last year's delivery operations:

Deliveries made	38,600
Direct labor	31,000 direct labor hours @ $14.00
Actual variable overhead	$157,700

Rostand employs a standard costing system. During the year, a variable overhead rate of $5.10 per hour was used. The labor standard requires 0.80 hour per delivery.

Exercise 10-56 Variable Overhead Variances, Service Company

OBJECTIVE ▸ 4

Refer to the information for Rostand Inc. above.

Required:

1. Compute the standard hours allowed for actual deliveries made last year.
2. Compute the variable overhead spending and efficiency variances.

Exercise 10-57 Fixed Overhead Variances

OBJECTIVE ▸ 4

Refer to the information for Rostand Inc. above. Assume that the actual fixed overhead was $403,400. Budgeted fixed overhead was $400,000, based on practical capacity of 32,000 direct labor hours.

Required:

1. Calculate the standard fixed overhead rate based on budgeted fixed overhead and practical capacity.
2. Compute the fixed overhead spending and volume variances.

Exercise 10-58 Overhead Variances

OBJECTIVE ▸ 4

At the beginning of the year, Lopez Company had the following standard cost sheet for one of its chemical products:

EXCEL

Direct materials (4 lbs. @ $2.80)	$11.20
Direct labor (2 hrs. @ $18.00)	36.00
FOH (2 hrs. @ $5.20)	10.40
VOH (2 hrs. @ $0.70)	1.40
Standard cost per unit	$59.00

Lopez computes its overhead rates using practical volume, which is 80,000 units. The actual results for the year are as follows: (a) Units produced: 79,600; (b) Direct labor: 158,900 hours at $18.10; (c) *FOH*: $831,000; and (d) *VOH*: $112,400.

(Continued)

Required:

1. Compute the variable overhead spending and efficiency variances.
2. Compute the fixed overhead spending and volume variances.

OBJECTIVE ▶ 4

Exercise 10-59 Overhead Application, Fixed and Variable Overhead Variances

Zepol Company is planning to produce 600,000 power drills for the coming year. The company uses direct labor hours to assign overhead to products. Each drill requires 0.75 standard hour of labor for completion. The total budgeted overhead was $1,777,500. The total fixed overhead budgeted for the coming year is $832,500. Predetermined overhead rates are calculated using expected production, measured in direct labor hours. Actual results for the year are:

Actual production (units)	594,000	Actual variable overhead	$928,000
Actual direct labor hours (*AH*)	446,000	Actual fixed overhead	$835,600

Required:

1. Compute the applied fixed overhead.
2. Compute the fixed overhead spending and volume variances.
3. Compute the applied variable overhead.
4. Compute the variable overhead spending and efficiency variances.

OBJECTIVE ▶ 4

Exercise 10-60 Understanding Relationships between Overhead Variances, Budgeted Amounts, and Actual Units Produced and Direct Labor Hours Worked

Last year, Gladner Company had planned to produce 140,000 units. However, 143,000 units were actually produced. The company uses direct labor hours to assign overhead to products. Each unit requires 0.9 standard hour of labor for completion. The fixed overhead rate was $11 per direct labor hour, and the variable overhead rate was $6.36 per direct labor hour.

The following variances were computed:

Fixed overhead spending variance	$24,000 *U*	Variable overhead spending variance	$9,196 *U*
Fixed overhead volume variance	29,700 *F*	Variable overhead efficiency variance	1,272 *U*

Required:

1. Calculate the total applied fixed overhead.
2. Calculate the budgeted fixed overhead.
3. Calculate the actual fixed overhead.
4. Calculate the total applied variable overhead.
5. Calculate the number of actual direct labor hours.
6. Calculate the actual variable overhead.

OBJECTIVE ▶ 4

Exercise 10-61 Performance Report for Variable Overhead Variances

Anker Company had the data below for its most recent year, ended December 31:

Actual costs:		Variable overhead standards:	
Indirect labor	$36,000	Indirect labor	0.15 hr. @ $24.00
Supplies	$3,800	Supplies	0.15 hr. @ $2.40
Actual hours worked	1,490 hours	Standard variable overhead rate	$26.40 per direct labor hour
Units produced	10,000 units		
Hours allowed for			
production	1,500 hours		

Required:

Prepare a performance report that shows the variances on an item-by-item basis.

PROBLEMS

Problem 10-62 Setting Standards and Assigning Responsibility

OBJECTIVE ▶ 1

Cabanarama Inc. designs and manufactures easy-to-set-up beach cabanas that families can set up for picnicking, protection from the sun, and so on. The cabanas come in a kit that includes canvas, lacing, and aluminum support poles. Cabanarama has expanded rapidly from a 2-person operation to one involving over a hundred employees. Cabanarama's founder and owner, Frank Love, understands that a more formal approach to standard setting and control is needed to ensure that the consistent quality for which the company is known continues.

Frank and Annette Wilson, his financial vice president, divided the company into departments and designated each department as a cost center. Sales, Quality Control, and Design report directly to Frank. Production, Shipping, Finance, and Accounting report to Annette. In the production department, one of the supervisors was assigned the materials purchasing function. The job included purchasing all raw materials, overseeing inventory handling (receiving, storage, etc.), and tracking materials purchases and use.

Frank felt that control would be better achieved if there were a way for his employees to continue to perform in such a way that quality was maintained and cost reduction was achieved. Annette suggested that Cabanarama institute a standard costing system. Variances for materials and labor could then be calculated and reported directly to her, and she could alert Frank to any problems or opportunities for improvement.

Required:

1. a. **CONCEPTUAL CONNECTION** When Annette designs the standard costing system for Cabanarama, who should be involved in setting the standards for each cost component?
   b. **CONCEPTUAL CONNECTION** What factors should be considered in establishing the standards for each cost component?
2. **CONCEPTUAL CONNECTION** Assume that Cabanarama develops the standards for materials use, materials price, labor use, and labor wages. Who will be assigned responsibility for each and for any resulting variances? Why?

Problem 10-63 Basics of Variance Analysis, Variable Inputs

OBJECTIVE ▶ 2 ▶ 4

Basuras Waste Disposal Company has a long-term contract with several large cities to collect garbage and trash from residential customers. To facilitate the collection, Basuras places a large plastic container with each household. Because of wear and tear, growth, and other factors, Basuras places about 200,000 new containers each year (about 20% of the total households). Several years ago, Basuras decided to manufacture its own containers as a cost-saving measure. A strategically located plant involved in this type of manufacturing was acquired. To help ensure cost efficiency, a standard cost system was installed in the plant. The following standards have been established for the product's variable inputs:

	Standard Quantity	Standard Price (rate in $)	Standard Cost
Direct materials	12 lbs.	$ 3.50	$42.00
Direct labor	1.70 hrs.	11.00	18.70
Variable overhead	1.70 hrs.	3.00	5.10
Total			$65.80

During the first week in January, Basuras had the following actual results:

Units produced	6,000
Actual labor costs	$118,800
Actual labor hours	10,800
Materials purchased and used	69,000 lbs. @ $3.55
Actual variable overhead costs	$39,750

(Continued)

The purchasing agent located a new source of slightly higher-quality plastic, and this material was used during the first week in January. Also, a new manufacturing process was implemented on a trial basis. The new process required a slightly higher level of skilled labor. The higher-quality material has no effect on labor utilization. However, the new manufacturing process was expected to reduce materials usage by 0.25 pound per container.

Required:

1. **CONCEPTUAL CONNECTION** Compute the materials price and usage variances. Assume that the 0.25 pound per container reduction of materials occurred as expected and that the remaining effects are all attributable to the higher-quality material. Would you recommend that the purchasing agent continue to buy this quality, or should the usual quality be purchased? Assume that the quality of the end product is not affected significantly.

2. **CONCEPTUAL CONNECTION** Compute the labor rate and efficiency variances. Assuming that the labor variances are attributable to the new manufacturing process, should it be continued or discontinued? In answering, consider the new process's materials reduction effect as well. Explain.

3. **CONCEPTUAL CONNECTION** Refer to Requirement 2. Suppose that the industrial engineer argued that the new process should not be evaluated after only one week. His reasoning was that it would take at least a week for the workers to become efficient with the new approach. Suppose that the production is the same the second week and that the actual labor hours were 9,000 and the labor cost was $99,000. Should the new process be adopted? Assume the variances are attributable to the new process. Assuming production of 6,000 units per week, what would be the projected annual savings? (Include the materials reduction effect.)

OBJECTIVE ▶ 1 ▶ 3

Problem 10-64 Setting Standards, Materials and Labor Variances

Tom Belford and Tony Sorrentino own a small business devoted to kitchen and bath granite installations. Recently, building contractors have insisted on up-front bid prices for a house rather than the cost-plus system that Tom and Tony had been using. They worry because natural flaws in the granite make it impossible to tell in advance exactly how much granite will be used on a particular job. In addition, granite can be easily broken, meaning that Tom or Tony could ruin a slab and would need to start over with a new one. Sometimes the improperly cut pieces could be used for smaller installations, sometimes not. All their accounting is done by a local certified public accounting firm headed by Charlene Davenport. Charlene listened to their concerns and suggested that it might be time to implement tighter controls by setting up a standard costing system.

Charlene reviewed the invoices pertaining to a number of Tom and Tony's previous jobs to determine the average amount of granite and glue needed per square foot. She then updated prices on both materials to reflect current conditions. The standards she developed for 1 square foot of counter installed were as follows:

Granite, per square foot	$50.00
Glue (10 oz. @ $0.15)	1.50
Direct labor hours:	
Cutting labor (0.10 hr. @ $15)	1.50
Installation labor (0.25 hr. @ $25)	6.25

These standards assumed that one seamless counter requires one sink cut (the space into which the sink will fit) as well as cutting the counter to fit the space available.

Charlene tracked the actual costs incurred by Tom and Tony for granite installation for the next 6 months. She found that they completed 50 jobs with an average of 32 square feet of granite installed in each one. The following information on actual amounts used and cost was gathered:

Granite purchased and used (1,640 sq. ft.)	$79,048
Glue purchased and used (16,000 oz.)	$2,560
Actual hours cutting labor	180
Actual hours installation labor	390

The actual wage rate for cutting and installation labor remained unchanged from the standard rate.

Required:

1. Calculate the materials price variances and materials usage variances for granite and glue for the past 6 months.
2. Calculate the labor rate variances and labor efficiency variances for cutting labor and installation labor for the past 6 months.
3. **CONCEPTUAL CONNECTION** Would it be worthwhile for Charlene to establish standards for atypical jobs (such as those with more than one sink cut or a wider than normal sink)?

Problem 10-65 Setting a Direct Labor Standard, Learning Curve Effects, Service Company

OBJECTIVE ◀ 1 ◀ 3

Mantenga Company provides routine maintenance services for heavy moving and transportation vehicles. Although the vehicles vary, the maintenance services provided follow a fairly standard pattern. Recently, a potential customer has approached the company, requesting a new maintenance service for a radically different type of vehicle. New servicing equipment and some new labor skills will be needed to provide the maintenance service. The customer is placing an initial order to service 150 vehicles and has indicated that if the service is satisfactory, several additional orders of the same size will be placed every 3 months over the next 3 to 5 years.

Mantenga uses a standard costing system and wants to develop a set of standards for the new vehicle. The usage standards for direct materials such as oil, lubricants, and transmission fluids were easily established. The usage standard is 25 quarts per servicing, with a standard cost of $4 per quart. Management has also decided on standard rates for labor and overhead. The standard labor rate is $15 per direct labor hour, the standard variable overhead rate is $8 per direct labor hour, and the standard fixed overhead rate is $12 per direct labor hour. The only remaining decision is the standard for labor usage. To assist in developing this standard, the engineering department has estimated the following relationship between units serviced and average direct labor hours used:

Units Serviced	Cumulative Average Time per Unit (hours)
40	2.500
80	2.000
160	1.600
320	1.280
640	1.024

As the workers learn more about servicing the new vehicles, they become more efficient, and the average time needed to service one unit declines. Engineering estimates that all of the learning effects will be achieved by the time that 320 units are produced. No further improvement will be realized past this level.

Required:

1. Assume that the average labor time is 0.768 hour per unit after the learning effects are achieved. Using this information, prepare a standard cost sheet that details the standard service cost per unit. (*Note:* Round costs to two decimal places.)
2. **CONCEPTUAL CONNECTION** Given the per-unit labor standard set, would you expect a favorable or an unfavorable labor efficiency? Explain. Calculate the labor efficiency variance for servicing the first 320 units.

(*Continued*)

3. **CONCEPTUAL CONNECTION** Assuming no further improvement in labor time per unit is possible past 320 units, explain why the cumulative average time per unit at 640 units is lower than the time at 320 units. Show that the standard labor time should be 0.768 hour per unit. Explain why this value is a good choice for the per-unit labor standard.

OBJECTIVE 1 3

EXCEL

Problem 10-66 Unit Costs, Multiple Products, Variance Analysis, Service Setting

The maternity wing of the city hospital has two types of patients: normal and cesarean. The standard quantities of labor and materials per delivery for 20X1 are:

	Normal	Cesarean
Direct materials (lbs.)	9.0	21.0
Nursing labor (hrs.)	2.5	5.0

The standard price paid per pound of direct materials is $10.00. The standard rate for labor is $16.00. Overhead is applied on the basis of direct labor hours. The variable overhead rate for maternity is $30.00 per hour, and the fixed overhead rate is $40.00 per hour.

Actual operating data for 20X1 are as follows:

a. Deliveries produced: normal, 4,000; cesarean, 8,000.
b. Direct materials purchased and used: 200,000 pounds at $9.50—35,000 for normal maternity patients and 165,000 for the cesarean patients; no beginning or ending raw materials inventories.
c. Nursing labor: 50,700 hours—10,200 hours for normal patients and 40,500 hours for the cesarean; total cost of labor, $580,350.

Required:

1. Prepare a standard cost sheet showing the unit cost per delivery for each type of patient.
2. Compute the materials price and usage variances for each type of patient.
3. Compute the labor rate and efficiency variances for each type of patient.
4. **CONCEPTUAL CONNECTION** Assume that you know only the total direct materials used for both products and the total direct labor hours used for both products. Can you compute the total materials usage and labor efficiency variances? Explain.
5. **CONCEPTUAL CONNECTION** Standard costing concepts have been applied in the healthcare industry. For example, diagnostic-related groups (DRGs) are used for prospective payments for Medicare patients. Select a search engine (such as Yahoo! or Google), and conduct a search to see what information you can obtain about DRGs. You might try "Medicare DRGs" as a possible search topic. Write a memo that answers the following questions:
   a. What is a DRG?
   b. How are DRGs established?
   c. How many DRGs are used?
   d. How does the DRG concept relate to standard costing concepts discussed in the chapter? Can hospitals use DRGs to control their costs? Explain.

OBJECTIVE 2 3

Problem 10-67 Control Limits, Variance Investigation

Buenolorl Company produces a well-known cologne. The standard manufacturing cost of the cologne is described by the following standard cost sheet:

Direct materials:	
Liquids (4.5 oz. @ $0.40)	$1.80
Bottles (1 @ $0.05)	0.05
Direct labor (0.2 hr. @ $15.00)	3.00
Variable overhead (0.2 hr. @ $5.00)	1.00
Fixed overhead (0.2 hr. @ $1.50)	0.30
Standard cost per unit	$6.15

Management has decided to investigate only those variances that exceed the lesser of 10% of the standard cost for each category or $20,000.

During the past quarter, 250,000 four-ounce bottles of cologne were produced. Descriptions of actual activity for the quarter follow:

a. A total of 1.35 million ounces of liquids was purchased, mixed, and processed. Evaporation was higher than expected. (No inventories of liquids are maintained.) The price paid per ounce averaged $0.42.
b. Exactly 250,000 bottles were used. The price paid for each bottle was $0.048.
c. Direct labor hours totaled 48,250, with a total cost of $733,000.

Normal production volume for Buenolorl is 250,000 bottles per quarter. The standard overhead rates are computed by using normal volume. All overhead costs are incurred uniformly throughout the year. (*Note:* Round unit costs to the nearest cent and total amounts to the nearest dollar.)

Required:

1. Calculate the upper and lower control limits for materials and labor.
2. Compute the total materials variance, and break it into price and usage variances. Would these variances be investigated?
3. Compute the total labor variance, and break it into rate and efficiency variances. Would these variances be investigated?

Problem 10-68 Control Limits, Variance Investigation   OBJECTIVE ▶ **2** ▶ **3**

The management of Golding Company has determined that the cost to investigate a variance produced by its standard cost system ranges from $2,000 to $3,000. If a problem is discovered, the average benefit from taking corrective action usually outweighs the cost of investigation. Past experience from the investigation of variances has revealed that corrective action is rarely needed for deviations within 8% of the standard cost. Golding produces a single product, which has the following standards for materials and labor:

Direct materials (8 lbs. @ $0.25)	$2	
Direct labor (0.4 hr. @ $7.50)	3	

Actual production for the past 3 months follows, with the associated actual usage and costs for materials and labor. There were no beginning or ending raw materials inventories.

	April	May	June
Production (units)	90,000	100,000	110,000
Direct materials:			
Cost	$189,000	$218,000	$230,000
Usage (lbs.)	723,000	870,000	885,000
Direct labor:			
Cost	$270,000	$323,000	$360,000
Usage (hrs.)	36,000	44,000	46,000

Required:

1. What upper and lower control limits would you use for materials variances? For labor variances?
2. Compute the materials and labor variances for April, May, and June. Identify those that would require investigation by comparing each variance to the amount of the limit computed in Requirement 1. Compute the actual percentage deviation from standard. Round all unit costs to four decimal places. Round variances to the nearest dollar. Round variance rates to three decimal places so that percentages will show to one decimal place.

(Continued)

3. **CONCEPTUAL CONNECTION** Let the horizontal axis be time and the vertical axis be variances measured as a percentage deviation from standard. Draw horizontal lines that identify upper and lower control limits. Plot the labor and material variances for April, May, and June. Prepare a separate graph for each type of variance. Explain how you would use these graphs (called *control charts*) to assist your analysis of variances.

OBJECTIVE **1** **3**

EXCEL

Problem 10-69 Standard Costing, Planned Variances

Phono Company manufactures a plastic toy cell phone. The following standards have been established for the toy's materials and labor inputs:

	Standard Quantity	Standard Price (rate in $)	Standard Cost
Direct materials	0.5 lb.	$ 1.50	$0.75
Direct labor	0.15 hr.	10.00	1.50

During the first week of July, the company had the following results:

Units produced	90,000
Actual labor costs	$138,000
Actual labor hours	13,400
Materials purchased and used	44,250 lbs. @ $1.55 per lb.

The purchasing agent located a new source of slightly higher-quality plastic, and this material was used during the first week in July. Also, a new manufacturing layout was implemented on a trial basis. The new layout required a slightly higher level of skilled labor. The higher-quality material has no effect on labor utilization. Similarly, the new manufacturing approach has no effect on material usage. (*Note:* Round all variances to the nearest dollar.)

Required:

1. **CONCEPTUAL CONNECTION** Compute the materials price and usage variances. Assuming that the materials variances are essentially attributable to the higher quality of materials, would you recommend that the purchasing agent continue to buy this quality, or should the usual quality be purchased? Assume that the quality of the end product is not affected significantly.
2. **CONCEPTUAL CONNECTION** Compute the labor rate and efficiency variances. Assuming that the labor variances are attributable to the new manufacturing layout, should it be continued or discontinued? Explain.
3. **CONCEPTUAL CONNECTION** Refer to Requirement 2. Suppose that the industrial engineer argued that the new layout should not be evaluated after only one week. His reasoning was that it would take at least a week for the workers to become efficient with the new approach. Suppose that the production is the same the second week and that the actual labor hours were 13,200 and the labor cost was $132,000. Should the new layout be adopted? Assume the variances are attributable to the new layout. If so, what would be the projected annual savings?

OBJECTIVE **1** **3**

EXCEL

Problem 10-70 Standard Costing

Botella Company produces plastic bottles. The unit for costing purposes is a case of 18 bottles. The following standards for producing one case of bottles have been established:

Direct materials (4 lbs. @ $0.95)	$ 3.80
Direct labor (1.25 hrs. @ $15.00)	18.75
Standard prime cost	$22.55

During December, 78,000 pounds of materials were purchased and used in production. There were 15,000 cases produced, with the following actual prime costs:

Direct materials	$74,000
Direct labor	$315,000 (for 22,500 hrs.)

Required:

1. Compute the materials variances.
2. Compute the labor variances.
3. **CONCEPTUAL CONNECTION** What are the advantages and disadvantages that can result from the use of a standard costing system?

Problem 10-71 *(Appendix 10A)* Variance Analysis, Revision of Standards, Journal Entries

OBJECTIVE 3 5

The Lubbock plant of Morril's Small Motor Division produces a major subassembly for a 6.0 horsepower motor for lawnmowers. The plant uses a standard costing system for production costing and control. The standard cost sheet for the subassembly follows:

Direct materials (6.0 lbs. @ $5)	$30.00
Direct labor (1.6 hrs. @ $12)	19.20

During the year, the Lubbock plant had the following actual production activity:
a. Production of subassemblies totaled 50,000 units.
b. A total of 260,000 pounds of raw materials was purchased at $4.70 per pound.
c. There were 60,000 pounds of raw materials in beginning inventory (carried at $5 per lb.). There was no ending inventory.
d. The company used 82,000 direct labor hours at a total cost of $1,066,000.
The Lubbock plant's practical activity is 60,000 units per year. Standard overhead rates are computed based on practical activity measured in standard direct labor hours.

Required:

1. **CONCEPTUAL CONNECTION** Compute the materials price and usage variances. Of the two materials variances, which is viewed as the more controllable? To whom would you assign responsibility for the usage variance in this case? Explain.
2. **CONCEPTUAL CONNECTION** Compute the labor rate and efficiency variances. Who is usually responsible for the labor efficiency variance? What are some possible causes for this variance?
3. **CONCEPTUAL CONNECTION** Assume that the purchasing agent for the small motors plant purchased a lower-quality raw material from a new supplier. Would you recommend that the plant continue to use this cheaper raw material? If so, what standards would likely need revision to reflect this decision? Assume that the end product's quality is not significantly affected.
4. Prepare all possible journal entries.

Problem 10-72 Overhead Application, Overhead Variances

OBJECTIVE 4

Moleno Company produces a single product and uses a standard cost system. The normal production volume is 120,000 units; each unit requires 5 direct labor hours at standard. Overhead is applied on the basis of direct labor hours. The budgeted overhead for the coming year is as follows:

FOH	$2,160,000*
VOH	1,440,000
*At normal volume.	

(*Continued*)

During the year, Moleno produced 118,600 units, worked 592,300 direct labor hours, and incurred actual fixed overhead costs of $2,150,400 and actual variable overhead costs of $1,422,800.

Required:

1. Calculate the standard fixed overhead rate and the standard variable overhead rate.
2. Compute the applied fixed overhead and the applied variable overhead. What is the total fixed overhead variance? Total variable overhead variance?
3. **CONCEPTUAL CONNECTION** Break down the total fixed overhead variance into a spending variance and a volume variance. Discuss the significance of each.
4. **CONCEPTUAL CONNECTION** Compute the variable overhead spending and efficiency variances. Discuss the significance of each.

OBJECTIVE 4

EXCEL

Problem 10-73 Overhead Variance Analysis

The Lubbock plant of Morril's Small Motor Division produces a major subassembly for a 6.0 horsepower motor for lawn mowers. The plant uses a standard costing system for production costing and control. The standard cost sheet for the subassembly follows:

Direct materials (6.0 lbs. @ $5.00)	$30.00
Direct labor (1.6 hrs. @ $12.00)	19.20
VOH (1.6 hrs. @ $10.00)	16.00
FOH (1.6 hrs. @ $6.00)	9.60
Standard unit cost	$74.80

During the year, the Lubbock plant had the following actual production activity: (a) Production of motors totaled 50,000 units. (b) The company used 82,000 direct labor hours at a total cost of $1,066,000. (c) Actual fixed overhead totaled $556,000. (d) Actual variable overhead totaled $860,000.

The Lubbock plant's practical activity is 60,000 units per year. Standard overhead rates are computed based on practical activity measured in standard direct labor hours.

Required:

1. Compute the variable overhead spending and efficiency variances.
2. **CONCEPTUAL CONNECTION** Compute the fixed overhead spending and volume variances. Interpret the volume variance. What can be done to reduce this variance?

OBJECTIVE 2 3

Problem 10-74 Overhead Variances

Extrim Company produces monitors. Extrim's plant in San Antonio uses a standard costing system. The standard costing system relies on direct labor hours to assign overhead costs to production. The direct labor standard indicates that 4 direct labor hours should be used for every monitor produced. (The San Antonio plant produces only one model.) The normal production volume is 120,000 units. The budgeted overhead for the coming year is as follows:

FOH	$1,286,400
VOH	888,000*
*At normal volume.	

Extrim applies overhead on the basis of direct labor hours.

During the year, Extrim produced 119,000 units, worked 487,900 direct labor hours, and incurred actual fixed overhead costs of $1.3 million and actual variable overhead costs of $927,010.

Required:

1. Calculate the standard fixed overhead rate and the standard variable overhead rate.
2. Compute the applied fixed overhead and the applied variable overhead. What is the total fixed overhead variance? Total variable overhead variance?
3. **CONCEPTUAL CONNECTION** Break down the total fixed overhead variance into a spending variance and a volume variance. Discuss the significance of each.
4. **CONCEPTUAL CONNECTION** Compute the variable overhead spending and efficiency variances. Discuss the significance of each.

Problem 10-75 Understanding Relationships, Incomplete Data, Overhead Analysis

OBJECTIVE ▶ 4

Lynwood Company produces surge protectors. To help control costs, Lynwood employs a standard costing system and uses a flexible budget to predict overhead costs at various levels of activity. For the most recent year, Lynwood used a standard overhead rate of $18 per direct labor hour. The rate was computed using practical activity. Budgeted overhead costs are $396,000 for 18,000 direct labor hours and $540,000 for 30,000 direct labor hours. During the past year, Lynwood generated the following data: (a) Actual production: 100,000 units; (b) Fixed overhead volume variance: $20,000 U; (c) Variable overhead efficiency variance: $18,000 F; (d) Actual fixed overhead costs: $200,000; and (e) Actual variable overhead costs: $310,000.

Required:

1. Calculate the fixed overhead rate.
2. Determine the fixed overhead spending variance.
3. Determine the variable overhead spending variance.
4. Determine the standard hours allowed per unit of product.

Problem 10-76 Flexible Budget, Overhead Variances

OBJECTIVE ▶ 4

Shumaker Company manufactures a line of high-top basketball shoes. At the beginning of the year, the following plans for production and costs were revealed:

Pairs of shoes to be produced and sold	55,000
Standard cost per unit:	
Direct materials	$15
Direct labor	12
VOH	6
FOH	3
Total unit cost	$36

During the year, a total of 50,000 units were produced and sold. The following actual costs were incurred:

Direct materials	$775,000	VOH	$310,000
Direct labor	590,000	FOH	180,000

There were no beginning or ending inventories of raw materials. In producing the 50,000 units, 63,000 hours were worked, 5% more hours than the standard allowed for the actual output. Overhead costs are applied to production using direct labor hours.

Required:

1. Using a flexible budget, prepare a performance report comparing expected costs for the actual production with actual costs.
2. Determine the following: (a) Fixed overhead spending and volume variances and (b) Variable overhead spending and efficiency variances.

CASES

OBJECTIVE 1 ▶ 3

Case 10-77   Establishment of Standards, Variance Analysis

Paul Golding and his wife, Nancy, established Crunchy Chips in 1938. Over the past 60 years, the company has established distribution channels in 11 western states, with production facilities in Utah, New Mexico, and Colorado. In 1980, Paul's son, Edward, took control of the business. By 2017, it was clear that the company's plants needed to gain better control over production costs to stay competitive. Edward hired a consultant to install a standard costing system. To help the consultant establish the necessary standards, Edward sent her the following memo:

To:	Diana Craig, Certified Management Accountant
From:	Edward Golding, President, Crunchy Chips
Subject:	Description and Data Relating to the Production of Our Plain Potato Chips
Date:	September 28, 2017

The manufacturing process for potato chips begins when the potatoes are placed into a large vat in which they are automatically washed. After washing, the potatoes flow directly to an automatic peeler. The peeled potatoes then pass by inspectors, who manually cut out deep eyes or other blemishes. After inspection, the potatoes are automatically sliced and dropped into the cooking oil. The frying process is closely monitored by an employee. After the chips are cooked, they pass under a salting device and then pass by more inspectors, who sort out the unacceptable finished chips (those that are discolored or too small). The chips then continue on the conveyor belt to a bagging machine that bags them in 1-pound bags. After bagging, the bags are placed in a box and shipped. The box holds 15 bags.

The raw potato pieces (eyes and blemishes), peelings, and rejected finished chips are sold to animal feed producers for $0.16 per pound. The company uses this revenue to reduce the cost of potatoes. We would like this reflected in the price standard relating to potatoes.

Crunchy Chips purchases high-quality potatoes at a cost of $0.245 per pound. Each potato averages 4.25 ounces. Under efficient operating conditions, it takes four potatoes to produce one 16-ounce bag of plain chips. Although we label bags as containing 16 ounces, we actually place 16.3 ounces in each bag. We plan to continue this policy to ensure customer satisfaction. In addition to potatoes, other raw materials are the cooking oil, salt, bags, and boxes. Cooking oil costs $0.04 per ounce, and we use 3.3 ounces of oil per bag of chips. The cost of salt is so small that we add it to overhead. Bags cost $0.11 each and boxes $0.52 each.

Our plant produces 8.8 million bags of chips per year. A recent engineering study revealed that we would need the following direct labor hours to produce this quantity if our plant operates at peak efficiency:

Raw potato inspection	3,200
Finished chip inspection	12,000
Frying monitor	6,300
Boxing	16,600
Machine operators	6,300

I'm not sure that we can achieve the level of efficiency advocated by the study. In my opinion, the plant is operating efficiently for the level of output indicated if the hours allowed are about 10% higher.

The hourly labor rates agreed upon with the union are:

Raw potato inspectors	$15.20
Finished chip inspectors	10.30
Frying monitor	14.00
Boxing	11.00
Machine operators	13.00

Overhead is applied on the basis of direct labor dollars. We have found that variable overhead averages about 116% of our direct labor cost. Our fixed overhead is budgeted at $1,135,216 for the coming year.

Required:

1. Discuss the benefits of a standard costing system for Crunchy Chips.
2. Discuss the president's concern about using the result of the engineering study to set the labor standards. What standard would you recommend?
3. Form a group with two or three other students. Develop a standard cost sheet for Crunchy Chips' plain potato chips. Round all computations to four decimal places.
4. Suppose that the level of production was 8.8 million bags of potato chips for the year as planned. If 9.5 million pounds of potatoes were used, compute the materials usage variance for potatoes.

Case 10-78 Standard Costing, Ethical Behavior, Usefulness of Costing

OBJECTIVE ▶ 1 ◀ 2 ◀ 3

Pat James, the purchasing agent for a local plant of the Oakden Electronics Division, was considering the possible purchase of a component from a new supplier. The component's purchase price, $0.90, compared favorably with the standard price of $1.10. Given the quantity that would be purchased, Pat knew that the favorable price variance would help to offset an unfavorable variance for another component. By offsetting the unfavorable variance, his overall performance report would be impressive and good enough to help him qualify for the annual bonus. More importantly, a good performance rating this year would help him to secure a position at division headquarters at a significant salary increase.

Purchase of the part, however, presented Pat with a dilemma. Consistent with his past behavior, Pat made inquiries regarding the reliability of the new supplier and the part's quality. Reports were basically negative. The supplier had a reputation for making the first two or three deliveries on schedule but being unreliable from then on. Worse, the part itself was of questionable quality. The number of defective units was only slightly higher than that for other suppliers, but the life of the component was 25% less than what normal sources provided.

If the part were purchased, no problems with deliveries would surface for several months. The problem of shorter life would cause eventual customer dissatisfaction and perhaps some loss of sales, but the part would last at least 18 months after the final product began to be used. If all went well, Pat expected to be at headquarters within 6 months. He saw little personal risk associated with a decision to purchase the part from the new supplier. By the time any problems surfaced, they would belong to his successor. With this rationalization, Pat decided to purchase the component from the new supplier.

Required:

1. Do you agree with Pat's decision? Why or why not? How important was Pat's assessment of his personal risk in the decision? Should it be a factor?
2. Do you think that the use of standards and the practice of holding individuals accountable for their achievement played major roles in Pat's decision?
3. Review the discussion on corporate ethical standards in Chapter 1. Identify the standards that might apply to Pat's situation. Should every company adopt a set of ethical standards that apply to its employees, regardless of their specialty?
4. The usefulness of standard costing has been challenged in recent years. Some claim that its use is an impediment to the objective of continuous improvement (an objective that many feel is vital in today's competitive environment). Write a short paper (individually or in a

(Continued)

small group with two or three other students) that analyzes the role and value of standard costing in today's manufacturing environment. Address the following questions:

a. What are the major criticisms of standard costing?
b. Will standard costing disappear, or is there still a role for it in the new manufacturing environment? If so, what is the role?
c. Given the criticisms, can you explain why its use continues to be so prevalent? Will this use eventually change?

In preparing your paper, the following references may be useful; however, do not restrict your literature search to these references. They are simply to help you get started.

- Robin Cooper and Robert S. Kaplan, "Activity-Based Systems: Measuring the Costs of Resource Usage," *Accounting Horizons* (September 1992): 1–13.
- Forrest B. Green and Felix E. Amenkhienan, "Accounting Innovations: A Cross-Sectional Survey of Manufacturing Firms," *Journal of Cost Management* (Spring 1992): 59–64.
- Bruce R. Gaumnitz and Felix P. Kollaritsch, "Manufacturing Variances: Current Practice and Trends," *Journal of Cost Management* (Spring 1991): 59–64.
- Chris Guilding, Dane Lamminmaki, and Colin Drury, "Budgeting and Standard Costing Practices in New Zealand and the United Kingdom," *Journal of International Accounting, Vol.* 33, No. 5 (1998): 569–588.

OBJECTIVE **4**   **Case 10-79** Fixed Overhead Spending and Volume Variances, Capacity Management

Lorale Company, a producer of recreational vehicles, recently decided to begin producing a major subassembly for jet skis. The subassembly would be used by Lorale's jet ski plants and also would be sold to other producers. The decision was made to lease two large buildings in two different locations: Little Rock, Arkansas, and Athens, Georgia. The company agreed to an 11-year, renewable lease contract. The plants were of the same size, and each had 10 production lines. New equipment was purchased for each line, and workers were hired to operate the equipment. The company also hired production line supervisors for each plant. A supervisor is capable of directing up to two production lines per shift. Two shifts are run for each plant. The practical production capacity of each plant is 300,000 subassemblies per year. Two standard direct labor hours are allowed for each subassembly. The costs for leasing, equipment depreciation, and supervision for a single plant are as follows (the costs are assumed to be the same for each plant):

Supervision (10 supervisors @ $50,000)	$ 500,000
Building lease (annual payment)	800,000
Equipment depreciation (annual)	1,100,000
Total fixed overhead costs*	$2,400,000

*For simplicity, assume these are the only fixed overhead costs.

After beginning operations, Lorale discovered that demand for the product in the region covered by the Little Rock plant was less than anticipated. At the end of the first year, only 240,000 units were sold. The Athens plant sold 300,000 units as expected. The actual fixed overhead costs at the end of the first year were $2,500,000 (for each plant).

Required:

1. Calculate a fixed overhead rate based on standard direct labor hours.
2. Calculate the fixed overhead spending and volume variances for the Little Rock and Athens plants. What is the most likely cause of the spending variance? Why are the volume variances different for the two plants?
3. Suppose that from now on the sales for the Little Rock plant are expected to be no more than 240,000 units. What actions would you take to manage the capacity costs (fixed overhead costs)?
4. Calculate the fixed overhead cost per subassembly for each plant. Do they differ? Should they differ? Explain. Do ABC concepts help in analyzing this issue?

Making the Connection | INTEGRATIVE EXERCISE (CHAPTERS 5, 9, and 10)

Cost System Choices, Budgeting, and Variance Analyses for Sacred Heart Hospital

Chapters	Objectives	Examples
5	5-1	5-2
9	5-2	5-3
10	5-4	10-1
	9-1	10-3
	10-1	10-4
	10-3	10-5
	10-4	10-6
	10-5	

The purpose of this integrated exercise is to demonstrate how a change in the cost system's allocation base can result in significantly different reported costs for control purposes (e.g., the cost of various service lines), as well as significantly different budgeted costs for planning purposes (e.g., flexible budgets and variance analyses).

The Two Cost Systems

Sacred Heart Hospital (SHH) faces skyrocketing nursing costs, all of which relate to its two biggest nursing service lines—the Emergency Room (ER) and the Operating Room (OR). SHH's current cost system assigns total nursing costs to the ER and OR based on the number of patients serviced by each line. Total hospital annual nursing costs for these two lines are expected to equal $300,000. The table below shows expected patient volume for both lines.

Measure	ER	OR	Total
Number of patients (ER visits or OR surgeries)	1,000	1,000	2,000
Number of vital signs checks	2,000	4,000	6,000
Number of nursing hours	10,000	5,000	15,000

Required:

1. Using the current cost system, calculate the hospital-wide rate based on number of patients.

2. Calculate the amount of nursing costs that the current cost system assigns to the ER and to the OR.

3. Using the results from Requirement 2, calculate the cost per OR nursing hour under the current cost system.

After discussion with several experienced nurses, Jack Bauer (SHH's accountant) decided that assigning nursing costs to the two service lines based on the number of times that nurses must check patients' vital signs might more closely match the underlying use of costly hospital resources. Therefore, for comparative purposes, Jack decided to develop a second cost system that assigns total nursing costs to the ER and OR based on the number of times nurses check patients' vital signs. This system is referred to as the "vital-signs costing system." The earlier table also shows data for vital signs checks for lines.

4. Using the vital-signs costing system, calculate the hospital-wide rate based on the number of vital signs checks.

5. Calculate the amount of nursing costs that the vital-signs costing system assigns to the ER and to the OR.

6. Using the results from Requirement 5, calculate the cost per OR nursing hour under the vital-signs costing system.

Budgeting and Variance Analysis

In an effort to better plan for and control OR costs, SHH management asked Jack to calculate the flexible budget variance (i.e., flexible budget costs - actual costs) for OR nursing costs, including the price variance and efficiency variance. Given that Jack is interested in comparing the reported costs of both systems, he decided to prepare the requested OR variance analysis for both the current cost system and the vital-signs costing system. In addition, Jack chose to use each cost system's estimate of the cost per OR nursing hour as the standard cost per OR nursing hour. Jack collected the following additional information for use in preparing the flexible budget variance for both systems:

Actual number of surgeries performed = 950
Standard number of nursing hours allowed for each OR surgery = 5
Actual number of OR nursing hours used = 5,000
Actual OR nursing costs = $190,000

7. For the OR service line, use the information above and the cost per OR nursing hour under the current cost system to calculate the

   a. flexible budget variance. (*Hint:* Use your answer to Requirement 3 as the standard cost per OR nursing hour for the current cost system.)
   b. price variance.
   c. efficiency variance.

8. For the OR service line, use the information above and the cost per OR nursing hour under the vital-signs costing system to calculate the

   a. flexible budget variance. (*Hint:* Use your answer to Requirement 6 as the standard cost per OR nursing hour for the vital-signs costing system.)
   b. price variance.
   c. efficiency variance.

Discussion of Reported Costs and Variances from the Two Systems

9. Consider SHH's need to control its skyrocketing costs, Jack's discussion with experienced nurses regarding their use of hospital resources, and the reported costs that you calculated from each cost system. Based on these considerations, which cost system (current or vital-signs) should Jack choose? Briefly explain the reasoning behind your choice.

10. What does each of the calculated variances suggest to Jack regarding actions that he should or should not take with respect to investigating and improving each variance? Also, briefly explain why the variances differ between the two cost systems.

11

Performance Evaluation and Decentralization

After studying Chapter 11, you should be able to:

1. ▸ Explain how and why firms choose to decentralize.

2. ▸ Compute and explain return on investment.

3. ▸ Compute and explain residual income and economic value added.

4. ▸ Explain the role of transfer pricing in a decentralized firm.

5. ▸ *(Appendix 11A)* Explain the uses of the Balanced Scorecard, and compute cycle time, velocity, and manufacturing cycle efficiency.

Courtesy Herman Miller, Inc.

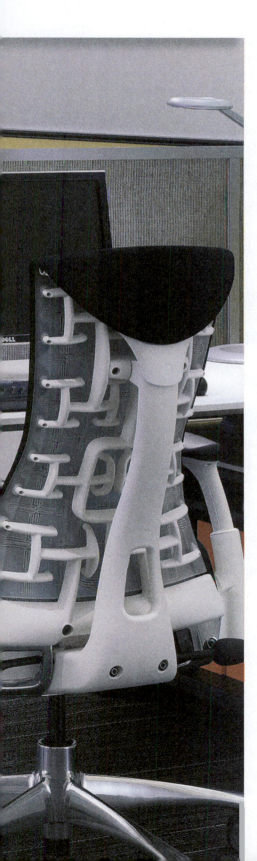

EXPERIENCE MANAGERIAL DECISIONS

with Herman Miller

The goal of performance evaluation is to provide information useful for assessing the effectiveness of past decisions so that future decisions can be improved. As you might guess, this goal is difficult to achieve because of the sheer quantity of information present in organizations and the complexity of the business environment in which most decisions are made. However, **Herman Miller, Inc.,** a large furniture manufacturer headquartered in western Michigan with business activities in over 100 countries, uses an increasingly popular performance evaluation technique—economic value added (EVA)—to help it make better decisions. For example, the entire office furniture market experienced a devastating slump in the early 2000s as a result of the dot-com bust and the 9/11 disaster. EVA measures provided Herman Miller with information beyond traditional accounting performance metrics that was critical to its dramatic and quick recovery from the negative operating margins it experienced during the slump to the near double-digit positive margins it enjoyed only a few years later. EVA identifies the return generated by the company's assets and then subtracts the cost of all capital, both debt (e.g., money raised from loans, leases, and bonds) and equity (e.g., money raised from investors), used by the company to finance those assets in order to determine whether value is being created or destroyed. More specifically, EVA helps Herman Miller to quantify the long-term financial benefits of carrying less inventory and employing fewer fixed assets in its business. As a result of such EVA analyses, Herman Miller makes fundamentally different strategic and operating decisions involving its furniture production processes than it would if it relied solely on traditional accounting metrics. The ability to impact decisions in such a positive fashion has catapulted EVA into a position of prominence in Herman Miller's successful performance evaluation system.

> "Herman Miller, Inc., a large furniture manufacturer headquartered in western Michigan with business activities in over 100 countries, uses an increasingly popular performance evaluation technique—economic value added—to help it make better decisions."

OBJECTIVE **1**

Explain how and why firms choose to decentralize.

DECENTRALIZATION AND RESPONSIBILITY CENTERS

In general, a company is organized along lines of responsibility. Traditional organizational charts illustrate the flow of responsibilities from the chief executive officer down through the vice presidents to middle- and lower-level managers. Today, most companies use a flattened hierarchy—emphasizing teams. This structure is consistent with decentralization. **GE Capital**, for example, is essentially a group of smaller businesses. Ideally, the responsibility accounting system mirrors and supports the structure of an organization.

Firms with multiple responsibility centers usually choose one of two decision-making approaches to manage their diverse and complex activities: *centralized* or *decentralized*.

- In centralized decision making, decisions are made at the very top level, and lower-level managers are charged with implementing these decisions.
- Decentralized decision making allows managers at lower levels to make and implement key decisions pertaining to their areas of responsibility. This practice of delegating decision-making authority to lower levels of management is called **decentralization**.

Exhibit 11.1 illustrates the difference between centralized and decentralized companies.

Exhibit 11.1

Centralization and Decentralization

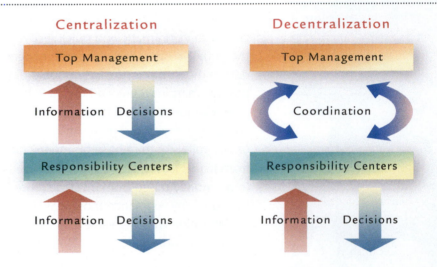

Organizations range from highly centralized to strongly decentralized. Most firms fall somewhere in between, with the majority tending toward decentralization. The reasons for the popularity of decentralization and the ways in which a company may choose to decentralize are discussed next.

Reasons for Decentralization

Firms decide to decentralize for several reasons, including the following:

- ease of gathering and using local information
- focusing of central management
- training and motivating of segment managers
- enhanced competition, exposing segments to market forces

Gathering and Using Local Information The quality of decisions is affected by the quality of information available. As a firm grows and operates in different markets and regions, central management may not understand local conditions. Lower-level managers, however, are in contact with immediate operating conditions (such as the strength and nature of local competition, the nature of the local labor force, and so on). As a result, they often are better positioned to make local decisions. For example, **McDonald's** has restaurants around the world. The tastes of people in China or France differ from those of people in the United States. So, McDonald's tailors its menu to different countries. The result is that the McDonald's in each country can differentiate to meet the needs of its local market. **Starbucks** also studied how the tastes and social habits of Indian culture differed from more Western cultures before it launched its first store in Mumbai in 2012.

Focusing of Central Management By decentralizing the operating decisions, central management is free to engage in strategic planning and decision making. The long-run survival of the organization should be of more importance to central management than day-to-day operations.

Training and Motivating of Managers Organizations always need well-trained managers to replace higher-level managers who leave to take advantage of other opportunities. What better way to prepare a future generation of higher-level managers than by providing them the opportunity to make significant decisions? These opportunities also enable top managers to evaluate local managers' capabilities and promote those who make the best decisions.

Enhanced Competition In a highly centralized company, overall profit margins can mask inefficiencies within the various subdivisions. Large companies now find that they cannot afford to keep a noncompetitive division. One of the best ways to improve performance of a division or factory is to expose it more fully to market forces. At **Koch Industries Inc.**, each unit is expected to act as an autonomous business unit and to set prices both externally and internally. Units whose services are not required by other Koch units may face possible elimination.

Divisions in the Decentralized Firm

Managers in a decentralized firm make and implement more decisions than do managers in a centralized firm. The benefit of decentralization is that decisions are more likely to be made by managers who have the specific local knowledge—not possessed by high-level managers—to use the firm's resources to maximize firm value. However, the cost of decentralization is that lower-level managers who have the knowledge to make the best decisions with the firm's resources are less likely to possess the same incentive as high-level managers to maximize firm value. Stated differently, as compared to high-level managers, lower-level managers are more likely to use the firm's resources for personal gain than for increasing the firm's stock value.

Decentralization usually is achieved by creating units called *divisions*. Divisions can be organized in a number of different ways, including the following:

- types of goods or services
- geographic lines
- responsibility centers

Types of Goods or Services

Divisions can be organized by product line. For example, divisions of **PepsiCo** include the Snack Ventures Europe Division (a joint venture with **General Mills**), **Frito-Lay Inc.**, and **Tropicana**, as well as its flagship soft-drink division. Exhibit 11.2 shows decentralized divisions of PepsiCo. These divisions are organized on the basis of product lines. Notice that some divisions depend on other divisions. For example, PepsiCo spun off its restaurant divisions to **YUM! Brands**. As a result, the cola served at **Pizza Hut**, **Taco Bell**, and **KFC** changed from Coke to Pepsi. In a

Exhibit 11.2

Decentralized Divisions

decentralized setting, some interdependencies usually exist; otherwise, a company would merely be a collection of totally separate entities.

Geographic Lines

Divisions may also be created along geographic lines. For example, **UAL Inc.** (parent of **United Airlines**) has a number of regional divisions: Asian/Pacific, Caribbean, European, Latin American, and North American. The presence of divisions spanning one or more regions creates the need for performance evaluation that can take into account differences in divisional environments.

Responsibility Centers

A third way divisions differ is by the type of responsibility given to the divisional manager. As a firm grows, top management typically creates areas of responsibility, known as responsibility centers, and assigns subordinate managers to those areas. A **responsibility center** is a segment of the business whose manager is accountable for specific activities. The four major types of responsibility centers are as follows:

- **Cost center**: Manager is responsible only for costs.
- **Revenue center**: Manager is responsible only for sales, or revenue.
- **Profit center**: Manager is responsible for both revenues and costs.
- **Investment center**: Manager is responsible for revenues, costs, and investments.

The choice of responsibility center depends on the actual situation and the type of information available to the manager. Information is the key to appropriately holding managers responsible for outcomes. For example, a production department manager is held responsible for departmental *costs* but not for sales. This responsibility choice occurs because the production department manager understands and directly controls some production costs but does not set prices. Any difference between actual and expected costs can best be explained at this level.

The marketing department manager sets the price and projected sales *revenue*. Therefore, the marketing department may be evaluated as a revenue center. Direct costs of the marketing department and overall sales are the responsibility of the sales manager.

In some companies, plant managers are given the responsibility for manufacturing and marketing their products. These plant managers control both *costs and revenues*, putting them in control of a profit center. Operating income is an important performance measure for profit center managers.

Finally, divisions may be investment centers. In addition to having control over cost and pricing decisions, these managers have the power to make *investment* decisions such as plant closings and openings and decisions to keep or drop a product line. As a result, both operating income and some type of return on investment are important performance measures for investment center managers. Exhibit 11.3 displays these centers along with the type of information that managers need to manage their operations. As the exhibit shows, investment centers represent the greatest degree of decentralization (followed by profit centers and finally by cost and revenue centers) because their managers have the freedom to make the greatest variety of decisions.

	Cost	Sales	Capital Investment	Other
Cost center	X			
Revenue center		X		
Profit center	X	X		
Investment center	X	X	X	X

Exhibit 11.3

Types of Responsibility Centers and Accounting Information Used to Measure Performance

It is important to realize that while the responsibility center manager has responsibility only for the activities of that center, decisions made by that manager can affect other responsibility centers. For example, the sales force at a floor care products firm routinely offers customers price discounts at the end of the month. Sales increase dramatically, which is good for revenue and the sales force. However, the factory is forced to institute overtime shifts to keep up with demand. These overtime shifts increase the costs of the factory as well as the cost per unit of product.

Organizing divisions as responsibility centers creates the opportunity to control the divisions through the use of responsibility accounting. Revenue center control is achieved by evaluating the efficiency and effectiveness of divisional managers on the basis of sales revenue. Cost center control is based on control of costs and frequently employs variance analysis, as described in Chapter 10. This chapter focuses on the evaluation of profit centers and investment centers.

Here's **Why It's important**

Here's How It's Used: IN THE SERVICE INDUSTRY

You have been chosen as the CEO of a new hospital. One important decision you face early is determining the optimal level of decentralization for your various levels of supporting management.

What factors should you consider as you decide how best to structure the hospital management?

There is no easy, one-size-fits-all answer. However, some of the top-ranked hospitals in the world, such as the **Cleveland Clinic**, recognize that much of the specific knowledge critically important for making the best patient care decisions resides with the hospital's physicians, surgeons, and nurses rather than with the chief executive officer or other "C-Suite" executives (e.g., chief financial officer, chief operations officer, chief integrity officer, etc.). Such hospitals choose a highly decentralized organizational structure so that many important decisions that affect patient treatment are made by individuals far removed from top management. The biggest challenge to effectively managing a highly

decentralized decision-making structure like this one is to create quantitative performance measures for the decision makers—in this case, the physicians, surgeons, and nurses—to assess the quality of their decisions. Furthermore, these performance measures need to be used as part of the decision makers' compensation packages to reward (or punish) their wise (or unwise) decisions that hopefully are taken in the best interest of the patients and, ultimately, the hospital. A growing number of publicly traded companies, such as **Starbucks**, offer lower-level employees—even part-time employees—incentives such as health care benefits and stock options to motivate them to take actions that are in the companies' best long-term interests.

In decentralized organizations, managerial accounting is important in designing effective performance measures and incentive systems to help ensure that lower-level managers use their decision-making authority to improve the organization's performance.

1. Think about summer jobs that you and your friends have held. To what extent did you or your friends work in a centralized or decentralized decision-making environment?

Answer:

If you worked at a **Taco Bell** or **Pizza Hut**, you were working for a decentralized company, **YUM! Brands**. This company owns many Taco Bells and Pizza Huts. Some decision making is pushed down to lower-level managers. On the other hand, suppose you worked for a small law or accounting firm that has only the local office. Then you were working for a centralized company, and the owner probably made all important operating and strategic decisions.

2. Reasons for decentralization do *not* include which of the following?
   a. Ease of gathering and using local information
   b. Enhanced competition and exposing segments to market forces
   c. Training and motivating managers
   d. Focusing of central management on strategic planning and decision making
   e. All of the above are reasons for decentralization.

Answer:

e

OBJECTIVE 2

Compute and explain return on investment.

MEASURING THE PERFORMANCE OF INVESTMENT CENTERS BY USING RETURN ON INVESTMENT

Typically, investment centers are evaluated on the basis of return on investment. Other common measures include residual income and economic value added.

Return on Investment

CONCEPT CLIP

Divisions that are investment centers have an income statement and a balance sheet. So, could those divisions be ranked on the basis of income? Suppose, for example, that a company has two divisions—Alpha and Beta. Alpha's income is $100,000, and Beta's income is $200,000. Did Beta perform better than Alpha? What if Alpha used an investment of $500,000 to produce the contribution of $100,000, while Beta used an investment of $2 million to produce the $200,000 contribution? Does your response change? Clearly, it does. Relating the reported operating profits to the assets used to produce them is a more meaningful measure of performance.

One way to relate operating profits to assets employed is to compute the **return on investment (ROI)**, which is the profit earned per dollar of investment. ROI is the most common measure of performance for an investment center. It can be defined as follows:

$$ROI = \text{Operating Income/Average Operating Assets}$$

Operating income refers to earnings before interest and taxes. **Operating assets** are all assets acquired to generate operating income, including cash, receivables, inventories, land, buildings, and equipment. Average operating assets is computed as follows:

$$\text{Average Operating Assets} = (\text{Beginning Assets} + \text{Ending Assets})/2$$

Opinions vary regarding how long-term assets (plant and equipment) should be valued (e.g., gross book value vs. net book value or historical cost vs. current cost). Most firms use historical cost and net book value.[1]

Going back to our example, Alpha's ROI is 0.20, calculated as:

$$\text{Operating Income/Average Operating Assets} = \$100,000/\$500,000$$

Beta's ROI is only 0.10 ($200,000/$2,000,000). The formula for ROI is quick and easy to use.

Margin and Turnover

A second way to calculate ROI is to separate the formula (Operating Income/Average Operating Assets) into margin and turnover. **Margin** is the ratio of operating income to sales. It tells how many cents of operating income result from each dollar of sales. It expresses the portion of sales that is available for interest, taxes, and profit. Some managers also refer to margin as return on sales. **Turnover** is a different measure; it is found by dividing sales by average operating assets. Turnover tells how many dollars of sales result from every dollar invested in operating assets. It shows how productively assets are being used to generate sales.

CONCEPT CLIP

Margin	Turnover

$$\text{ROI} = \text{Operating Income/Sales} \times \text{Sales/Average Operating Assets}$$

Notice that "Sales" in the above formula can be cancelled out to yield the original ROI formula of Operating Income/Average Operating Assets.

Suppose, for example, that Alpha had sales of $400,000. Then, margin would be 0.25, calculated as

$$\text{Operating Income/Sales} = \$100,000/\$400,000$$

Turnover would be 0.80, calculated as

$$\text{Sales/Average Operating Assets} = \$400,000/\$500,000$$

Alpha's ROI would still be 0.20 (0.25 × 0.80). **Example 11.1** shows how to calculate these ratios.

Celimar Company's Western Division earned operating income last year as shown in the following income statement:

Sales	$ 480,000
Cost of goods sold	(222,000)
Gross margin	$ 258,000
Selling and administrative expense	(210,000)
Operating income	$ 48,000

At the beginning of the year, the value of operating assets was $277,000. At the end of the year, the value of operating assets was $323,000.

Required:

For the Western Division, calculate the following: (1) average operating assets, (2) margin, (3) turnover, and (4) return on investment.

EXAMPLE 11.1

How to Calculate Average Operating Assets, Margin, Turnover, and Return on Investment

(Continued)

---

1 There is no one correct way to calculate ROI. The important thing is to be sure that one method is applied consistently, which allows the company to compare the ROI among divisions and over time.

EXAMPLE 11.1

(Continued)

Solution:

1. Average Operating Assets = (Beginning Assets + Ending Assets)/2
$$= (\$277,000 + \$323,000)/2$$
$$= \$300,000$$

2. Margin = Operating Income/Sales = $48,000/$480,000
$$= 0.10, \text{ or } 1\ \%$$

3. Turnover = Sales/Average Operating Assets = $480,000/$300,000 = 1.6

4. ROI = Margin × Turnover = 0.10 × 1.6 = 0.16, or 16%

   Note: ROI can also be calculated as:

   ROI = Operating Income/Average Operating Assets
$$= \$48,000/\$300,000$$
$$= 0.16, \text{ or } 16\%$$

While both approaches yield the same ROI, the calculation of margin and turnover gives a manager valuable information. To illustrate this additional information, consider the data presented in Exhibit 11.4. The Electronics Division improved its ROI from 18% in Year 1 to 20% in Year 2. The Medical Supplies Division's ROI, however, dropped from 18 to 15%. Computing the margin and turnover ratios for each division gives a better picture of what caused the change in rates. As with variance analysis, understanding the causes of managerial accounting measures (i.e., variances, margins, turnover, etc.) helps managers take actions to improve the division. These ratios also are presented in Exhibit 11.4.

Exhibit 11.4

Comparison of Divisional Performance

Comparison of ROI		
	Electronics Division	**Medical Supplies Division**
Year 1:		
Sales	$30,000,000	$117,000,000
Operating income	1,800,000	3,510,000
Average operating assets	10,000,000	19,510,000
ROI[a]	18%	18%
Year 2:		
Sales	$40,000,000	$117,000,000
Operating income	2,000,000	2,925,000
Average operating assets	10,000,000	19,500,000
ROI[a]	20%	15%

Margin and Turnover Comparisons				
	Electronics Division		**Medical Supplies Division**	
	Year 1	**Year 2**	**Year 1**	**Year 2**
Margin[b]	6.0%	5.0%	3.0%	2.5%
Turnover[c]	×3.0	×4.0	×6.0	×6.0
ROI	18.0%	20.0%	18.0%	15.0%

[a] Operating Income/Average Operating Assets
[b] Operating Income/Sales
[c] Sales/Average Operating Assets

Notice that the margins for both divisions dropped from Year 1 to Year 2. In fact, the divisions experienced the *same* percentage of decline (16.67%). A declining margin could be explained by increasing expenses, competitive pressures (forcing a decrease in selling prices), or both.

Despite the declining margin, the Electronics Division was able to increase its rate of return. The reason is that the increase in turnover more than compensated for the decline in margin. One explanation for the increased turnover could be a reduction in inventories. (Notice that the average assets employed remained the same for the Electronics Division, even though sales increased by $10 million.) The experience of the Medical Supplies Division was less favorable. Because its turnover rate remained unchanged, its ROI dropped. This division, unlike the Electronics Division, could not overcome the decline in margin.

Advantages of Return on Investment

At least three positive results stem from the use of ROI:

- It encourages managers to focus on the relationship among sales, expenses, and investment, as should be the case for a manager of an investment center.
- It encourages managers to focus on cost efficiency.
- It encourages managers to focus on operating asset efficiency.

These advantages are illustrated by the following three scenarios.

Illustrating Relationships: Focus on Return on Investment Relationships Della Barnes, manager of the Plastics Division, is mulling over a suggestion from her marketing vice president to increase the advertising budget by $100,000. The marketing vice president is confident that this increase will boost sales by $200,000. Della realizes that the increased sales will also raise expenses. She finds that the increased variable cost will be $80,000.

The division also will need to purchase additional machinery to handle the increased production. The equipment will cost $50,000 and will add $10,000 of depreciation expense. As a result, the proposal will add $10,000 ($200,000 − $80,000 − $10,000 − $100,000) to operating income. Currently, the division has sales of $2 million, total expenses of $1,850,000, and operating income of $150,000. Operating assets equal $1 million.

	Without Increased Advertising	With Increased Advertising
Sales	$2,000,000	$2,200,000
Less: Expenses	1,850,000	2,040,000
Operating income	$ 150,000	$ 160,000
Average operating assets	$1,000,000	$1,050,000

ROI:

$$\$150{,}000/\$1{,}000{,}000 = 0.15, \text{ or } 15\%$$

$$\$160{,}000/\$1{,}050{,}000 = 0.1524, \text{ or } 15.24\%$$

The ROI without the additional advertising is 15%. The ROI with the additional advertising and $50,000 investment in assets is 15.24%. Since ROI is increased by the proposal, Della decides to authorize the increased advertising. In effect, the current ROI, without the proposal, is the hurdle rate. **Hurdle rate** indicates the minimum ROI necessary to accept an investment.

Focus on Cost Efficiency Kyle Chugg, manager of Turner's Battery Division, groaned as he reviewed the projections for the last half of the current fiscal year. The recession was hurting his division's performance. Adding the projected operating income of $200,000 to the actual operating income of the first half produced expected annual earnings of $425,000. Kyle then divided the expected operating income by the division's average operating assets to obtain an expected ROI of 12.15%. "This is awful," muttered Kyle. "Last year our ROI was 16%. And I'm looking at a couple more bad years before business returns to normal. Something has to be done to improve our performance."

Kyle directed all operating managers to identify and eliminate nonvalue-added activities. As a result, lower-level managers found ways to reduce costs by $150,000 for the remaining half of the year. This reduction increased the annual operating income from $425,000 to $575,000, increasing ROI from 12.15% to 16.43% as a result. Interestingly, Kyle found that some of the reductions could be maintained after business returned to normal.

Focus on Operating Asset Efficiency The Electronic Storage Division prospered during its early years. In the beginning, the division developed portable external disk drives for storing data; sales and ROI were extraordinarily high. However, during the past several years, competitors had developed similar technology, and the division's ROI had plunged from 30 to 15%. Cost cutting had helped initially; but all of the fat had been removed, making further improvements from cost reductions impossible. Moreover, any increase in sales was unlikely—competition was too stiff. The divisional manager searched for some way to increase the ROI by at least 3 to 5%. Only by raising the ROI so that it compared favorably with that of the other divisions could the division expect to receive additional capital for research and development (R&D).

The divisional manager initiated an intensive program to reduce operating assets. Most of the gains were made in the area of inventory reductions. However, one plant was closed because of a long-term reduction in market share. By installing a just-in-time purchasing and manufacturing system, the division was able to reduce its asset base without threatening its remaining market share. Finally, the reduction in operating assets meant that operating costs could be decreased still further. The end result was a 50% increase in the division's ROI, from 15% to more than 22%.

Disadvantages of the Return on Investment Measure

Overemphasis on ROI can produce myopic behavior. Two negative aspects associated with ROI frequently are:

- It can produce a narrow focus on divisional profitability at the expense of profitability for the overall firm.
- It encourages managers to focus on the short run at the expense of the long run.

These disadvantages are illustrated by the following two scenarios.

Narrow Focus on Divisional Profitability A Cleaning Products Division has the opportunity to invest in two projects for the coming year. The outlay required for each investment, the dollar returns, and the ROI are as follows:

	Project I	Project II
Investment	$10,000,000	$4,000,000
Operating income	$1,300,000	$640,000
ROI	13%	16%

The division currently earns ROI of 15%, with operating assets of $50 million and operating income on current investments of $7.5 million. The division has approval to request up to $15 million in new investment capital. Corporate headquarters requires that all investments earn at least 10% (this rate represents the corporation's cost of acquiring the capital). Any capital not used by a division is invested by headquarters, and it earns exactly 10%.

The division manager has four alternatives: (1) invest in Project I, (2) invest in Project II, (3) invest in both Projects I and II, or (4) invest in neither project. The divisional ROI was computed for each alternative.

	Alternatives			
	Select Project I	Select Project II	Select Both Projects	Select Neither Project
Operating income	$8,800,000	$8,140,000	$9,440,000	$7,500,000
Operating assets	$60,000,000	$54,000,000	$64,000,000	$50,000,000
ROI	14.67%	15.07%	14.75%	15.00%

The divisional manager chose to invest only in Project II, since it would boost ROI from 15.00% to 15.07%.

While the manager's choice maximized divisional ROI, it did not maximize the profit the company could have earned. If Project I had been selected, the company would have earned $1.3 million in profits. By not selecting Project I, the $10 million in capital is invested at 10%, earning only $1 million (0.10 × $10,000,000). The single-minded focus on divisional ROI, then, cost the company $300,000 in profits ($1,300,000 − $1,000,000).

Encourages Short-Run Optimization Ruth Lunsford, manager of a Small Tools Division, was displeased with her division's performance during the first three quarters. Given the expected income for the fourth quarter, the ROI for the year would be 13%, at least 2 percentage points below where she had hoped to be. Such an ROI might not be strong enough to justify the early promotion she wanted. With only 3 months left, drastic action was needed. Increasing sales for the last quarter was unlikely. Most sales were booked at least 2 to 3 months in advance. Emphasizing extra sales activity would benefit next year's performance. What was needed were some ways to improve this year's performance.

After careful thought, Ruth decided to take the following actions:

- Lay off five of the highest paid salespeople.
- Cut the advertising budget for the fourth quarter by 50%.
- Delay all promotions within the division for 3 months.
- Reduce the preventive maintenance budget by 75%.
- Use cheaper raw materials for fourth-quarter production.

In the aggregate, these steps would reduce expenses, increase income, and raise the ROI to about 15.2% for the current year.

While Ruth's actions increase the profits and ROI in the short run, they have some long-run negative consequences. Laying off the highest-paid (and possibly the best) salespeople may harm the division's future sales-generating capabilities. Future sales could also be hurt by cutting back on advertising and using cheaper raw materials. Delaying promotions could hurt employee morale, which could, in turn, lower productivity and future sales. Finally, reducing preventive maintenance will likely increase downtime and decrease the life of the productive equipment.

Ethical Decisions

Ethical considerations also come into play when managers attempt to "game" ROI. Ruth's five top-earning salespeople probably were her best salespeople. Letting them go meant that sales probably would decrease, an outcome not in the best interest of the firm. Thus, her action is directly contrary to her obligation to take actions in the best interests of the company. The layoffs also might violate the implicit contract a company has with workers that outstanding work will lead to continued employment. ●

Check Point

1. **Since sales appears in the numerator of the margin ratio and the denominator of the turnover ratio, changing sales will have no effect on ROI. Is this statement true or false? Explain.**

   Answer:

   False. While sales in the numerator of margin and in the denominator of turnover does cancel out, sales also appears in the calculation of operating income. As long as the contribution margin ratio is greater than zero, increasing sales will increase ROI, assuming there is no change in fixed costs and assets.

2. **Think about some stores in your town, such as a jewelry store, fast-food outlet, and grocery store. How do you suppose their margins and turnover ratios compare with each other? Explain your thinking.**

   Answer:

   Fast-food outlets and grocery stores probably have low margins and high turnover. These financial characteristics exist because they deal in perishables and must have continual turnover or the food will go bad. A jewelry store, on the other hand, has high margin and relatively low turnover. These financial characteristics exist because the goods are not perishable and there is relatively less competition in this market. (The existence of competition, of course, changes as more jewelry stores enter a market and as consumers become more confident about buying jewelry online.)

   While both approaches yield the same ROI, the calculation of margin and turnover gives a manager valuable information. To illustrate this additional information, consider the data presented in Exhibit 11.4. The Electronics Division improved its ROI from 18% in Year 1 to 20% in Year 2. The Medical Supplies Division's ROI, however, dropped from 18 to 15%. Computing the margin and turnover ratios for each division gives a better picture of what caused the change in rates. As with variance analysis, understanding the causes of managerial accounting measures (i.e., variances, margins, turnover, etc.) helps managers take actions to improve the division. These ratios also are presented in Exhibit 11.4.

OBJECTIVE 3

Compute and explain residual income and economic value added.

MEASURING THE PERFORMANCE OF INVESTMENT CENTERS BY USING RESIDUAL INCOME AND ECONOMIC VALUE ADDED

 **Why It's important**

To compensate for the tendency of ROI to discourage investments that are profitable for the company but that lower a division's ROI, some companies have adopted alternative performance measures such as residual income.

Residual Income

Residual income is the difference between operating income and the minimum dollar return required on a company's operating assets:

> Residual Income = Operating Income − (Minimum Rate of Return × Average Operating Assets)

CONCEPT CLIP

Example 11.2 shows how to calculate residual income.

EXAMPLE 11.2

How to Calculate Residual Income

Celimar Company's Western Division earned operating income last year as shown in the following income statement:

Sales	$480,000
Cost of goods sold	222,000
Gross margin	$258,000
Selling and administrative expense	210,000
Operating income	$ 48,000

At the beginning of the year, the value of operating assets was $277,000. At the end of the year, the value of operating assets was $323,000. Celimar Company requires a minimum rate of return of 12%.

Required:

For the Western Division, calculate (1) average operating assets and (2) residual income.

Solution:

1. Average Operating Assets = (Beginning Assets + Ending Assets)/2

   = ($277,000 + $323,000)/2

   = $300,000

2. Residual Income = Operating Income − (Minimum Rate of Return × Average Operating Assets

   = $48,000 − (0.12 × $300,000)

   = $48,000 − $36,000

   = $12,000

The minimum rate of return is set by the company and is the same as the hurdle rate (see the section on ROI). If residual income is greater than zero, then the division is earning more than the minimum required rate of return (or hurdle rate). If residual income is less than zero, then the division is earning less than the minimum required rate of return. Finally, if residual income equals zero, then the division is earning precisely the minimum required rate of return.

Advantage of Residual Income Recall that the manager of the Cleaning Products Division (page 601) rejected Project I because it would have reduced divisional ROI. However, that decision cost the company $300,000 in profits. The use of residual income as the performance measure would have prevented this loss. The residual income for each project is computed as follows:

Project I
Residual Income = Operating Income − (Minimum Rate of Return × Average Operating Assets)

   = $1,300,000 − (0.10 × $10,000,000)

   = $1,300,000 − $1,000,000

   = $300,000

Project II
Residual Income = $640,000 − (0.10 × $4,000,000)
$$= \$640,000 - \$400,000$$
$$= \$240,000$$

Notice that both projects have positive residual income. For comparative purposes, the divisional residual income for each of the four alternatives identified is as follows:

	Alternatives			
	Select Only Project I	**Select Only Project II**	**Select Both Projects**	**Select Neither Project**
Operating assets	$60,000,000	$54,000,000	$64,000,000	$50,000,000
Operating income	$ 8,800,000	$ 8,140,000	$ 9,440,000	$ 7,500,000
Minimum return*	6,000,000	5,400,000	6,400,000	5,000,000
Residual income	$ 2,800,000	$ 2,740,000	$ 3,040,000	$ 2,500,000

*0.10 × Operating Assets

As shown on page 601, selecting both projects produces the greatest increase in residual income. The use of residual income encourages managers to accept any project that earns a return that is above the minimum rate.

Disadvantages of Residual Income   Residual income, like ROI, can encourage a short-run orientation. If Ruth Lunsford (page 601) were being evaluated on the basis of residual income, she could have taken the same actions.

Another problem with residual income is that, unlike ROI, it is an absolute measure of profitability. Thus, direct comparison of the performance of two different investment centers becomes difficult, as the level of investment may differ. For example, consider the residual income computations for Division A and Division B where the minimum required rate of return is 8%.

	Division A	Division B
Average operating assets	$15,000,000	$2,500,000
Operating income	$ 1,500,000	$ 300,000
Minimum return[a]	(1,200,000)	(200,000)
Residual income	$ 300,000	$ 100,000
Residual return[b]	2%	4%

[a]0.08 × Operating Assets
[b]Residual Income/Operating Assets

It is tempting to claim that Division A is outperforming Division B, since its residual income is three times higher. Notice, however, that Division A is considerably larger than Division B and has six times as many assets. One possible way to correct this disadvantage is to compute both ROI and residual income and to use both measures for performance evaluation. ROI could then be used for interdivisional comparisons.

Economic Value Added (EVA)

Another financial performance measure that is similar to residual income is *economic value added*. **Economic value added (EVA)**[2] is after-tax operating income minus the dollar cost of

---

2 EVA was developed by Stern Stewart & Co. in the 1990s. Now Stern Value Management, more information can be found on the firm's website, http://sternvaluemanagement.com/consulting-services-strategy-governance-financial-policy-operations/eva-training/

capital employed. The dollar cost of capital employed is the actual percentage cost of capital[3] multiplied by the total capital employed, expressed as follows:

> EVA = After-Tax Operating Income − (Actual Percentage Cost of Capital × Total Capital Employed)

Example 11.3 shows how to calculate EVA.

EXAMPLE 11.3

How to Calculate Economic Value Added

Celimar Company's Western Division earned net income last year as shown in the following income statement:

Sales	$480,000
Cost of goods sold	222,000
Gross margin	$258,000
Selling and administrative expense	210,000
Operating income	$ 48,000
Less: Income taxes (@ 30%)	14,400
Net income	$ 33,600

Total capital employed equaled $300,000. Celimar Company's actual cost of capital is 10%.

Required:
Calculate EVA for the Western Division.

Solution:
EVA = After-Tax Operating Income − (Actual Percentage Cost of Capital × Total Capital Employed)
= $33,600 − (0.10 × $300,000)
= $33,600 − $30,000
= $3,600

Basically, EVA is residual income with the minimum rate of return equal to the actual cost of capital for the firm (as opposed to some minimum rate of return desired by the company for other reasons). If EVA is positive, then the company has increased its wealth during the period. If EVA is negative, then the company has decreased its wealth during the period. Consider the old saying, "It takes money to make money." EVA helps the company to determine whether the money it makes is more than the money it takes to make it. Over the long term, only those companies creating capital, or wealth, can survive.

As a form of residual income, EVA is a dollar figure, not a percentage rate of return. However, it does bear a resemblance to rates of return such as ROI because it links net income (return) to capital employed. The key feature of EVA is its emphasis on *after-tax* operating profit and the *actual* cost of capital. Residual income, on the other hand, uses a minimum expected rate of return.

Investors like EVA because it relates profit to the amount of resources needed to achieve it. A number of companies are evaluated on the basis of EVA. For example, companies such as **General Electric**, **Wal-Mart**, **Merck & Co.**, **IBM**, **Verizon Communications**, **Disney Company**, **JetBlue Airways Corp.**, and **Pixar** use EVA metrics in some capacity. One important caveat for EVA metrics is that their calculation is not based on generally accepted accounting principles (GAAP), which means that 10 different organizations likely will calculate EVA

---

3 The computation of a company's actual cost of capital is reserved for advanced accounting courses.

Here's How It's Used: AT HERMAN MILLER

Let's return briefly to **Herman Miller**'s use of EVA that was introduced at the beginning of the chapter. Before developing its EVA metrics (as part of its lean manufacturing initiative), Herman Miller would purchase or build in large batches to capture savings resulting from bulk transactions. For example, managers often would order a batch of 1,000 parts when only 200 actually were needed for custom orders. However, with the introduction of EVA, a capital charge was assessed on the fixed warehousing- and equipment-related assets required to process, transport, store, replace (in the event of

obsolescence), and repair (if damaged) these large quantities of excess inventory. In so doing, EVA helped managers quickly realize that the costs of processing excess inventory often outweigh any benefits of purchasing or building in unnecessarily large quantities. Manager behavior at Herman Miller has changed dramatically as a result of EVA, as each part in the production process now is produced or purchased to match the customer order, and that part moves through the entire process without significant delay, usually going out the door within a single day.

in 10 different ways, unlike GAAP metrics that must be calculated in the same manner by all organizations.

Behavioral Aspects of Economic Value Added   A number of companies have discovered that EVA helps to encourage the right kind of behavior from their divisions in a way that emphasis on operating income alone cannot. The underlying reason is EVA's reliance on the true cost of capital. In some companies, the responsibility for investment decisions rests with corporate management. As a result, the cost of capital is considered a corporate expense rather than an expense attributable to particular divisions. If a division builds inventories and investment, the cost of financing that investment is passed along to the overall income statement and does not show up as a reduction from that division's operating income as it would under an EVA analysis. Without an EVA analysis, the result is to make investment seem free to the divisions, and, of course, they want more.

Not surprisingly, research indicates that more firms continue to adopt EVA measures as part of their overall performance evaluation package.[4] It should be cautioned, however, that research also shows that some firms that collect EVA measures struggle to integrate these relatively complex measures into managerial decision making without considerable training for the managers.[5]

Check Point

1. **What are the differences and similarities between the basic residual income calculation and EVA?**

Answer:
Residual income can use either before-tax income (operating income) or after-tax income. In addition, residual income uses a minimum required rate of return set by upper management. EVA, on the other hand, uses after-tax income and requires the company to compute its actual cost of capital.

2. **If ROI is 12% and the hurdle rate is 10%, what can you say about residual income?**

Answer:
You can say that residual income will be positive. In fact, it will equal 2% (12% – 10%) times average operating assets.

---

4 Stern Stewart Research, "Stern Stewart's EVA Clients Outperform the Market and Their Peers," *EVAluation: Special Report* (October 2002).

5 Alexander Mersereau, "Pushing the Art of Management Accounting," *CMA Management*, Volume 79, Issue 9 (February 1, 2006).

TRANSFER PRICING

OBJECTIVE ▶ **4**

Explain the role of transfer pricing in a decentralized firm.

In many decentralized organizations, the output of one division is used as the input of another. For example, assume that one division of **Sony** manufactures batteries for its VAIO computers, which in turn sells the batteries to another Sony division that uses them to complete the computer manufacturing process. This internal transfer between two divisions within Sony raises an accounting issue. How is the transferred good valued? When divisions are treated as responsibility centers, they are evaluated on the basis of their contribution to costs, revenues, operating income, ROI, and residual income or EVA, depending on the particular center type. As a result, the value of the transferred good is revenue to the selling division and cost to the buying division. This value, or internal price, is called the *transfer price*. In other words, a **transfer price** is the price charged for a component by the selling division to the buying division of the same company. Transfer pricing is a complex issue and has an impact on divisions and the company as a whole.

Here's **Why It's important**

Impact of Transfer Pricing on Divisions and the Firm as a Whole

When one division of a company sells to another division, both divisions as well as the company as a whole are affected. The price charged for the transferred good affects both

- the costs of the buying division and
- the revenues of the selling division

Thus, the profits of both divisions, as well as the evaluation and compensation of their managers, are affected by the transfer price. Since profit-based performance measures of the two divisions are affected (e.g., ROI and residual income), transfer pricing often can be an emotionally charged issue. Exhibit 11.5 illustrates the effect of the transfer price on two divisions of ABC Inc. Division A produces a component and sells it to another division of the same company, Division C. The $30 transfer price is revenue to Division A; clearly, Division A wants the price to be as high as possible. Conversely, the $30 transfer price is cost to Division C, just like the cost of any raw material. Division C prefers as low a transfer price as possible.

Division A	Division C
Produces component and transfers it to C for transfer price of $30 per unit.	Purchases component from A at transfer price of $30 per unit and uses it in production of final product.
Transfer price = $30 per unit	Transfer price = $30 per unit
Revenue to A	Cost to C
Increases income	Decreases income
Increases ROI	Decreases ROI

Note: Transfer Price Revenue = Transfer Price Cost; zero dollar impact on ABC Inc.

Exhibit 11.5

Impact of Transfer Price on Transferring Divisions and the Company, ABC Inc., as a Whole

The actual transfer price nets out for the company *as a whole* in that total *pretax* income for the company is the same regardless of the transfer price. However, transfer pricing can affect the level of *after-tax* profits earned by the multinational company that operates in multiple countries with different corporate tax rates and other legal requirements set by the countries in which the various divisions generate income. For example, if the selling division operates in a low-tax country and the buying division operates in a high-tax country, the transfer price may be set quite high. Then, the high transfer price (a revenue for A) would increase profit in the division in the low-tax country, and the high transfer price (a cost for B) would decrease profit in the division in the high-tax country. This transfer pricing strategy reduces overall corporate income taxes. The international transfer pricing situation is examined in detail in more advanced courses.

Transfer Pricing Policies

Recall that a decentralized company allows much more authority for decision making at lower management levels. It would be counterproductive for the decentralized company to then decide on the actual transfer prices between two divisions. As a result, top management usually sets the transfer pricing policy, but the divisions still decide whether or not to transfer. For example, top management at Verybig Inc. may set the corporate transfer pricing policy at full manufacturing cost. Then, if Mediumbig Division wants to transfer a product to Somewhatbig Division, the transfer price would be the product cost. However, neither division is forced to transfer the product internally. The transfer pricing policy only says that *if* the product is transferred, it must be at cost.

Several transfer pricing policies are used in practice, including the following:

CONCEPT CLIP

- market price
- cost-based transfer prices
- negotiated transfer prices

Market Price If there is a competitive outside market for the transferred product, then the best transfer price is the market price. In such a case, divisional managers' actions will simultaneously optimize divisional profits and firmwide profits. Furthermore, no division can benefit at the expense of another. In this setting, top management will not be tempted to intervene.

Suppose that the Furniture Division of a corporation produces futons. The Mattress Division of that same corporation produces mattresses, including a mattress model that fits into the futon. If mattresses are transferred from the Mattress Division to the Furniture Division, a transfer pricing opportunity exists. In this case, the Mattress Division is the selling division, and the Furniture Division is the buying division. Suppose that the mattresses can be sold to outside buyers at $50 each; this $50 is the market price. Clearly, the Mattress Division would not sell the mattresses to the Furniture Division for less than $50 each. Just as clearly, the Furniture Division would not pay more than $50 for the mattresses. The transfer price is easily set at the market price.

The market price, if available, is the best approach to transfer pricing. Since the selling division can sell all that it produces at the market price, transferring internally at a lower price would make the division worse off. Similarly, the buying division can always acquire the good at the market price, so it would be unwilling to pay more for an internally transferred good.

Will the two divisions transfer at the market price? It really does not matter, since the divisions and the company as a whole will be as well off whether or not the transfer takes place internally. However, if the transfer is to occur, it will be at the market price.

Cost-Based Transfer Prices Frequently, there is no good outside market price. The lack of a market price might occur because the transferred product uses patented designs owned by the parent company. Then, a company might use a cost-based transfer pricing approach. For example, suppose that the Mattress Division uses a high-density foam padding in the futon mattress and that outside companies do not produce this type of mattress in the appropriate size. If the company has set a cost-based transfer pricing policy, then the Mattress Division will charge the full cost of producing the mattress. (Full cost includes the cost of direct materials, direct labor, variable overhead, and a portion of fixed overhead.) Suppose that the full cost of the mattress is as follows:

Direct materials	$15
Direct labor	5
Variable overhead	3
Fixed overhead	5
Full cost	$28

Now, the transfer price is $28 per mattress. This amount will be paid to the Mattress Division by the Furniture Division. Notice that this transfer price does not allow for any profit for the selling division (here, the Mattress Division). The Mattress Division may well try to scale back production of the futon mattress and increase production of mattresses available for sale to outside parties. To reduce this desire, top management may define cost as "cost plus." In this case, suppose that the company allows transfer pricing at cost plus 10%. Then, the transfer price is $30.80, calculated as:

$$\text{Transfer Price} + (\text{Transfer Price} + 10\%) = \$28 + (\$28 \times 0.10)$$

If the policy is cost-based transfer pricing, will the transfer take place? It depends. Suppose the Furniture Division wants to purchase lower-quality mattresses in the external market for $25 each. Then, no transfer will occur. Also, suppose the Mattress Division is producing at capacity and can sell the special mattresses for $40 each. The Mattress Division will refuse to transfer any mattresses to the Furniture Division and instead will sell all it can produce to outside parties.

Negotiated Transfer Prices Finally, top management may allow the selling and buying division managers to negotiate a transfer price. This approach is particularly useful in cases with market imperfections, such as the ability of an in-house division to avoid selling and distribution costs that external market participants would have to incur. Using a negotiated transfer price then allows the two divisions to share any cost savings resulting from avoided costs.

Using the example of the Mattress and Furniture divisions, suppose that the futon mattress typically sells for $50 and has full product cost of $28. Normally, a sales commission of $5 is paid to the salesperson, but that cost will not be incurred for any internal transfers. Now, a bargaining range exists. That range goes from the minimum transfer price to the maximum. The two divisions will negotiate the transfer price, deciding how much of the cost savings will go to each division.

- Minimum Transfer Price (Floor): The transfer price that would leave the selling division no worse off if the good were sold to an internal division than if the good were sold to an external party. This is sometimes referred to as the "floor" of the bargaining range.
- Maximum Transfer Price (Ceiling): The transfer price that would leave the buying division no worse off if an input were purchased from an internal division than if the same good were purchased externally. This is sometimes referred to as the "ceiling" of the bargaining range.

In the example, the minimum transfer price is $45:

$50 market price − $5 selling commission that can be avoided on internal sales

The maximum transfer price is $50, which is the outside market price that the Furniture Division would have to pay if the mattresses were bought externally. What is the actual transfer price? That depends on the negotiating skills of the Mattress and Furniture division managers. Any transfer price between $45 and $50 is possible. **Example 11.4** shows how to calculate several types of transfer prices.

EXAMPLE 11.4

How to Calculate Transfer Price

Omni Inc. has a number of divisions, including Alpha Division, a producer of circuit boards, and Delta Division, a heating and air-conditioning manufacturer. Alpha Division produces the cb-117 model that can be used by Delta Division in the production of thermostats that regulate heating and air-conditioning systems. The market price of the cb-117 is $14, and the full cost of the circuit board is $9.

(Continued)

EXAMPLE 11.4

(Continued)

Required:

1. If Omni has a transfer pricing policy that requires transfer at full cost, what will the transfer price be? Would the Alpha and Delta divisions choose to transfer at that price?

2. If Omni has a transfer pricing policy that requires transfer at market price, what would the transfer price be? Would the Alpha and Delta divisions choose to transfer at that price?

3. Assume Omni allows negotiated transfer pricing and Alpha Division can avoid $3 of selling expense by selling to Delta Division. Which division sets the minimum transfer price, and what is it? Which division sets the maximum transfer price, and what is it? Would the Alpha and Delta divisions choose to transfer somewhere in the bargaining range?

Solution:

1. The full cost transfer price is $9. Delta Division would be delighted with that price, but Alpha Division would refuse to transfer, since $14 could be earned in the outside market.

2. The market price is $14. Both Delta and Alpha divisions would transfer at that price (since neither would be worse off than if it bought/sold in the outside market).

3. Minimum transfer price = $14 − $3 = $11. This price is set by Alpha, the selling division.

   Maximum transfer price = $14. This price is the market price and is set by Delta, the buying division.

   Both divisions would accept a transfer price within the bargaining range. Precisely what the transfer price would be depends on the negotiating skills of the division managers.

Here's How It's Used: AT KICKER

Kicker's top management is closely involved in all aspects of the company, from design and development through production, sales, delivery, and aftermarket activities. Profit performance, as measured by periodic income statements, is an important measure, but Kicker also keeps track of a number of other measures of performance.

For example, financial information is very important. Financial statements are presented to the president and vice presidents every month. These are reviewed carefully for trends and are compared with the budgeted amounts. Worrisome increases in expenses or decreases in revenue are analyzed to see what the underlying factors might be.

Customer satisfaction is also continually measured. Kicker has two major types of customers—dealers who sell Kicker products and end users who have Kicker car speakers installed. Each customer type has specific needs. For example, dealers have the exclusive right to sell Kicker products, and Kicker offers a 1-year warranty on speakers sold through a dealer. However, end users want as low a price as possible and will occasionally find speakers available on the Internet

(called "gray market" speakers because the seller is not authorized to sell them).

In the past, no warranty was available on nondealer-sold speakers, but problems arose when customers purchased obviously new products through the Internet, and they were not covered under warranty when something went wrong. Kicker therefore decided to offer a shorter warranty for new products sold by unauthorized sellers in order to keep the customer base happy and increase satisfaction.

Kicker focuses on strategic objectives for the long term. For example, engineers in R&D take continuing education to stay current in their fields. When Kicker approached producing and selling original equipment manufacture (OEM) speakers to a major automobile maker, a number of employees had to learn International Organization for Standardization (ISO) quality concepts quickly. They took classes, met with consultants, and traveled to the site of other ISO-qualified firms to learn how to meet quality standards.

Check Point

1. Is the market price always the best transfer price?

Answer:

If there is a competitive outside market for the component to be transferred, market price is best. It leads to the optimization of divisional and firmwide profits. However, if there is no competitive outside market, market price cannot be used and another transfer pricing policy must be applied.

2. Suppose ABC Inc. requires all transfers to take place at full cost. A component made by Division A and used by Division B has full cost of $45 and a market price of $60. What is the transfer price? Will the component be transferred internally from Division A to Division B?

Answer:

The transfer price would be $45. However, Division A will refuse to transfer because it can sell all that it makes of the component in the outside market for $60.

APPENDIX 11A: THE BALANCED SCORECARD—BASIC CONCEPTS

OBJECTIVE ◀ **5**

Explain the uses of the Balanced Scorecard, and compute cycle time, velocity, and manufacturing cycle efficiency.

Here's **Why It's important**

Segment income, ROI, residual income, and EVA are important measures of managerial performance, but they lead managers to focus only on dollar figures, which may not tell the whole story for the company. In addition, lower-level managers and employees may feel helpless to affect income or investment. As a result, nonfinancial operating measures that look at such factors as market share, customer complaints, personnel turnover ratios, and personnel development have been developed. Letting lower-level managers know that attention to long-run factors is also vital reduces the tendency to overemphasize financial measures.

Managers in an advanced manufacturing environment are especially likely to use multiple measures of performance and to include nonfinancial as well as financial measures. For example, General Motors evaluated Robert Lutz, then head of product development, on the basis of 12 criteria. These criteria include how well he used existing parts in new vehicles and how many engineering hours he cut from the development process.[6]

The **Balanced Scorecard** is a strategic management system that defines a strategic-based responsibility accounting system. The Balanced Scorecard *translates* an organization's mission and strategy into operational objectives and performance measures for the following four perspectives:

- The **financial perspective** describes the economic consequences of actions taken in the other three perspectives.
- The **customer perspective** defines the customer and market segments in which the business unit will compete.
- The **internal business process perspective** describes the internal processes needed to provide value for customers and owners.
- The **learning and growth (infrastructure) perspective** defines the capabilities that an organization needs to create long-term growth and improvement. This perspective is concerned with three major *enabling factors:* employee capabilities, information systems capabilities, and employee attitudes (motivation, empowerment, and alignment).

Exhibit 11.6 shows a Balanced Scorecard for a typical hotel, let's call it Ashley Hotel, based on questionnaire data provided by a research survey of 3- and 4-star hotels.[7] The scorecard includes the four basic scorecard categories and objectives with key measures for each category.

---

6 David Welch and Kathleen Kerwin, "Rick Wagoner's Game Plan," *BusinessWeek* (February 10, 2003): 52–60.

7 N. Evans, "Assessing the Balanced Scorecard as a Management Tool for Hotels," *International Journal of Contemporary Hospitality Management,* Vol. 17 (Issue 4/5, 2005): 376–390.

Exhibit 11.6

Balanced Scorecard for Ashley Hotel*

Objective	Measure
Financial Perspective	
Operating Revenues	• Total daily operating revenue • Revenue per available room
Operating Costs	• Operating expenses relative to budget • Cost per occupant
Customer Perspective	
Customer Satisfaction	• Customer satisfaction ratings • Number of monthly complaints
Customer Loyalty	• Number of new reward club members • Percent of returning guests
Internal Perspective	
Employee Turnover	• Employee turnover rate • Number of employee complaints
Response to Customer Complaint	• Percentage of complaints receiving response • Average response time
Learning and Growth	
New Market Identification	• Growth in reward club membership for new demographic segments
Employee Training and Advancement	• Percentage of employees participating in training courses • Survey scores pre- and post-training sessions

*Measures are based on survey data reported from actual hotels—N. Evans, "Assessing the Balanced Scorecard as a Management Tool for Hotels," *International Journal of Contemporary Hospitality Management*, Vol. 17, Issue 4/5, (2005): 376–390.

Strategy Translation

Strategy, according to the creators of the Balanced Scorecard framework, is defined as:[8]

> . . . *choosing the market and customer segments the business unit intends to serve, identifying the critical internal and business processes that the unit must excel at to deliver the value propositions to customers in the targeted market segments, and selecting the individual and organizational capabilities required for the internal, customer, and financial objectives.*

Strategy specifies management's desired relationships among the four perspectives. *Strategy translation,* on the other hand, means specifying objectives, measures, targets, and initiatives for each perspective. Consider, for example, the financial perspective.

- Objective: For the financial perspective, a company's *objective* may be to grow revenues by introducing new products.
- Measure: The *performance measure* may be the percentage of revenues from the sale of new products.
- Target: The *target* or *standard* for the coming year for the measure may be 20% (i.e., 20% of the total revenues for the coming year must be from the sale of new products).
- Initiative: The *initiative* describes *how* this is to be accomplished. The "how," of course, involves the other three perspectives.

The company must now identify the customer segments, internal processes, and individual and organizational capabilities that will permit the realization of the revenue growth objective.

---

8 Robert S. Kaplan and David P. Norton, *The Balanced Scorecard* (Boston: Harvard Business School Press, 1996), p. 37.

This illustrates the fact that the financial objectives serve as the focus for the objectives, measures, and initiatives of the other three perspectives.

The Role of Performance Measures The Balanced Scorecard is not simply a collection of critical performance measures. The performance measures are derived from a company's vision, strategy, and objectives. These measures must be *balanced* between the following measures:

- performance driver measures (i.e., lead indicators of future financial performance) and outcome measures (i.e., lagged indicators of financial performance)
- objective and subjective measures
- external and internal measures
- financial and nonfinancial measures

Linking performance measures to the organization's strategy creates significant advantages. For example, each quarter, **Analog Devices**' senior managers discuss Balanced Scorecard results for the various divisions. On one occasion, managers noted problems with their new-product ratios—used to measure the effectiveness of R&D spending. They quickly discovered that one division lagged in developing new products. The division's manager focused heavily on R&D by investing more money and exploring new market segments, new product sales, and marketing strategies. Analog Devices' corporate vice president for marketing, quality, and planning noted that they wouldn't have been able to catch the problem so early if they just looked at financials.[9] Other companies, such as **Bank of Montreal**, **Hilton Hotels Corporation**, and **Duke University Children's Hospital**, have had similar success.

The rapid and widespread adoption of this strategic management system is a strong testimonial of its worth. For example, companies like **General Electric**, **Verizon**, and **Microsoft** have adapted their initial Balanced Scorecards into risk dashboards that contain key financial and nonfinancial measures pertaining to the important risks that threaten organizational success.[10] Other organizations, such as **Walmart**, adapt their Balanced Scorecards to include measures that help their suppliers focus on increasingly important sustainability issues like using less packaging materials and more effective packaging techniques.[11]

Linking Performance Measures to Strategy Balancing outcome measures with performance drivers is essential to linking with the organization's strategy. Performance drivers make things happen and are indicators of how the outcomes are going to be realized. Thus, they tend to be unique to a particular strategy. Outcome measures are also important because they reveal whether the strategy is being implemented successfully with the desired economic consequences. For example, if the number of defective products is decreased, does this produce a greater market share? Does this, in turn, produce more revenues and profits? These questions suggest that the most important principle of linkage is the usage of cause-and-effect relationships. In fact, a **testable strategy** can be defined as a set of linked objectives aimed at an overall goal. The testability of the strategy is achieved by restating the strategy into a set of cause-and-effect hypotheses that are expressed by a sequence of if-then statements.[12] Consider, for example, the following sequence of if-then statements that link quality training with increased profitability:

> *If design engineers receive quality training, then they can redesign products to reduce the number of defective units; if the number of defective units is reduced, then customer satisfaction will increase; if customer satisfaction increases, then market share will increase; if market share increases, then sales will increase; if sales increase, then profits will increase.*

9 Joel Kurtzman, "Is Your Company Off Course: Now You Can Find Out Why," *Fortune* (February 17, 1997). http://money.cnn.com/magazines/fortune/fortune_archive/1997/02/17/222180/index.htm (accessed December 13, 2006).

10 Ante Spencer, "Giving the Boss the Big Picture," *BusinessWeek* (February 13, 2006).

11 "Getting Leaner—Ahead of the Pack: Suppliers Adjust to New Packaging Priorities," *Retailing Today* (2006): 16–18.

12 Robert S. Kaplan and David P. Norton, *The Balanced Scorecard* (Boston: Harvard Business School Press, 1996), p. 149. Kaplan and Norton describe the sequence of if-then statements only as a strategy. Calling it a testable strategy distinguishes it from the earlier, more general definition offered, and, in our opinion, properly so.

Here's How It's Used: SUPPLIER SUSTAINABILITY SCORECARDS AT WALMART

Over the past decade, **Walmart** has developed a systematic approach to improving its sustainability initiatives. One area that has caused real change is its emphasis on improving supplier sustainability. Walmart has suppliers fill out a Supplier Sustainability Assessment, a series of questions on their use of materials, waste, and their own supply chain. Suppliers are ranked from best to worst in each subcategory, and these results are shared with Walmart buyers to use in their purchasing decisions. As a result, many suppliers have worked to decrease their waste. **Miller Coors**, for example, has worked with its barley farmers to decrease their use of water and pesticides.

Walmart has worked to reduce its carbon footprint through reductions in energy usage of the Walmart and **Sam's Club** truck fleets. Three opportunities for efficiency were optimizing how trailers are loaded and filled, reducing overall miles by optimizing routes, and technology improvements to improve efficiency and reduce emissions. Over a 5-year period, expected savings of $300 million per year were exceeded, with savings of almost $1 billion. Carbon dioxide emission avoidance of about 650,000 metric tons was achieved.

As the company announced today, it has achieved Lee Scott's fleet-efficiency goal. And Scott's cost-saving estimate turned out to be grossly underestimated. The combined efforts of changing loading, routing and driving techniques, as well as collaborating with tractor and trailer manufacturers on new technologies will save the company nearly $1 billion this fiscal year alone. Compared to a 2005 baseline, this is more than three times Scott's projection at the time. And it will avoid emissions of nearly 650,000 metric tons of carbon dioxide.

Sources: Mark Gunther, "Game On: Why Walmart Is Ranking Suppliers on Sustainability," *GreenBiz* (April 15, 2013). Taken from https://www.greenbiz.com/blog/2013/04/15/game-why-walmart-ranking-suppliers-sustainability. Joel Makower, "Walmart Sustainability at 10: An Assessment," *GreenBiz* (November 17, 2015). Taken from https://www.greenbiz.com/article/walmart-sustainability-10-assessment.

Exhibit 11.7 illustrates the quality improvement strategy described by a sequence of if-then statements. First, notice how each of the four perspectives is linked through the cause-and-effect relationships hypothesized:

- The learning and growth perspective is present through the training dimension.
- The internal perspective is represented by the redesign and manufacturing processes.
- The customer perspective is represented by customer satisfaction and market share.
- The financial perspective is present because of revenues and profits.

Exhibit 11.7

Testable Strategy Illustrated

Second, viability of the strategy is testable. Strategic feedback is available that allows managers to test the reasonableness of the strategy. Hours of quality training, the number of products redesigned, the number of defective units, customer satisfaction, market share, revenues, and profits all are observable measures. Thus, the claimed relationships can be checked to see if the strategy produces the expected results. If not, it could be due to one of two causes—implementation problems or an invalid strategy.

Implementation Problems It is possible that key *performance drivers* such as training and redesign of products did not achieve their targeted levels (i.e., fewer hours of training and fewer products redesigned than planned). In this case, the failure to produce the targeted *outcomes* for defects, customer satisfaction, market share, revenues, and profits could be merely an implementation problem.

Invalid Strategy If the targeted levels of performance drivers were achieved and the expected outcomes did not materialize, then the problem could very well lie with the strategy itself. This example depicts a *double-loop feedback*. Double-loop feedback occurs whenever managers receive information about both the *effectiveness* of strategy implementation as well as the *validity* of the assumptions underlying the strategy. In a functional-based responsibility accounting system, typically only *single-loop feedback* is provided. Single-loop feedback emphasizes only effectiveness of implementation. In single-loop feedback, actual results deviating from planned results are a signal to take corrective action so that the plan (strategy) can be executed as intended. The validity of the assumptions underlying the plan is usually not questioned.

The Four Perspectives and Performance Measures

The four perspectives define the strategy of an organization and provide the structure or framework for developing an integrated, cohesive set of performance measures. These measures, once developed, become the means for articulating and communicating the strategy of the organization to its employees and managers. The measures also serve the purpose of aligning individual objectives and actions with organizational objectives and initiatives.

The Financial Perspective The financial perspective establishes the long- and short-term financial performance objectives. The financial perspective is concerned with the global financial consequences of the other three perspectives. Thus, the objectives and measures of the other perspectives must be linked to the financial objectives. The financial perspective has three strategic themes—revenue growth, cost reduction, and asset utilization—which serve as the building blocks for the development of specific operational objectives and measures.

Revenue Growth Several possible objectives are associated with revenue growth, including the following:

- increase the number of new products
- create new applications for existing products
- develop new customers and markets
- adopt a new pricing strategy

Once operational objectives are known, performance measures can be designed. For example, possible measures for the above list of objectives (in the order given) are percentage of revenue from new products, percentage of revenue from new applications, percentage of revenue from new customers and market segments, and profitability by product or customer.

Cost Reduction Examples of cost reduction objectives include:

- reducing the cost per unit of product
- reducing the cost per customer
- reducing the cost per distribution channel

The appropriate measure is the cost per unit of the particular cost object. Trends in this measure will tell whether or not the costs are being reduced. For these objectives, the accuracy of cost assignments is especially important. Activity-based costing can play an essential measurement role, especially for selling and administrative costs—costs not usually assigned to cost objects like customers and distribution channels.

Asset Utilization Improving asset utilization is the principal objective. Financial measures such as ROI and EVA are used. The objectives and measures for the financial perspective are summarized in Exhibit 11.8.

Exhibit 11.8

Summary of Objectives and Measures: Financial Perspective

Objectives	Measures
Revenue Growth:	
Increase the number of new products	Percentage of revenue from new products
Create new applications	Percentage of revenue from new applications
Develop new customers and markets	Percentage of revenue from new sources
Adopt a new pricing strategy	Product and customer profitability
Cost Reduction:	
Reduce unit product cost	Unit product cost
Reduce unit customer cost	Unit customer cost
Reduce distribution channel cost	Cost per distribution channel
Asset Utilization:	
Improve asset utilization	Return on investment
	Economic value added

Customer Perspective The customer perspective is the source of the revenue component for the financial objectives. This perspective defines and selects the customer and market segments in which the company chooses to compete.

Core Objectives and Measures Once the customers and segments are defined, then *core objectives and measures* are developed. Core objectives and measures are those that are common across all organizations. The five key core objectives are as follows:

- increase market share
- increase customer retention
- increase customer acquisition
- increase customer satisfaction
- increase customer profitability

Possible core measures for these objectives, respectively, are market share (percentage of the market), percentage growth of business from existing customers and percentage of repeating customers, number of new customers, ratings from customer satisfaction surveys, and individual and segment profitability. Activity-based costing is a key tool in assessing customer profitability (Chapter 5). Notice that customer profitability is the only financial measure among the core measures. This measure, however, is critical because it emphasizes the importance of the *right* kind of customers. What good is it to have customers if they are not profitable? The obvious answer spells out the difference between being customer focused and customer obsessed.

Customer Value In addition to the core measures and objectives, measures are needed that drive the creation of *customer value* and, thus, drive the core outcomes. For example, increasing customer value builds customer loyalty (increases retention) and increases customer satisfaction. **Customer value** is the difference between realization and sacrifice, where realization is what the customer receives and sacrifice is what is given up in return. Realization includes such things as product functionality (features), product quality, reliability of delivery, delivery response time, image, and reputation. Sacrifice includes product price, time to learn to use the product, operating cost, maintenance cost, and disposal cost. The costs incurred by the customer *after* purchase are called **post-purchase costs**.

The attributes associated with the realization and sacrifice value propositions provide the basis for the objectives and measures that will lead to improving the core outcomes. The objectives for the sacrifice value proposition are the simplest:

- decrease price
- decrease post-purchase costs

Selling price and post-purchase costs are important measures of value creation. Decreasing these costs decreases customer sacrifice and, thus, increases customer value. Increasing customer value should impact favorably on most of the core objectives.

Similar favorable effects can be obtained by increasing realization. Realization objectives, for example, would include the following:

- improve product functionality
- improve product quality
- increase delivery reliability
- improve product image and reputation

Possible measures for these objectives include, respectively, feature satisfaction ratings, percentage of returns, on-time delivery percentage, and product recognition ratings. Of these objectives and measures, delivery reliability will be used to illustrate how measures can affect managerial behavior, indicating the need to be careful in the choice and use of performance measures.

Delivery reliability, or on-time delivery, is a commonly used operational measure of reliability. To measure on-time delivery, a firm sets delivery dates and then calculates on-time delivery performance by dividing the orders delivered on time by the total number of orders delivered. The goal, of course, is to achieve a ratio of 100%. Some, however, have found that use of this measure may produce undesirable behavioral consequences.[13] Specifically, plant managers were giving priority to filling orders not yet late over orders that were already late. The performance measure was encouraging managers to have one very late shipment rather than several moderately late shipments. A chart measuring the age of late deliveries could help mitigate this problem. Exhibit 11.9 summarizes the objectives and measures for the customer perspective.

Objectives	Measures
Core:	
Increase market share	Market share (percentage of market)
Increase customer retention	Percentage growth of business from existing customers
	Percentage of repeating customers
Increase customer acquisition	Number of new customers
Increase customer satisfaction	Ratings from customer surveys
Increase customer profitability	Customer profitability
Customer Value:	
Decrease price	Price
Decrease post-purchase costs	Post-purchase costs
Improve product functionality	Ratings from customer surveys
Improve product quality	Percentage of returns
Increase delivery reliability	On-time delivery percentage
	Aging schedule
Improve product image and reputation	Ratings from customer surveys

Exhibit 11.9

Summary of Objectives and Measures: Customer Perspective

13 Joseph Fisher, "Nonfinancial Performance Measures," *Journal of Cost Management* (Spring 1992): 31–38.

Internal (Process) Perspective The internal perspective typically focuses on identifying the organization's core internal business processes needed for creating customer and shareholder value to achieve the customer and financial objectives. To provide the framework needed for this perspective, a *process value chain* is defined. The **process value chain** is made up of three processes:

- The **innovation process** anticipates the emerging and potential needs of customers and creates new products and services to satisfy those needs. It represents what is called the *long-wave* of value creation.
- The **operations process** produces and delivers *existing* products and services to customers. It begins with a customer order and ends with the delivery of the product or service. It is the *short-wave* of value creation.
- The **post-sales service process** provides critical and responsive services to customers after the product or service has been delivered.

Innovation Process: Objectives and Measures Objectives for the innovation process include the following:

- increase the number of new products
- increase percentage of revenue from proprietary products
- decrease the time to develop new products

Associated measures are actual new products developed versus planned products, percentage of total revenues from new products, percentage of revenues from proprietary products, and development cycle time (time to market).

Operations Process: Objectives and Measures The three operations process objectives that typically are mentioned and emphasized include the following:

- increase process quality
- increase process efficiency
- decrease process time

Examples of process quality measures are quality costs, output yields (good output divided by good input), and percentage of defective units (good output divided by total output). Measures of process efficiency are concerned mainly with process cost and process productivity. Activity-based costing and process-value analysis facilitate measuring and tracking process costs. Common process time measures are cycle time, velocity, and manufacturing cycle efficiency (MCE).

CONCEPT CLIP

Cycle Time and Velocity The time to respond to a customer order is referred to as *responsiveness*. *Cycle time* and *velocity* are two operational measures of responsiveness. **Cycle time** is the length of time it takes to produce a unit of output from the time raw materials are received (starting point of the cycle) until the good is delivered to finished goods inventory (finishing point of the cycle). Thus, cycle time is the time required to produce a product (Time ÷ Units produced). **Velocity** is the number of units of output that can be produced in a given period of time (Units produced ÷ Time). **Example 11.5** shows how to compute cycle time and velocity.

EXAMPLE 11.5

How to Compute Cycle Time and Velocity

A company has the following data for one of its manufacturing cells:

Maximum units produced in a quarter (3-month period): 200,000 units

Actual units produced in a quarter: 160,000 units

Productive hours in one quarter: 40,000 hours

EXAMPLE 11.5

(*Continued*)

Required:

1. Compute the theoretical cycle time (in minutes).
2. Compute the actual cycle time (in minutes).
3. Compute the theoretical velocity in units per hour.
4. Compute the actual velocity in units per hour.

Solution:

1. Theoretical Cycle Time = (40,000 hours)(60 minutes per hour)/200,000 units

    = 12 minutes per unit

2. Actual Cycle Time = (40,000 hours)(60 minutes per hour)/160,000 units

    = 15 minutes per unit

3. Theoretical Velocity = 60 minutes per hour/12 minutes per unit

    = 5 units per hour

    (Or, 200,000 units per quarter/40,000 hours per quarter = 5 units per hour)

4. Actual Velocity = 60 minutes per hour/15 minutes per unit

    = 4 units per hour

    (Or 160,000 units per quarter/40,000 hours per quarter = 4 units per hour)

Incentives can be used to encourage operational managers to reduce manufacturing cycle time or to increase velocity, thus improving delivery performance. A natural way to accomplish this objective is to tie product costs to cycle time and reward operational managers for reducing product costs. For example, in a just-in-time (JIT) firm, conversion costs of the cell can be assigned to products on the basis of the time that it takes a product to move through the cell. Using the theoretical productive time available for a period (in minutes), a value-added standard cost per minute can be computed.

Standard Cost per Minute = Cell Conversion Costs/Minutes Available

To obtain the conversion cost per unit, this standard cost per minute is multiplied by the actual cycle time used to produce the units during the period. By comparing the unit cost computed using the actual cycle time with the unit cost possible using the theoretical or optimal cycle time, a manager can assess the potential for improvement. Note that the more time it takes a product to move through the cell, the greater the unit product cost. With incentives to reduce product cost, this approach to product costing encourages operational managers and cell workers to find ways to decrease cycle time or increase velocity.

Manufacturing Cycle Efficiency Another time-based operational measure calculates MCE (**manufacturing cycle efficiency**). MCE is measured as value-added time divided by total time. Total time includes both value-added time (the time spent efficiently producing the product) and nonvalue-added time (such as move time, inspection time, and waiting time). The formula for computing MCE is:

MCE = Processing Time/Processing Time + Move Time + Inspection Time + Waiting Time

In this equation, processing time is the time that it takes to convert raw materials into a finished good. The other activities and their times are viewed as wasteful, and the goal is to reduce those times to zero. If this is accomplished, the value of MCE will be 1.0, or 100%. As MCE improves (moves toward 1.0), cycle time decreases. Furthermore, since the only way MCE can improve is by decreasing waste, cost reduction must also follow. **Example 11.6** shows how to calculate MCE.

EXAMPLE 11.6
 	
How to Calculate Manufacturing Cycle Efficiency
	A company provided the following information:
	
	Maximum units produced in a quarter (3-month period): 200,000 units
	
	Actual units produced in a quarter: 160,000 units
	
	Productive hours in one quarter: 40,000 hours
	
	Actual cycle time = 15 minutes
	
	Theoretical cycle time = 12 minutes
	
	Required:
	1. Calculate the amount of processing time and the amount of nonprocessing time.
	2. Calculate MCE.
	
	Solution:
	1. Processing time is equal to theoretical cycle time. That is, if everything goes smoothly and there is no wasted time, it takes 12 minutes to produce one unit. Nonprocessing time, therefore, must be the difference between actual cycle time (which includes some waste) and theoretical cycle time.
	
	    Processing Time = Theoretical Cycle Time = 12 minutes
	    Nonprocessing Time = Actual Cycle Time − Theoretical Cycle Time
	    = 15 − 12 = 3 minutes
	
	2. MCE = Processing Time/(Processing Time + Nonprocessing Time)
	    = 12/(12 + 3) = 0.8, or 80%

Example 11.6 illustrates a fairly efficient process, as measured by MCE. Many manufacturing companies have MCEs less than 0.05.[14]

Post-sales Service Process: Objectives and Measures Increasing quality, increasing efficiency, and decreasing process time are also objectives that apply to the post-sales service process. Service quality, for example, can be measured by first-pass yields, where first-pass yields are defined as the percentage of customer requests resolved with a single service call. Efficiency can be measured by cost trends and productivity measures. Process time can be measured by cycle time, where the starting point of the cycle is defined as the receipt of a customer request, and the finishing point is when the customer's problem is solved. The objectives and measures for the process perspective are summarized in Exhibit 11.10.

Learning and Growth Perspective The fourth and final category in a typical Balanced Scorecard is the learning and growth perspective, which represents the source of the capabilities that enable the accomplishment of the other three perspectives' objectives. This perspective has three major objectives:

- increase employee capabilities
- increase motivation, empowerment, and alignment
- increase information systems capabilities

---

14 Robert S. Kaplan and David P. Norton, *The Balanced Scorecard* (Boston: Harvard Business School Press, 1996), p. 117.

Objectives	Measures
Innovation:	
Increase the number of new products	Number of new products vs. planned
Increase proprietary products	Percentage revenue from proprietary products
Decrease new product development time	Time to market (from start to finish)
Operations:	
Increase process quality	Quality costs
	Output yields
	Percentage of defective units
Increase process efficiency	Unit cost trends
	Output/input(s)
Decrease process time	Cycle time and velocity
	MCE
Post-Sales Service:	
Increase service quality	First-pass yields
Increase service efficiency	Costs trends
	Output/input
Decrease service time	Cycle time

Exhibit 11.10

Summary of Objectives and Measures: Internal Perspective

Employee Capabilities Three core *outcome* measurements for employee capabilities are employee satisfaction ratings, employee turnover percentages, and employee productivity (e.g., revenue per employee). Examples of lead measures or performance drivers for employee capabilities are hours of training and strategic job coverage ratios (percentage of critical job requirements filled). As new processes are created, new skills are often required. Training and hiring are sources of these new skills. Furthermore, the percentage of the employees needed in certain key areas with the requisite skills signals the capability of the organization to meet the objectives of the other three perspectives.

Motivation, Empowerment, and Alignment Employees must not only have the necessary skills, but they must also have the freedom, motivation, and initiative to use those skills effectively. The number of suggestions per employee and the number of suggestions implemented per employee are possible measures of motivation and empowerment. Suggestions per employee provide a measure of the degree of employee involvement, whereas suggestions implemented per employee signal the quality of the employee participation. The second measure also signals to employees whether or not their suggestions are being taken seriously.

Information Systems Capabilities Increasing information system capabilities means providing more accurate and timely information to employees so that they can improve processes and effectively execute new processes. Measures should be concerned with the *strategic information availability*. For example, possible measures include percentage of processes with real-time feedback capabilities and percentage of customer-facing employees with online access to customer and product information. Exhibit 11.11 summarizes the objectives and measures for the learning and growth perspective.

Exhibit 11.11

Summary of Objectives and Measures: Learning and Growth Perspective

Objectives	Measures
Employee Capabilities: Increase employee capabilities	Employee satisfaction ratings Employee productivity (Revenue/Employee) Hours of training Strategic job coverage ratio (percentage of critical job requirements filled)
Motivation: Increase motivation and alignment	Suggestions per employee Suggestions implemented per employee
Information Systems Capabilities: Increase information systems capabilities	Percentage of processes with real-time feedback capabilities Percentage of customer-facing employees with online access to customer and product information

Check Point

1. **A manufacturing cell could produce a maximum of 6,000 units per week using 2,000 productive hours. Last week, it produced 5,000 units. What is the theoretical cycle time? Actual cycle time?**

Answer:
Theoretical Cycle Time = (2,000 hours)(60 minutes per hour)/6,000 units = 20 minutes
Actual Cycle Time = (2,000 hours)(60 minutes per hour)/5,000 units = 24 minutes

2. **A manufacturing cell could produce a maximum of 6,000 units per week using 2,000 productive hours. Last week, it produced 5,000 units. What is the processing time? Nonprocessing time? MCE?**

Answer:
Processing Time – Theoretical Cycle Time = 20 minutes
Nonprocessing Time = Actual Cycle Time – Theoretical Cycle Time
$$= 24 - 20 = 4 \text{ minutes}$$
MCE = 20/(20 + 4) = 0.83, or 83%

SUMMARY OF LEARNING OBJECTIVES

LO1. Explain how and why firms choose to decentralize.
- In a decentralized organization, lower-level managers make and implement decisions. In a centralized organization, lower-level managers are responsible only for implementing decisions.
- Reasons why companies decentralize:
  - Local managers can make better decisions using local information.
  - Local managers can provide a more timely response.
  - It is impossible for one central manager to be fully knowledgeable about all products and markets.

- Decentralization can train and motivate local managers and free top management from day-to-day operating conditions so that they can spend time on long-range activities, such as strategic planning. Managerial accounting is important in designing effective performance measures and incentive systems to help ensure that managers in a decentralized organization use their decision-making authority to improve the organization's performance.
- Four types of responsibility centers are:
  - Cost centers—manager is responsible for costs.
  - Revenue centers—manager is responsible for price and quantity sold.
  - Profit centers—manager is responsible for costs and revenues.
  - Investment centers—manager is responsible for costs, revenues, and investment.

LO2. Compute and explain return on investment.
- ROI is the ratio of operating income to average operating assets.
- Margin is operating income divided by sales *or* margin multiplied by turnover.
- Turnover is sales divided by average operating assets.
- Advantage: ROI encourages managers to focus on improving sales, controlling costs, and using assets efficiently.
- Disadvantage: ROI can encourage managers to sacrifice long-run benefits for short-run benefits.

LO3. Compute and explain residual income and economic value added.
- Residual income is operating income minus a minimum percentage cost of capital multiplied by capital employed.
  - If residual income > 0, then the division is earning more than the minimum cost of capital.
  - If residual income < 0, then the division is earning less than the minimum cost of capital.
  - If residual income = 0, then the division is earning just the minimum cost of capital.
- Economic value added is *after-tax* operating profit minus the *actual* total annual cost of capital.
  - If EVA > 0, then the company is creating wealth (or value).
  - If EVA < 0, then the company is destroying wealth.

LO4. Explain the role of transfer pricing in a decentralized firm.
- Transfer price is charged by the selling division of a company to a buying division of the same company.
  - Increases revenue to the selling division
  - Increases cost to the buying division
- Common transfer pricing policies are:
  - Cost based (e.g., total product cost)
  - Market based (price charged in the outside market)
  - Negotiated (between the buying and selling divisions' managers)

LO5. *(Appendix 11A)* Explain the uses of the Balanced Scorecard, and compute cycle time, velocity, and manufacturing cycle efficiency.
- Balanced Scorecard is a strategic management system.
- Objectives and measures are developed for four perspectives:
  - financial perspective
  - customer perspective
  - internal perspective
  - learning and growth perspective
- Velocity is the number of units produced in a period of time.
- Cycle time is the time needed to produce one unit.
- MCE is measured as value-added time divided by total time. The higher the MCE, the greater the firm's efficiency.

SUMMARY OF IMPORTANT EQUATIONS

1. ROI = Operating Income/Average Operating Assets

2. Average Operating Assets = (Beginning Assets + Ending Assets)/2

               Margin   **Turnover**

3. ROI = Operating Income/Sales × Sales/Average Operating Assets

4. Residual Income = Operating Income − (Minimum Rate of Return × Average Operating Assets)

5. EVA = After-Tax Operating Income − (Actual Percentage Cost of Capital × Total Capital Employed)

6. MCE = Processing Time/Processing Time + Move Time + Inspection Time + Waiting Time

KEY TERMS

Balanced Scorecard, 611 *(Appendix 11A)*, a strategic management system that translates an organization's mission and strategy into operational objectives and performance measures.

Cost center, 594, part of an organization in which the manager is responsible only for costs.

Customer perspective, 611 *(Appendix 11A)*, defines the customer and market segments in which the business segments compete.

Customer value, 616 *(Appendix 11A)*, the difference between realization (what the customer receives) and sacrifice (what is given up in return).

Cycle time, 618 *(Appendix 11A)*, the length of time required to produce one unit of a product.

Decentralization, 592, the practice of delegating decision-making authority to lower levels of management.

Economic value added (EVA), 604, after-tax operating income minus the dollar cost of capital employed.

Financial perspective, 611 *(Appendix 11A)*, describes the economic consequences of actions taken in the other three Balanced Scorecard perspectives.

Hurdle rate, 600, the minimum ROI required to accept an investment.

Innovation process, 618 *(Appendix 11A)*, creates new products and services to satisfy emerging and potential customer needs.

Internal business process perspective, 611 *(Appendix 11A)*, describes the internal business processes needed to provide value for customers and owners.

Investment center, 594, part of an organization in which the manager is responsible for sales, costs, and investment.

Learning and growth (infrastructure) perspective, 611 *(Appendix 11A)*, defines the capabilities that an organization needs to create long-term growth and improvement, including employee capabilities, information systems capabilities, and employee attitudes.

Margin, 597, the ratio of operating income to sales.

MCE (manufacturing cycle efficiency), 619 *(Appendix 11A)*, value-added time divided by total time.

Operating assets, 596, all assets acquired to generate income.

Operating income, 596, earnings before interest and taxes.

Operations process, 618 *(Appendix 11A)*, produces and delivers existing products and services to customers.

Post-purchase costs, 617 *(Appendix 11A)*, costs incurred by the customer after purchase.

Post-sales service process, 618 *(Appendix 11A)*, provides services to customers after the product is produced and delivered.

Process value chain, 618 *(Appendix 11A)*, the innovation, operations, and post-sales service processes.

Profit center, 594, part of an organization in which the manager is responsible for both sales and costs.

Residual income, 603, the difference between income and the minimum dollar return required on a company's operating assets.

Responsibility center, 594, segment of a business in which a manager is accountable for a specific set of activities.

Return on investment (ROI), 596, the profit (earnings) per dollar of investment.

Revenue center, 594, part of an organization in which the manager is responsible only for sales.

Strategy, 612 *(Appendix 11A)*, choosing the market and customer segments the business unit intends to serve, and identifying the critical internal and business processes that the unit must excel at to deliver the value propositions to customers in the targeted market segments.

Testable strategy, 613 *(Appendix 11A)*, a set of linked objectives aimed at an overall goal.

Transfer price, 607, price charged for a component or service by the selling division to the buying division of the same company.

Turnover, 597, sales divided by average operating assets.

Velocity, 618 *(Appendix 11A)*, the number of units that can be produced in a given period of time (e.g., output per hour).

REVIEW PROBLEMS

I. ROI

Flip Flop Politics Inc. had gross margin of $550,000 and selling and administrative expense of $300,000 last year. Also, Flip Flop began last year with $1,400,000 of operating assets and ended the year with $1,100,000 of operating assets.

Required:

Calculate return on investment for Flip Flop Politics.

(Continued)

Solution:

Return on Investment = Operating Income/Average Operating Assets

Gross margin	$550,000
Selling and administrative expense	300,000
Operating income	$250,000

Average Operating Assets = (Beginning Operating Assets + Ending Operating Assets)/2

$$= (\$1,400,000 + \$1,100,000)/2$$
$$= \$2,500,000/2$$
$$= \$1,250,000$$

Therefore, Return on Investment = Operating Income/Average Operating Assets

$$= \$250,000/\$1,250,000$$
$$= 0.20, \text{ or } 20\%$$

II. Economic Value Added

El Suezo Inc. had sales of $5,000,000, cost of goods sold of $3,500,000, and selling and administrative expense of $500,000 for its most recent year of operations. El Suezo faces a tax rate of 40%. Also, El Suezo employed $2,000,000 of debt capital and $4,000,000 of equity capital in generating its return. Finally, the company's actual cost of capital is 8%.

Required:

1. Calculate after-tax operating income for El Suezo.
2. Calculate EVA for El Suezo.

Solution:

1.

Sales	$5,000,000
Cost of goods sold	3,500,000
Gross margin	$1,500,000
Selling and administrative expense	500,000
Operating income	$1,000,000
Income taxes (@ 40%)	400,000
Net income	$ 600,000

2. EVA = After-Tax Operating Income – (Actual Percentage Cost of Capital
        × Total Capital Employed)
$$= \$600,000 - [0.08 \times (\$2,000,000 + \$4,000,000)]$$
$$= \$600,000 - (0.08 \times \$6,000,000)$$
$$= \$600,000 - \$480,000$$
$$= \$120,000$$

III. Transfer Pricing

The Components Division produces a part that is used by the Goods Division. The cost of manufacturing the part follows:

Direct materials	$10
Direct labor	2
Variable overhead	3
Fixed overhead*	5
Total cost	$20

*Based on a practical volume of 200,000 parts.

Other costs incurred by the Components Division are as follows:

Fixed selling and administrative	$500,000
Variable selling (per unit)	1

The part usually sells for between $28 and $30 in the external market. Currently, the Components Division is selling it to external customers for $29. The division is capable of producing 200,000 units of the part per year. However, because of a weak economy, only 150,000 parts are expected to be sold during the coming year. The variable selling expenses are avoidable if the part is sold internally.

The Goods Division has been buying the same part from an external supplier for $28. It expects to use 50,000 units of the part during the coming year. The manager of the Goods Division has offered to buy 50,000 units from the Components Division for $18 per unit.

Required:

1. Determine the minimum transfer price that the Components Division would accept.
2. Determine the maximum transfer price that the manager of the Goods Division would pay.
3. Should an internal transfer take place? Why or why not? If you were the manager of the Components Division, would you sell the 50,000 components for $18 each? Explain.
4. Suppose that the average operating assets of the Components Division total $10 million. Compute the ROI for the coming year, assuming that the 50,000 units are transferred to the Goods Division for $21 each.

Solution:

1. The minimum transfer price is $15. The Components Division has idle capacity and so must cover only its incremental costs, which are the variable manufacturing costs. (Fixed costs are the same whether or not the internal transfer occurs; the variable selling expenses are avoidable.)
2. The maximum transfer price is $28. The Goods Division would not pay more for the part than it has to pay an external supplier.
3. Yes, an internal transfer should occur. The opportunity cost of the selling division is less than the opportunity cost of the buying division. The Components Division would earn an additional $150,000 profit ($3 × 50,000). The total joint benefit, however, is $650,000 ($13 × 50,000). The manager of the Components Division should attempt to negotiate a more favorable outcome for that division.
4. Income statement:

Sales [($29 × 150,000) + ($21 × 50,000)]	$ 5,400,000
Less: Variable cost of goods sold ($15 × 200,000)	(3,000,000)
Less: Variable selling expenses ($1 × 150,000)	(150,000)
Contribution margin	$ 2,250,000
Less: Fixed overhead ($5 × 200,000)	(1,000,000)
Less: Fixed selling and administrative	(500,000)
Operating income	$ 750,000

$$\text{ROI} = \text{Operating Income/Average Operating Assets}$$
$$= \$750,000/\$10,000,000$$
$$= 0.075$$

DISCUSSION QUESTIONS

1. Discuss the differences between centralized and decentralized decision making.
2. What is decentralization?
3. Explain why firms choose to decentralize.

4. What are margin and turnover? Explain how these concepts can improve the evaluation of an investment center.
5. What are the three benefits of ROI? Explain how each benefit can lead to improved profitability.
6. What is residual income? What is EVA? How does EVA differ from the general definition of residual income?
7. Can residual income or EVA ever be negative? What is the meaning of negative residual income or EVA?
8. What is a transfer price?
9. Briefly explain three common transfer pricing policies used by organizations.
10. *(Appendix 11A)* What is the Balanced Scorecard?
11. *(Appendix 11A)* Describe the four perspectives of the Balanced Scorecard.

MULTIPLE-CHOICE QUESTIONS

11-1 The practice of delegating authority to division-level managers by top management is

    a. decentralization.
    b. good business practice.
    c. centralization.
    d. autonomy.
    e. never done in business today.

11-2 Which of the following is *not* a reason for decentralizing?

    a. Training and motivating managers
    b. Unmasking inefficiencies in subdivisions of an overall profitable company
    c. Allowing top management to focus on strategic decision making
    d. Allowing top management to make all key operating decisions throughout the company
    e. All of these.

11-3 A responsibility center in which a manager is responsible only for costs is a(n)

    a. investment center.
    b. revenue center.
    c. profit center.
    d. cost center.

11-4 A responsibility center in which a manager is responsible for revenues, costs, and investments is a(n)

    a. investment center.
    b. revenue center.
    c. profit center.
    d. cost center.

11-5 If sales and average operating assets for Year 2 are identical to their values in Year 1, yet operating income is higher, Year 2 return on investment (compared with Year 1 ROI) will

    a. decrease.
    b. increase.
    c. stay the same.
    d. The direction of change in ROI cannot be determined by this information.

11-6 If sales and average operating assets for Year 2 are identical to their values in Year 1, yet operating income is higher, Year 2 turnover (compared with Year 1 turnover) will

    a. decrease.
    b. increase.
    c. stay the same.
    d. The direction of change in turnover cannot be determined by this information.

11-7 The key difference between residual income and EVA is that EVA

    a. uses the actual cost of capital for the company rather than a minimum required cost of capital.

    b. uses the minimum required cost of capital for a company rather than the actual percentage cost of capital.

    c. is a ratio rather than an absolute dollar amount.

    d. cannot be negative.

    e. There is no difference between residual income and EVA.

11-8 If ROI for a division is 15% and the company's minimum required cost of capital is 18%, then

    a. residual income for the division is negative.

    b. residual income for the division takes on a value between 0 and +1.

    c. residual income cannot be computed.

    d. EVA must be negative.

    e. residual income is positive.

> *Use the following information for Multiple-Choice Questions 11–9 and 11–10:*
> Division A manufactures an aircraft engine component with unit variable product cost of $38 and market price of $50. Division A incurs shipping costs of $3 per unit for sales to outside parties only. Division B uses this component in the manufacture of its own engine production activities. Top management allows negotiated transfer pricing.

11-9 Refer to the information above. If Division A is operating at full capacity, the maximum transfer price (the ceiling of the bargaining range) is

    a. $38.

    b. $50.

    c. $44.

    d. $47.

    e. There is no bargaining range.

11-10 Refer to the information above. If Division A is operating at less than full capacity, the minimum transfer price (the floor of the bargaining range) is

    a. $38.

    b. $50.

    c. $44.

    d. $47.

    e. There is no bargaining range.

11-11 *(Appendix 11A)* Which of the following is a perspective of the Balanced Scorecard?

    a. Learning and growth (infrastructure)

    b. Internal business process

    c. Customer

    d. Financial

    e. All of these.

11-12 *(Appendix 11A)* The length of time it takes to produce a unit of output from the time raw materials are received until the good is delivered to finished goods inventory is called

    a. velocity.

    b. cycle time.

    c. manufacturing cycle efficiency.

    d. theoretical cycle time.

    e. theoretical MCE.

BRIEF EXERCISES: SET A

Use the following information for Brief Exercises 11-13 through 11-15:

East Mullett Manufacturing earned operating income last year as shown in the following income statement:

Sales	$3,750,000
Cost of goods sold	2,250,000
Gross margin	$1,500,000
Selling and administrative expense	1,200,000
Operating income	$ 300,000
Less: Income taxes (@ 40%)	120,000
Net income	$ 180,000

At the beginning of the year, the value of operating assets was $1,600,000. At the end of the year, the value of operating assets was $1,400,000.

OBJECTIVE 2
Example 11.1

Brief Exercise 11-13 Calculating Average Operating Assets, Margin, Turnover, and Return on Investment

Refer to the information for East Mullett Manufacturing above. Round answers to two decimal places.

Required:

Calculate (1) average operating assets, (2) margin, (3) turnover, and (4) return on investment.

OBJECTIVE 3
Example 11.2

Brief Exercise 11-14 Calculating Residual Income

Refer to the information for East Mullett Manufacturing above. East Mullett requires a minimum rate of return of 5%.

Required:

Calculate (1) average operating assets and (2) residual income.

OBJECTIVE 3
Example 11.3

Brief Exercise 11-15 Calculating Economic Value Added

Refer to the information for East Mullett Manufacturing above. Total capital employed equaled $1,200,000. East Mullett's actual cost of capital is 4%.

Required:

Calculate the EVA for East Mullett Manufacturing.

OBJECTIVE 4
Example 11.4

Brief Exercise 11-16 Calculating Transfer Price

Burt Inc. has a number of divisions, including the Indian Division, a producer of liquid pumps, and Maple Division, a manufacturer of boat engines.

Indian Division produces the h20-model pump that can be used by Maple Division in the production of motors that regulate the raising and lowering of the boat engine's stern drive unit. The market price of the h20-model is $720, and the full cost of the h20-model is $540.

Required:

1. If Burt has a transfer pricing policy that requires transfer at full cost, what will the transfer price be? Do you suppose that Indian and Maple divisions will choose to transfer at that price?

2. If Burt has a transfer pricing policy that requires transfer at market price, what would the transfer price be? Do you suppose that Indian and Maple divisions would choose to transfer at that price?

3. Now suppose that Burt allows negotiated transfer pricing and that Indian Division can avoid $120 of selling expense by selling to Maple Division. Which division sets the minimum transfer price, and what is it? Which division sets the maximum transfer price, and what is it? Do you suppose that Indian and Maple divisions would choose to transfer somewhere in the bargaining range?

Use the following information for Brief Exercises 11-17 and 11-18:
Indy Company has the following data for one of its manufacturing plants:

Maximum units produced in a quarter (3-month period): 250,000 units
Actual units produced in a quarter (3-month period): 200,000 units
Productive hours in one quarter: 25,000 hours

Brief Exercise 11-17 *(Appendix 11A)* **Calculating Cycle Time and Velocity**

Refer to the information for Indy Company above.

OBJECTIVE ▶ 5
Example 11.5

Required:

Compute the (1) theoretical cycle time (in minutes), (2) actual cycle time (in minutes), (3) theoretical velocity in units per hour, and (4) actual velocity in units per hour.

Brief Exercise 11-18 *(Appendix 11A)* **Calculating Manufacturing Cycle Efficiency**

Refer to the information for Indy Company above. The actual cycle time for Indy Company is 7.5 minutes, and the theoretical cycle time is 6 minutes.

OBJECTIVE ▶ 5
Example 11.6

Required:

1. Calculate the amount of processing time and the amount of nonprocessing time.
2. Calculate the MCE. (Round to one decimal place.)

BRIEF EXERCISES: SET B

Use the following information for Brief Exercises 11-19 through 11-21:
Barnard Manufacturing earned operating income last year as shown in the following income statement:

Sales	$4,000,000
Cost of goods sold	2,100,000
Gross margin	$1,900,000
Selling and administrative expense	1,100,000
Operating income	$ 800,000
Less: Income taxes (@ 40%)	320,000
Net income	$ 480,000

At the beginning of the year, the value of operating assets was $2,700,000. At the end of the year, the value of operating assets was $2,300,000.

OBJECTIVE 2
Example 11.1

Brief Exercise 11-19 Calculating Average Operating Assets, Margin, Turnover, and Return on Investment

Refer to the information for Barnard Manufacturing on the previous page. Round answers to two decimal places.

Required:

Calculate (1) average operating assets, (2) margin, (3) turnover, and (4) return on investment.

OBJECTIVE 3
Example 11.2

Brief Exercise 11-20 Calculating Residual Income

Refer to the information for Barnard Manufacturing on the previous page. Barnard requires a minimum rate of return of 15%.

Required:

Calculate (1) average operating assets and (2) residual income.

OBJECTIVE 3
Example 11.3

Brief Exercise 11-21 Calculating Economic Value Added

Refer to the information for Barnard Manufacturing on the previous page. Total capital employed equaled $1,400,000. Barnard's actual cost of capital is 12%.

Required:

Calculate the EVA for Barnard Manufacturing.

OBJECTIVE 4
Example 11.4

Brief Exercise 11-22 Calculating Transfer Price

Teslum Inc. has a number of divisions, including the Machina Division, a producer of high-end espresso makers, and the Java Division, a chain of coffee shops.

Machina Division produces the EXP-100 model espresso maker that can be used by Java Division to create various coffee drinks. The market price of the EXP-100 model is $950, and the full cost of the EXP-100 model is $475.

Required:

1. If Teslum has a transfer pricing policy that requires transfer at full cost, what will the transfer price be? Do you suppose that Machina and Java divisions will choose to transfer at that price?
2. If Teslum has a transfer pricing policy that requires transfer at market price, what would the transfer price be? Do you suppose that Machina and Java divisions would choose to transfer at that price?
3. Now suppose that Teslum allows negotiated transfer pricing and that Machina Division can avoid $135 of selling expense by selling to Java Division. Which division sets the minimum transfer price, and what is it? Which division sets the maximum transfer price, and what is it? Do you suppose that Machina and Java divisions would choose to transfer somewhere in the bargaining range?

Use the following information for Brief Exercises 11-23 and 11-24:
Theta Company has the following data for one of its manufacturing plants:

Maximum units produced in a quarter (3-month period): 400,000 units
Actual units produced in a quarter (3-month period): 375,000 units
Productive hours in one quarter: 20,000 hours

OBJECTIVE 5
Example 11.5

Brief Exercise 11-23 *(Appendix 11A)* Calculating Cycle Time and Velocity

Refer to the information for Theta Company above.

Required:

Compute the (1) theoretical cycle time (in minutes), (2) actual cycle time (in minutes), (3) theoretical velocity in units per hour, and (4) actual velocity in units per hour. (Round units to the nearest whole unit.)

Brief Exercise 11-24 *(Appendix 11A)* Calculating Manufacturing Cycle Efficiency

OBJECTIVE ⟨5
Example 11.6

Refer to the information for Theta Company on the previous page. The actual cycle time for Theta Company is 3.2 minutes, and the theoretical cycle time is 3 minutes.

Required:

1. Calculate the amount of processing time and the amount of nonprocessing time.
2. Calculate the MCE. (Round to two decimal places.)

EXERCISES

Exercise 11-25 Types of Responsibility Centers

OBJECTIVE ⟨1

Consider each of the following independent scenarios:

a. Terrin Belson, plant manager for the laser printer factory of Compugear Inc., brushed his hair back and sighed. December had been a bad month. Two machines had broken down, and some factory production workers (all on salary) were idled for part of the month. Materials prices increased, and insurance premiums on the factory increased. No way out of it; costs were going up. He hoped that the marketing vice president would be able to push through some price increases, but that really wasn't his department.

b. Joanna Pauly was delighted to see that her ROI figures had increased for the third straight year. She was sure that her campaign to lower costs and use machinery more efficiently (enabling her factories to sell several older machines) was the reason why. Joanna planned to take full credit for the improvements at her semiannual performance review.

c. Gil Rodriguez, sales manager for ComputerWorks, was not pleased with a memo from headquarters detailing the recent cost increases for the laser printer line. Headquarters suggested raising prices. "Great," thought Gil, "an increase in price will kill sales and revenue will go down. Why can't the plant shape up and cut costs like every other company in America is doing? Why turn this into my problem?"

d. Susan Whitehorse looked at the quarterly profit and loss statement with disgust. Revenue was down, and cost was up—what a combination! Then she had an idea. If she cut back on maintenance of equipment and let a product engineer go, expenses would decrease—perhaps enough to reverse the trend in income.

e. Shonna Lowry had just been hired to improve the fortunes of the Southern Division of ABC Inc. She met with top staff and hammered out a 3-year plan to improve the situation. A centerpiece of the plan is the retiring of obsolete equipment and the purchasing of state-of-the-art, computer-assisted machinery. The new machinery would take time for the workers to learn to use, but once that was done, waste would be virtually eliminated.

Required:

For each of the above independent scenarios, indicate the type of responsibility center involved (cost, revenue, profit, or investment).

Exercise 11-26 Margin, Turnover, Return on Investment

OBJECTIVE ⟨2

Pelak Company had sales of $25,000,000, expenses of $17,500,000, and average operating assets of $10,000,000.

EXCEL

Required:

Compute the (1) operating income, (2) margin and turnover ratios, and (3) ROI.

OBJECTIVE ▶ **2** ▶

Exercise 11-27 Margin, Turnover, Return on Investment, Average Operating Assets

Elway Company provided the following income statement for the last year:

Sales	$1,040,000,000
Less: Variable expenses	700,250,000
Contribution margin	$ 339,750,000
Less: Fixed expenses	183,750,000
Operating income	$ 156,000,000

At the beginning of last year, Elway had $28,300,000 in operating assets. At the end of the year, Elway had $23,700,000 in operating assets.

Required:

1. Compute average operating assets.
2. Compute the margin and turnover ratios for last year. (*Note:* Round the answer for margin ratio to two decimal places.)
3. Compute ROI. (*Note:* Round answer to two decimal places.)
4. **CONCEPTUAL CONNECTION** Briefly explain the meaning of ROI.
5. **CONCEPTUAL CONNECTION** Comment on why the ROI for Elway Company is relatively high (as compared to the lower ROI of a typical manufacturing company).

OBJECTIVE ▶ **2** ▶

Exercise 11-28 Return on Investment, Margin, Turnover

Data follow for the Consumer Products Division of Kisler Inc.:

	Year 1	Year 2
Sales	$ 92,100,000	$ 98,750,000
Operating income	9,210,000	7,900,000
Average operating assets	307,000,000	493,750,000

(*Note:* Round all answers to two decimal places.)

Required:

1. Compute the margin and turnover ratios for each year.
2. Compute the ROI for the Consumer Products Division for each year.

OBJECTIVE ▶ **3** ▶

Exercise 11-29 Residual Income

The Avila Division of Maldonado Company had operating income last year of $136,400 and average operating assets of $1,900,000. Maldonado's minimum acceptable rate of return is 9%. (*Note:* Round all answers to two decimal places.)

Required:

1. Calculate the residual income for the Avila Division.
2. Was the ROI for the Avila Division greater than, less than, or equal to 9%?

OBJECTIVE ▶ **3** ▶

Exercise 11-30 Economic Value Added

Falconer Company had net (after-tax) income last year of $12,375,400 and total capital employed of $111,754,000. Falconer's actual cost of capital was 9%.

Required:

1. Calculate the EVA for Falconer Company.
2. **CONCEPTUAL CONNECTION** Is Falconer creating or destroying wealth?

Use the following information for Exercises 11-31 and 11-32:

Washington Company has two divisions: the Adams Division and the Jefferson Division. The following information pertains to last year's results:

	Adams Division	Jefferson Division
Net (after-tax) income	$ 605,000	$ 315,000
Total capital employed	4,000,000	3,250,000

Washington's actual cost of capital was 12%.

Exercise 11-31 Economic Value Added

OBJECTIVE ▸ 3

Refer to the information for Washington Company above.

Required:

1. Calculate the EVA for the Adams Division.
2. Calculate the EVA for the Jefferson Division.
3. **CONCEPTUAL CONNECTION** Is each division creating or destroying wealth?
4. **CONCEPTUAL CONNECTION** Describe generally the types of actions that Washington's management team could take to increase Jefferson Division's EVA?

Exercise 11-32 Residual Income

OBJECTIVE ▸ 3

Refer to the information for Washington Company above. In addition, Washington Company's top management has set a minimum acceptable rate of return equal to 8%.

Required:

1. Calculate the residual income for the Adams Division.
2. Calculate the residual income for the Jefferson Division.

Use the following information for Exercises 11-33 through 11-35

Aulman Inc. has a number of divisions, including a Furniture Division and a Motel Division. The Motel Division owns and operates a line of budget motels located along major highways. Each year, the Motel Division purchases furniture for the motel rooms. Currently, it purchases a basic dresser from an outside supplier for $40. The manager of the Furniture Division has approached the manager of the Motel Division about selling dressers to the Motel Division. The full product cost of a dresser is $29. The Furniture Division can sell all of the dressers it makes to outside companies for $40. The Motel Division needs 10,000 dressers per year; the Furniture Division can make up to 50,000 dressers per year.

Exercise 11-33 Transfer Pricing

OBJECTIVE ▸ 4

Refer to the information for Aulman Inc. above.

Required:

1. Which division sets the maximum transfer price? Which division sets the minimum transfer price?
2. Suppose the company policy is that all transfers take place at full cost. What is the transfer price?
3. **CONCEPTUAL CONNECTION** Do you think that the transfer will occur at the company-mandated transfer price? Why or why not?

OBJECTIVE 4 ▶   **Exercise 11-34 Transfer Pricing**

Refer to the information for Aulman Inc. on the previous page. Also, assume that the company policy is that all transfer prices are negotiated by the divisions involved.

Required:

1. What is the maximum transfer price? Which division sets it?
2. What is the minimum transfer price? Which division sets it?
3. **CONCEPTUAL CONNECTION** If the transfer takes place, what will be the transfer price? Does it matter whether or not the transfer takes place?

OBJECTIVE 4 ▶   **Exercise 11-35 Transfer Pricing**

Refer to the information for Aulman Inc. on the previous page. Also, although the Furniture Division has been operating at capacity (50,000 dressers per year), it expects to produce and sell only 40,000 dressers for $40 each next year. The Furniture Division incurs variable costs of $14 per dresser. The company policy is that all transfer prices are negotiated by the divisions involved.

Required:

1. What is the maximum transfer price? Which division sets it?
2. What is the minimum transfer price? Which division sets it?
3. Suppose that the two divisions agree on a transfer price of $35. What is the benefit for the Furniture Division? For the Motel Division? For Aulman Inc. as a whole?

OBJECTIVE 5 ▶   **Exercise 11-36 *(Appendix 11A)* Cycle Time and Velocity**

Prakesh Company has the following data for one of its manufacturing cells:

> Maximum units produced in a month: 50,000 units
> Actual units produced in a month: 40,000 units
> Hours of production labor in 1 month: 10,000 hours

Required:

Compute the (1) theoretical cycle time (in minutes), (2) actual cycle time (in minutes), (3) theoretical velocity (in units per hour), and (4) actual velocity (in units per hour).

OBJECTIVE 5 ▶   **Exercise 11-37 *(Appendix 11A)* Cycle Time and Velocity**

Lasker Company divided its tool production factory into manufacturing cells. Each cell produces one product. The cordless drill cell had the following data for last quarter:

> Maximum units produced in a quarter: 90,000 units
> Actual units produced in a quarter: 75,000 units
> Hours of cell production labor in a quarter: 30,000 hours

Required:

Compute the (1) theoretical cycle time (in minutes), (2) actual cycle time (in minutes), (3) theoretical velocity (in units per hour), and (4) actual velocity (in units per hour).

OBJECTIVE 5 ▶   **Exercise 11-38 *(Appendix 11A)* Manufacturing Cycle Efficiency**

Ventris Company found that one of its manufacturing cells had actual cycle time of 15 minutes per unit. The theoretical cycle time for this cell was 9 minutes per unit.

Required:

1. Calculate the amount of processing time per unit and the amount of nonprocessing time per unit.
2. Calculate the MCE.

Exercise 11-39 *(Appendix 11A)* Manufacturing Cycle Efficiency

OBJECTIVE ▶ 5

Kurena Company provided the following information on one of its factories:

> Maximum units produced in a quarter: 180,000 units
> Actual units produced in a quarter: 112,500 units
> Hours of cell production labor in a quarter: 30,000 hours
> Theoretical cycle time: 10 minutes per unit
> Actual cycle time: 16 minutes per unit

Required:

1. Calculate the amount of processing time per unit and the amount of nonprocessing time per unit.
2. Calculate the MCE (rounded to three significant digits).

PROBLEMS

Problem 11-40 Return on Investment and Investment Decisions

OBJECTIVE ◀ 2 ◀ 3

EXCEL

Leslie Blandings, division manager of Audiotech Inc., was debating the merits of a new product—a weather radio that would put out a warning if the county in which the listener lived were under a severe thunderstorm or tornado alert.

The budgeted income of the division was $725,000 with operating assets of $3,625,000. The proposed investment would add income of $640,000 and would require an additional investment in equipment of $4,000,000. The minimum required return on investment for the company is 12%. Round all numbers to two decimal places.

Required:

1. Compute the ROI of the:
   a. division if the radio project is not undertaken.
   b. radio project alone.
   c. division if the radio project is undertaken.
2. Compute the residual income of the:
   a. division if the radio project is not undertaken.
   b. radio project alone.
   c. division if the radio project is undertaken.
3. **CONCEPTUAL CONNECTION** Do you suppose that Leslie will decide to invest in the new radio? Why or why not?

Problem 11-41 Return on Investment, Margin, Turnover

OBJECTIVE ◀ 2

Ready Electronics is facing stiff competition from imported goods. Its operating income margin has been declining steadily for the past several years. The company has been forced to lower prices so that it can maintain its market share. The operating results for the past 3 years are as follows:

	Year 1	Year 2	Year 3
Sales	$10,000,000	$ 9,500,000	$ 9,000,000
Operating income	1,200,000	1,045,000	945,000
Average assets	15,000,000	15,000,000	15,000,000

For the coming year, Ready's president plans to install a JIT purchasing and manufacturing system. She estimates that inventories will be reduced by 70% during the first year of operations, producing a 20% reduction in the average operating assets of the company, which would remain unchanged without the JIT system. She also estimates that sales and operating income will be

(Continued)

restored to Year 1 levels because of simultaneous reductions in operating expenses and selling prices. Lower selling prices will allow Ready to expand its market share. (*Note:* Round all numbers to two decimal places.)

Required:

1. Compute the ROI, margin, and turnover for Years 1, 2, and 3.
2. **CONCEPTUAL CONNECTION** Suppose that in Year 4 the sales and operating income were achieved as expected, but inventories remained at the same level as in Year 3. Compute the expected ROI, margin, and turnover. Explain why the ROI increased over the Year 3 level.
3. **CONCEPTUAL CONNECTION** Suppose that the sales and net operating income for Year 4 remained the same as in Year 3 but inventory reductions were achieved as projected. Compute the ROI, margin, and turnover. Explain why the ROI exceeded the Year 3 level.
4. **CONCEPTUAL CONNECTION** Assume that all expectations for Year 4 were realized. Compute the expected ROI, margin, and turnover. Explain why the ROI increased over the Year 3 level.

OBJECTIVE ▶ 2 ▶ 3 ▶   **Problem 11-42** Return on Investment for Multiple Investments, Residual Income

The manager of a division that produces add-on products for the automobile industry has just been presented the opportunity to invest in two independent projects. The first is an air conditioner for the back seats of vans and minivans. The second is a turbocharger. Without the investments, the division will have average assets for the coming year of $28.9 million and expected operating income of $4.335 million. The outlay required for each investment and the expected operating incomes are as follows:

	Air Conditioner	Turbocharger
Outlay	$750,000	$540,000
Operating income	90,000	82,080

(*Note:* Round all numbers to two decimal places.)

Required:

1. Compute the ROI for each investment project.
2. Compute the budgeted divisional ROI for each of the following four alternatives:
   a. The air conditioner investment is made.
   b. The turbocharger investment is made.
   c. Both investments are made.
   d. Neither additional investment is made.
3. **CONCEPTUAL CONNECTION** Assuming that divisional managers are evaluated and rewarded on the basis of ROI performance, which alternative do you think the divisional manager will choose?
4. **CONCEPTUAL CONNECTION** Suppose that the company sets a minimum required rate of return equal to 14%. Calculate the residual income for each of the following four alternatives:
   a. The air conditioner investment is made.
   b. The turbocharger investment is made.
   c. Both investments are made.
   d. Neither additional investment is made.
   Which option will the manager choose based on residual income? Explain.
5. **CONCEPTUAL CONNECTION** Suppose that the company sets a minimum required rate of return equal to 10%. Calculate the residual income for each of the following four alternatives:
   a. The air conditioner investment is made.
   b. The turbocharger investment is made.

c. Both investments are made.

d. Neither additional investment is made.

Based on residual income, are the investments profitable? Why does your answer differ from your answer in Requirement 3?

Problem 11-43 Return on Investment and Economic Value Added Calculations with Varying Assumptions

OBJECTIVE ▶ 2 ◀ 3

EXCEL

Knitpix Products is a division of Parker Textiles Inc. During the coming year, it expects to earn income of $310,000 based on sales of $3.45 million. Without any new investments, the division will have average operating assets of $3 million. The division is considering a capital investment project—adding knitting machines to produce gaiters—that requires an additional investment of $600,000 and increases net income by $57,500 (sales would increase by $575,000). If made, the investment would increase beginning operating assets by $600,000 and ending operating assets by $400,000. Assume that the actual cost of capital for the company is 7%. (*Note:* Round all answers to four decimal places.)

Required:

1. Compute the ROI for the division without the investment.
2. Compute the margin and turnover ratios without the investment. Show that the product of the margin and turnover ratios equals the ROI computed in Requirement 1.
3. **CONCEPTUAL CONNECTION** Compute the ROI for the division with the new investment. Do you think the divisional manager will approve the investment?
4. **CONCEPTUAL CONNECTION** Compute the margin and turnover ratios for the division with the new investment. How do these compare with the old ratios?
5. **CONCEPTUAL CONNECTION** Compute the EVA of the division with and without the investment. Should the manager decide to make the knitting machine investment?

Problem 11-44 Transfer Pricing

OBJECTIVE ◀ 4

GreenWorld Inc. is a nursery products firm. It has three divisions that grow and sell plants: the Western Division, the Southern Division, and the Canadian Division. Recently, the Southern Division of GreenWorld acquired a plastics factory that manufactures green plastic pots. These pots can be sold both externally and internally. Company policy permits each manager to decide whether to buy or sell internally. Each divisional manager is evaluated on the basis of ROI and EVA.

The Western Division had bought its plastic pots in lots of 100 from a variety of vendors. The average price paid was $75 per box of 100 pots. However, the acquisition made Rosario Sanchez-Ruiz, manager of the Western Division, wonder whether or not a more favorable price could be arranged. She decided to approach Lorne Matthews, manager of the Southern Division, to see if he wanted to offer a better price for an internal transfer. She suggested a transfer of 3,500 boxes at $70 per box.

Lorne gathered the following information regarding the cost of a box of 100 pots:

Direct materials	$35
Direct labor	8
Variable overhead	10
Fixed overhead*	10
Total unit cost	$63

*Fixed overhead is based on $200,000/20,000 boxes.

Selling price	$75
Production capacity	20,000 boxes

(Continued)

Required:

1. **CONCEPTUAL CONNECTION** Suppose that the plastics factory is producing at capacity and can sell all that it produces to outside customers. How should Lorne respond to Rosario's request for a lower transfer price?
2. **CONCEPTUAL CONNECTION** Now assume that the plastics factory is currently selling 16,000 boxes. What are the minimum and maximum transfer prices? Should Lorne consider the transfer at $70 per box?
3. **CONCEPTUAL CONNECTION** Suppose that GreenWorld's policy is that all transfer prices be set at full cost plus 20%. Would the transfer take place? Why or why not?

OBJECTIVE ▶ **1** ▶ **4**   **Problem 11-45 Setting Transfer Prices—Market Price versus Full Cost**

Lansing Electronics Inc. manufactures a variety of printers, scanners, and fax machines in its two divisions: the PSF Division and the Components Division. The Components Division produces electronic components that can be used by the PSF Division. All the components this division produces can be sold to outside customers. However, from the beginning, nearly all of its output has been used internally. The current policy requires that all internal transfers of components be transferred at full cost.

Recently, Cam DeVonn, the chief executive officer of Lansing Electronics, decided to investigate the transfer pricing policy. He was concerned that the current method of pricing internal transfers might force decisions by divisional managers that would be suboptimal for the firm. As part of his inquiry, he gathered some information concerning Component Y34, which is used by the PSF Division in its production of a basic scanner, Model SC67.

The PSF Division sells 40,000 units of Model SC67 each year at a unit price of $42. Given current market conditions, this is the maximum price that the division can charge for Model SC67. The cost of manufacturing the scanner follows:

Component Y34	$ 6.50
Direct materials	12.50
Direct labor	3.00
Variable overhead	1.00
Fixed overhead	15.00
Total unit cost	$38.00

The scanner is produced efficiently, and no further reduction in manufacturing costs is possible.

The manager of the Components Division indicated that she could sell 40,000 units (the division's capacity for this part) of Component Y34 to outside buyers at $12 per unit. The PSF Division could also buy the part for $12 from external suppliers. She supplied the following details on the manufacturing cost of the component:

Direct materials	$2.50
Direct labor	0.50
Variable overhead	1.00
Fixed overhead	2.50
Total unit cost	$6.50

Required:

1. Compute the firmwide contribution margin associated with Component Y34 and Model SC67. Also, compute the contribution margin earned by each division.
2. Suppose that Cam DeVonn abolishes the current transfer pricing policy and gives divisions autonomy in setting transfer prices. Can you predict what transfer price the manager of the Components Division will set? What should be the minimum transfer price for this part? The maximum transfer price?

3. **CONCEPTUAL CONNECTION** Given the new transfer pricing policy, predict how this will affect the production decision of the PSF Division manager for Model SC67. How many units of Component Y34 will the manager of the PSF Division purchase, either internally or externally?

4. Given the new transfer price set by the Components Division and your answer to Requirement 3, how many units of Y34 will be sold externally?

5. **CONCEPTUAL CONNECTION** Given your answers to Requirements 3 and 4, compute the firmwide contribution margin. What has happened? Was Cam's decision to grant additional decentralization good or bad?

Problem 11-46 Full Cost-Plus Pricing and Negotiation

OBJECTIVE ◀ 4

Techno Inc. has two divisions: Auxiliary Components and Audio Systems. Divisional managers are encouraged to maximize ROI and EVA. Managers are essentially free to determine whether goods will be transferred internally and what the internal transfer prices will be. Headquarters has directed that all internal prices be expressed on a full cost-plus basis. The markup in the full cost pricing arrangement, however, is left to the discretion of the divisional managers. Recently, the two divisional managers met to discuss a pricing agreement for a subwoofer that would be sold with a personal computer system. Production of the subwoofers is at capacity. Subwoofers can be sold for $31 to outside customers. The Audio Systems Division can also buy the subwoofer from external sources for the same price; however, the manager of this division is hoping to obtain a price concession by buying internally. The full cost of manufacturing the subwoofer is $20. If the manager of the Auxiliary Components Division sells the subwoofer internally, $5 of selling and distribution costs can be avoided. The volume of business would be 250,000 units per year, which is well within the capacity of the producing division.

After some discussion, the two managers agreed on a full cost-plus pricing scheme that would be reviewed annually. Any increase in the outside selling price would be added to the transfer price by simply increasing the markup by an appropriate amount. Any major changes in the factors that led to the agreement could initiate a new round of negotiation. Otherwise, the full cost-plus arrangement would continue in force for subsequent years.

Required:

1. Calculate the minimum and maximum transfer prices.

2. Assume that the transfer price agreed on between the two managers is halfway between the minimum and maximum transfer prices. Calculate this transfer price. What markup over full cost is implied by this transfer price?

3. Refer to Requirement 2. Assume that in the following year, the outside price of subwoofers increases to $32. What is the new full cost-plus transfer price?

4. **CONCEPTUAL CONNECTION** Assume that 2 years after the initial agreement, the market for subwoofers has softened considerably, causing excess capacity for the Auxiliary Components Division. Would you expect a renegotiation of the full cost-plus pricing arrangement for the coming year? Explain.

Problem 11-47 (Appendix 11A) Cycle Time, Velocity, Conversion Cost

OBJECTIVE ◀ 5

The theoretical cycle time for a product is 30 minutes per unit. The budgeted conversion costs for the manufacturing cell are $2,700,000 per year. The total labor minutes available are 600,000. During the year, the cell was able to produce 1.5 units of the product per hour. Suppose also that production incentives exist to minimize unit product costs.

Required:

1. Compute the theoretical conversion cost per unit.

2. Compute the applied conversion cost per unit (the amount of conversion cost actually assigned to the product).

3. **CONCEPTUAL CONNECTION** Discuss how this approach to assigning conversion costs can improve delivery time performance.

OBJECTIVE 5

Problem 11-48 *(Appendix 11A)* Balanced Scorecard

The following list gives a number of measures associated with the Balanced Scorecard:

a. Number of new customers
b. Percentage of customer complaints resolved with one contact
c. Unit product cost
d. Cost per distribution channel
e. Suggestions per employee
f. Warranty repair costs
g. Consumer satisfaction (from surveys)
h. Cycle time for solving a customer problem
i. Strategic job coverage ratio
j. On-time delivery percentage
k. Percentage of revenues from new products

Required:

1. Classify each performance measure as belonging to one of the following perspectives: financial, customer, internal business process, or learning and growth.
2. Suggest an additional measure for each of the four perspectives.

OBJECTIVE 5

Problem 11-49 *(Appendix 11A)* Cycle Time and Velocity, Manufacturing Cycle Efficiency

A company like **Kicker** performs warranty repair work on speakers in a manufacturing cell. The typical warranty repair involves taking the defective speaker apart, testing the components, and replacing the defective components. The maximum capacity of the cell is 1,000 repairs per month. There are 500 production hours available per month.

Required:

1. Compute the theoretical velocity (per hour) and the theoretical cycle time (minutes per unit repaired).
2. Speaker repair uses 4 minutes of move time, 10 minutes of wait time, and 6 minutes of inspection time. Calculate the MCE.
3. Using the information from Requirement 2, calculate the actual cycle time and the actual velocity for speaker repair.

CASE

OBJECTIVE 2

Case 11-50 Return on Investment Ethical Considerations

Jason Kemp was torn between conflicting emotions. On the one hand, things were going so well. He had just completed 6 months as the assistant financial manager in the Electronics Division of Med-Products Inc. The pay was good, he enjoyed his coworkers, and he felt that he was part of a team that was making a difference in American health care. On the other hand, his latest assignment was causing some sleepless nights. Mel Cravens, his boss, had asked him to "refine" the figures on the division's latest project—a portable imaging device code—named ZM. The original estimates called for investment of $15.6 million and projected annual income of $1.87 million. Med-Products required an ROI of at least 15% for new project approval. So far, ZM's rate of return was nowhere near that hurdle rate. Mel encouraged him to show increased sales and decreased expenses in order to get the projected income above $2.34 million. Jason asked for a meeting with Mel to voice his concerns.

Jason: Mel, I've gone over the figures for the new project and can't find any way to get the income above $1.9 million. The salespeople have given me the most likely revenue figures, and production feels that the expense figures are solid.

Mel: Jason, those figures are just projections. Sales doesn't really know what the revenue will be. In fact, when I talked with Sue Harris, our sales vice president, she said that sales could range from $1.5 million to $2.5 million. Use the higher figure. I'm sure this product will justify our confidence in it!

Jason: I know the range of sales was that broad, but Sue felt the $2.5 million estimate was pretty unlikely. She thought that during the first 5 years or so that ZM sales would stay in the lower end of the range.

Mel: Again, Sue doesn't know for sure. She's just estimating. Let's go with the higher estimate. We really need this product to expand our line and to give our division a chance to qualify for sales-based bonuses. If ZM sells at all, our revenue will go up, and we'll all share in the bonus pool!

Jason: I don't know, Mel. I feel pretty bad signing off on ROI projections that I have so little confidence in.

Mel: (frustrated) Look, Jason, just prepare the report. I'll back you up.

Required:

1. What is the ROI of project ZM based on the initial estimates? What would ROI be if the income rose to $2.34 million?
2. **CONCEPTUAL CONNECTION** Do you agree that Jason has an ethical dilemma? Explain. Is there any way that Mel could ethically justify raising the sales estimates and/or lowering expense estimates?
3. What do you think Jason should do? Explain.

12

Capital Investment Decisions

After studying Chapter 12, you should be able to:

1 ▸ Explain the meaning of capital investment decisions, and distinguish between independent and mutually exclusive capital investment decisions.

2 ▸ Compute the payback period and accounting rate of return for a proposed investment, and explain their roles in capital investment decisions.

3 ▸ Use net present value analysis for capital investment decisions involving independent projects.

4 ▸ Use the internal rate of return to assess the acceptability of independent projects.

5 ▸ Explain the role and value of postaudits.

6 ▸ Explain why net present value is better than internal rate of return for capital investment decisions involving mutually exclusive projects.

7 ▸ (*Appendix 12A*) Explain the relationship between current and future dollars.

mary981/Shutterstock.com

EXPERIENCE MANAGERIAL DECISIONS

with Hard Rock International

Launched in 1971 in London, England, nearly everyone has visited, or at least seen T-shirts for, one of **Hard Rock International**'s world-famous cafe restaurants located around the globe, from the United States to Europe to Asia and Australia. What visitors likely appreciate most is Hard Rock's impressive collection of rock 'n' roll memorabilia and tasty fare. However, for Hard Rock's managerial accountants and the readers of this textbook, what is most likely to be appreciated is Hard Rock's masterful use of effective capital budgeting techniques to make decisions that are critical to the company's continued success. One of those decisions concerns the opening of new cafes all over the world from Mumbai, India, to Louisville, Kentucky.

New cafes require advanced planning concerning anticipated cash flows, both for future costs and revenues. Future cost-related cash flow projections include items such as labor and materials from different countries, licensing laws, utilities, kitchen and bar equipment, computers, construction, and audiovisual equipment. Future cash flows for food and beverage sales are even more difficult to project than costs because of uncertainties involving demographics, economic conditions, and competition. Another complicating factor is the challenge of estimating local awareness of the Hard Rock brand. Brand awareness is important because it drives Hard Rock's merchandise sales. Estimates of future cash flows for revenues and expenses are combined to calculate a proposed cafe's payback period and net present value. These metrics then are compared with Hard Rock's decision model requirements to help determine whether or not the proposed cafe is a wise decision.

> "New cafes require advanced planning concerning anticipated cash flows, both for future costs and revenues. ... Future cash flows for food and beverage sales are even more difficult to project than costs because of uncertainties involving demographics, economic conditions, and competition."

Another capital investment decision for Hard Rock surrounds the acquisition of its rock 'n' roll memorabilia. Hard Rock uses its memorabilia to generate food and merchandise revenues by attracting more customers into the cafe. The collection has grown from a single Eric Clapton guitar to more than 72,000 instruments, stage outfits, platinum and gold LPs, music and lyric sheets, and photographs.

All of these decisions require effective capital budgeting practices.

645

OBJECTIVE

Explain the meaning of capital investment decisions, and distinguish between independent and mutually exclusive capital investment decisions.

TYPES OF CAPITAL INVESTMENT DECISIONS

Organizations, such as **Hard Rock**, often are faced with the opportunity (or need) to invest in assets or projects that represent long-term commitments. New production systems, new plants, new equipment, new product development, and, in the case of Hard Rock, new cafes are examples of assets and projects that fit this category. Usually, many alternatives are available. Hard Rock, for example, may be faced with the decision of whether or not to develop a new cafe in a certain location. Manufacturing firms, on the other hand, may need to decide whether to invest in a flexible manufacturing system or to continue with an existing traditional manufacturing system. These long-range decisions are examples of *capital investment decisions*.

Capital investment decisions are concerned with the process of planning, setting goals and priorities, arranging financing, and using certain criteria to select long-term assets. Because capital investment decisions place large amounts of resources at risk for long periods of time and simultaneously affect the future development of the firm, they are among the most important decisions made by managers. Poor capital investment decisions can be disastrous. For example, a failure to invest in automated manufacturing when other competitors do so may result in significant losses in market share because of the inability to compete on the basis of quality, cost, and delivery time. Making the right capital investment decisions is absolutely essential for long-term survival.

Independent and Mutually Exclusive Projects

The process of making capital investment decisions often is referred to as **capital budgeting**. Two types of capital budgeting projects will be considered: *independent projects* and *mutually exclusive projects*.

- **Independent projects** are projects that, if accepted or rejected, do not affect the cash flows of other projects. For example, a decision by **Hard Rock** to develop a cafe in Argentina is not affected by its decision to build a new cafe in Singapore. These are independent capital investment decisions.
- **Mutually exclusive projects** are those projects that, if accepted, preclude the acceptance of all other competing projects. For example, each time **Hard Rock** develops a new cafe, it installs kitchen and bar equipment. Some equipment uses standard technology, while other options offer advanced technology for energy efficiency. Once one type of equipment is chosen, the other type is excluded; they are mutually exclusive.

Making Capital Investment Decisions

In general terms, a sound capital investment will earn back its original capital outlay over its life and, at the same time, provide a reasonable return on the original investment. After making this assessment, managers must decide on the acceptability of independent projects and compare competing projects on the basis of their economic merits.

But what is meant by reasonable return? Generally, any new project must cover the opportunity cost of the funds invested. For example, if a company takes money from a money market fund that is earning 4% and invests it in a new project, then the project must provide at least a 4% return (the return that could have been earned had the money been left in the money market fund). In reality, funds for investment often come from different sources—each representing a different opportunity cost. The return that must be earned is a blend of the opportunity costs of the different sources. Thus, if a company uses two sources of funds, one with an opportunity cost of 4% and the other with an opportunity cost of 6%, then the return that must be earned is somewhere between 4 and 6%, depending on the relative amounts used from each source. Furthermore, it is usually assumed that managers should select projects that maximize the wealth of the firm's owners.

To make a capital investment decision, a manager must:

- estimate the quantity and timing of cash flows
- assess the risk of the investment
- consider the impact of the project on the firm's profits

Hard Rock has little difficulty estimating what a new cafe will cost (the investment required). However, estimating future cash flows is much more challenging. For example, Hard Rock projects sales for a new cafe by first looking at sales from existing cafes with a similar size and location. Next, local factors such as demographics, economic conditions, competition, and awareness of the Hard Rock brand are considered. After taking all these factors into account, two sets of sales estimates are made for a 10-year horizon: (1) a likely scenario and (2) a worst-case scenario. Sales are also broken out into four sources: Restaurant, Catering, Bar, and Retail. This breakout is important because each revenue area has a different labor and materials cost structure. This facilitates the estimating of operating costs. Given the estimated revenues and costs, the future cash flows can then be calculated. Obviously, as the accuracy of cash flow forecasts increases, the reliability of the decision improves.

Managers must set goals and priorities for capital investments. They also must identify some basic criteria for the acceptance or rejection of proposed investments. In this chapter, we will study four basic methods to guide managers in accepting or rejecting potential investments. The methods include both nondiscounting and discounting decision approaches (two methods are discussed for each approach). The discounting methods are applied to investment decisions involving both independent and mutually exclusive projects.

Note that, for simplicity, although forecasting future cash flows is a critical part of the capital investment process, we will reserve discussions of forecasting methodologies for more advanced courses. Furthermore, the cash flows projected must be *after-tax cash flows*. Taxes have an important role in developing cash flow assessments. Here, however, tax effects either are assumed away or the cash flows can be thought of as after-tax cash flows. Consequently, after-tax cash flows are assumed to be known and the focus in this chapter will be on making capital investment decisions *given* these cash flows.

Check Point

1. **What is the difference between independent and mutually exclusive investments?**

Answer:

Acceptance or rejection of an independent investment does not affect the cash flows of other investments. Acceptance of a mutually exclusive investment precludes the acceptance of any competing project.

2. **A sound capital investment must:**
   (a) **earn back most of its original outlay.**
   (b) **cover the opportunity cost of the funds invested.**
   (c) **have a high level of risk.**
   (d) **not affect a company's profits.**

Answer:

(b).

NONDISCOUNTING MODELS: PAYBACK PERIOD AND ACCOUNTING RATE OF RETURN

OBJECTIVE ◄ 2

Compute the payback period and accounting rate of return for a proposed investment, and explain their roles in capital investment decisions.

The basic capital investment decision models can be classified into two major categories: *nondiscounting models* and *discounting models*:

- **Nondiscounting models** ignore the time value of money.
- **Discounting models** explicitly consider the time value of money.

Although many accounting theorists disparage the nondiscounting models because they ignore the time value of money, many firms continue to use these models in making capital investment decisions. However, a large majority of the firms use discounting models as the primary evaluation method. Nonetheless, most firms seem to use both types.[1] This pattern suggests that both categories—nondiscounted and discounted—supply useful information to managers as they struggle to make a capital investment decision.

Payback Period

One type of nondiscounting model is the *payback period*. The **payback period** is the time required for a firm to recover its original investment. It is often used to assess things such as (1) financial risk, (2) impact of an investment on liquidity, (3) obsolescence risk, and (4) impact of investment on performance measures.

If the cash flows of a project are an equal amount each period, then the following formula can be used to compute its payback period:

$$\text{Payback Period} = \frac{\text{Original Investment}}{\text{Annual Cash Flow}}$$

If, however, the cash flows are unequal, the payback period is computed by adding the annual cash flows until such time as the original investment is recovered. If a fraction of a year is needed, it is assumed that cash flows occur evenly within each year. **Example 12.1** shows how payback analysis is done for both even and uneven cash flows.

EXAMPLE 12.1	
How to Calculate Payback	Suppose that a new car wash facility requires an investment of $100,000 and either has (a) even cash flows of $50,000 per year or (b) the following expected annual cash flows: $30,000, $40,000, $50,000, $60,000, and $70,000.

Required:
Calculate the payback period for each case.

Solution:

a. Payback Period = Original Investment/Annual Cash Flow

    = $100,000/$50,000 = 2 years

b.

Year	Unrecovered Investment (beginning of year)	Annual Cash Flow	Time Needed for Payback (years)
1	$100,000	$30,000	1.0
2	70,000	40,000	1.0
3	30,000	50,000	0.6*
4	0	60,000	0.0
5	0	70,000	0.0
			2.6

*At the beginning of Year 3, $30,000 is needed to recover the investment. Since a net cash flow of $50,000 is expected, only 0.6 year ($30,000/$50,000) is needed to recover the remaining $30,000, assuming a uniform cash inflow throughout the year.

---

1 John R. Graham and Campbell R. Harvey, "Theory and Practice of Corporate Finance: Evidence from the Field," *Journal of Financial Economics*, 60:2,3 (May/June 2001): 183–244.

Using the Payback Period to Assess Risk One way to use the payback period is to set a maximum payback period for all projects and to reject any project that exceeds this level. Why would a firm use the payback period in this way? Some analysts suggest that the payback period can be used as a rough measure of risk, with the notion that the longer it takes for a project to pay for itself, the riskier it is. Also, firms with riskier cash flows in general could require a shorter payback period than normal. Additionally, firms with liquidity problems would be more interested in projects with quick paybacks. Another critical concern is obsolescence. In some industries, the risk of obsolescence is high. Firms within these industries, such as computer and MP3 player manufacturers, would be interested in recovering funds rapidly.

Ethical Decisions

Another reason, less beneficial to the firm, may also be involved. Many managers in a position to make capital investment decisions may choose investments with quick payback periods out of self-interest. If a manager's performance is measured using such short-run criteria as annual net income, projects with quick paybacks may be chosen to show improved net income and cash flow as quickly as possible. Consider that divisional managers often are responsible for making capital investment decisions and are evaluated on divisional profit. The tenure of divisional managers, however, is typically short—3 to 5 years on average. Consequently, an incentive exists for self-interested managers to shy away from investments that promise healthy long-run returns but relatively meager returns in the short run. New products and services that require time to develop a consumer following fit this description. However, ethical managers would avoid responding to these types of incentives. Corporate budgeting policies and a budget review committee can mitigate these problems by clearly communicating expected behaviors. ●

Using the Payback Period to Choose Among Alternatives The payback period can be used to choose among competing alternatives. Under this approach, the investment with the shortest payback period is preferred over investments with longer payback periods. However, this use of the payback period is less defensible because this measure suffers from two major deficiencies:

- It ignores the cash flow performance of the investments beyond the payback period.
- It ignores the time value of money.

These two significant deficiencies are easily illustrated. Assume that an engineering firm is considering two different types of computer-aided design (CAD) systems: CAD-A and CAD-B. Each system requires an initial outlay of $150,000, has a 5-year life, and displays the following annual cash flows:

Investment	Year 1	Year 2	Year 3	Year 4	Year 5
CAD-A	$90,000	$ 60,000	$50,000	$50,000	$50,000
CAD-B	40,000	110,000	25,000	5,000	5,000

Both investments have payback periods of 2 years. In other words, if a manager uses the payback period to choose among competing investments, the two investments would be equally desirable. In reality, however, the CAD-A system should be preferred over the CAD-B system for two reasons:

- The CAD-A system provides a much larger dollar return for Years 3, 4, and 5 beyond the payback period ($150,000 vs. $35,000).

- The CAD-A system returns $90,000 in the first year, while CAD-B returns only $40,000. The extra $50,000 that the CAD-A system provides in the first year could be put to productive use, such as investing in another project. It is better to have a dollar now than to have it one year from now, because the dollar in hand can be invested to provide a return one year from now.

In summary, the payback period provides information to managers that can be used as follows:

- To help control the risks associated with the uncertainty of future cash flows.
- To help minimize the impact of an investment on a firm's liquidity problems.
- To help control the risk of obsolescence.
- To help control the effect of the investment on performance measures.

However, the method suffers significant deficiencies. It ignores a project's total profitability and the time value of money. While the computation of the payback period may be useful to a manager, relying on it solely for a capital investment decision would be foolish.

Accounting Rate of Return

Here's **Why It's important**

The *accounting rate of return* is the second commonly used nondiscounting model. The **accounting rate of return (ARR)** measures the return on a project in terms of income, as opposed to using a project's cash flow. Unlike the payback period, the accounting rate of return considers the profitability of an investment; however, like the payback period, it ignores the time value of money. It may be useful as a screening measure to ensure that a new investment does not adversely affect debt covenants (covenants may use accounting ratios that can be affected by the income reported and the level of long-term assets).

The accounting rate of return is computed by the following formula:

$$\text{Accounting Rate of Return} = \frac{\text{Average Income}}{\text{Initial Investment}}$$

Here's How It's Used: **IN YOUR LIFE**

Kent Shorts just graduated from pharmacy school and has accepted a position that requires him to travel to three different pharmacies, located in different communities. He expects to average about 24,000 miles per year. He is considering converting his new truck (which averages 15 miles per gallon) so that it can run on either compressed natural gas (CNG) or conventional fuel (a bi-fuel conversion). One of the incentives for conversion for Kent is the favorable impact that CNG usage would have on the environment. CNG is a cleaner fuel than gasoline and would reduce greenhouse emissions by 30 to 40%. Kent also hopes to save money on his fuel costs. The cost of CNG would be about half the cost of gasoline. He estimates that the cost for gasoline would average about $3.40 per gallon over the next 5 years, and that the cost per gallon for CNG would be $1.65.

However, the cost of conversion is about $8,000. The mechanic offering the conversion package also tells Kent that the state offers a $2,400 tax credit for alternative fuels. Intrigued, Kent wonders whether the conversion would be economical. He decides to consult with Lisa Powell, his fiancée and a CPA. She offers Kent the following analysis:

"Kent, at 15 mpg, you would use 1,600 gallons per year. CNG would save you $1.75 per gallon or $2,800 per year. With the tax credit, your net cost of conversion would be $5,600 ($8,000 − $2,400). It only takes 2 years ($5,600/$2,800) to recover your conversion cost from the fuel cost savings. That is not a bad payback period. Not only do you benefit the environment, but after the first 2 years, you pocket $2,800 per year in savings."

CONCEPT CLIP

Income is not equivalent to cash flows because of accruals and deferrals used in its computation. The average income of a project is obtained by adding the net income for each year of the project and then dividing this total by the number of years. **Example 12.2** shows how to calculate the accounting rate of return.

An investment requires an initial outlay of $100,000 and has a 5-year life with no salvage value. The yearly cash flows are $50,000, $50,000, $60,000, $50,000, and $70,000.

EXAMPLE 12.2

How to Calculate the Accounting Rate of Return

Required:

1. Calculate the annual net income for each of the 5 years.

2. Calculate the accounting rate of return.

Solution:

1. Yearly Depreciation Expense = ($100,000 – $0)/5 years = $20,000
   Annual Net Income = Net Cash Flow – Depreciation Expense
   Year 1 Net Income = $50,000 – $20,000 = $30,000
   Year 2 Net Income = $50,000 – $20,000 = $30,000
   Year 3 Net Income = $60,000 – $20,000 = $40,000
   Year 4 Net Income = $50,000 – $20,000 = $30,000
   Year 5 Net Income = $70,000 – $20,000 = $50,000

2. Total Net Income (5 Years) = $180,000
   Average Net Income = $180,000/5 = $36,000

   Accounting Rate of Return = $36,000/100,000 = 0.36

Limitations of Accounting Rate of Return Unlike the payback period, the ARR does consider a project's profitability. However, the ARR has other potential drawbacks, including the following:

- *Ignoring Time Value of Money:* Like the payback period, it ignores the time value of money. Ignoring the time value of money is a critical deficiency in this method as well. It can lead a manager to choose investments that do not maximize profits. The ARR and payback model are referred to as *nondiscounting models* because they ignore the time value of money.
- *Dependency on Net Income:* ARR is dependent upon net income, which is the financial measure most likely to be manipulated by managers. Some of the reasons for manipulating net income include debt contracts (i.e., debt covenants) and bonuses. Often, debt contracts require that a firm maintain certain financial accounting ratios, which can be affected by the income reported and by the level of long-term assets. Accordingly, the ARR may be used as a screening measure to ensure that any new investment will not adversely affect these ratios.
- *Managers' Incentive:* Additionally, because bonuses to managers often are based on accounting income or return on assets, managers may have a personal interest in seeing that any new investment contributes significantly to net income. A manager seeking to maximize personal income is likely to select investments that return the highest net income per dollar invested, even if the selected investments are not the ones that produce the greatest cash flows and return to the firm in the long run.

OBJECTIVE

Use net present value analysis for capital investment decisions involving independent projects.

DISCOUNTING MODELS: THE NET PRESENT VALUE METHOD

Discounting models use **discounted cash flows** which are future cash flows expressed in terms of their present value. The use of discounting models requires an understanding of the present value concepts. Present value concepts are reviewed in Appendix 12A (p. 667). Review these concepts and make sure that you understand them before studying capital investment discount models. Present value tables [Exhibits 12B.1 (p. 670) and 12B.2 (p. 671)] are presented in Appendix 12B (p. 669). These tables are referred to and used throughout the rest of this chapter. Two discounting models will be considered: *net present value* and *internal rate of return*.

Net Present Value Defined

Net present value (NPV) is the difference between the present value of the cash inflows and outflows associated with a project:

$$NPV = \left[\sum CF_t / (1+i)^t\right] - I$$
$$= \left[\sum CF_t df_t\right] - I$$
$$= P - I$$

where

I = The present value of the project's cost (usually the initial cash outlay)
CF_t = The cash inflow to be received in period t, *with* $t = 1 \ldots n$
i = The required rate of return
t = The time period
P = The present value of the project's future cash inflows
df_t = $1/(1 + i)^t$, the discount factor

Here's **Why It's important**

NPV measures the profitability of an investment. A positive NPV indicates that the investment increases the firm's wealth. Thus, projects with a positive (negative) NPV should be accepted (rejected). To use the NPV method, a *required rate of return* must be defined. The **required rate of return** is the minimum acceptable rate of return. It also is referred to as the *discount rate, hurdle rate*, and *cost of capital*. In theory, if future cash flows are known with certainty, then the correct required rate of return is the firm's **cost of capital**. In practice, future cash flows are uncertain, and managers often choose a discount rate higher than the cost of capital to deal with the uncertainty. However, if the rate chosen is excessively high, it will bias the selection process toward short-term investments. Because of the risk of being overly conservative, it may be better to use the cost of capital as the discount rate and find other approaches to deal with uncertainty.

Once the NPV for a project is computed, it can be used to determine whether or not to accept an investment:

- If the NPV is greater than zero, the investment is profitable and, therefore, acceptable. A positive NPV signals that (1) the initial investment has been recovered, (2) the required rate of return has been recovered, and (3) a return in excess of (1) and (2) has been received.
- If the NPV equals zero, the decision maker will find acceptance or rejection of the investment equal.
- If the NPV is less than zero, the investment should be rejected. In this case, it is earning less than the required rate of return.

Net Present Value Illustrated

Brannon Company has developed new MP3-player earphones that it believes are superior to anything on the market. The earphones have a projected product life cycle of 5 years. Although the marketing manager is excited about the new product's prospects, a decision to manufacture the new product depends on whether it can earn a positive NPV given the company's required rate of return of 12%. In order to make a decision regarding the earphones, two steps must be taken:

Step 1: The cash flows for each year must be identified.
Step 2: The NPV must be computed using the cash flows from Step 1.

Example 12.3 shows how to assess cash flows and calculate the NPV.

EXAMPLE 12.3

How to Assess Cash Flows and Calculate Net Present Value

A detailed market study revealed expected annual revenues of $300,000 for new earphones. Equipment to produce the earphones will cost $320,000. After 5 years, the equipment can be sold for $40,000. In addition to equipment, working capital is expected to increase by $40,000 because of increases in inventories and receivables. The firm expects to recover the investment in working capital at the end of the project's life. Annual cash operating expenses are estimated at $180,000. The required rate of return is 12%.

Required:
Estimate the annual cash flows, and calculate the NPV.

Solution:

STEP 1. CASH FLOW IDENTIFICATION

Year	Item	Cash Flow
0	Equipment	$ (320,000)
	Working capital	(40,000)
	Total	$ (360,000)
1–4	Revenues	$ 300,000
	Operating expenses	(180,000)
	Total	$ 120,000
5	Revenues	$ 300,000
	Operating expenses	(180,000)
	Salvage	40,000
	Recovery of working capital	40,000
	Total	$ 200,000

(Continued)

EXAMPLE 12.3

(Continued)

STEP 2A. NPV ANALYSIS

Year	Cash Flow[a]	Discount Factor[b]	Present Value
0	$(360,000)	1.00000	$(360,000)
1	120,000	0.89286	107,143
2	120,000	0.79719	95,663
3	120,000	0.71178	85,414
4	120,000	0.63552	76,262
5	200,000	0.56743	113,486
Net present value			$ 117,968

STEP 2B. NPV ANALYSIS

Year	Cash Flow	Discount Factor[c]	Present Value
0	$(360,000)	1.00000	$(360,000)
1–4	120,000	3.03735	364,482
5	200,000	0.56743	113,486
Net present value			$ 117,968

[a] From Step 1.

[b] From Exhibit 12B.1.

[c] Years 1–4 from Exhibit 12B.2; Year 5 from Exhibit 12B.1.

In Example 12.3, notice that Step 2 offers two approaches for computing NPV. Step 2A computes NPV by using discount factors from Exhibit 12B.1 (p. 670). Step 2B simplifies the computation by using a single discount factor from Exhibit 12B.2 (p. 671) for the even cash flows occurring in Years 1 through 4.

Illustrating Relationships: NPV, Discount Rates, and Cash Flows

Estimating cash flows is often difficult and certainly a major source of risk for capital budgeting decisions. The discount rate is the minimum acceptable required rate of return and, under certainty, would correspond to the firm's cost of capital. Because of uncertain future cash flows, firms may use a higher discount rate than its cost of capital. It is also common to provide pessimistic and most likely cash flow scenarios to help assess a project's risk (as **Hard Rock** does). As

Here's How It's Used: IN YOUR LIFE

Kent Shorts is still considering the investment in a CNG conversion for his truck. His fiancée, Lisa Powell, calculated the cash flows and the payback period for him and recommended the investment. He has one additional concern—he knows the $5,600 net investment could earn 5% annually in his savings account. At the end of 5 years, he would have the $5,600 plus the interest earned. Before making a final decision, he decides to consult with Lisa once again to see what she thinks. Below is the text message she sends him in response:

NPV analysis answers your question. The CNG conversion costs $5,600 and produces $2,800 savings per year in fuel costs. If your required rate of return is 5%, then using the same 5-year horizon we used for the payback analysis, you would have a net increase in your current financial wealth of about $6,523. This number is called the net present value. It is the value of the 5-year stream of savings (what you would have to invest at 5% to get the $2,800 per year for 5 years) less the $5,600 actually needed to produce those savings. In other words, in effect, you get back your $5,600 plus an additional $6,523. This CNG conversion is a great deal for you!

CONCEPT CLIP

the discount rate increases, the present value of future cash flows decreases, making it harder for a project to achieve a positive NPV. Alternatively, providing pessimistic and likely assessments of cash flows also allows managers to see the effect of differences in cash flow estimates on project viability as measured by NPV. Illustrating the relationship between the discount rate and cash flows affords rich insight about the economic feasibility of a project.

For purposes of illustration, suppose that an amusement park is considering an investment in a new ride that has the following data:

Investment	$3,500,000
Likely annual cash flow	$1,200,000
Pessimistic annual cash flow	$800,000
Discount rate range	0.08 to 0.18, in increments of 0.02
Expected cost of capital	0.10
Project life	6 years

Using this information, the NPV is calculated and plotted as the discount rate varies (increasing by increments of 0.02 for the range indicated) for each series of cash flows. Exhibit 12.1 illustrates the relationships. For the likely cash flow scenario, the project has a positive NPV for all discount rates. For the worst-case scenario, the NPV is negative for the four highest discount rates, about zero (actually slightly negative) for the 10% rate, and positive only for the 8% rate.

Exhibit 12.1 NPV, Discount Rates, and Cash Flow

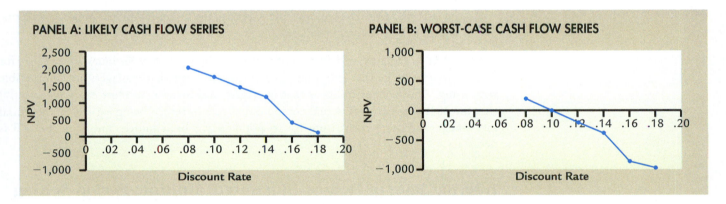

Knowing these relationships, what decision should be made? For the expected cost of capital of 10%, the worst prediction is an NPV of about zero (−$16,000). Thus, it appears to be a fairly safe investment, since there seems to be very little likelihood of losing on the project. Using both Panels A and B provides good insight into the risk and economic viability of the proposed project.

Check Point

1. **Suppose that the NPV of an investment is $2,000. Why does this mean that the investment should be accepted?**

   Answer:
   An NPV greater than zero means that the investment recovers its capital while simultaneously earning a return in excess of the required rate.

2. **Explain why the required rate of return is sometimes chosen to be greater than a firm's cost of capital.**

   Answer:
   In practice, future cash flows are uncertain, and managers often choose a discount rate higher than the cost of capital to deal with the uncertainty.

INTERNAL RATE OF RETURN

Another discounting model is the *internal rate of return* method.

Internal Rate of Return Defined

The **internal rate of return (IRR)** is defined as the interest rate that sets the present value of a project's cash inflows equal to the present value of the project's cost. In other words, the IRR is the interest rate (discount rate) where NPV = 0. Acceptable investments should have an IRR greater than the required rate of return (cost of capital).

The following equation can be used to determine a project's IRR:

$$I = \sum \left[CF_t / (1+i)^t \right]$$

where $t = 1, ..., n$

The right side of this equation is the present value of future cash flows, and the left side is the investment. I, CF_t, and t are known. Thus, the IRR (the interest rate, i, in the equation) can be found using trial and error. Once the IRR for a project is computed, it is compared with the firm's required rate of return:

- If the IRR is greater than the required rate of return, the project is deemed acceptable.
- If the IRR is less than the required rate of return, the project is rejected.
- If the IRR is equal to the required rate of return, the firm is indifferent between accepting or rejecting the investment proposal.

The IRR is the most widely used of the capital investment techniques. One reason for its popularity may be that it is a rate of return, a concept that managers are comfortable with using. Another possibility is that managers may believe (in most cases, incorrectly) that the IRR is the true or actual compounded rate of return being earned by the initial investment. Whatever the reasons for its popularity, a basic understanding of the IRR is necessary.

Internal Rate of Return Illustrated: Multiple-Period Setting with Uniform Cash Flows

Assume initially that the investment produces a series of uniform cash flows. Since the series of cash flows is uniform, a single discount factor from the present value table in Exhibit 12B.2 (p. 671) can be used to compute the present value of the annuity. Letting *df* be this discount factor and *CF* be the annual cash flow, the IRR equation assumes the following form:

$$I = CF(df)$$

Solving for *df*, we obtain:

$$df = I/CF$$
$$= \frac{\text{Investment}}{\text{Annual Cash Flow}}$$

Assume that the investment (I) is $100 and that it produces a single-period cash flow of $110. The discount factor is $I/CF = \$100/\$110 = 0.90909$. Looking in Exhibit 12B.2, a discount factor of 0.90909 for a single period corresponds to a rate of 10%, which is the IRR. In general, once the discount factor is computed, go to Exhibit 12B.2 (p. 671) and find the row corresponding to the life of the project, then move across that row until the computed discount factor is found. The interest rate corresponding to this discount factor is the IRR. **Example 12.4** illustrates how to calculate the IRR for multiple-period uniform cash flows.

EXAMPLE 12.4

How to Calculate Internal Rate of Return with Uniform Cash Flows

Assume that a hospital has the opportunity to invest $205,570.50 in a new ultrasound system that will produce net cash inflows of $50,000 at the end of each of the next 6 years.

Required:
Calculate the IRR for the ultrasound system.

Solution:

$$df = I/CF$$
$$= \$205,570.50/\$50,000$$
$$= 4.11141$$

Since the life of the investment is 6 years, find the sixth row in Exhibit 12B.2 and then move across this row until $df = 4.11141$ is found. The interest rate corresponding to 4.11141 is 12%, which is the IRR.

Exhibit 12B.2 does not provide discount factors for every possible interest rate. To illustrate, assume that the annual cash inflows expected by the hospital (in Example 12.4) are $51,000 instead of $50,000. The new discount factor is 4.03079 ($205,570.50/$51,000). Going once again to the sixth row in Exhibit 12B.2, it is clear that the discount factor—and thus the IRR—lies between 12 and 14%. Although it is possible to approximate the IRR by interpolation, for simplicity, we can identify the range for the IRR as indicated by the table values. In practice, business calculators or spreadsheet programs like Excel can provide the values of IRR without the use of tables such as Exhibit 12B.2.

Internal Rate of Return Illustrated: Multiple-Period Setting with Uneven Cash Flows

If the cash flows are not uniform, then the IRR equation must be used. For a multiple-period setting, this equation can be solved by trial and error or by using a business calculator or a spreadsheet program. To illustrate the solution by trial and error, assume that a $10,000 investment in a PC system produces clerical savings of $6,000 and $7,200, respectively, for the 2 years. The IRR is the interest rate that sets the present value of these two cash inflows equal to $10,000:

$$P = [\$6,000/(1+i)] + [\$7,200/(1+i)^2]$$
$$= \$10,000$$

To solve this equation by trial and error, start by selecting a possible value for i. Given this first guess, the present value of the future cash flows is computed and then compared with the initial investment. If the present value is greater than the initial investment, then the interest rate is too low. If the present value is less than the initial investment, then the interest rate is too high. The next guess is adjusted accordingly.

Assume that the first guess is 18%. Using i equal to 0.18, the present value table in Exhibit 12B.1 (p. 670) yields the following discount factors: 0.84746 and 0.71818. These discount factors produce the following present value for the two cash inflows:

$$P = (0.84746 \times \$6{,}000) + (0.71818 \times \$7{,}200)$$
$$= \$10{,}256$$

Since P is greater than $10,000, the interest rate selected is too low. A higher guess is needed. If the next guess is 20%, we obtain the following:

$$P = (0.83333 \times \$6{,}000) + (0.69444 \times \$7{,}200)$$
$$= \$9{,}999.95$$

Since this value is very close to $10,000, we can say that the IRR is 20%. (The IRR is, in fact, exactly 20%. The present value is slightly less than the investment because the discount factors found in Exhibit 12B.1 have been rounded to five decimal places.)

Here's How It's Used: SUSTAINABILITY, IRR, AND UNCERTAINTY

As a manager of a plant producing cooking oils and margarines, you are concerned about the emission of contaminated water effluents. On a regular basis, your plant violates its discharge permit and dumps many times the allowable waste (organic solids) into a local river. This practice is beginning to draw increased attention and criticism from the state environmental agency. You are considering the acquisition and installation of a zero-discharge, closed-loop system with an expected life of 10 years and a required investment of $250,000. The closed-loop system is expected to produce the following expected annual savings:

Water (from the ability to recycle the water)	$20,000
Materials (from the ability to use extracted materials)	5,000
Avoidance of fines and penalties	15,000
Reduction in demand for laboratory analysis	10,000
Total savings	$50,000

To accept any project, the IRR must be greater than the cost of capital, which is 10%.

Upon calculating the IRR, you find that it is about 15%, significantly greater than the 10% benchmark rate. However, upon seeking approval for the project from the divisional manager, he asks you how certain you are about the projected cash savings. He also questions the estimated life, arguing that based on his experience the expected life of the particular closed-loop system is usually closer to 8 years than 10.

How would you address the divisional manager's concerns about projected cash savings and estimated life?

The concerns of the divisional manager relate to the uncertainty surrounding both the cash flow and project life estimates. The savings from recycling water and the fines and penalties probably have very little uncertainty attached to them. The same may also be true of the lab costs, especially if the analysis is outsourced. The major source of uncertainty probably is attached to the quantity of organic solids that once extracted can be used to produce additional margarines and cooking oils. Assuming that the extraction process does not produce any usable organic solids, the annual savings would be $45,000 ($50,000 − $5,000), yielding the worst-case scenario for cash flows. This uncertainty in the cash flows can be dealt with by first calculating the minimum annual cash savings that must be realized to earn a rate equal to the firm's cost of capital and then comparing this minimum cash savings with the cash flows of the worst-case scenario ($45,000). Calculating this minimum cash flow for an 8-year life simultaneously addresses the project life issue.

The minimum cash flow is calculated as follows (where df is the discount factor for 8 years and 10%, from Exhibit 12B.2, p. 671):

$$I = CF(df)$$
$$CF = I/df$$
$$= \$250{,}000/5.33493$$
$$= \$46{,}861 \text{ (rounded)}$$

In the worst-case scenario, the project will not meet the minimum cash savings requirement. The cash savings from the extraction of organic solids can only be off by about 20% to retain project viability. As a plant manager, you might argue that there is a likely *underestimation* of future fines and penalties resulting from the increased political attention to polluting of the local river. Also, there may be a positive benefit, not included in the savings, of a more favorable public image (e.g., increased sales because of the favorable environmental action). Taken together, you should have a strong position for winning approval of the project.

Sensitivity analysis thus provides a powerful tool for assessing the impact of uncertainty in capital investment analysis.

CONCEPT CLIP

1. **What is the definition of IRR?**

Answer:

IRR is defined as the interest rate that sets the present value of a project's cash inflows equal to the present value of the project's cost or, in other words, the discount rate that sets NPV = 0.

2. **Suppose that a project requires an investment of $20,000, and it produces a single period cash flow of $25,000. What is the IRR of the project?**

Answer:

$df = I/CF = \$20,000/\$25,000 = 0.8$. From Exhibit 12B.2 (p. 671), IRR = 25%.

POSTAUDIT OF CAPITAL PROJECTS

A key element in the capital investment process is a follow-up analysis of a capital project once it is implemented. This analysis is called a *postaudit*. A **postaudit** compares the actual benefits with the estimated benefits and actual operating costs with estimated operating costs. It evaluates the overall outcome of the investment and proposes corrective action if needed. The following real-world case illustrates the usefulness of a postaudit activity.

Postaudit Illustrated

Allen Manesfield and Jenny Winters were discussing a persistent and irritating problem present in the process of producing intravenous (IV) needles. Allen and Jenny are employed by Honley Medical, which specializes in the production of medical products and has three divisions: the IV Products Division, the Critical Care Monitoring Division, and the Specialty Products Division. Allen and Jenny are associated with the IV Products Division—Allen as the senior production engineer and Jenny as the marketing manager.

The IV Products Division produces needles of five different sizes. During one stage of the manufacturing process, the needle itself is inserted into a plastic hub and is bonded by using epoxy glue. According to Jenny, the use of epoxy to bond the needles was causing the division all kinds of problems. In many cases, the epoxy wasn't bonding correctly. The rejects were high and the division was receiving a large number of complaints from its customers. Corrective action was needed to avoid losing sales. After some discussion and analysis, a recommendation was made to use induction welding in lieu of epoxy bonding. In induction welding, the needles are inserted into the plastic hub, and an RF generator is used to heat the needles. The RF generator works on the same principle as a microwave oven. As the needles get hot, the plastic melts and the needles are bonded.

Switching to induction welding required an investment in RF generators and the associated tooling. The investment was justified by the IV Products Division based on the savings associated with the new system. Induction welding promised to reduce the cost of direct materials by eliminating the need to buy and use epoxy. Savings of direct labor costs also were predicted because the welding process is more automated. Adding to these savings were the avoidance of daily cleanup costs and the reduction in rejects. Allen presented a formal NPV analysis showing that the welding system was superior to the epoxy system. Headquarters approved its purchase.

One year later, Allen and Jenny had the following conversation regarding the induction welding decision.

Jenny: Allen, I'm quite pleased with induction welding for bonding needles. In the year since the new process was implemented, we've had virtually no complaints from our customers. The needles are firmly bonded.

Allen: I wish that positive experience were true for all other areas as well. Unfortunately, implementing the process has uncovered some rather sticky and expensive problems that I didn't anticipate. The internal audit department recently completed a postaudit of the project, and now my feet are being held to the fire.

Jenny: That's too bad. What's the problem?

Allen: You mean problems. Let me list a few for you. One is that the RF generators interfered with the operation of other equipment. To eliminate this interference, we had to install filtering equipment. But that's not all. We also discovered that the average maintenance person doesn't know how to maintain the new equipment. Now we're faced with the need to initiate a training program to upgrade the skills of our maintenance people. Upgrading skills implies higher wages. Although the RF bonding process is less messy, it is more complex. The manufacturing people complained to the internal auditors about that. They maintain that a simple process, even if messy, is preferred—especially now that demand for the product is increasing by leaps and bounds.

Jenny: What did the internal auditors conclude?

Allen: They concluded that many of the predicted savings did take place but that significant costs were not foreseen. Because of these unforeseen problems, they recommended that I look carefully at the possibility of moving back to using epoxy. They indicated that NPV analysis using actual data appears to favor that process. With production expanding, the acquisition of additional RF generators and filtering equipment plus the necessary training is simply not as attractive as returning to epoxy bonding. This conclusion is reinforced by the fact that the epoxy process is simpler and by the auditors' conclusion that the mixing of the epoxy can be automated, avoiding the quality problem we had in the first place.

Jenny: Well, Allen, you can't really blame yourself. You had a real problem and took action to solve it. It's difficult to foresee all the problems and hidden costs of a new process.

Allen: Unfortunately, the internal auditors don't agree. In fact, neither do I. I probably jumped too quickly. In the future, I intend to think through new projects more carefully.

In the case of the RF bonding decision for Honley Medical, some of the estimated capital investment benefits did materialize: complaints from customers decreased, rejects were fewer, and direct labor and materials costs decreased. However, the investment was greater than expected because filtering equipment was needed, and actual operating costs were much higher because of the increased maintenance cost and the increased complexity of the process. Overall, the internal auditors concluded that the investment was a poor decision. The corrective action that they recommended was to abandon the new process and return to epoxy bonding. Based on this recommendation, the firm abandoned inductive welding and returned to epoxy bonding, which was improved by automating the mix.

Postaudit Benefits

Firms that perform postaudits of capital projects experience a number of benefits, including the following.

- *Resource Allocation:* By evaluating profitability, postaudits ensure that resources are used wisely. If the project is doing well, it may call for additional funds and additional attention. If the project is not doing well, corrective action may be needed to improve performance or abandon the project.
- *Positive Impact on Managers' Behavior:* If managers are held accountable for the results of a capital investment decision, they are more likely to make such decisions in the best interests of the firm. Additionally, postaudits supply feedback to managers that should help to improve future decision making. Consider Allen's reaction to the postaudit of the RF bonding process. Certainly, we would expect him to be more careful and more thorough in making future investment recommendations. In the future, Allen will probably consider more than

one alternative, such as automating the mixing of the epoxy. Also, for those alternatives being considered, he will probably be especially alert to the possibility of hidden costs, such as increased training requirements for a new process.

- *Independent Perspective:* For Honley Medical, the postaudit was performed by the internal audit staff. Generally, more objective results are obtainable if the postaudit is done by an independent party. Since considerable effort is expended to ensure as much independence as possible for the internal audit staff, that group is usually the best choice for this task.

Postaudit Limitations

Postaudits, however, are costly. Moreover, even though they may provide significant benefits, they have other limitations. Most obvious is the fact that the assumptions driving the original analysis may often be invalidated by changes in the actual operating environment. Accountability must be qualified to some extent by the impossibility of foreseeing every possible eventuality.

Check Point

1. Why do a postaudit?

Answer:

Postaudits allow a company to assess the quality of capital investment decisions and also produce corrective actions where some of the initial assumptions prove to be wrong. They also encourage managerial accountability and provide useful information for improving future capital budgeting decisions.

2. Explain how postaudits improve managerial decision making.

Answer:

First, being held accountable for a capital investment decision provides an incentive for managers to make decisions that are good for the company. Second, postaudits provide feedback that will help produce better decisions in the future.

MUTUALLY EXCLUSIVE PROJECTS

OBJECTIVE 6

Explain why net present value is better than internal rate of return for capital investment decisions involving mutually exclusive projects.

Up to this point, we have focused on independent projects. Many capital investment decisions deal with mutually exclusive projects. How NPV analysis and IRR are used to choose among competing projects is an interesting question. An even more interesting question to consider is whether NPV and IRR differ in their ability to help managers make wealth-maximizing decisions in the presence of competing alternatives. For example, we already know that the nondiscounting models can produce erroneous choices because they ignore the time value of money. Because of this deficiency, the discounting models are judged superior. Similarly, it can be shown that the NPV model is generally preferred to the IRR model when choosing among mutually exclusive alternatives.

Net Present Value Compared with Internal Rate of Return

NPV and IRR both yield the same decision for independent projects. For example, if the NPV is greater than zero, then the IRR is also greater than the required rate of return. Both models signal the correct decision. However, for competing projects, the two methods can produce different results. Intuitively, we believe that for mutually exclusive projects, the project with the highest NPV or the highest IRR should be chosen. Since it is possible for the two methods to produce different rankings of mutually exclusive projects, the method that consistently reveals the wealth-maximizing project is preferred.

NPV differs from IRR in two major ways:

- The NPV method assumes that each cash inflow received is reinvested at the required rate of return, whereas the IRR method assumes that each cash inflow is reinvested at the computed IRR. Reinvesting at the required rate of return is more realistic and produces more reliable results when comparing mutually exclusive projects.
- The NPV method measures profitability in absolute terms, whereas the IRR method measures it in relative terms. NPV measures the amount by which the value of the firm changes.

These differences are summarized in Exhibit 12.2.

Exhibit 12.2

Net Present Value Compared with
Internal Rate of Return

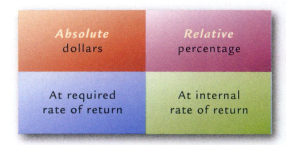

	NPV	IRR
Type of measure	*Absolute* dollars	*Relative* percentage
Cash flow reinvestment assumption	At required rate of return	At internal rate of return

Here's **Why It's important**

Since NPV measures the impact that competing projects have on the value of the firm, choosing the project with the largest NPV is consistent with maximizing the wealth of shareholders. On the other hand, IRR does not consistently result in choices that maximize wealth. IRR, as a relative measure of profitability, has the virtue of measuring accurately the rate of return of funds that remain internally invested. However, maximizing IRR will not necessarily maximize the wealth of firm owners because it cannot, by nature, consider the absolute dollar contributions of projects. In the final analysis, what counts are the total dollars earned—the absolute profits—not the relative profits. Accordingly, NPV, not IRR, should be used for choosing among competing, mutually exclusive projects or competing projects when capital funds are limited.

An independent project is acceptable if its NPV is positive. For mutually exclusive projects, the project with the largest NPV is chosen. There are three steps in selecting the best project from several competing projects:

Step 1: Assess the cash flow pattern for each project.
Step 2: Compute the NPV for each project.
Step 3: Identify the project with the greatest NPV.

NPV Analysis for Mutually Exclusive Projects Illustrated

Bintley Corporation has committed to improving its environmental performance. One environmental project identified a manufacturing process as being the source of both liquid and gaseous residues. After 6 months of research activity, the engineering department announced that it is possible to redesign the process to prevent the production of contaminating residues. Two different process designs (A and B) that prevent the production of contaminants are being considered. Both process designs are more expensive to operate than the current process. However, because the designs prevent production of contaminants, significant annual benefits are created. These benefits stem from eliminating the need to operate and maintain expensive pollution control equipment, treat and dispose of toxic liquid wastes, and pay the annual fines for exceeding allowable contaminant releases. Increased sales to environmentally conscious customers also are factored into the benefit estimates. **Example 12.5** shows how NPV and IRR analyses are carried out for this setting.

Consider two pollution prevention designs: Design A and Design B. Both designs have a project life of 5 years. Design A requires an initial outlay of $180,000 and has a net annual after-tax cash inflow of $60,000 (revenues of $180,000 minus cash expenses of $120,000). Design B, with an initial outlay of $210,000, has a net annual cash inflow of $70,000 ($240,000 − $170,000). The after-tax cash flows are summarized as follows:

CASH FLOW PATTERN

Year	Design A	Design B
0	$(180,000)	$(210,000)
1	60,000	70,000
2	60,000	70,000
3	60,000	70,000
4	60,000	70,000
5	60,000	70,000

The cost of capital for the company is 12%.

Required:
Calculate the NPV and the IRR for each project.

Solution:

DESIGN A: NPV ANALYSIS

Year	Cash Flow	Discount Factor*	Present Value
0	$(180,000)	1.00000	$(180,000)
1–5	60,000	3.60478	216,287
Net present value			$ 36,287

DESIGN A: IRR ANALYSIS

Discount Factor = Initial Investment/Annual Cash Flow
= $180,000/$60,000
= 3.00000

From Exhibit 12B.2 (p. 671), df = 3.00000 for 5 years implies that IRR ≈ 20%.

DESIGN B: NPV ANALYSIS

Year	Cash Flow	Discount Factor*	Present Value
0	$(210,000)	1.00000	$(210,000)
1–5	70,000	3.60478	252,335
Net present value			$ 42,335

DESIGN B: IRR ANALYSIS

Discount Factor = Initial Investment/Annual Cash Flow
= $210,000/$70,000
= 3.00000

From Exhibit 12B.2, df =3.00000 for 5 years implies that IRR ≈ 20%.
*From Exhibit 12B.2.

Based on the NPV analysis in Example 12.5, Design B is more profitable; it has the larger NPV. Accordingly, the company should select Design B over Design A. Interestingly, Designs A and B have identical internal rates of return. As shown by Example 12.5, both designs have a discount factor of 3.00000. From Exhibit 12B.2, it is seen that a discount factor of 3.00000 and a life of 5 years yields an IRR of about 20%. Even though both projects have an IRR of 20%, the firm should not consider the two designs to be equally desirable. The analysis demonstrates that Design B produces a larger NPV and, therefore, will increase the value of the firm more than Design A. Design B should be chosen. This illustrates the conceptual superiority of NPV over IRR for analysis of competing projects.

Special Considerations for Advanced Manufacturing Environment

For advanced manufacturing environments, like those using automated systems, capital investment decisions can be more complex because they must take special considerations into account.

How Investment Differs   Investment in automated manufacturing processes is much more complex than investment in the standard manufacturing equipment of the past. For standard equipment, the direct costs of acquisition represent virtually the entire investment. For automated manufacturing, the direct costs can represent as little as 50 or 60% of the total investment. Software, engineering, training, and implementation are a significant percentage of the total costs. Thus, great care must be exercised to assess the actual cost of an automated system. It is easy to overlook the peripheral costs, which can be substantial.

How Estimates of Operating Cash Flows Differ   Estimates of operating cash flows from investments in standard equipment typically have relied on directly identifiable tangible benefits, such as direct savings from labor, power, and scrap. However, when investing in

Here's How It's Used: At Kicker

CONCEPT CLIP

During the period of 2001–2003, **Stillwater Designs** experienced high sales of its **Kicker** products. As a result, the levels of inventory filled all storage areas to capacity. Consequently, Stillwater Designs began plans to add another building with 50,000 square feet of capacity. This new facility on existing property had an estimated construction cost between $1 and $1.5 million. During this preliminary planning phase, a shipping strike placed extra storage demands on existing facilities, and Stillwater Designs began looking for a warehousing facility that could be leased on a short-term basis.

It identified a 250,000-square-foot facility on 22 acres that was owned by **Moore Business Forms**. This facility was an attractive leasing option, and it quickly became a competing alternative to adding the 50,000-square-foot facility to Stillwater's current complex. In fact, the company began looking at the possibility of buying and renovating the Moore

facility and moving all of its operations into the one facility. Renovation required such actions as installing a new HVAC system, bringing the building up to current fire codes, painting and resealing the floor, and adding a large number of offices. After careful financial analysis, Stillwater Designs decided that the buy-and-renovate option was more profitable than adding the 50,000-square-foot building to its current complex. Two economic factors affecting the decision were (1) selling the current complex of five buildings to help pay for the needed renovations and (2) the purchase cost of the nonrenovated Moore facility being less than the cost of building the 50,000-square-foot facility.

automated systems, the intangible and indirect benefits can be material and critical to the viability of the project. Greater quality, more reliability, reduced lead time, improved customer satisfaction, and an enhanced ability to maintain market share all are important intangible benefits of an advanced manufacturing system. Reduction of labor in support areas such as production scheduling and stores are indirect benefits. More effort is needed to measure these intangible and indirect benefits in order to assess more accurately the potential value of investments.

Consider, for example, Zielesch Manufacturing, which is evaluating a potential investment in a flexible manufacturing system (FMS). The choice facing the company is to continue producing with its traditional equipment, expected to last 10 years, or to switch to the new system, which also is expected to have a useful life of 10 years. Zielesch's discount rate is 12%. The data pertaining to the investment are presented in Exhibit 12.3. Notice that for Zielesch, the *incremental cash flows* are used to compare the new project with the old. Instead of calculating the NPV for each alternative and comparing, an equivalent approach is to calculate the NPV of the incremental cash flows of the new system (cash flows of new system minus cash flows of old system). If the NPV for the incremental cash flows is positive, then the new equipment is preferred to the old.

	FMS	Status Quo
Investment (current outlay):		
Direct costs	$10,000,000	—
Software, engineering	8,000,000	—
Total current outlay	$18,000,000	—
Net after-tax cash flow	$ 5,000,000	$1,000,000
Less: After-tax cash flows for status quo	1,000,000	n/a
Incremental benefit	$ 4,000,000 ←	n/a
Incremental Benefit Explained		
Direct benefits:		
Direct labor	$ 1,500,000	
Scrap reduction	500,000	
Setups	200,000	
	$ 2,200,000	
Intangible benefits (quality savings):		
Rework	$ 200,000	
Warranties	400,000	
Maintenance of competitive position	1,000,000	
	$ 1,600,000	
Indirect benefits:		
Production scheduling	$ 110,000	
Payroll	90,000	
	$ 200,000	
Total	$ 4,000,000 ←	

Exhibit 12.3

Investment Data; Direct, Intangible, and Indirect Benefits

Using the incremental data in Exhibit 12.3, the NPV of the proposed system can be computed as follows:

Present value ($4,000,000 × 5.65022*)	$22,600,880
Investment	18,000,000
NPV	$ 4,600,880

*This number is the discount factor for an interest rate of 12% and a life of 10 years (see Exhibit 12B.2, p. 671).

The NPV is positive and large in magnitude, and it clearly signals the acceptability of the FMS. This outcome, however, is strongly dependent on explicit recognition of both intangible and indirect benefits. If those benefits are eliminated, then the direct savings total $2.2 million, and the NPV is negative:

Present value ($2,200,000 × 5.65022)	$12,430,484
Investment	18,000,000
NPV	$ (5,569,516)

The rise of activity-based costing has made identifying indirect benefits easier with the use of cost drivers. Once they are identified, they can be included in the analysis if they are material.

Examination of Exhibit 12.3 reveals the importance of intangible benefits. One of the most important intangible benefits is maintaining or improving a firm's competitive position. A key question is what will happen to the cash flows of the firm if the investment is not made. That is, if Zielesch chooses to forgo an investment in technologically advanced equipment, will it be able to continue to compete with other firms on the basis of quality, delivery, and cost? (The question becomes especially relevant if competitors choose to invest in advanced equipment.) If the competitive position deteriorates, Zielesch's current cash flows will decrease.

If cash flows will decrease if the investment is not made, this decrease should show up as an incremental benefit for the advanced technology. In Exhibit 12.3, Zielesch estimates this competitive benefit as $1,000,000. Estimating this benefit requires some serious strategic planning and analysis, but its effect can be critical. If this benefit had been ignored or overlooked, then the NPV would have been negative and the investment alternative rejected:

Present value ($3,000,000 × 5.65022)	$16,950,660
Investment	18,000,000
NPV	$ (1,049,340)

Check Point

1. Why is NPV better than IRR for choosing among competing projects?

Answer:
NPV uses a more realistic reinvestment assumption (reinvests at the cost of capital), and its signal is consistent with maximizing the wealth of firm owners (IRR does not measure absolute profits).

2. What are the three steps for using NPV to choose among competing projects?

Answer:
1. Estimate cash flows for each project.
2. Calculate NPV for each project.
3. Choose the project with the largest NPV.

APPENDIX 12A: PRESENT VALUE CONCEPTS

An important feature of money is that it can be invested and can earn interest. A dollar today is not the same as a dollar tomorrow. This fundamental principle is the backbone of discounting methods. Discounting methods rely on the relationships between current and future dollars. Thus, to use discounting methods, we must understand these relationships.

Future Value

Suppose that a bank advertises a 4% annual interest rate. If a customer invests $100, he or she would receive, after 1 year, the original $100 plus $4 interest [$100 + (0.04) ($100)] = (1 + 0.04)$100 = (1.04)($100) = $104. This result can be expressed by the following equation, where F is the future amount, P is the initial or current outlay, and i is the interest rate:

$$F = P(1 + i)$$

For the example, $F = \$100(1 + 0.04) = \$100(1.04) = \$104$.

Now suppose that the same bank offers a 5% rate if the customer leaves the original deposit, plus any interest, on deposit for a total of 2 years. How much will the customer receive at the end of 2 years? Again assume that a customer invests $100. Using the future value equation, the customer will earn $105 at the end of Year 1:

$$F = \$100(1 + 0.05) = \$100(1.05) = \$105$$

If this amount is left in the account for a second year, this equation is used again with P now assumed to be $105. At the end of the second year, then, the total is $110.25:

$$F = \$105(1 + 0.05) = \$105(1.05) = \$110.25$$

In the second year, interest is earned on both the original deposit and the interest earned in the first year. The earning of interest on interest is referred to as **compounding of interest**. The value that will accumulate by the end of an investment's life, assuming a specified compound return, is the **future value**. The future value of the $100 deposit in the second example is $110.25.

A more direct way to compute the future value is possible. Since the first application of the future value equation can be expressed as $F = \$105 = \$100(1.05)$, the second application can be expressed as $F = \$105(1.05) = \$100(1.05)(1.05) = \$100(1.05)^2 = P(1 + i)^2$. This suggests the following compounding interest formula for computing amounts for n periods into the future:

$$F = P(1 + i)^n$$

Present Value

Often, a manager needs to compute not the future value but the amount that must be invested now in order to yield some given future value. The amount that must be invested now to produce the future value is known as the **present value** of the future amount. For example, how much must be invested now in order to yield $363 two years from now, assuming that the interest rate is 10%? Or, put another way, what is the present value of $363 to be received two years from now?

In this example, the future value, the years, and the interest rate are all known. We want to know the current outlay that will produce that future amount. In the compounding interest equation, the variable representing the current outlay (the present value of F) is P. Thus, to compute the present value of a future outlay, all we need to do is solve the compounding interest equation for P:

$$P = F/(1 + i)^n$$

Using this present value equation, we can compute the present value of $363:

$$P = \$363/(1 + 0.1)^2$$
$$= \$363/1.21$$
$$= \$300$$

The present value, $300, is what the future amount of $363 is worth today. All other things being equal, having $300 today is the same as having $363 two years from now. Put another way, if a firm requires a 10% rate of return, the most the firm would be willing to pay today is $300 for any investment that yields $363 two years from now.

The process of computing the present value of future cash flows is often referred to as **discounting**. Thus, we say that we have discounted the future value of $363 to its present value of $300. The interest rate used to discount the future cash flow is the **discount rate**. The expression $1/(1 + i)^n$ in the present value equation is the **discount factor**. By letting the discount factor, called df, equal $1/(1 + i)^n$, the present value equation can be expressed as $P = F\,(df)$. To simplify the computation of present value, a table of discount factors is given for various combinations of i and n [refer to Exhibit 12B.1 (p. 670) in Appendix 12B]. For example, the discount factor for $i = 10\%$ and $n = 2$ is 0.82645 (go to the 10% column of the table and move down to the second row). With the discount factor, the present value of $363 is computed as follows:

$$P = F\,(df)$$
$$= \$363 \times 0.82645$$
$$= \$300 \text{ (rounded)}$$

Present Value of an Uneven Series of Cash Flows

Exhibit 12B.1 can be used to compute the present value of any future cash flow or series of future cash flows. A series of future cash flows is called an **annuity**. The present value of an annuity is found by computing the present value of each future cash flow and then summing these values. For example, suppose that an investment is expected to produce the following annual cash flows: $110, $121, and $133.10. Assuming a discount rate of 10%, the present value of this series of cash flows is computed in Exhibit 12A.1.

Exhibit 12A.1

Present Value of an Uneven Series of Cash Flows

Year	Cash Receipt	Discount Factor	Present Value*
1	$110.00	0.90909	$100.00
2	121.00	0.82645	100.00
3	133.10	0.75131	100.00
		2.48685	$300.00

*Rounded.

Present Value of a Uniform Series of Cash Flows

If the series of cash flows is even, the computation of the annuity's present value is simplified. For example, assume that an investment is expected to return $100 per year for 3 years. Using Exhibit 12B.1 and assuming a discount rate of 10%, the present value of the annuity is computed in Exhibit 12A.2.

Year	Cash Receipt*	Discount Factor	Present Value
1	$100	0.90909	$ 90.91
2	100	0.82645	82.65
3	100	0.75131	75.13
		2.48685	$248.69

*The annual cash flow of $100 can be multiplied by the sum of the discount factors (2.48685) to obtain the present value of the uniform series ($248.69).

Exhibit 12A.2

Present Value of an Annuity

As with the uneven series of cash flows, the present value in Exhibit 12A.2 was computed by calculating the present value of each cash flow separately and then summing them. However, in the case of an annuity displaying uniform cash flows, the computations can be reduced from three to one as described in the footnote to the exhibit. The sum of the individual discount factors can be thought of as a discount factor for an annuity of uniform cash flows. A table of discount factors that can be used for an annuity of uniform cash flows is available in Exhibit 12B.2.

Check Point

1. **How much will you receive in 2 years if you invest $100 with an interest rate of 10%?**

Answer:
$F = (1 + 0.10)^2(\$100) = 1.21(\$100) = \$121$

2. **What is meant by discount rate?**

Answer:
The discount rate is the interest rate used to discount a future cash flow.

APPENDIX 12B: PRESENT VALUE TABLES

The present value tables are found on pages 670 and 671.

Appendix 12B: Present Value Tables

Exhibit 12B.1 Present Value of a Single Amount*

n/i	1%	2%	3%	4%	5%	6%	7%	8%	9%	10%	12%	14%	16%	18%	20%	25%	30%
1	0.99010	0.98039	0.97087	0.96154	0.95238	0.94340	0.93458	0.92593	0.91743	0.90909	0.89286	0.87719	0.86207	0.84746	0.83333	0.80000	0.76923
2	0.98030	0.96117	0.94260	0.92456	0.90703	0.89000	0.87344	0.85734	0.84168	0.82645	0.79719	0.76947	0.74316	0.71818	0.69444	0.64000	0.59172
3	0.97059	0.94232	0.91514	0.88900	0.86384	0.83962	0.81630	0.79383	0.77218	0.75131	0.71178	0.67497	0.64066	0.60863	0.57870	0.51200	0.45517
4	0.96098	0.92385	0.88849	0.85480	0.82270	0.79209	0.76290	0.73503	0.70843	0.68301	0.63552	0.59208	0.55229	0.51579	0.48225	0.40960	0.35013
5	0.95147	0.90573	0.86261	0.82193	0.78353	0.74726	0.71299	0.68058	0.64993	0.62092	0.56743	0.51937	0.47611	0.43711	0.40188	0.32768	0.26933
6	0.94205	0.88797	0.83748	0.79031	0.74622	0.70496	0.66634	0.63017	0.59627	0.56447	0.50663	0.45559	0.41044	0.37043	0.33490	0.26214	0.20718
7	0.93272	0.87056	0.81309	0.75992	0.71068	0.66506	0.62275	0.58349	0.54703	0.51316	0.45235	0.39964	0.35383	0.31393	0.27908	0.20972	0.15937
8	0.92348	0.85349	0.78941	0.73069	0.67684	0.62741	0.58201	0.54027	0.50187	0.46651	0.40388	0.35056	0.30503	0.26604	0.23257	0.16777	0.12259
9	0.91434	0.83676	0.76642	0.70259	0.64461	0.59190	0.54393	0.50025	0.46043	0.42410	0.36061	0.30751	0.26295	0.22546	0.19381	0.13422	0.09430
10	0.90529	0.82035	0.74409	0.67556	0.61391	0.55839	0.50835	0.46319	0.42241	0.38554	0.32197	0.26974	0.22668	0.19106	0.16151	0.10737	0.07254
11	0.89632	0.80426	0.72242	0.64958	0.58468	0.52679	0.47509	0.42888	0.38753	0.35049	0.28748	0.23662	0.19542	0.16192	0.13459	0.08590	0.05580
12	0.88745	0.78849	0.70138	0.62460	0.55684	0.49697	0.44401	0.39711	0.35553	0.31863	0.25668	0.20756	0.16846	0.13722	0.11216	0.06872	0.04292
13	0.87866	0.77303	0.68095	0.60057	0.53032	0.46884	0.41496	0.36770	0.32618	0.28966	0.22917	0.18207	0.14523	0.11629	0.09346	0.05498	0.03302
14	0.86996	0.75788	0.66112	0.57748	0.50507	0.44230	0.38782	0.34046	0.29925	0.26333	0.20462	0.15971	0.12520	0.09855	0.07789	0.04398	0.02540
15	0.86135	0.74301	0.64186	0.55526	0.48102	0.41727	0.36245	0.31524	0.27454	0.23939	0.18270	0.14010	0.10793	0.08352	0.06491	0.03518	0.01954
16	0.85282	0.72845	0.62317	0.53391	0.45811	0.39365	0.33873	0.29189	0.25187	0.21763	0.16312	0.12289	0.09304	0.07078	0.05409	0.02815	0.01503
17	0.84438	0.71416	0.60502	0.51337	0.43630	0.37136	0.31657	0.27027	0.23107	0.19784	0.14564	0.10780	0.08021	0.05998	0.04507	0.02252	0.01156
18	0.83602	0.70016	0.58739	0.49363	0.41552	0.35034	0.29586	0.25025	0.21199	0.17986	0.13004	0.09456	0.06914	0.05083	0.03756	0.01801	0.00889
19	0.82774	0.68643	0.57029	0.47464	0.39573	0.33051	0.27651	0.23171	0.19449	0.16351	0.11611	0.08295	0.05139	0.04308	0.03130	0.01441	0.00684
20	0.81954	0.67297	0.55368	0.45639	0.37689	0.31180	0.25842	0.21455	0.17843	0.14864	0.10367	0.07276	0.05139	0.03651	0.02608	0.01153	0.00526
21	0.81143	0.65978	0.53755	0.43883	0.35894	0.29416	0.24151	0.19866	0.16370	0.13513	0.09256	0.06383	0.04430	0.03094	0.02174	0.00922	0.00405
22	0.80340	0.64684	0.52189	0.42196	0.34185	0.27751	0.22571	0.18394	0.15018	0.12285	0.08264	0.05599	0.03819	0.02622	0.01811	0.00738	0.00311
23	0.79544	0.63416	0.50669	0.40573	0.32557	0.26180	0.21095	0.17032	0.13778	0.11168	0.07379	0.04911	0.03292	0.02222	0.01509	0.00590	0.00239
24	0.78757	0.62172	0.49193	0.39012	0.31007	0.24698	0.19715	0.15770	0.12640	0.10153	0.06588	0.04308	0.02838	0.01883	0.01258	0.00472	0.00184
25	0.77977	0.60953	0.47761	0.37512	0.29530	0.23300	0.18425	0.14602	0.11597	0.09230	0.05882	0.03779	0.02447	0.01596	0.01048	0.00378	0.00142
26	0.77205	0.59758	0.46369	0.36069	0.28124	0.21981	0.17220	0.13520	0.10639	0.08391	0.05252	0.03315	0.02109	0.01352	0.00874	0.00302	0.00109
27	0.76440	0.58586	0.45019	0.34682	0.26785	0.20737	0.16093	0.12519	0.09761	0.07628	0.04689	0.02908	0.01818	0.01146	0.00728	0.00242	0.00084
28	0.75684	0.57437	0.43708	0.33348	0.25509	0.19563	0.15040	0.11591	0.08955	0.06934	0.04187	0.02551	0.01567	0.00971	0.00607	0.00193	0.00065
29	0.74934	0.56311	0.42435	0.32065	0.24295	0.18456	0.14056	0.10733	0.08215	0.06304	0.03738	0.02237	0.01351	0.00823	0.00506	0.00155	0.00050
30	0.74192	0.55207	0.41199	0.30832	0.23138	0.17411	0.13137	0.09938	0.07537	0.05731	0.03338	0.01963	0.01165	0.00697	0.00421	0.00124	0.00038

*$P_n = A/(1 + i)^n$

Exhibit 12B.2   Present Value of an Annuity*

n/i	1%	2%	3%	4%	5%	6%	7%	8%	9%	10%	12%	14%	16%	18%	20%	25%	30%
1	0.99010	0.98039	0.97087	0.96154	0.95238	0.94340	0.93458	0.92593	0.91743	0.90909	0.89286	0.87719	0.86207	0.84746	0.83333	0.80000	0.76923
2	1.97040	1.94156	1.91347	1.88609	1.85941	1.83339	1.80802	1.78326	1.75911	1.73554	1.69005	1.64666	1.60523	1.56564	1.52778	1.44000	1.36095
3	2.94099	2.88388	2.82861	2.77509	2.72325	2.67301	2.62432	2.57710	2.53129	2.48685	2.40183	2.32163	2.24589	2.17427	2.10648	1.95200	1.81611
4	3.90197	3.80773	3.71710	3.62990	3.54595	3.46511	3.38721	3.31213	3.23972	3.16987	3.03735	2.91371	2.79818	2.69006	2.58873	2.36160	2.16624
5	4.85343	4.71346	4.57971	4.45182	4.32948	4.21236	4.10020	3.99271	3.88965	3.79079	3.60478	3.43308	3.27429	3.12717	2.99061	2.68928	2.43557
6	5.79548	5.60143	5.41719	5.24214	5.07569	4.91732	4.76654	4.62288	4.48592	4.35526	4.11141	3.88867	3.68474	3.49760	3.32551	2.95142	2.64275
7	6.72819	6.47199	6.23028	6.00205	5.78637	5.58238	5.38929	5.20637	5.03295	4.86842	4.56376	4.28830	4.03857	3.81153	3.60459	3.16114	2.80211
8	7.65168	7.32548	7.01969	6.73274	6.46321	6.20979	5.97130	5.74664	5.53482	5.33493	4.96764	4.63886	4.34359	4.07757	3.83716	3.32891	2.92470
9	8.56602	8.16224	7.78611	7.43533	7.10782	6.80169	6.51523	6.24689	5.99525	5.75902	5.32825	4.94637	4.60654	4.30302	4.03097	3.46313	3.01900
10	9.47130	8.98259	8.53020	8.11090	7.72173	7.36009	7.02358	6.71008	6.41766	6.14457	5.65022	5.21612	4.83323	4.49409	4.19247	3.57050	3.09154
11	10.36763	9.78685	9.25262	8.76048	8.30641	7.88687	7.49867	7.13896	6.80519	6.49506	5.93770	5.45273	5.02864	4.65601	4.32706	3.65640	3.14734
12	11.25508	10.57534	9.95400	9.38507	8.86325	8.38384	7.94269	7.53608	7.16073	6.81369	6.19437	5.66029	5.19711	4.79322	4.43922	3.72512	3.19026
13	12.13374	11.34837	10.63496	9.98565	9.39357	8.85268	8.35765	7.90378	7.48690	7.10336	6.42355	5.84236	5.34233	4.90951	4.53268	3.78010	3.22328
14	13.00370	12.10625	11.29607	10.56312	9.89864	9.29498	8.74547	8.24424	7.78615	7.36669	6.62817	6.00207	5.46753	5.00806	4.61057	3.82408	3.24867
15	13.86505	12.84926	11.93794	11.11839	10.37966	9.71225	9.10791	8.55948	8.06069	7.60608	6.81086	6.14217	5.57546	5.09158	4.67547	3.85926	3.26821
16	14.71787	13.57771	12.56110	11.65230	10.83777	10.10590	9.44665	8.85137	8.31256	7.82371	6.97399	6.26506	5.66850	5.16235	4.72956	3.88741	3.28324
17	15.56225	14.29187	13.16612	12.16567	11.27407	10.47726	9.76322	9.12164	8.54363	8.02155	7.11963	6.37286	5.74870	5.22233	4.77463	3.90993	3.29480
18	16.39827	14.99203	13.75351	12.65930	11.68959	10.82760	10.05909	9.37189	8.75563	8.20141	7.24967	6.46742	5.81785	5.27316	4.81219	3.92794	3.30369
19	17.22601	15.67846	14.32380	13.13394	12.08532	11.15812	10.33560	9.60360	8.95011	8.36492	7.36578	6.55037	5.87746	5.31624	4.84350	3.94235	3.31053
20	18.04555	16.35143	14.87747	13.59033	12.46221	11.46992	10.59401	9.81815	9.12855	8.51356	7.46944	6.62313	5.92884	5.35275	4.86958	3.95388	3.31579
21	18.85698	17.01121	15.41502	14.02916	12.82115	11.76408	10.83553	10.01680	9.29224	8.64869	7.56200	6.68696	5.97314	5.38368	4.89132	3.96311	3.31984
22	19.66038	17.65805	15.93692	14.45112	13.16300	12.04158	11.06124	10.20074	9.44243	8.77154	7.64465	6.74294	6.01133	5.40990	4.90943	3.97049	3.32296
23	20.45582	18.29220	16.44361	14.85684	13.48857	12.30338	11.27219	10.37106	9.58021	8.88322	7.71843	6.79206	6.04425	5.43212	4.92453	3.97639	3.32535
24	21.24339	18.91393	16.93554	15.24696	13.79864	12.55036	11.46933	10.52876	9.70661	8.98474	7.78432	6.83514	6.07263	5.45095	4.93710	3.98111	3.32719
25	22.02316	19.52346	17.41315	15.62208	14.09394	12.78336	11.65358	10.67478	9.82258	9.07704	7.84314	6.87293	6.09709	5.46691	4.94759	3.98489	3.32861
26	22.79520	20.12104	17.87684	15.98277	14.37519	13.00317	11.82578	10.80998	9.92897	9.16095	7.89566	6.90608	6.11818	5.48043	4.95632	3.98791	3.32970
27	23.55961	20.70690	18.32703	16.32959	14.64303	13.21053	11.98671	10.93516	10.02658	9.23722	7.94255	6.93515	6.13636	5.49189	4.96360	3.99033	3.33054
28	24.31644	21.28127	18.76411	16.66306	14.89813	13.40616	12.13711	11.05108	10.11613	9.30657	7.98442	6.96066	6.15204	5.50160	4.96967	3.99226	3.33118
29	25.06579	21.84438	19.18845	16.98371	15.14107	13.59072	12.27767	11.15841	10.19828	9.36961	8.02181	6.98304	6.16555	5.50983	4.97472	3.99381	3.33168
30	25.80771	22.39646	19.60044	17.29203	15.37245	13.76483	12.40904	11.25778	10.27365	9.42691	8.05518	7.00266	6.17720	5.51681	4.97894	3.99505	3.33206

*$P_n = (1/i)[1 - 1/(1 + i)^n]$

SUMMARY OF LEARNING OBJECTIVES

LO1. Explain the meaning of capital investment decisions, and distinguish between independent and mutually exclusive capital investment decisions.

- Capital investment decisions are concerned with the acquisition of long-term assets and usually involve a significant outlay of funds.
- The two types of capital investment projects are independent and mutually exclusive.
- Independent projects are projects that, whether accepted or rejected, do not affect the cash flows of other projects.
- Mutually exclusive projects are projects that, if accepted, preclude the acceptance of all other competing projects.

LO2. Compute the payback period and accounting rate of return for a proposed investment, and explain their roles in capital investment decisions.

- Managers make capital investment decisions by using formal models to decide whether to accept or reject proposed projects.
- These decision models are classified as nondiscounting and discounting, depending on whether they address the question of the time value of money.
- The two nondiscounting models are the payback period and the ARR.
- The payback period is the time required for a firm to recover its initial investment. For even cash flows, it is calculated by dividing the investment by the annual cash flow. For uneven cash flows, the cash flows are summed until the investment is recovered. If only a fraction of a year is needed, then it is assumed that the cash flows occur evenly within each year.
- The payback period ignores the time value of money and the profitability of projects because it does not consider the cash inflows available beyond the payback period. The payback period is useful for assessing and controlling risk, minimizing the impact of an investment on a firm's liquidity, and controlling the risk of obsolescence.
- The ARR is computed by dividing the average income expected from an investment by either the original or average investment.
- Unlike the payback period, the ARR does consider the profitability of a project; however, it ignores the time value of money.
- The ARR may be useful to managers for screening new investments to ensure that certain accounting ratios are not adversely affected (specifically, accounting ratios that may be monitored to ensure compliance with debt covenants).

LO3. Use net present value analysis for capital investment decisions involving independent projects.

- NPV is the difference between the present value of future cash flows and the initial investment outlay.
- To use the NPV model, a required rate of return must be identified (usually, the cost of capital). The NPV method uses the required rate of return to compute the present value of a project's cash inflows and outflows.
- If the present value of the inflows is greater than the present value of the outflows, then the NPV is greater than zero, and the project is profitable. If the NPV is less than zero, then the project is not profitable and should be rejected.

LO4. Use the internal rate of return to assess the acceptability of independent projects.

- The IRR is computed by finding the interest rate that equates the present value of a project's cash inflows with the present value of its cash outflows.
- If the IRR is greater than the required rate of return (cost of capital), then the project is acceptable; if the IRR is less than the required rate of return, then the project should be rejected.

LO5. Explain the role and value of postaudits.
- Postauditing of capital projects is an important step in capital investment.
- Postaudits evaluate the actual performance of a project in relation to its expected performance.
- A postaudit may lead to corrective action to improve the performance of the project or to abandon it.
- Postaudits also serve as an incentive for managers to make capital investment decisions prudently.

LO6. Explain why net present value is better than internal rate of return for capital investment decisions involving mutually exclusive projects.
- In evaluating mutually exclusive or competing projects, managers have a choice of using NPV or IRR.
- When choosing among competing projects, the NPV model correctly identifies the best investment alternative.
- IRR may choose an inferior project. Thus, since NPV always provides the correct signal, it should be used.

LO7. *(Appendix 12A)* Explain the relationship between current and future dollars.
- The value of an investment at the end of its life is called its future value.
- Present value is the amount that must be invested now to yield some future value.
- Present value is computed by discounting the future value using a discount rate. The discount rate is the interest rate used to discount the future amount.
- An annuity is a series of future cash flows. If the annuity is uneven, then each future cash flow must be discounted using individual discount rates. (The present value for each cash flow is calculated separately and then summed.) For even cash flows, a single discount rate, which is the sum of each discount rate for each cash flow, can be used.

SUMMARY OF IMPORTANT EQUATIONS

1. $\text{Payback Period} = \dfrac{\text{Original Investment}}{\text{Annual Cash Flow}}$

2. $\text{Accounting Rate of Return} = \dfrac{\text{Average Income}}{\text{Initial Investment}}$

3. $NPV = \left[\sum CF_t / (1+i)^t\right] - I$

   $ = \left[\sum CF_t df_t\right] - I$

   $ = P - I$

4. $I = \sum\left[CF_t / (1+i)^t\right]$

5. $I = CF(df)$

6. $df = I / CF$

   $ = \dfrac{\text{Investment}}{\text{Annual Cash Flow}}$

7. $F = P(1 + i)^n$

8. $P = F / (1 + i)^n$

KEY TERMS

Accounting rate of return (ARR), 650, the rate of return obtained by dividing the average accounting net income by the original investment.

Annuity, 668 *(Appendix 12A)*, a series of future cash flows.

Capital budgeting, 646, the process of making capital investment decisions.

Capital investment decisions, 646, the process of planning, setting goals and priorities, arranging financing, and identifying criteria for making long-term investments.

Compounding of interest, 667 *(Appendix 12A)*, paying interest on interest.

Cost of capital, 653, the cost of investment funds, usually viewed as a weighted average of the costs of funds from all sources.

Discount factor, 668 *(Appendix 12A),* the factor used to convert a future cash flow to its present value.

Discount rate, 668 *(Appendix 12A)*, the rate of return used to compute the present value of future cash flows.

Discounted cash flows, 652, future cash flows expressed in present value terms.

Discounting, 668 *(Appendix 12A)*, the act of finding the present value of future cash flows.

Discounting models, 647, capital investment models that explicitly consider the time value of money in identifying criteria for accepting and rejecting proposed projects.

Future value, 667 *(Appendix 12A)*, the value that will accumulate by the end of an investment's life if the investment earns a specified compounded return.

Independent projects, 646, projects that, if accepted or rejected, will not affect the cash flows of another project.

Internal rate of return (IRR), 656, the rate of return that equates the present value of a project's cash inflows with the present value of its cash outflows (i.e., it sets the NPV equal to zero). Also, the rate of return being earned on funds that remain internally invested in a project.

Mutually exclusive projects, 646, projects that, if accepted, preclude the acceptance of competing projects.

Net present value (NPV), 652, the difference between the present value of a project's cash inflows and the present value of its cash outflows.

Nondiscounting models, 647, capital investment models that identify criteria for accepting or rejecting projects without considering the time value of money.

Payback period, 648, the time required for a project to return its investment.

Postaudit, 659, a follow-up analysis of an investment decision, comparing actual benefits and costs with expected benefits and costs.

Present value, 667 *(Appendix 12A),* the current value of a future cash flow. It represents the amount that must be invested now if the future cash flow is to be received, assuming compounding at a given rate of interest.

Required rate of return, 652, the minimum rate of return that a project must earn in order to be acceptable. Usually corresponds to the cost of capital.

REVIEW PROBLEMS

I. Basics of Capital Investment

Kenn Day, manager of Day Laboratory, is investigating the possibility of acquiring some new test equipment. The equipment requires an initial outlay of $300,000. To raise the capital, Kenn will sell stock valued at $200,000 (the stock pays dividends of $24,000 per year) and borrow $100,000. The loan for $100,000 would carry an interest rate of 6%. Kenn figures that his weighted average cost of capital is 10% $[(2/3 \times 0.12) + (1/3 \times 0.06)]$. This weighted cost of capital is the discount rate that will be used for capital investment decisions.

Kenn estimates that the new test equipment will produce a cash inflow of $50,000 per year. Kenn expects the equipment to last for 20 years.

Required:

1. Compute the payback period.
2. Assuming that depreciation is $14,000 per year, compute the ARR (on total investment).
3. Compute the NPV of the test equipment.
4. Compute the IRR of the test equipment.
5. Should Kenn buy the equipment?

Solution:

1. The payback period is $300,000/$50,000, or 6 years.
2. The ARR is ($50,000 − $14,000)/$300,000, or 12%.
3. From Exhibit 12B.2 (p. 671), the discount factor for an annuity with *i* at 10% and *n* at 20 years is 8.51356. Thus, the NPV is (8.51356 × $50,000) − $300,000, or $125,678.
4. The discount factor associated with the IRR is 6.00000 ($300,000/$50,000). From Exhibit 12B.2, the IRR is between 14 and 16% (using the row corresponding to Period 20).
5. Since the NPV is positive and the IRR is greater than Kenn's cost of capital, the test equipment is a sound investment. This, of course, assumes that the cash flow projections are accurate.

II. Capital Investments with Independent Projects

A hospital is considering the possibility of two new purchases: new X-ray equipment and new biopsy equipment. Each project would require an investment of $750,000. The expected life for each is 5 years with no expected salvage value. The net cash inflows associated with the two independent projects are as follows:

(Continued)

Year	X-Ray Equipment	Biopsy Equipment
1	$375,000	$ 75,000
2	150,000	75,000
3	300,000	525,000
4	150,000	600,000
5	75,000	675,000

Required:

1. Compute the net present value of each project, assuming a required rate of 12%.
2. Compute the payback period for each project. Assume that the manager of the hospital accepts only projects with a payback period of 3 years or less. Offer some reasons why this may be a rational strategy, even though the NPV computed in Requirement 1 may indicate otherwise.

Solution:

1. X-ray equipment:

Year	Cash Flow	Discount Factor	Present Value
0	$(750,000)	1.00000	$(750,000)
1	375,000	0.89286	334,823
2	150,000	0.79719	119,579
3	300,000	0.71178	213,534
4	150,000	0.63552	95,328
5	75,000	0.56743	42,557
NPV			$ 55,821

Biopsy equipment:

Year	Cash Flow	Discount Factor	Present Value
0	$(750,000)	1.00000	$(750,000)
1	75,000	0.89286	66,965
2	75,000	0.79719	59,789
3	525,000	0.71178	373,685
4	600,000	0.63552	381,312
5	675,000	0.56743	383,015
NPV			$ 514,766

2. X-ray equipment:

Payback Period =	$375,000	1.00 year
	150,000	1.00
	225,000	0.75 ($225,000/$300,000)
	$750,000	2.75 years

Biopsy equipment:

Payback Period =	$ 75,000	1.00 year
	75,000	1.00
	525,000	1.00
	75,000	0.13 ($75,000/$600,000)
	$750,000	3.13 years

This might be a reasonable strategy because payback is a rough measure of risk. The assumption is that the longer it takes a project to pay for itself, the riskier the project is. Other reasons might be that the firm might have liquidity problems, the cash flows might be risky, or there might be a high risk of obsolescence.

DISCUSSION QUESTIONS

1. Explain the difference between independent projects and mutually exclusive projects.
2. Explain why the timing and quantity of cash flows are important in capital investment decisions.
3. The time value of money is ignored by the payback period and the ARR. Explain why this is a major deficiency in these two models.
4. What is the payback period? Compute the payback period for an investment requiring an initial outlay of $80,000 with expected annual cash inflows of $30,000.
5. Name and discuss three possible reasons that the payback period is used to help make capital investment decisions.
6. What is the accounting rate of return? Compute the ARR for an investment that requires an initial outlay of $300,000 and promises an average net income of $100,000.
7. The NPV is the same as the profit of a project expressed in present dollars. Do you agree? Explain.
8. Explain the relationship between NPV and a firm's value.
9. What is the cost of capital? What role does it play in capital investment decisions?
10. What is the role that the required rate of return plays in the NPV model? In the IRR model?
11. Explain how the NPV is used to determine whether a project should be accepted or rejected.
12. The IRR is the true or actual rate of return being earned by the project. Do you agree or disagree? Discuss.
13. Explain what a postaudit is and how it can provide useful input for future capital investment decisions, especially those involving advanced technology.
14. Explain why NPV is generally preferred over IRR when choosing among competing or mutually exclusive projects. Why would managers continue to use IRR to choose among mutually exclusive projects?
15. Suppose that a firm must choose between two mutually exclusive projects, both of which have negative NPVs. Explain how a firm can legitimately choose between two such projects.

MULTIPLE-CHOICE QUESTIONS

12-1   Capital investments should

 a. always produce an increase in market share.
 b. only be analyzed using the ARR.
 c. earn back their original capital outlay plus a reasonable return.
 d. always be done using a payback criterion.
 e. None of these.

12-2   To make a capital investment decision, a manager must

 a. estimate the quantity and timing of cash flows.
 b. assess the risk of the investment.
 c. consider the impact of the investment on the firm's profits.
 d. choose a decision criterion to assess viability of the investment (such as payback period or NPV).
 e. All of these.

12-3 Mutually exclusive capital budgeting projects are those that

  a. if accepted or rejected do not affect the cash flows of other projects.
  b. if accepted will produce a negative NPV.
  c. if rejected preclude the acceptance of all other competing projects.
  d. if accepted preclude the acceptance of all other competing projects.
  e. if rejected imply that all other competing projects have a positive NPV.

12-4 An investment of $6,000 produces a net annual cash inflow of $2,000 for each of 5 years. What is the payback period?

  a. 2 years
  b. 1.5 years
  c. Unacceptable
  d. 3 years
  e. Cannot be determined

12-5 An investment of $1,000 produces a net cash inflow of $500 in the first year and $750 in the second year. What is the payback period?

  a. 1.67 years
  b. 0.50 year
  c. 2.00 years
  d. 1.20 years
  e. Cannot be determined

12-6 The payback period suffers from which of the following deficiencies?

  a. It is a rough measure of the uncertainty of future cash flows.
  b. It helps control the risk of obsolescence.
  c. It ignores the uncertainty of future cash flows.
  d. It ignores the financial performance of a project beyond the payback period.
  e. Both c and d.

12-7 The ARR has one specific advantage *not* possessed by the payback period in that it

  a. considers the time value of money.
  b. measures the value added by a project.
  c. is always an accurate measure of profitability.
  d. is more widely accepted by financial managers.
  e. considers the profitability of a project beyond the payback period.

12-8 An investment of $2,000 provides an average net income of $400. Depreciation is $40 per year with zero salvage value. The ARR using the original investment is

  a. 44%.
  b. 22%.
  c. 20%.
  d. 40%.
  e. None of these.

12-9 If the NPV is positive, it signals

  a. that the initial investment has been recovered.
  b. that the required rate of return has been earned.
  c. that the value of the firm has increased.
  d. All of these.
  e. Both a and b.

12-10 NPV measures

a. the profitability of an investment.
b. the change in wealth.
c. the change in firm value.
d. the difference in present value of cash inflows and outflows.
e. All of these.

12-11 NPV is calculated by using

a. the required rate of return.
b. accounting income.
c. the IRR.
d. the future value of cash flows.
e. None of these.

12-12 Using NPV, a project is rejected if it is

a. equal to zero.
b. negative.
c. positive.
d. equal to the required rate of return.
e. greater than the cost of capital.

12-13 If the present value of future cash flows is $4,200 for an investment that requires an outlay of $3,000, the NPV

a. is $200.
b. is $1,000.
c. is $1,200.
d. is $2,200.
e. cannot be determined.

12-14 Assume that an investment of $1,000 produces a future cash flow of $1,000. The discount factor for this future cash flow is 0.80. The NPV is

a. $0.
b. $110.
c. ($200).
d. $911.
e. None of these.

12-15 Which of the following is *not* true regarding the IRR?

a. The IRR is the interest rate that sets the present value of a project's cash inflows equal to the present value of the project's cost.
b. The IRR is the interest rate that sets the NPV equal to zero.
c. The popularity of IRR may be attributable to the fact that it is a rate of return, a concept that is comfortably used by managers.
d. If the IRR is greater than the required rate of return, then the project is acceptable.
e. The IRR is the most reliable of the capital budgeting methods.

12-16 Using IRR, a project is rejected if the IRR

a. is equal to the required rate of return.
b. is less than the required rate of return.
c. is greater than the cost of capital.
d. is greater than the required rate of return.
e. produces an NPV equal to zero.

12-17 A postaudit

    a. is a follow-up analysis of a capital project, once implemented.

    b. compares the actual benefits with the estimated benefits.

    c. evaluates the overall outcome of the investment.

    d. proposes corrective action, if needed.

    e. All of these.

12-18 Postaudits of capital projects are useful because

    a. they are not very costly.

    b. they have no significant limitations.

    c. the assumptions underlying the original analyses are often invalidated by changes in the actual working environment.

    d. they help to ensure that resources are used wisely.

    e. All of these.

12-19 For competing projects, NPV is preferred to IRR because

    a. maximizing IRR maximizes the wealth of the owners.

    b. in the final analysis, relative profitability is what counts.

    c. choosing the project with the largest NPV maximizes the wealth of the shareholders.

    d. assuming that cash flows are reinvested at the computed IRR is more realistic than assuming that cash flows are reinvested at the required rate of return.

    e. All of these.

12-20 Assume that there are two competing projects, A and B. Project A has an NPV of $1,000 and an IRR of 15%. Project B has an NPV of $800 and an IRR of 20%. Which of the following is true?

    a. Project A should be chosen because it has a higher NPV.

    b. Project B should be chosen because it has a higher IRR.

    c. It is not possible to use NPV or IRR to choose between the two projects.

    d. Neither project should be chosen.

    e. None of these.

BRIEF EXERCISES: SET A

OBJECTIVE 2
Example 12.1

Brief Exercise 12-21 Payback Period

Payson Manufacturing is considering an investment in a new automated manufacturing system. The new system requires an investment of $1,200,000 and either has (a) even cash flows of $300,000 per year or (b) the following expected annual cash flows: $150,000, $150,000, $400,000, $400,000, and $100,000.

Required:

Calculate the payback period for each case.

OBJECTIVE 2
Example 12.2

Brief Exercise 12-22 Accounting Rate of Return

Uchdorf Company invested $9,000,000 in a new product line. The life cycle of the product is projected to be 7 years with the following net income stream: $360,000, $360,000, $600,000, $1,080,000, $1,200,000, $2,520,000, and $1,444,000.

Required:

Calculate the ARR.

Brief Exercise 12-23 Net Present Value

OBJECTIVE ▸ 3
Example 12.3

Snow Inc. has just completed development of a new cell phone. The new product is expected to produce annual revenues of $1,400,000. Producing the cell phone requires an investment in new equipment, costing $1,500,000. The cell phone has a projected life cycle of 5 years. After 5 years, the equipment can be sold for $180,000. Working capital is also expected to increase by $200,000, which Snow will recover by the end of the new product's life cycle. Annual cash operating expenses are estimated at $820,000. The required rate of return is 8%.

Required:

1. Prepare a schedule of the projected annual cash flows.
2. Calculate the NPV using only discount factors from Exhibit 12B.1 (p. 670).
3. Calculate the NPV using discount factors from both Exhibits 12B.1 and 12B.2 (p. 671).

Brief Exercise 12-24 Internal Rate of Return

OBJECTIVE ▸ 4
Example 12.4

Lisun Company produces a variety of gardening tools and aids. The company is examining the possibility of investing in a new production system that will reduce the costs of the current system. The new system will require a cash investment of $4,607,200 and will produce net cash savings of $800,000 per year. The system has a projected life of 9 years.

Required:

Calculate the IRR for the new production system.

Brief Exercise 12-25 NPV and IRR, Mutually Exclusive Projects

OBJECTIVE ▸ 6
Example 12.5

Hunt Inc. intends to invest in one of two competing types of computer-aided manufacturing equipment: CAM X and CAM Y. Both CAM X and CAM Y models have a project life of 10 years. The purchase price of the CAM X model is $3,600,000, and it has a net annual after-tax cash inflow of $900,000. The CAM Y model is more expensive, selling for $4,200,000, but it will produce a net annual after-tax cash inflow of $1,050,000. The cost of capital for the company is 10%.

Required:

1. Calculate the NPV for each project. Which model would you recommend?
2. Calculate the IRR for each project. Which model would you recommend?

BRIEF EXERCISES: SET B

Brief Exercise 12-26 Payback Period

OBJECTIVE ▸ 2
Example 12.1

Folsom Advertising, Inc. is considering an investment in a new information system. The new system requires an investment of $1,800,000 and either has (a) even cash flows of $750,000 per year or (b) the following expected annual cash flows: $450,000, $225,000, $600,000, $600,000, and $150,000.

Required:

Calculate the payback period for each case.

Brief Exercise 12-27 Accounting Rate of Return

OBJECTIVE ▸ 2
Example 12.2

Cannon Company invested $8,000,000 in a new product line. The life cycle of the product is projected to be 8 years with the following net income stream: $400,000, $300,000, $700,000, $800,000, $1,100,000, $2,000,000, and $1,100,000.

Required:

Calculate the ARR.

OBJECTIVE **3**
Example 12.3

Brief Exercise 12-28 Net Present Value

Talmage Inc. has just completed development of a new printer. The new product is expected to produce annual revenues of $2,700,000. Producing the printer requires an investment in new equipment costing $2,880,000. The printer has a projected life cycle of 5 years. After 5 years, the equipment can be sold for $360,000. Working capital is also expected to increase by $360,000, which Talmage will recover by the end of the new product's life cycle. Annual cash operating expenses are estimated at $1,620,000. The required rate of return is 8%.

Required:

1. Prepare a schedule of the projected annual cash flows.
2. Calculate the NPV using only discount factors from Exhibit 12B.1 (p. 670).
3. Calculate the NPV using discount factors from both Exhibits 12B.1 and 12B.2 (p. 671).

OBJECTIVE **4**
Example 12.4

Brief Exercise 12-29 Internal Rate of Return

Richins Company produces automobile engine parts. The company is examining the possibility of investing in a new production system that will reduce the costs of the current system. The new system will require a cash investment of $11,551,968 and will produce net cash savings of $1,800,000 per year. The system has a projected life of 10 years.

Required:

Calculate the IRR for the new production system.

OBJECTIVE **6**
Example 12.5

Brief Exercise 12-30 NPV and IRR, Mutually Exclusive Projects

Techno Inc. intends to invest in one of two competing types of flexible manufacturing systems: FLEX-1K and FLEX-2Z. Both systems have a project life of 10 years. The purchase price of the FLEX-1K system is $9,600,000, and it has a net annual after-tax cash inflow of $2,400,000. The FLEX-2Z is more expensive, selling for $11,200,000, but it will produce a net annual after-tax cash inflow of $2,800,000. The cost of capital for the company is 12%.

Required:

1. Calculate the NPV for each system. Which system would you recommend?
2. Calculate the IRR for each system. Which system would you recommend?

EXERCISES

Round all present value calculations to the nearest dollar and payback periods to two decimal places.

OBJECTIVE **1 ▶ 2**

EXCEL

Exercise 12-31 Payback Period

Each of the following scenarios is independent. Assume that all cash flows are after-tax cash flows.

a. Colby Hepworth has just invested $400,000 in a book and video store. She expects to receive a cash income of $120,000 per year from the investment.

b. Kylie Sorensen has just invested $1,400,000 in a new biomedical technology. She expects to receive the following cash flows over the next 5 years: $350,000, $490,000, $700,000, $420,000, and $280,000.

c. Carsen Nabors invested in a project that has a payback period of 4 years. The project brings in $960,000 per year.

d. Rahn Booth invested $1,300,000 in a project that pays him an even amount per year for 5 years. The payback period is 2.5 years.

Required:

1. What is the payback period for Colby?
2. What is the payback period for Kylie?
3. How much did Carsen invest in the project?
4. How much cash does Rahn receive each year?

Exercise 12-32 Accounting Rate of Return

OBJECTIVE ◄ 1 ◄ 2

EXCEL

Each of the following scenarios is independent. Assume that all cash flows are after-tax cash flows.

a. Cobre Company is considering the purchase of new equipment that will speed up the process for extracting copper. The equipment will cost $3,600,000 and have a life of 5 years with no expected salvage value. The expected cash flows associated with the project are as follows:

Year	Cash Revenues	Cash Expenses
1	$6,000,000	$4,800,000
2	6,000,000	4,800,000
3	6,000,000	4,800,000
4	6,000,000	4,800,000
5	6,000,000	4,800,000

b. Emily Hansen is considering investing in one of the following two projects. Either project will require an investment of $75,000. The expected cash revenues minus cash expenses for the two projects follow. Assume each project is depreciable.

Year	Project A	Project B
1	$22,500	$22,500
2	30,000	30,000
3	45,000	45,000
4	75,000	22,500
5	75,000	22,500

c. Suppose that a project has an ARR of 30% (based on initial investment) and that the average net income of the project is $120,000.

d. Suppose that a project has an ARR of 50% and that the investment is $150,000.

Required:

1. Compute the ARR on the new equipment that Cobre Company is considering.
2. **CONCEPTUAL CONNECTION** Which project should Emily Hansen choose based on the ARR? Notice that the payback period is the same for both investments (thus equally preferred). Unlike the payback period, explain why ARR correctly signals that one project should be preferred over the other.
3. How much did the company in Scenario c invest in the project?
4. What is the average net income earned by the project in Scenario d?

OBJECTIVE ▶ 1 ▶ 3

Exercise 12-33 Net Present Value

Each of the following scenarios is independent. Assume that all cash flows are after-tax cash flows.

a. Campbell Manufacturing is considering the purchase of a new welding system. The cash benefits will be $480,000 per year. The system costs $2,700,000 and will last 10 years.

b. Evee Cardenas is interested in investing in a women's specialty shop. The cost of the investment is $270,000. She estimates that the return from owning her own shop will be $52,500 per year. She estimates that the shop will have a useful life of 6 years.

c. Barker Company calculated the NPV of a project and found it to be $63,900. The project's life was estimated to be 8 years. The required rate of return used for the NPV calculation was 10%. The project was expected to produce annual after-tax cash flows of $135,000.

Required:

1. Compute the NPV for Campbell Manufacturing, assuming a discount rate of 12%. Should the company buy the new welding system?
2. **CONCEPTUAL CONNECTION** Assuming a required rate of return of 8%, calculate the NPV for Evee Cardenas' investment. Should she invest? What if the estimated return was $135,000 per year? Would this affect the decision? What does this tell you about your analysis?
3. What was the required investment for Barker Company's project?

OBJECTIVE ▶ 1 ▶ 4

Exercise 12-34 Internal Rate of Return

Each of the following scenarios is independent. Assume that all cash flows are after-tax cash flows.

a. Cuenca Company is considering the purchase of new equipment that will speed up the process for producing flash drives. The equipment will cost $7,200,000 and have a life of 5 years with no expected salvage value. The expected cash flows associated with the project follow:

Year	Cash Revenues	Cash Expenses
1	$8,000,000	$6,000,000
2	8,000,000	6,000,000
3	8,000,000	6,000,000
4	8,000,000	6,000,000
5	8,000,000	6,000,000

b. Kathy Shorts is evaluating an investment in an information system that will save $240,000 per year. She estimates that the system will last 10 years. The system will cost $1,248,000. Her company's cost of capital is 10%.

c. Elmo Enterprises just announced that a new plant would be built in Helper, Utah. Elmo told its stockholders that the plant has an expected life of 15 years and an expected IRR equal to 25%. The cost of building the plant is expected to be $2,880,000.

Required:

1. Calculate the IRR for Cuenca Company. The company's cost of capital is 16%. Should the new equipment be purchased?
2. Calculate Kathy Short's IRR. Should she acquire the new system?
3. What should be Elmo Enterprises' expected annual cash flow from the plant?

Exercise 12-35 Net Present Value and Competing Projects

OBJECTIVE ◀1◀6

EXCEL

Spiro Hospital is investigating the possibility of investing in new dialysis equipment. Two local manufacturers of this equipment are being considered as sources of the equipment. After-tax cash inflows for the two competing projects are as follows:

Year	Puro Equipment	Briggs Equipment
1	$320,000	$120,000
2	280,000	120,000
3	240,000	320,000
4	160,000	400,000
5	120,000	440,000

Both projects require an initial investment of $560,000. In both cases, assume that the equipment has a life of 5 years with no salvage value.

Required:

1. Assuming a discount rate of 12%, compute the net present value of each piece of equipment.
2. A third option has surfaced for equipment purchased from an out-of-state supplier. The cost is also $560,000, but this equipment will produce even cash flows over its 5-year life. What must the annual cash flow be for this equipment to be selected over the other two? Assume a 12% discount rate.

Exercise 12-36 Payback, Accounting Rate of Return, Net Present Value, Internal Rate of Return

OBJECTIVE ◀1◀2◀3◀4

Blaylock Company wants to buy a numerically controlled (NC) machine to be used in producing specially machined parts for manufacturers of tractors. The outlay required is $384,000. The NC equipment will last 5 years with no expected salvage value. The expected after-tax cash flows associated with the project follow:

Year	Cash Revenues	Cash Expenses
1	$510,000	$360,000
2	510,000	360,000
3	510,000	360,000
4	510,000	360,000
5	510,000	360,000

Required:

1. Compute the payback period for the NC equipment.
2. Compute the NC equipment's ARR. Round the percentage to one decimal place.
3. Compute the investment's NPV, assuming a required rate of return of 10%.
4. Compute the investment's IRR.

Exercise 12-37 Payback, Accounting Rate of Return, Present Value, Net Present Value, Internal Rate of Return

OBJECTIVE ◀1◀2◀3◀4

All scenarios are independent of all other scenarios. Assume that all cash flows are after-tax cash flows.

a. Kambry Day is considering investing in one of the following two projects. Either project will require an investment of $20,000. The expected cash flows for the two projects follow. Assume that each project is depreciable.

(Continued)

Year	Project A	Project B
1	$ 6,000	$ 6,000
2	8,000	8,000
3	10,000	10,000
4	10,000	3,000
5	10,000	3,000

b. Wilma Golding is retiring and has the option to take her retirement as a lump sum of $450,000 or to receive $30,000 per year for 20 years. Wilma's required rate of return is 6%.

c. David Booth is interested in investing in some tools and equipment so that he can do independent drywalling. The cost of the tools and equipment is $30,000. He estimates that the return from owning his own equipment will be $9,000 per year. The tools and equipment will last 6 years.

d. Patsy Folson is evaluating what appears to be an attractive opportunity. She is currently the owner of a small manufacturing company and has the opportunity to acquire another small company's equipment that would provide production of a part currently purchased externally. She estimates that the savings from internal production will be $75,000 per year. She estimates that the equipment will last 10 years. The owner is asking $400,000 for the equipment. Her company's cost of capital is 8%.

Required:

1. **CONCEPTUAL CONNECTION** What is the payback period for each of Kambry Day's projects? If rapid payback is important, which project should be chosen? Which would you choose?

2. **CONCEPTUAL CONNECTION** Which of Kambry's projects should be chosen based on the ARR? Explain why the ARR performs better than the payback period in this setting.

3. Assuming that Wilma Golding will live for another 20 years, should she take the lump sum or the annuity?

4. Assuming a required rate of return of 8% for David Booth, calculate the NPV of the investment. Should David invest?

5. Calculate the IRR for Patsy Folson's project. Should Patsy acquire the equipment?

OBJECTIVE ▶ **3** ▶

Exercise 12-38 Net Present Value, Basic Concepts

Wise Company is considering an investment that requires an outlay of $600,000 and promises an after-tax cash inflow of $693,000 one year from now. The company's cost of capital is 10%.

Required:

1. Break the $693,000 future cash inflow into three components: (a) the return of the original investment, (b) the cost of capital, and (c) the profit earned on the investment. Now compute the present value of the profit earned on the investment.

2. **CONCEPTUAL CONNECTION** Compute the NPV of the investment. Compare this with the present value of the profit computed in Requirement 1. What does this tell you about the meaning of NPV?

OBJECTIVE ▶ **1** ▶ **3** ▶ **4** ▶

Exercise 12-39 Solving for Unknowns

Each of the following scenarios is independent. Assume that all cash flows are after-tax cash flows.

a. Thomas Company is investing $120,000 in a project that will yield a uniform series of cash inflows over the next 4 years.

b. Video Repair has decided to invest in some new electronic equipment. The equipment will have a 3-year life and will produce a uniform series of cash savings. The NPV of the equipment is $1,750, using a discount rate of 8%. The IRR is 12%.

c. A new lathe costing $60,096 will produce savings of $12,000 per year.
d. The NPV of a project is $3,927. The project has a life of 4 years and produces the following cash flows:

Year 1	$10,000	Year 3	$15,000
Year 2	$12,000	Year 4	?

The cost of the project is two times the cash flow produced in Year 4. The discount rate is 10%.

Required:

1. If the internal rate of return is 14% for Thomas Company, how much cash inflow per year can be expected?
2. Determine the investment and the amount of cash savings realized each year for Video Repair.
3. For Scenario c, how many years must the lathe last if an IRR of 18% is realized?
4. For Scenario d, find the cost of the project and the cash flow for Year 4.

Exercise 12-40 Net Present Value versus Internal Rate of Return

OBJECTIVE 6

Skiba Company is thinking about two different modifications to its current manufacturing process. The after-tax cash flows associated with the two investments follow:

Year	Project I	Project II
0	$(100,000)	$(100,000)
1	—	63,857
2	134,560	63,857

Skiba's cost of capital is 10%.

Required:

1. Compute the NPV and the IRR for each investment.
2. **CONCEPTUAL CONNECTION** Explain why the project with the larger NPV is the correct choice for Skiba.

PROBLEMS

Round all present value calculations to the nearest dollar and payback periods to two decimal places.

Problem 12-41 Basic Net Present Value Analysis

OBJECTIVE 1 3

Jonathan Butler, process engineer, knows that the acceptance of a new process design will depend on its economic feasibility. The new process is designed to improve environmental performance. On the negative side, the process design requires new equipment and an infusion of working capital. The equipment will cost $1,200,000, and its cash operating expenses will total $270,000 per year. The equipment will last for 7 years but will need a major overhaul costing $120,000 at the end of the fifth year. At the end of 7 years, the equipment will be sold for $96,000. An increase in working capital totaling $120,000 will also be needed at the beginning. This will be recovered at the end of the 7 years.

On the positive side, Jonathan estimates that the new process will save $400,000 per year in environmental costs (fines and cleanup costs avoided). The cost of capital is 12%.

(*Continued*)

Required:

1. Prepare a schedule of cash flows for the proposed project. (*Note:* Assume that there are no income taxes.)
2. Compute the NPV of the project. Should the new process design be accepted?

OBJECTIVE ▶ 1 ▶ 3

Problem 12-42 Net Present Value Analysis

Emery Communications Company is considering the production and marketing of a communications system that will increase the efficiency of messaging for small businesses or branch offices of large companies. Each unit hooked into the system is assigned a mailbox number, which can be matched to a telephone extension number, providing access to messages 24 hours a day. Up to 20 units can be hooked into the system, allowing the delivery of the same message to as many as 20 people. Personal codes can be used to make messages confidential. Furthermore, messages can be reviewed, recorded, cancelled, replied to, or deleted all during the same message playback. Indicators wired to the telephone blink whenever new messages are present.

To produce this product, a $1.75 million investment in new equipment is required. The equipment will last 10 years but will need major maintenance costing $150,000 at the end of its sixth year. The salvage value of the equipment at the end of 10 years is estimated to be $100,000. If this new system is produced, working capital must also be increased by $90,000. This capital will be restored at the end of the product's 10-year life cycle. Revenues from the sale of the product are estimated at $1.65 million per year. Cash operating expenses are estimated at $1.32 million per year.

Required:

1. Prepare a schedule of cash flows for the proposed project. (*Note:* Assume that there are no income taxes.)
2. Assuming that Emery's cost of capital is 12%, compute the project's NPV. Should the product be produced?

OBJECTIVE ▶ 1 ▶ 4

Problem 12-43 Basic Internal Rate of Return Analysis

Julianna Cardenas, owner of Baker Company, was approached by a local dealer of air-conditioning units. The dealer proposed replacing Baker's old cooling system with a modern, more efficient system. The cost of the new system was quoted at $339,000, but it would save $60,000 per year in energy costs. The estimated life of the new system is 10 years, with no salvage value expected. Excited over the possibility of saving $60,000 per year and having a more reliable unit, Julianna requested an analysis of the project's economic viability. All capital projects are required to earn at least the firm's cost of capital, which is 8%. There are no income taxes.

Required:

1. Calculate the project's IRR. Should the company acquire the new cooling system?
2. Suppose that energy savings are less than claimed. Calculate the minimum annual cash savings that must be realized for the project to earn a rate equal to the firm's cost of capital.
3. Suppose that the life of the new system is overestimated by 2 years. Repeat Requirements 1 and 2 under this assumption.
4. **CONCEPTUAL CONNECTION** Explain the implications of the answers from Requirements 1, 2, and 3.

OBJECTIVE ▶ 1 ▶ 3

Problem 12-44 Net Present Value, Uncertainty

EXCEL

Ondi Airlines is interested in acquiring a new aircraft to service a new route. The route will be from Tulsa to Denver. The aircraft will fly one round-trip daily except for scheduled maintenance days. There are 15 maintenance days scheduled each year. The seating capacity of the aircraft is 150. Flights are expected to be fully booked. The average revenue per passenger per flight (one-way) is $235. Annual operating costs of the aircraft follow:

Fuel	$1,750,000
Flight personnel	750,000
Food and beverages	100,000
Maintenance	550,000
Other	100,000
Total	$3,250,000

The aircraft will cost $120,000,000 and has an expected life of 20 years. The company requires a 12% return. Assume there are no income taxes.

Required:

1. Calculate the NPV for the aircraft. Should the company buy it?
2. In discussing the proposal, the marketing manager for the airline believes that the assumption of 100% booking is unrealistic. He believes that the booking rate will be somewhere between 70 and 90%, with the most likely rate being 80%. Recalculate the NPV by using an 80% seating capacity. Should the aircraft be purchased?
3. Calculate the average seating rate that would be needed so that NPV will equal zero. Round the seating rate to the nearest percent.
4. **CONCEPTUAL CONNECTION** Suppose that the price per passenger could be increased by 10% without any effect on demand. What is the average seating rate now needed to achieve an NPV equal to zero? What would you now recommend? Round the seating rate to the nearest percent.

Problem 12-45 Review of Basic Capital Budgeting Procedures

OBJECTIVE ◀1 ◀2 ◀3 ◀4

EXCEL

Dr. Whitley Avard, a plastic surgeon, had just returned from a conference in which she learned of a new surgical procedure for removing wrinkles around eyes, reducing the time to perform the normal procedure by 50%. Given her patient-load pressures, Dr. Avard is excited to try out the new technique. By decreasing the time spent on eye treatments or procedures, she can increase her total revenues by performing more services within a work period. In order to implement the new procedure, special equipment costing $74,000 is needed. The equipment has an expected life of 4 years, with a salvage value of $6,000. Dr. Avard estimates that her cash revenues will increase by the following amounts:

Year	Revenue Increases
1	$19,800
2	27,000
3	32,400
4	32,400

She also expects additional cash expenses amounting to $3,000 per year. The cost of capital is 12%. Assume that there are no income taxes.

Required:

1. Compute the payback period for the new equipment.
2. Compute the ARR. Round the percentage to two decimal places.
3. **CONCEPTUAL CONNECTION** Compute the NPV and IRR for the project. Use 14% as your first guess for IRR. Should Dr. Avard purchase the new equipment? Should she be concerned about payback or the ARR in making this decision?
4. **CONCEPTUAL CONNECTION** Before finalizing her decision, Dr. Avard decided to call two plastic surgeons who have been using the new procedure for the past 6 months. The conversations revealed a somewhat less glowing report than she received at the conference. The new procedure reduced the time required by about 25% rather than the advertised 50%. Dr. Avard estimated that the net operating cash flows of the procedure would be

(Continued)

cut by one-third because of the extra time and cost involved (salvage value would be unaffected). Using this information, recompute the NPV of the project. What would you now recommend?

Problem 12-46 Net Present Value and Competing Alternatives

Stillwater Designs has been rebuilding Model 100, Model 120, and Model 150 **Kicker** subwoofers that were returned for warranty action. Customers returning the subwoofers receive a new replacement. The warranty returns are then rebuilt and resold (as seconds). Tent sales are often used to sell the rebuilt speakers. As part of the rebuilding process, the speakers are demagnetized so that metal pieces and shavings can be removed. A demagnetizing (demag) machine is used to achieve this objective. A product design change has made the most recent Model 150 speakers too tall for the demag machine. They no longer fit in the demag machine.

   Stillwater Designs is currently considering two alternatives. First, a new demag machine can be bought that has a different design, eliminating the fit problem. The cost of this machine is $600,000, and it will last 5 years. Second, Stillwater can keep the current machine and sell the 150 speakers for scrap, using the old demag machine for the Model 100 and 120 speakers only. A rebuilt speaker sells for $295 and costs $274.65 to rebuild (for materials, labor, and overhead cash outlays). The $274.65 outlay includes the annual operating cash effects of the new demag machine. If not rebuilt, the Model 150 speakers can be sold for $4 each as scrap. There are 10,000 Model 150 warranty returns per year. Assume that the required rate of return is 10%.

Required:

1. Determine which alternative is the best for Stillwater Designs by using NPV analysis.
2. **CONCEPTUAL CONNECTION** Determine which alternative is best for Stillwater Designs by using an IRR analysis. Explain why NPV analysis is a better approach.

Problem 12-47 Basic Net Present Value Analysis, Competing Projects

Kildare Medical Center, a for-profit hospital, has three investment opportunities: (1) adding a wing for in-patient treatment of substance abuse, (2) adding a pathology laboratory, and (3) expanding the outpatient surgery wing. The initial investments and the net present value for the three alternatives are as follows:

	Substance Abuse	Laboratory	Outpatient Surgery
Investment	$1,500,000	$500,000	$1,000,000
NPV	150,000	140,000	135,000

Although the hospital would like to invest in all three alternatives, only $1.5 million is available.

Required:

1. Rank the projects on the basis of NPV, and allocate the funds in order of this ranking. What project or projects were selected? What is the total NPV realized by the medical center using this approach?
2. **CONCEPTUAL CONNECTION** Assume that the size of the lot on which the hospital is located makes the substance abuse wing and the outpatient surgery wing mutually exclusive. With unlimited capital, which of those two projects would be chosen? With limited capital and the three projects being considered, which projects would be chosen?
3. **CONCEPTUAL CONNECTION** Form a group with two to four other students, and discuss qualitative considerations that should be considered in capital budgeting evaluations. Identify three such considerations.

OBJECTIVE 1 2 3 4 6

EXCEL

Problem 12-48 Payback, Net Present Value, Internal Rate of Return, Intangible Benefits, Inflation Adjustment

Foster Company wants to buy a numerically controlled (NC) machine to be used in producing specially machined parts for manufacturers of trenching machines (to replace an existing manual system). The outlay required is $3,500,000. The NC equipment will last 5 years with no expected salvage value. The expected incremental after-tax cash flows (cash flows of the NC equipment minus cash flows of the old equipment) associated with the project follow:

Year	Cash Benefits	Cash Expenses
1	$3,900,000	$3,000,000
2	3,900,000	3,000,000
3	3,900,000	3,000,000
4	3,900,000	3,000,000
5	3,900,000	3,000,000

Foster has a cost of capital equal to 10%. The above cash flows are expressed without any consideration of inflation.

Required:

1. Compute the payback period.
2. Calculate the NPV and IRR of the proposed project.
3. **CONCEPTUAL CONNECTION** Inflation is expected to be 5% per year for the next 5 years. The discount rate of 10% is composed of two elements: the real rate and the inflationary element. Since the discount rate has an inflationary component, the projected cash flows should also be adjusted to account for inflation. Make this adjustment, and recalculate the NPV. Comment on the importance of adjusting cash flows for inflationary effects.

Problem 12-49 Cost of Capital, Net Present Value

OBJECTIVE 3

Leakam Company's product engineering department has developed a new product that has a 3-year life cycle. Production of the product requires development of a new process that requires a current $100,000 capital outlay. The $100,000 will be raised by issuing $60,000 of bonds and by selling new stock for $40,000. The $60,000 in bonds will have net (after-tax) interest payments of $3,000 at the end of each of the 3 years, with the principal being repaid at the end of Year 3. The stock issue carries with it an expectation of a 17.5% return, expressed in the form of dividends at the end of each year (with $7,000 in dividends expected for each of the next 3 years). The sources of capital for this investment represent the same proportion and costs that the company typically has. Finally, the project will produce after-tax cash inflows of $50,000 per year for the next 3 years.

Required:

1. Compute the cost of capital for the project. (*Hint*: The cost of capital is a weighted average of the two sources of capital, where the weights are the proportion of capital from each source.)
2. **CONCEPTUAL CONNECTION** Compute the NPV for the project. Explain why it is not necessary to subtract the interest payments and the dividend payments and appreciation from the inflow of $50,000 in carrying out this computation.

Problem 12-50 Capital Investment, Advanced Manufacturing Environment

OBJECTIVE 1 6

"I know that it's the thing to do," insisted Pamela Kincaid, vice president of finance for Colgate Manufacturing. "If we are going to be competitive, we need to build this completely automated plant."

(*Continued*)

"I'm not so sure," replied Bill Thomas, CEO of Colgate. "The savings from labor reductions and increased productivity are only $4 million per year. The price tag for this factory—and it's a small one—is $45 million. That gives a payback period of more than 11 years. That's a long time to put the company's money at risk."

"Yeah, but you're overlooking the savings that we'll get from the increase in quality," interjected John Simpson, production manager. "With this system, we can decrease our waste and our rework time significantly. Those savings are worth another million dollars per year."

"Another million will only cut the payback to about 9 years," retorted Bill. "Ron, you're the marketing manager—do you have any insights?"

"Well, there are other factors to consider, such as service quality and market share. I think that increasing our product quality and improving our delivery service will make us a lot more competitive. I know for a fact that two of our competitors have decided against automation. That'll give us a shot at their customers, provided our product is of higher quality and we can deliver it faster. I estimate that it'll increase our net cash benefits by another $2.4 million."

"Wow! Now that's impressive," Bill exclaimed, nearly convinced. "The payback is now getting down to a reasonable level."

"I agree," said Pamela, "but we do need to be sure that it's a sound investment. I know that estimates for construction of the facility have gone as high as $48 million. I also know that the expected residual value, after the 20 years of service we expect to get, is $5 million. I think I had better see if this project can cover our 14% cost of capital."

"Now wait a minute, Pamela," Bill demanded. "You know that I usually insist on a 20% rate of return, especially for a project of this magnitude."

Required:

1. Compute the NPV of the project by using the original savings and investment figures. Calculate by using discount rates of 14% and 20%. Include salvage value in the computation.
2. Compute the NPV of the project using the additional benefits noted by the production and marketing managers. Also, use the original cost estimate of $45 million. Again, calculate for both possible discount rates.
3. Compute the NPV of the project using all estimates of cash flows, including the possible initial outlay of $48 million. Calculate by using discount rates of 14% and 20%.
4. **CONCEPTUAL CONNECTION** If you were making the decision, what would you do? Explain.

OBJECTIVE ▶ 5 ▶ 6   **Problem 12-51** **Postaudit, Sensitivity Analysis**

Newmarge Products Inc. is evaluating a new design for one of its manufacturing processes. The new design will eliminate the production of a toxic solid residue. The initial cost of the system is estimated at $860,000 and includes computerized equipment, software, and installation. There is no expected salvage value. The new system has a useful life of 8 years and is projected to produce cash operating savings of $225,000 per year over the old system (reducing labor costs and costs of processing and disposing of toxic waste). The cost of capital is 16%.

Required:

1. Compute the NPV of the new system.
2. One year after implementation, the internal audit staff noted the following about the new system: (1) the cost of acquiring the system was $60,000 more than expected due to higher installation costs, and (2) the annual cost savings were $20,000 less than expected because more labor cost was needed than anticipated. Using the changes in expected costs and benefits, compute the NPV as if this information had been available one year ago. Did the company make the right decision?

3. **CONCEPTUAL CONNECTION** Upon reporting the results mentioned in the postaudit, the marketing manager responded in a memo to the internal audit department indicating that cash inflows also had increased by a net of $60,000 per year because of increased purchases by environmentally sensitive customers. Describe the effect that this has on the analysis in Requirement 2.

4. **CONCEPTUAL CONNECTION** Why is a postaudit beneficial to a firm?

Problem 12-52 Discount Rates, Automated Manufacturing, Competing Investments

OBJECTIVE ▶ 6

Patterson Company is considering two competing investments. The first is for a standard piece of production equipment. The second is for computer-aided manufacturing (CAM) equipment. The investment and after-tax operating cash flows follow:

EXCEL

Year	Standard Equipment	CAM Equipment
0	$(500,000)	$(2,000,000)
1	300,000	100,000
2	200,000	200,000
3	100,000	300,000
4	100,000	400,000
5	100,000	400,000
6	100,000	400,000
7	100,000	500,000
8	100,000	1,000,000
9	100,000	1,000,000
10	100,000	1,000,000

Patterson uses a discount rate of 18% for all of its investments. Patterson's cost of capital is 10%.

Required:

1. Calculate the NPV for each investment by using a discount rate of 18%.
2. Calculate the NPV for each investment by using a discount rate of 10%.
3. **CONCEPTUAL CONNECTION** Which rate should Patterson use to compute the NPV? Explain.

Problem 12-53 Quality, Market Share, Automated Manufacturing Environment

OBJECTIVE ▶ 6

Fabre Company, Patterson Company's competitor, is considering the same investments as Patterson. Refer to the data in **Problem 12-52** above. Assume that Fabre's cost of capital is 14%.

Required:

1. Calculate the NPV of each alternative by using the 14% rate.
2. **CONCEPTUAL CONNECTION** Now assume that if the standard equipment is purchased, the competitive position of the firm will deteriorate because of lower quality (relative to competitors who did automate). Marketing estimates that the loss in market share will decrease the projected net cash inflows by 50% for Years 3 through 10. Recalculate the NPV of the standard equipment given this outcome. What is the decision now? Discuss the importance of assessing the effect of intangible benefits.

CASES

OBJECTIVE **3**

Case 12-54 Capital Investment and Ethical Behavior

Manny Carson, certified management accountant and controller of Wakeman Enterprises, has been given permission to acquire a new computer and software for the company's accounting system. The capital investment analysis showed an NPV of $100,000. However, the initial estimates of acquisition and installation costs were made on the basis of tentative costs without any formal bids. Manny now has two formal bids, one that would allow the firm to meet or beat the original projected NPV and one that would reduce the projected NPV by $50,000. The second bid involves a system that would increase both the initial cost and the operating cost.

Normally, Manny would take the first bid without hesitation. However, Todd Downing, the owner of the firm presenting the second bid, is a close friend. Manny called Todd and explained the situation, offering Todd an opportunity to alter his bid and win the job. Todd thanked Manny and then made a counteroffer.

Todd: Listen, Manny, this job at the original price is the key to a successful year for me. The revenues will help me gain approval for the loan I need for renovation and expansion. If I don't get that loan, I see hard times ahead. The financial stats for loan approval are so marginal that reducing the bid price may blow my chances.

Manny: Losing the bid altogether would be even worse, don't you think?

Todd: True. However, if you award me the job, I'll be able to add personnel. I know that your son is looking for a job, and I can offer him a good salary and a promising future. Additionally, I'll be able to take you and your wife on that vacation to Hawaii that we've been talking about.

Manny: Well, you have a point. My son is having an awful time finding a job, and he has a wife and three kids to support. My wife is tired of having them live with us. She and I could use a vacation. I doubt that the other bidder would make any fuss if we turned it down. Its offices are out of state, after all.

Todd: Out of state? All the more reason to turn it down. Given the state's economy, it seems almost criminal to take business outside. Those are the kind of business decisions that cause problems for people like your son.

Required:

Evaluate the ethical behavior of Manny. Should Manny have called Todd in the first place? Would there have been any problems if Todd had agreed to meet the lower bid price? Identify the parts of the Statement of Ethical Professional Practice (Chapter 1) that Manny may be violating, if any.

OBJECTIVE **2** **3** **4**

Case 12-55 Payback, Net Present Value, Internal Rate of Return, Effects of Differences in Sales on Project Viability

Shaftel Ready Mix is a processor and supplier of concrete, aggregate, and rock products. The company operates in the intermountain western United States. Currently, Shaftel has 14 cement-processing plants and a labor force of more than 375 employees. With the exception of cement powder, all materials (e.g., aggregates and sand) are produced internally by the company. The demand for concrete and aggregates has been growing steadily nationally. In the West, the growth rate has been above the national average. Because of this growth, Shaftel has more than tripled its gross revenues over the past 10 years.

Of the intermountain states, Arizona has been experiencing the most growth. Processing plants have been added over the past several years, and the company is considering the addition of yet another plant to be located in Scottsdale. A major advantage of another plant in Arizona is the ability to operate year round, a feature not found in states such as Utah and Wyoming.

In setting up the new plant, land would have to be purchased and a small building constructed. Equipment and furniture would not need to be purchased. These items would be transferred from a plant that opened in Wyoming during the oil boom period and closed a few years after the end of that boom. However, the equipment needs some repair and modifications before it can be used. The equipment has a book value of $200,000, and the furniture has a book value of $30,000. Neither has any outside market value. Other costs, such as the installation of a silo, well, electrical hookups, and so on, will be incurred. No salvage value is expected. The summary of the initial investment costs by category is as follows:

Land	$ 20,000
Building	135,000
Equipment:	
Book value	200,000
Modifications	20,000
Furniture (book value)	30,000
Silo	20,000
Well	80,000
Electrical hookups	27,000
General setup	50,000
Total	$582,000

Estimates concerning the operation of the Scottsdale plant follow:

Life of plant and equipment	10 years
Expected annual sales (in cubic yards of cement)	35,000
Selling price (per cubic yard of cement)	$45.00
Variable costs (per cubic yard of cement):	
Cement	$ 12.94
Sand/gravel	6.42
Fly ash	1.13
Admixture	1.53
Driver labor	3.24
Mechanics	1.43
Plant operations (batching and cleanup)	1.39
Loader operator	0.50
Truck parts	1.75
Fuel	1.48
Other	3.27
Total variable costs	$ 35.08
Fixed costs (annual):	
Salaries	$135,000
Insurance	75,000
Telephone	5,000
Depreciation	58,200*
Utilities	25,000
Total fixed costs	$298,200

*Straight-line depreciation is calculated by using all initial investment costs over a 10-year period, assuming no salvage value.

After reviewing these data, Karl Flemming, vice president of operations, argued against the proposed plant. Karl was concerned because the plant would earn significantly less than the normal 8.3% return on sales. All other plants in the company were earning between 7.5 and 8.5% on sales. Karl also noted that it would take more than 5 years to recover the total initial outlay of

(Continued)

$582,000. In the past, the company had always insisted that payback be no more than 4 years. The company's cost of capital is 10%. Assume that there are no income taxes.

Required:

1. Prepare a variable-costing income statement for the proposed plant. Compute the ratio of net income to sales. Is Karl correct that the return on sales is significantly lower than the company average?

2. Compute the payback period for the proposed plant. Is Karl right that the payback period is greater than 4 years? Explain. Suppose you were told that the equipment being transferred from Wyoming could be sold for its book value. Would this affect your answer?

3. Compute the NPV and the IRR for the proposed plant. Would your answer be affected if you were told that the furniture and equipment could be sold for their book values? If so, repeat the analysis with this effect considered.

4. Compute the cubic yards of cement that must be sold for the new plant to break even. Using this break-even volume, compute the NPV and the IRR. Would the investment be acceptable? If so, explain why an investment that promises to do nothing more than break even can be viewed as acceptable.

5. Compute the volume of cement that must be sold for the IRR to equal the firm's cost of capital. Using this volume, compute the firm's expected annual income. Explain this result.

Making the Connection

Relevant Costing, Cost-Based Pricing, Cost Behavior, and Net Present Value Analysis for NoFat

Chapters	Objectives	Examples
3	3-1	5-2
5	5-1	8-2
8	8-2	8-9
12	8-4	12-3
	12-1	12-5
	12-3	
	12-6	

The purpose of this integrated exercise is to demonstrate how a special sales-relevant decision analysis relies on knowledge of cost behavior (including variable, fixed, and batch costs) and how the adoption of a long-term time horizon can affect the final decision.

Special Sales Offer Relevant Analysis

NoFat manufactures one product, olestra, and sells it to large potato chip manufacturers as the key ingredient in nonfat snack foods, including Ruffles, Lays, Doritos, and Tostitos brand products. For each of the past 3 years, sales of olestra have been far less than the expected annual volume of 125,000 pounds. Therefore, the company has ended each year with significant unused capacity. Due to a short shelf life, NoFat must sell every pound of olestra that it produces each year. As a result, NoFat's controller, Allyson Ashley, has decided to seek out potential special sales offers from other companies. One company, Patterson Union (PU)—a toxic waste cleanup company—offered to buy 10,000 pounds of olestra from NoFat during December for a price of $2.20 per pound. PU discovered through its research that olestra has proven to be very effective in cleaning up toxic waste locations designated as Superfund Sites by the U.S. Environmental Protection Agency. Allyson was excited, noting that "This is another way to use our expensive olestra plant!"

The annual costs incurred by NoFat to produce and sell 100,000 pounds of olestra are as follows:

Variable costs per pound:	
Direct materials	$ 1.00
Variable manufacturing overhead	0.75
Sales commissions	0.50
Direct manufacturing labor	0.25
Total fixed costs:	
Advertising	$ 3,000
Customer hotline service	4,000
Machine setups	40,000
Plant machinery lease	12,000

In addition, Allyson met with several of NoFat's key production managers and discovered the following information:

- The special order could be produced without incurring any additional marketing or customer service costs.

- NoFat owns the aging plant facility that it uses to manufacture olestra.

- NoFat incurs costs to set up and clean its machines for each production run, or batch, of olestra that it produces. The total setup costs shown in the previous table represent the production of 20 batches during the year.

- NoFat leases its plant machinery. The lease agreement is negotiated and signed on the first day of each year. NoFat currently leases enough machinery to produce 125,000 pounds of olestra.

- PU requires that an independent quality team inspects any facility from which it makes purchases. The terms of the special sales offer would require NoFat to bear the $1,000 cost of the inspection team.

Required:

1. Conduct a relevant analysis of the special sales offer by calculating the following:

   a. The relevant revenues associated with the special sales offer
   b. The relevant costs associated with the special sales offer
   c. The relevant profit associated with the special sales offer

2. Based solely on financial factors, explain why NoFat should accept or reject PU's special sales offer.

3. Describe at least one qualitative factor that NoFat should consider, in addition to the financial factors, in making its final decision regarding the acceptance or rejection of the special sales offer.

Cost-Based Pricing

Assume for this question that NoFat rejected PU's special sales offer because the $2.20 price suggested by PU was too low. In response to the rejection, PU asked NoFat to determine the price at which it would be willing to accept the special sales offer. For its regular sales, NoFat sets prices by marking up *variable costs* by 10%.

4. If Allyson decides to use NoFat's 10% markup pricing method to set the price for PU's special sales offer,

   a. Calculate the price that NoFat would charge PU for each pound of olestra.
   b. Calculate the relevant profit that NoFat would earn if it set the special sales price by using its markup pricing method. (*Hint:* Use the estimate of relevant costs that you calculated in response to Requirement 1b.)
   c. Explain why NoFat should accept or reject the special sales offer if it uses its markup pricing method to set the special sales price.

Incorporating a Long-Term Horizon into the Decision Analysis

Assume for this question that Allyson's relevant analysis reveals that NoFat would earn a positive relevant profit of $10,000 from the special sale (i.e., the special sales alternative). However, after conducting this traditional, short-term relevant analysis, Allyson wonders whether it might be more profitable over the long term to downsize the company by reducing its manufacturing capacity (i.e., its plant machinery and plant facility). She is aware that downsizing requires a multiyear time horizon because companies usually cannot increase or decrease fixed plant assets every year. Therefore, Allyson has decided to use a 5-year time horizon in her long-term decision analysis. She has identified the following information regarding capacity downsizing (i.e., the downsizing alternative):

- The plant facility consists of several buildings. If it chooses to downsize its capacity, NoFat can immediately sell one of the buildings to an adjacent business for $30,000.

- If it chooses to downsize its capacity, NoFat's annual lease cost for plant machinery will decrease to $9,000.

Therefore, Allyson must choose between these two alternatives: Accept the special sales offer each year and earn a $10,000 relevant profit for each of the next 5 years *or* reject the special sales offer and downsize as described above.

5. Assume that NoFat pays for all costs with cash. Also, assume a 10% discount rate, a 5-year time horizon, and all cash flows occur at the end of the year. Using an NPV approach to discount future cash flows to present value,

   a. Calculate the NPV of accepting the special sale with the assumed positive relevant profit of $10,000 per year (i.e., the special sales alternative).
   b. Calculate the NPV of downsizing capacity as previously described (i.e., the downsizing alternative).
   c. Based on the NPV of Requirements 5a and 5b, identify and explain which of these two alternatives is best for NoFat to pursue in the long term.

13 Emerging Topics in Managerial Accounting

After studying Chapter 13, you should be able to:

1. Explain enterprise risk management and its importance for achieving strategy.

2. Understand the role of managerial accounting in business sustainability.

3. Define quality costs and describe the approaches used for reporting and controlling quality costs.

4. Describe the basics of lean manufacturing and lean accounting.

5. Explain the role of the management accountant in the international environment.

6. Explain the role of the management accountant in fraud and forensic accounting.

CARL COURT/Stringer/Getty Images

EXPERIENCE MANAGERIAL DECISIONS

with UPS

This chapter provides an overview of several important emerging business issues and their exciting impact on managerial accounting. **UPS** exemplifies how managerial accounting plays an increasingly vital role in these emerging areas to help improve decision-making and create shareholder value. For example, UPS' business model is based on its ability to drive trucks and fly planes across the globe delivering packages. High quality delivery service is critical for UPS. By delivering packages on time and without damage, UPS can satisfy both the retailers and distributors who are shipping their goods and the customers who are buying those goods. However, for UPS, finding cost-efficient ways to provide high service quality is also vital for its financial success. Thus, searching for ways to eliminate waste and become a lean service provider is an integral part of the UPS business model. In fact, it is fully compatible with the company's original slogan: "Best service and lowest rates."

In providing its delivery services, UPS employs nearly 450,000 workers, handles almost 70 million daily tracking requests, and uses approximately 105,000 vehicles (cars, vans, trucks, and motorcycles) and 650 planes to deliver over 4.7 billion packages and documents annually. The continued success of UPS' business model necessitates that managerial accountants provide executives with information to help them understand and manage key risks, such as carbon emissions. Companies refer to this emerging business area as enterprise risk management. UPS also faces numerous opportunities to innovate the company's delivery fleet options, such as decreasing carbon emissions and saving money through materials and end-of-life fleet recycling, alternative fuel technologies, and GPS and telematics technologies for maximizing route efficiencies. Identifying these types of opportunities to create economic, social or environmental value for the organization represents the rapidly emerging area of business sustainability.

As a global company, UPS faces international issues in business every day. The various currencies in which it deals require sophisticated knowledge of currency risk and ways to mitigate it. The use of the internet by customers requires UPS to employ fraud prevention and detection. Customer account numbers and payment methods must be secured and financial information protected.

As illustrated throughout this chapter, managerial accountants are well suited to support business decision making in these varied emerging areas.

> "The continued success of UPS' business model necessitates that managerial accountants provide executives with information to help them understand and manage key risks, such as carbon emissions. Companies refer to this emerging business area as enterprise risk management."

This chapter provides an overview of several important emerging business issues and their impact on management accounting. Each issue uses relatable examples to illustrate management accounting's increasingly important role within organizations and how it improves decision making across these issues.

ENTERPRISE RISK MANAGEMENT

Managers often make business decisions that require them to consider future events, such as the success or failure of new products or services under development, regulatory actions, economic conditions, the actions of competitors, and employee talent pools. Such future events usually involve considerable uncertainty as to how they will actually play out in reality. As a result, companies face considerable risks that must be effectively managed. For example, of the 500 companies that appeared on the first Fortune 500 list of the world's biggest companies (as measured by sales revenue) in 1955, only 11% remain in business, including **General Motors, Coca-Cola, IBM,** and **General Electric.** In other words, eighty-nine percent of the original Fortune 500 companies have failed to manage their risks in a successful enough manner to remain in business!

Not surprisingly, most investors do not like uncertainty. As a result, companies that are able to make more effective decisions in the face of uncertainty often are rewarded by key stakeholders in various ways, such as with a lower cost of borrowing (i.e., interest rates), more success in hiring and retaining top talent (i.e., employees), attracting additional investor capital (e.g., from investors who share the company's shareholder return time horizon), or relatively less regulatory scrutiny (e.g., fewer regulatory requirements, lower fines for any violations, etc.).

Here's **Why It's important**

Enterprise risk management helps an organization make better decisions in uncertain business environments and, most importantly, to achieve its chosen strategy (e.g., to create the most innovative products or services; to provide the lowest cost products or services; to offer the highest quality products or services). Specifically, **enterprise risk management (ERM)** is the formal process of aligning an organization's overall desired level of risk taking with its strategy, and then managing its top risks in a manner that maintains this alignment. Over 90% of large organizations (i.e., sales revenues > $1 billion) engage in some type of ERM, ranging from having a complete, formal ERM process in place to investigating the concept of ERM. However, despite such widespread adoption, the complexity and relative newness of ERM mean that most organizations have yet to perfect their ERM systems.[1] As such, as reported in CFO surveys and illustrated throughout this section, ERM represents a growing area of importance and opportunity for management accountants to create value within organizations.[2]

Exhibit 13.1 presents an overview of the key steps within the ERM process examined in this chapter.

Exhibit 13.1

Key Steps within the ERM Process

- **Risk Appetite Determination:** Determine the organization's desired overall level of risk taking that should be pursued to generate the financial returns expected by shareholders and other key stakeholders.
- **Risk Identification:** Identify top risks.
- **Risk Assessment:** Assess top risks at the inherent level.
- **Risk Response:** Using a portfolio perspective, identify, evaluate, and implement the best response alternatives for inherent risks that bring the portfolio of residual risks into alignment with the organization's risk appetite.
- **Risk Monitoring:** Continually search for new emerging risks, reevaluate accuracy of risk assessments, and consider more effective risk response alternatives.

---

1   Mark Beasley, Bruce Branson, and Bonnie Hancock, *The State of Risk Oversight: An Overview of Enterprise Risk Management Practices,* 7th Edition (American Institute of Certified Public Accountants, April 2016). Taken from https://www.aicpa.org/InterestAreas/BusinessIndustryAndGovernment/Resources/ERM/DownloadableDocuments/AICPA_ERM_Research_Study_2016.pdf

2   David McCann, "Finance and Accounting Skills Gap Vexes CFOs: The Wish List of Traits Desired in Entry-Level Finance and Management Accounting Staff Continues to Expand," *CFO.com* (February 4, 2015). Taken from http://ww2.cfo.com/training/2015/02/you-just-cant-get-good-help-anymore-accounting-skills-gap/.

Determining Risk Appetite

An organization's overall desired level of risk taking is referred to as its **risk appetite**. Risky Business Company manufactures Adirondack chairs with a strategy of providing the highest quality chairs for use in luxury beach and vacation homes. Panel A of Exhibit 13.2 shows Risky Business Company's risk appetite as the line that connects the horizontal axis (i.e., likelihood) and the vertical axis (i.e., impact). The company's risk appetite can be considered moderate in nature because it is neither very near nor very far from the origin but rather connects the midpoints of the likelihood and impact axes.

Exhibit 13.2 Key Elements of a Portfolio Risk Management Perspective

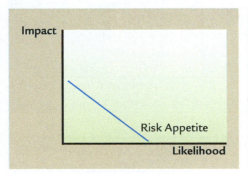

Panel A: Risk Appetite

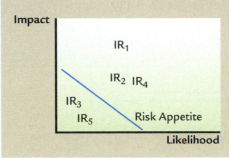

Panel B: Inherent Risks

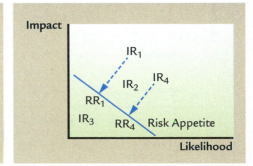

Panel C: Residual Risks

Identifying Top Risks

After determining its risk appetite, a company next identifies its most important risks. Some managers or board of director members refer to these most important risks as a Top 10 list or, more casually, as the risks that "keep them up at night." Risk identification requires input from a cross-functional team to capture all of the perspectives of the organization to understand the threats—or risks—to the organization. Most companies separate identified risks into various categories, such as strategic risk, operational risk, compliance risk, financial reporting risk, etc., that can be further tailored to the specifics of a particular company or industry. Each top risk is assigned a "risk owner" who has responsibility for overseeing the successful management of that risk throughout the ERM process.

Assessing Inherent Risks

After being identified, management must assess top risks at the inherent level. An **inherent risk** is the risk that exists absent of any risk management action to reduce or avoid the risk. Most ERM programs assess, or estimate, two aspects of uncertainty for inherent risks— (1) the *likelihood*, or probability P, of an event occurring and (2) the *impact*, or magnitude, on the company should an event actually occur. Probability P is measured as falling between 0 (no chance of occurring) and 1 (will occur for sure)—(i.e., $0 \leq P \leq 1$). Impact can be measured in qualitative terms (e.g., company reputation), in nonfinancial quantitative terms (e.g., percentage of quality defects), or financial quantitative terms (e.g., additional costs incurred or revenues lost). Both probability and impact are difficult to quantify. Managers increasingly rely on the measurement expertise of management accountants to estimate these amounts. Panel B of Exhibit 13.2 plots Risky Business Company's five most important inherent risks (IR) shown as IR_1 through IR_5.

Here's How It's Used: AT ADIDAS GROUP

ERM analyses contain extremely confidential internal information and, as a result, companies rarely share them publicly. However, the chart below displays an excerpt from **adidas Group**'s annual report that illustrates how this large (over $18 billion in annual sales) international sports apparel and equipment company considers the impact and likelihood of its most critical risks.[3]

02 CORPORATE RISK EVALUATION CATEGORIES

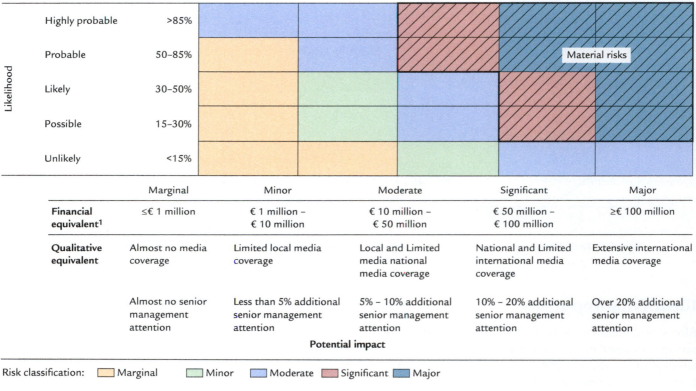

		Marginal	Minor	Moderate	Significant	Major
Financial equivalent[1]		≤€ 1 million	€ 1 million – € 10 million	€ 10 million – € 50 million	€ 50 million – € 100 million	≥€ 100 million
Qualitative equivalent		Almost no media coverage	Limited local media coverage	Local and Limited media national media coverage	National and Limited international media coverage	Extensive international media coverage
		Almost no senior management attention	Less than 5% additional senior management attention	5% – 10% additional senior management attention	10% – 20% additional senior management attention	Over 20% additional senior management attention

Potential impact

Risk classification: ☐ Marginal ☐ Minor ☐ Moderate ☐ Significant ☐ Major

1 Based on operating profit, financial, result or tax expenses.

The axis labels are flipped from that of Exhibit 13.2. Nevertheless, the risk chart is interpreted in the same basic manner—the further from the origin, the greater the risk as measured by likelihood of occurrence and the potential impact should it occur. In addition to its adidas Originals, Sports Performance, and Sports Styles brands, the Group also owns the Reebok and TaylorMade brands. The adidas Group has a risk and opportunity management system for carrying out an ERM process similar to the one examined in this chapter. For example, its annual report states that the "risk and opportunity management system ensures risk-aware, opportunity-oriented and informed actions in a dynamic business environment in order to guarantee the competitiveness and sustainable success of the adidas Group." Examples of top risks identified and managed by its Risk and Opportunity Management System include strategic risks (e.g., product distribution risks, competition risks, and sociopolitical and regulatory risks), operational risks (e.g., personnel risks, business partner risks, IT risks, and inventory risks), legal and compliance risks (e.g., customs and tax regulations), and financial risks (e.g., currency risks, impairment of intangible assets, liquidity risks, and credit risks). With an effective and transparent ERM process, adidas Group more effectively pursues its mission to "strive to be the best sports company in the world, with brands built on a passion for sports and a sporting lifestyle!"

---

3 From adidas Group's 2015 Annual Report, p. 158. Taken from http://www.adidas-group.com/media/filer_public/ e9/73/e973acf3-f889-43e5-b3c0-bc870d53b964/2015_gb_en.pdf.

Responding to Risks Using a Portfolio Perspective

Once management assesses its top risks at an inherent level, the next step in the ERM process is to decide how best to manage, or respond, to each top risk. A **residual risk** is the risk that remains after any risk management action has been taken. ERM uses a portfolio perspective to help decide how to respond to each top inherent risk in the most effective manner. A **portfolio ERM perspective** is the practice of managing the company's most important risks in a collective (or portfolio) fashion, such that the residual risks that remain align with the company's risk appetite.

Generally, there are three alternatives for responding to an inherent risk: (1) accept, (2) avoid, or (3) reduce. To *accept* an inherent risk means that the company does nothing in response—it simply continues conducting business as normal. Many risks are managed this way simply because companies do not have enough money and personnel resources to reduce all of their top risks. With this response, the residual risk is the same as the inherent risk because no response action is taken.

CONCEPT CLIP

To *avoid* an inherent risk means that the company ceases to perform the activity that gave rise to the risk. Some top risks are avoided because the company cannot reduce the risk in a cost-beneficial manner and it is unwilling to allow the risk to remain at its current inherent level. With this response, there is no residual risk because the risk itself is removed from the company as a result of the company no longer performing the activity that caused the inherent risk to exist. For example, companies might sell off a business unit or product or service line if management believes it cannot manage the associated risk(s) in a cost-beneficial manner.

Finally, to *reduce* an inherent risk means that the company enacts some particular procedure to decrease the inherent risk to a lower residual risk level. Possible risk reduction procedures include a specific activity or internal control (e.g., separation of duties), insurance policy (e.g., a fire or other catastrophic event insurance policy on a warehouse facility), strategic alliance (e.g., a product toy tie-in between Disney's Pixar and McDonald's restaurants), or even an entire business process (i.e., a collection of related business activities, such as brand management or barista training for Starbucks). With this response, the residual risk will be lower than the inherent risk as a result of the chosen risk reduction alternative.

Net Benefit of Risk Response   Each risk response alternative produces a benefit. **Risk response benefit** can be defined as the difference between the inherent risk and the residual risk produced by the particular risk response. Inherent risk is the probability (or likelihood) of a

---

Here's How It's Used: AT GOOGLE

China has more than twice as many people using the Internet as the United States has citizens, and yet Google elected to exit its Chinese search engine business in 2010, thereby losing a tremendously large market.[4] Google chose this *avoidance* action to avoid the risk of censorship from the Chinese government, whose impact was measured by cyber attacks that targeted the company from within the country, as well as dozens of other companies and even various Chinese human rights activists. Given that Google had invested 4 years in developing its Chinese market offering, management undoubtedly considered a risk reduction response action instead. However, the incremental direct and indirect costs of reducing these negative impacts appeared to outweigh the benefits of doing business in this large, emerging market. The end risk response result—at least for a number of years—was risk avoidance by exiting the market.

---

4   Kaveh Waddell, "Why Google Quit China—and Why It's Heading Back," *The Atlantic* (January 19, 2016). Taken from http://www.theatlantic.com/technology/archive/2016/01/why-google-quit-china-and-why-its-heading-back/424482/.

risk occurring multiplied by the impact should it actually occur, which in essence is an expected value calculation. Residual risk is calculated in the same manner, except that the equation uses the probability and the impact that are expected to exist *after* the risk response in question has been implemented (i.e., the residual amounts).

Risk Response Benefit = Inherent Risk – Residual Risk

Most risk responses also incur a cost in order to be implemented. **Risk response cost** can be defined as the incremental cost incurred by the company to implement the given risk response. This incremental cost (see Chapter 8 for a discussion of incremental, or relevant, costs) can include both direct and indirect costs (see Chapter 4 for a discussion of direct and indirect costs) and often is quite challenging to estimate accurately.[5] Management accountants can add tremendous value to organizations by accurately estimating the incremental costs of each risk response alternative under consideration.

Effective ERM requires that management evaluate and implement the most appropriate risk response to each top risk—in other words, the response that generates the greatest positive net benefit. **Risk response net benefit** is measured as the benefit of risk response minus the cost of risk response.

Risk Response Net Benefit = Response Benefit – Response Cost

Here's **Why It's important**

Only after risk response costs have been accurately estimated and subtracted from the response benefit can management estimate the net benefit of each risk response alternative and select the best course of action (i.e., the alternative with the greatest positive net benefit). Management must understand how to evaluate multiple risk response alternatives and select the one that best manages the given risk in a cost-effective manner. **Example 13.1** illustrates how net benefit can be used to evaluate and select between risk response alternatives.

Returning to Risky Business Company, Panel C of Exhibit 13.2 (p. 703) plots Risky's residual risks (RR) shown in orange as RR_1 and RR_4. Assume that IR_1 represents the inherent risk of poor-quality wooden materials being purchased and used in the production of its Adirondack chairs. Panel C shows that Risky Business management chose to reduce IR_1 down to the lower RR_1 level to be in alignment with the company's risk appetite. Similarly, Panel C shows that management also chose to reduce IR_4 down to the lower RR_4 level. Furthermore, management chose to avoid IR_5, as evidenced by the absence of either an IR_5 or a RR_5 from Panel C. In other words, IR_5 was deemed too significant simply to accept (i.e., do nothing), and yet also was too costly to reduce to a point where its residual risk aligned with the company's overall risk appetite. Finally, when considered in isolation, IR_2 is too risky (i.e., it exceeds the risk appetite) and IR_3 is not risky enough (i.e., it falls below the risk appetite line—investors will demand a higher return than what will be generated by this overly conservative position). However, IR_2 exceeds the risk appetite line by approximately the same amount that IR_3 falls short of the risk appetite line. When considered from a portfolio perspective, IR_2 and IR_3

Here's **Why It's important**

offset each other and, thus, together align with the company's risk appetite line. ERM uses a portfolio perspective to ensure that the organization's most important residual risks are aligned with its risk appetite, thereby helping the organization achieve its strategy. The final risk plots shown in Panel C show that Risky Business Company's portfolio of residual risks align with its risk appetite.

---

5 B. Ballou, D. Heitger, and T. Schultz, Measuring the Costs of Responding to Business Risks. *Management Accounting Quarterly*, Vol. 10, No. 2 (2009): 1–11.

Swift Ascent Backpacking Company provides various outdoor adventure services to climbers visiting Mount Rainer National Park. One of its most popular services is a guided 12-mile hike from Paradise Lodge to the main Base Camp where climbers can make their final ascent to the summit of the mountain. Swift Ascent's management is concerned about the additional costs the company would incur from potential lawsuits and fines resulting from injured climbers. The chart below contains a description of this top risk, an inherent risk assessment, three risk response alternatives, and a residual risk assessment for each response alternative.

EXAMPLE 13.1

How to Use Net Benefit to Evaluate Risk Response Alternatives

	Inherent Risk		Risk Response	Residual Risk	
Risk	**Likelihood**	**Impact (operating costs)**	**Alternatives**	**Likelihood**	**Impact (operating costs)**
Climbers become either sick or injured during their 12-mile hike from Paradise Lodge to Base Camp, resulting in costly lawsuits from climbers and fines from the National Park Service (both of which increase operating costs for Swift Ascent)	20%	$10,000,000	A—Require an intensive day-long training and education seminar for all climbers the day before their climb	10%	$ 6,000,000
			B—Form an alliance with the leading outdoor gear company that guarantees climbers use the best performing gear (boots, ice picks, oxygen masks, etc.) on the market	15%	$ 5,000,000
			C—Take no action in response to possible new lawsuits or fines	20%	$10,000,000

Swift Ascent's management accountants estimate that the incremental cost of implementing risk response A is $550,000 and the incremental cost of implementing risk response B is $300,000.

Required:

1. Calculate the inherent risk for Swift Ascent.

2. Calculate the residual risk for Swift Ascent associated with each of the three risk response alternatives A, B, and C.

3. Calculate the benefit for Swift Ascent associated with each of the three risk response alternatives A, B, and C.

4. Calculate the net benefit for Swift Ascent associated with each of the three risk response alternatives A, B, and C.

5. Using net benefit as the criterion, which risk response should Swift Ascent choose to implement?

Solution:

1. The inherent risk for Swift Ascent equals the likelihood of the risk occurring multiplied by the impact that is expected should the risk actually occur.

   Therefore, the inherent risk (IR) is:

   = 0.20 (likelihood) × $10,000,000 (impact) = $2,000,000

(Continued)

EXAMPLE 13.1

(Continued)

2. The residual risk associated with a particular risk response alternative equals the likelihood that remains after the alternative is implemented multiplied by the impact that remains after the alternative is implemented.

   Therefore, residual risk (RR) for response alternative A is:

   = 0.10 (likelihood) × $6,000,000 (impact) = $600,000

   Therefore, residual risk (RR) for response alternative B is:

   = 0.15 (likelihood) × $5,000,000 (impact) = $750,000

   Therefore, residual risk (RR) for response alternative C is:

   = 0.20 (likelihood) × $10,000,000 (impact) = $2,000,000

3. The benefit associated with a particular risk response alternative equals the inherent risk (IR) minus the residual risk (RR).

   Therefore, the benefit for risk response alternative A is:

   = $2,000,000 (IR) – $600,000 (RR) = $1,400,000

   Therefore, the benefit for risk response alternative B is:

   = $2,000,000 (IR) – $750,000 (RR) = $1,250,000

   Therefore, the benefit for risk response alternative C is:

   = $2,000,000 (IR) – $2,000,000 (RR) = $0

4. The net benefit associated with a particular risk response alternative equals the benefit minus the cost.

   Therefore, the net benefit for risk response alternative A is:

   = $1,400,000 (benefit) – $550,000 (cost) = $850,000

   Therefore, the net benefit for risk response alternative B is:

   = $1,250,000 (benefit) – $300,000 (cost) = $950,000

   Therefore, the net benefit for risk response alternative C is:

   = $0 (benefit) – $0 (cost) = $0

5. Using net benefit as the criterion, Swift Ascent should select and implement risk response alternative B because this option has the greatest positive net benefit, $950,000, as compared to alternative A, $850,000, or alternative C, $0.

Monitoring the ERM Process

Finally, risk monitoring means that management proceeds through the ERM process in an iterative fashion, continually looking for ways to improve any and all steps along the way. One common mistake made by management in implementing ERM is treating it as a checklist that simply requires one-time consideration. Instead, management should initially proceed through the complete ERM process and then return each year to begin the process again.

Well-run companies continuously look for ways to improve their ERM process and turn to management accountants to play an important role in providing key inputs into each step of the ERM process. For example, management accountants can help continually reevaluate key inputs, such as identifying emerging—yet previously ignored—risks and reassessing the stated risk appetite to verify that it aligns with the company's strategy and expectations from key stakeholders. Furthermore, from a measurement perspective, management accountants should play an important role in more creatively and accurately estimating inherent risks, the incremental cost of specific risk response alternatives, the residual risk that is expected to be achieved from the selected risk response plan, and the residual risk that actually is achieved after the selected risk response plan has been implemented. Finally, risk correlation—the extent to which one risk or risk response is associated with other risks—represents a growing challenge for management accountants to employ data analytics to substantially improve the ERM process.

Check Point

1. **Which step within the ERM process should occur immediately after risk assessment?**

Answer:

Risk response follows risk assessment and involves the identification, evaluation, and implementation of the best risk response alternatives for the organization's top inherent risks.

2. **The decision to form a strategic alliance with a new business partner to respond to the risk of low product quality represents an example of which risk response alternative?**
   a. **Accept**
   b. **Avoid**
   c. **Reduce**
   d. **None of these.**

Answer:

c. A strategic alliance is an example of a risk reduction alternative as it attempts to reduce the likelihood, the impact, or both of the given inherent risk.

BUSINESS SUSTAINABILITY

OBJECTIVE ▸ **2**

Understand the role of managerial accounting in business sustainability.

The term "sustainability" is one of the most often used, yet misunderstood, terms in business. For example, some managers equate sustainability with environmental issues, such as greenhouse gas emissions or other "green" initiatives. While such environmental issues are important, many additional issues are equally—if not more—important to an organization's overall performance. For this chapter, as well as for most successful organizations, sustainability actually refers to *business* sustainability. **Business sustainability is the practice of creating long-term organizational value through internally understanding, measuring, and managing the key threats and opportunities to achieving the organization's strategy and then externally reporting to key stakeholders on the successes and failures of such efforts.**

𝓗ere's **Why It's important**

This section focuses on the important and growing role of management accounting in helping organizations practice business sustainability. The business sustainability cycle, shown in

Exhibit 13.3, highlights the interconnectivity of the key management accounting areas within business sustainability.[6]

These areas include (1) organizational strategy, (2) stakeholder engagement, (3) risk management, (4) financial and nonfinancial performance measurement, (5) sustainability reporting and, finally, (6) sustainability assurance. The remainder of this section explores these areas and how they build upon one another to help make a business more sustainable.

Here's **Why It's important**

Strategy Business sustainability begins first and foremost with the company's strategy. Selecting the company's strategy is an important decision usually made by the CEO. However, perhaps even more important than selecting the best strategy is *implementing* the selected strategy in an effective manner. Effective strategy implementation requires management to make business sustainability-oriented decisions that support, rather than conflict with, strategy. For example, as the business sustainability cycle illustrates, effectively carrying out **Apple**'s strategy of continually designing innovative products in a high profile manner requires management to engage with key stakeholders, measure and manage risks, and finally report and assure sustainability information in a very different manner as compared to implementing **Costco**'s strategy of driving sales, using a no-frills approach without advertising. Apple's strategy leads its management to be more concerned with convincing investors that its various decisions promote an innovative product design culture, whereas Costco's strategy leads management to focus more on providing quality products at a price lower than competitors' prices.

Stakeholder Engagement **Stakeholders** are those individuals or groups that (1) are affected by an organization's pursuit of its strategy or (2) can affect an organization's ability to achieve its strategy. In other words, the relationship between key stakeholders and the organization is a two-way street. Stakeholders can include investors, creditors, customers, employees, regulators, suppliers, competitors, lobbyists, community members, and nongovernment organizations (e.g., **Sierra Club**, **American Red Cross**). Investors (or shareholders) represent the ultimate stakeholder.

---

6 Exhibit 13.4 is adapted from B, Ballou, D. Heitger, and C. Landes, *Accounting for the Sustainability Cycle: How the Accounting Profession Can Add Value to Sustainability-Oriented Activities* (American Institute of Certified Public Accountants, October 2013). Taken from https://www.aicpa.org/InterestAreas/FRC/AssuranceAdvisoryServices/DownloadableDocuments/Sustainability/Whitepaper_Accounting_for_the_Sustainability_Cycle.pdf.

Here's How It's Used: AT DE BEERS

Business sustainability involves many functions and varies across businesses and industries. One decision that likely will change your life one day regards marriage and the selection of a diamond engagement ring. You might consider the life cycle of the ring's diamond—it almost surely has traveled a great distance and involved a large number of key stakeholders along the way. For example, founded in 1888, **De Beers** is one of the world's best-known diamond companies. De Beers extracts, or recovers, the majority of its diamonds from Botswana, South Africa, Canada, and Namibia.[7] Exhibit 13.4 displays a variety of De Beers' various business sustainability issues (both threats and opportunities) along its entire value chain. De Beers' value chain spans from research and development Exploration (e.g., the positive and negative political, economic, and social impacts that occur as a result of the countries where De Beers chooses to explore for diamonds) through customer service Brands/Retail (e.g., changes in De Beers' reputation for exclusivity and quality resulting from the prices it charges and the retail establishments it uses to sell its diamonds).

Exhibit 13.4 Business Sustainability Issues throughout the Value Chain

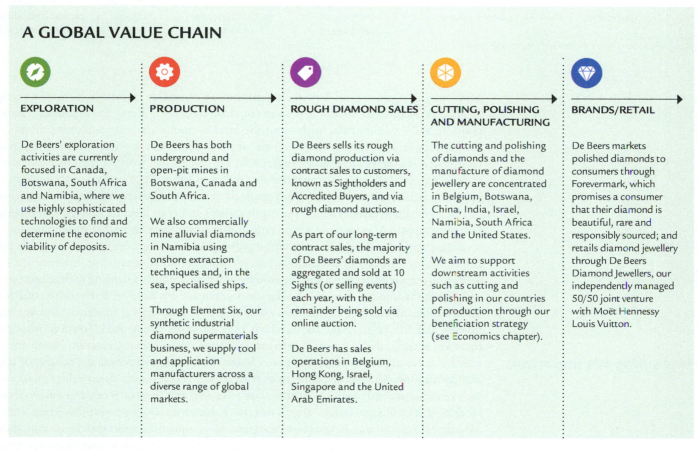

A GLOBAL VALUE CHAIN

EXPLORATION

De Beers' exploration activities are currently focused in Canada, Botswana, South Africa and Namibia, where we use highly sophisticated technologies to find and determine the economic viability of deposits.

PRODUCTION

De Beers has both underground and open-pit mines in Botswana, Canada and South Africa.

We also commercially mine alluvial diamonds in Namibia using onshore extraction techniques and, in the sea, specialised ships.

Through Element Six, our synthetic industrial diamond supermaterials business, we supply tool and application manufacturers across a diverse range of global markets.

ROUGH DIAMOND SALES

De Beers sells its rough diamond production via contract sales to customers, known as Sightholders and Accredited Buyers, and via rough diamond auctions.

As part of our long-term contract sales, the majority of De Beers' diamonds are aggregated and sold at 10 Sights (or selling events) each year, with the remainder being sold via online auction.

De Beers has sales operations in Belgium, Hong Kong, Israel, Singapore and the United Arab Emirates.

CUTTING, POLISHING AND MANUFACTURING

The cutting and polishing of diamonds and the manufacture of diamond jewellery are concentrated in Belgium, Botswana, China, India, Israel, Namibia, South Africa and the United States.

We aim to support downstream activities such as cutting and polishing in our countries of production through our beneficiation strategy (see Economics chapter).

BRANDS/RETAIL

De Beers markets polished diamonds to consumers through Forevermark, which promises a consumer that their diamond is beautiful, rare and responsibly sourced; and retails diamond jewellery through De Beers Diamond Jewellers, our independently managed 50/50 joint venture with Moët Hennessy Louis Vuitton.

As De Beers illustrates, business sustainability requires that management considers the numerous stakeholders, as well as threats and opportunities, involved with major decisions throughout the company.

However, many organizations increasingly realize that understanding, measuring, and responding to key stakeholder concerns in an effective and logical manner generally creates smoother and greater increases in shareholder returns than ignoring stakeholders and their concerns.

Exhibit 13.5 presents results from **PricewaterhouseCooper**'s survey of 1,409 CEOs from across 83 countries who were asked to list the stakeholders who had the greatest impact on their

---

7 Excerpt from De Beers' "Building Forever: Report to Society" (2015). Taken from https://www.debeersgroup.com/content/dam/de-beers/corporate/documents/BuildingForever/Report%20to%20Society%202015.pdf.

organization's strategy.[8] Customers, regulators, competitors, employees, supply chain partners, and investors are the stakeholders with the largest impact on organizational strategy.

Exhibit 13.5   The Relationship Between Stakeholders and Strategy

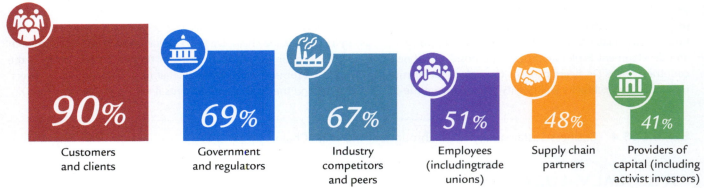

| 90% | 69% | 67% | 51% | 48% | 41% |
| Customers and clients | Government and regulators | Industry competitors and peers | Employees (includingtrade unions) | Supply chain partners | Providers of capital (including activist investors) |

Note: Respondents who indicated high or very high impact

Most managers understand how their organization can affect its stakeholders. For example, **Walmart**'s decision to build a new store (or close an existing store) has significant financial, political, and environmental impacts on the local economy, citizens, employees, utility companies, suppliers, and competitors. These impacts oftentimes are referred to as footprints. Conversely, managers increasingly realize that the impact can work in the other direction as stakeholders can influence the organization's ability to achieve its strategy. For example, current or potential customers can refuse to buy products as a result of boycotting the opening or closing of a store, which negatively affects the organization's ability to meet its strategic and other performance targets. Management accountants can estimate these and other stakeholder impacts on organizational performance involving a growing or shrinking workforce, more or less qualified employees, the cost of electricity, water, pollution, or other externalities, more or less stringent regulatory requirements, and the amount and cost of equity financing or debt borrowings.

Given the impacts that stakeholders and organizations have on one another, one of the most important business sustainability challenges for managers is to understand key stakeholders and the exact issues about which they are most concerned. However, identifying these key stakeholder concerns is extremely difficult unless the organization has an effective stakeholder engagement process in place. **Stakeholder engagement** is the process by which an organization's management interacts with its key stakeholders. Stakeholder engagement varies from casual, impromptu, informal conversations all the way to regular, structured interactions where both parties exchange data and expectations about one another's performance. Managerial accountants can play an important role in quantifying stakeholders' expectations about the organization and estimating the extent to which such expectations can impact (either positively or negatively) the organization's future earnings, cash flows, or other performance measures.

Exhibit 13.6 is an excerpt from **Eli Lilly and Company**'s integrated annual report that showcases its key stakeholders and the channels Eli Lilly employs to engage them.[9]

Note the variety of measures and approaches used by management to understand key stakeholders and their concerns.

Here's **Why It's important**

---

8   Excerpt from PricewaterhouseCooper's 19th annual CEO survey entitled "Redefining Business Success in a Changing World" (2016). Taken from https://www.pwc.com/gx/en/ceo-survey/2016/landing-page/pwc-19th-annual-global-ceo-survey.pdf.

9   Excerpt from Eli Lilly and Company's "Integrated Report" (2015). Taken from https://www.lilly.com/_assets/pdf/integrated-report.pdf.

Exhibit 13.6 Stakeholder Engagement Activities at Eli Lilly

Stakeholder Groups and Examples of Engagement Channels

Healthcare Professionals
› Online medical information resources
› Disease-state educational programs
› Advisory boards
› Sales force interactions
› Direct-mail communications
› The Lilly Answers Center telephone line
› Medication guides and package inserts
› Online registries
› Publications (manuscripts, posters, and abstracts)
› Medical letters
› Patient support programs
› Lilly-sponsored symposia and scientific exchange meetings
› Medical and commercial booths at congresses
› Interactions with Lilly physicians, scientists, and medical liaisons
› Clinical trial investigation contracting
› Lilly-sponsored mobile applications that provide physicians with easy-to-access research and clinical trial information

Patients
› Healthcare provider discussions
› Educational materials and programs
› Product package inserts and medication guides
› Patient advocacy groups
› Patient support and assistance programs
› Online product resources
› The Lilly Answers Center telephone line

Public and Private Healthcare Administrators
› Account-manager interactions
› Disease-state educational programs
› Advisory boards
› The Lilly Answers Center telephone line
› Online medical information resources

Community Members
› Employee service on boards and committees of local organizations
› Participation in local volunteer opportunities
› Employee-directed philanthropy

Investors
› Daily interactions through our investor relations function
› Industry investor conferences
› Meetings in Indianapolis and major global cities
› Quarterly earnings communications
› Annual meeting of shareholders
› Annual report and other financial disclosures
› Periodic investment community update meetings
› Corporate governance discussions facilitated by the corporate secretary's office

Suppliers
› Green procurement program
› Product stewardship standard
› Supplier self-assessments and qualifications
› Supplier audits that Lilly performs
› Supplier risk-assessment process
› Policy advocacy conversations with vendors

Employees[1]
› Live "global town hall" meetings
› Intranet social collaboration/networking tools, including CEO blog
› Employee resource groups
› Employee surveys
› Electronic newsletters
› Hotline for ethics, compliance, and privacy questions/concerns

Non-Governmental Organizations
› Partnerships to support patients and families
› Partnerships to raise awareness about certain diseases
› Advisory board participation
› Participation in annual conferences/exhibitions
› Company communications
› Memberships

Government and Regulatory Organizations
› Policy education materials
› Published policy research
› Responses to written requests for information
› Oral and written testimony
› Written comments on proposed regulations
› Policy discussions
› Advisory boards
› Meetings and conferences
› Communication of studies
› Lobbying activities
› Educational briefings
› Direct legislator and policy-maker engagement

With strong roots in minimizing risk, facilitating governance, and strengthening relationships, our Office of Alliance Management has been conducting "Voice of Alliance" surveys for the past 15 years. Data is regularly collected from Lilly and alliance partner employees to assess the strategic, cultural, and operational fit of each partnership and determine how the collaborations can be improved.

1 Approximately 41,000 employees as of December 31, 2015.

Risk Management As discussed earlier, an organization's selected strategy plays a large part in determining which stakeholders are most important to the organization. Stakeholders usually have concerns or expectations about the organization's performance. Stakeholder concerns can be thought of as the risks and opportunities that either hurt or help the organization's ability to achieve its selected strategy (i.e., stakeholder concerns equal organizational risks/opportunities). An effective stakeholder engagement process is extremely helpful in identifying these stakeholder concerns and recognizing the risks and opportunities they pose to the organization more quickly than if no such process exists.

More specifically, these risks (or threats) and opportunities vary widely across organizations and can relate to many different key stakeholder groups and performance areas, including economic, social, environmental, political, financial, legal, reputational, and regulatory. Some organizations use acronyms, such as TBL (triple bottom line of economic, environmental, and social factors) or ESG (environmental, social, and governance factors), to categorize some of the most common risks and areas of stakeholder concern. Therefore, risk management (discussed in the previous section) plays a critical role within the business sustainability cycle because it helps managers focus more clearly on exactly which issues should be measured and managed internally and, subsequently, communicated to key external stakeholders to increase organizational value.

Performance Measurement For investors and other key stakeholders, financial measures, such as future cash flows and earnings streams, usually serve as the ultimate means for evaluating the effectiveness with which managers make decisions that involve numerous—and often conflicting—stakeholder concerns. However, organizations have limited resources and cannot please all key stakeholders all of the time. Thus, managers must make trade-offs when deciding on which risks and opportunities they choose to address and how to address them.

Here's **Why It's important**

Here's How It's Used: SUSTAINABILITY

UPS illustrates the important connection between stakeholders, risks, and performance measurement. In essence, UPS's business model is predicated on its ability to drive trucks and fly planes all over the globe delivering packages. In so doing, UPS employs over 444,000 workers, handles an average of 69.4 million daily tracking requests, and uses approximately 105,000 vehicles (cars, vans, tractors, and motorcycles) and 650 planes to deliver over 4.7 billion packages and documents annually.[10] As an indication of its environmental footprint, the company touts that its Orion delivery routing technology will reduce the distance its vehicles drive each year by 100 million miles. The UPS graph in Exhibit 13.7—with importance to stakeholders shown on the vertical axis and influence on business success shown on the horizontal axis—shows the relationship between the company's stakeholder concerns and its business sustainability.

Exhibit 13.7   The Relationship between Stakeholder Concerns and Business Success at UPS

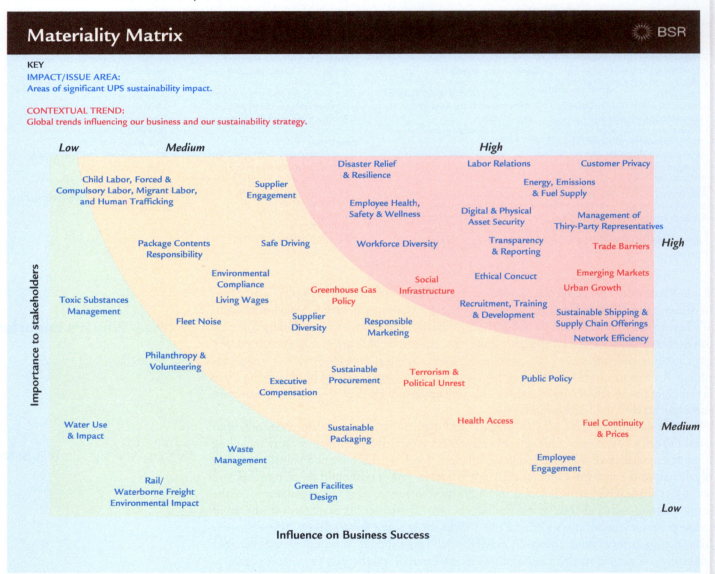

Not surprisingly, as evidenced by its inclusion in the upper right-hand corner, UPS's performance measurement system ranks Energy, Emissions & Fuel Supply as one of its most important risks, given its extreme importance to stakeholders and influence on UPS's performance. From this point, UPS accountants can perform more in-depth analyses to estimate how the most important stakeholder issues shown in the graph translate into impacts on the organization's most critical performance measures.

---

10 From UPS's "Fact Sheet." Taken from https://pressroom.ups.com/assets/pdf/pressroom/fact%20sheet/UPS_General_Fact_Sheet_5_18_2016.pdf.

One of the most common complaints from managers concerning business sustainability is the lack of financial analysis that compares and contrasts the short- and long-term effects that would result from various decisions involving key stakeholder concerns. The good news for managerial accountants is that this complaint creates an opportunity for managerial accountants to add significant value to the organization. Business sustainability is valuable because it improves decision making by helping managers understand how their various decisions involving risks and opportunities (i.e., stakeholder issues) relate to important performance measures, such as future cash flow and earnings streams.

Here's **Why It's important**

As one example of business sustainability trade-offs, consider the various issues and stakeholder concerns involved with an organization's overseas manufacturing plants. Would the organization be better served by spending its limited resources to reduce child labor, increase worker safety, more carefully inspect raw materials quality, patrol for intellectual property theft (i.e., local workers stealing patented technology and producing competing inexpensive "knockoff" products), verify that its suppliers follow the agreed-upon Code of Conduct, train workers not to offer or accept bribes in order to comply with the U.S. Foreign Corrupt Practices law, or reduce waste and associated product costs? Each of these potential decisions would impact key stakeholders, but management likely cannot address them all or give them all equal priority. Increasingly, management accountants play an important role in helping managers better understand the connection between specific decisions and key stakeholder concerns. Understanding these connections gives managers the ability to measure concerns such as employee safety, environmental emissions, regulatory scrutiny, economic constraints, and investor pressures in common financial terms. As a result, management can make these trade-off decisions in a financially informed manner rather than randomly responding to the stakeholders who "yell the loudest" and hoping for the best.

Sustainability Reporting **Corporate sustainability reporting (CSR)** refers to the voluntary public disclosure of qualitative and/or quantitative information about an organization's performance on one or more financial and/or nonfinancial dimensions. For example, common types of information disclosed in CSRs include the TBL and ESG issues discussed earlier. Other terms for corporate sustainability reporting include corporate responsibility reporting, citizenship reporting, corporate accountability reporting, and nonfinancial reporting. CSR is a relatively recent, yet very impactful reporting phenomenon, both for the organization issuing the CSR and for the multitude of external stakeholders that make various decisions based on the information contained within the CSR.

Exhibits 13.8, 13.9, and 13.10 contain excerpts from **KPMG**'s global survey of corporate sustainability reporting practices.[11] In Exhibit 13.8, the green circles represent data from the world's largest (by sales revenue) 250 companies. The purple circles represent data from the largest (by sales revenue) 100 companies in each of 45 different countries (i.e., 4,500 total companies represented). Exhibit 13.8 displays how CSR has changed since its inception in the mid-1990s. Perhaps the most striking observation is the extremely rapid growth—from 0 to 92%—in the percentage of organizations that prepare and issue some form of CSR. This growth has transpired over a relatively short 20-year time period.

Here's **Why It's important**

All data in Exhibit 13.9 are from the largest (by sales revenue) 100 companies in each of 45 different countries (i.e., 4,500 total companies represented—the purple represents 2015 and the green represents 2013). Furthermore, Exhibits 13.9 (page 716) and 13.10 (page 717) display the widespread adoption of CSR across nearly every industry and in countries across the globe, respectively. These observations are important because they further support the notion that CSR is not a temporary "hot topic" that will quickly fizzle out, but instead has deep roots and anticipated benefits for the majority of organizations around the world.

---

11 From KPMG's "Currents of Change: The KPMG Survey of Corporate Responsibility Reporting" (2015). Taken from https://www.kpmg.com/CN/en/IssuesAndInsights/ArticlesPublications/Documents/kpmg-survey-of-corporate-responsibility-reporting-2015-O-201511.pdf.

Exhibit 13.8   Rapid Growth in Corporate Sustainability Reporting Since Its Inception

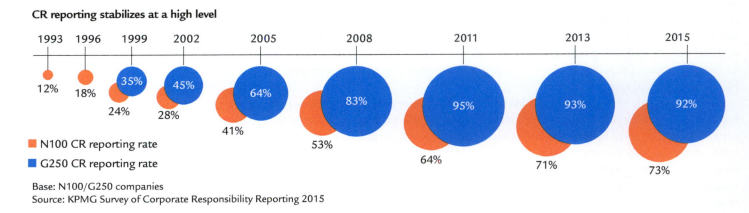

CR reporting stabilizes at a high level

■ N100 CR reporting rate
■ G250 CR reporting rate

Base: N100/G250 companies
Source: KPMG Survey of Corporate Responsibility Reporting 2015

Exhibit 13.9   Widespread Adoption of Corporate Sustainability Reporting across Industries

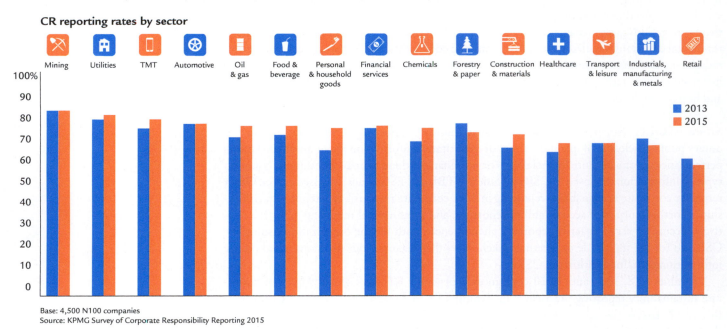

CR reporting rates by sector

Base: 4,500 N100 companies
Source: KPMG Survey of Corporate Responsibility Reporting 2015

Corporate sustainability reporting differs from traditional financial reporting (i.e., the 10-K annual report in general and financial statements in particular) in three major ways. In *most* countries and business environments, sustainability reporting is (1) voluntary, (2) not required to follow any particular set of rules when preparing the information contained within the report (i.e., unlike traditional financial reporting that must adhere to generally accepted accounting principles), and (3) not required to have the report contents verified by an independent third party (i.e., unlike traditional financial reporting that must be assured by an independent third party). It should be noted that the Global Reporting Initiative and the Sustainability Accounting Standards Board each have published reporting standards that organizations often choose to adopt when preparing their CSRs. However, neither of these sets of CSR standards has been widely recognized as "generally accepted," nor (as noted above) is the use of any standard required in most places.

These differences might surprise some financial market participants. On the one hand, it would be hard to imagine publicly traded organizations issuing financial statements that are voluntary in nature, or free from following any set of rules, or without any form of verification from an independent third party (i.e., auditor)—let alone all three, as is the case with CSR! On the other hand, one must remember that traditional financial reporting regulations have been under

Exhibit 13.10 The Global Phenomenon of Corporate Sustainability Reporting

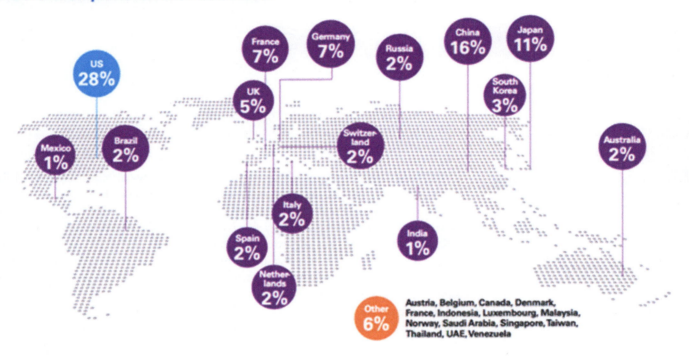

development since the early 1930s, when the stock market crash and the Great Depression led to the first meaningful financial reporting regulations (e.g., Securities Acts of 1933 and 1934). These rules have continued to evolve over the past 80 years to include current generally accepted accounting principles. By comparison, CSR has been employed by a majority of large organizations since only the mid-2000s. Therefore, while far from perfect, CSR is in its infancy relative to financial reporting and likely will continue to experience significant and frequent changes for the foreseeable future.

Sustainability Assurance **Sustainability assurance** is the external verification that an independent party provides concerning the content of a corporate sustainability report and/or the process used in preparing a corporate sustainability report. As noted earlier, in most countries and financial markets, CSRs are not required to be verified (e.g., assured) by independent third parties. Traditionally, most organizations have found it much easier to estimate the costs of CSR assurance than the benefits. As a result, only a small percentage of CSRs was assured during the earliest years of CSR.

However, Exhibit 13.11 shows the slow, yet steady, increase in the percentage of organizations that have their CSRs assured in some capacity. For example, from 2005 to 2015, those organizations that had their CSR information assured changed from being in the minority (only 30%) to the majority (63%). In this exhibit, the purple line represents the world's largest (by sales revenue) 250 companies, and the green line represents the largest 100 companies in 45 different countries across the globe (i.e., 4,500 total companies represented).

Exhibit 13.11

Growth in Independent Assurance
of Corporate Sustainability
Information

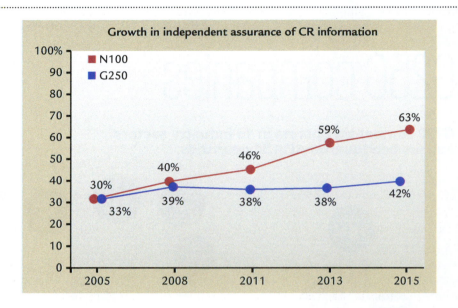

Growth in independent assurance of CR information

Here's **Why It's important**   The most significant benefit of having a CSR assured by an independent third party is that assurance can increase the believability of the CSR's content for external stakeholders. In other words, people are more likely to trust qualitative and quantitative CSR information if it has been verified by an unbiased party that is unrelated to the reporting organization (i.e., the CSR issuer). Most managers and external stakeholders agree that CSR assurance is beneficial, although they acknowledge that measuring the exact size of such a benefit is very challenging. However, managerial accountants can provide valuable insights by estimating the benefits (and costs) of CSR assurance with increasing accuracy.

The cost of CSR assurance can be considerable. For example, some managers complain that assuring only a small part of the CSR can cost more than preparing the entire CSR. Several factors contribute to these costs. One factor is that the lack of a generally accepted set of reporting standards for preparing CSRs leads to higher assurance costs because of the various ways that organizations prepare them. Another factor is the forward-looking nature of CSRs, which means that they contain information with far greater uncertainty—and thus less accuracy—than traditional financial reports, which also increases assurance costs. Specifically, assurance firms worry that stakeholders might pursue legal action against them if stakeholders make decisions or enter into contracts based on assured CSR information that subsequently is discovered to be materially inaccurate.

The Challenge of Communicating an Organization's Business Sustainability "Story" Many organizations fail to adequately understand the link between changes in measures of stakeholder concerns (i.e., risks and opportunities) and their eventual financial impact as measured by costs, revenues, net income, cash flows, or stock price. In other words, organizations struggle internally to understand their business sustainability "story" as captured via their most important performance measures. Yet at the same time, many organizations face extreme pressure to release large quantities of information to satisfy external stakeholders (e.g., regarding geographic sourcing of materials or ingredients, workforce diversity, executive and employee compensation, overseas factory working conditions, carbon footprint, etc.).

In a rush to respond to this growing stakeholder demand for greater disclosure, many organizations prematurely release large quantities of sustainability-oriented information. This reactionary approach often results in a "cart before the horse" problem in that CSRs suffer from information overload (e.g., many CSRs exceed 100 pages) without explaining to key stakeholders how the company measures and manages its most important risks to achieve strategy. Additionally, some CSRs do not follow optional reporting rules, thereby resulting in reports that fail to consider information characteristics such as relevance, reliability, materiality, and consistency that are highly important to stakeholders interested in evaluating the organization's performance. Finally, many CSRs are not audited, thereby resulting in stakeholder skepticism regarding the quality or believability of their contents. For example, **greenwashing** occurs when stakeholders believe that an organization's corporate sustainability report contains environmental (or other types of) information that is materially biased in favor of the reporting organization. Such greenwashing rarely results in positive organizational benefits over the long run.

Therefore, starting with the organization's strategy and then proceeding through the business sustainability cycle—as described throughout this section—helps managers understand the organization's business sustainability story and effectively communicate it with key external stakeholders. Interestingly, in a transformational change in reporting practices, some organizations are moving to the use of integrating reporting to communicate their story. **Integrated reporting** occurs when an organization combines its annual report (i.e., 10-K) with its sustainability report to form one combined (or integrated) report for all stakeholders, including investors. The organization can reap significant benefits as a result of communicating its business sustainability story. The benefits to organizations include more effectively capturing investor capital, securing a lower cost of borrowing, attracting and retaining better employees, working with higher-quality suppliers, receiving more favorable treatment from regulators and lawmakers, and eliciting more welcoming treatment from the local communities in which they operate.

Here's **Why It's important**

Check Point

1. **Which area within the business sustainability cycle immediately follows risk management?**
   a. **Strategy**
   b. **Performance measurement**
   c. **Sustainability assurance**
   d. **Carbon emissions testing**

   Answer:
   b.

2. **For the world's largest companies, how does the percentage of organizations that issue corporate sustainability reports compare to the percentage of organizations that have their corporate sustainability reports externally assured?**

   Answer:
   According to **KPMG**'s survey of corporate responsibility reporting referenced in Exhibits 13.8 through 13.11, as of 2015, ninety-two percent of the world's largest organizations (i.e., G250) issue a sustainability report, while only 63% of these companies have their corporate sustainability report externally assured.

QUALITY COST MANAGEMENT

OBJECTIVE 3

Define quality costs and describe the approaches used for reporting and controlling quality costs.

A **quality product or service** is one that meets or exceeds customer expectations. Customers expect a product to be reliable, durable, fit for use and essentially perform well. In effect, they expect a product to conform to specifications. In fact, many quality experts believe that **quality of conformance** is the best operational definition of quality. Implicitly, a conforming product is reliable, durable, fit for use and performs well. The product should be produced as the design specifies it, and specifications should be met. Conformance is the basis for defining what is meant by a nonconforming, or *defective*, product. A **defective product** is one that does not conform to specifications. **Zero defects** means that all products conform to specifications.

Costs of Quality

Whenever a product fails to conform to specifications (i.e., "poor quality" exists), costs are incurred. Moreover, actions taken to prevent nonconformance also cause costs. Thus, **costs of quality** are costs that exist because poor quality may or does exist. Quality costs can be substantial *in size* and a source of significant savings *if managed effectively*. Improving quality can increase market share and sales, while simultaneously decreasing costs. The overall effect enhances a firm's financial and competitive position. There are numerous quality-related activities, all of which consume resources that determine *the level of quality incurred by a firm*. Inspecting or testing parts, for example, is a quality appraisal activity that has the objective of detecting bad products. Detecting bad products and correcting them before they are sent to customers is usually less expensive than letting them be acquired by customers. The objective of quality cost management is to find ways to reduce total quality costs to 2 to 4% of sales, the optimal range recommended by quality experts. To achieve this objective, a more detailed understanding of quality costs is needed. Quality costs can be categorized as *control costs* and *appraisal costs*.

Control costs   **Control costs** are the costs of preventing or detecting poor quality. These costs are incurred because poor quality may exist. Control costs can be further subdivided into prevention and appraisal costs.

Prevention costs are incurred to prevent poor quality in the products or services being produced. As prevention costs increase, we would expect the costs of failure to decrease. Examples of prevention costs are quality engineering, quality training programs, quality planning, quality reporting, supplier evaluation and selection, quality audits, quality circles, field trials, and design reviews.

Appraisal costs are incurred to determine whether products and services are conforming to their requirements. The main objective of the appraisal function is to prevent nonconforming goods from being shipped to customers. Examples include inspecting and testing raw materials, packaging inspection, supervising appraisal activities, product acceptance, process acceptance, measurement (inspection and test) equipment, and outside endorsements. Two of these terms require further explanation. *Product acceptance* involves sampling from batches of finished goods to determine whether they meet an acceptable quality level. If so, the goods are accepted. *Process acceptance* involves sampling goods while in process to see if the process is in control and producing nondefective goods. If not, the process is shut down until corrective action can be taken.

Failure costs   **Failure costs** are the costs incurred because products or services do not conform to specifications. These costs tend to be most significant and, like control costs, have two major subdivisions.

Internal failure costs are incurred when products and services do not conform to specifications, and this nonconformance is detected *before* the bad products or services are shipped or delivered to outside parties. These are the failures detected by appraisal activities. Examples of internal failure costs are scrap, rework, downtime (due to defects), reinspection, retesting, and design changes. These costs disappear if no defects exist.

External failure costs are incurred when products and services fail to conform to requirements or satisfy customer needs *after* being delivered to customers. Of all the costs of quality, this category can be the most devastating. For example, costs of recalls can run into the hundreds of millions of dollars. Other examples include lost sales because of poor product performance, returns and allowances because of poor quality, warranties, repairs, product liability, customer dissatisfaction, lost market share, and complaint adjustment. External failure costs, like internal failure costs, disappear if no defects exist.

Exhibit 13.12 summarizes the four quality cost categories and lists specific examples of costs. Each of the costs could have been expressed as the cost of quality-related activities, such as the cost of certifying vendors, inspecting incoming materials, or adjusting complaints.

Prevention Costs	Appraisal (Detection) Costs
Quality engineering	Inspection of materials
Quality training	Packaging inspection
Recruiting	Product acceptance
Quality audits	Process acceptance
Design reviews	Field testing
Quality circles	Continuing supplier verification
Marketing research	
Prototype inspection	
Vendor certification	

Internal Failure Costs	External Failure Costs
Scrap	Lost sales (performance-related)
Rework	Returns/allowances
Downtime (defect-related)	Warranties
Reinspection	Discounts due to defects
Retesting	Product liability
Design changes	Complaint adjustment
Repairs	Recalls

Exhibit 13.12

Examples of Quality Costs by Category

Reporting Quality Costs

Improving quality can increase firm value because it increases a firm's profitability. Improving quality can increase profitability in at least two ways: (1) by increasing customer demand and (2) by decreasing the costs of providing goods and services. A quality cost reporting system is essential to an organization serious about improving and controlling quality costs. The first and simplest step in creating such a system is assessing current actual quality costs. A detailed listing of actual quality costs by category can provide two important insights. First, it reveals the magnitude of the quality costs in each category, allowing managers to assess their financial impact. Second, it shows the distribution of quality costs by category, allowing managers to assess the relative importance of each category. When quality costs reach the optimal range of 2 to 4% of sales, control costs typically account for about 80 to 85% of total quality costs.

Here's **Why It's important**

Example 13.2 illustrates a quality cost report for Auger Company.

EXAMPLE 13.2

How to Prepare a Quality Cost Report

Auger Company had total sales of $10,000,000 for the fiscal year ending on December 31, 20X1. Auger's costs of quality are as follows:

Recalls	$500,000
Scrap	350,000
Quality engineering	90,0000
Reinspection	250,000
Quality training	10,000
Product acceptance	120,000
Materials inspection	80,000
Product liability	600,000

(Continued)

EXAMPLE 13.2

(Continued)

Required:

1. Prepare a quality cost report, classifying costs by category and expressing each category as a percentage of sales. What message does the cost report provide?

2. Prepare a bar graph and pie chart that illustrate each category's relative contribution to total quality costs. Comment on the significance of the distribution.

Solution:

1.

Auger Company
Quality Cost Report
For the Year Ended December 31, 20X1

	Quality Costs		Percentage of Sales[a]
Prevention costs:			
Quality training	$ 10,000		
Quality engineering	90,000	$ 100,000	1.00%
Appraisal costs:			
Materials inspection	$ 80,000		
Product acceptance	120,000	200,000	2.00
Internal failure costs:			
Scrap	$350,000		
Reinspection	250,000	600,000	6.00
External failure costs:			
Recalls	$500,000		
Product liability	600,000	1,100,000	11.00
Total quality costs		$2,000,000	20.00%[b]

[a] Actual sales of $10,000,000.
[b] $2,000,000/$10,000,000 = 20%

The report clearly indicates that quality costs are too high, as 20% of sales is much greater than the desired 2 to 4% of sales that prevails for companies with good quality performance.

2. See Exhibit 13.13. The graphs reveal that failure costs are 85% of the total quality costs, suggesting that Auger needs to invest more in control activities to drive down failure costs.

The financial significance of quality costs can be assessed more easily by expressing these costs as a percentage of actual sales. The quality cost report in Example 13.2 reports Auger Company's quality costs as representing 20% of sales for fiscal year 20X1. Given the rule of thumb that quality costs should be no more than about 2 to 4% of sales, Auger Company has ample opportunity to improve profits by decreasing quality costs through improving quality. The quality cost report encourages managers to identify the various costs that should appear in a performance report, to identify the current quality performance level of the organization, and to begin thinking about the level of quality performance that should be achieved.

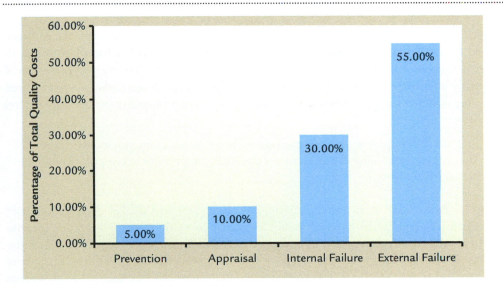

Exhibit 13.13

Quality Cost Categories: Relative Contribution by Category

Exhibit 13.13

Quality Cost Categories: Relative Contribution by Category

Percentage of Total Quality Costs

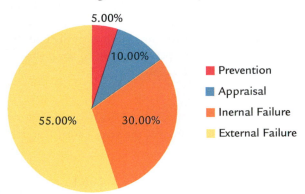

Here's How It's Used: AT ALCOA

In 2011, an executive leadership team of **Alcoa Power and Propulsion (APP)**, a unit of **Alcoa, Inc.**, decided to take steps to improve product quality, reduce waste, and decrease costs. The business unit was experiencing a high incidence of scrap, rework, and returns (internal and external failure costs). Customer satisfaction was low as indicated through customer satisfaction surveys (60% of respondents held an unfavorable or neutral view of the unit).

The initial focus was on the nine foundries that had the highest scrap rates. The strategy was to develop a sustainable and continuous process improvement approach that would achieve the desired improvement goals (e.g., a 10% annual reduction in scrap). Processes were studied and analyzed to determine which ones offered the greatest potential for savings. It was determined that the wax, shell, and cast manufacturing operations had the most potential savings. These processes were then mapped, benchmarking studies were performed,

shop-floor interviews were done, and brainstorming sessions held. Potential solutions were identified and then implemented using a three-stage plan: first, the process improvements were implemented in a pilot plant; and then in fast-follower plants; finally, they were extended to the broader business unit. Quality audits and management reviews were used to ensure process improvement sustainability.

Thus, by using prevention activities such as process management, quality audits, and management reviews, APP was able to significantly reduce scrap, rework, and returns. APP easily exceeded the initial goal of reducing scrap by 10% per year and saved more than $20 million from improvements in the wax, shell, and cast operations. For example, a subprocess of one plant's cast operation reduced scrap and rework costs by more than 30%, which saved $750,000 per year.[12]

CONCEPT CLIP

---

12 Janet Jacobsen, "Process Management Approach Reduces Scrap, Saves Alcoa Millions," *Making the Case for Quality* (May 2016): 1–5.

Controlling Quality Costs

Improving quality and reducing quality costs require that quality costs be reported and controlled. Control enables managers to compare actual outcomes with standard outcomes to gauge performance and take any necessary corrective actions. Performance reports are essential to quality improvement programs. Quality performance reports measure the progress realized by an organization's quality improvement program. Two types of quality performance reports are useful:

1. Progress with respect to a current-period standard or goal (an interim standard report)
2. The progress trend since the inception of the quality improvement program (a multiple-period trend report)

Here's **Why It's important**

Interim Standard Reports Identifying the quality standard is a key element in a quality performance report. The standard should emphasize cost reduction opportunities. **Interim quality standards** express quality goals for the year. The organization must establish an interim quality standard each year and make plans to achieve this targeted level. Often, the interim quality standard is simply the quality costs incurred in the previous year, adjusted for reductions expected from planned quality improvements. Since quality costs are a measure of quality, the targeted level can be expressed in dollars budgeted for each category of quality costs and for each cost item within the category. At the end of the period, the **interim quality performance report** compares the actual quality costs for the period with the budgeted costs. This report measures the progress achieved within the period relative to the planned level of progress for that period. **Example 13.3** illustrates such a report.

EXAMPLE 13.3

How to Prepare an Interim Quality Performance Report

The actual quality costs of Auger Company, for the years ended December 31, 20X1 and 20X2, are provided below.

	20X1	20X2
Prevention costs:		
Quality training	$ 10,000	$ 12,000
Quality engineering	90,000	108,000
Appraisal costs:		
Materials inspection	80,000	98,000
Process acceptance	120,000	145,000
Internal failure costs:		
Scrap	350,000	294,000
Reinspection	250,000	203,000
External failure costs:		
Recalls	500,000	410,000
Product liability	600,000	530,000

At the end of 20X1, management decided to increase its investment in control costs by 20% for each category's items, with the expectation that failure costs would decrease by 20% for each item of the failure categories. Sales were $10,000,000 for both 20X1 and 20X2.

Required:

1. Calculate the budgeted costs for 20X2, and prepare an interim quality performance report.
2. Comment on the significance of the report. How much progress has Auger made?

Solution:

1.

EXAMPLE 13.3

(*Continued*)

Auger Company
Interim Standard Performance Report: Quality Costs
For the Year Ended June 30, 20X2

	Actual Costs	Budgeted Costs	Variance
Prevention costs:			
Quality training	$ 12,000	$ 12,000[a]	$ 0
Quality engineering	108,000	108,000[a]	0
Total prevention costs	$ 120,000	$ 120,000	$ 0
Appraisal costs:			
Materials inspection	$ 98,000	$ 96,000[a]	$ 2,000 U
Process acceptance	145,000	144,000[a]	1,000 U
Total appraisal costs	$243,000	$ 240,000	$ 3,000 U
Internal failure costs:			
Scrap	$ 294,000	$ 280,000[b]	$ 14,000 U
Reinspection	203,000	200,000[b]	3,000 U
Total internal failure costs	$ 497,000	$ 480,000	$ 17,000 U
External failure costs:			
Recalls	$ 530,000	$ 480,000[b]	$ 50,000 U
Product liability	410,000	400,000[b]	10,000 U
Total external failure costs	$ 940,000	$ 880,000	$ 60,000 U
Total quality costs	$1,800,000	$1,720,000	$ 80,000 U
Percentage of sales	18.0%	17.2%	0.8% U

[a] 20X1 actual control cost × 1.20 (e.g., quality training = $10,000 × 1.20 = $12,000)
[b] 20X1 actual failure cost × 0.80 (e.g., scrap = $350,000 × 0.80 = $280,000)

2. Auger has come close to meeting the planned outcomes. Quality costs dropped from 20% of sales to 18.0%, falling 0.8% short of the expected percentage. Management's belief that investing an additional 20% in control costs would produce a 20% reduction in failure costs was somewhat overstated, but the overall outcome is good.

Multiple-Period Trend Reports The interim quality report provides management with information concerning the within-period progress measured relative to specific goals. Also useful is a picture of how the quality improvement program has been doing since its inception. Is the multiple-period trend—the overall change in quality costs—moving in the right direction? Are significant quality gains being made each period? Answers to these questions can be given by providing a chart or graph that tracks the change in quality from the beginning of the program to the present. Such a graph is called a **multiple-period quality trend report**. Trend in quality costs as a percentage of sales reveals the effects of quality improvement initiatives over time. Expressing these trends by quality cost category provides insight concerning the effect of quality improvement initiatives on the relative distribution of quality costs.

Here's Why It's important

Example 13.4 provides a detailed example of multiple-period trend reporting.

EXAMPLE 13.4

How to Prepare Multiple-Period Quality Trend Reports

Assume that Auger Company has experienced the following:

Year	Quality Costs	Actual Sales	Costs as a Percentage of Sales
20X1	$2,000,000	$10,000,000	20.0%
20X2	1,800,000	10,000,000	18.0
20X3	1,680,000	12,000,000	14.0
20X4	1,440,000	12,000,000	12.0
20X5	1,400,000	14,000,000	10.0

By cost category as a percentage of sales for the same period of time:

Year	Prevention	Appraisal	Internal Failure	External Failure
20X1	1.00%	2.00%	6.00%	11.00%
20X2	1.20	2.43	4.97	8.60
20X3	3.00	3.00	3.00	5.00
20X4	4.00	3.00	2.50	2.50
20X5	4.50	1.25	2.25	2.00

Required:

1. Prepare a bar graph that reveals the trend in quality cost as a percentage of cost (time on the horizontal axis and percentages on the vertical axis). Comment on the message of the graph.

2. Prepare a bar graph for each cost category as a percentage of sales. What does this graph tell you?

Solution:

1. See Exhibit 13.14. From Exhibit 13.14, it is clear that there has been a steady downward trend in quality costs as a percentage of sales (dropping from 20 to 10%). The graph also reveals that there is still ample room for improvement.

2. See Exhibit 13.15. From Exhibit 13.15, we can see that Auger has had dramatic success in reducing internal and external failure costs. More money is being spent on prevention. Also, appraisal costs have increased and then decreased, suggesting that Auger is becoming more confident in its prevention initiatives.

Exhibit 13.14

Multiple-Period Trend Graph: Total Quality Costs

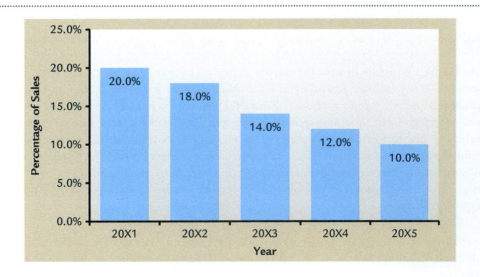

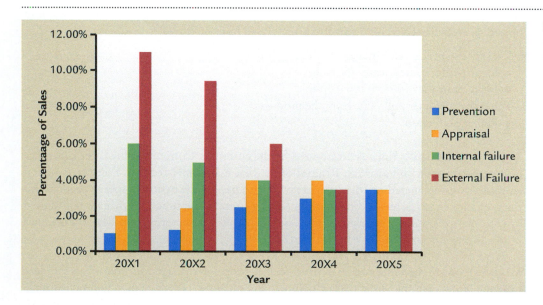

Exhibit 13.15
Multiple-Period Trend Graph:
Individual Quality Cost Categories

Check Point

1. **Which of the following is an internal failure cost?**
   a. **Training production worker in new quality procedures**
   b. **Sampling a batch of goods to determine if the batch has an acceptable defect rate**
   c. **Processing and responding to customer complaints**
   d. **Retesting a reworked product**

Answer:

d. Internal failure is the cost incurred when a defective product is discovered prior to an external sale.

2. **What purposes are served by preparing a quality cost report?**

Answer:

A quality cost report reveals the magnitude of quality costs and also shows the relative distribution of the quality cost categories. The relative distribution allows the manager to assess the importance of the various categories and to determine where quality improvement emphasis is needed.

LEAN MANUFACTURING AND LEAN ACCOUNTING

OBJECTIVE ◀ **4**

Describe the basics of lean manufacturing and lean accounting.

Lean manufacturing is concerned with eliminating waste in manufacturing processes. Promised benefits include such outcomes as reduced lead times, improved quality, improved on-time deliveries, less inventory, less space, less human effort, lower costs, and increased profitability. *Lean accounting* is a simplified approach to costing that supports lean manufacturing with both financial and nonfinancial measures.

Lean Manufacturing

Lean manufacturing is an approach designed to eliminate waste and maximize customer value. It is characterized by delivering the right product, in the right quantity, with the right quality (zero defects), at the exact time the customer needs it, and at the lowest possible cost. These lean objectives are achieved by following five principles of lean thinking:[13]

- Precisely specify value by each particular product.
- Identify the "value stream" for each.
- Make value flow without interruption.
- Let the customer pull value from the producer.
- Pursue perfection.

Value by Product Value is determined by the customer. Customer value is the difference between realization and sacrifice. Realization is what a customer receives. Sacrifice is what a customer gives up, including what they are willing to pay for the basic and special product features, quality, brand name, and reputation. Adding features and functions that are not wanted by customers is a waste of time and resources. Furthermore, attempting to market features and products that customers don't want is a waste of time and resources.

Value Stream The **value stream** is made up of all processes that a product must pass through, from the initial customer order to the delivery to the customer. The most common value stream is called the *order fulfillment value stream.* The order fulfillment value stream focuses on providing current products to current customers. A value stream reflects all that is done—both good and bad—to bring the product to a customer. Thus, analyzing the value stream, called value-stream mapping, allows management to identify waste. Activities within the value stream are value-added or nonvalue-added. Nonvalue-added activities are the source of waste. They are of two types: (1) activities avoidable in the short run and (2) activities unavoidable in the short run due to current technology or production methods. The first type is most quickly eliminated, while the second type requires more time and effort. Exhibit 13.16 visually portrays an order fulfillment value stream. This particular value stream only has one manufacturing cell. Other value streams may have several cells.

Exhibit 13.16

Order Fulfillment Value Stream

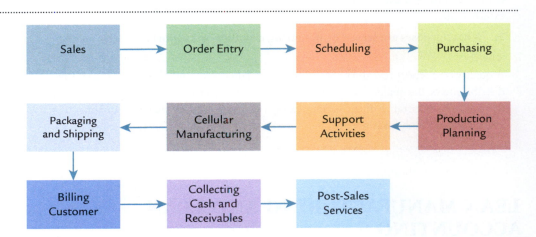

A value stream may be created for every product; however, it is more common to group products that use common processes into the same value stream (families of similar products). Once value streams are identified, then the next step is to assign people and resources to the value streams. As much as possible, the people, the machines, the manufacturing processes, and the support activities need to be dedicated to the value streams. This allows a sense of ownership and provides a means of direct accountability. It also simplifies and facilitates product costing. In a sense, the value stream is its own independent company, a factory within a factory, and the value-stream team is responsible for its improvement, growth, and profitability.

---

13 James Womack and Daniel Jones, *Lean Thinking* (New York: Free Press, 2003).

Value Flow In a traditional manufacturing setup, production is organized by function into departments and products are produced in large batches, moving from department to department. There is significant move time and wait time as each batch *moves* from one department to another and *waits* for its turn if there is a batch in process in front of it. Batches must wait for a preceding batch and a subsequent setup *before* beginning a process. Once a batch starts a process, units are processed sequentially. As units are finished, they must wait for other units in the batch to be finished before the entire batch moves to the next process. Thus, there is pre-process waiting and post-process waiting. Exhibit 13.17 illustrates a traditional batch production process, with the presence of both wait and move times.

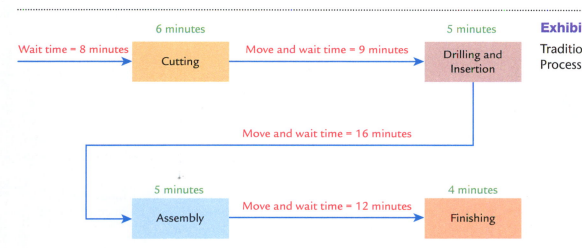

Exhibit 13.17

Traditional Batch Production Process

Color Code:
Red = Nonvalue-added move and pre-process wait time
Green = Value-added process time

Reduced Setup/Changeover Times Lean manufacturing reduces wait and move times dramatically and allows the production of small batches (low volume) of differing products (high variety). The key factors in achieving these outcomes are lower setup times and cellular manufacturing. Reducing the time to configure equipment to produce a different type of product enables *smaller batches in greater variety* to be produced. It also decreases the time it takes to produce a unit of output, thus increasing the ability to respond to customer demand. Customers do not value changeover and therefore it represents waste. While reducing setup times is important, even more critical is the use of cellular or continuous flow manufacturing.

Cellular Manufacturing Lean manufacturing uses a series of cells to produce families of similar products. A lean manufacturing system replaces the traditional plant layout with a pattern of manufacturing cells. Cell structure is chosen over departmental structure because it reduces lead time, decreases product cost, improves quality, and increases on-time delivery. **Manufacturing cells** contain all the operations in close proximity that are needed to produce a family of products. The machines used are typically grouped in a semicircle. The reason for locating processes close to one another is to minimize move time and to keep a continuous flow between operations while maintaining zero inventory between any two operations. The cell is usually dedicated to producing products that require similar operations. Exhibit 13.18 shows a proposed cellular manufacturing structure. Notice that by grouping processes closely together and dedicating the cell to a family of products, the move and wait times are essentially eliminated. Example 13.18 illustrates the value of cellular manufacturing relative to the traditional departmental approach.

Here's **Why It's important**

Exhibit 13.18
Proposed Manufacturing Cell

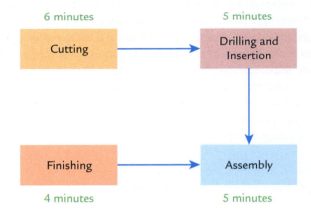

EXAMPLE 13.5

How to Calculate Production Time for Traditional and Cellular Manufacturing

See Exhibits 13.17 and 13.18.

Required:

1. Using Exhibit 13.17, calculate the total time it takes to produce a batch of 12 units, using the traditional departmental structure.

2. Now refer to Exhibit 13.18. With cellular manufacturing, how much time is saved producing the same batch of 12 units? Assuming the cell operates continuously, what is the production rate? Which process controls this production rate?

3. If the processing time of machining is reduced from 6 to 5 minutes, what is the production rate now, and how long will it take to produce a batch of 12 units?

Solution:

1. Total lead time for a batch of 12 units:

    Processing time
Cutting	72 minutes
Drilling and insertion	60 minutes
Assembly	60 minutes
Finishing	48 minutes
Total processing	240 minutes
Move and wait times	45 minutes
Total batch time	285 minutes

2.

    Processing time (12 units):
First unit	20 minutes
Second unit	26 minutes (processing begins 6 minutes after the first)
Twelfth unit	86 minutes (total processing time)

    Time saved over traditional manufacturing: 240 minutes – 86 minutes = 154 minutes

    If the cell is processing continuously, then a unit is produced every 6 minutes after the start-up unit. Thus, the production rate is 10 units per hour (60/6). The *bottleneck* process (the one with the longest per-unit processing time) controls the production rate.

3. Five minutes is now the longest per-unit processing time, and so the production rate is 60/5 = 12 units per hour. Producing 12 units will take 60 minutes.

Pull Value Many firms produce for inventory and then try to sell the excess goods they have produced (*demand-push* system). Efforts are made to create demand for the excess goods—goods that customers probably may not even want. Lean manufacturing uses a *demand-pull* system. Lean manufacturing eliminates waste by producing a product only when it is needed and only in the quantities demanded by customers. Demand pulls products through the manufacturing process. Each operation produces only what is necessary to satisfy the demand of the succeeding operation. Low setup times and cellular manufacturing are the major enabling factors for producing on demand.

A companion to a demand-pull system is *JIT purchasing.* **JIT purchasing** requires suppliers to deliver parts and materials just in time to be used in production, eliminating the need for materials inventories. Supply of parts must be linked to production, which is linked to demand. Lean manufacturers emphasize long-term contracts with suppliers that stipulate prices and acceptable quality levels.

Pursue Perfection Zero setup times, zero defects, zero inventories, zero waste, producing on demand, increasing a cell's production rates, minimizing cost, and maximizing customer value represent ideal outcomes that a lean manufacturer seeks. As the process of becoming lean begins to unfold and improvements are realized, the possibility of achieving perfection becomes more believable. The relentless and continuous pursuit of these ideals is fundamental to lean manufacturing. As production flow increases and processes begin to improve, more hidden waste tends to be exposed. The objective is to produce the highest-quality, lowest-cost products in the least amount of time.

Lean Accounting

Lean manufacturing changes structural and procedural activities, and these changes, in turn, lead to changes in traditional cost management practices. In fact, traditional costing and operational control approaches like standard costing and departmental budgetary variances may encourage overproduction and work against the demand-pull system needed in lean manufacturing. Furthermore, distorted product costs can signal failure for lean manufacturing, even when significant improvements may be occurring. To avoid obstacles and false signals, changes in both product-costing and operational control approaches are needed when moving to a value-stream-based lean manufacturing system.[14]

Focused Value Streams and Traceability of Overhead Costs Creating a value stream for every product within a plant (focused value streams) means that many overhead costs previously assigned to products using either driver tracing or allocation are now directly traceable to products. For example, equipment in a focused value stream is now dedicated to the production of a single product. In this case, depreciation is now a directly traceable product cost. The same is true of other resources such as multiskilled workers, decentralized services, and workers with specialized skills (e.g., industrial engineers and production schedulers). Typically, implementing the value-stream structure does not require an increase in the number of people needed. Lean manufacturing eliminates wasteful activities, reducing the demand for people. For example, when production planning is reduced significantly because of an efficiently functioning demand-pull system, some of those working in production planning can be cross-trained to perform value-added activities within the value stream, such as purchasing and quality control. Exhibit 13.19 is a visual summary of value-stream cost assignments.

---

14 Much of the material on lean accounting is based on two sources: Frances A. Kennedy and Jim Huntzinger, "Lean Accounting: Measuring and Managing the Value Stream," *Cost Management* (September/October 2005): 31–38, and Brian Maskell and Bruce Baggaley, *Practical Lean Accounting* (New York: Productivity Press, 2004).

Exhibit 13.19

Value-Stream Cost Assignments

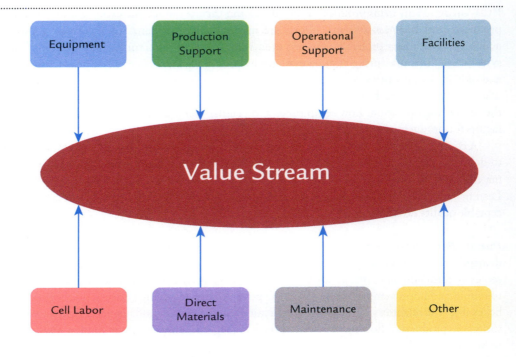

As Exhibit 13.19 shows, most costs are assigned directly to the value stream; however, some costs such as facility costs are assigned to each value stream using cost drivers. Facility costs are assigned using a cost per square foot (total cost/total square feet). If a value stream uses less square feet, it receives less cost. Thus, the purpose of this assignment is to motivate value-stream managers to find ways to occupy less space. As space is made available, it can be used for new product lines or to accommodate increased sales. For example, suppose that the facility costs are $450,000 per year for a plant occupying 30,000 square feet. The cost per square foot is $15. A value stream occupying 10,000 square feet would be assigned a cost of $150,000. If the value-stream manager figures out how to do the same tasks with 5,000 square feet, the cost would be reduced to $75,000. Any unabsorbed facility cost would be deducted from revenue as a separate item.

Limitations   Initially, it may not be possible to assign all the people needed exclusively to a value stream. There may be some individuals working in more than one value stream. The cost of these shared workers can be assigned to individual value streams in proportion to the time spent in each stream. It is also true that even in the most ideal circumstances, some individuals will remain outside any particular value stream (the plant manager, for example). However, with multiple value streams, the unassigned costs are likely to be a very small percentage of the total costs. Finally, in reality, having a value stream for every product is not practical. The usual practice is to organize value streams around a family of products.

Value-Stream Costing

Here's **Why It's important**

Product Costing: Single-product (Focused) Value Stream   In a focused value stream, all value-stream costs belong exclusively to the product that the stream produces and, therefore, are assigned to a product using direct tracing. Value streams increase the number of directly traceable costs and therefore increase the accuracy of product costing. Focused value streams provide simple and accurate product costing. Typically, unit costs are calculated weekly and are based on actual costs, using the following formula:

Value-Stream Product Cost = Total Actual Value-Stream Costs/Units Shipped

Using units shipped in the unit cost calculation instead of units produced motivates managers to reduce inventories. If more units are shipped than produced, then the weekly unit cost will decrease and inventories will reduce. If more is produced than shipped, then the unit cost will increase (because the production costs of the units produced and not shipped are added to the numerator), creating a disincentive to produce for inventory.

Product Costing: Multiple-Product Value Stream Many value streams are formed around products with common processes. Manufacturing cells within a value stream are thus structured to make a family of products or parts that require the same manufacturing sequence. The weekly unit product cost for multiple-product value streams is the sum of each unit's materials cost and the average conversion cost:

Here's **Why It's important**

Value-Stream Product Cost = Unit Materials Cost + Average Conversion Cost

where

Unit Materials Cost (for each product) = Actual Materials Cost/Units Shipped

Average Conversion Cost = Total Actual Conversion Costs/Units Shipped

Here's How It's Used: IN YOUR LIFE

Emily recently joined a large law firm fresh out of law school. She discovered that the 50 employees of the law firm eat lunch every Friday at a popular pizza restaurant. They eat in a separate reserved room. They are served individual bowls of salad ($2.80 each). A two-topping pizza costs $20 and is divided into 10 slices. For drinks, the restaurant provides complimentary tea and water. Each member of the law firm has to pay an assessed amount for the lunch. Since the food had to be ordered in advance, the managing partner gave Emily the assignment to determine how much food to order and how much to charge each individual of the firm for the lunch.

Emily surveyed the members of the firm and compiled the following table that reflected eating preferences (divided into four subgroups):

Group	Number in Each Group	Slices per Person	Total Slices
A	10	1	10
B	10	2	20
C	15	4	60
D	15	6	90
Totals	50	N/A	180

Based on the survey, Emily ordered 18 pizzas (180/10) and noted that the expected cost would be $360 ($20 × 18), with an average pizza cost per person of $7.20 ($360/50). Thus, she

would need to collect $10 ($2.80 + $7.20) from each person to pay for the lunch. This approach is like having one value stream with four products (four different eating patterns). The cost of materials (salads in this case) is assigned directly to each product, and the average conversion cost (average pizza cost) is added to the direct materials cost to obtain a total product cost.

Emily noted, however, that the eating patterns were quite different among the groups. For Group A, the total pizza cost is simply $20 (only one pizza is needed) and the pizza cost per person is $2.00, which when added to the $2.80 gives a lunch cost of $4.80. On the other hand, for Group D, the average pizza cost per person is $12, which when added to the salad cost gives a lunch cost of $14.80. Groups B and C would have lunch costs of $6.80 and $10.80, respectively. Charging by groups is more accurate. Each group would be analogous to a focused value stream.

Another possibility for Emily is to group the employees into a "family of products," where employees with similar eating habits are grouped together. Groups A and B, for example, could form a light-eaters value stream, and Groups C and D would form a heavy-eaters value stream. The light-eaters lunch cost would be $5.80 ($2.80 for salad plus an average pizza cost of $3.00). The heavy-eaters lunch cost would be $12.80 each. Forming value streams has a lot to do with trading off complexity and accuracy. Sometimes simplicity outweighs the issue of accuracy.

CONCEPT CLIP

The materials costs are assigned accurately as they are directly traced to each product. However, all products in the value stream receive the same average conversion cost per unit. The accuracy of the resulting average conversion cost depends on how homogeneous the products are. If they are very similar, then using the average conversion cost will approximate quite closely the individual product cost. Using the average conversion cost is useful provided the products are similar and consume resources in approximately the same proportions. If products are quite similar, the resulting product cost will approximate the individual product costs. Furthermore, if the product mix is stable, then the trend in the average product cost over time is a reasonable measure of changes in economic efficiency. If, however, the products are heterogeneous or reflect a great deal of variety through custom designing, then using average conversion cost is not a good measure for tracking changes in value-stream efficiency. Also, there is no clear indication of what the cost of individual products is. In this case, other product cost calculation approaches are needed—approaches that provide a much better level of accuracy.

Features and Characteristics Costing   An approach called *features and characteristics costing* is recommended (albeit reluctantly) by those advocating the simple average costing approach. This approach recognizes that some product components take more effort (time) to make than others and thus cost more. Differences in features and characteristics cause cost differences. An adjustment is made to the average product cost that reflects this complexity difference. Value streams with heterogeneous products find themselves in the same cost-distortion dilemma as plants with multiple products and plantwide overhead rates. ABC solves the distortion problem using causal tracing. ABC could, of course, be used within a value stream; however, the argument is that ABC is too complex and too data intensive for a lean setting. Yet, there is no compelling evidence that features and characteristics costing provides simplicity with accuracy. A relatively new costing approach, called *duration-based costing* seems to offer both simplicity and accuracy and, thus, may be well suited for multiple-product value streams.

Here's **Why It's important**

Duration-Based Costing   **Duration-based costing (DBC)** uses a single rate to assign conversion costs and approximates a comprehensive ABC system based in duration drivers.[15] To apply DBC to a value stream, first calculate a weekly value-stream conversion cost rate as follows:

$$\text{Conversion Cost Rate} = \text{Total Actual Conversion Costs/Total Net Production Hours}$$

The net total production hours are the *total hours available* for work of all primary activities (activities consumed by products) whether the activities are value- or nonvalue-added. Net hours mean that such things as break times and expected stoppages are excluded and thus correspond to the practical capacity for each activity. Once the rate is calculated, the unit conversion cost is calculated by multiplying the rate by the cycle time for each product:

$$\text{Conversion Cost per Unit} = \text{Conversion Cost Rate} \times \text{Cycle Time}$$

Cycle time is the time that a unit of product spends in the value stream, from start to finish. It is not the same as the production rate.

The actual costs and production hours for a value stream with two products in Holland Company are shown in Exhibit 13.20 for the week ending October 8. Using this information, **Example 13.6** illustrates product costing for single- and multiple-product value streams.

---

15 Adapted from the methodology described in Anne-Marie T. Lelkes and Donald R. Deis, "Using the Production Cycle Time to Reduce the Complexity of ABC," *Journal of Theoretical Accounting Research*, Vol. 9, Issue 1 (Fall 2013): 57–84.

Exhibit 13.20 Value-Stream Costs and Production Hours: Models X12 and Y35

			Holland Company This Week, October 8			
	Net Hours	**Materials**	**Salaries/Wages**	**Machining**	**Other**	**Total Cost**
Order processing	800		$ 18,000			$ 18,000
Production planning	50		2,000			2,000
Purchasing	400		11,000			11,000
Cutting	1,000	$100,000	37,500	$36,000	$18,000	191,500
Welding and drilling	1,200	50,000	42,000	42,000	12,000	146,000
Assembly	250	75,000	25,000	10,000	15,000	125,000
Testing	300		8,500		2,000	10,500
Packaging and shipping	300		9,000			9,000
Invoicing	700		12,000			12,000
Totals	5,000	$225,000	$165,000	$88,000	$47,000	$525,000

EXAMPLE 13.6

How to Calculate Value-Stream Product Costs

See Exhibit 13.20. During the week of October 8, Holland Company produced and shipped 2,000 units of Model X12 and 8,000 units of Model Y35, for a total of 10,000 units. Model X12 has a cycle time of 1.04 hours, and Model Y35 has a cycle time of 0.34 hour.

Required:

1. Assume that the value-stream costs and total units shipped apply only to one model (a single-product value stream). Calculate the unit cost, and comment on its accuracy.

2. Assume that Model X12 is responsible for 50% of the materials cost. Calculate the unit cost for Models X12 and Y35, and comment on its accuracy. Explain the rationale for using units shipped instead of units produced in the calculation.

3. Calculate the unit cost for the two models, using DBC. Explain when and why this cost is more accurate than the unit cost calculated in Requirement 2.

Solution:

1. Unit cost = $525,000/10,000 = $52.50 per unit. The cost is very accurate, as the value stream is dedicated to one product and its costs all belong to that product.

2. First, the unit materials cost is calculated separately:

   Model X12: $112,500*/2,000 = $56.25
   Model Y35: $112,500/8,000 = $14.06

   *50% × $225,000

   Next, the average unit conversion cost is calculated: $300,000*/10,000 = $30.

   *Conversion Cost = Total Cost − Materials Cost
   = $525,000 − $225,000 = $300,000

   Finally, the unit cost is computed (sum of materials and average conversion cost):

   Model X12: $56.25 + $30 = $86.25
   Model Y35: $14.06 + $30 = $44.06

   The accuracy of the unit cost depends on the accuracy of the average unit conversion cost, which depends on the homogeneity of the products within the value stream. Using units shipped for the unit calculation motivates managers to reduce inventories.

(Continued)

EXAMPLE 13.6

(Continued)

3. First, calculate the conversion cost rate:

Conversion Cost Rate = Conversion Cost/Total Net Production Hours
= $300,000/5,000
= $60 per hour

Next, calculate the unit conversion cost for each product:

Conversion Cost per Unit = Conversion Rate × Cycle Time

Model X12: $60 × 1.04 = $62.40
Model Y35: $60 × 0.34 = $20.40

Finally, add the unit materials cost:

Model X12 = $56.25 + $62.40 = $118.65
Model Y35 = $14.06 + $20.40 = $34.46

DBC should be used if the products are not homogeneous products. It is more accurate, as it approximates ABC assignments.

Value-Stream Operational Control

The lean control system replaces the traditional standard costing approach with a Box Scorecard that compares operational, capacity, and financial metrics with prior week performances and with a future desired state. Trends over time and the expectation of achieving some desired state in the near future are the means used to motivate constant performance improvement. Thus, the lean control uses a mixture of financial and nonfinancial measures for the value stream. The future desired state reflects targets for the various measures. Operational, nonfinancial measures are also used at the cell level. A typical value-stream Box Scorecard is shown in Exhibit 13.21 (metrics and format can vary).

Exhibit 13.21

Holland Company Value-Stream Box Scorecard

	For 10/8/20X1 Last Week	This Week (10/8/20X1)	Planned Future State (01/31/20X2)
Operational			
Units sold per person	500	520	540
On-time delivery	88%	90%	95%
Dock-to-dock days	19.5	19.0	17.0
First-time through	65%	75%	85%
Average product cost	$55.00	$52.50	$50.00
Accounts receivable days	28	27	26
Capacity			
Productive	31%	35%	37%
Nonproductive	45%	40%	35%
Available	24%	25%	28%
Financial			
Weekly sales	$950,000	$875,000	$1,250,000
Weekly material cost	$250,000	$225,000	$310,000
Weekly conversion cost	$396,000	$300,000	$365,000
Weekly value-stream profit	$304,000	$325,000	$625,000
ROS	32%	40%	46%

For the operational measures, units sold per person is a partial labor productivity measure and is therefore a measure of labor *efficiency*. Dock-to-dock days is the *time* it takes for a product to be manufactured from the moment the materials arrive at the receiving dock until the finished product is shipped from the shipping dock and thus includes wait time and inventory time. First-time through is a measure of *quality* and is simply the percentage of product that made it through production without being defective and thus needing to be rejected or reworked. For multiple-product value streams, average product cost may be supplemented (or perhaps replaced) with individual product cost information. Capacity is labeled as *productive* (value-added), *nonproductive* (nonvalue-added—used but wasteful), and *available* (unused). The financial measures are also important and are self-explanatory.

The scorecard measures are expected to improve over time and to be helpful in managing and bringing about improvement. For example, from the Box Scorecard in Exhibit 13.21, we see that the nonproductive capacity is targeted to go from 45% (current state) to 35% (future state), with productive capacity increasing from 31 to 37% and available capacity increasing from 24 to 28%. As waste is eliminated, the nonproductive capacity converts into available capacity. The machines, people, and other resources used for wasteful activities are now available for more productive work. For financial performance to improve, some decisions must be made with respect to the increase in available capacity. The most sensible and practical approach is to commit to use the freed-up resources to expand the business. One possibility is to add new product lines. Another possibility is to transfer the resources to other value streams that are in a high-growth state with increasing resource demands. Another is to realize cost reductions by reducing headcount and eliminating resources. This latter approach is the least desirable. It makes it hard to gain the cooperation and involvement of employees with the transformation into a lean workforce if their suggestions and actions are going to lead to the loss of their jobs or the jobs of their friends and coworkers.

Check Point

1. **A manufacturing cell within a value stream is structured with four processes and associated unit processing times:**

   Molding: 7 minutes

   Grinding: 15 minutes

   Polishing: 4 minutes

   Finishing: 2 minutes

   How many units can the cell produce per hour on a continuous running basis (production rate)?

   Answer:
   Using the bottleneck process (Grinding), the production rate is 4 units per hour (60/15).

2. **Suppose a value stream has two products with materials costs of $20,000 and $60,000, respectively, for a given week. The conversion costs for the week are $120,000. The units produced for the first product are 11,000, with 10,000 shipped to customers. For the second product, 20,000 units were produced and shipped. What is the cost per unit for the first product?**

   Answer:
   Unit Cost = Unit Materials Cost + Average Unit Conversion Cost
   = $20,000/10,000 units shipped + ($120,000/30,000 units shipped)
   = $2.00 + $4.00 = $6.00 per unit

OBJECTIVE **5**

Explain the role of the management accountant in the international environment.

INTERNATIONAL ISSUES IN MANAGEMENT ACCOUNTING

In an increasingly global economy, the management accountant provides crucial financial and business expertise. Good training, education, and staying abreast of changes in one's field are important to any accountant. However, the job of the management accountant in the international firm is made more challenging by the ambiguous and ever-changing nature of global business. Since much of the management accountant's job is to provide relevant information to management, staying up to date requires reading books and articles in a variety of business areas, including information systems, marketing, management, politics, and economics. In addition, the management accountant must be familiar with the financial accounting rules of the countries in which the firm operates.

Types of Involvement in the International Economy

Here's Why It's important

Companies can participate in the international environment in a number of ways. Some of the choices are importing and exporting, wholly owned subsidiaries, joint ventures, and the **multinational corporation (MNC)**. Each of these offers both costs and benefits for the company and the management accountant must be aware of them in order to help decision makers determine which, if any, involvement in international trade is best.

Importing and Exporting A relatively simple form of multinational involvement is importing and exporting. Even such simple transactions as importing and exporting can present new risks and opportunities for companies. A company may import materials for use in production. While this transaction may seem identical to the purchase of materials from domestic suppliers, U.S. tariffs add complexity and cost. In accounting for materials, freight-in is a materials cost. An imported part may have a tariff, or duty, in addition to freight-in cost. A **tariff,** or **duty,** is a tax on imports levied by the federal government. In accounting, we treat this tax as part of the cost of the materials. The amount of tax may be decreased sometimes if domestic content is added (making a new product or material) or if the importation of the material occurs in a foreign trade zone.

The U.S. government has set up **foreign trade zones**, which are areas near a customs port of entry that are physically on U.S. soil but are considered to be outside U.S. commerce. San Antonio, New Orleans, and the Port of Catoosa, Oklahoma, are examples of cities with foreign trade zones. Some U.S. companies have set up manufacturing plants within the foreign trade zones. Goods imported into a foreign trade zone are duty-free until they leave the zone for sale in the United States. This has important implications for manufacturing firms that import materials. Since tariffs are not paid until the imported materials leave the zone as part of a finished product, the company can postpone payment of duty and any associated loss of working capital. Additionally, the company does not pay duty on defective materials or on inventory that has not yet been included in finished products. The management accountant must be aware of the costs of importing materials. He or she should also be able to evaluate the potential benefits of the foreign trade zone in considering the location of satellite plants.

Let's take a closer look at two companies. Roadrunner, Inc., operates a petrochemical plant located in a foreign trade zone and imports volatile materials (e.g., chemicals that experience substantial evaporation loss during processing) for use in production. Wilycoyote, Inc., operates an identical plant just outside the foreign trade zone. Each plant imported $400,000 of crude oil for use in chemical production. About 30% of the oil is lost through evaporation during production. Duty is assessed at 6% of cost, and carrying cost is 12% per year. Both companies purchase the material and process it. They sell the finished product 8 months later. What is the amount of duty paid and carrying costs incurred for each company?

Wilycoyote pays duty, at the point of purchase, of $24,000 ($0.06 \times $400,000$). Wilycoyote also has carrying costs associated with the duty payment of 12% per year times the portion of the year that the oil is in materials or finished goods inventory, in this case, 8 months. Total duty-related carrying cost is $1,920 ($0.12 \times 8/12 \times \$24,000$). Total duty and duty-related carrying costs are $25,920. Roadrunner, on the other hand, pays duty at the time of sale because it is in a foreign trade zone, and imported goods do not incur duty until (or unless) they are moved out of the zone. Since 70% of the original imported oil remains in the final product, duty equals $16,800 ($0.70 \times \$400,000 \times 0.06$). There are no carrying costs associated with the duty. A summary of the duty-related costs for the two companies follows:

	Roadrunner	Wilycoyote
Duty paid at purchase	$ 0	$24,000
Carrying costs of duty	0	1,920
Duty paid at sale	16,800	0
Total duty and duty-related cost	$16,800	$25,920

Clearly, Roadrunner has saved $9,120 ($25,920 - $16,800) on just one purchase of imported materials by locating in the foreign trade zone.

Exporting Exporting is the sale of a company's products in foreign countries. However, exporting is usually more complex than the sale of finished goods within the home country. Foreign countries have a variety of import and tariff regulations. The job of complying with the foreign rules and regulations often falls to the controller's office, just as compliance with U.S. tax regulations is an accounting function. Alternatively, a U.S. company may choose to work with an experienced distributor familiar with the legal complexities of the other countries.

Trade treaties between countries affect the tariffs charged. For example, the North American Free Trade Agreement (NAFTA) allows importers in the United States, Mexico, and Canada to pay reduced tariffs on goods produced in the three countries. The Trans-Pacific Partnership (TPP) will charge tariff rates and require member countries to adhere to regulations on human trafficking, child labor, minimum wages, and working conditions. If Vietnam joins the TPP, **Nike** will be able to import shoes without payment of tariff (currently ranging from 8 to 15%). U.S. companies will have improved protection of intellectual property and the ability to sue in international court if the companies feel they are treated worse than Vietnamese companies.[16]

Management accountants must be aware of the customs regulations and ensure that adequate recordkeeping and internal control mechanisms exist.

Wholly Owned Subsidiaries A company may choose to purchase an existing foreign company, making the purchased company a wholly owned subsidiary of the parent. This strategy has the virtue of simplicity. The foreign company has established an outlet for the product and has the production and distribution facilities already set up.

Outsourcing of technical and professional jobs is becoming an important issue for cost-conscious U.S. firms. **Outsourcing** is the payment by a company for a business function formerly done in house. For example, **Levi Strauss** outsourced 10 of its inventory and financial functions to **Wipro**, a Banglore, India, consulting firm, as part of a move designed to save up to $200 million in costs.[17]

Outsourcing is done by foreign firms as well. **Lexus** opened its Kentucky manufacturing plant in 2015. Building cars in the United States allows Lexus to reduce transportation costs as well as currency conversion risk.[18]

---

16 Lydia DePillis, "How More Business with Nike Could Affect Workers in Vietnam," *The Washington Post* (May 8, 2015). Taken from https://www.washingtonpost.com/news/wonk/wp/2015/05/08/how-more-business-with-nike-could-help-workers-in-vietnam/.
17 Kimberly S. Johnson, "Levi Strauss to Outsource Finance Unit," *The Wall Street Journal* (July 13, 2015). Taken from http://blogs.wsj.com/cfo/2015/07/13/levi-strauss-to-outsource-finance-unit/.
18 Aaron M. Kessler, "With a Hush, an American Lexus Plant Goes to Work," *New York Times* (November 12, 2015). Taken from http://www.nytimes.com/2015/11/13/business/with-a-hush-an-american-lexus-plant-goes-to-work.html.

Joint Ventures   Sometimes, companies with the expertise needed by MNCs do not exist or are not for sale. In this case, a joint venture may work. A **joint venture** is a type of partnership in which investors co-own the enterprise.

Sometimes, a joint venture is required because of restrictive laws. In China, for example, MNCs are not allowed to purchase companies or set up their own subsidiaries. Joint ventures with Chinese firms are required. Similarly, India and Thailand demand local ownership. Loctite, maker of Super Glue, runs joint ventures in both India and Thailand for that reason.

A special case of joint venture cooperation is the maquiladora. A **maquiladora** is a manufacturing plant, located in Mexico, that processes imported materials and reexports them to the United States. Originally designed to encourage U.S. firms to invest in Mexico, the program has now expanded to include other foreign firms, such as Nissan Motor and Sony. Basically, the maquiladora enjoys special status in both Mexico, which grants operators an exemption from Mexican laws governing foreign ownership, and the United States, which grants exemptions from or reductions in customs duties levied on reexported goods. The structure of the maquiladora is flexible. Mexico permits different levels of involvement. The minimal level combines low risk with low cost savings. In this case, the U.S. firm transfers materials to an existing Mexican firm and imports them back in finished form. All hiring and operating of the Mexican plant is handled by the Mexican owners. The highest level of involvement offers both high risk and high cost savings. At this level, the U.S. firm owns the Mexican subsidiary and oversees all the operations.

Foreign investment has moved well beyond the border cities to a broad band of northern Mexico. Improvements in the Mexican infrastructure (e.g., roads and communications) have enticed companies further into the interior, lowering nonlabor costs. U.S. companies were originally drawn to the maquiladoras for the cheap labor. Now, both wage rates and other benefits have risen.

U.S. firms have also found other benefits to investment in maquiladoras. For example, Ford's plant in Chihuahua was built to satisfy export requirements for doing business in Mexico. Now, it supports Ford's sales to Mexico, establishing a marketing reason for the plant's presence.

No matter which structure the MNC takes, it faces issues of foreign trade. An important issue is foreign currency exchange, which is addressed in the next section.

Foreign Currency Exchange

When a company operates only in its home country, only one currency is used, and exchange issues never arise. However, when a company begins to operate in the international arena, it may use foreign currencies. These foreign currencies can be exchanged for the domestic currency using **exchange rates.** If the exchange rates never changed, problems would not occur. Exchange rates do change, however, and often on a daily basis. Thus, a dollar that could be traded for 115 yen one day may be worth only 105 yen on another day. Currency rate fluctuations add considerably to the uncertainty of operating in the international arena.

The management accountant plays an important role in managing the company's exposure to risk of currency fluctuations. **Transaction risk** refers to the possibility that future cash transactions will be affected by changing exchange rates. **Economic risk** refers to the possibility that a firm's present value of future cash flows will be affected by exchange rate fluctuations. **Translation** (or **accounting**) **risk** is the degree to which a firm's financial statements are exposed to exchange rate fluctuation. Let's look more closely at these three components of currency risk and ways in which the accountant can manage the company's exposure to them.

Managing Transaction Risk   Currencies may be traded for one another, depending on the exchange rate in effect at the time of the trade. The **spot rate** is the exchange rate of one currency for another for immediate delivery (i.e., today). For example, on June 1, 2017, the spot rate of dollars for euros was $1 = €1.117 and of dollars for yen was $1 = ¥109.5471. You can easily find the spot rates for any currency, using the Internet. Changes in the spot rates can affect the value of a company's future cash transactions, posing transaction risk. Let's first get a feel for currency appreciation and depreciation before we go on to exchange gains and losses.

Here's How It's Used: IN YOUR LIFE

Luisa has been planning all year to spend a summer abroad studying art in Italy. She can join a program with her university that will cover airfare, room and board, and credit for her classes. She's been told that she will need about $3,000 extra for optional side trips within Italy and for food and entertainment outside of the school. In November 2017, when Luisa first began planning her trip, the exchange rate was $1 = €1.07. At that rate, her $3,000 would buy €3,210. In mid-June 2018, Luisa left for Italy. The exchange rate was $1 = €1.27 and her $3,000 could buy €3,810. Luisa was delighted that the dollar had strengthened against the euro, making purchases in euros relatively less expensive and enabling her to buy more.

Luisa's friend Paul also planned a study-abroad trip, but his trip was to Japan. When he began planning in November 2017, the exchange rate was $1 = ¥123.48, and his estimated $3,000 extra amount needed would have equaled ¥370,440. Unfortunately for Paul, the dollar weakened against the yen. By mid-June 2018, the exchange rate was $1 = ¥106.07 and his $3,000 for incidentals only equaled ¥318,210.

When one country's currency strengthens relative to another country's currency, **currency appreciation** occurs, and one unit of the first country's currency can buy more units of the second country's currency. Conversely, **currency depreciation** means that one country's currency has become relatively weaker and buys fewer units of another currency. For example, in the summer of 2015, a weak euro made summer travel to many European countries a relative bargain. Conversely, exports from U.S. firms have decreased due to the weak global economy and a strong dollar that makes American goods more expensive.[19]

CONCEPT CLIP

Let's examine the impact of changes in exchange rates on the sale of goods from a local company to a customer in another country. Example 13.7 shows the effect of currency rate changes on the transaction.

EXAMPLE 13.7

How to Calculate the Value of an Exchange in Another Currency

SuperTubs, Inc., based in Oklahoma, sells its line of whirlpool tubs at home and to foreign distributors. On January 15, Bonbain, a French distributor of luxury plumbing fixtures, orders 100 tubs at a price of $1,000 per tub, to be delivered immediately, and to be paid in euros on March 15. On January 15, the rate of exchange is $1 = €0.80.

Required:

1. Using the January 15 rate of exchange, how many euros will Bonbain pay SuperTubs upon completion of the order? What is the value in dollars?

2. Suppose that on March 15 the rate of exchange was $1 = €0.90. What is the value in dollars of Bonbain's payment in euros?

3. What is the exchange gain (loss) on the order?

4. Now suppose that on March 15, the rate of exchange was $1 = €0.70. What is the value in dollars of Bonbain's payment in euros? What is the exchange gain (loss) on the order?

Solution:

1. Euros to be paid by Bonbain = $100,000 × 0.80 = €80,000

2. Value of Bonbain's payment = €80,000/0.90 = $88,889 (rounded)

3. SuperTubs has realized an exchange loss = $100,000 − $88,889 = $11,111

4. Value of Bonbain's payment = €80,000/0.70 = $114,286 (rounded)

   SuperTubs has realized an exchange gain = $114,286 − $100,000 = $14,286

---

19 Heather Long, "Europe Is on Sale for American Travelers," *CNN Money* (January 27, 2015). Taken from http://money.cnn.com/2015/01/27/investing/europe-cheap-travel-euro-11-year-low/. Jeffry Bartash, "U.S. Exports Fall in 2015 for First Time Since Recession," *Market Watch* (February 5, 2016). Taken from http://www.marketwatch.com/story/us-exports-fall-in-2015-for-first-time-since-recession-2016-02-05.

An **exchange gain** is the gain on the exchange of one currency for another due to appreciation of the home currency. An **exchange loss** is a loss on the exchange of one currency for another due to depreciation of the home currency.

Transaction risk also affects the purchase of commodities from foreign companies. Suppose that on February 20, AmeriMon, Inc. (based in Big Timber, Montana) purchases computers from **NEC** (located in Japan) for $50,000, payable in yen on May 20. Assume the spot rate for yen is 130 per dollar on February 20. It is easy to see that AmeriMon's true payable is for 6,500,000 yen ($50,000 × 130). If the spot rate for yen is 135 on May 20, it will cost AmeriMon only $48,148 (6,500,000/135) to get enough yen to pay NEC:

Liability in dollars on February 20	$50,000
Liability in dollars on May 20	48,148
Exchange gain	$ 1,852

As we can see, the more favorable May 20 spot rate has resulted in an exchange gain. Clearly, transaction risk caused by the movement of foreign currency against the dollar must be taken into account by managers, as it affects the prices paid and received for goods. If the company does not want to be involved in gambling on exchange rates, the management accountant can either encourage the company to make all imports/exports in dollars or can engage in hedging (a form of insurance against transaction risk). Typically, a forward exchange contract is used as a hedge. The **forward contract** requires the buyer to exchange a specified amount of a currency at a specified rate (the **forward rate**) on a specified future date. For example, suppose AmeriMon is concerned that the rate of yen for dollars will decrease, from 130 yen per dollar on January 15 to potentially 120 yen per dollar on May 20. If the forward rate is ¥128 = $1, the company can purchase a contract to lock in that rate. The 2-yen difference between the spot rate of 130 and the forward rate of 128 is the premium that AmeriMon pays the exchange dealer on the transaction. Think of it as an insurance premium.

Managing Economic Risk   Dealing in different currencies can introduce an economic dimension into currency exchange transactions. Recall that economic risk was defined as the impact of exchange rate fluctuations on the present value of a firm's future cash flows. The risk can affect the relative competitiveness of the firm, even if it never participates directly in international trade. Take a simple example based on the market for heavy equipment.

Suppose that U.S. consumers can choose to purchase heavy equipment from either **Caterpillar** (based in the United States) or from **Komatsu** (based in Japan). Assume the price of one type of equipment is $80,000 from both makers. However, while Caterpillar truly means $80,000, Komatsu really is interested in ¥10,400,000, its own currency. At an exchange rate of $1 = ¥130, the price of $80,000 is set. Now suppose that the value of the dollar strengthens against the yen and the exchange rate becomes $1 = ¥140. To get the same ¥10,400,000, Komatsu requires a price of only $74,286. The cost structures of the two firms have not changed nor has customer demand, but because of currency fluctuations, the Japanese firm has become more "competitive." Of course, as the dollar weakens, the position is reversed, and U.S. exports become relatively cheaper to foreign customers.

How does the accountant manage the company's exposure to economic risk? Most importantly, he or she must be aware of it by understanding the position of the firm in the global economy. As we can see in the Caterpillar–Komatsu example, the two firms were competitors and were linked through their customers' participation in the global marketplace. The accountant provides financial structure and communication for the firm. In preparing the master budget, for example, budgeted sales must take into account potential strengthening or weakening of the currencies of competitors' countries. Often, the controller's office is responsible for forecasting foreign exchange movements.

Transfer Pricing and the Multinational Firm

For the multinational firm, transfer pricing must accomplish two objectives: performance evaluation and optimal determination of income taxes.

Performance Evaluation Divisions are frequently evaluated on the basis of income and return on investment. As is the case for any transfer price, the selling division wants a high transfer price that will raise its income, and the buying division wants a low transfer price that will raise its income. But transfer prices in multinational companies are frequently set by the parent company, making the use of ROI and income suspect. Because they are not under the control of divisional managers, they may no longer serve as good indicators of management performance.

Income Taxes and Transfer Pricing If all countries had the same tax structure, then transfer prices would be set independently of taxes. However, this does not happen. Instead, there are high-tax countries (like the United States) and low-tax countries (such as the Cayman Islands). As a result, multinational companies may use transfer pricing to shift costs to high-tax countries and shift revenues to low-tax countries.

Exhibit 13.22 illustrates this concept as two transfer prices are set. The first transfer price is $100 as title for the goods passes from the Belgian subsidiary to the reinvoicing center in Puerto Rico. Because the first transfer price is equal to full cost, profit is zero, and taxes on zero profit also equal zero. The second transfer price is set at $200 by the reinvoicing center in Puerto Rico. The transfer from Puerto Rico to the United States does result in profit, but this profit does not result in any tax because Puerto Rico has no corporate income taxes. Finally, the U.S. subsidiary sells the product to an external party at the $200 transfer price. Again, price equals cost, so there is no profit on which to pay income taxes.

Action	Tax Impact
Belgian subsidiary of parent company produces a component at a cost of $100 per unit. Title to the component is transferred to a reinvoicing center* in Puerto Rico at a transfer price of $100 per unit.	42% tax rate $100 revenue − $100 cost = $0 Taxes paid = $0
Reinvoicing center in Puerto Rico, also a subsidiary of parent company, transfers title of component to U.S. subsidiary of parent company at a transfer price of $200 per unit.	0% tax rate $200 revenue − $100 cost = $100 Taxes paid = $0
U.S. subsidiary sells component to external company at $200 each.	35% tax rate $200 revenue − $200 cost = $0 Taxes paid = $0

*A reinvoicing center takes title to the goods but does not physically receive them. The primary objective of a reinvoicing center is to shift profits to divisions in low-tax countries.

Exhibit 13.22

Use of Transfer Pricing to Affect Taxes Paid

Consider what would have happened without the reinvoicing center. The goods would have gone directly from Belgium to the United States. If the transfer price was set at $200, the profit in Belgium would have been $100, subject to the 42% tax rate. Alternatively, if the transfer price set was $100, no Belgian tax would have been paid, but the U.S. subsidiary would have realized a profit of $100 and that would have been subject to the U.S. corporate income tax rate of 35%.

U.S.-based multinationals are subject to Internal Revenue Code Section 482 on the pricing of intercompany transactions. This section gives the IRS the authority to reallocate income and deductions among divisions if it believes that such reallocation will reduce potential tax evasion. Basically, Section 482 requires that sales be made at "arm's length." That is, the transfer price set should match the price that would be set if the transfer were being made by unrelated parties, adjusted for differences that have a measurable effect on the price. There are four potential transfer prices sanctioned by the IRS. Their discussion is reserved to more advanced courses.

Managers may legally avoid taxes. They may not evade them. The distinction is important. Unfortunately, the difference between avoidance and evasion is less a line than a blurry gray area. While the situation depicted in Exhibit 13.22 is clearly abusive, other tax-motivated actions are not. For example, a multinational company may legally decide to establish a needed research and development center within an existing subsidiary in a high-tax country, since the costs are deductible. Multinational companies may also use tax-planning information systems that attempt to accomplish global tax minimization. This is not an easy task.

Ethical Decisions

Business ethics pose difficulties in a single-country context, but they pose far more problems in a global context. Given these difficulties, how does the modern corporation conduct business in an ethical manner? Is each country different? Is there a baseline? Some research indicates that human societies do share an ethical basis. However, there are some prerequisites for the establishment of an ethical business environment. These include basic societal stability, legitimacy and accountability of government, legitimacy of private ownership and personal wealth, confidence in one's own and society's future, confidence in the ability to provide for one's family, and knowledge of how the system works and how to participate. ●

A strong underlying system is important for enforcing contracts and provides the basis for confidence in ethical dealings. For some countries (e.g., the United States and Western European countries), that system is legal, with deviations punishable by law. For others (e.g., Japan and countries in the Middle East), it is cultural, and deviations are punished at least as severely by loss of honor.

Other ethical problems with differing business laws exist. U.S. companies that contract with overseas firms may find themselves the target of unfavorable publicity on use of child labor. During the 1990s, Nike was criticized for low wages (as little as $0.14 per hour in Indonesia), unsafe working conditions, and the use of child labor. Protests outside Niketown stores and rampant bad publicity led Nike CEO Phil Knight to announce a turnaround. Nike would raise wages, enforce U.S. clean air standards in the workplace, and raise the minimum age of workers. Nike audits its overseas factories and publishes its standards and audit data in annual reports. The company also banded together with other apparel and sporting goods companies to address poor conditions in overseas factories.[20]

---

20 Max Nisen, "How Nike Solved Its Sweatshop Problem," *Business Insider* (May 9, 2013). Taken from http://www.businessinsider.com/how-nike-solved-its-sweatshop-problem-2013-5.

Check Point

1. A company builds a manufacturing plant in a foreign trade zone. Materials costing $1 million each month are imported. The duty is 8%. About 10% of the materials are defective and disposed of as waste. What is the savings to the company of locating inside a foreign trade zone?

Answer:

Each month, the company pays a duty of $72,000 ($1,000,000 × 0.9 × 0.08), since only 90% of the material is good and can be sold. If the company were located outside the foreign trade zone, a duty of $80,000 ($1,000,000 × 0.08) would be paid. The savings is $8,000 per month.

2. Casey Company purchases pottery from Mexico for resale in its southwestern gift shops. Purchases must be made in pesos. On May 1, Casey purchased goods costing 50,000 pesos and agreed to pay, in pesos, on June 1. The spot rates of dollars for pesos are as follows:

   May 1 $1 = 18.25

   June 1 $1 = 18.84

   How many pesos does Casey expect to pay on June 1? What is the dollar value of the cost on May 1? On June 1? Did Casey have an exchange gain or an exchange loss?

   Now suppose the exchange rate of dollars for pesos on June 1 is $1 to 18 pesos. How many dollars must Casey pay to cover the 50,000 peso cost of the merchandise? Did Casey have an exchange gain or an exchange loss?

Answer:

Casey has agreed to pay 50,000 pesos on June 1. On May 1, Casey thinks that will cost $2,739.73 (50,000 pesos/18.25). On June 1, Casey must actually pay $2,653.93 (50,000 pesos/18.84) to get 50,000 pesos. There has been an exchange gain on the transaction.

Now with a June 1 spot rate of $1 = 18 pesos, Casey must still make a 50,000 pesos payment on June 1; however, it will cost $2,777.78 (50,000 pesos/18) to buy that amount of pesos. There is an exchange loss on the transaction.

THE ROLE OF COST AND MANAGERIAL ACCOUNTING IN FRAUD AND FORENSIC ACCOUNTING

OBJECTIVE ◀ 6

Explain the role of the management accountant in fraud and forensic accounting.

Fraud and forensic accounting are new, growing areas of importance for the management accountant. The management accountant is involved in fraud prevention and detection. The management accountant is also involved with **forensic accounting**, which is the application of accounting knowledge in legal or other cases to help resolve different types of disputes. Successful fraud and forensic accountants have strong technical expertise in all areas of accounting, good investigative skills, and excellent communications skills.

Here's **Why It's important**

Fraud and Management Accounting

Fraud is defined as wrongful or criminal deception intended to result in financial or personal gain. Fraud committed by employees is occupational fraud and is often tied to the fraud triangle. According to the Association of Certified Fraud Examiners (ACFE), the **fraud triangle** is a model that explains the factors causing someone to commit fraud. The three components are:

- Perceived unshareable financial need
- Perceived opportunity
- Ability to rationalize the commission of fraud

Basically, it is more likely that a person will engage in fraud if they feel financial need, think they can successfully get away with fraud, and can lead themselves to believe the fraud is acceptable—even if only to themselves. Note that all three components must occur to encourage the individual to commit fraud. The fraud triangle helps explain how previously stellar employees can be led to commit fraud.

The fraud triangle also suggests the importance of stopping fraud. Most companies work hard to minimize opportunity and have policies that make it hard to commit successful fraud. For example, some companies require all employees to take at least some vacation each year. Many types of fraud would be discovered if the employee was not on site to continue the cover-up. Mandatory vacation means that another employee will fill in—possibly discovering anomalies. (Note that in the following Here's How It's Used box, Rita Crundwell's fraud was discovered while she was on vacation and another employee took over her duties during the interim.) Companies may require two signatures on any check or payment over a particular amount. Companies also try to understand human weaknesses and vulnerabilities. Human resources may make it a policy to check for sudden changes in an employee's situation, such as a sudden illness in the family. The HR department can help employees find sources of additional funds or outside help during the problem times. Fraud hotlines help employees report anything that seems strange, and then management and management accountants can follow up.

Fraud is discovered in a number of ways.

- Tips: about 45%
- Accident: about 15%
- Internal audit: about 15%
- Internal controls: about 15%
- External audit: about 10%

Here's How It's Used: EMBEZZLEMENT IN A SMALL TOWN

A notorious case in Dixon, Illinois, involved the town's comptroller and treasurer, Rita Crundwell. Over a period of 22 years, she embezzled over $53 million from the town coffers. Her scheme was simple and highly successful. She opened a secret bank account called the RSCDA (Reserve Sewer Capital Development Account) which she made to appear to be a city account—with herself as the only signatory. City funds were deposited into another city account (the Capital Development Fund) and then false invoices were used to support checks written on that account to "Treasurer" and then deposited in the RSCDA. Crundwell then used the money to support her American quarter horse breeding operation as well as a lavish lifestyle.

How did that amount of embezzlement go unnoticed for so long? Crundwell was well thought of as an employee and did a good job covering her tracks. She also had ready answers for questions on the bare-bones budget required of city departments and draconian cuts in services. The fraud eventually came to light while Crundwell was on an extended vacation. Another employee, acting in her stead, discovered the secret account and the numerous checks written on it. She went to higher-ups and alerted the FBI. A 6-month investigation—kept secret from Crundwell—discovered the extensive fraud. Crundwell was indicted and admitted to wire fraud and money laundering. She is currently serving time in a federal correctional facility, and is scheduled for release in 2030.

Note that over half the cases of fraud are discovered through tips and by accident. Something is strange and an individual asks management about it. In one instance, an employee of a local chamber of commerce got a manicure at a local salon. The manicurist mentioned that the chamber was a great employer—why just recently, another employee (let's call her Cindy) paid for her manicure with a check drawn on the chamber—given to her, she said, as a birthday present. The problem is that the first employee did not get that birthday present. She checked with the chamber CEO who asked for an audit of the financial records to see what was going on. A $20,000+ fraud was discovered, documented, and reported to authorities. This is an example of the investigative abilities of the management accountant. Here, the accountant sat down with the books and combed through them for anything unusual. One thing that jumped out was the number of checks written to the **U.S. Post Office**. The accountant asked the CEO: Do you send out that many packages or mailings? The answer was "No." Further investigation revealed that the checks had been written by Cindy to herself and when the bank statements came in, Cindy—responsible for reconciliation—altered the payee after the fact and recorded the "new" check. Additionally, Cindy used the chamber credit card for personal purposes. While some purchase were legitimate, such as paper products and plastic cups for chamber receptions, others were not. Notably, the card was used to buy dog food and the chamber had no pets.

Prevention is as important as detection. The most important thing for companies or nonprofit entities to do is to stay aware of financial matters. A small veterinary practice in the Midwest found that its office manager had embezzled over $100,000 during a 2-year period. If the veterinarians/owners had been more aware of their financial situation and understood their costs and revenues, they would have noticed the shortfall much sooner and stopped the losses. It should have been a simple matter to do a quick calculation of the revenue earned each week by multiplying the average amount charged by the number of patients seen. While the office manager was caught and sent to jail, that did not get the practice's money back—it had been spent.

Ethical Decisions

Clearly, this section on fraud demonstrates ethical lapses. The bottom line is that fraud requires lying and deception. The fraud, by nature, is not supposed to happen. So the fraudster must lie continually to make it work. Those with access to funds must be aware of the opportunity and ability to rationalize. Many employees do not believe they are getting paid what they are worth. It's a short leap to believing they have the right to make up for it by taking something when possible. The way to nip this in the bud is to recognize one's own ability and potential desire to rationalize and stop it. One good way might be to envision Rita Crundwell, in prison until 2030. ●

The ACFE is the largest provider of antifraud training and education. The association sponsors the **Certified Fraud Examiner (CFE)** credential. CFEs have undertaken academic and professional requirements and have passed the Certified Fraud Examiner exam. This exam tests the applicant's knowledge of the four main areas of fraud examination: fraud prevention and deterrence, financial transactions and fraud schemes, investigation, and the law. Its website (www.acfe.com) gives details on membership and CFE requirements.

Forensic Accounting in Management Accounting

Nearly all cases in fraud and forensic accounting involve the identification and quantification of financial damages resulting from the issues raised in the case. The plaintiff in a case attempts to prove that some amount of financial damages did occur, while the defendant attempts to prove that either no or minimal damages occurred. Each party in the case uses cost/managerial concepts to support and defend their damage estimates. The major areas of forensic practice involve fraud, litigation support, and business valuations.

Important managerial accounting concepts include incremental/differential costs, relevant costs, activity-based costing, cost behavior, cost-volume-profit analysis, and the matching principle. Just as important as understanding and applying these concepts is the ability to explain them clearly and persuasively to opponents, judges, and a jury. This requires that the forensic accounting expert be very knowledgeable and skilled in defending these concepts. Exhibit 13.23 shows the use of various cost and management accounting concepts in forensic accounting.

Exhibit 13.23

Applying Different Types of Accounting Knowledge to Forensic Accounting

- *Cost behavior* is used in almost all damage calculations to determine the amount of financial harm that resulted from the liability found by the court. Cost behavior is also an important determinant of whether predatory pricing has occurred in an antitrust case.
- *Differential/incremental costs* are used in the calculation of damages in answering questions about the type and amount of costs to include in the damage calculation. Frequently, the issue in a breach of contract case is the determination of which costs are different as a result of the contract breach. The concept of *relevant costs* is useful in determining which costs relate to the issues being litigated. For example, lost wages are relevant in measuring damages in a wrongful discharge case, but value of lost household services would not be relevant in calculating damages.
- The *matching concept* is useful in determining which costs logically should be matched with contract revenue in a breach of contract case.
- *Consistency* is a useful concept in evaluating whether a company has changed accounting policy or practices in measuring costs that should be charged under a contract. For example, in a cost-based government contract, a frequent question that arises pertains to the appropriateness of a company using accelerated depreciation to charge the government for its share of facility deprecation costs when the company uses straight-line depreciation for all other purposes.

Source: Taken from Lester E. Heitger and Dan L. Heitger, "Incorporating Forensic Accounting and Litigation Advisory Services into the Classroom," *Issues in Accounting Education* (November 2008): 561–572. Used with permission.

The nature of forensic accounting activities is both interesting and challenging. For example, some common characteristics of forensic accounting practice include detective work and problem solving, its adversarial nature, a range of answers rather than one correct answer, and the importance of excellent communications skills.

Detective work and problem solving: Because there is conflict in most cases, some data and information are not clear or readily available. The accountant must use his/her knowledge and skills to find, assemble, and present the relevant information in the best and most understandable way possible.

Adversarial nature: Because virtually all court cases involve conflict of some sort, the accounting expert must learn to work, analyze, and present information for the court in an adversarial environment. Because there are differences of opinion about case issues, accounting issues, and measurements in the case, forensic accountants must be effective in an adversarial environment.

Range of potential answers: Often, there is not a correct answer, but only better or more persuasive answers. Many cases have legitimate differences of opinion. A forensic accountant must decide what is the better, more logical, and more persuasive solution to the dispute, given the information and issues. The accountant uses his/her best judgment to determine the best answer to the issues in the case.

Excellent communication skills: Strong communications skills, both written and oral, are essential. Accountants often need to explain the financial information to laypeople because judges and juries typically know very little about accounting concepts. In addition, the adversarial nature of the work means that the opposing side will be doing its best to argue against the tack taken by the forensic accountant. Thus, the forensic accountant must both explain concepts and rebut the opposing views. Written communications skills are essential, as the accountant must write reports that explain accounting concepts as well as the value determined.

It is difficult to overstate the value of the role of managerial/cost accounting in litigating and resolving cases. Whether criminal fraud, litigation, valuations, or any other type of dispute, the crucial issues of how much the damages are typically can only be resolved by accurate and defendable cost/managerial measurements. Even the liability side of a trial may be impacted by the knowledge and testimony of forensic accounting cost experts. For example, determining whether or not "predatory pricing" took place in an antitrust case is determined by whether or not a company priced products or services below their average variable costs. In summary, managerial/cost accountants play a crucial role in the world of forensic accounting.

Check Point

1. What are the three legs of the fraud triangle?

Answer:

They are financial need, opportunity, and ability to rationalize.

2. Jim Alberts is majoring in accounting at the local college. Jim is highly intelligent and very knowledgeable about all areas of accounting. He would like to go into forensic accounting. Jim is not a skilled writer or speaker, but he feels that is no problem, since most accountants work in solitude anyway. Is he right? What advice would you give him in order to maximize his chances of working in forensic accounting?

Answer:

Communications skills are vital to the forensic accountant. Jim will need to be able to explain accounting concepts clearly and succinctly to judges and juries. He will need both written and oral communications skills.

SUMMARY OF LEARNING OBJECTIVES

LO1. Explain enterprise risk management and its importance for achieving strategy.
- The most important reason for using enterprise risk management is to help the organization achieve its strategy through identifying, measuring, and managing its most important risks and opportunities.
- Determining an organization's desired level of risk taking, or risk appetite, is necessary to ensure that its portfolio of risks and opportunities aligns with the returns expected from shareholders and other key stakeholders.
- After determining risk appetite, enterprise risk management involves identifying the top risks, assessing risks at the inherent level, and managing (or responding to) risks such that the remaining residual risks align with the organization's risk appetite.
- Risk monitoring is the final step in the iterative enterprise risk management process, whereby management continually searches for emerging risks, reevaluates the accuracy of its risk assessments, and considers more effective risk response alternatives.

LO2. Understand the role of managerial accounting in business sustainability.
- Business sustainability focuses on creating long-term organizational value through internally understanding, measuring, and managing the key threats and opportunities to achieving the organization's strategy and then externally reporting to key stakeholders on the successes and failures of such efforts.

- The important aspects of business sustainability can be characterized in the business sustainability cycle, which includes strategy, stakeholder engagement, risk management, performance measurement, stakeholder reporting, and sustainability assurance.
- Managerial accounting plays an increasingly important role in the business sustainability cycle, including areas such as in quantifying the results of stakeholder engagement activities, providing critical inputs to the enterprise risk management process, creating nonfinancial and financial performance measures relevant to the organization's top risks and opportunities, and communicating the organization's overall business sustainability "story", both qualitatively and quantitatively.

LO3. Define quality costs and describe the approaches used for reporting and controlling quality costs.
- Quality costs are the costs of preventing or detecting poor quality.
- There are four categories of quality costs: prevention, appraisal, internal failure, and external failure.
- A quality cost report is prepared by listing costs for each item within each of the four major quality cost categories.
- Knowing total quality costs allows managers to assess their financial importance.
- Knowing the distribution of quality costs by category allows managers to assess the relative importance of each category.
- An interim quality cost report compares actual quality costs with budgeted quality costs and allows managers to assess the effectiveness of its quality improvement efforts for the period.
- A multiple-period trend report provides a trend graph for several years and allows managers to assess the direction and change of quality costs since the inception of its quality improvement program.

LO4. Describe the basics of lean manufacturing and lean accounting.
- Lean manufacturing is characterized by lean thinking—focusing on customer value, value streams, production flow, demand-pull, and perfection.
- Value streams are made up of all activities, both value-added and nonvalue-added, required to bring a product group or service from its starting point (e.g., customer order or concept for a new product) to a finished product in the hands of the customer.
- Value-stream analysis allows waste to be identified and eliminated.
- Lean accounting is an approach designed to support and encourage lean manufacturing.
- Average costing and the expanded use of nonfinancial measures for operational control are typical lean accounting approaches.
- The average product cost is the total value-stream cost of the period divided by the units shipped in the period.
- Lean control uses a mix of operational, capacity, and financial metrics to monitor and improve performance.

LO5. Explain the role of the management accountant in the international environment.
- The management accountant provides financial and business expertise and must stay up to date on the ever-changing international business environment.
- Companies involved in international business may engage in import and export activities, purchase wholly owned subsidiaries, or participate in joint ventures.
- Three types of foreign currency risk are transaction risk, economic risk, and translation risk.
- Multinational companies with subsidiaries in both high- and low-tax countries may use transfer pricing to shift costs to the high-tax countries (where their deductibility will lower tax payments) and to shift revenues to low-tax countries.

LO6. Explain the role of the management accountant in fraud and forensic accounting.
- Fraud is wrongful or criminal deception intended to result in financial or personal gain.
- The triangle is a model that explains what makes someone commit fraud. Its components are:
  - Perceived unshareable financial need
  - Perceived opportunity
  - Ability to rationalize the commission of fraud
- Forensic accounting is the application of accounting knowledge in legal or other cases to help resolve different types of disputes.
  - Fraud
  - Litigation support
  - Business valuation
- Many cost concepts are critical in determining valuation.

SUMMARY OF IMPORTANT EQUATIONS

1. Risk Response Benefit = Inherent Risk − Residual Risk

2. Risk Response Net Benefit = Response Benefit − Response Cost

3. Value-Stream Product Cost = Total Actual Value-Stream Costs/Units Shipped

4. Value-Stream Product Cost = Unit Materials Cost + Average Conversion Cost

5. Unit Materials Cost (for each product) = Actual Materials Cost/Units Shipped

6. Average Conversion Cost = Total Actual Conversion Costs/Units Shipped

7. Conversion Cost Rate = Total Actual Conversion Costs/Total Net Production Hours

8. Conversion Cost per Unit = Conversion Cost Rate × Cycle Time

EXAMPLE 13.1	How to use net benefit to evaluate risk response alternatives, page 707
EXAMPLE 13.2	How to prepare a quality cost report, page 721
EXAMPLE 13.3	How to prepare an interim quality performance report, page 724
EXAMPLE 13.4	How to prepare multiple-period quality trend reports, page 726
EXAMPLE 13.5	How to calculate production time for traditional and cellular manufacturing, page 730
EXAMPLE 13.6	How to calculate value-stream product costs, page 735
EXAMPLE 13.7	How to calculate the value of an exchange in another currency, page 741

KEY TERMS

Appraisal costs, 720, cost incurred to determine whether products and services are conforming to requirements.

Business sustainability, 709, the practice of creating long-term organizational value through internally understanding, measuring, and managing the key threats and opportunities to achieving the organization's strategy and then externally reporting to key stakeholders on the successes and failures of such efforts.

Certified Fraud Examiner (CFE), 747, a premier credential for the forensic accountant, administered by the Association of Certified Fraud Examiners.

Control costs, 720, the costs of preventing or detecting poor quality.

Corporate sustainability reporting (CSR), 715, the voluntary public disclosure of qualitative and/or quantitative information about an organization's performance on one or more financial and/or nonfinancial dimensions.

Costs of quality, 720, costs that exist because poor quality may or does exist.

Currency appreciation, 741, when one country's currency strengthens relative to another country's currency.

Currency depreciation, 741, when one country's currency weakens relative to another country's currency.

Cycle time, 734, the length of time required to produce one unit of a product.

Defective product, 719, a product or service that does not conform to specifications.

Duration-based costing (DBC), 734, uses a single rate to assign conversion costs and approximates a comprehensive ABC system based in duration drivers.

Economic risk, 740, the possibility that a firm's present value of future cash flows will be affected by exchange rate fluctuations.

Enterprise risk management (ERM), 702, the formal process of aligning an organization's overall desired level of risk taking with its strategy and then managing its top risks in a manner that maintains this alignment.

Exchange gain, 742, the gain on the exchange of one currency for another due to appreciation of the home currency.

Exchange loss, 742, the loss on the exchange of one currency for another due to depreciation of the home currency.

Exchange rates, 740, the rate at which one unit of a currency can be traded for another currency.

External failure costs, 720, costs incurred because products fail to conform to requirements after being sold to outside parties.

Failure costs, 720, the costs incurred by an organization because failure activities are performed.

Foreign trade zones, 738, areas near a customs port of entry that are physically on U.S. soil but are considered by the U.S. government to be outside U.S. commerce. Goods entering a foreign trade zone are not subject to duty until they leave the zone.

Forensic accounting, 745, the application of accounting knowledge in legal or other cases to help resolve different types of disputes.

Forward contract, 742, requires the buyer to exchange a specified amount of a currency at a specified rate (the forward rate) on a specified future date.

Forward rate, 742, the currency exchange rate specified for a particular future date.

Fraud, 745, wrongful or criminal deception intended to result in financial or personal gain.

Fraud triangle, 746, a model that explains the factors causing someone to commit fraud. The factors are: opportunity, perceived need, and ability to rationalize the fraudulent actions.

Greenwashing, 719, a situation in which stakeholders believe that an organization's corporate sustainability report contains environmental information that is materially biased in favor of the reporting organization.

Inherent risk, 703, the risk that exists absent of any risk management action to reduce or avoid the risk.

Integrated reporting, 719, the combination of an organization's annual report (i.e., 10-K) with its sustainability report to form one combined (or integrated) report for all stakeholders, including investors.

Interim quality performance report, 724, a comparison of current actual quality costs with short-term budgeted quality costs.

Interim quality standards, 724, a standard based on short-run quality goals.

Internal failure costs, 720, costs incurred because products and services fail to conform to requirements where lack of conformity is discovered prior to external sale.

JIT purchasing, 731, a system that requires suppliers to deliver parts and materials just in time to be used in production.

Joint venture, 740, a type of partnership in which investors co-own the enterprise.

Lean manufacturing, 727, an approach designed to eliminate waste and maximize customer value.

Manufacturing cells, 729, a plant layout where all the operations (machines) that are needed to produce a family of products are grouped in close proximity, typically in a semicircle.

Maquiladora, 740, a manufacturing plant, located in Mexico, that processes imported materials and re-exports them to the United States.

Multinational corporation (MNC), 738, a company with divisions in more than one country.

Multiple-period quality trend report, 725, a graph that plots quality costs (as a percentage of sales) against time.

Outsourcing, 739, the payment by a company for a business function formerly done in house.

Portfolio ERM perspective, 705, the practice of managing a company's most important risks in a collective (or portfolio) fashion, such that the residual risks that remain align with the company's risk appetite.

Prevention costs, 720, costs incurred to prevent or detect poor quality.

Quality of conformance, 719, a product or service that conforms to its design requirements or specifications.

Quality product or service, 719, a product or service that meets or exceeds customer expectations.

Residual risk, 705, the risk that remains after any risk management action has been taken.

Risk appetite, 703, an organization's overall desired level of risk taking.

Risk response benefit, 705, the difference between the inherent risk and the residual risk produced by the particular risk response.

Risk response cost, 706, the incremental cost incurred by the company to implement the given risk response.

Risk response net benefit, 706, the benefit of the risk response minus the cost of risk response.

Spot rate, 740, the exchange rate of one currency for another for immediate delivery.

Stakeholder engagement, 712, the process by which an organization's management interacts with its key stakeholders.

Stakeholders, 710, those individuals or groups that (1) are affected by an organization's pursuit of its strategy *or* (2) can affect an organization's ability to achieve its strategy.

Sustainability assurance, 717, the external verification that an independent party provides concerning the content of a corporate sustainability report and/or the process used in preparing a corporate sustainability report.

Tariff (duty), 738, a tax on imports levied by the federal government.

Transaction risk, 740, the possibility that future cash transactions will be affected by changing exchange rates.

Translation (or accounting) risk, 740, the degree to which a firm's financial statements are exposed to exchange rate fluctuation.

Value stream, 728, all processes that a product must pass through, from the initial customer order to the delivery to the customer.

Zero defects, 719, means that all products conform to specifications.

REVIEW PROBLEMS

I. Quality Cost Classification, Quality Improvement, and Profitability

At the beginning of 20X2, Landing Company initiated a quality improvement program. Because of the quality improvement efforts, the number of defective units decreased compared to the previous year. By the end of 20X2, scrap and rework had both decreased. The president of the company was pleased to hear of the success but wanted some assessment of the financial impact of the improvements. To make this assessment, the following financial data were collected for the current year (20X2) and the preceding year, 20X1:

	20X1	20X2
Sales	$15,000,000	$15,000,000
Scrap	600,000	450,000
Rework	900,000	600,000
Product inspection	150,000	200,000
Vendor certification	60,000	150,000
Product warranty	1,200,000	900,000
Process acceptance	90,000	100,000

Required:

1. Classify the costs as prevention, appraisal, internal failure, or external failure.
2. Compute quality cost as a percentage of sales for each of the two years. By how much has profit increased because of quality improvements? Assuming that quality costs can be reduced to 3% of sales, how much additional profit is available through quality improvements (assuming that sales revenues will remain the same)?

Solution:

1. Prevention costs: Vendor certification;
   Appraisal costs: Product inspection and process acceptance
   Internal failure costs: Scrap and rework
   External failure costs: Product warranty

2. Year 20X1: total quality costs: $3,000,000; percentage of sales: 20% ($3,000,000/$15,000,000). Year 20X2: total quality costs: $2,400,000; percentage of sales: 16% ($2,400,000/$15,000,000). Profit has increased by $600,000 [(0.20 − 0.16) × $15,000,000)]. If quality costs drop to 3% of sales, another $1,950,000 of profit improvement is possible ($2,400,000 − $450,000).

II. Foreign Trade Zones; Foreign Currency Exchange

Golo, Inc., has two manufacturing plants, one in Singapore and the other in San Antonio. The San Antonio plant is located in a foreign trade zone. On March 1, Golo received a large order from a Japanese customer. The order is for 10,000,000 yen to be paid on receipt of the goods, scheduled for June 1. Golo assigned this order to the San Antonio plant; however, one necessary component for the order is to be manufactured by the Singapore plant. The component will be transferred to San Antonio on April 1, using a cost-plus transfer price of $10,000 (U.S. dollars). Typically, two percent of the Singapore parts are defective. The U.S. tariff on the component parts is 30%. The carrying cost for Golo is 15% per year.

The following spot rates for $1 U.S. are as follows:

	Exchange Rates of $1 for	
	Yen	**Singapore Dollars**
March 1	107.00	1.60
April 1	107.50	1.55
June 1	107.60	1.50

Required:

1. What is the total cost of the imported parts from Singapore to the San Antonio plant in U.S. dollars?
2. Suppose that the San Antonio plant were not located in a foreign trade zone; what would be the total cost of the imported parts from Singapore?
3. How much does Golo expect to receive from the Japanese customer in U.S. dollars, using the spot rate at the time of the order?
4. How much does Golo expect to receive from the Japanese customer in U.S. dollars, using the spot rate at the time of payment?

Solution:

1.

Transfer price	$10,000
Tariff ($9,800 × 0.3)	2,940
Total cost	$12,940

The transfer price was set in U.S. dollars, so there is no currency exchange involved for the San Antonio plant.
The San Antonio plant is in a foreign trade zone, so the 30% tariff is paid only on the good parts, costing $9,800 ($10,000 × 0.98).

2. If the San Antonio plant were located outside the foreign trade zone, the cost of the imported parts would be as follows:

Transfer price	$10,000
Tariff ($10,000 × 0.3)	3,000
Carrying cost of tariff*	75
Total cost	$13,075

*$3,000 × 2/12 × 0.15 = $75

3. On March 1, Golo expects to receive $93,458 (10,000,000/107.00).
4. On June 1, Golo expects to receive $92,937 (10,000,000/107.60).

DISCUSSION QUESTIONS

1. What is the most important reason for an organization to use enterprise risk management?
2. What is the difference between inherent risk and residual risk?
3. Why should the incremental cost of a risk response alternative be considered when deciding how best to respond to an important risk?
4. How is business sustainability different from environmental sustainability?
5. Explain how performance measurement can help improve an organization's business sustainability efforts.
6. Identify and discuss the four kinds of quality costs.
7. Discuss the benefits of quality cost reports that simply list the quality costs for each category.
8. What is a focused value stream?
9. Why are units shipped used to calculate the value-stream cost?
10. When will the average unit cost be used for value streams?
11. How do international issues affect the role of the management accountant?
12. What is a foreign trade zone, and what advantages does it offer U.S. companies?
13. Define outsourcing, and discuss why companies may outsource various functions.
14. Define *forensic accounting*.
15. Define the *fraud triangle*.

MULTIPLE-CHOICE QUESTIONS

13-1 A fire insurance policy on a manufacturing plant is an example of a risk reduction alternative that would reduce which component of the inherent risk of a plant fire?

    a. Likelihood only
    b. Impact only
    c. Both likelihood and impact
    d. Neither likelihood nor impact

13-2 An organization's overall desired level of risk taking is referred to as its

    a. riskiness.
    b. inherent risk.
    c. monitoring ability.
    d. risk appetite.

13-3 A common way to assess the likelihood of an inherent risk is to measure its

    a. incremental cost.
    b. probability.
    c. lost revenues.
    d. company reputation.

13-4 Which of the following risk response items would *not* be affected by an increase in the cost of managing a strategic alliance partnership that was formed to reduce a top organizational risk?

    a. Risk response net benefit
    b. Risk response cost
    c. Risk response benefit
    d. All of these.
    e. None of these.

13-5 Beginning with strategy, which of the following items lists the areas of the business sustainability cycle in the correct order in which they should be performed? (*Note:* Not all areas are contained in each list.)

a. Sustainability assurance, sustainability reporting, risk management, performance measurement

b. Performance measurement, risk management, sustainability reporting, stakeholder engagement

c. Stakeholder engagement, risk management, sustainability assurance, performance measurement

d. Risk management, stakeholder engagement, sustainability reporting, sustainability assurance

e. Stakeholder engagement, risk management, performance measurement, sustainability reporting

13-6 In which areas of an organization's value chain can important business sustainability risks or opportunities arise?

I.   Research & Development   II. Customer Service
III. Manufacturing   IV. Warehousing & Distribution

a. I only
b. II only
c. III only
d. II and IV
e. I, II, III, and IV

13-7 Exhibit 13.8 contains results from **KPMG**'s survey of corporate responsibility reporting,[21] showing how the percentage of the world's 250 largest companies (i.e., the larger green bubbles) that issue corporate responsibility reports has changed over the years. According to Exhibit 13.8, when was the *first* year in which a *majority* (i.e., more than 50%) of these companies issued corporate responsibility reports?

a. 1999
b. 2002
c. 2005
d. 2008
e. 2011

13-8 Which of the following items *correctly* describes an important difference (in most countries and business environments) between traditional financial reporting and corporate sustainability reporting?

a. Corporate sustainability reporting is required, while traditional financial reporting is not required.

b. Corporate sustainability reporting is voluntary, but the contents of any such report are required to be verified by an independent third party, whereas traditional financial reporting is required and its contents must be verified by an independent third party.

c. No published reporting standards exist for organizations to follow when preparing and issuing corporate sustainability reports, whereas published reporting standards do exist for organizations to follow when preparing and issuing traditional financial reports.

d. None of these.

---

21 From KPMG's "Currents of Change: The KPMG Survey of Corporate Responsibility Reporting" (2015). Taken from https://www.kpmg.com/CN/en/IssuesAndInsights/ArticlesPublications/Documents/kpmg-survey-of-corporate-responsibility-reporting-2015-O-201511.pdf.

13-9 Which of the following is a prevention cost?

    a. Inspection of materials
    b. Continuing supplier verification
    c. Prototype inspection
    d. Recalls

13-10 Which of the following is an external failure cost?

    a. Design reviews
    b. Warranties
    c. Field testing
    d. Vendor certification

13-11 Internal failure costs are incurred

    a. to prevent poor quality in the products or services being produced.
    b. because products or services do not conform to requirements after being delivered to the customer.
    c. to determine whether products and services are conforming to their requirements.
    d. because products and services do not conform to specifications or customer needs prior to the product being shipped or the service being rendered to outside parties.

13-12 Lean manufacturing seeks to achieve all of the following except for

    a. zero defects.
    b. maximizing customer value.
    c. zero inventories.
    d. waiting.

13-13 When materials costs differ significantly among products in a value stream, the value-stream product cost is calculated by which of the following?

    a. Unit Materials Cost + Value-Stream Costs/Units Shipped
    b. Unit Materials Cost + Value-Stream Conversion Costs/Units Shipped
    c. Value-Stream Costs/Units Produced
    d. Value-Stream Costs/Units Shipped

13-14 A manufacturing cell within a value stream has three processes and the following associated processing times:

Drilling: 12 minutes
Inserting: 6 minutes
Finishing: 2 minutes

How many units can the cell produce per hour (on a continuous running basis)?

    a. 10 units per hour
    b. 3 units per hour
    c. 5 units per hour
    d. 30 units per hour

13-15 Which of the following is *true* regarding foreign trade zones?

    a. They are pieces of land physically located in foreign countries that are subject to the laws of the United States.
    b. They must be located near seaports.
    c. Goods that enter a foreign trade zone are not subject to tariff until they leave the zone for destinations in the United States.
    d. Goods sold in a foreign trade zone are not subject to U.S. income taxes.
    e. All of these.

13-16 A manufacturing plant located in Mexico that processes imported materials and reexports them to the United States is called a(n)

a. maquiladora.
b. foreign trade zone.
c. joint venture.
d. exchange venture.
e. foreign transaction.

13-17 The following spot rates for $1 in terms of yen and pounds were in effect for June 1 and November 1.

	June 1	November 1
Japanese yen	115.0	118.0
British pound	0.699	0.650

Did the U.S. dollar appreciate or depreciate against these currencies between June 1 and November 1?

	Japanese Yen	British Pound
a.	appreciate	appreciate
b.	appreciate	depreciate
c.	depreciate	depreciate
d.	depreciate	appreciate
e.	Cannot tell from the information given	

13-18 The premier credential for the forensic accountant is the

a. CPA.
b. CFE.
c. CMA.
d. CIA.
e. None of these.

13-19 Which of the following is *not* true of forensic accounting?

a. Many cases are adversarial in nature.
b. Excellent written and oral communications skills are required.
c. The forensic accountant must be able to explain basic accounting concepts to nonaccountants.
d. The forensic accountant is trained to determine the correct answer for each case.
e. The forensic accountant may earn specialized certification.

BRIEF EXERCISES: SET A

Brief Exercise 13-20 Using Net Benefit to Evaluate Risk Response Alternatives

OBJECTIVE ◄ 1
Example 13.1

Cooper Movie Studio Corp. makes movies and is interested in lowering its operating costs for the following year, while maintaining the high quality and appeal of its movies. Cooper's management is concerned about the additional costs the company would have to incur if new industry regulation is passed by Congress. The chart at the top of the next page contains a description of this top risk, an inherent risk assessment, three risk response alternatives, and a residual risk assessment for each response alternative.

(Continued)

Risk	Inherent Risk		Risk Response	Residual Risk	
	Likelihood	Impact (on operating costs)	Alternatives	Likelihood	Impact (on operating costs)
Poor behavior by others in the industry results in Congress passing costly new legislation that regulates the behavior of all movie studios.	30%	$80,000,000	A—Share Cooper's effective marketing processes with competitors to help mitigate poor industry behavior	20%	$80,000,000
			B—Lobby Congress on behalf of the movie industry generally and Cooper in particular	15%	$50,000,000
			C—Take no action in response to possible new regulation	30%	$80,000,000

Finally, Cooper's management accountants estimate that the incremental cost of implementing risk response A is $3,000,000 and the incremental cost of implementing risk response B is $13,000,000.

Required:

1. Calculate the inherent risk for Cooper.
2. Calculate the residual risk for Cooper associated with each of the three risk response alternatives A, B, and C.
3. Calculate the benefit for Cooper associated with each of the three risk response alternatives A, B, and C.
4. Calculate the net benefit for Cooper associated with each of the three risk response alternatives A, B, and C.
5. Using net benefit as the criterion, which risk response should Cooper choose to implement?

OBJECTIVE 3
Example 13.2

Brief Exercise 13-21 Quality Cost Report

Whitley Company had total sales of $1,000,000 for the year ending 20X1. The costs of quality are given below.

Returns/allowances	$50,000
Design changes	60,000
Prototype inspection	13,000
Downtime	40,000
Quality circles	2,000
Packaging inspection	14,000
Field testing	6,000
Complaint adjustment	65,000

Required:

1. Prepare a quality cost report, classifying costs by category and expressing each category as a percentage of sales. What message does the cost report provide?
2. Prepare a bar graph and pie chart that illustrate each category's contribution to total quality costs. Comment on the significance of the distribution.

Brief Exercise 13-22 Interim Quality Performance Report

OBJECTIVE ◀ **3**

Example 13.3

Andresen Company had the following quality costs for the years ended June 30, 20X1 and 20X2:

	20X1	20X2
Prevention costs:		
Quality audits	$ 30,000	$ 45,000
Vendor certification	60,000	90,000
Appraisal costs:		
Product acceptance	45,000	67,500
Process acceptance	37,500	54,750
Internal failure costs:		
Retesting	51,000	45,000
Rework	108,000	90,000
External failure costs:		
Recalls	75,000	60,000
Warranty	165,000	150,000

At the end of 20X1, management decided to increase its investment in control costs by 50% for each category's items, with the expectation that failure costs would decrease by 20% for each item of the failure categories. Sales were $6,000,000 for both 20X1 and 20X2.

Required:

1. Calculate the budgeted costs for 20X2, and prepare an interim quality performance report.
2. Comment on the significance of the report. How much progress has Andresen made?

Brief Exercise 13-23 Quality Trend Report Objective

OBJECTIVE ◀ **3**

Example 13.4

Norris Company implemented a quality improvement program and tracked the following for the 5 years:

	Quality Costs	Actual Sales	Costs as a Percentage of Sales
20X1	$880,000	$4,000,000	22.00%
20X2	840,000	4,200,000	20.00
20X3	765,000	4,500,000	17.00
20X4	700,000	5,000,000	14.00
20X5	594,000	5,400,000	11.00

By cost category as a percentage of sales for the same period of time:

	Prevention	Appraisal	Internal Failure	External Failure
20X1	1.50%	2.50%	6.50%	11.50%
20X2	2.75	3.25	4.00	10.00
20X3	3.00	5.00	2.75	6.25
20X4	3.50	3.50	2.00	5.00
20X5	3.75	2.25	1.50	3.50

Required:

1. Prepare a bar graph that reveals the trend in quality cost as a percentage of sales (time on the horizontal axis and percentages on the vertical). Comment on the message of the graph.

(Continued)

2. Prepare a bar graph for each cost category as a percentage of sales. What does this graph tell you?

OBJECTIVE 3
Example 13.5

Brief Exercise 13-24 Continuous Flow vs. Departmental Manufacturing

Mabbut Company has the following departmental manufacturing layout for one of its plants:

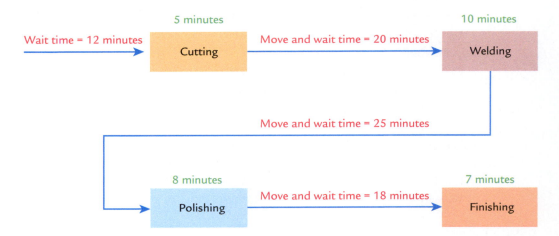

A consulting firm recommended a value stream with the following manufacturing cell:

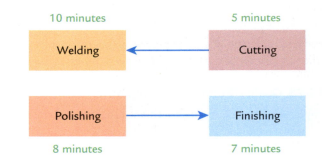

Required:

1. Calculate the total time it takes to produce a batch of 10 units using the traditional departmental manufacturing layout.
2. Using cellular manufacturing, how much time is saved producing the same batch of 10 units? Assuming the cell operates continuously, what is the production rate? Which process controls this production rate?
3. Assume the processing time of Welding is reduced to 6 minutes, while the times of the other processes stay the same. What is the production rate now, and how long will it take to produce a batch of 10 units if the cell is in a continuous production mode?

OBJECTIVE 3
Example 13.6

Brief Exercise 13-25 Value Stream Product Costing

During the week of May 10, Hyrum Manufacturing produced and shipped 16,000 units of its aluminum wheels: 4,000 units of Model A and 12,000 units of Model B. The cycle time for

Model A is 1.09 hours and for Model B is 0.47 hour. The following costs and production hours were incurred:

Hyrum Manufacturing
Value-Stream Costs and Production Hours
This Week, May 10

	Net Hours	Materials	Salaries/Wages	Machining	Other	Total Cost
Order processing	1,600		$ 18,000			$ 18,000
Production planning	100		36,000			36,000
Purchasing	800		27,000			27,000
Stamping	2,000	$267,000	145,500	$36,000	$18,000	466,500
Welding	2,400	100,000	42,000	42,000	12,000	196,000
Cladding	500	75,000	50,000			125,000
Inspection	600		10,500			10,500
Packaging and shipping	600		9,000			9,000
Invoicing	1,400		12,000			12,000
Totals	10,000	$442,000	$350,000	$78,000	$30,000	$900,000

Required:

1. Assume that the value-stream costs and total units shipped apply only to one model (a single-product value stream). Calculate the unit cost, and comment on its accuracy.
2. Assume that Model A is responsible for 40% of the materials cost. Calculate the unit cost for Models A and B, and comment on its accuracy. Explain the rationale for using units shipped instead of units produced in the calculation.
3. Calculate the unit cost for the two models, using DBC. Explain when and why this cost is more accurate than the unit cost calculated in Requirement 2.

Brief Exercise 13-26 Exchange Gains and Losses

OBJECTIVE ◄ 5

Example 13.7

On March 1, Friedle Import-Export Company purchased merchandise costing 70,100 Mexican pesos. Payment was due, in pesos, on June 1. The exchange rates of pesos for $1 were as follows:

March 1	$1 = 10.9 pesos
June 1	$1 = 11.4 pesos

Round all answers to the nearest dollar.

Required:

1. What is the liability in dollars on March 1?
2. What is the liability in dollars on June 1?
3. If Friedle pays on June 1, is there an exchange gain or loss? If so, how much is it?

BRIEF EXERCISES: SET B

Brief Exercise 13-27 Using Net Benefit to Evaluate Risk Response Alternatives

OBJECTIVE ◄ 1

Example 13.1

Palakiko's Fish Taco Hut is a small start-up restaurant in Hanalei. Palakiko recently completed an online risk management course and has identified food safety as his restaurant's top risk. Specifically, he is concerned that the potential of spoiled food resulting from inadequate refrigeration and food preparation techniques could drastically increase restaurant costs. The chart

(Continued)

below contains a description of this top risk, an inherent risk assessment, three risk response alternatives, and a residual risk assessment for each response alternative.

	Inherent Risk		Risk Response	Residual Risk	
Risk	Likelihood	Impact (on operating costs)	Alternatives	Likelihood	Impact (on operating costs)
Inadequate refrigeration and food preparation techniques result in costly food spoilage problems for Palakiko.	40%	$1,000,000	A—Invest in new and larger refrigeration units	15%	$325,000
			B—Design and implement new and improved food preparation training techniques for all employees	35%	$300,000
			C—Take no action in response to possible new regulation	40%	$1,000,000

Finally, Palakiko estimates that the cost of implementing risk response A is $201,250, and the cost of implementing risk response B is $195,000.

Required:

1. Calculate the inherent risk for Palakiko.
2. Calculate the residual risk for Palakiko associated with each of the three risk response alternatives A, B, and C.
3. Calculate the benefit for Palakiko associated with each of the three risk response alternatives A, B, and C.
4. Calculate the net benefit for Palakiko associated with each of the three risk response alternatives A, B, and C.
5. Using net benefit as the criterion, which risk response should Palakiko choose to implement?

Brief Exercise 13-28 Quality Cost Report

Loring Company had total sales of $2,400,000 for fiscal 20X1. The costs of quality-related activities are given below.

Discounts due to defects	$100,000
Retesting	30,000
Vendor certification	14,000
Rework	120,000
Marketing research	6,000
Process acceptance	14,000
Field testing	16,000
Product liability	200,000

Required:

1. Prepare a quality cost report, classifying costs by category and expressing each category as a percentage of sales. What message does the cost report provide?
2. Prepare a bar graph and pie chart that illustrate each category's contribution to total quality costs. Comment on the significance of the distribution.

Brief Exercise 13-29 Interim Quality Performance Report

OBJECTIVE ◀ 3
Example 13.3

Cassara, Inc., had the following quality costs for the years ended December 31, 20X1 and 20X2:

	20X1	20X2
Prevention costs:		
Design reviews	$ 60,000	$ 83,000
Prototype inspection	120,000	168,000
Appraisal costs:		
Field testing	90,000	126,000
Packaging inspection	75,000	106,000
Internal failure costs:		
Scrap	100,000	76,200
Repairs	220,000	166,800
External failure costs:		
Lost sales	160,000	122,000
Product liability	360,000	277,000

At the end of 20X1, management decided to increase its investment in control costs by 40% for each category's items, with the expectation that failure costs would decrease by 25% for each item of the failure categories. Sales were $12,000,000 for both 20X1 and 20X2.

Required:

1. Calculate the budgeted costs for 20X2, and prepare an interim quality performance report.
2. Comment on the significance of the report. How much progress has Cassara made?

Brief Exercise 13-30 Quality Trend Report

OBJECTIVE ◀ 3
Example 13.4

Pintura Company implemented a quality improvement program and tracked the following for the five years:

	Quality Costs	Actual Sales	Costs as a Percentage of Sales
20X1	$750,000	$3,000,000	25.00%
20X2	690,000	3,000,000	23.00
20X3	680,000	3,400,000	20.00
20X4	510,000	3,400,000	15.00
20X5	480,000	4,000,000	12.00

By cost category as a percentage of sales for the same period of time:

	Prevention	Appraisal	Internal Failure	External Failure
20X1	1.00%	1.50%	9.50%	13.00%
20X2	2.00	2.00	8.50	10.50
20X3	2.50	3.00	7.50	7.00
20X4	3.00	3.50	4.50	4.00
20X5	3.50	3.50	2.50	2.50

Required:

1. Prepare a bar graph that reveals the trend in quality cost as a percentage of sales (time on the horizontal axis and percentages on the vertical). Comment on the message of the graph.
2. Prepare a bar graph for each cost category as a percentage of sales. What does this graph tell you?

OBJECTIVE 4
Example 13.5

Brief Exercise 13-31 Continuous Flow vs. Departmental Manufacturing

Gumbrecht Company has the following departmental manufacturing layout for one of its plants:

A consulting firm has recommended a value stream with the following manufacturing cell:

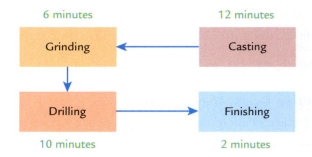

Required:

1. Calculate the total time it takes to produce a batch of 20 units using the traditional departmental manufacturing layout.
2. Using cellular manufacturing, how much time is saved producing the same batch of 20 units? Assuming the cell operates continuously, what is the production rate? Which process controls this production rate?
3. Assume the processing time of Casting is reduced to 9 minutes, while the times of the other processes stay the same. What is the production rate now, and how long will it take to produce a batch of 20 units if the cell is in a continuous production mode?

OBJECTIVE 4
Example 13.6

Brief Exercise 13-32 Continuous Flow vs. Departmental Manufacturing

During the week of August 21, Parley Manufacturing produced and shipped 4,000 units of its machine tools: 1,500 units of Tool SK1 and 2,500 units of Tool SK3. The cycle time for SK1 is 0.73 hour, and the cycle time for SK3 is 0.56 hour. The following costs were incurred:

Parley Manufacturing
Value-Stream Costs and Production Hours
This Week, August 21

	Net Hours	Materials	Salaries/ Wages	Machining	Other	Total Cost
Order processing	400		$ 4,500			$ 4,500
Production planning	50		9,000			9,000
Purchasing	200		6,750			6,750
Casting	500	$ 66,750	36,375	$ 9,000	$4,500	116,625
Grinding	600	25,000	10,500	10,500	3,000	49,000
Drilling	125	18,750	12,500			31,250
Inspection	150		2,625			2,625
Packaging and shipping	150		2,250			2,250
Invoicing	325		3,000			3,000
Totals	2,500	$110,500	$87,500	$19,500	$7,500	$225,000

Required:

1. Assume that the value-stream costs and total units shipped apply only to one model (a single-product value stream). Calculate the unit cost, and comment on its accuracy.
2. Assume that Tool SK1 is responsible for 60% of the materials cost. Calculate the unit cost for Tool SK1 and Tool SK3, and comment on its accuracy. Explain the rationale for using units shipped instead of units produced in the calculation.
3. Calculate the unit cost for the two models, using DBC. Explain when and why this cost is more accurate than the unit cost calculated in Requirement 2.

Brief Exercise 13-33 Exchange Gains and Losses

OBJECTIVE 5
Example 13.7

On March 1, Friedle Import-Export Company sells merchandise costing 75,000 Mexican pesos. Payment will be made in pesos, on June 1. The exchange rates of pesos for $1 were as follows:

March 1	$1 = 10.9 pesos
June 1	$1 = 11.4 pesos

Round all answers to the nearest dollar.

Required:

1. What is the receivable in dollars on March 1?
2. What is the dollar value of the amount paid in pesos on June 1?
3. If Friedle is paid on June 1, is there an exchange gain or loss? If so, how much is it?

EXERCISES

Exercise 13-34 Managing Risks Using a Portfolio Perspective

OBJECTIVE 1

Barolo Company manufactures laptop stickers for Italian sports teams. Barolo's risk management team has identified the company's top five inherent risks and plans to manage them using a typical ERM portfolio perspective (i.e., align the portfolio of residual risks with the company's risk appetite) . Specifically, the team has decided to accept inherent risk 2 (IR_2) and inherent risk 3 (IR_3) as they approximately offset each other. The team also decided to accept inherent risk 1 (IR_1) because it is very close to the company's risk appetite. In addition, the team decided to reduce inherent risk 4. Barolo's risk graph shown below depicts its portfolio of risks after the team has implemented its risk responses.

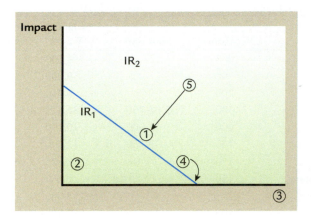

Required:

Refer to Barolo's risk graph and match the numbers (①–⑤) on the graph with the correct lettered descriptions (A–G).

① = _____   A. Inherent risk 3 (IR_3)

② = _____   B. Residual risk 4 (RR_4)

③ = _____   C. Net benefit

④ = _____   D. Inherent risk 4 (IR_4)

⑤ = _____   E. Likelihood

                                                 F. Board of directors

                                                 G. Risk appetite

OBJECTIVE 1 ▶   **Exercise 13-35 Managing Risks Using a Portfolio Perspective**

Brunello Winery produces expensive wines. Brunello's enterprise risk management team has chosen its particular risk response to each of its top five inherent risks. The risk graph below shows Brunello's risks *after* all of the team's risk responses have been enacted.

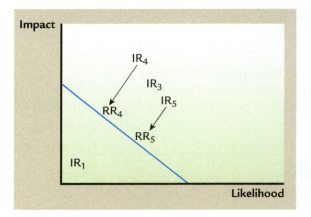

Required:

Refer to Brunello's risk graph and determine the particular risk response alternative (Accept, Avoid, or Reduce) that the team chose to implement for each of the company's inherent risks 1 (IR_1) through 5 (IR_5).

Exercise 13-36 Using Net Benefit to Evaluate Risk Response Alternatives

OBJECTIVE ◄ 1

Crazy Fan Guard Company provides security services to popular live sporting event venues. Crazy Fan management has identified one of its top risks as the possibility that restrictions on premium close seating options will severely decrease its sales revenue by lessening the demand for its security services. The table below displays a description of this top risk, an inherent risk assessment, three risk response alternatives, and finally, a residual risk assessment.

	Inherent Risk		Risk Response	Residual Risk	
Risk	Likelihood	Impact (on lost revenues)	Alternatives	Likelihood	Impact (on lost revenues)
Premium close seating at future popular live sporting events is discontinued due to viewer outrage over previous on-field security violations (e.g., fans rushing court or field and making physical contact with the athletes).	25%	$10,000,000	A—Invest in a business process that focuses on managing improved fan behavior at popular live sporting events	10%	$5,000,000
			B—Form an alliance with another security organization to more effectively (e.g., quickly and forcefully) remove fans who rush the field	15%	$10,000,000
			C—Take no action	25%	$10,000,000

Crazy Fan Guard's management accounting team estimates that the incremental cost of implementing response A is $2,200,000, and the incremental cost of implementing response B is $700,000.

Required:

1. Calculate the benefit of each risk response alternative A through C.
2. Calculate the net benefit of each risk alternative A through C.
3. **CONCEPTUAL CONNECTION** Using net benefit as the criterion, explain the best risk response alternative that Crazy Fan Guard Company management should implement.

Exercise 13-37 Incorporating Stakeholder Impacts into Business Sustainability Analyses and Decisions

OBJECTIVE ◄ 2

Jack's Apps Company researches, develops, and sells traditional applications (i.e., apps) for middle-aged mobile phone device users. In an attempt to tap into the large young adult app market to boost sales and advertising revenues, Jack's CFO, Daniel, is considering hiring students from area high schools and universities to drastically increase the innovativeness of the company's apps. Specifically, Daniel hopes that Jack's new student employee pool will make Jack's next wave of phone apps inventions popular with young adults by providing innovative services, such as exchanging payments for late-night food deliveries, arranging informal dating and other social gatherings, exchanging perspectives on different professors, and identifying unusual debit card purchase patterns to assist with early fraud detection notification. Based on cost estimates from Jack's finance team and surveys of its new target customers (i.e., New Customer Financial Survey), Daniel estimates that this new customer market would increase Jack's annual net income by $10,000,000.

(Continued)

In addition to the New Customer Financial Survey, Jack's management team conducted a Business Sustainability Analysis. Specifically, the stakeholder engagement portion of the Business Sustainability Analysis revealed that four of Jack's most important stakeholder groups (advertisers, regulators, employees, and customers) would react strongly—some favorably and others unfavorably—to the decision to push its app business in the direction of the young adult market. Specifically, ten percent of its existing advertisers would drop Jack's as a client, thereby reducing its annual advertising revenue of $10,000,000. Also, confidential discussions with competitors suggest that the new fraud detection app would require sensitive customer information that Jack's would be unable to protect perfectly from data hackers, thereby resulting in annual fines of $1,500,000 from regulators. In addition, employee engagement meetings indicated that they would strongly favor the expansion into the young adult market. Daniel estimates that improved employee morale would significantly increase their productivity and creativity, thereby increasing annual sales revenue by $2,000,000. Finally, focus groups with existing customers revealed that they would highly value the increased workforce diversity of Jack's hiring a large number of talented young female employees with an expertise in technology. Daniel estimates that this positive customer sentiment would translate into an additional $3,000,000 in annual traditional apps sales.

Required:

1. Using the New Customer Financial Survey and the Business Sustainability Analysis, calculate the net change in Jack's Apps Company's net income that would be expected from pursuing the young adult app market.
2. Based on the calculation in Requirement 1, should Jack's Apps pursue the young adult app market? Explain your answer.
3. **CONCEPTUAL CONNECTION** Describe two additional considerations that Jack's Apps Company management might be wise to consider before making a final decision on whether or not to pursue the young adult apps market.

OBJECTIVE 2

Exercise 13-38 Stakeholder Engagement in Business Sustainability

Apple Inc. is a multinational technology company that designs, develops, manufactures, and sells innovative consumer electronics products and services around the globe. Its products include laptop (e.g., MacBook) and desktop (e.g., iMac) computers, mobile phones (e.g., iPhone), MP3 players (e.g., iPod nano), tablets (e.g., iPad), and various other devices (e.g., Apple Watch, Apple TV, etc.). Its services include personalized, onsite (e.g., at Apple Store) group and individual training sessions, fitness notifications (e.g., from Apple Watch), audio and video streaming, and online and phone help services. Founded in Cupertino, California, in 1976, Apple has been a success as measured by almost any standard. As one example, Apple recently reported the largest ever recorded quarterly profit by a single public corporation! While a history of such amazing performance is admirable, publicly traded companies must always focus on the future and convince investors, and various other key stakeholders, that they will maintain—or even improve—performance in the future.

Required:

1. **CONCEPTUAL CONNECTION** Identify the five most important stakeholders for **Apple Inc.** Briefly explain how you selected these five stakeholders and why they are important to Apple.
2. **CONCEPTUAL CONNECTION** Describe the specific approach you believe **Apple**'s management team should employ to engage with each of the five stakeholders you identified in Requirement 1. For each stakeholder engagement approach, briefly explain

the type of information or performance measures that Apple's management team should provide to the stakeholder (or receive from the stakeholder) to improve the effectiveness of the engagement.

Exercise 13-39 Linking Risk Management and Performance Measurement in Business Sustainability

OBJECTIVE ▶ 2

Princeville Paradise Ice Cream Shoppe manufactures and sells premium ice cream in a unique Hawaiian environment. Princeville Paradise's management performed a stakeholder engagement exercise to identify its most important stakeholders, given its strategy to "*Provide tourists and residents with the best ice cream experience in the islands.*" The exercise revealed that Princeville Paradise's top four stakeholders are customers, employees, local suppliers, and regulators.

Required:

1. **CONCEPTUAL CONNECTION** For each stakeholder, list and briefly describe a *risk* that the stakeholder poses to Princeville Paradise achieving its strategy.
2. **CONCEPTUAL CONNECTION** For each risk described in Requirement 1, list and briefly describe one *nonfinancial performance metric* that Princeville Paradise management should use to measure how effectively this associated risk is being managed.
3. **CONCEPTUAL CONNECTION** For each nonfinancial performance metric in Requirement 2, list and briefly describe one *financial performance metric* that Princeville Paradise management should use to measure in financial terms (i.e., to investors) how the management of the associated risk ultimately affects the company's financial performance.

Exercise 13-40 Quality Cost Classification

OBJECTIVE ▶ 3

Classify the following quality costs as prevention costs, appraisal costs, internal failure costs, or external failure costs:

1. Scrap (created by defective units)
2. Certifying a vendor to ensure that quality parts are provided
3. Stopping work to control process malfunction
4. Replacing a defective product for a customer
5. Goods returned because they were defective
6. Inspecting a subassembly
7. Inspecting and testing prototypes
8. Reinspecting a reworked product
9. Packaging inspection
10. Lost sales because of recalled products
11. Recall to repair defective products
12. Process acceptance
13. Internal audit to ensure that quality guidelines and processes are being followed
14. Repairing products in the field
15. Providing engineering assistance to selected suppliers to improve their product quality
16. Correcting a design error discovered during product development
17. Settling a bodily injury lawsuit caused by a defective product
18. Customer complaint department
19. Quality control circles
20. Continuing supplier verification
21. Redesigning a product to eliminate a product defect
22. Lost sales because of product quality concerns

Exercise 13-41 Quality Cost Report

Bradshaw Company reported sales of $5,000,000 in 20X1. At the end of the fiscal year (June 30, 20X1), the following quality costs were reported:

Vendor certification	$ 43,500
Warranty	100,000
Rework	125,000
Field testing	54,000
Quality training	56,500
Process acceptance	40,000
Scrap	75,000
Recalls	90,000
Product inspection	46,000
Returned goods	70,000

Required:

1. Prepare a quality cost report.
2. Prepare a graph (pie chart or bar graph) that shows the relative distribution of quality costs, and comment on the distribution.
3. Assuming sales of $5,000,000, by how much would profits increase if quality improves so that quality costs are only 3% of sales?

Exercise 13-42 Multiple-Year Trend Reports

The controller of Emery, Inc. has computed quality costs as a percentage of sales for the past 5 years (20X1 was the first year the company implemented a quality improvement program). This information is as follows:

	Prevention	Appraisal	Internal Failure	External Failure	Total
20X1	1%	3%	9%	12%	25%
20X2	3	4	7	9	23
20X3	4	5	4	6	19
20X4	5	4	3	5	17
20X5	6	3	1	2	12

Required:

1. Prepare a trend graph for total quality costs. Comment on what the graph has to say about the success of the quality improvement program.
2. Prepare a graph that shows the trend for each quality cost category. What does the graph have to say about the success of the quality improvement program? Does this graph supply more insight than the total cost trend graph does?
3. Prepare a graph that compares the trend in relative control costs versus relative failure costs. Comment on the significance of this trend.

Exercise 13-43 Traditional vs. Cellular Manufacturing

OBJECTIVE ▶ 4

Erba Inc. has the following departmental layout for producing an herbal supplement:

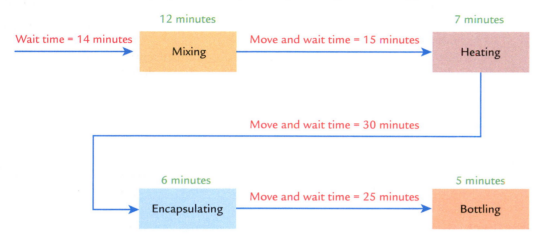

After a detailed study, the head of the plant's industrial engineering department recommended that the following cellular manufacturing layout replace the current departmental structure:

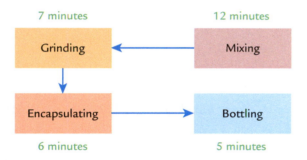

Required:

1. Calculate the time required to produce a batch of 12 bottles using a batch processing departmental structure.
2. Calculate the time to process 12 units using cellular manufacturing.
3. How much manufacturing time will the cellular manufacturing structure save for a batch of 12 units?
4. How many units can the cell produce per hour, assuming the cell is producing on a continuous basis?
5. What must happen so that the cell can produce 12 units per hour, assuming the cell produces on a continuous basis?

Exercise 13-44 Value-Stream Average Costing, ABC, DBC

OBJECTIVE ▶ 4

A value stream has three activities and two products. The units produced and shipped per week are 50 of the limited model (Model K), characterized by special additional features, and 150 of the regular model (Model R), with only basic features. The conversion cost resource consumption patterns are shown as follows:

	Model K	Model R	Costs of Value-Stream Activities
Cell manufacturing	2,700 minutes	2,100 minutes	$19,200
Engineering	65 hours	15 hours	3,400
Testing	25 hours	55 hours	3,000
Total			$25,600

(Continued)

Required:

1. Calculate the ABC product cost (conversion cost) for Models K and R.
2. Calculate the value-stream average product cost (conversion cost). Assuming reasonable stability in the consumption patterns of the products and product mix, assess how well the products are grouped, based on similarity.
3. Calculate the cycle time for each product by dividing the total hours used for each product by the units produced of each product. Now calculate the DBC cost for each product. Comment on the significance of DBC for this setting.

OBJECTIVE **4** ▶ **Exercise 13-45** Box Scorecard

A Box Scorecard was prepared for a value stream:

	Last Week	This Week (1/7/20X1)	Planned Future State (12/31/20X1)
Operational			
Units sold per person	150	162	175
On-time delivery	80%	85%	96%
Dock-to-dock days	10	9	8
First-time through	70%	73%	85%
Average product cost	$100	$99	$97
Capacity			
Productive	35%	36%	37%
Nonproductive	60%	67%	45%
Available	15%	17%	38%
Financial			
Weekly sales	$1,200,000	$1,237,500	$1,400,000
Weekly material cost	$480,000	$495,000	$570,000
Weekly conversion cost	$420,000	$420,360	$460,000
Weekly value-stream profit	$300,000	$325,000	$450,000
ROS	25%	26%	32%

Required:

1. How many nonfinancial measures are used to evaluate performance? Why are nonfinancial measures used?
2. Classify the operational measures as time-based, quality-based, or efficiency-based. Discuss the significance of each category for lean manufacturing.
3. What is the role of the Planned Future State column?
4. Discuss the capacity category and explain the meaning of each measure and its significance.
5. Discuss the relationship between the financial measures and the measures in the operational and capacity categories.

OBJECTIVE **5** ▶ **Exercise 13-46** Types of Involvement in International Trade

Match each term in Column A with its related definition in Column B.

Column A

1. _____ Maquiladora
2. _____ Import
3. _____ Joint venture
4. _____ Export
5. _____ MNC

Column B
   a. A company that does business in more than one country in such volume that its well-being and growth rest in more than one country.
   b. A company purchases materials or parts from another company that is located in a foreign country.
   c. A company sells its product to purchasers located in foreign countries.
   d. A type of partnership in which investors from one country co-own the enterprise with investors from another country.
   e. A manufacturing plant located in Mexico that processes imported materials and reexports them to the United States.

Exercise 13-47 Foreign Currency Exchange

OBJECTIVE ▸ 5

Match each term in Column A with its related definition in Column B.

Column A

1. _____ Spot rate
2. _____ Currency appreciation
3. _____ Translation risk
4. _____ Transaction risk
5. _____ Exchange rate

Column B

   a. The rate at which one currency can be traded for another currency.
   b. The possibility that future cash transactions will be affected by changing exchange rates.
   c. A month ago, $1 U.S. was worth 8.5 Mexican pesos. Today, $1 is worth 9.0 Mexican pesos. The U.S. dollar has undergone what?
   d. The degree to which a firm's financial statements are exposed to exchange rate fluctuation.
   e. The exchange rate of one currency for another for immediate delivery (today).

Exercise 13-48 Payment of Duty and Duty-Related Carrying Cost

OBJECTIVE ▸ 5

Kamber, Inc., owns a factory located close to, but not inside, a foreign trade zone. The plant imports volatile chemicals that are used in the manufacture of chemical reagents for laboratories. Each year, Kamber imports about $14,200,000 of chemicals subject to a 30% tariff when shipped into the United States. About 15% of the imported chemicals are lost through evaporation during the manufacturing process. In addition, Kamber has a carrying cost of 10% per year associated with the duty payment. On average, the chemicals are held in inventory for 9 months.

Required:

   1. How much duty is paid annually by Kamber?
   2. What is the carrying cost associated with the payment of duty?

Exercise 13-49 Payment of Duty and Duty-Related Carrying Cost

OBJECTIVE ▸ 5

Refer to Exercise 13-48. Suppose that Kamber is considering building a new plant inside a foreign trade zone to replace its chemical manufacturing plant.

Required:

   1. How much duty will be paid per year by the factory located inside the foreign trade zone?
   2. How much in duty and duty-related carrying costs will be saved by relocating inside the foreign trade zone?

OBJECTIVE **6**

Exercise 13-50 Fraud Concepts

Consider each of the following situations. Is there a potential problem? Which part of the fraud triangle is involved, if any?

A. Susan is an accounts payable clerk. She sets up creditors in a financial database and pays invoices as they come in. Last year, she won employee of the year and is a valued employee. Through the grapevine, Susan's boss just learned that Susan's brother has a gambling problem.

B. Now suppose that Susan from situation A is now secretary for the head of the marketing department. She keeps track of the vice president of marketing's schedule and handles the correspondence.

C. Keith has been employed for 6 months as a teller at a community bank. All is going well, and his cash drawer has had shortages only twice (of less than $10). The shortages were traced and the problems corrected.

D. At the company Memorial Day picnic and golf outing last week, Nancy notice that June moved her ball to a better lie when she thought no one was looking. There were no prizes for a low score, and June did not benefit from the lower score that resulted.

PROBLEMS

OBJECTIVE **1**

Problem 13-51 Using Net Benefit to Evaluate Risk Response Alternatives

Rocket Motors manufactures sterndrive engines for pleasure craft boats. Rocket's management is concerned about increasing competition in its industry, resulting from a very large international boat motor manufacturer that appears to be seriously considering entering the same customer market served by Rocket. Specifically, management is most worried about the sales revenue it might lose should this international competitor enter Rocket's market. The chart below contains a description of Rocket's top risk, an inherent risk assessment, three risk response alternatives, and a residual risk assessment for each response alternative.

	Inherent Risk		Risk Response	Residual Risk	
Risk	Likelihood	Impact (on lost revenues)	Alternatives	Likelihood	Impact (on lost revenues)
A large international competitor enters the same market served by Rocket, thereby significantly decreasing Rocket's annual sales revenue.	50%	$60,000,000	A—Sign long-term sales contracts with its five biggest customers before the competitor enters the market	25%	$50,000,000
			B—Invest in a new quality program to significantly increase the performance and quality of its engines beyond the level achieved by the new competitor	40%	$15,000,000
			C—Take no action in response to possible new regulation	50%	$60,000,000

Finally, Rocket's management accounting team estimates that Rocket would need to spend $10,000,000 in product giveaways on each of its five biggest customers in order to convince them to sign long-term sales contracts with Rocket. Also, the team believes that Rocket would incur $8,500,000 in additional sales staff travel to complete the long-term contracts. Further, the team estimates that the new quality program would cost $15,000,000 in order to attain the higher level of performance quality necessary to set Rocket apart from its potential new competitor. Finally, Rocket forecasts that it would need to spend an additional $5,000,000 on advertising to sufficiently spread the word to customers regarding its significantly improved performance quality.

Required:

1. Calculate the net benefit for each of Rocket's three risk response alternatives (A, B, and C) under consideration.
2. **CONCEPTUAL CONNECTION** Which risk response alternative should Rocket select? Explain your reasoning.
3. **CONCEPTUAL CONNECTION** Under what conditions would risk response alternative C be the preferred alternative?

Problem 13-52 Incorporating Stakeholder Impacts into Business Sustainability Analyses and Decisions

OBJECTIVE ▶ 2

Stylz Company, a recent start-up fashion retailer based in the United States, is deciding between opening its first sales presence in either Italy's Tuscany Region or Spain's Matarrana Region. Stylz's financial group surveyed potential customers in both markets and has compiled a business plan that estimates the financial impact for the first 5 years. This 5-year financial plan estimates that entering Tuscany would generate $9,000,000 of operating income for Stylz in the first year, which would increase by 10% per year throughout the plan period. The plan also estimates that entering Matarrana would generate $5,000,000 of operating income for Stylz in the first year, which would increase by 50% per year throughout the plan period.

In addition, after completing its 5-year financial plan focusing on operating income, Stylz's management decided also to conduct a business sustainability analysis. Based on Stylz's strategy, management identified the company's four most important stakeholders for its initial sales region decision to be suppliers, employees, regulators, and the local community (in addition to investors and customers whose insights drove the results of the 5-year financial plan). The results of management's stakeholder engagement analysis, including additional insights with respect to how each stakeholder is expected to impact Stylz's performance measures, are as follows:

Suppliers: Suppliers carry out the sourcing of Stylz's products in the chosen sales region. The existing supplier network in Tuscany is mature and already works with other fashion companies in the region; thus, Stylz could connect with this supplier network at a negligible cost. However, the existing supplier network in Matarrana is much less established because there are fewer competing fashion retailers in the region. While less competition offers greater growth opportunities for Stylz, the Matarrana region's less established supplier network will require Sytlz to spend approximately $5,000,000 during each of its first 2 years in the region in order to create adequate supply chain quality and reliability.

Employees: Employees affect the existence and quality of Stylz's workforce in the new sales region. The stakeholder engagement interaction revealed that the regions have a very similar cost of living (and, therefore, very similar wage rates), as well as sufficient numbers of potential hourly store employees. However, the Tuscany region has significantly fewer potential store managers. As a result, Stylz expects that choosing Tuscany would lead the company to spend an additional $2,000,000 annually to train and develop its store managers that it would not need to spend if it chose the Matarrana region.

Regulators: Regulators affect the cost of Stylz complying with any applicable existing or new regulations. The stakeholder engagement sessions revealed an atmosphere of growing pressure on regulators to increase the number of environmental regulations for companies operating

(Continued)

in the region. Stylz management estimates that it would need to spend $1,000,000 annually in the Tuscany region to comply with these fully expected new environmental regulations that it would not face in the Matarrana region. Alternately, stakeholder engagement sessions in the Matarrana region revealed a surprisingly lax atmosphere in which it is commonplace to pay bribes to secure deals and contracts with various necessary business partners in the region. As a result, Stylz management estimates that it would need to spend an additional $3,000,000 annually on training its own employees, as well as many of its business partners, on how to conduct business ethically and in compliance with the Foreign Corrupt Practices Act (FCPA, which is required for all U.S.-based companies). This training would help the company avoid intentional or unintentional unethical activity. Stylz management does not believe it would need to incur this additional FCPA training cost if it chose Tuscany.

Local Community: The local community reflects the general attitude of the underlying population toward a particular company and its policies. Stakeholder engagement sessions suggested that Stylz generally would have the support of the Tuscan community. However, these sessions also revealed a strong undercurrent of resentment among many local residents in the Matarrana region from those residents who do not want a U.S.-based fashion retailer placing its economic, social, or environmental footprint within its community. However, Stylz management believes that its footprint will be significantly positive as it will hire and train local workers, give back to the community through various programs and new community parks, and employ state-of-the-art environmental policies throughout its value chain that will have a net-zero impact on the environment. Stylz management estimates that it would need to spend $1,500,000 each year to convince the Matarrana community of its significantly positive footprint. In addition, if the Matarrana region is chosen, Stylz management believes it would need to spend an additional $3,500,000 in the first year only in order to win the approval of the most influential activist group in the community.

Required:

1. Considering *only* the results of Stylz financial group's initial 5-year financial plan (i.e., ignore the business sustainability analysis for this requirement), estimate the operating income over the 5-year period for each sales region—Tuscany and Matarrana. Based solely on the operating income from this 5-year financial plan, which region should Stylz Company management select in order to maximize its estimated total operating income? Explain your answer.

2. Next consider *only* the results of Stylz management's business sustainability analysis (i.e., ignore the 5-year financial plan for this requirement) that incorporated the findings from the stakeholder engagement sessions with Stylz's four key stakeholders—suppliers, employees, regulators, and the local community. Based solely on this business sustainability analysis, estimate the impact that the four stakeholders would have on Stylz Company's operating income over the 5-year period. Explain your answer.

3. Now considering *both* the initial 5-year financial plan AND the business sustainability analysis, estimate the total operating income over the 5-year period for each sales region. Based on this combined analysis, which region should Stylz Company management select in order to maximize its estimated total operating income over the 5-year period? Explain your answer.

4. **CONCEPTUAL CONNECTION** Identify one important qualitative factor that you believe Stylz management should consider in making its initial sales region decision. Explain how this qualitative factor could potentially change your quantitative answer to Requirement 3.

OBJECTIVE ▶ **2** ▶   **Problem 13-53** Creating Corporate Sustainability Reports

Dorsey Scott MU Company manufactures and bottles a collection of health-oriented fruity beverages. Dorsey's CFO, Rozella, recently signed a series of new contracts with several dozen large universities to serve as the sole external beverage supplier on these campuses. Although the company has never internally conducted or externally disclosed any sustainability activities, Dorsey's CEO, Les, has a strong hunch that the company would be wise to look into the idea of sustainability, given its recent significant growth in the university market. Therefore, Les and Rozella assigned Dorsey's team of five interns to spend their summer internships creating Dorsey's first corporate sustainability report.

Required:

1. **CONCEPTUAL CONNECTION** Briefly explain the most likely reason(s) that Les believes Dorsey would be wise to begin looking into sustainability at this time.
2. **CONCEPTUAL CONNECTION** List and describe three *challenges* that the internship team might face in creating Dorsey's first corporate sustainability report.
3. **CONCEPTUAL CONNECTION** List and describe three *benefits* that Dorsey or its key stakeholders might enjoy as a result of Dorsey creating and issuing its first corporate sustainability report.

Problem 13-54 **Quality Cost Summary**

OBJECTIVE **3**

Danna Wise, president of Tidwell Company, recently returned from a conference on quality and productivity. At the conference, she was told that many American firms have quality costs totaling 20 to 30% of sales. The quality experts at the conference convinced her that a company could increase its profitability by improving quality. However, she was of the opinion that the quality of Tidwell Company was much less than 20%—probably more in the 4 to 6% range. However, because the potential for increasing profits was so great if she was wrong, she decided to request a preliminary estimate of the total quality costs currently being incurred. She asked her controller for a summary of quality costs, with the costs classified into four categories: prevention, appraisal, internal failure, or external failure. She also wanted the costs expressed as a percentage of both sales and profits. The controller had his staff assemble the following information from the past year, 20X1:

a. Sales revenue, $37,240,000; net income, $4,000,000.
b. During the year, customers returned 40,000 units needing repair. Repair cost averages $9 per unit.
c. Twelve inspectors are employed, each earning an annual salary of $80,000. The inspectors are involved only with final inspection (product acceptance).
d. Total scrap is 200,000 units. Of this total, ninety percent is quality related. The cost of scrap is about $10 per unit.
e. Each year, approximately 800,000 units are rejected in final inspection. Of these units, seventy-five percent can be recovered through rework. The cost of rework is $1.80 per unit.
f. A customer cancelled an order that would have increased profits by $600,000. The customer's reason for cancellation was poor product performance.
g. The company employs 10 full-time employees in its complaint department. Each earns $48,600 a year.
h. The company gave sales allowances totaling $180,000 due to substandard products being sent to the customer.
i. The company requires all new employees to take its 4-hour quality training program. The estimated annual cost of the program is $120,000.

Required:

1. Prepare a simple quality cost report classifying costs by category.
2. Compute the quality cost-sales ratio. Also, compare the total quality costs with total profits. Should Danna be concerned with the level of quality costs?
3. Prepare a pie chart for the quality costs. Discuss the distribution of quality costs among the four categories. Are they properly distributed? Explain.

(*Continued*)

4. Discuss how the company can improve its overall quality and at the same time reduce total quality costs.
5. By how much will profits increase if quality costs are reduced to 3% of sales?

OBJECTIVE 3

Problem 13-55 Quality Cost Performance Reporting; One-Year Trend, Long-Range Analysis

In 20X2, Clarkson Inc. initiated a full-scale, quality improvement program. At the end of the year, Tony Ming, the president, noted with some satisfaction that the defects per unit of product had dropped significantly compared to the prior year. He was also pleased that relationships with suppliers had improved and defective materials had declined. The new quality training program was also well accepted by employees. Of most interest to the president, however, was the impact of the quality improvements on profitability. To help assess the dollar impact of the quality improvements, the actual sales and the actual quality costs for 20X1 and 20X2 are as follows by quality category:

	20X1	20X2
Sales	$12,000,000	$15,000,000
Appraisal costs:		
Packaging inspection	480,000	450,000
Product acceptance	60,000	42,000
Prevention costs:		
Quality circles	6,000	60,000
Design reviews	3,000	30,000
Quality improvement projects	3,000	150,000
Internal failure costs:		
Scrap	420,000	360,000
Rework	540,000	480,000
Yield losses	240,000	150,000
Retesting	300,000	240,000
External failure costs:		
Returned materials	240,000	240,000
Allowances	180,000	210,000
Warranty	600,000	660,000

All prevention costs are fixed (by discretion). Assume all other quality costs are unit-level variable.

Required:

1. Compute the relative distribution of quality costs for each year and prepare a pie chart. Do you believe that the company is moving in the right direction in terms of the balance among the quality cost categories? Explain.
2. Prepare a 1-year trend performance report for 20X2 (comparing the actual costs of 20X2 with those of 20X1, adjusted for differences in sales volume). How much have profits increased because of the quality improvements made by Clarkson Inc.?
3. Estimate the additional improvement in profits if Clarkson Inc. ultimately reduces its quality costs to 3% of sales revenues (assume sales of $15 million).

OBJECTIVE 3

Problem 13-56 Trend Analysis, Quality Costs

In 20X1, Don Blackburn, president of Price Electronics, received a report indicating that quality costs were 31% of sales. Faced with increasing pressures from imported goods, Don resolved to take measures to improve the overall quality of the company's products. After hiring a consultant in 20X1, the company began an aggressive program of total quality control. At the end of 20X5, Don requested an analysis of the progress the company had made in reducing and controlling quality costs. The accounting department assembled the following data:

	Sales	Prevention	Appraisal	Internal Failure	External Failure
20X1	$1,000,000	$ 10,000	$20,000	$160,000	$120,000
20X2	1,200,000	50,000	30,000	120,000	100,000
20X3	1,400,000	70,000	60,000	70,000	50,000
20X4	1,200,000	80,000	30,000	50,000	40,000
20X5	1,000,000	100,000	10,000	24,000	16,000

Required:

1. Compute the quality costs as a percentage of sales by category and in total for each year.
2. Prepare a multiple-year trend graph for quality costs, both by total costs and by category. Using the graph, assess the progress made in reducing and controlling quality costs. Does the graph provide evidence that quality has improved? Explain.
3. Using the 20X1 quality cost relationships (assume all costs are variable), calculate the quality costs that would have prevailed in 20X4. By how much did profits increase in 20X4 because of the quality improvement program? Repeat for 20X5.

Problem 13-57 Value-Stream Product Costing, ABC, and DBC   OBJECTIVE ◄ 4

Brasher Company is transitioning to a lean manufacturing system and has just finalized two order fulfillment value streams. One of the value streams has two products, and the other has four products. The two-product value stream produces precision machine parts and the four-product value stream produces machine tools. Before moving to the value-stream structure, Brasher had a well-developed ABC system (one that used all duration drivers) and had experienced good success with the more accurate product costs. Management wanted to be sure that the average costing approach of value-stream costing did not produce distorted product costs. Accordingly, expected weekly activity data were provided for the two-product value streams to see how well average costing worked (see below); however, management did not want to continue using ABC because of its intense data demands and the cost of updating as changes unfolded due to lean practices. In the table below, the driver for each activity is a duration driver. Order processing, for example, uses hours available for processing orders; purchasing uses hours available for processing purchases, etc.

Machine Parts Value Stream
For the Coming Week

Activity	Conversion Cost	Part M15 (hours used)	Part M78 (hours used)	Total Activity Hours
Order processing	$ 36,000	600	1,800	2,400
Purchasing	72,000	200	300	500
Lathe	108,000	480	320	800
Milling	200,000	800	1,200	2,000
Drilling	144,000	720	1,680	2,400
Assembly	40,000	1,200	800	2,000
Inspection	20,000	800	200	1,000
Shipping	18,000	600	200	800
Invoicing	32,000	700	800	1,500
Totals	$670,000	6,100	7,300	13,400

During the week, the machine parts value stream expects to produce and ship 10,000 units of M15 and 30,000 units of M78. Since materials cost is calculated separately, the main concern is with the unit conversion cost.

(Continued)

Required:

1. Calculate the average unit conversion cost for the two machine parts.
2. Calculate the conversion cost per unit for each part, using ABC. Comparing ABC unit cost with the average cost, what would you recommend?
3. Calculate the conversion cost per unit, using DBC (first calculating the cycle time for each product). Based on this outcome, what would you recommend to the management of Brasher Company?

OBJECTIVE 4

Problem 13-58 Box Scorecard

Merkley Company, a manufacturer of machine parts, implemented lean manufacturing at the end of 20X1. Three value streams were established: one for new product development and two order fulfillment value streams. One of the value streams set a goal to increase its ROS to 45% of sales by the end of the year. During the year, the value stream made significant improvements in several areas. The Box Scorecard below was prepared, with performance measures for the beginning of the year, midyear, and end of year. Although the members of the value stream were pleased with their progress, they were disappointed in the financial results. They were still far from the targeted ROS of 45%. They were also puzzled as to why the improvements made did not translate into significantly improved financial performance.

	January 1, 20X2	June 30, 20X2	December 31, 20X2
Operational			
Revenue per person	$25,000	$25,000	$25,000
On-time delivery	78%	85%	93%
Dock-to-clock days	13	8	6
First-time through	70%	70%	92%
Average product cost	$90	$90	$88.50
Capacity			
Productive	42%	42%	42%
Nonproductive	48%	30%	12%
Available	10%	28%	46%
Financial			
Weekly sales	$1,200,000	$1,200,000	$1,200,000
Weekly material cost	$390,000	$390,000	$360,000
Weekly conversion cost	$450,000	$450,000	$450,000
Weekly value-stream profit	$360,000	$360,000	$390,000
ROS	35%	35%	38%

Required:

1. From the scorecard, what was the focus of the value-stream team for the first 6 months? The second 6 months? What are the implications of these changes?
2. Using information from the scorecard, offer an explanation for why the financial results were not as good as expected.

OBJECTIVE 5

Problem 13-59 Exporting, Maquiladoras, Foreign Trade Zones

Paladin Company manufactures plain paper fax machines in a small factory in Minnesota. Sales have increased by 50% in each of the past 3 years, as Paladin has expanded its market from the United States to Canada and Mexico. As a result, the Minnesota factory is at capacity. Beryl Adams, president of Paladin, has examined the situation and developed the following alternatives:

1. Add a permanent second shift at the plant. However, the semiskilled workers who assemble the fax machines are in short supply, and the wage rate of $15 per hour would probably have to be increased across the board to $18 per hour in order to attract sufficient workers from out of town. The total wage increase (including fringe benefits) would amount to $125,000. The heavier use of plant facilities would lead to increased plant maintenance and small tool cost.
2. Open a new plant and locate it in Mexico. Wages (including fringe benefits) would average $3.50 per hour. Investment in plant and equipment would amount to $300,000.
3. Open a new plant and locate it in a foreign trade zone, possibly in Dallas. Wages would be somewhat lower than in Minnesota, but higher than in Mexico. The advantages of postponing tariff payments on imported parts could amount to $50,000 per year.

Required:

Advise Beryl of the advantages and disadvantages of each of her alternatives.

Problem 13-60 **Currency Exchange Rates**   OBJECTIVE 5

Custom Shutters, Inc., manufactures plantation shutters according to customer order. The company has a reputation for producing excellent quality shutters that fit virtually any size or shape of window. Sales are made in all 50 states. On July 1, Custom Shutters received orders from contractors in Switzerland and Japan. Lee Mills, president and co-owner of Custom Shutters, was delighted. The Swiss order is for shutters priced at $64,000. The order is due in Geneva on September 1, with payment due in full on October 1. The Japanese order is for shutters priced at $124,000. It is due in Tokyo on August 1, with payment due in full on October 1. Both orders are to be paid in the customer's currency. The Swiss customer has a reputation in the industry for late payment, and it could take as long as 6 months. Lee has never received payment in foreign currency before. He had his accountant prepare the following table of exchange rates:

	Exchange Rate for $1	
	Swiss Franc	Yen
Spot rate	1.2360	117.70
30-Day forward rate	1.2450	117.68
90-Day forward rate	1.2590	117.70
180-Day forward rate	1.2708	117.66

Required:

1. If the price of the shutters is set using the spot rate as of July 1, how many francs does Lee expect to receive on October 1? How many yen does he expect on October 1?
2. Using the number of francs and yen calculated in Requirement 1, how many dollars does Lee expect to receive on October 1? Will he receive that much? What is the value of hedging in this situation?

Problem 13-61 **Forensic Accounting and Business Valuation**   OBJECTIVE 6

You have just opened your own printing business. A large sports franchise is beginning an important advertising campaign in order to attract more fans to the sport. The purchasing officer of the company calls and asks you to make a bid on printing 5,000 high-quality posters that are to be given out to important boosters. He asks you to come by his office to talk about the job. There, he tells you that he would like to help you get started in your new business. He says that he has already asked for bids, and the lowest is for $25,000. He continues by suggesting that you come in with a bid for $24,000 and give him $500 in cash so that you get the bid. Your immediate reaction is to be flattered because you know that this could lead to many more contracts. You go back to your office and calculate your costs. You are pleased to see that you will make about $6,000 on the project, which you really need.

Required:

Is the deal suggested by the purchasing officer fraud? Explain.

CASES

OBJECTIVE ▶ 2

Case 13-62 Examining Corporate Sustainability Reports

Corporate sustainability reports vary greatly across companies and industries. Select two companies that interest you and conduct an online search to find their corporate sustainability report. (If one or both of the companies you selected do not issue a corporate sustainability report, then select a different company that does issue such a report.) You can either scroll through the corporate sustainability reports for the two companies you selected or you can download them onto your computer and scroll through the downloaded reports.

Required:

1. Identify and briefly explain three *similarities* between the two corporate sustainability reports.
2. Identify and briefly explain three *differences* between the two corporate sustainability reports.
3. **CONCEPTUAL CONNECTION** What do you believe is the greatest *strength* of each corporate sustainability report?
4. **CONCEPTUAL CONNECTION** What do you believe is the greatest *weakness* of each corporate sustainability report?
5. **CONCEPTUAL CONNECTION** Assume that you are able to provide the executive team at each company with *one suggestion for improving* its next corporate sustainability report. Briefly explain your suggestion for each company's executive team.

OBJECTIVE ▶ 3

Case 13-63 Quality Cost Performance Reports

Luna Company is a printing company and a subsidiary of a large publishing company. Luna is in its fourth year of a 5-year, quality improvement program. The program began in 20X1 as a result of a report by a consulting firm that revealed that quality costs were about 20% of sales. Concerned about the level of quality costs, Luna's top management began a 5-year plan in 20X1 with the objective of lowering quality costs to 10% of sales by the end of 20X5. Sales and quality costs for each year are as follows:

	Sales Revenues	Quality Costs
20X1	$30,000,000	$6,000,000
20X2	30,000,000	5,400,000
20X3	33,000,000	5,445,000
20X4	33,857,000	4,740,000
20X5	36,000,000	3,960,000

Quality costs by category are expressed as a percentage of sales as follows:

	Prevention	Appraisal	Internal Failure	External Failure
20X1	1.0 %	2.0 %	7.0 %	10.0 %
20X2	2.0	3.0	6.0	7.0
20X3	2.5	4.0	4.0	6.0
20X4	3.0	4.0	3.5	3.5
20X5	3.5	3.5	2.0	2.0

The detail of the 20X5 budget for quality costs is also provided.

Quality planning	$ 450,000
Quality training	180,000
Quality improvement (special project)	430,000
Quality reporting	260,000
Proofreading	860,000
Other inspection	480,000
Correction of typos	375,000
Plate revisions	125,000
Press downtime	221,000
Waste (because of poor work)	125,000
Returns/allowances	450,000
Lost sales	235,000
Rework (because of customer complaints)	195,000
Total quality costs	$4,386,000

Actual quality costs for 20X4 and 20X5 are as follows:

	20X5	20X4
Quality planning	$450,000	$440,000
Quality training	160,000	250,000
Special project	390,000	150,000
Quality reporting	260,000	240,000
Proofreading	800,000	860,000
Other inspection	460,000	580,000
Correction of typos	350,000	200,000
Plate revisions	100,000	380,000
Press downtime	200,000	260,000
Waste	70,000	120,000
Returns/allowances	400,000	620,000
Lost sales	200,000	330,000
Rework	120,000	310,000

Required:

1. Prepare an interim quality cost performance report for 20X5 that compares actual quality costs with budgeted quality costs. Comment on the firm's ability to achieve its quality goals for the year.
2. Prepare a single-period quality performance report for 20X5 that compares the actual quality costs of 20X4 with the actual costs of 20X5. How much did profits change because of improved quality?
3. Prepare a graph that shows the trend in total quality costs as a percentage of sales since the inception of the quality improvement program.
4. Prepare a graph that shows the trend for all four quality cost categories for 20X1 through 20X5. How does this graph help management know that the reduction in total quality costs is attributable to quality improvements?
5. Assume that the company is preparing a second 5-year plan to reduce quality costs to 2.5% of sales. Prepare a long-range quality cost performance report that compares the costs for 20X5 with those planned for the end of the second 5-year period. Assume sales of $45 million at the end of 5 years. The final planned relative distribution of quality costs is as follows: proofreading, 50%; other inspection, 13%; quality training, 30%; and quality reporting, 7%. Assume that all prevention costs are fixed and all other costs are variable (with respect to sales).

Case 13-64 Ethical Considerations

Lindell Manufacturing embarked on an ambitious quality program that is centered on continual improvement. This improvement is operationalized by declining quality costs from year to year. Lindell rewards plant managers, production supervisors, and workers with bonuses ranging from $1,000 to $10,000 if their factory meets its annual quality cost goals.

Len Smith, manager of Lindell's Boise plant, felt obligated to do everything he could to provide this increase to his employees. Accordingly, he has decided to take the following actions during the last quarter of the year to meet the plant's budgeted quality cost targets:

a. Decrease inspections of the process and final product by 50% and transfer inspectors temporarily to quality training programs. Len believes this move will increase the inspectors' awareness of the importance of quality; also, decreasing inspection will produce significantly less downtime and less rework. By increasing the output and decreasing the costs of internal failure, the plant can meet the budgeted reductions for internal failure costs. Also, by showing an increase in the costs of quality training, the budgeted level for prevention costs can be met.

b. Delay replacing and repairing defective products until the beginning of the following year. While this may increase customer dissatisfaction somewhat, Len believes that most customers expect some inconvenience. Besides, the policy of promptly dealing with customers who are dissatisfied could be reinstated in 3 months. In the meantime, the action would significantly reduce the costs of external failure, allowing the plant to meet its budgeted target.

c. Cancel scheduled worker visits to customers' plants. This program, which has been very well received by customers, enables Lindell workers to see just how the machinery they make is used by the customer and also gives them first-hand information on any remaining problems with the machinery. Workers who went on previous customer site visits came back enthusiastic and committed to Lindell's quality program. Lindell's quality program staff believes that these visits will reduce defects during the following year.

Required:

1. Evaluate Len's ethical behavior. In this evaluation, consider his concern for his employees. Was he justified in taking the actions described? If not, what should he have done?
2. Assume that the company views Len's behavior as undesirable. What can the company do to discourage it?
3. Assume that Len is a CMA and a member of the IMA. Refer to the ethical code for management accountants in Chapter 1. Were any of these ethical standards violated?

Case 13-65 Transfer Pricing and Ethical Issues

Paterson Company,* a U.S.-based company, manufactures and sells electronic components worldwide. Virtually all its manufacturing takes place in the United States. The company has marketing divisions throughout Europe, including France. Debbie Kishimoto, manager of this division, was hired from a competitor 3 years ago. Debbie, recently informed of a price increase in one of the major product lines, requested a meeting with Jeff Phillips, marketing vice president. Their conversation follows.

Debbie: "Jeff, I simply don't understand why the price of our main product has increased from $5.00 to $5.50 per unit. We negotiated an agreement earlier in the year with our manufacturing division in Philadelphia for a price of $5.00 for the entire year. I called the manager of that division. He said that the original price was still acceptable—that the increase was a directive from headquarters. That's why I wanted to meet with you. I need some explanations. When I was hired, I was told that pricing decisions were made by the divisions. This directive interferes with this decentralized philosophy and will lower my division's profits. Given current market

---
*This scenario is based on the experiences of an actual firm. Names have been changed to preserve confidentiality.

conditions, there is no way we can pass on the cost increase. Profits for my division will drop at least $600,000 if this price is maintained. I think a midyear increase of this magnitude is unfair to my division."

Jeff: "Under normal operating conditions, headquarters would not interfere with divisional decisions. But as a company, we are having some problems. What you just told me is exactly why the price of your product has been increased. We want the profits of all our European marketing divisions to drop."

Debbie: "What do you mean that you want the profits to drop? That doesn't make any sense. Aren't we in business to make money?"

Jeff: "Debbie, what you lack is corporate perspective. We are in business to make money, and that's why we want European profits to decrease. Our U.S. divisions are not doing well this year. Projections show significant losses. At the same time, projections for European operations show good profitability. By increasing the cost of key products transferred to Europe—to your division, for example—we increase revenues and profits in the United States. By decreasing your profits, we avoid paying taxes in France. With losses on other U.S. operations to offset the corresponding increase in domestic profits, we avoid paying taxes in the United States as well. The net effect is a much-needed increase in our cash flow. Besides, you know how hard it is in some of these European countries to transfer out capital. This is a clean way of doing it."

Debbie: "I'm not so sure that it's clean. I can't imagine the tax laws permitting this type of scheme. There is another problem, too. You know that the company's bonus plans are tied to a division's profits. This plan could cost all of the European managers a lot of money."

Jeff: "Debbie, you have no reason to worry about the effect on your bonus—or on our evaluation of your performance. Corporate management has already taken steps to ensure no loss of compensation. The plan is to compute what income would have been if the old price had prevailed and base bonuses on that figure. I'll meet with the other divisional managers and explain the situation to them as well."

Debbie: "The bonus adjustment seems fair, although I wonder if the reasons for the drop in profits will be remembered in a couple of years when I'm being considered for promotion. Anyway, I still have some strong ethical concerns about this. How does this scheme relate to the tax laws?"

Jeff: "We will be in technical compliance with the tax laws. In the United States, Section 482 of the Internal Revenue Code governs this type of transaction. The key to this law, as well as most European laws, is evidence of an arm's-length price. Since you're a distributor, we can use the resale price method to determine such a price. Essentially, the arm's-length price for the transferred good is backed into by starting with the price at which you sell the product and then adjusting that price for the markup and other legitimate differences, such as tariffs and transportation."

Debbie: "If I were a French tax auditor, I would wonder why the markup dropped from last year to this year. Are we being good citizens and meeting the fiscal responsibilities imposed on us by each country in which we operate?"

Jeff: "Well, a French tax auditor might wonder about the drop in markup. But, the markup is still within reason, and we can make a good argument for increased costs. In fact, we've already instructed the managers of our manufacturing divisions to legitimately reassign as many costs as they can to the European product lines. So far, they have been very successful. I think our records will support the increase that you are receiving. You really do not need to be concerned with the tax authorities. Our tax department assures me that this has been carefully researched—it's unlikely that a tax audit will create any difficulties. It'll all be legal and above board. We've done this several times in the past with total success."

(Continued)

Required:

1. Do you think that the tax-minimization scheme described to Debbie Kishimoto is in harmony with the ethical behavior that should be displayed by top corporate executives? Why or why not? What would you do if you were Debbie?

2. Apparently, the tax department of Paterson Company has been strongly involved in developing the tax-minimization scheme. Assume that the accountants responsible for the decision are CMAs and members of the IMA, subject to the IMA standards of ethical conduct. Review the IMA standards for ethical conduct in Chapter 1. Are any of these standards being violated by the accountants in Paterson's tax department? If so, identify them. What should these tax accountants do if requested to develop a questionable tax-minimization scheme?

14 Statement of Cash Flows

After studying Chapter 14, you should be able to:

1 Explain the basic elements of a statement of cash flows.

2 Prepare a statement of cash flows using the indirect method.

3 Calculate operating cash flows using the direct method.

4 Prepare a statement of cash flows using a worksheet approach.

testing/Shutterstock.com

EXPERIENCE MANAGERIAL DECISIONS

with Google

You probably are familiar with the famous business phrase "Cash Is King." In fact, cash is so important that it has its own financial statement—the statement of cash flows. Cash flows, particularly their source and timing, are especially important for high-growth companies.

Google has been one of the fastest growing companies in U.S. history. Many companies are pleased with double-digit growth (e.g., at least 10%). But from 2006 through 2009, Google's revenue grew at a triple-digit annualized rate. In addition, its stock price skyrocketed from its initial public offering price of $85 in 2004 to over $600 per share by the end of 2009, making the two founders multibillionaires.[1] How did Google grow at such an amazing pace, and what are some of the impacts of this growth on the company?

Google's statement of cash flows contained in its annual report helps answer this question.[2] The statement shows that Google's cash balance increased during 2009 from a beginning balance of $8,656,670,000 to an ending balance of $10,197,590,000. The statement of cash flows breaks this total cash flow amount into three categories: operating, investing, and financing. Google's impressive growth is reflected partly in its cash flows from operating activities. Driven by soaring sales, Google's net cash *provided* by *operating* activities almost quadrupled from 2005 through 2009, increasing from $2,459,400,000 to $9,316,200,000. Also, the statement shows that heavy investments in marketable and nonmarketable securities explain the company's relatively large net cash outflows, as represented by the net amount of cash *used* for *investing* activities of $8,019,210,000. Finally, the statement of cash flows indicates that the company issued stock in 2009 that added $90,270,000 of cash from financing activities. Other financing activities provided $143,140,000. Therefore, these three important categories of cash inflows and outflows—operating, investing, and financing—go a long way in helping to explain Google's business activities and their impact on the king of all measures—cash!

> "Google has been one of the fastest growing companies in U.S. history. Many companies are pleased with double-digit growth; but from 2006 through 2009, Google's revenue grew at a triple-digit annualized rate."

1 http://moneycentral.msn.com/investor/charts/chartdl.aspx?Symbol=US%3aGOOG provides historical stock prices for Google (accessed July 5, 2010).

2 http://moneycentral.msn.com/companyreport?Symbol=US%3agoog provides the statement of cash flows for the years 2005 to 2009 (accessed July 5, 2010).

OBJECTIVE

Explain the basic elements of a statement of cash flows.

OVERVIEW OF THE STATEMENT OF CASH FLOWS

The cash information provided by **Google** illustrates that management needs to understand the sources and uses of cash within its own company to assess its financing capabilities. Google has tremendous cash resources which enable the company to easily invest in new product developments and expand its revenue-generating capability. In general, management should raise a number of questions relating to cash management. For example, can the company make necessary purchases or investments using cash generated from operations? Will the company need to borrow all or some of the cash it needs for various purposes? If borrowing is necessary, can the debt be serviced? Can some or all of the cash be raised by issuing additional capital stock?

Answers to these questions and others like them are not available in a company's income statement or balance sheet. A third financial statement—the statement of cash flows—does provide this information. All firms that are registered with the U.S. Securities and Exchange Commission (SEC) must issue a statement of cash flows.

Cash Defined

Cash is defined as both currency and cash equivalents. **Cash equivalents** are highly liquid investments, such as treasury bills, money market funds, and commercial paper. Many firms, as part of their cash management programs, invest their excess cash in these short-term securities. Because of their high liquidity, these short-term investments are treated as cash for the statement of cash flows. For example, suppose that a company has $100,000 of cash and $200,000 of marketable securities on its beginning balance sheet. The total cash at the beginning of the year would be measured as $300,000.

Sources and Uses of Cash

The **statement of cash flows** provides information regarding the sources and uses of a firm's cash (as illustrated in Exhibit 14.1). Activities that increase cash are sources of cash and are referred to as **cash inflows**. Activities that decrease cash are uses of cash and referred to as **cash outflows**.

Here's **Why It's important**

The statement provides additional information by classifying cash flows into three categories: cash flows from operating activities, cash flows from investing activities, and cash flows from financing activities.

Exhibit 14.1

Sources and Uses of Cash

Sources of Cash

Operating Activities
• Collection of sales revenue

Investing Activities
• Sale of long-term asset

Financing Activities
• Issuance of long-term debt or stock

Uses of Cash

Operating Activities
• Payment of operating expenses

Investing Activities
• Purchase of long-term asset

Financing Activities
• Retirement of long-term debt
• Treasury stock purchases
• Dividends

- **Operating activities** are the ongoing, day-to-day, revenue-generating activities of an organization. Typically, operating cash flows involve increases or decreases in either current assets or current liabilities. Cash inflows from operating activities come from the collection of sales revenues. Cash outflows are caused by payment for operating costs. The difference between the two produces the net cash inflow (outflow) from operations.
- **Investing activities** are those activities that involve the acquisition or sale of long-term assets. Long-term assets may be productive assets (e.g., acquiring new equipment) or long-term activities (e.g., acquiring stock in another company).
- **Financing activities** are those activities that raise (provide) cash from (to) creditors and owners. Although interest payments could be seen as financing outflows, the statement includes these payments in the operating section.

This classification, referred to as the **activity format**, is the format that should be followed in preparing the statement of cash flows.

Example 14.1 shows how activities can be classified into the three categories and identified as sources or uses of cash.

Methods for Calculating Operating Cash Flows

The two approaches for calculating operating cash flows are the *indirect method* and the *direct method*. The two methods differ only on how the cash flows from *operating activities* are calculated.

- The **indirect method** computes operating cash flows by *adjusting net income* for noncash items, nonoperating gains and losses, and accruals.
- The **direct method** computes operating cash flows by *adjusting each line on the income statement* to reflect cash flows.

For example, revenue on an accrual basis is adjusted to reflect only cash revenue. If the direct method is used, companies must also provide a supplementary schedule that shows how net income is reconciled with operating cash flows. This requirement means that direct method users must also provide the information associated with the indirect method. On the other hand, if the indirect method is used, there is no need to provide a line-by-line adjustment as found in the direct method. Not surprisingly, the indirect method is by far the most widely used.

EXAMPLE 14.1

How to Classify Activities and Identify Them as Sources or Uses of Cash

During the last 2 years of operation, Wiggum Company engaged in the following activities:

1. issuing long-term debt
2. paying cash dividends
3. reporting unprofitable operations
4. issuing capital stock
5. reducing long-term debt
6. retiring capital stock
7. selling long-term assets (e.g., plant, equipment, and securities)
8. reporting profitable operations
9. purchasing long-term assets

Required:
Classify each of these activities as belonging to the operating, investing, or financing categories and identify them as sources or uses of cash.

Solution:

1. financing, source of cash
2. financing, use of cash
3. operating, use of cash
4. financing, source of cash
5. financing, use of cash
6. financing, use of cash
7. investing, source of cash
8. operating, source of cash
9. investing, use of cash

Individuals also engage in operating, investing, and financing activities in much the same way as businesses. Consider John Wilkinson, a newly employed chemical engineer. His day-to-day activities as an engineer produce an annual salary of $72,000 (an operating cash inflow). He also has day-to-day activities that cause cash outflows, such as transportation, food, housing, federal and state income taxes, social security taxes, and health insurance. The difference between the operating cash inflows and operating cash outflows gives John his net cash from his personal operating activities.

During the year, John also acquired and sold long-term assets (investing activities). For example, John sold some real estate inherited from his grandfather and bought some shares of a mutual fund. He also bought his first home as he began his career as an engineer. All three are investing activities. Two of the investing activities involve uses of cash (buying stock and buying the home), and one is a source of cash (selling the inherited real estate).

John also had a financing activity for the year. First, he took out a 30-year mortgage (to help finance the acquisition of the home). This activity raised cash from a creditor that allowed him to acquire the house in which he lives. The interest expense on this mortgage is viewed as an operating expense and is part of the cash outflow in the operating section.

Finally, John and his brother-in-law agreed to a trade of assets: John traded a truck (also part of his recent inheritance) for a car that his brother-in-law owned. This is an example of a noncash exchange, and including this transaction in his personal statement of cash flows illustrates the all-financial-resources approach.

CONCEPT CLIP

Noncash Exchanges

Occasionally, investing and financing activities take place without affecting cash. These are referred to as **noncash investing and financing activities**. A direct exchange of noncurrent balance sheet items may occur. For example, land may be exchanged for common stock. These noncash transactions must also be disclosed in a supplementary schedule attached to the statement. The requirement to report noncash financing and investing activity is essentially an "all-financial-resources approach." Since the major purpose of the statement is to provide cash flow information, the noncash nature of these transactions should be identified and highlighted in the supplementary schedule.

Check Point

1. **Explain why disclosing the sources and uses of cash is so important for potential users of a statement of cash flows.**

Answer:
Knowing the sources of cash—especially from operating activities—provides a user with a good idea of a company's financial strength and its long-term viability. The decision to invest in a company is much safer if a potential investor—be it a bank or buyer—knows how much cash is being produced, where it is coming from, and the requirements for using cash. A firm's value is inextricably tied to its cash flows.

2. **Raising cash by issuing a long-term bond is an example of**
   (a) a financing activity.
   (b) an investing activity.
   (c) an operating activity.
   (d) All of these.

Answer:
(a)

Ethical Decisions

The need to report a strong cash position for obtaining loans and equity capital may invite potential abuse. For example, at the end of a fiscal year, early deliveries of goods sold on credit (to reduce inventories) coupled with deliberate one-time special arrangements for secretive cash side payments by a third party to cover the increase in accounts receivables would show a stronger cash position than a company really has. Of course, such behaviors are deceptive and unethical. Ethical professional practices require fair, objective, and accurate reporting. ●

PREPARATION OF THE STATEMENT: INDIRECT METHOD

OBJECTIVE ◀ **2**

Prepare a statement of cash flows using the indirect method.

Five basic steps are followed in preparing a statement of cash flows:

Step 1: *Compute the change in cash for the period.* This figure is the difference between the ending and beginning cash balances shown on the balance sheets. It must equal the net cash inflow or outflow shown on the statement of cash flows.

Step 2: *Compute the cash flows from operating activities.* Use the period's beginning and ending balance sheets and information about other events and transactions to adjust the period's income statement to an operating cash flow basis.

Step 3: *Identify the cash flows from investing activities.* Use the period's beginning and ending balance sheets and information about other events and transactions to identify the cash flows associated with the sale and purchase of long-term assets.

Step 4: *Identify the cash flows from financing activities.* Use the period's beginning and ending balance sheets to identify the cash flows associated with long-term debt and capital stock.

Step 5: *Prepare the statement of cash flows based on the previous four steps.*

Here's **Why It's important**

Exhibit 14.2 provides comparative balance sheets for the Lemmons Company. These comparative balance sheets provide essential information for preparing a statement of cash flows.

Exhibit 14.2

Balance Sheets: Lemmons Company

Lemmons Company Comparative Balance Sheets At December 31, 20X1 and 20X2			Net Changes	
	20X1	**20X2**	**Debit**	**Credit**
Assets				
Cash	$ 70,000	$175,000	$105,000	
Accounts receivable	140,000	112,500		$ 27,500
Inventories	50,000	60,000	10,000	
Plant and equipment	400,000	410,000	10,000	
Accumulated depreciation	(200,000)	(210,000)		10,000
Land	200,000	287,500	87,500	
Total assets	$660,000	$835,000		
Liabilities and stockholders' equity				
Accounts payable	$120,000	$ 95,000	25,000	
Mortgage payable		100,000		100,000
Common stock	75,000	75,000		
Paid-in capital in excess of par	100,000	100,000		
Retained earnings	365,000	465,000		100,000
Total liabilities and stockholders' equity	$660,000	$835,000	$237,500	$237,500

Step 1: Compute the Change in Cash

Example 14.2 shows how to compute the change in cash.

EXAMPLE 14.2

How to Compute the Change in Cash

Exhibit 14.2 showed the following information on cash and cash equivalents for Lemmons Company:

			Net Changes	
Assets	20X2	20X1	Debit	Credit
Cash	$175,000	$70,000	$105,000	—

Required:
Calculate the change in cash.

Solution:

$$\text{Change in Cash} = \text{Ending Cash Balance} - \text{Beginning Cash Balance}$$
$$= \$175,000 - \$70,000 = \$105,000$$

In **Example 14.2**, notice that the change in cash flow is simply the change in cash, which for Lemmons is an increase of $105,000 from 20X1 to 20X2. This number serves as a control figure for the statement of cash flows. The sum of the operating, investing, and financing cash flows must equal $105,000.

Step 2: Compute Operating Cash Flows

Here's **Why It's important**

Income statements are prepared on an accrual basis. Thus, revenues and expenses that involve no cash inflows and outflows might be recognized. Also, cash inflows and outflows that are not recognized on the income statement might occur. The accrual income statement can be converted to an operating cash flow basis by making four adjustments to net income:

a. Add to net income any increases in current liabilities and decreases in noncash current assets.
b. Deduct from net income any decreases in current liabilities and increases in noncash current assets.
c. Add to or deduct from net income the remaining net income items that do not affect cash flows (e.g., add back noncash expenses).
d. Eliminate any income items that belong in either the investing or financing section.

Example 14.3 lists these four types of adjustments and illustrates how to calculate the operating cash flows that use them.

EXAMPLE 14.3

How to Calculate Operating Cash Flows Using the Indirect Method

Exhibit 14.2 (p. 795) showed the following information on current assets and liabilities for Lemmons Company:

			Net Changes	
	20X1	20X2	Debit	Credit
Current assets				
Accounts receivable	$140,000	$112,500		$27,500
Inventories	50,000	60,000	$10,000	
Current liabilities				
Accounts payable	120,000	95,000	25,000	

EXAMPLE 14.3

The income statement for Lemmons Company follows:

Lemmons Company
Income Statement
For the Year Ended December 31, 20X2

Revenues	$ 480,000
Gain on sale of equipment	20,000
Cost of goods sold	(260,000)
Depreciation expense	(50,000)
Interest expense	(10,000)
Net income	$ 180,000

Required:

Compute operating cash flows using the indirect method.

Solution:

Net income	$180,000	
Add (deduct) adjusting items:		
Decrease in accounts receivable	27,500	(Type A adjustment)
Decrease in accounts payable	(25,000)	(Type B adjustment)
Increase in inventories	(10,000)	(Type B adjustment)
Depreciation expense	50,000	(Type C adjustment)
Gain on sale of equipment	(20,000)	(Type D adjustment)
Net cash from operating activities	$202,500	

Five adjusting items are used to compute operating cash flows for Lemmons Company. These five entries exhibit each of the four types of adjustments.

Decrease in Accounts Receivable (Example of Type A Adjustment) From **Example 14.3**, operating income is increased by a $27,500 decrease in accounts receivable. A decrease in accounts receivable represents a decrease in a noncash current asset. It indicates that cash collections from customers were greater than the revenues reported on the income statement by the amount of the decrease. Thus, to compute the operating cash flow, the decrease must be added to net income. To understand fully why this amount is added back to net income, consider the cash collection activity of Lemmons.

At the beginning of the year, Lemmons reported accounts receivable of $140,000 (Exhibit 14.2, p. 795). This beginning balance represents revenues recognized during 20X1 but not collected. During 20X2, additional operating revenues of $480,000 were earned and recognized on the income statement. Lemmons, therefore, had a total cash collection potential of $620,000 ($140,000 + $480,000). Since the ending balance of accounts receivable was $112,500, the company collected cash totaling $507,500 ($620,000 − $112,500). The cash collected from operations was $27,500 greater than the amount recognized on the income statement ($507,500 vs. $480,000), an amount exactly equal to the decrease in accounts receivable. Thus, the change in accounts receivable can be used to adjust revenues from an accrual to a cash basis.

Decrease in Accounts Payable and Increase in Inventories (Examples of Type B Adjustment) **Example 14.3** shows that the second adjusting item in the operating section reflects a decrease in accounts payable of $25,000 and the third an increase in inventories of $10,000. Taken together, these two items adjust the cost of goods sold to a cash basis. A decrease in accounts payable means that cash payments to creditors were larger than the purchases made during the period. The difference is the amount that accounts payable decreased. The total cash payment made to creditors, therefore, is equal to the purchases plus the decrease in accounts payable. Since inventories increased, purchases are larger than the cost of goods sold by the amount that inventories increased. Thus, by deducting both the decrease in accounts payable and the increase in inventories, the cost of goods sold figure is increased to reflect the cash outflow for goods during the period.

Using information from Exhibit 14.2, the following statement of costs of goods sold can be prepared for Lemmons. (In this statement, goods available for sale and purchases are obtained by working backwards from cost of goods sold.)

Beginning inventory	$ 50,000
Purchases	270,000
Goods available for sale	$320,000
Ending inventory	(60,000)
Cost of goods sold	$260,000

Adding purchases to the beginning balance in accounts payable (from Exhibit 14.2, p. 795) yields the total potential payments to creditors: $390,000 ($270,000 + $120,000). Subtracting the ending balance of accounts payable (Exhibit 14.2) from the total potential payments gives the total cash payments for the year: $295,000 ($390,000 − $95,000). By deducting the decrease in accounts payable ($25,000) and the increase in inventories ($10,000), the cost of goods sold figure increases to $295,000 ($260,000 + $35,000). This amount equals the total cash payments for goods during 20X2.

Depreciation Expense (Example of Type C Adjustment) While depreciation expense is a legitimate deduction from revenues to arrive at net income, it does not require any cash outlay. As a noncash expense, it should be added back to net income as part of the adjustment needed to produce operating cash flow.

Gain on the Sale of Equipment (Example of Type D Adjustment) The sale of long-term assets is a nonoperating activity and should be classified in the section that reveals the firm's investing activities. Furthermore, the gain on the sale of the equipment does not reveal the total cash received. It gives only the cash received in excess of the equipment's book value. The correct procedure is to deduct the gain and report the full cash inflow from the sale in the investing section of the statement of cash flows.

Step 3: Compute Investing Cash Flows

Here's **Why It's important**

Investing activities include the purchase and sale of long-term assets (plant and equipment, land, and long-term securities). **Example 14.4** shows how to compute investing cash flows for Lemmons. The company had three investing transactions in 20X2, which are summarized in the investing section.

EXAMPLE 14.4	Equipment with a book value of $50,000 was sold for $70,000 (original purchase cost of $90,000). New equipment was purchased. Exhibit 14.2 showed the following information
How to Compute Investing Cash Flows	on investing transactions for Lemmons Company:

			Net Changes	
Long-Term Assets	**20X1**	**20X2**	**Debit**	**Credit**
Plant and equipment	$ 400,000	$ 410,000	$10,000	
Accumulated depreciation	(200,000)	(210,000)		$10,000
Land	200,000	287,500	87,500	

Required:
Calculate the investing cash flows.

EXAMPLE 14.4

(*Continued*)

Solution:

Sale of equipment	$ 70,000[a]
Purchase of equipment	(100,000)[b]
Purchase of land	(87,500)[c]
Net cash from investing activities	$(117,500)

[a] The sale of long-term assets is an investing activity. Thus, the receipt of the $70,000 should be reported in the investing section.

[b] There is no explicit information concerning the purchase price of equipment. The purchase price is inferred from the comparative balance sheet information as well as the information about the equipment originally costing $90,000 that was sold and removed from the books. The purchase price of the new equipment can be computed by the following procedure:

Beginning plant and equipment	$400,000
Purchase of equipment	?
Sale of equipment	(90,000)
Ending balance, plant, and equipment	$410,000

The "plug figure" for the equipment purchase must be $100,000. (*Note:* $40,000 of accumulated depreciation was deducted from the books, removing the accumulated depreciation associated with the equipment that was sold, and $50,000 was added to reflect the depreciation expense for 20X2, giving a net increase of $10,000.)

[c] The comparative balance sheets reveal that land was purchased for $87,500. This transaction also should appear in the investing section.

Step 4: Compute Financing Cash Flows

Issuance of long-term debt or capital stock can produce cash inflows. Retirement of debt or stock and payment of dividends produce cash outflows. Dividends represent a return on the funds provided by stockholders. **Example 14.5** shows how to compute the financing cash flows for Lemmons.

Here's **Why It's important**

EXAMPLE 14.5

**How to Compute
Financing Cash Flows**

In 20X2, net income of $180,000 was earned, and dividends of $80,000 were paid. Exhibit 14.2 showed the following information on financing transactions for Lemmons Company:

			Net Changes	
	20X1	20X2	Debit	Credit
Mortgage payable		$100,000		$100,000
Common stock	$ 75,000	75,000		
Paid-in capital in excess of par	100,000	100,000		
Retained earnings	365,000	465,000		100,000

Required:
Compute the financing cash flows for 20X2.

EXAMPLE 14.5

(Continued)

Solution:

Issuance of mortgage	$100,000[a]
Payment of dividends	(80,000)[b]
Net cash from financing activities	$ 20,000

[a] The comparative balance sheets show that the only change in long-term debt and capital stock accounts is the apparent issue of a mortgage during 20X2. The proceeds from this mortgage should be shown as a source of cash in the financing section.

[b]

Retained earnings, end of 20X1	$365,000
Net income (20X2)	180,000
Total	$545,000
Less retained earnings, end of 20X2	465,000
Dividends paid in 20X2	$ 80,000

Step 5: Prepare the Statement of Cash Flows

The outcomes of Steps 2 through 4 correspond to the individual sections needed for the statement of cash flows. The statement of cash flows summarizes the flows for operating, investing, and financing activities.

Here's **Why It's important**

Example 14.5 shows how to prepare this statement.

EXAMPLE 14.6

How to Prepare the Statement of Cash Flows

Refer to the information for Lemmons Company in Examples 14.2 (p. 796) through 14.5.

Required:

Prepare a statement of cash flows for Lemmons.

Solution:

Lemmons Company
Statement of Cash Flows
For the Year Ended December 31, 20X2

Cash flows from operating activities:		
Net income	$ 180,000	
Add (deduct) adjusting items:		
Decrease in accounts receivable	27,500	
Decrease in accounts payable	(25,000)	
Increase in inventories	(10,000)	
Depreciation expense	50,000	
Gain on sale of equipment	(20,000)	
Net cash from operating activities		$202,500
Cash flows from investing activities:		
Sale of equipment	$ 70,000	
Purchase of equipment	(100,000)	
Purchase of land	(87,500)	
Net cash from investing activities		(117,500)
Cash flows from financing activities:		
Issuance of mortgage	$ 100,000	
Payment of dividends	(80,000)	
Net cash from financing activities		20,000
Net increase in cash		$105,000

Notice that the change in cash flow computed in Step 1 from the comparative balance sheets corresponds to the net increase in cash identified in the statement of cash flows. The computation produced by Step 1 serves as a control on the accuracy of Steps 2 through 4.

Here's How It's Used: AT KARABEKIAN COMPANY

You are the vice president of finance for **Karabekian** Company. Terry Kitchen, the CEO, calls a meeting with you and Kilgore Trout, the vice president of operations. Kitchen is very interested in acquiring Flemington, a small, private company that manufactures a component used in the construction of Karabekian's major product. Kitchen expresses his view that the small company appears to be a good buy and will contribute to the long-run objective of vertical integration. He is curious, though, why the owner now appears eager to sell when, the last time he was approached, he was strongly opposed to any deal. He wonders whether the company might now be having cash flow problems.

Trout doubts that this could be the case and points out that the income statements for the past several years show stable profits. Moreover, the most recent balance sheet shows a small but positive cash balance and the working capital appears to be fairly stable. Kitchen then turns to you and asks the following:

Do you agree with this analysis? Does this financial evidence mean there is no cash flow problem? If not, then what do we need to know?

Your response to the first question is definitely no. You then make the following comments: "The positive cash balance on the balance sheet doesn't say much about cash flows—nothing about the sources and uses of cash during the reporting period is known. Furthermore, we need to be very cautious about interpreting stable profits and working capital. Many companies have reported stable profits and working capital for several periods and then have gone bankrupt in spite of these signals. In answer to the second question, before we commit formally to any acquisition, we need to evaluate Flemington's current cash flows and assess its future cash flow potential. If the firm is in a current cash crisis, acquiring it will cost a great deal more than the purchase price. Also, if the firm is in a cash crisis, we still may be able to work out a deal but on much more favorable terms. I suggest that we obtain a statement of cash flows for the last 5 years. This statement should show cash flows from operations as well as cash flows from the firm's financing and investing activities."

CONCEPT CLIP

Check Point

1. Retained earnings were $120,000 at the beginning of the year and $160,000 at the end of the year. Net income for the current year was $$100,000. Calculate the dividends paid and explain why they are presented in the financing section of the statement of cash flows.

Answer:
Dividends paid = $120,000 + $100,000 – $160,000 = $60,000. Dividends represent a return on funds provided by stockholders and so should appear in the financing section.

2. Explain why "gain on sale of equipment" is subtracted from net income in calculating operating cash flows.

Answer:
The sale of long-term assets is a nonoperating activity. The correct procedure is to deduct the gain and report the full cash inflow from the sale in the investing section of the statement of cash flows.

THE DIRECT METHOD: AN ALTERNATIVE APPROACH

OBJECTIVE 3

Calculate operating cash flows using the direct method.

The section of operating cash flows in **Example 14.3** (p. 796) computes cash flows by adjusting net income for items that do not affect cash flows. This approach is known as the indirect method. Some individuals prefer to show operating cash flows as the difference between cash receipts and cash payments. To do so, each item on the accrual income statement is adjusted to reflect cash flows. Either approach to computing and presenting operating cash flows may be

Here's How It's Used: AT KICKER

The statement of cash flows is a report required of all SEC-registered firms. **Stillwater Designs**, however, is not a public company and therefore is not subject to the requirement to produce a statement of cash flows. The management of Stillwater Designs does not see any value in producing this statement; therefore, the accounting department does not produce it. A daily cash position report is provided to management. Furthermore, it is a very easy matter to identify the source of the cash flows—either they come from operating, investing, or financing activities. Thus, if this information is ever explicitly needed, it can be provided.

Interestingly, Stillwater Designs' creditors have not demanded this statement as information needed for granting loans. Income statements and balance sheets have provided the needed information. Stillwater Designs' chief accountant, Jeanne Snyder, noted that bank officers tend to be much more interested in assets that can act as collateral, such as accounts receivable and inventory.

used. Which to use is a matter of preference. However, if a company chooses the direct method, it must also present the indirect method in a separate schedule.

Here's Why It's important

The same adjustments and the same reasoning are used to produce the operating cash flows for both the direct and indirect methods. However, the presentation of the information is different. The direct method calculates operating cash flows by adjusting each line of the income statement to produce a cash flow income statement.

Example 14.7 shows how to compute operating cash flows using this approach for Lemmons.

EXAMPLE 14.7

How to Calculate Operating Cash Flows Using the Direct Method

Exhibit 14.2 (p. 795) showed the following information on current assets and liabilities for Lemmons Company:

	20X1	20X2	Net Changes Debit	Net Changes Credit
Current assets				
Accounts receivable	$140,000	$112,500		$27,500
Inventories	50,000	60,000	$10,000	
Current liabilities				
Accounts payable	120,000	95,000	25,000	

The income statement for Lemmons follows:

Lemmons Company
Income Statement
For the Year Ended December 31, 20X2

Revenues	$ 480,000
Gain on sale of equipment	20,000
Cost of goods sold	(260,000)
Depreciation expense	(50,000)
Interest expense	(10,000)
Net income	$ 180,000

Required:

Calculate operating cash flows using the direct method.

EXAMPLE 14.7

Solution:

(Continued)

	Income Statement	Adjustments	Cash Flows
Revenues	$ 480,000	$ 27,500[a]	$ 507,500
Gain on sale of equipment	20,000	(20,000)	
Cost of goods sold	(260,000)	(25,000)[b]	
		(10,000)[c]	(295,000)
Depreciation expense	(50,000)	50,000	
Interest expense	(10,000)		(10,000)
Net income	$ 180,000		
Net cash from operating activities			$ 202,500

[a] Decrease in accounts receivable.
[b] Decrease in accounts payable.
[c] Increase in inventories.

Check Point

1. What is the difference between the indirect method and the direct method for calculating operating cash flows?

Answer:

The indirect method arrives at operating cash flows by making adjustments to net income for noncash items, nonoperating items, and accruals. The direct method computes operating cash flows by adjusting each line on the income statement to reflect cash flows, effectively producing a cash-based income statement.

2. Is a company required to use the direct method?

Answer:

No, a company can use either method. If the direct method is used, then the indirect method must also be presented in a supplemental schedule.

WORKSHEET APPROACH TO THE STATEMENT OF CASH FLOWS

OBJECTIVE 4

Prepare a statement of cash flows using a worksheet approach.

As transactions increase in number and complexity, a worksheet becomes a useful and almost necessary aid in preparing the statement of cash flows. The approach minimizes confusion and allows careful consideration of all the details underlying an analysis of cash flows. One advantage of a worksheet is the fact that it uses a spreadsheet format, allowing the preparer to use a computer and spreadsheet software like Excel. Furthermore, a worksheet offers the user an efficient, logical means to organize the data needed to prepare a statement of cash flows. Although the worksheet itself is not the statement of cash flows, the statement can be easily extracted from the worksheet. To illustrate, refer to the comparative balance sheets of Portermart Company presented in Exhibit 14.3 (p. 804).

Here's **Why It's important**

Example 14.8 shows how to prepare a worksheet for Portermart's statement of cash flows. Notice that the worksheet (p. 805) is divided into two major sections: one corresponding to the balance sheet classifications and one corresponding to the statement of cash flows classifications.

Exhibit 14.3

Balance Sheets: Portermart Company

			Net Changes	
Portermart Company **Comparative Balance Sheets** **At December 31, 20X1 and 20X2**				
	20X1	**20X2**	**Debit**	**Credit**
Assets				
Cash	$ 90,000	$183,000	$ 93,000	
Accounts receivable	55,000	60,000	5,000	
Inventory	80,000	55,000		$ 25,000
Plant and equipment	130,000	100,000		30,000
Accumulated depreciation	(65,000)	(60,000)	5,000	
Land	25,000	65,000	40,000	
Total assets	$315,000	$403,000		
Liabilities and stockholders' equity				
Accounts payable	$ 40,000	$ 60,000		20,000
Wages payable	5,000	3,000	2,000	
Bonds payable	30,000	20,000	10,000	
Preferred stock (no par)	5,000	15,000		10,000
Common stock	50,000	60,000		10,000
Paid-in capital in excess of par	50,000	80,000		30,000
Retained earnings	135,000	165,000		30,000
Total liabilities and stockholders' equity	$315,000	$403,000	$155,000	$155,000

Four columns are needed: two for the beginning and ending balances of the balance sheet and two to analyze the transactions that produced the changes in cash flows. The columns for the analysis of transactions are the focus of the worksheet approach. Generally, a debit or credit in a balance sheet column produces a corresponding credit or debit in a cash flow column. Once all changes are accounted for, the statement of cash flows can be prepared (by using the lower half of the worksheet).

EXAMPLE 14.8

How to Prepare a Statement of Cash Flows Using a Worksheet Approach

Refer to the comparative balance sheets for Portermart Company in Exhibit 14.3. Other (20X2) transactions include the following:

a. Cash dividends of $10,000 were paid.

b. Equipment was sold for $8,000. It had an original cost of $30,000 and a book value of $15,000. The loss is included in operating expenses.

c. Land with a fair market value of $40,000 was acquired by issuing common stock with a par value of $10,000.

d. One thousand shares of preferred stock (no par) were sold for $10 per share.

The income statement for Portermart for 20X2 follows:

Sales	$ 400,000
Cost of goods sold	(250,000)
Gross margin	$ 150,000
Operating expenses	(110,000)
Net income	$ 40,000

EXAMPLE 14.8

(*Continued*)

Required:

Prepare a worksheet for Portermart Company.

Solution:

Worksheet: Portermart Company

	20X1		Debit		Credit	20X2
			Transactions			
Assets						
Cash	$ 90,000	(1)	$93,000			$183,000
Accounts receivable	55,000	(2)	5,000			60,000
Inventory	80,000			(3)	$25,000	55,000
Plant and equipment	130,000			(4)	30,000	100,000
Accumulated depreciation	(65,000)	(4)	15,000	(5)	10,000	(60,000)
Land	25,000	(6)	40,000			65,000
Total assets	$315,000					$403,000
Liabilities and stockholders' equity:						
Accounts payable	$ 40,000			(7)	20,000	$ 60,000
Wages payable	5,000	(8)	2,000			3,000
Bonds payable	30,000	(9)	10,000			20,000
Preferred stock (no par)	5,000			(10)	10,000	15,000
Common stock	50,000			(11)	10,000	60,000
Paid-in capital in excess of par	50,000			(11)	30,000	80,000
Retained earnings	135,000	(13)	10,000	(12)	40,000	165,000
Total liabilities and stockholders' equity	$315,000					$403,000
Cash flows from operating activities:						
Net income		(12)	40,000			
Depreciation expense		(5)	10,000			
Loss on sale of equipment		(4)	7,000			
Decrease in inventory		(3)	25,000			
Increase in accounts payable		(7)	20,000			
Increase in accounts receivable				(2)	5,000	
Decrease in wages payable				(8)	2,000	
Cash flows from investing activities:						
Sale of equipment		(4)	8,000			
Cash flows from financing activities:						
Reduction in bonds payable				(9)	10,000	
Payment of dividends				(13)	10,000	
Issuance of preferred stock		(10)	10,000			
Net increase in cash				(1)	93,000	
Noncash investing and financing activities:						
Land acquired with common stock		(11)	40,000	(6)	40,000	

Analysis of Transactions

The summary transactions on the worksheet will be explained by examining the items on the worksheet in order of their appearance (essentially equivalent to the numerical order of the entries). The entries are developed by considering each balance sheet item and the associated supplementary information.

Change in Cash   Entry (1) identifies the total change in cash during 20X2.

(1)	Cash	93,000	
	Net Increase in Cash		93,000

The actual cash balance increased from the beginning to the end of the year by $93,000.

Change in Accounts Receivable   Entry (2) reflects the increase in accounts receivable.

(2)	Accounts Receivable	5,000	
	Operating Cash		5,000

Increasing accounts receivable means that revenues were recognized on the income statement but not collected. Thus, net income must be adjusted to show that cash inflows from revenues were less by this amount.

Decrease in Inventory   Entry (3) reflects the effect of a decrease in inventory on operating cash flow.

(3)	Operating Cash	25,000	
	Inventory		25,000

Operating cash should be increased since a decrease in inventory would be included in the cost of goods sold but would not represent a cash outflow.

Sale of Equipment   The sale of equipment affects two balance sheet accounts and two cash flow accounts. The effect is captured in Entry (4).

(4)	Operating Cash	7,000	
	Cash from Investing Activities	8,000	
	Accumulated Depreciation	15,000	
	Plant and Equipment		30,000

Operating cash shows an increase because the loss on the sale is a noncash expense and should be added back to net income to arrive at the correct cash provided by operating activities. The equipment is sold for $8,000. This sale produces a cash inflow that is recognized as a cash flow from investing activities. The other two entries reflect the fact that the original cost of the equipment and the accumulated depreciation have been removed from the company's books.

Depreciation Expense   Entry (5) shows an increase in operating cash flow because depreciation expense, a noncash expense, is added back to net income.

(5)	Operating Cash	10,000	
	Accumulated Depreciation		10,000

Although the amount of depreciation expense is not explicitly given, it can be easily computed. The net decrease in the accumulated depreciation account is $5,000 (Exhibit 14.3, p. 804). The sale of the equipment decreased accumulated depreciation by $15,000. (Accumulated depreciation removed is equal to original cost minus book value, or $30,000 − $15,000.) Thus, the amount of depreciation expense recognized for the period must be $10,000. Depreciation expense increases accumulated depreciation. An increase of $10,000 and a decrease of $15,000 produce a net decrease of $5,000.

Land for Common Stock Three balance sheet accounts are affected in the noncash transaction that acquires land in exchange for common stock. To balance transactions columns, two separate entries [(6) and (11)] are needed.

(6)	Land	40,000	
	Noncash Investing Activities		40,000
(11)	Noncash Investing Activities	40,000	
	Common Stock		10,000
	Paid-In Capital in Excess of Par		30,000

Accounts Payable Entry (7) provides the adjusting entry for an increase in accounts payable.

(7)	Operating Cash	20,000	
	Accounts Payable		20,000

An increase in accounts payable means that some of the purchases were not acquired through the use of cash. Accordingly, the amount of the increase needs to be added back to net income.

Wages Payable Wages payable decreased by $2,000 during 20X2. This decrease means that the company had a cash outflow $2,000 larger than the wage expense recognized on the income statement. Entry (8) reflects this $2,000 decrease.

(8)	Wages Payable	2,000	
	Operating Cash		2,000

Bonds Payable Bonds payable decreased by $10,000, indicating a cash outflow belonging to the financing section. Entry (9) recognizes the reduction of debt and the associated cash outflow.

(9)	Bonds Payable	10,000	
	Cash Flow from Financing Activities		10,000

Preferred Stock Entry (10) reflects the cash inflow that resulted from the issuance of preferred stock.

(10)	Cash Flow from Financing Activities	10,000	
	Preferred Stock		10,000

Net Income Net income is assigned to the operating cash flow section by Entry (12).

(12)	Operating Cash	40,000	
	Retained Earnings		40,000

Payment of Dividends The payment of dividends is given in Entry (13).

(13)	Retained Earnings	10,000	
	Cash Flow from Financing Activities		10,000

The Final Step

The statement of cash flows for Portermart, derived from the worksheet, is shown in Exhibit 14.4.

Once the worksheet is completed, the final step in preparing the statement of cash flows is relatively straightforward. The lower half of the worksheet contains all of the sections needed.

Exhibit 14.4

Worksheet-Derived Statement of Cash Flows for Portermart Company

Cash flows from operating activities:		
Net income	$40,000	
Add (deduct) adjusting items:		
Depreciation expense	10,000	
Loss on sale of equipment	7,000	
Decrease in inventory	25,000	
Increase in accounts payable	20,000	
Increase in accounts receivable	(5,000)	
Decrease in wages payable	(2,000)	
Net cash from operating activities		$ 95,000
Cash flows from investing activities:		
Sale of equipment		$ 8,000
Cash flows from financing activities:		
Reduction in bonds payable		$(10,000)
Payment of dividends		(10,000)
Issuance of preferred stock		10,000
Net cash from financing activities		$(10,000)
Net increase in cash		$ 93,000
Noncash investing and financing activities:		
Acquisition of land issuing common stock		$ 40,000

The debit column provides the cash inflows, and the credit column provides the cash outflows. The noncash section is an exception; either column may be used to provide the information. The only additional effort needed is to compute subtotals for each section.

Check Point

1. **What are the advantages of a worksheet approach for preparing the statement of cash flows?**

Answer:
A worksheet reduces confusion, provides a ready way to track the details of a cash flow analysis, and allows the use of spreadsheet programs.

2. **Explain how selling manufacturing equipment for a loss can affect both operating and investing cash.**

Answer:
The loss is a noncash expense added back to obtain an operating cash effect. The money coming in from the sale is a source of cash for the investing activity.

SUMMARY OF LEARNING OBJECTIVES

LO1. Explain the basic elements of a statement of cash flows.
- Knowing a company's cash flows enables managers, investors, creditors, and others to assess the economic strength and viability of a company by evaluating its current cash flows and by assessing future cash flow potential.
- The Financial Accounting Standards Board (FASB), recognizing the need for cash flow information, recommended that all firms prepare a statement of cash flows.

- The activity format for a statement of cash flows has three sections: cash flows from operating activities, cash flows from investing activities, and cash flows from financing activities. Noncash financing and investing activities also are reported.
- The change in cash for a period is the difference between the beginning and ending balances of the cash account. The change in cash equivalents also is included in the change in cash.
- Operating activities are the main revenue-generating activities engaged in by the organization.
- Operating cash flows are computed by adjusting the period's net income for noncash expenses, accrual effects, and nonoperating revenues or expenses.
- Investing activities involve the acquisition and sale of long-term assets.
- Financing activities involve raising outside capital through the issuance of debt and capital stock. Financing activities also involve the retirement of debt and capital stock.

LO2. Prepare a statement of cash flows using the indirect method.
- Compute the change in cash.
- Compute operating cash flows by adjusting net income for items that do not affect cash flows.
- Identify investing cash flows.
- Identify financing cash flows.
- Assemble the data into a statement of cash flows.
- Preparation of the statement relies on the beginning and ending balance sheets and information regarding other activities and events that may not be fully apparent from the balance sheets themselves.

LO3. Calculate operating cash flows using the direct method.
- Compute the change in cash.
- Compute operating cash flows by adjusting each line on the income statement to reflect cash flows.
- Identify investing cash flows.
- Identify financing cash flows.
- Assemble the data into a statement of cash flows.
- Preparation of the statement relies on the beginning and ending balance sheets and information regarding other activities and events that may not be fully apparent from the balance sheets themselves.

LO4. Prepare a statement of cash flows using a worksheet approach.
- Worksheets can be used to organize the data for the statement of cash flows.
- Worksheets offer increased efficiency in form and the added convenience of spread-sheet software packages.

EXAMPLE 14.1	How to classify activities and identify them as sources or uses of cash, page 793
EXAMPLE 14.2	How to compute the change in cash, page 796
EXAMPLE 14.3	How to calculate operating cash flows using the indirect method, page 796
EXAMPLE 14.4	How to compute investing cash flows, page 798
EXAMPLE 14.5	How to compute financing cash flows, page 799
EXAMPLE 14.6	How to prepare the statement of cash flows, page 800
EXAMPLE 14.7	How to calculate operating cash flows using the direct method, page 802
EXAMPLE 14.8	How to prepare a statement of cash flows using a worksheet approach, page 804

KEY TERMS

Activity format, 793, a format for the statement of cash flows that reports cash flows for three categories: (1) cash flows from operating activities, (2) cash flows from investing activities, and (3) cash flows from financing activities.

Cash equivalents, 792, highly liquid investments, such as treasury bills, money market funds, and commercial paper.

Cash inflows, 792, activities that increase cash and are sources of cash.

Cash outflows, 792, activities that decrease cash and are uses of cash.

Direct method, 793, method that assigns support department costs *only* to the producing departments. No cost from one support department is given to another support department; thus, it ignores support department interaction.

Financing activities, 793, those activities that raise (provide) cash from (to) creditors and owners.

Indirect method, 793, computes operating cash flows by *adjusting net income* for noncash items, nonoperating gains and losses, and accruals.

Investing activities, 793, those activities that involve the acquisition or sale of long-term assets.

Noncash investing and financing activities, 794, investing and financing activities that take place without affecting cash.

Operating activities, 793, the ongoing, day-to-day, revenue-generating activities of an organization.

Statement of cash flows, 792, a statement that provides information regarding the sources and uses of a firm's cash.

REVIEW PROBLEMS

I. Statement of Cash Flows: Indirect Method

The following balance sheets are taken from the records of Golding Inc.:

	20X1	20X2
Assets		
Cash	$130,000	$150,000
Accounts receivable	25,000	20,000
Plant and equipment	50,000	60,000
Accumulated depreciation	(20,000)	(25,000)
Land	10,000	10,000
Total assets	$195,000	$215,000
Liabilities and equity		
Accounts payable	$ 10,000	$ 5,000
Bonds payable	8,000	18,000
Common stock	120,000	120,000
Retained earnings	57,000	72,000
Total liabilities and equity	$195,000	$215,000

Additional information is as follows: Equipment costing $10,000 was purchased at year-end. No equipment was sold. Net income for the year was $25,000, and $10,000 in dividends were paid.

Required:

Prepare a statement of cash flows using the indirect method.

Solution:

1. Cash flow change: $150,000 – $130,000 = $20,000
2. Operating cash flows:

Net income	$25,000
Add (deduct):	
Decrease in accounts receivable	5,000
Depreciation expense	5,000
Decrease in accounts payable	(5,000)
Net cash from operating activities	$30,000

3. Cash from investing activities for purchase of equipment is $(10,000).
4. Cash from financing activities:

Payment of dividends	$(10,000)
Issuance of bonds	10,000
Net cash from financing activities	$ 0

5.

Golding Inc.
Statement of Cash Flows
For the Year Ended December 31, 20X2

Cash flows from operating activities:		
Net income	$ 25,000	
Add (deduct) adjusting items:		
Decrease in accounts receivable	5,000	
Depreciation expense	5,000	
Decrease in accounts payable	(5,000)	
Net cash from operating activities		$ 30,000
Cash flows from investing activities:		
Purchase of equipment		(10,000)
Cash flows from financing activities:		
Payment of dividends	$(10,000)	
Issuance of bonds	10,000	
Net cash from financing activities		0
Net increase in cash		$ 20,000

II. Statement of Cash Flows: Direct Method

The following balance sheets are taken from the records of Golding:

	20X1	20X2
Assets		
Cash	$130,000	$150,000
Accounts receivable	25,000	20,000
Plant and equipment	50,000	60,000
Accumulated depreciation	(20,000)	(25,000)
Land	10,000	10,000
Total assets	$195,000	$215,000

(Continued)

	20X1	20X2
Liabilities and equity		
Accounts payable	$ 10,000	$ 5,000
Bonds payable	8,000	18,000
Common stock	120,000	120,000
Retained earnings	57,000	72,000
Total liabilities and equity	$195,000	$215,000

Additional information is as follows: Equipment costing $10,000 was purchased at year-end. No equipment was sold. Net income for the year was calculated as follows:

Revenues	$ 500,000
Cost of goods sold	(375,000)
Depreciation expense	(5,000)
Other expenses	(95,000)
Net income	$ 25,000

Dividends paid were $10,000.

Required:

Prepare a statement of operating cash flows using the direct method.

Solution:

Cash flows from operating activities:

	Income Statement	Adjustments	Cash Flows
Revenues	$ 500,000	$ 5,000[a]	$ 505,000
Cost of goods sold	(375,000)	(5,000)[b]	(380,000)
Depreciation expense	(5,000)	5,000[c]	
Other expenses	(95,000)		(95,000)
Net cash from operating activities			$ 30,000

[a] Decrease in accounts receivable.
[b] Decrease in accounts payable.
[c] Add back depreciation (noncash expense).

DISCUSSION QUESTIONS

1. What are cash equivalents? How are cash equivalents treated in preparing a statement of cash flows?
2. The activity format calls for three categories on the statement of cash flows. Define each category.
3. Of the three categories on the statement of cash flows, which do you think provides the most useful information? Explain.
4. Explain the all-financial-resources approach to reporting financing and investing activities.
5. Why is it better to report the noncash investing and financing activities in a supplemental schedule rather than to include these activities on the body of the statement of cash flows?
6. What are the five steps for preparing the statement of cash flows? What is the purpose of each step?
7. Explain how a company can report a positive net income and yet still have a negative net operating cash flow.
8. Explain how a company can report a loss and still have a positive net operating cash flow.
9. In computing the period's net operating cash flows, why are increases in current liabilities and decreases in current assets added back to net income?
10. In computing the period's net operating cash flows, why are decreases in liabilities and increases in current assets deducted from net income?

11. In computing the period's net operating cash flows, why are noncash expenses added back to net income?

12. Explain the reasoning for including the payment of dividends in the financing section of the statement of cash flows.

13. What are the advantages in using worksheets when preparing a statement of cash flows?

14. Explain how the statement of cash flows can be prepared using the worksheet approach.

MULTIPLE-CHOICE QUESTIONS

14-1 Cash inflows from operating activities come from

    a. payment for raw materials.

    b. gains on the sale of operating equipment.

    c. collection of sales revenues.

    d. issuing capital stock.

    e. issuing bonds.

14-2 Cash outflows from operating activities come from

    a. collection of sales revenues.

    b. payment for operating costs.

    c. acquisition of operating equipment.

    d. retirement of bonds.

    e. None of these.

14-3 Raising cash by issuing capital stock is an example of

    a. a financing activity.

    b. an investing activity.

    c. an operating activity.

    d. a noncash transaction.

    e. None of these.

14-4 Sources of cash include

    a. profitable operations.

    b. the issuance of long-term debt.

    c. the sale of long-term assets.

    d. the issuance of capital stock.

    e. All of these.

14-5 Uses of cash include

    a. cash dividends.

    b. the sale of old equipment.

    c. the purchase of long-term assets.

    d. only a and b.

    e. only a and c.

14-6 The difference between the beginning and ending cash balances shown on the balance sheet

    a. is added to net income to obtain total cash inflows.

    b. serves as a control figure for the statement of cash flows.

    c. is deducted from net income to obtain net cash inflows.

    d. is the source of all investing and financing activities.

    e. is both c and d.

14-7 Which of the following adjustments helps to convert accrual income to operating cash flows?

    a. Deduct from net income all noncash expenses.
    b. Add to net income a decrease in inventories.
    c. Add to net income a decrease in accounts payable.
    d. Deduct from net income an increase in accounts payable.
    e. None of these.

14-8 Which of the following adjustments to net income is needed to obtain cash flows?

    a. Eliminate gains on sale of equipment.
    b. Deduct from net income all noncash expenses (e.g., depreciation and amortization).
    c. Deduct from net income any increases in current liabilities.
    d. Add to net income any increases in inventories.
    e. All of these.

14-9 An increase in accounts receivable is deducted from net income to obtain operating cash flows because

    a. cash collections increased due to increasing sales.
    b. cash collections from customers were less than the revenues reported.
    c. cash collections decreased due to declining sales.
    d. cash collections from customers were greater than the revenues reported.
    e. None of these.

14-10 An increase in inventories is deducted from net income to arrive at operating cash flow because

    a. cash payments to customers were larger than the purchases made during the period.
    b. purchases are larger than the cost of goods sold by the amount that inventories increased.
    c. cash payments to customers were less than the purchases made during the period.
    d. purchases are less than the cost of goods sold by the amount that inventories increased.
    e. All of these.

14-11 The gain on sale of equipment is deducted from net income to arrive at operating cash flows because

    a. the sale of long-term assets is an operating activity.
    b. the gain reveals the total cash received.
    c. all of the cash received from the sale is reported in the operating section.
    d. All of these.
    e. None of these.

14-12 Which of the following is an investing activity?

    a. Issuance of a mortgage
    b. Increase in accounts receivable
    c. Purchase of land
    d. Increase in inventories
    e. All of these.

14-13 Which of the following is a financing activity?

    a. Increase in inventories
    b. Purchase of land
    c. Increase in accounts receivable
    d. Issuance of a mortgage
    e. All of these.

14-14 Which method calculates operating cash flows by adjusting the income statement on a line-by-line basis?

    a. Direct method
    b. Indirect method
    c. Working paper approach
    d. Income method
    e. None of these.

14-15 A worksheet approach to preparing the statement of cash flows

    a. is a useful aid.
    b. uses a spreadsheet format.
    c. offers an efficient and logical way of organizing the data.
    d. allows an easy extraction of the needed data.
    e. All of these.

14-16 In a completed worksheet,

    a. the debit column contains the cash inflows.
    b. the debit column contains the cash outflows.
    c. the credit column contains the cash inflows.
    d. the credit column contains only operating cash flows.
    e. None of these.

BRIEF EXERCISES: SET A

Brief Exercise 14-17 Activity Classification

OBJECTIVE 1
Example 14.1

During the last 2 years of operations, Haws Company had the following transactions:

    a. Reported a loss for the year ($800,000).
    b. Reported profits of $6,000,000 for the most recent year.
    c. Issued bonds with a 6-year maturity date for $2,000,000.
    d. Retired a mortgage bond.
    e. Sold a 20% interest in a company.
    f. Paid cash dividends of $2,000,000.
    g. Sold equipment for $500,000.
    h. Purchased a new manufacturing system for $6,000,000.
    i. Issued preferred stock for $2,000,000.

Required:

Classify each of these transactions as an operating activity, an investing activity, or a financing activity and indicate whether the activity is a source of cash or a use of cash.

Brief Exercise 14-18 Change in Cash

OBJECTIVE 2
Example 14.2

Swasey Company provided the following information:

Swasey Company
Comparative Balance Sheets
At December 31, 20X1 and 20X2

	20X1	20X2
Cash	$1,400,000	$2,260,000

Required:

1. Calculate the change in cash.
2. Explain the role of the change in cash in the statement of cash flows.

OBJECTIVE **2**

Example 14.3

Brief Exercise 14-19 Operating Cash Flows: Indirect Method

Swasey Company provided the following partial comparative balance sheets and the income statement for 20X2

Swasey Company
Comparative Balance Sheets
At December 31, 20X1 and 20X2

	20X1	20X2
Current assets:		
Accounts receivable	$1,500,000	$1,165,000
Inventories	600,000	640,000
Current liabilities:		
Wages payable	1,400,000	1,030,000

Swasey Company
Income Statement
For the Year Ended December 31, 20X2

Revenues	$ 6,000,000
Gain on sale of equipment	200,000
Cost of goods sold	(3,840,000)
Depreciation expense	(540,000)
Interest expense	(20,000)
Net income	$ 1,800,000

Required:

Compute operating cash flows using the indirect method.

OBJECTIVE **2**

Example 14.4

Brief Exercise 14-20 Cash Flows from Investing Activities

During the year, Swasey Company sold equipment with a book value of $560,000 for $760,000 (original purchase cost of $960,000). New equipment was purchased.

Swasey provided the following comparative balance sheets:

Swasey Company
Comparative Balance Sheets
At December 31, 20X1 and 20X2

	20X1	20X2
Long-Term Assets:		
Plant and equipment	$ 4,400,000	$ 4,300,000
Accumulated depreciation	(2,400,000)	(2,540,000)
Land	(2,000,000)	(2,875,000)

Required:

Calculate the investing cash flows for the current year.

OBJECTIVE **2**

Example 14.5

Brief Exercise 14-21 Cash Flows from Financing Activities

Swasey Company earned net income of $1,800,000 in 20X2. Swasey provided the following information:

Swasey Company
Comparative Balance Sheets
At December 31, 20X1 and 20X2

	20X1	20X2
Bonds payable	$ —	$ 770,000
Mortgage payable	200,000	—

Swasey Company
Comparative Balance Sheets
At December 31, 20X1 and 20X2

	20X1	20X2
Common stock	750,000	750,000
Paid-in capital in excess of par	560,000	560,000
Retained earnings	3,650,000	4,650,000

Required:

Compute the financing cash flows for the current year.

Brief Exercise 14-22 Statement of Cash Flows

OBJECTIVE 2
Example 14.6

Refer to the information provided in **Brief Exercises 14-19, 14-20**, and **14-21**.

Required:

1. Prepare a statement of cash flows for Swasey for 20X2.
2. What is the relationship between the statement of cash flows and the change in cash calculated in **Brief Exercise 14-18**?

Brief Exercise 14-23 Operating Cash Flows: Direct Method

OBJECTIVE 3
Example 14.7

Tidwell Company has provided the following partial comparative balance sheets and the income statement for 20X2.

Tidwell Company
Comparative Balance Sheets
At December 31, 20X1 and 20X2

	20X1	20X2
Current assets:		
Accounts receivable	$700,000	$563,000
Inventories	250,000	300,000
Current liabilities:		
Accounts payable	600,000	475,000

Tidwell Company
Income Statement
For the Year Ended December 31, 20X2

Revenues	$ 2,400,000
Gain on sale of equipment	100,000
Cost of goods sold	(1,300,000)
Depreciation expense	(250,000)
Interest expense	(50,000)
Net income	$ 900,000

Required:

Compute operating cash flows using the direct method.

Brief Exercise 14-24 Worksheet Approach

OBJECTIVE 4
Example 14.8

During 20X2, Norton Company had the following transactions:

a. Cash dividends of $20,000 were paid.
b. Equipment was sold for $9,600. It had an original cost of $36,000 and a book value of $18,000. The loss is included in operating expenses.

(Continued)

c. Land with a fair market value of $50,000 was acquired by issuing common stock with a par value of $12,000.

d. One thousand shares of preferred stock (no par) were sold for $14 per share.

Norton provided the following income statement (for 20X2) and comparative balance sheets:

Sales	$ 492,000
Cost of goods sold	(300,000)
Gross margin	$ 192,000
Operating expenses	(132,000)
Net income	$ 60,000

Norton Company
Comparative Balance Sheets
At December 31, 20X1 and 20X2

	20X1	20X2
Assets		
Cash	$108,000	$ 222,000
Accounts receivable	66,000	73,600
Inventory	96,000	66,000
Plant and equipment	156,000	120,000
Accumulated depreciation	(78,000)	(72,000)
Land	30,000	80,000
Total assets	$378,000	$ 489,600
Liabilities and stockholders' equity		
Accounts payable	$ 48,000	$ 72,000
Wages payable	6,000	3,600
Bonds payable	36,000	22,000
Preferred stock (no par)	6,000	20,000
Common stock	60,000	72,000
Paid-in capital in excess of par	60,000	98,000
Retained earnings	162,000	202,000
Total liabilities and stockholders' equity	$378,000	$ 489,600

Required:

Prepare a worksheet for Norton Company.

BRIEF EXERCISES: SET B

Brief Exercise 14-25 Activity Classification

During the last 2 years of operations, Lelkes Company had the following transactions:

a. Purchased land for $1,000,000.

b. Issued bonds with a 5-year maturity date for $3,000,000.

c. Reported a loss of $2,000,000 for the most recent year.

d. Bought equipment for $500,000.

e. Issued common stock for $2,000,000.

f. Bought a 30% interest in a company.

g. Retired a long-term note payable.

h. Reported a profit for the year ($500,000).

i. Paid dividends of $1,000,000.

Required:

Classify each of these transactions as an operating activity, an investing activity, or a financing activity and indicate whether the activity is a source of cash or a use of cash.

Brief Exercise 14-26 **Change in Cash**

Roberts Company provided the following information:

OBJECTIVE ◄ 2

Example 14.2

Roberts Company
Comparative Balance Sheets
At December 31, 20X1 and 20X2

	20X1	20X2
Cash	$350,000	$565,000

Required:

1. Calculate the change in cash.
2. Explain the role of the change in cash flow in the statement of cash flows.

Brief Exercise 14-27 **Operating Cash Flows: Indirect Method**

Roberts Company provided the following partial comparative balance sheets and the income statement for 20X2.

OBJECTIVE ◄ 2

Example 14.3

Roberts Company
Comparative Balance Sheets
At December 31, 20X1 and 20X2

	20X1	20X2
Current assets:		
Accounts receivable	$375,000	$291,250
Inventories	150,000	160,000
Current liabilities:		
Wages payable	350,000	257,500

Roberts Company
Income Statement
For the Year Ended December 31, 20X2

Revenues	$1,500,000
Gain on sale of equipment	50,000
Cost of goods sold	(960,000)
Depreciation expense	(135,000)
Interest expense	(5,000)
Net income	$ 450,000

Required:

Compute operating cash flows using the indirect method.

Brief Exercise 14-28 **Cash Flows from Investing Activities**

During the year, Roberts Company sold equipment with a book value of $140,000 for $190,000 (original purchase cost of $240,000). New equipment was purchased.

Roberts provided the following comparative balance sheets:

OBJECTIVE ◄ 2

Example 14.4

Roberts Company
Comparative Balance Sheets
At December 31, 20X1 and 20X2

	20X1	20X2
Long-Term Assets:		
Plant and equipment	$1,100,000	$1,075,000
Accumulated depreciation	(300,000)	(635,000)
Land	(500,000)	(718,750)

(Continued)

Required:

Calculate the investing cash flows for the current year.

OBJECTIVE `2`
Example 14.5

Brief Exercise 14-29 **Cash Flows from Financing Activities**

Roberts Company earned net income of $450,000 in 20X2. Roberts provided the following information:

Roberts Company
Comparative Balance Sheets
At December 31, 20X1 and 20X2

	20X1	20X2
Bonds payable	$ —	$ 192,500
Mortgage payable	50,000	—
Common stock	187,500	187,500
Paid-in capital in excess of par	190,000	190,000
Retained earnings	912,500	1,162,500

Required:

Compute the financing cash flows for the current year.

OBJECTIVE `2`
Example 14.6

Brief Exercise 14-30 **Statement of Cash Flows**

Refer to the information provided in **Brief Exercises 14-27, 14-28**, and **14-29**.

Required:

1. Prepare a statement of cash flows for Roberts Company for 20X2.
2. What is the relationship between the statement of cash flows and the change in cash calculated in Brief Exercise 14-26?

OBJECTIVE `3`
Example 14.7

Brief Exercise 14-31 **Operating Cash Flows: Direct Method**

Belnap Company has provided the following partial comparative balance sheets and the income statement for 20X2.

Belnap Company
Comparative Balance Sheets
At December 31, 20X1 and 20X2

	20X1	20X2
Current assets:		
Accounts receivable	$140,000	$112,600
Inventories	50,000	24,000
Current liabilities:		
Accounts payable	120,000	95,000

Belnap Company
Income Statement
For the Year Ended December 31, 20X2

Revenues	$ 480,000
Gain on sale of equipment	20,000
Cost of goods sold	(260,000)
Depreciation expense	(50,000)
Interest expense	(10,000)
Net income	$ 180,000

Required:

Compute operating cash flows using the direct method.

Brief Exercise 14-32 Worksheet Approach

OBJECTIVE ◀ 4

Example 14.8

During 20X2, Evans Company had the following transactions:

a. Cash dividends of $6,000 were paid.
b. Equipment was sold for $2,880. It had an original cost of $10,800 and a book value of $5,400. The loss is included in operating expenses.
c. Land with a fair market value of $15,000 was acquired by issuing common stock with a par value of $3,600.
d. One thousand shares of preferred stock (no par) were sold for $4.20 per share.

Evans provided the following income statement (for 20X2) and comparative balance sheets:

Sales	$147,600
Cost of goods sold	(90,000)
Gross margin	$ 57,600
Operating expenses	(39,600)
Net income	$ 18,000

Evans Company
Comparative Balance Sheets
At December 31, 20X1 and 20X2

	20X1	20X2
Assets		
Cash	$ 32,400	$ 66,600
Accounts receivable	19,800	22,080
Inventory	28,800	19,800
Plant and equipment	46,800	36,000
Accumulated depreciation	(23,400)	(21,600)
Land	9,000	24,000
Total assets	$113,400	$146,880
Liabilities and stockholders' equity		
Accounts payable	$ 14,400	$ 21,600
Wages payable	1,800	1,080
Bonds payable	10,800	6,600
Preferred stock (no par)	1,800	6,000
Common stock	18,000	21,600
Paid-in capital in excess of par	18,000	29,400
Retained earnings	48,600	60,600
Total liabilities and stockholders' equity	$113,400	$146,880

Required:

Prepare a worksheet for Evans Company.

EXERCISES

Exercise 14-33 Activity Classification

OBJECTIVE ◀ 1

Stillwater Designs is a private company and outsources production of its **Kicker** speaker lines. Suppose that Stillwater Designs provided you the following transactions:

a. Sold a warehouse for $750,000.
b. Reported a profit of $100,000.
c. Retired long-term bonds.
d. Paid cash dividends of $350,000.

(Continued)

e. Obtained a mortgage for a new building from a local bank.
f. Purchased a new robotic system.
g. Issued a long-term note payable.

h. Purchased a 40% interest in a company.
i. Reported a loss for the year.
j. Negotiated a long-term loan.

Required:

Classify each of these transactions as an operating activity, an investing activity, or a financing activity. Also, indicate whether the activity is a source of cash or a use of cash.

OBJECTIVE 2   **Exercise 14-34 Adjustments to Net Income**

Consider the following independent events:

a. Gain on sale of an asset
b. Increase in accounts receivable
c. Decrease in prepaid insurance
d. Amortization expense
e. Increase in accounts payable

f. Uncollectible accounts expense
g. Decrease in wages payable
h. Increase in inventories
i. Depreciation expense

Required:

Indicate whether each event will be added to or deducted from net income in order to compute cash flow from operations.

OBJECTIVE 2   **Exercise 14-35 Adjustment for Prepaid Rent**

Jarem Company showed $189,000 in prepaid rent on December 31, 20X1. On December 31, 20X2, the balance in the prepaid rent account was $226,800. Rent expense for 20X2 was $472,500.

Required:

1. What amount of cash was paid for rent in 20X2?
2. **CONCEPTUAL CONNECTION** What adjustment in prepaid expenses is needed if the indirect method is used to prepare Jarem's statement of cash flows?

OBJECTIVE 2   **Exercise 14-36 Operating Cash Flows**

During the year, Hepworth Company earned a net income of $61,725. Beginning and ending balances for the year for selected accounts are as follows:

	Account	
	Beginning	**Ending**
Cash	$108,000	$126,600
Accounts receivable	67,500	99,750
Inventory	36,000	52,500
Prepaid expenses	27,000	30,000
Accumulated depreciation	81,000	91,500
Accounts payable	45,000	55,125
Wages payable	27,000	15,000

There were no financing or investing activities for the year. The above balances reflect all of the adjustments needed to adjust net income to operating cash flows.

Required:

1. Prepare a schedule of operating cash flows using the indirect method.

2. Suppose that all the data are used in Requirement 1 except that the ending accounts payable and cash balances are not known. Assume also that you know that the operating cash flow for the year was $20,475. What is the ending balance of accounts payable?

3. **CONCEPTUAL CONNECTION** Hepworth has an opportunity to buy some equipment that will significantly increase productivity. The equipment costs $25,000. Assuming exactly the same data used for Requirement 1, can Hepworth buy the equipment using this year's operating cash flows? If not, what would you suggest be done?

Exercise 14-37 Cash Flow from Investing Activities

OBJECTIVE ▶ 2

During 20X1, Craig Company had the following transactions:

a. Purchased $300,000 of 10-year bonds issued by Makenzie Inc.
b. Acquired land valued at $105,000 in exchange for machinery.
c. Sold equipment with original cost of $810,000 for $495,000; accumulated depreciation taken on the equipment to the point of sale was $270,000.
d. Purchased new machinery for $180,000.
e. Purchased common stock in Lemmons Company for $82,500.

Required:

1. Prepare the net cash from investing activities section of the statement of cash flows.
2. **CONCEPTUAL CONNECTION** Usually, the net cash from investing activities is negative. How can Craig cover this negative cash flow? What other information would you like to have to make this decision?

Exercise 14-38 Cash Flow from Financing Activities

OBJECTIVE ▶ 2

Tidwell Company experienced the following during 20X1:

a. Sold preferred stock for $480,000.
b. Declared dividends of $150,000 payable on March 1, 20X2.
c. Borrowed $575,000 from a bank on a 2-year note.
d. Purchased $80,000 of its own common stock to hold as treasury stock.
e. Repaid 5-year bonds issued for $400,000 that mature and are due in December.

Required:

Prepare the net cash from financing activities section of the statement of cash flows.

Use the following information for Exercises 14-39 and 14-40:
Oliver Company provided the following information for the years 20X1 and 20X2:

Oliver Company
Income Statement
For the Year Ended December 31, 20X2

Sales	$ 75,000
Cost of goods sold	(20,000)
Depreciation expense	(2,000)
Other expenses	(13,000)
Net income	$ 40,000

(Continued)

Oliver Company
Comparative Balance Sheets
At December 31, 20X1 and 20X2

	20X1	20X2
Assets		
Cash	$ 24,600	$ 64,600
Accounts receivable	5,400	9,200
Inventory	8,000	6,000
Property, plant, and equipment	160,000	175,000
Accumulated depreciation	(18,000)	(20,000)
Land	20,400	47,000
Total assets	$200,400	$281,800
Liabilities and equity		
Accounts payable	$ 8,600	$ 10,000
Mortgage payable	—	40,000
Stockholders' equity	191,800	231,800
Total liabilities and equity	$200,400	$281,800

OBJECTIVE 2

Exercise 14-39 **Operating Cash Flows**

Refer to the information for Oliver Company above and on the previous page.

Required:

1. Calculate the change in cash flows that serves as the control figure for the statement of cash flows.
2. Prepare a schedule that provides operating cash flows for the year 20X2 using the indirect method.
3. Assume that you have all the information provided for Requirement 1 except that you only know the beginning balance of accounts receivable for 20X2. Given this information and assuming that the operating cash flows for 20X2 are $41,000, calculate the ending balance for accounts receivable.

OBJECTIVE 3

Exercise 14-40 **Operating Cash Flows**

Refer to the information for Oliver Company above and on the previous page.

EXCEL

Required:

Prepare a schedule that provides operating cash flows for the year 20X2 using the direct method.

OBJECTIVE 1

Exercise 14-41 **Classification of Transactions**

Consider the following independent activities:

a. Payment of a cash dividend
b. Amortization of intangible asset
c. Gain on disposal of equipment
d. Exchange of common stock for land
e. Increase in accrued wages
f. Retirement of preferred stock
g. Purchase of a new plant
h. Depreciation expense
i. Decrease in accounts payable

j. Increase in accounts receivable
k. Proceeds from the sale of land
l. Increase in prepaid expenses
m. Retirement of a bond
n. Purchase of a 60% interest in another company

Required:

Classify these transactions as operating activities, investing activities, financing activities, or financing/investing not affecting cash. If an activity is an operating activity, indicate whether it will be added to or deducted from net income to compute cash from operations.

Use the following information for Exercises 14-42 and 14-43:

The income statement for Piura Merchandising Corporation is as follows:

Piura Merchandising Corporation
Income Statement
At December 31, 20X1

Sales		$ 1,500,000
Cost of goods sold		
Beginning inventory	$ 400,000	
Purchases	800,000	
Ending inventory	(200,000)	
		(1,000,000)
Depreciation expense		(100,000)
Amortization of patent		(20,000)
Wages expense		(80,000)
Insurance expense		(40,000)
Income before taxes		$ 260,000
Income taxes (all current)		(104,000)
Net income		$ 156,000

Other information is as follows:

a. Accounts payable decreased by $20,000 during the year.
b. Accounts receivable increased by $20,000.
c. All wages were paid at the beginning of the year; at the end of the year, wages payable had a balance of $12,000.
d. Prepaid insurance increased by $24,000 during the year.

Exercise 14-42 Operating Cash Flows
OBJECTIVE ◄ 2

Refer to the information for Piura Merchandising Corporation above.

Required:

Prepare a schedule that provides the operating cash flows for the year using the indirect method.

Exercise 14-43 Operating Cash Flows, Direct Method
OBJECTIVE ◄ 3

Refer to the information for Piura Merchandising Corporation above.

Required:

Prepare a schedule of operating cash flows using the direct method.

EXCEL

PROBLEMS

Use the following information for Problems 14-44 and 14-45:
Solpoder Corporation has the following comparative financial statements:

Solpoder Corporation
Comparative Balance Sheets
At December 31, 20X1 and 20X2

	20X1	20X2
Assets		
Cash	$ 49,500	$ 81,000
Accounts receivable, net	135,000	108,000
Inventory	27,000	54,000
Plant and equipment	180,000	180,000
Accumulated depreciation	(36,000)	(45,000)
Total assets	$355,500	$378,000
Liabilities and equity		
Accounts payable	$ 57,600	$ 18,000
Common stock	190,800	207,000
Retained earnings	107,100	153,000
Total liabilities and equity	$355,500	$378,000

Solpoder Corporation
Income Statement
For the Year Ended December 31, 20X2

Sales		$ 297,000
Cost of goods sold		(175,500)
Gross margin		$ 121,500
Operating expenses		(58,500)
Net income		$ 63,000

Dividends of $17,100 were paid. No equipment was purchased or retired during the current year.

OBJECTIVE 2

Problem 14-44   Statement of Cash Flows, Indirect Method

Refer to the information for Solpoder Corporation above and on the previous page.

Required:

Prepare a statement of cash flows using the indirect method.

OBJECTIVE 3

Problem 14-45   Statement of Cash Flows, Direct Method

Refer to the information for Solpoder Corporation above and on the previous page.

Required:

Prepare a statement of cash flows using the direct method.

Use the following information for Problems 14-46 and 14-47:
The following financial statements were provided by Roberts Company:

Roberts Company
Balance Sheets
At September 30, 20X1 and 20X2

	20X1	20X2
Assets		
Cash	$ 23,000	$ 7,000
Accounts receivable	7,600	9,600
Inventory	20,800	18,000
Plant and equipment	40,000	60,000
Accumulated depreciation	(10,000)	(16,000)
Total assets	$ 81,400	$ 78,600
Liabilities and equity		
Accounts payable	$ 4,800	$ 3,200
Wages payable	1,200	800
Common stock	50,000	50,000
Retained earnings	25,400	24,600
Total liabilities and equity	$ 81,400	$ 78,600

Roberts Company
Income Statement
For the Year Ended September 30, 20X2

Sales		$ 40,000
Cost of goods sold:		
Beginning inventory	$ 20,800	
Purchases	26,000	
Ending inventory	(18,000)	(28,800)
Wages expense		(4,000)
Advertising		(2,000)
Depreciation expense		(6,000)
Net income (loss)		$ (800)

At the end of 20X2, Roberts purchased some additional equipment for $20,000.

Problem 14-46 Statement of Cash Flows, Indirect Method   OBJECTIVE ▸ 3

Refer to the information for Roberts Company above and on the previous page.

Required:

Prepare a statement of cash flows using the indirect method.

Problem 14-47 Statement of Cash Flows, Direct Method   OBJECTIVE ▸ 3

Refer to the information for Roberts Company above and on the previous page.

Required:

Calculate operating cash flows using the direct method.   **EXCEL**

Use the following information for Problems 14-48 and 14-49:
Booth Manufacturing has provided the following financial statements.

Booth Manufacturing
Comparative Balance Sheets
At December 31, 20X1 and 20X2

	20X1	20X2
Assets		
Cash	$ 112,500	$ 350,000
Accounts receivable	350,000	281,250
Inventories	125,000	150,000
Plant and equipment	1,000,000	1,025,000
Accumulated depreciation	(500,000)	(525,000)
Land	500,000	718,750
Total assets	$1,587,500	$2,000,000
Liabilities and equity		
Accounts payable	$ 300,000	$ 237,500
Mortgage payable	—	250,000
Common stock	75,000	75,000
Paid-in capital in excess of par	300,000	300,000
Retained earnings	912,500	1,137,500
Total liabilities and equity	$1,587,500	$2,000,000

Booth Manufacturing
Income Statement
For the Year Ended December 31, 20X2

Revenues	$1,200,000
Gain on sale of equipment	50,000
Cost of goods sold	(640,000)
Depreciation expense	(125,000)
Interest expense	(35,000)
Net income	$ 450,000

Other information includes: (a) equipment with a book value of $125,000 was sold for $175,000 (original cost was $225,000) and (b) dividends of $225,000 were declared and paid.

OBJECTIVE 1 2

Problem 14-48 Statement of Cash Flows, Indirect Method

Refer to the information for Booth Manufacturing above.

EXCEL

Required:

1. Calculate the cash flows from operations using the indirect method.
2. Prepare a statement of cash flows.
3. **CONCEPTUAL CONNECTION** Search the Internet to find a statement of cash flows. Which method was used—the indirect method or the direct method? How does the net income reported compare to the operating cash flows? To the change in cash flows?

OBJECTIVE 1 3

Problem 14-49 Statement of Cash Flows, Direct Method

Refer to the information for Booth Manufacturing above.

EXCEL

Required:

Calculate operating cash flows using the direct method.

Use the following information for Problems 14-50 and 14-51:

The following balance sheets and income statement were taken from the records of Rosie-Lee Company:

Rosie-Lee Company
Comparative Balance Sheets
At June 30, 20X1 and 20X2

	20X1	20X2
Assets		
Cash	$270,000	$333,000
Accounts receivable	126,000	144,000
Investments	—	54,000
Plant and equipment	180,000	189,000
Accumulated depreciation	(54,000)	(57,600)
Land	36,000	54,000
Total assets	$558,000	$716,400
Liabilities and equity		
Accounts payable	$ 72,000	$ 90,000
Mortgage payable	108,000	—
Bonds payable	—	90,000
Preferred stock	36,000	—
Common stock	180,000	288,000
Retained earnings	162,000	248,400
Total liabilities and equity	$558,000	$716,400

Rosie-Lee Company
Income Statement
For the Year Ended June 30, 20X2

Sales	$ 920,000
Cost of goods sold	(620,000)
Gross margin	$ 300,000
Operating expenses	(177,600)
Net income	$ 122,400

Additional transactions were as follows:

a. Sold equipment costing $21,600, with accumulated depreciation of $16,200, for $3,600.
b. Issued bonds for $90,000 on December 31.
c. Paid cash dividends of $36,000.
d. Retired mortgage of $108,000 on December 31.

Problem 14-50 Direct and Indirect Methods

OBJECTIVE ▸2 ▸3

Refer to the information for Rosie-Lee Company above.

Required:

1. Prepare a schedule of operating cash flows using (a) the indirect method and (b) the direct method.
2. Prepare a statement of cash flows using the indirect method.

Problem 14-51 Statement of Cash Flows, Worksheet

OBJECTIVE ▸4

Refer to the information for Rosie-Lee Company above.

(Continued)

Required:

Prepare a statement of cash flows using a worksheet similar to the one shown in Example 14.8 (p. 804). Use the indirect method to prepare the statement.

Use the following information for Problems 14-52 and 14-53:
Balance sheets for Brierwold Corporation follow:

	Beginning Balances	Ending Balances
Assets		
Cash	$ 100,000	$ 150,000
Accounts receivable	200,000	180,000
Inventory	400,000	410,000
Plant and equipment	700,000	690,000
Accumulated depreciation	(200,000)	(245,000)
Land	100,000	150,000
Total assets	$1,300,000	$1,335,000
Liabilities and equity		
Accounts payable	$ 300,000	$ 250,000
Mortgage payable	—	110,000
Preferred stock	100,000	—
Common stock	240,000	280,000
Paid-in capital in excess of par	360,000	420,000
Retained earnings	300,000	275,000
Total liabilities and equity	$1,300,000	$1,335,000

Additional transactions were as follows:

a. Purchased equipment costing $50,000.
b. Sold equipment costing $60,000, with a book value of $25,000, for $40,000.
c. Retired preferred stock at a cost of $110,000. (The premium is debited to Retained Earnings.)
d. Issued 10,000 shares of common stock (par value, $4) for $10 per share.
e. Reported a loss of $15,000 for the year.
f. Purchased land for $50,000.

OBJECTIVE **1** **2**   **Problem 14-52 Statement of Cash Flows, Indirect Method**

Refer to the information for Brierwold Corporation above.

Required:

Prepare a statement of cash flows using the indirect method.

OBJECTIVE **3** **4**   **Problem 14-53 Statement of Cash Flows, Worksheet**

Refer to the information for Brierwold Corporation above.

Required:

Prepare a statement of cash flows using the worksheet approach. Use the indirect method to prepare the statement.

Problem 14-54 Schedule of Operating Cash Flows, Indirect Method

OBJECTIVE ▶ 1 ◀ 2

The income statement for Mendelin Corporation is as follows:

Revenues		$ 380,000
Cost of goods sold:		
Beginning inventory	$ 50,000	
Purchases	200,000	
Ending inventory	(34,000)	(216,000)
Patent amortization		(20,000)
Advertising		(12,000)
Depreciation expense		(60,000)
Wages expense		(30,000)
Insurance expense		(10,500)
Bad debt expense		(6,400)
Interest expense		(7,600)
Net income		$ 17,500

Additional information is as follows:
a. Interest expense includes $1,800 of discount amortization.
b. The prepaid insurance expense account decreased by $2,000 during the year.
c. Wages payable decreased by $3,000 during the year.
d. Accounts payable increased by $7,500. (This account is for purchase of merchandise only.)
e. Accounts receivable increased by $10,000 (net of allowance for doubtful accounts).
f. Inventory decreased by $16,000.

Required:

Prepare a schedule of operating cash flows using the indirect method.

Problem 14-55 Statement of Cash Flows, Indirect Method

OBJECTIVE ▶ 1 ◀ 2

The following balance sheets are taken from the records of Golding Company (numbers are expressed in thousands):

	20X1	20X2
Assets		
Cash	$130,000	$150,000
Accounts receivable	25,000	20,000
Plant and equipment	50,000	60,000
Accumulated depreciation	(20,000)	(25,000)
Land	10,000	10,000
Total assets	$195,000	$215,000
Liabilities and equity		
Accounts payable	$ 10,000	$ 5,000
Bonds payable	8,000	18,000
Common stock	120,000	120,000
Retained earnings	57,000	72,000
Total liabilities and equity	$195,000	$215,000

Additional information is as follows: (a) equipment costing $10,000,000 was purchased at year-end; no equipment was sold; and (b) net income for the year was $25,000,000, and $10,000,000 in dividends were paid.

(Continued)

Required:

1. Prepare a statement of cash flows using the indirect method.
2. **CONCEPTUAL CONNECTION** Assess Golding's ability to use cash to acquire Lemmons Company. Consider the information in Exhibit 14.2 (p. 795) and Example 14.6 (p. 800) as part of your analysis.

Use the following information for Problems 14-56 and 14-57:
The following balance sheets were taken from the records of Blalock Company:

At the Years Ended December 31

	20X1	20X2
Assets		
Cash	$150,000	$ 185,000
Accounts receivable	70,000	80,000
Investments	—	30,000
Plant and equipment	100,000	105,000
Accumulated depreciation	(30,000)	(32,000)
Land	20,000	30,000
Total assets	$310,000	$ 398,000
Liabilities and equity		
Accounts payable	$ 40,000	$ 50,000
Bonds payable	60,000	—
Mortgage payable	—	50,000
Preferred stock	20,000	—
Common stock	100,000	160,000
Retained earnings	90,000	138,000
Total liabilities and equity	$310,000	$ 398,000

Additional transactions were as follows:

a. Sold equipment costing $12,000, with accumulated depreciation of $9,000, for $2,000.
b. Retired bonds at a price of $60,000 on December 31.
c. Earned net income for the year of $68,000; paid cash dividends of $20,000.

OBJECTIVE 4 ▶

Problem 14-56 Statement of Cash Flows

Refer to the information for Blalock Company above.

Required:

Prepare a statement of cash flows using the indirect method.

OBJECTIVE 4 ▶

Problem 14-57 Statement of Cash Flows, Worksheet

Refer to the information for Blalock Company above.

Required:

Prepare a statement of cash flows using the worksheet approach. Use the indirect method to prepare the statement.

CASES

Case 14-58 **Direct and Indirect Methods**

The comparative balance sheets and income statement of Piura Manufacturing follow.

Piura Manufacturing
Comparative Balance Sheets
For the Years Ended June 30, 20X1and 20X2

	20X1	20X2
Assets		
Cash	$ 72,000	$ 146,400
Accounts receivable	44,000	48,000
Inventory	64,000	44,000
Plant and equipment	104,000	112,000
Accumulated depreciation	(52,000)	(48,000)
Land	20,000	20,000
Total assets	$252,000	$ 322,400
Liabilities and equity		
Accounts payable	$ 32,000	$ 48,000
Wages payable	4,000	2,400
Bonds payable	24,000	16,000
Preferred stock (no par)	4,000	12,000
Common stock	30,000	36,000
Paid-in capital in excess of par	50,000	76,000
Retained earnings	108,000	132,000
Total liabilities and equity	$252,000	$ 322,400

Piura Manufacturing
Income Statement
For the Year Ended June 30, 20X2

Sales	$ 320,000
Cost of goods sold	(200,000)
Gross margin	$ 120,000
Operating expenses	(88,000)
Net income	$ 32,000

Additional transactions for 20X2 were as follows:
a. Cash dividends of $8,000 were paid.
b. Equipment was acquired by issuing common stock with a par value of $6,000. The fair market value of the equipment is $32,000.
c. Equipment with a book value of $12,000 was sold for $6,000. The original cost of the equipment was $24,000. The loss is included in operating expenses.
d. Two thousand shares of preferred stock were sold for $4 per share.

Required:

1. Prepare a schedule of operating cash flows using (a) the indirect method and (b) the direct method.
2. Prepare a statement of cash flows using the indirect method.
3. Prepare a statement of cash flows using a worksheet similar to the one shown in Example 14.8 (p. 804).

(Continued)

4. Form a group with two to four other students, and discuss the merits of the direct and indirect methods. Which do you think investors might prefer? Should the FASB require all companies to use the direct method?

OBJECTIVE 1 2 3

Case 15-59 **Management of Statement of Cash Flows, Ethical Issues**

Fred Jackson, president and owner of Bailey Company, is concerned about the company's ability to obtain a loan from a major bank. The loan is a key factor in the firm's plan to expand its operations. Demand for the firm's product is high—too high for the current production capacity to handle. Fred is convinced that a new plant is needed. Building the new plant, however, will require an infusion of new capital. Fred calls a meeting with Karla Jones, financial vice president.

Fred: Karla, what is the status of our loan application? Do you think that the bank will approve?

Karla: Perhaps, but at this point, there is a real risk. The loan officer has requested a complete set of financials for this year and the past 2 years. He has indicated that he is particularly interested in the statement of cash flows. As you know, our income statement looks great for all 3 years, but the statement of cash flows will show a significant increase in receivables, especially for this year. It will also show a significant increase in inventory, and I'm sure that he'll want to know why inventory is increasing if demand is so great that we need another plant. Both of these effects show decreasing cash flows from operating activities.

Fred: Well, it is certainly true that cash flows have been decreasing. One major problem is the lack of operating cash. This loan will solve that problem. Bill Lawson has agreed to build the plant for the amount of the loan but will actually charge me for only 95% of the stated cost. We get 5% of the loan for operating cash. Bill is willing to pay 5% to get the contract.

Karla: The loan may help with operating cash flows, but we can't get the loan without showing some evidence of cash strength. We need to do something about the increases in inventory and receivables that we expect for this year.

Fred: The increased inventory is easy to explain. We had to work overtime and use subcontractors to take care of one of our biggest customers. That inventory will be gone by the first of next year.

Karla: The problem isn't explaining the inventory. The problem is that the increase in inventory decreases our operating cash flows, and this shows up on the statement of cash flows. This effect, coupled with the increase in receivables, depicts us as being cash poor. It'll definitely hurt our chances.

Fred: I see. Well, this can be solved. The inventory is for a customer that I know well. She'll do me a favor. I'll simply get her to take delivery of the inventory early, before the end of our fiscal year. She can pay me next year as originally planned.

Karla: Fred, all that will do is shift the increase from inventory to receivables. It'll still report the same cash position.

Fred: No problem. We'll report the delivery as a cash sale, and I'll have Bill Lawson advance me the cash as a temporary loan. He'll do that to get the contract to build our new plant. In fact, we can do the same with some of our other receivables. We'll report them as collected, and I'll get Bill to cover. If he understands that this is what it takes to get the loan, he'll cooperate. He stands to make a lot of money on the deal.

Karla: Fred, this is getting complicated. The bank will have us audited each year if this loan is approved. If an audit were to reveal some of this manipulation, we could be in big trouble, particularly if the company has any trouble in repaying the loan.

Fred: The company won't have any trouble. Sales are strong, and the problem of collecting receivables can be solved, especially given the extra time that the 5% of the loan proceeds will provide.

Required:

1. Form a group with two to four other students. Discuss the propriety of the arrangement that Fred has with Bill Lawson concerning the disbursement of the proceeds from the loan.

2. In your group, discuss the propriety of the actions that Fred is proposing to improve the firm's statement of cash flows. Suppose that there is very little risk that the loan will not be repaid. Does this information affect your assessment?

3. Assume that Karla is subject to the Institute of Management Accountant's (IMA) code of ethics. Look up this code, and identify the standards of ethical conduct that will be violated, if any, by Karla should she agree to cooperate with Fred's scheme.

4. Using the IMA code of ethics, if you were in Karla's position, what would you do (supposing that Fred insists on implementing his plan)? Now, answer the question, assuming that Fred is willing to consider alternative ways to solve the company's problems.

15 Financial Statement Analysis

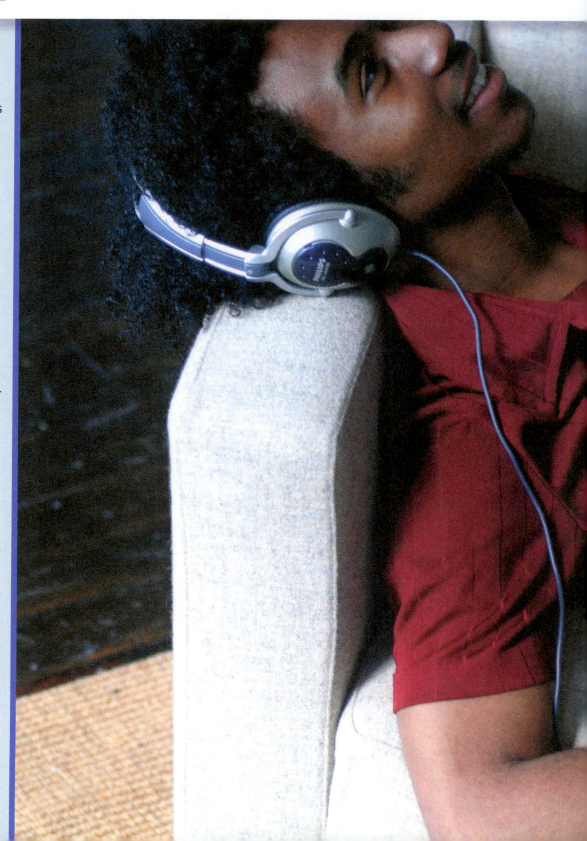

After studying Chapter 15, you should be able to:

1 ▶ Analyze financial statements using two forms of common-size analysis: horizontal analysis and vertical analysis.

2 ▶ Explain why historical standards and industrial averages are important for ratio analysis.

3 ▶ Calculate and use liquidity ratios to assess the ability of a company to meet its current obligations.

4 ▶ Calculate and use leverage ratios to assess the ability of a company to meet its long- and short-term obligations.

5 ▶ Calculate and use profitability ratios to assess the extent to which a company's resources are being used efficiently.

EXPERIENCE MANAGERIAL DECISIONS

with Apple

Apple represents one of the most successful companies in history, as measured by its product innovations, market penetration, and "coolness" factor that many consumers feel toward its reputation. For example, Apple offers numerous successful products, such as Apple TV, iPad Air, iPad Pro, iPad mini, iPad touch, Apple Watch, iMac, and iPhone series. Several popular financial statement ratios provide insight into Apple's remarkable performance.

First, the current ratio of 1.11—a common liquidity ratio—indicates that Apple had $1.11 of current assets for every $1 of current liabilities.[1] Given that it has more current assets than current liabilities, as well as significant cash resources (over $21 billion), it appears as though Apple is in a position to remain liquid and meet its short-term obligations.

Apple's inventory turnover, another liquidity ratio, shows that the company turned over its inventory 62.8 times during that year, which also means that on average its inventory sat on the shelf for only 5.8 days before being sold! Turning inventory into cash so quickly is very beneficial to the company because it can reinvest the cash back into the business, such as for research and development of the next generation of Apple products.

> "Apple had its best quarter ever by recording nearly $76 billion in revenue by selling over 74 million iPhones, 16 million iPads, and 5 million Macs!"

Apple's debt ratio is 0.59, indicating that 59% of its assets are financed using some form of debt, while the remaining 41% are financed using equity. In addition, only 47% of Apple's liabilities are current in nature. Interestingly, these measures reflect in part Apple's decision in recent years to increase its liabilities significantly—almost doubling its long-term debt in just 1 year! Apple uses the proceeds from its debt offerings to help pay for dividends to its shareholders, as well as to repurchase large quantities of its own stock (i.e., a $200 billion stock buyback program)!

Finally, the company's return on sales of 0.23, a profitability ratio, indicates that $0.23 of every $1.00 in sales revenue was left over as profit after accounting for all expenses.

In summary, several common financial statement ratios suggest that Apple is able to perform so effectively, in part, because of its impressive ability to turn inventory into cash quickly and raise significant capital through stock issuances to investors and bond issuances to creditors. Therefore, the next time you stream or download a song, television episode, or movie from the iTunes Store, you can appreciate Apple's performance on these key financial statement ratios and be thankful for its part in revolutionizing the entertainment industry.

1 Information compiled from Apple's 2015 Annual Report.

Financial statement analysis provides useful information for many users and purposes.

- **Creditors:** By using ratio analysis, common-size analysis, and other techniques, loan managers can assess the creditworthiness of potential customers. The formal analysis of financial statements can also provide a means to exercise control over outstanding loans.
- **Investors:** Investors need to analyze financial statements to assess the attractiveness of a company as a potential investment.
- **Managers:** Managers need to analyze their own financial statements to assess profitability, liquidity, debt position, and progress toward organizational objectives.

The analysis of financial statements is designed to reveal relationships among items on the financial statements and trends of individual items over time. By knowing these relationships and trends, users are in a better position to exercise sound judgment regarding the current or future performance of a company. The two major techniques for financial analysis are common-size analysis and ratio analysis.

Here's How It's Used: IN YOUR LIFE

One of the most significant financial decisions you face in your young adult life is whether and when to purchase versus rent the residence (e.g., house, condominium, etc.) where you live. If you wish to start building home equity, deduct interest payments on your taxes, or simply develop a sense of "ownership," you might decide to purchase a home. However, unless you were born with or married into extreme wealth, you likely will need to borrow a considerable amount of money in order to fulfill your home ownership dream. The bank (or other lender) will rely heavily on accounting ratios to evaluate (1) *whether* or not they will loan you money, (2) *how much* money they will loan you, (3) the *rate of interest* they will charge you, and (4) the size of the *down payment* they will require from you. Much like companies use leverage ratios—such as the debt ratio—to evaluate their debt-carrying ability, individuals also use ratios for important personal financial decisions. One of the most

common ratios banks use to assess individuals is the debt-to-income ratio. This ratio helps the bank measure your ability to meet monthly loan payments, along with other recurring discretionary expenditures and required monthly payments. Recurring discretionary expenditures include items like food, utilities, and insurance. More significantly, required monthly payments might be for cars, student loans, and credit card balances. While you correctly should be very excited with your debt-to-income denominator (i.e., your salary), the bank will be equally interested in your numerator (i.e., your required monthly payments). Specifically, the bank will require that your debt-to-income ratio be below a certain threshold, such as 0.43, before it will move forward with a loan. Therefore, when contemplating your own financial decisions, such as when to purchase a home, be sure to consider how the other actions in your life will affect your debt-to-income ratio, so that this exciting moment proceeds as smoothly as possible!

OBJECTIVE 1

Analyze financial statements using two forms of common-size analysis: horizontal analysis and vertical analysis.

COMMON-SIZE ANALYSIS

A simple first step in financial statement analysis is comparing two financial statements. For example, the income statement for this year could be compared with the income statement for last year. To make the analysis more meaningful, percentages can be used. **Common-size analysis** expresses line items or accounts in the financial statements as percentages. The two major forms of common-size analysis are horizontal analysis and vertical analysis. Exhibit 15.1 illustrates horizontal and vertical analysis.

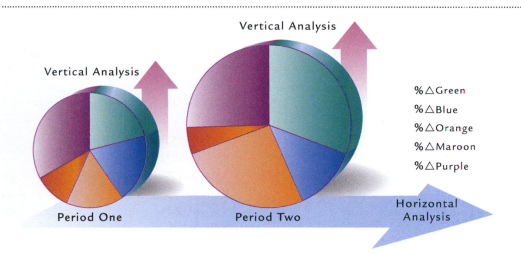

Vertical Analysis

Vertical Analysis

% △ Green

% △ Blue

% △ Orange

% △ Maroon

% △ Purple

Period One

Period Two

Horizontal Analysis

Exhibit 15.1
Common-Size Analysis

Horizontal Analysis

Also called *trend analysis*, **horizontal analysis** expresses a line item as a percentage of some prior-period amount. This approach allows the trend over time to be assessed. In horizontal analysis, line items are expressed as a percentage of a base period amount. The base period can be the immediately preceding period, or it can be a period further in the past.

By comparing a given financial statement line item, such as sales or various expenses, as a percentage of some prior-period amount, managers can better identify trends in performance. **Example 15.1** shows how to prepare common-size income statements by using the first year as the base period.

Here's **Why It's important**

EXAMPLE 15.1

How to Prepare Common-Size Income Statements Using Base Period Horizontal Analysis

Simpson Company provided the following income statements for its first 3 years of operation:

	Year 1	Year 2	Year 3
Net sales	$100,000	$120,000	$132,000
Less: Cost of goods sold	(60,000)	(75,000)	(81,000)
Gross margin	$ 40,000	$ 45,000	$ 51,000
Less:			
Operating expenses	(20,000)	(24,000)	(29,000)
Income taxes	(8,000)	(9,000)	(10,000)
Net income	$ 12,000	$ 12,000	$ 12,000

Required:
Prepare common-size income statements by using Year 1 as the base period.

Solution:
Year 1 is the base year. Therefore, every dollar amount in Year 1 is 100% of itself.

Percent for a Line Item = (Dollar Amount of Line Item/Dollar Amount of Base Year Line Item) × 100

Percent Year 1 Net Sales = ($100,000/$100,000) × 100 = 100%
Percent Year 2 Net Sales = ($120,000/$100,000) × 100 = 120%
Percent Year 3 Net Sales = ($132,000/$100,000) × 100 = 132%

(Continued)

EXAMPLE 15.1

(Continued)

	Year 1		Year 2		Year 3	
	Dollars	**Percent**	**Dollars**	**Percent**	**Dollars**	**Percent**
Net sales	$100,000	100%	$120,000	120.0%	$132,000	132.0%
Less: Cost of goods sold	(60,000)	100	(75,000)	125.0	(81,000)	135.0
Gross margin	$ 40,000	100	$ 45,000	112.5	$ 51,000	127.5
Less:						
Operating expenses	(20,000)	100	(24,000)	120.0	(29,000)	145.0
Income taxes	(8,000)	100	(9,000)	112.5	(10,000)	125.0
Net income	$ 12,000	100	$ 12,000	100.0	$ 12,000	100.0

Since the base year in Example 15.1 is Year 1, all line amounts in subsequent years are compared with the amount in the base year. For example, Year 3 sales are expressed as a percentage of Year 1 sales. By comparing each subsequent amount with the base period, trends can be seen. The data reveal that sales have increased by 32% over the 3 years. With such a large increase in sales, many would expect net income to experience a significant increase also. The percentage analysis, however, shows that net income has shown no change from the base period. Net income has stayed flat because expenses and taxes have also increased: cost of goods sold has increased by 35%, operating expenses by 45%, and taxes by 25%. As a result of the percentage analysis, the manager of the company might decide to focus more attention on controlling costs.

Vertical Analysis

While horizontal analysis involves relationships among items over time, vertical analysis is concerned with relationships among items within a particular time period. **Vertical analysis** expresses the line item as a percentage of some other line item for the same period. With this approach, within-period relationships can be assessed. Line items on income statements often are expressed as percentages of net sales. Items on the balance sheet often are expressed as a percentage of total assets.

Here's **Why It's important**

By comparing a given financial statement line item as a percentage of some other line item (such as sales or total assets) for the same time period, managers can better understand the relative size and importance of each item. **Example 15.2** shows how to perform vertical analysis with the same example used in Example 15.1 (p. 839).

EXAMPLE 15.2

How to Prepare Income Statements Using Net Sales as the Base: Vertical Analysis

Simpson Company provided the following income statements for its first 3 years of operation:

	Year 1	Year 2	Year 3
Net sales	$100,000	$120,000	$132,000
Less: Cost of goods sold	(60,000)	(75,000)	(81,000)
Gross margin	$ 40,000	$ 45,000	$ 51,000
Less:			
Operating expenses	(20,000)	(24,000)	(29,000)
Income taxes	(8,000)	(9,000)	(10,000)
Net income	$ 12,000	$ 12,000	$ 12,000

EXAMPLE 15.2

(*Continued*)

Required:

Prepare common-size income statements by using net sales as the base.

Solution:

Since the analysis is based on net sales, net sales in each year equals 100% of itself. Then, every line item on the income statement is expressed as a percent of that year's net sales.

Percent for a Line Item = (Dollar Amount of Line Item/Dollar Amount of
                 That Year's Sales) × 100
Percent Year 1 Net Sales = ($100,000/$100,000) × 100 = 100%
Percent Year 2 Net Sales = ($120,000/$120,000) × 100 = 100%
Percent Year 3 Net Sales = ($132,000/$132,000) × 100 = 100%

	Year 1		Year 2		Year 3	
	Dollars	**Percent***	**Dollars**	**Percent***	**Dollars**	**Percent***
Net sales	$100,000	100%	$120,000	100.0%	$132,000	100.0%
Less: Cost of goods sold	(60,000)	60	(75,000)	62.5	(81,000)	61.4
Gross margin	$ 40,000	40	$ 45,000	37.5	$ 51,000	38.6
Less:						
Operating expenses	(20,000)	20	(24,000)	20.0	(29,000)	22.0
Income taxes	(8,000)	8	(9,000)	7.5	(10,000)	7.6
Net income	$ 12,000	12	$ 12,000	10.0	$ 12,000	9.1

*Percentages are rounded to one decimal place.

In Example 15.2, sales are used as the base for computing percentages. Although the main purpose of vertical analysis is to highlight relationships among components of a company's financial statements, changes in these relationships over time can also be informative. For example, Example 15.1 (p. 839) reveals large increases in cost of goods sold and operating expenses over time. Over the 3-year period, cost of goods sold has increased by 35% ($21,000/$60,000), and operating expenses have increased by 45% ($9,000/$20,000). Example 15.2 compares these expenses with sales. This comparison reveals that much of the increase may be tied to increased sales. That is, Year 1 operating expenses represented 20% of sales, whereas in Year 3, they represented 22% of sales.

Percentages and Size Effects

The use of common-size analysis makes comparisons more meaningful because percentages eliminate the effects of size. For example, if Heisman Company earns $100,000 and Casciani Company earns $1 million, which company is more profitable? The answer depends to a large extent on the assets employed to earn the profits. If Heisman used an investment of $1 million to earn the $100,000, then the return expressed as a percentage of dollars is 10% ($100,000/$1,000,000). If Casciani used an investment of $20 million to earn its $1 million, the percentage return is only 5% ($1,000,000/$20,000,000). By using percentages, it is easy to see that the first firm is relatively more profitable than the second.

Check Point

1. Horizontal analysis also is referred to as
   a. vertical analysis.
   b. sideways analysis.
   c. longways analysis.
   d. trend analysis.
   e. numerical analysis.

Answer:

d.

2. Hornsby Company's net income is $1,000 one year and $1,500 the following year. Grabowski Company's net income is $10,000 one year and $12,000 the following year. What is the percentage increase from one year to the next for each company? Which company is performing better?

Answer:

Hornsby's net income has increased by 50%, while Grabowski's net income has increased by 20%. It is difficult to say which company is performing better. Because percentages abstract from size, users must exercise caution in their interpretation, particularly when the numbers involved are small. If the base is small, small changes in line items can produce large percentage changes. The percentage increase in net income is larger for Hornsby than for Grabowski. However, Hornsby increased its total earnings by only $500, while Grabowski increased its total earnings by $2,000.

OBJECTIVE 2

Explain why historical standards and industrial averages are important for ratio analysis.

RATIO ANALYSIS

Ratio analysis is the second major technique for financial statement analysis. Ratios are fractions or percentages computed by dividing one account or line-item amount by another. For example, operating income divided by sales produces a ratio that measures the profit margin on sales.

Standards for Comparison

Ratios by themselves tell little about the financial well-being of a company. For meaningful analysis, the ratios should be compared with a standard. Only through comparison can someone

Here's How It's Used: AT KICKER

Every month, **Kicker** holds a companywide meeting of all employees. In addition to the introduction of new employees and general announcements, Kicker's owner shares financial information. Then, graphs showing the trend in sales and profits are posted on the bulletin board in the break room. Employees can check trends in financial information at their leisure. This information is important to Kicker employees because all of them are part of a comprehensive profit-sharing plan. Robust monthly sales and income will result in a bonus check to every employee that month. Yearly profits lead to another bonus check at year-end. Finally, Kicker also contributes to employees' 401(K) accounts. Since all of this is dependent on net income, each employee has a vested interest in keeping costs down and sales up.

KICKER
Livin Loud

using a financial statement assess the financial health of a company. Two standards commonly used are the past history of the company and industrial averages. Exhibit 15.2 illustrates the way a company might view both types of ratio comparison.

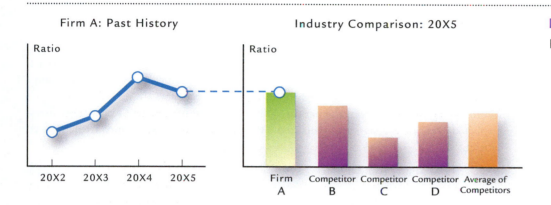

Firm A: Past History   Industry Comparison: 20X5

Exhibit 15.2

Ratio Analysis

Past History One way to detect progress or problems is to compare the value of a ratio over time. Doing so allows trends to be assessed. For example, ratios measuring liquidity may be dropping over time, signaling a deteriorating financial condition. The company's management can use this information to take corrective action. Investors and creditors, on the other hand, may use this information to decide whether or not to invest money in the company.

Industrial Averages Additional insight can be gained by comparing a company's ratios with the same ratios for companies in the same business. To facilitate the comparison, a number of annual publications provide industrial figures. For example, **Dun and Bradstreet** reports the median, upper quartile, and lower quartile for 14 commonly used ratios for more than 900 lines of business. The titles and publishers of some of the more common sources of industrial ratios are as follows:

- *Key Business Ratios*, **Dun and Bradstreet**
- *NetAdvantage*, **Standard & Poor's**
- *Annual Statement Studies*, **Risk Management Association**
- *The Almanac of Business and Industrial Financial Ratios*, **Wolters Kluwer**

A number of online sources are also useful for obtaining competitive information on a company's ratios. Some of these are:

- www.bizstats.com
- www.fidelity.com
- http://money.msn.com
- http://biz.yahoo.com/r/

Even though the industrial figures provide a useful reference point, they should be used with care. Companies within the same industry may use different accounting methods, which diminishes the validity of the average. Other problems, such as small sample sizes for the industrial report, different labor markets, the impact of extreme values, and terms of sale, can produce variations among companies within the same industry. The industrial statistics should not be taken as absolute norms but rather as general guidelines for purposes of making comparisons.

Classification of Ratios

Ratios generally are classified into one of three categories: liquidity, borrowing capacity or leverage, and profitability.

- **Liquidity ratios** measure the ability of a company to meet its current obligations.
- **Leverage ratios** measure the ability of a company to meet its long- and short-term obligations. These ratios provide a measure of the degree of protection provided to a company's creditors.
- **Profitability ratios** measure the earning ability of a company. These ratios allow investors, creditors, and managers to evaluate the extent to which invested funds are being used efficiently.

Some of the more common and popular ratios for each category will be defined and illustrated. Exhibits 15.3 and 15.4 (p. 845) provide an income statement, a statement of retained earnings, and comparative balance sheets for Payne Company, a manufacturer of glassware. These financial statements provide the basis for subsequent analyses.

Exhibit 15.3

Income Statement and Statement of Retained Earnings for Payne Company for Year 2

Payne Company
Income Statement
For the Year Ended December 31, Year 2
(dollars in thousands)

	Amount	Percent
Net sales	$ 50,000	100.0%
Less: Cost of goods sold	(35,000)	70.0
Gross margin	$ 15,000	30.0
Less: Operating expenses	(10,000)	20.0
Operating income	$ 5,000	10.0
Less: Interest expense	(400)	0.8
Income before taxes	$ 4,600	9.2
Less: Income taxes (50%)*	(2,300)	4.6
Net income	$ 2,300	4.6

*Includes both state and federal taxes.

Payne Company
Statement of Retained Earnings
For the Year Ended December 31, Year 2

Balance, beginning of period	$ 5,324
Net income	2,300
Total	$ 7,624
Less: Preferred dividends	(224)
Dividends to common stockholders	(1,000)
Balance, end of period	$ 6,400

Payne Company
Comparative Balance Sheets
For the Years Ended December 31, Year 1 and Year 2
(dollars in thousands)

Assets

	Year 2	Year 1
Current assets:		
Cash	$ 1,600	$ 2,500
Marketable securities	1,600	2,000
Accounts receivable (net)	8,000	10,000
Inventories	10,000	3,000
Other	800	1,500
Total current assets	$22,000	$19,000
Property and equipment:		
Land	$ 4,000	$ 6,000
Building and equipment (net)	6,000	5,000
Total long-term assets	$10,000	$11,000
Total assets	$32,000	$30,000

Liabilities and Stockholders' Equity

	Year 2	Year 1
Current liabilities:		
Notes payable, short term	$ 3,200	$ 3,000
Accounts payable	6,400	5,800
Current maturity of long-term debt	400	400
Accrued payables	2,000	1,876
Total current liabilities	$12,000	$11,076
Long-term liabilities:		
Bonds payable, 10%	4,000	4,000
Total liabilities	$16,000	$15,076
Stockholders' equity:		
Preferred stock, $25 par, 7%	$ 3,200	$ 3,200
Common stock, $2 par	1,600	1,600
Additional paid-in capital*	4,800	4,800
Retained earnings	6,400	5,324
Total equity	$16,000	$14,924
Total liabilities and stockholders' equity	$32,000	$30,000

*For common stock only.

Exhibit 15.4

Comparative Balance Sheets for Payne Company for Years 1 and 2

Check Point

1. **Which one of the following items is NOT a category into which ratios generally are placed?**
   a. **Performance ratios**
   b. **Profitability ratios**
   c. **Liquidity ratios**
   d. **Leverage ratios**

Answer:
a.

(*Continued*)

2. **Which of the three ratio categories is most important?**

Answer:

The answer depends on exactly what question is being asked. For example, a bank creditor that is considering loaning money to a company likely will be most interested in the company's (as the potential borrower) ability both to repay the principal (i.e., the amount borrowed) and to make the required interest payments on a timely basis. The bank will look very closely at the company's liquidity ratios to determine whether the company appears to have sufficient current assets to settle its current liabilities, such as periodic interest payments. However, the bank also will examine the company's leverage ratios to assess its ability to meet both long- and short-term obligations. For example, if the company already has a large amount of debt (e.g., loans), then the bank likely will either charge a greater rate of interest to compensate for the company's greater riskiness or perhaps even decide not to approve the loan. Finally, the bank should consider the company's profitability ratios to ensure that it appears to have a healthy financial future, such as increasing sales and/or lowering expenses, to be in business long enough to repay the loan by the maturity date. Therefore, these three categories of ratios usually are considered collectively to assess the overall health of a company or an industry.

OBJECTIVE

Calculate and use liquidity ratios to assess the ability of a company to meet its current obligations.

LIQUIDITY RATIOS

Liquidity ratios are used to assess the short-term debt-paying ability of a company. If a company does not have the short-term financial strength to meet its current obligations, it is likely to have difficulty meeting its long-term obligations. Accordingly, evaluation of the short-term financial strength of a company is a good starting point in financial analysis. Although there are numerous liquidity ratios, only the most common ones will be discussed in this section. These liquidity ratios are:

- current ratio
- quick or acid-test ratio
- accounts receivable turnover ratio
- inventory turnover ratio

Current Ratio

The **current ratio** is a measure of the ability of a company to pay its short-term liabilities out of short-term assets. The current ratio is computed as follows:

> Current Ratio = Current Assets/Current Liabilities

Since current liabilities must be paid within an operating cycle (usually within a year) and current assets can be converted to cash within an operating cycle, the current ratio provides a direct measure of the ability of a company to meet its short-term obligations. Payne Company's current ratio for Year 2 is computed as follows, using data from Exhibit 15.4:

$$\text{Current Ratio} = \$22,000,000/\$12,000,000$$
$$= 1.83$$

Here's How It's Used: AT MACY'S

You are a finance manager at **Macy's**, an international retailing company. One of your primary duties is management of the company's cash position.

Which financial ratios would you most likely use in managing Macy's cash position? In addition to these ratios, what other factors would you consider?

While numerous ratios are important in managing a company's cash position, the ones you might consider first would be the liquidity ratios because they address a company's ability to meet current obligations as they come due. For example, Macy's current ratio is a critical indicator of the extent to which the company has enough current assets to settle its current liabilities. Typically, having a current ratio greater than 1.0 is an important benchmark because it indicates that current assets exceed current liabilities. Looking at the quick ratio would add incremental insights into Macy's cash position because it focuses on the company's most liquid current assets—cash, marketable securities, and receivables. Examining the current and quick ratios in tandem, along with any other pertinent information such as the timing of cash inflows and outflows,

paints a more complete picture of the company. For instance, a retailer might experience a seasonal preholiday decrease in its quick ratio as it builds inventory, while accounts payable simultaneously increases faster than sales. These ratios would change again as the holiday season progresses and inventory is sold (increasing accounts receivable and eventually cash) and current liabilities are paid using cash generated from holiday sales.

Additional factors to consider include the company's customer credit-granting policies, which affects credit sales and accounts receivable. Loosening credit policies usually increases credit sales and accounts receivable. However, if bad debts (i.e., customer payment defaults) increase as a result of selling on credit to customers with poor credit ratings, then such information should supplement the current and quick ratio analyses to best predict the company's future cash position.

Effective cash management is particularly important during severe economic downturns. Some companies even go so far as to prepare daily liquidity reports.

But what does a current ratio of 1.83 mean? Does the ratio of 1.83 signal good or poor debt-paying ability? Additional information is needed to interpret it. Many creditors use the rule of thumb that a 2.0 ratio is needed to provide good debt-paying ability. Based on this assessment, Payne does not have sufficient liquidity.

However, this rule has many exceptions. For example, the industrial norm might be less than 2.0. Suppose that the upper quartile, median, and lower quartile values of the current ratio for the glassware industry are 2.2, 1.7, and 1.3, respectively. Payne's current ratio of 1.83 is above the median ratio for its industry, suggesting that Payne does not have liquidity problems. More than half of the firms in its industry have lower current ratios. Information on the ratio's trend is also helpful. It is possible, for example, that Payne's current ratio for Year 2 is representative of what usually happens. By comparing this year's ratio with ratios for prior years, some judgment about whether or not it is representative can be made. For example, if the ratio in prior years has been reasonably stable with values in the 1.7 to 1.9 range, this year's ratio is representative. If the ratio has been declining for the past several years, the company's financial position could be deteriorating.

A declining current ratio is not necessarily bad, particularly if it is falling from a high value. A high current ratio may signal excessive investment in current resources. Some of these current resources may be more productively employed by reducing long-term debt, paying dividends, or investing in long-term assets. Thus, a declining current ratio may signal a move toward more efficient utilization of resources. But a declining current ratio coupled with a current ratio lower than that of other firms in the industry supports the judgment that a company is having liquidity problems.

Quick or Acid-Test Ratio

For many companies, inventory represents 50% or more of total current assets. For example, Payne Company's inventory represents 45% of its total current assets. The liquidity of inventory often is less than that of accounts receivable, marketable securities, and cash. Inventory may be slow moving, nearly obsolete, or even pledged in part to creditors. Because including inventory may produce a misleading measure of liquidity, it is often excluded in computing liquidity ratios. For similar reasons, other current assets, such as miscellaneous assets, also are excluded.

The **quick or acid-test ratio** is a measure of liquidity that compares only the most liquid assets with current liabilities. Excluded from the quick ratio are nonliquid current assets such as inventories. The numerator of the quick ratio includes only the most liquid assets (cash, marketable securities, and accounts receivable).

> Quick Ratio = (Cash + Marketable Securities + Accounts Receivable)/Current Liabilities

For Payne Company, the quick ratio is calculated as follows (using data from Exhibit 15.4, p. 845 for Year 2):

$$\text{Quick Ratio} = (\$1,600,000 + \$1,600,000 + \$8,000,000)/\$12,000,000$$
$$= \$11,200,000/\$12,000,000$$
$$= 0.93$$

Payne's quick ratio reveals that it does not have the capability to meet its current obligations with its most liquid assets. A ratio of 1.0 is the usual standard. Payne's quick ratio is not far below the standard level, and perhaps some attention should be paid to raise it somewhat.

Here's **Why It's important**   The current ratio measures a company's liquidity by showing how many dollars of current assets it possesses relative to current liabilities. The quick ratio provides an even more direct assessment of liquidity by including in the numerator only the three assets that already are cash or typically are converted to cash most quickly. **Example 15.3** shows how to calculate the current ratio and the quick ratio.

EXAMPLE 15.3	Bordner Company has current assets equal to $120,000. Of these, $15,000 is cash, $30,000 is accounts receivable, and the remainder is inventories. Current liabilities total $50,000.

How to Calculate the Current Ratio and the Quick (or Acid-Test) Ratio

Required:

1. Calculate the current ratio.
2. Calculate the quick ratio (acid-test ratio).

Solution:

1. Current Ratio = Current Assets/Current Liabilities
$$= \$120,000/\$50,000$$
$$= 2.40$$

2. Quick Ratio = (Cash + Marketable Securities + Accounts Receivable)/Current Liabilities
$$= (\$15,000 + \$0 + \$30,000)/\$50,000$$
$$= 0.90$$

Accounts Receivable Turnover Ratio

The extent of Payne's liquidity problem can be further investigated by examining the liquidity of its receivables, or how long it takes the company to turn its receivables into cash. A low liquidity of receivables signals more difficulty, since the quick ratio would be overstated. The liquidity of receivables is measured by the **accounts receivable turnover ratio**, computed as follows:

Accounts Receivable Turnover Ratio = Net Sales/Average Accounts Receivable

Average accounts receivable is defined as follows:

Average Accounts Receivable = (Beginning Receivables + Ending Receivables)/2

The average accounts receivable is based on the beginning and ending balances of accounts receivable because this matches the account to the period that corresponds to the income statement measure.

Payne Company's accounts receivable turnover is computed as follows (using data from Exhibits 15.3, p. 844 and 15.4, p. 845):

$$\text{Accounts Receivable Turnover Ratio} = \$50,000,000/\$9,000,000^*$$
$$= 5.56 \text{ times per year}$$

*Average Receivables = ($10,000,000 + $8,000,000)/2

The accounts receivable turnover ratio can be taken further to determine the number of days the average balance of accounts receivable is outstanding before being converted into cash, which is calculated as follows:

Accounts Receivable Turnover in Days = 365/Accounts Receivable Turnover Ratio

Payne Company's accounts receivable turnover in days is computed as follows (using data from Exhibits 15.3, p. 844, and 15.4, p. 845):

$$\text{Accounts Receivable Turnover in Days} = 365/5.56 = 65.6 \text{ days}$$

Payne's receivables are held for almost 66 days before being converted to cash.

Whether this is good or bad depends to some extent on what other companies in the industry are experiencing. The low turnover ratio suggests a need for Payne's managers to modify credit and collection policies to speed up the conversion of receivables to cash. This need is particularly acute if a historical analysis shows a persistent problem or a trend downward. Note that net sales were used to compute the turnover ratio. Technically, credit sales should be used. However, external financial reports do not usually break net sales into credit and cash components. Consequently, if a turnover ratio is to be computed by external users, net sales must be used. For many firms, most sales are credit sales, and the computation is a good approximation. If sales are mostly for cash, liquidity is not an issue. In that case, the ratio provides a measure of the company's operating cycle.

The accounts receivable ratios assess the speed at which a company converts its accounts receivables into cash. **Example 15.4** shows how to calculate the average accounts receivable, the accounts receivable turnover ratio, and the accounts receivable turnover in days.

Here's **Why It's important**

EXAMPLE 15.4

How to Calculate the Average Accounts Receivable, the Accounts Receivable Turnover Ratio, and the Accounts Receivable Turnover in Days

Last year, Shuster Company had net sales of $750,000 and cost of goods sold of $400,000. Shuster had the following balances:

	January 1	December 31
Accounts receivable	$98,500	$101,500
Inventories	83,000	87,000

Required:

1. Calculate the average accounts receivable.
2. Calculate the accounts receivable turnover ratio.
3. Calculate the accounts receivable turnover in days.

(*Continued*)

EXAMPLE 15.4

(Continued)

Solution:

1. Average Accounts Receivable = (Beginning Receivables + Ending Receivables)/2

$$= (\$98,500 + \$101,500)/2 = \$100,000$$

2. Accounts Receivable Turnover Ratio = Net Sales/Average Accounts Receivable

$$= \$750,000/\$100,000 = 7.5 \text{ times}$$

3. Accounts Receivable Turnover in Days = Days in a Year/Accounts Receivable Turnover Ratio

$$= 365/7.5 = 48.7 \text{ days}$$

Note: Answer is rounded to one decimal place.

Inventory Turnover Ratio

Inventory turnover is also an important liquidity measure. The **inventory turnover ratio** is computed as follows:

Inventory Turnover Ratio = Cost of Goods Sold/Average Inventory

Average inventory is found as follows:

Average Inventory = (Beginning Inventory + Ending Inventory)/2

This ratio tells an analyst how many times the average inventory turns over, or is sold, during the year. The number of days inventory is held before being sold can be computed as follows:

Inventory Turnover in Days = 365/Inventory Turnover Ratio

The inventory turnover ratio for Payne Company is computed as follows, using data from Exhibits 15.3 (p. 844) and 15.4 (p. 845):

$$\text{Inventory Turnover} = \$35,000,000/\$6,500,000^*$$
$$= 5.38 \text{ times per year, or every } 67.8 \text{ days } (365/5.38)$$

*Average Inventory = (\$3,000,000 + \$10,000,000)/2

Suppose that the glassware industry revealed the upper quartile, median, and lower quartile turnover figures in days to be 34, 57, and 79, respectively. Payne's turnover ratio is midway between the median and the lower quartile. The evidence seems to indicate that the turnover ratio is lower than it should be. A low turnover ratio may signal the presence of too much inventory or sluggish sales. More attention to inventory policies and marketing activities may be in order.

Here's **Why It's important**   The inventory ratios assess the speed at which a company converts its inventory into cash. **Example 15.5** shows how to calculate the average inventory, the inventory turnover ratio, and the inventory turnover in days.

EXAMPLE 15.5

How to Calculate the Average Inventory, the Inventory Turnover Ratio, and the Inventory Turnover in Days

Last year, Shuster Company had net sales of $750,000 and cost of goods sold of $400,000. Shuster had the following balances:

	January 1	December 31
Accounts receivable	$98,500	$101,500
Inventories	83,000	87,000

Required:

1. Calculate the average inventory.
2. Calculate the inventory turnover ratio.
3. Calculate the inventory turnover in days.

Solution:

1. Average Inventory = (Beginning Inventory + Ending Inventory)/2

   = ($83,000 + $87,000)/2

   = $85,000

2. Inventory Turnover Ratio = Cost of Goods Sold/Average Inventory

   = $400,000/$85,000

   = 4.7 times

3. Inventory Turnover in Days = Days in a Year/Inventory Turnover Ratio

   = 365/4.7

   = 77.7 days

Note: Answers are rounded to one decimal place.

Here's How It's Used: AT APPLE

Let's return briefly to **Apple**, which was the focus of the chapter's opening vignette. Apple always has displayed mastery in successfully launching new products. For example, it sold 1 million first-generation iPhones during the first 74 days after launch. Was this successful launch performance a one-time aberration, or was it indicative of a trend that would continue with future product launches? The next several big launches provided clear insights on this question, as Apple subsequently launched its initial iPad and sold 1 million units in only 28 days, which continued with a total of 3 million iPad unit sales during its first 80 days. Even more impressive was Apple's sales of 1.7 million iPhone 4 units during its first *3 days* on the market. More recently, Apple broke its previous record by selling approximately 75 million iPhones in the fourth quarter alone! Following Apple's inventory turnover surrounding such astounding product launches provides insights regarding its ability to successfully sell its products after the initial "wow" factor subsides at some point after launch. In addition, Apple's inventory turnover of 62.8 means that its inventory sits on the shelf for less than a week—5.8 days to be exact—before being sold. Apple's inventory turnover has remained high (i.e., or a low average number of days on hand), which is particularly impressive, given that the majority of Apple's inventory consists of at least moderately expensive merchandise that customers likely retain for relatively long periods. In other words, to maintain such large inventory turnover results, Apple has succeeded in attracting customers to purchase multiple Apple products, sometimes of the same type (e.g., multiple laptops, iPads, or iPhones for the entire family).

CONCEPT CLIP

Impact of the Just-in-Time Manufacturing Environment

In the just-in-time (JIT) manufacturing environment, reducing inventories and increasing quality are critical activities. Both activities are essential for many companies to retain their competitive ability. Accordingly, users of financial statements should have a special interest in ratios that measure a company's progress in achieving the goals of zero inventories and total quality. As a company reduces its inventory, the inventory turnover ratio should increase dramatically. Traditionally, high inventory turnovers have had a negative connotation. It was argued that a high inventory turnover ratio might signal such problems as stockouts and disgruntled customers. In the JIT manufacturing environment, however, a high turnover ratio is viewed positively. High turnover is interpreted as a signal of success—of achieving the goal of zero inventories with all of the efficiency associated with that state.

As inventory levels drop, the current ratio also is affected. Without significant inventories, the current ratio will drop. In fact, it will approach the value of the quick ratio. Since many lenders require a 2.0 current ratio to grant and control a loan, some reevaluation of the use of this ratio is needed for customers with a JIT system. It may be necessary to rely more on the quick ratio or other alternative ratios (such as cash flow divided by current maturities of long-term debt).

A ratio that says something about quality also is desirable for JIT firms. The usual approach is to express quality costs as a percentage of sales. External users, however, may not have access to quality costs as a separate category. Warranty costs, returns and allowances, unfavorable materials quantity variances, and other quality costs that are readily identifiable from the financial statements can be added. This sum can then be divided by sales to give the external users some idea of the company's capability in this important area. Tracking this ratio over time will reveal the progress that the company is making. As quality improves, quality costs as a percentage of sales should decline.

Check Point

1. This year, Bellows Company has the same level of current assets and current liabilities as last year. However, last year current assets were 50% cash and accounts receivable, while this year current assets are 75% inventories. How will the change in the current asset mix affect this year's current ratio? Quick ratio?

Answer:
The current ratio will be unaffected (i.e., this year's current ratio will equal last year's current ratio). The quick ratio will be lower this year than last year because cash and accounts receivable are lower than last year. *Hint:* Sometimes it helps to put numbers into this type of a question. For example, you can choose to let last year's (as well as this year's) current assets equal $2,000 and to let last year's (as well as this year's) current liabilities equal $1,000. Then, the current ratio last year will be $2,000/$1,000, or 2. This year's current ratio is the same. The quick ratio for last year will be 1 ($1,000/$1,000), while this year's quick ratio will be 0.5 ($500/$1,000).

2. Which of the following four liquidity ratios contains an item that appears on the income statement? (*Hint:* There could be more than one.)

   I. Quick ratio   II. Accounts receivable turnover ratio

   III. Current ratio   IV. Inventory turnover ratio
   a. I and III
   b. III only
   c. II and III
   d. IV only
   e. II and IV

Answer:
e.

LEVERAGE RATIOS

OBJECTIVE 4

Calculate and use leverage ratios to assess the ability of a company to meet its long- and short-term obligations.

When a company incurs debt, it has the obligation to repay the principal and the interest. Holding debt increases the riskiness of a company. Unlike other sources of capital (e.g., retained earnings or proceeds from the sale of capital stock), debt carries with it the threat of default foreclosure and bankruptcy if income does not meet projections. Both potential investors and creditors need to evaluate a company's debt position. A potential creditor may find that the amount of debt and debt-servicing requirements of a company make it too risky to grant further credit. Similarly, the company may be too risky for some potential investors. Leverage ratios can help an individual to evaluate a company's debt-carrying ability.

Times-Interest-Earned Ratio

The first leverage ratio uses the income statement to assess a company's ability to service its debt. This ratio, called the **times-interest-earned ratio**, is computed as follows:

Times-Interest-Earned Ratio = (Income Before Taxes + Interest Expense)/Interest Expense

Income before taxes must be recurring income; thus, unusual or infrequent items appearing on the income statement should be excluded in order to compute the ratio. Recurring income is used because it is the income that is available each year to cover interest payments.

The times-interest-earned ratio for Payne Company is computed as follows, using data from Exhibit 15.3 (p. 844):

$$\text{Times-Interest-Earned Ratio} = (\$4,600,000 + \$400,000)/\$400,000$$
$$= \$5,000,000/\$400,000$$
$$= 12.5 \text{ times}$$

Since the assumed upper quartile for the glassware industry is 10.0, Payne's times-interest-earned ratio is among the highest in its industry. Payne does not have a significant interest expense burden.

Times-interest-earned is a profitability ratio that compares a company's earnings to its interest expense to assess how well the company can service its debt. **Example 15.6** shows how to calculate the times-interest-earned ratio.

Here's **Why It's important**

EXAMPLE 15.6

How to Calculate the Times-Interest-Earned Ratio

Calvin Company provided the following income statement for last year:

Sales	$900,000
Cost of goods sold	350,000
Gross margin	$550,000
Operating expenses	270,000
Operating income	$280,000
Interest expense	15,000
Income before taxes	$265,000
Income taxes	80,000
Net income	$185,000

Required:

Calculate the times-interest-earned ratio.

Solution:

Times-Interest-Earned Ratio = (Income Before Taxes + Interest Expense)/Interest Expense
$$= (\$265,000 + \$15,000)/\$15,000$$
$$= 18.7 \text{ times}$$

Note: Answer is rounded to one decimal place.

Ratios help tell the story of a company's performance, both in comparison to itself over time (e.g., past history) and in comparison to competitors at a given point in time (e.g., industrial averages). As discussed throughout this chapter, ratios involve data. The more data that are available, the more potential ratios a company, or an industry, can compute, analyze, and share with investors. However, even experienced internal executives and external analysts face limitations with respect to their ability to sift through the increasing quantities of available data in order to utilize the most useful ratios for assessing company performance. These limitations create significant opportunities for individuals and companies that can properly utilize data analytics (or big data) to help detect meaningful patterns in data, either financial or nonfinancial in nature.[2] Increasingly, managerial accountants and accounting firms use data analytics to more effectively describe past performance, predict future performance, and guide improved decision making. Using data analytics requires some level of understanding in various areas beyond accounting, including statistics, computer programming, operations, and communications. As noted by accounting firms, such as **Grant Thornton**, managerial accountants armed with an understanding of data analytics and ratio analysis can more effectively recognize business trends and pinpoint root causes of problems (i.e., specific practices to cease or correct) and successes (i.e., specific practices to continue or even expand). Without question, the combined use of data analytics and ratio analysis will grow in importance in the future.

Debt Ratio

Investors and creditors are the two major sources of capital. As the percentage of assets financed by creditors increases, the riskiness of the company increases. The **debt ratio** measures this percentage and is computed as follows:

$$\text{Debt Ratio} = \text{Total Liabilities}/\text{Total Assets}$$

Since total liabilities are compared with total assets, the ratio measures the degree of protection afforded creditors in case of insolvency. Creditors often impose restrictions on the percentage of liabilities allowed. If this percentage is exceeded, the company is in default, and foreclosure can take place.

The debt ratio for Payne Company is calculated as follows, using data from Exhibit 15.4 (p. 845):

$$\text{Debt Ratio} = \$16,000,000/\$32,000,000$$
$$= 0.50$$

Payne's debt ratio indicates that 50% of its assets are financed by creditors.

Is this percentage good or bad? How much risk will the stockholders allow? Will creditors be willing to provide more capital? For guidance, we again turn to industrial figures. The upper quartile, median, and lower quartile figures are 0.47, 0.55, and 0.69, respectively. With respect to industrial performance, Payne's debt ratio is not out of line. In fact, Payne is close to the upper quartile figure of 0.47. This position might indicate that Payne still has the capability to use additional credit.

Another ratio useful in assessing the leverage used by a company is the debt-to-equity ratio. This ratio compares the amount of debt that is financed by stockholders and is calculated as follows:

$$\text{Debt-to-Equity Ratio} = \text{Total Liabilities}/\text{Total Stockholder' Equity}$$

For Payne Company, the debt-to-equity ratio is calculated as follows, using data from Exhibit 15.4:

$$\text{Debt-to-Equity Ratio} = \$16,000,000/\$16,000,000$$
$$= 1.00$$

2   Matt Unterman, Mary Foster, and Anthony Pember, "Utilizing Data Analytics to Improve Performance," *Grant Thornton* (March 31, 2016). Taken from https://www.grantthornton.com/issues/library/whitepapers/nfp/2016/SoNFP/Data-analytics-improve-performance.aspx.

Creditors would like this ratio to be relatively low, indicating that stockholders have financed most of the assets of the firm. Stockholders, on the other hand, may wish this ratio to be higher because that indicates that the company is more highly leveraged and stockholders can reap the return of the creditors' financing.

The debt ratio and debt-to-equity ratio provide insights into the capital structure (i.e., debt or equity) used by a company to finance its assets. **Example 15.7** shows how to calculate the debt ratio and the debt-to-equity ratio.

Here's **Why It's important**

EXAMPLE 15.7

How to Calculate the Debt Ratio and the Debt-to-Equity Ratio

Jemell Company's balance sheet shows total liabilities of $450,000, total stockholders' equity of $300,000, and total assets of $750,000.

Required:

1. Calculate the debt ratio for Jemell.
2. Calculate the debt-to-equity ratio for Jemell.

Solution:

1. Debt Ratio = Total Liabilities/Total Assets

    = $450,000/$750,000

    = 0.60, or 60%

2. Debt-to-Equity Ratio = Total Liabilities/Total Stockholders' Equity

    = $450,000/$300,000

    = 1.50

Check Point

1. **Quickly estimate your total debts and your total assets. Calculate your own debt ratio. Do you expect it to change over the next 5 years? Why or why not?**

Answer:

Answers will vary. As a student, your debt ratio is likely high because you are incurring student loan costs and/or living expenses, probably without full-time employment. However, this scenario likely will change in the future when you graduate and are more likely to begin paying off debt (and then hopefully saving at least small amounts of money), instead of continuing to accrue it.

2. **How would a company's debt-to-equity ratio change if it were to raise capital by issuing common stock (assume nothing else changes)?**
    a. **Increase**
    b. **Decrease**
    c. **Remain the same**
    d. **Impossible to determine**

Answer:

b. Issuing common stock represents an increase in stockholders' equity. Specifically, the transaction would be an increase to cash (i.e., what the investor pays the company for purchasing ownership shares in the company) and an increase to common stock (and probably also an addition to additional paid-in capital, which is part of stockholders' equity). Therefore, the decision to issue common stock increases total assets and increases stockholders equity, with no effect on liabilities. Therefore, the numerator does not change, while the denominator increases, which causes the debt-to-equity ratio to decrease.

OBJECTIVE 5

Calculate and use profitability ratios to assess the extent to which a company's resources are being used efficiently.

PROFITABILITY RATIOS

Investors earn a return through the receipt of dividends and appreciation of the market value of their stock. Both dividends and market price of shares are related to the profits generated by companies. Since they are the source of debt-servicing payments, profits also are of concern to creditors. Managers also have a vested interest in profits. Bonuses, promotions, and salary increases often are tied to reported profits. Profitability ratios, therefore, are given particular attention by both internal and external users of financial statements.

Return on Sales

Return on sales is the profit margin on sales. It represents the percentage of each sales dollar that is left over as net income after all expenses have been subtracted. **Return on sales** is one measure of the efficiency of a firm and is computed as follows:

$$\text{Return on Sales} = \text{Net Income/Sales}$$

Here's **Why It's important**

Return on sales computes the cents from each sales dollar that remain after subtracting all expenses. **Example 15.8** shows how to calculate the return on sales for Payne Company for Year 2.

EXAMPLE 15.8

How to Calculate the Return on Sales

Refer to the information for Payne Company in Exhibit 15.3 (p. 844).

Required:
Calculate the return on sales.

Solution:
$$\text{Return on Sales} = \$2{,}300{,}000/\$50{,}000{,}000$$
$$= 0.046, \text{ or } 4.6\%$$

Return on Total Assets

Return on assets measures how efficiently assets are used by calculating the return on total assets used to generate profits. **Return on total assets** is computed as follows:

$$\text{Return on Total Assets} = \{\text{Net Income} + [\text{Interest Expense}(1 - \text{Tax Rate})]\}/\text{Average Total Assets}$$

Average total assets is found as follows:

$$\text{Average Total Assets} = (\text{Beginning Total Assets} + \text{Ending Total Assets})/2$$

By adding back the after-tax cost of interest, this measure reflects only how the assets were employed. It does not consider the manner in which they were financed (interest expense is a cost of obtaining the assets, not a cost of *using* them).

Here's **Why It's important**

Return on assets is a popular ratio that assesses the efficiency with which assets generate earnings. **Example 15.9** computes the return on assets for Payne Company for Year 2.

Refer to the information for Payne Company in Exhibits 15.3 (p. 844) and 15.4 (p. 845).

EXAMPLE 15.9

How to Calculate the Average Total Assets and the Return on Assets

Required:

1. Calculate the average total assets.
2. Calculate the return on total assets.

Solution:

1. Average Total Assets = ($30,000,000 + $32,000,000)/2
   = $31,000,000

2. Return on Total Assets = {$2,300,000 + [$400,000(1 − 0.50)]}/$31,000,000
   = ($2,300,000 + $200,000)/$31,000,000
   = $2,500,000/$31,000,000
   = 0.0806, or 8.06%

Note: The $400,000 of interest expense in the return on total assets numerator is given in Exhibit 15.3. Alternately, it can be calculated as follows:

   $4,000,000 of Bonds Payable (as shown in Exhibit 15.4) × 10% = $400,000.

Note: Answer is rounded to four decimal places.

Return on Common Stockholders' Equity

Return on total assets is measured without regard to the source of invested funds. For common stockholders, however, the return that they receive on their investment is of paramount importance. Of special interest to common stockholders is how they are being treated relative to other suppliers of capital funds. The **return on stockholders' equity** provides a measure that can be used to compare against other return measures (e.g., preferred dividend rates and bond rates) and is computed as follows:

> Return on Stockholders' Equity = (Net Income − Preferred Dividends)/
> Average Common Stockholders' Equity

For Payne Company, the beginning and ending common stockholders' equity require further calculations because the company has preferred stock. The preferred stock must be backed out of the total equity to get the common stockholders' equity. For Payne, the beginning and ending common stockholders' equity is calculated as follows:

   Beginning Common Stockholders' Equity = $14,924,000 − $3,200,000
   = $11,724,000

   Ending Common Stockholders' Equity = $16,000,000 − $3,200,000
   = $12,800,000

   Average Common Stockholders' Equity = ($12,800,000 + $11,724,000)/2
   = $12,262,000

Return on stockholders' equity is a popular ratio among investors, showing the earnings generated per dollar of stockholders' equity. **Example 15.10** calculates the return on stockholders' equity for Payne Company.

Here's **Why It's important**

EXAMPLE 15.10

How to Calculate the Average Common Stockholders' Equity and the Return on Stockholders' Equity

Refer to the information for Payne Company in Exhibits 15.3 (p. 844) and 15.4 (p. 845).

Required:

1. Calculate the average common stockholders' equity.
2. Calculate the return on stockholders' equity.

Solution:

1. Average Common Stockholders' Equity = ($11,724,000 + $12,800,000)/2

   $$= \$12,262,000$$

   Note: Common stockholders' equity for each year is calculated by summing common stock, additional paid-in capital, and retained earnings (all three of which are shown in Exhibit 15.4). Therefore, common stockholders' equity for Year 1 = $1,600,000 + $4,800,000 + $5,324,000 = $11,724,000.

2. Return on Stockholders' Equity = ($2,300,000 − $224,000)/$12,262,000

   $$= \$2,076,000/\$12,262,000$$

   $$= 0.1693, \text{ or } 16.93\%$$

   Note: Preferred dividends = $3,200,000 of preferred stock × 7% preferred dividend rate = $224,000 (as shown in Exhibits 15.3 and 15.4).

   Note: Answer is rounded to four decimal places.

CONCEPT CLIP

As we can see in Example 15.10, compared with the bond return of 10% and the preferred dividend rate of 7%, common stockholders are faring quite well. Furthermore, since the industrial average is about 14%, the rate of return provided common stockholders is above average.

Here's How It's Used: AT COCA-COLA

Companies use ratio analysis to communicate their financial performance to investors and other interested stakeholders. **Coca-Cola** in its integrated annual report discloses numerous ratios, including the most popular profitability ratio of all—earnings per share (EPS).[3] The company also shares more complex financial measures, such as the opex ratio (operating expenses divided by net sales revenue—29.2%) and return on invested capital (net operating profit after tax divided by the capital employed in the business—8.8%). However, in order to convey a more complete picture of its overall performance, Coca-Cola also chooses to disclose less common ratios involving nonfinancial data of interest to various key stakeholders. For example, these additional ratios include the water use ratio (liters of water used per liter of produced beverage—2.00), operational water footprint (billions of liters used—18.4), energy use ratio (megajoules of energy used per liter of produced beverage—0.44), CO_2 ratio (scope 1, 2, and 3 emissions for its carbon footprint as measured by grams of CO_2 per liter of produced beverage—353), safety rate ratio (number of lost time accidents longer than 1 day per 100 employees—1.14), and landfill waste ratio (grams per liter of produced beverage—0.76). The company believes that the benefit of disclosing these ratios, including current performance and future target performance, outweighs the costs of collecting, verifying, and compiling the data required to create these voluntary ratios.

---

3 Coca-Cola: Hellenic Bottling Company's "Refreshing Business 2015 Integrated Annual Report." Taken from http://coca-colahellenic.com/en/investors/reports/2015-integrated-annual-report/.

Earnings per Share

Investors also pay considerable attention to a company's profitability on a per-share basis. **Earnings per share** is computed as follows:

Earnings per Share = (Net Income – Preferred Dividends)/Average Common Shares

Average common shares outstanding is computed by taking a weighted average of the common shares for the period under study. For example, assume that a company has 8,000 common shares at the beginning of the year. At the end of the first quarter, 4,000 additional shares are issued. No other transactions take place during the period. The weighted average is computed as follows:

	Outstanding Shares	Weight	Weighted Shares
First quarter	8,000	3/12	2,000
Last three quarters	12,000	9/12	9,000
Average common shares outstanding			11,000

Earnings per share is the ratio most frequently cited by the majority of investors because it calculates the earnings generated per share of common stock. **Example 15.11** shows how to compute earnings per share for Payne Company.

Here's **Why It's important**

EXAMPLE 15.11

How to Compute Earnings per Share

Refer to the information for Payne Company in Exhibits 15.3 (p. 844) and 15.4 (p. 845).

Required:

1. Compute the number of common shares.
2. Compute earnings per share for Payne Company.

Solution:

1. Number of Common Shares = $1,600,000/$2 = 800,000 shares
2. Earnings per Share = ($2,300,000 – $224,000)/800,000

   = $2,076,000/800,000

   = $2.60

Since the median value for the industry is about $3.47 per share, Payne's earnings per share is somewhat low and may signal a need for management to focus on increasing earnings.

Price-Earnings Ratio

The **price-earnings ratio** is calculated as follows:

Price-Earnings Ratio = Market Price per Share/Earnings per Share

Price-earnings ratios are viewed by many investors as important indicators of stock values. If investors believe that a company has good growth prospects, then the price-earnings ratio should be high. If investors believe that the current price-earnings ratio is low based on their view of future growth opportunities, the market price of the stock may be bid up. However, the price-earnings ratio should be interpreted with caution, as it is comprised of stock price—a highly volatile measure that is influenced by numerous factors, including investor psychology—and earnings—a number that can be manipulated to meet certain targets involving analyst expectations, managerial bonuses, and other organizational goals.

Here's **Why It's important**

The price-earnings ratio varies widely across companies and compares the market price per share of stock to the earnings generated per share of common stock. **Example 15.12** shows how to compute the price-earnings ratio for Payne Company.

EXAMPLE 15.12	Assume that the price per common share for Payne Company is $15.
How to Compute the Price-Earnings Ratio	**Required:** Compute the price-earnings ratio. **Solution:** Price-Earnings Ratio = $15.00/$2.60 = 5.7692, or 5.77 *Note:* Refer to Example 15.11 for an explanation of how to calculate the $2.60 earnings per share. *Note:* Answer is rounded to two decimal places.

As Example 15.12 shows, Payne's stock is selling for 5.8 times its current earnings per share. This ratio compares with an industry median value of 6.3. Thus, Payne's price-earnings ratio is lower than more than half of the firms in the industry.

Dividend Yield and Payout Ratios

The profitability measure called **dividend yield** is computed as follows:

Dividend Yield = Dividends per Common Share/Market Price per Common Share

By adding the dividend yield to the percentage change in stock price, a reasonable approximation of the total return accruing to an investor can be obtained.

The **dividend payout ratio** is computed as follows:

Dividend Payout Ratio = Common Dividends/(Net Income – Preferred Dividends)

The payout ratio tells an investor the proportion of earnings that a company pays in dividends. Investors who prefer regular cash payments instead of returns through price appreciation will want to invest in companies with a high payout ratio. Investors who prefer gains through appreciation will generally prefer a lower payout ratio.

Here's **Why It's important**

The dividend yield and dividend payout ratios compare the amount of dividends a company declares relative to other popular measures of its profitability, such as the market price per share of common stock or earnings. **Example 15.13** computes the dividend yield and dividend payout ratio for Payne Company.

Assume that the market price per common share is $15. Refer to the information for Payne Company in Exhibits 15.3 (p. 844) and 15.4 (p. 845).

Required:

1. Compute the dividends per share.
2. Compute the dividend yield.
3. Compute the dividend payout ratio.

Solution:

1. Dividends per Share = $1,000,000/800,000 = $1.25
2. Dividend Yield = $1.25/$15.00

    $$= 0.0833, \text{ or } 8.33\%$$

3. Dividend Payout Ratio = $1,000,000/($2,300,000 − $224,000)

    $$= \$1,000,000/\$2,076,000$$

    $$= 0.4817$$

    Note: Answer is rounded to four decimal places.

The Summary of Important Equations section at the end of the chapter (pages 863–864) provides an overview of the ratios discussed in this chapter.

The Importance of Profitability Ratios to External Users of the Financial Statements

Of course, for ratio analysis to be useful, it is critically important that the underlying financial information be accurate. The purpose of financial statements prepared for outside users is to fairly represent the underlying economic position of the firm. Many external users, such as investors in the stock market, banks, and public agencies, rely on financial statements to provide necessary information. A look back at the recent past shows many instances in which corporate heads, knowing the importance of various ratios, took unethical steps to make the information fit the desired ratio results rather than letting the ratios come from fairly generated information. For example, ratio analysis can be very beneficial in identifying potential fraudulent corporate behavior, such as seeing sales revenue or net income skyrocket without adequate explanation or accompanying underlying operational data.

Ethical Decisions

Enron provides an excellent example of top management's obsession with ratio "doctoring." The focus of Enron top management was the company's stock price. In order to convince the stock market that Enron was a strong company, worthy of supporting the price set by the market, Enron officials took steps to report increasing income, even when income was decreasing. Of course, when the facts about Enron's actual earnings came out, the stock price tumbled, and the company resorted to bankruptcy. The demise of this company, one of the largest companies in the United States, had serious consequences for Enron investors and employees, as well as their families. In a separate fraud in a different industry, **Diamond Foods Inc.** paid $5 million to settle civil charges that it mislead investors by lying about its direct materials cost (i.e., walnut costs). This lie caused the company's timing of net income to differ such that it reported higher net income, thereby beating analysts' expectations about Diamond's critically important EPS across several years. The company's subsequent earnings restatement the following year caused its stock to tumble from a high of $90 per share to only $17 per share.[4] ●

Check Point

1. **Which of the following ratios contains both balance sheet and income statement accounts?**
   a. **Dividend yield**
   b. **Return on common stockholders' equity**
   c. **Return on sales**
   d. **Price-earnings ratio**

Answer:

b. Of the four ratios listed, only return on common stockholders' equity includes items from both the balance sheet (common stockholders' equity) and the income statement (net income). Return on sales contains only income statement items. Dividend yield contains dividends (on the statement of retained earnings) and market price per common share (with shares recorded in stockholders' equity at par value when issued). Finally, nothing in the price-earnings ratio appears on the balance sheet.

2. **Briefly explain why earnings per share is important to investors.**

Answer:

Earnings per share (EPS) likely is the ratio to which investors and stock market analysts pay the most attention. EPS reflects the amount of net income a company generates for each share of common stock that has been issued and remains outstanding (i.e., has not been repurchased by the company in a stock buyback program—see "Here's How It's Used: At Apple" feature earlier in the chapter). Generally speaking, higher EPS is preferred to lower EPS. However, investors should take care in interpreting EPS, as this ratio can be manipulated by certain actions. For example, some companies buy back shares of their common stock toward the end of the year, which decreases the denominator (Average Common Shares), thereby increasing EPS. In addition, investors should be wary of the "earnings game," whereby companies try extremely hard to have their *actual* EPS meet or exceed *expected* (either from themselves or from stock market analysts) EPS. Therefore, EPS is an extremely important ratio that investors should use with the proper degree of caution.

---

4 "Diamond Foods to Pay $5 mln to Settle SEC Accounting Fraud Case," *Reuters* (January 9, 2014). Taken from http://www.reuters.com/article/2014/01/09/us-diamond-sec-accountingfraud-idUSL2N0KJ1OP20140109.

SUMMARY OF LEARNING OBJECTIVES

LO1. Analyze financial statements using two forms of common-size analysis: horizontal analysis and vertical analysis.
- Common-size analysis expresses accounts or line items in financial statements as percentages.
- Horizontal analysis compares line items from one period with another period, to assess trends.
- Vertical analysis compares one line item with another line item from the same time period, to assess relationships among financial statement items.

LO2. Explain why historical standards and industrial averages are important for ratio analysis.
- Ratios can be compared with a standard.
- The most common standards are historical values and industrial values.

LO3. Calculate and use liquidity ratios to assess the ability of a company to meet its current obligations.
- Liquidity ratios are used to assess the short-term debt-paying ability of a company.
- These ratios include the current ratio, the quick or acid-test ratio, the accounts receivable turnover ratio, and the inventory turnover ratio.

LO4. Calculate and use leverage ratios to assess the ability of a company to meet its long- and short-term obligations.
- Leverage ratios measure the ability of a company to meet long-term debt obligations.
- These ratios include the times-interest-earned ratio and the debt ratio.

LO5. Calculate and use profitability ratios to assess the extent to which a company's resources are being used efficiently.
- Profitability ratios relate the firm's earnings to the resources used to create those earnings.
- Profitability ratios include return on sales, return on total assets, earnings per share, the price-earnings ratio, dividend yield, and the dividend payout ratio.

SUMMARY OF IMPORTANT EQUATIONS

Liquidity ratios:

1. Current Ratio = Current Assets/Current Liabilities

2. Quick Ratio = (Cash + Marketable Securities + Accounts Receivable)/Current Liabilities

3. Accounts Receivable Turnover Ratio = Net Sales/Average Accounts Receivable

4. Average Accounts Receivable = (Beginning Receivables + Ending Receivables)/2

5. Accounts Receivable Turnover in Days = 365/Accounts Receivable Turnover Ratio

6. Inventory Turnover Ratio = Cost of Goods Sold/Average Inventory

7. Average Inventory = (Beginning Inventory + Ending Inventory)/2

8. Inventory Turnover in Days = 365/Inventory Turnover Ratio

9. Times-Interest-Earned Ratio = (Income Before Taxes + Interest Expense)/Interest Expense

10. Debt Ratio = Total Liabilities/Total Assets

11. Debt-to-Equity Ratio = Total Liabilities/Total Stockholder' Equity

Profitability ratios:

12. Return on Sales = Net Income/Sales

13. Return on Total Assets = {Net Income + [Interest Expense(1 − Tax Rate)]}/Average Total Assets

14. Average Total Assets = (Beginning Total Assets + Ending Total Assets)/2

15. Return on Stockholders' Equity = (Net Income − Preferred Dividends)/Average Common Stockholders' Equity

16. Earnings per Share = (Net Income − Preferred Dividends)/Average Common Shares

17. Price-Earnings Ratio = Market Price per Share/Earnings per Share

18. Dividend Yield = Dividends per Common Share/Market Price per Common Share

19. Dividend Payout Ratio = Common Dividends/(Net Income − Preferred Dividends)

KEY TERMS

Accounts receivable turnover ratio, 848, a ratio that measures the liquidity of receivables. It is computed by dividing net sales by average accounts receivable.

Common-size analysis, 838, a type of analysis that expresses line items or accounts in the financial statements as percentages.

Creditors, 838, loan managers who assess the creditworthiness of potential customers through ratio analysis, common-size analysis, and other techniques.

Current ratio, 846, a measure of the ability of a company to pay its short-term liabilities out of short-term assets.

Debt ratio, 854, the ratio that measures the percentage of a company's risk as the percentage of its assets financed by creditors increases. It is computed by dividing a company's total liabilities by its total assets.

Dividend payout ratio, 860, a ratio that is computed by dividing the total common dividends by the earnings available to common stockholders.

Dividend yield, 860, a profitability measure that is computed by dividing the dividends received per unit of common share by the market price per common share.

Earnings per share, 859, earnings per share is computed by dividing net income less preferred dividends by the average number of shares of common stock outstanding during the period.

Horizontal analysis, 839, also called trend analysis, this type of analysis expresses a line item as a percentage of some prior-period amount.

Inventory turnover ratio, 850, a ratio that is computed by dividing the cost of goods sold by the average inventory.

Investors, 838, those who analyze financial statements to assess the attractiveness of a company as a potential investment.

Leverage ratios, 844, ratios that measure the ability of a company to meet its long- and short-term obligations. These ratios provide a measure of the degree of protection provided to a company's creditors.

Liquidity ratios, 844, ratios that measure the ability of a company to meet its current obligations.

Managers, 838, those individuals who analyze their own financial statements to assess profitability, liquidity, debt position, and progress toward organizational objectives.

Price-earnings ratio, 859, the price-earnings ratio is found by dividing the market price per share by the earnings per share.

Profitability ratios, 844, ratios that measure the earning ability of a company. These ratios allow investors, creditors, and managers to evaluate the extent to which invested funds are being used efficiently.

Quick or acid-test ratio, 848, a measure of liquidity that compares only the most liquid assets to current liabilities.

Return on sales, 856, a measure of the efficiency of a firm that is computed by dividing net income by sales.

Return on stockholders' equity, 857, a measure that can be used to compare against other return measures (e.g., preferred dividend rates and bond rates). It is computed by dividing net income less preferred dividends by the average common stockholders' equity.

Return on total assets, 856, the result of dividing net income plus the after-tax cost of interest by the average total assets.

Times-interest-earned ratio, 853, a leverage ratio that uses the income statement to assess a company's ability to service its debt. It is computed by dividing net income before taxes and interest by interest expense.

Vertical analysis, 840, a type of analysis that expresses the line item as a percentage of some other line item for the same period.

REVIEW PROBLEM

I. Financial Statement Analysis

Shera Company just completed its second year of operations. The comparative income statements for these years are as follows:

(Continued)

	20X1	20X2
Sales revenue	$500,000	$800,000
Cost of goods sold	300,000	464,000
Gross margin	$200,000	$336,000
Operating expenses	(80,000)	(164,000)
Interest expenses	(20,000)	(20,000)
Income before taxes	$100,000	$152,000
Income taxes	34,000	51,680
Net income	$ 66,000	$100,320

Selected information from the balance sheet for 20X1 is also given.

Current assets	$100,000
Long-term assets	400,000
Total assets	$500,000
Current liabilities	$ 80,000
Long-term liabilities	220,000
Total liabilities	$300,000
Common stock	$100,000
Retained earnings	100,000
Total equity	$200,000

Shera had 100,000 shares of stock outstanding. At the end of 20X2, a share had a market value of $1.80. The shares outstanding have not changed since the original issue. Dividends of $30,000 were paid in 20X2. Total assets have not changed during 20X2.

Required:

1. Using 20X1 as a base period, express all line items of the income statements as a percentage of the corresponding base period item.
2. Express each line item of the two income statements as a percentage of sales.
3. Comment on the trends revealed by the computations in Requirements 1 and 2.
4. Compute the following ratios for 20X2: (a) current ratio, (b) debt ratio, (c) return on total assets, (d) times-interest-earned ratio, (e) earnings per share, and (f) dividend yield.

Solution:

1. Horizontal analysis:

	20X1	Percent	20X2	Percent
Sales revenue	$500,000	100.0%	$800,000	160.0%
Cost of goods sold	300,000	100.0	464,000	154.7
Gross margin	$200,000	100.0	$336,000	168.0
Operating expenses	(80,000)	100.0	(164,000)	205.0
Interest expense	(20,000)	100.0	(20,000)	100.0
Income before taxes	$100,000	100.0	$152,000	152.0
Income taxes	34,000	100.0	51,680	152.0
Net income	$ 66,000	100.0	$100,320	152.0

2. Vertical analysis:

	20X1	Percent	20X2	Percent
Sales revenue	$500,000	100.0%	$ 800,000	100.0%
Cost of goods sold	300,000	60.0	464,000	58.0
Gross margin	$200,000	40.0	$ 336,000	42.0
Operating expenses	(80,000)	16.0	(164,000)	20.5
Interest expense	(20,000)	4.0	(20,000)	2.5
Income before taxes	$100,000	20.0	$ 152,000	19.0
Income taxes	34,000	6.8	51,680	6.5
Net income	$ 66,000	13.2	$ 100,320	12.5

3. The trends reflected by both the horizontal and vertical analyses are basically favorable. Sales have increased and, with the notable exception of operating expenses, expenses have not increased as rapidly as sales and have declined as a percentage of sales. Operating expenses, however, have more than doubled from 20X1 to 20X2 and have also increased as a percentage of sales.

4. a. Current Ratio = $100,000/$80,000 = 1.25
   b. Debt Ratio = $300,000/$500,000 = 0.60, or 60%
   c. Return on Total Assets = {$100,320 + [$20,000(0.66)]}/$500,000 = 0.227, or 22.7%
   d. Times-Interest-Earned Ratio = $172,000/$20,000 = 8.6
   e. Earnings per Share = $100,320/100,000 = $1.00 per share
   f. Dividend Yield = $0.30/$1.80 = 0.167, or 16.7%

DISCUSSION QUESTIONS

1. Name the two major types of financial statement analysis discussed in this chapter.
2. What is horizontal analysis? Vertical analysis? Should both horizontal and vertical analyses be done? Why?
3. Explain how creditors, investors, and managers can use common-size analysis as an aid in decision making.
4. What are liquidity ratios? Leverage ratios? Profitability ratios?
5. Identify two types of standards used in ratio analysis. Explain why it is desirable to use both types.
6. What information does the quick ratio supply that the current ratio does not?
7. Suppose that the accounts receivable turnover ratio of a company is low when compared with other firms within its industry. How would this information be useful to the managers of a company?
8. A high inventory turnover ratio provides evidence that a company is having problems with stockouts and disgruntled customers. Do you agree? Explain.
9. A loan agreement between a bank and a customer specified that the debt ratio could not exceed 60%. Explain the purpose of this restrictive agreement.
10. A manager decided to acquire some expensive equipment through the use of an operating lease, even though a capital budgeting analysis showed that it was more profitable to buy than to lease. However, the purchase alternative would have required the issuance of some bonds. Offer some reasons that would explain the manager's choice.
11. Explain why an investor would be interested in a company's debt ratio.
12. Assume that you have been given the responsibility to invest some funds in the stock market to provide an annuity to an individual who has just retired. Explain how you might use the dividend yield and the dividend payout ratio to help you with this investment decision.

13. Explain how an investor might use the price-earnings ratio to value the stock of a company.

14. When a company participates in a stock buyback program, it means that the company is buying shares of its own stock and taking them off the market. With this simple definition in mind, how would a company's stock buyback program affect its Earnings per Share?

15. Explain the significance of the inventory turnover ratio in a JIT manufacturing environment.

16. In a JIT manufacturing environment, the current ratio and the quick ratio are virtually the same. Do you agree? Why?

MULTIPLE-CHOICE QUESTIONS

15-1 In examining Luke Company's current-period income statement, you notice that research and development expenses are 62% of sales revenue. Luke has most likely provided

    a. a horizontal analysis.

    b. a vertical analysis using sales as the base.

    c. a horizontal analysis using sales as the base.

    d. a vertical analysis using net income as the base.

    e. none of these.

15-2 An advantage of common-size analysis is that

    a. the size of dollar amounts impact the analysis.

    b. larger companies will have higher common-size percentages.

    c. it focuses only on vertical analysis.

    d. the effects of size are eliminated.

    e. it focuses only on horizontal analysis.

15-3 Fractions or percentages computed by dividing one account or line-item amount by another are called

    a. returns.

    b. industry averages.

    c. common-size statements.

    d. dividend yields.

    e. ratios.

15-4 The measures of the ability of a company to meet its current obligations are called

    a. ratios.

    b. liquidity ratios.

    c. leverage ratios.

    d. profitability ratios.

    e. percentage changes.

15-5 Pedee Company's inventory turnover in days is 80 days. Which of the following actions could help to improve that ratio?

    a. Increase the sales price.

    b. Increase manufacturing costs.

    c. Reduce the cost of goods sold.

    d. Reduce average inventory.

    e. All of these.

15-6 Etchey Company shows that 46% of its assets are financed by creditors. Which of the following shows this result?

a. Current ratio
b. Times-interest-earned ratio
c. Debt ratio
d. Inventory turnover in days
e. Return on sales

15-7 Profitability ratios are used by which of the following groups?

a. Company managers
b. Creditors
c. Lenders
d. Investors
e. All of these.

15-8 Fred and Torrie Jones are a retired couple looking for income. They are currently rebalancing their portfolio of stocks to include more with high dividends. Fred and Torrie will be most interested in which of the following?

a. Current ratio
b. Dividend payout ratio
c. Return on assets
d. Price-earnings ratio
e. Dividend yield

15-9 A small pizza restaurant, founded and owned by the Martinelli sisters, would be expected to have which of the following?

a. Low inventory turnover and high gross margin
b. Low accounts receivable turnover and low gross margin
c. High price-earnings ratio
d. High inventory turnover and low gross margin
e. All of these.

15-10 The after-tax cost of interest expense is used in calculating which of the following?

a. Times-interest-earned ratio
b. Return on assets
c. Debt ratio
d. Inventory turnover ratio
e. All of these.

BRIEF EXERCISES: SET A

Use the following information for Brief Exercises 15-11 and 15-12:
Scherer Company provided the following income statements for its first 3 years of operation:

	Year 1	Year 2	Year 3
Net sales	$1,000,000	$1,100,000	$1,300,000
Less: Cost of goods sold	(300,000)	(310,000)	(364,000)
Gross margin	$ 700,000	$ 790,000	$ 936,000
Less: Operating expenses	(421,000)	(484,000)	(591,000)
Income taxes	(111,600)	(122,400)	(137,800)
Net income	$ 167,400	$ 183,600	$ 207,200

OBJECTIVE **1**
Example 15.1

Brief Exercise 15-11 Preparing Common-Size Income Statements by Using Base Period Horizontal Analysis

Refer to the information for Scherer Company on the previous page.

Required:

Prepare common-size income statements by using Year 1 as the base period. (*Note:* Round answers to the nearest whole percentage.)

OBJECTIVE **1**
Example 15.2

Brief Exercise 15-12 Preparing Income Statements by Using Net Sales as the Base: Vertical Analysis

Refer to the information for Scherer Company on the previous page.

Required:

Prepare common-size income statements by using net sales as the base. (*Note:* Round answers to the nearest whole percentage.)

OBJECTIVE **3**
Example 15.3

Brief Exercise 15-13 Calculating the Current Ratio and the Quick (or Acid-Test) Ratio

Chen Company has current assets equal to $5,000,000. Of these, $1,000,000 is cash, $2,250,000 is accounts receivable, $500,000 is inventory, and the remainder is marketable securities. Current liabilities total $4,000,000.

Required:

Note: Round answers to two decimal places.
1. Calculate the current ratio.
2. Calculate the quick ratio (acid-test ratio).

Use the following information for Brief Exercises 15-14 and 15-15:
Last year, Nikkola Company had net sales of $2,299,500,000 and cost of goods sold of $1,755,000,000. Nikkola had the following balances:

	January 1	December 31
Accounts receivable	$142,650,000	$172,350,000
Inventory	54,374,200	62,625,800

OBJECTIVE **3**
Example 15.4

Brief Exercise 15-14 Calculating the Average Accounts Receivable, the Accounts Receivable Turnover Ratio, and the Accounts Receivable Turnover in Days

Refer to the information for Nikkola Company above.

Required:

Note: Round answers to one decimal place.
1. Calculate the average accounts receivable.
2. Calculate the accounts receivable turnover ratio.
3. Calculate the accounts receivable turnover in days.

OBJECTIVE **3**
Example 15.5

Brief Exercise 15-15 Calculating the Average Inventory, the Inventory Turnover Ratio, and the Inventory Turnover in Days

Refer to the information for Nikkola Company above.

Required:

Note: Round answers to one decimal place.

1. Calculate the average inventory.
2. Calculate the inventory turnover ratio.
3. Calculate the inventory turnover in days.
4. **CONCEPTUAL CONNECTION** Based on these ratios, does Nikkola appear to be performing well or poorly?

Brief Exercise 15-16 Calculating the Times-Interest-Earned Ratio

OBJECTIVE ◀ 4
Example 15.6

Paxton Company provided the following income statement for last year:

Sales	$87,021,000
Cost of goods sold	62,138,249
Gross margin	$24,882,751
Operating expenses	19,371,601
Operating income	$ 5,511,150
Interest expense	875,400
Income before taxes	$ 4,635,750
Income taxes	1,854,300
Net income	$ 2,781,450

Required:

Calculate the times-interest-earned ratio. (*Note:* Round the answer to one decimal place.)

Brief Exercise 15-17 Calculating the Debt Ratio and the Debt-to-Equity Ratio

OBJECTIVE ◀ 4
Example 15.7

Ernst Company's balance sheet shows total liabilities of $32,500,000, total stockholders' equity of $8,125,000, and total assets of $40,625,000.

Required:

Note: Round answers to two decimal places.
1. Calculate the debt ratio.
2. Calculate the debt-to-equity ratio.

Use the following information for Brief Exercises 15-18 through 15-23:
The income statement, statement of retained earnings, and balance sheet for Somerville Company are as follows:

Somerville Company
Income Statement
For the Year Ended December 31, 20X2

	Amount	Percent
Net sales	$ 8,281,989	100.0%
Less: Cost of goods sold	(5,383,293)	65.0
Gross margin	$ 2,898,696	35.0
Less: Operating expenses	(1,323,368)	16.0
Operating income	$ 1,575,328	19.0
Less: Interest expense	(50,000)	0.6
Income before taxes	$ 1,525,328	18.4
Less: Income taxes (40%)*	(610,131)	7.4
Net income	$ 915,197	11.0

*Includes both state and federal taxes.

(*Continued*)

Somerville Company
Statement of Retained Earnings
For the Year Ended December 31, 20X2

Balance, beginning of period	$1,979,155
Net income	915,197
Total	$2,894,352
Preferred dividends	(80,000)
Dividends to common stockholders	(201,887)
Balance, end of period	$2,612,465

Somerville Company
Comparative Balance Sheets
At December31, 20X1 and 20X2

	20X1	20X2
Assets		
Current assets:		
Cash	$2,875,000	$2,580,000
Marketable securities	800,000	700,000
Accounts receivable (net)	939,776	690,000
Inventories	490,000	260,000
Other	93,000	74,261
Total current assets	$5,197,776	$4,304,261
Property and equipment:		
Land	$1,575,000	$1,067,315
Building and equipment (net)	1,348,800	1,150,000
Total long-term assets	$2,923,800	$2,217,315
Total assets	$8,121,576	$6,521,576
Liabilities and Stockholders' Equity		
Current liabilities:		
Notes payable, short term	$1,170,127	$ 543,641
Accounts payable	298,484	101,500
Current maturity of long-term debt	3,000	2,000
Accrued payables	200,000	57,780
Total current liabilities	$1,671,611	$ 704,921
Long-term liabilities:		
Bonds payable, 10%	500,000	500,000
Total liabilities	$2,171,611	$1,204,921
Stockholders' equity:		
Preferred stock, $25 par, 8%	$1,000,000	$1,000,000
Common stock, $1.50 par	337,500	337,500
Additional paid-in capital*	2,000,000	2,000,000
Retained earnings	2,612,465	1,979,155
Total stockholders' equity	$5,949,965	$5,316,655
Total liabilities and stockholders' equity	$8,121,576	$6,521,576

*For common stock only.

Brief Exercise 15-18 Calculating the Return on Sales

OBJECTIVE 5

Example 15.8

Refer to the information for Somerville Company on the previous pages.

Required:

Calculate the return on sales. (*Note:* Round the answer to three decimal places.)

Brief Exercise 15-19 Calculating the Average Total Assets and the Return on Assets

OBJECTIVE 5

Example 15.9

Refer to the information for Somerville Company on the previous pages. Assume a tax rate of 40%.

Required:

Note: Round answers to four decimal places.
1. Calculate the average total assets.
2. Calculate the return on assets.

Brief Exercise 15-20 Calculating the Average Common Stockholders' Equity and the Return on Stockholders' Equity

OBJECTIVE 5

Example 15.10

Refer to the information for Somerville Company on the previous pages.

Required:

Note: Round answers to four decimal places.
1. Calculate the average common stockholders' equity.
2. Calculate the return on stockholders' equity.

Brief Exercise 15-21 Computing Earnings per Share

OBJECTIVE 5

Example 15.11

Refer to the information for Somerville Company on the previous pages.

Required:

Note: Round answers to two decimal places.
1. Compute the number of common shares.
2. Compute earnings per share.

Brief Exercise 15-22 Computing the Price-Earnings Ratio

OBJECTIVE 5

Example 15.12

Refer to the information for Somerville Company on the previous pages. Also, assume that the price per common share for Somerville is $8.10.

Required:

Compute the price-earnings ratio. (*Note:* Round the answer to two decimal places.)

Brief Exercise 15-23 Computing the Dividend Yield and the Dividend Payout Ratio

OBJECTIVE 5

Example 15.13

Refer to the information for Somerville Company on the previous pages. Also, assume that the market price per common share is $8.10.

Required:

Note: Round answers to four decimal places.
1. Compute the dividends per share.
2. Compute the dividend yield.
3. Compute the dividend payout ratio.

BRIEF EXERCISES: SET B

> Use the following information for Brief Exercises 15-24 and 15-25:
> Jasmine Company provided the following income statements for its first 3 years of operation:
>
> | | Year 1 | Year 2 | Year 3 |
> |---|---|---|---|
> | Net sales | $ 5,000,000 | $ 4,500,000 | $ 4,000,000 |
> | Less: Cost of goods sold | (3,000,000) | (3,250,000) | (3,600,000) |
> | Gross margin | $ 2,000,000 | $ 1,250,000 | $ 400,000 |
> | Less: Operating expenses | (1,420,000) | (800,000) | (165,000) |
> | Income taxes | (232,000) | (180,000) | (134,000) |
> | Net income | $ 348,000 | $ 270,000 | $ 101,000 |

OBJECTIVE ▶ **1**
Example 15.1

Brief Exercise 15-24 Preparing Common-Size Income Statements by Using Base Period Horizontal Analysis

Refer to the information for Jasmine Company above.

Required:

Prepare common-size income statements by using Year 1 as the base period. (*Note:* Round answers to the nearest whole percentage.)

OBJECTIVE ▶ **1**
Example 15.2

Brief Exercise 15-25 Preparing Income Statements by Using Net Sales as the Base: Vertical Analysis

Refer to the information for Jasmine Company above.

Required:

Prepare common-size income statements by using net sales as the base. (*Note:* Round answers to the nearest whole percentage.)

OBJECTIVE ▶ **3**
Example 15.3

Brief Exercise 15-26 Calculating the Current Ratio and the Quick (or Acid-Test) Ratio

LoLo Lemon Company has current assets equal to $500,000. Of these, $300,000 is cash, $75,000 is accounts receivable, $125,000 is inventory, and the remainder is marketable securities. Current liabilities total $425,000.

Required:

Note: Round answers to two decimal places.
1. Calculate the current ratio.
2. Calculate the quick ratio (acid-test ratio).

> Use the following information for Brief Exercises 15-27 and 15-28:
> Last year, Toby's Hats had net sales of $45,000,000 and cost of goods sold of $29,000,000. Toby's had the following balances:
>
> | | January 1 | December 31 |
> |---|---|---|
> | Accounts receivable | $5,500,000 | $6,500,000 |
> | Inventories | 3,000,000 | 2,800,000 |

Brief Exercise 15-27 Calculating the Average Accounts Receivable, the Accounts Receivable Turnover Ratio, and the Accounts Receivable Turnover in Days

OBJECTIVE ▶ 3
Example 15.4

Refer to the information for Toby's on the previous page.

Required:

Note: Round answers to one decimal place.
1. Calculate the average accounts receivable.
2. Calculate the accounts receivable turnover ratio.
3. Calculate the accounts receivable turnover in days.

Brief Exercise 15-28 Calculating the Average Inventory, the Inventory Turnover Ratio, and the Inventory Turnover in Days

OBJECTIVE ▶ 3
Example 15.5

Refer to the information for Toby's on the previous page.

Required:

Note: Round answers to one decimal place.
1. Calculate the average inventory.
2. Calculate the inventory turnover ratio.
3. Calculate the inventory turnover in days.
4. **CONCEPTUAL CONNECTION** Based on these ratios, does Toby's appear to be performing well or poorly?

Brief Exercise 15-29 Calculating the Times-Interest-Earned Ratio

OBJECTIVE ▶ 4
Example 15.6

Alessandra Makeup Manufacturers provided the following income statement for last year:

Sales	$51,350,000
Cost of goods sold	19,250,000
Gross margin	$32,100,000
Operating expenses	6,200,000
Operating income	$25,900,000
Interest expense	9,500,000
Income before taxes	$16,400,000
Income taxes	6,560,000
Net income	$ 9,840,000

Required:

Calculate the times-interest-earned ratio. (*Note:* Round the answer to one decimal place.)

Brief Exercise 15-30 Calculating the Debt Ratio and the Debt-to-Equity Ratio

OBJECTIVE ▶ 4
Example 15.7

Klynveld Company's balance sheet shows total liabilities of $94,000,000, total stockholders' equity of $75,000,000, and total assets of $169,000,000.

Required:

Note: Round answers to two decimal places.
1. Calculate the debt ratio.
2. Calculate the debt-to-equity ratio.

Use the following information for Brief Exercises 15-31 through 15-36:

The income statement, statement of retained earnings, and balance sheet for Santiago Systems are as follows:

Santiago Systems
Income Statement
For the Year Ended December 31, 20X2

	Amount	Percent
Net sales	$ 5,345,000	100.0%
Less: Cost of goods sold	(3,474,250)	65.0
Gross margin	$ 1,870,750	35.0
Less: Operating expenses	(1,140,300)	21.3
Operating income	$ 730,450	13.7
Less: Interest expense	(27,000)	0.5
Income before taxes	$ 703,450	13.2
Less: Income taxes (40%)*	(281,380)	5.3
Net income	$ 422,070	7.9

*Includes both state and federal taxes.

Santiago Systems
Statement of Retained Earnings
For the Year Ended December 31, 20X2

Balance, beginning of period	$1,205,500
Net income	422,070
Total	$1,627,570
Preferred dividends	(40,000)
Dividends to common stockholders	(150,000)
Balance, end of period	$1,437,570

Santiago Systems
Comparative Balance Sheets
At December 31, 20X1 and 20X2

	20X1	20X2
Assets		
Current assets:		
Cash	$1,900,000	$2,100,000
Marketable securities	350,000	400,000
Accounts receivable (net)	625,000	675,000
Inventories	230,000	240,000
Other	50,000	50,000
Total current assets	$3,155,000	$3,465,000
Property and equipment:		
Land	$ 900,000	$ 900,000
Building and equipment (net)	1,240,800	1,192,800
Total long-term assets	$2,140,800	$2,092,800
Total assets	$5,295,800	$5,557,800

Liabilities and Stockholders' Equity

Current liabilities:

Notes payable, short term	$ 247,300	$ 256,230
Accounts payable	240,000	250,000
Current maturity of long-term debt	3,000	4,000
Accrued payables	150,000	160,000
Total current liabilities	$ 640,300	$ 670,230
Long-term liabilities:		
Bonds payable, 9%	300,000	300,000
Total liabilities	$ 940,300	$ 970,230
Stockholders' equity:		
Preferred stock, $25 par, 8%	$ 500,000	$ 500,000
Common stock, $1.00 par	150,000	150,000
Additional paid-in capital*	2,500,000	2,500,000
Retained earnings	1,205,500	1,437,570
Total stockholders' equity	$4,355,500	$4,587,570
Total liabilities and stockholders' equity	$5,295,800	$5,557,800

*For common stock only.

Brief Exercise 15-31 Calculating the Return on Sales

Refer to the information for Santiago Systems above.

OBJECTIVE 5
Example 15.8

Required:

Calculate the return on sales. (*Note:* Round the answer to three decimal places.)

Brief Exercise 15-32 Calculating the Average Total Assets and the Return on Assets

Refer to the information for Santiago Systems above. Assume a tax rate of 40%.

OBJECTIVE 5
Example 15.9

Required:

Note: Round answers to four decimal places.
1. Calculate the average total assets.
2. Calculate the return on assets.

Brief Exercise 15-33 Calculating the Average Common Stockholders' Equity and the Return on Stockholders' Equity

Refer to the information for Santiago Systems above.

OBJECTIVE 5
Example 15.10

Required:

Note: Round answers to four decimal places.
1. Calculate the average common stockholders' equity.
2. Calculate the return on stockholders' equity.

Brief Exercise 15-34 Computing Earnings per Share

Refer to the information for Santiago Systems above.

OBJECTIVE 5
Example 15.11

(Continued)

Required:

Note: Round answers to two decimal places.
1. Compute the number of common shares.
2. Compute earnings per share.

OBJECTIVE 5
Example 15.12

Brief Exercise 15-35 Computing the Price-Earnings Ratio

Refer to the information for Santiago Systems on the previous pages. Also, assume that the price per common share for Santiago is $20.

Required:

Compute the price-earnings ratio. (*Note:* Round the answer to two decimal places.)

OBJECTIVE 5
Example 15.13

Brief Exercise 15-36 Computing the Dividend Yield and the Dividend Payout Ratio

Refer to the information for Santiago Systems on the previous pages. Also, assume that the market price per common share is $20.

Required:

Note: Round answers to four decimal places.
1. Compute the dividends per share.
2. Compute the dividend yield.
3. Compute the dividend payout ratio.

EXERCISES

Use the following information for Exercises 15-37 and 15-38:
Sundahl Company's income statements for the past 2 years are as follows:

Sundahl Company
Income Statements
For the Years 1 and 2

	Year 1	Year 2
Sales	$ 2,000,000	$ 1,800,000
Less: Cost of goods sold	(1,400,000)	(1,200,000)
Gross margin	$ 600,000	$ 600,000
Less operating expenses:		
Selling expenses	(300,000)	(300,000)
Administrative expenses	(100,000)	(110,000)
Operating income	$ 200,000	$ 190,000
Less: Interest expense	(50,000)	(40,000)
Income before taxes	$ 150,000	$ 150,000

OBJECTIVE 1

Exercise 15-37 Horizontal Analysis

Refer to the information for Sundahl Company above.

Required:

Prepare a common-size income statement for Year 2 by expressing each line item for Year 2 as a percentage of that same line item from Year 1. (*Note:* Round percentages to the nearest tenth of a percent.)

Exercise 15-38 Vertical Analysis

OBJECTIVE ▶ 1

Refer to the information for Sundahl Company on the previous page.

Required:

1. Prepare a common-size income statement for Year 1 by expressing each line item as a percentage of sales revenue. (*Note:* Round percentages to the nearest tenth of a percent.)
2. Prepare a common-size income statement for Year 2 by expressing each line item as a percentage of sales revenue. (*Note:* Round percentages to the nearest tenth of a percent.)

Use the following information for Exercises 15-39 and 15-40:

Cuneo Company's income statements for the last 3 years are as follows:

Cuneo Company
Income Statements
For the Years 1, 2, and 3

	Year 1	Year 2	Year 3
Sales	$1,000,000	$1,200,000	$ 1,700,000
Less: Cost of goods sold	(700,000)	(700,000)	(1,000,000)
Gross margin	$ 300,000	$ 500,000	$ 700,000
Less operating expenses:			
Selling expenses	(150,000)	(220,000)	(250,000)
Administrative expenses	(50,000)	(60,000)	(120,000)
Operating income	$ 100,000	$ 220,000	$ 330,000
Less: Interest expense	(25,000)	(25,000)	(25,000)
Income before taxes	$ 75,000	$ 195,000	$ 305,000

Exercise 15-39 Horizontal Analysis

OBJECTIVE ▶ 1

Refer to the information for Cuneo Company above.

Required:

1. Prepare a common-size income statement for Year 2 by expressing each line item for Year 2 as a percentage of that same line item from Year 1. (*Note:* Round percentages to the nearest tenth of a percent.)
2. Prepare a common-size income statement for Year 3 by expressing each line item for Year 3 as a percentage of that same line item from Year 1. (*Note:* Round percentages to the nearest tenth of a percent.)

Exercise 15-40 Vertical Analysis

OBJECTIVE ▶ 1

Refer to the information for Cuneo Company above.

EXCEL

Required:

1. Prepare a common-size income statement for Year 1 by expressing each line item as a percentage of sales revenue. (*Note:* Round percentages to the nearest tenth of a percent.)
2. Prepare a common-size income statement for Year 2 by expressing each line item as a percentage of sales revenue. (*Note:* Round percentages to the nearest tenth of a percent.)
3. Prepare a common-size income statement for Year 3 by expressing each line item as a percentage of sales revenue. (*Note:* Round percentages to the nearest tenth of a percent.)

OBJECTIVE **3**

EXCEL

Exercise 15-41 **Current Ratio and Quick (Acid-Test) Ratio**

Jordan Company provided the following information:

Current assets:	
Cash	$12,450,000
Accounts receivable	8,740,000
Inventories	8,150,000
Total current assets	$29,340,000
Current liabilities	$16,300,000

Required:

Note: Round answers to one decimal place.
1. Compute the current ratio.
2. Compute the quick (acid-test) ratio.

OBJECTIVE **3**

Exercise 15-42 **Current Ratio and Quick (Acid-Test) Ratio**

Upton Company has current assets equal to $3,600,000. Of these, $1,100,000 is cash, $1,300,000 is accounts receivable, and the remainder is inventories. Current liabilities total $3,000,000.

Required:

Note: Round answers to two decimal places.
1. Compute the current ratio.
2. Compute the quick (acid-test) ratio.

OBJECTIVE **3**

Exercise 15-43 **Average Accounts Receivable, Accounts Receivable Turnover Ratio, Accounts Receivable Turnover in Days**

Montalcino Company had net sales of $54,000,000. Montalcino had the following balances:

	January 1	December 31
Accounts receivable	$5,000,000	$7,000,000
Inventories	1,200,000	1,500,000

Required:

Note: Round answers to one decimal place.
1. Calculate the average accounts receivable.
2. Calculate the accounts receivable turnover ratio.
3. Calculate the accounts receivable turnover in days.

OBJECTIVE **3**

Exercise 15-44 **Average Accounts Receivable, Accounts Receivable Turnover Ratio, Accounts Receivable Turnover in Days**

Whalen Company had net sales of $125,500,250,000. Whalen had the following balances:

	January 1	December 31
Accounts receivable	$2,500,500,000	$2,750,000,000
Inventories	1,500,000,000	1,600,000,000

Required:

Note: Round answers to two decimal places.
1. Calculate the average accounts receivable.
2. Calculate the accounts receivable turnover ratio.
3. Calculate the accounts receivable turnover in days.

Exercise 15-45 **Average Inventory, Inventory Turnover Ratio, Inventory Turnover in Days**

Belt Company had net sales of $2,225,500,000 and cost of goods sold of $1,557,850,000. Belt had the following balances:

	January 1	December 31
Inventories	$335,000,000	$350,000,000

Required:

Note: Round answers to two decimal places.
1. Calculate the average inventory.
2. Calculate the inventory turnover ratio.
3. Calculate the inventory turnover in days.

Exercise 15-46 **Average Inventory, Inventory Turnover Ratio, Inventory Turnover in Days**

Delater Company had sales of $3,948,340 and a gross margin of $1,859,260. Delater had beginning inventory of $53,420 and ending inventory of $62,640.

Required:

Note: Round answers to one decimal place.
1. Calculate the average inventory.
2. Calculate the inventory turnover ratio.
3. Calculate the inventory turnover in days.

Exercise 15-47 **Profitability Ratios**

EXCEL

Bryce Company manufactures pet supplies. However, Bryce's electronic accounting system recently crashed and, unfortunately, only a partial recovery of the company's year-end accounting records (which included several profitability ratios) was possible. As a result, Bryce's controller, a bright young CMA named Jeanette, must compute various lost financial account balances using the recovered information listed below.

- Long-term liabilities: $1,500,000
- Ending inventory is the same as beginning inventory.
- Gross margin: $3,000,000
- Net sales: $8,000,000
- Accounts receivable turnover: 50
- Ending accounts receivable is the same as beginning accounts receivable.
- Total liabilities: $2,000,000
- Current ratio: 2.5
- Cash: $600,000
- Quick ratio: 2.0
- Inventory turnover in days: 3.65

Required:

1. Calculate current liabilities.
2. Calculate current assets.
3. Calculate average accounts receivable
4. Calculate marketable securities.
5. Calculate average inventory.

OBJECTIVE ▶ **4** ▶   **Exercise 15-48**   **Times-Interest-Earned**

Tsao Company provided the following income statement for last year:

Sales	$16,250,000
Cost of goods sold	6,500,000
Gross margin	$ 9,750,000
Operating expenses	3,750,000
Operating income	$ 6,000,000
Interest expense	500,000
Income before taxes	$ 5,500,000
Income taxes	1,650,000
Net income	$ 3,850,000

Required:

Calculate the times-interest-earned ratio.

OBJECTIVE ▶ **4** ▶   **Exercise 15-49**   **Debt Ratio, Debt-to-Equity Ratio**

Busch Company's balance sheet shows total liabilities of $510,900, total equity of $126,000, and total assets of $636,900.

Required:

Note: Round answers to two decimal places.
1. Calculate the debt ratio.
2. Calculate the debt-to-equity ratio.
3. **CONCEPTUAL CONNECTION** Based on the ratios calculated in Requirements 1 and 2, comment on the riskiness of Busch's financing decisions.

Use the following information for Exercises 15-50 through 15-52:
Juroe Company provided the following income statement for last year:

Sales	$11,300,000
Cost of goods sold	3,000,000
Gross margin	$ 8,300,000
Operating expenses	3,800,000
Operating income	$ 4,500,000
Interest expense	1,000,000
Income before taxes	$ 3,500,000
Income taxes	1,400,000
Net income	$ 2,100,000

Juroe's balance sheet as of December 31 last year showed total liabilities of $10,250,000, total equity of $6,150,000, and total assets of $16,400,000.

OBJECTIVE ▶ **4** ▶   **Exercise 15-50**   **Times-Interest-Earned Ratio, Debt Ratio, Debt-to-Equity Ratio**

Refer to the information for Juroe Company above.

Required:

Note: Round answers to two decimal places.
1. Calculate the times-interest-earned ratio.
2. Calculate the debt ratio.
3. Calculate the debt-to-equity ratio.

Exercise 15-51 Return on Sales

Refer to the information for Juroe Company on the previous page.

Required:

1. Calculate the return on sales. (*Note*: Round the percent to two decimal places.)
2. **CONCEPTUAL CONNECTION** Briefly explain the meaning of the return on sales ratio, and comment on whether Juroe's return on sales ratio appears appropriate.

Exercise 15-52 Average Total Assets, Return on Assets

Refer to the information for Juroe Company on the previous page. Also, assume that Juroe's total assets at the beginning of last year equaled $17,350,000 and that the tax rate applicable to Juroe is 40%.

Required:

Note: Round answers to two decimal places.
1. Calculate the average total assets.
2. Calculate the return on assets.

Use the following information for Exercises 15-53 through 15-55:
Rebert Inc. showed the following balances for last year:

	January 1	December 31
Stockholders' equity:		
Preferred stock, $100 par, 8%	$ 4,000,000	$ 4,000,000
Common stock, $3 par	3,000,000	3,000,000
Additional paid-in capital*	4,800,000	4,800,000
Retained earnings	4,000,000	4,250,000
Total stockholders' equity	$15,800,000	$16,050,000

*For common stock only.

Rebert's net income for last year was $3,182,000.

Exercise 15-53 Average Common Stockholders' Equity, Return on Stockholders' Equity

Refer to the information for Rebert Inc. above.

Required:

1. Calculate the average common stockholders' equity.
2. Calculate the return on stockholders' equity.

Exercise 15-54 Earnings per Share, Price-Earnings Ratio

Refer to the information for Rebert Inc. above. Also, assume that the market price per share for Rebert is $51.50.

Required:

1. Compute the dollar amount of preferred dividends.
2. Compute the number of common shares.
3. Compute earnings per share. (*Note:* Round to two decimals.)
4. Compute the price-earnings ratio. (*Note:* Round to the nearest whole number.)

Exercise 15-55 Dividend Yield Ratio, Dividend Payout Ratio

Refer to the information for Rebert Inc. above. Also, assume that the dividends paid to common stockholders for last year were $2,600,000 and that the market price per share of common stock is $51.50.

(Continued)

Required:

1. Compute the dividends per share.
2. Compute the dividend yield. (*Note*: Round to two decimal places.)
3. Compute the dividend payout ratio. (*Note:* Round to two decimal places.)

PROBLEMS

OBJECTIVE ▶ **3**

EXCEL

Problem 15-56 Liquidity Analysis

The following selected information is taken from the financial statements of Arnn Company for its most recent year of operations:

Beginning balances:	
Inventory	$200,000
Accounts receivable	300,000
Ending balances:	
Inventory	250,000
Accounts receivable	400,000
Cash	100,000
Marketable securities (short-term)	200,000
Prepaid expenses	50,000
Accounts payable	175,000
Taxes payable	85,000
Wages payable	90,000
Short-term loans payable	50,000

During the year, Arnn had net sales of $2.45 million. The cost of goods sold was $1.3 million.

Required:

Note: Round all answers to two decimal places.
1. Compute the current ratio.
2. Compute the quick or acid-test ratio.
3. Compute the accounts receivable turnover ratio.
4. Compute the accounts receivable turnover in days.
5. Compute the inventory turnover ratio.
6. Compute the inventory turnover in days.

OBJECTIVE **2** **4**

EXCEL

Problem 15-57 Leverage Ratios

Grammatico Company has just completed its third year of operations. The income statement is as follows:

Sales	$2,460,000
Less: Cost of goods sold	1,410,000
Gross profit margin	$1,050,000
Less: Selling and administrative expenses	710,000
Operating income	$ 340,000
Less: Interest expense	140,000
Income before taxes	$ 200,000
Less: Income taxes	68,000
Net income	$ 132,000

Selected information from the balance sheet is as follows:

Current liabilities	$1,000,000
Long-term liabilities	1,500,000
Total liabilities	$2,500,000
Common stock	$4,000,000
Retained earnings	750,000
Total stockholders' equity	$4,750,000

Required:

Note: Round answers to two decimal places.
1. Compute the times-interest-earned ratio.
2. Compute the debt ratio.
3. **CONCEPTUAL CONNECTION** Assume that the lower quartile, median, and upper quartile values for debt and times-interest-earned ratios in Grammatico's industry are as follows:

Time-interest-earned	2.4, 5.4, 16.1
Debt	0.3, 0.8, 2.4

How does Grammatico compare with the industrial norms? Does it have too much debt?

Problem 15-58 Profitability Ratios

OBJECTIVE ▶ **2** ◀ **5**

The following information has been gathered for Malette Manufacturing:

Net income	$ 5,000,000	Common dividends	$1,200,000
Interest expense	400,000	Average common shares outstanding	800,000 shares
Average total assets	60,000,000	Average common stockholders' equity	$20,000,000
Preferred dividends	400,000	Market price per common share	$40

Assume that the firm has no common stock equivalents. The tax rate is 34%.

Required:

1. Compute the return on assets.
2. Compute the return on common stockholders' equity.
3. Compute the earnings per share.
4. Compute the price-earnings ratio.
5. Compute the dividend yield.
6. Compute the dividend payout ratio.

> *Use the following information for Problems 15-59 through 15-63:*
> Mike Sanders is considering the purchase of Kepler Company, a firm specializing in the manufacture of office supplies. To be able to assess the financial capabilities of the company, Mike has been given the company's financial statements for the 2 most recent years.

(Continued)

Kepler Company
Comparative Balance Sheets

	This Year	Last Year
Assets		
Current assets:		
Cash	$ 50,000	$ 100,000
Accounts receivable, net	300,000	150,000
Inventory	600,000	400,000
Prepaid expenses	25,000	30,000
Total current assets	$ 975,000	$ 680,000
Property and equipment, net	125,000	150,000
Total assets	$1,100,000	$ 830,000
Liabilities and Stockholders' Equity		
Current liabilities:		
Accounts payable	$ 400,000	$ 290,000
Short-term notes payable	200,000	60,000
Total current liabilities	$ 600,000	$ 350,000
Long-term bonds payable, 12%	100,000	150,000
Total liabilities	$ 700,000	$ 500,000
Stockholders' equity:		
Common stock (100,000 shares)	200,000	200,000
Retained earnings	200,000	130,000
Total liabilities and stockholders' equity	$1,100,000	$ 830,000

Kepler Company
Comparative Income Statements

	This Year	Last Year
Sales	$950,000	$900,000
Less: Cost of goods sold	500,000	490,000
Gross margin	$450,000	$410,000
Less: Selling and administrative expenses	275,000	260,000
Operating income	$175,000	$150,000
Less: Interest expense	12,000	18,000
Income before taxes	$163,000	$132,000
Less: Income taxes	65,200	52,800
Net income	$ 97,800	$ 79,200
Less: Dividends	27,800	19,200
Net income, retained	$ 70,000	$ 60,000

OBJECTIVE 1 ▶  **Problem 15-59** Horizontal Analysis

Refer to the information for Kepler Company above.

EXCEL

Required:

Note: Round all percentages to one decimal place.

1. Compute the percentage change for each item in the balance sheet and income statement.
2. **CONCEPTUAL CONNECTION** Comment on any significant trends.

Problem 15-60 Vertical Analysis

OBJECTIVE ▶ 1

Refer to the information for Kepler Company on the previous page.

Required:

Note: Round all percentages to one decimal place.
1. Express each item in the asset section of the balance sheet as a percentage of total assets for each year.
2. Express each item in the liabilities and equity section as a percentage of total liabilities and equity for each year.
3. Express each item in the income statement as a percentage of sales for each year.

Problem 15-61 Liquidity Ratios

OBJECTIVE ▶ 2 ▶ 3

Refer to the information for Kepler Company on the previous page.

Required:

Note: Round all answers to two decimal places.
1. Compute the following ratios for each year: (a) current ratio, (b) quick ratio, (c) accounts receivable turnover (in days), and (d) inventory turnover (in days).
2. **CONCEPTUAL CONNECTION** Has the liquidity of Kepler improved over the past year? Explain why industrial liquidity performance would be useful information in assessing Kepler's liquidity performance.

Problem 15-62 Leverage Ratios

OBJECTIVE ▶ 2 ▶ 4

Refer to the information for Kepler Company on the previous page.

Required:

Note: Round all answers to two decimal places.
1. Compute the following for each year: (a) the times-interest-earned ratio and (b) the debt ratio
2. **CONCEPTUAL CONNECTION** Does Kepler have too much debt? What other information would help in answering this question?

Problem 15-63 Profitability Ratios

OBJECTIVE ▶ 2 ▶ 5

Refer to the information for Kepler Company on the previous page. Also, assume that for last year and for the current year, the market price per share of common stock is $2.98. In addition, for last year, assets and equity were the same at the beginning and end of the year.

Required:

Note: Round all answers to two decimal places.
1. Compute the following for each year: (a) return on assets, (b) return on stockholders' equity, (c) earnings per share, (d) price-earnings ratio, (e) dividend yield, and (f) dividend payout ratio.
2. **CONCEPTUAL CONNECTION** Based on the analysis in Requirement 1, would you invest in the common stock of Kepler?

Problem 15-64 Profitability Analysis

OBJECTIVE ▶ 5

Albion Inc. provided the following information for its most recent year of operations. The tax rate is 40%.

(Continued)

Sales	$100,000	Preferred dividends	$300
Cost of goods sold	45,000	Common dividends (paid December 31)	$8,000
Net income	10,500	Common shares outstanding—January 1	30,000 shares
Interest expense	350	Common shares outstanding—December 31	40,000 shares
Assets—beginning balance	120,000	Average common stockholders' equity	$55,000
Assets—ending balance	126,000	Market price per common share	$12

Required:

1. Compute the following: (a) return on sales, (b) return on assets, (c) return on stockholders' equity, (d) earnings per share, (e) price-earnings ratio, (f) dividend yield, and (g) dividend payout ratio.
2. **CONCEPTUAL CONNECTION** If you were considering purchasing stock in Albion, which of the above ratios would be of most interest to you? Explain.

OBJECTIVE ▶ **3**

Problem 15-65 Analysis of Accounts Receivable and Credit Policy

Based on customer feedback, Ted Pendleton, manager of Gray Company, which produces photo supplies, decided to grant more liberal credit terms. Ted chose to allow customers to have 60 days before full payment of the account was required. From 20X2 through 20X4, Gray's credit policy for sales on account was 2/10, n/30. In 20X5, the policy of 2/10, n/60 became effective. By the end of 20X6, Gray was beginning to experience cash flow problems. Although sales were strong, collections were sluggish, and the company was having a difficult time meeting its short-term obligations. Ted noted that the cash flow problems materialized after the credit policy was changed and wondered if there was a connection. To help assess the situation, he gathered the following data pertaining to the collection of accounts receivable. (Balances are end-of-year balances. The 20X2 balance was the same as that in 20X1.)

	20X2	20X3	20X4	20X5	20X6
Accounts receivable	$100,000	$120,000	$100,000	$150,000	$190,000
Net credit sales	500,000	600,000	510,000	510,000	520,000

Required:

Note: Round answers to two decimal places.

1. Compute the number of times that accounts receivable turned over per year for each of the 5 years. Also express the turnover in days instead of times per year.
2. **CONCEPTUAL CONNECTION** Based on your computation in Requirement 1, evaluate the effect of the new credit policy. Include in this assessment the impact on the company's cash inflows.
3. **CONCEPTUAL CONNECTION** Assume that the industry has an average receivables turnover of six times per year. If this knowledge had been available in 20X4, along with knowledge of the company's accounts receivable turnover rate, do you think that Ted Pendleton would have liberalized his company's credit policy?

OBJECTIVE ▶ **5**

Problem 15-66 Profitability Analysis for an Investment Decision

Suppose that you are considering investing in one of two companies, each in the same industry. The most recent income statements for each company and other relevant information are as follows:

Income Statements (in thousands)

	McGregor Company	Fasnacht Company
Sales	$50,000	$40,000
Less: Cost of goods sold	30,000	26,000
Gross margin	$20,000	$14,000
Less: Selling and administrative expenses	15,000	7,000
Operating income	$ 5,000	$ 7,000
Less: Interest expense	1,000	3,000
Income before taxes	$ 4,000	$ 4,000
Less: Income taxes	1,360	1,360
Net income	$ 2,640	$ 2,640
Retained earnings	8,000	6,000
	$10,640	$ 8,640
Less: Dividends	840	1,040
Ending retained earnings	$ 9,800	$ 7,600
Average total assets	$20,000,000	$22,000,000
Average common equity	$10,000,000	$13,000,000
Average common shares	1,000,000 shares	1,200,000 shares
Average preferred shares*	300,000 shares	100,000 shares
Market price per common share	$5.00	$9.80

*For both McGregor and Fasnacht, the preferred dividend is $1 per share.

Required:

Note: Round answers to two decimal places.
1. Compute the following for each company: (a) earnings per share, (b) dividend yield, (c) dividend payout ratio, (d) price-earnings ratio, (e) return on assets, and (f) return on stockholders' equity.
2. **CONCEPTUAL CONNECTION** In which of the two companies would you invest? Explain.

CASES

Case 15-67 Manipulation of Ratios and Ethical Behavior

OBJECTIVE ▸ 2 ▸ 3 ▸ 4

Pete Donaldson, president and owner of Donaldson Mining Supplies, was concerned about the firm's liquidity. He had an easy time selling supplies to the local coal mines, but had a difficult time collecting the receivables. He had even tried offering discounts for prompt payment. The outcome wasn't as expected. The coal mines still took as long to pay as before, but took the discount as well. Although he had complained about the practice, he was told that other suppliers would provide the supplies for the same terms. Collections were so slow that he was unable to pay his own payables on time and was receiving considerable pressure from his own creditors.

The solution was a line of credit that could be used to smooth his payment patterns. Getting the line of credit was another matter, however. One bank had turned him down, indicating that he already had too much debt and that his short-term liquidity ratios were marginal. Pete had begun the business with $5,000 of his own capital and a $30,000 loan from his father-in-law. He was making interest payments of $3,000 per year to his father-in-law, with a promise to pay the principal back in 5 years (3 years from now).

While mulling over his problem, Pete suddenly saw the solution. By changing accountants, he could tell the next accountant that the $30,000 had been donated to the business and

(Continued)

therefore would be reclassified into the equity section. This would dramatically improve the debt ratio. He would simply not disclose the $3,000 annual payment—or he could call it a dividend. Additionally, he would not tell the next accountant about the $6,000 of safety gear that was now obsolete. That gear could be added back, and the current ratio would also improve. With an improved financial statement, the next bank would be more likely to grant the needed line of credit.

Required:

1. Evaluate Pete Donaldson's ethical behavior.
2. Suppose that you have been hired as the chief finance officer for Donaldson Mining Supplies. You have been told that the $30,000 has been donated to the company. During the second week of your employment, the father-in-law drops in unexpectedly and introduces himself. He then asks you how the company is doing and wants to know if his $30,000 loan is still likely to be repaid in 3 years. Suppose also that on the same day you overhear an employee mention that the safety equipment is no longer usable because regulations now require a newer and different model.
   a. Assume that you have yet to prepare the financial statements for the loan application. What should you do?
   b. Suppose that the financial statements have been prepared and submitted to the bank. In fact, that morning, you had received a call from the bank, indicating that a decision was imminent and that the line of credit would likely be approved. What should you do under these circumstances?
3. Suppose that Pete invites you in as a consultant. He describes his problem to you. Can you think of a better solution?

OBJECTIVE ▶ **2** ▶ **3** ▶ **4** ▶ **5**

Case 15-68 Interpreting the Meaning of Ratios from the Financial Statements

Using the Internet, locate the most recent financial statements for two companies from the same industry. Find (or calculate) the ratios listed below, and compare the two companies. (If you cannot calculate a particular ratio, explain why.) Which company do you think is performing better? Why?

a. Current ratio
b. Quick ratio
c. Accounts receivable turnover ratio
d. Inventory turnover ratio
e. Turnover in days
f. Times-interest-earned ratio
g. Debt ratio
h. Debt-to-equity ratio
i. Return on sales
j. Return on assets
k. Return on stockholders' equity
l. Earnings per share
m. Price-earnings ratio
n. Dividend yield
o. Dividend payout ratio

Glossary

A

absorption costing   assigns *all* manufacturing costs to the product and includes direct materials, direct labor, variable overhead, and fixed overhead.

accounting rate of return (ARR)   the rate of return obtained by dividing the average accounting net income by the original investment.

accounts receivable turnover ratio   a ratio that measures the liquidity of receivables. It is computed by dividing net sales by average accounts receivable.

accumulating costs   the way that costs are measured and recorded.

activity   action taken or work performed by equipment or people for other people.

activity analysis   the process of identifying, describing, and evaluating the activities an organization performs.

activity-based costing (ABC) system   a cost assignment approach that first uses direct and driver tracing to assign costs to activities and then uses drivers to assign costs to cost objects.

activity-based management   a systemwide, integrated approach that focuses management's attention on activities with the objective of improving customer value and the profit achieved by providing this value. It includes driver analysis, activity analysis, and performance evaluation, and draws on activity-based costing as a major source of information.

activity dictionary   a list of activities described by specific attributes such as name, definition, classification as primary or secondary, and activity driver.

activity drivers   factors that measure the consumption of activities by products and other cost objects.

activity elimination   the process of eliminating nonvalue-added activities.

activity format   a format for the statement of cash flows that reports cash flows for three categories: (1) cash flows from operating activities, (2) cash flows from investing activities, and (3) cash flows from financing activities.

activity inputs   the resources consumed by an activity in producing its output. (They are the factors that enable the activity to be performed.)

activity output   the result or product of an activity.

activity output measure   the number of times an activity is performed. It is the quantifiable measure of the output.

activity reduction   decreasing the time and resources required by an activity.

activity selection   the process of choosing among sets of activities caused by competing strategies.

activity sharing   increasing the efficiency of necessary activities by using economies of scale.

actual cost system   an actual cost system uses only actual costs of direct materials, direct labor, and overhead to determine unit cost.

adjusted cost of goods sold   normal cost of goods sold (actual direct materials, actual direct labor, and applied overhead) is adjusted for the overhead variance. Underapplied overhead is added back; overapplied overhead is subtracted. This is an expense on the income statement.

administrative costs   all costs associated with research, development, and general administration of the organization that cannot reasonably be assigned to either selling or production.

allocation   when an indirect cost is assigned to a cost object using a reasonable and convenient method.

annuity   a series of future cash flows.

applied overhead   calculated by multiplying the predetermined overhead rate by the actual amount of the base or driver used.

appraisal costs   cost incurred to determine whether products and services are conforming to requirements.

assigning costs   the way that a cost is linked to some cost object.

B

Balanced Scorecard   a strategic management system that translates an organization's mission and strategy into operational objectives and performance measures.

beginning work-in-process (BWIP)   incomplete units on hand at the beginning of a period. Work done on these partially completed units represents prior-period work, with the costs assigned to them being prior-period costs.

break-even point   the point at which total revenue equals total cost (both fixed and variable cost). At break-even, profit is zero.

budget committee   the group that reviews the budget, provides policy guidelines and policy goals, resolves differences that arise as the budget is prepared, approves the final budget, and monitors the actual performance of the organization as the year unfolds.

budget director   typically the controller, this is the person responsible for directing and coordinating the organization's overall budgeting process.

budgetary slack   padding the budget, which occurs when a manager deliberately underestimates revenues or overestimates costs in order to make budgeted expectations more easily achievable in the future.

budgets   financial plans for the future.

business sustainability   the practice of creating long-term organizational value through internally understanding, measuring, and managing the key threats and opportunities to achieving the organization's strategy and then externally reporting to key stakeholders on the successes and failures of such efforts.

C

capital budgeting   the process of making capital investment decisions.

capital investment decisions   the process of planning, setting goals and priorities, arranging financing, and identifying criteria for making long-term investments.

cash budget   a budget that shows budgeted cash inflows and outflows for the time period so that managers can determine any expected cash excess or deficiency.

cash equivalents   highly liquid investments, such as treasury bills, money market funds, and commercial paper.

cash inflows   activities that increase cash and are sources of cash.

cash outflows   activities that decrease cash and are uses of cash.

causal factors   drivers that are directly associated with the actual use of the services.

Certified Fraud Examiner (CFE)   a premier credential for the forensic accountant, administered by the Association of Certified Fraud Examiners.

Certified Internal Auditor (CIA)   has passed a comprehensive examination designed to ensure technical competence and has 2 years of experience.

Certified Management Accountant (CMA)   has passed a rigorous qualifying examination, met an experience requirement, and participates in continuing education.

Certified Public Accountant (CPA)   has passed a national examination and must be licensed by the state in which he or she wishes to practice accounting (e.g., in audit, tax, etc.).

coefficient of determination (R2)   the percentage of total variability in a dependent variable that is explained by an independent variable. It assumes a value between 0 and 1.

committed fixed costs   a fixed cost that cannot be easily changed.

common costs   the costs of resources shared by two or more services or products.

common fixed expenses   fixed expenses that cannot be traced to individual segments or products. They will continue to exist even if one segment or product is eliminated.

common-size analysis   a type of analysis that expresses line items or accounts in the financial statements as percentages.

compounding of interest   paying interest on interest.

constraints   mathematical expressions that express resource limitations.

consumption ratio   the proportion of an overhead activity consumed by a product.

continuous budget   a moving 12-month budget. As one month expires, another month in the future is added.

continuous improvement   searching for ways to increase the overall efficiency and productivity of activities by decreasing waste, increasing quality, and reducing costs.

contribution margin   the difference between total sales and total variable costs on a total basis, or price minus unit variable cost on a per-unit basis. Total contribution margin is the amount left over from sales to contribute to covering fixed costs and profit.

contribution margin income statement   the cost behavior-based income statement. Costs are separated into fixed and variable categories. First, total variable cost is subtracted from sales to get the contribution margin. Next, total fixed expenses are subtracted to get operating

income (profit).

contribution margin ratio   the ratio of total contribution margin to sales or of unit contribution to price. Contribution margin ratio is also computed as 1 (100%) minus the variable cost ratio. It represents the percentage of each sales dollar available to contribute to fixed cost and profit.

control costs   the costs of preventing or detecting poor quality.

control limits   the maximum allowable deviation from a standard.

controllable costs   costs whose level a manager can influence or control.

controller   the chief accounting officer in an organization.

controlling   the managerial activity of monitoring a plan's implementation and taking corrective action as needed.

conversion cost   the sum of direct labor cost and overhead cost.

corporate sustainability reporting (CSR)   the voluntary public disclosure of qualitative and/or quantitative information about an organization's performance on one or more financial and/or nonfinancial dimensions.

cost   the amount of cash or cash equivalent sacrificed for goods and/ or services that are expected to bring a current or future benefit to the organization.

cost behavior   the way in which a cost changes when the level of output changes.

cost center   part of an organization in which the manager is responsible only for costs.

cost driver   a causal factor that measures the output of the activity that leads (or causes) costs to change.

cost object   any item such as products, customers, departments, projects, and so on, for which costs are measured and assigned.

cost of capital   the cost of investment funds, usually viewed as a weighted average of the costs of funds from all sources.

cost of goods manufactured   the total product cost of goods completed during the current period.

cost of goods sold   the total product cost of goods sold during the period.

cost of goods sold budget   a budget that shows the expected production cost of the units budgeted to be sold during the period.

cost reconciliation   the final section of the production report that compares costs to account for with the costs accounted for to ensure that they are equal.

cost structure   the company's relative mix of fixed to variable costs. It is useful in determining operating leverage.

cost-volume-profit (CVP) analysis   estimates how changes in costs (both variable and fixed), sales volume, and price affect profit.

cost-volume-profit graph   a graph showing the relationships among cost, volume (units sold), and profit using a total cost line and a total revenue line. The intersection of the total cost line with the total revenue line is the break-even point.

costs of quality   costs that exist because poor quality may or does exist.

creditors   loan managers who assess the creditworthiness of potential customers through ratio analysis, common-size analysis, and other techniques.

currency appreciation   when one country's currency strengthens relative to another country's currency.

currency depreciation   when one country's currency weakens relative to another country's

currency.

current ratio   a measure of the ability of a company to pay its short-term liabilities out of short-term assets.

customer perspective   defines the customer and market segments in which the business segments compete.

customer value   the difference between realization (what the customer receives) and sacrifice (what is given up in return).

cycle time   the length of time required to produce one unit of a product.

D

debt ratio   the ratio that measures the percentage of a company's risk as the percentage of its assets financed by creditors increases. It is computed by dividing a company's total liabilities by its total assets.

decentralization   the practice of delegating decision-making authority to lower levels of management.

decision making   the process of choosing among competing alternatives.

decision model   a specific set of procedures that, when followed, produces a decision.

defective product   a product or service that does not conform to specifications.

degree of operating leverage (DOL)   shows the degree to which fixed costs are used to obtain a higher percent change in profits as sales change. DOL is equal to the total contribution margin divided by operating income.

departmental overhead rate estimated overhead for a department divided by the estimated activity level for that same department. There are as many rates as there are producing departments. This allows firms to more accurately cost products that only pass through a few departments.

dependent variable a variable whose value depends on the value of another variable.

differential cost the difference in total cost between the alternatives in a decision.

direct costs costs that can be easily and accurately traced to a cost object.

direct fixed expenses fixed costs that are directly traceable to a given segment and, consequently, disappear if the segment is eliminated.

direct labor the labor that can be directly traced to the goods or services being produced.

direct labor budget the budget showing the expected number of direct labor hours to be worked and the total cost of direct labor for the budget period.

direct materials materials that are a part of the final product and can be directly traced to the goods or services being produced.

direct materials purchases budget a budget that shows the amount and cost of every type of raw material to be purchased in each time period.

direct method method that assigns support department costs *only* to the producing departments. No cost from one support department is given to another support department; thus, it ignores support department interaction.

discount factor the factor used to convert a future cash flow to its present value.

discount rate the rate of return used to compute the present value of future cash flows.

discounted cash flows future cash flows expressed in present value terms.

discounting the act of finding the present value of future cash flows.

discounting models capital investment models that explicitly consider the time value of money in identifying criteria for accepting and rejecting proposed projects.

discretionary fixed costs fixed costs that can be changed relatively easily in the short run at management discretion.

discretionary variable costs variable costs that can be changed or avoided relatively easily in the short run at management discretion.

dividend payout ratio a ratio that is computed by dividing the total common dividends by the earnings available to common stockholders.

dividend yield a profitability measure that is computed by dividing the dividends received per unit of common share by the market price per common share.

driver analysis the effort expended to identify those factors that are the root causes of activity costs.

duration-based costing (DBC) uses a single rate to assign conversion costs and approximates a comprehensive ABC system based in duration drivers.

dysfunctional behavior individual behavior that is in basic conflict with the goals of the organization.

E

earnings per share earnings per share is computed by dividing net income less preferred dividends by the average number of shares of common stock outstanding during the period.

economic risk the possibility that a firm's present value of future cash flows will be affected by exchange rate fluctuations.

economic value added (EVA) after-tax operating income minus the dollar cost of capital employed.

ending finished goods inventory budget budget that shows the cost of units budgeted to be in ending finished goods inventory.

ending work-in-process (EWIP) incomplete units on hand at the end of a period. The work and costs assigned to these partially completed units are carried over to the next period.

enterprise risk management (ERM) the formal process of aligning an organization's overall desired level of risk taking with its strategy and then managing its top risks in a manner that maintains this alignment.

equivalent units of output complete units that could have produced, given the total amount of manufacturing effort expended during the period.

ethical behavior choosing actions that are right, proper, and just.

exchange gain the gain on the exchange of one currency for another due to appreciation of the home currency.

exchange loss the loss on the exchange of one currency for another due to depreciation of the home currency.

exchange rates the rate at which one unit of a currency can be traded for another currency.

expenses costs that are used up (expired) in the production of revenue.

external failure costs costs incurred because products fail to conform to requirements after being sold to outside parties.

F

failure costs the costs incurred by an organization because failure activities are performed.

favorable (F) variances variances produced whenever the actual amounts are less than the budgeted or standard allowances.

FIFO costing method a process-costing method that separates units in beginning inventory from those produced during the current period. Unit costs include only current-period costs and production.

financial accounting a type of accounting focused primarily on the creation of financial information for external users.

financial budgets budgets that detail the inflows and outflows of cash and the overall financial position of the firm.

financial perspective describes the economic consequences of actions taken in the other three Balanced Scorecard perspectives.

financing activities those activities that raise (provide) cash from (to) creditors and owners.

fixed costs costs that, in total, are constant within the relevant range as the level of output increases or decreases.

fixed overhead spending variance the difference between the actual fixed overhead (AFOH) and the budgeted fixed overhead (BFOH).

fixed overhead volume variance the difference between budgeted fixed overhead (BFOH) and applied fixed overhead.

flexible (variable) budget budget that shows expected costs for a particular activity level. A before-the-fact flexible budget gives expected costs for a range of activity levels. An after-the-fact flexible budget gives expected costs for the actual level of activity.

flexible budget variance the difference between the budgeted costs and actual costs for the chosen level of activity.

foreign trade zones areas near a customs port of entry that are physically on U.S. soil but are considered by the U.S. government to be outside U.S. commerce. Goods entering a foreign trade zone are not subject to duty until they leave the zone.

forensic accounting the application of accounting knowledge in legal or other cases to help resolve different types of disputes.

forward contract requires the buyer to exchange a specified amount of a currency at a specified rate (the forward rate) on a specified future date.

forward rate   the currency exchange rate specified for a particular future date.

fraud   wrongful or criminal deception intended to result in financial or personal gain.

fraud triangle   a model that explains the factors causing someone to commit fraud. The factors are: opportunity, perceived need, and ability to rationalize the fraudulent actions.

future value   the value that will accumulate by the end of an investment's life if the investment earns a specified compounded return.

G

goal congruence   the alignment of managerial and organizational goals.

greenwashing   a situation in which stakeholders believe that an organization's corporate sustainability report contains environmental information that is materially biased in favor of the reporting organization.

gross margin   the difference between sales revenue and cost of goods sold.

H

high-low method   a method for separating mixed costs into fixed and variable components by using just the high and low data points. [*Note*: The high (low) data point corresponds to the high (low) output level.]

horizontal analysis   also called trend analysis, this type of analysis expresses a line item as a percentage of some prior-period amount.

hurdle rate   the minimum ROI required to accept an investment.

I

independent projects   projects that, if accepted or rejected, will not affect the cash flows of another project.

independent variable   explains changes in the dependent variable and, as such, its value does not depend on the value of another variable.

indifference point   the point at which two different operating systems produce the same income.

indirect costs   costs that cannot be easily and accurately traced to a cost object.

indirect method   computes operating cash flows by *adjusting net income* for noncash items, nonoperating gains and losses, and accruals.

inherent risk   the risk that exists absent of any risk management action to reduce or avoid the risk.

innovation process   creates new products and services to satisfy emerging and potential customer needs.

integrated reporting   the combination of an organization's annual report (i.e., 10-K) with its sustainability report to form one combined (or integrated) report for all stakeholders, including investors.

intercept   the fixed cost, representing the point where the cost formula intercepts the vertical axis.

interim quality performance report   a comparison of current actual quality costs with short-term budgeted quality costs.

interim quality standards   a standard based on short-run quality goals.

internal business process perspective   describes the internal business processes needed to provide value for customers and owners.

internal failure costs   costs incurred because products and services fail to conform to requirements where lack of conformity is discovered prior to external sale.

internal rate of return (IRR)   the rate of return that equates the present value of a project's cash inflows with the present value of its cash outflows (i.e., it sets the NPV equal to zero). Also, the rate of return being earned on funds that remain internally invested in a project.

investing activities   those activities that involve the acquisition or sale of long-term assets.

investment center   part of an organization in which the manager is responsible for sales, costs, and investment.

inventory turnover ratio   a ratio that is computed by dividing the cost of goods sold by the average inventory.

investors   those who analyze financial statements to assess the attractiveness of a company as a potential investment.

J

JIT purchasing   a system that requires suppliers to deliver parts and materials just in time to be used in production.

job   one distinct unit or set of units. The costs for that unit are unique and must be kept track of on an individual job basis.

job-order cost sheet   document prepared for every job; it is subsidiary to the work-in-process account and is the primary document for accumulating all costs related to a particular job.

job-order costing system   a costing system in which costs are accumulated by job.

joint products   products that are inseparable prior to a split-off point. All manufacturing costs up to the split-off point are joint costs.

joint venture   a type of partnership in which investors co-own the enterprise.

K

keep-or-drop decisions   relevant costing analyses that focus on keeping or dropping a segment of a business.

L

labor efficiency variance (LEV)   the difference between the actual direct labor hours used and the standard direct labor hours allowed multiplied by the standard hourly wage rate.

labor rate variance (LRV)   the difference between the actual hourly rate paid and the standard hourly rate multiplied by the actual hours worked.

lean accounting   an accounting practice that organizes costs according to the value chain to help managers eliminate waste and, ultimately, reduce costs and improve financial performance.

lean manufacturing   an approach designed to eliminate waste and maximize customer value.

learning and growth (infrastructure) perspective   defines the capabilities that an organization needs to create long-term growth and improvement, including employee capabilities, information systems capabilities, and employee attitudes.

leverage ratios   ratios that measure the ability of a company to meet its long- and short-term obligations. These ratios provide a measure of the degree of protection provided to a company's creditors.

line positions   positions that have direct responsibility for the basic objectives of an organization.

liquidity ratios   ratios that measure the ability of a company to meet its current obligations.

M

make-or-buy decisions   relevant costing analyses that focus on whether a component should be made internally or purchased externally.

managerial accounting   a type of accounting focused primarily on providing internal users with the necessary financial and nonfinancial information to help them make the best possible decisions for the company.

managers   those individuals who analyze their own financial statements to assess profitability, liquidity, debt position, and progress toward organizational objectives.

manufacturing cells   a plant layout where all the operations (machines) that are needed to produce a family of products are grouped in close proximity, typically in a semicircle.

manufacturing cycle efficiency (MCE)   value-added time divided by total time.

manufacturing organization   an organization that produces tangible products.

manufacturing overhead   all product costs other than direct materials and direct labor. In a manufacturing firm, manufacturing overhead also is known as factory burden or indirect manufacturing costs. Costs are included as manufacturing overhead if they cannot be traced to the cost object of interest (e.g., unit of product).

maquiladora   a manufacturing plant, located in Mexico, that processes imported materials and re-exports them to the United States.

margin   the ratio of operating income to sales.

margin of safety   the number of units sold or the amount of sales revenue earned above the break-even point.

markup   the percentage applied to a base cost; it includes desired profit and any costs not included in the base cost.

master budget   the comprehensive financial plan for the organization as a whole. It covers a fiscal year.

materials price variance (MPV)   the difference between the actual price paid per unit of materials and the standard price allowed per unit multiplied by the actual quantity of materials purchased.

materials requisition form   a source document that assigns the cost of direct materials to a job.

materials usage variance (MUV)   the difference between the direct materials actually used and the direct materials allowed for the actual output multiplied by the standard price.

method of least squares (regression)   a statistical method to find the best-fitting line through a set of data points. It is used to break out the fixed and variable components of a mixed cost.

mixed costs   costs that have both a fixed and a variable component.

monetary incentives   monetary rewards used to control a manager's tendency to shirk and waste resources by tying budgetary performance to salary increases, bonuses, and promotions.

multinational corporation (MNC)   a company with divisions in more than one country.

multiple-period quality trend report   a graph that plots quality costs (as a percentage of sales) against time.

mutually exclusive projects   projects that, if accepted, preclude the acceptance of competing projects.

myopic behavior   when a manager takes actions that improve budgetary performance in the short run but bring long-run harm to the firm.

N

net present value (NPV)   the difference between the present value of a project's cash inflows and the present value of its cash outflows.

noncash investing and financing activities   investing and financing activities that take place without affecting cash.

nondiscounting models   capital investment models that identify criteria for accepting or rejecting projects without considering the time value of money.

nonmonetary incentives   rewards that include job enrichment, increased responsibility and autonomy, and recognition programs.

nonunit-level activity drivers   factors that measure the consumption of nonunit-level activities by products and other cost objects.

nonvalue-added activities   all activities other than those that are absolutely essential to remain in business.

nonvalue-added costs   costs that are caused either by nonvalue-added activities or by the inefficient performance of value-added activities.

normal cost of goods sold   cost of goods sold before any adjustment for an overhead variance.

normal cost system   a system in which the cost of production consists of actual direct materials, actual direct labor, and applied (not actual) overhead.

O

operating activities   the ongoing, day-to-day, revenue-generating activities of an organization.

operating assets   all assets acquired to generate income.

operating budgets   budgets that describe the income-generating activities of a firm, sales, production, and finished goods inventories, ending with the budgeted income statement.

operating income   earnings before interest and taxes.

operating leverage   occurs when fixed costs are used to obtain higher change in profits as sales change.

operations process   produces and delivers existing products and services to customers.

opportunity cost   the benefit given up or sacrificed when one alternative is chosen over another.

outsourcing   the payment by a company for a business function formerly done in house.

overapplied overhead   overhead that occurs when the applied overhead is greater than the actual overhead.

overhead budget   a budget that shows the expected cost of all production costs other than direct materials and direct labor.

overhead variance   difference between applied overhead and actual overhead.

P

parallel processing   a processing pattern in which two or more sequential processes are required to produce a finished product.

participative budgeting   type of budgeting that allows subordinate managers considerable say in how the budgets are established.

payback period   the time required for a project to return its investment.

performance report   a form that compares actual costs with budgeted costs.

period costs   costs that are not product costs (i.e., all areas of the value chain except for production).

physical flow schedule   a schedule that reconciles units to account for with units accounted for. The units are not adjusted for percent of completion.

planning   a management activity that involves the detailed formulation of action to achieve a particular end.

plantwide overhead rate   a single overhead rate calculated by using all estimated overhead for a factory divided by the estimated activity level across the entire factory.

portfolio ERM perspective   the practice of managing a company's most important risks in a collective (or portfolio) fashion, such that the residual risks that remain align with the company's risk appetite.

postaudit   a follow-up analysis of an investment decision, comparing actual benefits and costs with expected benefits and costs.

post-purchase costs   costs incurred by the customer after purchase.

post-sales service process   provides services to customers after the product is produced and delivered.

predetermined overhead rate   the overhead rate calculated at the beginning of the year by dividing the total estimated annual overhead by the total estimated level of associated activity or cost driver.

present value   the current value of a future cash flow. It represents the amount that must be invested now if the future cash flow is to be received, assuming compounding at a given rate of interest.

prevention costs   cost incurred to prevent or defect poor quality.

price   the revenue per unit.

price-earnings ratio   the price-earnings ratio is found by dividing the market price per share by the earnings per share.

price (rate) variance   the difference between the actual and standard unit price of an input multiplied by the number of inputs used.

price standards   the amount that *should be paid* per unit of the input to be used.

prime cost   the sum of direct materials cost and direct labor cost.

process-costing system   a costing system that accumulates production costs by process or by department for a given period of time. Unit costs are computed by dividing the process costs for the given period by the output of the period.

process-value analysis   an approach that focuses on processes and activities and emphasizes systemwide performance instead of individual performance.

process value chain   the innovation, operations, and post-sales service processes.

producing departments   departments in a factory or service firm that make the product or service that is sold to customers.

product (manufacturing) costs   costs of producing a product in a manufacturing firm or of acquiring a product in a merchandising firm and preparing it for sale. Product costs include direct materials, direct labor, and manufacturing overhead.

product diversity   the situation present when products consume overhead in different proportions.

production budget   a budget that details the number of units of each product to be produced in the coming year, in order to satisfy sales and desired ending inventory needs.

production report   a document that summarizes the manufacturing activity that takes place in a process department for a given period of time.

products   goods produced by converting raw materials through the use of labor and indirect manufacturing resources, such as the manufacturing plant, land, and machinery.

profit center   part of an organization in which the manager is responsible for both sales and costs.

profitability ratios   ratios that measure the earning ability of a company. These ratios allow investors, creditors, and managers to evaluate the extent to which invested funds are being used efficiently.

pseudoparticipation   when top management has total control of the budgeting process, allowing only superficial participation from lower-level managers.

Q

quality of conformance   a product or service that conforms to its design requirements or specifications.

quality product or service   a product or service that meets or exceeds customer expectations.

quantity standards   the amount of input that *should be used* per unit of output.

quick or acid-test ratio   a measure of liquidity that compares only the most liquid assets to current liabilities.

R

reciprocal method   a support department allocation method that recognizes all interactions among support departments.

relevant costs   future costs that change across alternatives.

relevant range   the range of output over which an assumed cost relationship is valid for the normal operations of a firm.

required rate of return   the minimum rate of return that a project must earn in order to be acceptable. Usually corresponds to the cost of capital.

residual income   the difference between income and the minimum dollar return required on a company's operating assets.

residual risk   the risk that remains after any risk management action has been taken.

resource drivers   factors that measure the consumption of resources by activities.

responsibility center   segment of a business in which a manager is accountable for a specific set of activities.

return on investment (ROI)   the profit (earnings) per dollar of investment.

return on sales   a measure of the efficiency of a firm that is computed by dividing net income by sales.

return on stockholders' equity   a measure that can be used to compare against other return measures (e.g., preferred dividend rates and bond rates). It is computed by dividing net income less preferred dividends by the average common stockholders' equity.

return on total assets   the result of dividing net income plus the after-tax cost of interest by the average total assets.

revenue center   part of an organization in which the manager is responsible only for sales.

risk appetite   an organization's overall desired level of risk taking.

risk response benefit   the difference between the inherent risk and the residual risk produced by the particular risk response.

risk response cost   the incremental cost incurred by the company to implement the given risk response.

risk response net benefit   the benefit of the risk response minus the cost of risk response.

S

sales budget   a budget that describes expected sales in units and dollars for every product or service sold.

sales mix   the relative combination of products sold by a company. Sales mix is usually expressed in the lowest whole units. For example, a sales mix of 3:2 means that for every 3 units of Product A sold, 2 units of Product B are sold.

Sarbanes-Oxley Act (SOX)   passed in response to revelations of misconduct and fraud by several well-known firms, this legislation established stronger governmental regulation of public companies in the United States, from enhanced oversight (PCAOB) to increased auditor independence and tightened regulation of corporate governance.

scattergraph method   a method to fit a line to a set of data using two points that are selected by judgment. It is used to break out the fixed and variable components of a mixed cost.

segment   a subunit of a company of sufficient importance to warrant the production of performance reports.

segment margin   the contribution a segment makes to cover common fixed costs and provide for profit after direct fixed costs and variable costs are deducted from the segment's sales revenue.

sell-or-process-further decision   relevant costing analysis that focuses on whether a product should be processed beyond the split-off point.

selling and administrative expenses budget   a budget that shows the expected costs for nonmanufacturing costs of selling and administration.

selling costs   those costs necessary to market, distribute, and service a product or service.

semi-variable costs   a cost that is variable in nature but whose rate of change is not constant (i.e., total cost increases at either a decreasing or an increasing rate) as output increases.

sensitivity analysis   a "what-if" technique used to see what impact a change in an underlying variable has on the answer.

sequential (or step) method   a support department allocation method that recognizes that interactions among support departments occur, but does not fully account for support department interaction.

sequential processing   a processing pattern in which units pass from one process to another in a set (sequential) order.

service organization   an organization that produces intangible products.

services   tasks or activities performed for a customer or an activity performed by a customer using an organization's products or facilities.

slope   the variable cost per unit of activity usage.

special-order decisions   relevant costing analyses that focus on whether a specially priced order should be accepted or rejected.

split-off point   the point at which products become distinguishable after passing through a common process.

spot rate   the exchange rate of one currency for another for immediate delivery.

staff positions   positions that are supportive in nature and have only indirect responsibility for an organization's basic objectives.

stakeholder engagement   the process by which an organization's management interacts with its key stakeholders.

stakeholders   those individuals or groups that (1) are affected by an organization's pursuit of its strategy *or* (2) can affect an organization's ability to achieve its strategy.

standard cost per unit   the per-unit cost that should be achieved, given materials, labor, and overhead standards.

standard cost sheet   a listing of the standard costs and standard quantities of direct materials, direct labor, and overhead that should apply to a single product.

standard hours allowed (SH)   the direct labor hours that should have been used to produce the actual output (Unit labor standard × Actual output).

standard quantity of materials allowed (SQ)   the quantity of materials that should have been used to produce the actual output (Unit materials standard × Actual output).

statement of cash flows   a statement that provides information regarding the sources and uses of a firm's cash.

static budget   a budget created in advance for a particular level of activity.

step cost   a cost that displays a constant level of total cost for a range of output and then jumps to a higher level of total cost at some point, where it remains for a similar range of output.

strategic plan   a plan that plots a direction for an organization's future activities and operations; it generally covers at least 5 years. The overall strategy is then translated into the long- and short-term objectives that form the basis of the budget.

strategy   choosing the market and customer segments the business unit intends to serve, and identifying the critical internal and business processes that the unit must excel at to deliver the value propositions to customers in the targeted market segments.

sunk costs   costs for which the outlay has already been made and that cannot be affected by a future decision.

support departments   departments that provide essential services for producing departments, but do not actually make the product or service being sold.

sustainability assurance   the external verification that an independent party provides concerning the content of a corporate sustainability report and/or the process used in preparing a corporate sustainability report.

T

target cost   the difference between the sales price needed to achieve a projected market share and the desired per-unit profit.

target costing   a method of determining the cost of a product or service based on the price (target price) that customers are willing to pay.

tariff (duty)   a tax on imports levied by the federal government.

testable strategy   a set of linked objectives aimed at an overall goal.

time ticket   a source document that records time spent on each job by each employee. It is used to assign direct labor costs to jobs.

times-interest-earned ratio   a leverage ratio that uses the income statement to assess a company's ability to service its debt. It is computed by dividing net income before taxes and interest by interest expense.

total budget variance   the difference between the actual cost of an input and its planned cost.

total quality management   a management philosophy in which manufacturers strive to create an environment that will enable workers to manufacture perfect (zero-defect) products.

transaction risk   the possibility that future cash transactions will be affected by changing exchange rates.

transfer price   price charged for a component or service by the selling division to the buying division of the same company.

transferred-in costs   costs transferred from a prior process to a subsequent process.

translation (or accounting) risk   the degree to which a firm's financial statements are exposed to exchange rate fluctuation.

treasurer   the individual responsible for the finance function; raises capital and manages cash and investments.

turnover   sales divided by average operating assets.

U

underapplied overhead   overhead that occurs when the applied overhead is less than the actual overhead.

unfavorable (U) variances   variances produced whenever the actual input amounts are greater than the budgeted or standard allowances.

unit-level activities   activities that are performed each time a unit is produced.

unit-level activity drivers   factors that measure the consumption of unit-level activities by products and other cost objects.

usage (efficiency) variance   the difference between standard quantities and actual quantities multiplied by standard price.

V

value-added activities   activities that are necessary for a business to achieve corporate objectives and remain in business.

value-added costs   costs caused by value-added activities.

value chain   the set of activities required to design, develop, produce, market (and deliver), and service products and services to customers.

value stream   all processes that a product must pass through, from the initial customer order to the delivery to the customer.

variable cost ratio   the ratio of total variable cost to sales or of unit variable cost to price. Variable cost ratio is also computed as 1 (100%) minus the contribution margin ratio. It represents the percentage of each sales dollar used to cover variable cost.

variable costing   assigns all variable manufacturing costs to the product and includes direct materials, direct labor, and variable overhead.

variable costs   costs that, in total, vary in direct proportion to changes in output within the relevant range.

variable overhead efficiency variance   the difference between the actual direct labor hours used and the standard hours allowed multiplied by the standard variable overhead rate.

variable overhead spending variance   the difference between the actual variable overhead and the budgeted variable overhead based on actual hours used to produce the actual output.

velocity   the number of units that can be produced in a given period of time (e.g., output per hour).

vertical analysis   a type of analysis that expresses the line item as a percentage of some other line item for the same period.

W

weighted average costing method   a process-costing method that combines beginning inventory costs with current-period costs to compute unit costs. Costs and output from the current period and the previous period are averaged to compute unit costs.

work distribution matrix   identifies the amount of labor consumed by each activity and is derived from the interview process (or a written survey).

work in process (WIP)   the cost of the partially completed goods that are still being worked on at the end of a time period.

Z

zero defects   means that all products conform to specifications.

Check Figures

Check Figures are given for selected problems.

Chapter 2

2-51 1. Total direct materials = $7,810
2. Net income = $6,120

2-52 1. Total owed by Natalie = $30
2. Total cost for Mary = $17.50

2-53 2. Total manufacturing cost for July = $236,450
3. Cost of goods manufactured = $224,950

2-54 1. Total product cost = $9,200,000
2. Operating income = $2,000,000
3. Gross margin = $2,860,000

2-55 1. Cost of goods manufactured = $24,725
2. Cost of goods sold = $27,160

2-57 1. Direct materials used in production = $50,000

2-58 3. Operating income = $332,100

2-60 2. Magazine total prime costs = $4,500
4. Operating income = $2,010

Chapter 3

3-60 2. Fixed receiving cost = $6,600
3. Receiving cost for the year = $295,200

3-61 2. Receiving cost = $25,180

3-62 2. Supplies variable rate = $6.50
4. Charge per hour = $75.69

3-63 2. Plan 2 unused minutes = 75
3. Plan 2 minutes used = 90

3-64 3. Variable rate = $4.50

3-66 1. Total cost ending inventory = $28,353
2. Operating income = $73,569

3-67 1. 10 months' data intercept = 3,212

3-68 2. Variable power cost = $1.125 (rounded)

3-69 2. Fixed rate = $1,349 (rounded)

Chapter 4

4-53 2. Total cost Job 741 = $148,230
4. Cost of goods sold = $234,882

4-54 1. Total = $10,575

4-55 2. Total cost of Carter job = $2,179
4. Gross margin = $3,309

4-56 1. Overhead rate per machine hour = $6
2. Department B overhead rate per machine hour = $4.125

4-57 2. Finishing overhead rate = $75 per machine hour
2. Total manufacturing cost Job 2 = $24,139

4-58 1. Total Ed's Job = $234

4-59 2. Ending Work in Process = $16,526

4-60 2. Total Job 519 = $3,448

4-61 1. Overhead rate = 175% of direct labor cost
3. Cost of goods manufactured = $245,000

4-62 2. Applied overhead = $3,024
5. Adjusted cost of goods sold = $634,340

4-63 2. Total Job 703 = $41,220
4. Ending balance Work in Process = $40,900

4-64 1. Direct Total (laboratory) = $664,500
2. Sequential Total (laboratory) = $663,825

4-65 1. Drilling rate = $15.30 per machine hour (direct); $16.23 (sequential)

4-66 2. May overhead assigned = $200
3. Total cost = $475

Chapter 5

5-53 1. Unit cost = $0.60
2. Duffel bags unit cost = $2.40 per unit
3. Total per unit of Backpacks = $0.80 per unit

5-54 1. Model B overhead cost per unit = $6.75
2. Model B overhead per unit = $7.49
3. Model B overhead cost per unit = $8.38

5-55 1. Total cost = $120,000
2. Basic unit cost = $87.50

5-56 1. Cost per patient day = $277
2. Cost per patient day (complications) = $658

5-57 1. Average monthly fee = $6.78
2. Cost per account (low) = $87.37
3. Profit per account (high-balance) = $112.50

5-58 2. Category I per-unit ordering cost = $0.08
3. Total cost reduction = $4,950,000

5-59 1. Watson unit cost = $1,096.60

5-60 2. Potential reduction per unit = $7.10
4. Total potential unit reduction = $8.35
5. Greatest benefit = $12 price

5-61 1. Total nonvalue cost = $1,204,800
2. Materials nonvalue-added cost = $164,000 U

5-62 1. Theoretical cycle time = 8 minutes
2. Actual cycle time = 9.6 minutes
3. Reduction = $16.67 per telescope

Chapter 6

6-56 1. Units completed = 384,000
2. Total units = 480,000
3. Total units = 51,000

6-57 1. Total units to account for = 180,000
2. Equivalent units, conversion = 156,000
3. Total cost per equivalent unit = $320
4. Cost of Ending WIP = $7,440,000

6-58 1. Total cost per equivalent unit = $320

6-59 1. Total units to account for = 160,000
2. Equivalent Units in Ending WIP = 24,000

6-60 Cost per equivalent unit = $5.20

6-61 1. Units to account for = 50,000
2. Ending WIP = 1,250
4. Cost of EWIP = $750

6-62 Cost per equivalent unit = $12.00

6-63 Cost per equivalent unit = $10.1994

6-64 1. Total equivalent units = 500,000
2. Unit cost = $23.225
3. Goods transferred out = $11,148,000
5. Unit paraffin cost = $6.74

6-65 1. Unit cost = $5.7405

6-66 1. Total cost of units transferred out = $161,044

6-67 1. Total cost of goods transferred out = $17,349
2. Total cost of goods transferred out = $23,400

6-68 1. Cost of units started and completed = $15,573
2. Cost of units started and completed = $23,174

Chapter 7

7-51 1. Unit contribution margin = $6.00
4. Current units = 85,000

7-52 2. Break-even units = 47,699

7-53 1. Break-even sales revenue = $11,538,731
3. Profits underestimated = $642,900
5. Operating leverage = 5.32

7-54 2. Break-even basic sleds = 39,680
3. Increase in total contribution margin = $320,000

7-55 1. Break-even units = 68,400
2. Operating income = $11,220
4. Operating income = $58,140

7-56 4. New contribution margin = $276,180

7-57 1. Break-even sales revenue = $450,000
2. Desk lamps = 9,000 (rounded)

7-58 2. Contribution margin = $180,000
3. Trim kits = 32,444

7-59 1. Break-even units = 21,429
3. Variable cost = $548,100

7-60 1. Variable cost ratio = 78%
4. Contribution margin from increased sales = $2,640

7-61 1. Variable cost = $100,800

7-62 1. Contribution margin ratio = 0.25
2. Break-even units = 32,000
3. Variable cost = $147,000
5. New operating income = $18,200

7-63 1. Macduff degree of operating leverage = 9
2. Duncan break-even point = $250,000
3. Macduff increase in profits = 270%

7-64 1. May current year contribution margin ratio = 0.5489
2. May prior year break-even sales = $24,590
3. May current year margin of safety = $6,522

7-65 1. Grade I sales = 224 cabinets
2. Grade II break-even in units = 392
3. Additional contribution margin = $73,602
4. Increase in operating income = $25,365

7-66 1. First process break-even units = 5,000 cases
2. Units for equal profit = 25,000 cases

Chapter 8

8-54 1. Variable overhead = $300,000

8-55 1. Total operating income = $200,000
3. Total operating income = $235,000

8-56 2. Contribution margin = $10,000

8-57 1. Cost to make = $367,000
4. Cost to make = $598,000

8-58 2. Additional income per pound = $21.025

8-59 1. Operating income = $6,100
2. Operating income = $16,558
3. Total segment margin = $29,620

8-60 1. Increase Pat's profit = $18,400
2. Increase Steve's profit = $15,200

8-61 2. Total cost = $4,200

8-62 1. Standard contribution margin per machine hour = $20

8-63 1. Loss per box = ($0.05)

8-64 1. Operating profit = $40,000

8-66 1. Differential amount to process further = $4,900

8-67 1. Monthly cost for Community Bank = $5,773

Chapter 9

9-65 Total cash, September = $203,462

9-66 1. i. Budgeted income before taxes = $4,971,260
j. Cash budget ending balance (March) = $2,686,004

9-67 1. 40,000 direct labor hours
2. Total fixed costs = $139,750

9-68 1. 20% lower = 32,000 direct labor hours
2. 10% higher total overhead costs = $271,750

9-69 1. 47,000 direct labor hours
2. Total variance = $1,850 U

9-70 1. Total assets = $562,750
2. Cash budget ending cash balance (Sept.) = $12,005
3. Total assets = $565,605

9-72 Ending cash balance = $24,722

9-73 10. Income before taxes = $16,105,000

9-74 1. December materials to be purchased = 5,150 yards

9-75 1. September total cash = $79,446

Chapter 10

10-63 1. MUV = $10,500 F
2. LRV = $0
3. LEV = $13,200 F

10-64 2. LEV, Cutting = $300 U

10-65 1. Standard cost per unit = $126.88
2. LEV = $2,457.60 U

10-66 1. Standard cost (normal) = $305 per patient day
2. MUV (cesarean) = $30,000 F
3. LEV (normal) = $3,200 U
4. LEV = $11,200 U

10-67 1. UCL (labor) = $770,000
2. Total liquid variance = $117,000 U
3. LEV = $26,250 F

10-68 1. June UCL (labor) = $372,600 (price standard)
2. May LEV = $30,000 U (10%)

10-69 1. MPV = $2,213 U
2. LEV = $1,000 F
3. LRV = $0

10-70 1. MUV = $17,100 U
2. LEV = $56,250 U

10-71 1. MUV = $100,000 U
2. LEV = $24,000 U
3. Net effect = $46,000 U

10-72 1. SFOR = $3.60
2. Total FOH variance = $15,600 U
3. Volume variance = $25,200 U
4. VOH efficiency variance = $1,680 F

10-73 1. VOH efficiency = $20,000 U
2. FOH spending = $20,000 F

10-74 1. Standard variable overhead rate = $1.85
3. Volume variance = $10,720 U
4. Efficiency variance = $22,015 U

10-75 3. Standard hours = 26,667

10-76 1. Total variance = $40,000 U
2. Fixed volume variance = $15,000 U;
   Variable efficiency variance = $15,000 U

Chapter 11

11-40 1. ROI of radio project alone = 0.16
2. Residual income of division with radio = $450,000

11-41 1. ROI Year 3 = 6.30%
3. Turnover = 0.75
4. Turnover = 0.83

11-42 1. Turbocharger ROI = 15%
4. Residual income with neither = $289,000

11-43 2. Turnover = 1.15
4. Margin = 9.13%
5. EVA with investment = $122,500

11-44 2. Minimum price = $53

11-45 1. Model SC67 contribution margin = $760,000
5. Contribution margin = $320,000

11-46 2. Markup percentage = 42.5%

11-47 1. Theoretical rate = $4.50/minute

11-49 1. Theoretical cycle time = 30 minutes
3. Actual cycle time = 50 minutes

Chapter 12

12-41 2. Present value year 7 = $97,708

12-42 2. Present value year 10 = $167,424

12-43 2. Discount factor = 6.71008
3. Minimum CF = $58,991

12-44 1. Annual cash flow = $21,425,000
3. Daily revenue = $55,187
4. Seats to be sold = 107

12-45 2. Average cash revenue = $27,900
3. IRR = 14% (approximately)
4. Present value year 1 = $10,000

12-46 1. NPV (scrap alternative) = $151,632

12-48 1. Annual cash flow = $900,000
2. NPV = $(88,289)
3. Present value year 5 = $713,222

12-49 1. Bond cost = 5%

12-50 1. NPV (20% rate) = $(25,391,280)
3. NPV (14%) = $1,374,962

12-51 1. Present value years 1-8 cash flow = $977,308
2. Present value years 1-8 cash flow = $890,436
3. Present value years 1-8 cash flow = $260,615

12-52 1. NPV (standard) = $190,719
2. NPV (CAM) = $761,686

12-53 1. NPV (CAM) = $198,560

Chapter 13

13-51 1. Benefit for A = $17,500,000
1. Net Benefit for B = $4,000,000

13-52 1. Cumulative Operating Income from Five-Year Financial Plan
   (only) for Tuscany = $54,945,900
2. Cumulative Business Sustainability Analysis (only) for
   Matarrana = ($36,000,000)

13-54 1. Internal failure costs = 7.73% of sales
3. External failure = 29.1% of total quality costs

13-55 1. External failure = 33.20% of total in 20x1; 36.13% in 20X2
2. Profits increased by $765,000

13-56 3. Profits increased by $172,000 in 20X4

13-57 2. Unit conversion cost (M15) = $29.42
3. Unit Conv. Cost (M15) = $30.50 per unit

13-60 1. Japanese order = 14,594,800 yen
2. Oct. 1 receipt from Swiss in dollars = $62,831

Chapter 14

14-44 Net cash from operating activities = $32,400

14-46 Net cash from operating activities = $4,000

15-48 1. Net cash from operating activities = $506,250
2. Net cash from investing activities = $(293,750)

14-50 1. Net cash from operating activities = $144,000

14-52 1. Net cash from operating activities = $10,000; net cash from investing activities = $(60,000)

14-54 Net cash from operating activities = $111,800

14-55 1. Net cash from operating activities = $30,000,000; net cash flow from investing activities = $(10,000,000)

14-56 Net cash from operating activities = $80,000; net cash from investing activities = $(55,000)

Chapter 15

15-56 1. Current ratio = 2.50
3. Average receivables = $350,000
5. Average inventory = $225,000

15-57 2. Total assets = $7,250,000

15-58 3. Earnings per share = $5.75
5. Dividends per common share = $1.50

15-59 1. Percent change total assets = 32.5%

15-60 1. This year percent total current assets = 88.6%
2. Last year percent total liabilities = 60.2%
3. This year percent net income after tax = 10.3%

15-61 1. b. Last year quick ratio = 0.71
d. Last year turnover in days = 296.75

15-62 1. b. Last year debt ratio = 0.60

15-63 1. a. Last year return on assets = 0.11
f. Last year dividend payout = 0.24

15-64 1. b. Return on assets = 8.7%

15-65 1. 20X2 accounts receivable turnover = 5.00
20X5 accounts receivable turnover = 4.08

15-66 1. a. McGregor EPS = $2.34
b. Fasnacht dividends per common share = $0.78
e. McGregor return on assets = 0.17

Index

903

Summary of Important Equations

Chapter 2

1. Total Product Cost = Direct Materials + Direct Labor + Manufacturing Overhead
2. Per-Unit Product Cost = Total Product Cost/Number of Units Produced
3. Prime Cost = Direct Materials + Direct Labor
4. Conversion Cost = Direct Labor + Manufacturing Overhead
5. Beginning Inventory of Materials + Purchases − Direct Materials Used in Production = Ending Inventory of Materials
6. Gross Margin = Sales Revenue − Cost of Goods Sold
7. Operating Income = Gross Margin − Selling and Administrative Expense

Chapter 3

1. Total Variable Costs = Variable Rate × Units of Output
2. Total Cost = Total Fixed Cost + Total Variable Cost
3. Total Cost = Total Fixed Cost + (Variable Rate × Units of Output)
4. Variable Rate = (High Point Cost − Low Point Cost)/(High Point Output − Low Point Output)
5. Fixed Cost = Total Cost at High Point − (Variable Rate × Output at High Point)
6. Fixed Cost = Total Cost at Low Point − (Variable Rate × Output at Low Point)
7. Absorption Costing Product Cost = Direct Materials + Direct Labor + Variable Overhead + Fixed Overhead
8. Variable Costing Product Cost = Direct Materials + Direct Labor + Variable Overhead

Chapter 4

1. Predetermined Overhead Rate = $\dfrac{\text{Estimated Annual Overhead}}{\text{Estimated Annual Activity Level}}$
2. Applied Overhead = Predetermined Overhead Rate × Actual Activity Level
3. Total Normal Product Costs = Actual Direct Materials + Actual Direct Labor + Applied Overhead
4. Overhead Variance = Actual Overhead - Applied Overhead
5. Adjusted COGS = Unadjusted COGS ± Overhead Variance

   (*Note*: Applied Overhead > Actual Overhead means Overapplied Overhead, subtract from Unadjusted COGS; Applied Overhead < Actual Overhead means Underapplied Overhead, add to Unadjusted COGS)
6. Departmental Overhead Rate = $\dfrac{\text{Estimated Department Overhead}}{\text{Estimated Departmental Activity Level}}$

Chapter 5

1. Consumption Ratio = $\dfrac{\text{Amount of Activity Driver per Product}}{\text{Total Driver Quantity}}$
2. Overhead Rate = $\dfrac{\text{Total Overhead Costs}}{\text{Total Direct Labor Hours}}$
3. Cycle Time = Time/Units Produced
4. Velocity = Units Produced/Time

Chapter 6

1. Unit Cost = Total Cost/Equivalent Units
2. Units Started and Completed = Total Units Completed - Units in BWIP

   Units Started = Units Started and Completed + Units in EWIP

Chapter 7

1. Unit Contribution Margin = Price − Unit Variable Cost

   Total Contribution Margin = Sales − Total Variable Cost
2. Operating Income = (Price × Number of Units Sold) − (Variable Cost per Unit × Number of Units Sold) − Total Fixed Cost
3. Break-Even Units = Total Fixed Cost/Unit Contribution Margin
4. Sales Revenue = Price × Units Sold
5. Variable Cost Ratio = Total Variable Cost/Sales
6. Variable Cost Ratio = Unit Variable Cost/Price
7. Contribution Margin Ratio = Total Contribution Margin/Sales
8. Contribution Margin Ratio = Unit Contribution Margin/Price
9. Break-Even Sales = Total Fixed Expenses/Contribution Margin Ratio
10. Margin of Safety = Sales − Break-Even Sales
11. Degree of Operating Leverage = Total Contribution Margin/Operating Income
12. Percentage Change in Profits = Degree of Operating Leverage × Percent Change in Sales

Chapter 8

1. Contribution Margin per Unit of Scarce Resource =

   (Selling Price per Unit − Variable Cost per Unit)/Required Amount of Scarce Resource per Unit
2. Price Using Markup = Cost per Unit + (Cost per Unit × Markup Percentage)
3. Target Cost = Target Price − Desired Profit

Chapter 9

1. Units to Be Produced = Expected Unit Sales + Units in Desired Ending Inventory (EI) − Units in Beginning Inventory (BI)
2. Purchases = Direct Materials Needed for Production + Direct Materials in Desired Ending Inventory − Direct Materials in Beginning Inventory
3. Cash Available = Beginning Cash Balance + Expected Cash Receipts
4. Ending Cash Balance = Cash Available − Expected Cash Disbursements

Chapter 10

Abbreviations:

FOH = Fixed Overhead

VOH = Variable Overhead

$BFOH$ = Budgeted FOH

AH = Actual Direct Labor Hours

SH = Direct Labor Hours That *Should Have Been Worked* for Actual Units Produced

SQ = Quantity of Materials That *Should Have Been Used* for Actual Units Produced

AP = Actual Price per Unit

SP = Standard Price per Unit

$SFOR$ = Standard Fixed Overhead Rate

$SVOR$ = Standard Variable Overhead Rate

1. Cost per Unit = Total Cost/Total Units
2. Standard Cost per Unit = Quantity Standard × Price Standard
3. SQ = Unit Quantity Standard × Actual Output
4. SH = Unit Labor Standard × Actual Output
5. Total Variance = Actual Cost − Planned Cost = $(AP \times AQ) − (SP \times SQ)$
6. Total Materials Variance = Actual Cost − Planned Cost = $(AP \times AQ) − (SP \times SQ)$
7. $MPV = (AP − SP) \times AQ$
8. $MUV = (AQ − SQ) \times SP$
9. $MPV = (AP \times AQ) − (SP \times AQ)$
10. $MUV = (SP \times AQ) − (SP \times SQ)$
11. Total Labor Variance = $(AR \times AH) − (SR \times SH)$
12. Total Labor Variance = Labor Rate Variance + Labor Efficiency Variance
13. $LRV = (AR \times AH) − (SR \times AH)$
14. $LRV = (AR − SR) \times AH$
15. $LEV = (SR \times AH) − (SR \times SH)$
16. $LEV = (AH − SH) \times SR$
17. Target Cost per Unit = Expected Sales Price per Unit − Desired Profit per Unit
18. VOH Spending Variance = Actual VOH − $(AH \times SVOR)$
19. VOH Efficiency Variance = $(AH − SH) \times SVOR$
20. Practical Capacity at Standard = SH_p
21. $SFOR = BFOH/SH_p$
22. Applied $FOH = SH \times SFOR$
23. Total FOH Variance = Actual FOH − Applied FOH
24. FOH Spending Variance = $AFOH − BFOH$
25. Volume Variance = $BFOH$ − Applied FOH
    = $BFOH − (SH \times SFOR)$

Chapter 11

1. ROI = Operating Income/Average Operating Assets
2. Average Operating Assets = (Beginning Assets + Ending Assets)/2
3.   **Margin**   **Turnover**
   ROI = Operating Income/Sales × Sales/Average Operating Assets
4. Residual Income = Operating Income − (Minimum Rate of Return × Average Operating Assets)
5. EVA = After-Tax Operating Income − (Actual Percentage Cost of Capital × Total Capital Employed)
6. MCE = Processing Time/(Processing Time + Move Time + Inspection Time + Waiting Time)

Chapter 12

1. Payback Period = $\dfrac{\text{Original Investment}}{\text{Annual Cash Flow}}$
2. Accounting Rate of Return = $\dfrac{\text{Average Income}}{\text{Initial Investment}}$
3. $NPV = \left[\sum CF_t / (1+i)^t \right] − I$
   $= \left[\sum CF_t df_t \right] − I$
   $= P − I$

4. $I = \sum \left[CF_t / (1+i)^t \right]$
5. $I = CF(df)$
6. $df = I/CF$
   $= \dfrac{\text{Investment}}{\text{Annual Cash Flow}}$
7. $F = P(1 + i)^n$
8. $P = F/(1 + i)^n$

Chapter 13

1. Risk Response Benefit = Inherent Risk − Residual Risk
2. Risk Response Net Benefit = Response Benefit − Response Cost
3. Value-Stream Product Cost = Total Actual Value-Stream Costs/Units Shipped
4. Value-Stream Product Cost = Unit Materials Cost + Average Conversion Cost
5. Unit Materials Cost (for each product) = Actual Materials Cost/Units Shipped
6. Average Conversion Cost = Total Actual Conversion Costs/Units Shipped
7. Conversion Cost Rate = Total Actual Conversion Costs/Total Net Production Hours
8. Conversion Cost per Unit = Conversion Cost Rate × Cycle Time

Chapter 15

Liquidity ratios:

1. Current Ratio = Current Assets/Current Liabilities
2. Quick Ratio = (Cash + Marketable Securities + Accounts Receivable)/Current Liabilities
3. Accounts Receivable Turnover Ratio = Net Sales/Average Accounts Receivable
4. Average Accounts Receivable = (Beginning Receivables + Ending Receivables)/2
5. Accounts Receivable Turnover in Days = 365/Accounts Receivable Turnover Ratio
6. Inventory Turnover Ratio = Cost of Goods Sold/Average Inventory
7. Average Inventory = (Beginning Inventory + Ending Inventory)/2
8. Inventory Turnover in Days = 365/Inventory Turnover Ratio
9. Times-Interest-Earned Ratio = (Income Before Taxes + Interest Expense)/Interest Expense
10. Debt Ratio = Total Liabilities/Total Assets
11. Debt-to-Equity Ratio = Total Liabilities/Total Stockholder' Equity

Profitability ratios:

12. Return on Sales = Net Income/Sales
13. Return on Total Assets = {Net Income + [Interest Expense(1 − Tax Rate)]}/Average Total Assets
14. Average Total Assets = (Beginning Total Assets + Ending Total Assets)/2
15. Return on Stockholders' Equity = (Net Income − Preferred Dividends)/Average Common Stockholders' Equity
16. Earnings per Share = (Net Income − Preferred Dividends)/Average Common Shares
17. Price-Earnings Ratio = Market Price per Share/Earnings per Share
18. Dividend Yield = Dividends per Common Share/Market Price per Common Share
19. Dividend Payout Ratio = Common Dividends/(Net Income − Preferred Dividends)

Examples